S0-BTD-061

338.9009 Ros
Rostow.
Theorists of economic growth
from David Hume to the ...

The Lorette Wilmot Library
Nazareth College of Rochester

Theorists of Economic Growth
from David Hume to the Present

Theorists of Economic Growth from David Hume to the Present

With a Perspective on the Next Century

W. W. ROSTOW

Including a Mathematical Appendix by
MICHAEL KENNEDY AND THE AUTHOR

New York   Oxford
OXFORD UNIVERSITY PRESS
1990

DISCARDED

NAZARETH COLLEGE

Oxford University Press

Oxford   New York   Toronto
Delhi   Bombay   Calcutta   Madras   Karachi
Petaling Jaya   Singapore   Hong Kong   Tokyo
Nairobi   Dar es Salaam   Cape Town
Melbourne   Auckland

and associated companies in
Berlin   Ibadan

Copyright © 1990 by Oxford University Press, Inc.

Published by Oxford University Press, Inc.,
200 Madison Avenue, New York, New York 10016

Oxford is a registered trademark of Oxford University Press

All rights reserved. No part of this publication may be reproduced,
stored in a retrieval system, or transmitted, in any form or by any means,
electronic, mechanical, photocopying, recording, or otherwise,
without the prior permission of Oxford University Press.

Library of Congress Cataloging-in-Publication Data
Rostow, W. W. (Walt Whitman), 1916–
Theorists of economic growth from David Hume to the present : with
a perspective on the next century / W. W. Rostow ; including a
mathematical appendix by Michael Kennedy and the author.
p.   cm.
Bibliography: p.
Includes index.
ISBN 0-19-505837-2
1. Economists—History.   2. Economic development—History.
I. Kennedy, Michael.   II. Title.
HB75.R6724   1990
338.9'009—dc20   89-32560 CIP

3 5 7 9 8 6 4 2

Printed in the United States of America
on acid-free paper

338.9009
Ros

To the Economists of the Next Generation:
in the hope that, without abandoning modern tools
of analysis, they may bridge the chasm of 1870 and reestablish
continuity with the humane, spacious, principled tradition
of classical political economy.

Preface

This is a book about theories of economic growth and the men and women who formulated them. It is also about the vicissitudes of the world economy over the past two and a half centuries as they helped shape those theories. And it has something to say about the future—the future of the world economy, of political economy, and of public policy. Thus, it begins in the middle of the eighteenth century with David Hume and ends with a look into the next century.

The first three parts discuss chronologically the contributions of the major thinkers who have shaped the evolution of theories of economic growth. The fourth part assesses some unresolved questions in growth theory and sets out a policy agenda that will not only determine the course of the world economy but also will influence profoundly the issue of war or peace in the several generations ahead. An introductory chapter provides a more detailed overview of the book and an exposition of the analytic approach brought to bear.

This book was written with an acute sense of the danger of the undertaking. For an economist, a review of the work of some of his most distinguished predecessors and contemporaries is an engaging exercise. The task proved so seductive to Joseph Schumpeter that he never got around to the synthesis of dynamic economics he had in mind when he began what proved to be nine years of labor on his *History of Economic Analysis*. Even at that, the historical section of the book was uncompleted when he died. My purpose in entering this beguiling but somewhat treacherous terrain is, at once, narrower than Schumpeter's and wider. It deals with fewer economists, but more economic history, and with some major present and foreseeable issues of public policy, as well.

I had long been planning a final, substantial work on economic growth, but the proximate impetus to begin and the ultimate structure of the book were affected by an experience that may be worth recording. It runs counter to a view held by many in the academic world that undergraduate teaching and research are competing rather than mutually reinforcing.

During the academic year 1983–84 I was invited to teach an upper-level seminar in Plan II at the University of Texas. Plan II is a vital liberal arts enclave—some 600 extremely talented undergraduate students in a university of more than 45,000—granted great flexibility but held to rigorous standards. I was asked to teach on a topic of my own choice. In a lighthearted mood, I created a course entitled "Historical Insights into the Present State of the World Economy." I built the course around the following five questions:

1. Are we in the second, third, fourth, or fifth Industrial Revolution?
2. Are we in the Fifth Kondratieff Upswing or Fourth Kondratieff Downswing?
3. Will the gap between the rich and the poor nations narrow or widen?

4. Will that old devil Diminishing Returns get us in the end?

5. The quantity theory of money: philosopher's stone or misleading tautology?

Each question was dealt with on a triangular basis: relevant economic theory, historical background, and the current scene. With respect to the quantity theory, for example, the students read some Ricardo and Tooke, Friedman and Rostow; examined the sweep of historical price, interest rate, and monetary trends; and then looked at the curious goings on in the world economy since Bretton Woods was abandoned in 1971.

The course turned out to be a lively, cheerful exercise. The experience also drove home certain propositions that helped to shape this book. First, the extent to which economic theories are related to the time and place where they are first formulated. Second, the Faustian Bargain—to steal a phrase from David Landes—made by most mainstream economists after 1870 in which they traded away their capacity to deal endogenously with technological change as well as with the noneconomic dimensions of economic growth for the illusory elegance of partial and general equilibrium analysis. Third, the centrality and the wide-ranging consequences—economic and noneconomic—of the process by which latecomers to economic growth catch up with early comers. This proposition yields an odd result in the book's final chapter. David Hume is judged to have articulated better than any of his successors the problem likely to dominate the world scene over the next several generations; that is, the completion of the drive to technological maturity by what I call the Fourth Graduating Class. (See Figure 19.1, p. 446.)

Reflecting on the palpable challenges posed by the world economy over the next several generations, I became increasingly concerned with the poverty and substantial irrelevance of how we now teach economics to the young. One purpose of this book is to suggest to the next generation of economists and economic historians how rich a heritage lies behind them and how much was lost when mainstream economics abandoned the spacious tradition of classical political economy. Thus the dedication.

One further word about those who, from David Hume to the present, concerned themselves with growth theory. In writing this book I made a list of quotations that had impressed me in the course of this enterprise. Reviewing that list at the end, I stopped with this statement of David Ricardo's: "[T]he friends of humanity cannot but wish that in all countries the labouring classes should have a taste for comforts and enjoyments, and they should be stimulated by all legal means in their exertions to procure them. There cannot be a better security against a superabundant population." By and large, the men and women who move across this stage were driven less by Stephen Leacock's paraphrase of Adam Smith* ("[S]elfishness was bound to pay, of all your doctrine that was the pith, wasn't it, wasn't it, wasn't it, Smith?") than by the opening sentence of *The Theory of Moral Sentiments:* "How selfish soever man may be supposed, there are evidently some principles in his nature, which interest him in the fortune of others, and render their happiness necessary to him, though he derives nothing from it, except the pleasure of seeing it." Taken as a whole, theorists of economic growth over these two and a half centuries belong among "the friends of humanity."

In writing this book I incurred many debts to colleagues. In large ways and small, they turned from their own work to help: Moses Abramovitz, Loring Allen, Francis Bator, William J. Baumol, Frank D. Bean, Woodrow W. Bledsoe, Herbert Block, Arthur F. Burns, Alexander Cairncross, Robert L. Causey, Sukhamoy Chakravarty, Hollis Chenery, Colin Clark, Harry Cleaver, A. W. Coats, Solomon Fabricant, C. H. Feinstein,

---

Hellements of Hickonomics (New York: Dodd, Mead, 1936).

James S. Fishkin, James K. Galbraith, Vincent Geraci, William P. Glade, Saul Eduardo Gonzalez, Ronald Haymen, Samuel Hollander, Istvan Hont, F. Tomasson Jannuzi, Nicholas Kaldor, David Kendrick, Michael Kennedy, Sophie Kim, Charles P. Kindleberger, George Kozmetsky, Edith Kuznets, Douglas Lanat, David Landes, Bruce Larson, Leon S. Lasdon, W. Arthur Lewis, Hans Mark, Edward S. Mason, Standish Meacham, Gerald Meier, Yugandhar Raj Nallari, Duncan Newton, Franz Oppenheimer, Dwight Perkins, Nicholas T. Phillipson, Dudley L. Poston, John M. Robson, Paul M. Romer, Nathan Rosenberg, Henry Rosovsky, Elspeth D. Rostow, Eugene V. Rostow, Victoria Rostow, Carl Rubino, Zhang Ruizhaung, Paul A. Samuelson, Thomas K. Seung, Claudia Siegel, David L. Sills, Raymond W. Smilor, Robert Solow, Henry V. Spiegel, Douglas S. Tharp, Sten Thore, John K. Whitaker, Jeffrey G. Williamson, Shen Xiaoli, and Peter Yelovich.

The following provided invaluable detailed observations on particular sections of the draft text: Messrs. Abramovitz, Baumol, Cairncross, Cleaver, Coats, Hollander, Galbraith, Kendrick, Kennedy, Kindleberger, Robson, Spiegel, and Whitaker.

Loring Allen and Bruce Larson graciously made available before publication manuscripts of their work on Schumpeter and Bickerdike, respectively.

The Swedish Embassy in Washington went to extraordinary lengths to track down an obscure, but necessary, piece of information.

Mrs. Mickey Russell typed the various drafts, ran down innumerable books and journal articles in the University of Texas library; but also spotted relevant materials on her own that enriched the text.

Timothy Martin, as manager of Project Mulhall—a computerized economic history data base—produced a good many useful tables and charts.

Victor Hauser labored on the reader's behalf with extraordinary devotion to correct minor errors and inconsistencies in the printed text.

Lois Nivens, my assistant in all manner of adventures since January 1961, coordinated the various facets of the project and, as always, served as a meticulous editor.

The Administration of the University of Texas made possible the valuable collaboration of Michael Kennedy in the appendix. IC^2 Institute—a research institute of the University, of which I am a Fellow—generously supported the study with research assistance and in other important ways. I wish, in particular, to thank Gerhard Fonken, Robert King, George Kozmetsky, and William Livingston, as well as the authorities at RAND who permitted Kennedy to divert a part of his time from other responsibilities.

My editors at Oxford University Press—Herbert J. Addison and Ann Fishman—were, simply, the ablest and most congenial I have encountered in publishing some thirty books.

Although she no doubt often felt I was bringing home an endless parade of professional colleagues—starting with David Hume—my wife, Elspeth Davies Rostow, backed the enterprise with amused enthusiasm and was at once my most unsparing and most constructive critic, as she has been for getting on to a half century.

Austin, Texas

W. W. R.

Contents

Figures

Tables

Theorists of Economic Growth
from David Hume to the Present

1

Introduction

Purpose

The purpose of this study is to explore how a sequence of growth theorists, beginning in the middle of the eighteenth century and stretching up to the present day, chose to deal (or not deal) with an array of variables and problems that are, in my view, inevitably posed by the dynamics of economic growth. The book discusses the ideas of many economists with all the sympathetic understanding I can muster. But I have not tried to hide my own views along the way. The reader should be aware of some of these views at the outset, and I will have something to say about them later in this chapter and in Chapter 18. First, however, it may be useful to provide an overview of the book as a kind of road map.

The Structure of the Book

Parts I, II, and III survey growth theory from the mid-eighteenth century to the 1980s. Part IV concludes the book by taking stock of what I judge to be the major unsolved problems of growth theory and then looks broadly at the prospects and problems of growth itself over the next several generations and the choices they present to governments and citizens.

Each of the first three parts is organized by a set of questions posed of growth theorists that I will describe later in this chapter. These questions provide an important element of continuity to the analysis in the three historical sections. But these parts are organized in strikingly different ways, and the differences were imposed by the evolution of growth theory itself.

Part I argues that there is unmistakable continuity in the century beginning with David Hume and Adam Smith and ending with J. S. Mill and Karl Marx: continuity in the questions posed, the concepts and methods applied, and a consciousness that economists were working within an evolving tradition. This holds even for Marx, despite his compulsion to shape history in another direction. Above all, for our purposes, they all placed growth at the center of their analyses; and they all understood that the performance of economies was inextricably bound up with the character of the societies of which they were a part. There were a good many more characters I might have brought on stage in both the eighteenth and nineteenth centuries, in France as well as Britain; and the story might well have been pushed back to some of the seventeenth-century founders of political arithmetic to whom I only briefly refer. But I concluded that the essential points I wished to make would emerge if I dealt with the six figures whose growth analyses constitute the subject of Part I.

The problem from 1870 to 1939 imparts a quite different structure to Part II. There is, in the broad classical sense, only one major growth economist in this period, and my designation may surprise some: Alfred Marshall. There are a few others who took growth (or aspects of growth) seriously: Schumpeter, Colin Clark, Kuznets, Walther Hoffmann, and, at the end—and after a curious fashion—Roy Harrod. But there are a great many who, as a byproduct of other concerns, had something of interest to say about economic growth. To bring some sort of order to a consideration of their oblique contributions, I finally fell back on the basic matrix used to bind this book into a reasonably coherent structure. Thus after the lengthy consideration of Marshall as a growth economist (Chapter 6), we move forward under the familiar headings of population and the working force, investment and technology, business cycles, and so on.

The problem in Part III (1939–1988) is, again, quite distinctive but much easier to resolve. Out of clearly identifiable pre-1939 origins, three virtually independent types of growth analysis emerge after 1945: neo-Keynesian growth modeling derived proximately from Roy Harrod's work, with antecedents, in turn, traced out in Part II; statistical analyses of growth patterns in which Colin Clark was unambiguously the great pioneer; and the analysis of and prescription for developing countries, where there is no single pioneering figure but antecedents from Hume and Adam Smith through J. S. Mill to Vera Anstey and R. H. Tawney. Thus, the tripartite structure for Part III was quite natural. The problem was that each ring of the circus was, for a time, very crowded indeed. The task was to try to capture and assess the main strands of thought without excessive cluttering. Readers will have to judge for themselves how well the balance was struck.

In Part IV the closing chapters are addressed to certain unsolved problems in the analysis of growth (Chapter 20) and to the challenges and opportunities that the processes of growth in the world economy are likely to place on the global agenda down to the middle of the next century (Chapter 21). The mathematical appendix was developed jointly with Michael Kennedy, but the mathematical exposition was executed wholly by him. It permits key propositions that shape this volume to be examined in sharp focus—though, as with most such analyses, at a high cost in oversimplification. Despite the severe limitation of mathematics as a language in economics, we regard this appendix as a useful supplement to the book.

The Analytic Perspective

I would underline three limitations in this exposition that distinguish it from a conventional history of economic doctrine. First, the economists dealt with are a highly selective group. In a narrow analytic effort of this kind, there is clearly no need to be exhaustive. Second, the sharp focus on the problem of economic growth means that many other aspects of the work of the economists discussed are set aside. For example, of the seven striking contributions to knowledge Keynes (with Edgeworth's assistance) attributed to Marshall, there is hardly reference to five of his innovations. On the other hand, Marshall emerges in Chapter 6 as a major growth theorist. Finally, even with respect to theories of growth, the purpose here is primarily to indicate the variables and problems economists found most relevant, rather than to present a full exposition of their views on economic growth. From the rather special perspective of this review, I am more interested in each economist's angle of vision than the substance or provenance of their doctrine, or, indeed, in whether I judge their views to have been, in some sense, correct or flawed; although a certain amount of debate with one's intellectual ancestors and contemporaries is inevitable in an enterprise of this kind.

Wherever possible, I pose a uniform sequence of questions to these theorists and their propositions:

- Were their views framed by or related to a definable, reasonably explicit philosophic, psychological, moral, or other noneconomic doctrine?
- Were their views shaped significantly by the passages of economic history that they observed closely at the time their doctrines took shape?
- Did they use, explicitly or implicitly, the basic growth equation; if so, what was distinctive in their particular formulations of it?

Here we pause for a moment. A central proposition that runs through this book is that, from the eighteenth century to the present, growth theories have been based on one formulation or another of a universal equation or production function. This is how I expressed it in *The Process of Economic Growth* (1952):[1]

> The argument hinges on one version of a simple, classical relationship. Output is taken as determined by the scale and productivity of the working force and of capital. Included within capital, for purposes of this analysis, is land and other natural resources, as well as scientific, technical, and organizational knowledge. The rate of growth of an economy is thus viewed as a function of changes in two enormously complex variables. . . .
>
> It is central to the perspective of this book that the economic decisions which determine the rate of growth and productivity of the working force and of capital should not be regarded as governed by the strictly economic motives of human beings. Economic action is judged the outcome of a complex process of balancing material advance against other human objectives. Further, both history and contemporary events indicate that actions which result in economic advance need not be motivated by economic goals. . . . The present purpose . . . may be defined as an effort to introduce into formal economic analysis variables which incorporate the human response to the challenges and material opportunities offered by the economic environment. These variables are designed to constitute a link between the domain of the conventional economist on the one hand, and the sociologist, anthropologist, psychologist, and historian on the other. . . .
>
> The device chosen for this linkage consists of six propensities:
>
> - The propensity to develop fundamental science (physical and social)
> - The propensity to apply science to economic ends
> - The propensity to accept innovations
> - The propensity to seek material advance
> - The propensity to consume
> - The propensity to have children

In her *Theories of Economic Growth and Development* (1961)[2] Irma Adelman embraces the same set of variables in the production function:

$$Y_t = f(K_t, N_t, L_t, S_t, U_t)$$

where K_t denotes the services flowing from an economy's capital stock; N_t, from natural resources; L_t, the labor force; S_t represents the society's fund of applied knowledge; U_t, the sociocultural milieu within which the economy operates. This latter variable, U_t, is a kind of generalized set of the propensities that are disaggregated in *The Process of Economic Growth.* The purpose of that disaggregation was to focus what Adelman calls "the social-cultural milieu" on specific variables determining the rate of growth of the working force, the rate of investment, and the productivity of investment; for "the social-cultural milieu" of different societies not only differs at a moment of time or over time but those differences do not have their impact uniformly on the key specific growth variables. Therefore a single, aggregate "social-cultural milieu" variable will simply not do except to remind us that noneconomic variables are inescapably relevant to the analysis of economic growth.

Something like the basic equation is embedded equally in Hume's economic essays, Adam Smith's *The Wealth of Nations,* the latest neoclassical growth model, and virtually every formulation in between. But this checklist of basic variables is the beginning, not the end, of the matrix applied to the array of growth economists examined in this book. A set of further questions are posed to all that relate directly to the growth model that underlies this critique.

- What population theory did they accept, and what, if anything, did they have to say about the quality and productivity of the working force?
- What did they identify as the determinants of the level and productivity of investment? Did they treat investment as an undifferentiated aggregate or did they disaggregate and distinguish investment in different directions? If so, what was the extent of their disaggregation?
- What did they have to say about machinery and other forms of new technology? Did they examine the forces tending to generate and diffuse new technology?
- How, if at all, did they deal with business cycles? Did they relate them to the growth process? Did they distinguish cycles of different length? If so, on the basis of what criteria?
- Did they distinguish the prospects for productivity as between raw produce and manufacturing, to use the classical terms? How, if at all, did they deal with diminishing and increasing returns, relative price movements, and their consequences for other variables relevant to growth and the distribution of income?
- Did they distinguish countries or regions at different levels of real income per capita or stage of growth? If so, on the basis of what criteria?
- How, if at all, did they deal with the limits to growth? Did they regard the economic system as headed toward acceleration, deceleration, a steady state, or decline? What variables did they believe would determine the outcome? What were their time horizons?
- What, if anything, did they have to say about the noneconomic variables? If introduced, how were the noneconomic variables linked to the economic performance of societies?

These questions are neither random nor neutral. They reflect a conviction that an economic theory useful for either historical or contemporary analysis of the world that has emerged since the eighteenth century must: embrace endogenously the demographic transition; treat science and invention as investment subsectors and the capacity to innovate as a creative task distinguishable from profit maximization with fixed or incrementally changing production functions; account for the tendency of major innovations to cluster rather than spread randomly through time; demonstrate the intimate linkage between growth and cyclical fluctuations of differing periodicity with major innovations and the generation of the requisite inputs of food and raw materials accounted as endogenous to the system. Such a theory must also cope with the variables that determine when and at what pace particular societies absorb efficiently the backlog of relevant, then-existing technologies and plough back the profits thus generated into further investment and growth. Finally, I would hold, this dynamic, disaggregated system must be linked to conventional macroeconomic analysis, a task of "organized complexity" in Warren Weaver's phrase.[3]

Evidently, every one of these imperatives requires a weaving together of noneconomic and economic variables.

The system that emerges does incorporate the notion of a dynamic, moving equilibrium although, as shall later emerge, the system inherently lurches through time, overshooting and undershooting its optimum sectoral (and, therefore, aggregate) paths. It is also a non-linear (or chaos) system marked by irreversible change where stable equilibrium is ruled out and disequilibrium drives the sectors toward equilibrium paths passed through but never sustained.

This book does not constitute a formal exposition of this system, a task undertaken elsewhere. But the underlying perspective that informs the system is reflected throughout and sketched mathematically in the appendix.

The Link to Economic History

Readers may find more economic history here than in conventional studies of the history of economic doctrine. As I worked forward in this story, I found it increasingly important to relate writers to the particular times in which their views were formed and, sometimes, to the particular narrow interval when they set down a line of argument. The various growth formulations clearly bear the marks of particular passages of economic history intimately observed by their authors. As Alfred Marshall wrote to John Neville Keynes in 1891:[4] "I hold that the 'classical' economists knew their facts—but only put an abstract of them in their shop front. Also I don't think they were nearly as abstract as you do." The post-1870 economists were not all as knowledgeable as their pioneering predecessors; but, taken as a whole, their views also constitute a rather striking vindication of four similar propositions:[5] Confucius's identification of the age of 30 as the time a person's way of thinking was "established"; Walter Bagehot's observation (relative to Malthus) that "scarcely any man who has evolved a striking and original conception of a subject ever gets rid of it"; and the well-known peroration of J. M. Keynes's *General Theory*: ". . . in the field of economic and political philosophy there are not many who are influenced by new theories after they are twenty-five or thirty years of age. . . ." We shall also find that Schumpeter, who shared this perspective, refers often to an economist's twenties as the "sacred decade" when "the vision" of his task was defined.

I am inclined to take the Confucius–Bagehot–Keynes–Schumpeter proposition seriously, but not too seriously, recalling, if necessary, that François Quesnay published his

Table 1.1. When Their Visions Took Shape

Major economic growth theorist	Year when economist was 30	Year when economist set down his major doctrine
David Hume (1711–1776)	1741	1739 (*A Treatise of Human Nature*)
Adam Smith (1723–1790)	1753	1748–1751 (Edinburgh Lectures)
T. R. Malthus (1766–1834)	1796	1798 (*An Essay on the Principle of Population* [first edition])
David Ricardo (1772–1823)	1802	1817 (*Principles of Political Economy*)
J. S. Mill (1806–1873)	1836	1829–1830 (*Some Unsettled Questions* [Not published until 1844])
Karl Marx (1818–1883)	1848	1848 (*Communist Manifesto*)

first article on an economic problem when he was 62 years old. Nevertheless, here are the relevant data for the leading characters of Part I (Table 1.1).

The only authentic exception among the six classical figures of Part I to the Confucius–Bagehot–Keynes–Schumpeter theory may be Ricardo; although even his case is not certain. He did not retire definitively from business until 1819, but he was already a central figure in the bullion controversy of 1809–1810. And Ricardo certainly began to formulate his views on economics before his thirtieth year. Starting in 1797, at the age of 25, he devoted some of his leisure time to mathematics and the physical sciences; but 2 years later, while in Bath with his wife, he accidentally came upon *The Wealth of Nations*. From quite reliable testimony, some of his leisure time was regularly allocated thereafter to political economy.[6]

Adam Smith is a less clear-cut exception, and probably not an exception at all. He was teaching at the University of Edinburgh as early as 1748–1751 where he began his association with David Hume (1750) and his bridging of moral philosophy and political economy. He became a professor at the University of Glasgow in 1751. We have notes on the substance of his lectures as delivered in 1762; but he was certainly engaged earlier in formulating his thoughts on the economic process, a good many of which are reflected in his *Theory of Moral Sentiments* (1759). The major biographer of this period of Smith's life in fact dates his transition to political economy in the period 1748–1751; that is, in Smith's late twenties.[7]

The moderately serious reason for this rather playful bit of biographical arithmetic is that the perspective on the economic process reflected in various theories of growth does appear to be influenced strongly by the course of economic events observed at a relatively early stage of each economist's career. We shall find an interesting example of this linkage when we examine in Part III a sampling of development economists who mainly came to that field late—as a kind of second marriage. But the mark of their earlier commitments can generally be detected. Circumstances in the outer world change, and our economists address themselves to them; but they tend to do so in continuity with the concepts that had crystallized in earlier times. To use Schumpeter's phrase, their ''vision'' usually comes early, and their subsequent work tends to be an elaboration of that vision. The implications of this judgment will emerge recurrently as we move forward in time.

Even a review as narrowly focused as this deals, perforce, with many factors beyond contemporary economic events that left—or may have left—their mark on the doctrines of the economists whose views we examine. But it is true of the history of economic thought, as of other dimensions of intellectual history, that the story cannot be told simply as an insulated series of theoretical elaborations and changes by men and women trying to improve in some abstract, scientific sense the formulations they inherited from their professional predecessors. There is a powerful contrapuntal strand: the effort of each generation to solve the problems of its time.

Personalities: Do They Matter?

The noneconomic variables brought to bear here include, of course, the moral as well as political and social judgments that these economists brought, consciously or otherwise, to their analyses. Thereby one is led to try, in degree at least, to establish in one's mind an answer to the question: What sort of human being was (or is) this?

One thoughtful observer, Sir Peter Medawar, has counseled against the effort. And although Schumpeter's characterization of Quesnay ("He . . . must have been an awful bore") cannot be generalized to all economists, Medawar's view should not be hastily set aside:[8]

> The lives of scientists, considered as Lives, almost always make dull reading. . . . Academics can only seldom lead lives that are spacious or exciting in a worldly sense. They need laboratories or libraries in the company of other academics. Their work is in no way made deeper or more cogent by privation, distress or worldly buffetings. Their private lives may be unhappy, strangely mixed up or comic, but not in ways that tell us anything special about the nature or direction of their work. Academics lie outside the devastation area of the literary convention according to which the lives of artists and men of letters are intrinsically interesting, a source of cultural insight in themselves. If a scientist were to cut his ear off, no one would take it as evidence of a heightened sensibility; if a historian were to fail (as Ruskin did) to consummate his marriage, we should not suppose that our understanding of historical scholarship had somehow been enriched.

And in most cases I concluded either Medawar was right, or I didn't have enough information to decide if he was right or wrong, or the analysis would be distorted by going into the necessary detail. Charles Babbage and John Rae, for example, were, in thoroughly different ways, quite fascinating characters. But, given their ancillary supporting roles in the story, I suppressed my impulse to elaborate on the kind of men they were. At the other end of the spectrum, Adam Smith, from what we know, is a case study in Medawar's proposition. His dislike of Oxford does leave its mark on his views; but the kidnapping as a child, an alleged unrequited love, a deep attachment to his mother, and an extreme case of absentmindedness do not greatly illuminate his writings.

Thus I have not tried to establish and pursue a uniform pattern in this matter. With respect to the six classic political economists of Part I, I introduced personal material when I thought it relevant and appropriate—as in the obvious cases of David Hume, J. S. Mill, and Karl Marx. The importance of the Malthus–Ricardo friendship and their unresolved intellectual conflict requires something of this dimension; and Ricardo's faceless, austere image among neoclassical mainstream economists who think well of him deserves a bit of softening; for he was evidently a vital, humane person with a quality not endemic among economists—a sense of humor.

In Part II the stage is too crowded for much of this kind of thing. Alfred Marshall was, on the surface, almost a prototype Medawar scientist; but it is important, I believe, to catch something of the moral passion that led him, against his will, into economics. Not many of those who regarded him as a stuffy Victorian wandered the streets in working class districts looking into the faces of the poor, enjoyed such comfortable relations with workers and labor leaders, or, indeed, made bolder proposals to mitigate poverty.

Schumpeter comes nearer to vindicating Medawar's proposition. We now know through Loring Allen's fine biography a great deal about the recurrent traumatic and even tragic events that marked his life. But it is hard to trace the impact of these incidents and circumstances on his work as an economist except, perhaps, in the failure to complete his *History of Economic Analysis.*

As for Part III, there is some mild indulgence in personal observations in dealing with the nine development pioneers, all of whom, except Colin Clark, I have known; but these strands are introduced only when relevant to their approach to development problems.

Ideas come first in this book, but when ideas appear to have been shaped or tempered by the personalities of these growth theorists I have not hesitated to let them emerge as human beings too.

I

SIX CLASSICAL ECONOMISTS: DAVID HUME TO KARL MARX

2

David Hume
and Adam Smith

The Setting

Classical economics took its start in the eighteenth century—with some earlier anticipations—from a much larger enterprise: the protracted effort to discover and install the natural laws that should govern man in society, shifting the Heavenly City "to earthly foundations."[1] Here is Carl Becker's evocation of the climate of opinion in the thirteenth century from which the transition begins:[2]

> . . . it was an unquestioned fact that the world and man in it had been created in six days by God the Father, an omniscient and benevolent intelligence, for an ultimate if inscrutable purpose. Although created perfect, man had through disobedience fallen from grace into sin and error, thereby incurring the penalty of eternal damnation. Yet happily a way of atonement and salvation had been provided through the propitiatory sacrifice of God's only begotten son. Helpless in themselves to avert the just wrath of God, men were yet to be permitted, through his mercy, and by humility and obedience to his will, to obtain pardon for sin and error. Life on earth was but a means to this desired end, a temporary probation for the testing of God's children. In God's appointed time, the Earthly City would come to an end, the earth itself be swallowed up in flames. On that last day good and evil men would be finally separated. For the recalcitrant there was reserved a place of everlasting punishment; but the faithful would be gathered with God in the Heavenly City, there in perfection and felicity to dwell forever.
>
> Existence was thus regarded by the medieval man as a cosmic drama, composed by the master dramatist according to a central theme and on a rational plan. . . . The duty of man was to accept the drama as written, since he could not alter it; his function, to play the role assigned. . . . Intelligence was essential, since God had endowed men with it. But the function of intelligence was strictly limited. . . . [T]o reconcile diverse and pragmatic experience with the rational pattern of the world as given in faith.

The transformation that followed over the subsequent five centuries—yielding, in effect, the modern world—is, as every student in an undergraduate course in Western Civilization knows, a complex, many-sided story. It embraces the revival of Greek and Roman learning and the Renaissance in the broader sense; the slow, uneven break-up of feudalism; the rise of towns and of lively urban societies; the scientific revolution from Copernicus to Newton, with all its oblique, pervasive consequences; the emergence of Protestantism; the voyages of discovery and the commercial revolution; the bloody triumph of nation states and their struggles for power and profit; then the Enlightenment of the eighteenth century from which, among many other things, modern economic theory and doctrine emerged, substantially from Scotland, oddly enough, at Europe's northwest periphery.

It is inevitable that this extraordinary kaleidoscopic saga should be viewed, generation after generation, from many perspectives no one of which can claim to be inclusive or definitive.[3] Peter Gay, for example, thus defines his view of the philosophes of the Enlightenment, a relatively small cadre within which he includes Adam Smith as well as David Hume, evidently one of its truly major figures:[4]

> There were many philosophes in the eighteenth century, but there was only one Enlightenment. A loose, informal, wholly unorganized coalition of cultural critics, religious skeptics, and political reformers from Edinburgh to Naples, Paris to Berlin, Boston to Philadelphia, the philosophes made up a clamorous chorus, and there were some discordant voices among them, but what is striking is their general harmony, not their occasional discord. The men of the Enlightenment united on a vastly ambitious program, a program of secularism, humanity, cosmopolitanism, and freedom, above all, freedom in its many forms—freedom from arbitrary power, freedom of speech, freedom of trade, freedom to realize one's talents, freedom of aesthetic response, freedom, in a word, of moral man to make his own way in the world. In 1784, when the Enlightenment had done most of its work, Kant defined it as man's emergence from his self-imposed tutelage, and offered as its motto *Sapere aude*—"Dare to know": take the risk of discovery, exercise the right of unfettered criticism, accept the loneliness of autonomy.* Like the other philosophes—for Kant only articulated what the others had long suggested in their polemics—Kant saw the Enlightenment as man's claim to be recognized as an adult, responsible being.

The secularism of the Enlightment took the form, for some, of a direct assault on organized Christianity. Gay has this to say about Hume's protracted campaign against religion.[5]

> Despite the difficulty of his thought . . . despite the profusion of his output and the range of his interests, neither critic nor admirer—neither Christian nor unbeliever—had the slightest hesitation in placing Hume among the most radical of radical philosophes. . . . [The philosophes] admired Hume's writings, loved his person, and cherished him as a leader in the common cause.
>
> Not without reason: in his intellectual pedigree, in his intentions, and in his very world view Hume belongs with the philosophes, no matter how amiable his disposition, individual his argumentation, and unexpected his conclusions. . . . It is true that Hume had marked if grudging respect for man's

*"Beantwortung der Frage: Was Ist Aufklarung?" *Werke*, IV, 169.

ability to resist rational argument and had little confidence that the liberation from superstition was either continuous or inevitable. But if the mischief that his writings did was limited, that was not for want of trying. Hume devoted his best energies to elaborating his critique of religion in the hope that some men at least would listen and (I am convinced) to satisfy an irrepressible need of his own.

There are other treatments of the protagonists at quite different levels: for example, Louis Loeb's highly technical study of their perspectives as professional philosophers.[6]

Nearer to the major concerns of this book is the ferment stirred by John Pocock. His *The Machiavellian Moment* gave impetus to the re-study of the Scottish Enlightenment[7] and, thereby, a fresh look at Hume, Adam Smith, and their contemporaries.

Pocock's argument, elaborated with loving detail and sophistication, is, at its core, quite simple. The Machiavellian proposition, derived from the Greco-Roman world, was that the fate of a political unit (*Fortuna*) depended, in an inherently uncertain and treacherous world, on civic virtue (*Virtù*). Virtue, in this context, demanded a body of citizen-warriors, equal in status, holders of landed property, totally devoted to the interests of the state, living an austere life whose satisfaction was substantially defined in terms of an absolute commitment to the state, transcending Christian morality, as it confronted the succession of dangers history generated as its *Fortuna*. On this spartan view, wealth and the pursuit of wealth, luxury, and idleness were paramount corrupting forces:[8] "It was possible . . . to restate the vision of history as an *anakuklōsis* [cycle], in which republics were transformed into empires by their own *virtù* and then corrupted and destroyed by the subsequent luxury."

This was a not quite satisfactory doctrine for eighteenth-century Scotland. With the salutary course of British political and economic affairs after 1660, including the 1707 Act of Union with Scotland, things began to change in Edinburgh as well as London:[9]

> With the defeat of . . . advocacy of a federal rather than an incorporating Union, came the realization that Scottish participation in the English *Wirtschaftwunder* had been bought by the sacrifice of civic virtue, and that an alternative form of virtue was an ideological and practical necessity. This was met by the massive and rapid adoption of an Addisonian Whig political, or rather social, culture; Edinburgh saw a proliferation of Spectatorial clubs and societies, practising the virtues of polite conversation and enlightened taste while discussing the economic, cultural and even—given an age in which manners seemed no unimportant part of morality—the moral improvement of Scottish life. The locus of virtue shifted decisively from the civic to the civil, from the political and military to that blend of the economic, cultural and moral which we call the social for short.

From one perspective, this was the setting in which Hume and Adam Smith evolved, and their work can be regarded as a fully elaborated reply to the older conception of civic virtue. But to his credit, Pocock is quite aware that his rather stylish portrait of the transformation of Florentine civic virtue to the "immensely rich and multi-faceted concept of civil or social humanism" doesn't quite cover the ground.[10] He cites respectfully, for example, a quite different source of transformation: the continental elaboration of civil jurisprudence "as a principal mode of organizing great traditions of moral, social, and political philosophy."[11] And, no doubt he would accept, as a matter of course, the role of

Newtonian science in stimulating the search for the natural laws that should govern men in society. He thus wisely leaves much open for future scholarship and reflection.

But he poses at the end a question with which this book is much concerned, down to the last page of its text:[12] "How did the complex synthesis of 'moral sentiment' with 'the wealth of nations' evolve or degenerate into the science of classical economics; how did it come to be denounced as cold, mechanical and dismal, founded on a restrictive and reductionist theory of the human personality it had sought to liberate from classical restraints?" As will emerge, the turning point comes around 1870, when, dazzled by marginal analysis and the calculus, political economy becomes, for most professionals, economics. But in the time of Hume and Adam Smith it was a vital part of a great human and social enterprise: in Becker's phrase, shifting the Heavenly City "to earthly foundations." Central to that enterprise were fundamental moral values, purposes, and dilemmas that suffused political economy over its first century and a quarter and, to a degree, down to the present. The question is: To what extent were the moral values of the Enlightenment Christianity in disguise? Carl Becker's is the most straightforward and unambiguous view:[13]

> . . . we find that at every turn the *Philosophes* betray their debt to medieval thought without being aware of it. They denounced Christian philosophy, but rather too much, after the manner of those who are but half emancipated from the "superstitions" they scorn. They had put off the fear of God, but maintained a respectful attitude toward the Deity. They ridiculed the idea that the universe had been created in six days, but still believed it to be a beautifully articulated machine designed by the Supreme Being according to a rational plan as an abiding place for mankind. . . . They renounced the authority of church and Bible, but exhibited a naive faith in the authority of nature and reason. . . . They denied that miracles ever happened but believed in the perfectibility of the human race. . . . [T]here is more of Christian philosophy in the writings of the *Philosophes* than has yet been dreamt of in our histories.

At first sight, Peter Gay's interpretation of the Enlightenment, with its subtitle, *The Rise of Modern Paganism,* is at the other end of the spectrum. But his study is shot through—almost haunted—by an effort to sort out a credible response to the question Becker posed.[14] His conclusion is captured in the following:[15]

> . . . the philosophes have been sarcastically commended for "merely" secularizing religious ideas and caricatured as medieval clerks in modern dress, ungrateful and forgetful heirs of the Christian tradition who combated the pious wish for salvation in the name of a secular salvation disguised as progress; who denied the immortality of the soul only to substitute the immortality of reputation; who laughed at religious idolatry but had their own saints—Bacon, Newton, and Locke; who excommunicated their heretics— Rousseau; and even made pilgrimages—to Ferney.

Such analogies are seductive and even telling: they draw attention to origins the philosophes did not like to remember. There was some point after all, in the derisive observation that the Enlightenment was a derivative, vulgarized restatement of traditional Christian values: the new philosophy a secularized faith, optimism a secularized hope, humanitarianism a secularized charity.

. . . But from the vantage point of each camp the same set of facts takes on two very different shapes. What Christians saw, with some justice, as an act of imitation, the philosophes saw, with greater justice, as an act of repudiation or, at best, of exploitation. . . . The origins of ideas may be a clue to their function, they do not determine it. Christianity made a substantial contribution to the philosophes' education, but of the definition of the Enlightenment it forms no part.

In less sophisticated terms a good many intellectual figures of the era hedged their bets. Edmund Halley, in his ode on the title page of Newton's *Principia,* was quite orthodox, as was appropriate given Newton's serious commitment to religion.

> Here ponder too the laws which God,
> Framing the universe, set not aside
> But made the fixed foundations of His Work.

In the next century, however, Alexander Pope, rather successfully, has it both ways:

> Nature and Nature's laws lay hid in night;
> God said, Let Newton be! and all was light.

Accepting this ambiguity among the philosophes, Gay nevertheless isolates clearly the strand he regards as most distinctive and admirable in the Enlightenment and finds it crystallized in Hume. The final section of his text is entitled "David Hume: The Complete Modern Pagan." It concludes as follows with a statement that may constitute as well Gay's own creed:[16]

> For David Hume was both courageous and modern; he understood the implications of his philosophy and did not shrink from them. He was so courageous that he did not have to insist on his courage; he followed his thinking where it led him, and he provided through his own life (and, Samuel Johnson to the contrary, in the face of death) a pagan ideal to which many aspired but which few realised. He was willing to live with uncertainty, with no supernatural justifications, no complete explanations, no promise of permanent stability, with guides of merely probable validity; and what is more, he lived in his world without complaining, a cheerful Stoic. Hume, therefore, more decisively than many of his brethren in the Enlightment, stands at the threshold of modernity and exhibits its risks and its possibilities. Without melodrama but with the sober eloquence one would expect from an accomplished classicist, Hume makes plain that since God is silent, man is his own master: he must live in a disenchanted world, submit everything to criticism, and make his own way.

In probing this question I also consulted Professor Nicholas T. Phillipson. In a letter of October 14, 1987, he responded with a somewhat different emphasis than Gay: "You ask where Hume and Smith got their moral philosophy from. So far as Hume is concerned, part of my answer would be, from Cicero." Hume reports in his autobiographical essay that, as a very young man, it was Virgil and Cicero he was "secretly devouring" when he should have been reading law. Phillipson saw in Cicero the root of Hume's judgment that people were social animals: preoccupied with justice and social approval; pursuing happiness in common life rather than in the life hereafter; defining morality in civic terms.

It is neither necessary nor appropriate for me to try to pronounce definitively on the links between the Roman world, Christianity, and the moral principles Hume and Adam Smith brought to bear in their prescriptions for "a great society," to use Smith's phrase. What is essential is that Hume and Smith understood quite clearly that their mission as political economists was to try to analyze and solve a set of essentially moral, social, and political rather than narrowly economic problems; and whatever their route of derivation might have been, the values they brought to bear were congruent with much of the longer classical and Christian past.

In particular, four large problems concerned them. First, the problem of good and evil. Clearly, Hume and Smith viewed man as capable of "sin and error," translated into avarice and greed in the life of the economy. They saw in man's need for social approval and sense of kinship with others a tempering force defined as "sympathy"; but they did not rely wholly on sympathy to hold avarice within civilized bounds. Nor, except over a narrow range—notably, in guaranteeing the sanctity of property—did they rely on the state. They viewed open competition as the most effective reconciling force.

Second, they were deeply concerned with the moral problems posed by simultaneous existence of abject poverty and unearned affluence—again a concern deeply rooted in the Christian tradition. As Hont and Ignatieff have reminded us: "the central commitment of Hume and Smith was to justice."[17] The *Wealth of Nations* begins with the paradox that British society of the mid-eighteenth century, relatively affluent by historical and contemporary standards, was marked by both morally disturbing patterns of income distribution and a higher standard of living for the working poor than had ever been achieved in more egalitarian primitive societies. In the continued expansion of the wealth of nations they saw a solvent for the poor to which their successors added a limitation of family size sufficient, in effect, to render labor rather than land the scarcest factor of production.

Third, they were concerned with the impact of the economy on the social and political life of their nation. Here the linkage to religous values was real but focused rather sharply on English society, post-1688, and on Scotland, post-1707. They saw affluence as the friend of civil liberty and, on balance, a civilizing agent over a wide front.

Finally, both Hume and Smith were enemies of the barbarities of mercantilism abroad as well as at home. In his day it was no small thing for Hume to "pray for the flourishing commerce of . . . even France itself" (following, p. 30) and for Smith to oppose a regime of colonies. The underlying principle, as in domestic life, was that the avarice of nations as well as men could be tempered by open and free competitive commerce.[18]

However real David Hume's atheism may have been, his work reflects sytematically this array of large moral considerations.

David Hume (1711–1776)

David Hume has a quite strong—but not exclusive—claim to being the first modern economist. But as virtually every commentator notes, his work as a philosopher, psychologist, and historian tends to overshadow his quality as an economist. It follows directly from the view developed in this book, however, that Hume's claim to distinction as an economist lies, in good part, in his insistence on placing economic analysis in this broad human and societal setting and keeping it there. His views on economics and economic policy are suffused, even more than those of Adam Smith, by his wider assessment of the human condition and the dynamics of history. And as a psychologist, he observed:[19]

"These principles of human nature, you'll say are contradictory: but what is man but a heap of contradictions."

Hume's economic man is, then, no simple profit or relative utility maximizer. In analyzing the motives for effective economic action ("causes of labor"), Hume did, indeed, include avarice and the desire for gain,[20] but he also introduced the desire for "pleasure," "action," and "liveliness."[21] In projecting this multidimensional image of human beings, Hume allowed for differences in preferences among individuals but suggested that, in general, the greatest happiness lay in achieving a balance among the contending human impulses governed by the law of diminishing relative marginal utility; i.e., the more of any one form of satisfaction a human being enjoyed the less he valued each additional unit of it relative to other forms of satisfaction. And he applied this notion of diminishing relative marginal utility to real income itself and to income distribution:[22] "Every person, if possible, ought to enjoy the fruits of his labour, in a full possession of all the necessaries, and many of the conveniencies of life. No one can doubt, but such an equality is most suitable to human nature, and diminishes much less from the *happiness* of the rich than it adds to that of the poor."

The basic concepts that Hume elaborated from 1739 to 1776 were certainly formed by the earlier date. He belongs, therefore, in the phase of remarkable ferment that followed the Glorious Revolution (1688) and, for a Scot, the Act of Union (1707). It was also a period when people became fully conscious of the revolutionary changes brought about in the two centuries since the world economy was extended by the voyages of discovery and the subsequent commercial revolution. There was sufficient common knowledge for comparative judgments to be formed and communicated about contemporary China, India, and the American colonies as well as about ancient Greece, Rome, and Egypt, from an earlier heritage.

In reflecting on the processes set in motion by the commercial revolution, Hume, like a good many of his contemporaries, was contending against the earlier policy doctrines that we group together under the rubric of mercantilism. His tight brief essays in economics, running to some 107 pages, are all sharply pointed policy pamphlets. (I exclude Hume's monograph "Of the Populousness of Ancient Nations," of some 75 pages, although it, too, contains some reflections bearing on policy.) His expositions are shaped by that operational purpose and are quite different in their emphasis and balance than if he had set out to write a systematic treatise on economics—which he might have done if his youthful *Treatise of Human Nature* had not been, in his view, such a dramatic initial failure. In the end, his economic concepts come through quite clearly. They form a reasonably coherent and consistent theory of the dynamics of growth; but issues not in policy contention are skimped (e.g., investment) whereas key issues in the running debate on mercantilism are quite fully expounded (e.g., the economic significance of the trade balance).

Hume's argument also reflects clearly the economic state of affairs in, roughly, the second quarter of the eighteenth century. In broad terms, the British economy in the period during which Hume's basic ideas crystallized (and Adam Smith's as well) can be characterized as follows:[23]

- The period 1713–1738 was peaceful, by eighteenth century standards, after the great exertions of the War of Spanish Succession (1701–1713); but hostilities resumed with the War of Jenkins' Ear (1739) and of the Austrian Succession (1740–1748), the latter never reaching the scale of the conflict earlier in the century or of

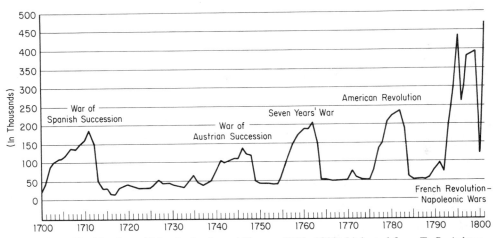

Figure 2.1. The Number of Men in the Armed Forces, 1700–1800. [Adapted from T. S. Ashton, *Economic Fluctuations in England 1700–1800* (Oxford: at the Clarendon Press, 1959), p. 187.]

the later wars of 1756–1763, 1775–1783, and 1793–1815 (see Figure 2.1). Hume accepted as a fact of life the need for the state to be able to divert resources quickly from peace to war; but he believed this was best accomplished by building up in peacetime a surplus above minimum necessaries, to be taxed away in time of war, rather than by accumulating a bullion hoard.[24]

- Except for the bad harvest years 1728–1729, Britain was, throughout Hume's formative years, a net exporter of wheat and flour (see Figure 2.2). Phyllis Deane notes that in 1750 (the peak year for the century) England's grain export was equivalent to the subsistence requirements of roughly a quarter of the total population of England.[25] Up to mid-century the trend of grain prices was mildly downward. The interval 1720–1750, in particular, was one of cheap food, distinctly easier than preceding and following periods. It is not surprising, then, that there is little Malthusian anxiety in Hume and that he argued in his monograph, "Of the Populousness of Ancient Nations," that an abundant population was the reflection of a prosperous economy presided over by a "wise, just and mild government."[26] As nearly as we know, the population of England in the first half of the eighteenth century fluctuated about a relatively constant level, with an increase beginning perhaps in the 1740s.[27]

- Both physical output and foreign trade trended slowly but distinctly upward during this period, the latter at about twice the pace of the former.[28] The best measure we have of the rate of growth of output per head suggests that improvement was less than half of 1% per annum—perhaps higher than that (say, 0.7% per annum) for the period 1740–1760.[29] On the other hand, British observers of the economic scene were conscious that England enjoyed, relative to others, a high standard of living and that the period since the end of the War of Spanish Succession had seen economic progress along a broad front.

- Down to 1760 technological change was exceedingly slow. Ashton's dictum holds: "In the period 1700–60 Britain experienced no revolution, either in the technique of production, the structure of industry, or the economic and social life of the people."[30] A distinct surge in the 1760s came in the pace of invention, as in the

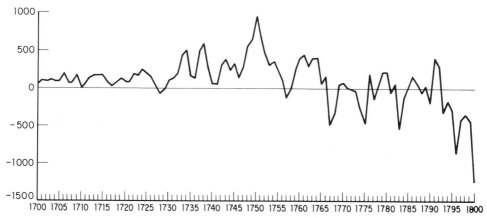

Figure 2.2. Net Exports of Wheat (Including Flour): Net Imports (−). [Adapted from T. S. Ashton, *Economic Fluctuations in England: 1700–1800* (Oxford: at the Clarendon Press, 1959), p. 183.]

now famous schoolboy's phrase, a "wave of gadgets swept over England."[31] The acceleration of major innovations comes in the 1780s.

It is possible, then to describe the English economy during the critical years of Hume's life as being well along in what I call the preconditions for takeoff but not yet in the final pre-takeoff phase, which begins in the 1760s, or in the takeoff that clearly begins in the 1780s. The emphasis on foreign trade in Hume (and Smith) is justified by its role in their time as the major dynamic force at work on the British economy.

Against this background, we turn to our standard array of questions designed to expose Hume's view of the dynamics of economic growth and to permit easy comparison with the views of others.

The Basic Growth Equation

Hume backs into the growth equation. He was contending against the view that a favorable balance of trade was of transcendent importance for a nation's political economy; that a low rate of interest was caused by the bullion surplus earned by a favorable trade balance; and that both at home and abroad the control over the use of resources should be regarded as a zero-sum game in which what one country gained another lost. With national interest thus at stake policy should, evidently, be determined by governments. Hume, like a good many of his contemporaries, was in revolt against this doctrine. He saw trade as a transaction of mutual advantage. In the domestic society he was in revolt against the doctrine that what the state required for its purposes could only be amassed at the expense of its citizens. His definitions of the true determinants of prosperity and the resources available to the state emerge, therefore, as a by-product of the policy debate. His central assertion was that real factors, rather than the acquisition of bullion through a favorable trade balance, determined a nation's prosperity; and that such prosperity, rather than a bullion hoard, was the only sure foundation for the security of the state. Hume's real factors emerge, tersely stated, in his famous peroration to the essay "Of the Balance of Trade:"[32] ". . . a government has great reason to preserve with care its people and its manufacturers. Its money, it may safely trust to the course of human affairs, without fear or jealousy. Or if it ever give attention to this latter circumstance, it ought only to be so far as it affects the former.'' But there was more to his growth equation than "people and manufactures.'' He linked manufactures and agriculture in a rather subtle way. It is the attractions of manufactured consumer goods that constitute the incentive for those in agriculture "to increase their skill and industry:"[33] "When a nation abounds in manufactures and mechanic arts, the proprietors of land, as well as the farmers, study agriculture as a science, and redouble their industry and attention."[34]

If Hume regarded the availability of manufactures as the necessary incentive for the exertion of proprietor and farmer alike (and the urban working force as well), what engine drove manufactures? His answer was:[35]

> Foreign trade, by its imports, furnishes materials for new manufactures; and by its exports, it produces labour in particular commodities, which could not be consumed at home. . . . If we consult history we shall find, that in most nations, foreign trade has preceded any refinement in home manufactures, and given birth to domestic luxury.

Like all men and, especially, women of his time, Hume was conscious of the quite extraordinary and, ultimately, revolutionary impact on Europe of the expansion, despite inhibitions, of Indian cotton textile imports, starting around 1670. The memorable contemporary description of the impact on French women of Indian calicoes early in the eighteenth century holds generally for Western Europe:[36] "Fruit défendu, les toiles deviennent la passion de toutes les filles d'Eve françaises.'' ("Forbidden fruit, cotton cloth became the passion of every French daughter of Eve.'') About half the people of France were said to have worn cottons at this time, and the evidence is that the passion did not abate until 1757, when the French government finally abandoned its rigorous but smuggling-ridden inhibitions on cotton imports. But there could be no more vivid or historically important illustration of Hume's doctrine. Foreign trade did yield an attractive luxury; the demonstration effect set in motion a "fermentation" in Western Europe (and a profit incentive) that finally resulted in the textile machinery required to manufacture the cotton yarn that European hands were too clumsy to produce by methods long used in India. There is a serious sense in which the British industrial revolution of the late eighteenth century was the first import-substitution takeoff.

In a more general passage, Hume describes the central creative function of the merchant in terms that embrace domestic as well as foreign trade:[37]

> But when men's industry encreases, and their views enlarge, it is found, that the most remote parts of the state can assist each other as well as the more contiguous, and that this intercourse of good offices may be carried on to the greatest extent and intricacy. Hence the origin of *merchants,* one of the most useful races of men, who serve as agents between those parts of the state, that are wholly unacquainted, and are ignorant of each other's necessities. Here are in a city fifty workmen in silk and linen, and a thousand customers; and these two ranks of men, so necessary to each other, can never rightly meet, till one man erects a shop, to which all the workmen and all the customers repair. In this province, grass rises in abundance: The inhabitants abound in cheese, and butter, and cattle; but want bread and corn, which, in a neighbouring province, are in too great abundance for the use of the inhabitants. One man

discovers this. He brings corn from the one province and returns with cattle; and supplying the wants of both, he is, so far, a common benefactor.

The dynamics of comparative advantage, at home as well as abroad, thus plays in Hume the role of virtually identical concepts in Adam Smith: the widening of the market and specialization of function.

Output in Hume's system, then, is a function of labor, land, and manufactures; the productivity of labor and land is determined by the scale of manufactures; and the scale of manufactures is determined by the scale of trade, foreign and domestic, and the productivity increases provided by the exploitation of comparative advantage. But, as always, Hume suffuses his argument with his particular view of the human motives that drive the economic variables. The productivity increases reflect the increased human effort induced, in the first instance, by the availability of a widened range of "luxuries" and, then, by the cumulative experience of merchant, worker, farmer, and manufacturer operating within a progressively more diversified economy, offering both heightened challenges and rewards that, in Hume's view, were the optimum setting within which men stretched their capacities to the limit and came to prefer frugality and gain to the immediacy of pleasure.

But what about capital in Hume's version of the basic equation? The most systematic references to savings and the supply of capital in Hume appear in his essay "Of Interest." There he argues that it is the general prosperity of a country, not the money supply, that yields low rates of interest; that rates of interest are a product of demand and supply; and in generating the necessary supply of savings, once again the merchant emerges as hero, this time as miser rather than that exploiter of comparative advantage:[38]

> There is no craving or demand of the human mind more constant and insatiable than that for exercise and employment; and this desire seems the foundation of most of our passions and pursuits. . . . But if the employment you give him be lucrative, especially if the profit be attached to every particular exertion of industry, he has gain so often in his eye, that he acquires, by degrees, a passion for it, and knows no such pleasure as that of seeing the daily encrease of his fortune.[39] And this is the reason why trade encreases frugality, and why, among merchants, there is the same overplus of misers above prodigals, as, among the possessors of land, there is the contrary.

In his observations on interest, Hume reflects the fact that a good deal of borrowing to be observed in his time was to sustain the accustomed levels of consumption of prodigal landlords. But Hume's writings also contain references to borrowing for productive purposes; e.g., to build a house.[40] And there is an important observation on the critical role of capital (and long leases) in rendering British agriculture profitable.[41] But it is fair to conclude that Hume's polemical purposes, combined with the essentially premodern economies that concerned him, yielded less concern with the investment process than is to be found in his successors. Hume's active, miserly merchants were clearly capable of generating their own resources for investment; and it was plowback investment by merchants to exploit comparative advantage that drove Hume's system along its expansionist track. That kind of investment Hume could take for granted, once "fermentation" was set in motion by an expansion of trade and the demonstration effect of "luxuries"—introduced primarily by foreign trade whose rapid expansion was evidently the most dynamic feature of the English (and Scottish) economy in the formative years of his life.

Thus Hume could concentrate on the contemporary debate that focused on the determinants of the rate of interest rather than on all the determinants of the rate of investment.

Population and the Working Force

As already noted, the comfortable population–food balance of Britain in the first half of the century yielded a rather complacent perspective on the contemporary state of population. This view flowed from his central proposition that population accommodated itself to the resources available for its support:[42]

> All our later improvements and refinements, have they done nothing towards the easy subsistence of men, and consequently towards their propagation and encrease? Our superior skill in mechanics; the discovery of new worlds, by which commerce has been so much enlarged; the establishment of posts; and the use of bills of exchange: These seem all extremely useful to the encouragement of art, industry, and populousness. Were we to strike off these, what a check should we give to every kind of business and labour, and what multitudes of families would immediately perish from want and hunger?

But, looking back at the population history of other societies in other times, Hume understood clearly the initial Malthusian insight; that is, the geometric potential of the human species (which Hume estimated could, if unrestrained, yield a doubling every generation) usually held in check by plague, slavery, war, infanticide, and other limits that "poverty and necessity" may impose.[43]

As for the quality of the working force, Hume begins by evoking the marginal life of the landless peasant in "rude unpolished nations, where the arts are neglected, all labour is bestowed on the cultivation of the ground. . . . [Vassals and tenants] are necessarily dependent, and fitted for slavery and subjection; especially where they possess no riches, and are not valued for their knowledge in agriculture, as must always be the case where the arts are neglected."[44] As in his general theory of growth, the low-level trap is broken by the demonstration effect of diversified consumers goods. "But where luxury nourishes commerce and industry, the peasants, by a proper cultivation of the land, become rich and independent; while the tradesmen and merchants acquire a share of the property, and draw authority and consideration to that middling rank of men, who are the best and firmest basis of public liberty."[45]

In short, Hume envisaged the emergence of higher productivity in the working force as a joint outcome of the motivation generated by the availability of "luxuries" and the practical experience of production in the diversified setting of a commercial, manufacturing, and sophisticated agricultural society.

Investment and Technology

If there are few references to investment in Hume, there are even fewer to machinery or technology. I believe it to be the case that Hume's only explicit reference to a particular technology is the following:[46] "Can we expect, that a government will be well modelled by a people, who know not how to make a spinning-wheel, or to employ a loom to advantage?" The index to Rotwein's valuable edition of Hume's economic writing reflects the matter well. There is no entry for investment; the entry for industry is: "See Art and Industry; Commerce." The entry for Art and Industry is: "See, Commerce, Luxury." The reason for this neglect is, again, the particular issues of policy that Hume addressed in his systematic attack on mercantilist doctrine. Investment was certainly a lower proportion of GNP than it was to become in the last two decades of the eighteenth century; probably under 5%.[47] Nevertheless, it is palpable that the kind of intensely commercial, premodern manufacturing, and reasonably high productivity agricultural society that England had achieved in the second quarter of the eighteenth century (and to which Scotland aspired) required a good deal of investment: for working capital in a quite rapidly expanding domestic and foreign trade; to build ships and docks, houses and shops; to meet requirements for depreciation and for modest expansion in manufactures and, above all, in agriculture. Although Britain was to become an increasingly import-dependent agricultural country in the second half of the eighteenth century, the vitality of its agricultural, as well as its commercial and industrial sectors was critical to its industrialization and, indeed, its victory over Napoleon. After all, something like 5% of GNP allocated to investment is not a trivial figure. As for Hume all one can usefully say is that, having disposed to his satisfaction of the mercantilist doctrine on the rate of interest, he was content to leave savings and investment in the hands of his passionately acquisitive and miserly merchants who would plow back their expanding profits. And he could assume that, in stimulating diversified manufactures by the exploitation of comparative advantage, the "mechanic arts" would flourish and even his normally prodigal proprietors of land would divert some of their surplus from consumption to investment and "study agriculture as a science, and redouble their industry and attention."

One fundamental and abiding proposition relating to technology was, however, enunciated by Hume with clarity: "necessity . . . is the great spur to industry and invention."[48]

Business Cycles

See pp. 41–42, below.

Relative Prices

Hume's history of England devotes a good deal of space to economic matters, including observations on price trends.[49] At several points Hume introduces what was later to become a major theme of classical economics, reemerging for two centuries at times when the relative prices of food and raw materials were high; that is, technical progress in manufactures tends to be more rapid than in agriculture. Therefore, he concluded, the prices of basic commodities relative to manufactures would rise over time. Here, for example, are two of Hume's observations on the course of events since the sixteenth century.[50]

> Labour and commodities have certainly risen since the discovery of the West-Indies; but not so much in every particular as is generally imagined. . . . [T]he additional art employed in the finer manufactures has even made some of these commodities fall below their former value. . . . The commodities whose price has chiefly risen, are butchers meat, fowl, and fish (especially the latter), which cannot be much augmented in quantity by the increase of art and industry.

> The arts of manufacture were much more advanced in other European
> countries than in England; and even in England these arts had made greater
> progress than the knowledge of agriculture; a profession which of all mechan-
> ical employments requires the most reflection and experience.

The trend of price and relative price movements over the period during which Hume's
basic concepts formed up were not calculated to stir significant controversy except,
perhaps, the role of low grain prices in stimulating the gin mania, which did not end
definitively until strong public policy measures were taken in 1751. After a period of
shortage and high prices toward the close of the War of Spanish Succession, the wheat
price fell and remained in a low range down to mid-century except for occasional bad
harvest years (Figure 2-2). Bread was cheap and spirits as well. The trend in wool prices
was also downward. Import prices (e.g., for sugar, tea, bar iron) fluctuated strongly with
phases of war and peace but were also generally lower at mid-century than in the first
decade. Hume discusses prices in his economic essays primarily in short-run terms related
to his exposition of the quantity theory of money, including his application of it to forces
making for equilibrium in foreign trade—a theme that still earns Hume an honored place
in elementary economics textbooks.

The Stages of and Limits to Growth

Early in the first of Hume's economic essays (''Of Commerce'') there is a brief, rather
conventional reference to historical stages of economic growth, as well as a faint anticipation of Colin Clark *et al.* on the shift in the distribution of the working force as growth
proceeds.[51]

> The bulk of every state may be divided into husbandmen and manufactur-
> ers. . . . As soon as men quit their savage state, where they live chiefly by
> hunting and fishing, they must fall into these two classes; though the arts of
> agriculture employ at first the most numerous parts of society. Time and
> experience improve so much these arts, that the land may easily maintain a
> much greater number of men, than those who are immediately employed in its
> culture, or who furnish the more necessary manufactures to such as are so
> employed.

But Hume's interest was not in elaborating historical stages of growth. His interest lay
in a vital contemporary, cross-sectional problem stemming from differences in stages of
growth. Indeed, the most striking aspect of Hume's economic writing is his treatment of
the ''rich country–poor country'' problem; that is, the dynamics of countries or regions at
different phases of growth in an era before the first takeoff had occurred or, to use
Kuznets's vocabulary, before modern economic growth began in Great Britain.[52] Hume's
treatment of the rich country–poor country problem, before major technological innovation had become a more or less regular flow, led directly to his contemplation of the limits
to growth.

Three circumstances made this subject a matter of absorbing interest in the eighteenth
century.[53]

First, the voyages of discovery and the founding of colonies in America and Asia had
acquainted thoughtful Europeans with a new, widened array of societies for comparative
analysis and posed a fresh set of questions to be addressed to the societies of contemporary

Europe and, retrospectively, of the classical world. All of this was intellectually exciting at a time when men were consciously reaching for new ways of looking at the human and social condition.

Second, the wide spectrum of societies available for examination posed a dynamic question as well as a field for comparative static analysis. Would the richer countries, applying more sophisticated technologies and more complex patterns of specialization and trade, be able to hold their lead; or would the poor countries with lower money wages catch up with them in time? The question related to both recent history and critical contemporary problems: the dramatic economic decline of Spain in the seventeenth century and the equally dramatic rise of the Dutch Republic; the relative rise of Britain and France in the eighteenth century *vis-à-vis* the Dutch Republic; the protracted struggle in which Britain and France were locked; the dramatic differences between the British colonies in North America and the Iberian colonies to the south. How one judged the relative prospects of the currently rich and poor societies raised issues over a wide range of domestic as well as foreign economic policy, including policy toward colonies. Above all, it raised the issue of whether it was the interest of a richer nation to frustrate, if it could, the rise of poor nations; was it a matter of indifference; or was it a positive interest of the rich nations to encourage the development of the poor?

Third, there was a narrower but even more sharply focused question: What would be the fate of Scotland, locked since 1707 into a common market with an econo.. ically more advanced England?

Neither Hume nor Smith was a parochial Scotsman. They were both men of the essentially international world of ideas, comfortable in Paris and London as well as Glasgow and Edinburgh. They drew on direct observation as well as reading over a wide front. But they were no doubt also influenced, to a degree, by the course of the economy of Scotland in the period when their major concepts took shape.

In dealing with this linkage, we are fortunate to have a recent, directly relevant essay: T. C. Smout's "Where Had the Scottish Economy Got to by the Third Quarter of the Eighteenth Century?"[54] Table 2.1 summarizes the statistical data available on the Scottish economy for five year intervals covering the period 1750–1754 to 1770–1774.

Since I am suggesting that Hume's and Smith's ideas may have crystallized by, say, 1750, it is helpful that Smout also provided a broad sketch of how the Scottish economy had evolved since the Act of Union of 1707.

It is useful to begin by noting a persistent characteristic of the Scottish economy in the early eighteenth century that leaves its mark on Hume's and Smith's view of the food–population problem. Except for years of extremely bad harvests when famine was posble—which occurred as late as the 1690s—Scotland was a food surplus region with difficulty in finding export markets. Unmarketable agricultural surplus, rather than chronic dearth, was part of the local background out of which Hume and Smith emerged.

Down to mid-century, three positive elements in Scottish economic development can be observed: progress in administration, expanded transport facilities, and modest improvements in agricultural productivity converged to end the danger of famine in bad harvest years; Glasgow became a vital center for the tobacco trade, which expanded strongly from the 1730s until the American War of Independence with spreading effects in the whole west-central region more substantial than earlier analyses had suggested; and the important rural handicraft linen industry entered a 20-year period of modest expansion in the mid-1740s.

From that time, in fact, the pace of progress quickens over a wide front. The rate of

Table 2.1. Scottish Economic Data, 1750–1774
(by quinquennia, index numbers 1755–1759 = 100)

Prices	1750–4	1755–9	1760–4	1765–9	1770–4
1 East Lothian oats	99	100	104	124	130
2 Lanark oatmeal	100	100	101	131	133
3 Perth oatmeal	93	100	105	127	143
4 Kintyre bullocks	135	100	103	151	146
5 Kintyre cows	133	100	100	133	143
Wages					
6 Midlothian day labourer (money)	88	100		125	
7 Midlothian day labourer (oatmeal equivalent)	95	100		101	
Taxes					
8 Yield of 'old duty' on beer	103	100	101	81	71
9 Yield of 'old duty' on malt	118	100	103	94	92
Industrial production					
10 Paper	71	100	163	228	271
11 Linen (volume)	89	100	126	134	129
12 Linen (value)	100	100	133	158	140
13 Flax imports	—	100	131	161	164
Trade (official values)					
14 Home-produced exports	—	100	119	121	142
15 Tobacco imports	—	100	158	182	253
16 Other imports	—	100	133	185	200
Agricultural change					
17 Land surveyors	75	100	134	168	235

Source: T. C. Smout, Chapter 2 in Istvan Hont and Michael Ignatieff (eds.), *Wealth and Virtue, The Shaping of Political Economy in the Scottish Enlightenment,* p. 53, where original sources are given. Smout also supplies (p. 52) the absolute data, rather than index numbers.

population increase, probably negligible in the first half of the century, averages .5% per annum between 1755 and 1775, with the population of Scotland's five large towns rising by 30%; cattle exports to England increase by 50% between 1740 and 1770; and, in a remarkable surge, bank assets increase almost tenfold between 1744 and 1772, the note issue, 16-fold. As Table 2.1 demonstrates, agricultural prices rise, the increase in industrial production and foreign trade accelerates, and real wages just about hold their own. The markedly increased activity of land surveyors suggests a phase of agricultural prosperity validated by nonstatistical evidence.

Smout concludes:[55] "By 1800 . . . Scotland . . . had . . . reached the stage of take-off. But that position had not been reached in Scotland in the quarter-century prior to the publication of the *Wealth of Nations.*" The economy of Scotland, like England's, was in an active stage of preconditions for takeoff in the period when Hume's and Smith's ideas were formed and elaborated; but not as far forward as England in that wide-ranging dynamic process.

It is quite natural, then, that Hume, living in an economy that was moving forward vigorously from, say, the second half of the 1740s, but which was clearly lagging its more advanced and much larger neighbor, should have been drawn to speculate on how the relations between dynamic richer and poorer countries would evolve with the passage of time. But, again, it should be underlined that Hume and Smith were in no sense tightly bound by the Scottish experience.

In fact, Hume's analysis of the rich country–poor country problem can only be understood in a larger context: as part of his systematic contention against three doctrines of his time—a contention we have already observed. In that sense his analysis of the rich country–poor country problem constitutes a kind of synthesis of his theory of economic growth.

The three doctrines that Hume challenged were these:

- That virtue in societies was associated with austerity, if not poverty; luxury and wealth, with corruption and decay.[56]
- That an influx of bullion, derived from a favorable trade balance would assure the strength and trading advantage of a rich country.
- That the economic rise of poor countries could only be at the expense of rich countries.

Hume's response can be summarized as follows:

1. Wealth is the friend of virtue. The process of developing ''luxuries,'' requiring the systematic exploitation of comparative advantage, is central to economic growth; and economic growth and prosperity are fundamental to the security of the state, a civilized social life, political liberty, and, above all, to the creative fulfillment of individual talents and of other legitimate sources of human satisfaction.
2. The demonstration of the possibility of economic growth sets in motion both within societies and among them a ''fermentation'' that yields similar efforts to cultivate commerce, industry, and refinements in the mechanical arts.
3. In particular, poor nations have the capacity to catch up with the rich nations because they enjoy, in their period of transition, the advantage of lower money wages as well as a backlog of hitherto unapplied technology.

But what of the fate of rich nations in the face of the rise to riches of the poor? Before the debate was finished, Hume would produce several answers, but here is the most fundamental, building up to what was, at a time of chronic mercantilist confrontation between Britain and France, a rather dramatic climax:[57]

> It ought . . . to be considered, that, by the encrease of industry among the neighbouring nations, the consumption of every particular species of commodity is also encreased; and though foreign manufactures interfere with them in the market, the demand for their product may still continue, or even encrease. And should it diminish, ought the consequence to be esteemed so fatal? If the spirit of industry be preserved, it may easily be diverted from one branch to another; and the manufacturers of wool, for instance, be employed in linen, silk, iron, or any other commodities, for which there appears to be a demand. We need not apprehend, that all the objects of industry will be exhausted, or that our manufactures, while they remain on an equal footing with those of our neighbours, will be in danger of wanting employment. The emulation among rival nations serves rather to keep industry alive in all of

them. And any people is happier who possess a variety of manufactures, than
if they enjoyed one single great manufacture, in which they are all employed.
Their situation is less precarious; and they will feel less sensibly those revolutions and uncertanties, to which every particular branch of commerce will
always be exposed. . . . I shall therefore venture to acknowledge, that, not
only as a man but as a British subject, I pray for the flourishing commerce of
Germany, Spain, Italy and even France itself. I am at least certain, that Great
Britain, and all those nations, would flourish more, did their sovereigns and
ministers adopt such enlarged and benevolent sentiments towards each other.

But Hume's full treatment of the problem did not conclude on so unambiguously
confident a note. His further discussion of the catching-up process included some observations that plunged him into controversy; for he was too good a historian not to note
that prosperity of countries and regions could prove transitory:[58] "Manufactures . . . gradually shift their places, leaving those countries and provinces which they
have already enriched, and flying to others, whither they are allured by the cheapness of
provisions and labour; till they have enriched there also, and are again banished by the
same causes.''

When challenged on this apparently gloomy prospect for the rich, by two able contemporaries (James Oswald and Josiah Tucker), Hume argued that what he had in mind was a
division of manufacturing according to comparative advantage; that is, the rich would
concentrate on production of capital- and skill-intensive manufactures; up-and-coming
countries and provinces would concentrate on simpler and more labor-intensive manufactures.[59] As Tucker perceived, Hume's clarification left dangling the question of whether
this division of effort would persist; or whether relative wages and prices would move to
equality between a rich and formerly poor country when the "fermentation" had yielded a
full exploitation of comparative advantage. And in a phrase in a letter of 1758 to Lord
Kames, Hume does, indeed, indicate that poorer nations would be expected to move on
from "coarser" manufactures to the "more elaborate" with the passage of time.[60]

In fact, Hume did not rule out the possibility that the dynamics of the rich country–poor
country problem might in time yield a decline in foreign trade:[61] ". . . a nation may lose
most of its foreign trade, and yet continue a great a powerful people. If strangers will not
take any particular commodity of ours, we must cease to labour in it. The same hands will
turn themselves towards some refinement in other commodities, which may be wanted at
home." Here Hume has China explicitly in mind; but an implication of his argument
might be that there could be circumstances when tariff protection might be justified. The
bulk of Hume's analysis, however, envisages an expansionist, liberal trade policy.

The debate on these issues also generated a modification of Hume's well-known specie
flow–price level hypothesis. His central argument was that an inflow of bullion derived
from a favorable trade balance would correct itself. It would raise the price level but not
output, since the latter was determined by the real factors at work, and full employment of
those resources was implicitly assumed; the rise in prices would inhibit exports, encourage imports; and the trade balance would shift unfavorably. Hume acknowledged, however, a kind of Keynesian transitional exception:[62]

[S]ome time is required before the money circulates through the whole state,
and makes its effect be felt on all ranks of people. At first, no alteration is
perceived; by degrees the price rises, first of one commodity then another; till
the whole at least reaches a just proportion with the new quantity of specie

which is in the kingdom. In my opinion, it is only in this interval or intermediate situation, between the acquisition of money and rise of prices, that the encreasing quantity of gold and silver is favourable to industry.

Hume's view appears, then, to have been this. Latent in a system of primitive, low productivity agricultural economies there lay the potentiality for much higher levels of real incomes for all, if the potentialities of comparative advantage were exploited by domestic and foreign commerce. In a sense, Hume came to appreciate that substantial idle capacity existed within such a system. The process of bringing this idle capacity into play could be set in motion by the example of one or more countries that had been stirred, probably by foreign trade, into demonstrating the attractive products the latent potentialities of the system might yield and how they could be exploited. The engines of exploitation were the three human "causes of labour" which were strengthened both by the initial demonstration effect of the "luxuries" introduced into the system and the stimulus provided by the challenges and rewards involved in closing the gap itself. Hume's was thus a truly dynamic, psychological theory of economic growth. Production under conditions where comparative advantage was being exploited increased human skills, the arts of manufacture, and the capital stock. An expansion in the money supply might have an ancillary, transitional real effect.

But a flow of major technological innovations does not appear in Hume's system; for it had not yet happened. He did not, therefore, believe in unlimited growth. His final dictum on the limits to growth, within the technological possibilities he could perceive, clearly acknowledged that a limit did exist:[63] "The growth of everything, both in arts and nature, at last checks itself." But one gets the impression that Hume was not much interested in driving this argument about the long-run future of the various economies of the world to a dogmatic conclusion. As a historian and philosopher, he understood well the complexity and impenetrability of the forces that would determine the ultimate outcome in a world subject to endless change. And besides, he was conscious that one could project man's fate only on the basis of an inadequate few thousand years of recorded history. The opening passage in "Of the Populousness of Ancient Nations" probably reflects most accurately his net judgment:[64]

> There is very little ground either from reason or observation to conclude the world eternal or incorruptible. The continual and rapid motion of matter, the violent revolutions with which every part is agitated, the changes remarked in the heavens, the plain traces as well as tradition of an universal deluge, or in general confusion of the elements; all these prove strongly the mortality of this fabric of the world, and its passage, by corruption or disolution, from one state or order to another.

But this mild, long-run philosophic pessimism about the staying power of greatness in a single country does not capture Hume's inherently cheerful and activist temper. He was primarily concerned to use his qualities of mind and character to move the world and time of which he was a part toward more civilized policies; and this he did.

Noneconomic Factors

It is appropriate that Part I of this book begins with David Hume and ends with Karl Marx. Of all the classical economists, these two insisted most strongly on embedding economics in the study of the dynamics of whole societies as they moved through history. Moreover, both saw economic growth as a powerful agent in social, political, and cultural change. On the other hand, their views of human beings and their motivations, of the optimum organization of societies and their economies, differ about as radically as is possible for social scientists of the same culture. In part, those differences reflect the century's revolutionary change that separates their formative years. But, at bottom, it is Hume's view of human beings in society that most sharply separates him from Marx.

From beginning to end, Hume saw human beings as complex units trying to find satisfying balances among contradictory impulses. Societies—their political, social, and economic organization and their culture—determined the choices open to men in express-ing their impulses; but, in a dynamic process, societies were themselves shaped by the choices men made earlier among the options they then perceived to be open.

In this way of proceeding to study the dynamics of man in society, Hume was directly in the line from Plato to Freud.[65] Plato analyzed the problem of balancing the "spirited" side of man, "appetite" and "reason"; and he linked psychology and politics by defining these three powerful contending forces as "the state within us." The roughly analogous human elements for Freud were, of course, the id, ego, and superego, which become societal variables in his *Civilization and Its Discontents*.

What were the equivalent primal impulses identified by Hume? It will be recalled that he defined the "causes of labour" as "action, pleasure, and indolence." As developed by Hume, the satisfactions generated by "action" can be broadly linked to Plato's spirited side of man and Freud's id. In Hume's sense, "action" constitutes the exercise of physical, mental, or artistic talent in a setting of challenge, for some practical purpose. Hume's wide-ranging definition of "pleasure" surely parallels Plato's appetite and Freud's ego. "Indolence" emerges not as a positive cause of labor but a requirement of respite from the pursuit of action or pleasure.

What, then, of reason and the superego, the balance wheels that lead man to discipline his energies and ambitions, passions and appetites to the requirements of organized social life? The nearest equivalent in Hume is his concept of "sympathy" that links the indi-vidual to his fellow men and women and heightens the virtues required for a good society. This is how Rotwein describes Hume's linkage:[66]

> As the vehicle for the growth of a sense of morality it [sympathy] would appear to be operative in a twofold fashion. Most generally . . . the evocation of a benevolent response to others depends in a large measure on the vivacity of our perception of their emotions. . . . Most fundamentally, then, the en-couragement given to "humanity" by the development of a more closely knit society may be traced to its influence in a widening basis for the association of "self" with others. . . . Also, as Hume recognizes, we "sympathise with others in the sentiments they entertain of us." Thus, nourished by a growing concern over our reputation in society, "this constant habit of surveying ourselves, as it were in reflection, keeps alive all the sentiments of right and wrong, and begets, in noble natures a certain reverence for themselves as well as others, which is the surest guardian of every virtue."

If we assume—as we should—that, in seeking to evoke the basic components of human motivation, Plato, Hume, and Freud are, at their best, not scientists but evocative philosopher-poets, "sympathy" does bear a family relation to the healing and stabilizing role of Plato's "reason" and Freud's "superego." It is meant to capture the process by which human beings internalize the values necessary for societies to operate in a reasonably civilized way.

Hume's view of human nature, however, was not simple or mechanical. In Rotwein's good summation, Hume's "analysis conveys an appreciation of the ineffable density of human behavior and an understanding of the opposing forces on which it rests."[67] More vividly than Adam Smith, Hume perceived the interaction among the irreducible elements of human nature he could discern; the complexities embedded in the concepts he defined, and even the wild card of inexplicable irrationality that often characterized human behavior.

Nevertheless, from this matrix of competing, interacting, often contradictory human impulses, Hume fashioned a quite straightforward operational economic doctrine. The expansion and diversification of manufactures and the increase in agricultural productivity brought about by the expansion of commerce and the exploitation of comparative advantage not only enriches private life, by expanding the range of choices open for the pursuit of action and pleasure, but also has wide-ranging, benign social consequences for the noneconomic dimensions of society, including provision of the foundation for free democratic government.[68]

In short, Hume's analysis of the economic process and his prescriptions for policy are simply part of his vision of the good life for individuals and societies; he saw economic change as fundamental to social and political change; but he also saw economic change as dependent rather more on noneconomic than economic human motives.

A final word is appropriate about Hume the man because there was a clear linkage between his personality and his view of the human condition. He was famous in his time, much observed, written about then and subsequently. We have his own terse autobiography and Adam Smith's moving account of Hume's final days.[69] In what he called his own "funeral oration," Hume described himself as "a man of mild dispositions, of command of temper, of an open, social, and cheerful humour, capable of attachment, but little susceptible of enmity, and of great moderation in all of my passions. Even my love of literary fame, my ruling passion, never soured my temper, notwithstanding my frequent disappointments." The testimony of his contemporaries and the researches of biographers do not significantly alter this self-portrait; although there is, no doubt, something stylized and studied in *le bon David* which emerges.[70]

This personality—wise and balanced, ironic, sceptical, but committed to the cause of humanity—contributed to the breadth of vision that made his essays "The Cradle of Political Economy" and led one of Adam Smith's biographers to conclude: ". . . but for Hume, Smith could never have been."[71]

Adam Smith (1723–1790)

Like his older friend David Hume, Adam Smith spent his professional life formulating and articulating the natural laws governing people in society. His teaching and writing embrace not only psychology and philosophy, politics and economics, sociology, law, and history, but astronomy and even poetry, the theater, and other branches of culture. Smith's *Theory of Moral Sentiments* and *Wealth of Nations* were, in Bagehot's words, "a fragment of the immense design of showing the origin and development of cultivation and law; or, as we may perhaps put it, not inappropriately, of saying how, from being a savage, man rose to be a Scotchman.''[72] The design was never completed; but the framework of Smith's approach to economics was no less than the dynamics of human beings as social animals.

In his *Theory of Moral Sentiments* (1759) Smith, like Hume, recognizes that humans may be stirred to increased economic effort by the attraction of consumers goods beyond the bare necessities.[73] Hume regarded such luxuries tolerantly, not only as a stimulant but as softening the harshness of life; but Smith viewed these ''trifling conveniences'' as ''in the highest degree contemptible.''[74] Nevertheless, the willingness of humans to pursue these illusory satisfactions was an essential element in the workings of ''an invisible hand'' that, as Hollander points out, appears first in his *Theory of Moral Sentiments,* 17 years before *The Wealth of Nations.*[75] And, in general, Adam Smith's view of the human race, including men of commerce and manufacturing, let alone profligate landowning country gentlemen and Oxford dons, was often not flattering. There is a strand of almost Restoration good cheer in Hume's perspective on the human condition notably lacking in the complex, ambivalent perspective of his dour younger friend. Nevertheless, when Smith turned to economics, the individual appeared as a somewhat simpler character than Hume's central figure who found Aristotelian happiness in the full exercise of his powers in a setting that combined challenge with potentially useful results. There is considerable justice in the observation of an anonymous wit that Smith thought ''there was a Scotchman inside every man.''[76] For mainstream modern economists, Smith's economic man, unconsciously doing public good by doggedly pursuing private advantage, is, on the whole, a comfortable and familiar character.

But that image is too comfortable and too familiar; for Adam Smith's view of human motivation was much more complex than is often credited. His *Theory of Moral Sentiments* opens with the following not sufficiently quoted sentence: ''How selfish soever man may be supposed, there are evidently some principles in his nature, which interest him in the fortune of others, and render their happiness necessary to him, though he derives nothing from it, except the pleasure of seeing it.''

The Wealth of Nations is more nearly a conventional treatise than Hume's selective, brief tracts for the times; and it is almost ten times the size of Hume's collected economic essays. *The Wealth of Nations* does not march forward with quite the well-honed mainstream logic of a modern economics textbook. There are many passages of illustration from history and the contemporary scene that would now be widely regarded as diversionary. But it's all there. Smith's theory of economic growth, for example, lends itself quite easily to mathematical formulation in the modern style; and a good many have tried their hand.[77] And, as shall emerge, Smith had something to say about almost every variable on our standard checklist.

Smith was 12 years younger than Hume; but Britain's economic setting in his formative years did not differ significantly from that of his great friend and predecessor. Specifically, by 1753, when Smith was 30 years old, Britain was still a net grain exporter and operating its lively commercial and proto-industrial economy with premodern technology. On the other hand, Smith lived until 1790, and the fifth and final edition of *The Wealth of Nations* was published in the previous year. It contains virtually nothing to suggest an awareness of the three great economic developments since mid-century: the gathering pressure of population increase on the food supply, yielding a rise in grain prices and an erratic shift of England from a net grain export to a net grain import position; marked acceleration of inventive activity from 1760 forward; and the coming on stage in the 1780s of three major innovations that virtually define the first Industrial Revolution: machine and factory manufactured cotton textiles; Watt's more effective steam engine; and Cort's method for fabricating iron with coke.[78]

The Basic Growth Equation

In Hume's version of the basic growth equation, capital formation (saving-investment) appears virtually as a by-product of the expansion of trade and the plowback of the creative but miserly merchant's profits. In Smith, labor, land, and capital are unambiguously the three factors of production; but the system is driven forward, as in Hume, by the savings of the frugal, who are assumed to invest all savings, without leakage. Leakage, as we shall see, occurs when the rich and government indulge in expenditures that employ "unproductive" labor. In Hume, capital made possible the exploitation of regional or international relative advantage; in Smith, capital permits the widening of the market and, thereby, the division of labor. Capital is mainly envisaged as working capital supplying labor with necessaries, raw materials, and simple tools. "Machines" appear somewhat more explicitly in Smith than in Hume, but they come to much the same thing as Hume's "mechanic arts." In explaining how the division of labor increases productivity, Smith identifies three forces:[79] the worker's increase in dexterity; the saving of the worker's time as he concentrates on a single task rather than moves from one task to another; and "the invention of a great number of machines which facilitate and abridge labour, and enable one man to do the work of many." These significant refinements of familiar technologies he distinguishes from occasional, rare major technological breakthroughs—an important distinction to the best of my knowledge not to be found earlier in the literature of economics.

Smith's self-reinforcing growth process—in which increased capital investment permits the expansion of the market which, in turn, generates increased profits and further investment—does not proceed indefinitely. A limit is set by a nation's "soil and climate, and its situation with respect to other countries" as well as by its "laws and institutions." This statement would appear to imply diminishing returns to agriculture and to efforts to expand markets by geographic extension.

We shall explore the components of Smith's version of the basic equation in greater detail below. Here, we simply note that, in its framework, it is quite familiar and, in a sense, modern, although it is applied to a society with premodern technology in both agriculture and manufacturing. Productivity increases mainly via an incremental refinement of old, familiar technologies to exploit the potentialities of widened markets and specialization rather than via the successive introduction of major innovations creating new industries or radically altering methods of production in old industries. From the 1780s, innovation altered in both character and scale. Smith's concept of mainly incremental technological change, brought about by inventive craftsmen in the workshop, could no longer suffice; although it was so convenient that some economists clung to it for two centuries. After the 1780s Smith's occasional major inventions became an uneven flow of changing composition; but this phenomenon, yielding endless disequilibrium, was so inconvenient for post-1870 mainstream economists that they have still not found a credible way to deal with it.

Table 2.2. Great Britain: Trade in Wheat, 1750–1789

	Net exports (including flour) annual average	Net imports (−) (in thousand quarters)
1750–1759	312	
1760–1769	136	
1770–1779		−43
1780–1789		−23

SOURCE: T. S. Ashton, *Economic Fluctuations in England 1700–1800* (Oxford: at the Clarendon Press, 1959), p. 183.

Population and the Working Force

Like Hume, Smith reflects no special anxiety about the population-food balance in Britain; although the trend of the wheat price (Table 3.1) and net wheat and flour exports and imports (Table 2.2) clearly justified some attention in the 4 decades before his death in 1790.[80] The average figure for the 1790s was net imports of 198,000 quarters (the British imperial quarter equaled 8 bushels), and the setting was ripe for the first edition, at least, of Malthus on population.

Smith's population doctrine is more explicit than, if quite consistent with, Hume's; and it exhibits some subtle features.[81] It can be summarized as follows:

1. Population size is determined by the availability of means of subsistence.
2. The rate of change of population is determined by the difference between the market and the subsistence wage rate. If the difference is positive, population will increase; negative, decrease; equal, population will be constant.
3. The market wage rate is a function of the rate of increase in the demand for labor, which, in turn, depends on the rate of increase in the capital stock that determines the pace at which the market widens, specialization of function proceeds, and the national wealth increases.
4. A period of rapid increase in capital formation and growth could thus, via high money wages relative to the subsistence wage, set in motion (through early marriages and falling infant mortality) a rise in population and the working force that would, in time, tend to bring down the market wage rate.

Thus Smith's famous conclusion:[82]

> It is not the actual greatness of national wealth, but its continual increase, which occasions a rise in the wages of labour. It is not, accordingly, in the richest countries, but in the most thriving, or in those which are growing rich the fastest, that the wages of labour are highest. England is certainly, in the present times, a much richer country than any part of North America. The wages of labour, however, are much higher in North America than in any part of England.
>
>   . . . it is in the progressive state, while the society is advancing to the further acquisition, rather than when it has acquired its full complement of riches, that the condition of the labouring poor, of the great body of the

people, seem to be the happiest and the most comfortable. It is hard in the stationary, and miserable in the declining state. The progressive state is in reality the cheerful and the hearty state to all the different orders of the society. The stationary is dull; the declining melancholy.

In Smith's judgment, the American colonies were in a progressive state; relatively rich China, stationary; Bengal, declining.

Smith also had a good deal to say about high and low wages, relative to the subsistence level, the quality of the work force, and the effective effort put forward by the worker. His observations were not always consistent. In his *Lectures,* for example, Smith evoked vividly the costs of specialization of function (on which Marx was to build), including a backward sloping supply curve for labor:[83]

> When the greater part of people are merchants, they always bring probity and punctuality into fashion, and these, therefore, are the principal virtues of a commercial nation.
>
> There are some inconveniences, however, arising from a commercial spirit. The first we shall mention is that it confines the views of men. Where the division of labour is brought to perfection, every man has only a simple operation to perform; to this his whole attention is confined, and few ideas pass in his mind but what have an immediate connexion with it. . . . It is remarkable that in every commercial nation the low people are exceedingly stupid. The Dutch vulgar are eminently so, and the English are more so than the Scotch. The rule is general; in towns they are not so intelligent as in the country, nor in a rich country as in a poor one.
>
> Another inconvenience attending commerce is that education is greatly neglected. In rich and commercial nations the division of labour, having reduced all trades to very simple operations, affords an opportunity of employing children very young. . . . But, besides this want of education, there is another great loss which attends the putting boys too soon to work. . . . When he is grown up he has no ideas with which he can amuse himself. . . . Their work through half the week is sufficient to maintain them, and through want of education they have no amusement for the other, but riot and debauchery.

In *The Wealth of Nations* Smith's view of the impact of progress on "the common people" is, on balance, more positive, although there are still echoes of the backward sloping supply curve as representing the minority response to a rise in wages.[84] "The liberal reward of labour, as it encourages the propagation, so it increases the industry of the common people. . . . Some workmen, indeed, when they can earn in four days what will maintain them through the week, will be idle the other three. This however, is by no means the case with the greater part."

One of the most interesting anticipatory strands in Adam Smith's view of the economic development process is his emphasis on the importance of education not merely for the working force but also for "people of some rank and fortune." The latter observations clearly reflect Smith's dissatisfactions with his 6 years at Oxford (1740–1746), and his view that the university then grossly failed to train the youth for a productive role in English society. Smith strongly urged that, at public expense, there be established "in every parish or district a little school, where children may be taught for a reward so moderate, that even a common labourer may afford it. . . ."[85] His emphasis on the need for popular education, generously financed, was linked to his sense that government should take pains to prevent the degenerative and alienating consequences of the division of labor.[86]

A further and fundamental aspect of Smith's treatment of the working force is his distinction between productive and unproductive labor. The distinction was familiar from the work of the physiocrats who viewed only labor employed in agriculture as productive. Smith widened the concept out to embrace all "labour which adds to the value of the subject upon which it is bestowed. . . . It is, as it were, a certain quantity of labour stocked and stored up to be employed, if necessary, upon some other occasion."[87] Menial servants are Smith's prime example of unproductive labor, but there are others as well:[88]

> The sovereign, for example, with all the officers both of justice and war who serve under him, the whole army and navy, are unproductive labourers. They are the servants of the public, and are maintained by a part of the annual produce of the industry of other people. Their service, how honourable, how useful, or how necessary soever, produces nothing for which an equal quantity of service can afterwards be procured.

From this passage Smith moves directly into his formulation of what came later to be narrowed down to a corn growth model in which the rate of growth in a given year is determined by the supply of corn left over from the previous year allocated as working capital, to sustain productive labor and provide seeds for next year's output.[89]

> Both productive and unproductive labourers, and those who do not labour at all, are all equally maintained by the annual produce of the land and labour of the country. This produce, how great soever, can never be infinite, but must have certain limits. According, therefore, as a smaller or greater proportion of it is in any one year employed in maintaining unproductive hands, the more in the one case and the less in the other will remain for the productive, and the next year's produce will be greater or smaller accordingly; the whole annual produce, if we except the spontaneous productions of the earth, being the effect of productive labour.

Smith plainly understood that servants and kings all commanded a market price for their services and were, in some sense, "useful." As a development economist (rather than an equilibrium market economist) whose model was driven by the rate of savings-investment, Smith palpably resented the diversion of potential investment resources allocated to "unproductive" services. But he was quite capable of stating his doctrine with cool professional lucidity:[90]

> The annual produce of the land and labour of any nation can be increased in its value by no other means, but by increasing either the number of its productive labourers, or the productive powers of those labourers who had before been employed. The number of its productive labourers, it is evident, can never be much increased, but in consequence of an increase of capital, or of the funds destined for maintaining them. The productive powers of the same number of labourers cannot be increased, but in consequence either of some addition and improvement to those machines and instruments which

facilitate and abridge labour; or of a more proper division and distribution of employment. In either case an additional capital is almost always required.

Investment and Technology

The process of capital investment thus plays a central role in Adam Smith's scheme of things as it is bound to do in any serious theory of economic growth. But, unlike Hume, Smith devotes a great deal of space and care to the elaboration of his doctrine: "Of the Nature, Accumulation, and Employment of Stock" (Book II, about 100 pages) as well as "Of the Profits of Stock" (dealt with in Chapters IX and X of Book I).

Like the rest of *The Wealth of Nations,* Smith's exposition of capital investment "has its errors, its gaps, its ambiguities and its bias."[91] And these have led to criticisms, differences of interpretation, and elaborate exigeses. But his essential argument is reasonably clear and can be summarized in three fairly complex propositions.

1. *All savings are invested;* the motive for savings is profit, taking account of risk; savings will rise with the level of income.
2. *Enlarged investment is the basis for growth* because it is required for (a) enlarging the market; (b) equipping labor to perform increasingly specialized functions; and (c) increasing wages above subsistence necessary to induce the population increase, which will increase effective demand and the scale of the market while also generating the labor necessary to supply the needs of the expanded market. Because savings-investment rises with the increase in income, a cumulative process is set in motion by an initial rise in the investment rate.
3. *However, the benign upward spiral is constrained.* The rate of profit will decline as capital accumulates, income rises, and an economy approaches its "full complement of riches"; but the potentialities for increases in productivity are greater in manufactures than in the primary production sectors.[92] "It is the natural effect of improvement . . . to diminish gradually the real price of almost all manufactures." Investment will continue so long as the profit rate (including the risk premium) exceeds the minimum rate necessary to induce men to save.

Smith's theory of investment is closely linked to his distinction between productive and unproductive labor, thus inducing much aggravated prose among later commentators. But what Smith had in mind—who the heroes and villains were—is quite clear:[93]

> What is annually saved is as regularly consumed as what is annually spent, and nearly in the same time too; but it is consumed by a different set of people. That portion of his revenue which a rich man annually spends, is in most cases consumed by idle guests, and menial servants, who leave nothing behind them in return for their consumption. That portion which he annually saves is immediately employed as a capital, is consumed in the same manner, and nearly in the same time too, but by a different set of people, by labourers, manufacturers, and artificers, who re-produce with a profit the value of their annual consumption. . . .
>
> The prodigal perverts it in this manner. By not confining his expense within his income, he encroaches upon his capital. . . .
>
> This expence . . . not being in foreign goods, and not occasioning any

exportation of gold and silver, the same quantity of money would remain in the country as before. But if the quantity of food and clothing, which were thus consumed by unproductive, had been distributed among productive hands, they would have re-produced, together with a profit, the full value of their consumption. The same quantity of money would in this case equally have remained in the country, and there would besides have been a reproduction of an equal value of consumable goods. There would have been two values instead of one.

There is a kind of multiplier built into Smith's view of the process induced by parsimony-savings-investment; but there is no accelerator at work to enlarge investment if profligate, unproductive expenditures increase, even if there is no leakage via imports.

With respect to consumption expenditures, as well, Smith makes a sharp distinction between the virtue of outlays on durable versus nondurable consumers goods.[94]

> As the one mode of expence is more favourable than the other to the opulence of an individual, so is it likewise to that of a nation. The houses, the furniture, the clothing of the rich, in a little time, become useful to the inferior and middling ranks of people. They are able to purchase them when their superiors grow weary of them. . . .
>
> The expence, besides, that is laid out in durable commodities, gives maintenance, commonly, to a greater number of people, than that which is employed in the most profuse hospitality. . . . I would not, however, by all this be understood to mean, that the one species of expence always betokens a more liberal or generous spirit than the other. . . . All that I mean is, that the one sort of expence, as it always occasions some accumulation of valuable commodities, as it is more favourable to private frugality, and, consequently, to the increase of the public capital, and as it maintains productive, rather than unproductive hands, conduces more than the other to the growth of public opulence.

Smith, in passages such as these, which apparently reject the ultimate legitimacy of consumer's sovereignty, is writing as a moralist at least as much as a market analyst. He saw life around him as an uncertain struggle in which the moderate, beer-drinking, hardworking poor had to compensate for the profligate, gin-drinking, lazy poor; in which "private frugality and good conduct" among the well-to-do had "to compensate" not only for "the private prodigality and misconduct" of individuals but also for "the public extravagance of government."[95] When Smith addresses himself to these themes one cannot miss the strand of authentic passion that suffuses the text. He felt the balance between salvation and perdition was close.

Smith's distinction between productive and unproductive labor brings him also to a lucid sectoral disaggregation of investment and the notion of sectoral capital-labor and capital-output ratios. For an analyst of economic growth the following is one of the most striking passages in *The Wealth of Nations:*[96]

> Though all capitals are destined for the maintenance of productive labour only, yet the quantity of that labour, which equal capitals are capable of putting into motion, varies extremely according to the diversity of their employment; as does likewise the value which that employment adds to the annual produce of the land and labour of the country.

A capital may be employed in four different ways: either, first, in procuring the rude produce annually required for the use and consumption of society; or, secondly, in manufacturing and preparing that rude produce for immediate use and consumption; or, thirdly, in transporting either the rude or manufactured produce from the places where they abound to those where they are wanted; or, lastly, in dividing particular portions of either into such small parcels as suit the occasional demands of those who want them. In the first way are employed the capitals of all those who undertake the improvement or cultivation of lands, mines, or fisheries; in the second, those of all master manufacturers; in the third, those of all wholesale merchants; and in the fourth, those of all retailers. It is difficult to conceive that a capital should be employed in any way which may not be classed under some one or other of those four.

Each of those four methods of employing a capital is essentially necessary either to the existence or extension of the other three, or to the general conveniency of the society.

Here we have something akin to the Clark-Kuznets disaggregation of economic activity into primary, secondary, and tertiary sectors; an assertion that all are "essentially necessary" for the maintenance or expansion of output; and an awareness that the productivity of investment outlays in the several sectors may differ, however necessary the expansion of all may be for balanced growth. Although Smith aligned himself against government intrusion into the investment process, where private incentives were adequate, here is the beginning of a framework for development planning.

As noted earlier, Smith had something more to say than Hume about invention and innovation, fixed capital and machinery; but, like Hume, the general thrust of his doctrine suggested invention and innovation as an incremental improvement in ways of doing things, evoked by profit possibilities that almost automatically accompanied the widening of the market and the division of labor. He did recognize, however, that over long periods of time one could identify a few major technological innovations whose high productivity constituted an identifiable discontinuity helping to explain a long period decline in price. For example, surveying the woolen industry over 3 centuries, since the time of Edward IV, he identifies "three very capital improvements":[97] the exchange of rock and spindle for the spinning wheel; machines for winding and arranging the yarn before being put into the loom; and the fulling mill which supplanted treading in water to thicken the cloth. Both in his *Lectures* and *The Wealth of Nations* Smith drew a distinction between inventions contrived by those who actually operated the machines—a kind of incremental learning by doing—and those created by "philosophers" [scientists] that involved "new powers not formerly applied."[98] He cites the water wheel, fire machines, [steam engines, Newcomen vintage], and wind and water mills as examples of major discontinuous inventions. In making this distinction, Smith clearly foreshadows Schumpeter.

Although he left open the possibility of major inventive breakthroughs, Smith, like Hume, envisaged productivity improvements mainly within the framework of existing, essentially familiar technologies.

Business Cycles

Neither Hume nor Smith exhibited an awareness of more or less regular cyclical fluctuations in trade and manufactures. The data on pre-1783 Britain, at first sight, do suggest that fairly regular fluctuations occurred.[99] Between 1700 and 1783, cycles with an average length of 5.25 years can be identified as well as five building cycles averaging 17.4 years. Examined closely, however, eighteenth-century British fluctuations in trade and manufactures are closely linked to the course of the harvests and the timing of wars; and, as always, building fluctuations are extremely sensitive to the timing and intensity of wars. In addition the relative immobility of the labor force and wide variations in regional economic circumstances make generalizations in terms of the national economy of Great Britain uncertain. Finally, the modest role of fixed capital outlays in manufactures reduces the potential role of what was later to be a major variable in business cycles.

There is, nevertheless, some evidence for an inventory cycle in the British foreign trade statistics for the period 1701–1801. Twenty-one cycles in British export volume can be marked off, averaging 3.8 years, as opposed to a 4-year average for the period 1783–1860.[100] This *ex post* identification of an element of inventory fluctuations due to time lags inherent in foreign trade is not reflected in contemporary literature. But there is one passage in Smith where, in discussing the "scarcity of money," he comes close to isolating the key elements, including overoptimistic expectations and time lags, that imparted an authentic cyclical element to the eighteenth-century international trading arena:[101]

> When the profits of trade happen to be greater than ordinary, over-trading becomes a general error both among great and small dealers. They do not always send more money abroad than usual, but they buy upon credit both at home and abroad, an unusual quantity of goods, which they send to some distant market, in hopes that the returns will come in before the demand for payment. The demand comes before the returns, and they have nothing at hand with which they can either purchase money, or give solid security for borrowing. It is not any scarcity of gold and silver, but the difficulty which such people find in borrowing, and which their creditors find in getting payment, that occasions the general complaint of the scarcity of money.

It was only the major cycle expansion peaking in 1792, with its substantial component of fixed capital investment, (and the unemployment to be observed in 1793–1794) that a sequence of (approximately) 9-year major cycles began. These were initially so interwoven with war and immediate postwar events that Karl Marx, for example, wrongly dated the first major cycle as that peaking in 1825 (p. 92). With Hume and Smith, however, we are dealing with economists who assumed in their day that full employment was normal and that all savings were directly invested. They recognized the reality of various kinds of perturbation in the system—notably, wars and harvest fluctuations; but they regarded them, essentially, as random. Nevertheless, Smith, with his consciousness of the role of expectations, time lags, and credit, captures some essential elements required in cyclical analysis.

Relative Prices

Again, Smith's view of the prospects for the intersectoral terms of trade was wholly consistent with Hume's fragmentary observations but much more explicit. Clearly, Smith believed that in the natural course of events, the prices of manufactures would fall relative to prices of basic commodities:[102]

It is the natural effect of improvement, however, to diminish gradually the real price of almost all manufactures. . . . In consequence of better machinery, of greater dexterity, and of a more proper division and distribution of work, all of which are the natural effects of improvement, a much smaller quantity of labour becomes requisite for executing any particular piece of work; and though, in consequence of the flourishing circumstances of the society, the real price of labour should rise very considerably, yet the great diminution of the quantity will generally much more than compensate the greatest rise which can happen in the price.

Smith here asserts, then, that the rise in unit wage will be outweighed in manufactures by the reduction in unit labor requirements—one of the most fundamental propositions in *The Wealth of Nations*. He then goes on:

There are, indeed, a few manufactures, in which the necessary rise in the real price of the rude materials will more than compensate all the advantages which improvement can introduce into the execution of the work. In carpenters and joiners work, and in the coarser sort of cabinet work, the necessary rise in the real price of barren timber, in consequence of the improvement of land, will more than compensate all the advantages which can be derived from the best machinery, the greatest dexterity, and the most proper division and distribution of work.

But in all cases in which the real price of the rude materials either does not rise at all, or does not rise very much, that of the manufactured commodity sinks very considerably.

Smith's assertion of increasing returns to manufactures is, essentially, a simple, straightforward proposition.* His analysis of the possible and probable course of productivity and prices in basic commodities ("rude produce") is differentiated and rather complex:[103]

These different sorts of rude produce may be divided into three classes. The first comprehends those which it is scarce in the power of human industry to multiply at all. The second, those which it can multiply in proportion to the demand. The third, those in which the efficacy of industry is either limited or uncertain. In the progress of wealth and improvement, the real price of the first may rise to any degree of extravagance, and seems not to be limited by any certain boundary. That of the second, though it may rise greatly, has, however, a certain boundary beyond which it cannot well pass for any considerable time together. That of the third, though its natural tendency is to rise in the progress of improvement, yet in the same degree of improvement it may sometimes happen even to fall, sometimes to continue the same, and sometimes to rise more or less, according as different accidents render the efforts of human industry in multiplying this sort of rude produce, more or less successful.

---

*I use the term "increasing returns" here and elsewhere to embrace systematically falling costs due not merely to "economies of scale" but, also, to technological change, whether incremental or discontinuous.

He then proceeds for some twenty-five pages to examine each of his three categories with rich illustrations from history and the contemporary scene. For our purposes a full paraphrase of his argument is not required; but the following points are worth noting.

1. Smith illustrates his first category, where an expansion of supply is virtually impossible, with scarce birds and fish; and second, where economic progress reduces supply and increases price, with the rise in the price of cattle as a hitherto uncultivated but fertile region brings its excess land into food production, reducing the acreage hitherto used without opportunity cost for grazing; the third, where the real cost of a basic commodity rises irregularly in the course of economic progress, with the evolution of prices for wool, hides, meat, and fish.

2. In accounting for historical price trends for particular commodities, Smith adduces changes in both demand and supply. He does not sharply focus on diminishing returns although there are a good many references to more or less productive lands and mines, as well as the likelihood of disproportionate price increases as the intensity of fishing a given area rises. His general proposition is that the relative price of all basic commodities except food will rise, as an economy's real income increases; e.g., textile raw materials, building materials, minerals, precious metals, and stones.

3. Quite possibly because his image was of an ample grain supply, supported in the eighteenth century by considerable improvements in agricultural technology, which he cites, Smith does not assert in general terms the operation of diminishing returns to raw produce; but, on balance, it is quite clear that he viewed the prospects for productivity increases in such sectors with less optimism than in manufactures, and he expected, therefore, that the relative prices of manufactures would fall. It is, in fact, difficult to make sense of his inclusion of "soil and climate" among the determinants of the limits to growth without introducing diminishing returns to agriculture at some point in the expansion process.

The Stages of and Limits to Growth

Smith's discussion of the stages of growth appears at first glance, paradoxical if not mildly schizophrenic. He begins by asserting the central importance of commerce between town and country in "every civilized society" and "the mutual and reciprocal" gains derived from that commerce, including both the impulse for the division of labor in urban manufactures and for higher productivity agriculture in the countryside.[104] He then proceeds to define a sequence for development that would conform to "the natural inclinations of man:"[105] that is, agriculture, manufactures, and foreign trade. He asserts that:

> This order of things is so very natural, that in every society that had any territory, it has always, I believe, been in some degree observed. Some of their lands must have been cultivated before any considerable towns could be established, and some sort of coarse industry of the manufacturing kind must have been carried on in those towns, before they could well think of employing themselves in foreign commerce.
>
> But though this natural order of things must have taken place in some degree in every such society, it has, in all the modern states of Europe, been, in many respects, entirely inverted. The foreign commerce of some of their

cities has introduced all their finer manufactures, or such as were fit for distant sale; and manufactures and foreign commerce together, have given birth to the principal improvements of agriculture. The manners and customs which the nature of their original government introduced, and which remained after that government was greatly altered, necessarily forced them into this unnatural and retrograde order.

Smith here appears to argue that the course of political and military history had violated and degraded the natural sequence of things despite his awareness that, of its nature, agriculture required a broad spectrum of, essentially, urban supporters:[106] "Smiths, carpenters, wheel-wrights, and plough-wrights, masons, and bricklayers, tanners, shoe-makers, and taylors. . . . The butcher, the brewer, and the baker, soon join them, together with many other artificers and retailers, necessary or useful for supplying their occasional wants, and who contribute still further to augment the town." But he finds an attractive, somewhat nostalgic sequence at work in the uncorrupted North American colonies where good land is so plentiful, and the psychological attractions of life as an independent landowning farmer so strong, that the successful artificer does not move on to manufacture "for distant sale" but buys land and becomes a planter.[107] Only where good cheap land is not available does he become a manufacturer who produces for widening markets. This is by no means the only apparent clash in *The Wealth of Nations* between Smith's somewhat romantic attachment to physiocratic doctrines and his Humeian awareness that, in the end, the wealth of nations, including the productivity of agriculture, depended on the widening of the market and the exploitation of increasing returns in manufactures.[108] The ultimate reconciliation of Smith's apparently dualistic view lay in his perception that a sound and sturdy process of economic development required productivity-increasing investment in agriculture as well as in manufactures and commerce; and that mercantilist doctrine and policy were biased against agriculture.

This emphasis on the importance of agriculture, as opposed to the mercantilist priority for manufacture and commerce, appears in Smith's "Introduction and Plan of Work;"[109] and it becomes quite clear when Smith turns from his discussion of stages and sequences of growth to the rich country–poor country debate that Hume had heightened with his attack on the beggar-thy-neighbor thrust of mercantilist conceptions and policies.[110]

Like Hume, Smith believed the more advanced countries could continue to thrive in an environment of free trade in which the less developed countries and regions (e.g., the North American colonies and Scotland[111]) came forward more rapidly than the richer countries. Although his argument differed somewhat from Hume's, he also confronted some difficulty when he dealt with the limits to growth.

Here are the key elements in Smith's position on the rich country–poor country debate.

1. A rich country had a number of inherent advantages over a poor country that ought to permit it to retain its lead, barring failure to conduct correct policies.
2. These advantages included lower unit labor costs, despite higher real wage rates, resulting from the greater division of labor, in turn made possible by the abundance and cheapness of capital. They included also a more elaborate and efficient transport system reducing the relative prices of basic commodities.
3. Therefore, a rich country could afford to move toward free trade where it would enjoy the advantages of a large and productive commerce with its partners in the world economy, even with its potential military adversaries.

The flavor of Smith's view is well captured in the following two quotations:[112]

> The more opulent therefore the society, labour will always be so much dearer and work so much cheaper, and if some opulent countries have lost several of their manufactures and some branches of their commerce by having been undersold in foreign markets by the traders and artisans of poorer countries, who were contented with less profit and smaller wages, this will rarely be found to have been merely the effect of the opulence of one country and the poverty of the other. Some other cause, we may be assured, must have concurred. The rich country must have been guilty of some error in its police [policy].

> A nation that would enrich itself by foreign trade, is certainly most likely to do so when its neighbours are all rich, industrious, and commercial nations. A great nation surrounded on all sides by wandering savages and poor barbarians might, no doubt, acquire riches by the cultivation of its own lands, and by its own interior commerce, but not by foreign trade.

The question then arose, as with Hume, of what would happen in the long run if there were limits to growth. Would not the poor latecomers catch up with the initially richer nations if the latter came to a steady state?

Smith was not quite capable of envisaging that his "philosophers" could generate a sufficient flow of profitable major inventions and innovations over long periods of time that the rich could exploit in a forehanded way to maintain their place at the front of the queue. There were, therefore, limits to the extent that the expansion of the capital stock could expand the market and reap for nations the benefits of the progressive division of labor. In a famous passage he explicitly acknowledged that there was, for each country, a ceiling on real income per capita.[113]

> In a country which had acquired that full complement of riches which the nature of its soil and climate, and its situation with respect to other countries, allowed it to acquire; which could, therefore, advance no further, and which was not going backwards, both the wages of labour and the profits of stock would probably be very low. . . .

> But perhaps no country has ever yet arrived at this degree of opulence. China seems to have been long stationary, and had probably long ago acquired that full complement of riches which is consistent with the nature of its laws and institutions. . . . A country which neglects or despises foreign commerce, and which admits the vessels of foreign nations into one or two of its ports only, cannot transact the same quantity of business which it might do with different laws and institutions.

In Smith's judgment Holland, which did not neglect or despise foreign commerce, was nearer to its full complement of riches than China.[114]

Again, like Hume, Smith did not try seriously to resolve the logical contradiction between the short- and medium-run mutual advantages of free trade between rich and poor countries (and regions) and a long-run prospect of steady state stagnation. The latter concept could not exclude the poor achieving levels of wealth and productivity that might challenge the rich when all had achieved their "full complement of riches" and, according to his analysis of this steady state (and the case of China), wages declined. Smith could and did argue that, with sound policy, the rich ought to be able to look after themselves; but, in fact, his interest was not in the long run but in his "very violent" attack on current British and continental economic policy. In a world where market forces were permitted (with a few specified exceptions) to work their will, colonies permitted to go their way, and investment in agriculture (as well as manufactures and commerce) not discouraged, the prospects were good that a high level of income per capita could be sustained in Britain and elsewhere. Here, as Hont points out, wealth and virtue are brought together by Smith's central proposition that high productivity (low unit labor costs) induced by the triple impact of the widening of the market can reconcile high wages and low costs in manufactures.[115]

Noneconomic Factors

In concluding the discussion of Hume, I focused primarily on the manner in which his view of the complexities of the human condition suffused his economic analysis. As noted at the beginning of the treatment of Smith, his interest in the many dimensions of human society tended to fall away when he dealt with strictly economic matters, as in the following often-quoted passage.[116]

> [M]an has almost constant occasion for the help of his brethern, and it is in vain for him to expect it from their benevolence only. He will be more likely to prevail if he can interest their self-love in his favour, and shew them that it is for their own advantage to do for him what he requires of them. Whoever offers to another a bargain of any kind, proposes to do this. Give me that which I want, and you shall have this which you want, is the meaning of every such offer; and it is in this manner that we obtain from one another the far greater part of those good offices which we stand in need of. It is not from the benevolence of the butcher, the brewer, or the baker, that we expect our dinner, but from their regard to their own interest. We address ourselves not to their humanity but to their self-love, and never talk to them of our own necessities but of their advantages.

Passages like these comfort greatly those who find relative utility and profit maximization a satisfactory basis for the elaboration of an essentially mathematical economic theory.

Nevertheless, *The Wealth of Nations* is shot through with passages in which the economic outcome is affected, both negatively and positively, by noneconomic human motives. Many of these concern Smith's (and Hume's) favorite target, the rent-collecting large landowners, who dissipated their rents (and part of the nation's investible surplus) by surrounding themselves with nonproductive servants. But read closely, it is clear that Smith tried to introduce noneconomic variables quite systematically when he believed them relevant. For example, in dealing with the motives for having children and in seeking to delineate the negative as well as positive consequences for productivity and human welfare of the specialized division of labor, he evokes the potentially healing role of widespread elementary education.[117]

Smith provided another and rather engaging example of the role of noneconomic factors in the course of the economy in discussing the favorable impact of the rise of towns on the countryside:[118]

> Merchants are commonly ambitious of becoming country gentlemen, and when they do, they are generally the best of all improvers. A merchant is

accustomed to employ his money chiefly in profitable projects; whereas a mere country gentleman is accustomed to employ it chiefly in expence. . . . Those different habits naturally affect their temper and disposition in every sort of business. A merchant is commonly a bold; a country gentleman, a timid undertaker. . . . Whoever has had the fortune to live in a mercantile town situated in an unimproved country, must have frequently observed how much more spirited the operations of merchants were in this way, than those of mere country gentlemen. The habits, besides, of order, economy and attention, to which mercantile business naturally forms a merchant, render him much fitter to execute, with profit and success, any project of improvement.

More generally, Smith was conscious of the extent to which the impulse to pursue self-interest could be frustrated, deflected, or heightened by the realities of social life. There is shrewdness as well as compassion in his assessment of the degree to which recipients of rent, wages, and profits are capable of understanding and pressing forward their interests, with the generators of profits clearly in the most advantageous position.[119] Under these circumstances, virtually the only effective recourse, in Smith's view, was to insist on the strictest possible application of competition. But his view of the correct role of the state was not wholly negative. Indeed, the detail and explicitness of Smith's treatment of public policy is a major distinctive characteristic of his work as compared to that of his contemporaries. Despite his central negative objective of attacking the "commercial or mercantile system," his analysis of the legitimate functions of government and their financing is lengthy (some 250 pages), positive, and principled. Smith begins with a lucid statement of the irreducible minimum tasks of government under a regime of "natural liberty":[120]

> According to the system of natural liberty, the sovereign has only three duties to attend to; three duties of great importance, indeed, but plain and intelligible to common understandings: first, the duty of protecting the society from the violence and invasion of other independent societies; secondly, the duty of protecting, as far as possible, every member of the society from the injustice or oppression of every other member of it, or the duty of establishing an exact administration of justice; and, thirdly, the duty of erecting and maintaining certain public works and certain public institutions, which it can never be for the interest of any individual, or small number of individuals, to erect and maintain; because the profit could never repay the expence to any individual or small number of individuals, though it may frequently do much more than repay it to a great society.

Smith's recommendations for economic policy relate easily to these three functions.[121] Recognizing the legitimacy of the military functions of the state, he defended, for example, the Navigation Acts as providing a reserve of seamen for the navy in times of war; and, with a bit less conviction, he was prepared to countenance bounties in the export of British made sailcloth and gunpowder. With respect to the second function of government, he supported a considerable array of measures that would positively strengthen the workings of the free competitive economy. He commended: security of property, above all; control over primogeniture and entailing of estates, which he regarded as a hindrance to agricultural investment; a Naderesque supervision of the purity of metals and the quality of cloth; and the regulation of public health. Smith was also prepared to defend usury laws, fixing maximum interest rates, to prevent desperate debtors from bidding away resources from productive investment. As for the third function, Smith envisaged education and a wide array of infrastructure investments as legitimate. Indeed, in his otherwise laudatory essay on the occasion of Adam Smith's bicentenary Milton Friedman suggested the master may have gone too far with his definition of the third legitimate function of government.[122] But Peter Bauer, let alone Milton Friedman, can feel content with Smith's dictum on sectoral investment planning:[123]

> What is the species of domestic industry which his capital can employ, and of which the produce is likely to be of the greatest value, every individual, it is evident, can, in his local situation, judge much better than any statesman or lawgiver can do for him. The statesman, who should attempt to direct private people in what manner they ought to employ their capitals, would not only load himself with a most unnecessary attention, but assume an authority which could safely be trusted, not only to no single person, but to no council or senate whatever, and which would nowhere be so dangerous as in the hands of a man who had folly and presumption enough to fancy himself fit to exercise it.

Both Hume and Smith, however, were acutely conscious of external economies that government should assure were exploited and external diseconomies that government should prevent. Anticipating Smith on the needs of "a great society," Hume had argued in *A Treatise on Human Nature* that a large number of individuals would find it impossible to agree to concert and execute a project of public interest; but "political societies" find it easy to proceed:[124]

> . . . Thus, bridges are built, harbours opened, ramparts raised, canals formed, fleets equipped, and armies disciplined, everywhere, by the care of government, which, though composed of men subject to all human infirmities, becomes, by one of the finest and most subtle inventions imaginable, a composition which is in some measure exempted from all these infirmities.

Similarly, Smith breaks off his disquisition on paper money to supply two examples of legitimate government intervention to fend off undesirable consequences of an unmodulated system of natural liberty:[125]

> To restrain private people, it may be said, from receiving in payment the promissory notes of a banker, for any sum whether great or small, when they themselves are willing to receive them; or, to restrain a banker from issuing such notes, when all his neighbours are willing to accept of them, is a manifest violation of that natural liberty which it is the proper business of law, not to infringe, but to support. Such regulations may, no doubt, be considered as in some respect a violation of natural liberty. But those exertions of the natural liberty of a few individuals, which might endanger the security of the whole society, are, and ought to be, restrained by the laws of all governments; of the most free, as well as of the most despotical. The obligation of building party walls, in order to prevent the communication of fire, is a violation of natural liberty, exactly of the same kind with the regulations of the banking trade which are here proposed.

In terms of development theory of the 1950s and 1960s Hume and Smith might not fully qualify as ''structuralists;'' but it is clear that they did not believe competitive market economics would, without government intervention, maximize the wealth of nations, and they would have understood with sympathy Paul Rosenstein-Rodan's case for a Big Push to expand infrastructure in an underdeveloped economy (to follow, pp. 409ff.).

3

T. R. Malthus
and David Ricardo

T. R. Malthus (1766–1834)

The close human ties between Hume and Smith and between Malthus and Ricardo are a splendid strand in the inheritance of professional economists. Hume and Smith first met in 1739; but their friendship dates from the early 1750s running on to Hume's death in 1776. They were each other's literary executors, a function Smith carefully fulfilled. Their published works indicate that they did not always agree; but, excepting Hume's amiable letter of April 1, 1776, expressing pleasure at the publication of *The Wealth of Nations* but also disagreement with Smith's theory of rent (and with a lesser point), we have no formal record of their exchanges on economic matters.[1] Things are quite different in the even more remarkable friendship of Ricardo and Malthus. There exist ninety-two letters from Ricardo to Malthus, seventy-five from Malthus to Ricardo.[2] They run from 1811 to 1823; that is, from their first meeting (June 1811) to Ricardo's death. Their exchanges constitute 30% of all Ricardo's preserved correspondence on economic and political matters. Malthus's *Principles of Political Economy* (1820) was, in good part, a response to Ricardo's *Principles of Political Economy and Taxation* (1817). But there are also Ricardo's elaborate book-length and mainly critical notes on Malthus's text.[3]

Although Hume and Smith had predecessors and contemporaries who made serious contributions to economic thought, they crystallized a coherent body of theory and doctrine. They can be properly regarded as the key figures of the first generation of modern economists. Hume may have been more original, but Smith's claim to primacy exceeds his because of the more systematic and spacious character of *The Wealth of Nations* and its widespread and abiding influence. Malthus and Ricardo are, evidently, the key figures of the second generation. They viewed themselves as part of a living and accepted tradition. They felt no need, for example, to reexamine the psychological and philosophical assumptions in which Hume and Smith rooted their basic economic propositions. Ricardo's *Political Economy* begins with a brisk bow to Smith and other predecessors; an assertion that they had not correctly defined "the principles of rent" and, more generally, the laws determining distribution; and he's off and running with a highly technical effort to refine and elaborate a received doctrine whose basic presuppositions about human beings in society he largely took for granted.[4]

Malthus was, to a degree, a different case. His work on population and an appropriate stance on the issue of poverty plunged him deeply into an assessment of basic human drives and needs. And his later more empirical analysis of population dynamics led him back systematically to noneconomic variables. But as the intense wartime pressures of population increase on the food supply eased after 1812, Malthus focused on a wider agenda. His *Political Economy* (1820) begins with a discussion of the nature and limits of the scientific method as applied to his subject. He, too, indicates respectfully his judgment that some of Adam Smith's propositions require correction and refinement. And when he comes to Book II, "On the Progress of Wealth," he acknowledges in two brief pages the importance of institutional, moral, and religious factors, and then goes to work on the variables "directly within the province of political economy."[5] And, indeed, he was the first professor of political economy at Haileybury, the college of the East India Company.

For good or ill, then, we observe in the work of Malthus and Ricardo an emergence from the spacious Big Sky setting of Hume and Adam Smith into a narrowing intellectual terrain more nearly approximating contemporary mainstream economics.

We know in great detail that Malthus and Ricardo differed substantially on issues of both theory and policy. There is something extraordinarily engaging about the image of Malthus peacefully reading portions of his manuscript to Ricardo, at the latter's country house, Gatcomb Park—a manuscript directly addressed to answering Ricardo "without giving my work a controversial air."[6] They held stubbornly to their respective views; but they appear to have so respected the integrity of each other's pursuit of truth, and so combined doggedness with humility in the face of the large problems they sought to solve, that their mutual affection was unaffected or, perhaps, deepened. Their achievement in this respect is not unique but less common than it might be in the world of ideas; although it must be added that, despite mutual respect, affection, and an almost compulsive flow of communication, their exchanges constitute virtually a dialogue of the deaf. This is the case because the most important issue in contention between Malthus and Ricardo was, almost certainly, an issue of method rooted ultimately in temperament and cast of mind, as Keynes suggests.[7]

Both men were ultimately concerned with public policy. Here is Schumpeter's memorable description of how Ricardo went about his business.[8]

> His [Ricardo's] interest was in the clear-cut result of direct, practical significance. In order to get this he cut that general system to pieces, bundled up as large parts of it as possible, and put them in cold storage—so that as many things as possible should be frozen and "given." He then piled one simplifying assumption upon another until, having really settled everything by these assumptions, he was left with only a few aggregative variables between which, given these assumptions, he set up simple one-way relations so that, in the end, the desired results emerged almost as tautologies. For example, a famous Ricardian theory is that profits "depend upon" the price of wheat. And under his implicit assumptions and in the particular sense in which the terms of the proposition are to be understood, this is not only true, but undeniably, in fact trivially, so. Profits could not possibly depend upon anything else, since everything else is "given," that is, frozen. It is an excellent theory that can never be refuted and lacks nothing save sense. The habit of applying results of this character to the solution of practical problems we shall call the Ricardian Vice.

The best description of Malthus's less elegant but more complex approach to political economy is his own in which he contrasts those under strong compulsion to simplify and generalize (clearly, Ricardo) with those willing to put their propositions to the test of experience at the cost of admitting "limitations and exceptions" (clearly, himself).[9]

> The principal cause of error, and of the differences which prevail at present among the scientific writers on political economy, appears to me to be a precipitate attempt to simplify and generalize. While their more practical opponents draw too hasty inferences from a frequent appeal to partial facts, these writers run into a contrary extreme, and do not sufficiently try their theories by a reference to that enlarged and comprehensive experience which, on so complicated a subject, can alone establish their truth and utility. . . .
>
> In political economy the desire to simplify has occasioned an unwillingness to acknowledge the operation of more causes than one in the production of particular effects. . . .
>
> The same tendency to simplify and generalize, produces a still greater disinclination to allow of modifications, limitations, and exceptions to any rule or proposition, than to admit the operation of more causes than one. . . .
>
> The first business of philosophy is to account for things as they are. . . . Where unforeseen causes may possibly be in operation, and the causes that are foreseen are liable to great variations in their strength and efficacy, an accurate yet comprehensive attention to facts is necessary, . . .

Ricardo's explanations of their cross purposes is related but distinct, focusing on the difference between forces operating over long and short periods of time—the clue on which Alfred Marshall built the bulk of his formal analysis.

The work of Malthus and Ricardo was shaped not merely by their role as second-generation refiners and elaborators, not merely by their marked differences in temperament and method, but also by radical changes in the British economy, the problems it confronted, and the international setting in which it operated. Malthus and Ricardo were 25 to 30 years of age in the decade ending in 1802: strictly speaking, 1791–1796 for Malthus, 1797–1802 for Ricardo. But the five essential changes they both inescapably observed were not sensitive to fine-tuned distinctions.

First of course, Britain was at war with revolutionary France, from 1793 forward, excepting 1802, an interval that Malthus exploited for an important trip to the continent to test his theory of population. The Revolution and the war left their marks on the formulations of both men.

Second, the population of England and Wales, virtually stagnant from 1710 to 1740, increasing at .58% per annum from 1740 to 1780, accelerated approximately as follows in the next 20 years.[10]

1780–1785	.64%
1785–1790	.98
1790–1795	1.05
1795–1800	1.16

Third, there was in the 1790s an extraordinary acceleration in the rise in the price of wheat, which had begun around mid-century. The acceleration is well captured in the following table, Table 3.1, from Deane and Cole and in Figure 3.1. The latter exhibits

LORETTE WILMOT LIBRARY
NAZARETH COLLEGE

Table 3.1. Index Numbers of the Price of Wheat 1695–1805

1695–1705	122	1750–1760	101
1700–1710	105	1755–1765	106
1705–1715	121	1760–1770	117
1710–1720	109	1765–1775	141
1715–1725	92	1770–1780	136
1720–1730	99	1775–1785	132
1725–1735	94	1780–1790	142
1730–1740	84	1785–1795	148
1735–1745	86	1790–1800	196
1740–1750	84	1795–1805	250
1745–1755	90		

SOURCE: Phyllis Deane and W. A. Cole, *British Economic Growth, 1688–1959,* 2d ed.
(Cambridge: at the University Press, 1969), p. 91.

also the post-1812 decline in the wheat price.[11] These movements had, of course, a
profound impact on agricultural rents, urban living costs, and real wages, which greatly
influenced the work of Malthus and Ricardo.[12]

Fourth, the industrial revolution asserted itself unmistakably in the 1780s and 1790s
with the astonishing rise of the factory-based cotton industry, the progressive diffusion of
Watt's steam engine, and the emergence of Cort's steam-powered, coke-using forges for
fabricating iron. The impact of machinery on income distribution and employment began
to force itself on economists. Even more important, the first modern business cycle
expansion peaked in 1792 with a substantial component of investment in fixed industrial
capital. It was followed by a sharp recession during which, perhaps, the first substantial
period of cyclical industrial unemployment occurred.[13] And despite the vicissitudes and
erratic shocks of a protracted major war, the cyclical rhythm continued to 1815 and, of
course, beyond (Figure 3.2).[14] Thus, full employment could no longer be assumed
without challenge, and the question of gluts, underconsumption, and overproduction was
raised not only by Malthus but also by a good many others.[15]

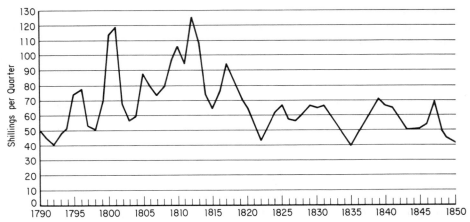

Figure 3.1. Gazette Price of Wheat, 1790–1850. [Adapted from A. D. Gayer *et al., The Growth
and Fluctuation of the British Economy, 1790–1850,* Vol. II (Oxford: at the Clarendon Press,
1953), p. 826.]

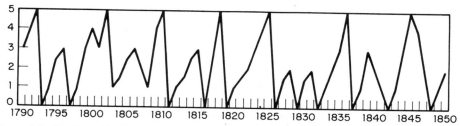

Figure 3.2. Business Cycle Pattern, Great Britain, 1790–1850. [Adapted from Arthur D. Gayer, W. W. Rostow, and Anna Jacobson Schwartz, with the assistance of Isaiah Frank, *The Growth and Fluctuation of the British Economy, 1790–1850,* Vol. I (Oxford: at the Clarendon Press, 1953), p. 355.]

Finally, wartime inflation (with the bullion standard suspended after 1797) and postwar deflation stimulated analysis and debate on monetary theory, international monetary equilibrium, and the role of monetary and real variables in determining price movements. The propositions crystallized and the positions taken have significantly affected the contours of economic theory down to the present. Indeed, the causes of war and postwar price movements are still debated.[16]

These changes in the British economy left clear-cut marks on the growth theories and controversies of the second generation, including a marked shift in the focus of attention from the pre-1815 to the post-1815 years. It is against the background of these changes in setting that we turn to the views on growth of the two major figures of the second generation.

The Basic Growth Equation

Malthus's theory of growth is essentially a variation on Adam Smith's. Its distinctive elements can be traced through the sequence of his writings beginning with the first edition (1798) of his *Essay on the Principle of Population.* He presented his analysis of the determinants of growth in its most complete and systematic form in Book II ("On the Progress of Wealth") of his *Principles of Political Economy* (1820, second edition 1836). We shall here use the second edition, published 2 years after his death, as representing his final reflections on the subject.[17] He begins by acknowledging but setting aside the noneconomic forces that determine a society's rate of growth. He isolates the economic from the noneconomic variables as follows.[18]

> It is obviously true that there are many countries, not essentially different either in the degree of security which they afford to property, or in the moral and religious instruction received by the people, which yet, with nearly equal natural capabilities, make a very different progress in wealth. It is the principal object of the present inquiry to explain this. . . . If the actual riches of a country not subject to repeated violences and a frequent destruction of produce, be not after a certain period in some degree proportioned to its power of producing riches, this deficiency must have arisen from the want of an adequate stimulus to continued production. The practical question then for our consideration is, what are the most immediate and effective stimulants to the creation and progress of wealth.

He proceeds to deal with each now-familiar element in the classic growth equation in the following sequence: the rate of growth of population; capital formation; land and its fertility; and laborsaving inventions. Then follows his most distinctive contribution: a disquisition on the role of demand as well as supply in determining the rate of growth entitled ''Of the Necessity of a Union of the Powers of Production with the Means of Distribution, in Order to Ensure a Continued Increase of Wealth.'' Although Malthus's insight on the significance of effective demand can be traced back to brief but lucid passages in Chapters V and XVI in his first *Essay on Population* (1798), almost 60% of the exposition of growth theory in his *Political Economy* is incorporated in this section of the text, which he introduces as follows.[19]

> The three great causes most favourable to production are accumulation of capital, fertility of soil, and inventions to save labor. They all act in the same direction; and as they all tend to facilitate supply, without reference to demand, it is not probable that they should either separately or conjointly afford an adequate stimulus to the continued increase of wealth.

In dealing with these variables, a concern with effective demand suffused each dimension of Malthus's argument. His claim to originality in this respect does not depend on the *ex post* identification of a few precociously anticipatory passages suggestive of Keynesian doctrine. His central theme, as will emerge, is in fact post-Keynesian. It is that dynamic equilibrium in a growing economy requires an endless correct proportioning and balancing of supply and demand.

Population and the Working Force

Perhaps because he had already written so much about population, perhaps because the pressure of British population increase on the food supply had eased, Malthus's discussion in Book Two of his *Political Economy* runs only to three pages. He argues, simply, that while ''an increase in population is a powerful and necessary element of increasing demand,'' it is not a sufficient condition for the progress of wealth. He refers briefly in passing to ''the natural tendency of population to increase beyond the funds destined for its maintenance,'' but his central objective is to drive home the following proposition that one might well find in a modern text on development economics:[20] ''[T]he slowest progress in wealth is often made where the stimulus arising from population alone is the greatest.'' He cites Spain, Portugal, Poland, Hungary, and Turkey, as well as ''nearly the whole of Asia and Africa and the greatest part of America.''

Malthus asserted, however, a number of propositions about the productivity of labor in the context of his discussion of wages rather than the progress of wealth. In the following passage he comes close, in fact, to evoking a kind of demographic transition in which an initial increase in real wages is not overwhelmed by a surge in population but yields a regime of civil and political liberty, security of property, popular education, ''prudential habits,'' and, thus, a reduced birth rate and a progressive increase in real wages.[21]

> From high real wages, or the power of commanding a large portion of the necessaries of life, two very different results may follow; one, that of a rapid increase of population, in which case the high wages are chiefly spent in the maintenance of large and frequent families; and the other, that of a decided improvement in the modes of subsistence, and the conveniences and comforts

enjoyed, without a proportionate acceleration in the rate of increase. . . . In an inquiry into the causes of these different habits, we shall generally be able to trace those . . . which make them [the lower classes] unable or unwilling to reason from the past to the future, and ready to acquiesce, for the sake of present gratification, in a very low standard of comfort and respectability; and those which . . . tend to . . . make them act as beings who look before and after, and who consequently cannot acquiesce patiently in the thought of depriving themselves and their children of the means of being respectable, virtuous, and happy.

Among the circumstances which contribute to the character first described, the most efficient will be found to be despotism, oppression, and ignorance: among those which contribute to the latter character, civil and political liberty, and education.

Here we have a glimmering of the calculus that has operated in a good many developing societies in the second half of the twentieth century to help bring down birthrates; that is, an awareness that a limitation of family size can improve the prospects for each individual child in the smaller family "being respectable, virtuous, and happy."

In his treatment of the forces determining the attitude of husbands and wives toward family size, Malthus introduces a rather subtle notion of the dynamic interplay between material circumstances and social behavior:[22]

It rarely happens, however, that either of them remains fixed for any great length of time together. The rate at which the funds for the maintenance of labour increase is, we well know, liable, under varying circumstances, to great variation; and the habits of a people though not so liable, or so necessarily subject to change, can scarcely ever be considered as permanent. In general, their tendency is to change together. When the funds for the maintenance of labour are rapidly increasing, and the labourer commands a large portion of necessaries, it is to be expected that if he has the opportunity of exchanging his superfluous food for conveniences and comforts, he will acquire a taste for these conveniences, and his habits will be formed accordingly. On the other hand, it generally happens that, when the funds for the maintenance of labour become nearly stationary, such habits, if they ever have existed, are found to give away; and, before the population comes to a stop, the standard of comfort is essentially lowered. . . . The effect . . . certainly becomes in its turn a cause; and there is no doubt, that if the continuance of low wages for some time, should produce among the labourers of any country habits of marrying with the prospect only of a mere subsistence, such habits, by supplying the quantity of labour required at a low rate, would become a constantly operating cause of low wages.

Thus, Malthus envisaged social attitudes and behavior ("habits") as subject to change by the protracted operation of economic forces; but he also envisaged the economy, in turn, shaped by the "habits" operative at a given time.

Malthus's view of the backward-sloping supply curve for labor was one reflection of this interactive economic-social dynamics. Like Smith, he was conscious that human beings could become so fatalistic about the prospects for a long-run improvement in their lot or that of their children that a short-run rise in real wages caused a reduction in the amount of labor supplied. But his observations also convinced him that the social behavior of labor could alter if its range of perceived choice were widened by education and the responsibilities of increased political freedom. Explicitly following Smith, he judged the facilities for popular education in England deplorable:[23]

> It is surely a great national disgrace, that the education of the lower classes of people in England should be left merely to a few Sunday schools, supported by a subscription from individuals, who can give to the course of instruction in them any kind of bias which they please. . . .
>
> The principal argument which I have heard advanced against a system of national education in England is, that the common people would be put in a capacity to read such works as those of Paine, and that the consequences would probably be fatal to government. But on this subject I agree most cordially with Adam Smith in thinking that, an instructed and well-informed people would be much less likely to be led away by inflammatory writings, and much better able to detect the false declamation of interested and ambitious demagogues, than an ignorant people.

It is in this chapter ("Of the Modes of Correcting the Prevailing Opinions on Population") that Malthus comes closest to foreshadowing the possibility of a demographic transition with the birth rate declining not only as the result of wider popular education but also—in anticipation of J. S. Mill—a "greater degree of respect and personal liberty to single women" and other measures that would underline the connection between individual well-being and reduced family size.

Investment and Technology

Malthus's basic proposition about capital investment is simple and orthodox:[24]

> It is certainly true that no permanent and continued increase of wealth can take place without a continued increase of capital; and I cannot agree with Lord Lauderdale in thinking that this increase can be effected in any other way than by saving from the stock which might have been destined for consumption, and adding it to that which is to yield a profit; or in other words, by the conversion of revenue into capital.

But the balance of Malthus's treatment of investment is devoted to other matters, notably his protracted argument with Ricardo, Jean Baptiste Say, and James Mill about the possibility of a "general glut"; that is, a phase of widespread unemployment of labor and capital marked by a piling up of unsold manufactures. This strand in Malthus's writing is, aside from his work on population, his most memorable contribution to economic thought; and, since Keynes's essay on Malthus (1933), it is the most discussed.[25]

Malthus, as several of his *ex post* critics have noted, did not produce a formal, self-contained theory of underemployment equilibrium. He did, however, introduce into his argument certain variables that were later perceived to be important in modern income analysis and growth models; for example, the relative insensitivity of money wages to a decline in demand for labor,[26] and the possibility of changes in the savings-investment rate, and therefore, the demand for consumer goods, as the level of income changes. In addition, Malthus adduced a possible variable that might limit the expansion of the economy and yield, for a time at least, general oversupply; that is, a backward-sloping curve for labor in which, beyond a certain point, leisure (as well as saving) is preferred to additional goods and services with a rise in real income. Malthus succinctly summed up both dynamic strands in his argument as follows:[27] "We should constantly keep in mind that the tendency to expenditure in individuals has most formidable antagonists in love of indolence, and in the desire of saving, in order to better their condition and provide for a family. . . ."

But the heart of Malthus's case against Ricardo and Say was much less abstruse than these incomplete foreshadowings of modern macro-theory. It lay in his interpretation of two severe cyclical depressions in the aftermath of the Napoleonic Wars.[28] They extended from a peak in March 1815 to a trough in September 1816 and from a peak in September 1818 to a trough 1 year later.[29]

The first was marked by a convergence of agricultural and industrial depression that made 1815–1816 one of the most difficult periods in the history of the British economy. Unemployment was widespread, and contemporary journals are full of accounts of riots, strikes, and arrests under the Combination Acts. The fall in the prices of foodstuffs in 1814 and 1815 had eased the position of labor somewhat; but the rise in 1816 turned the rioters' anger against bakers and millers.

The second year of crisis, 1819, saw perhaps the most serious labour disturbances of the entire period 1790–1850. Wages in many districts were reduced, and unemployment again was severe. A distinctive character was imparted to the discontent by its distinct political overtones. Meetings begun over wage decreases ended with petitions for parliamentary reform. The movement had its center in Manchester, and reached its climax with the meeting at St. Peter's Field on 16 August. Somewhere between 50,000 and 80,000 persons gathered. A deputy constabulary, frightened by the mob, lost its head and charged. Eleven persons were killed, about 400 injured. The government, feeling revolution in the air, overrode a distinguished opposition to pass the famous Six Acts, which virtually suppressed freedom of speech, of the press, of free assembly. But most significant were the banners carried at the Peterloo meeting: they forecast the direction of reform agitation during the following years—"No Corn Laws," "Vote by Ballot," "Equal Representation or Death."

A turning-point came in 1820 in the fortunes of both industry and labour. A further sharp fall in living costs aided the working classes, as did the mild trade revival that set in during the year. The great boom that peaked in 1825 was underway.

The final section of Malthus's *Principles*, written in 1820, is addressed to these painful postwar phenomena: "Application of Some of the Preceding Principles to the Distresses of the Labouring Classes since 1815, with General Observations." It is the most lucid and effective statement of Malthus's differences with Ricardo with respect to both theory and policy—the latter including monetary as well as tax and tariff policy.

Ricardo's responses to this section are rather peripheral except for a blunt and at least mildly irritated statement of their most profound difference:[30] "Mr. Malthus never appears to remember that to save is to spend, as surely, as what he exclusively calls spending."

Malthus's interpretation of the period 1815–1820 is of particular relevance here because it is set out in terms that relate his theory of growth to short-run fluctuations of the economy. Centered as his argument was on the contrast between a wartime boom and what appeared in 1820 to be a chronic period of overcapacity and high unemployment, it inevitably evokes the post-World War I setting out of which Keynes's views emerged. Malthus's thesis as of 1820 may be summarized as follows.

1. The protracted period of war from 1793 to 1815, accompanied by "prodigious public expenditure" constituted a "violent stimulant" yielding an "unnatural" high rate of growth. Specifically, it generated in all its ramifications high agricultural prices, an expansion of acreage into hitherto submarginal land, increased application of capital to both existing and new acreage, and a setting of rural prosperity that accelerated the growth of population. Unlike the situation during the American (1775–1783) and earlier wars, unlike the situation envisaged by Hume and Adam Smith, who believed a small increase in the public debt would cause bankruptcy, there was "a more rapid and successful progress in the use of machinery than was ever before known"; and the "vast increase of productive power" thus generated permitted the burdens of war to be carried while the nation's capital and real income per capita increased. (Malthus does not deal with the probable decline in urban real wages during the war years due to chronically high food prices.)

2. Chronic postwar distress was the direct result of the radical decline in public expenditure and the fall in agricultural prices, as normal international trade in grain was resumed.[31] Agricultural prices fell by nearly a third, reducing the purchasing power of landlords and farmers:[32] "The failure of home demand filled the warehouses of the manufacturers with unsold goods, which urged them to export more largely at all risks."

3. In taking this view, Malthus deals explicitly with other explanations of this distinctly uncomfortable phase of British economic and social history. He deals, in particular, with those who argued that British distress was caused by prior cultivation of low-grade land, high tariffs, and high taxes. His response has the élan of a political pamphlet, which, essentially, he was writing:[33]

   > . . . I find it very difficult to admit a theory of our distresses so inconsistent with the theory of our comparative prosperity. While the greatest quantity of our poor lands were in cultivation; while there were more than usual restrictions upon our commerce, and very little corn was imported; and while taxation was at its height, the country confessedly increased in wealth with a rapidity never known before. Since some of our poorest lands have been thrown out of cultivation; since the peace has removed many of the restrictions upon our commerce, and, notwithstanding our corn laws, we have imported a great quantity of corn; and since seventeen millions of taxes have been taken off from the people, we have experienced the greatest degree of distress, both among capitalists and labourers.

4. Turning to remedy for the pains of "transition from war to peace," Malthus makes clear that he is not, of course, advocating a return to high taxes, large military expenditures, and the imposition of high protective tariffs on grain; although he quotes Adam Smith on the need for gradualism in reducing tariffs. He also opposes a radical increase in the issuance of paper money on grounds that empirical analysts from Thomas Tooke to Philip Cagan have confirmed:[34]

In the history of our paper transactions, it will be found that the abundance or scantiness of currency has generally followed and aggravated high or low prices, but seldom or never led them; and it is of the utmost importance to recollect that, at the end of the war, the prices failed before the contraction of the currency began. It was, in fact, the failure of the prices of agricultural produce, which destroyed the country banks, and shewed us the frail foundations on which the excess of our paper currency rested.

Malthus's positive proposals flow from the following simple but powerful dictum:[35] ". . . the progress of wealth depends upon proportions." He applies this principle to what he takes to be the central task of adjusting from war to peace; that is, "a union of the means of distribution with the powers of production."[36] He rejects increased saving as an initial method for stimulating demand and, in fact, finds it counterproductive at a time of idle capacity and severe unemployment. He then examines three other possibilities for inducing "an increased national revenue": the division of landed property; the extension of domestic and foreign trade; and the maintenance of "such a proportion of unproductive consumers as is best adapted to the powers of production."[37] He concludes that all are either unsatisfactory, slow, or marginal: the abolition of primogeniture "would produce more evil than good," as a device for increasing national revenue; a desirable but modest increase of international trade might be brought about by a gradual reduction in tariffs; and "the maintenance of unproductive consumers" (e.g., service jobs) might, at most, slow the reduction of national revenue. Then comes his famous call for public (and private) works accompanied by reference to the possibility of chronic rather than transitional unemployment:[38]

It is also of importance to know that, in our endeavours to assist the working classes in a period like the present, it is desirable to employ them in those kinds of labour, the results of which do not come for sale into the market, such as roads and public works. The objection to employing a large sum in this way, raised by taxes, would not be its tendency to diminish the capital employed in productive labour; because this, to a certain extent, is exactly what is wanted; but it might, perhaps, have the effect of concealing too much the failure of the national demand for labour, and prevent the population from gradually accommodating itself to a reduced demand. This however might be, in a considerable degree, corrected by the wages given. . . .

And as soon as the capitalists can begin to save from steady and improving profits, instead of from diminished expenditure, that is, as soon as the national revenue, estimated in bullion, and in the command of this bullion over labour, begins yearly and steadily to increase, we may then begin safely and effectively to recover our lost capital by the usual process of saving a portion of our increased revenue to add to it.

Thus the heart of Malthus's reply to Ricardo's central question about saving and spending is that a significant margin of investment based on saving is the result of a high marginal rate of plowback from an expanding national revenue; and that if other forces are at work depressing national revenue (e.g., a decline in agricultural prices or inventory overstocking in export markets) increased private savings may not result in increased investment. On the other hand, at such a time, a purposeful policy of increased public (or private) outlays might set in motion an increase in national revenue that would render increased savings a public as well as private virtue. An accelerator as well as a multiplier is clearly latent in his analysis.

Malthus's analysis of the low level of activity in the British economy as of 1819–1820, and its short-run prospects, was in this part of his exposition incomplete. Britain in 1820 was just beginning a major sustained expansion that ran down to an explosive peak in 1825.[39] And, although the subsequent quarter century was clearly marked by a strong cyclical pattern, with recurrent years of severe unemployment, the overall British growth rate was higher than during the war years; and the trend movement of urban real wages more favorable.[40] The reason was that British growth was carried forward by two forces of which Malthus was clearly aware but that he did not identify as at work in 1820: the dynamism of an expanding world economy, to which the dynamism of the British economy itself significantly contributed; and the emergence, since the 1780s, of new technology as an accelerating flow. At this stage Britain was not only the most important single source of new technology in the world economy (reflected, for example, in the declining price of its cotton exports), not only a rapidly expanding market for exports of other countries, but also the major source of international long-term capital, notably in the expansions of 1817–1818, the mid-1820s, and the mid-1830s.[41] Thus, at first glance, Malthus's macroeconomic propositions relate rather better to the cyclical than to the trend phenomena of the period.

But his analysis takes on a quite different cast when he turns to machinery. As should have been the case, Malthus was much more conscious of the role of machinery in capital formation and growth than Adam Smith; and, quite particularly, he was, unlike Smith, acutely conscious of the dramatic evolution of the cotton textile industry since 1783.[42]

The title of Malthus's section on machinery is: "Of Inventions to Save Labour, Considered as a Stimulus to the Continued Increase of Wealth." Malthus begins with the already well-established dictum that inventions are, in the usual case, induced; that is, an endogenous response to "a decided demand" for them.[43] But he moves immediately to assert that the new powers of supply will be "accompanied by an adequate extension of the market" taking into account both the price elasticity of demand and what I call lateral spreading effects.[44]

> This effect has been very strikingly exemplified in the cotton machinery of this country. The consumption of cotton goods has been so greatly extended both at home and abroad, on account of their cheapness, that the value of the whole of the cotton goods and twist now made exceeds, beyond comparison, their former value; while the rapidly increasing population of the towns of Manchester, Glasgow, &c. during the last thirty years, amply testifies that, with a few temporary exceptions, the demand for the labour concerned in the cotton manufactures, in spite of the machinery used, has been increasing very greatly.

Malthus then examines a case where demand is inelastic with respect to price. Labor-saving machinery then yields unemployment and some idleness in "the old fixed capital." He allows for a shift of idle labor and capital to new employments; but is sceptical that they will be as productive in their new uses as the old. The net loss must be set off against the gain from the initial use of the new laborsaving machinery. The outcome is inconclusive.

Malthus proceeds to drive home his point with a marginal case. He assumes machinery that might permit all home-manufactured commodities to be produced with one-third the labor currently employed, and in an evocation of something akin to Hume's stimulating effect of foreign luxuries, concludes as follows:[45]

> . . . if only an increase of domestic commodities could be obtained, there is every reason to fear that the exertions of industry would slacken. The peasant, who might be induced to labour an additional number of hours for tea or tobacco, might prefer indolence to a new coat. The tenant or small owner of land, who could obtain the common conveniences and luxuries of life at one third of their former price, might not labour so hard to procure the same amount of surplus produce from the land. And the trader or merchant, who would continue in his business in order to be able to drink and give his guests claret and champagne, might think an addition of homely commodities by no means worth the trouble of so much constant attention.

Pursuing the argument that the impact of machinery on national income hinged on a widening of foreign as well as domestic markets Malthus cites and reflects on some dramatic evidence for 1817, a year of cyclical expansion.[46] He finds that three machinery-intensive manufactures dominate exports: cottons, woolens, and hardware. On the other hand, 60% of imports consist of items that cannot be produced in Britain: coffee, indigo, sugar, tea, silks, tobacco, wines, and raw cotton:

> Now I would ask how we should have obtained these valuable imports, if the foreign markets for our cottons, woolens, and hardware had not been extended with the use of machinery? And further, where could we have found substitutes at home for such imports, which would have been likely to have produced the same effects, in stimulating the cultivation of the land, the accumulation of capital, and the increase of population?

And he draws a general lesson: "In the actual state of things therefore, there are great advantages to be looked forward to, and little reason to apprehend any permanent evil from the increase of machinery."

Clarity about the concepts of price and income elasticity of demand came to economic theory only long after Malthus's time; but, by making the widening of the market a function of cost and price reduction permitted by the invention of machinery—a kind of inversion of Adam Smith—Malthus captured essential elements of the interplay between the British and world economies in his time.

Business Cycles

I observed earlier that Malthus's analysis as of 1820, while couched in terms of a structural transition from war to peace, was linked quite particularly to two intervals of deep cyclical depression: 1816 and 1819. I concluded that his insights into macro-theory related rather more to short-run cyclical theory than to the trend prospects for the British economy in war and peace. But there is virtually no reference to regular cyclical fluctuations in Malthus. I say virtually because he twice refers to fluctuations of "eight to ten years": once in 1817; and then in the final page of his *Principles*. (The major cycle peaks in his time, on an annual basis, were 1792, 1800 [or 1802], 1810, 1818, and 1825.[47] These two passages deserve further explanation.

The first is in Malthus's response to a thoughtful observation of Ricardo's that seeks to isolate "the great cause of our difference in opinion."[48] Ricardo finds the cause in Malthus's concern with "immediate and temporary effects" whereas he [Ricardo] puts them aside and fixes his "whole attention on the permanent state of things which will result from them. Perhaps you estimate these temporary effects too highly, whilst I am too much disposed to under-value them. To manage the subject quite right they should be carefully distinguished and mentioned, and the due effects ascribed to each." In the course of his response Malthus observes: "I really think that the progress of society consists of irregular movements, and that to omit the consideration of causes which for eight or ten years will give a great *stimulus* to production and population, or a great *check* to them, is to omit the causes of the wealth and poverty of nations—the grand object of all enquiries in Political Economy."

The second reference is the following:[49]

> . . . eight or ten years, recurring not unfrequently, are serious spaces in human life. They amount to a serious sum of happiness or misery, according as they are prosperous or adverse, and leave the country in a very different state at their termination. In prosperous times the mercantile classes often realize fortunes, which go far towards securing them against the future; but unfortunately the working classes, though they share in the general prosperity, do not share in it so largely as in the general adversity. They may suffer the greatest distress in a period of low wages, but cannot be adequately compensated by a period of high wages. To them fluctuations must always bring more evil than good; and, with a view to the happiness of the great mass of society, it should be our object, as far as possible, to maintain peace, and an equable expenditure.

But beyond these two elusive references, I have not been able to find any discussion of regular business cycles in Malthus. What we do have is a systematic emphasis on the role of effective demand in determining alterations in the rate of increase in national income. We also have two empirical observations that have played an important part in the evolution of Keynesian income analysis. First, as indicated earlier, he envisages the possibility of sticky money wages and a decline in the demand for labor yielding unemployment rather than reduced wages:[50] "We know from repeated experience that the money price of labour never falls till many workmen have been for some time out of work." And, contrary to an assertion of George Stigler, Malthus did introduce the concept of hoarding.[51] It appears, in fact, in the first edition of his *Essay on Population*:[52] ". . . the avaricious man of Mr. Godwin locks his wealth in a chest, and sets in motion no labour of any kind, either productive or unproductive." The possibility of savings not invested stayed with Malthus throughout his life. In 1820, for example, he pounces on an admission of Say's that a good deal of savings that could not, at that time, find productive use as conceding "all that I contend for."[53] In *The Principles* he also evoked "redundant capital . . . glutting the markets of Europe . . ." in the wake of the coming of peace.[54] And here, with a kind of accelerator—the possibility of inadequate effective demand playing back on the motive for investment—we come to the main thrust of Malthus's theory. H. W. Spiegel quotes the following passage to suggest that Malthus anticipated Oskar Lange's notion (1938) of an optimum propensity to consume.[55]

> If consumption exceed production, the capital of the country must be diminished and its wealth must be gradually destroyed from its want of power to

produce; if production be in a great excess above consumption, the motive to accumulate and produce must cease from the want of an effectual demand in those who have the principal means of purchasing. The two extremes are obvious; and it follows that there must be some intermediate point, though the resources of political economy may not be able to ascertain it, where, taking into consideration both the power to produce and the will to consume, the encouragement to the increase of wealth is the greatest.

D. P. O'Brien argues effectively that Malthus's is a post-Keynesian "stock-adjustment" model:[56]

> . . . the first and fundamental point to grasp is that it is not a Keynesian model with which Malthus is dealing. It is not a case of savers being unable to find an outlet for their savings so that *ex ante* saving is greater than *ex ante* investment. Saving is realized—it is not mere hoarding—but this is what causes the trouble. What we have here is in fact a *post*-Keynesian model—a capital-stock-adjustment model. . . .
>
> Of course it is possible to be critical of Malthus's handling of all this. His neglect of the multiplier effects of the investment spending is important. But he had latched on to an intellectual problem of some size: It really was a capital stock adjustment problem which concerned him—his constant references to "proportionality" between productive and unproductive activity, and between consumption and investment, show this very clearly—and if we need post-Keynesian economics to understand what he was after, this is not entirely his fault.

One might add that, in his emphasis on the need for an appropriate "proportionality" between investment and consumption Malthus anticipates Marx's two-sector model of the second volume of *Capital* (following, p. 138) and the subsequent long sequence of those who sought to define equilibrium growth in these terms.

Malthus did not produce a fully articulated macro-theory, nor did he apply his insights satisfactorily to the business cycle. (Nor, for that matter, did Keynes in the *General Theory*). Thomas Tooke captured the dynamics of cyclical fluctuations of this period better than Malthus or, indeed, any other economist of the day. But Malthus did relate his macro-theory to the years of acute post-1815 depression. His insights go far deeper than the simple underconsumptionist doctrine of which he is sometimes accused and constitute, in effect, essential components in any viable theory of growth and fluctuations.[57]

George Stigler concludes his relative evaluation of Malthus and Ricardo with the following counter-weight to Keynes's judgment:[58] "The triumph of Ricardo over Malthus cannot be regretted by the modern economist: it is more important that good logic win over bad than good insight win over poor." Even if there was not more good logic in Malthus's position than Stigler is willing to grant, his *bon mot* is rather more a stricture on modern mainstream economics than on Malthus.

Relative Prices

The argument here is, then, that Malthus's direct observation of economic affairs over the span of his mature life generated important insights into the dynamics of fluctuations in real national income. Here we suggest an equally remarkable *tour de force;* namely, a

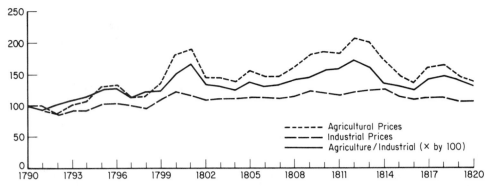

Figure 3.3. Indexes of Agricultural and Industrial Prices: Great Britain, 1790–1820 (1790=100). [Adapted from W. W. Rostow, *World Economy: History and Prospect* (University of Texas, 1978), p. 114, illustration derived from Glenn Hueckel, "War and the British Economy, 1793–1815: A General Equilibrium Analysis," *Explorations in Economic History,* Vol. 10, No. 4 (Summer 1973), p. 388.]

rough modelling of the dynamics set in motion by changes in the relative prices of agricultural products and manufactures that bring him within sight of a 40-year cycle along the lines of the Kondratieff cycle.[59] The fact is, of course, that Malthus lived through the First Kondratieff Upswing (say, 1790–1815); and, by the time of his death in 1834, he had observed a good part of the First Kondratieff Downswing (say, 1815–1848). But, as we shall see, it took a rather special kind of imagination in 1820 for Malthus casually to toss out the suggestion that the early years of the twentieth century might be a time of war, high interest rates, rapidly expanding international trade, and relatively high-priced agricultural commodities—which they turned out to be.

Malthus's exposition of the dynamics of the intersectoral terms of trade begins with a doctrine rooted in the founding fathers of political economy but heightened by the experience of the war years, when basic commodity prices rose much more rapidly than those of manufactured goods (Figure 3.3). On an index number basis (1790 = 100) agricultural prices rose to a peak of 206 (1812), whereas industrial prices peaked at 126 (1814).[60] So powerful were the cost-reducing technological changes at work in certain sectors that the price of British cotton exports (and domestic commodity exports as a whole) peaked out in 1799 and declined thereafter. British bar iron prices peaked out 2 years later and also subsequently declined.

Here is Malthus's enunciation of the classic view of relative prices:[61]

> The elementary cost of manufactures, or the quantity of labour and other conditions of the supply necessary to produce a given quantity of them, has a constant tendency to diminish; while the quantity of labour and other conditions of the supply necessary to procure the last addition which has been made to the raw produce of a rich and advancing country, has a constant tendency to increase.

The acceptance of this doctrine did not lead Malthus into predictions of an early stage of stagnation or worse. He was, on balance, quite optimistic about the prospects for sustaining productivity and profits in agriculture. He cites, in particular: improved agricultural machinery, methods of cropping and managing the land, and increased personal exertion by farm labor, noting wide international variations in labor efficiency; the possibility of a rise in domestic prices damped by increased imports; and a decline in the price of manufactures due to improved machinery, which may permit a rise in the money price of agricultural produce without a proportional rise in the money wage rate. Malthus concluded, in fact, that diminishing returns in agriculture might be fended off "for some centuries to come."[62] He could, therefore, argue against the Ricardian doctrine that the rate of profit was doomed regularly to decline because it depended "on the fertility of the last land taken into cultivation."[63] Profits, Malthus argued, could vary around a fairly stable norm depending on "the relative abundance or scarcity of capital, and the demand for [agricultural] produce compared with the supply."[64]

It is evident that Malthus was, in part at least, led to this conclusion by contemplating a succession of three periods as they were then understood.[65] First, a long stretch of the eighteenth century (excluding intervals of war) in which profits and interest rates were low (the latter about 3%) and agricultural supplies ample. In this interval profits also declined and the prices of manufactures fell relative to wage rates. Then came the 20 years 1792–1812 when the convergence of war and a surge in agricultural prices, profits, and investment yielded an average market rate of interest "rather above than below 5%."[66] This is Malthus's description of the forces at work:[67]

> In the first place, there can be no doubt of the improvements in agriculture which were going forward during these twenty years, both in reference to the general management of the land, and the instruments which are connected with cultivation, or which in any way tend to facilitate the bringing of raw produce to market. Secondly, the increasing practice of task-work during these twenty years, together with the increasing employment of women and children, unquestionably occasioned a great increase of personal exertion; and more work was done by the same number of persons and families than before.
>
> . . . to these two causes of the increased productiveness of the powers of labour we [must] add a fall in the prices of manufactures from improved machinery, and a rise in the price of corn from increased demand, unaccompanied by a proportionate rise of most foreign, and many home commodities. . . .

Then, as we have already seen, (preceding, p. 60) comes Malthus's view of the third period—of post-1815 agricultural distress, a glut of capital, with low interest rates, profits, and rents, as well as a declining price level.

From his examination of these three historical episodes Malthus does not generate an explicit theory of long cycles. And, clearly, the role of war and peace is important in his interpretation, as it was in fact. But there is more to his view than war and peace. He was conscious of the importance of lags in the economic process. As indicated in note 61, he was sensitive to the slower response of agriculture than manufactures to an increase in demand. In the *Principles* there is a second passage that captures in a demographic setting the likelihood of disequilibrium in economic growth due to time lags:[68]

> . . . it appears from experience that while the productive powers of labour remain nearly the same, the supplies of labour and the supplies of capital and produce do not always keep pace with each other. Practically, they are often separated at some distance, and for a considerable period; and sometimes population increases faster than capital and produce, and at other times capital and produce increase faster than population.

It is obvious, for instance, that from the very nature of population, and the time required to bring full-grown labourers into the market, a sudden increase of capital and produce cannot effect a proportionate supply of labour in less than sixteen or eighteen years. On the other hand, when capital and produce are nearly stationary from the want of will to accumulate, it is well known that population in general is apt to increase faster than the produce which is to support it, till the wages of labour are reduced to that standard which, with the actual habits of the country, are no more than sufficient to maintain a stationary population.

These periods, in which population and produce do not keep pace with each other, are evidently of sufficient extent, essentially to alter the proportion which goes to pay wages of labour; and consequently, to influence essentially the rate of profits.

Malthus's view of the possibility of long cycles rooted in shifts in the relative prices of basic commodities is, of course, not fully developed. It contains for example, some but not all the elements I deploy in my exposition of Kondratieff cycles.[69] It comes closest to Colin Clark's sequence of "capital-hungry" and "capital-sated" periods that also are related to wars, to periods of relative scarcity and abundance of agricultural products, and to periods of more and less rapid expansion of foreign trade.[70] In any case, Malthus proved capable of the following rather remarkable projection based on historical analogy and reflection.[71]

I should feel no doubt, for instance, of an increase in the rate of profits in this country for twenty years together, at the beginning of the twentieth century, compared with the twenty years which are now coming on; provided this near period were a period of profound tranquillity and peace and abundant capital, and the future period were a period in which capital was scanty in proportion to the demand for it owing to a war, attended by the circumstances of an increasing trade, and an increasing demand for agricultural produce similar to those which were experienced from 1793 to 1813.

Ricardo's response to this passage dramatizes his instinct to drive for a single overriding and fundamental cause in the face of complex phenomena:[72] "What a number of conditions! the only one of importance is the abundance or scarcity of capital compared with the demand for it, . . ."

Behind what appears to be a somewhat wild flight of imagination, based on reckoning from a flimsy empirical base, Malthus is earnestly seeking to resolve his difference with Ricardo on the determination of profits. He recognizes the legitimacy of the long-run theory of rent, profit, and the stationary state argued by Ricardo; but he recognizes also that it is likely to be overwhelmed in its effect by the operation of forces of great power and persistence that, he feels, cannot be dismissed as simply short-run or transitory:[73]

. . . when cultivation is pushed to its extreme practical limits, that is, when the labour of a man on the last land taken into cultivation will scarcely do more than support such a family as is necessary to maintain a stationary population, it is evident that no other cause or causes can prevent profits from sinking to the lowest rate required to maintain the actual capital. But though this principle is finally of the very greatest power, yet its progress is extremely slow and gradual; and while it is proceeding with scarcely perceptible steps to its final destination, the second cause is producing effects which entirely overcome it, and often for twenty or thirty, or even 100 years together, make the rate of profits take a course absolutely different from what it ought to be according to the first cause.

The Stages of and Limits to Growth

Malthus's view of the stages of and limits to growth is, in effect, an exercise in the relative power of his "first" and "second" causes in the quotation above. The first is to be seen at work, in immense variety, in the empirical sections of his second (and subsequent) edition of the *Essay on Population*. Using the already conventional stages of hunting-gathering, stock-raising, agriculture, commerce-manufacturing, he sets out the positive and, where they exist, preventive checks to population increase in more than 30 societies from "the wretched inhabitants of Tierra del Fuego" to "the beggars of Teshoo Loomboo" (Tibet); and from ancient Greece to contemporary Europe and the United States. Exploiting some 102 authorities within the existing literature and his own travels, Malthus produced an impressive and coherent study in what might be called comparative demographic anthropology.[74] The bulk of the cases he examines represent, in one fashion or another, the operation of his first cause; that is, the inexorable expansion of population up to the point where the means of subsistence, whatever the form of the economy, can maintain at best a stationary population at a minimum level. But Malthus finds some exceptional cases; for example, Norway, where he judged (perhaps inaccurately) that military service and a lively communal sense of limitations of the environment discourage early marriages.[75] And, of course, he finds a happy state of affairs in contemporary United States and, for transitional periods, in previous societies blessed for a time with extremely favorable resource–population balances. But, as in his first edition of the *Essay on Population,* Malthus's "checks to population" constitute a catalogue of horrors as various forms of misery and vice act "positively."

When Malthus turns to the prospects for Britain, however, he is back in the world of his second cause; that is, the extent to which diminishing returns can be fended off, aided by benign preventive checks to the population. Here some shift in Malthus's views can be detected. For example, in responding to Godwin's technological optimism about the future, Malthus expresses in the first edition of the *Essay on Population* a cautionary scepticism, including observations on the probable limitations of the telescope that were short of prescient.[76] And, when Malthus, like Hume and Adam Smith before him, gets into the rich-country–poor-country problem, again his view is more measured and less sanguine than those of his predecessors.[77] The result stems, in part, from a shift in the framework of debate. Hume and Smith were arguing against mercantilist protectionists; Malthus was arguing against extreme Free Traders.

He begins the discussion with a lucid statement of the Free Trader's point of view:[78]

> A country which excels in commerce and manufactures may purchase corn from a great variety of others; and it may be supposed, perhaps, that, proceeding upon this system, it may continue to purchase an increasing quantity, and to maintain a rapidly increasing population, till the lands of all the nations with which it trades are fully cultivated. As this is an event necessarily at a

great distance, it may appear that the population of such a country will not be checked from the difficulty of procuring subsistence till after the lapse of a great number of ages.

Malthus then adduces a series of circumstances that could make difficulty long before fertile land in surrounding countries had run out:

- "Advantages which depend exclusively upon capital and skill, and the present position of particular channels of commerce, cannot in their nature be permanent."[79]
- Domestic competition of the kind experienced in the highly successful cotton industry is also capable of driving down profits and wages to levels that would constitute "a check on population" that "no ingenuity of machinery which was not continually progressive" could prevent.
- A country dependent on both food and raw material imports to sustain its people and industry is vulnerable to a wide variety of forces that might reduce its capacity to import from its suppliers; indolence or bad management of resources in the supplying nation; an unfavorable shift in the terms of trade; or, a virtually certain shift in the supplying nation from agricultural and raw material production to manufacturing. Malthus concludes that a balanced system of both agriculture and commerce is optimal:[80]

> . . . it is the union of the agricultural and commercial systems, and not either of them taken separately, that is calculated to produce the greatest national prosperity; that a country with an extensive and rich territory, the cultivation of which is stimulated by improvements in agriculture, manufactures, and foreign commerce, has such a various and abundant resources that it is extremely difficult to say when they will reach their limits. That there is, however, a limit, which, if the capital and population of a country continue increasing, they must ultimately reach and cannot pass: and that this limit, upon the principle of private property, must be far short of the utmost power of the earth to produce food.

Passages like that just quoted have yielded a somewhat belated revisionist literature.[81] Malthus (and Ricardo as well) is associated in much of the literature on the history of economic theory with pessimistic views about the prospects for the world economy. The popular image of economics as "the dismal science" owes a good deal to what many have believed were the practical conclusions of Malthus and Ricardo on population and diminishing returns. And the first edition of Malthus's *Essay on Population,* written in the 1790s in a setting of chronic strain on the food supply, contending against the ardent optimism of William Godwin, certainly contains some blood-curdling passages. Indeed, Malthus's own evaluation in the Preface is: "The view which he [the author] has given of human life has a melancholy hue. . . ." And it is wholly understandable that a rather urgent limits-to-growth strand should enter the writings of close observers in the 1790s as they projected, in an excessively linear way, the apparent implications of rising food prices, years of true food shortage mitigated only by large income subsidies to the poor, despite vastly increased agricultural investment in hitherto submarginal land. As we shall see, such pessimism was to recur in each of the other Kondratieff upswings of the next 2 centuries.

Moreover, both Malthus and Ricardo used the stationary state as an expositional device to illustrate the operation of certain abstract forces; and as Frederic Kolb has emphasized,

Ricardo's dedicated disciples, James Mill and J. R. McCulloch, by suggesting the early arrival of the stationary state, created considerable confusion.[82]

I am inclined to think that an additional factor at work flows from the timing of Malthus's observations and writing. The somewhat more hopeful second edition of Malthus's *Essay on Population* was written in an interval of remission from the acute population–food pressures of 1795–1796 and 1799–1801 (see Figure 3.3, above). From a peak in March 1801 the price of wheat fell from 154s to 50s per quarter in March 1804.[83] The next acute phase of pressure on the food supply came in the period 1809–1812, notably the extremely difficult years 1811–1812. From a peak in August 1812 grain prices declined erratically to a trough in 1822, after which they oscillated about a stable average level for 30 years. It was in precisely this interval, 1813–1822, when the First Kondratieff Downswing had begun and the agricultural interests were clamoring for protection, that Malthus and Ricardo formulated their final temperately optimistic judgments on how long man's ingenuity and the exploitation of comparative advantage could keep that old devil Diminishing Returns at bay.[84]

Noneconomic Factors

Noneconomic factors play a more important role in Malthus's analysis of economic growth than in Adam Smith's, and a somewhat different role than in Hume's.

The population issue inescapably introduced noneconomic variables in both the rather stark formulation of the first edition of the *Essay* and the more nuanced second edition containing in Volume I its treatise in comparative demography.

The first edition takes its start, of course, from the state of heightened excitement, tension, and speculation evoked by the revolution that had been unfolding in France since 1789. The dialogue, as Malthus saw it, was between "the advocate for the perfectibility of man" and "the defender of establishments."[85] The major contenders, Malthus judged, neither listened to each other nor fairly judged each other's motives. In defining the difficulties that impeded the perfectibility of man, Malthus sought to contribute to the amelioration of the human condition. But, from the beginning of his inquiry he found himself inevitably dealing with dimensions of the human condition beyond the conventional terrain of political economy. After all, the second of his two basic postulates, about which he has a good deal to say, is:[86] ". . . the passion between the sexes is necessary, and will nearly remain in its present state." And even in his first edition, the passages on "the preventive check" consist of a series of shrewd sociological observations on why men ranging from "the highest rank" in society to "servants who live in gentlemen's families" may choose to postpone marriage or never marry at all.[87] Despite a bit of the pomposity of both youth and the ministry, there is also a strand of Jane Austen in Malthus.

His handling of the greatly enlarged, empirical materials in the second edition is much more professional. The two books of Volume One of the 1803 edition, surveying systematically "The Checks to Population" in ancient, primitive, and less developed societies and, then, in contemporary Europe, are a *tour de force* of general social science. Demographic statistical calculations are interwoven with social, political, psychological, anthropological, and economic analysis. It all permits him a less dramatic and more comforting conclusion—at least for Europe—than the first edition:[88] ". . . it appears that in modern Europe the positive checks to population prevail less and the preventive checks more than in past times, and in the more uncivilized parts of the world."

The ascendancy of the preventive over the positive checks to population was linked, as we saw earlier (p. 57) to large conclusions about the appropriate shape societies should assume.[89] It will be recalled that Hume and Smith argued that a lively commercial and manufacturing society, built by and strengthening a strong middle class, sedulously protecting private property, would tend also to generate institutions of civil and political freedom. In a similar but not identical vein, Malthus argued that the nurturing of those institutions plus the cultivation of popular education would maximize the strength of preventive checks to population by teaching "the lower classes of society to respect themselves by obliging the higher classes to respect them. . . ."[90]

As a personality, Malthus differs from his two greatest predecessors. David Hume emerges, it will be recalled, as a sanguine, humorous, somewhat stylized eighteenth-century figure, perhaps masking his frustrations and disappointments, but pretty much the wise, humane companion his friends describe, capable of going about in a black-spotted yellow coat and, as mortal illness closed in, mounting on July 4, 1776, a cheerful farewell dinner for those closest to him. Adam Smith is less penetrable, the absent-minded bachelor professor who, in Hume's commendation, was a "man of true merit, though perhaps his sedentary recluse life may have hurt his air and appearance as a man of the world." Smith was said to have had one great passion in his life; but for unknown reasons nothing came of it. He never married, nor did she.[91] What we do know is that his father died before he was born and he was closely attached to his mother, with whom he lived for 60 years and after whose death he went into a rapid decline. But, Adam Smith remains in recorded memory about as pure a scholar-teacher as one is likely to find.

It is somewhat different with Malthus. His complexities are more exposed. For one thing, he carried the burden of a cleft palate and a hare lip. As a curate of the Church of England and, later, professor of the East India College at Hailebury, he was never truly affluent. Indeed, he was only able to marry because in 1803, when he was 38, the rectorship of the parish of Walesby became open through the death of the incumbent and was granted to him with a reasonably comfortable living.[92]

There is every evidence that, on balance, Malthus was "a mild and benevolent person."[93] But these qualities were sustained by inner discipline; for Malthus was clearly driven by a complex of authentic passions, and there are often flashes of white heat in his prose.

From all accounts, he fell deeply in love with Harriet Echersall in 1802; but they could not marry without losing his income from his Cambridge fellowship and had to wait two nerve-wracking years for the opening at Walesby. He was clearly a man who felt compassion for the unfortunate poor, even for unmarried mothers ("so natural a fault"); but logic and what he felt was scientific integrity led him to oppose the Poor Laws as they were then administered. Above all, in writing so vividly about issues of great sensitivity, Malthus was plunged into controversies that shadowed the rest of his life. These focused around matters of maximum intensity of feeling: religion, sex, and the treatment of the poor.[94] Controversy was heightened because Malthus's formulation of his position often left him vulnerable—sometimes because his judgments were unwise, often because they were expressed in unguarded and provocative language and always without humor. It did not matter that his central hypothesis was to be found in Hume and Smith or that his argument was buttressed by an impressive body of evidence.

The irony of all this is that of the four great classical figures—Hume, Smith, Malthus, and Ricardo—I would guess that Malthus felt most deeply and personally—least abstractly—the reality of human misery among the poor and found the greatest difficulty in reconciling that reality with belief in a just God.

David Ricardo (1772–1823)

In setting the background for Malthus, we dealt, inevitably, with aspects of the life and work of Ricardo. They were linked not only by their ties of professional association, friendship, and respect, but also by their bafflement at the unresolvable differences that flowed from their respective approaches to political economy. They were also linked by an awareness that they stood as leaders of a second generation, operating in the wake of Adam Smith and *The Wealth of Nations*. And they were linked by the dramatic sequence of problems confronted by the British economy in their time that set their working agenda as political economists: the pressure of an accelerated population increase on the food supply during the years of war and its dramatic easing in the postwar years; a period of sustained agricultural expansion and high profitability followed, after 1812, by a dramatic fall in grain prices, agricultural distress, and a sharp debate on agricultural protection; wartime inflation, with detachment from a bullion standard and a floating exchange rate after 1797, and then return to a gold standard in 1821 in a contentious setting of falling prices; and, asserting itself progressively in the background, the first round of the industrial revolution, making possible the financing of the war against Napoleon in good part via cotton exports, generating also an enlarged and increasingly assertive industrial and commercial middle class and a volatile urban working class sensitive to fluctuations in the cost of living and employment. In the last years of Ricardo's life, when he was a member of Parliament (1819–1823), the issue of electoral reform was actively on the agenda; and he addressed himself to it.

Ricardo's education was distinctly not in the mainstream of his time.[95] His first two years' schooling was in Holland, from which his father had come and with which his family maintained close ties; then a common school education until his father took his eldest son, aged 14, into his firm as a Stock Exchange broker. There David exhibited remarkable capacity for the business in hand and a precocious maturity, which his father recognized by granting him responsibilities beyond his years. On his brother's credible account, David also exhibited "a taste for abstract and general reasoning [and] . . . a propensity to go to the bottom of the subjects by which [his mind] was attracted . . ."[96] The capacity to hold strong, independent views against opposition, but without rancor—exhibited so markedly in his relations with Malthus—appears early and may have been strengthened by his relations with his parents. Ricardo's father, as described by David's brother, Moses, was a man of strong prejudices rooted in "the opinions of his forefathers in points of religion, politics, education, etc."[97] He expected his children to accept these "upon faith and without investigation. . . . [H]is son [David], however, never yielded his assent on any important subject, until after he had thoroughly investigated it. It was perhaps in opposing these strong prejudices, that he was first led to that freedom and independence of thought for which he was so remarkable. . . ."[98]

Conflict in the family came to a head with Ricardo's marriage in December 1793 to Priscilla Wilkinson, daughter of a Quaker surgeon. The details of what must have been a nerve-wracking sequence are not firmly known. The evidence suggests a period of gradual loosening of Ricardo's commitment to Judaism as a religion;[99] a formal break enforced by the Sephardic view of marriage outside the faith; a mother so offended that she insisted that her eldest son be driven from their home and separated from the family business; a reconciliation between father and son 8 years later after the mother's death. Ricardo did, indeed, have to set himself up in business independently when he married. Although only

21 he had already acquired a sufficient reputation to be backed as a broker by an eminent firm (Lubbochs and Forster), which remained his bank for the rest of his life.

Ricardo's withdrawal from Judaism never went further than Unitarianism. There is some justice in an observation not meant to be friendly of Lord Wilberforce in his diary in the wake of a speech in Parliament in which Ricardo said at one point:[100]

> He must now inform the House, that after a long and attentive consideration of the question, he had made up his mind that prosecutions ought never be instituted for religious opinions. All religious opinions, however absurd and extravagant, might be conscientiously believed by some individuals. Why, then, was one man to set up his ideas on the subject as the criterions from which no other was to be allowed to differ with impunity? Why was one man to be considered infallible, and all his fellow men as frail and erring creatures? Such a doctrine ought not to be tolerated: it savoured too much of the Inquisition to be received as genuine in a free country like England.

In Parliament, Wilberforce observed judiciously: ". . . the hon. member for Portarlington seemed to carry into more weighty matters those principles of free trade he had so successfully expounded." Wilberforce's diary entry after the debate reads: "I had hoped that _____ had become a Christian; I see now that he has only ceased to be a Jew." (The dash was inserted by cautious editors of the diary, but the reference to Ricardo is clear.)

Ricardo was active in Unitarian circles, his wife maintained a connection with the Quakers. He also kept close ties to most of his own and his wife's brothers and sisters.

Despite the homeric efforts of Sraffa and Dobb there is still a good deal we do not know about David Ricardo. At times, his universally attested competence, modesty, moderation, independence, integrity, and commitment to the common good fail to combine into a portrait of a recognizable human being. In part, this is probably the case because he was, by temperament and tempering, a highly self-disciplined person living in an age of stylized manners and language. But there are enough glimpses of him offstage and even off-balance to render credible his virtues and his humanity.

Although Maria Edgeworth's testimony in a letter to her stepmother during a visit to Gatcomb Park characterizes Ricardo's style in discourse along familiar lines, it arises from a fresh report of a particular conversation on a given day and carries perhaps more conviction than *ex post* generalizations:[101]

> We had delightful conversation, both on deep and shallow subjects. Mr. Ricardo, with a very composed manner, has a continual life of mind, and starts perpetually new game in conversation. I never argued or discussed a question with any person who argues more fairly or less for victory and more for truth. He gives full weight to every argument brought against him, and seems not to be on any side of the question for one instant longer than the conviction of his mind on that side. It seems quite indifferent to him whether you find the truth, or whether he finds it, provided it be found. One gets at something by conversing with him; one learns either that one is wrong or that one is right, and the understanding is improved without the temper being ever tried in the discussion. . . .

And three days later Maria Edgeworth is reporting to her sister a rollicking evening of charades with Ricardo appearing as a coxcomb, a monk, and a monkey.[102] We see a good deal more of an agreeable, cheerful, and affectionate family man in his letters home from the continental grand tour of 1822, including commiseration with his son Osman over Eton's loss to Harrow at cricket.

These personal documents also tell a good deal about Ricardo's view of money. His operations on the Stock Exchange made him a very rich man in an astonishingly short time. When detached from his father's firm in 1793 he had £800 to his name. When he died in 1823 he was worth something like £725,000.[103] His estate would convert to something like $42.5 million (as of the third quarter of 1987), yielding an annual income of about $1,780,000.

Ricardo began his withdrawal from business in 1814 to live the life of a country gentleman and completed the process in 1819. There is no reason to doubt his 1814 letter to Malthus observing ". . . I shall not sigh after the Stock Exchange and its enjoyments."[104] And there is a good deal of evidence that he generously helped members of his family and his wife's when they were in need. This was not without embarrassment. He had to deal with what he felt to be overeffusive thanks;[105] but two of his sisters, in fact, returned some money he sent them in what must have involved pain at both ends of the frustrated transaction.[106]

Ricardo was apparently driven in his known (and no doubt many unknown) philanthropies by two reflections: that, by chance, he was "one of Fortune's chief favorites" with respect to making money;[107] and it was a source of satisfaction to see sums, which meant so little to him, used by those to whom it might make an important difference. He was acutely aware of how different the relative marginal utility of money could be among individuals in different circumstances.

But perhaps the most revealing insight into Ricardo's character are the occasions when he was moved by moral outrage and expressed it forcefully. There are three striking examples. First, an extraordinary letter written to his father-in-law when the latter was 75, Ricardo 31. Dr. Wilkinson was, by all accounts, a tyrant whose behavior drove his children to break with him. The occasion of the letter was the departure of Ricardo's sister-in-law Fanny to live with her brothers.

Ricardo begins by evoking the heavy-handed discipline Wilkinson imposed on his children:[108] ". . . no enjoyments, no comforts, no pleasures were to be obtained by the highest or lowest in y^r family unless they emanated from you. Y^r system was that of an eastern monarch ruling over abject slaves. . . ." Ricardo then reminds his father-in-law of the successive escape from his tyranny of three of his children: Josiah, Priscilla, and Fanny. Speaking then for the family as a whole he says its members bear him no ill will and ask nothing of him except to ". . . trust every thing to affection and exact nothing. Come among us as a friend and a father and confide in our willingness to sooth your cares and contribute to your happiness,—so shall the remainder of your days be passed in comfort and peace. . . ."

Ricardo's chivalrous strand emerged again in the unfortunate Cumberland affair. Briefly, Mrs. Ricardo dismissed a young maidservant, Catherine Harrison, believed by the Ricardos to be of good character. Returning by stagecoach to her family home in Burford she met a young man, Sydney Cumberland, and proceeded with him to London at her suggestion. Cumberland, it seemed, left her at a house of ill-repute presided over by a Mrs. Whiting. Ricardo got wind of the girl's failure to return to Burford and enlisted a brother in London to establish the facts. It first appeared that Sydney Cumberland had a hand in bringing Miss Harrison to London. On the basis of this report, Ricardo wrote an evidently outraged letter to him. Cumberland denied strongly any wrongdoing. His father

George Cumberland was soon in the act. As the facts unfolded, it appeared that Ricardo's information had been wrong and Miss Harrison was a duplicitous young woman, if not simply "the bad girl" evoked by George Cumberland. Ricardo was forced to apologize. He did this handsomely and without equivocation but defended the honor and veracity of his brother. He also posed this revealing question:[109] "If you had been as firmly persuaded as I was of the girls innocence and virtue; if . . . you had heard that the writer [Sydney Cumberland] had conveyed her to such a house as Mrs. Whiting's . . . [w]ould not your conclusions have been very similar to those I formed? and would not your indignation have broken out in language as severe as mine?"

Ricardo's capacity for indignation emerges, finally, in the positions he adopted in Parliament. As noted earlier he was flatly for freedom of religious expression; but the occasion was calculated to heighten Ricardo's rhetoric.[110] One Mary Ann Carlile had been prosecuted by the Society for the Suppression of Vice for selling a copy of *An Appendix to the Theological Works of Thomas Paine* and had been sentenced for blasphemous libel to a year's imprisonment and a fine of £500 or to be imprisoned until the fine was paid. When her term of imprisonment expired, she was kept in jail because she could not pay the fine. She then petitioned Parliament through a member [Mr. Hume] and thus launched the debate.

It may or may not be significant, but in all three cases of rather passionate moral outrage Ricardo was reacting to what he felt was the mistreatment of women: his sister-in-law Fanny; Catherine Harrison before her true character was revealed; and the proselytizing Mary Ann Carlile.

In a more conventional mood of dissatisfaction in the face of inequity, Ricardo was a steady advocate of parliamentary reform and vote by ballot.[111] Two major papers published posthumously in the *Scotsman* in 1824 were on those two themes.[112]

Correctly reflecting his time, then, Ricardo, emerged after the Napoleonic Wars as a man of the nineteenth rather than the eighteenth century. He did not concern himself explicitly with the large issues of philosophical and social science analysis that engaged Hume and Smith and framed their propositions in political economy. Unlike Malthus, his work was ahistorical. He focused sharply on the unfolding operational agenda of an increasingly industrialized Britain: free trade, parliamentary reform, an appropriate policy toward the poor, and, as we shall see, the impact on labor of the introduction of machinery. Ricardo, in fact, reflected more accurately than Malthus what was to become mainstream nineteenth-century economic policy. Malthus's reserved views on free trade had an eighteenth-century cast, his obsession with effective demand foreshadowed the twentieth century. Moreover, Malthus's early identification with population theory put him, in the public mind, in a rather special category. In any case, the fact that Ricardo's theoretical formulations, however abstract, were geared to increasingly popular political policies, enlarged his stature as an economist, at least down to the mid-nineteenth century.

Thus, as Schumpeter perceived in his evocation of "the Ricardian vice," the most abstract and formal of the classical theorists was also sharply focused and, in a sense, controlled by his concern with policy.

His drift toward public affairs, as the grip of the Stock Exchange gradually loosened, yielded an important advantage for students of his basic concepts and propositions. In Parliament and in giving evidence before public commissions Ricardo's positions were systematically rooted in his theories; but he was, in those circumstances, terse and lucid. One can find in his policy statements clear and unambiguous formulations of most of his theoretical doctrines.

There is one more thing to be said about Ricardo: like Hume, but unlike the other four classical economists considered in Part I, he had a lively, often self-deprecating sense of humor. His letters to his friend Hutches Trower, for example, were shot through with quiet observations scoring off himself and, occasionally, others.[113] This sense of proportion and perspective also permitted him without apparent pain to admit the possibility of error:[114]

> The bullionists, and I among the number, considered gold and silver as less variable commodities than they really are, and the effect of war on the prices of these metals were certainly very much underrated by them. The fall in the price of bullion on the peace in 1814, and its rise again on the renewal of the war on Bonaparte's entry into Paris are remarkable facts, and should never be neglected in any future discussion on this subject.

The Basic Growth Equation

Clearly foreshadowed in his earlier work, Ricardo's central theme when he came to write his treatise was not the determinants of the wealth of nations but its distribution. As the first sentence of the opening passage from the Preface of his *On the Principles of Political Economy and Taxation* indicates, he took for granted the terms of the already classical basic equation of economic growth.[115]

> The produce of the earth—all that is derived from its surface by the united application of labour, machinery, and capital, is divided among three classes of the community; namely, the proprietor of the land, the owner of the stock or capital necessary for its cultivation, and the labourers by whose industry it is cultivated.
>
> But in different stages of society, the proportions of the whole produce of the earth which will be allotted to each of these classes, under the names of rent, profit, and wages, will be essentially different; depending mainly on the actual fertility of the soil, on the accumulation of capital and population, and on the skill, ingenuity, and instruments employed in agriculture.
>
> To determine the laws which regulate this distribution, is the principal problem in Political Economy: much as the science has been improved by the writings of Turgot, Stuart, Smith, Say, Sismondi, and others, they afford very little satisfactory information respecting the natural course of rent, profit, and wages.

Evidently, Ricardo's theory of distribution was intimately interwoven with his concept of the process of economic growth. Quite complete and internally consistent Ricardian growth models have therefore not been difficult to construct.[116] Ricardo provides observations on each of the variables in the basic growth equation, although in several cases those observations are a bit thin.

As the passage quoted above implies, Ricardo, like his predecessors and successors, asserts that output is a function of land, capital, and labor. Machinery is introduced in quasi-independent status from the beginning with the implication that "capital is to be viewed as the food and the necessaries supplied, via wages, to the worker during the production process."

Ricardo managed to generate by misadventure a great deal of harmless controversy by sharpening (or appearing to sharpen) Adam Smith's corn growth model (preceding, p. 38) into a general paradigm for the growth process.[117] The simplification was beguiling because the fact that corn could be regarded as both circulating capital and output permitted the wage rate, productivity, and the profit rate to be measured in real terms. But it turned out that the model was a bit more Sraffa's than Ricardo's, in part because, as Ricardo was aware (and Malthus pointed out), wage goods consisted of more than corn (e.g., cotton textiles); and the value problem could not be evaded. Thus, as Sraffa indicates, the critical function of the labor theory of value in Ricardo's *Principles* is as an alternative device for measuring the key economic variables in uniform, comparable terms.[118]

Putting aside these controversies and refinements, Ricardo's original model is worth noting briefly. It was presented in his *Essay on Profits,* a pamphlet published in 1815.[119] The *Essay* marked Ricardo's movement from the bullionist debate to a wider terrain in political economy. As often in the history of economic theory, the occasion was an intense controversy about policy brought on by a quite particular economic situation. The situation was the dramatic decline in the price of wheat from a peak of 152s per quarter in August 1812 to 75s in December 1813, after which it drifted erratically downward to a trough early in 1815.[120] Ricardo's pamphlet was published in a comfortable interval; between Napoleon's initial defeat and his return from Elba (March 1, 1815). Prices then bounded up moderately until the outcome of the Battle of Waterloo (June 18). What Ricardo was trying to do (along with Malthus, West, Torrens, and other pamphleteers of the time) was to influence the forthcoming debate in the House of Commons on the following subject: Should a tariff be imposed on imported grain to protect the agricultural interests of Britain against the halving of the wheat prices which had occurred? To capture the temper and focus of the occasion it is worth, before examining the growth model involved, to quote the peroration of Ricardo's pamphlet that evoked the debating device of *reductio ad absurdum* to oppose agricultural protection.[121]

> . . . If the interests of the landlord be of sufficient consequence, to determine us not to avail ourselves of all the benefits which would follow from importing corn at a cheap price, they should also influence us in rejecting all improvements in agriculture, and in the implements of husbandry; for it is as certain that corn is rendered cheap, rents are lowered, and the ability of the landlord to pay taxes, is for a time, at least, as much impaired by such improvements, as by the importation of corn. To be consistent then, let us by the same act arrest improvement, and prohibit importation.

The model Ricardo uses to arrive at his polemical conclusion is rooted, of course, in a theory of rent based on diminishing returns to land. In the course of the war years Britain had experienced a relative rise in agricultural prices and rents accompanied by both increased application of capital to existing land and the extension of production into new land. In both cases rents rose as the marginal return on the application of additional labor and capital declined.[122]

Ricardo's argument marches forward as follows:

1. The operation of diminishing returns in a long-settled and developed country can only be held off by improved agricultural technology or increased agricultural imports at prices cheaper than the cost of growing grain at home.
2. Assuming these possibilities are not available and that ''capital and population

advance in proper proportion so that the real wages of labor remain constant,''[123] the expansion of population and income will yield rising real costs in agriculture; that is, increased labor and capital will be required to produce additional units of physical output.

3. The result will be an increase in rents and a decline of profits in agriculture and elsewhere in the economy.
4. Ricardo then relaxed his assumption about fixed wages.[124] He notes that a fall in real wages could raise profits; and this introduces, tersely stated, his theory of population.[125]

> The rise or fall of wages is common to all states of society, whether it be the stationary, the advancing, or the retrograde state. In the stationary state, it is regulated wholly by the increase or falling off of the population. In the advancing state, it depends on whether the capital or the population advance, at the more rapid course. In the retrograde state, it depends on whether population or capital decrease with the greater rapidity.
>
> As experience demonstrates that capital and population alternately take the lead, the wages in consequence are liberal or scanty, nothing can be positively laid down, respecting profits, as far as wages are concerned.
>
> But I think it may be most satisfactorily proved, that in every society advancing in wealth and population, independently of the effect produced by liberal or scanty wages, general profits must fall, unless there be improvements in agriculture, or corn can be imported at a cheaper price.
>
> It seems the necessary result of the principles which have been stated to regulate the progress of rent.

5. Finally, Ricardo argues his thesis at some length that the long-run profit rate throughout the economy is set by "the profits on agriculture."[126]

Ricardo's *Essay* was, quite explicitly, a pamphlet for the times with its objective lucidly explained on its first page; namely, to demonstrate that the linkage of rent and profits combined with the law of diminishing returns lead directly to support for "the policy of leaving the importation of corn unrestricted by law."[127]

His *Principles* flows in time and inspiration directly from the *Essay;* but, under the prodding of James Mill and the dynamics of working on a broader canvas, it is much more nearly a general treatise, despite the allocation of about half the text to the subject of taxation.[128] As noted earlier, despite its focus on distribution rather than the determinants of the wealth of nations, it contains observations on virtually all the elements in the basic growth equation. It is possible, then, to proceed directly to examine Ricardo's view of its major components.

Population and the Working Force

In the quotation on wages from Ricardo's *Essay on Profits* (above, this page) he took the view that the rate of growth of population was closely linked to the rate of growth of investment; that the link was not stable through time, yielding periods when wages were "liberal" or "scanty."[129] In *The Principles* this proposition becomes, more formally, that the rate of population increase is a function of the difference between the market and natural rate of wages; that a market rate above the natural rate discourages investment, reduces thereby the demand for labor, and thus tends to bring the market wage rate back to the natural wage rate.

The operation of diminishing returns in agriculture tended ultimately to constrain the natural wage rate as well as the expansion of the economy; but Ricardo introduces quite formally a proposition latent in Malthus's 1803 and later editions of his *Essay on Population*:[130]

> . . . the natural price of labour, estimated even in food and necessaries, . . . varies at different times in the same country, and very materially differs in different countries. It essentially depends on the habits and customs of the people. An English labourer would consider his wages under their natural rate, and too scanty to support a family, if they enabled him to purchase no other food than potatoes, and to live in no better habitation than a mud cabin; yet these moderate demands of nature are often deemed sufficient in countries where "man's life is cheap," and his wants easily satisfied.
> . . . The friends of humanity cannot but wish that in all countries the labouring classes should have a taste for comforts and enjoyments, and they should be stimulated by all legal means in their exertions to procure them. There cannot be a better security against a superabundant population.

And in Ricardo's view, "a diminished rate of increase in population" was, along with improvements in agricultural technology and food imports cheaper than domestic production, one of the basic instruments for fending off the operation of diminishing returns to agriculture.

On the other hand, without population restraint induced by a rise in the natural wage rate due to elevated popular tastes, without improved agriculture technology or increased imports, a rise in the market wage rate brought about via diminishing returns and the increased real cost of producing additional food would prove self-defeating: profits and investment would be reduced; and the excessive population perhaps brought into being by the prior phase of high wages would be painfully reduced in the manner of Malthus's first edition of the *Essay*.

Essentially, Ricardo's theory of population and wages derived from Smith and, to a degree, from Malthus. His innovation—and it is a truly major innovation—lies in the clarity with which he defined the minimum or natural wage in social rather than physiological terms, i.e., in terms of "habits and customs" and "a taste for comforts and enjoyments." His other deviation from Adam Smith (and his own earlier work) with respect to labor lies in his admittance, in the third edition of *The Principles*, of the possibility of new technology resulting in a net decline in the demand for labor (following, pp. 81–83).

Investment and Technology

Ricardo recognized explicitly that capital represented a spectrum of degrees of durability, that the types of capital could be combined in different proportions with each other and with labor.[131] For purposes of exposition, however, he generally assumed that circulating and fixed capital moved in fixed relation to each other except in the special analysis of machinery and unemployment. Circulating capital is the fund from which wages are paid and, therefore, the demand for labor determined.

In this system where the demand for labor is geared to the value of investment, the latter is determined by the rate of savings which, in turn, flows "either in consequence of increased revenue, or of diminished consumption."[132] As already noted in his exchanges with Malthus (preceding, pp. 58–59), Ricardo assumed that all saving was invested.[133] Saving-investment, in turn was assumed to depend on two factors. First, profits; i.e., "net income" above the allocation of resources necessary to maintain labor at its subsistence level. Second, on the impulse to save that Ricardo assumed would vary with the expected rate of profit. Low profits combined with the inescapable risks of investment would induce the capitalist or landowner to expand his consumption rather than increase his savings. Diminishing returns in agriculture decree that ultimately profits will decline by a process Ricardo described as follows:[134]

> . . . when poor lands are taken into cultivation, or when more capital and labour are expended on the old land, with a less return of produce, the effect must be permanent. A greater proportion of that part of the produce which remains to be divided, after paying rent, between the owners of stock and the labourers, will be apportioned to the latter. Each man may, and probably will, have a less absolute quantity; but as more labourers are employed in proportion to the whole produce retained by the farmer, the value of a greater proportion of the whole produce will be absorbed by wages, and consequently the value of a smaller proportion will be devoted to profits. This will necessarily be rendered permanent by the laws of nature, which have limited the productive powers of the land.
>
> Thus we again arrive at the same conclusion which we have before attempted to establish:—that in all countries, and all times profits depend on the quantity of labour requisite to provide necessaries for the labourers, on that land or with that capital which yields no rent.

Here, as at every opportunity, Ricardo drives home his lesson for policy.[135]

> However extensive a country may be where the land is of a poor quality, and where the importation of food is prohibited, the most moderate accumulations of capital will be attended with great reductions in the rate of profit, and a rapid rise in rent; and on the contrary a small but fertile country, particularly if it freely permits the importation of food, may accumulate a large stock of capital without any great diminution in the rate of profits, or any great increase in the rent of the land.

But free trade in grain was not the only instrument Ricardo envisaged for fending off diminishing returns:[136]

> This tendency, this gravitation as it were of profits, is happily checked at repeated intervals by the improvements in machinery, connected with the production of necessaries, as well as by discoveries in the science of agriculture which enables us to relinquish a portion of labour before required, and therefore to lower the price of the prime necessary of the labourer.

Ricardo's position on capital investment, related as it is to diminishing returns in agriculture, relative price trends, wages, rents, profits, and the prospect for long-run stagnation of investment and growth, is elaborated further below. A word is required here, however, about his position on machinery in the third edition of the *Principles,* and on the possibility of technological unemployment. This is the case not because his position was particularly wise or prescient, but because it was the analytic basis for Marx's famous prediction of a reserve army of the unemployed under capitalism.

Ricardo starts with a micro-case and then generalizes the result to the economy as a whole.[137] The case is of an entrepreneur who produces both food and manufactured "necessaries"; that is, manufactures consumed by labor. He then assumes that the entrepreneur diverts in a given year half his working force to manufacturing a new machine. Once the machine is in operation his fixed capital expands, but he now operates regularly with only half the circulating capital formerly used and, in Ricardo's system, therefore, half the level of employment. Thus, the machine throws some workers out of their jobs. They would have less to spend on the manufactured "necessaries." Output would decline because of reduced workers' incomes, but profits would be maintained because the entrepreneur would have fewer workers to pay.

Ricardo aimed to demonstrate that net income to the entrepreneur (net of depreciation, but including replacement of circulating capital) could be maintained while gross income (including circulating capital used to pay labor) could decline. He had hitherto regarded the two variables as firmly linked and, therefore, had ruled out the possibility of technological unemployment.

He concluded:[138]

> In this case, then, although the net produce will not be diminished in value, although its power of purchasing commodities may be greatly increased, the gross produce will have fallen . . . and as the power of supporting a population, and employing labour, depends always on the gross produce of a nation, and not on its net produce, there will necessarily be a diminution in the demand for labour, population will become redundant, and the situation of the labouring classes will be that of distress and poverty.
>
> . . . All I wish to prove, is, that the discovery and use of machinery may be attended with a diminution of gross produce; and whenever that is the case, it will be injurious to the labouring class, as some of their number will be thrown out of employment, and population will become redundant, compared with the funds which are to employ it.

But Ricardo concluded this passage on a more hopeful note:

> . . . if the improved means of production, in consequence of the use of machinery, should increase the net produce of a country in a degree so great as not to diminish the gross produce . . . then the situation of all classes will be improved. The landlord and capitalist will benefit, not by an increase of rent and profit, but by the advantages resulting from the expenditure of the same rent, and profit, on commodities, very considerably reduced in value [i.e., price], while the situation of the labouring classes will also be considerably improved; 1st, from the increased demand for menial servants; 2dly, from the stimulus to savings from revenue, which such an abundant net produce will afford; and 3dly, from the low price of all articles of consumption of which their wages will be expended.

Ricardo evidently felt his special case should be taken seriously. But he goes on immediately to describe a case where "there would not necessarily be any redundancy of people" and, a bit later, he expresses the hope that his "statements . . . will not . . . lead to the inference that machinery should not be encouraged."[139] He argues in effect that machinery and more capital-intensive production processes are an inevitable consequence of the long-term rise in the price of food (due to diminishing returns) and, in any case, the diffusion of machinery will be required to sustain the balance of payments and employment in export industries. He is also quite conscious throughout that the profits enlarged by labor-saving inventions could, in time, result in an expansion in savings, investment, and, thus, employment.

Despite these softening passages, Ricardo's blunt and lucidly acknowledged change of position on machinery and employment has generated since 1821 a substantial body of analysis and debate. It starts with Malthus who explicitly assumed a high elasticity of demand for the product of machines (as in the case of cotton textiles), rejected Ricardo's conclusion, and found, as we saw, a quite different explanation for post-1815 unemployment.[140] Among other arguments that have underlined the special assumptions required to yield Ricardo's conclusion are these:[141]

- Ricardo's assumptions about labor requirements in the old production process, the building of the new machine, and the new production process are quite arbitrary; and the outcome he suggests depends on particular assumptions of dubious reality.
- Ricardo's neglect of the employment multiplier effects of the investment in machinery required for the new, more capital-intensive process.
- Ricardo's assumption that an entrepreneur would accept the risks of investing in new fixed capital to produce less at the same profit has been challenged.

Ricardo refers explicitly to John Barton's essay on the *Condition of the Labouring Classes of Society* (1817), disagreeing with some of his observations but noting that his work "contains much valuable information." To some (disputed) degree Barton may well have influenced Ricardo. But I suspect Ricardo felt the need to deal with the possibility of technological unemployment by contemplating the reality of the severe depression of 1819, marked by heavy unemployment, riots, and machine breaking by workers. As we have seen, both Malthus and Ricardo were deeply concerned to explain this phenomenon as well as the sharp decline in agricultural prices. And in the latter's notes on Malthus's *Principles,* written in 1820, there is a clear foreshadowing of the machinery case of the third edition of Ricardo's *Principles* published the next year.[142]

Ricardo was reacting to a passage in Malthus's chapter "Of the Wages of Labour."[143] Malthus argued that, in the general case, when a greater quantity of fixed capital is introduced gradually into agriculture ("the only way in which we can suppose it practically to take place") the result would be benign for labor despite an immediately reduced requirement for labor in agriculture. This happy outcome would flow from the increased demand for labor in manufactures and commerce, an increase made possible by higher agricultural productivity. Malthus went on to assert in general that there was ". . . no occasion . . . to fear that the introduction of fixed capital . . . will diminish the effective demand for labour . . ."; although he allowed for an interval of possible distress if the timing of increased productivity and output was not matched by "an adequate market . . . for the more abundant supplies."

Against the background of this general view—based on an appropriate dynamic proportionality between the rates of increase of capital, output, and effective demand—Malthus suggested that even in the marginal case of a substitution of horses for manpower in agriculture, labor, on balance, gains.[144] At this point Ricardo comes sharply to life with a comment foreshadowing his machinery doctrine:[145]

> If it might be possible to do almost all the work performed by men with horses, would the substitution of horses in such case, even if attended with a

greater produce, be advantageous to the working classes, would it not on the contrary very materially diminish the demand for labor? All I mean to say is that it *might* happen with a cheaper mode of cultivation the demand for labour *might* diminish, and with a dearer it might increase.

As we have seen, in his elaboration of the machinery case, Ricardo never specified satisfactorily the conditions under which the overall demand for labor would be diminished by a "cheaper mode of cultivation." Malthus, much influenced by the indirect as well as direct expansion of employment induced by the new cotton textile machinery, was a long-run optimist about fixed capital; but he allowed for the possibility of a net reduction in the demand for labor if the shift in factor proportions was sudden. Formally, Malthus's analysis of the machinery case is, essentially, macro, Ricardo's micro; although Ricardo's concluding, more hopeful observations on the longer run impact of machinery embrace structural changes in employment and relate to the economy as a whole. Despite the formal character of their efforts, both were brought to confront the problem by the reality of severe unemployment and a Luddite machine-breaking mood in the working force, notably in the years 1816 and 1819.

Contrary to Hicks's view that Ricardo's case may have captured a critical secular time lag between the initiation of innovation and a rise in real wages,[146] I am inclined to believe that Ricardo and Hicks (and Malthus as well) mistook a cyclical for a structural phenomenon. In the course of 1820 Britain moved toward tranquility as the great expansion of 1819–1825 began.[147] The next phase of labor volatility occurred in 1824–1825 when a combination of rising food prices and great labor leverage led to strikes and other demands for higher money wages. But with the sharp depression of 1826 we are back in the difficult world of 1819 with cotton operatives taking out "their resentment on the newly installed power looms."[148] And that is the episodic, cyclical pattern in which tensions unfolded down to mid-century and, even, beyond.[149]

What, then, did Ricardo have to say about economic fluctuations?

Business Cycles

The answer is: not much. He reacted to the problems posed by the severe economic and social distress of 1816 and 1819, but he did not interpret the course of events from 1815 to 1819 in cyclical terms. The bulk of Ricardo's reflections on economic fluctuations is confined to Chapter XIX in *Principles,* "On Sudden Changes in the Channels of Trade." There are also passages bearing on the problem in his earlier *Essay on Profits,* speeches in Parliament, and his correspondence with Malthus.

As the title of Chapter XIX suggests, Ricardo regarded the major source of fluctuations in his time as resulting from the transition from peace to war, with subsequent vicissitudes in wartime trade, and, then, the transition from war to peace. As a first approximation he viewed the analysis of the two transitions as an exercise in movement from one more or less stable growth pattern to another, as the following passage suggests:[150]

> The commencement of war after a long peace, or of peace after a long war, generally produces considerable distress in trade. It changes in a great degree the nature of the employments to which the respective capitals of countries were before devoted; and during the interval while they are settling in the situations which new circumstances have made the most beneficial, much

fixed capital is unemployed, perhaps wholly lost, and labourers are without full employment. . . .

From contingencies of this kind, though in an inferior degree, even agriculture is not exempted. War . . . interrupts the commerce of States, frequently prevents the exportation of corn from countries where it can be produced with little cost, to others not so favourably situated. At the termination of the war, the obstacles to importation are removed, and a competition destructive to the home-grower commences. . . . The best policy of the State would be, to lay a tax, decreasing in amount from time to time, on the importation of foreign corn, for a limited number of years, in order to afford to the home-grower an opportunity to withdraw his capital gradually from the land.

Ricardo concludes with his major policy theme; namely, the need to move the British economy to Free Trade in grain as fast as a decent transition for landowners permitted. This proposal plus his advocacy of a return to the gold standard and the retirement of the national debt by a capital levy constituted Ricardo's program for postwar Britain. He understood well the structural changes in manufacturing that had been brought about during the war years; and he believed that Britain was on a secular path of expansion likely to persist for a long time. But neither he nor Malthus grasped clearly the notion that the British economy had been for some time in the grip of a regular business cycle pattern; although Malthus had some glimmering of this possibility. A consciousness of cyclical fluctuations gradually emerged in the course of the next generation after Ricardo's and Malthus's work was done,[151] in response to cumulative evidence of regularity in the timing of dramatic financial crises; e.g., 1815, 1825, 1836, 1847, etc. Before 1815, however, the cycles were linked in popular perception with wartime events, even though, in most cases, their timing and causation were more strictly economic than appeared. For example, the crisis of 1793 came after a long-sustained commercial expansion with a concentration of long-term investment in its final stage quite typical of successor major cycle upswings. There is in 1792 evidence of strain in financial markets, increased bankruptcies, and other phenomena typical toward the end of a period of sustained expansion. Although there would almost certainly have been a financial crisis in 1793, the one that actually occurred was, in fact, associated with the outbreak of war with revolutionary France on February 1. The crisis of 1797, which led to the suspension of the bullion standard, was, indeed, the product of a mass rush for liquidity induced by false rumors of an impending French invasion. It came after a serious period of financial strain had been successfully weathered in 1795–1796—a strain induced by large grain imports, heavy war-related remittances abroad, and a French return to a metallic standard.

In the normal rhythm of things, the expansion from the trough in 1797 would have peaked about 1800; but there was, in fact, a double peak: 1800 and 1802. The normal downturn of 1800–1801 was interrupted by the brief Peace of Amiens and a transient foreign trade boom. The expansion of 1808–1810, driven by exports to Latin America, in the face of a quite effective phase of Napoleon's commercial blockade of the continent, was essentially an exploitation of the consequences of the Peninsular War for the transformation of Brazil in particular, Latin America in general. The break up of the Continental System, the War of 1812 with the United States, the initial defeat of Napoleon, his return and final defeat at Waterloo, all left their marks on the course of the British economy.

Then came the typically overoptimistic surge of British exports to the peacetime markets and the subsequent collapse of 1815–1816. It is wholly understandable under these circumstances that Ricardo's Chapter XIX should be entitled "On Sudden Changes in the Channels of Trade."

A second reason for failing to perceive the cyclical pattern operating beneath the "sudden changes" of war and peace is that while manufactures and trade in manufactures were rapidly expanding as a component of the British economy they seemed less dramatic to observers of a still heavily agricultural society, with much of the population poor or close to the means of subsistence, than the dramatic upward and downward trends in agricultural prices; the emergence of phases of what appeared acute pressure of population on the food supplies available; and short-term movements in agricultural prices of great amplitude, responding to the luck of the harvests and the uncertain grain supply lines from the Baltic.

In addition, there was the postwar debate on the return to a metallic standard. Britain had slipped into nonconvertibility in the midst of a wartime liquidity panic; and, in retrospect, it is possible to question whether the move was necessary.[152] But the return to convertibility was an intensely debated issue at the time posing many abiding issues on the relation of the money supply to other forces affecting prices and output.[153] In short, agricultural protection versus free trade and the question of the monetary standard and monetary policy were at the center of the post-1815 debate on policy rather than counter-cyclical policy; and it was on these that Ricardo mainly brought his theoretical apparatus to bear—an apparatus, in fact, significantly shaped by those issues.

Relative Prices

As is already clear, Ricardo held quite unambiguously to the view that diminishing returns operated in the production of raw produce, increasing returns in manufactures.[154]

> The natural price of all commodities, excepting raw produce and labour, has a tendency to fall, in the progress of wealth and population; for though, on one hand, they are enhanced in real value, from the rise in the natural price of the raw material of which they are made, this is more than counterbalanced by the improvements in machinery, by the better division and distribution of labour, and by the increasing skill, both in science and art, of the producers. . . .
>
> From manufactured commodities always falling, and raw produce always rising, with the progress of society, such a disproportion in their relative value is at length created, that in rich countries a labourer, by the sacrifice of a very small quantity only of his food, is able to provide liberally for all his other wants.

Ricardo judged that machinery and scientific progress were relevant to agriculture as well as manufacture;[155] but he believed the potentialities were less in the former than the latter sector. With respect to agriculture, he distinguished two types of improvements: those that increased the productive powers of the land, such as "the more skilful rotation of crops; or the better choice of manure;" and those that permit the same output from a given piece of land with less labor, such as "[i]mprovements in agricultural implements, such as the plough and thrashing machine, economy in the use of horses employed in husbandry, and a better knowledge of the veterinary art. . . ."[156]

One does not have to dig for passages suggesting diminishing and increasing returns in Ricardo. The two concepts are pillars of his analytic system. And the reasons are obvious: the situation of British agriculture during the wars with France dramatized the reality of diminishing returns; the acceleration of invention and innovation from the 1780s, including the remarkable decline in cotton textile prices after the turn of the century, in an otherwise inherently inflationary period, made clear the potential power of increasing returns. But, as in other important respects, the decline in grain prices after 1812 altered Ricardo's perspective on the future.

The Stages of and Limits to Growth

The race between diminishing and increasing returns played a central role in Ricardo's view of the stages of development and the long-run prospects for Britain and other advanced economies; but with the passage of time his view of those prospects became increasingly optimistic. Indeed, it is not too much to say that, as with Malthus, his initial Schumpeterian "vision" changed rather radically.

Unlike those of Hume, Smith, and Malthus, Ricardo's exposition is almost bare of references to economies other than that of Great Britain. There is virtually no historical dimension to his writing or allusions to Greece, Rome, China, India, Latin America, or the less advanced economies of Eastern Europe. The index of his *Principles* contains several references to the colonial trade in a sustained passage reexamining the views of Adam Smith; a reference to Spain drawn from *The Wealth of Nations;* a reference to the past effect of the discovery of the new mines in America on the price of precious metals. There is also a reference to the relative attractiveness of substituting machinery for labor in America as opposed to England, not indexed. Ricardo's difference in this respect from Hume, Smith, and Malthus emerges in his *Notes* on the latter's *Principles*. Malthus at one point disputes a Ricardian generalization by reference to early British history, to which Ricardo replies:[157] "The observation was applied to this country and not to countries only half civilized." Malthus's references to Spanish America[158] and Ireland[159] evoked even more exasperated responses from Ricardo.

Despite this strand of candid parochialism—his sharp focus on contemporary Britain and, indeed, on certain quite specific policy issues of his time—Ricardo's theoretical model was inherently dynamic and bore on certain broad issues of development and, most particularly, on the limits to growth.

Ricardo allowed quite explicitly for a socially determined and rising subsistence ("natural") wage and related it to the possibility of reduced population pressure. He distinguished, for example, actual wages from a true minimum subsistence wage; and, in new countries with much good land and relatively few people, was prepared to regard high money wages as containing "part of the profits of stock."[160]

He perceived that in countries with cheap food and abundant labor, the incentive to introduce machinery would be weak.[161] And one analyst has drawn from Ricardo's third edition treatment of machinery and unemployment an explicit conclusion for contemporary developing countries; i.e., "industrialization without growing domestic savings or foreign capital can quite easily aggravate unemployment or accentuate the price inflation."[162]

One can find a good many *ad hoc* references to economies at different stages of development, often in exchanges with Malthus; and, in an important passage, Ricardo

distinguished three quite different stages* of growth where population comes to press
against the means of subsistence or actually does so:[163]

> In new settlements, where the arts and knowledge of countries far advanced
> in refinement are introduced, it is probable that capital has a tendency to
> increase faster than mankind: and if deficiency of labourers were not supplied
> by more populous countries, this tendency would very much raise the price of
> labour. . . . [Although] it will not long continue so; for the land being limited
> in quantity, and differing in quality, with every increased portion of capital
> employed on it, there will be a decreased rate of production, whilst the power
> of population continues always the same.
>
> In those countries where there is abundance of fertile land, but where, from
> the ignorance, indolence, and barbarism of the inhabitants, they are exposed
> to all the evils of want and famine . . . a very different remedy should be
> applied. . . . To be made happier they require only to be better governed and
> instructed, as the augmentation of capital, beyond the augmentation of peo-
> ple, would be the inevitable result. . . .
>
> With a population pressing against the means of subsistence, the only
> remedies are either a reduction of people, or a more rapid accumulation of
> capital. In rich countries, where all the fertile land is already cultivated, the
> latter remedy is neither very practicable nor very desirable, because its effect
> would be, if pushed very far, to render all classes equally poor.

But there is not in Ricardo's work even a routine reference to the sequence from hunting
and gathering to agriculture to domestic and foreign commerce and the expansion of
technological virtuosity. Ricardo moved into political economy rather late in life, and he
found the systematic exposition of his views difficult. He did not command knowledge of
other societies or the facility of exposition a classical education of the late eighteenth
century might have provided. He was, in a sense, forced to focus his talents on what he
regarded as most important in his time and place. As he wrote to Trower in 1815, he
wished "to concentrate all the talent I possess" on the principles governing rent, profits,
and wages, where his opinions differed from those of Adam Smith, Malthus, and others,
and to draw "important deductions from them."[164] In one sense, he was, from his own
perspective, mainly a pamphleteer for free trade in grain.

With his attention focused on Britain in, essentially, its second generation after takeoff,
certainly the most important deductions Ricardo drew from his examination of the determinants of the distribution of output related to the future prospects of dynamic economies.
Like Malthus, Ricardo was judged in his own time and in retrospect to be a pessimistic
oracle of a coming stationary state. And, again as in Malthus, there are passages, as
Ricardo elaborates the formal consequences of diminishing returns, that appear to justify
the view that he contributed to the image of economics as the dismal science; for
example:[165]

> With every increased difficulty of producing additional supplies of raw
> produce from the land, corn, and the other necessaries of the labourer, would
> rise. Hence wages would rise. A real rise of wages is necessarily followed by
> a real fall of profits, and, therefore, when the land of a country is brought to
> the highest state of cultivation, when more labour employed upon it will not

yield in return more food than what is necessary to support the labourer so employed, that country is come to the limit of its increase both of capital and population.

And, indeed, with diminishing returns to agriculture taken to be the central economic phenomenon, it followed that the real cost of sustaining the working force at a minimum level would rise. But the rents of the passive landlord would also rise. A reduced proportion of output would thereby be available for profits and thus investment. Under the assumptions he laid down, Ricardo's formal model was a rather pure exercise in limits to growth analysis. Hume and Adam Smith in the end had also accepted the notion that economies, like trees, did not grow to the sky; but Ricardo's method of utilizing abstract, simple cases to illuminate his basic propositions rendered the stationary state (or worse) more vivid and, apparently, inescapable. Besides, Ricardo, in seeking to establish the ultimate principles at work, was often fuzzy about timing. What, for him, were principles governing an undated long-run outcome could seem mighty vivid and immediate, like the fires of Hell in a fundamentalist Baptist sermon.

But the fact is that he became systematically sanguine—not pessimistic—about Britain's prospects. Ricardo's net conclusion flowed directly from his analysis, not from visceral optimism. His theory led to the conclusion that the timing of the arrival of the stationary state depended on three variables: the pace at which new technology—both machinery and relevant scientific knowledge—was generated and applied; the extent to which a policy of free imports of grain was adopted, and other aspects of comparative advantage exploited; the extent to which the workers, through education and rising aspirations, elevated their measure of the subsistence wage and, thereby, reduced family size and the rate of population growth. In addition, since he regarded all savings as automatically invested, he argued that a reduction in government expenditure and wise policies of taxation would help postpone the stationary state that diminishing returns ultimately decreed.

On the whole he was optimistic about the probable course of all these variables, once the war was over and the grain price continued on the erratic downward course which had begun in the second half of 1812. As noted earlier, all the optimistic quotations deployed by Kolb in making his case against Ricardo as a pessimist come from the period of Napoleon's time on Elba or after his defeat at Waterloo. What gave Ricardo confidence was not so much the pace of technological advance, where his direct knowledge was extremely limited; nor firmly established evidence on the upward trend of working-class norms of minimum consumption; nor authentic confidence in the capacity of government to constrain expenditures, of which he had little. What lifted his hopes for the future was the fall in the price of grain. As the following passage from a letter of Trower of 5 February 1816 shows, his theory of rent made the circumstances of the time a moment of rejoicing, despite his personal status as landowner and landlord:[166]

> The low price of corn is an evil to the landed gentlemen which no decrease of charges can wholly compensate—they must submit to a fall of rents and they ought to rejoice in the evidence which the low price of produce affords of the yet unexhausted state of the resources of the country. High rents are always a symptom of an approach to the stationary state—we are happily yet in the progressive state, and may look forward with confidence to a long course of prosperity. It is difficult to persuade the country gentlemen that the

fall of rents, unaccompanied by loss of capital and population, will essentially contribute to the general welfare, and that their interest and that of the public are frequently in direct opposition.

And, more positively, this general prognosis as of 1819—a year in which it required a rather deeply rooted long-run philosophic perspective to express what proved to be a quite realistic optimism:[167]

> The richest country in Europe is yet far distant from that degree of improvement [The Stationary State], but if any had arrived at it, by the aid of foreign commerce, even such a country could go on for an indefinite time increasing in wealth and population, for the only obstacle to this increase would be the scarcity, and consequent high value, of food and other raw produce. Let these be supplied from abroad in exchange for manufactured goods, and it is difficult to say where the limit is at which you would cease to accumulate wealth and to derive profit from its employment.

Noneconomic Factors

Whatever human sympathies might have been stirred in Ricardo by accounts of peoples elsewhere or in other times, impoverished by poor government or poor soil, indolence or thoughtless procreation, or by some combination of them all, Ricardo as a political economist was focused sharply on those noneconomic factors relevant to his time and place: chancellors of the exchequer who milked the sinking fund and otherwise diverted savings from productive investment; economists and politicians who argued the case for agricultural protection; compassionate but wrong-headed advocates of a poor law that, in Ricardo's view, would perpetuate rather than reduce poverty. But there was also his argument that, in the common interest, "the labouring classes should have a taste for comforts and enjoyments, and that they should be stimulated by all legal means in their exertions to procure them." And, in and out of Parliament he fought redoubtably for electoral reform and religious freedom. In a phrase he himself evoked, Ricardo, the model-builder whose exceedingly abstract theories were, in fact, tracts for the times, belongs clearly among "the friends of humanity."

4

J. S. Mill
and Karl Marx

John Stuart Mill (1806–1873)

The linkage of David Hume and Adam Smith in Chapter 2 and of Robert Malthus and David Ricardo in Chapter 3 was easy to defend. In the case of each pairing, the two men were friends whose professional perspectives were shaped by essentially the same forces in the society around them. They exchanged views on problems that deeply engaged them. Their professional views were by no means identical; but their wider perspectives on the nature of a good society were pretty much of a piece.

Evidently, this was not the case with Mill and Marx. The latter went in 1849 to London believing he was a transient political refugee; but, in fact, England was his home until his death in 1883. As nearly as we know, the two men never met. And there is no indication that Mill ever read anything Marx had written.[1] Marx did read Mill, quoted from him selectively when it suited his purpose, but generally treated him with the compulsive polemical scorn that Marx systematically accorded those with whom he disagreed. He did, however, distinguish Mill from "the herd of vulgar economic apologists" with the following economium:[2] "On the level plain, simple mounds look like hills; and the imbecile flatness of the present bourgeoisie is to be measured by the altitude of its great intellects." And, on the face of it, the man whom Gladstone called "the Saint of Rationalism," the author of *On Liberty* as well as the most popular text on political economy in the mid- and late-Victorian capitalist world, does not pair easily with the impoverished revolutionary zealot working away in the British Museum with total dedication to the task of destroying the economic, social, and political system around him.[3]

There are, nevertheless, six serious reasons for treating them together in the present context.[4]

First, the technical economic foundations of both Mill and Marx are rooted in the work of their predecessors in British political economy over the previous century, David Ricardo in particular. Both men modified received economic doctrine in important respects; and both were concerned with social science as a whole and with public policy rather than economics in the narrow sense. But in this, too, they were part of the classical tradition in political economy.

Second, their views of the British and continental economies were formed in the post-1815 period of peace, in an interval of relatively low agricultural prices, before the drama of the Irish potato famine (1845–1847), the doubling of the wheat price in 1852–1854, and the mass migration from Scandinavia and Germany as well as from Ireland. Mill devoted a good deal of thought (and space in his *Principles*) to the population question. But, in fact, he was less urgently concerned with the pressure of population on the food supply than Malthus and Ricardo. The rate of increase in the British population was decelerating from the 1820s on; for example, the inter-census rate of increase for the period ending 1821 for England was 18.06%, for the period ending 1861, 11.90%.

The limitation of family size remains in Mill's work a major factor determining the real income of workers; an important element in the liberation of women, to which he attached great importance; and a critical condition for the benign stationary state he evoked as a vision of the future. Unlike Malthus, Mill felt more or less free, at least as a young man, to advocate and distribute literature advocating birth control. He was, in fact, haled before a magistrate for the latter offense, an incident that might have cost him his newly acquired post in the East India Company if it had not been handled with discretion by the authorities.[5] But there is in Mill an underlying confidence that, so far as Britain and continental Western Europe were concerned, the problem of the population–food balance would not be apocalyptic. For good reasons, he was even more of an optimist than post-1812 Malthus and Ricardo. From 1846 Britain was a Free Trade country, a position consolidated in the 1850s by access to the wheat fields in the American West being rapidly opened up with railroads and migrants from Northern Europe. And, shocking as the Irish famine was in 1845–1847, migration was possible to Glasgow, Liverpool, and Boston. Put another way, the deep concern with excess population in Mill is the foundation not so much for the avoidance of raw human tragedy as for the creation of a more civilized society in which labor overcomes its primal instinct to render itself redundant and, by prudent restraint, renders labor rather than land the scarce factor of production.

Marx would have no truck with Malthusian doctrines. He sought to explain the alleged downward pressure of the labor market on real wages by seizing upon and generalizing one special case from Ricardo's reflections on the introduction of machinery. Thus, the concept of the reserve army of the unemployed.

Third, as the British economy moved forward in the postwar years, with Belgium, France, Germany, and the United States soon demonstrating a capacity to follow in its footsteps, it became clear that a new kind of economic system had been created in the North Atlantic world. This sense of an ongoing system was heightened in the 1840s—a critical decade for both men—by the multiple railway booms of that decade: in the American Northeast, Great Britain, Belgium, Germany, and France. Both Mill and Marx brooded about the larger implications for society of this system, including two of its central characteristics: the introduction into the economy of inventions not as occasional events but as a more or less regular flow; and the tendency of the system to move cyclically, generating recurrent financial crises as well as intervals of unemployment and idle industrial capacity. For Marx the British crisis of 1825 was viewed as a benchmark in economic history, although, as noted earlier, the first modern major cycle peaked in September 1792 with its associated financial crisis coming, as was typical, later (February 1793). Mill, on the basis of Tooke's work (p. 108), was aware of the earlier crises.

Fourth, both recognized that the new system was being accompanied by a remarkable shift in the locus of political power. Charles Babbage, author of a book which significantly influenced both Mill and Marx (*On the Economy of Machinery and Manufactures*), made a memorable reference to the Reform Bill of 1832. By enfranchising the newly emergent industrial middle class, it clearly constituted a turning point in British political history. In explaining the remarkable success of the first edition of his book, Babbage adduced as a major reason ". . . the increasing desire to become acquainted with the pursuits and interests of that portion of the people which has recently acquired so large an accession of political influence."[6] Mill, in Schumpeter's phrase, was "a man palpably out of sympathy with the scheme of values of the industrial bourgeoisie";[7] while Marx was at war to the death with the emerging capitalist industrial system. But both men recognized that they lived in a time when change was possible; and each, in his own way, aimed to bring about the changes he believed were desirable.

Fifth, in contemplating the inequities of the industrial capitalism that had emerged, both Mill and Marx were drawn to Socialism. Their notions of Socialism were, of course, quite different; but the following passage from Mill's *Autobiography* is a useful reminder that he was moved toward Socialism by some of the same aspects of the system that appear to have moved Marx; while the emphasis on individual liberty in this passage also underlines the central point of difference between the prescriptions of the two men.[8]

> While we repudiated with the greatest energy that tyranny of society over the individual which most Socialistic systems are supposed to involve, we yet looked forward to a time when society will no longer be divided into the idle and the industrious; when the rule that they who do not work shall not eat, will be applied not to paupers only, but impartially to all; when the division of the produce of labour, instead of depending, as in so great a degree it now does, on the accident of birth, will be made by concert on an acknowledged principle of justice; and when it will no longer either be, or be thought to be, impossible for human beings to exert themselves strenuously in procuring benefits which are not to be exclusively their own, but to be shared with the society they belong to. The social problem of the future we considered to be, how to unite the greatest individual liberty of action, with a common ownership in the raw material of the globe, and an equal participation of all in the benefits of combined labour.

There are also, as we shall see, parallels between Mill's vision of a benign quasi-stationary state and Marx's utopian vision of communism.

Finally, there is a connection between Mill and Marx that is fundamental to the argument of this book and, indeed, to its structure. Taken together, the publication in 1848 of Mill's *Principles* and Marx and Engels' *Communist Manifesto,* against the background of multiple revolutions and deep cyclical depression, constitutes a kind of hinge on which political economy shifts from one set of priorities to another. Roughly speaking, 1848 marks the end of a century that begins with Hume's *Treatise of Human Nature* (1739) and Adam Smith's Edinburgh lectures on political economy (1748–1751), a century in which economic growth and policy to maximize growth and to postpone the victory of diminishing returns hold the center of the stage. The classical economists of the first round were sensitive to the palpable inequity of contemporary income distribution; but they looked primarily to economic development (growth plus education, an elevation of taste, etc.) to improve the lot of the majority.

But taken together, what Mill and Marx had to say in 1848 also marks the beginning of a century and more in which the clash between the imperatives of efficiency, in a competitive private enterprise system of changing technologies, and the imperatives of human welfare, rooted in western culture and its religions, dominate the agenda of political economy and politics. In addressing the issues they did, both were creatures of their time. Reviewing a book entitled *The Claims of Labor; an Essay on the Duties of the Employers to the Employed,* Mill wrote in 1845: "The claims of labor have become the question of the day."[9] Those claims led to the protracted struggle not only over income distribution, as affected by the tax policies and organization of labor, but also over policies to mitigate the harshness and vicissitudes of modern industrial society; e.g., unemployment insurance and a wide range of welfare policies. The passage of the Ten-Hour Bill in Britain in 1847 is a symbolic opening trumpet for the next century just as the coming of Free Trade in the previous year is a suitable symbolic conclusion of the century of British political economy that begins with Hume and Smith. The conventional dating of the watershed in the technical and policy focus of political economy is 1870 (following, pp. 153–154), but the late 1840s is a useful anticipatory benchmark.

Excepting Hume, no great economist ever spent less time on economics than John Stuart Mill. And the ultimate reason, articulated on the first page of the Preface to all editions of his *Principles,* deserves to be repeated daily wherever economics is taught or applied: "Except on matters of mere detail, there are perhaps no practical questions, even among those which approach nearest to the character of purely economical questions, which admit of being decided on economical premises alone."

Mill was concerned with the well-being of men and women in society. He recognized the relevance of political economy to the outcome but judged its role to be limited. This perspective flowed naturally from his quite incredible education, under James Mill's, his father's, direct tutelage. It begins at the age of 3 with Greek and comes to an important stage at 14, when the boy goes off for a happy year to France.[10] Only in the final year of his father's teaching—that is, at the age of 13—was he introduced to political economy.[11] The first edition of Ricardo's *Principles* was the basis for his father's elucidation of the subject; but young Mill read Adam Smith and, no doubt, others as well.

Political economy became a permanent part of his intellectual life, but its center initially was the utilitarian doctrine of Jeremy Bentham, which he adopted with fervor about 1822 when, after his return from France, he was 15:[12]

> . . . I had become a different being. The principle of utility . . . fell exactly into its place as the keystone which held together the detached and fragmentary component parts of my knowledge and beliefs. It gave unity to my conceptions of things. I now had opinions; a creed, a doctrine, a philosophy; in one among the best sense of the word, a religion; the inculcation and diffusion of which could be made the principal outward purpose of a life. And I had a grand conception laid before me of changes to be effected in the condition of mankind through that doctrine.

On his seventeenth birthday, in 1823—the earliest possible moment by company rule—he went to work in the London office of the East India Company, where his father had found regular employment 4 years earlier. With this base established, he made common cause with a lively group of like-minded young men, formed the Utilitarian Society, and, in his own phrase, became a "youthful propagandist." At this stage he was generally in step with his father, with the *Westminister Review* emerging in 1824 as a major instrument for disseminating the Radical Benthamite view. Mill's first published work consisted of two letters in defense of Ricardo that the latter did not particularly welcome.[13] It is clear from his own account that freedom of religious belief and expression, political and legal reform, including women's rights, and birth control, generated in him more emotional fervor. This was a phase when he "had what might truly be called an object in life; to be a reformer in the world."[14] Economic reform—notably, Free Trade—was part of the agenda; but four of his five *Essays on Some Unsettled Questions of Political Economy,* written in 1829–1830, were not published until 1844, by which time his *Logic* had achieved considerable success.

Then, in the autumn of 1826, at the age of 20, Mill suffered what can be regarded either as a precocious kind of mid-life crisis; or a sophisticated version of a typical young man's passage to maturity, including the taking of distance from his father; or, as some have argued, a quite rational but transient reaction to the gloom of a British winter:[15]

> I was in a dull state of nerves, such as everybody is occasionally liable to; unsusceptible to enjoyment or pleasurable excitment; one of those moods when what is pleasure at other times, becomes insipid or indifferent; the state, I should think, in which converts to Methodism usually are, when smitten by their first "conviction of sin." In this frame of mind it occurred to me to put the question directly to myself: "Suppose that all your objects in life were realized; that all the changes in institutions and opinions which you are looking forward to, could be completely effected at this very instant: would this be a great joy and happiness to you?" And an irrepressible self-consciousness distinctly answered, "No!" At this my heart sank within me: the whole foundation on which my life was constructed fell down. All my happiness was to have been found in the continual pursuit of this end. The end had ceased to charm, and how could there ever again be any interest in the means? I seemed to have nothing left to live for.

Mill has described his crisis and its resolution so vividly that one hesitates to paraphrase or characterize its nature and evolution; although it has generated a quite substantial literature, including psychiatric interpretations. Essentially, he suddenly concluded that the Benthamite creed and method were excessively narrow; that the habit of analysis in which he had been sedulously trained by his father "has a tendency to wear away the feelings";[16] and, quite particularly, he felt drained of a capacity to derive joy from the round of life, doomed to an "ever present sense of irremediable wretchedness."[17] The cloud began to lift when he found he was capable of being moved to tears by a story told in Marmontel's *Memoires*—a story with patricidal overtones. He then discovered increasing satisfaction in music and poetry (notably, in Wordsworth), in closer association with those who were not rigid Benthamites, and in sympathetic but not uncritical examination of the views of British and French socialists, the latter of whom were to play an important role also in the emergence of Marx in the 1840s as a political economist. Mill summed up as follows:[18]

> If I am asked, what system of political philosophy I substituted for that which, as a philosophy, I had abandoned, I answer, no system: only a conviction that the true system was something much more complex and many-sided than I had previously had any idea of, and that its office was to supply, not a set of model institutions, but principles from which the institutions suitable to any given circumstances might be deduced.

Mill also concluded, true to his analytic training, that he had identified the fatal flaw in his father's method and moved on to his work in logic, notably on the Logic of the Moral [social] Sciences.

In human terms, however, Mill at last was freed to let the strong romantic strands in his personality, straitjacketed by his early Benthamite commitment, express themselves. He was evidently ripe for his meeting with Harriet Taylor and the extraordinary merging thereafter of his emotional and intellectual life.

From our narrow perspective, the story of Mill's rite of passage bears on two characteristics of his political economy including his theory of growth. First, it led to his ". . . great readiness and eagerness to learn from everybody, and to make room in my opinion for every new acquisition by adjusting the old and the new to one another. . . ."[19] As Schumpeter justly says, the mature Mill "was the opposite of a zealot."[20] This does not mean his work is a shapeless, eclectic amalgam. But neither is it a simple, powerful Ricardian or Marxist system. By "learning from everybody" Mill turns some of the abiding critical problems of political economy and social philosophy around in his hand and exposes lucidly their inherent complexity. His efforts at resolution may not now be judged wholly satisfactory; but, in some cases, almost a century and a half after the publication of Mill's *Principles,* we have still not found agreed answers to some of the technical, social, and institutional issues he dealt with. In the mid-1980s, for example, we are still debating the impact of the introduction of laborsaving machinery on the level of employment; the appropriate balance between competition and public control of the economy; how to reconcile societies that cherish human rights and wide political freedom with effective government and avoidance of tyranny by the majority; to what extent can voluntary association be cultivated to fulfill large social purposes? Although historians of economic theory tend to view Mill primarily as the economist who summarized the cumulative technical achievement of the previous century, the subtitle of his *Political Economy* is seriously meant, indeed: *with some of their applications to social philosophy.*

Second, Mill's crisis and its resolution, later strengthened by his association with Harriet Taylor, led him to take democratic socialism with increasing seriousness as a system that might, in time, reconcile efficiency in an ongoing industrial system with equity. Typical of the mature Mill, his vision of socialism was qualified in a good many directions: by the need to protect the individual from the overbearing power of the state; by a continued belief in the efficacy of competition where competition was possible; by the need to assure that democracy did not lead to a tyranny of the majority, a strand of concern introduced by Mill's reading of Alexis de Tocqueville's *Democracy in America;* and, above all, by the need to generate over time a citizenry much better educated and better prepared to assume responsibility in social institutions.

Before turning to the substance of Mill's views on economic growth, mainly as expounded in his *Principles,* that book itself deserves a few words. It was written in less than a year and a half in the period 1845–1847. While writing this treatise of about 1,000 pages, Mill carried forward his work at India House and barely slackened the pace at which he turned out articles and editorials for journals and the press.[21] Two contemporary events are reflected in the book. The great British railway boom, accompanied by "the speculative madness of 1845," peaked and turned down while he was composing *The Principles,*[22] and these were, of course, also the years of the Irish potato famine. There are a number of passages in *The Principles* devoted to the problems of Ireland; and, indeed, Mill took time off in the period October 1846–January 1847 to write 43 leaders for the *Morning Chronicle* on Irish affairs. Under the pressure of the second successive potato crop failure in Ireland, an inadequate British wheat harvest, and similar conditions on the Continent, the British wheat price rose erratically from 46s. per quarter in August 1846 to 93s. per quarter in June 1847.[23]

Although touched by these events and other contemporary concerns, Mill's purpose related to a much longer horizon. He sought to write for his own time a successor to Adam Smith's *Wealth of Nations*, published some 70 years earlier,

> . . . similar in its object and general conception to that of Adam Smith, but adapted to the extended knowledge and improved ideas of the present age. . . . No attempt . . . has yet been made to combine his practical mode of treating his subject with the increased knowledge since acquired of its theory, or to exhibit the economical phenomena of society in the relation in which they stand to the best social ideas of the present time.[24]

The book achieved an instant success and remained a widely used text for a half century and more.[25] Aside from the correctness of Mill's judgment on the gap that existed in the literature of political economy, the book's popularity flowed from the author's gift for lucid, logical exposition. James Mill had systematically trained his son to summarize in writing as well as to expound what he had read. When Mill was about 15, after his return from France, his father had him write a short abstract of every paragraph of the former's *Elements of Political Economy*, to assist the author in improving the character of his exposition. J. S. Mill's text remains notable for the clarity with which its structure is delineated.

But perhaps even more important for the success of his text, Mill wrote well. By the time he composed *The Principles*, he was just about 40 years old. He had been writing for journals for a quarter-century and writing the disciplined memoranda of an East India Company official for almost as long.

There is a final observation to be made about Mill's classic text. I believe it helps explain both its continued vitality for those prepared to read it as well as the bafflement and frustration of some of Mill's contemporaries and successors. W. S. Jevons for example, said of Mill: ". . . however it arose, Mill's mind was essentially illogical."[26] Joseph Schumpeter came closer to the special character of *The Principles* with this observation:[27]

> What looks like so many tergiversations or what gives the impression, energetically voiced by Marx, that Mill never says a thing without also saying its opposite is in part due to this cause. But to a greater part it is due to Mill's judicial habit of mind that forced him to consider all aspects of each question. Also, it is due to something that is still more creditable. He was a man of strong preferences. But he also was incorruptibly honest. He would not twist either facts or arguments if he could help it. When the preferences—his social sympathies—did assert themselves all the same, he was not slow to apply the pruning knife. Hence many an inconclusive result, or even many a contradiction.

I would put it a bit differently. Mill was, like all interesting people, a household of quite different characters.[28] In his case, three of these characters are all hard at work in *The Principles:* a gifted economic theorist; a romantic warm-hearted preacher; and, which is often forgotten, a shrewd, hard-minded man of affairs.

With respect to the latter, I quote at length the following passage from Mill's *Autobiography* because it articulates well a significant strand in his experience and approach to problems not usually given much weight.[29]

. . . the opportunity which my official position gave me of learning by personal observation the necessary conditions of the practical conduct of public affairs, has been of considerable value to me as a theoretical reformer of the opinions and institutions of my time. Not, indeed, that public business transacted on paper, to take effect on the other side of the globe, was of itself calculated to give much practical knowledge of life. . . . As a speculative writer, I should have had no one to consult but myself, and should have encountered in my speculations none of the obstacles which would have started up whenever they came to be applied to practice. But as a Secretary conducting political correspondence, I could not issue an order or express an opinion, without satisfying various persons very unlike myself, that the thing was fit to be done. . . . I learnt how to obtain the best I could, when I could not obtain everything; . . . to bear with complete equanimity the being overruled altogether. I have found, through life, these acquisitions to be of the greatest possible importance for personal happiness, and they are also a very necessary condition for enabling any one, either as theorist or as practical man, to effect the greatest amount of good compatible with his opportunities.

Thus, in a serious study of one aspect or another of the human condition, one should not expect logical consistency of the kind Jevons had in mind; and one should view simple, powerful, logical systems with great reserve as the basis for action. One should be prepared for inconclusive results and contradictions; for David Hume was certainly correct with his expostulation: "These principles of human nature, you'll say, are contradictory. But what is man but a heap of contradictions." In general, I believe, economists have been somewhat deceived by taking at face value Mill's rather modest prefatory statement of his purpose. He emerges as a more subtle and original political economist than his method of appearing to refine and update Smith and Ricardo would suggest.

The Basic Growth Equation

Mill's version of the basic growth equation begins in Book I ("Production") with a thoroughly professional reassertion of the conventional wisdom of political economy, accumulated over the previous century, in the form of the most coherent exposition of the basic growth equation to be found among our six classical economists. He deals successively with labor, land ("appropriate natural objects"), and capital; then the "degree of productiveness" of his three production agents; finally, he turns to a consideration of the factors determining the rate of increase of each major variable in his production function and the determinants of the overall rate of increase in production. The orderliness of his sequence emerges from this preliminary passage in Chapter X as he turns from the determinants of the level of output to the rate of growth:[30]

We may say, then, . . . that the requisites of production are Labour, Capital, and Land. The increase of production, therefore depends on . . . the increase either of the elements themselves, or of their productiveness. The law of the increase of production must be a consequence of the laws of these elements; the limits to the increase of production must be the limits, whatever they are, set by those laws. We proceed to consider the three elements successively, with reference to this effect; or in other words, the law of the increase of production, viewed in respect of its dependence, first on Labour, secondly on Capital, and lastly on Land.

Mill introduces "the limited quantity and limited productiveness of land" as "the real limits to production."[31] Diminishing returns is introduced as "the most important proposition in political economy";[32] and then, the "antagonist principle": "the progress of improvements in production."[33] He deals with the accelerated decline in the cost and prices of manufactures due to "the mechanical inventions of the last seventy or eighty years" which he judges to be "susceptible of being prolonged and extended beyond any limit which it would be safe to specify."[34] But he deals also at greater length than any of his major predecessors with the full range of inventions and innovations capable of exercising "an antagonist influence to the law of diminishing return to agricultural labour."[35] Among these innovations are improved education of the working force, improved systems of taxation and land tenure, and "more solid instruction" of the "rich and idle classes" that would increase their "mental energy," generate "stronger feelings of conscience, public spirit, or philanthropy: and qualify them for roles of constructive social as well as economic innovation."[36]

Mill concludes this initial restatement and elaboration of the classical model by discussing the remedies available to postpone the time when diminishing returns definitively asserts its sway: population restraint; free trade in food; emigration. He also has something to say about generating growth "in countries where the principle of accumulation is as weak as it is in the various nations of Asia . . . and . . . the less civilized and industrious parts of Europe, as Russia, Turkey, Spain, and Ireland."[37]

Mill appears to draw a quite sharp line between production, determined in his view by firmly established scientific principles, and distribution, determined by law, custom, and other human institutions.

Later commentators have criticized Mill—sharply or gently—for failing to unify the analysis of price determination with the analysis of wage, interest, rent, and profit determination, viewed as market phenomena. Looked at closely, however, Mill did not draw a sharp line between the rules governing production and distribution. He is quite aware of the market process at work in determining income distribution. But he had a further serious point to make in Book II. It is that a whole array of quite specific human and social institutions in fact do affect income distribution; e.g., private property, inheritance laws, custom as it affects rents, slavery, and land tenure, to which he devotes three chapters (84 pages), in part to promote the program of reform for Ireland that he advocated.

When Mill comes to wages, the role of custom, etc., does not disappear, but he states flatly:[38] "Competition . . . must be regarded, in the present state of society, as the principal regulator of wages, and custom or individual character only as a modifying circumstance, and that in a comparatively slight degree." His treatment of rent and profits is equally linked to the market process. Indeed, he concluded the discussion of profits by referring to its later, fuller treatment under "Value and Price," and goes on to deal with rent in Book II only "so far as it admits being treated independently of considerations of value. . . ."[39]

Similarly, in dealing with the variables determining the level and rate of increase of production, Mill introduces nonmarket variables such as levels of education and the extent to which custom and institutions provide strong or weak incentives.

I conclude that the fault here is Mill's, to the extent that certain highly quotable passages are distinctly misleading; for example:[40] "The laws and conditions of production of wealth partake of the character of physical truths. There is nothing optional or arbitrary in them. . . . It is not so with the distribution of wealth. That is a matter of human institution solely.'' The conventional caricature of his view is also the product of rather careless reading[41]; for it is a purposeful characteristic of Mill's *Principles* that the role of noneconomic factors, as reflected in law, custom, etc., is regularly interwoven with conventional economic analysis. And in insisting that the political, social, and legal framework of the economy was subject to change with the passage of time, Mill was certainly correct. The organization of Mill's Book II in relation to Book III (and, indeed, Book I in relation to Book IV) may or may not be judged felicitous. But his basic argument deserves examination on its merits.

This digression is relevant to any serious evaluation of Mill because one's judgment of his role and stature and contemporary relevance depends greatly on one's image of what economics as a social science should aim to be. In Mill's treatment of each of the variables in the production function, one can observe not only his capacity to take into account narrowly technical views generated by others in the post-Ricardian period but also a steady insistence that the noneconomic variables relevant to growth are not only subject to change but also are legitimate, indeed, inescapable objectives of economic development policy.

Population and the Working Force

There is something of a paradox in Mill's treatment of population. On the one hand, he notes that since the British census of 1821, its rate of increase was decelerating; and that the birth rate was declining in France.[42] The corn laws had been repealed in Britain, the railways and improved transoceanic travel permitted easier emigration to countries and regions where food was cheap and abundant.[43] But in Mill's view, these developments only granted ''to this over-crowded country a temporary breathing time, capable of being employed in accomplishing those moral and intellectual improvements in all classes of people, the very poorest included, which would render improbable any relapse into the over-peopled state.''[44]

Here we have clearly the elements of what is distinctive in Mill. His basic position is rooted, of course, in Malthus and Ricardo and the earlier political economists who foreshadowed the concept of diminishing returns to agriculture and the tendency of population to press against the means of subsistence. In particular, he accepts the probability that diminishing returns will, on balance, triumph despite all the likely postponing devices of human ingenuity, the opening of virgin lands, emigration, free trade, etc.

More specifically, he accepts Ricardo's model that, *ceteris paribus,* a market wage rate higher than the natural rate has two simultaneous contrary effects: it induces an increase in population, and it discourages investment and reduces thereby the demand for labor. Under the dual impact of those consequences, increasing the supply and decreasing the demand for labor, the market wage rate declines back to the natural rate and, painfully, population declines. That model was a sufficient basis for Ricardo to make his case for free trade; and, indeed, Ricardo includes among his conditions for fending off the operation of diminishing returns to agriculture ''a diminished rate of increase in population.'' This minor strand in Ricardo's analysis becomes the major thrust in Mill's. He puts to himself the question beyond: What permanently might avoid ''an over-peopled state'' with its attendant marginally low wages, poverty, ignorance, and a degradation particularly acute for women? His answer is a sustained public policy to encourage smaller families; greatly enlarged efforts in popular education; and, ultimately, movement to a higher income per capita stationary state.

In one sense, this comparison suggests why the charge that Mill wrote "a readable Ricardo" is, to a degree, sustainable.[45] The formal apparatus underpinning Mill's theory of population is substantially (not wholly) derivative. But, in fact, no one can read carefully the four major passages in Mill bearing on population and the working force without realizing that a distinctly different perspective is at work. Mill deals with the subject under the headings of population increase as a determinant of the rate of increase of production[46]; the determination of wages[47]; the characteristics of the stationary state[48]; and in his reflections on the "Probable Futurity of the Labouring Classes."[49] Taken together these passages are an often passionate plea for the limitation of family size as a necessary condition for a civilized society; a society where the real wages of labor were high, education was universal, women were accorded equal rights by custom as well as law; and the members of the working class were not a servile mass to be governed "in a tutelary manner," but full and dignified citizens capable of taking their destinies into their own hands. Mill's powerful argument is for something more than a rise in real income per capita above the subsistence level:[50]

There is room in the world, no doubt, and even in old countries, for a great increase of population, supposing the arts of life to go on improving, and capital to increase. But even if innocuous, I confess I see very little reason for desiring it. The density of population necessary to enable mankind to obtain, in the greatest degree, all the advantages both of cooperation and of social intercourse, has, in all the most populous countries, been attained. A population may be too crowded, though all be amply supplied with food and raiment. It is not good for man to be kept perforce at all times in the presence of his species. A world from which solitude is extirpated, is a very poor ideal. Solitude, in the sense of being often alone, is essential to any depth of meditation or of character; and solitude in the presence of natural beauty and grandeur, is the cradle of thoughts and aspirations which are not only good for the individual, but which society could ill do without. Nor is there much satisfaction in contemplating the world with nothing left to the spontaneous activity of nature; with every rood of land brought into cultivation, which is capable of growing food for human beings; every flowery waste or natural pasture ploughed up, all quadrupeds or birds which are not domesticated for man's use exterminated as his rivals for food, every hedgerow or superfluous tree rooted out, and scarcely a place left where a wild shrub or flower could grow without being eradicated as a weed in the name of improved agriculture. If the earth must lose that great portion of its pleasantness which it owes to things that the unlimited increase of wealth and population would extirpate from it, for the mere purpose of enabling it to support a larger, but not a better or a happier population, I sincerely hope, for the sake of posterity, that they will be content to be stationary, long before necessity compels them to it.

It is scarcely necessary to remark that a stationary condition of capital and population implies no stationary state of human improvement. There would be as much scope as ever for all kinds of mental culture, and moral and social progress; as much room for improving the Art of Living, and much more likelihood of its being improved, when minds ceased to be engrossed by the art of getting on. Even the industrial arts might be as earnestly and as success-fully cultivated, with this sole difference, that instead of serving no purpose but the increase of wealth, industrial improvements would produce their legit-imate effect, that of abridging labour. Hitherto it is questionable if all the mechanical inventions yet made have lightened the day's toil of any human being. They have enabled a greater population to live the same life of drudg-ery and imprisonment, and an increased number of manufacturers and others to make fortunes. They have increased the comforts of the middle classes. But they have not yet begun to effect those great changes in human destiny, which it is in their nature and in their futurity to accomplish. Only when, in addition to just institutions, the increase of mankind shall be under the deliberate guidance of judicious foresight, can the conquests made from the powers of nature by the intellect and energy of scientific discoverers, become the com-mon property of the species, and the means of improving and elevating the universal lot.

There is in Mill's vision something in common with those of an unlikely pair: with Karl Marx's vision of Communism (following, p. 123); and that evoked almost a century later (1930) by J. M. Keynes in his "Economic Possibilities for Our Grandchildren."[51]

Mill embraced in the quoted passage the underlying Malthusian argument but clearly moved beyond. And he moved beyond, as well, with respect to birth control. He was what is known chastely in the demographic literature as a neo-Malthusian; that is, a believer in birth control. But the logic of Malthus's latter-day arguments virtually qualify him as a neo-Malthusian (preceding, pp. 56–57). There are a number of passages in Mill's *Principles* that argue so strongly for the limitation of family size that one expects support for birth control to become explicit. For example:[52]

> . . . While there is a growing sensitiveness to the hardships of the poor and a ready disposition to admit claims in them upon the good offices of other people, there is an all but universal unwillingness to face the real difficulty of their position, or advert at all to the conditions which nature has made indis-pensable to the improvement of their physical lot. . . . [T]here is a tacit agreement to ignore totally the law of wages, or to dismiss it in a parenthesis, with such terms as "hard-hearted Malthusianism"; as if it were not a thou-sand times more hard-hearted to tell human beings that they may, than that they may not, call into existence swarms of creatures who are sure to be miserable, and most likely to be depraved. . . .

Despite the lack of any explicit reference to contraception in Mill's published work, it is clear that he remained a supporter of birth control throughout his life. Norman E. Himes, an admirable sleuth in this rather complex matter, concludes:[53]

> (1) that John Stuart Mill as a young man played at least a passive, if not an active, role in the distribution of practical literature and that he was active in the early propaganda, at least to the extent of writing on the subject with the purpose in mind of influencing the working classes; and (2) that Mill accepted in mature life the Neo-Malthusian principle, but entertained it diffidently as a private opinion, preferring not to embark upon any public advocacy.

As noted earlier (p. 92) there is no doubt that Mill was associated as a young man of 17 or 18 with the distribution of birth control literature and was haled before a magistrate.

Himes goes further and concludes that he was also "the author of some of the most brilliant essays on Neo-Malthusianism written in that early period."[54] His subsequent reticence was broken on only one known occasion. In 1868, five years before his death, he was sent a privately printed pamphlet on *The Marriage Problem* dealing with the medical and physiological aspects of contraception. He replied to the author, in effect, that the issue was a matter of private judgment for the married people concerned and that the requisite information should be made available by professional medical persons.[55]

Aside from the specific reasons for reticence arrayed by Himes (note 53), and the inhibitions on the public discussion of matters relating to sex in nineteenth-century British society, Petersen adduced the following:[56] ". . . another and often more important reason for the isolation of neo-Malthusians was that they were in the main the type of people who expounded unpopular opinion of all kinds." He goes on to document the "recurrent association of neo-Malthusianism with every heterodox or crackpot idea" from atheism to free love; but he judges progress was inhibited by "the hostility between it [neo-Malthusianism] and socialism, two competitors in utopian wares."

The intensity of the issue is suggested by the fact that the London *Times* published a "particularly malevolent" review of Mill's career on the occasion of his death.[57] The writer of the obituary notice, Abraham Hayward, not only recalled the charge that Mill was associated since his youth with the birth control movement, but also circulated to a substantial group of public figures a more explicit version of this charge, thereby launching a public controversy as Mill's friends rallied round to defend his name. It was, thus, no small thing for Mill in his day to support—like his father—contraception as an additional potential ''negative'' restraint on population increase.

From Mill's point of view, however, the most distinctive strand in his treatment of labor as a factor of production was not his semicovert support for birth control but his extensive examination of the forces determining the productivity of the working force. He introduces, of course, the factors of production with which labor must combine: e.g., the quality and availability of the soil and sources of raw materials, as well as the scale and quality of capital equipment. But he goes on to explore questions like these: What determines the capacity and willingness of labor to engage in "steady and regular bodily and mental exertion''?[58] In what ways do the workers of various European countries differ with respect to skill, adaptability, and moral character?[59] How does the degree of security of property affect productivity?[60] What have we learned about the potentialities and limits of the division of labor since Adam Smith and his parable of pin manufacture?[61] Then, later, in speculating on the future of the working classes: What effects can be anticipated on the size, quality, and composition of the working force from the expansion of popular education and the movement of women toward equal rights?[62] What is the evidence on the relation between labor productivity and profit-sharing schemes?[63] What about producer's cooperatives?[64]

To refer back to Irma Adelman's version of the production function (preceding, p. 6), Mill deals more fully than any of his predecessors with the impact of U_t ("the sociocultural milieu") on L_t ("the employment of the labor force"), although it was a consistent strand in the classical tradition that sociocultural forces be taken into account.

Investment and Technology

The distinctive elements in Mill's treatment of capital and technology are candidly derivative; and they do not reflect his central concerns as a reformer in quite the same way as his expositions of population dynamics, the labor supply, and labor productivity. It is not unfair to say that Mill helped elevate two authors into conventional histories of economic thought. One was Charles Babbage, whose *On the Economy of Machinery and Manufactures* (1841) is quoted substantially, and sometimes at length, on eight occasions by Mill; the other, John Rae, whose *Statement of Some New Principles on the Subject of Political Economy* (1834) is quoted on four occasions, including passages fundamental to Mill's conclusions on saving and capital formation.[65] Mill says of Rae, then virtually unknown: "In no other book known to me is so much light thrown, both from principle and history, on the causes which determine the accumulation of capital."[66] Mill's chapter "Of the Law of the Increase of Capital" is, almost literally, a paraphrase of a part of Rae's doctrine. The central proposition, quite original in its time, is that all accumulation involves the sacrifice of a present for the sake of a future good. The forces making for weakness or strength in the process of accumulation are then reviewed mainly on the basis of specific illustrations drawn from Rae. Mill then arrays the reasons for the peculiarly strong British propensity to save and invest: exemption from the ravages of war; a long tradition of security of property; a geographical setting that lent itself to commerce rather than war; the early decline of feudalism; and the social prestige and political influence of the wealthy. The conclusion of this passage—worthy of G. B. Shaw—reminds us that Mill was, after all, of a Scottish family and never lost his warm association with France.[67]

> To get out of one rank in society into the next above it, is the great aim of English middle-class life, and the acquisition of wealth the means. . . . These causes have, in England, been greatly aided by that extreme incapacity of the people for personal enjoyment, which is a characteristic of countries over which puritanism has passed. But if accumulation is, on one hand, rendered easier by the absence of a taste for pleasure, it is, on the other, made more difficult by the presence of a very real taste for expense. So strong is the association between personal consequence and the signs of wealth, that the silly desire for the appearance of a large expenditure has the force of a passion, among large classes of a nation which derive less pleasure than perhaps any other in the world from what it spends.

Rae combines his analysis of the motives for accumulation with a quite original and complex analysis of the human impulses which yield invention and the impact of the flow of invention on the capital stock.[68] It is difficult to do justice to his extended and richly illustrated argument in summary. But briefly, he asserts that the normal instinct of men in society is to imitate and "amalgamate with the mass"; deviants and inventors are rarely rewarded; but revolutionary change imposed from the outside or the emergence of "necessity" for new options can stimulate invention and render it acceptable. He sensed in his time a decline in the barriers to change. Little of this is reflected in Mill except a passing reference: ". . . it is a just remark of Mr. Rae, that nothing has a greater tendency to promote improvements in any branch of production, than its trial under a new set of conditions."[69]

With respect to machinery and technology, Mill relies heavily on Babbage. Indeed, despite multiple references to Babbage's work, Mill appears to have assumed his readers were familiar with its argument. And he had some reason to do so. The first edition of Babbage's book on machinery and manufactures sold some 3,000 copies in 2 months—the equivalent of about 40,000 copies in the United States of the mid-1980s. Two further printings shortly followed.

It is a curious best-seller. The author was a professor of mathematics at Cambridge. He achieved a permanent place in the history of technology by designing and working long to complete a Calculating Engine, as he called it, clearly based on principles underlying the modern electronic computer. It was the engineering, not the scientific, problems that held him up. In seeking to solve them, Babbage moved about England and Western Europe for 10 years studying machinery and its relation to manufacturing. Thus he "was insensibly led to apply to them [the various sources of mechanical art] those principles of generalization to which my other pursuits had naturally given rise."[70] This by-product of his work on the computer is his major monument because, in 1842, the government of Sir Robert Peel refused the further support for the project recommended by the Royal Society.[71]

Babbage's study of machinery and manufactures is remarkable because it combines scientific and engineering expertise with detailed knowledge of production processes, business practice, and basic economic principles. It is, in these respects, a unique study. The closing sections of his third edition dramatize its range: Babbage moves from a philosophic discussion of the critical linkages between basic science, invention, and manufacture (plus an attack on the election of the Duke of Sussex to be President of the Royal Society) to some recent innovations including a vivid and detailed account of how the horse-slaughtering houses at Montfaucon, near Paris, manage "the profitable conversion of substances apparently of little value"—including maggots and rats.

Although Babbage's best-seller was a rather special product, it was clearly part of a phase of heightened self-consciousness about the scale, momentum, and scope of the technological revolution under way. Edward Baines's excellent *History of the Cotton Manufacture* was published in 1835, as was Andrew Ure's *The Philosophy of Manufactures*.[72] Knowledge of what was going on was greatly enlarged by the testimony laid before the parliamentary Select Committee on Manufactures, Commerce, and Shipping (1833). Here is how I characterized in another context the period between the cyclical peak in 1825 and the time the Select Committee was set up:[73]

> Although evidence on the state of British industry suggests that there was no major cyclical movement from 1827 to 1832 [there were two minor cycles], the character of these years can be clearly defined. Evidence before the Committee of 1833—on cotton, wool, iron, and shipping—is remarkably unanimous in designating the period as one of falling prices and profits, increasingly severe competition, rising output. Fixed plant had been expanded in all directions in the boom which ended in 1825; and, even in the following years, there was a strong cost-reducing incentive to take advantage of new technical possibilities. The cost of machinery and construction, moreover, was falling, and long-established firms faced the competition of new plants, better equipped and more cheaply constructed. For many manufacturers they were extremely difficult years. A falling value for fixed capital had steadily to be accepted.

> These were the underlying trends from 1815, and perhaps earlier. They lie at the heart of the secular process called the Industrial Revolution. An extraordinarily inflated state of demand was required in the middle twenties, thirties, and forties to yield, and then only briefly, rising prices and profit margins.

Testimony before the Committee dramatized the manner in which new cost-reducing technologies were flowing into many manufacturing sections, permitting forehanded entrepreneurs to survive but exerting pressure on the profits of laggards, and creating a general setting of idle capacity. All this colored analyses of the early 1830s, before the majestic boom of 1833–1836 got under way. Babbage, for example, includes a chapter "On Over-Manufacturing." The Committee also generated a large body of information on which Babbage, Baines, and others drew.

Mill exploited Rae and Babbage, with generous acknowledgement; but in neither case did he fully absorb and develop their insights. With respect to Rae, for example, Mill accepted the notion of saving as overcoming the time discount of present over future satisfaction; but he does not deal with Rae's insight that a lengthening of the period of production of a capital good increases its productivity—an anticipation of Bohm–Bawerk and the Austrians.[74] And, in a weakness shared by classical and neoclassical economists for the better part of $2\frac{1}{2}$ centuries, Mill fails to exploit the reflections of both Rae and Babbage on the generation of inventions.[75] But it should be immediately added that, perhaps reinforced by Babbage's vigorous views on the subject, Mill did strongly advocate generous public support for scientific (and other) research in universities:[76]

> It is highly desirable . . . that there should be a mode of insuring to the public the services of scientific discoverers, and perhaps of some other classes of savants, by affording them the means of support consistently with devoting a sufficient portion of time to their peculiar pursuits. . . . The most effectual plan, and at the same time least liable to abuse, seems to be that of conferring Professorships, with duties of instruction attached to them. . . . [T]he greatest advances which have been made in the various sciences, both moral and physical, have originated with those who were public teachers of them; from Plato and Aristotle to the great names of the Scotch, French, and German Universities. I do not mention the English, because until very lately their professorships have been, as is well known, little more than nominal.

Putting aside the issue posed by the innovations of Rae and Babbage, Mill's treatment of investment and machinery can be seen as an orderly elaboration of the structure of thought inherited from his great predecessors, most notably Ricardo.

As with respect to labor, Mill proceeds by viewing capital first as a factor of production; then as one source of income (profits). Finally, explicitly abandoning Statics for Dynamics, he moves to consider capital in Book IV, in the context of "The Influence of the Progress of Society on Production and Distribution."

Mill starts his exposition of the role of capital in production in sound textbook style: with a set of rather elaborate definitions; six fundamental propositions; and a detailed exploration of the distinction between fixed and working capital. In dealing with the "degree of productiveness" of factors of production he exploits Babbage on machinery and manufacturing and then introduces a fresh note of some importance:[77]

> The use of machinery is far from being the only mode in which the effects of knowledge in aiding production are exemplified. In agriculture and horticulture, machinery is only now beginning to show that it can do anything of importance, beyond the invention and progressive improvement of the plough and a few other simple instruments. The greatest agricultural inventions have consisted in the direct application of more judicious processes to the land itself, and to the plants growing on it: such as rotation of crops, to avoid the necessity of leaving the land uncultivated for one season in every two or three; improved manures, to renovate its fertility when exhausted by cropping;

ploughing and draining the subsoil as well as the surface; conversion of bogs and marshes into cultivable land; such modes of pruning, and of training and propping up plants and trees, as experience has shown to deserve the preference; in the case of the more expensive cultures, planting the roots or seeds further apart, and more completely pulverizing the soil in which they are placed, &c. In manufactures and commerce, some of the most important improvements consist in economizing time; in making the return follow more speedily upon the labour and outlay. There are others of which the advantage consists in economy of material.

In the course of the 1830s the emergence of new technologies began to hold out the hope of rendering British farming profitable again after the long period of declining and stagnant agricultural prices that started in 1812, but it was only from about 1837 that the application of the new methods began to yield substantial results and create a new mood.[78] By the time Mill's *Principles* was published it was clear that British agriculture would profitably survive, despite the repeal of the Corn Laws.

In dealing with profits more generally he distinguishes three components: interest; insurance against risk; and wages of superintendence. He then considers the determinants of the minimum profit rate; variations; and the tendency of profits in various sectors toward equality. He concludes with the following clarification of Ricardo:[79]

We thus arrive at the conclusion of Ricardo and others, that the rate of profits depends on wages; rising as wages fall, and falling as wages rise. In adopting, however, this doctrine, I must insist upon making a most necessary alteration in its wording. Instead of saying that profits depend on wages, let us say (what Ricardo really meant) that they depend on the cost of labour.

He thus allows for the possibility of a decline in unit labor costs with rising wage rates.

So far as machinery is concerned, however, Mill flatly rejects Ricardo's judgment that a shift toward fixed at the expense of circulating capital might be at the worker's expense:[80]

. . . the conversion of circulating capital into fixed, whether by railways, or manufactories, or ships, or machinery, or canals, or mines, or works of drainage and irrigation, is not likely in any rich country, to diminish the gross produce or the amount of employment for labor. . . . There is hardly any increase of fixed capital which does not enable the country to contain eventually a larger circulating capital . . . for there is hardly any creation of fixed capital which, when it proves successful, does not cheapen the articles on which wages are habitually expended. . . . All these improvements make the labourers better off with the same money wages, better off if they do not increase their rate of multiplication.

In particular, the British railroad boom of the 1840s, with its massive expansion in fixed capital, and diffuse, strong, and positive effects on employment, output, and productivity, made it clear to Mill and others that Ricardo's proposition about machinery was valid only under extremely restricted assumptions—a view Ricardo himself held.

Nevertheless, Mill's view of the investment process was incomplete. Schumpeter, for example, took Mill to task as follows.[81]

In agreement with all the English "classics"—perhaps we might say, with the spirit of his age—he greatly underrated the importance in economic development of the element of personal initiative and, correspondingly, he greatly overemphasized the importance of mere increase in physical producers' goods. And in this again, he overemphasized the importance of saving. . . . He took it for granted that the important thing was to have something to invest: the investment itself did not present additional problems either as to promptness—it was *normally* sure to be immediate—or as to direction—it was sure to be guided by investment opportunities that were equally obvious to all and existed independently of the investing man. Saving, then, was the powerful lever of economic development.

Mill's depersonalized entrepreneurs and what Schumpeter later calls his "Colorless Saving" are related in a way Schumpeter does not quite drive home in the preceding quoted passage; and the linkage is, in my view, fundamental to growth analysis. In a world of rapidly changing production functions, of the kind, for example, Babbage described, the entrepreneur is caught up in a competitive, creative struggle in which two things are likely to be true. First, his profits and the rate of growth of his firm are likely to depend on a correct assessment of the risks of absorbing a new technology as well as his skill in introducing it efficiently. These are skills distinct from profit maximation with fixed technology. Second, the level of saving in the economy will depend heavily on the aggregate success of entrepreneurs in these functions; for a critical component of saving is the plowback of profits. In a sense, the level of saving-investment becomes substantially a function not of private frugality but the pace of absorption of technology which, in turn, helps determine the rate of growth of output and the size of profits in particular sectors. Of all of Mill's major predecessors, Hume came closest to capturing the role of the plowback of profits with his avaricious merchants exploiting the potentialities of widened markets (preceding, p. 23). By the mid-nineteenth century the creative, innovative performance of the industrial entrepreneur had become critical to the saving-investment process; and Schumpeter was correct in his judgment that Mill does not fully capture the multi-faceted industrial and transport revolution proceeding around him which was to be well dramatized in the Crystal Palace Exposition of 1851, 3 years after the publication of his *Principles*.

Business Cycles

Mill had more to say about the business cycle than any of his predecessors or contemporaries except Thomas Tooke. Indeed, he acknowledges that he learned a good deal from Tooke.[82] Mill's first discussion of the subject—and the most vivid—is in his essay on the commercial distress of 1826, written when he was 20 years old. He returned to the theme a few years later in the second of his *Essays on Some Unsettled Questions of Political Economy*, entitled "Of the Influence of Consumption on Production."[83] And he has something to say in his *Principles* when dealing with credit, the possibilities of excess supply, the rate of interest, profits, and the "tendency of profits to a minimum." But his major judgments on the subject were clearly formed during the dramatic financial crisis of 1825 and the sharp cyclical depression of 1826, the first such sequence he was in a position to observe closely in reasonable maturity.

Mill's concept of the business cycle was firmly anchored in a theory of irrational expectations:[84]

> . . . the cause of the evil [cycles and depression] is one which legislation cannot reach—the universal propensity of mankind to over-estimate the chances in their own favour. While this propensity subsists, every event which stimulates hopes, will give rise to extensive miscalculation; and every miscalculation upon a sufficiently extensive scale, will terminate in the ruin of multitudes. All that we are entitled to hope is, that as the world grows older it may grow wiser; [and] . . . that traders may one day acquire sufficient prudence to abstain from risking their own property in *rash* speculations, and sufficient probity to abstain from risking in *any* speculations the property of others.

Mill makes clear that his generalization applies not merely to 1824–1826 but to other "calamitous" periods that he identifies as 1784, 1793, 1810–1811, 1814–1815, and 1819. In a passage as full of insight as any in 2 centuries of business-cycle theory, Mill distinguished three distinct forms of irrational expectations.[85] First were those arising from fraudulent projects. These, while dramatic, were generally exposed rather promptly and resulted in only modest losses. Second were those arising from an underestimate of the time required for investment projects to yield "adequate renumeration." Mill judged many such projects would prove viable in time, although returns on them would not fulfill the exaggerated hopes entertained at the peak of the boom. Third was speculation in commodities or "over-trading," a process that Mill traces through a sequence of self-reinforcing stages yielding a "frenzy" when:[86]

> . . . prices at length rise to such a height, as to induce a considerable number of the holders to think of realizing. Then commences the fall of prices. This operates as a signal to all the other holders to hurry their stocks to market, in order to secure what they can before the price relapses to its original level. The recoil is hence almost instantaneous. Not only do prices fall to the level from which they rose, but, from the increased quantity which has been imported or produced, they fall lower; commonly much lower. . . . The failure of a few great commercial houses occasions the ruin of many of their numerous creditors. A general alarm ensues, and an entire stop is put for the time to all dealings upon credit: many persons are thus deprived of their usual accommodation, and are unable to continue their business.

In his "Paper Currency and Commercial Distress," Mill then goes on to criticize the monetary remedies for this process discussed in the parliamentary sessions of 1826. Table 4.1 exhibits the movement of some key commodities in the period of intense speculation, crisis, and depression.

A few years later, however, Mill was forced by events to deal not merely with the process of boom and bust but also with the problem of chronic excess capacity in the system. In a sense, he was plunged back into the world of 1815–1820, which had produced the Malthus–Ricardo debate on whether a "general glut" was real or a theoretical possibility (preceding, pp. 60–62).

The whole period 1826–1832 was one framed by declining trends in prices and profits (preceding, p. 105). There was some overall expansion in the volume of exports and some

Table 4.1. Selected Commodity Price Movements, Great Britain, 1823–1826

	Raw cotton (exc. duty) d. per lb.	British pig iron £'s per ton	British manufactured copper	Jamaica Sugar Inc. duty d. per lb.
1823	8.6	62.0	113.0	58.0
1824	8.2	76.7	112.0	56.0
1825	12.2	106.9	137.0	65.0
1826	7.2	81.2	124.0	61.0

SOURCE: A. D. Gayer *et al.*, *Growth and Fluctuation*, microfilmed supplementary data, Table 128.

continuing technological change, including the invention of the hot blast, which made possible the commercial exploitation of the hitherto unusable blackband ironstone deposits of Scotland. And it was in this interval that commercial railway construction began in earnest, if on a relatively small scale. But in general, this was a time of idle industrial capacity, and investment prospects were bleak:[87]

> British investment, from 1827 to 1832, presents a strange contrast to the optimistic development which preceded 1825. Foreign loans and mining ventures virtually disappear from the market; railways and joint-stock companies were put forward on a much reduced scale; statistics of brick production, from 1827, fluctuate irregularly about a level well below the peak of 1824–5. The long-term interest rate tended to fall. A *Circular to Bankers,* in 1832, commented as follows: "The general absence of speculation in the commercial affairs of England is, from the extraordinary length in which it has been manifest, the most remarkable feature in the history of commerce of the present time."

In a manner quite typical of Mill's mode of exposition, he approaches the question of general glut in his *Essays* by first reaffirming strongly the Ricardian position:[88]

> . . . it was triumphantly established by political economists, that consumption never needs encouragement. All which is produced is already consumed, either for the purpose of reproduction or of enjoyment. The person who saves his income is no less a consumer than he who spends it: he consumes it in a different way; it supplies food and clothing to be consumed, tools and materials to be used, by productive labourers.
> . . . What is consumed for mere enjoyment, is gone; what is consumed for reproduction, leaves commodities of equal value, commonly with the addition of a profit.

Having reasserted orthodoxy, he then turns to the problem of how to explain the palpable reality of idle capacity. He emerges with two propositions that, in fact, take him some distance in a Malthusian direction. First, that the division of labor inherently results in chronic idle capacity, because of the time lag between the completion of production and sale. Capital previously laid out for production is "locked up" in inventories, transit, etc.; and it is "not disposable." His dictum:[89] "This perpetual non-employment of a large proportion of Capital, is the price we pay for the division of labour. The purchase is worth what it costs; but the price is considerable."

Then a proposition which brings him back to irrational expectations and cycles:[90]

> . . . the calculations of producers and traders being of necessity imperfect, there are always some commodities which are more or less in excess, as there always some which are in deficiency. . . . The commonest cause of such delusion is some general, or very extensive rise of prices . . . which persuades all dealers that they are growing rich. . . . But when the delusion vanishes and the truth is disclosed, those whose commodities are relatively in excess must diminish their production or be ruined: and if during the high prices they have built mills and erected machinery, they will be likely to repent at leisure. . . .
>
> In this last case, it is commonly said that there is a general superabundance. . . . An overstocked state of the market is always temporary, and is generally followed by a more than common briskness of demand. . . .
>
> The essentials of the doctrine are preserved[;] . . . there cannot be permanent excess of production, or of accumulation; though it be at the same time admitted, that . . . there may be a temporary excess of . . . commodities generally, not in consequence of over-production, but of a want of commercial confidence.

By the time Mill wrote his *Principles* Britain had experienced two further major business cycles, peaking in 1836 and 1845, with an intervening period of quite severe chronic idle capacity (1839–1842).[91] His discussion of cycles follows along much the same lines as his two previous efforts; but it includes some special features:

- An analysis of the difference between the crises of 1825 and 1845.[92]
- A discussion of "a glut of commodities" that introduces more explicitly than earlier the role of a rush to liquidity.[93]
- A further attack on the underconsumptionist strand in Malthus, Chalmers, and Sismondi, including a tribute to his father's writing on this problem.[94]
- A rather sophisticated discussion of the forces determining the cyclical behavior of the interest rate:[95]

  > Fluctuations in the rate of interest arise from variations either in the demand for loans or in the supply. The supply is liable to variation, though less so than the demand. The willingness to lend is greater than usual at the commencement of a period of speculation, and much less than usual during the revulsion which follows. . . . During the revulsion, . . . interest always rises inordinately, because, while there is a most pressing need on the part of many persons to borrow, there is a general disinclination to lend. This disinclination, when at its extreme point, is called a panic. . . .
  >
  > In the intervals between commercial crises, there is usually a tendency in the rate of interest to a progressive decline, from the gradual process of accumulation. . . . and this diminution of interest tempts the possessor to incur hazards in the hopes of a more considerable return.

- Finally, there is Mill's rather odd doctrine that "commercial revulsions" help prevent the rate of profit from falling to a minimum and, thereby, postpone the arrival of the stationary state. His exposition includes a vivid account of what happens in a cyclical depression and the forces that, in time, yield a revival.[96]

It is clear, then, that Mill had a lively sense that an "almost periodical" cyclical process had been underway since the 1780s; that its roots lay in the systematic tendency of the investment process to proceed on the basis of overoptimistic and overpessimistic expectations; that important time lags helped account for this process, which was the form economic growth inevitably assumed in a system exploiting specialization of function and in which investment decisions were made by individuals operating without full knowledge of the investment decisions of others but in fact all acting in response to the same signals of future profit or loss.

Relative Prices

Like most of Mill's exposition, his treatment of diminishing returns to agriculture, increasing returns to manufactures is classical—but with some distinctive features of his own.

On diminishing returns, he begins once again on a Ricardian note:[97] "The general law of agricultural industry is the most important proposition in political economy. Were the law different, nearly all the phenomena of the production and distribution of wealth would be other than they are." Diminishing returns to inferior new land or in the more intensive cultivation of old land is then expounded.

Mill then turns to "certain explorations and limitations" of the basic principle.

- He notes that "usages connected with property in land and the tenure of farms" may cause actual practice in farming to fall short of the productivity that might result from commercially viable best practice.[98]
- In taking account of the view of the American economist H. C. Carey, he notes that the latter indeed had established the possibility that the best land might not be the first cultivated in a new undeveloped country, but he asserts that this exception does not subvert the long-run validity of the principle of diminishing returns.[99]
- And, as noted earlier, he devotes more attention to the potentialities for improving agricultural technology and practice than his predecessors. And he observes, quite explicitly, that the increase in "agricultural skill" since 1830 had reduced the real cost of producing food in England and Scotland despite the rise in population; the repeal of the Corn Laws had intensified the pressure to increase agricultural productivity; and emigration and colonization of new fertile areas was working in the same direction.[100] But he concludes with the proposition that ultimately determines his acceptance as inevitable the coming of the stationary state.[101]

   To resume; all natural agents which are limited in quantity, are not only limited in their ultimate productive power, but, long before that power is stretched to the utmost, they yield to any additional demands on progressively harder terms. This law may however be suspended, or temporarily controlled, by whatever adds to the general power of mankind over nature; and especially by any extension of their knowledge, and their consequent command, of the properties and powers of natural agents.

After then enunciating increasing returns in manufactures as "a probable and usual, but not a necessary consequence" of expanded production, he brings the two principles together and predicts as follows the likely long-run shift in the intersectoral terms of trade against manufactures.[102]

As manufactures, however, depend for their materials either upon agriculture, or mining, or the spontaneous produce of the earth, manufacturing industry is subject, in respect of one of its essentials, to the same law as agriculture. But the crude material generally forms so small a portion of the total cost, that any tendency which may exist to a progressive increase in that single item, is much over-balanced by the diminution continually taking place in all the other elements; to which diminution it is impossible at present to assign any limit. . . .

[I]t follows that the exchange values of manufactured articles, compared with the products of agriculture and of mines, have, as population and industry advance, a certain and decided tendency to fall.

There is no Malthusian inkling in Mill of cycles in relative prices, although he emphasizes strongly what he regarded as the transient nature of the pre-1848 postponement of diminishing returns to agriculture. His optimism about agricultural technology and relevant scientific knowledge, the opening of new areas, and migration was more solidly based than the post-1815 optimism of Malthus and Ricardo. And the later editions of the *Principles* (the seventh and last of which was published in 1871) could reflect the opening of the American West with railroads and the massive transatlantic emigration of the 1850s and the post-1865 years. Similarly the economies induced by new technology and the increased scale of manufacturing units, as well as multiple revolutions in transport and communications, clearly strengthened Mill's confidence about the future as he looked out on a rapidly diversifying industrial system. Like Alfred Marshall, Mill never fully abandoned the root Ricardian doctrine that diminishing returns would ultimately prevail; but, as we shall see, he looked on the stationary state in a somewhat different way than his predecessors.

The Stages of and Limits to Growth

By bringing together various scattered passages in Mill's *Principles* one can construct a quite coherent manual on the stages of economic growth including policy prescriptions for both underdeveloped and advanced industrial countries. It would have four components.

First is the extended passage in "Preliminary Remarks" that deals with the stages of growth over the long sweep of human history, concluding that one could find in the world economy of the mid-nineteenth century approximations of virtually every stage.[103] His array is based on the degree to which each stage generates and depends on a stock of capital; and the stages flow, one from the other, not easily or automatically but from "the spontaneous course of events."

Mill begins with a marginal case—a community living wholly on "the spontaneous produce of vegetation." Next are tribes that live "almost exclusively" on "the produce of hunting and fishing." "The first great advance" beyond this state of poverty, lacking virtually all forms of fixed working capital, comes with "the domestication of the more useful animals" and a diet based not on hunting but "on milk and its products, and on the annual increase of flocks and herds." Inequality as among families and tribes emerges, as well as leisure time, the handicraft manufacture of textiles and other consumers goods, and even the beginnings of scientific observation.

The pressure of expanding population and herds leads some communities to begin to till the ground; the struggle between the nomads and the farmers (noted as far back as

Aristotle) begins with the initial military advantages of the ruder, hardier nomads; but, in time, the farmers learn how to defend themselves and their crops, and the invading nomads "were obliged also to become agricultural communities."

Mill then turns to the various forms of agricultural-based societies to be observed in both history and in his contemporary world: some generating great empires, in which the collection of relatively small margins of revenue (or output) from large numbers of peasants permits rulers to conduct major military campaigns, to build great monuments, and to enjoy lives of opulence; some starting as small egalitarian communities but, in a complex, dynamic process, emerging as the city-states, republics, and empires of the Mediterranean world, ultimately overcome by the nomads from the North to generate the chaos out of which came the Middle Ages, the states of Europe, and "the great communities which have been founded beyond the Atlantic by the descendents of Europeans."

He brings this *tour de force* of highly compressed and stylized history to the following conclusion:[104]

> The world now contains several extensive regions, provided with the various ingredients of wealth in a degree of abundance of which former ages had not even the idea. . . .
>
> But in all these particulars, characteristic of the modern industrial communities, those communities differ widely from one another. . . . The diversities in the distribution of wealth are still greater than in the production. There are great differences in the condition of the poorest class in different countries; and in the proportional numbers and opulence of the classes which are above the poorest. . . .

Mill then notes that in the contemporary world of his day it was possible to observe all the historical economic stages of the past:

> . . . Hunting communities still exist in America, nomadic in Arabia and the steppes of Northern Asia; Oriental society is in essentials what it has always been; the great empire of Russia is even now, in many respects, the scarcely modified image of feudal Europe. Every one of the great types of human society, down to that of the Esquimaux or Patagonians, is still extant.

He concludes:

> . . . In so far as the economical condition of nations turns upon the state of physical knowledge, it is a subject for the physical sciences, and the arts founded on them. But in so far as the causes are moral or psychological, dependent on institutions and social relations, or on the principles of human nature, their investigation belongs not to physical, but to moral and social science, and is the object of what is called Political Economy.

Mill's second proposition about the stages of growth concerned the linkage of science to the economy. He took the general view that the "cultivation of speculative knowledge" was "one of the most useful of all employments" and deserved the financial support of the state.[105] And, as the preceding quotation suggests, he saw clearly the link between "the economical condition of nations" and "the physical sciences, and the arts founded on them." But, in a self-denying ordinance costly to economics, he treated these matters as exogenous[106]: as variables "Political Economy does not investigate, but assumes. . . ." On the other hand, without investigating their origins, Mill was quite clear that a fundamental turning point had occurred in Britain with "the great mechanical inventions of Watt, Arkwright, and their contemporaries. . . ."[107] Mill marks the introduction of these technologies as inaugurating a period when the forces contending against diminishing returns in agriculture gained ground, the real wages of labor held their own and, in Mill's view, would have increased if there had not been so large an increase in population. In my vocabulary, Mill correctly identified the timing and proximate cause of the British takeoff; and, so far as I can make out, he was the first of the major economists to do so.

The third strand in Mill's exposition of the stages of growth is the most familiar: his distinctive view of the stationary state. It emerges from Book IV, "Influence of the Progress of Society on Production and Distribution" certainly the most innovative feature of Mill's *Principles,* explicitly presented as "adding a theory of motion to our theory of equilibrium—the Dynamics of political economy to the Static," which were taken up in Books I, II, and III.[108]

He begins with an evocation of the potentialities of science and invention that, in itself, suggests endless progress rather than a stationary state:[109] "[I]t is impossible not to look forward to a vast multiplication and long succession of contrivances for economizing labour and increasing its produce; and to an ever wider diffusion of the use and benefit of those contrivances." Despite this optimistic vision of science, invention, and labor productivity, Mill did not quite conceive of invention as a flow. In a critical passage he concludes:[110] "Inventions and discoveries, too, occur only occasionally, while the increase of population and capital are continuous agencies." This assessment is central to his envisioning an ultimate stationary state.

But another positive factor is at work. Reinforcing the improvements in technology would be, in Mill's view, a progressive improvement in "the security of person and prosperity" that he regarded as fundamental to "industry and frugality."[111]

He then rings the changes on five cases in which three variables in the basic growth equation are assumed to behave in different ways: the rate of population increase; the rate of increase in the capital stock; and "the arts of production."[112] At considerable risk of oversimplifying a rather remarkable exercise in dynamic analysis, Mill's cases can be summarized as follows:

Case 1. *Population increases; capital and the arts of production stationary.* Real wages will decline due to diminishing returns to agriculture as population increases; an initial tendency of profits to rise, due to cheaper unit labor costs, may be countered in time by a rise in the total wage bill as more labor is drawn to agriculture to meet rising food requirements under conditions of diminishing returns. Rents rise. Mill implies that the fall in real wages is met by a reduction in workers' "indulgences" or "habitual standard" rather than the dire consequences of a sub-subsistence wage. Therefore, this case does not set in motion a population decrease.

Case 2. *Population stationary; capital increasing; arts of production stationary.* Real wages rise. In consequence, the demand for food increases under conditions of diminishing returns. Rents rise, but profits fall:[113] "What the Capitalists lose, above what the labourers gain, is partly transferred to the landlord, and partly swallowed up in the cost of growing food on worse land or by a less productive process."

Case 3. *Population and capital increasing equally, the arts of production stationary.* Real wages remain constant in the face of a rise in both agricultural prices and money wages. The profit rate will fall, although gross profits may rise. Once again, rents rise.

Case 4. *Population and capital stationary; the arts of production progress.* Mill elaborates this case in three forms: a sudden increase in agricultural productivity; a gradual increase in agricultural productivity; and an increase in the productivity of manufactures consumed by workers. A sudden improvement in agricultural productivity would raise real wages, lower rents, and leave profits unchanged. This assumes the rise in real wages took the form of relatively constant money wages and a falling price trend for wage goods, as indeed had happened in Britain between 1812 and 1848. The longer run outlook was seen to depend on whether the rise in real wages elevated the "habitual standard" of the workers' consumption or induced an increase of population at the old, existing standard. In the latter case, money wages would fall as the labor supply increased, the rate of profit would rise. In the former case—where the intent to maintain a higher standard induced a prudent restraint on family size—labor rendered itself the scarce factor, preserving the higher real wage at the expense of rents and profits.

Case 5: *Population, capital, and the arts of production increase together.* Here, Mill argues, only rent would increase:[114] "There is a greater aggregate production, a greater produce divided among the labourers, and a larger gross profit; but the wages being shared among a larger population, and the profits spread over a larger capital, no labourer is better off, nor does any capitalist derive from the same amount of capital a larger income."

He then goes on to conclude his highly Ricardian exercise:[115]

> The result of this long investigation may be summed up as follows. The economical progress of a society constituted of landlords, capitalists, and labourers, tends to the progressive enrichment of the landlord class; while the cost of the labourer's subsistence tends on the whole to increase, and profits to fall. Agricultural improvements are a counteracting force to the two last effects; but the first, though a case is conceivable in which it would be temporarily checked, is ultimately in a high degree promoted by those improvements; and the increase of population tends to transfer all the benefits derived from agricultural improvement to the landlords alone.

As noted earlier, Mill proceeds to argue that, with a fixed "field of employment," profits must tend toward the minimum rate required to induce savings and productive investment, taking risk into account as well as the time discount of future against present income. The descent to the minimum can be postponed by the destructive effect of "commercial revulsions," improvements in production, the import of cheaper food and capital goods, and capital exports.

With these analytic tools in hand, Mill, like his four predecessors, confronts the limits to growth and the stationary state. Here, most self-consciously, he breaks with "political economists of the old school":[116] they regarded the stationary state as an "unpleasing and discouraging prospect." Mill, in the quotation noted earlier (pp. 101–102), takes a more cheerful view. And, in the first edition of *The Principles,* he added this passage, withdrawn from later editions in the wake of the North's Civil War performance he greatly respected:[117]

> The northern and middle states of America are a specimen of this stage of civilization in very favourable circumstances; having, apparently, got rid of all social injustices and inequalities that affect persons of Caucasian race and of the male sex, while the proportion of population to capital and land is such as to ensure abundance to every able-bodied member of the community who

does not forfeit it by misconduct. They have the six points of Chartism, and they have no poverty: and all that these advantages do for them is that the life of the whole of one sex is devoted to dollar-hunting, and of the other to breeding dollar-hunters.

But Mill's positive acceptance of the virtues of the stationary state did not stem simply from a revulsion against materialism. It was rooted technically in the possibilities opened up in general by the elevation of the intellectual and social position of the working class, and in particular, by birth control. J. R. Hicks put the matter succinctly:[118]

> If the population can once be controlled, there is no need for the economy to go on expanding, in order that wages should be above the subsistence level. Instead of land being the main fixed factor, so that (as in the Ricardian stationary state) surplus production is swallowed up in rent, it is labour that becomes the main fixed factor, so that surplus production can be made to go, at least in large measure, to wages. This is an altogether different, and much more agreeable, picture. The Stationary State is no longer a horror. It becomes an objective at which to aim.

Clearly, Mill was premature in asserting this proposition in the mid-nineteenth century.[119] All classes in the "most advanced" as well as "backward" countries still had a great deal more to ask of the economic system as the flow of new technologies expanded its potentialities for goods and services, including a remarkable lengthening of life. But Mill, building explicitly on "the juster and more hopeful anticipations" of Malthus's later editions, comes closer to foreshadowing the demographic transition of the second half of the nineteenth and twentieth centuries than any of his predecessors or contemporaries. He anticipates, as well, strands of thought and aspiration that began to appear in the third quarter of the twentieth century as a margin of the population in the most affluent countries appeared to reject further striving for a higher real income per capita, defined in conventional material terms. Mill was the first major environmentalist. But it should be underlined that his stationary state implies only a fixed population: technological change could proceed elevating real income per capita.[120]

Noneconomic Factors

As Hont and Ignatieff have dramatized afresh, *The Wealth of Nations* is, in part, an effort to reconcile a paradox enunciated by Adam Smith on the second page in his book: how to explain the fact that in primitive egalitarian societies, where all work, all are poor whereas in advanced societies, marked by great differences in wealth and income, and much idleness, the poorest worker enjoys a standard of life beyond the reach of a savage ruler.[121] From Hume and Adam Smith forward political economy has acknowledged the inequity—for some, the immorality—of those living in affluent idleness on the basis of inherited wealth or enjoying the rising rents induced by an inelastic demand for the product of a factor of production subject to diminishing returns or otherwise rendered increasingly scarce. In general, the classical political economists rather disliked the money-grubbing capitalist and were (perhaps excepting Malthus) often outraged at the profligate rent-collecting landlord. The economists' advocacy of rigorous competition, including Free Trade, was designed, in part, to discipline the innate avarice of entrepreneur and landowner and force them, against their natural bent, to serve the public interest.

This ambivalence in defense of a system of private property, inherited wealth, and competitive capitalism reached an acute stage with Mill.

On the one hand, his overriding concern was with the maximum feasible freedom of thought and action for a society of diverse unique individuals. This is the central theme of *On Liberty:*[122]

> The object of this Essay is to assert one very simple principle . . . that the sole end for which mankind are warranted, individually or collectively, in interfering with the liberty of action of any of their number, is self-protection. . . . His own good, either physical or moral, is not a sufficient warrant. . . . In the part which merely concerns himself, his independence is, of right, absolute. Over himself, over his own body and mind, the individual is sovereign.

This commitment to the libertarian creed runs through Mill's *Principles* as well.

But, as he fully acknowledged, the reconciliation of that need with the imperatives of organized society—assuring that one person's liberty did not harm another—was often a complex calculus. The final two chapters of the *Principles* are devoted to sorting out the interferences of government grounded in erroneous theories as opposed to those Mill judged to be legitimate.[123] But, as in *On Liberty, laissez-faire* was "the general rule" against which exceptions should be cautiously and sceptically measured. And in this spirit he sanctions:

- Cases in which the consumer is an incompetent judge of the commodity and of which education is the major example cited.
- Cases of persons exercising power over others, notably the protection of young persons and the insane.
- Cases of contracts in perpetuity in which an individual is not in a position to judge his interest at some future and distant time.
- Cases of delegated management where public surveillance and limited powers over joint-stock companies are judged legitimate to assure that inherently monopoly powers are not abused. Mill judged public ownership and operation of economic units to be "jobbing, careless, and ineffective"; but he thought private joint-stock companies little better, if better at all.
- Cases where public intervention is required to achieve a broadly agreed objective; for example, the reduction of hours of work which, if not accomplished by law, could be disrupted by a minority of workers or factory owners. Mill also cites the control over the disposition of land in land-rich, population-poor colonial areas.
- Poor laws, where it is necessary to reconcile the need to aid the destitute with the need to avoid generating habitual reliance on such aid.
- Colonization, where it is necessary to reconcile the legitimate private interests of those planting or developing colonies with "a deliberate regard to the permanent welfare of the nations afterwards to arise from these small beginnings."[124]
- Support for enterprises, installations, or institutions clearly in the public interest but not capable of generating adequate private support; e.g., voyages of discovery, light houses, scientific research in universities, etc. And similar public activities in areas where private agencies "would be more suitable" but where the society has not developed the experience and habits of private cooperative action; e.g., roads, docks, harbors, canals, etc.

The question then arises: How did Mill, rooted in the individualist utilitarian creed, believing that each individual was the best judge of his or her own interest, carefully and reluctantly rationing out exceptions to *laissez-faire,* end up a qualified socialist of sorts?

He begins his discussion of socialism with precisely the issue Adam Smith confronts at the beginning of *The Wealth of Nations:* the uneven distribution of wealth.[125] He notes the complex and violent history that yielded the distribution of property in contemporary Europe and the legitimacy of questioning the appropriateness of that distribution:[126]

> In an age like the present, when a general reconsideration of all first principles is felt to be inevitable, and when more than at any former period of history the suffering portions of the community have a voice in the discussion, it was impossible but that ideas of this nature should spread far and wide. The late revolutions in Europe [in 1848] have thrown up a great amount of speculation of this character, and an unusual share of attention has consequently been drawn to the various forms which these ideas have assumed: nor is this attention likely to diminish, but on the contrary, to increase more and more.

In his typically fair-minded way, Mill turns then to the case for socialism (or communism, which he uses interchangeably), and to the arguments conventionally made against it. He concludes:

1. Putting degrees of efficiency aside, production with collective (or state) ownership of property is practical.

2. As for evasion of work, the problem of generating maximum effort with fixed salaries is real; but it exists as well in private enterprise systems. His net judgment is:[127]

> If communistic labour might be less rigorous than that of a peasant proprietor, or a workman labouring on his own account, it would probably be more energetic than that of a labourer for hire, who has no personal interest in the matter at all. . . . Undoubtedly, as a general rule, remuneration by fixed salaries does not in any class of functionaries produce the maximum of zeal; and this is as much as can be reasonably alleged against communistic labour.

3. He acknowledges as real the problem of allocating labor equitably to the tasks for which it is best fitted; but asserts that any system that aimed at equality would be superior to "the inequality and injustice" of the prevailing system.

4. In general, the balance sheet tips towards the idea of communism when set against current reality:[128]

> If, therefore, the choice were to be made between Communism with all its chances, and the present state of society with all its sufferings and injustices; if the institution of private property necessarily carried with it as a consequence, that the produce of labour should be apportioned as we now see it, almost in inverse ratio to the labour—the largest portions to those who have never worked at all, the next largest to those whose work is almost nominal, and so in a descending scale, the remuneration dwindling as the work grows harder and more disagreeable, until the most fatiguing and exhausting bodily labour cannot count with certainty on being able to earn even the necessaries of life; if this or Communism were the alternative, all the difficulties, great or small, of Communism would be but dust in the balance.

5. But that, Mill argues, is not the appropriate comparison.[129] ". . . to make the comparison applicable, we must compare Communism at its best, with the regime of individual property, not as it is, but as it might be made." He then evokes the possibilities open to a capitalist society to render its distribution of income and wealth more equitable. It is here that we come back to the author of *On Liberty:*[130]

> If a conjecture may be hazarded, the decision will probably depend mainly on one consideration, *viz.* which of the two systems is consistent with the greatest amount of human liberty and spontaneity. After the means of subsistence are assured, the next in strength of the personal wants of human beings is liberty; and (unlike the physical wants, which as civilization advances become more moderate and more amenable to control) it increases instead of diminishing in intensity, as the intelligence and the moral faculties are more developed.

Returning unreconstructed to the spirit of Adam Smith, he adds, later on, a vigorous defense of competition:[131]

> . . . I utterly dissent from the most conspicuous and vehement part of their [socialists'] teaching, their declamations against competition. . . . They forget that wherever competition is not, monopoly is; and that monopoly, in all its forms, is that taxation of the industrious for the support of indolence, if not of plunder. . . . Instead of looking upon competition as the baneful and antisocial principle which it is held to be by the generality of Socialists, I conceive that, even in the present state of society and industry, every restriction of it is an evil, and every extension of it, even if for the time injuriously affecting some class of labourers, is always an ultimate good.

One can understand that some readers have found Mill on this and other issues a kind of Hamlet of the social sciences. But the fact is that he defined with remarkable clarity the dilemmas with which the political process of the presently advanced industrial countries have wrestled over the past 140 years—and with which they continue to wrestle.

Socialist countries have, indeed, demonstrated that they can operate a modern economy; but they have paid a heavy price in "jobbing, careless, and ineffective" enterprises and for the lack of strong individual incentives. And some have even turned to forms of competition to stimulate sluggish economies overburdened with heavy, self-serving bureaucracies.

Politically democratic countries have, indeed, sought to temper the inequity of wealth and income distribution as decreed by history through devices of taxation and a wide range of measures to grant a better approximation of equality of opportunity as well as welfare cushions against the vicissitudes of modern industrial life.

And, although the ultimate verdict of history has not yet been rendered, it is altogether possible—even likely—that the choice between communism and democracy may well hinge on "which of the two systems is consistent with the greatest amount of human liberty and spontaneity."

Looking to the past as well as the future, it is clear that Mill foreshadowed a great deal not merely in the ideology of social democracy but of virtually universal consensus in the Atlantic world of the late nineteenth and twentieth centuries; and he identified with considerable precision the increasingly intense internal contradictions that have changed and are changing the character of socialist regimes as the twentieth century moves toward its close.

Karl Marx (1818–1883)

In a study of this kind one is tempted to shear away the noneconomic aspects of Marx's doctrine (and the enormous body of polemical argument that surrounds it) and focus narrowly on his theory of economic growth. In that spirit Joan Robinson once observed:[132] ". . . there is no need to turn him [Marx], as many seek to do, into an inspired prophet. He regarded himself as a serious thinker, and it is as a serious thinker that I have endeavored to treat him. . . ." In the end, however, virtually all commentators on Marx (including Robinson) are driven to deal with him on a broader basis. The reason is quite technical: Marx's economics in general and his theory of economic growth in particular are the engine that drives his theory of history to its appointed conclusion; and, as he was quite aware, his theory of history was designed as a revolutionary weapon. Marx's own identification of his key innovations is quite accurate if one suspends judgment on the word *prove:*[133]

> . . . no credit is due to me for discovering the existence of classes in modern society or the struggle between them. Long before me bourgeois historians had described the historical development of this class struggle and bourgeois economists the economic anatomy of the classes. What I did that was new was to prove: 1. that the *existence of classes* is only bound up with *particular historical phases in the development of production,* 2. that the class struggle necessarily leads to the *dictatorship of the proletariat,* 3. that this dictatorship itself only constitutes the transition to the *abolition of all classes* and to a *classless society.*

The fact that Marx was a general theorist of society, advocated its transformation in quite specific directions, and regarded his writing as an operational instrument for that purpose does not, in itself, distinguish him from the five other growth theorists thus far considered. With the partial exception of Ricardo, all were general social scientists conducting their analyses from more or less explicit philosophical and value premises; and all, including Ricardo, sought to bring about quite radical changes in policies, institutions, and in the balance of political power.

What distinguishes Marx from the other classical growth economists is the Hegelian philosophic framework on which he built and the view of the individual in relation to society it incorporated. The line from Hume to J. S. Mill was rooted in a view that accorded the uniqueness of the individual a high priority in the organization of communities, despite the inescapable disciplines the latter required. Indeed, the sense of community was traced back by Hume and Smith to the quality of "sympathy" as among unique individuals, not to the imperatives of an anonymous "state" or an anonymous "class." In tracing the stages through which societies and economies had passed and in looking to the future, the progressive widening of political and social freedom for the individual was a central touchstone of historical progress and a fundamental rationale for enlarging and diffusing the wealth of nations. Nothing better characterizes the vision of the classical economists than Mill's judgment that the ultimate decision as between capitalism and socialism would depend on which "is consistent with the greatest amount of human liberty and spontaneity." For Hegel and Marx history was a more abstract process in which large forces endlessly contended, and the individual receded from the center of the stage, finding "freedom" in acting in accordance with the laws of history. In Hegel's case, the clash was between nation states each embodying a distinct culture or idea. Out of the ferment of the critical phase of Marx's intellectual life—in Paris and Brussels in 1843–1847, between the ages of 25 and 29—the following alternative emerged that Marx himself described, looking back from 1859:[134]

> The general result at which I arrived and which, once won, served as a guiding thread for my studies, can be briefly formulated as follows: In the social production of their life, men enter into definite relations that are indispensable and independent of their will, relations of production which correspond to a definite stage of development of their material productive forces. The sum total of these relations of production constitutes the economic structure of society, the real foundation, on which rises a legal and political superstructure and to which correspond definite forms of social consciousness. The mode of production of material life conditions the social, political and intellectual life process in general. It is not the consciousness of men that determines their being, but, on the contrary, their social being that determines their consciousness. At a certain stage of their development, the material productive forces of society come in conflict with the existing relations of production, or—what is but a legal expression for the same thing— with the property relations within which they have been at work hitherto. From forms of development of the productive forces these relations turn into their fetters. Then begins an epoch of social revolution. . . . No social order ever perishes before all the productive forces for which there is room in it have developed; and new, higher relations of production never appear before the material conditions of their existence have matured in the womb of the old society itself. . . . In broad outlines Asiatic, ancient, feudal, and modern bourgeois modes of production can be designated as progressive epochs in the economic formation of society. The bourgeois relations of production are the last antagonistic form of the social process of production—antagonistic not in the sense of individual antagonism, but of one arising from the social conditions of life of the individuals; at the same time the productive forces developing in the womb of bourgeois society create the material conditions for the solution of that antagonism. This social formation brings, therefore, the prehistory of human society to a close.

Thus, Hegel's thesis, antithesis, and synthesis become dynamic sequences in which the imperatives of changing technology and modes of production generate conflicts with the existing organization and institutions of society yielding revolutionary change. And the sequence that obsessed Marx was the overthrow of capitalism by the proletariat; the installation of socialism; and the ultimate dream of communism.

This marriage of Hegelian philosophy and historical materialism when buttressed with Marx's theory of growth under capitalism constituted "scientific socialism." Marx scorned socialists who came to their convictions by assessing life under capitalism as inequitable or immoral. He insisted that the correct view was that the destruction of capitalism was historically inevitable; that it must and would take place by force;[135] and, besides, the canons of equity and morality applied by such deviant socialists were, themselves, a by-product of bourgeois capitalism.

Here we come to one of several deeply rooted paradoxes in Marx's doctrine. His expositions—notably those for widespread public consumption, but his more technical writings as well—are shot through with language designed to evoke outrage at real or alleged violations of bourgeois concepts of equity and morality; and, no doubt, in his day and beyond, it was the convergence of moral outrage and the alleged inevitability of the historical outcome that gave his doctrine its appeal. In short, Marx tried to have it both ways; and, to a degree, his posture as the morally outraged scientist of society was successful.

In terms of stages of growth the bloody sequence Marx envisaged—including the overthrow of capitalism by force and a dictatorship of the new ruling class, the proletariat—dissolves, in a romantic Hegelian synthesis, into true communism.[136]

> When, in the course of development, class distinctions have disappeared, and all production has been concentrated in the hands of a vast association of the whole nation, the public power will lose its political character. Political power, properly so called, is merely the organised power of one class for oppressing another. If the proletariat during its contest with the bourgeoisie is compelled, by the force of circumstances, to organise itself as a class, if, by means of a revolution, it makes itself the ruling class, and, as such, sweeps away by force the old conditions of production, then it will, along with these conditions, have swept away the conditions for the existence of class antagonisms and of classes generally, and will thereby have abolished its own supremacy as a class.
>
> In place of the old bourgeois society, with its classes and class antagonisms, we shall have an association, in which the free development of each is the condition for the free development of all.
>
> In a higher phase of communist society, after the enslaving subordination of the individual to the division of labour, and therewith also the antithesis between mental and physical labour, has vanished; after labour has become not only a means of life but life's prime want; after the productive forces have also increased with the all-round development of the individual, and all the springs of cooperative wealth flow more abundantly—only then can the narrow horizon of bourgeois right be crossed in its entirety and society inscribe on its banner: From each according to his ability, to each according to his needs!

In the end, Marx's image of human beings "wise, creative, and free,"[137] released from scarcity and the brutalizing imperatives of the class struggle, bears a family relationship, at least, to J. S. Mill's Stationary State. Both were deeply rooted in the humane values of Western culture and religion. Mill, however, understood well that in the life of societies the results achieved are not independent of the means used to achieve them. One derivation of Marx from Hegel was a separation of ends and means.

There are other paradoxes and contradictions embedded in Marx's doctrine; and, accepting Hume's dictum about the inherent complexity of human character, this is no surprise. Like Mill—and all of us—Marx was a household of personalities. In part, he was a mid-nineteenth century German bourgeois, taking his family on Sunday picnics and reading poetry for his own and their pleasure, deeply suspicious and critical of bohemians. In part, he was a well-trained scholar, with a gift for creative synthesis, but also driven to pursue erudite details. He was quite easily diverted from his main task. For example, he turned to learning Russian and Turkish when he should have been completing Volumes II and III of *Capital*;[138] but he was in addition a vivid and sometimes ruthless simplifier and popularizer. Perhaps above all, he was, in his father's phrase, driven by "a demonic egoism."[139] This dimension of his character suffuses a good many aspects of his style: a determination to leave his mark on history, which carried him through years of poverty and deprivation for himself and his long-suffering family; a compulsion to demand total loyalty or to denounce those whose views deviated from his own; an uncontrollable impulse to use vulgar and destructive language in intellectual and political controversy.

I have long been skeptical of psychobiography and will, therefore, note but not try to explain a curious characteristic of Marx. Out of a childhood and youth without apparent frustration or denial he emerges as a profoundly lonely, self-isolated man driven, in part, by a strand of violence, hatred, and aggression. In his sensitive essay on Marx's life and personality, Isaiah Berlin evokes his early days: a kindly, supportive if sometimes anxious father; success at school; a neighbor and family friend, Freiherr Ludwig von Westphalen, a distinguished government official who befriended the young scholar and consented to the marriage of Marx to his daughter Jenny. Berlin concludes:[140]

> Speaking of Westphalen in later life Marx, whose judgements of men are not noted for their generosity, grew almost sentimental. Westphalen had humanized and strengthened that belief in himself and his own powers which was at all periods Marx's single most outstanding characteristic. He is one of the rare revolutionaries who were neither thwarted nor persecuted in their early life. Consequently, in spite of his abnormal sensitiveness, his *amour-propre,* his vanity, his aggressiveness and his arrogance, it is a singularly unbroken, positive and self-confident figure that faces us during forty years of illness, poverty and unceasing warfare.

We shall come later (pp. 148–149) to a view of Marx as a less self-confident, more consciously frustrated figure; but Berlin does capture one of the several profound puzzlements in Marx's personality and performance.

In turning now to Marx's theory of growth—the engine that would cause capitalism to self-destruct and create the setting for socialism and then communism—two points should be noted. First there was a quite particular respect in which Marx was Mill's polar opposite. Mill, in his own phrase, was ready and eager "to learn from everybody, . . . adjusting the old and the new to one another" Marx also read "everybody"; but, once his system crystallized in the 1840s, he read only to derive data and concepts to support and elaborate that system. Everything else was set aside or explicitly denounced. To his daughter Laura on April 11, 1868, he wrote:[141] "I am a machine, condemned to devour them [books] and then, throw them, in a changed form, on a dunghill of history." This means that despite the special vocabulary manufactured by Marx we are dealing with concepts quite familiar and very much in the classical tradition. They are, however, employed in a highly selective and exploitative way for a predetermined purpose.

Marx and the study of Marx pose a second problem anyone now writing about his work inescapably confronts. From one perspective he constitutes a classic example of the Confucius–Bagehot–Keynes–Schumpeter proposition: his "vision" was fully formed by the age of 30 when the *Communist Manifesto* was published; and with almost incredible single-mindness he devoted the rest of his life to provide it with a scientific foundation and, until discouraged by the failure of the First International, to bring it politically to life. The simple, brute fact is that he found it impossible, despite prodigious efforts, to build a scientific foundation consistent with the argument of the Manifesto. He experimented with various lines of approach; but, somehow subliminally aware that things didn't add up, he never finished the task. Volumes II and III of *Capital* were laboriously constructed by Engels from Marx's notes. Potentially significant ideas are developed but remain unlinked or unreconciled with others to which they inherently relate. After a century and more of adulatory and critical exegesis, there remains a great deal of obscurity and contradiction in Marx's writing. Critics anxious to free Marx of charges of crude under-consumptionism can find attacks on that doctrine written by him; but there are also distinctly underconsumptionist passages in his writing. Similarly, without question Marx allowed for the possibility of a rise in the real wages of labor; but elsewhere, with great eloquence, he portrays the balance of power between capitalist and worker as so skewed in favor of the former as to make the outcome appear virtually a literal subsistence wage—although that is not Marx's doctrine. Then there is the "youthful Marx" ploy. Some writers argue that the ardent young man who mainly authored the *Communist Manifesto* should not be confused with the mature scholar of *Capital* and other writings. But his later work is still suffused with his youthful vision as well as with contradictions and passages of passionate, sometimes violent prose.

There are, in fact, times when Marx's writing recalls an anecdote told to his graduate seminar at Yale in 1938–1939 by Professor Alvin Johnson. It concerns Thorstein Veblen. Johnson, as a graduate student, attended a seminar taught by Veblen, who spoke in so a low a voice that he could often not be understood. Johnson was deputized by his colleagues to confront Veblen on the matter and request politely that he speak up. Johnson did so. Veblen listened, looked up, and said quite clearly: "Johnson, if you wish to create a cult, mumble."[142]

But mumbles, distortions derived from his polemical purposes, confusion, and major errors do not alter the fact that Marx wove from the corpus of classical economics a powerful and original projection of the dynamics of capitalism, profoundly flawed and incomplete as it proved to be.[143]

The Basic Growth Equation

I shall begin with a terse summary of Marx's initial theory of growth set out according to the usual headings employed in our pattern of exposition, with minimum attention at this stage to Marx's changes of position, contradictions, and refinements.

1. Strictly speaking, Marx developed no theory of population beyond the proposition that every mode of production—and the society built upon it—generates its own laws of population. This proposition lay behind his impassioned rejection of Malthusian doctrines. But Marx does include the notion of a minimum wage that provides subsistence for the workers and the children who will succeed them. And, like Ricardo, Marx provides for an "historical and moral element" in the determination of the minimum wage, reflecting "the habits and degree of comfort in which the class of free labourers has been formed."[144] But Marx is concerned not with population but with the size, productivity, negotiating leverage, and remuneration of the working force. All these variables derive from his view of the process of capital accumulation that decrees a supply curve for labor of, essentially, infinite elasticity except during the most intense phase of business expan-

sions. Thus in his most typical formulation the wage rate oscillates cyclically around the societally defined subsistence and reproduction minimum, but there are other passages consistent with the hypothesis that Marx did not rule out a secular rise in the real wage rate.[145]

2. As on many other subjects, Marx said a good many things about wages, not all consistent. The variations in his position are suggested a bit later in this analysis (p. 130). In general, his view can be stated as follows: No rule governs wage rates except the bargaining power of worker and capitalist, evidently subject to change. He was quite aware that wages varied as among national economies and over time within those economies.[146] On balance, however, Marx's portrait of the worker under capitalism is one where bargaining power is tipped heavily in favor of the capitalist's interest: "antagonistic conditions of distribution . . . reduce the consumption of the bulk of society to a minimum varying within more or less narrow limits. . . ." (following, p. 130). This is the case because the process of capital accumulation normally generates from three sources an excess supply of labor: farm labor displaced from the land; handicraft labor displaced by factories; and, in a derivation from Ricardo on machinery, a progressive capital-intensive bias in the investment process that displaces labor from the factories. Thus, Marx's famous "reserve army of the unemployed" that not only permitted the capitalist to keep real wages at a depressed level but also provided him with a pool of labor to deploy from one sector to another as the dynamics of growth (including the flow of new technologies) shifted the locus of profitability. Marx even rejected Mill's counsel for labor to increase its market leverage by reducing the rate of population increase on the ostensible grounds that the deploying of such leverage would merely increase the incentive of capitalists to substitute machinery for labor and thus enlarge the reserve army of the unemployed. Marx wanted to leave the worker no way out except his kind of revolution.

3. The process of accumulation as a whole is rooted, however, not simply in the capitalist's desire for more profits, income, and wealth but in a kind of satanic version of Hume's judgment that man seeks "action" and "liveliness." Psychological satisfaction and social compulsion drive Marx's concept of capitalist accumulation; although the profit motive in a more conventional sense also appears. The resources available to the compulsively accumulating capitalist for investment derive from "surplus value"; that is, profits, interest, and rents—the difference between total revenue and the amount paid out by the capitalist in wages. Following certain usages in the classics, Marx viewed wage payments as the provision of variable (or working) capital. He also accepted from the classics and used for his own purposes the notion that all value derived ultimately from labor—a proposition he regarded as a tautology. Constant (or fixed) capital was defined as plant, machinery, and raw materials used in the production process. The "rate of exploitation" of labor was the proportion of surplus value to wage payments, which Marx assumed was a constant. The rate of profit was the proportion of surplus value to both variable and constant capital. In a powerful hypothesis at the center of capitalism's self-destructing engine, Marx asserted that the proportion of constant to variable capital (the "organic composition of capital") would rise with the passage of time. Thus, with the rate of exploitation fixed (the proportion of surplus value to variable capital) and the proportion of constant to variable capital rising, the rate of profit, by Marx's definition, must fall.[147]

4. Since, in Marx's scheme, accumulation is not sensitive to the profit rate, capital investment continues despite the fall in the profit rate. This produces two results that

finally lead the system to self-destruct: a progressive concentration of production and capital in the hands of a narrowing circle of industrial and banking monopolists, and a progressive increase in the organic composition of capital. The concentration of labor and its impoverishment in the face of the self-emasculated but growing powers of capitalist production generate finally the overthrow of capitalism by workers painfully educated by their experiences to perform the task.

5. Like Mill, Marx has a good deal to say about business cycles. His view is not systematic, and it is not linked in a firm and unambiguous way to his theory of growth. It is, however, connected to three significant elements in his argument: the reserve army of the unemployed whose size (and labor's wage rate) fluctuates inversely (positively) with the business cycle; the falling rate of profit, linked to the rising organic composition of capital; and the tendency, as the increase in the organic composition of capital proceeds, for a gap to widen between the enlarging productive power of the system and the workers' constrained (but not necessarily static) capacity to consume. Crises and depressions brought on by business cycles played a large part not only in Marx's theoretical view of the mechanics of capitalism's self-destruction but also in his sporadic role as a revolutionary political tactician.

6. Marx rejected diminishing returns to agriculture and raw materials production much as he rejected Malthusian population doctrines.[148] He foresaw all production as technically subject to increasing returns as the new technologies were applied and the organic composition of capital rose in both industry and agriculture. Marx had relatively little to say about agriculture in the *Communist Manifesto,* but he foresaw under socialism "[c]ombination of agriculture with manufacturing industries; gradual abolition of the distinction between town and country, by a more equable distribution of the population over the country."[149] In dealing with agriculture and rent, Marx's central analytic purpose was to reduce if not eliminate the classic distinction between the basic commodity and industrial sectors.

7. Although Marx refers to earlier forms of societal organization (e.g., primitive communism and slave systems), his basic stages are feudalism, capitalism, socialism, and communism. Each presocialist stage gives way to the next as the result of dynamic forces shifting the balance of power among contending classes. Within capitalism there were countries at various stages of advancement and ripeness for revolution. And, as we shall see, Marx made some *ad hoc* observations on India and other underdeveloped countries of his day. His descriptions of how societies and their economies would actually be organized and operate under communism were exceedingly sketchy.

8. Marx's basic proposition relating noneconomic factors to his theory of growth is, evidently, that social, political, and cultural life derives from the technical characteristics of the economic system at a given period of time and the property relationships it generates. In Marx's writing—and those of his followers—one finds this linkage elaborated with various degrees of sophistication. And Engels, at least, late in life allowed quite explicitly for interaction between the economic base and the societal superstructure.[150] But the heart of Marx's charge against capitalism was that it left "no other nexus between man and man than naked self-interest, than callous 'cash payment' ";[151] and he viewed contemporary European politics, religion, marriage, and other social institutions as, essentially, operational instruments of the capitalist bourgeoisie.

With this stylized map of Marx's youthful vision before us, we turn to a somewhat more detailed review of its components, as they were subsequently elaborated.

Population and the Working Force

There is no Marxist law of population, but there is an observation drawn from his general doctrine of historical materialism:[152] "This [Malthus's] is a law of population peculiar to the capitalist mode of production; and in fact every special historic mode of production has its own special laws of population, historically valid within its limits alone. An abstract law of population exists for plants and animals only, and only in so far as man has not interfered with them." On the basis of this relativistic view, Marx and Engels systematically denounced Malthus in the most extravagant terms, of which "baboon" was among the mildest.[153] Behind this drumfire of vituperation there appears to have been several quite lucid and understandable objectives. First, to provide the economic foundations for the vision of past, present, and future incorporated in the *Communist Manifesto,* Marx needed to avoid accepting any economic laws that transcended the stages of evolution he envisaged. In the world of socialism and then communism he wanted no carryover from capitalism of a law of population. He set aside diminishing returns to material resources for the same reason, a concept Marx correctly perceived was fundamental to Malthusian doctrine as originally formulated. Second, the Malthusian view clashed head-on with his doctrine of the reserve army of the unemployed generated, in turn, by his assumption of the rising organic composition of capital. The latter assumption was critical to the self-destructing character of capitalism. Malthus was, therefore, a rather dangerous competitor and, like competing socialists, had to be destroyed. Third, Malthus's examination of family limitation in various societies in the second and subsequent editions of his *Essay on Population,* his increased emphasis on the possibilities of raising the real wages of labor by prudence and education, and his increasing post-1815 optimism about fending off diminishing returns in agriculture suggested a gradual and ameliorative path from the harshness of life in early industrial Britain that challenged at its core Marx's vision of the necessity for violent revolutionary change. Engels suggests this uneasiness in the following passage:[154]

> . . . even if Malthus were altogether right, it would still be necessary to carry out this reorganization [socialism] immediately, since only this reorganization, only the enlightment of the masses which it can bring with it, can make possible that moral restraint upon the instinct for reproduction which Malthus himself puts forward as the easiest and most effective countermeasure against over-population.

What if capitalist societies could generate enlightenment leading to moral restraint and falling birthrates?

In its own way Malthus's more mature view of the forces determining the rate of increase of population was quite as relativistic as Marx's, but it was linked to an array of stages and types of societies much more diversified than Marx's narrower categories (preceding, p. 69). It was, therefore, quite important for Marxists to present Malthus falsely as one who "presupposes bourgeois conditions as a whole, and then proves that every part of them is a necessary part—and therefore an 'eternal law.' "[155]

It should be noted that Marx's view of the population question in Western Europe—like Mill's—was colored by the experience of relatively cheap food after the Napoleonic Wars and the palpable availability of the vast resources of the American West after the railway boom of the 1850s.

I do not propose here to enter at any length into the so-called transformation problem;[156] that is, the problem posed by the need to translate Marx's use of the labor theory of value and surplus value into terms of conventional prices, interest, profits, and rent. It is not essential to our purpose; and, to a substantial degree, the debate has been resolved as between Marxists and non-Marxists of our times. For example, William Fellner concluded:[157] "The main function of the labour-value theory in Marx'[s] work is that of linking a set of hypotheses to a 'creed' in which the judgment is prominent that all nonlabour income results from 'exploitation' and hence is objectionable." Joan Robinson, a more friendly but independent analyst of Marx, observed:[158]

> The awkwardness of reckoning in terms of *value,* while commodities and labour-power are constantly changing in *value,* accounts for much of the obscurity of Marx's exposition, and none of the important ideas which he expresses in terms of the concept of *value* cannot be better expressed without it.
>
> But the terminology which Marx employs is important because of its suggestive power. No school of economics has ever used a perfectly colourless terminology. Overtones ring in the mind of the reader, even if the writer believes himself to be coldly scientific.

Robinson then cites Marshall on interest as a legitimate reward for capitalists' "waiting" (not "abstinence") and Pigou on "exploitation" with respect to real wages under monopoly versus free competition as also mobilizing the suggestive power of language.

Paul Sweezy, a sophisticated orthodox Marxist, validates, in his own language, Fellner's and Robinson's assessments:[159]

> It may be urged that the whole set of problems concerned with value calculation and the transformation of values into prices is excess baggage. The real world is one of price calculation; why not deal in price terms from the outset?
>
> A Marxist can safely concede something to this point of view. . . .
>
> One might be tempted to go farther and concede that from the formal point of view it is possible to dispense with value calculation even in the analysis of the behavior of the system as a whole. There is, however, a weighty reason for believing that this would be a mistaken view. The entire social output is the product of human labor. Under capitalist conditions, a part of this social output is appropriated by that group in the community which owns the means of production. This is not an ethical judgment, but a method of describing the really basic economic relation between social groups. It finds its most clear-cut theoretical formulation in the theory of surplus value. As long as we retain value calculation, there can be no obscuring of the origin and nature of profits as a deduction from the product of total social labor. The translation of pecuniary categories into social categories is greatly facilitated.

Paul Samuelson, dealing with the labor theory of value in strictly economic terms, is less charitable:[160] "Marxolaters, to use [George Bernard] Shaw's term, should heed the basic economic precept valid in all societies: Cut your losses!"

If the transformation problem reduces, in the end, to a matter of doctrine, creed, persuasion, propaganda, or social morality, Marx's judgment about and projection of real wages under capitalism is a matter of fundamental importance. The remarkable rise in real wages (as well a social services) from the Napoleonic Wars trough of, say, 1812 constitutes the greatest technical and, in the end, political failure of Marx's vision of capitalism and its future.

Here are the two memorable passages in the *Communist Manifesto* bearing on the prospect for real wages:[161]

> Owing to the extensive use of machinery and to division of labour, the work of the proletarians has lost all individual character, and consequently, all charm for the workman. He becomes an appendage of the machine, and it is only the most simple, most monotonous, and most easily acquired knack, that is required of him. Hence, the cost of production of a workman is restricted, almost entirely, to the means of subsistence that he requires for his maintenance, and for the propagation of his race. But the price of a commodity, and therefore also of labour, is equal to its cost of production. In proportion, therefore, as the repulsiveness of the work increases, the wage decreases. Nay more, in proportion as the use of machinery and division of labour increases, in the same proportion the burden of toil also increases, whether by prolongation of the working hours, by increase of the work exacted in a given time or by increased speed of the machinery, etc.

> The modern labourer . . . instead of rising with the progress of industry, sinks deeper and deeper below the conditions of existence of his own class. He becomes a pauper, and pauperism develops more rapidly than population and wealth.

In *Capital* itself, despite its technical character, there are passages of equal emotional intensity that also imply that real wages of labor will be held to a socially conventional subsistence minimum.[162] But there are other passages in which Marx's view of real wages is less clear cut. For example, it is possible to interpret the following as asserting that real wages might rise to a degree so long as they didn't reduce profits in such a way as to destroy the impulse to accumulate; and, in Marx's view, it was very hard indeed to destroy the capitalist's impulse to accumulate:[163]

> Wages, as we have seen, by their very nature, always imply the performance of a certain quantity of unpaid labour on the part of the labourer. Altogether, irrespective of the case of a rise of wages with a falling price of labour, &c., such an increase only means at best a quantitative diminution of the unpaid labour that the worker has to supply. This diminution can never reach the point at which it would threaten the system itself. Apart from violent conflicts as to the rate of wages (and Adam Smith has already shown that in such a conflict, taken on the whole, the master is always master), a rise in the price of labour resulting from accumulation of capital implies the following alternative.
>
> Either the price of labour keeps on rising, because its rise does not interfere with the progress of accumulation. . . . In this case it is evident that a diminution in the unpaid labour in no way interferes with the extension of the domain of capital. —Or, on the other hand, accumulation slackens in consequence of the rise in the price of labour, because the stimulus of gain is blunted. . . . The price of labour falls again to a level corresponding with the needs of the self-expansion of capital, whether the level be below, the same as, or above the one which was normal before the rise of wages took place.

Table 4.2. Trends in Real Adult Male Full-time Earnings for Selected Groups of Workers, 1755–1851 (1851 = 100)

Benchmark year	Farm labourers	Middle group	Artisans	All blue collar	White collar	All workers
1755	65.46	47.54	56.29	56.50	23.93	42.74
1781	61.12	46.19	48.30	50.19	22.24	39.24
1797	74.50	52.54	46.73	53.61	23.45	42.48
1805	74.51	52.96	42.55	51.73	20.82	40.64
1810	67.21	51.54	42.73	50.04	19.97	39.41
1815	75.51	57.81	52.18	58.15	25.49	46.71
1819	73.52	54.35	50.26	55.68	27.76	46.13
1827	75.86	70.18	66.39	69.25	39.10	58.99
1835	91.67	85.97	78.62	83.43	66.52	78.69
1851	100.00	100.00	100.00	100.00	100.00	100.00

Percentage Change, 1781–1851, under the three sets of cost-of-living weights and price assumptions:

	Farm labourers	Middle group	Artisans	All blue collar	White collar	All workers
Most pessimistic	31.6%	75.1%	68.0%	61.8%	294.5%	103.7%
"Best guess"	63.6%	116.5%	107.0%	99.2%	349.6%	154.8%
Most optimistic	107.0%	175.3%	164.2%	154.4%	520.3%	220.3%

SOURCES AND NOTES: The most pessimistic and most optimistic variants are based on relatively unrealistic cost of living indices, selected as extreme cases from 16 alternatives. The most pessimistic used a cost-of-living index combining northern urban expenditure weights with Tucker's institutional clothing prices and Trentham cottage rents, while the most optimistic used an index combining northern rural weights with export clothing prices and no rents. Again, we prefer the "best guess" index, combining southern urban weights with export clothing prices and Trentham rents.

The 1755 figures are derived by relying on the Phelps Brown-Hopkins index to extend our 1781–1850 series (Table 4) backwards.

SOURCE: Peter H. Lindert and Jeffrey G. Williamson, "English Workers' Living Standards During the Industrial Revolution: A New Look," *Economic History Review*, Vol. 36, No. 1 (February 1983), p. 13.

But the more general impression one gets from Marx's technical writing, taken as a whole, is that the capitalists' power to expand the reserve army of the unemployed is so great that real wages oscillate cyclically about a level close to the subsistence minimum in a protracted power struggle, which will end only when capitalism is overthrown.[164]

As the quotations already cited in this chapter indicate, however, Marx's bill of particulars against capitalism transcends stagnant or inequitably constrained real wages. He vividly evokes long working hours; soul-destroying repetitive tasks rendering men, women, and children the slaves of machines; poor conditions of housing, sewerage, and water supply; and vulnerability to unemployment. Moreover, he distinguished the situation of various categories within the working force, some doing rather well, others trapped in abject poverty. It is on these aspects of Marx's exposition that contemporary Marxists are inclined to focus increasingly as the weight of evidence slowly gathers that the trend of real wages in Britain was erratically upward from the closing years of the Napoleonic Wars.

Indeed, one unambiguous achievement of Marx's was to stimulate a protracted scholarly debate, running down to the 1980s, on what actually happened to British real wages during the Industrial Revolution.[165] Table 4.2 and Figure 4.1 present the best estimates now available for the trend of British real wages for several sectors of the working force.

Overall, the story is reasonably clear.

- Even before the French Revolutionary and Napoleonic Wars, British real wages

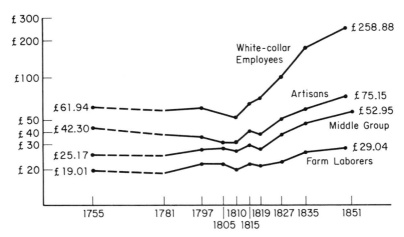

Figure 4.1. Adult Male Average Full-time Earnings for Selected Groups of Workers, 1755–1851, at Constant Prices. [Adapted from Lindert and Williamson, "English Workers' Living Standards," p. 12.]

came under downward pressure as the rise in population converted Britain into an increasingly regular net grain importer from, say, the late 1760s.

- There was a clear deterioration of real wages during the war years and a quite sharp postwar recovery, broken by two exceedingly bad years: 1816 and 1819.
- The trend thereafter—from, say 1820—was erratically upward to 1850 and beyond.

It has taken a great deal of painstaking scholarship, sharpened by sometimes heated debate, to achieve such confidence as we have in these propositions. Looking back at Marx's time, the resources available to him, and his strongly asserted sympathy with the plight of the industrial worker, one should, in my view, not be excessively critical of his failure to detect and measure the trend of real wages after 1815. Figure 4.2 sharpens the point. In the period 1840–1880, when Marx's views were formed and his mature work written, British, French, and United States real wages oscillated a good deal in the 1840s and 1850s with no firmly detectable trend; and they move up unmistakably only after the U.S. Civil War and the flood of cheap grain that came to Europe from the American West when its railway net was completed.

It is, then, understandable that Marx, in his time, would have formulated a theory of wages that, in effect, yielded cyclical oscillations about a relatively static level as the pool of unemployed contracted and expanded. After all, whether accurate or not, Mill also concluded and Marx quoted:[166] "It is questionable if all the mechanical inventions yet made have lightened the day's toil of any human being." And as a compulsive reader of the Factory Inspectors Reports and other descriptions of the round of life of workers of the time, it is also understandable that Marx should have reacted strongly—as many of his contemporaries did—to the human and social costs of the maturing industrial system.

Nevertheless, Marx's analysis can be criticized on two grounds: one relatively minor, the other of fundamental importance.

First, he does not recognize that both short-term as well as trend movements in real wages were, in this period, much more a result of movements in the cost of living than in money wage rates—a point illustrated vividly in Figure 4.3. Money wages in some other

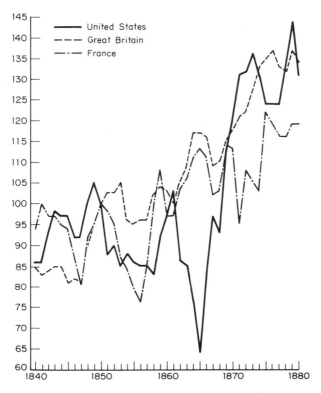

Figure 4.2. Real Wages: Great Britain, France, and the United States, 1840–1880 (1850=100). Col. I, 1840–1850, R. S. Tucker, "Real Wages of Artisans in London"; 1850–1880, G. H. Wood, real wages at full work (in Walter T. Layton and Geoffrey Crowther, *An Introduction to the Study of Prices* [London: Macmillan, 1938], p. 273); col. 2, Jean Lhomme, "Le Pouvoir d'achat de l'ouvrier français au cours d'un siècle: 1840–1940," *Le Mouvement Social,* no. 63 (April–June 1968), p. 46; col. 3, Hansen, "Factors Affecting the Trend of Real Wages," p. 32.

sectors were, no doubt, more volatile than in the London Building trade. But the greater amplitude of fluctuations in cost of living than in money wage rates is well documented for Britain in this period.[167]

Second, Marx's failure to predict rising real wages as a long-run feature of capitalism reflects a profound error in theory as well as a failure of imagination. As suggested earlier, Marx drove himself into a *cul de sac* with the now universally acknowledged incompatibility of his argument that real wages would remain more or less constant and profits decline (preceding, p. 126).[168] As Samuelson notes:[169] ". . . modern Marxians increasingly turn to that part of the sacred writings more consistent with last century's tremendous rise in workers' real wage rates." And there are passages that suggest that real wages might rise so long as the profit rate remained sufficient to induce a continued flow of investment. But that is not a doctrine likely to bring workers pouring into the streets with revolutionary fervor. Marx's failure to predict firmly and lucidly that rising real wages was the likely outcome of the capitalist process is important because it illustrates a characteristic of Marx that can be observed quite systematically: he tended to project in a rather linear way situations and trends observable in his own times. This is an odd failing

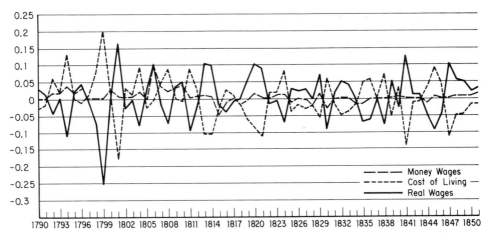

Figure 4.3. Comparison of Money Wages, Cost of Living, and Real Wages: London Artisans, 1790–1850. [Adapted from Rufus S. Tucker, "Real Wages of Artisans in London, 1729–1935," *Journal of the American Statistical Association,* Vol. XXXI, 1936, pp. 78–79.]

for a man who regarded himself correctly as a Hegelian theorist of history rather than an economist; but, it is a failure that recurs.

A final point to be underlined about labor. Just as Marx had no general theory of population he had no general theory of wages. The same reason prevailed: wage rates were the product of historically determined circumstances rooted in technologies, property relations, the institutions surrounding them, and the contention of the classes they created. In most formulations Marx regarded wage rates under capitalism as determined by a raw struggle for power in which the deck was stacked in favor of the employers, against the worker. Only the capitalist's interest in keeping the worker and his children alive set a limit on his avarice in enlarging surplus value at the workers expense. Behind the power struggle lay the perception that, under relatively full employment, the bargaining power of labor would increase and wages would rise at the expense of profits. A cyclical depression—enlarging the pool of unemployed workers and generating labor-saving inventions raising the organic composition of capital—emerges as a key instrument for whipping labor back into line.

Thus, as one might expect in dealing with an author whose major book is entitled *Capital,* Marx's view of the position of labor flows, like all else, from his analysis of the investment process, including the generation and diffusion of technology.

Investment and Technology

Marx's theory of growth, like all others, comes to rest on the process of capital formation; but his need to produce a self-destructing growth process gives his system a special character. The impulse of capitalists to accumulate is sometimes presented in terms of an overriding social compulsion, independent of the profit motive, but, Marx's argument generally runs in terms of the exploitation of perceived profit possibilities under conditions of ruthless competition.

At its core, Marx's theory of investment envisages three related processes: the progressive increase in the proportion of fixed capital to labor (a rise in the organic composition of capital); the progressive concentration of industry and banking in increasingly large units; and the increase in the reserve army of the unemployed, as labor-saving machinery is progressively introduced in agriculture as well as industry.

The flavor of Marx's exposition of each process is captured in the following quotations from *Capital*.[170]

THE RISING ORGANIC COMPOSITION OF CAPITAL.

. . . [T]he growing extent of the means of production, as compared with the labour-power incorporated with them, is an expression of the growing productiveness of labour. . . . [T]his growth in the mass of means of production, as compared with the mass of the labour-power that vivifies them, is reflected again in . . . the increase of the constant constituent of capital at the expense of its variable constituent. . . .

THE PROGRESSIVE CONCENTRATION OF CAPITAL.

Capital grows in one place to a huge mass in a single hand, because it has in another place been lost by many. This is a centralization proper, as distinct from accumulation and concentration. . . .

The world would still be without railways if it had had to wait until accumulation had got a few individual capitals far enough to be adequate for the construction of a railway. Centralisation, on the contrary, accomplished this in the twinkling of an eye, by means of joint-stock companies. . . .

THE PROGRESSIVE EXPANSION OF THE RESERVE ARMY OF THE UNEMPLOYED.

The additional capitals formed in the normal course of accumulation . . . serve particularly as vehicles for the exploitation of new inventions and discoveries, and industrial improvements in general. . . .

On the one hand . . . the additional capital formed in the course of accumulation attracts fewer and fewer labourers in proportion to its magnitude. On the other hand, the old capital periodically reproduced with change of composition, repells more and more of the labourers formerly employed by it. . . .

The industrial reserve army, during the periods of stagnation and average prosperity, weighs down the active labour-army; during the periods of overproduction and paroxysm, it holds its pretensions in check . . . as soon as, by Trades' Unions, &c., they try to organise a regular co-operation between employed and unemployed in order to destroy or weaken the ruinous effects of this natural law of capitalistic production on their class, so soon capital and its sycophant, Political Economy, cry out at the infringement of the "eternal" and so to say "sacred" law of supply and demand.

So far as I am aware, Marx visited only one factory—near Karlsbad.[171] But he was, evidently, fascinated by machinery; and, like Mill, he drew heavily on Babbage, as well as on others writing in this phase of increasing awareness of the ongoing revolution that had unfolded since the 1780s. And he went further back into the history of machinery in earlier times. Marx viewed machinery as a great achievement of capitalism, as a satanic instrument for keeping labor in subjection, and, ultimately, as a major instrument for capitalism's undoing, via the forces set in motion by the rising organic composition of capital.

Marx's ambivalence towards machinery is well reflected in the following passage in which he begins with an evocation of invention as the business of generating practical applications from science and ends with an analogy from Goethe in which labor is sexually possessed by machinery.[172]

> [Machinery] is, firstly, the analysis and application of mechanical and chemical laws, arising directly out of science, which enables the machine to perform the same labour as that previously performed by the worker. However, the development of machinery along this path occurs only when large industry has already reached a higher stage, and all the sciences have been pressed into the service of capital; and when, secondly, the available machinery itself already provides great capabilities. Invention then becomes a business, and the application of science to direct production itself becomes a prospect which determines and solicits it. But this is not the road along which machinery, by and large, arose, and even less the road on which it progresses in detail. This road is, rather, dissection . . . through the division of labour, which gradually transforms the workers' operations into more and more mechanical ones, so that at a certain point a mechanism can step into their places. Thus, the specific mode of working here appears directly as becoming transferred from the worker to capital in the form of the machine, and his own labour capacity devalued thereby. Hence the workers' struggle against machinery. What was the living worker's activity becomes the activity of the machine. Thus the appropriation of labour by capital confronts the worker in a coarsely sensuous form; capital absorbs labour into itself—"as though its body were by love possessed."*

Building on observations in Adam Smith relating to the negative as well as positive consequences of the division of labor (preceding, p. 37), Marx elaborated in great detail his view of the destructive psychological and social consequences of machinery. It is a recurrent theme that suffuses much of his writing. In particular Chapter XV of Volume I *Capital*, "Machinery and Modern Industry," is a sustained polemic of 136 pages. It concludes with one of Marx's most eloquent attacks on the consequences of technology for life under capitalism including agricultural life:[173]

> . . . In agriculture as in manufacture, the transformation of production under the sway of capital, means, at the same time, the martyrdom of the producer. . . . Moreover, all progress in capitalistic agriculture is a progress in the art, not only of robbing the labourer, but of robbing the soil; all progress in increasing the fertility of the soil for a given time, is a progress towards ruining the lasting sources of that fertility. . . . Capitalist production, therefore, develops technology, and the combining together of various processes into a social whole, only by sapping the original sources of all wealth—the soil and the labourer.

Despite Marx's profound interest in and almost obsession with invention and machinery, and despite his awareness of the link between science and invention, his analysis of the historical transition to modern industrial capitalism is curiously incomplete, and his linkage of technology to capital formation excessively simple. Historically, he moves from the widening of international markets, the "primitive accumulation" brought about

---

*"als hätt' es Lieb im Leibe," Goethe, *Faust*, Pt. I, Act 5, "Auerbach's Cellar in Leipzig."

by colonization, the slave trade, the expansion of the public debt, and other mercantilist policies, to the diversion of this pool of resources—"dripping from head to foot, from every pore, with blood and dirt"—to machinery and the expansion of fixed capital.[174] There is no role in this story for the scientific revolution, Newton, and the new perception of the human capacity to understand and manipulate nature to his advantage.[175] Somewhat similarly, in dealing with the technological change in modern industrial capitalism, Marx subsumes the generation and diffusion of new technology in the whole process of accumulation.[176] In a sense Marx shared with his classical predecessors and his successors in mainstream economics a tendency to structure his analysis of capital formation in ways that obscured the complex interplay of science, invention, and innovation despite the critical role it played in his system.[177]

Marx's view of the dynamics of capital formation, with its alleged technological bias toward laborsaving innovations, led him to the following basic conclusions about the future of capitalism:

- Real wages would oscillate cyclically around a socially determined subsistence level—his predominant but not exclusive doctrine.
- The pool of unemployed, relative to the working force, would expand and contract cyclically, but increase as a matter of trend; and at least once he asserted that business cycles would progressively increase in their amplitude.
- The social and psychological costs of capitalism for the worker would progressively increase whatever the trend in real wages might be.
- The capital–labor ratio in industry would rise, the profit rate would fall, but the volume of profits would rise with the absolute increase in fixed capital.
- The degree of concentration of industry would rise.
- By implication income distribution would become increasingly skewed.

Looking back over the more than 140 years since 1848 (or more than 120 years since 1867, when the first volume of *Capital* was published), none of these predictions has come about. As Samuelson notes in his centenary talk on *Das Kapital,* one can understand with sympathy writers in the 1930s believing that elements in Marx's predictions had come true.[178] Indeed, Marxists have perked up a good deal with the economic discomfiture of the noncommunist world of the 1970s and 1980s.[179] But, evidently, the real-enough problems of the years since the wheat and oil price explosions of 1972–1973 are not significantly illuminated by Marx's analysis of the dynamics of capitalism.

Surveying Marx's undistinguished record in prognostication, Eltis makes this observation:[180] "Marx's argument commands far more attention when it is applied to the century and a half prior to the publication of *Capital.* He kept close to known facts and his propositions derive from them." I would not wholly agree with this proposition because Marx as a historian was notably selective in his use of the facts available to him. In constructing his capitalist self-destruction machine to give scientific substance to the predictions of the *Communist Manifesto,* he did not place a high premium on organizing a judicious, well-balanced argument. He searched his predecessor political economists, government papers, contemporary journals, and pamphlets for validating evidence or argument, confident that his youthful vision of the future was essentially correct. As suggested earlier, in considering his view of the prospects for real wages, his flaw as a social scientist was familiar and pedestrian: he predicted in a linear way. The future was a rather unimaginative extension of the dynamics of the present and recent past, as he saw it.

A final brief note is necessary on the two-sector growth model that emerges in Volume II of *Capital*.[181] Marx poses as follows his central question, derived from François Quesnay's *Tableau Économique*:[182] "How is the capital *consumed* in production replaced in value out of the annual product and how does the movement of this replacement intertwine with the consumption of the surplus-value by the capitalists and of the wages of the labourers?" Marx first elaborates a circular-flow model with two sectors: Department I, Capital Goods; Department II, Consumers Goods. Output in each sector is then apportioned as between variable capital, in support of workers; constant capital, to meet depreciation; and surplus-value. After considering the intersectoral flows required for this system to sustain itself, without net investment, Marx moves on to begin to elaborate a dynamic system in which both fixed capital and the working force expand, an exercise he entitles "Accumulation and Reproduction on an Extended Scale." This interesting, if incomplete, exercise stimulated some of Marx's successors to elaborate further the extended-scale model for two purposes: to demonstrate the incapacity of capitalism to keep capital goods and consumers goods production in dynamic equilibrium and to develop models of cyclical crises created systematically by underconsumption.[183] If one takes into account Quesnay's role in stimulating Marx to develop a two-sector growth model, Samuelson's ungrudging but modulated tribute is just.[184]

> First, we can make a deposition—as the lawyers say—that Marx did, in his posthumous Volume II, innovate two-sector models of reproduction and growth. These are useful anticipations of work done in our day by Harrod, Domar, Leontief, Solow, Robinson, Uzawa, Pasinetti, Kaldor, Findlay, and many others. I do not honestly think that modern developments were much influenced, directly or indirectly, by Marxian writings; instead they grew naturally out of a marriage of the Clark–Bickerdike accelerator and the Keynes multiplier, and out of earlier works by Von Neumann and Frank Ramsey that show no Marxian influence. But still we all might well have benefited earlier from study of the Marx Tableaux.

I would add that painful as it might be to Marx and Marxists, Malthus's concept of "Proportionality" between production and consumption (preceding, p. 65). belongs somewhere between Quesnay and Marx. In the special perspective of this study—which, in the end, would treat business cycles as an endogenous aspect of the process of economic growth—it is Marx's extensive but, again, incomplete and unresolved work on business cycles that his schemes of reproduction are most usefully deployed.

Business Cycles

Marx was interested in business cycles in two respects, the first no doubt heightening the second. As a revolutionary politician he saw cyclical crises and deep depressions as potential catalytic occasions for the destruction of capitalism to be succeeded by a socialist dictatorship of the proletariat, a doctrine already proclaimed in the *Communist Manifesto*. As P. F. Bell and Harry Cleaver correctly conclude:[185] "Marx and Engels studied economic crisis, not as academic theorists but as militants[,] . . . an integral part of their attempt to determine optimal working class strategy." The end of the 1840s was for Marx a time of high hopes, intensive political activity, and, after his 1849 exile to London, somber reflection. There was a revival of hope a decade later. Isaiah Berlin notes:[186] "The great economic crisis, the severest yet experienced in Europe, which began in 1857, was warmly welcomed both by him and by Engels as likely to breed discontent and rebellion. . . ." There is no clear reflection in Marx's political stance of the British recession of 1866–1868, which was a good deal milder than those of the 1850s and late 1870s.[187] In addition, the cyclical phases of the major industrial powers were somewhat different in their timing.[188] By 1873 the First International had broken up, the Paris Commune had failed, and Bismarck had triumphantly created the German Empire. Nevertheless, Marx anticipated with relish the evidently coming crisis of 1873, but appeared by that time to expect no more than it would teach the arrogant Prussian "mushroom-upstarts" a bit of "dialectics."[189]

Isaiah Berlin observes that 1867 when[190]

> . . . the first volume [*Capital*] appeared marks not a turning but a breaking-point in Marx's life. His views during the remaining sixteen years of his life altered little; he added, revised, corrected, wrote pamphlets and letters, but published nothing that was new; he reiterated the old position tirelessly, but the tone is milder; a faint note almost of querulous self-pity, totally absent before, is now discernible. His belief in the proximity, even in the ultimate inevitability of a world revolution, diminished. His prophecies had been disappointed too often. . . .

But down to 1867 and even beyond, Marx had a second continuing reason to interest himself deeply in business cycles. If, as a revolutionary politician, he was not to see the destruction of capitalism in his lifetime, he aimed to provide the scientific underpinning for the *Communist Manifesto*'s confident prediction of capitalism's inevitable self-destruction. Here crises were, evidently, of central importance. Besides, like Mill, Marx lived his formative years in a time when the phenomenon of roughly decadal major cycles, marked by dramatic crises in the wake of their upper turning points, was inescapable; and as a political economist his attention was inevitably drawn to them.

In dealing formally with cycles, however, Marx faced a problem he never successfully resolved. His long-run vision of the dynamics of capitalism was based on the capitalists' socially and culturally determined impulse to accumulate. As Joan Robinson points out, this proposition denied him a consistent underconsumptionist theory of the business cycle:[191]

> If capitalists were always prepared to invest their surplus in capital goods, without regard to the prospect of profit, the output of capital goods would fill the gap between consumption and maximum potential output. Thus to clinch the [Marx's] argument it is necessary to show that investment depends upon the rate of profit, and that the rate of profit depends, in the last resort, upon consuming power. . . .
>
> This Marx fails to do. . . .

But, on a detailed *ad hoc* basis, Marx provides in Volume III of *Capital* some observations that clearly evoke Malthus's focus on lack of "proportionality" between consumption and investment as the basis for unemployment and "general glut":[192]

> . . . The entire mass of commodities . . . must be sold. . . . The conditions of direct exploitation, and those of realising it, are not identical. . . . The first are only limited by the productive power of society, the latter by the proportional relation of the various branches of production and the consumer

power of society. . . . The more productiveness develops, the more it finds itself at variance with the narrow basis on which the conditions of consumption rest.

. . . a crisis could only be explained as the result of a disproportion of production in various branches of the economy, and as a result of disproportion between the consumption of the capitalists and their accumulation. . . .

But Marx also propounded a quite different theory of crisis under capitalism that ran counter to the conventional underconsumptionist argument of his day; that is, crises flowing from a falling rate of profit induced by the rise in wages during the latter stage of a business cycle expansion (preceding, p. 130). It was this sort of pressure on profits, Marx believed, that not only reduced investment in the short run but induced the invention and diffusion of laborsaving machinery, increasing the organic composition of capital and guaranteeing the perpetuation of the reserve army of the unemployed. Thus Marx scores off Rodbertus and other contemporary underconsumptionist theorists:[193] "It is sheer tautology to say that crises are caused by the scarcity of effective consumption, or of effective consumers. The capitalist system does not know any other modes of consumption than effective ones, except that of *sub forma pauperis* or of the swindler.''

Aside from heading off at the pass a line of thought that might lead to the amelioration of capitalism, Marx is evoking here part of the process by which the dynamics of business expansion brings on crisis and depression. Rising money wages, due to a tightened labor market, lowers the expected rate of return over cost that initially led to the increase in investment that helped set in motion the expansion. Other constraining forces tended to operate in the same direction toward the peak of an expansion; e.g., rising commodity prices, rising interest rates, and a fall in expected rates of return as the products of increased investment earlier in the boom begin coming on the market, increasing supply in the leading sectors and reducing expected profitability in those sectors.

Clearly, then, Marx had no theory of business cycles that fitted coherently his theory of growth; and his long-run theory of falling profits, based on the assumption of a constant rate of surplus value, was of no help to him here, or, indeed, on other economic problems. But from his own observations and study, as well as from the writing of others, Marx did generate some significant insights. His best writing on the business cycle is less pretentiously theoretical, chronicling the phases and timing of cyclical fluctuations and relating them in a rough-and-ready way to the growth process. For example:[194]

> The enormous power, inherent in the factory system, of expanding by jumps, and the dependence of that system on the markets of the world, necessarily beget . . . a series of periods of moderate activity, prosperity, over-production, crisis and stagnation. The uncertainty and instability to which machinery subjects the employment . . . of the operatives become normal. . . . Except in the periods of prosperity, there rages between the capitalists the most furious combat for the share of each in the markets. This share is directly proportional to the cheapness of the product. . . . [T]here . . . comes a time in every industrial cycle, when a forcible reduction of wages beneath the value of labour-power is attempted for the purpose of cheapening commodities.

A necessary condition, therefore, to the growth of the number of factory hands, is a proportionally much more rapid growth of the amount of capital invested in mills. This growth, however, is conditioned by the ebb and flow of the industrial cycle. It is, besides, constantly interrupted by the technical progress that at one time virtually supplies the place of new workmen, at another, actually displaces old ones. . . . The workpeople are thus continually both repelled and attracted, hustled from pillar to post, while, at the same time, constant changes take place in the sex, age, and skill of the levies.

This passage is followed by a detailed account of fluctuations in the cotton textile industry from 1815 to 1863.[195]

The weaving of laborsaving technology into the cyclical process—with the impulse to generate or diffuse such technology at its maximum when wages rise toward the peak of a boom—evokes something of Gerhard Mensch's contemporary doctrine.[196] Mensch argues that inventions generated in depression form the basis of the ensuing expansion (see following, pp. 457–458). Marx has little or nothing to say about the process of invention; and, indeed, his work, like Mill's, is vulnerable to Schumpeter's charge that the creative process of innovation is underrated (preceding, p. 108). Quite specifically, Marx does not explore the time lags that might exist between a strong cyclical impulse to generate laborsaving machinery and the availability of such new devices.

Time lags do, however, enter Marx's evocation of the possibility of "periodic crises" due to "interconnected turnovers" related to the length of life of capital goods.[197] This concept emerges in the elaboration of his two-sector circular-flow model without net investment (preceding, p. 138). Marx envisages the need for periodic replacement of fixed capital, as it becomes obsolescent, implying that its original installation was concentrated in a short period rather than smoothly spread through time.

One Marxist scholar has even demonstrated that one can find in Marx and Engels some scattered passages that suggest an awareness of the possibility of a long cycle.[198] These fragmentary passages are not wholly consistent; but, in general, they would fall within the framework of an innovational conception of the long cycle rather than one centered on movements in the relative prices of basic commodities and industrial products.

Relative Prices

Marx rejected the concept of diminishing returns to agricultural and raw material production as he did the related Malthusian population doctrine (preceding, p. 127).[199] Marx's basic perception was that, under capitalism, the same forces were at work in agriculture as in industry. As he says in the *Grundrisse*:[200] "Agriculture more and more becomes a branch of industry, and is entirely dominated by capital." To simplify but not distort his argument, Marx was content to assume in Volume I of *Capital* that no part of surplus value was paid to the landlord as rent;[201] but he does devote a few pages to suggesting certain differences as well as similarities between modern industry and agriculture.[202]

In Volume III of *Capital,* however, Marx turns directly and at length (200 pages) to the determination of rent under conditions of industrial capitalism.[203] Essentially his effort here is to bring the analysis of agriculture in general and rent payments in particular into the general orbit of his analysis of production, accumulation, surplus-value, and profits. Prices enter into the analysis only as Marx considers the effects on rent of rising, falling, or constant prices in a regime of agriculture where capital investment and the application of technology (including chemical fertilizers) can alter productivity. So far as diminishing returns is concerned, his central theme is:[204] "The soil . . . if properly treated, improves all the time. The advantage of the soil, permitting successive investments of capital to bring gains without loss of previous investments, implies the possibility of differences in yield from these successive investments of capital.'' He admits the possibility of an increase in production requiring more than ''can be supplied with the help of this natural power ['a free gift of Nature's productive power'],''[205] but he regards this situation not as diminishing returns but as a requirement for additional capital ''in order to secure the same output. All other circumstances remaining the same, a rise in the price of production takes place.''[206] A part of this effort at generalizing the problem of diminishing returns out of existence is Marx's insistence that manufacturing, as well as agriculture or mining, exploits natural forces; e.g., waterfalls, the capacity for water to turn into steam when boiled, etc.

There is also in Volume III of *Capital* an extended, if somewhat shorter, treatment of the effects of raw material price fluctuations on the rate of profit.[207] It will be recalled that raw materials, by Marx's definition, are a component of constant (c), not variable capital (v). The rate of profit is defined as $s/(c + v)$. Therefore, by definition, a rise or fall in raw materials prices, either random or cyclical, will raise or lower the profit rate, other things remaining equal. Marx rings the changes on this proposition but includes, from his own times, examples of market adjustment where other things did not remain equal; e.g., the response of non-American raw cotton producers to the cotton famine caused and high prices induced by the Civil War.

Stages of and Limits to Growth

Down to the modern industrial phase of capitalism Marx's notion of the stages of growth in the long sweep of history conforms to the conventional sequence set out in the earlier classics of political economy: hunters and gatherers; primitive agriculture; feudalism; commercial expansion and premodern manufacture. He devotes a good deal of his exposition to slavery in Greece and elsewhere, partly as a basis for analogy to the worker under capitalism. What distinguishes Marx's treatment of these familiar stages is, of course, his theory of how changes in methods of production generated revolutionary class conflicts within each stage out of which a new stage emerged with its own technologies, property relations, institutions, antagonistic classes, and latent capacity for self destruction:[208] ''We see, therefore, how the modern bourgeoisie is itself the product of a long course of development, of a series of revolutions in the modes of production and of exchange.''

In a broad sense, Marx is also quite specific and vivid about the dynamics that would lead to the self-destruction of industrial capitalism: the progressive concentration of industry and banking as increasingly efficient labor-saving methods are introduced in response to the competitive struggle among capitalists and their shared interest in restraining wage rates; the increased concentration and self-consciousness of the proletariat. To the latter Marx added a technological dimension:[209] ''And that union, to attain which the burghers of the Middle Ages, with their miserable highways, required centuries, the modern proletarians, thanks to railways, achieve in a few years.''

Examined more closely, however, the mechanics of the breakdown of capitalism is less clear in Marx's technical analysis than the familiar litany of the *Communist Manifesto* would suggest. Paul Sweezy, for example, in reviewing ''The Breakdown Controversy'' among Marxists indicates the various lines of thought Marx himself brought to bear on the problem but concludes:[210] ''. . . nowhere in his work is there to be found a doctrine of the specifically economic breakdown of capitalist production. . . . [I]t is clear that his treatment of the problem, both in its positive and its negative aspects, prepared the ground for a long-drawn-out controversy which cannot be regarded as fully settled to this day.''

Marx's stages of growth proceed from controversy to obscurity when one moves from the breakdown of capitalism to socialism. Technically, Marx defined socialism in terms of a straightforward concept: abolition of private property; or, more operationally, as Engels put it: ''The proletariat seizes political power and turns the means of production into state property.''[211] From that act there follows ''an unbroken, constantly accelerated development of productive forces, and therewith for a practically unlimited increase of production itself.''[212]

The *Communist Manifesto* is lucid and candid on a 10-point program to complete the destruction of the bourgeoisie after the proletariat has seized power but before power is fully consolidated; and, indeed, something quite close to that program of consolidation has been followed by Communist parties in their early days in authority. But there is in Marx virtually nothing on the economics of socialism or, indeed, communism. In evoking the day when labor became ''life's prime want'' (preceding, p. 123), Marx did not appear to appreciate that, in a stable affluent society that had already brought the workweek down to, say, 40 hours, the decision to seek no further increase in real income per capita would provide only about an extra half-day per week in leisure. This assumes zero net investment but the need to allocate something like 8%–10% of GNP to meet depreciation of the capital stock as opposed to, say, 16%–20% for gross investment at present. The same proposition would hold for Mill's affluent Stationary State, although he did not rule out continued technological progress and net investment. There is, in general, a tendency for economists (including Keynes) to become somewhat romantic in contemplating the world of affluence that the persistence of compound interest might bring about; but the maintenance of high levels of affluence per capita will not be quite as effortless as their visions suggest.

In short, Marx failed to anticipate the real-enough problems of socialism with respect to pricing, planning, incentives, wage setting, etc.; and he never replied satisfactorily to his contemporary critics who identified those problems. Mill, in fact, was more lucid and responsive than Marx in setting out his case for socialism (preceding, pp. 119–121). The stages of socialism and communism thus remain, in Marx's economic writing, part of a vision rather than an operational program. One derives the impression that neither temperamentally nor intellectually was Marx much interested in the happy times after victory had been gained and consolidated over the bourgeoisie. As Engels said of Marx in his graveside speech: ''Fighting was his element.'' For whatever reason, he was obsessed with the objective of destroying the bourgeoisie.

With respect to the noneconomic aspects of socialism, however, Marx was quite explicit in the *Manifesto,* responding to criticism of his program with respect to culture, the family, the social training of children, the status of women, marriage, nationalism, and religion. In each of the relevant paragraphs of the *Manifesto* he tells off the bourgeoisie with evident relish. He is definitely still ''fighting'' rather than describing soberly and professionally how these critical social and cultural dimensions of society would be organized under socialism.

The most interesting of Marx's observations on the character of socialist society, however, are his annotated replies to Bakunin's criticism of Marxism in *Statehood and Anarchy* (1873).[213] Bakunin pressed hard on the proposition that the proletariat, organized as the ruling class, would generate an elite ruling group that would oppress farmers,

Slavs (on the assumption the revolution would first succeed in Germany), and, indeed, the workers themselves. Bakunin's charge has a certain contemporary resonance: ". . . the so-called people's state will be nothing other than the quite despotic administration of the masses of the people by a new and very nonnumerous aristocracy of real and supposed learned ones. . . . So, to liberate the masses of the people they first have to be enslaved. . . . [W]e answer: no dictatorship can have any other aim than to perpetuate itself. . . ." Marx replied, at three levels. First, with invective: "schoolboy drivel," "the ass," "democratic nonsense," "political windbaggery," etc. Second, by repeating in a rather wooden way his dogma about the exclusively class character of politics; for example:[214]

> The character of elections depends not on these designations but on the economic foundations, on the economic ties of the voters amongst one another, and from the moment these functions cease being political (1) no governmental functions any longer exist; (2) the distribution of general functions takes on a business character and involves no domination; (3) elections completely lose their present political character.

Third, he asserts Bakunin's is, in the end, a counsel of passivity: ". . . Bakunin deduces that it's best for the proletariat not to undertake any action but to sit and await—the day of *general liquidation,* the Last Judgement."

Readers have and will assess these exchanges in different ways. It is my impression, at least, that Marx was not at all convinced that the state would "fall away after liberation" in quite the easy way he argued it would from the simple principles of dialectical materialism; that he had no clear notion of what kind of political system might operate in the stages of socialism and communism; and that a dictatorship in the name of the proletariat, run by men with his vision of history, would be, in fact, quite an acceptable outcome. I believe Bakunin was essentially correct in identifying Marx as a "state worshipper"; a political and ideological rather than economic determinist when it came to action rather than historical analysis; in short, a Hegelian rather than a Marxist.

In any case, Marx's response to Bakunin is the kind of passage that justifies Schumpeter's observation:[215]

> . . . a reader who wishes for anything other than indoctrination must, of course, learn to distinguish both facts and logically valid reasoning from the ideological mirage. Marx himself helps us in this: sometimes, becoming semiconscious of ideological delusion, he rises, in defense, to the heights of his vituperative rhetoric, which therefore serves to indicate the spots at which there is something wrong.

So far as a formal model of stages of and limits to growth is concerned, what Marx's system asserted was that, under socialism, the economy would be organized to exploit science and invention in a steady flow; cycles would be eliminated along with "the senseless extravagance of the ruling classes;" output and real wages would increase up to the point where the society would decide, through some unspecified mechanism, that enough is enough; and income distribution would proceed on the principle of "from each according to his ability, to each according to his need." It is not diminishing returns but diminishing relative marginal utility that brings Marx's system to a more or less steady state, and this is also essentially true of Mill's vision and, later, Keynes's.

On the stages of growth in the contemporary world rather than in a postrevolutionary future Marx's views were generally formulated in terms of the prospects for revolution in particular countries and, especially, on the stages through which they would have to pass before they were officially ripe for revolution. Like some of his writing for the *New York Tribune* and other journals, in which Engels often played a significant part, these observations appear in letters, pamphlets, and other occasional settings. In general, they are more flexible than Marx's expositions in *Capital,* and often full of liveliness and insight. Marx begins his pamphlet on Louis Bonaparte, for example, by extending Hegel's observation that great historical personages appear twice by adding: "the first time as tragedy, the second as farce." In an article in the *New York Tribune* he characterizes India as a "strange combination of Italy and Ireland, of a world of voluptuousness and of a world of woes. . . ."[216] He judged that India, having experienced under British rule both "the annihilation of old Asiatic society, and the laying of the material foundations of Western society . . ." would have to proceed through a stage of bourgeois capitalism before achieving socialism. On Russia, which Marx and Engels had viewed for most of their lives as a center of reaction and hopelessly backward, Marx (but not Engels) began to alter his view late in life. He was responding, in part, to the strong positive reaction of a good many Russian middle-class intellectuals to the publication in Russian of *Capital:*[217]

> Letters reached him from Danielson in Russia, and from the exiles Lavrov and Vera Zassulich, begging him to apply himself to specific problems presented by the peculiar organization of the Russian peasants into primitive communes, holding land in common, and in particular to state his view on propositions derived from Herzen and Bakunin and widely accepted by Russian radicals, which asserted that a direct transition was possible from such primitive communes to developed communism, without the necessity of passing through the intermediate stage of industrialism and urbanization, as had happened in the West. Marx, who had previously treated this hypothesis with contempt . . . was by now sufficiently impressed by the intelligence, seriousness, and, above all, the fanatical and devoted socialism of the new generation of Russian revolutionaries to reexamine the issue. . . . Marx wrote two lengthy letters in which he made considerable doctrinal concessions. He admitted that if a revolution in Russia should be the signal of a common rising of the entire European proletariat, it was conceivable and even likely that communism in Russia could be based directly upon the semi-feudal communal ownership of land by the village as it existed at the time; but this could not occur if capitalism continued among its nearest neighbours, since this would inevitably force Russia in sheer economic self-defence along the path already traversed by the more advanced countries of the West.

But, in general, despite this glimmer of hope to the East, Marx's closing years were not cheerful. German socialism turned toward ameliorative measures and political democracy in the conventional sense. In Britain and other industrial countries, the urban workers experienced a rise in real income as food prices fell and new technologies continued to cut the cost of manufactures and transport. Socialist and other movements of protest against the inequities and harshness of capitalist industrial society gathered strength on both sides of the Atlantic, but they generally did not validate Marx's vision of the scientific laws that would inevitably determine the unfolding of history.

In retrospect, the machine that Marx tried to construct to validate his youthful vision was a kind of Ptolmeic instrument in a Copernican world. As he confronted reality in his years of research, he found the pieces did not fit well together. By Copernicus's day, followers of Ptolemy (who argued that the earth is the center of the Solar system) had to create more than 80 spheres "to save appearances"; i.e., to account for observed movements of the planets.[218] Marx left that task to later Marxists. He went on with his research but was often diverted and never finished the second and third volumes of *Capital*.

It is worth asking why this extraordinary effort dribbled off into the sand?

Noneconomic Factors

In George Santayana's evocative phrase, all human beings are destined to try to deal with "crude facts and pressing issues" in "paper money of our own stamping, the legal tender of the mind."[219] It is, therefore, not enough to describe Marx's "paper money" as arbitrary. One must try to account for its special character.

Marx's engine of capitalism's self-destruction was evidently built up, piece by piece, by careful selection from the corpus of classical economics. From certain passages in Adam Smith, for example, he derives the image of the worker dehumanized by specialization of function, setting aside other passages that suggest the advantages that the worker might derive from the process. He generalizes by simple assertion Ricardo's special case of unemployment caused by the introduction of machinery and generates thereby the reserve army of the unemployed, setting aside Ricardo's conclusion on the net advantage to the worker of the introduction of the machinery (preceding, p. 82) as well as the counterarguments of Malthus, Mill, and others. From Quesnay and, quite possibly, from the hated Malthus he derives the notion of a possible disproportion in the expansion of capital and consumption goods sectors; but he rejects ameliorative policies that might restore the balance.

It is systematic selectivity with respect to both ideas and facts that renders Marx's analysis essentially a caricature of reality. It contains elements that command recognition; but the portrait as a whole is a vast distortion of both the life he could observe and its destined future. The economic and technical distortions in Marx's analysis, however, are evidently a product of his determination to generate a theory of growth that would fulfill his larger vision of the past and the future. One must, therefore, try to establish what it is that distorted this larger vision. I believe it was his view of the individual and his relation to society and, indeed, to history. Marx asserted, and may well have believed, that all previous forms of culture would, in a sense, be repealed by the revolutionary overthrow of capitalism, the consolidation of socialism, and an ending, once and for all, of class struggles. One of the most interesting passages in the *Communist Manifesto* bears on this question. Marx begins:[220]

> The charges against Communism made from a religious, a philosophical, and, generally, from an ideological standpoint, are not deserving of serious examination. . . .
>
> What else does the history of ideas prove, than that the intellectual production changes its character in proportion as material production is changed? The ruling ideas of each age have ever been the ideas of its ruling class.

But he then goes on to take the matter quite seriously, indeed:

> Undoubtedly, it will be said, religious, moral, philosophical and juridical ideas have been modified in the course of historical development. But re-

ligion, morality, philosophy, political science, and law, constantly survived this change.

There are, besides, eternal truths, such as Freedom, Justice, etc., that are common to all states of society. But Communism abolishes eternal truths, it abolishes all religion, and all morality, instead of constituting them on a new basis; it therefore acts in contradiction to all past historical experience.

What does this accusation reduce itself to? The history of all past society has consisted in the development of class antagonisms, antagonisms that assumed different forms at different epochs.

But whatever form they may have taken, one fact is common to all past ages, *viz.*, the exploitation of one part of society by the other. No wonder, then, that the social consciousness of past ages, despite all the multiplicity and variety it displays, moves within certain common forms, or general ideas, which cannot completely vanish except with the total disappearance of class antagonisms.

The extraordinary hypothesis asserted here is that because conflicting class interests of one kind or another existed in all past societies, the continuity of certain concepts of justice, morality, and religion must be associated with those conflicts. If nothing else, Marx's appeal to those concepts in generating outrage at the ills of capitalism suggests that something is wrong with his *non sequitur*. And his error is underlined by a further 140 years of history, including considerable experience with consolidated socialist rule during which the abiding character of certain fundamental political, social, and economic problems has asserted itself as well as the continuity of important moral, cultural, and, even, religious values.

The error—shared in much post-1870 mainstream economics—is that human beings are much more complex units than Marx credited, filled with conflicting impulses, as the philosophers and religious leaders, poets, and storytellers of every culture have perceived. A Copernican system for societies must begin with human beings in their full complexity. In the *Communist Manifesto*—and occasionally elsewhere—Marx built his view of human beings around the "cash nexus"—the crudest kind of materialistic motivation. In more mature passages, he allowed for a wider range of human impulses, although always rooted in values and interests determined by the technological and economic structure of particular societies at particular periods of time.

In comparing my own stages of economic growth with Marx's, I found our ultimate difference in this economically determined view of human beings—whether crude or sophisticated.[221]

In the stages-of-growth sequence human beings seek not merely economic advantage but also power, leisure, adventure, continuity of experience, and security; they are concerned with their family, the familiar values of a regional and national culture, and a bit of fun down at the local or some other congenial gathering place. And beyond these diverse homely attachments, human beings are also capable of being moved by a sense of connection with their fellows everywhere, who, they recognize, share an ultimately common human experience and destiny. In short, net human behavior is seen not directly or obliquely as economically determined, but as an act of balancing alternative and often conflicting human objectives—often abiding and universal objectives—in the face of the range of choices men and women perceive to be open to them.

This notion of balance among alternatives perceived to be open is, of course, more complex and difficult than a simple maximization proposition; and it does not lead to a series of rigid, inevitable stages of history. It leads to patterns of choice made within the framework permitted by the changing setting of society; a setting itself the product both of objective real conditions and of the prior choices made by men that help determine the current setting that men confront.

The sectors of a society interact: cultural, social, and political forces, reflecting different facets of human beings, have their own authentic, independent impact on the performance of societies, including their economic performance. Thus, the policy of nations and the total performance of societies—like the behavior of individuals—represent acts of balance rather than a simple maximization procedure.

On this view it matters greatly how societies go about making their choices and balances. Capitalism, which is the center of Marx's account of the postfeudal phase, is thus an inadequate analytic basis to account for the performance of Western societies. One must look directly at the full mechanism of choice among alternative policies, including the political process—and, indeed, the social and religious processes—as quasi-independent arenas for making decisions and choices.

It was on this inherently complex view of human beings and societies that the line from Hume to Mill was built. And a respect for that complexity lies behind the forces that drove Western societies progressively to build their political systems around universal suffrage, multiple parties, and the secret ballot. The Reform Bill of 1867 was, in part, a conventional maneuver in two-party politics; but it was also a "leap in the dark" voted by men concerned with more than the cash nexus, moved by forces deeply rooted in the values of a society committed to democracy. The widening of the electorate was a major force in achieving over the next century many of the objectives Marx professed to seek for the worker in his *magnum opus* published the same year. And it is not inappropriate that Marx died in the year (1883) that Bismarck put through major health insurance legislation, responding to conventional political pressures from a social democratic party whose unity and ameliorative program Bismarck feared but Marx had bitterly opposed in 1875.

But an analysis of Karl Marx in a book on theorists of growth should not end here. He was both a polemicist and a social scientist. His vision of the dynamics of history, of capitalism, its demise and supersession by socialism and then communism was fully formed by 1848. It yielded in the *Communist Manifesto* a powerful call to arms, appealing with some success both to the conscience of the Western European middle class and the frustration of the worker. And a part of his life was subsequently devoted to the politics of bringing that vision to life. But he committed most of his life to an almost inhuman effort to underpin that vision with a scientific foundation. Writing in 1867 of *Capital,* in explanation of failure to correspond with a friend, he wrote:[222] "I therefore [because of illness] had to use *every* moment in which I was capable of working in order to complete my book, to which I have sacrificed my health, my happiness, and my family."

A recent biographer concludes and cites a striking image Marx evoked of his own dilemma:[223]

> The drama of Marx's life was the confrontation of theory and reality, thought and the world. The struggle was powerful because its stage was the whole of human history, and because each of the two protagonists—intellectual vision and actual experience—was equally clothed with the full intensity of Marx's commitment to it. This double devotion was Marx's dilemma and his glory. His life had all the character and dimensions of tragedy.

In the 1860s Marx found a literary image of his own plight in a story of Balzac. Paul Lafargue wrote:

> One of Balzac's psychological studies, "The Unknown Masterpiece" . . . made a great impression on him because it was in part a description of his own feelings. A talented painter tries again and again to limn the picture which has formed itself in his brain; touches and retouches his canvas incessantly; to produce at last nothing more than a shapeless mass of colors; which nevertheless to his prejudiced eye seems a perfect reproduction of the reality in his own mind.

Lafargue's testimony is the only evidence that Marx regarded Balzac's character as an image of his own dilemma, but Marx recommended the story to Engels as a "masterpiece" in February 1867, just at the time Volume One was going to the printer.

. . . Some features of Balzac's painter recall Marx's own literary creation, the Democritus of his doctoral dissertation. Driven by the contrast between the light in his mind and the pale reflection of his vision reality offered, Democritus had also traveled the world in search of evidence. Cicero calls him a *vir eruditus*. He is competent in physics, ethics, mathematics, in the encyclopedic disciplines, in every art. So did Marx become a *vir eruditus*, extending his learning to some of the same disciplines Democritus had cultivated. His notebooks and manuscripts bulged with accumulated knowledge. He did not, like Democritus, travel through half the world in order to exchange experiences, pieces of knowledge, and observations, but he learned new languages and constantly expanded the scope of his reading. He wrote to friends at various times that *Capital* could not be completed until he had at hand one more piece of information—from Belgium, or Russia, or the United States. Marx's self-induced illnesses were less radical and violent than Democritus' blinding himself, but their self-destructiveness served a similar purpose, preserving the theoretical vision underlying *Capital* from the threatened revelation that the empirical reality of market relations might not correspond to it.

Marx clearly failed to fulfill the coherent but romantic destiny he defined for himself in his "sacred decade." (But, then, neither did Hume nor Adam Smith nor Marshall nor Schumpeter—to name four who set themselves tasks beyond their reach.) As Marx well knew, his system as a whole did not capture economic, social, and political reality as it progressively unfolded after 1848. But along the way he generated a range of insights—often inconsistent and derivative as they were—that will continue to make him a major figure among classical economists—a designation that a part, at least, of his exceedingly complex personality might not have resented.

II

GROWTH THEORY MOVES TO THE PERIPHERY, 1870–1939

5

The Setting

The period considered in Part II runs from, roughly, 1870 to the outbreak of the Second World War. As the analysis of Part I makes clear, 1848—when the *Communist Manifesto* and the first edition of Mill's *Principles* were published—might be taken as the end of the classical century of growth analysis, in terms of intellectual history, although it evidently took some time for the attitudes they reflected and their doctrines to diffuse. The more conventional benchmark date of 1870 comes closer to the time when Jevons (1871), Menger (1871), and Walras (1874) published their respective formulations of marginal analysis, although Jevons's "coefficient of utility" dates back to 1862. I would add that also about this time (1873) almost a quarter-century of secular price decline began, which had important effects on the contours of economic theory as well as of the world economy. In addition, the date approximates 1867 when the first volume of *Capital* appeared (and Marshall began his serious study of economics); it is close enough to 1871 when the seventh edition of Mill's *Principles*, the last edited by the author, was published; and it was just about the time when chairs of political economy began to be established in the leading American universities, foreshadowing the emergence, in the next generation, of U.S. and British economic associations and learned journals. As turning points go, then, 1870 is a reasonable if somewhat arbitrary symbol.

Note 1 to this chapter incorporates characterizations of the 1870 watershed by nine historians of economic thought.[1] Broadly speaking, they underline the shift from a focus on growth to social reform and welfare; a new emphasis on the refinement of analysis; a heightened concern with the optimum allocation of resources, in terms of marginal analysis; and the emergence of economics throughout the Atlantic world as an academic profession.

While accepting as legitimate virtually all the insights set out in Note 1, my own formulation of what happened to political economy after 1870 would distinguish, rather sharply, as do some historians of doctrine, the period down to 1914 from the interwar years. In the $4\frac{1}{2}$ decades before the First World War, the earlier relative convergence of the formal theoretical concepts of mainstream economists with the great issues in political and social contention was weakened. The advanced industrial societies of that era began to come seriously to grips with problems of welfare, income distribution, monopoly power, and other contentious matters that forced themselves to the center of the political stage. Operationally, these issues were posed by the rise of new political forces: the Populists, Grangers, and Progressives in the United States; the Labour Party and the invigorated

Liberals in Britain; the socialists on the Continent; the labor unions everywhere; and, down to the mid-1890s, the embattled American farmers. These developments were quite consistent with the critical questions to which Mill and Marx had addressed themselves.

Mill's *Principles* reigned as the mainstream textbook down to the 1890s when Marshall's *Principles* began to take over, in the Anglo-Saxon world at least. Marshall, quite consciously in Mill's tradition, took problems of welfare very seriously indeed, regarded himself as a socialist for some time, and rejected socialism only after protracted soul-searching. But mainstream economics, as a formal method of analysis, moved in a quite different direction. True to Malthus's insight (p. 581, n. 9), the calculus proved capable of expressing with precision certain fundamental economic propositions and, especially, defining, under strict limiting assumptions, conditions of stable equilibrium in both specific markets and for an economy as a whole. The major economic figures—in Britain, on the Continent, and in the United States—were caught up in the authentic adventure of refining market analysis for both final output and factors of production under what came to be known as Marshallian short-period assumptions—excluding the dynamic supply forces, as well as changing incomes and tastes, at work in the process of economic growth. Without these complications, pure theories of production and distribution could be brought together in splendid symmetry, but political economy gave way to economics. The discipline became the evolving methods of analysis, not the great problems demanding solution in the active world; and the increasingly refined methods of analysis led, in most—not all—cases, away from, rather than toward, the issues in active contention in the political arena. What John Williams had to say after an exhaustive test of the classical theory of foreign trade could be said of mainstream economics as a whole in the wake of the revolution of 1870 and after:[2] "The classical theory assumes as fixed, for purposes of reasoning, the very things which, in my view, should be chief objects of study. . . ." And Alfred Marshall, at once major architect and major critic of mainstream economics in its second century, would agree.

Moral and ethical issues did not, of course, disappear from economics, and economists certainly did not abandon the right to hold strong personal views on issues of policy and social justice. Even Léon Walras was an advocate of wide-ranging economic and social reform; but this stance was clearly divorced from his work as an analyst of general equilibrium. Economists did not become less concerned with the fate of their societies; but the linkage of theoretical formulation to problems of policy was attenuated by the seductive elegance of the new concepts and methods of analysis.

The gap between theoretical formulation and the complexities of current economic and social life were sometimes dealt with by including within general treatises a good deal of empirical material in the tradition of Adam Smith and J. S. Mill. This is true, for example, of Marshall's *Principles,* discussed in in Chapter 6. But there is a sense in which the intellectual underpinnings of the movement for what we might broadly call welfare reform were quite precisely related to the gaps between the formal assumptions underlying post-1870 mainstream economics and reality.

The central propositions of mainstream economic theory assumed perfect competition and steady full employment; the dissidents dramatized the reality of monopolies and severe cyclical unemployment. Formal theory linked income distribution to the net marginal value product of the economic functions performed by individuals, the dissidents dramatized (as had Mill) the institutions, patterns of land ownership, inheritance law, relative access to education, and other noneconomic determinants of income distribution emerging from the history of particular societies.

Among the inequities they identified was the asymmetry in the labor market of the individual worker vis-à-vis the more concentrated power of the employer, operating individually or collectively. The market-oriented theory of distribution in its pure form was silent on such vicissitudes as accidents at the workplace, health facilities and educational opportunity for the poor, and old-age insurance. By one form of argument or another, the dissidents dragged these issues toward the center of the political arena. The examples could go on to embrace Henry George's powerful polemic built on an interpretation of the Malthus–Ricardo theory of rent; Thorstein Veblen on conspicuous consumption, the monopolistic corporation, and technology; Upton Sinclair on the Chicago slaughterhouses; the American institutionalists; the Fabians, including Shaw; the German and British historical schools, including R. H. Tawney. And then—sometimes overlapping these examples and categories—there were various kinds of socialists, including some writing and arguing in the tradition of Marx as they chose to interpret him.

I would emphasize again that the mainstream economists did not universally and systematically oppose the measures that arose from these heterodox sources. Some, in fact, supported them. But the formal constructs of mainstream economics were a poor basis for crusading zeal; and the social welfare movement, which progressively gathered momentum down to the First World War, was, in fact, nourished mainly by an array of iconoclasts who were crusading not only on behalf of the less advantaged but also against the inadequacies they thought they perceived in mainstream economics.

It does not follow that the quiet acknowledgment of the inhumanities of capitalism, the exploration of possible remedies, and authentic concern for the less advantaged that motivated Mill, Marshall, Pigou, and others in that nonpolemical tradition were unimportant in democratic societies. They did not provide the banners and rhetoric for the ardent reformers. But they helped persuade the critically important "moderate, decent, conservative margin" in the middle of the political spectrum that major reforms were legitimate and necessary.[3]

On one point, central to this book, both orthodox and heterodox economic analysts of the 1870–1914 period—with a few exceptions noted later—more or less silently agreed: the analysis of economic growth could be dropped from the agenda. Both groups assumed the existence of an ongoing, viable, expanding economic system. Although the lines between them were not sharp, one group was devoted primarily to refining theoretical knowledge of how it worked, the other to diagnosing and remedying, in more or less radical ways, its inhumanities. But by and large the theory of economic growth was placed by both groups on protracted holiday. The political process came to concentrate on a more or less civilized struggle over the division of a pie virtually all contestants assumed would continue to expand as a matter of trend. That struggle determined the shape of democratic politics in advanced industrial societies for about a century.

One aspect of the history of the world economy did generate fresh, creative thought in the 40 pre-1914 years: the powerful declining price trend from 1873 to about 1896; the subsequent rising trend that was to be exacerbated by the First World War, reaching a peak in 1920. The declining price trend from 1873 to the mid-1890s was the occasion for extended analysis by virtually all the major pre-1914 and interwar monetary theorists, including Cassel, Fisher, Giffen, Keynes, Layton, Marshall, Pierson, Wells, and Wicksell.[4] In the case of Marshall, his written and oral testimony before the Royal Commission on the Depression of Trade and Industry (1886), and the Royal Commission on the Values of Gold and Silver (1887–1888), were the occasion to crystallize and present the monetary doctrines that he had generated in his teaching and that had become part of the oral

tradition at Cambridge. In his lengthy biographical essay on Marshall, Keynes observes:[5]
"It was an odd state of affairs that one of the most fundamental parts of monetary theory should, for about a quarter of a century, have been available to students nowhere except embedded in the form of question-and-answer before a Government Commission interested in a transitory practical problem."

There was more than the falling price trend of 1873 to the mid-1890s that affected the contours of political economy in the pre-1914 era.

- The world arena of power was reshaped: in part, by the emergence of Bismarck's German Empire in 1871 and, at about the same time, a unified United States bound together by a continental railway net; in part, by the movement into takeoff of Sweden in the 1870s, Japan and Denmark in the 1880s, Russia and Italy in the 1890s, with regional takeoffs in parts of the Austro-Hungarian Empire. Germany, Japan, Russia, and Italy bestirred themselves to assert imperial claims in Africa and East Asia before all options were closed, while the nationalist strains within the Ottoman and Austro-Hungarian Empires became more intense. Analysis of imperialism became a popular subject; and the multiple minor wars of this period all relate to the new impulses at work: the Italian campaign in Africa; the Sino–Japanese and Russo-Japanese wars; the Boer war; the Spanish–American war; and two Balkan wars.

- The upward shift in the relative prices of agricultural products and raw materials after the mid-1890s imposed a severe check on the trend rise in real wages in the advanced industrial countries that had marked the previous quarter-century. The political forces that had been gathering in support of expanded welfare measures rapidly increased in strength as urban workers turned to politics for redress against the forces operating on prices in the world economy. German social insurance dates from the 1870s: against accidents (1871,1884); sickness (1883); and old age and invalidity (1888). A measurable increase in social outlays as a proportion of GNP occurred in the Atlantic world in the pre-1914 generation (Table 5.1), although the increase was modest compared to that which took place during the interwar years.[6]

- Although, on the whole, business cycles were of modest amplitude from the mid-1890s to 1914, this was the period when systematic study of the business cycle began, and many of the fundamental pioneering studies were published.

- The relatively high prices of basic commodities and favorable terms of trade in agricultural and raw material producing regions after 1896 led to phases of rapid development, including large flows of capital and immigrants, expanded investment in infrastructure as well as export commodities, and, in two cases at least (Canada and Australia), movement into takeoff.[7]

These developments were, to a degree, reflected in the writings of mainstream economists; but the barrier between formal theory and the problems of the active world was heightened by an institutional development to which Heilbroner refers (Note 1): economics became an academic discipline throughout the Atlantic world. That meant professors, learned journals, doctoral (or fellowship) theses, specialized fields within the discipline, and the emergence of schools of economic thought and method.[8]

One consequence of these developments was considerable continuity of thought that transcended the great chasm of the First World War—and, to a degree, even the Second. Table 5.2 is meant to suggest, with no pretense to completeness, the rough—very rough —grouping of five of the major schools of the period 1870–1939.

Table 5.1. Social Service Expenditures as a Percentage of GNP: 1890–1932 (all levels of government)

	United States	United Kingdom	Germany
1890	1.8%	1.9%	—
1900	1.9	2.6	—
1913	2.1	4.1	5.1%
1932	6.3	12.9	19.3

SOURCE: Richard A. Musgrave, *Fiscal Systems* (New Haven: Yale University Press, 1969), pp. 94–95 (Table 4-1). Social services include education, welfare programs, and housing as well as social insurance. There are no estimates for total German social expenditures for 1890 and 1913. The more narrow category of social insurance expenditures appears to have increased as follows as a proportion of GNP. 1891, 0.7%; 1901, 1.3%; 1913, 1.8%. (Calculated from Supan Andic and Jindrich Veverka, "The Growth of Government Expenditure in German Since the Unification," *Finanzarchiv*, Vol. 23, No. 2, January 1964, pp. 199–200 (per capita total budget expenditures in constant [1900] prices and per capita social insurance as % of total expenditure; p. 238 [population]; and p. 241 [GNP at 1900 prices].)

They reflect many anomalies. None kept vitality and even approximate continuity for more than three generations; Schumpeter, although a devoted pupil of Wieser and Böhm-Bawerk, went off in his own direction, influenced more by Walras—and perhaps even more by Marx—than by his Vienna teachers. The Stockholm School, in its first two generations, was marked by intense sibling rivalries. Leontief, although clearly building on Walras, emerged as a young man not from Lausanne but from the Soviet Union of the 1920s. And a good many economists of distinction absorbed elements from various traditions and schools; in England, for example, Roy Harrod, John R. Hicks, and Lionel Robbins. The American economists were notably diverse. J. B. Clark (1847–1938)

Table 5.2. Five Major Schools of Economists

Austrian School
Carl Menger (1840–1921)
Friedrich von Weiser (1851–1926)   Eugen von Böhm-Bawerk (1851–1914),
Ludwig von Mises (1881–1973)   Joseph A. Schumpeter (1883–1950),
Friedrich von Hayek (1899–)

Stockholm School
Knut Wicksell (1851–1926)   Gustav Cassel (1866–1945),
Johan Äkerman (1896–1982)   Erik Lindahl (1891–1960),
Gunnar Myrdal (1898–1987)   Bertil Ohlin (1899–1979)

Lausanne School
Leon Walras (1834–1910)   Wilfred Pareto (1848–1923)
[Wassily Leontief (1906–)]

Cambridge School
Alfred Marshall (1842–1924)
Arthur C. Pigou (1877–1959)   John M. Keynes (1883–1946)
Dennis H. Robertson (1890–1963)   Joan Robinson (1903–1985)

American Institutionalists
Thorstein Veblen (1857–1929)   Herbert J. Davenport (1861–1931)
John R. Commons (1862–1945)   Wesley C. Mitchell (1874–1948)
Walton Hamilton (1881–1958)   Clarence Ayres (1891–1972)

reflected in his work the German historical school and British socialism; but his most memorable contribution was in applying marginal productivity analysis to distribution theory. Irving Fisher (1867–1947) began, like Marshall, as a mathematician but moved over to economics under the influence of William Graham Sumner and studied in Germany and France in 1893–1894; but, essentially, Fisher was a school unto himself despite his gracious acknowledgment of debts to others. Frank Taussig (1859–1940), on the other hand, elaborated and sought to test empirically the British classical theory of foreign trade, although Schumpeter notes a bit of Böhm-Bawerk in his theory of distribution.

One is dealing, then, in the 44 years before the First World War, with an increasingly complex, diversified professional field, rooted in universities, its widening content fed by a number of distinctive streams of thought, interpenetrating with the passage of time. But there was also a substantial cacophonous chorus of critical dissidents; notably, the German and British historical schools, the British Fabians, the American Institutionalists, and an assortment of not-always-harmonious socialists.

From the present perspective, the central fact about the period 1914–1939 is that the conceptual barriers between mainstream economic theory and problems of public policy were notably lowered as the apparently solid institutional framework of the world economy was shattered, first by war, then by an unexampled sequence of acute problems: chronic unemployment, extreme trade and payments disequilibrium, a sharp relative decline after 1920 in basic commodity prices, a great depression, and a neo-mercantilist fragmentation of the world economy, as a second world war became a virtual certainty. Figure 5.1 seeks to capture something of this discontinuity for Great Britain.

On both sides of the Atlantic the First World War drew a good many economists into government, confronting them with circumstances where the normal operation of competitive markets palpably did not suffice. That experience, however, left less profound marks on economic theory and analysis than the array of decisions of public policy posed initially by reparations and war debts, and by the subsequent sequence of traumatic problems confronted in the Atlantic world over the next generation.

These urgent problems forced the pace of both theoretical and empirical work. Intensified efforts were concentrated, in particular, on the transfer problem, the intersectoral and international terms of trade, optimum exchange rates, and, above all, on unemployment in general and the business cycle in particular, where the foundations for theoretical analysis had been laid before 1914. Keynes's reshaping of macroeconomic theory to capture the theoretical possibility of chronic high unemployment and the direction of its remedy was simply the most dramatic of a number of forced-draft theoretical responses to a world economy deeply troubled for a more protracted interval than any since 1815.

In these areas the impulse to produce conclusions promptly useful for policy was evidently strong; but more influential than a sense of short-run urgency was the fact that the conventional theoretical structures applied to these problems were generally set up under Marshallian short-run assumptions. Thus, neither the economic and political environment of the interwar years nor the reigning structures of mainstream economics led the major figures in economics to place the analysis of economic growth at the center of the stage. Nevertheless, important insights related to economic growth emerged as a kind of by-product of work induced by the pressure of current problems. The state of growth analysis in the 1980s cannot be understood without reference to these oblique interwar contributions.

Gathering momentum even before 1914, but greatly heightened by the interwar imperatives, was a development that ranks in importance with major creativity in theory; that is,

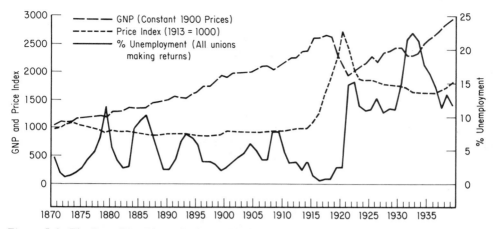

Figure 5.1. The Inter-War Discontinuity: British Historical Data, 1870–1939. [Adapted from B. R. Mitchell, *Abstract of British Historical Statistics* (Cambridge: at the University Press, 1971).]

the systematic amassing of reasonably reliable statistical data. The power of the Keynesian revolution depended, in fact, on the parallel emergence of national income accounting that matched its terms, although early national income estimates were mainly designed to establish patterns of income distribution.

Meanwhile, a few substantial figures marched to the beat of their own drummers, of whom four certainly belong in any review of theories of economic growth: Joseph Schumpeter, Simon Kuznets, Colin Clark, and Roy Harrod. None generated a theory of growth covering what I regard here as all the relevant variables. None approached growth in the broad societal terms of Marshall and the century of classics on which he built. Nevertheless, each in different ways carried the analysis of growth beyond the classics. And there were others on the periphery who, under one impulse or another, made significant contributions to growth analysis.

How, then, should one organize an account of growth theory from 1870 to 1939? Evidently, one cannot again pick six commanding figures, analyze them along the lines of the heroes of Part I, and feel one has an approximate account of how growth theory evolved. There is a paradox here: on the one hand, a good many economists made contributions to growth analysis as by-products arising from work addressed primarily to other problems; on the other hand, there are not even six major figures who can be regarded primarily as analysts of growth.

Under these circumstances, I begin with a chapter on what Marshall had to say about the long-run and economic growth (Chapter 6). It is longer than I initially planned but presented without apology. I found Marshall had a great deal to say about the key economic growth variables. He by no means solved all the problems he defined, but neither have his successors. I concluded he is still worth reading as a growth economist, and I hope Chapter 6 will encourage a reexamination of his views in those terms. The balance of Part II is built around the key variables used as the matrix for Part I: population and the working force (Chapter 7); investment and technology (Chapters 8 and 9); the business cycle and growth (Chapters 10 and 11); relative prices and Kondratieff cycles (Chapter 12); and the stages of and limits to growth (Chapter 13). The contributions of such major figures as Schumpeter, Kuznets, and Colin Clark are woven into these functional chapters.

6

Alfred Marshall
(1842–1924)

I once entitled a piece on the evolution of theories of economic development, including my own, "Development: The Political Economy of the Marshallian Long Period."[1] What I had in mind was this, among a number of similar passages from Marshall:[2]

> The theory of stable equilibrium of normal demand and supply helps indeed to give definiteness to our ideas; and in its elementary stages it does not diverge from the actual facts of life, so far as to prevent its giving a fairly trustworthy picture of the chief methods of action of the strongest and most persistent group of economic forces. But when pushed to its more remote and intricate logical consequences, it slips away from the conditions of real life. In fact we are here verging on the high theme of economic progress; and here therefore it is especially needful to remember that economic problems are imperfectly presented when they are treated as problems of statical equilibrium, and not of organic growth. For though the statical treatment alone can give us definiteness and precision of thought, and is therefore a necessary introduction to a more philosophic treatment of society as an organism; it is yet only an introduction.
>
> . . . [I]t is barely even an introduction to the study of the progress and development of industries which show a tendency to increasing return. Its limitations are so constantly overlooked, especially by those who approach it from an abstract point of view, that there is a danger in throwing it into definite form at all. But, with this caution, the risk may be taken; and a short study of the subject is given in Appendix H.

Appendix H then demonstrates that under conditions of increasing returns (decreasing costs)—the normal condition of many firms and sectors in an economy regularly absorbing new technologies—no single stable equilibrium position exists for price and output; when "a casual disturbance" results in a substantial increase in capacity and output (and, thereby, lower costs), a cessation of that disturbance does not result in a return to the initial capacity-output-cost position; and, with respect to demand, a sharp reduction in costs and price may result not merely in increased purchases but an irreversible outward shift of the demand curve as consumers become accustomed to the commodity whose price has been greatly reduced.[3] A reversal in cost and price will, under these circumstances, not return the demand curve to its initial equilibrium position. Thus, not only do both demand and supply curves slope downward but they cease to be independent of each other; and conventional equilibrium microeconomics becomes inoperative.

Although, as J. K. Whitaker notes, Marshall may have been given to occasional hyperbole, he reflected a powerful and recurrent obsession when, in a letter to N. G. Pierson, the Dutch economist, he wrote:[4]

> . . . [T]he book [*Principles*] was written to express one idea; & one only. That idea is that whereas Ricardo & Co. maintain that value is determined by Cost of production, & Malthus, Macleod, Jevons & (in a measure) the Austrians that it is determined by utility, each was right in what he affirmed but wrong in what he denied. They none of them paid, I think, sufficient attention to the element of *Time*. That I believe holds the key of all the paradoxes w^h. this long controversy has raised. When Ricardo spoke of Cost of production as determining value he had in mind periods as to which cost of production is the dominant force; when Jevons emphasized utility, he had in mind shorter periods. The attempt to work all existing knowledge on the subject of value into one Continuous & harmonious whole, by means of a complex study of the element of Time permeates every Book almost every page of my volume. It is the backbone of all that, from a scientific point of view, I care to say.

But Marshall was acutely aware that he had not fully met his own challenge and woven the element of time into a continuous and harmonious whole. At the close of Appendix H in the *Principles* he reflects on "the imperfection of our analytical methods" and, as often, throws out a clue as to how progress might be made in dealing scientifically with the long run; i.e., by dating the time a certain volume of production became "normal." In one sense, the large body of historical and empirical material in Marshall's three major volumes reflects the extraordinarily high goal (or Schumpeterian vision) he set for himself. It was to produce a set of principles that matched reality in its full complexity. Unlike Marx, he visited many factories, met many businessmen, labor leaders, and workers. He understood and often said that the study of "organic growth," which lay at the center of the problem of time in economic theory, was a biological field, not a derivative of or parallel to Newtonian Physics.

But the technical tools Marshall inherited and substantially refined did not permit him to come to grips in a systematic way with "society as an organism." Writing retrospectively, Marshall said:[5] ". . . the purely analytical work in Book V of my *Principles*, with a part of Book III, were the kernel from which my volume expanded backwards and forwards to its present shape." Most of Book V and, almost certainly, the parts of Book III to which Marshall referred are susceptible of formulation in mathematical terms with supply–demand equilibrium conditions defined under short-period assumptions. On the other hand, Book IV ("The Agents of Production")—Marshall's most extended treatment of the determinants of growth—is of quite different, more descriptive texture without an explicitly stated theoretical bone structure. In fact, Marshall did make notes that constitute a quite lucid approximation of an aggregate neoclassical growth model; but, like those later models, Marshall's did not bring him very close to the reality he sought to evoke. And of this he was quite aware.

The dichotomy between the rigorous exposition of "introductory" propositions and the evocation of the interacting, irreversible dynamics of economic, social, and political processes in the active world persisted in Marshall's mind and exposition to the end. The

1920 Preface to the last edition of the *Principles* he edited (the eighth) contained these two passages that capture the divergent strands in Marshall's work:[6]

> The main concern of economics is thus with human beings who are impelled, for good and evil, to change and progress. Fragmentary statical hypotheses are used as temporary auxiliaries to dynamical—or rather biological—conceptions: but the central idea of economics, even when its Foundations alone are under discussion, must be that of living force and movement.
>
> . . . It [the differential calculus] is still in its infancy; it has no dogmas, and no standard of orthodoxy. It has not yet had time to obtain a perfectly settled terminology; and some differences as to the best use of terms and other subordinate matters are but a sign of healthy life. In fact however there is a remarkable harmony and agreement on essentials among those who are working constructively by the new method; and especially among such of them as have served an apprenticeship in the simpler and more definite, and therefore more advanced, problems of physics. Ere another generation has passed, its dominion over that limited but important field of economic inquiry to which it is appropriate will probably be no longer in dispute.

The harmonization of these two perspectives—Darwinian and Newtonian—has not proved easy over the subsequent 7 decades nor the achievement of consensus on the limited but important field of economic inquiry to which the differential calculus is appropriate.

It was this clash between Marshall's vision of what economics should be and the partial equilibrium analysis of competitive markets under short-run assumptions—in which Marshall excelled—that accounts for his curious attitude toward the use of mathematics in economics. It was the field in which he was trained as a Cambridge undergraduate, emerging with distinction as Second Wrangler. Whitaker argues, not unpersuasively, that this achievement, in itself, does not mean that he was "a born mathematician."[7] Whitaker points to others who excelled in the Cambridge Mathematical Tripos of the period who did not go on with mathematics and, more cogently, to the fact that the examinations at that time were more a test of endurance, memory, and rapid manipulation than of a capacity for research in mathematics. This is an issue I am certainly not qualified to settle. But the fact is that Marshall's "awkwardness and hesitancy" in mathematical economics as opposed to the evident greater "comfort" of Jevons and Edgeworth, despite their inferior technical training, were the product of Marshall's more acute sense that the use of mathematics in economics could be dangerously limiting as well as helpful. In a statement with overtones of Francis Bacon (following, p. 331), Marshall concluded that the principal legitimate use of mathematics was extremely limited. It was to clear the way to the center of the "difficult problems" in economic theory that neither in his time nor in ours, lend themselves to mathematical resolution.[8]

Like professors since history took note of them, Marshall was not above a bit of professional rivalry—although he struggled stoutly against it; and he was certainly quintessentially English, despite his oft-acknowledged intellectual links as a social scientist to Cournot, von Thünen, Roscher, and Hegel. But Walras missed something, so far as Marshall was concerned, when he despaired of the insuperable insularity of "MM. les économistes Anglais."[9] Marshall deeply believed that economics as a Moral Science should aim higher than the elegant elaboration of essentially static theory, abstracted from the evolving political and institutional life as well as the technological base of the societies of which they were a part. After all, the first sentence of the *Principles* reads: "Economic conditions are constantly changing, and each generation looks at its own problems in its own way." The acceptance of that dictum is not calculated to lead an economist to be satisfied with a world of Walrasian equilibrium.

This central proposition relates to the third source of tension—and distinction—in Marshall's work. He came to economics by a route that led him from mathematics to metaphysics to ethics, and, finally, without enthusiasm, to political economy. The heart of his dedication to economics lay in a deeply-rooted desire to lift from the working classes the degrading burden of poverty.[10] There is something in Clark Kerr's observation that, with all their differences, Marshall and Marx shared the view that "the transformation of the working class" was "the key to Utopia."[11] Thus, in the first edition of the *Principles* (1890), ". . . the study of the causes of poverty is the study of the causes of the degradation of a large part of mankind";[12] in his Preface to *Money, Credit, and Commerce* (written about 1917):[13] "Its [psychology's] fascinating inquiries into the possibilities of the higher and more rapid development of human faculties brought me into touch with the question: How far do the conditions of life of the British (and other) working classes generally suffice for the fullness of life?"; and, reminiscing near the end of his life:[14]

> So I read Mill's *Political Economy* and got much excited about it. I had doubts about the propriety of inequalities of *opportunity,* rather than of material comfort. Then, in my vacations I visited the poorest quarters of several cities and walked through one street after another, looking at the faces of the poorest people. Next, I resolved to make as thorough study as I could of Political Economy.

It was "the quality of life" with which Marshall was ultimately concerned.[15] Keynes's toast of 1945 to the Royal Economic Society was thus much in the Marshallian tradition, with echoes reaching, through Mill, back to Hume and Adam Smith: ". . . to economics and economists who are the trustees not of civilization but of the possibility of civilization."[16]

A final introductory observation is required on Marshall's systematic emphasis on the continuity of change in the life of societies, an observation crystallized in the quotation on the title page of the *Principles*: "*Natura non facit saltum.*" In the prefaces to the first and eighth editions he states quite clearly what he had in mind:[17]

> The notion of continuity with regard to development is common to all modern schools of economic thought, whether the chief influences acting on them are those of biology, as represented by the writings of Herbert Spencer; or of history and philosophy, as represented by Hegel's *Philosophy of History.* . . . These two kinds of influences have affected, more than any other, the substance of the views expressed in the present book; but their form has been most affected by mathematical conceptions of continuity, as represented in Cournot's *Principes Mathématiques de la Théorie des Richesses.* He taught that it is necessary to face the difficulty of regarding the various elements of an economic problem—not as determining one another in a chain of causation, A determining B, B determining C, and so on—but as all mutually determining one another." [First edition.]

> Economic evolution is gradual. Its progress is sometimes arrested or reversed by political catastrophes: but its forward movements are never sudden. . . . And though an inventor, or an organizer, or a financier of genius may seem to have modified the economic structure of a people almost at a stroke; yet . . . his influence . . . is found on inquiry to have done little more than bring to a head a broad constructive movement which had long been in preparation. . . .
>
> The Mecca of the economist lies in economic biology rather than in economic dynamics. [Eighth edition.]

This view was rooted, in part, in Marshall's analysis of the interacting process at work between man and his environment. It is summarized as follows by Whitaker:[18]

> One of its themes is . . . the effect of economic conditions on human character, particularly "the influence which the daily occupations of men exert on their character." Since character is intimately related to ethical beliefs, this leads to Marshall's major theme: the mutual interdependence between economic conditions and ethical progress.

Marshall uses this proposition as the framework for reflections on his visit to the United States in 1875 and, especially, his analysis of the origins and implications of the higher degree of mobility in American than in European society.

Clearly, Marshall was driven to his view of the primacy of incremental change by a convergence of what he derived from his study of mathematics and philosophy, psychology and economics. He was prepared to reaffirm his judgment in October 1920 in the wake of the First World War, but before the chronic pathology of the interwar period asserted itself. One can not, of course, be sure; but one is tempted to consider that Marshall's doctrine of the power of environment on human perspectives might be applied to himself—a social scientist whose basic ideas took shape in the 1860s and 1870s, who lived almost all his life in a century of uniquely peaceful, incremental change from an Englishman's point of view. The century 1815–1914 might not have seemed quite so peaceful and incremental to citizens of Russia or Japan, China or Mexico, or the Ottoman Empire, or even France, Germany, Italy, or the United States. Be that as it may, Marshall's vision of the process of change suffuses what he had to say about economic growth.

The Basic Growth Equation

In his survey of development theories, Lionel Robbins notes that, unlike his major contemporaries, "Marshall's focus was upon growth" and, in that sense, his *Principles* is "akin to that of the earlier nineteenth century economists."[19] This is not a surprising outcome for a man who began as an economist by translating some of Ricardo's and Mill's key propositions into mathematical formulae and geometric diagrams.[20] So far as the theory of economic growth is concerned, Whitaker mobilizes persuasive circumstantial evidence that Marshall was strongly influenced by Book IV and parts of Book I (bearing on population and labor efficiency) from Mill's *Principles;*[21] and he began with a set of exploratory exercises, focused around the determinants of income distribution, based on a highly recognizable aggregate growth model whose five equations are set out in the notes.[22] Here is how Marshall introduces his model with its two driving variables: the rate of saving and the rate of increase in the size and efficiency of the working force:[23]

The gross real income of a country depends on (*i*) the number and average efficiency of the workers in it, (*ii*) the amount of its accumulated wealth, (*iii*) the extent, richness and convenience of situation of its natural resources, (*iv*) the state of the arts of production, [and] (*v*) the state of public security and the assurance to industry and capital of the fruits of their labour and abstinence. . . .

The total net income available for saving is the excess of this gross income over what is required to provide the necessaries of life; that is those things which are required for sustaining the efficiency of the several grades of industry [i.e., labor]; and the price which has to be paid in taxes for the maintenance of public security. No separate allowance need be made for the taxes levied for maintaining public works, or education. . . .

The extent to which the country makes use of the power of saving which this net income gives, or in other words the rate of growth of its wealth, depends on (*i*) the amount of this net income, (*ii*) the willingness of its inhabitants to sacrifice present enjoyment for future, (*iii*) the strength of family affections among them (since it is not a man's own future enjoyment but that of his family which is generally the chief motive of his saving) and (*iv*) the rate of interest on capital, which affords a premium to saving. . . .

The rates of increase of the number and efficiency of the working population of a country depend, broadly speaking, on (*i*) the number and efficiency of the population already existing, (*ii*) the gross real income that there is to be distributed among the different classes of the nation, (*iii*) the evenness of the distribution of that income (for an increase of income of a less wealthy class at the expense of an equal aggregate loss to a more wealthy class generally promotes the increase of the number and efficiency of the population, providing it is obtained without injury to public security), (*iv*) on the strength of the family affections in so far as they incline people to lead a domestic life and to incur trouble and expense on bringing up their children, and (*v*) their willingness to sacrifice present and immediate enjoyment for more distant enjoyment (this counting in two ways, leading them on the one hand to delay marriage so as to retain a high Standard of Comfort, and on the other to think highly of the advantages of a good education). In addition, the growth of the efficiency of the population depends on the magnitude of the reward that in the existing state of the arts of production can be obtained by industrial ability. . . .

The rate of interest depends on the labour which can be got in exchange for a given amount of the produce of past labour. This depends on (*i*) the amount of wealth already accumulated, (*ii*) the number and efficiency of the people, (*iii*) the scope that the arts of production offer for the use of machinery and other forms of capital, and (*iv*) the relative importance of the future enjoyments as it appears on the one hand to spendthrifts and others who borrow wealth for the purposes of immediate enjoyment, and on the other to their creditors.

After probing at several ways this structure might be elaborated, Marshall set it aside, apparently "discouraged."[24] And it is not difficult to understand why this should have been so. Even in this exercise in notation and simplification, Marshall insisted on including so many variables as relevant to the determination of the rate of saving and the rate of interest—including variables difficult or impossible to measure—that he forced himself, as it were, into a wide-ranging descriptive, institutional mode of exposition.

Until these mathematical notes were discovered, no one had deduced from Marshall's passages on income distribution in *The Economics of Industry* and those on growth and income distribution in the *Principles* that he had formulated a quite straightforward and rather complex formal growth model. If one turns back to those passages, however, one can perceive that their elemental bone structure might well have lent itself to such formal treatment. But one also perceives that Marshall's practical interests forced him to leave mathematics behind: interests in the complex, intensely human determinants of the rate of saving and the efficiency of the working force; in the efficacy of various forms of industrial organization and the pros and cons of labor unions; and, in the end, like Mill, the pros and cons of capitalism and socialism.

Marshall's view of the prospects for growth seen through the spectrum of the basic growth equation can be briskly stated.

So far as population is concerned, he perceived a decelerating trend in marriage, birth, and death rates. In Britain, these trends were accompanied by rising real wages. The bulk of his analysis was devoted to the full array of forces that determined efficiency, including not only diet and education but "hopefulness, freedom, and change." After surveying the negative as well as positive forces at work, again his conclusion was temperately optimistic:[25]

> . . . [I]f the strength and vigour of the race improves, the increase of numbers will not for a long time to come cause a diminution of the average real income of the people.
>
> Thus then the progress of . . . medical science, the ever-growing activity and wisdom of Government in all matters relating to health, and the increase of material wealth, all tend to lessen mortality and to increase health and strength, and to lengthen life. On the other hand, vitality is lowered and the death-rate raised by the rapid increase of town life, and by the tendency of the higher strains of the population to marry later and to have fewer children than the lower.
>
> . . . [T]he two sets hold one another very nearly in balance, the former slightly preponderating. While the population of England is growing nearly as fast as ever, those who are out of health in body or mind are certainly not an increasing part of the whole: the rest are much better fed and clothed. . . .
> The average duration of life both for men and women has been increasing steadily for many years.

Behind this relatively hopeful prospect lay his conclusion on increasing versus diminishing returns. He found increasing returns widely at work in most of industry and transport; while diminishing returns was held off by Britain's access to cheap food and raw materials from fertile sources throughout the world. But Marshall concluded with a warning:[26]

> . . . England's foreign supplies of raw produce may at any time be checked by changes in the trade regulations of other countries, and may be almost cut off by a great war, while the naval and military expenditure which would be

necessary to make the country fairly secure against this last risk, would appreciably diminish the benefits that she derives from the action of the law of increasing return.

Marshall came to think diminishing returns would reassert itself in the world economy (pp. 183–184, following), but, unlike Mill, he saw that British and other workers had still too much to ask of the economic system for diminishing relative marginal utility for real income itself to decree a stationary state from the side of demand:[27]

> There seems to be no good reason for believing that we are anywhere near a stationary state in which there will be no new important wants to be satisfied; in which there will be no more room for profitably investing present effort in providing for the future, and in which the accumulation of wealth will cease to have any reward. The whole history of man shows that his wants expand with the growth of his wealth and knowledge.

Nor did he envisage stagnation from the side of the productivity of investment. In the advanced industrial countries he noted the decline of interest rates from 1873 to the mid-1890s; but he did not judge the trend decline in interest rates would lead, along with all the other determinants of saving, to a cessation of investment and a stationary state.

But Marshall, in concluding his discussion of value and utility, does permit himself, "as a preacher and pastor of men" (in Keynes's phrase), to go beyond the expansion of conventional goods and services:[28]

> Laws against luxury have been futile; but it would be a gain if the moral sentiment of the community could induce people to avoid all sorts of display of individual wealth. There are indeed true and worthy pleasures to be got from wisely ordered magnificence: but they are at their best . . . when they centre round public buildings, public parks, public collections of the fine arts, and public games and amusement.
>
> . . . The world would go much better if everyone would buy fewer and simpler things, and would take trouble in selecting them for their real beauty; being careful of course to get good value in return for his outlay, but preferring to buy a few things made well by highly paid labour rather than many made badly by low paid labour.

This is not quite Mill's stationary state with high quality of life, but bears a family relationship to it. Although there is something of Mill in these reflections, Marshall is more typically realistic in noting that:[29]

> The Englishman Mill bursts into unwonted enthusiasm when speaking . . . of the pleasures of wandering alone in beautiful scenery: and many American writers give fervid descriptions of the growing richness of human life as the backwoodsman finds neighbours settling around him, as the backwoods settlement develops into a village, the village into a town, and the town into a vast city.

Marshall tended, in the end, to focus on "practical conclusions" of more immediate relevance to the future of Britain. Thus *Principles* ends not with a portrait of the remote outcome for society of an era of sustained compound interest but a summation of his views on the issue he regarded as central in his time: the situation of and prospects for labor. He starts with a historical sketch of the forces that had made for an increased standard of life in Britain in the second half of the nineteenth century.[30] He then goes on to explore a range of variables bearing on the future of real wages, including hours of work; the effect of excessively high wages on the direction of investment, including investment abroad; the positive and negative effects of labor unions; and an evaluation of income inequities. He concludes that, on balance, ". . . there is no real necessity, and therefore no moral justification for extreme poverty side by side with great wealth."[31] The summation ends with an analysis of capitalism versus socialism. What distinguishes these passages is Marshall's effort to use economic analysis to the limit in exploring these large questions while acknowledging in the end:[32] "We have reached very few practical conclusions; because it is generally necessary to look at the whole of the economic, to say nothing of the moral and other aspects of a practical problem before attempting to deal with it at all. . . ."

Population and the Working Force

Marshall's treatment of population and the working force in the *Principles* illustrates well his central doctrine about method in economics:[38] "Economics affords no scope for long chains of deductive reasoning. . . . Constructive imagination is the dominant force in scientific work: its strength is shown not in developing abstract hypotheses, but in correlating the multitudinous influences of real economic forces acting over a wide area."

Marshall devotes three successive chapters covering 46 pages in Book IV ("The Agents of Production") to the forces governing the growth of population, its health and strength, its skill and mobility.[34]

Marshall begins with a general proposition:[35]

> In the animal and vegetable world the growth of numbers is governed by the tendency of individuals to propagate their species on the one hand, and on the other hand by the struggle for life which thins out the young before they arrive at maturity. In the human race alone the conflict of these two opposing forces is complicated by other influences. On the one hand regard for the future induces many individuals to control their natural impulses; sometimes with the purpose of worthily discharging their duties as parents; sometimes, as for instance at Rome under the Empire, for mean motives. And on the other hand society exercises pressure on the individual by religious, moral and legal sanctions, sometimes with the object of quickening, and sometimes with that of retarding, the growth of population.

He then summarizes evidence from the rapidly emerging professional field of demography, as well as from older historical sources bearing on: the forces making for pro- and anti-natalist public policies at various times and places; the forces that had determined the evolution of the English birth rate and death rate down to the early years of the twentieth century (eighth edition). Along the way he deals with the impact on short-run population movements of oscillations in the cost of living, the business cycle, and emigration.

Turning to the health and strength of the population, again Marshall begins with a general proposition:[36]

> The marriage-rate, the birth-rate and the death-rate are diminishing in almost every country. But the general mortality is high where the birth-rate is

high. For instance, both are high in Slavonic countries, and both are low in the North of Europe. The death-rates are low in Australasia, and the "natural" increase there is fairly high, though the birth-rate is low and falling very fast.

The following review of determining variables embraces, *inter alia,* innate muscular strength, climate, race, food (and the quality of its preparation), clothing, shelter, the fuel supply, rest, and "three closely allied conditions of vigour, namely, hopefulness, freedom, and change."[37] He then examines the influence of occupation on health, strength, and mortality, as well as the reasons for higher death rates in the towns and cities and other social forces operating on the vitality of the population, including the following:[38]

> In the later stages of civilization the rule has indeed long been that the upper classes marry late, and in consequence have fewer children than the working classes, and the vigour of the nation that is tending to be damped out among the upper classes is thus replenished by the fresh stream of strength that is constantly welling up from below.

Marshall then casts up the balance sheet of positive and negative forces at work on the health and strength of the population—quite aware but unembarrased because they are quantitative in their influence but not measurable—and emerges with a temperately optimistic judgment on British prospects.

In the third chapter, Marshall turns to all the substantial forces he can perceive that affect what he calls "industrial training"; that is, the capacity to sustain efficiency in modern factory work. Once again he insists on ranging over an extraordinary spectrum of relevant variables: the generational time lags in the perception of a dynamic current reality;[39] the extent to which rapid technological change creates a premium for generalized rather than specialized working-force skills; the influences, starting with mothers, that determine whether innate abilities will be developed; British education policy in the light of the increasing scientific capacity being generated by the German educational system, building up to this powerful statement:[40]

> There is no extravagance more prejudicial to the growth of national wealth than that wasteful negligence which allows genius that happens to be born of lowly parentage to expend itself in lowly work. No change would conduce so much to a rapid increase of material wealth as an improvement in our schools, and especially those of the middle grades, provided it be combined with an extensive system of scholarships, which will enable the clever son of a working man to rise gradually from school to school till he has the best theoretical and practical education which the age can give.

Clearly, Marshall regarded increased outlays for education in England of his day as a form of investment subject to increasing returns. His analysis—and its predecessor analyses back to Hume and Adam Smith—makes it difficult to regard the emergence of investment in "human capital" in post-1945 development economics as a pioneering revelation.

Marshall's analysis goes on to reflect on the importance of and relations between education in art and industrial design; the indirect as well as direct virtues of education to a society; the irreducible responsibilities of parents with respect to education. He concludes by returning to the linkage in classical economics between wages and the size and vigor of the population, concluding that the answer was difficult to predict because the critical variables were "the ethical, social and domestic habits of life" which were influenced, in turn, by economic causes operating over long periods of time by routes difficult to trace.[41] In facing up to this lagged interplay between economic and noneconomic forces, Marshall is returning to a relationship identified by Malthus (preceding, p. 57, and note 22, p. 582).

Marshall's treatment of the determinants of the size and quality of the working force demonstrates how seriously and responsibly he went about the business of grappling with all the variables he perceived as relevant, mobilizing, in the best tradition of the great classical economists, everything he could derive from history, statistical analysis, and protracted direct observation of the society around him.

In terms of theory, then, Marshall regarded the size and quality of the population as an endogenous variable, if viewed from the perspective of the complex dynamics of societies as a whole. On balance, even more than Mill, he was aware that the rate of population growth in England was declining and that, in times of peace, the food supply was well assured; but looking much farther ahead, at world population as a whole, he was less sanguine, and the shadow of Malthusian anxiety reemerges:[42]

> Taking the present population of the world at one and a half thousand millions; and assuming that its present rate of increase (about 8 per 1000 annually, see Ravenstein's paper before the British Association in 1890) will continue, we find that in less than two hundred years it will amount to six thousand millions; or at the rate of about 200 to the square mile of fairly fertile land (Ravenstein reckons 28 million square miles of fairly fertile land, and 14 millions of poor grass lands. The first estimate is thought by many to be too high; but, allowing for this, if the less fertile land be reckoned in for what it is worth, the result will be about thirty million square miles as assumed above.) Meanwhile there will probably be great improvements in the arts of agriculture; and, if so, the pressure of population on the means of subsistence may be held in check for about two hundred years, but no longer.

The jury is still out on Marshall's prediction, although it appears that modern medicine and public health will take almost a century off Ravenstein's predicted arrival of a global population of 6 billion.

Capital and Technology

Marshall's treatment of capital investment and technology is governed by two considerations. First, by the question he takes as central to a macro theory of growth: Does the productivity of each factor of production—its "power of productive work"—increase or decrease with the "volume of work" it is called upon to perform? Second, by a determination to link his macro-analysis of growth to his micro-analysis of the case of increasing return to business firms and industries. Thus, the following two passages from the concluding chapter of Book IV:[43]

> At the beginning of this Book we saw how the extra return of raw produce which nature affords to an increased application of capital and labour, other things being equal, tends in the long run to diminish. In the remainder of the Book . . . we have . . . seen how man's power of productive work increases with the volume of the work that he does. . . . [E]very increase in the physical, mental and moral vigour of a people makes them more likely, other

things being equal, to rear to adult age a large number of vigorous children. Turning next to the growth of wealth, we observed how every increase of wealth tends in many ways to make a greater increase more easy than before. And lastly we saw how every increase of wealth and every increase in the numbers and intelligence of the people increased the facilities for a highly developed industrial organization, which in its turn adds much to the collective efficiency of capital and labour.

Meanwhile an increase in the aggregate scale of production of course increases those economies, which do not directly depend on the size of individual houses of business. The most important of these result from the growth of correlated branches of industry which mutually assist one another, perhaps being concentrated in the same localities, but anyhow availing themselves of the modern facilities for communication offered by steam transport, by the telegraph and by the printing-press. The economies arising from such sources as this, which are accessible to any branch of production, do not depend exclusively upon its own growth: but yet they are sure to grow rapidly and steadily with that growth; and they are sure to dwindle in some, though not all respects, if it decays.

Behind this quite sophisticated linking of macro- and micro-analysis is Marshall's hard-won knowledge that the process of technological change cannot be well understood as an aggregate phenomenon but must be related to particular sectors at particular phases of their evolution, and his acute awareness that the case of increasing returns—on which growth analysis depends—is extremely difficult to handle formally with the conventional tools of economics.

In dealing with diminishing returns Marshall illustrates vividly how Capital, Knowledge, and Organization can hold off the day when equal doses of inputs yield less than proportional increases in output; but he concludes that—from Abraham's parting from Lot[44] down to the early twentieth century and into the foreseeable future—diminishing returns will, in the end, assert itself:[45] ". . . whatever may be the future developments of the arts of agriculture, a continued increase in the application of capital and labour to land must ultimately result in a diminution of the extra produce which can be obtained by a given amount of capital and labour."

Most of Book IV, however, including important aspects of Marshall's treatment of the determinants of the quality of the working force, is devoted to the complex forces making for increasing returns.

He begins by noting changes in the sources of British savings since the early nineteenth century, introducing along the way a quite radical conclusion on the relation between income distribution, investment, and growth:[46]

. . .[E]arly in the present century, the commercial classes in England had much more saving habits than either the country gentlemen or the working classes. These causes combined to make English economists of the last generation regard savings as made almost exclusively from the profits of capital.

But even in modern England rent and the earnings of professional men and hired workers are an important source of accumulation: and they have been the chief source of it in all the earlier stages of civilization. Moreover, the middle and especially the professional classes have always denied themselves much in order to invest capital in the education of their children; while a great part of the wages of the working classes is invested in the physical health and strength of their children. The older economists took too little account of the fact that human faculties are as important a means of production as any other kind of capital; and we may conclude, in opposition to them, that any change in the distribution of wealth which gives more to the wage receivers and less to the capitalists is likely, other things being equal, to hasten the increase of material production, and that it will not perceptibly retard the storing-up of material wealth. Of course other things would not be equal if the change were brought about by violent methods which gave a shock to public security. . . .

A people among whom wealth is well distributed, and who have high ambitions, are likely to accumulate a great deal of public property; and the savings made in this form alone by some well-to-do democracies form no inconsiderable part of the best possessions which our own age has inherited from its predecessors. The growth of the co-operative movement in all its many forms, of building societies, friendly societies, trades-unions, of working men's savings-banks, etc., shows that, even so far as the immediate accumulation of material wealth goes, the resources of the country are not, as the older economists assumed, entirely lost when they are spent in paying wages.

In a manner foreshadowed in his early aggregate macro-growth model Marshall explores various motives for saving, focusing mainly, in the end, on family affection and the rate of interest. Referring explicitly to sardonic Marxist criticisms of interest as the reward for abstinence, Marshall identifies it as a reward for waiting.[47] He concludes by introducing once again his doctrine of the high rate of return associated with working-class education:[48] "From the national point of view the investment of wealth in the child of the working man is as productive as its investment in horses or machinery."

Thus far Marshall's argument is, essentially, a modernized version of the classical theory of saving. There follow, however, five chapters on industrial organization in which he seeks to identify and examine all the elements that enter into the net increase of productivity with the expansion of output in industry. Out of his sustained empirical examination of the industrial process Marshall perceived that the net tendency toward increasing returns was not a simple matter of the enlargement of the market, specialization of function, and the progressive introduction of laborsaving machinery. At every point he identifies negative as well as positive forces at work: in some cases, extreme specialization increases efficiency, in others, not; machinery has both good and bad effects on the quality of human life; advantages are identified for large over small factories, but also, under specified circumstances, for small over large production units. Similarly, Marshall was acutely sensitive to the fact that economic progress was not linear for either firms or industries. His analysis of why sons rarely succeed in carrying forward successfully the family firm is perceptive sociology much in the vein of Thomas Mann's *Buddenbrooks*.[49] He notes: ". . . creative ideas and experiments in business technique, and in business organization, to be very rare in Governmental undertakings, and not very common in private enterprise which have drifted towards bureaucratic methods as the result of their great age and large size."[50] In more conventional economic passages Marshall cites the differential effects on employment of technological progress in steel versus textiles, in steamships versus docks.[51]

In dealing with the dynamics of industrial progress, Marshall analyzes with considerable subtlety, anticipating the later conclusions of Colin Clark and Simon Kuznets, the proportionate shift of the labor force out of agriculture, the relative constancy (since 1851) of the proportion in manufactures, and the relative rise of service employment, due primarily to the comparative lack of technological progress in the latter.[52]

On balance, then, Marshall saw no end to the operation of increasing returns, although he perceived the costs as well as benefits of the complex process involved. But the continued net progress of the system required, in his own famous image, that new trees rise in the forest as the great old trees reach their natural limits, "lose vitality; and one after another give place to others, which, though of less material strength, have on their side the vigour of growth."[53] And of all the forces Marshall perceived as necessary to sustain the forest—or to assure its continued expansion—investment in the talented young of the working classes appeared to be the most important.

One fundamental weakness in Marshall's analysis of the long period should be underlined. He created various devices for dealing with increasing returns—the trees in the forest, the representative firm, internal and external economies, a historic succession of short-period cost curves moving downward through time in response to improving technology but permitting a definition of equilibrium at a moment of time. With these he could more or less cope with the analysis of firms in existing industries. But Marshall never found a way to deal formally with what he knew to be a major characteristic of technological history; namely, the emergence from time to time of inventions so radical as to create new industries (e.g., the railroad and electricity) or profoundly to transform old industries (e.g., cotton textiles and steel). Moreover, Marshall was extremely sensitive to the fact that, at any particular period of time in a given country, there were fast-growing, slow-growing, and declining sectors; and that their pace was often related to the historical stages of their underlying technologies. But he never generated a sectoral theory that might have linked his macro- and micro-analysis. He could comfort himself with *Natura non facit saltum,* with its implication that all events were deeply rooted in the past, as he did in the Preface to the eighth edition of *Principles;*[54] but Marshall's failure to deal adequately with the role in increasing returns of Adam Smith's inventions by "Philosophers" produced evasive theoretical formulations (following, p. 336). It opened an area for intellectual innovation that Schumpeter launched with panache, but with imbalance in another direction (following, pp. 233–242).

Business Cycles

Marshall had something to say about business cycles in all four of the books he wrote as well as in the testimony he gave before the two Royal Commissions of the mid-1880s. But in his own mind his earliest analysis of the problems in *The Economics of Industry* (1879), was evidently judged the most important, because he referred back to it quite systematically.[55] Marshall had some observations to make on his early view if not quite second thoughts; but he evidently felt no fundamental modifications were necessary.

In considering Marshall's view of the business cycle, two facts should be kept in mind: his point of departure was Mill's analysis of the business cycle (preceding, pp. 108–112);[56] and Marshall's views crystallized during a major cycle (1868–1879) marked by an intense inflationary phase toward the end of the expansion (1871–1873), then by the protracted business decline of 1873–1879, accompanied by a dramatic and sustained decline in prices but with high levels of unemployment (over 5%) in only the final 2 years.

It is understandable, therefore, that he begins his treatment of the business cycle by focusing on changes in the price level rather than the level of unemployment. After a few observations on striking price changes in the more distant and more recent past, and the emergence during the nineteenth century of credit as the predominant form of money supply, Marshall launches into a quite recognizable account of the phases of the business cycle, in which his acknowledged debt to Mill is evident.[57]

First, expansion:

> The beginning of a period of rising credit is often a series of good harvests. Less having to be spent in food, there is a better demand for other commodities. . . . Employers compete with one another for labour; wages rise; and the employed in spending their wages increase the demand for all kinds of commodities. New public and private Companies are started to take advantage of the promising openings which shew themselves among the general activity. Thus the desire to buy and the willingness to pay increased prices grow together; Credit is jubilant, and readily accepts paper promises to pay. Prices, wages and profits go on rising: there is a general rise in the incomes of those engaged in trade: they spend freely, increase the demand for goods and raise prices still higher. Many speculators seeing the rise, and thinking it will continue buy goods with the expectation of selling them at a profit. . . . [A]nd every one who thus enters into the market as a buyer, adds to the upward tendency of prices, whether he buys with his own or with borrowed money.

Then tension and crisis:

> This movement goes on for some time, till . . . trade is in a dangerous condition. Those whose business it is to lend money are among the first to read the signs of the times; and they begin to think about contracting their loans. But they cannot do this without much disturbing trade. . . . Trading companies of all kinds have borrowed vast sums with which they have begun to build railways and docks and ironworks and factories; prices being high they do not get much building done for their outlay, and though they are not yet ready to reap profits on their investment, they have to come again into the market to borrow more capital. The lenders of capital already wish to contract their loans; and the demand for more loans raises the rate of interest very high. . . . Some speculators have to sell goods in order to pay their debts; and by so doing they check the rise of prices. This check makes all other speculators anxious, and many rush in to sell. . . . When a large speculator fails, his failure generally causes that of others who have lent their credit to him; and their failure again that of others. . . . As credit by growing makes itself grow, so when distrust has taken the place of confidence, failure and panic breed panic and failure. The commercial storm leaves its path strewn with ruin.

Depression descends:

> [W]hen it is over there is a calm, but a dull heavy calm. Those who have saved themselves are in no mood to venture again; companies, whose success is doubtful, are wound up; new companies cannot be formed. Coal, iron, and

the other materials for making Fixed capital fall in price as rapidly as they rose. Iron works and ships are for sale, but there are no buyers at any moderate price. . . . after a crisis the warehouses are overstocked with goods in almost every important trade; scarcely any trade can continue undiminished production so as to afford a good rate of profits to capital and a good rate of wages to labour. . . . [W]hen confidence has been shaken by failures, capital cannot be got to start new companies or extend old ones. . . . [T]here is but little occupation in any of the trades which make Fixed Capital. Those whose skill and capital is Specialised in these trades are earning little, and therfore buying little of the produce of other trades. . . . Thus disorganization spreads, the disorganization of one trade throws others out of gear, and they react on it and increase its disorganization.''

Finally, Marshall reflects on how the cycle bottoms out and expansion asserts itself again:

The chief cause of the evil is a want of confidence. The greater part of it could be removed almost in an instant if confidence could return, touch all industries with her magic wand, and make them continue their production and their demand for the wares of others. . . . But the revival of industry comes about through the gradual and often simultaneous growth of confidence among many various trades; it begins as soon as traders think that prices will not continue to fall; and with a revival of industry prices rise.

As with Mill, Marshall's analysis is an exercise in the economics and psychology of irrational expectations, suffusing the behavior of the short- and long-term capital markets. It recalls the marvelous simplicity of the title of Walter Bagehot's rather sophisticated rendition of his business cycle theory in Chapter VI of *Lombard Street*: "Why Lombard Street is Often Very Dull and Sometimes Extremely Excited." Marshall correctly captures the manner in which the boom spreads from the expansion of consumers goods industries to increased investment in fixed capital—an accelerator of sorts; how the expansion of investment increases competition for labor and those employed "increase the demand for all kinds of commodities''—a multiplier of sorts; how the boom itself (by raising the prices of raw materials, money-wage rates, and interest rates) lowers the initially calculated expected rate of return over cost for fixed investments, and, in the end, plunges the investment goods industries into a particularly deep depression, as a rush for liquidity follows a belated recognition of how the dynamics of the expansion itself has altered profit expectations.

There follow passages dealing with the relation between movements in prices, profits, output, and real wages in the course of the business cycle.[58] These foreshadow the kind of analyses that became quite conventional when the examination of the business cycle became a specialized professional sport in the pre-1914 generation and then between the wars (following, Chapters 10 and 11).

1. There is an important symmetry in the position of the entrepreneur in a period of rising and falling prices. In the former case, the price of his product is likely to rise more rapidly than those of the relevant raw materials and labor; his profits will expand; real wages will come under pressure, although employment will be high. In the latter case, the reverse is true.[59]

. . . thus a fall in prices lowers profits and impoverishes the manufacturer: while it increases the purchasing power of those who have fixed incomes. So again, it enriches creditors at the expense of debtors. . . . [A]nd it impoverishes those who make, as most business men have, considerable fixed money payments for rents, salaries, and other matters. When prices are ascending, the improvement is thought to be greater than it really is. . . . But statistics prove that the real income of the country is not very much less in the present time of low prices, than it was in the period of high prices that went before it. The total amount of the necessaries, comforts and luxuries which are enjoyed by Englishmen is but little less in 1879 than it was in 1872.

Marshall's analysis is essentially correct for the period 1872–1879; that is, the level of consumption was sustained by the radical fall in prices. Consumption only fell below the 1872 level in 1878–1879 when unemployment rose to 6.3% and 10.7%, respectively.[60] Real wages for those in full work, however, rose 7% between 1873 and 1879.

2. The amplitude of fluctuations in output and prices was greatest in capital goods industries.[61]

3. British imports were sustained better than exports in the period 1873–1879, in part because the radical decline in capital (and capital goods) exports, mainly for foreign railways, led to a switch in the direction of British investment towards the building trades at home that sustained the level of demand for imports, whereas major markets in which the boom of 1871–1873 had centered were more depressed than Britain and their demand for British exports radically reduced.

4. Wage increases and decreases systematically lag price (and profit) movements in the course of the business cycle. Wage movements are, therefore, not a primary cause of price fluctuations, and their amplitude of fluctuation is less than for prices and profits.[62]

Marshall was, of course, aware of the human and social costs of unemployment; and comments on these dimensions of the problem run through his work from beginning to end. He advocated credit policies in the banking system and wage policies by unions that would damp the amplitude of fluctuations. And he examined the proposals of others. In *The Economics of Industry,* for example, he rejects in what might be called indecisive puzzlement a socialist suggestion for using the powers of the state to damp cyclical oscillations:[63]

> The most plausible of all the plans that have been suggested by Socialists for the artificial organization of industry is one which aims at the "abolition of commercial risk." They propose that in times of depression Government should step forward, and, by guaranteeing each separate industry against risk, cause all industries to work, and therefore to earn and therefore to buy each other's products. Government, by running every risk at once, would, they think, run no risk. But they have not yet shewn how Government should tell whether a man's distress was really due to causes beyond his control, nor how its guarantee could be worked without hindering that freedom on which energy and the progress of invention depend.

The final sentence reflects Marshall's oft-repeated perception that technological change inevitably involved some short-term frictional unemployment.

Marshall was questioned at length in December 1887 before the Gold and Silver Commission about the impact of the post-1873 environment on the level of unemployment.[64] He dealt along the way with a number of structural changes affecting the level of unemployment and public perceptions of that level; e.g., the progressive movement of labor from households to factories, a large proportionate shift from unskilled to skilled labor, possible distortions in the unemployment statistics arising from the fact that they were generated from the records of labor unions, special technological changes that might affect the situation of iron founders, whose unemployment data tended to dominate the statistics available. Here is the climactic passage in which Marshall asserts his judgment that, averaged over decennial periods (to eliminate cyclical bias), the average level of unemployment had not increased in Britain:[65]

9823. Do you share the general opinion that during the last few years we have been passing through a period of severe depression?—*Yes, of severe depression of profits.*

9824. And that has been during a period of abnormally low prices?—*A severe depression of profits and of prices. . . . I cannot see any reason for believing that there is any considerable depression in any other respect. There is, of course, great misery among the poor; but I do not believe it is greater than it used to be. I do not mean that we should idly acquiesce in the existence of this misery, and regard it as inevitable. I hold rather extreme opinions in the opposite direction.*

9825. (*Chairman.*) Then I understand you to think that the depression in those three respects is consistent with a condition of prosperity?—*Certainly.*

9826. (*Mr. Chaplin.*) The depression of profits, does not that more or less affect all classes?—*No, I believe that a chief cause of the depression of profits is that the employer gets less and the employee more.*

9828. Can you speak as to the fact whether there has been a larger number of the working classes than usual unemployed altogether during this period of depression?—*My belief is that there have not been a larger number of people unemployed during the last ten years than during any other consecutive ten years. Of course there are many more unemployed now than there were in 1872–73.*

9830. Are you aware that we have had evidence given by gentlemen speaking with definite knowledge of a directly opposite nature to what you are stating now?—*I am aware that some persons actively engaged in business have given evidence that they believe there is an increasing unsteadiness of employment. But the facts which they bring forward are, in my opinion, outweighed by the statistical and other evidence in the opposite direction. . . . I have, however, omitted one thing of very great importance. . . . that is the transitional stage in which a great number of industries are. When an improvement is brought into an industry it benefits the public at once, and in the long run it is pretty sure to benefit even the trade into which it is introduced; but in many cases an improvement in the methods of the industry injures that industry, and throws people temporarily out of employment. Now, I do not think there has been any period in which there have been so many great changes. . . . The changes are, I think, chiefly due to the great fall, the unparalleled fall, in the cost of transport, which renders it worth while to do a great many things that it was not worth while to do before; but besides this there are an immense number of changes in all industries, chemical and mechanical. . . .*

9833. (*Mr. Barbour.*) You said that in so far as the fall of prices had tended to give the wage-earning classes more for their labour, it was a distinct gain?—*That is my opinion.*

When he came to publish his *Principles,* Marshall repeats again what he and his wife had to say in 1879 in *The Economics of Industry,* including a quotation from Mill on the impossibility of general overproduction marked by the not highly illuminating dictum: "what constitutes the means of payment for commodities is simply commodities." But in a footnote, after referring to the Mill quotation, Marshall expresses his uneasiness and his sense that, in this domain, economists had not brought their study to "successful issue:"[66]

> It is true that in times of depression the disorganization of consumption is a contributory cause to the continuance of the disorganization of credit and of production. But a remedy is not to be got by a study of consumption. . . . But the main study needed is that of the organization of production and of credit. And, though economists have not yet succeeded in bringing that study to a successful issue, the cause of their failure lies in the profound obscurity and ever-changing form of the problem. . . . Economics from beginning to end is a study of the mutual adjustments of consumption and production: when the one is under discussion, the other is never out of mind.

In *Money, Credit, and Commerce* a chapter is devoted to "Influences on the Stability of Employment Exerted by Development of Techniques" and a second on the relations of the money market to industrial and trade fluctuations;[67] but they contain little that was new, repeating once again themes and passages published 44 years earlier.

What explains Marshall's failure to come to grips with the business cycle and its amelioration? The *Principles* and Marshall's two subsequent major books conclude with many appendixes. Why not one on business cycles? Keynes, in his memoir, suggests that the failure lay in leaving until too late the writing of *Money, Credit, and Commerce* (originally *Money, Credit and Employment*).[68] Schumpeter asserts that, essentially, Marshall never went beyond Mill in dealing with the business cycle.[69]

I am inclined to think that, with respect to analysis, Marshall's problem with the business cycle was more substantive. It lay in the fact that there was no lucid linkage between the dynamic micro-analysis of production and prices he had evolved as his major theoretical achievement and the dynamic macro-analysis of production and prices he inherited in the form of the quantity theory of money. The latter he modified but reconciled only partially with his micro-analysis.

And there was another problem. He never reconciled the classic growth equation he formulated in mathematical terms as early as 1881–1882—and which, in effect, underpinned Book IV of the *Principles*—with his version of the quantity theory of money.

With respect to the first failure of linkage, it will be recalled that, in an effort to solve the problem of dynamic micro-analysis under conditions of changing technology and increasing returns, Marshall adopted the concept of "the representative firm" and the "normal supply price" or "expenses of production." For example:[70]

> These results [external economies] will be of great importance when we come to discuss the causes which govern the supply price of a commodity. . . , and for this purpose we shall have to study *the expenses of a representative* producer for that aggregate volume. . . . [O]ur representative firm must be

one which has had a fairly long life, and fair success, which is managed with normal ability, and which has normal access to the economies, external and internal, which belong to that aggregate volume of production.[71]

In terms of these concepts, Marshall envisaged that the volatility of human expectations led in the course of the boom—when confidence was excessive—to an overshooting of the normal supply price of the representative firm, a rise in profits, and to an expansion of output and employment that could not be sustained, because full employment brought with it an unexpected rise in expenses of production beyond the long-run normal level; i.e., in the prices of raw materials, in wage rates, and interest rates that had initially lagged the rise in the market price of output. A consequent decline in profits and loss of confidence led to an undershooting of the normal supply price of the representative firm and, with its costs relatively sticky, a further decline in profits and output.

Now, implicitly or explicitly, virtually all business-cycle theories involve an overshooting and undershooting of some conceptual dynamic "normal" or "optimum" path. Marshall's problem was that, while he defined a representative firm in an industry or sector whose normal path was linked to the positive or negative growth path of that sector, he did not define the determinants of sectoral growth paths. Thus, he oscillated analytically between the micro-analysis of firms and the macro-behavior of the monetary system implied by his overriding emphasis on "fluctuations of commercial credit," bypassing the critical processes proceeding in the sectors.

In Marshall's description of the cyclical upswing and downswing that clearly left on him the most powerful impression (upswing 1868–1873; downswing 1873–1879), he was quite aware that the cyclical pattern could not be explained without reference to its distinct sectoral characteristics: an extraordinary expansion of capital and capital goods exports in the boom, related to a surge in railway building abroad, which came to rest on a bottleneck in coal output and an exaggerated price inflation in the coal-iron-steel-engineering complex; a rapid subsidence from 1873 in capital and capital goods exports, cushioned in its impact on the overall behavior of the economy down to 1877, by a building boom—a sector crowded out by capital exports at high interest rates down to 1873. Marshall could—and did—discuss all this quite precisely in *ad hoc* terms. But there was no sectoral bone structure in his system; the representative firm did not fill the gap; and in Keynes's memorable description, Marshall was caught in a trap that bedeviled economics from the beginning and that by no means has been disposed of, despite Keynes's efforts, down to the present day:[72]

> So long as economists are concerned with what is called the Theory of Value, they have been accustomed to teach that prices are governed by the conditions of supply and demand; and, in particular, changes in marginal cost and the elasticity of short-period supply have played a prominent part. But when they pass in Volume II, or more often in a separate treatise, to the Theory of Money and Prices, we hear no more of these homely but intelligible concepts and move into a world where prices are governed by the quantity of money, by its income-velocity, by the velocity of circulation relatively to the volume of transactions, by hoarding, by forced saving, by inflation and deflation *et hoc genus omne;* and little or no attempt is made to relate these vaguer phrases to our former notions of the elasticities of supply and demand. . . . We have all of us become used to finding ourselves sometimes on the one side

of the moon and sometimes on the other, without knowing what route or journey connects them, related, apparently, after the fashion of our waking and our dreaming lives.

But the quantity theory of money—even with Marshall's cash balances modification— also proved an inadequate instrument for the serious analysis of either business cycles or price trends, both of which figured in the probing of the Royal Commissions of the mid-1880s. In each case the problem centered on the rate of growth of real output.

So far as the business cycle was concerned, Marshall's description of its phases implied that, in some sense, the generation of excessively optimistic expectations led to credit expansion, which pushed the system into inefficient overfull employment, striving for a level of output beyond its overall trend capacity. It so happened that the 1868–1873 expansion and, notably, its final highly inflationary phase, was a vivid illustration of Keynes's effort to make sense of the Quantity Theory of Money, under explicit restrictive assumptions:[73]

> Thus if there is perfectly elastic supply so long as there is unemployment, and perfectly inelastic supply so soon as full employment is reached, and if effective demand changes in the same proportion as the quantity of money, the Quantity Theory of Money can be enunciated as follows: "So long as there is unemployment, *employment* will change in the same proportion as the quantity of money; and when there is full employment, prices will change in the same proportion as the quantity of money."

To deal formally with a situation defined in such terms requires the concept of a maximum sustainable overall growth rate for output at full employment rooted in the rate of growth of the fundamental factors of production and their productivity embraced in Marshall's macro-growth model and Book IV of *Principles*. Marshall's description of the business cycle is wholly consistent with such a construct; and it is vivid, acute, and accurate. With the notion of a trend real-growth-rate ceiling (pretty well implied in Book IV) and an interacting multiplier-accelerator mechanism (not all that much beyond Marshall's description) he could have produced a fair approximation of a modern macro-economic business cycle. But the business cycle did not prove analytically manageable with the tools he had in hand, including those of his own fabrication.

Marshall was quite conscious that he left a great deal still to be done in monetary and business-cycle analysis. Schumpeter includes among Marshall's virtues his capacity to point in helpful directions with respect to tasks unfulfilled:[74]

> But there is something about Marshall's work that is much greater than anything he actually accomplished—something that assures immortality or, let us say, vitality far beyond the lifetime of any definite achievement. Over and above the products of his genius which he handed to us to work with and which inevitably wear out in our hands, there are in the *Principles* subtle suggestions or directions for further advance, manifestations of that quality of leadership that I have made an effort to define at the start.

Pigou, Robertson, and Keynes, among his other pupils, did indeed carry forward with Marshall's agenda influenced by the course of events around them as well as by the guidance of their respected master.

Relative Prices

In the case of the analysis of price trends, Marshall once again was in the position of holding a lucid, defensible view of the course of events without a solid, coherent theoretical base; once again the problem was embedded in how to deal with the real growth rate, and in this case his dilemma was heightened—indeed, openly acknowledged—because he was sharply questioned by members of the Gold and Silver Commission.

Although formally the issue he confronted was the determination of the general price level, in fact, the question of relative price movements was also involved. Specifically, two issues concerned the Commission. To what extent had the post-1873 declining price trend, only modestly interrupted in the 1879–1883 business expansion, been caused by a relative shortage of bullion in the world economy as opposed to a decline in real costs of production? To what extent could a shift of the British pound to a bimetallist base reverse the downward price trend, if that should be judged desirable? The evidence on these points generated by the Commission on the Depression in Trade and Industry (1886) had been so confusing and contradictory that a successor Royal Commission on Gold and Silver (1887–1888) was set up with a narrower focus. Marshall submitted written responses to questions from the first commission; responded in writing and appeared for extensive questioning before the second. The general character of his judgment about the period since 1873 is incorporated in the preceding quotation (pp. 177–178).

In explaining the concurrence of declining price trends, increased output, an acceleration in real wages, and a normal level of unemployment (averaged over major cycles), Marshall encountered two problems existing theory could not grip.[75] First was the problem of introducing into the quantity-theory framework the role of reduced costs, which, in Marshall's view, had played a decisive role in the price decline after 1873. All the quantity theory provided was a term for total output or, in the vocabulary Marshall used before the Commission, "the supply of commodities." But the supply of commodities could be increased by a number of factors, aside from reduced costs. How, then, to separate the effects of reduced costs from other factors affecting total output and avoid double counting? Marshall, in his written submission to the Commission on the Depression in Trade in May 1886, begins by quoting Thomas Tooke's cost-reduction explanation for the price decrease between 1814 and 1837, affirming that with a few technological additions it fitted rather well the price decline from 1873 to 1886. But Marshall adds a theoretical objection:[76]

> He [Tooke] has not made it clear that diminution of the cost of production of commodities must not be counted as an additional cause of a fall of prices, when its effects on increasing the supply of commodities relatively to gold have already been allowed for separately. This is a point of some difficulty, and its interest is theoretical rather than practical.

In fact, for the Commissioners the issue was highly practical because the economists' unlinked dual vocabulary for dealing with prices prevented an agreed answer to the second question that puzzled Marshall as well as the Commissioners: to what extent was the price decline a demand phenomenon, imposed by a gold shortage, as opposed to a supply phenomenon reflecting rapid technological change in industry and transport, the opening up of new overseas supplies of food and raw materials, and reduced interest rates?

Here, too, Marshall found his theoretical tools inadequate. He began bravely:[77] "I look with scepticism on any attempt to divide the recent fall of prices into that part which is due to changes in the supply of commodities and that which is due to the available gold supply.'' But the shrewd and persistent Commissioners, already knowledgeable and hardened by the conflicting answers they had heard, were not about to be put off by such purist academic scepticism. They insisted that Marshall try to trace out precisely how a scarcity of gold comes to affect prices—a process that Marshall acknowledged ''puzzles me down to this moment.''[78] The testimony then marches through the Bank of England's reserve position, its discount rate, and the consequences for the availability of credit. Marshall acknowledged that interest rates were lower in the post-1873 period than in the decade before but argued that, for four reasons, they should have been still lower: the growing international character of the money market; improved management of the Bank of England; a lack of wars; a lower long-term rate of interest.[79]

Marshall concluded that the major forces that caused the price decline were on the supply side but that ''the scarcity of supplies of gold have made themselves felt a little in the Bank parlour.''[80] But clearly this was a matter of personal judgment that could not be rigorously demonstrated.

In retrospect, Marshall's testimony on what had happened to the British economy since the crisis of 1873 was sensible and holds up quite well. He argued correctly that the trend decline in prices did not imply a chronic depression in employment or output; that the price decline had, on balance, accelerated the rise in real wages, shifting income distribution in favor of labor; that the pressure on profits had not been such as to restrict investment and innovation abnormally; that the major causes of the price decline were nonmonetary, technological, cost-reducing, and salutary; and that the government should not act radically with respect to bimetallism or any other monetary reform.

On the other hand, Marshall's testimony dramatized that as of the mid-1880s mainstream economics had not unified effectively micro- and macro-price analysis nor found an agreed method for isolating the impact of monetary forces from other variables at work in price determination. And, despite Keynes's effort in *The General Theory,* the same propositions can be asserted, a century later, as the awkwardness of macro-economists in dealing with fluctuations in oil prices over the period 1973–1989 suggests.

Strictly speaking, the analysis thus far does not conform to the title of this section; i.e., Relative Prices. And it is somewhat surprising that the question of relative prices—and, especially, the relative prices of British exports and imports—did not enter more explicitly into Marshall's testimony developed for the two Commissions. For a striking aspect of the period from 1873 down to the mid-1890s was a phenomenon that derived substantially from shifts in relative prices; namely, a sustained rise in real wages at a rate substantially in excess of that during the third quarter of the century and, in fact, in excess of the rate of growth of real output per capita.[81] Marshall took the opportunity of laying before the Committee on Indian Currency, in testimony presented in 1899, newly published data organized by Arthur Bowley that reinforced the position on the course of real wages he had taken 11 years earlier before the Gold and Silver Commission (Table 6.1).[82] Behind the almost revolutionary rise in real wages after 1873 was a decline in the British wheat price between 1873 and the trough in the 1890s of about 60%, only slightly less for barley and oats;[83] a decline in U.S. farm prices as a whole of 62%.[84] The best current estimate of the movement of British retail prices as a whole for this period was a decline of 32%.[85]

But as the 1890s wore on and gave way to the new century, by which time relative prices had begun to reverse, Marshall did come to grips with the issue. His approach was,

Table 6.1. Average Real and Nominal Wages in the United Kingdom, France, and the United States as Percentages of Those in 1891

Country	1844–1853	1854–1863	1864–1873	1874–1883	1884–1893	1891
United Kingdom						
Nominal	61	73	82	93	95	100
Real	53	51	59	82	97	100
France						
Nominal	52	65	73	86	95	100
Real	55	61	67	78	94	100
United States						
Nominal	53	58	72	86	95	100
Real	54	53	57	76	95	100

SOURCE: J. M. Keynes (ed.), *Official Papers of Alfred Marshall* (London: Macmillan, 1926), p. 287.

indeed, foreshadowed by passages in the *Principles* in which he argued, in considering the "General Influences of Economic Progress," that the greatest benefit to the British people from the technologies generated in the previous century derived not from the cheapened cost of manufactures but from the radically cheapening in the cost of transport by land and by sea. In a book on growth, this passage, ultimately concerned with the real (productivity) terms of trade, is worth extensive quotation including its evocative climax:[86]

> But though in the eighteenth century, as now, the real national dividend of England depended much on the action of the law of increasing return with regard to her exports, the mode of dependence has very much changed. Then England had something approaching to a monopoly of the new methods of manufacture; and each bale of her goods would be sold—at all events when their supply was artificially limited—in return for a vast amount of the produce of foreign countries. But partly because the time was not yet ripe for carrying bulky goods great distances, her imports from the far-east and the far-west consisted chiefly of comforts and luxuries for the well-to-do; they had but little direct effect in lowering the labour-cost of necessaries to the English workman. . . . [I]t had very little effect on the cost of his food; and that was left to rise under the tendency to diminishing return, which was called into action by the rapid increase of population in new manufacturing districts where the old customary restraints of a narrow village life did not exist. A little later the great French war, and a series of bad harvests, raised that cost to much the highest point it has ever reached in Europe.
>
> But gradually the influence of foreign trade began to tell on the cost of production of our staple food. As the population of America spread westward from the Atlantic, richer and still richer wheat soils have come under cultivation; and the economies of transport have increased so much, especially in recent years, that the total cost of importing a quarter of wheat from the farms on the outskirts of cultivation has diminished rapidly, though the distance of that margin has been increasing. And thus England has been saved from the need of more and more intensive cultivation. The bleak hill-sides, up which the wheat-fields were laboriously climbing in Ricardo's time, have returned to

pasture; and the ploughman works now only where land will yield plentiful returns to his labour: whereas if England had been limited to her own resources, he must have plodded over ever poorer and poorer soils, and must have gone on continually replough ing land that had already been well ploughed, in the hope of adding by this heavy toil an extra bushel or two to the produce of each acre.''

Marshall addressed himself most directly to the question of relative prices, however, in the context of a ''Memorandum on Fiscal Policy of International Trade,'' written in 1903 but not published until 1908 when members of the House of Commons prevailed upon him to permit its publication as a public paper after minor modification. The occasion was the debate on protectionism launched by the Conservative Party's position that, in an increasingly competitive world, Britain should abandon free trade and move toward a system of imperial preference.[87]

In responding to protectionist arguments, Marshall introduced the question of relative prices in both a short-run and long-run context. In the short run he noted clearly, but without alarm, that forces were generating in the United States—notably, the transition from ''pioneer wheat farming'' to diversified agriculture—likely to end the decline in the wheat price that had so strikingly benefited the British consumer.[88]

At a later point in his memorandum, Marshall introduces his long-run anxiety, which Keynes and D. H. Robertson were to echo down to 1920 (following, pp. 302–304):[89]

> . . . [T]he world is being peopled up very quickly. It is but a century since Britain accumulated her great Public Debt; and before another century has passed the scene may have changed. There may then remain but a few small areas of fertile soil, and of rich mineral strata, which are not so well supplied with both population and capital as to be able to produce most of the manufactured products which they require, and to be able to turn to a tolerably good account most of their raw products for their own use. When that time comes, those who have surplus raw products to sell will have the upper hand in all international bargains. Acting concurrently, whether by mutual agreement or not, they will be in the possession of an unassailable monopoly; and any taxes, however oppressive, which they may choose to impose on the only products which densely peopled countries can offer to them will be paid mainly by those countries. It is this consideration, rather than the prospect of any immediate danger, which makes me regard the future of England with grave anxiety.

Thus, in Marshall, much more than in Mill or Marx, diminishing returns reasserts itself as he contemplates the historical outcome of movement by a lengthening array of nations through the stages of growth.

Stages of and Limits to Growth

It was Marshall's acute sense of the relevance of time and place that forced him to suffuse all his substantial work with historical references and analyses. Joined with his conviction that history moved slowly, by small increments, this sense also lead him to the view that the study of history permits an estimate not only of the first but also of the second derivative of the course of events; that is, the manner in which the rate of change is changing:[90] ". . . [O]bservation of the present only shows what is perhaps its rate of movement: some guidance is needed also as to the rate of increase of movement. That can only be got by looking backwards."

Marshall looks backward and, cautiously, forward in four distinct contexts:

- Observations on stages of economic growth along the lines of the classical economists with some observations also on the more modern German stage theorists.
- Historical passages directly related to institutional or technical features of the contemporary scene; e.g., the evolution of banking, joint stock companies, and transport facilities as they influenced the grain supply for urban areas.
- The immediate challenge to British economic leadership mounted, notably, by Germany and the United States, including the competitive strengths and weaknesses of the contenders; and the longer run competive prospects for a wider group of potential economic leaders. Aside from continuing to elevate the level and quality of life of the working classes I would guess Marshall regarded this problem—with its echoes of Hume on the rich-country–poor-country problem—as the most important issue of political economy confronted by Britain in his time.
- Finally, once again, is Marshall's deeply rooted anxiety about the prices of food and raw materials relative to manufactures in the longer future.

What we might call the long sweep of stages of growth appears as early as 1879 in *The Economics of Industry,* Book I, Chapter VII.[91] In six pages Marshall takes his reader, in reasonably colorful style, from the egalitarian life of the savage through the early phases of the division of labor to the emergence of agricultural systems supported by specialized handicraft manufacture and other services in villages. After a diversion on societies rooted in slavery and serfdom he returns to the rise of towns, craft guilds, banking, trade—all associated with a marked increase in specialization of function. Without further explanation, machinery (along with "the train, the steamship, the printing press, and telegraph") appears and a curious parallel to Marx's rise in the organic Composition of Capital:[92] "The amount which a manufacturer devotes to the purchase of machinery increases much faster than the amount he spends on the hire of labour. In other words, Auxiliary capital is increasing at a greater rate than Remuneratory." The passage closes with emphasis on the increased mobility of labor and capital and the tendency towards equal profits in trades of "equal risks, discomforts, and exertions."

A more spacious version of this stylized passage of economic history is incorporated in Appendix A of the *Principles* entitled "The growth of free industry and enterprise," running to thirty pages. It begins, again, with the forces that determine the shape of primitive societies, covers the evolution of Europe down through medieval times, and the emergence of the powerful monarchies in Austria, Spain, and France. He then defines the critical turning point as follows:[93]

> Then the world might have gone backwards if it had not happened that just at that time new forces were rising to break up the bonds of constraint, and spread freedom over the broad land. Within a very short period came the invention of printing, the Revival of Learning, the Reformation, and the discovery of the ocean routes to the New World and to India. Any one of these events alone would have been sufficient to make an epoch in history; but coming together as they did, and working all in the same direction, they effected a complete revolution."

Marshall has a good deal more to say about the emergence of modern manufacturing than in his earlier account. He brings together several strands including the prior capitalist organization of agriculture, the impact of the Reformation, and the role of the nonconformist:[94]

> England's industrial and commercial characteristics were intensified by the fact that many of those who had adopted the new doctrines in other countries sought on her shores a safe asylum from religious persecution. By a sort of natural selection, those of the French and Flemings, and others whose character was most akin to the English, and who had been led by that character to study thoroughness of work in the manufacturing arts, came to mingle with them, and to teach them those arts for which their character had all along fitted them. During the seventeenth and eighteenth centuries, the court and the upper classes remained more or less frivolous and licentious; but the middle class and some parts of the working class adopted a severe view of life; they took little delight in amusements that interrupted work, and they had a high standard as to those material comforts which could be obtained only by unremitting, hard work.

The emergence of the factory system, its diffusion throughout Britain, to the Continent, and across the Atlantic is evoked, and the story ends with reflections, later to be much elaborated, on the industrial prospects for the United States, Germany, and others. In a footnote, he lucidly identifies the critical three initial innovations of the industrial revolution (Watt's steam engine, the new textile machinery, and the new method for manufacturing iron with coke) and enumerates some of those that followed.[95]

Two things are striking about this highly compressed essay in the sweep of economic history. First, Marshall obviously had read thoroughly the rapidly expanding professional literature in economic history, notably the writings in Germany and Britain. Second, he wove together easily factors deriving from climate and geography, custom and culture, social structure, legal systems, politics, religion, and a recurrent strand of emphasis on racial characteristics. Marshall's synthesis was distinctive, although what he had to say was not particularly original. For our purposes, however, what this appendix underlines is the wide range of variables Marshall correctly perceived as relevant to a serious analysis of the process of economic growth. No reader of Appendix A in the *Principles* will fail to understand why Marshall did not regard the refinement of his incipient neoclassical growth model (preceding, p. 167) as high-priority business. He believed the economist should, like the economic historian, be "saturated with a knowledge of the religious and moral, the intellectual and aesthetic, the political and social environment. . ."[96]

The same insistence on the relevance of history with all its dynamic complexity suffuses the two appendices that follow: B, "The Growth of Economic Science," and C, "The Scope and Method of Economics." Except for a brief, initial passage in *Money, Credit, and Commerce,* reaching back to medieval times, Marshall returned to the long sweep of stages of growth only once: in Appendix B of *Industry and Trade,* where he fences a bit with Roscher's three stages related to virtuosity in manufactures: total dependence on imports; simple manufactures; and sharing industrial leadership at the technological frontier.[97] There are also more conventional excursions into economic history in Appendix C ("England's Early Industry and Trade") as well as an essay (Appendix D) on "The English Mercantilists and Adam Smith."

This brings us to Marshall's second use of economic history—as an essential part of the setting for analyzing a contemporary economic problem. Here he was quite systematic. Starting with *The Economics of Industry,* Marshall provided wherever he judged it appropriate a historical prelude to his analysis of particular problems; for example, with respect to population,[98] land tenure,[99] and trade unions.[100] By the time the more spacious *Principles* was published, 11 years later, Marshall had elaborated the technique of appendices; but the text itself, notably Books IV and VI, contains a good many passages of throwback to earlier times.[101] The same two devices—appendices and historical introductions in the text—are used in *Industry and Trade* and *Money, Credit, and Commerce* to provide a stereoscopic, dynamic dimension to his analysis—a perspective he applied to the history of economic theory and doctrine, as well.

Perhaps Marshall's most striking use of the historical method was in framing the central issue dealt with in Book I of *Industry and Trade* which comes to rest on the future of industrial leadership in the world economy. One can observe in the sequence of Marshall's work—stretching over a half century—a gathering awareness that Britain's critical economic problem was how to meet the challenge posed by the rise to industrial maturity of the United States and Germany.

Marshall begins his most detailed consideration of the problem in *Industry and Trade* with three chapters that are, in effect, analytic essays in British history.[102] They cover the elements in the longer past that prepared the foundations for its pioneering of what Marshall calls "massive industry"; Britain's industrial leadership, which he dates proximately from the mechanization of the cotton industry in the late eighteenth century to 1873; the subsequent challenge to Britain's primacy, and the British response. Chapters follow on the special characteristics of French, German, and American industrialization. The genius of each, he found, respectively, in "fine goods, embodying some artistic feeling and individual judgment"; industries that can be nurtured by "academic training and laboratory work"; and "massive multiform standardization." He closes with "some slight speculations as to future homes of industrial leadership."

The first edition of *Industry and Trade* was published in 1919, the fourth and final edition in 1923. But, typical of Marshall's long periods of gestation, some of the book was set in type as early as 1904. His analysis of Britain's relative position and the intensity of the challenge it confronted reflects rather better the mood of 1904 than 1919 or 1923. The point is germane because the recommendations of Marshall to his countrymen are modest, and, like his analyses of France, Germany, and the United States, do not reflect the major economic consequences of the First World War and its aftermath; although he inserted references to wartime developments and notes that "Britain surprised the rest of the world, if not herself, by the energy which she has shown in the World War: and the English-speaking peoples of four continents have proved themselves to be united in spirit and truth."[103]

Specifically, Marshall commends to his countrymen an intensification of measures already belatedly underway: an expansion and improvement of popular education, a need recognized and acted upon starting in 1904;[104] an improvement of University education for "the well-to-do classes in England;"[105] an expansion of training in science and engineering as well as increased allocation of public resources for scientific research laboratories;[106] improved information about overseas markets and less conservative methods of industrial financing.[107] (The agenda does not greatly differ from prescriptions in the late 1980s for the United States in the face of challenges from within the Pacific Basin.)

Despite his sense that Britain was responding to the industrial challenge in appropriate directions and his evident pride in its redoubtable wartime performance the general tone of Marshall's view of the future is not unlike Hume's mild, long-run philosophic acceptance that manufactures tend to shift from countries and provinces they have already enriched and fly to others (preceding, pp. 29–31).

Marshall looks to some of the British Dominions assuming, in time, degrees of industrial leadership, but notes that they are likely to be more influenced by the experience of the United States than Britain.[108] His concluding reflections went beyond the Atlantic and English-speaking world and, on the whole, are prescient.[109]

> Passing away from European races, we find in Japan a bold claimant for leadership of the East on lines that are mainly Western. Her insular position, contiguous to a great Continent, is almost as well adapted for the development of industry and trade as that of Britain. She has learnt so much during the last thirty years, that she can hardly fail to become a teacher ere long. It seems indeed that stronger food than they now have will be required to enable her people to sustain continuous, severe, physical strain: but the singular power of self-abnegation, which they combine with high enterprise, may enable them to attain great ends by shorter and simpler routes than those which are pursued where many superfluous comforts and luxuries have long been regarded as conventionally necessary. Their quick rise to power supports the suggestion, made by the history of past times, that some touch of idealism, religious, patriotic, or artistic, can generally be detected at the root of any great outburst of practical energy.
>
> India, though less agile, is developing renewed vigour and independence in industry as in thought. She is the home of some of the greatest thoughts that have ever come to the world; and the originator of many of the subtlest and most artistic manual industries. She has suffered in the past from lack of unity, and a scarcity of power for manufactures and transport. But she may yet be found to have considerable stores of coal: and some of her regions may be enriched by electrical energy derived from water power. The rapid recent rise of her larger industries is a source of just pride to her, and of gladness to Britain.
>
> Great futures may also await Russia and China. Each is large, continuous and self-contained: each has enormous resources, which could not be developed so long as good access to ocean highways was a necessary condition for great achievement. Their populations differ in temperament; the persistence of the Chinese being complementary to the quick sensibility of the Russian: each has inherited great powers of endurance from many generations of ancestors who have suffered much. But recent events obscure the outlook.

Marshall does capture, in this passage, some of the principal actors (e.g., China and India) in what might be called the coming third round of adjustment of advanced industrial countries to the challenge of maturing latecomers: the first having been Britain's adjustment to the maturing of countries whose takeoffs began in the second quarter of the nineteenth century (Belgium, France, the United States, and Germany); the second, the adjustment of Western Europe and the United States to the maturing of countries whose takeoffs began in the 1880s and 1890s (Japan, Russia, and Italy).

As for the long-term prospect for growth in the world economy as a whole, Marshall was, as already noted, something of a limits-to-growth pessimist. Looking back and projecting forward the prospects for increase in population and the demands for food and raw materials, his sense was that, despite the potentialities of science, diminishing returns to natural resources would constrain the expansion of the world economy rather than diminishing relative marginal utility for real income itself, and he concluded that this constraint would prevail before the end of the twenty-first century. Thus, Marshall, on this point, was more kin to the older classical economists than to J. S. Mill and Marx.

Noneconomic Factors

In his remarkable essay on Marshall, Keynes portrays him as a man with a double nature: a preacher and pastor of men; and a scientist. Keynes goes on:[110]

> . . . [A]s a preacher and pastor of men he was not particularly superior to other similar natures. As a scientist he was, within his own field, the greatest in the world for a hundred years. Nevertheless it was to the first side of his nature that he himself preferred to give the preeminence. This self should be master, he thought; the second self, servant. The second self sought knowledge for its own sake; the first self subordinated abstract aims to the need for practical advancement. The piercing eyes and ranging wings of an eagle were often called back to earth to do the bidding of a moraliser.
>
> This double nature was the clue to Marshall's mingled strength and weakness; to his own conflicting purposes and waste of strength; to the two views which could always be taken about him; to the sympathies and antipathies he inspired.

In a subtle transition Keynes then links "the diversity of his nature" to a third quite distinctive characteristic of Marshall:[111]

> In another respect the diversity of his nature was pure advantage. The study of economics does not seem to require any specialised gifts of an unusually high order. Is it not, intellectually regarded, a very easy subject compared with the higher branches of philosophy and pure science? Yet good, or even competent, economists are the rarest of birds. An easy subject, at which very few excel! The paradox finds its explanation, perhaps, in that the master-economist must possess a rare *combination* of gifts. He must combine talents not often found together. He must be a mathematician, historian, statesman, philosopher—in some degree. He must understand symbols and speak in words. He must contemplate the particular in terms of the general, and touch abstract and concrete in the same flight of thought. He must study the present in the light of the past for the purposes of the future. No part of man's nature or his institutions must lie entirely outside his regard. He must be purposeful and disinterested in a simultaneous mood; as aloof and incorruptible as an artist, yet sometimes as near the earth as a politician. Much, but not all, of this ideal many-sidedness Marshall possessed.

This is the quality that emerges as paramount if one examines Marshall's work from the perspective of economic growth. He insisted on bringing to bear on every problem he confronted insights from history, sociology, psychology, philosophy, or any other discipline he judged might be relevant. Keynes's distinction between Marshall as a scientist and his multifaceted technique of analysis obscures an essential point. Marshall's method—with its introduction of noneconomic as well as economic forces interacting dynam-ically through time—was the essence of his vision of what the economist, as scientist, should be. At one point in his memorial essay, Keynes (with the assistance of notes from Edgeworth) lists seven of Marshall's striking contributions to knowledge.[112] Five of these are components of mainstream economics, some after considerable modification, down to the present day: (1) clarification of the respective roles of demand and cost of production in price determination in short-term partial equilibrium analysis; (2) the extension of this formulation to general equilibrium analysis, strengthened by the substitution of factors of production as well as consumers goods at the margin; (3) the concept of consumer's Rent or Surplus, notably its role in opening the way to welfare analysis; (4) the analysis of monopoly; and (5) clarification of the concept of the elasticity of demand.

This chapter has hardly referred to any of these innovations that constitute the bulk of what would be conventionally regarded as Marshall's "scientific" contribution, to accept for the moment Keynes's distinction.

The other two contributions referred to in the Keynes–Edgeworth array are: "the explicit introduction of the element of time as a factor in economic analysis";[113] and Marshall's large-scale mobilization of historical materials. With respect to time, Keynes notes the various devices Marshall created to try to give systematic order to the long period; but he notes that Marshall left much for his successors to do. With respect to economic history, Keynes can barely conceal his regret, if not irritation, that Marshall spent so much time and energy on the subject.[114]

The view here is, of course, that Marshall regarded historical analysis as one of the essential tools for dealing with the problem of time, the long period, and "organic growth." He (and his successors down to the present) did not devise the tools that would permit economists to deal with growth and the long period in as tidy a way as they would like; but it was a great scientific virtue of Marshall's that he insisted that growth be confronted in all its irreducible complexity—a decision heightened by knowledge that he formulated in the early 1880s a pretty fair approximation of a neoclassical growth model, and, after exploring its properties, set it aside for good reasons.

On the other hand, Marshall was quite conscious that, in insisting on the relevance to economic analysis of every facet of the human experience, no framework existed or was in sight that would order each dimension in relation to the others:[115] "It is vain to speak of the higher authority of a unified social science. No doubt if that existed Economics would gladly find shelter under its wing. But it does not exist; it shows no signs of coming into existence. There is no use waiting idly for it; we must do what we can with our present resources." Marshall was arguing here against the narrowness and excessive dogmatism of some of the British economists earlier in the century and of what he regarded as Comte's incorrect deduction from his correct insistence on the complexity of social phenomena. Marshall rejected Comte's notion that economic phenomena could not be studied separately. He insisted that they should be studied by induction as well as deduc-tion and with a biologist's willingness to take "organic growth" as the focus of attention.

He observed:[116] "The same bent of mind, that led our lawyers to impose English civil law on the Hindoos, led our economists to work out their theories on the tacit assumption that the world was made up of city men."[117] In this methodological dialectic Marshall held, then, a middle position and built his work systematically upon it. His wide-ranging, loose-jointed, societal approach to economic analysis was directly and quite consciously in the tradition of Mill and Smith. And this was the case, as well, for his role as "a preacher and pastor of men." The classical tradition in economics, even in its apparently most antiseptic, abstract Ricardian form, was inspired by moral values and objectives its practitioners were proud to proclaim and defend.

I have already cited a number of the unembarrassed moral judgments that suffuse Marshall's economic analysis; for example the moral basis for his initial dedication to economics (p. 163), his plea for greater craftsmanship in consumer goods (p. 167), his truly radical proposal for reducing the skewness of income distribution in Britain (following, p. 192). But a final word is required on Marshall's position with respect to socialism.

I begin with one of Schumpeter's barbs that Marshall's late-Victorian style appears to have generated in the former's Central European soul:[118] "Marshall professed to be in sympathy with the ultimate aims of socialism, though he expressed himself in so patronizing a way as to evoke nothing but irritation." Schumpeter may capture accurately the human reaction generated among contemporary socialists by Marshall—a reaction Schumpeter was in a position personally to observe.[119] But I do believe Marshall's sympathies with socialism were more deeply rooted than Schumpeter implies; his reservations grounded in serious issues of both method and substance; and, one can add, that whatever irritations Marshall may have stirred in socialist intellectuals, he got on well and easily with workers and labor leaders.

As for the depth of Marshall's concern for the poor, the evidence is abundant that he was drawn to economics by a compulsion to answer the question: "Are the opportunities of real life to be confined to a few?";[120] and the centrality of that question in his work remains to the end. In the best tradition of the classics—notably Smith and Mill—he was intensely aware of the imperfections, costs, and inequalities of capitalism. His formal analysis led him to refine and dramatize the proposition (at least as old as Hume) that "the same sum of money measures a greater pleasure for the poor than the rich," with its powerful implications for the scientific legitimacy of progressive taxation.[121] As noted earlier, Marshall opened the way for the modern analysis of monopolistic competition and welfare economics. And there is no reason to question his own testimony on the seriousness as well as the sympathy with which he read and considered socialist writings of his time.[122]

But he drew back in the end because he found the analytic methods of the socialists (and the German historical school) unpersuasive, and because he came to question whether socialism would, in fact, solve the problem of mass poverty that was his central concern. Here is his own articulation of both points, set down in third person for a German compilation of short autobiographical sketches of the lives of leading economists:[123]

> . . . [H]e was attracted towards the new views of economics taken by Roscher and other German economists; and by Marx, Lassalle and other Socialists. But it seemed to him that the analytical methods of the historical economists were not always sufficiently thorough to justify their confidence that the causes which they assigned to economic events were the true causes. He thought indeed that the interpretation of the economic past was almost as difficult as the prediction of the future. The Socialists also seemed to him to underrate the difficulty of their problems, and to be too quick to assume that the abolition of private property would purge away the faults and deficiencies of human nature. . . .

Marshall felt the historical method was philosophically inadequate:[124] ". . . [T]he facts by themselves are silent. Observation discovers nothing directly of the actions of causes, but only sequences in them." He knew that theory, explicit or implicit, was inescapable; and he felt no confidence that the explicit or implicit theories of history, on which socialist analyses of the contemporary scene and remedy for its ills were based, were valid. At one point in his inaugural lecture at Cambridge he compares the over-simplifications of the socialist historical school to "the careless sayings of the leaders of the Ricardian school in the last generation."[125]

As for Marx, the labor theory of value, surplus-value, and the structure he built on it, Marshall tartly observed:[126] ". . . [T]his assumption that the whole of this Surplus is the produce of labour, already takes for granted what they ultimately profess to prove by it— they make no attempt to prove it; and it is not true."

But, more fundamentally, he doubted that socialism would generate that expansion of output and increase in productivity on which the lifting of poverty ultimately depended; he was convinced its bureaucratic character would violate the inherent rights of individuals and inhibit their creativity; and he had faith that there was an alternative. He set out this argument most fully, in "Social Possibilities of Economic Chivalry" (1907).[127] The following extracts capture, I believe, Marshall's sometimes Veblenian line of argument, which amounts to a precise—even quantitative—case for the democratic welfare state:

> It is a common saying that we have more reason to be proud of our ways of making wealth than of our ways of using it. . . .
>
> Opinions are not likely to agree as to the amount of private expenditure which is to be regarded as socially wasteful from this point of view. Some may put it as high as four or even five hundred millions a year. But it is sufficient for the present that there is a margin of at least one or two hundred millions* which might be diverted to social uses without causing any great distress to those from whom it was taken; provided their neighbours were in a like position, and not able to make disagreeable remarks on the absence of luxuries and of conventional "necessaries for social propriety" which are of little solid advantage. . . . The Law of Diminishing Return is almost in-operative in Britain just now, but after a generation or two it may again be a powerful influence here and nearly all over the world. . . . There is an urgent duty on us to make even more rapid advance during this age of economic grace, for it may run out before the end of the [twentieth] century.
>
> Men of certain types of mind, which are not morbid, delight now, as in previous generations, in vehement indictments of existing social conditions. Their efforts may rouse a passing enthusiasm, which is invigorating while it lasts; but they nearly always divert energies from sober work for the public good, and are thus mischievous in the long run. . . .
>
> . . . I was a Socialist before I knew anything of economics; and indeed, it was my desire to know what was practicable in social reform by State and other agencies which led me to read Adam Smith and Mill, Marx and Lassalle, forty years ago. . . , and I have watched with admiration the stren-uous and unselfish devotion to social well-being that is shown by many of the able men who are leading the collectivist movement. I do not doubt that the paths, on which they would lead us, might probably be strewn with roses for some distance. But I am convinced that, so soon as collectivist control had spread so far as to narrow considerably the field left for free enterprise, the

*By Marshall's calculation U.K. annual income was £1.7 billion. His proposed additional social allocation would, therefore, be 5.9%–11.8% of national income.

pressure of bureaucratic methods would impair not only the springs of material wealth, but also many of those higher qualities of human nature, the
strengthening of which should be the chief aim of social endeavour. . . .
[U]nder collectivism there would be no appeal from the all-pervading bureaucratic discipline. . . . [W]e . . . need to face the difficulty . . . that those
improvements in method and in appliances, by which man's power over
nature has been acquired in the past, are not likely to continue with even
moderate vigour if free enterprise be stopped, before the human race has been
brought up to a much higher general level of economic chivalry than has ever
yet been attained. The world under free enterprise will fall far short of the
finest ideals until economic chivalry is developed. But until it is developed,
every great step in the direction of collectivism is a grave menace to the
maintenance even of our present moderate rate of progress. . . . [I]t seems
best that the difficulties of collectivism should be studied much more carefully, before the scope for creative enterprise is further narrowed by need-
lessly intruding collective administration into industries in which incessant
free initiative is needed for progress.

This was Marshall's reply to the question with which he challenged himself and his
generation in his inaugural lecture:[128] "Why should it be left for impetuous socialists and
ignorant orators to cry aloud that none ought to be shut out by the want of the material
means from the opportunity of leading a life that is worthy of man?" Today, 104 years
later, that reply is likely to be judged fresh and relevant in capitals of developing countries
from New Delhi to Brasilia, to say nothing of Beijing and Moscow.

As for the required method of transformation, he believed *Natura non facit saltum*—
nature doesn't make a jump—said it all: the technological, educational, social, and
political transformations required to achieve an opportunity for all to achieve the good life
would take time and unrelenting effort; progress would have to be slow—yet solid; he
could perceive no short cuts.

Here at the close of the *Principles* is his definition of the middle ground between
"impatient insincerity" and "moral torpor" on which he felt comfortable.[129]

. . . [T]he pessimist descriptions of our own age, combined with romantic
exaggerations of the happiness of past ages, must tend to the setting aside of
methods of progress, the work of which if slow is yet solid; and to the hasty
adoption of others of greater promise, but which resemble the potent medi-
cines of a charlatan, and while quickly effecting a little good, sow the seeds of
widespread and lasting decay. This impatient insincerity is an evil only less
great than that moral torpor which can endure that we, with our modern
resources and knowledge, should look on contentedly at the continued destruction of all that is worth having in multitudes of human lives, and solace
ourselves with the reflection that anyhow the evils of our own age are less
than those of the past.

7

Population and
the Working Force

The focus shifts now from major analysts of the growth process as a whole to the now-familiar key dimensions of the growth process as I have defined them. This phase of the story begins with a brief review of the evolution of population analysis in the period 1870–1939 as it relates to economic growth.

The Statistical Analysis of Population

For more than three centuries the study of population—fertility, mortality, migration—has had a statistical cast because public authorities, including the churches, generated a progressively widened range of interests in the size and character of populations under their political or spiritual dominion. Demographers were thus not unique, but they were rather special among social scientists in their early sense that they could fill their conceptual empty boxes with more or less reliable numbers.

This is not the occasion for even a short history of population analysis; but it is worth noting that the orderly use of statistics in the social sciences begins with John Gaunt's pamphlet, published in London in 1662: *Natural and Political Observations . . . Made upon the Bills of Mortality,* a study of weekly records of burials.[1] Gaunt was a close and influential friend of William Petty, whose wider, more imaginative, and less rigorous exercises in "Political Arithmetick" were published in the period of 1662–1676. Indeed, historians of demography trace Gaunt's influence directly and indirectly through a variety of seventeenth- and eighteenth-century figures down to Malthus and Darwin.[2] Among those on whom he left his mark was the German cleric, mercantilist, pro-natalist, and demographic pioneer, Johann Süssmilch (1707–1765).[3]

Although there were some European and colonial population enumerations in the seventeenth century, regular censuses begin in the eighteenth century: Sweden, Prussia, the United States; and then Great Britain and France in 1801.[4] By the time Malthus wrote his second edition there was a considerable body of material on which to call including some statistical data.

The controversy stirred up by Malthus's first edition did not immediately stimulate many empirical population studies and may, indeed, have discouraged them to a degree in

Britain.[5] Nevertheless it helped generate Michael Sadler's demographic study of Ireland and had, of course, a powerful long-run influence on population research and analysis. There was in the nineteenth century considerably more progress in studies of mortality than of fertility. The general rule governing the focus of demographic research as enunciated by Sauvy appears to have been a version of that determining the directions to which economists allocated their talent and energies:[6] "Just as a man is engrossed with the diseased or painful parts of his body, so demographic research was centered primarily around the points where some social malady was indicated. Thus, we see that demography was influenced directly by the very history of population or, more precisely, by anxieties which developed about it."

The range of anxieties varied, of course, with place and time. Official circles in mercantilist Europe focused on the link of population to military manpower. In France, for example, there was considerable concern about sluggish population trends starting in the late seventeenth century and running down to about 1780. Clearly, France did not experience as dramatic a population setback as Spain in the seventeenth century; but there was a widespread sense (engaging, for example, Montesquieu) that population had fallen and poverty increased, which reached a climax in 1756 with Mirabeau's *L'ami des hommes ou traité de la population,* which asserted that "the strength of the nation, dependent on the well-being of the peasants and workers, was being sapped away, as evidenced by the decline in population."[7] A good deal of empirical effort was stirred up by the subsequent controversy which, on the whole, established that births exceeded deaths, even modestly, in the latter half of the eighteenth century. Sauvy reports that "the national anxiety was less acute . . . after 1780. Economic demography . . . underwent an eclipse in the nineteenth century."[8] But the Prussian defeat of Austria in 1866 and France in 1870 revived demographic anxiety and research.

The flavor of the post-1870 debate, centered on the low French birth rate but reaching beyond, is well captured in a June 1904 article by E. Castelot.[9] It includes the following passage:[10] ". . . French publicists . . . insist on the indisputable fact that in 1860 Germany and France had the same population, that the former now has about 52 million inhabitants against only 38 for the latter, and this ominous difference goes on growing steadily and rapidly." A part of Castelot's discussion anticipates aspects of the secular stagnation argument of the 1930s.[11] The low French birth rate, regarded with relative complacency in France in the period 1815–1870, became the focus of a wide range of fertility studies in other countries.

From a quite different direction increasing concern of government authorities with public health and social welfare as well as the spread of life insurance stimulated studies of mortality as the century wore on. The late nineteenth-century wave of immigration from Eastern and Southern Europe generated studies in the United States of the comparative fertility of immigrant and native-born populations. Echoing Benjamin Franklin's 1751 concern that the immigrants would, in time, "eat the natives out," Francis Walker stirred not only controversy but also a refinement of methods for calculating the net impact of immigration on population.[12] As with fertility and mortality studies, migration studies gathered momentum and were consolidated in the monumental National Bureau of Economic Research project organized by Walter F. Willcox and Imre Ferenzi.[13]

These and other impulses derived from specific problems stimulated the empirical and theoretical study of population in government departments, international organizations, and universities. There were no regular population or demography departments in universities, but men and women were drawn to the study of population from a variety of directions: sociology, mathematics, the physical sciences, public health, economics, as well as business and government. The name *demography* was invented as early as 1855 by Achille Guillard; and, from 1882, when the Fourth International Conference on Hygiene gathered in Geneva, the demographers managed to get together under its tent and regularly to keep in touch thereafter. They read each other's work, argued with and learned from each other, and cumulatively built up an increasingly solid statistical base for their analyses.

By the mid-1930s, A. M. Carr-Saunders could publish estimates of past and current world population.[14] On foundations reaching back to the eighteenth-century work of Süssmilch and the Swiss mathematician Leonhard Euler, a sequence of major figures refined the conceptual and mathematical tools for analyzing the determinants of population changes; for example, A. L. Bowley, Louis I. Dublin, Alfred J. Lotka, Raymond Pearl, and Walter F. Willcox. As in economic theory, demographers found it clarifying to develop a concept of general equilibrium "as a limiting type toward which a closed population tends, given a constant schedule of age-specific fertility, and a constant sex ratio at birth."[15] An elegant general theory of population growth emerged by analogy with the dynamics of fruit flies in the limited environment of a milk bottle. It was incorporated in Pearl's *The Biology of Population Growth* (1925). The stretched out S-curve which Pearl derived from his fruit fly experiments bears a family relation both to Adam Smith's path of nations to their "full complement of riches" (preceding, pp. 46–47) and to the analyses of growth rates in relation to real income per capita in the third quarter of the twentieth century (following, pp. 363–365):[16]

> The long-run tendency of population growth can be represented by a curve which starting from a previously established stationary level, representing the supporting capacity of its region at the prevailing level of culture, productive technique, and standard of living—rises at first slowly, then at an increasing rate, finally leveling out as the curve approaches an upper asymptote which represents the supporting capacity of the environment at the last stage of culture development.

By the coming of the Second World War the study of population and its dynamics was a recognized multidisciplinary branch of the social sciences, with a good deal more confidence than other branches in its powers of prediction. That confidence was to be shaken by post-1945 population developments in various parts of the world, but demography had achieved a respectable degree of maturity since John Gaunt went to work on the London burial records.

Population and Growth Theory: Advanced Industrial Countries

There are essentially three linkages of population analysis to growth theory that had emerged with more or less clarity by 1939: the notion of an optimum population; the demographic transition; and the introduction of population–working-force variables in formal growth models.

The formal concept of an optimum population is usually associated with the publication in 1954 of Harvey Leibenstein's *A Theory of Economic-Demographic Development*. Spengler, however, asserts the concept was anticipated at least as early as 1848;[18] and I shall comment later on a rather sharp pre-1939 debate focused explicitly on the concept (following, p. 199). Detracting nothing from Leibenstein's important contribution, the fact is that an optimum population concept is latent in all but one of the six economists dealt with in Part I. Excepting Marx, they all had the notion, in one form or another, that population might be "too low" or "too high." Up to a point, for example, Adam Smith perceived that an increasing population was required both to expand the market and to supply the working force for the increasingly specialized manufactures necessary to supply that market. But since his growth process is constrained, life becomes "hard in the stationary and miserable in the declining state" (preceding, pp. 36–37). The optimum population ("the happiest and most comfortable") is, evidently, that found in "the progressive state, while the society is advancing to the further acquisition, rather than when it has acquired its full complement of riches. . . ." Smith did not envisage a more or less regular flow of inventions and innovations that might indefinitely frustrate the three determinants of his growth ceiling: soil, climate, and "situation with respect to other countries." But his criterion for the optimum is clear: an environment of rising real income per capita.

But this was all abstract: Smith felt no apparent anxiety about the level and rate of increase of population in Britain. With pre-1812 Malthus and Ricardo, we are dealing with analysts who felt population increase was dangerously excessive, again in terms of its impact on real income per capita. Thus their recommendations for postponed marriage, prudence, education, and a "subsistence" wage reflecting higher economic and social aspirations. Mill advocated a determined effort to limit family size to a point where population was constant. Technological innovation would continue, and real income per capita would increase in a setting where the physical environment was not under degrading pressure and the quality of life in every dimension could rise.

In the period 1870–1939 in the advanced industrial countries, the occasions for sharpest focus on optimum population were Britain, Sweden, and the United States, in the Great Depression of the 1930s.[19]

As Table 7.2 (following, p. 200) indicates, the fall in the British net reproduction rate brought it by the years of deep depression to virtually the same low point as Sweden's. Public concern was heightened by a consciousness of the population loss of the First World War and, as the 1930s wore on, by the likelihood of a second great military conflagration.

Keynes's *General Theory,* and the sharp recession of 1937–1938 long before full employment had been achieved in Britain and the United States, spurred speculation about secular stagnation in which the possibility of a declining population generally figured. Keynes's only reference to the economics of population decline in the *General Theory* relates to its negative impact on investment; but it is set in the context of business-cycle analysis rather than secular stagnation:[20]

> . . . [T]he interval of time, which will have to elapse before the shortage of capital through use, decay and obsolescence causes a sufficiently obvious scarcity to increase the marginal efficiency, may be a somewhat stable function of the average durability of capital in a given epoch. If the characteristics of the epoch shift, the standard time-interval will change. If, for example, we pass from a period of increasing population into one of declining population, the characteristic phase of the cycle will be lengthened.

In a subsequent article published in *The Eugenics Review* Keynes discussed population in the context of his then view of secular stagnation.[21] So far as I can make out it is the occasion when he comes closest to stating lucidly his version of the classic growth equation. His argument is as follows:

- The demand for capital is a function of three variables: the rate of growth of population, the rate of growth of "the standard of life," and the rate of increase and character of technology.
- Putting aside the other two variables, a positive rate of population increase enlarges the demand for capital by diffusing a hopeful—even excessively hopeful—set of expectations among investors; but such errors of overoptimism are rapidly corrected. The errors of pessimism induced by a falling population correct themselves more slowly, and the changeover from optimistic to pessimistic expectations, rooted in population projections, can be "very disastrous."
- In an interesting combination of conventional British and Austrian analyses of capital, Keynes argues that, as compared to the long sweep of the past, inventions are getting less capital intensive, with a lower "average period of production," due to the high income elasticity of demand for services.
- Projecting forward on the basis of considerable confidence a stationary or declining population "in a very short time" plus a decline in the capital intensity of new inventions plus an assumed 1% per annum limit on the rise in per capita consumption ("standard of life"), Keynes concluded that "to ensure equilibrium conditions of prosperity over a period of years it will be essential, *either* that we alter . . . the distribution of wealth [to reduce the savings rate] . . . *or* reduce the rate of interest sufficiently to make profitable very large changes in technique . . . or . . . as would be wisest . . . both policies to a certain extent."

Keynes closed by recalling that Malthus focused his work successively around two anxieties: the early Malthus, around the dangers of excessive population (P); the later Malthus, of chronic unemployment (U): "When devil P . . . is chained up we are free of one menace; but we are more exposed to the other devil U. . . . I only wish to warn you that the chaining up of one devil may, if we are careless, only serve to loose another still fiercer and more intractable."

Technically, Keynes's argument, whose basic assumptions were to be mainly belied in the post-1945 quarter-century, is an interesting exercise in the use of comparative statics to draw dynamic policy conclusions centered around an implicit notion of an optimum population growth rate.

W. B. Reddaway's *The Economics of a Declining Population,* first published in 1939, reflects the best systematic prewar British thought on the economic implications of the potential population decline implicit in a net reproduction rate close to .7.[22] His argument—and the British discussion in general—is rather narrowly economic as compared to the concurrent debate in Sweden; and, as one would expect, it is colored strongly by Keynesian analysis. Reddaway argues that the level of investment will fall with population retardation and decline, but capital per head will increase. His balance sheet for an economy experiencing population decline is set out in Table 7.1:[23] But he identifies "the skeleton in the cupboard" in terms similar to Keynes's in the *General Theory* (see note 20): "the increased risk of slumps."[24] His proposed remedies, therefore, come to rest on those commonly recommended at the time "to avoid general unemployment," to use Reddaway's phrase.

Sweden is the most interesting case of anxiety about a stagnant or falling population for two reasons. First, its greatest and most influential economist, Knut Wicksell (1851–

Table 7.1. Factors Influencing the Real National Income
per Person Employed

Factor	Absolute effect	Relative effect
Capital Supply	Very favorable	Favorable
Technical Progress etc.	Favorable	Nil
Age-Composition	Perhaps slightly favorable	Unimportant
Scale of Production	Unimportant	Unfavorable, but not very important
International Trade	May be unfavorable but probably not very important	Unfavorable

SOURCE: W. B. Reddaway, *The Economics of a Declining Population* (London: Allen and Unwin, 1946), p. 152.

1926), was led into economics through an interest in population and related social questions—an interest he never lost.[25] In this matter he shares, in fact, a distinction with J. S. Mill: they both got in trouble with the legal authorities over the issue. Wicksell was arrested (and sent to prison in 1909) for what Lionel Robbins delicately refers to as "strong utterances on certain of its [population's] non-economic aspects."[26] Aside from his redoubtable public advocacy of birth control, Wicksell explicitly explored the considerations bearing on the definition of an optimum population. He acknowledged that circumstances of underpopulation might exist but he leaned, like J. S. Mill, toward population limitation as a way of increasing real income per capita and elevating the quality of life. His dictum:[27] "The densest population (the maximum) is the most unfavorable (the pessimum) for a country."

Sweden is also of considerable interest because the radical fall in the net reproduction rate set in motion during the 1930s generated a major national debate on the population question; sophisticated analyses by first-class economists and sociologists; policy recommendations from a Swedish Population Commission; and pro-natalist legislation passed in the 1937 session of the Swedish Parliament known as "the mothers and babies session." Table 7.2 suggests why concern in Sweden was particularly intense. As of the mid-1930s it was at the bottom of the net reproduction league—by a bare margin beneath England and Wales.

What was thought and done about population at this time are well captured in books by Gunnar and Alva Myrdal.[28] Gunnar Myrdal's 1938 Godkin lectures at Harvard linked demographic, economic, social, political, and psychological analysis in ways extremely rare in social science, foreshadowing his great study of the race issue in the United States, *An American Dilemma* (1940). He rejects the theory of optimum population as it had evolved in the wake of Mill's *Principles,* including Wicksell's formulation;[29] specifies the economic and social forces making for a falling population trend in Sweden; analyzes in detail the dynamic degenerative effects of a falling population trend on savings and investment, unemployment and poverty; and concludes that a set of positive economic and social policies redistributing income in favor of those with large families is required that would "take away the obstacles preventing ordinary persons from following their natural urge to marry and to have children."[30] Since the objective was to improve the quality as well as to sustain the size of the population, Myrdal proposes a wide range of social legislation to achieve the required redistribution of income.

Table 7.2. Net Reproduction Rates, Selected Advanced Industrial Countries: 1935–1939, 1955–1959, and 1975–1979

	1935–1939	1955–1959	1975–1979
Austria	—	1.12	0.80 (1975–1979)
Belgium	0.96 (1939)	1.14	0.80 (1978)
Bulgaria	—	1.03	1.05 (1976)
Canada	1.16	1.82	0.84 (1978)
Czechoslovakia	—	1.23	1.16 (1975)
Denmark	0.94	1.19	0.82 (1975–1979)
Finland	0.99 (1936–1939)	1.31	0.79 (1978)
France	0.86 (1936–1937)	1.27 (1956–1960)	0.88 (1978)
Germany (Federal Republic)	—	1.04	0.65 (1978)
Germany (GDR)	—	1.11 (1959)	0.90 (1978)
Hungary	1.04 (1930–1931)	1.07	0.97 (1978)
Italy	1.18 (1936–1939)	1.08 (1959)	0.91 (1977)
Japan	1.49	0.96	0.86 (1977)
Luxembourg	—	0.98	0.70 (1978)
Netherlands	1.15	1.46	0.76 (1978)
Norway	0.81	1.32	0.88 (1975–1979)
Poland	1.15 (1932–1934)	1.52	1.05 (1977)
Sweden	0.78 (1936–1939)	1.06	0.81 (1975–1979)
United Kingdom (England and Wales)	0.79	1.13	0.83 (1978)
United States	0.96	1.73	0.86 (1978)
USSR	1.53 (1938–1939)	1.29 (1958–1959)	1.07 (1978–1979)
Yugoslavia	—	1.55 (1950–1954)	1.00 (1977)

SOURCE: *Population Index*, April 1973, April 1974, April 1975, April 1976, and Summer 1981.

In effect, Myrdal argued that the classic optimum population was defined statically at the point where real income per capita was at a maximum, after the benefits of increasing returns were exploited, before they began to be overwhelmed by diminishing returns. Myrdal's optimum—roughly, a constant population with rising real income—requires an active and purposeful social and economic policy for its achievement and maintenance.

Alva Myrdal's later study elaborates the argument with special attention to the measures taken in Sweden with respect to education, family planning, housing, nutrition, health, and social security.

Clearly, the anxiety about population trends was used by the Myrdals—not without considerable legitimacy—to heighten the case for the welfare state.

In the United States the concern about the falling net reproduction rate emerged mainly in the 1930s as part of the view that the country was in the grip of secular stagnation; that investment opportunities had diminished for technological as well as demographic and geographical reasons; and that a radical and systematic Keynesian stimulus to consumption would be required for the long pull to bring the economy back to full employment and keep it there. We shall return to this argument as a whole, as expounded by Alvin Hansen in Chapter 13 (pp. 321–323).

Population entered this argument in terms of a decelerating demand for housing and the package of durable consumers goods which had become a standard feature of American family formation in the 1920s. Alvin Hansen for example, cites the following table showing the decennial increase in U. S. population.[31] His image of secular stagnation in the 1930s also included—even in retrospect—a natural deceleration in the innovational

Table 7.3. U.S. Population Increase: by Decades, 1900–1909
to 1940–1949

Decade	Increase
1900–1909	16,000,000
1910–1919	13,700,000
1920–1929	17,000,000
1930–1939	8,900,000
1940–1949	18,000,000

SOURCE: Alvin Hansen, *Business Cycles and National Income* (New York: W. W. Norton,
1951), p. 76. n. 23.

leading sectors of what I am inclined to call the Third Industrial Revolution (p. 456),
yielding in the 1930s a cyclical depression of peculiar depth, analogous to that of the
1890s when, he believed, the Second Industrial Revolution had run its course.[32]

Like Leibenstein's lucid crystallization of the concept of the optimum population, the
concept of the demographic transition is, in its present standard form, a post-1939 phenomenon enunciated notably by Frank Notestein ("Population: The Long View",
1945)[33] and Warren S. Thompson (*Plenty of People,* 1948). In its usual formulation,
approximating the population dynamics of the West, the demographic transition is as in
Figure 7.1 a movement from a static equilibrium population at a high level of birth and
death rates to a low-level equilibrium with a great population surge induced by the initially
more rapid decline of death than birth rates. Something like this form of transition is
implicit in Pearl's S-shaped population growth curve; and with real GNP per capita plotted
along the horizontal axis, is quite well empirically established on the basis of data drawn
from the period 1950–1970 (Figure 7.2), which will be discussed in Chapter 20 (following, pp. 450–451).

The pre-1939 foreshadowings of this concept are to be found in the work of Walter
Willcox (ed.) (*International Migration,* 1931) and A. M. Carr-Saunders (*World Population,* 1936). The latter's plotting of birth and death rates over considerable time periods
for a variety of countries, and his discussion of them, constitute, in effect, an exercise in
the analysis of the demographic transition.[34]

The third linkage of population to growth analysis is, in a sense, the least sophisticated;
i.e., the *pro forma* introduction of the rate of population increase in two-sector growth
models. Again, the heyday of such models comes after 1945 (following, pp. 332–351).
But they are clearly foreshadowed in the period we are now considering. Indeed, their
lineage can be traced from Quesnay, through Malthus, Marx, and forward. Here we shall

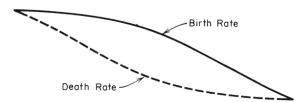

Figure 7.1. The Demographic Transition: Abstract (The Modern Cycle). [Adapted from Donald O.
Cowgill, "The Theory of Population Growth Cycles," *American Journal of Sociology,* Vol. LV,
1949, pp. 163–170, reprinted in P. M. Hauser and O. D. Duncan, *Study of Population,* p. 298.]

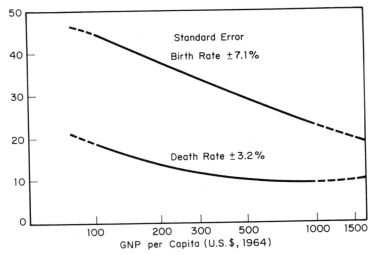

Figure 7.2. The Demographic Transition: A Cross-sectional View (1950–1970): Birth and Death Rates per Thousand; GNP per Capita. {Adapted from Hollis B. Chenery and Moises Syrquin, assisted by Hazel Elkington, *Patterns of Development, 1950–1970* (London: Oxford University Press [for the World Bank], 1975), p. 57.}

briefly note the manner in which population and/or the working force, including the quality of the working force, appears in the principal formal growth models generated between 1870 and 1939.

1. *Marshall.* As noted earlier, Marshall formulated but did not persevere with a quite recognizable growth model (preceding, pp. 165–166), reflecting his early study of Mill and the original strands in his *Economics of Industry*. The working force and its rate of increase are, of course, variables in his growth equation. He also introduces labor efficiency and calculates the working force in efficiency units. In his most fully elaborated case, he envisaged that the rate of increase of both the working force and its efficiency depended on the same array of variables:[35]

$$\frac{dn}{dt} = f_4(n, e, g, E, A', D)$$

$$\frac{de}{dt} = f_5(n, e, g, E, A', D)$$

In these equations n = number of workers; e = labor efficiency; g = gross income; E = degree of equality of income distribution; A' = strength of family affections; and D = rate of discount at which people on the average discount future enjoyments.

In a further version of his growth equation the rate of population increase is set out in a simpler, more classic form:[36]

$$\frac{dn}{dt} = F_4(n, w, s)$$

Where w = the wage rate and s = the standard of comfort (the socially defined subsistence wage).

2. *J. B. Clark.* J. B. Clark's *Essentials of Economic Theory* (1907) might well be

regarded, like Marshall's four volumes, as an exception to the general view that growth moved after 1870 from the center of the stage. Clark's other major studies reflect the conventional post-1870 shift in priority; e.g., *The Philosophy of Wealth* (1885), *The Distribution of Wealth* (1899), and *The Problem of Monopoly* (1904). But the *Essentials,* while reflecting the current concerns of political economists of his generation is, in the end, structured like a classic treatise with the dynamics of growth at its core. Here, for example, is how he sums up:[37]

> The laws which govern progress—which cause the social norm to take a different character from decade to decade, and cause actual society to hover near it in its changes—are the subject of Social Economic Dynamics. We have made a study of the more general economic changes which affect the social structure, and they stand in this order:
>
> 1. Increase of population, involving increase in the supply of labor.
> 2. Increase in the stock of productive wealth.
> 3. Improvements in method.
> 4. Improvements in organization.

Here we focus on one narrow aspect of Clark's exposition. In a chapter devoted to the law of population, Clark argues that contrary to Malthus's initial fears, the increase in wages, accompanied by social changes he specifies, have produced "a retarded growth of population."[38] He concludes that a strand of Malthusianism may operate cyclically—in the short period—but in the long run the socially defined subsistence wage (Marshall's Standard of Comfort) will rise:[39]

> . . . [T]he general result of this uneven advance of the general prosperity may be expressed by the following figure:
>
> The line AC measures time in decades and indicates, by the figures ranging from 1 to 10, the passing of a century. AB represents the rate of wages which, on the average, are needed for maintaining the standard of living at the beginning of the century; and CD measures the amount that is necessary at the end. The dotted line which crosses and recrosses the line BD describes the actual pay of labor, ranging now above the standard rate and now below it.

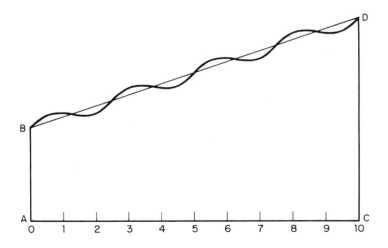

As was natural for an economist writing in the United States in the midst of the great wave of pre-1914 immigration, Clark also reflects on the manner in which the flow of immigrants was offsetting—and more—the retardation in the growth of the native population. In another of his abstract historical diagrams he acknowledges that the consequent increase in the labor supply may have damped the rise in real wages but asserts that, on balance, the increase in the supply of capital had more than compensated for this factor:[40]

> We may represent the resultant of the actual growth of population and of capital by the following figure:
>
> Measuring time by decades along the horizontal base line and the rate of wages at the beginning of a century by the line AB, we represent the increase in the pay of labor which would be brought about by an increase of capital not counteracted by any other influence by the dotted line BC, and the reduction which would be caused by an increase of population by the dotted line BE. The line BD describes the resultant effect of these two changes acting together, on the supposition that during the latter part of the century the growth of population is somewhat retarded and that the increase of capital is the predominating influence.

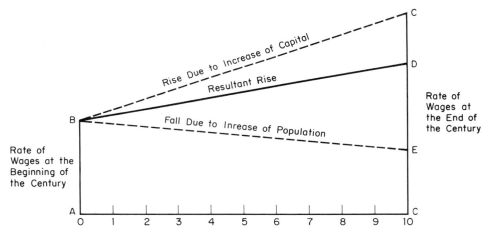

3. *Gustav Cassel.* In his *The Theory of Social Economy,* first published in German in 1918, Gustav Cassel included a rather striking two sections in his first chapter entitled: "The Stationary State" and "The Uniformly Progressing State," followed, 100 or so pages later, by a prose description of an essentially mathematical model generating increased output per capita.[41] These passages, covering about twenty pages, belong among the fairly long list of forerunners to post-1945 growth models considered in Chapter 15.

The heart of Cassel's initial dynamic system—in which population expands but real income per capita remains constant—is a savings rate that will permit the supply of circulating and fixed (real) capital to expand at the assumed rate of progress; i.e., the rate of population increase.[42]

> It is necessary to widen the conception of real income for the purposes of the progressive state. *Real income* must, in this context, be defined, in harmony with the common use of phrase, as the *total real income serving for purposes of consumption plus the increase of real capital during the income period selected.* . . .

It follows that if income is to grow in this way, the formation of capital must also grow in the same way. . . .

In that particular type of progressive state . . . in which progress merely consists of an expansion of economic processes in proportion to the growth of population, the sacrifice of saving is undergone purely for the benefit of the increasing population. . . .

First and foremost, new houses must be built for the new population, but under modern conditions the economic system must also be equipped with additional transport facilities, factories, machines, etc., in proportion to the growth in population. The productive resources used for this increase of real capital cannot be used for the satisfaction of daily wants, so that, at any moment, less wants will be satisfied than could have been without the increase in population.

This initial model requires, then, for dynamic equilibrium a kind of Malthusian "proportion" between saving and consumption to match the system's production requirements for the maintenance of the capital stock as well as increases in capital and consumers goods to match the assumed rate of population increase. At a later point, Cassel describes a dynamic model with income per capita increasing, with the ratio of allocations to purchase consumers goods and capital goods determining the rate of progress.

Cassel's further rather perfunctory comments on population are to be found in his chapter on wages for which he was taken to task (among a good many other matters) in the famous critical review of Knut Wicksell.[43]

Harrod's pioneering highly aggregated dynamic growth model (following, pp. 254–256) contains literally one sentence on population in its penultimate paragraph asserting that a stagnant population, by lowering the natural growth rate, increased the tendency of the system to lapse into depression before full employment is reached. The mechanism envisaged is that movement from an expanding to a stagnant population creates or enlarges the gap between the warranted and natural growth rates.

One final linkage of population dynamics to the economy should be noted. The period 1870–1939, with its mounting attention to business cycle analysis, generated studies of the statistical relationship between marriage, birth, and death rates and cyclical fluctuations as well as research on patterns of migration in relation to business cycles.[44]

Population and Development

Whereas the statistical data base for population studies was progressively expanded, the tools for demographic analysis refined, and the link between demography and the life of the more advanced industrial economies explored, some—but relatively little—thought was given to population problems and prospects in Latin America, Africa, the Middle East, and Asia. The issue of relative degrees of development arose, of course, in migration studies; but there was a beginning, at least, of modern demographic analysis in a few cases in which population was related to the problem of development.

Of these, India had probably moved further down the road toward modern demography and with speculation, at least, about an appropriate population policy. There is evidence of sophisticated census techniques in India back to the fourth century B.C.; and under Akbar's strong unified rule (1556–1605) economic as well as population data were collected. But regular censuses begin under British rule, on an all-India basis, only from

1881.[45] Demography got caught up, however, in the debate in India over British rule and the struggle for independence:[46]

> The setting was hardly suitable for the development of a scientific attitude toward the census, for the population problem had then become a political question. The British administrators were prone to point out that the large size of the population of India was the cause of India's poverty, while Indians imbued with the spirit of nationalism were eager to maintain the contrary and to show that the British rule was the cause of poverty in India. According to them, the relatively slow growth of the population was in itself a reflection on the British administration. Thus the inhibiting effect of the political situation was a fundamental handicap in the development of demography until at least the third decade of the present century.

Under the impact of the growing intensity and increasing refinement of demographic studies in the West and the growing sophistication of Indian social scientists, serious discussion on demographic issues began in the mid-1930s with population conferences in 1936 in Lucknow and 1938 in Bombay. The latter touched off an intense debate on the probable outcome of the 1941 census between those who estimated a low versus those who envisaged an "alarming" increase in population over the decade. At about this time two studies were published, one linking the prospect of a population of 400 million to agricultural policy (Radhakamal Mukerjee, *Food Planning for Four Hundred Millions*, 1938, and Gyan Chand's *India's Teeming Millions*, 1939). But without question the most important symbol of the acceptance of excessive population as an obstruction to development was this passage from a 1938 resolution of the National Planning Committee chaired by Pandit Jawaharlal Nehru:[47]

> In the interests of social economy, family happiness, and national planning, family planning and a limitation of children are essential; and the State should adopt a policy to encourage these. It is desirable to lay stress on self-control, as well as to spread knowledge of cheap and safe methods of birth control. Birth Control Clinics should be established and other necessary measures taken in this behalf and to prevent the use or advertisement of harmful methods.

Meanwhile in 1929, a classic, pioneering study had been published in London by Vera Anstey, *The Economic Development of India*.[48] Mrs. Anstey had lived in Bombay for 7 years (1914–1920), where her husband was principal of the Sydenham College of Commerce. After his death in India, she taught at the London School of Economics and wrote her study of India's stage of development and its prospects. Its structures and substance are examined in Chapter 13. Here it is sufficient to note that her study includes a quietly impassioned section on population; and, in her conclusions, she judged the population problem the first of the three great obstacles to Indian economic development.[49] After tracing briefly the evidence on the growth of Indian population since 1872, and noting an acceleration since 1921, she concludes:[50]

> No definite trend in population growth can be discerned, but it seems quite clear that in the past the population has been prevented from growing still more rapidly mainly owing to the operation of "positive" checks—i.e., poverty, disease, misery, and vice. Prudential checks, such as deferring the age of marriage, limiting the size of the family and contraceptive practices, have not yet been adopted in India to an extent which effectively limits the

rate of increase, except in so far as intervals between births are prolonged by continuation of suckling. In other words, India is still at that stage, through which most Western countries have recently passed, characterized by a high death- and a high birth-rate. This stage is necessarily accompanied by terrible waste of life, and moral and economic misery. . . .

The high density of population (especially in rural areas), the fact that a rapid increase in population has taken place in areas where prosperity has been rather suddenly increased, and the experience of other countries where high birth- and death-rates have usually been accompanied by a low standard of life, all tend to the conclusion that the population of India tends to increase at an uneconomic rate, and that the mass of the people would be better off if this tendency could be checked.

She then examines the religious and social foundations of Indian life, concluding:[51] "The economic results of the customs and institutions that have just been described can be summarized by saying that they tend towards over-population, improvidence, the checking of economic enterprise, and the prevalence of a poor standard of mental and physical development, particularly in the case of women." Her final assessment was unambiguous:[52] "The population problem lies at the root of the whole question of India's economic future, and it is useless to try to bilk the fact." What Anstey saw in India was a society almost literally medieval in European terms. She drew, in fact, on the work of Eileen Power, her distinguished contemporary at The London School of Economics, in making certain analogies between medieval attitudes and social structure and India in the first quarter of the twentieth century.[53] In terms of Adam Smith's concept of stages of growth, Anstey was describing a society that had come to its "full complement of riches," where population had expanded to the limit and lived literally at the margin of subsistence, pushed periodically beneath it by famine and plague. Life was "dull" if not "melancholy." But this outcome was the product of two conflicting forces. One, which Smith did not envisage, was the positive force of the post-1780s technologies already at work in enclaves of modern industrial activity in India, which Anstey describes in detail: notably, cotton textiles, iron and steel, and the railroads. These kept India from the declining state Smith judged Bengal to be caught up in during the third quarter of the eighteenth century. But the power of the new technologies was damped and frustrated by the noneconomic factors that Smith evoked under the heading of "laws and institutions," which, he judged, kept eighteenth-century China from a "full complement of riches" higher than it had, in fact, achieved. So far as India was concerned the impact of those noneconomic factors on population was critical.

A second distinguished study of development during this period is Tawney's *Land and Labour in China,* which is also examined in more detail in Chapter 13.[54] His general conclusions on population are much like Anstey's on India:[55]

The fundamental fact, it is urged, is of a terrible simplicity. It is that the population of China is too large to be supported by existing resources. While, in China as a whole, its mean density is low compared with that of most western countries, in certain areas it is appalling. Whole provinces, as large as European states, may properly be described as congested districts. The struggle of a swarm of human beings for a bare physical existence is an ever-present reality. All the phenomena of rural distress—minute holdings, tiny incomes, female infanticide, starvation—are the unavoidable result of it. . . .

It is true that the population attempting to live by agriculture is in China excessive; the practical proof is that so many persons die. . . . It is true that Chinese habit and doctrine put a premium on the growth of population, which appears to western eyes unnatural and artificial. Sentiment, hallowed by immemorial tradition, makes it a duty to leave sons, and the communism of the patriarchal family dissociates the production of children from responsibility for their maintenance. Hence prudential restraints act with less force than elsewhere; and population, instead of being checked by the gradual tightening of economic pressure on individuals, plunges blindly forward, till whole communities go over the precipice. Apart from the improvement of methods of agriculture, the principal expedients adopted elsewhere, though extremely various, may be reduced to three—migration, the development of alternative sources of livelihood, and the deliberate limitation of the size of families. The question is how far any or all of them are applicable to China, and what, if applied, their effect would be.''

Tawney reviews in turn each remedy; finds potentialities in each; but concludes that the achievement of effective political unity, efficient administration, and a larger, more modern educational system are the overriding requirements.

One specific potentiality examined was Chinese migration to sparsely populated Manchuria. Before Tawney's book was published, the Japanese had occupied Manchuria, and China faced 18 years of war and civil war before the development issues Tawney discerned so well could return to a high place on that nation's agenda.

Lillian Knowles's *Economic Development of the British Overseas Empire* (1924)[56] is also among the few empirical studies of economic development between 1870 and 1939. It contains a few observations on population problems, notably with respect to public health policy and its achievements; but demographic patterns in various parts of the empire are not systematically examined.

An Interim Conclusion

The study of population, as a distinct discipline linked with many others, gathered momentum and came to a highly professional maturity between 1870 and 1939. The scope and quality of data improved, including estimates of population over long time periods; population growth dynamics was refined, fertility as well as death rates came under careful examination; the rather sophisticated concept of the net reproduction rate was established as a useful foreshadowing of the future, if other things remained equal; the demographic transition was defined, and the concept of an optimum population debated.

Before 1939, three distinct links of demography to development were identified and expounded: in the advanced industrial countries, the relation of population retardation, stagnation, or decline to investment, growth, and unemployment rates and to prospects for real income per capita; the kinds of public policies, including social policies, best calculated to return the net reproduction rate to unity; in India and China, the nature, causes, and cures for the raw operation of Malthusian ''positive'' population restraint, in a setting of bare subsistence income levels.

The pride of demographers in their empirical and conceptual progress was palpable as they looked back from the late 1930s; but they—and everyone else—were in for some demographic surprises in the world that emerged after 1945.

8

Investment and Technology, Part One: The Emergence of National Income Accounting

The Statisticians Blow Their Trumpets—Again

In the course of the 1920s the statisticians, conscious of their growing skills and the proliferation of governmental statistical series, conscious also that new and puzzling problems were shaking the complacency of the mainstream economists, unfurled their flags and asserted with confidence a major role in the further development of the social sciences. One could quote various Americans and Britons to this effect (as well as Norwegian, Dutch, and other econometricians); but in Britain Sir Josiah Stamp captures the spirit in which the statisticians, with more than two centuries of professionality behind them, staked out a new enlarged area on the turf of economics.[1]

> Science sans experience
> N'apporte pas grande assurance.
> —Paré's Canon (1510–90)*

Anyone who reflects upon the troubles and problems of the civilized world to-day must realize that questions are constantly put to economic science to which no clear answer, and sometimes no answer at all, is being given. If we are satisfied that no body of knowledge is worthy [of] the name of science unless it has a capacity for development to meet such new needs, we shall be looking around to see upon what lines growth and change in economics must take place. Will the old methods of inquiry and proof suffice, or must we seek new ones, not necessarily "better," but more adapted to cope with the fresh problem and to unfold hidden secrets?

It is my view that the analytical method in the line of Ricardo, Mill, and Marshall has, for the time being, at any rate, reached the limit of its usefulness, and that no striking advance can be made thereby from the ground now occupied. I do not think, moreover, that the refinements and extension of

*"Science without experiment does not provide great confidence."

it in the mathematical or Cambridge School is likely to lead to important results. Certainly inductions by the Historical School must be so broad, and so lacking in touch with modern data, that they will yield only a small contribution to the constructive problems of the moment.

I believe that for the next advance we must depend upon realistic statistical investigation and verification, and that we stand on the threshold of a new method, which is of general application.

Although Stamp and his colleagues appear unaware of their predecessors, they were echoing almost precisely the arguments and ambitions articulated a century earlier when there was great ferment on the subject of statistics on both sides of the Channel.[2] The Statistical Society of London (later the Royal Statistical Society) was organized with Malthus and Babbage among its founding members. Like their counterparts in France, they were stirred to concern and measurement by "the troubles and problems" of the emerging industrial societies. In Britain, as a century later, there was a conscious effort to escape from the limits of "the abstract, deductive style of Ricardian economics."[3]

Having blown again their ideological trumpets, with renewed hope and conviction, the post-1918 statisticians went to work. Their most significant interwar achievement was in filling the empty boxes of national income accounts with reasonably reliable numbers. Out of the interplay of the related concerns of governments and economists, Britain and the United States possessed, on the eve of the Second World War, fairly reliable estimates of national income (or gross national product) and its components. They were used for the first time as major instruments of policy analysis during the war years; and such estimates diffused to virtually all national states quite promptly after 1945. The components came to include estimates for investment and yielded inevitably a comparison of investment proportions to GNP and GNP growth rates. Thus emerged the marginal capital-output ratio, a rough, black-box, aggregate measure of the rate of productivity increase associated with investment; that is, the proportion of GNP invested required to produce a 1% increase in real GNP.

Keynesian income analysis, as clarified after the 1936 publication of *The General Theory*, heightened and helped shape national income analysis; but it is fair to say that the Keynesian doctrine would not have attained the influence it did without the generation of statistical data to fill its empty boxes. But the process of generating national income estimates was set in motion by a concern with quite different issues; and the first substantive section of this chapter seeks to identify the impulses that led to the creation of these powerful tools for both the short-run and long-run analysis of economic growth.

The cumulative and sustained efforts that took place in Britain and the United States between say, 1900 and the end of the Second World War, set the pattern for such calculations since 1945. But the British and American economists and statisticians were by no means alone. There were pioneering calculations of national income in Australia and Canada, and significant work in Germany and elsewhere on the European continent. Writing in 1933 Simon Kuznets was able to cite more or less reputable national income estimates for fifteen countries (following, p. 222, and note 56).

The British Story:

From William Petty to Richard Stone

As in the case of the statistical analysis of population, national income accounting can be traced back to Britain in the second half of the seventeenth century—to the writings and calculations of William Petty and Gregory King.[4] Like most statistical calculations, those generated after 1660 reflected not scientific enquiry but concern with public policy. As Petty's late nineteenth-century editor concludes:[5]

> His writings then are not conscious elaborations of some economic system, more or less clearly conceived. Each of them, on the contrary, was prompted by some circumstances of the times, and addresses itself, in fact if not in form, to some question of the day. The "Treatise of Taxes" the most systematic of them all, grows out of the changes in the revenue which the Restoration occasioned. The "Verbum Sapienti" is due to the costliness of the first Dutch war, the "Quantulumcunque" to the recoinage projects of Halifax. The moral of the "Political Arithmetik," implicit but clearly implied, is that Charles II may, if he will, make himself independent of the bribes of Louis XIV. . . . The "Essays in Political Arithmetick" instruct James, wavering on the verge of an independent policy, that London is more considerable than the two best cities of the French monarchy.

Even Petty's trenchant observation on the disproportionate role of religious minorities in the conduct of trade concludes operationally:[6] ". . . from whence it follows, that for the advancement of Trade, (if that be a sufficient reason) Indulgence must be granted in matters of Opinion. . . ."

Two eighteenth-century figures, Joseph Massie and Arthur Young, were stirred to calculate British national income in the third quarter of the eighteenth century but it has proved difficult to reconcile their approximations to each other or to Gregory King's estimates a century earlier.[7] It was not until the convergence of the industrial surge in last two decades of the century with the radical rise in agricultural prices and the imposition of the wartime income tax that analysts again turned seriously to estimating British income and wealth. Led by Patrick Colquhoun, estimates for British national income were made for 1800–1801, 1803, 1812; and in the postwar years, 1822, 1823, 1833, with some half-dozen further estimates down to midcentury.[8] The latter calculations were generated for a variety of purposes. First and perhaps most important was a desire to measure "The Progress of the Nation," to use the title of G. R. Porter's 1847 statistical compilation. Second, there was a growing interest in income distribution and, especially, the extent to which British workers shared or failed to share in the palpable expansion of the economy. After 1870, with the increasing professionalization of both statistical and economic analysis, and the rise of the democratic socialist movement in Britain and on the continent, the latter issue was extensively explored. For example, Robert Giffen, a major national income and wealth analyst, delivered his presidential address before the Statistical Society in 1883 on "The Progress of the Working Classes in the Last Half Century."[9] From 1873 to the mid-1890s the declining trend in interest rates and palpable rise in real wages as the cost of living fell, yielded a shift in income distribution in favor of urban workers; and this was duly captured by the statisticians.[10] By 1892, that extraordinary if somewhat untamed statistician and collector of statistics, Michael G. Mulhall, could present a table purporting to show "the annual earnings or income" of eighteen nations: fourteen in Europe plus the United States, Canada, Australia, and Argentina.[11] Nine categories of earnings are calculated by the method described in Note 8 as well as average income per capita in British pounds.

None of the calculations cited provided estimates of investment rates; although Mulhall estimated foot-tons in use per inhabitant (hand, horse, and steam) that yielded a rough index of capital intensity;[12] and his wealth figures included breakdowns for land, cattle, houses, railways, ships, etc.[13] But the consequences of growth for national welfare and income distribution rather than the mechanics and dynamics of growth itself were the principal motives for national income calculations in Britain down to the end of the nineteenth century. And this continued to be the case for some time as two major figures emerged: A. L. Bowley and A. C. Pigou. One was a first-class statistician, the other, Marshall's successor, a first-class theorist.[14] Bowley's work over a 40-year span is well summarized, and its central focus accurately reflected, in his *Wages and Income in the United Kingdom since 1860*.[15] Bowley's estimates of national income were, in the first instance, a by-product of his concern to establish the extent to which the real income of British workers had increased or failed to increase; and whether income distribution had shifted in favor of the wage earner or against him. The outcome turned out to hinge substantially on forces set in motion by movements in relative prices and the British terms of trade. But it was from Bowley's estimates of British national income in 1924 (done with Josiah Stamp) that Colin Clark's work in this field takes its start.[16]

It will be recalled (preceding, p. 192) that Marshall used not only the concept of national income but boldly estimated the proportion of that income that might be diverted from "socially wasteful" to constructive social uses "without causing great distress," thus adding to the community's welfare. Pigou shared fully his conviction that the purpose of economics was to enrich the lives of human beings by lifting from them the burden of poverty. In Pigou's vivid phrases:[17] "It is . . . the social enthusiasm which revolts from the sordidness of mean streets and the joylessness of withered lives, that is the beginning of economic science." Pigou greatly extended Marshall's effort to identify circumstances where the social and private net product of an economic activity can be distinguished.[18] In elaborating his argument, Pigou used the concepts of "economic welfare" and the "national dividend," devoting a good deal of attention to refining the latter and exploring the problems involved in its measurement.[19]

Colin Clark's initial interest in national income and its measurement flowed quite explicitly from Pigou's *Economics of Welfare,* whose purposes Clark paraphrased in his own way:[20]

> . . . [to] discover methods which will advance, and counsel the rejection of proposals which will hinder, the following three objects:
>
> 1. To increase the average national dividend.
> 2. To regularise its flow through time.
> 3. To equalise its distribution between persons.
>
> The student of economics soon becomes aware that proposals which may advance one of these objects will injure another, and it is the duty of the economists to attempt to find methods for balancing the gains and losses of human welfare caused thereby.

Clark began his studies as a natural scientist and, as he turned to economics, brought with him a bias he defined in retrospect as follows:[21] "It has always been my profound conviction that economics should be based on empirical observation and classification of what has actually been happening, with theory occupying only a secondary position." After receiving his B.A. from Oxford in 1928 he took part in a social survey of Merseyside and was on the staff of the British Economic Advisory Council in 1930–1931. This body was chaired by Keynes, who recommended Clark for the post of University

Lectureship in Economic Statistics at Cambridge. There Clark worked from 1931 to 1937, from the ages of 26 to 32, when, in classic style, the major themes of his subsequent work crystallized.

He began by carrying British national income estimates forward from 1924 to 1931[22] from the welfare perspective of Bowley and Pigou; but his 1937 study, *National Income and Outlay,* reflects a reaching beyond with considerable originality in four directions all relevant to the analysis of growth:[23] capital investment in relation to economic growth; changes in the components of national income, including investment, in the course of a business cycle; the impact of changing relative prices (and the terms of trade) on real wages, investment, and employment; and the statistical measurement of growth and its structure over long periods, and as among nations, coming to rest on the conditions of economic progress.

For the limited purposes of this portion of our exposition it is sufficient to note two aspects of Clark's analysis of investment. First, he concluded with a proposition whose implications might be widely accepted in principle—over, say, a faculty club lunch—but have still not been fully absorbed in macroeconomic theory; namely, that growth is determined by a complex of factors rather than by the amount of capital invested that "seems to be an effect rather than a cause."[24] He arrived at this conclusion by comparing the British economy in the pre-1914 decade with its position in the 1920s. In the early years of the century the average level of unemployment was low, the terms of trade deteriorating, productivity increase decelerating, real wages static or slightly declining, and an enormous volume of British savings flowing abroad. In the interwar years, on the contrary, British productivity was much higher than earlier and increasing, and the terms of trade were favorable; but the gains from these sources were dissipated in high unemployment. Looking back at his analysis of this period Clark rephrased his conclusion as follows:[25] "At that time, and for many years afterwards, it was believed that the key factor in economic growth was the accumulation of capital. As early as 1937 I began profoundly to question this doctrine. . . . [W]e know now that such an accumulation is a *necessary* but not a *sufficient* condition for economic progress, an important logical distinction."

In *National Income and Outlay* (1937) Clark brought together the factors he judged, in fact, to be critical, in the following rather striking passage:[26]

> If technical knowledge had then been better, or the quality of the population; or if British industries had been able to work for a larger market at home or abroad, and to enjoy further economies of increasing returns, without suffering diminishing returns in their supply of food-stuffs and raw materials, the general level of productivity might have been greater. But these three factors between them seem to have been the consideration, setting an upper limit to which the curve of productivity was tending. We have now broken through that particular limit, largely, I think through improvement in our technical knowledge, and, what is equally important from the point of view of the national productivity, the growing up of a generation of trained and experienced workers and technicians who can apply this knowledge.
>
> I have stated above a positive view of the conditions dominating the long-term possibilities of an increase in productivity, because I believe the facts have destroyed the view up till now generally prevalent, i.e., that the rate of economic growth was primarily dependent upon the rate at which capital

could be accumulated. The very rapid expansion in productivity at the present time is taking place at a time of heavily diminishing capital accumulation.

Clark perceived clearly the key determinants of growth, with one exception: the specific, sectoral character of the flow of innovations that he viewed in aggregate form as "improvement in our technical knowledge." In any case, he never attempted to bring his variables together in a formal exposition of growth, although he was certainly one of the few major analysts of growth between 1870 and the Second World War.

Clark captured a narrower point related to investment in his detailed analysis of British business cycle fluctuations, 1929–1936.[27] In the course of this exercise he subjected to empirical analysis R. F. Kahn's famous analysis of the investment multiplier.[28] Clark found the propensities to save and to consume to be rather more complex than the simple notion of a consumption function would suggest:[29]

> We have already shown that during recent years impersonal saving through undistributed company profits and local-authority sinking funds accounted for the greater part of the observed total of investment. During the last few years, it appeared that private saving by the rich had altogether disappeared or even became negative. . . . . The key factor in the situation would therefore seem to be the propensity (if that word may be used) of company officials to distribute in dividends, or not to distribute in dividends, any given increment of income. . . . . The analysis is delightfully simple. The data for the period 1924–35 lie almost exactly along a straight line, indicating a more or less constant propensity to save on the part of company authorities. Of each additional £1 of income, whether starting from a low level or a high level, on the average £0.46 will be distributed in dividends and the remainder added to reserves.*
>
> The remarkable constancy of this relation probably explains the closeness with which the multiplier 2 is adhered to in the relation between investment and national income.

Clark's *National Income and Outlay* already reflects the impact on national income analysis of the publication in 1936 of Keynes's *General Theory*. Book II of the *General Theory* had dealt at some length with definitions of income, saving, and investment;[30] and, at a later point, Keynes relates his discussion of capital depreciation (gross and net investment) to the statistical calculations of Colin Clark and Simon Kuznets. As the Keynesian concepts were clarified they were increasingly linked to national income statistics that, as noted earlier, had been evolving in Britain out of an array of welfare concerns rather than the sharp Keynesian focus on the problem of chronic high unemployment.

But the crisis in Europe soon turned Keynes's thought towards the economics of war: first, the question of commodity stockpiling; then, from October–November 1939, how to pay for the war.[31] He outlined in letters to the *Times* (and in an *Economic Journal* article of December) a plan to contain wartime inflation by compulsory saving; and he published in February 1940 a short book, *How to Pay for the War*, which may well have been the first occasion when double-entry national accounts were used as a framework for expounding a major policy position. Although Britain used taxation and rationing rather than the large-scale forced saving Keynes commended, the British budget presented by the

---

*In other words, as the proverb goes, "£1 for the company and £1 for the shareholders."

Chancellor of the Exchequer in April 1941, with its supplementary income and expenditure analysis, represented a kind of irreversible triumph of the Keynesian revolution with which Keynes and two of his disciples—James Meade and Richard Stone—were personally connected.[32] Within, say, 10 years, the setting of public finance in the context of national income data and analysis had become an almost universal political convention.

C. K. Hobson and Paul Douglas

Before turning to the quite distinctive but parallel evolution of national income estimates in the United States, two studies of British investment data should be noted: C. K. Hobson's *The Export of Capital* and Paul Douglas's "An Estimate of the Growth of Capital in the United Kingdom, 1865–1909."[33]

Hobson's work was a doctoral thesis at the University of London that, in addition to its valuable and much-used statistical calculations on British capital exports, reviewed the history of the flow, its institutional mechanisms, and its links to emigration and the domestic state of the British economy. He concluded with a judicious but tentative evaluation of the net effects of capital exports on British national income and real wages:[34]

> . . . [W]here the amount of capital exported is small, so that the rate of interest at home is practically unaffected, the loss to home production, resulting from the fact that the capital is not invested at home (or is withdrawn from home investment), is measured by the income which would have been obtained from the home investment. If the rate of interest at home is materially increased as the immediate result of foreign investment, the loss to home production is greater than the amount of income which would have been obtained from home investment. But, in either case, the amount of the national income from all sources is presumably increased by the higher return obtained from investment abroad, except in so far as the amount of labour at home tends to mean that a larger share of the home output goes to capital, and a smaller share to labour. . . . [I]n the long run, foreign investment tends to produce an improvement in the economic lot of the wage earner—an increased demand for work-people, as well as for capital at home—which may outweigh the injurious effects of a high rate of interest upon those who own no considerable amount of capital. The benefit which British capital invested abroad confers on foreign countries may, however, possibly be greater than the advantage which it brings to British wage-earners. In this case the inducement to emigrate may increase, despite the improvement in their position at home.

Hobson's analysis captures all the relevant considerations except, perhaps the most important; i.e., the substantial pre-1914 role of British capital exports in opening up overseas supplies of foodstuffs and raw materials thus improving in the long run the British terms of trade and thereby damping the rise in the British cost of living.

Douglas was concerned to establish, from estimates of the British domestic capital stock at different periods, and from Hobson's estimates of the export of capital, an answer to this question: How does the supply of capital relate to trend movements in the rate of interest and in real wages?

The period for which Douglas made his estimates saw, on balance, a decline in the rate of interest; although the trough for the rate of interest (the yield on consols) came in 1896–1898, after which the rate rose with the rise in the price level. Douglas was aware of the problem of the real rate of interest in periods of falling and rising price trend, but made no correction.[35] And, indeed, given the unambiguous result yielded by his data, no such refinement was required.[36]

> These figures show an increase of 78 per cent in the amount of real capital per capita within the United Kingdom during this period, while, if foreign investments are also included, the increase was 90 per cent. . . .
>
> It is apparent . . . that capital has increased much faster than the quantity of labor. Since the hours of work have decreased during this period, this increase has been appreciably greater than that indicated by the relative capital per capita.
>
> This greater increase, it should be remembered, occurred during a period in which the interest rate was on the whole falling,* while real wages were rising. The fact that capital thus increased at an appreciably faster rate than labor indicated that, during this period of industrial advance at least, its supply was, historically speaking, much more elastic than was that of labor.

The emergence of national income estimation in the United States, as compared to Great Britain, is an essay in the comparative sociology of innovation. In Britain, the older society, such estimates run back to the end of the seventeenth century. From the beginning they reflect a sequence of efforts to illuminate and, usually, to provide a basis for advice on public policy; whether it was post-Restoration rulers confronting France, the estimation of the tax base for the struggle against Napoleon, or the pattern of income distribution as, in Mill's phrase, "the claims of labour [became] the question of the day" in the second half of the nineteenth and early twentieth centuries. Driven on by these welfare concerns, a handful of men, mainly centered at Cambridge, built the concepts, and amassed and disciplined the awkward data required for more or less rigorous national income estimates: Bowley, Stamp, Pigou, Clark, Keynes, and, recruited into the Treasury during the war, James Meade and Richard Stone. The critical link to the Treasury came when Keynes, without stipend, was given a Treasury office in a vaguely defined role as wartime advisor. He and a good many major economists of the interwar years had seen government service in the First World War and, as the crisis with Hitler intensified, turned their minds to the economic dimensions of the struggle ahead. Once in the Treasury, Keynes helped put together and encourage the small team that produced the national income supplement to the April 1941 budget, setting a pattern for regular analysis of the economy and projection in national income terms that was to continue into the postwar period. The saga has the character of an old-boy, family affair, with an illusory, casual, amateur quality to it.

The American Story

From George Tucker to Simon Kuznets

There are strong similarities and differences in the American story. The latter also begins proximately with pre-1914 efforts to clarify the facts about income distribution, a concern

---

*The change in the value of the principal resulting from the movement of the price level is, however, a complicating fact which makes it difficult to determine what the "real" rates of interest were.

that persisted into the 1920s and was heightened by the issues posed in the Great Depression of the 1930s. It was in the context of depression that the initial link was forged between the American government and the research community engaged in building national income estimates; but, as in Britain, the use of such calculations to frame wartime economic policy, within the intellectual matrix of Keynesian income analysis, consolidated the empirical foundations for implementing the mandate of the Employment Act of 1946. From its creation in 1946, the Council of Economic Advisers placed national income and its components at the center of its analyses.

As one would expect, there was a relatively short and thin history of national income estimates in the United States, in part because, unlike Britain and Germany, the income tax was only introduced in 1913. Mulhall cites one estimate by George Tucker for 1840 that he judged to be inaccurate.[37] Mulhall arrays estimates of national wealth, however, starting in 1790, based on census returns by states.[38]

In the pre-1914 generation, the damping pressure of cost-of-living increases on real wages stimulated further estimates, centered on possible shifts in income distribution against labor. A major pioneer of modern U. S. national income estimates, Willford I. King, identified, for example, two reputable predecessors to his 1915 *The Wealth and Income of the People of the United States:* Charles B. Spahr's *The Present Distribution of Wealth in the United States* (1896); and Frank H. Steightoff's *The Distribution of Incomes in the United States* (1912).[39] Problems of finance during the First World War heightened interest in the subject.

The first estimate of national income within the government was done by Adolph C. Miller, an economist serving on the Board of Governors of the Federal Reserve in 1917. Anticipating British and U. S. calculations in World War II, he sought to estimate the surplus (above minimum consumption and capital maintenance) available for the conduct of the war.[40] Miller's proposed method did not take hold, however, until issues of welfare asserted themselves in the wake of the Armistice.

The issue of national income estimates was brought to a head in a manner reflecting three abiding aspects of the American operating style at its most effective: an important role for individuals who take on themselves the responsibility for trying to solve a large problem; the building of a wide-based communal consensus; the creation, on the basis of that consensus, of an institutional mechanism to carry forward on a regular basis.

The process was instigated by two men: Malcolm Rorty and Nahum Stone, respectively a business statistician and a labor arbitrator. These characters, of modest hierarchical stature, felt something should be done to clarify the facts "on controversial economic issues of great public interest," starting with the issue of income distribution.[41] They had in mind, in particular, the controversial 1916 estimate of Scott Nearing—a socialist—that U. S. national income was divided 50–50 between what Nearing defined as "property" and "service" income. Although one of the two protagonists was associated with business, the other with labor arbitration—and they had differed on other occasions—they were both sceptical of Nearing's calculations. One, (Rorty) assumed the role of innovator; the outcome was the creation of an institution: The National Bureau of Economic Research (NBER). It was envisaged from the beginning and, in fact, organized as a communal venture. It was to have embraced "well-known economists representing every school of economic thought from extreme conservative to extreme radical who should associate with them representatives of all the important organized interests in the country: Financial, industrial, agricultural, labor, etc;"[42] but in fact the extremes got lopped off. Note 11 provides some of the details of this process of institutional invention and innovation climaxed by the launching of the NBER in 1920 with the estimation of national income and its distribution already determined to be its first task, the analysis of business cycles to follow (following, pp. 286–294). The brief but intense phase of U. S. war mobilization in 1917–1918 had widened the community of economists with experience of public policy and strengthened the consensus that an institution like the NBER was desirable.

Within 2 years a two-volume study of national income and its distribution was completed.[43] Willford I. King was primarily responsible for the national income estimates by sources of production; Oswald Knauth, for estimates by incomes received; Frederick Macaulay, for estimates of personal income distribution. The short summary volume is firmly integrated and clearly bears the mark of the editor and NBER research director, Wesley C. Mitchell. Before publication, the directors of the NBER, representing a wide range of academic and other perspectives, but chosen also for their "judicious temperaments," had reviewed the study for possible bias and judged it, unanimously, "fair and unbiased and reasonably close to the truth." Altogether the study (and the NBER) closely approximated the shared vision of Messrs. Stone and Rorty (both on the board of directors) when they had thought the whole thing up.

The project was financed mainly by two philanthropic private foundations with additional modest contributions from individuals and business firms. The high-minded spirit of the enterprise was well symbolized by the fact that office space was donated by a theological seminary. It is not difficult to understand the acerbic tone of Colin Clark's 1937 comment comparing his hard-pressed situation to that of his American and German brethren:[44]

> . . . I have had to do the entire work of investigation and calculation for this book with the exception of such clerical assistance as I paid for out of my own pocket. The more detailed investigations, which are needed to bring our knowledge of this subject to the extent and precision to which it has been brought in America and Germany, cannot be made by individual investigators. If the saying is true, that economics is eventually capable of benefiting the human race as much as the other sciences put together, it must be equipped not only with the scientific spirit, but also with the financial resources, of the older sciences.

Work on national income estimates continued at the NBER as it moved simultaneously to come to grips with systematic analysis of business cycles. Four further national income studies were published, climaxed in 1930 by King's review of the 1921–1922 volumes based on the cumulative results of continuing research, *The National Income and Its Purchasing Power*. Its special feature was the inclusion of a detailed analysis of corporate dividends paid to stockholders in relation to profits earned. The National Industrial Conference Board (NICB) entered the field in 1927 with a method for keeping national income estimates—usually available only after considerable delay—reasonably current. The estimates were moved forward from a base year in accordance with changes in six readily accessible indexes reflecting the gross value of output.

In the life of the NBER and, indeed, in the history of economic thought and doctrine, 1930 was a significant year. It was then that Wesley Mitchell asked Simon Kuznets to take over the work on national income. As Solomon Fabricant notes, it was a decision Kuznets made with "some hesitation,"[45] for it took him away from one approach to economic analysis and committed him, for the rest of his professional life, to another.

In 1930, Kuznets, a student of Mitchell's, had published his *Secular Movements in Production and Prices, Their Nature and Their Bearing upon Cyclical Fluctuations,* a study begun 5 years earlier, completed in 1927, recommended for publication the next year by the Hart, Schaffner, and Marx Committee.[46] Like Colin Clark, Kuznets, born in 1901, fulfills the Confucius–Bagehot–Keynes insight about when one is likely to formulate one's most creative ideas and guiding Schumpeterian "vision." *Secular Movements* is one of the few studies almost wholly directed to the process of economic growth published between 1870 and 1939. It recognized three factors as the key dynamic "pushing" forces in growth: the growth of population; changes in demand; and technical changes, including both mechanical or engineering progress, and improvements in business organization.[47] Technical change was judged the most important of the three variables. Its patterns and consequences for growth and cyclical fluctuations in individual sectors of the economy is the subject of the book; although Kuznets's "Concluding Notes," and a few other passages contain a vision of the link between his initial sectoral findings and the process of economic growth as a whole. Kuznets clearly understood that a high degree of disaggregation was necessary to study technical change. And his *Secular Movements* is examined later as one of the major works of this period bearing on technology (following, pp. 242–246). For the moment the simple point to be made is that in moving as Mitchell requested to the field of national income analysis, Kuznets shifted to estimation in an inevitably more highly aggregated world. In that world, in which he was a second generation figure succeeding King's pioneering work, he became the acknowledged intellectual leader in the further development of national income estimates in the United States, and, after the Second World War, the leader in a great international effort to generate and use such data for the analysis of economic growth. But he was never able to link the important sectoral insights concerning technological change in *Secular Movements* to his later highly aggregated national income growth analysis—a grave matter for an analyst who understood the central role of innovation in the process of growth.[48]

Nevertheless, with Kuznets in command at the NBER, national income analysis prospered in the United States. On June 8, 1932, a not trivial if not quite earth-shaking event occurred in American political history—Senator Robert La Follette of Wisconsin introduced the following resolution:[49]

> Resolved, that the Secretary of Commerce is requested to report to the Senate of the United States on or before December 15, 1933, estimates of the total national income of the United States for each of the calendar years 1929, 1930, and 1931, including estimates of the portions of the national income originating from agriculture, manufacturing, mining, transportation, and other gainful industries and occupations, and estimates of the distribution of the national income in the form of wages, rents, royalties, dividends, profits, and other types of payments. These estimates shall be prepared by the Bureau of Foreign and Domestic commerce, and the bureau shall use available official and unofficial statistics and such relevant data as may be in the possession of the various departments, bureaus, and independent establishments of the Federal Government.

> Mr. LA FOLLETTE. . . . "May I say, Mr. President, that for a number of years there has been no study of the very important question of national income, its distribution, and its sources. The only available data on this

question have been furnished by unofficial agencies, particularly the Bureau of National Economic Research. That bureau has, however, not made any study since the years prior to 1929.

In the consideration of legislation in the future, I believe that the data to be compiled under the authorization of the resolution introduced by me will be of very great importance in helping Congress to determine policies relating to fiscal affairs of the Government, as well as to other legislation which is economic in character.

A vote was delayed to permit consultation with the Department of Commerce; but on June 13 the link between the federal government and national income analysis was forged without dissent. The Department of Commerce turned to Kuznets for help in designing the unit responsible for making the new official estimates on a regular basis.[50]

Behind Senator La Follette's initiative lay not only an awareness of the work going forward on national income at the NBER but also the convergence of two groups within the government also actively interested in the development of improved statistics on purchasing power as well as national income. One group was centered in the Research Division of the Bureau of Foreign and Domestic Commerce, in the Department of Commerce, and included at the time Willard L. Thorp and J. Frederick Dewhurst. The other group was directly associated with Senator LaFollette and included Isador Lubin and Paul Webbink. These two groups made common cause and were, proximately, the lobbyists behind the Senate resolution. But Carol Carson is no doubt correct in underlining the retrospective judgment of several of the participants in this initiative:[51]

> . . . [A]ny one person's role in initiating the official work on national income should not be exaggerated. Such a step was in the air, for it was a convenient and logical method of broadening our knowledge of the national economy, considering the crisis situation existing at that time and the almost complete lack of reliable data upon which to make major policy decisions regarding what the government could and should to do improve the economic outlook.

Having helped the National Income Section in the Department of Commerce come to life with its initial response to the La Follette Resolution,[52] Kuznets was able to see it turned over, in time, to one of his students and friends, Robert R. Nathan, who directed it down to December 1940 when he joined the Defense Advisory Commission.[53]

Before getting caught up in the Second World War, Kuznets, back at the NBER, completed three major national income studies: *National Income and Capital Formation* (1938); *Commodity Flow and Capital Formation* (1938); and *National Income* (1941). Kuznets's work in capital formation incorporated the highly original studies of capital consumption of Solomon Fabricant, at the NBER from 1930, presented in detail in his *Capital Consumption and Adjustment* (1938). From the perspective of this portion of our analysis these studies have a special importance: they focused sharply, as NBER Director David Friday had counseled in 1933, on ''The division of income as between these two categories of capital formation and consumption'' with the explicit purpose of providing the data which would permit a damping of the extreme amplitude of fluctuations in capital formation.[54] Friday was an economist of imagination and substance as well as a major figure in the Social Science Research Council and an NBER director.

These pre-war years also saw the bringing together of economists working this terrain in the NBER, universities, and government—through the creation of the Conference on Research in National Income and Wealth. The meetings held yielded several volumes of studies in income and wealth in which unsolved problems were identified, solutions explored and debated. Kuznets was clearly the leader in this enterprise.

In the period 1942–1944 Kuznets brought his now-matured expertise to the War Production Board, where he served as Associate Director of the Bureau of Planning and Statistics, a function reflected in his *National Product in Wartime* (1945).

Kuznets and Nathan were closely involved, on the same side, in a sharp bureaucratic conflict of some general historical interest but particularly relevant here because it forced—unfortunately for a transient interval—the linking of national income to sectoral analysis. The conflict appears in the literature as "The Feasibility Dispute."[55]

Briefly, the story appears to have unfolded as follows:

- In mid-1941, with the likelihood of full U. S. involvement in the war increasingly accepted in Washington, The Supply, Priorities, and Allocation Board (SPAB) was directed to formulate a Victory Program on the basis of requirements submitted by the military departments and other agencies. The existence of the enterprise represented the triumph of the group in Washington that, against considerable resistance, had advocated a maximum U. S. military production effort in 1940–1941. That included the redoubtable Frenchman Jean Monnet, a member of the British Supply Mission, who lobbied at both ends of the communications lines between the White House and 10 Downing Street.
- The Victory Program was directed by Robert Nathan, then chief planner for SPAB. It contained requirements for planes, tanks, ships, etc., in terms of aggregate expenditures, ($150 billion by September 1943), as well as in terms of steel, copper, aluminum, etc. The exercise was completed in December 1941 and became Roosevelt's production response to Pearl Harbor and the German declaration of war on the United States.
- Once war was on, the military departments began to request (and Congress to acquiesce in) radically expanded production programs. Nathan and his colleagues (now the Planning Committee of the War Production Board) judged that these uncoordinated, enlarged programs might not all prove feasible and, if attempted simultaneously, could produce considerable confusion and inefficiency. They therefore undertook a preliminary feasibility study, completed in March 1942, which indicated the likelihood that the programs would not prove compatible in the time period planned. Kuznets was brought in, and he played an important part in this study. In May, again with Kuznets's active participation, a 4-month study was launched that examined the feasibility of production plans in terms of national income aggregates, raw materials, industrial equipment, and labor supply. Again, the need to stretch the program out over a longer time period than was originally envisaged was demonstrated.
- Bureaucratic conflict arose when the Army's Chief of Services and Supplies, General Brehon B. Somervell, urged that the Planning Committee's initial feasibility report be suppressed and that the civilian busybodies get out of his way. Somervell lost this battle but, apparently, never quite forgave his adversaries.

The exercise reflects not only the important analytic role of national income accounting as a tool for war production planning but also the manner in which that kind of planning forced a bringing together of macro- and sectoral analysis that, in the United States, at least—but not immediate postwar France—were subsequently permitted to go their separate ways.

Kuznets's major published work down to the end of the Second World War was focused sharply on the elaboration and refinement of national income estimates for the United States. But one of his most impressive pieces of work—still something of a classic— written early in his research on national income, foreshadows his later concern with national income estimates on an international basis: the essay on "National Income" in Volume Eleven of the *Encyclopedia of the Social Sciences* (1933).[56] It explores the problems, difficulties, and choices inevitably confronted in national income estimates including philosophical, theoretical, and institutional problems. It also includes a table arraying pre- and post-World War I total per-capita real income estimates for fifteen countries as well as the most complete international bibliography of national income estimates of that time.[57]

It would be satisfying to be able to record that the refinement of national income estimates from 1930 forward and then their incorporation after 1932 in the routine work of the Department of Commerce had a significant and constructive impact on United States economic policy in the prewar decade. But, useful as these developments were and proved to be over the long run, they do not appear to have had substantial consequences for policy in the 1930s. It is almost certainly true, as in Great Britain, that national income estimates played their first substantial policy role in providing a coherent framework for problems of the war economy.

The buildup of national income estimates between 1870 and 1941, in the United States as in Great Britain, clearly took place, then, as a by-product of concerns with urgent problems other than long-run economic growth; notably, income distribution, welfare, unemployment, and, finally, the economic conduct of a great war. Nevertheless, the process generated data indispensable for the long-run analysis of growth, as national income series were, with increasing difficulty, pushed backward into the historical past. Above all, it became possible to estimate the level of gross and net investment, its relation to gross and net national product, and its changing components.

As both Colin Clark and Kuznets were aware, growth analysis required a great deal more than analysis of the investment rate. It was necessary to understand what was happening to technology and to productivity, which did not relate in a simple, straightforward way to the current level of investment. A good deal of work on technology and productivity was done between 1870 and 1939, including the mobilization of more or less relevant statistical data. After some reflection, I have decided the statistical materials generated by analyses that embraced technological change should be treated along with those analyses, to which we now turn.

9

Investment and Technology, Part Two: Growth Theory

With certain partial exceptions (e.g., Colin Clark, W. G. Hoffmann, Kuznets, and Schumpeter), contributions to growth analysis, like early national income estimates, are by-products—sometimes unintended by-products—of interest in other problems. With the diffusion and professionalization of economics, the stage gets progressively more crowded. There is a danger of losing the thread of analysis in a catalog of worthy names and cryptic references. Moreover, in terms of the basic growth variables, a good many contributions overlap. Kuznets's *Secular Movements* and Schumpeter's *Business Cycles*, for example, deal with both technology in the process of growth and cyclical fluctuations in output and prices. Some of the studies of the transfer problem (e.g., those of John Williams, Jacob Viner, and Alexander Cairncross) involve the dynamics of growth in both capital-exporting, advanced industrial countries and in capital-importing, developing countries. I have, therefore, made arbitrary decisions on where to comment on particular economists. For example, I shall have something to say about studies of the transfer problem in this section, but I have allocated Hoffmann's *The Growth of Industrial Economies* and Colin Clark's *Condition of Economic Progress* to the section on the stages of and limits to growth. That section also contains references to the 1930s literature on secular stagnation, even though it might well have been treated along with other analyses of technology and growth.

Aside from these arbitrary allocations I have resolved the by-product problem by grouping the contributors to growth analysis of this period around certain major issues that did not dominate but significantly affected the focus of their work; and resolved the second problem—the over-crowded stage—by concentrating attention on one or two major figures and making no pretense to a full "review of the troops." We proceed, therefore, with six subsections and their key figures, as follows:

A. Defending the legitimacy of interest: Böhm-Bawerk.
B. The interest rate and price trends: Fisher and Wicksell.
C. The transfer problem: Williams and Cairncross.
D. Technology and growth: Kuznets and Schumpeter.

E. Two unorthodox views: Adams and Veblen.
F. Formal growth models: Bickerdike and Harrod.

Defending the Legitimacy of Interest: Böhm-Bawerk

The Austrian School commands a respectable and substantial place in conventional histories of economic doctrine mainly but not exclusively as one of the concurrently emerging centers of marginal analysis. The School embraces not only Wieser, Böhm-Bawerk, Mises, and Hayek but leaves its mark in Sweden via Wicksell and Cassel, Britain via Wicksteed, Robbins, and the London School of Economics, and across the Atlantic via Frank Taussig and Irving Fisher, whose *Theory of Interest* is dedicated to John Rae (preceding, p. 104) as well as to Böhm-Bawerk.

In his *Capital and Interest,* Böhm-Bawerk reviewed exhaustively the debates about interest that run from the time of Aristotle through the attack on usury by the medieval church to the controversies of the late nineteenth century stirred up by Marx's surplus-value and other socialist assertions that interest was the immoral product of the raw exploitation of labor.[1] His own theory of interest is briefly outlined in this volume and fully elaborated in his *The Positive Theory of Capital.*[2] In the present perspective only one of his three famous determinants of interest is relevant: his "third reason."

Like Marshall, Böhm-Bawerk focused sharply on the question of time as it related to the phenomenon of interest. In Marshall, interest was the reward for waiting. In Böhm-Bawerk there were three time-related factors: two stemmed from human psychology, one was linked to productivity. Psychologically, human beings place a premium on present over future goods because, in Schumpeter's terse but authoritative paraphrase, "the possession of present goods permits provision both for alternative present as well as future wants."[3] With respect to productivity, interest exists in Böhm-Bawerk's formulation "because 'time-consuming' roundabout production is more efficient, that is, a given quantity of original means of production yields a larger physical product when applied first to the production of intermediate products (e.g., tools) and then to the production of consumer's goods, than when they are applied entirely to the direct production of consumers' goods."[4] As critics were quick to note, this proved a somewhat unsatisfactory way to deal with the productivity of investment since, in fact, all technical improvements do not require greater roundaboutness. Moreover, lumping together roundaboutness of different degrees into an aggregate average period of production for all forms of investment explained little about what, in fact, determined the productivity of investment. And there were a good many other objections to Böhm-Bawerk's "third reason."[5]

In Irving Fisher's hands, however Böhm-Bawerk's argument was powerfully and elegantly simplified. His *Theory of Interest* reduced Böhm-Bawerk's two psychological factors to "income impatience" and roundaboutness to "opportunity" or the rate of return over cost.[6] Fisher was thus a kind of parent to Keynes's marginal efficiency of capital, as Keynes acknowledged, just as Fisher acknowledged his debt to John Rae and Böhm-Bawerk. As for the latter's "average period of production," it emerges in a more manageable form in modern growth models as the capital-output ratio; although the latter also turns out to be a black box that obscures as much as it illuminates (following, p. 454).

Nevertheless, the effort to clarify the somewhat untidy inheritance of the classics on interest and to meet the socialist challenge led to clarification and some moderately useful tools of both short- and long-run analysis of the investment process.

The Interest Rate and Price Trends: Fisher and Wicksell

In Chapter 6 I noted that the secular price decline in the world economy from 1873 to the mid-1890s and its upward trend down to 1914 captured the attention of an impressive array of contemporary economists. Writing of the major analyses of the price decline from 1873 to 1896, I once divided the types of theory applied into the following categories:[7]

1. Those that argued directly from gold to the price level.
2. Those that took into account changes in $M'V'$, dealing explicitly with the monetary and banking system.
3. Those that looked explicitly to the interest rate as the lever by which price movements were achieved.
4. Those that explained movements in the general price level in terms of a supply–demand analysis of individual prices.
5. Finally, there were three efforts to combine the various strands into a consistent general explanation: those of Marshall, Wicksell, and Keynes in the *Treatise*.

We have already considered Marshall's interesting but indecisive grappling with this question (preceding, pp. 181–182). For our purposes here, Fisher's version of the first and third categories and Wicksell's somewhat more complex analysis of the third type will suggest how concern with this problem bore on (or failed to bear on) the analysis of growth. Keynes's view in the *Treatise on Money* adds little to the arguments of Fisher and Wicksell.[8] As a kind of coda to this section, I shall, however, report Keynes's retrospective view of the price decline, in the post-*General Theory* period.

Fisher's general proposition relating interest rates and the price level is summarized in his usual clear manner in *The Theory of Interest*.[9]

> We have found evidence general and specific, from correlating P' [the price level] with both bond yields and short-term interest rates, that price changes do, generally and perceptibly, affect the interest rate in the direction indicated by *a priori* theory [that is, they move in the same direction]. But since forethought is imperfect, the effects are smaller than the theory requires and lag behind price movements, in some periods, very greatly. When the effects of price changes upon interest rates are *distributed* over several years, we have found remarkably high co-efficients of correlation, thus indicating that interest rates follow price changes closely in degree, though rather distantly in time.
>
> The final result, partly due to foresight and partly to the lack of it, is that price changes do after several years and with the intermediation of changes in profits and business activity affect interest very profoundly. In fact, while the main object of this book is to show how the rate of interest would behave if the purchasing power of money were stable, there has never been any long period of time during which this condition has been even approximately fulfilled. When it is not fulfilled, the money rate of interest, and still more the real rate of interest, is more affected by the instability of money than by those

more fundamental and more normal causes connected with income impatience, and opportunity, to which this book is chiefly devoted.

As Fisher was aware, his conclusion that price changes affect interest rates with a lag ran counter to the view of Wicksell and others that interest rates influenced price movements. But when Fisher came to deal directly with the price decline from 1873 to 1896, his argument was not in terms of a lag of a falling rate of interest behind a still more rapidly falling "natural" rate but in these rather conventional quantity theory terms.[10]

> Between 1873 and 1896 prices fell. This fall was presumably due to the slackening in the production of gold; to the adoption of the gold standard by nations previously on a silver basis, and the consequent withdrawal of gold by these new users from the old, to the arrest of the expansion of silver money consequent on the closure of the mints to silver; to the slackening in the growth of banking; and to the ever-present growth of trade. . . . It is not that the left-hand side of the equation did not increase, but that it did not increase so fast as trade. . . . It will be seen that the history of prices has in substance been the history of a race between the increase in the media of exchange (M and M') and the increase in trade (T), while (we assume) the velocities of circulation were changing in a much less degree.

In both the *Purchasing Power of Money* and the *Theory of Interest* Fisher explored the relation between the interest rate and price movements; yet, in a so-called statistical verification, he finds a correlation between gold stocks and price-level movements a sufficient test.[11] There is no investigation of capital market conditions calculated to reveal whether, in fact, the money rate was lagging behind the "real" rate of interest. As for production and employment, Fisher, like monetarists down to and including Milton Friedman—and in the spirit of the Ricardian vice—makes a powerful and somewhat evasive simplifying assumption:[12] "Knowing little of the variations in the development of trade, we may tentatively assume a steady growth, and pay chief attention to the variations of circulating media." The fact is that steady growth rates have not been a characteristic of modern economies; and to assume they were yields inaccurate assessments of the determinants of price movements.

But there is a quite different—almost Schumpeterian—dimension to Fisher that flows from his concept of Opportunity. In his *Theory of Interest* he explores in the spirit of John Rae the relation between interest rates and discovery and invention.[13] His central argument is that the emergence of a major innovation (in the broad Schumpeterian sense) has the initial effect of raising the rate of interest, but in the longer run, as the innovation matures, its particular impact on the rate of interest is to lower it. An extended discussion of the growing institutionalization of the invention-innovation process, focused on the United States in the 1920s, follows. In concluding and summarizing his analysis of fluctuations of Opportunity (the rate of return over cost) Fisher writes:[14]

> . . . [T]he invention of the automobile, and the inventions and discoveries in electricity and chemistry have succeeded the railroads as a field for investment and have required new sacrifices of immediate income for the sake of future income. Thus, as fast as the first effect of any one invention, tending to raise interest, wears off and is succeeded by its secondary effect in lowering

interest, this secondary effect is likely to be offset by the oncoming of new inventions.

In his firm grasp on the real forces at work on the rate of interest (and on the capital markets as a whole) Fisher stands unique among those often classed as monetarists; but he never united his real and monetary perspectives on the economy as fully, say, as D. H. Robertson. Fisher came closest in the 1930 version of his analysis of the determinants of the interest rate.

Wicksell's argument is interesting because he reverses the quantity theory explanation for price movements, attributes them to lags between the "natural" and money rates of interest, and, somewhat like Malthus in his debate with Ricardo on the post-1815 decline in British prices (preceding, pp. 60–61), views the supply of money primarily as reflecting price changes rather than causing them, without wholly ruling out a role for independent monetary factors. His key theoretical passage is worth quotation:[15]

> . . . [T]he explanation suggested by the Quantity Theory—that rising prices are due to an excess of money, falling prices to a scarcity—does not accord with actually observed movements of the rate of interest. If it were correct, we should expect that at a time of rising prices there would be a temporary reduction in the rate of interest, at a time of falling prices a temporary increase; and that when prices had become accommodated to the change in the stocks of precious metal, the rate of interest would once again return to its normal position. Observation teaches us, however, that when prices are rising there is a continual *rise* in rates of interest, and that when prices are falling there is a continual *fall* in rates of interest.
>
> All these difficulties and complications at once disappear when it is changes, brought about by independent factors, in the *natural rate of interest on capital* that are regarded as the essential cause of such movements. These changes can be regarded as the cause, not only of the movement of prices, but indirectly of the analogous but somewhat later alteration, in the money rate of interest. Abundance or scarcity of money, and in particular the quantity of cash held by the banks, is now imbued with a merely secondary importance. Such factors are to be regarded as consequences of changes in the demand for instruments of exchange brought about by changes in the level of prices. It still remains true, however, that they *may* take their origin in independent causes (the production of precious metals, issue of paper money, development of the credit system, etc.), and that they then have an independent significance in regard to movements of prices, in so far as they accelerate or retard the movement of the money rate of interest to the new position of the natural rate (they may even cause the money rate to move in the opposite direction to the natural rate).

Wicksell applies this theory to the movement of British prices over the century starting in the 1790s in a chapter entitled "Actual Price Movements in the Light of Preceding Theory."[16] His conclusion on the price decline from the early 1870s to the mid-1890s centered on a fall in the natural rate of interest, as the railway age waned, real wages rose, and a surge in savings confronted "a considerable lack of really profitable openings" for investment.[17] He then argues that, although the interest rate fell, it didn't fall far enough due to increased monetary demand for gold and a decelerating supply. At this point, he brings himself up short by noting that the gold shortage could not have been important because the banks had large idle reserves. This statement does center attention on the changed direction of investment. It is developed, moreover, in a set of unified terms, but fails to indicate that the type of investment "increasing real capital, serving to raise real wages," would, in itself, lower prices whether a lag in the money rate of interest behind the real rate caused a chronic deflation of demand or not. Unless Wicksell contemplated two separate pressures downward on prices—one from the side of supply ("increasing real capital, lowering costs and prices, raising real wages"), the other from the side of demand ("a lagging money rate of interest")—there is a real conflict here.

It should be underlined that Wicksell's central concern was not growth but an alternative to the Quantity Theory of Money. He sympathized with Tooke's criticism of the monetarists but felt that Tooke had not supplied a fully unified and coherent theoretical alternative.[18] Wicksell's alternative coming to rest on the relation between the natural and money rates of interest was used by him to suggest policies to achieve the objective that then concerned him: a stable price level.[19]

Wicksell presented his theory as a tentative and somewhat uncertain hypothesis. It soon became the object of acute criticism and modification including (or especially) criticisms by his respected friend, David Davidson, and his most devoted disciples: Eric Lindahl, Gunnar Myrdal, and Bertil Ohlin. But there has rarely been a more fruitful formulation. It led on directly to the anticipation in Sweden of much of Keynes's analysis in *The General Theory;* and Wicksell's concept of the progressive, cumulative processes set in motion by natural interest rates above and below the money rate were brought to bear in Myrdal's *Monetary Equilibrium* not on the objective of a stable price level but "the mitigation of business fluctuations" which Myrdal regarded as "the main objective."[20] Even more remarkable, a direct line can be traced from Wicksell's cumulative processes to one of the major tools of analysis in Myrdal's study of the race problem in the United States, *An American Dilemma.*[21]

In the present perspective it was Wicksell's awareness of the technological and other forces determining the productivity of investment and the demand for capital in the century he analyzed that made him a contributor to growth analysis when he was mainly focused on the problem of the determinants of price trends. But his basic insight—that the source of price and monetary movements was to be sought on the right hand (output) rather than the left hand (money supply) side of the Quantity Equation—rendered him a growth analyst despite himself.

Now a brief note on Keynes's view of this problem after he abandoned *The Treatise on Money* and had written *The General Theory,* for it relates a bit to Wicksell's natural rate of interest, Fisher's rate of return over cost, as well as to the concept of secular stagnation to which we shall return (following, pp. 321–325). This is what Keynes wrote in 1940.[22]

> Reading about my own opinions as set forth in the Treatise does indeed feel like an historical exercise! One of the many elements which I entirely omitted then and certainly should stress now is the greatly increased volume of investment required to produce full employment, as the years went by after 1870, owing to the great growth in wealth. The opportunities for profitable investment have not merely to keep pace with what they had been formerly, but to increase far beyond that, if they are to match a greatly increased volume of savings, corresponding to full employment in a much richer community.

In my view, Keynes still had it wrong. He persisted, as in the *Treatise,* in looking for an explanation of the trend decline in prices after 1873 primarily to the demand rather than the supply side—a mistake Marshall did not make.

The Transfer Problem: Williams and Cairncross

The manner in which work on a quite different problem generated insights for growth analysis is rather vividly illustrated by historical studies of capital exports conducted during the interwar years. The issue arose, in fact, before the First World War in the context of the unfavorable trend movement in the British terms of trade. We shall consider analyses of such trend movements in Chapter 13 (Relative Prices). Here we are concerned with a related but distinct problem: how it came about that analyses of the capital transfer problem became part of the literature of economic growth.

The convergence of two distinct experiences account for the surge of interest in the transfer problem after the First World War. First, was the intense debate over the German capacity to pay reparations heightened by the publication of Keynes's *Economic Consequences of the Peace* in 1919. Central to his argument was a proposition, derived from classical foreign trade theory; i.e., that the effort to pay reparations—in effect large capital exports—would turn the terms of trade against Germany and still further impoverish the country. Keynes's anxiety was reinforced by his concern with a long period factor rooted in the classical theory of production but not embraced in conventional foreign trade theory; namely, that diminishing returns had been operating on the relative prices of the food and raw materials industrial Europe imported in the period from the mid-1890s to 1914.[23] Keynes assumed that this trend would continue to operate on the European terms of trade after the war, and that the transfer problem involved in the payment of war debts to the United States would put a dangerous strain on all of western Europe, not merely Germany. Second, some analysts of the reparations transfer problem were conscious that the extraordinary pre-1914 flows of capital to Argentina, Canada, and Australia, as well as the experience of French reparations payments after the Franco-Prussian war provided an opportunity to establish the relevance of the classical analysis of the transfer problem.

It is, indeed, something of a paradox that the testing of that analysis should have contributed to growth analysis; for as John H. Williams once vividly pointed out, trade theory was formulated under assumptions that quite literally, excluded the process of growth.[24]

> . . . [T]he English classical theory of international trade. . . has always rested mainly upon the distinction made by Ricardo between external and internal mobility of economic factors. It abstracts too, for simplicity's sake, from cost of transport. Less obviously, perhaps, it assumes for each trading country fixed quantums of productive factors, already existent and employed, and asks how, subject to the assumptions, these may be most effectively applied under conditions of international trade.
>
> . . . The classical theory assumes as fixed, for purposes of reasoning, the very things which, in my view, should be the chief objects of study if what we wish to know is the effects and causes of international trade, so broadly regarded that nothing of importance in the facts shall fail to find its place in the analysis.

It is the writer's [Williams] view:

1. that the premises are inaccurate in sufficient degree to raise serious question of the soundness of the theory, or at least of the range of its useful application to the trade of the world;
2. that the relation of international trade to the development of new resources and productive forces is a more significant part of the explanation of the present status of nations, of incomes, prices, well-being, than is the cross-section value analysis of the classical economists, with its assumption of given quantums of productive factors, already existent and employed;
3. that the international movement of productive factors has significance relative to comparative prices, incomes, positions of nations, at least equal to that of the trade in goods . . . .
4. that international trade in goods, cost of transport, and mobility of economic factors—externally and internally—continually react upon each other; and by investigating these interactions—in this actual, growing, changing world—we may hope to throw light upon the causes and effects of international economic contacts, upon market and productive organisation, upon prices and price processes, upon incomes and general well-being, and finally upon the wisdom or unwisdom of international commercial, financial and labour policies.

In short, Williams came to believe the transfer problem should be studied in the context of economic growth, with all the Marshallian long period factors in play. He earned his right to this judgment the hard way. His was one of the historical studies, mainly fostered by Frank Taussig, in an admirable effort to subject the classical theory of the transfer process to empirical test. Note 25 lists the major such studies published before 1939.[25]

Under Taussig's inspiration, Williams undertook to test the doctrine of classic international trade theory under a depreciated paper money standard; that is, with gold abandoned and driven from circulation. Williams posed his problem lucidly in terms David Hume, in effect, pioneered (preceding, p. 30):[26]

Summed up baldly, the bases of the usual statement of the theory of international trade and foreign exchange are as follows:

1. The trading countries are on a gold basis.
2. Through the mechanism of the specie points, gold flows freely between the trading countries.
3. When gold flows out of a country the level of prices within that country falls, and in consequence exports increase and imports diminish: and conversely, when gold flows in, the price level rises, so that imports are encouraged, and exports discouraged.

Given this mechanism, a comparatively slight disturbance of the balance of international payments, as for example an increase in borrowings, will set the machinery in motion and effect a change in the merchandise imports and exports. A disturbance sufficiently marked would result in an overturn of the trade balance.

But how explain such an overturn without the mechanism?

Argentina from 1880 to 1900 was an admirable laboratory in which to seek an answer because it was on a depreciated paper standard for most of the period; and it suffered a dramatic "overturn of the trade balance" in the wake of the Baring crisis of 1890.

The result of Williams's enquiry was a sophisticated analysis of Argentina during the first of the two great turning points in its economic history—the second being its surge into the first phase of serious industrialization in the form of its import substitution drive of the 1930s. As Williams says, as of 1930:[27] "The decade from 1880 to 1890 is the great 'boom' period of Argentine economic history. It is not too much to say that in those ten years Argentina underwent a greater economic development than in all the preceding decades of the century." The boom was based on capital imports on a scale relative to the size of the importing country rarely seen in economic history, permitting rising imports despite rising interest payments. Then comes the great Baring crisis of 1890–1891 and a period of painful readjustment down to the mid-1890s as capital imports cease, goods imports collapse, exports hold up but in an environment of falling world prices. Finally, there is, from 1894, a surge of production and the volume of exports, soon reinforced by rising world prices for Argentine exports; the trade surplus permits imports to expand despite interest payments that exceed foreign borrowings; a conversion law is passed in 1899 ending the gold premium; capital imports revive; and Argentina is launched on its great pre-1914 boom.

All this is quite clear in Williams's account, although the distortion imposed by his narrowly defined task forces him to put one of his most important pieces of analysis in an extended footnote.[28] Williams put the conclusions of this thesis in narrow unrevolutionary terms although the bases for his later apostasy are clear.[29]

> Since the exports are of an agricultural character, they are subject, as we have seen, to the uncontrollable vagaries of nature. Natural irregularities occur which are in no wise connected with domestic monetary and price conditions, but which interfere profoundly with any set of forces which are dependent on conditions of money and prices. On the other hand, the imports, being manufactured goods and drawn from a variety of foreign sources, are relatively unaffected by fluctuating natural conditions. Again, since the exports form only a minor part of the world's supply. . . fluctuations in the world price. . . affect the total value of exports far more deeply than does the effect of a fluctuating gold premium upon domestic paper prices. . . .
>
> In other words, it would seem probable that as regards agricultural countries "other things" are more apt to remain "equal" in the case of imports than in the case of exports.

One can not easily deduce the strong general attack on classical foreign trade theory in Williams's 1929 article cited in note 24 from the conclusions of his study of Argentina, except for his arraying of multiple forces that act on the export prices of agricultural countries and the unlikelihood that "other things" will remain "equal."

What struck Williams as he looked back at his study—and what led, one suspects, to his 1929 broadside—is what also strikes the modern reader; that is, the most interesting passages in the book have nothing directly to do with foreign trade theory. They explain why the boom of the 1880s happened; why forces in London as well as Argentina generated the extraordinary flow of capital; why the flow could not be sustained, Baring collapsed and had to be rescued by a consortium organized by the Bank of England; how the investments of the 1880s—in large part railways—plus a massive flow of immigrants generated, with a painful time lag, the output and exports that carried Argentina forward triumphantly from the mid-1890s to 1914. Williams remains loyal to the outline he set himself in conducting a laboratory test of the theory of international trade; i.e., the interrelations of depreciated paper money, foreign borrowings, and foreign trade. But in accounting for the dynamics of these three variables and how they interacted, he wrote a still-relevant tract on a fast-moving passage in a nation's development and the role of capital imports in that development. In the end it is not difficult to understand his later conclusion (preceding, p. 229):[30] "The classical theory assumes as fixed, for purposes of reasoning the very things which, in my view, should be the chief objects of study. . . .''

Across the Atlantic, in the other Cambridge, much the same impulses we have just examined appear to have led Alexander Cairncross to address himself in the 1930s to his studies in capital accumulation, later published as *Home and Foreign Investment, 1870–1913:*[31]

> . . . [T]he origin was an undergraduate thesis on "Capital Transfer and the Terms of Trade." Reared on Keynes and Taussig, I thought that I detected both of the masters in confusion in their treatment of reparations and its consequences and was moved by so unaccustomed a spectacle to develop my own ideas on the subject. My interest in foreign investment and the dynamics of international trade gradually widened and eventually focused on two relationships: between foreign investment and home investment on the one hand, and between the migration of capital and of labour on the other.

In a sense Cairncross was more fortunate than Taussig's pupils at Harvard. The latter were led to begin their research by testing the classical theory of the transfer problem. And that is where Cairncross also began in his undergraduate thesis; notably, because he developed the tentative judgment that capital movements responded to shifts in the terms of trade rather than causing them. But it is clear he felt himself to be on looser rein; and as his Preface indicates he had the benefit and advice of scholars with interests that ranged far beyond the classical theory of international trade; for example, Keynes and D. H. Robertson.

The upshot was that Cairncross did not feel constrained to spend his time and energy establishing precisely the extent to which classical trade theory was helpful, misleading, or wrong. He proceeded directly to a series of pioneering studies—which he regarded as a prolegomenon to later research—of the scale, character, and fluctuations of British investment in the period 1870–1914. Cairncross does touch on the behavior of the terms of trade during the capital transfer process; and he found the same lack of consistency as Taussig's pupils.[32] While his interest was not, initially, growth itself, his head-on approach to capital accumulation, nevertheless, led him to touch on many aspects of the process of growth in both advanced industrial and developing countries; for example:

- Investment and migration.[33]
- The institutional structure of the pre-1914 capital market,[34] and the changing sectoral composition of investment.[35]
- Cyclical fluctuations in British domestic and foreign investment.[36]
- Relative prices and the terms of trade from the perspective of capital exporter[37] and capital importer.[38]
- The dynamics of the Canadian takeoff.[39]

Evidently, we have here another example of a substantial oblique contribution to growth analysis.

In addition, Cairncross in a thoughtful penultimate chapter reflects on the question: Did foreign investment pay?[40] Like Hobson, Cairncross concludes, on balance, that it did up to 1914: by stimulating the export industries; generating and spreading information on profitable outlets for further British investment; cheapening food imports and thereby raising real wages. Cairncross's cost-benefit assessment of capital exports after World War I was distinctly less sanguine.

It should be recalled that these essays were a preliminary exploration by a young scholar of ground he might later cultivate systematically. Cairncross did not attempt to integrate his findings into a general theory of investment and growth in an international economy subject to cyclical fluctuations. But his willingness to question Taussig and Keynes on the transfer problem yielded a quite rich haul in terms of growth analysis.

Technology and Growth:
J. A. Schumpeter and the Early Simon Kuznets

Loring Allen closes his excellent biography of Joseph Schumpeter with the following summation:[41]

> He wore many garments in the course of his life, and as disparate as they were, all seemed somehow tailor-made. His 67 years saw him play countless, yet natural, roles—those of inspired student, enfant terrible, government minister, bank president and businessman, and above all, professor; pretender to aristocracy, true elitist, and gentleman of manners; public speaker, scholar, writer, and counsellor; art historian, horseman, and traveller; complainer, critic, and ebullient entertainer; historian, theoretician, and secret worshipper to a private God. All these roles intertwined to make a multi-faceted man of paradox. His life raises questions as to how a man can persevere in the face of repeated tragedy and disappointment; how a great romanticism can coexist with a deep commitment to science; how a man eaten up with grief, guilt, and inner torment can produce a life's work that overwhelms in sheer volume, erudition, and span of knowledge; and how a man who viewed himself as a failure could reach the pinnacle of his profession and still be haunted by the belief that it wasn't enough. A deep melancholy pervaded Schumpeter's life and character, self-doubt dogged his every turn, and his quest for knowledge left him frustrated and despairing.
>
> Yet he suffered silently so that he could do what he did best: teach. Committed to opening doors, he devoted himself to unlocking that "sacred decade" within others, always convinced that answers to the mysteries of how and why the world works as it does could be found, understood, and acted upon. Schumpeter's work is there for anyone to study, confirming his reputation as one of this century's great economists and social scientists. And his public life stands as an open testament to the rewards of seemingly boundless energy and deep conviction. His interior life, however, must remain in shadows, illuminated here and there, but ultimately so paradoxical that it con-

founds and confuses. This is, perhaps, the way Schumpeter would have wanted it.

This book deals only with the various dimensions of Schumpeter's work on economic growth. But even there one can not wholly escape the persistently paradoxical strands in his character and performance. Like all of us, but perhaps a little more so, Schumpeter confirmed Hume's dictum: ". . . [W]hat is man except a heap of contradictions".

From the perspective of growth analysis it is clear that one of the few major theoretical works published between 1870 and 1939 is the youthful Schumpeter's *The Theory of Economic Development* (1911). He reports that "some of the ideas submitted . . . go back as far as 1907; all of them had been worked out by 1909. . . ."[42] In the latter year Schumpeter became 26. Once again we are dealing with a classic case of a "vision" articulated in the "sacred decade";[43] for his subsequent work, excepting the *History of Economic Analysis,* is an elaboration of propositions rooted in *The Theory of Economic Development.*

As for originality, no addition to knowledge is wholly without antecedents. Indeed, in a rough parallel to Myrdal's later exposition of *Monetary Equilibrium* embedded within a Wicksellian framework, Schumpeter begins explicitly with Walras and Menger, Wieser and Böhm-Bawerk, notably the latter.[44] But these acknowledgments are somewhat illusory. In fact, he seized a nettle none of his predecessors and virtually none of his successors in mainstream economics was willing to grasp; namely, that the processes of invention and innovation were not always exogenous nor incremental; although clear that all innovations were undertaken because of their believed profitability, he was of two minds on the extent to which they were, strictly speaking, an endogenous response to "necessity."[45] In his own words, he asserted innovation was "spontaneous and discontinuous."

Schumpeter does not tell us what led him to make major discontinuous innovations generated by economic incentives the center of his system.[46] Perhaps he didn't know. But, objectively, we can identify three suggestive antecedents:

- Adam Smith's distinction between incremental inventions contrived by those who actually operated the machines and those created by "philosophers" that involved "new powers not formerly applied" (preceding, p. 41).
- Karl Marx's exposition of a circular flow and, then, a dynamic economic model at the opening of Volume II of *Capital* (preceding, p. 138).
- Alfred Marshall's explicit recognition—even dramatization—of the case of increasing returns, the severe theoretical problems it posed, and his effort to resolve them, a recognition Schumpeter respected while regarding Marshall's solution as unsatisfactory.

As an economist, Schumpeter's formal commitment and highest praise went to Léon Walras, mathematical expositor of static general equilibrium who separated his reformist zeal from his scientific effort. But, taking Schumpeter's work as a whole, I am inclined to feel, without firm evidence, that it was the challenge posed by Karl Marx's historical, theoretical, and polemical analysis of the dynamics of capitalism that most profoundly influenced Schumpeter.[47]

Schumpeter begins his exposition in *Economic Development* with a particular version of a static equilibrium Walrasian (or Marxian) system in a state of circular flow. He introduces (or accepts from Walras) a powerful simplifying assumption; namely, that "we shall primarily think of a commercially organized state, one in which private property, division of labor, and free competition prevail."[48] The acceptance of this assumption blocked off Schumpeter throughout his career from the analysis of the process of growth from underdeveloped beginnings, and thereby limited his range as a growth economist. Put another way, Schumpeter was a rather parochial economist of the advanced industrial world, above all, of post-takeoff Germany, Britain, and the United States. It was logical that his initial insight should lead him, in the end, to speculate on the probable fate of capitalism rather than on the emerging problems of growth and modernization in the developing world or, in the Hume–Smith tradition, on the relation between the more and less developed nations.

Schumpeter's circular flow system is, however, not quite as static as it might at first appear. It does not imply that "year after year 'the same things' happen."[49] It allows for incremental changes in technology that displace the equilibrium point of the system so marginally as to permit new equilibrium positions to be reached from the old "by infinitesimal steps" with which unimaginative managers (as opposed to heroic innovating entrepreneurs) can deal.[50] It also allows for changes in response to powerful exogenous events with economic implications; e.g., bad harvests, wars, revolutions.

Chapter II ("The Fundamental Phenomenon of Economic Development") focuses with great clarity—and a foreshadowing of chaos theory—on the one concept that distinguishes development from circular flow—the concept that remained the core of Schumpeter's subsequent work:[51]

> Development in our sense is a distinct phenomenon, entirely foreign to what may be observed in the circular flow or in the tendency toward equilibrium. It is spontaneous and discontinuous change in the channels of the flow, disturbance of equilibrium, which forever alters and displaces the equilibrium state previously existing. . . .
>
> This concept covers the following five cases: (1) the introduction of a new good—that is one with which consumers are not yet familiar—or of a new quality of a good. (2) The introduction of a new method of production, that is one not yet tested by experience in the branch of manufacture concerned, which need by no means be founded upon a discovery scientifically new, and can also exist in a new way of handling a commodity commercially. (3) The opening of a new market, that is a market into which the particular branch of manufacture of the country in question has not previously entered, whether or not this market has existed before. (4) The conquest of a new source of supply of raw materials or half-manufactured goods, again irrespective of whether this source already exists or whether it has first to be created. (5) The carrying out of the new organisation of any industry, like the creation of a monopoly position (for example through trustification) or the breaking up of a monopoly position.

Schumpeter was quite conscious that his assumption that the major economic changes of the capitalist epoch occurred in an irreversible revolutionary way rather than by continuous adaptation was theoretically explosive. He referred, for example, to Marshall's failure to overcome "the difficulties which surround the problem of increasing return."[52] But he proceeded forward courageously to explore the implications of his proposition that "spontaneous and discontinuous changes in the channel of the circular flow" were the heart of capitalist development.

The two broad implications Schumpeter derived from this exploration in his *Theory of Development* were these:

- Particularly creative individuals—entrepreneurs as opposed to managers—were required to respond effectively to the potentialities for profitable innovation generated within the system. In a remarkably sensitive human passage Schumpeter evokes the lonely creativity involved when an innovating entrepreneur, with imperfect information, steps off uncertainly into the dark to do something new:[53] "Carrying out a new plan and acting according to a customary one are things as different as making a road and walking along it."
- To finance the early stage of their creative endeavors, the entrepreneurs require that capitalists grant them credit. Since Schumpeter assumes full employment in his circular flow model, the granting of credit from capitalist to entrepreneurs is inherently inflationary, because innovation takes time.

Although Schumpeter's break away from his contemporaries in Vienna, Lausanne, Sweden, Britain, and the United States was serious and dramatic, he was still, in part of his being, a loyal product of the Austrian School. This fact is reflected not only in his respectful obeisance to Wieser, Menger, and Böhm-Bawerk but, more important, in the fact that he elaborated his breakthrough around three of the issues that obsessed that school, i.e., the nature of capital, profit, and interest on capital. Only a few of Schumpeter's major points in this portion of his exposition (Chapters III, IV, and V) need concern us here:

- Profit (as opposed to "Wages of Management" in the static circular flow system) is the excess of total receipts over total costs induced by innovation and its consequences for development throughout the system.[54]
- The consequences include a "clustering" of entrepreneurship around the new innovation once truly pioneering entrepreneurs demonstrate profit possibilities, as well as "creative destruction" of activities superseded and rendered unprofitable by the diffusing innovation.[55]
- Capital investment and the expansion of wealth derive mainly from the plowback of profits associated with innovation.[56]
- Schumpeter's theory of interest, which led to considerable controversy, is fairly complex in its full exposition, but essentially, like the rest of his argument, quite simple. It can be reduced to three propositions. First:[57] "Interest is a premium on present over future purchasing power." Second, certain forms of interest payment are unrelated to development and could exist "in the circular flow";[58] e.g., interest on consumptive loans, on distress loans, and loans to governments. Third, otherwise interest would not exist in the circular flow economy; but it exists throughout a dynamic, innovational economy because productive loans are "an offshoot" of profits on innovational ventures that have an impact "over the whole economic system."[59]

After a long and rather laborious elaboration of the third proposition, Schumpeter emerges with a demand–supply formulation that bears a family relation to both Fisher's intersection of a "rate of return over cost" demand curve and a savings supply curve and to Keynes's intersection of a liquidity preference demand curve and the supply of money decreed by the monetary authorities generating a rate of interest that confronts the marginal efficiency of capital demand curve to determine the level of investment.[60] The critical players in Schumpeter's capital market are the demanding entrepreneurs and the supplying capitalists.[61]

Schumpeter finally puts his system to work on the business cycle with a dictum that I regard as the most important proposition to be asserted in this field:[62] cycles are viewed as "the form economic development takes in the era of capitalism." Schumpeter does not claim originality for this proposition. Indeed, he introduces it by indicating he shares this perspective with Spiethoff.[63] But no one asserted it more lucidly or built his analysis more systematically around it.

This quality is heightened in *The Theory of Economic Development* because Schumpeter does not attempt there a full analysis of the business cycle but rather presents "a torso" that links his view of the business cycle to his theory of development. The sequence of his argument can be paraphrased in the following propositions.

1. The question to be answered is: Why does economic development proceed not in "a smooth line" but in cycles?
2. The fundamental answer is that innovations—"new combinations"—are not "evenly distributed through time . . . but appear . . . discontinuously in groups or swarms."
3. Swarming occurs because the appearance of a few entrepreneurs who meet success induces a progressively widened circle of entrepreneurs, of progressively diminishing creative talent and spirit, to try to exploit the newly revealed possibilities for profit.
4. The concentration of entrepreneurial talent is heightened because "every normal boom starts in one or a few branches of industry (railway building, electrical and chemical industries, and so forth), and that it derives its character from the innovations in the industry where it begins." Thus, in Schumpeter the business cycle is basically a sectoral phenomenon with macroeconomic manifestations.

Schumpeter concludes:[64]

> . . . [T]he swarm-like appearance of new combinations easily and necessarily explains the fundamental features of periods of boom. It explains why increasing capital investment is the very first symptom of the coming boom, why industries producing means of production are the first to show supernormal stimulation, above all why the consumption of iron increases. It explains the appearance of new purchasing power in bulk, thereby the characteristic rise in prices during booms, which obviously no reference to increased need or increased costs alone can explain. Further, it explains the decline of unemployment and the rise of wages, the rise in the interest rate, the increase in freight, the increasing strain on bank balances and bank reserves, and so forth, and, as we have said, the release of secondary waves—the spread of prosperity over the whole economic system.

But, Schumpeter goes on to argue, the swarming entrepreneurs in the innovational sectors also produce, via three routes, the crisis and the slump: by expanding the demand for means of production, using credits, and thus raising costs and imposing losses on firms "which belong to the circular flow";[65] by expanding supply, when the period of gestation is complete ("after a few years or sooner") and thereby inducing a tendency for prices to decline;[66] and by inducing "a credit deflation, because entrepreneurs are now in a position—and have every incentive—to pay off their debts; and . . . no other borrowers step into their place."[67]

In my vocabulary, Schumpeter is asserting that, out of its lagged dynamics, the boom brings down the expected rate of return over costs in the leading sectors by raising costs and lowering the expected rate of return and, thereby, induces a tendency for prices to fall both from the side of supply and demand.

In his growth-oriented theory of the business cycle Schumpeter takes, on the whole, a benign view of the depression. It is "normally" a time of "resorption and liquidation."[68] This process is required because the boom, led by one or a few innovational sectors, inherently produces "disproportionality" in output and prices among the sectors. But the depression also leads to "a new equilibrium position" as innovations are "digested," and "it fulfills what the boom promised" with a long-term decline in costs and prices.[69] He acknowledges, nevertheless, in a vivid but passing phrase, that unemployment "is a great and under certain circumstances annihilating misfortune for those concerned."[70]

It is here that Schumpeter is most redoubtably Austrian as he was to be in opposing what might be broadly called Keynesian measures in the interwar years including the Great Depression of the 1930s. But, as the concluding paragraph in *The Theory of Economic Development* indicates, Schumpeter had his eyes fastened firmly on the sometimes painful but creative dynamics of a capitalist society:[71]

> . . . [N]o therapy can permanently obstruct the great economic and social process by which businesses, individual positions, forms of life, cultural values and ideals, sink in the social scale and finally disappear. In a society with private property and competition, this process is the necessary complement of the continual emergence of new economic and social forms and of continually rising real incomes of all social strata. The process would be milder if there were no cyclical fluctuations, but it is not wholly due to the latter and it is completed independently of them. These changes are theoretically and practically, economically and culturally, much more important than the economic stability upon which all analytical attention has been concentrated for so long. And in their special way both the rise and the fall of families and firms are much more characteristic of the capitalist economic system, of its culture and its results, than any of the things that can be observed in a society which is stationary in the sense that its processes reproduce themselves at a constant rate.

Before moving on to Schumpeter's later work it may be helpful to make a few observations on his system from the perspective of my own theory of economic growth.

First, it is incomplete—"a torso"—as Schumpeter was quite aware.[72] It lacks, for example, a theory relating birth and death rates to development, including population-related investment in housing, infrastructure, and agriculture; it lumps the opening of a new source of supply for raw materials with technological and institutional change without examining its special features, including prior shifts in relative prices and typically longer periods of gestation than industrial investment; it does not deal with the complex interactions of science, invention, and innovation; it does not deal with the stages of and limits to growth. Schumpeter clings fiercely to his initial distinction between the world of static circular flow and innovational entrepreneurship when his own analysis suggests that one is, in fact, dealing at a moment of time, with a spectrum of degrees of creative entrepreneurship as among sectors and firms. Above all, Schumpeter's theory of growth and its related business cycle analysis is set in the wrong matrix. He counterposes the erratic disproportionate cyclical form innovation actually assumes in history with his static, circular flow Walrasian system. In my view, his theory implicitly assumes—and should be matched against—a system with all its sectors moving forward in dynamic sectoral equilibrium at different rates (following, pp. 429–431). Some of these limitations yielded an essentially false analogy between Schumpeter's theory of the major conventional business cycle and the Kondratieff cycle that mars his later *Business Cycles.* But taken on its own terms, in its own time, *The Theory of Economic Development* is a powerful, creative landmark in the history of economic thought. Subsequent mainstream economics is a good deal less than it might have been if its practitioners had not acted in terms of a *bon mot* attributed to Winston Churchill:[73] "Men often stumble over the truth, but most manage to pick themselves up and hurry off as if nothing had happened." But, as Marshall's indecisive work on increasing returns demonstrated, and the later efforts of others (following, pp. 454 and 470), it is not easy to bring together technological change and either mainstream micro- or macroeconomics as they emerged after 1870.

Schumpeter's *Business Cycles* was published in 1939, some 30 years after he had arrived at the basic concepts that form the substance of his *Theory of Economic Development.* The later study is a massive two-volume work of 1100 pages, almost four times the size of the earlier book. But as Schumpeter's Preface makes clear, the central theme is the same:[74] "Analyzing business cycles means neither more nor less than analyzing the economic process of the capitalist era. . . . [C]ycles are . . . like the beat of the heart, of the essence of the organism that displays them." The titles of the two works do reflect some change of emphasis and environment. The early study is of development, with business cycles dealt with in a final incomplete but suggestive chapter. The later study focuses on business cycles, although Schumpeter notes "the subtitle really renders what I have tried to do":[75] *A Theoretical Historical and Statistical Analysis of the Capitalist Process.* One suspects that a convergence of enforced attention to business cycles in the depressed 1930s and the character of the literature he felt impelled to take into account explains the shift in focus. But, on the whole, there can be few examples of an economist so faithfully trying to turn the "scaffolding" of his youth "into a house."[76]

The bulk of the first five chapters of *Business Cycles* elaborates, with one important exception, themes familiar from *The Theory of Development:* the stationary flow equilibrium model; external and endogenous sources of change; innovation and the role of the entrepreneur; innovation, credit creation, and the capital market; the cyclical process starting from an initial position of assumed full employment; the critical role of the plowback of entrepreneurial profits in capital formation seen, in turn, as the generation, diffusion, and absorption of innovations. Along this beaten path there are many more references to the views of others than in the earlier study, and a few refinements. But the only substantial change introduced is the notion of three concurrent cycles: The Kondratieff (say, 55 years); the Juglar (9–10 years); the Kitchin (40 months). *The Theory of Development* only recognized the Juglar.

This introduction of interacting multiple cycles builds up to a climactic synthesis in which the three cycles are combined in a single abstract chart.[77] As I have pointed out on a number of other occasions, Kondratieff demonstrated that there were rough long cycles in prices, interest rates, and money wages reaching back to, say, 1790; but he failed in his effort to associate them with cycles in rates of real growth or unemployment.[78] Schumpeter's synthesis is based on the assumption that the Kondratieff cycle was, essentially, the Juglar writ large; that is, a cycle in employment and rate of growth of output as well as in prices. For example, Schumpeter, responding to an observation of Wesley Mitchell's, asserts that "those movements [long waves] are associated (to say the least) with definite historical processes in industry which are of the same nature and produce the same symptoms as those which are responsible for and produce the symptoms of cycles which are universally recognized as such [presumably decennial Juglars]."[79] This conclusion leads Schumpeter to accept rather blindly, for example, evidence of this kind:[80]

> Summing up earlier work of his, Professor A. Spiethoff showed in his monograph on cycles (*Krisen in Handwörterbuch der Staatwissenschaften,* 4th ed., 1923) that there are epochs in which prosperities and other epochs in which depressions are relatively more marked, and these epochs he considered as bigger units without, however, combining them into cycles containing an upgrade and a downgrade and also without going beyond a statement to the effect that they were probably due to other causes than what he was prepared to call *cycles.* Applying his criterion of iron consumption he found that for England the period from 1822 to 1842 constitutes such a span of (prevalence of) depression (Stockungsspanne) and that for Germany the years 1843 to 1873 and 1895 to 1913 make up spans of (prevalence of) prosperity (Aufschwungsspanne), while from 1874 to 1894 we have a span of depression.

Spiethoff (and Schumpeter) introduces an inadmissible distortion: in defining his prosperous periods he is measuring from cyclical (Juglar) troughs to peaks; his depressed periods, from cyclical peaks to troughs.[81] And there are other factors to be taken into account in Spiethoff's figures, e.g., the precise timing of the coming of the railroad in Germany relative to Britain and the United States; the length and intensity of Juglar upswings in relation to subsequent downswings, etc.

With respect to Kitchins, Schumpeter notes that he did not have time to investigate each short cycle but he assumes tentatively that it also is related to the same innovational process that suffuses the Kondratieff and Juglar. He therefore felt reasonably comfortable in producing an abstract composite "three-cycle schema," each cycle distinguished by "the periods of gestation and absorption" of the innovational investment taking place.[82] This analysis builds up to a climactic chart combining the three types of cycles in the form of sine curves, with time (57 years) on the horizontal axis and (implicitly) unemployment and/or the rate of growth of output on the vertical axis.[83]

Schumpeter exhibits an awareness of the complexity of the relationships assumed in his stylized three-cycle schema; and, at a later stage, he goes into detail, covering some 250 pages, to explore empirically, within the considerable limits of the evidence, what actually happened between the 1780s and 1914 to prices, growth rates in output, levels of unemployment, the behavior of major individual prices, wages, the capital supply, and interest rates.

These passages, which reflect much accumulated scholarship by others and a good many debates about both theory and history, are peculiarly indecisive. Schumpeter is reported to have said late in life that he regretted that he was not an economic historian. There is a certain derivative akwardness in the historical sections of *Business Cycles;* and he was quite aware that they did not firmly support the initial abstract presentation of his vision. They are however, a tribute to his energy and his awareness that a dynamic economic theory must, in the end, be a theory about history. This inadequacy explains the seriousness of this passage in Schumpeter's preface to *Business Cycles.*[84]

It took longer than I thought to turn that scaffolding into a house, to embody the results of my later work, to present the historical and statistical complement, to expand old horizons. Nevertheless I doubt whether the result warrants that simile. The house is certainly not a finished and furnished one— there are too many glaring lacunae and too many unfulfilled desiderata. The restriction to the historical and statistical material of the United States, England, and Germany, though serious, is not the most serious of all the shortcomings. The younger generation of economists should look upon this book merely as something to shoot at and to start from—as a motivated program for further research. Nothing, at any rate, could please me more.

Schumpeter's brief treatment of developments in agriculture and raw material supply (6 pages) is particularly inadequate. He focuses mainly on the playback of innovations (notably the railroad and farm machinery) on expansion and cost-reduction in agriculture from the 1780s to 1914 rather than the whole more complex process of opening up new agricultural areas.[85]

The analytic historical sections of *Business Cycles,* dealing with Germany, Britain, and the United States (1787–1913), cover some 230 pages with a further 350 pages for the period from 1919 to the late 1930s. Again, as in the analytic confrontation of his theory with the behavior of long-time series, Schumpeter reflects a prodigous effort to master historical materials—matched among economists only by Hume, Smith, and Marshall— and a good deal of integrity in acknowledging the failure of history neatly to fit his model. Despite the space devoted to the project and its conceptual grandeur, most of these historical passages remain a collection of terse references to complicated phenomena linked loosely and episodically to Schumpeter's theory of the cyclical character of growth. The one element in his scheme that comes through persuasively is the three periods of relative concentration of major innovations: cotton textiles, good iron from coke, and Watt's steam engine starting in the 1780s; the railroads, starting (awkwardly for the Kondratieff cycle) in the 1830s and 1840s, leading on to steel, in the late 1860s; and then, round about the turn of the century, electricity, a batch of new chemicals, and the internal combustion engine.

This is a bit different from *The Theory of Development,* where the primary emphasis is on the heroic innovator in a given sector rather than on the tendency of certain groups of leading sectors to move from invention to innovation at about the same time. The latter phenomenon is discussed later, pp. 459–460.

Schumpeter's extended analysis of the interwar years emphasizes, of course, the great power of exogenous forces in shaping economic events, but sees also a good many characteristics of a Kondratieff downswing. He concludes with an important argument bearing on technology and innovation. It starts by reviewing the technical case made, in the late 1930s, for the arrival of secular stagnation. The expansion of the U.S. economy between 1933 and 1937 still left 14% unemployed at the peak of what Schumpeter called "The Disappointing Juglar."[86] Then came the partially self-inflicted wound of the sharp American recession of 1937–1938. In the latter year Alvin Hansen published his *Full Recovery and Stagnation.* The substance of the debate belongs with the discussion of limits to growth. For present purposes, what is significant is that Schumpeter argued that in no objective, technical sense had investment opportunities diminished.[87] "Nor can it be urged that fundamentally new opportunities of first-rate magnitude are not in prospect. Barring the question whether that is so, it is sufficient to reply that in the eighteen-twenties hardly anybody can have foreseen the impending railroad revolution or, in the eighteen-seventies, electrical developments and the motor car.'' After making his case that cap-italism was imperiled not by a waning of investment opportunities but by a hostile political, social, and intellectual environment plus self-generated degenerative forces, Schumpeter concludes:[88] ''. . .[I]f our schema is to be trusted, recovery and prosperity should be more, and recession and depression phases less strongly marked during the next three decades than they have been in the last two. But the sociological drift can not be expected to change.'' That was a quite remarkable prognosis to make in 1939, even if the period of extraordinary prosperity occurred in a Kondratieff downswing (1951–1973) and the sociological drift towards socialism began to reverse from, roughly, the mid-1970s (following, pp. 483–484). Schumpeter's deeply rooted Central European pessimism would have been astonished by the rapidly rising and widely diffusing respect for com-petitive private enterprise and the price system in the 1980s.

Simon Kuznets's *Secular Movements in Prices and Production* (1930) shares with Schumpeter's *Theory of Economic Development* and *Business Cycles* a few striking similarities and is marked by several equally striking differences.

Like *Economic Development, Secular Movements* is a young man's book incorporating a large vision of the terrain the author intended to explore in his professional career and a definition of his proposed strategy.[89] Both Schumpeter and Kuznets aimed to contribute to the generation of intimately linked, dynamic theories of economic growth and business cycles that would combine historical and statistical analysis with theory. Above all, they identified innovation as the critical dimension of growth; they perceived the inherent unevenness of the process of innovation as key to an understanding of cycles of differing lengths; they accepted that the pursuit of these insights required not merely aggregate analysis but detailed analysis of the sectors where innovation actually happened; and they based their analyses on the inescapable path of deceleration followed by a sector caught up in radical innovational change.

In building on these insights both men broke away from the mainstream preoccupations of their day; although Kuznets had available Schumpeter's *Economic Development;* and, in *Business Cycles,* Schumpeter had available Kuznets's *Secular Movements.*[90]

The first of their differences lay in the theoretical hypotheses which framed their work. Schumpeter was trained in the Austrian School, which was suffused by a conscious commitment to theory. It had conducted against the German historical school a protracted debate about method. Moreover, Schumpeter was strongly drawn to the elegance of Walras's general equilibrium system, which is his point of departure.[91]

Kuznets emerged from a different intellectual matrix with a bias towards the primacy of facts over theory. He was a pupil of Wesley C. Mitchell, who belonged with the pragmat-ic philosophical tradition of Charles Pierce (1839–1914), William James (1842–1910), and John Dewey (1859–1952). As an economist Mitchell was influenced by but was less iconoclastic than Thorstein Veblen. Mitchell (and Kuznets) did not reject the use of economic theory. They did not belong, say, with the German historical school, of which they were explicitly critical. Indeed, Mitchell regularly taught a course in the history of economic thought at Columbia. But the institutionalist tradition on Morningside Heights of the 1920s was less rigorous with respect to theory, more flexible and eclectic than Schumpeter's Vienna in the first decade of the century; and, above all, it was more acutely focussed on the facts which, it was believed, the conventional theorists ignored. Thus, Schumpeter begins in his *Theory of Development* with a static (or incrementally expand-ing) circular flow equilibrium model of an economic system into which he introduces his disruptive, creative, innovating entrepreneur. Kuznets begins with a set of observations on the empirical evidence.[92]

> The picture of economic development suffers a curious change as we examine it first in a rather wide sphere, then in a narrower one. If we take the world from the end of the eighteenth century, there unrolls before us a process of uninterrupted and seemingly unslackened growth. . . .
>
> But if we single out the various nations or the separate branches of industry, the picture becomes less uniform. Some nations seem to have led the world at one time, others at another. Some industries were developing most rapidly at the beginning of the century, others at the end. . . . Great Britain has relinquished the lead in the economic world because its own growth, so vigorous through the period 1780–1850, has slackened. She has been overtaken by rapidly developing Germany and the United States. . . . As we observe the various industries within a given national system, we see that the lead in development shifts from one branch to another. The main reason for this shift seems to be that a rapidly developing industry does not continue its vigorous growth indefinitely, but slackens its pace after a time, and is overtaken by industries whose period of rapid development comes later. Within any country we observe a succession of different branches of activity leading the process of development, and in each mature industry we notice a conspicuous slackening in the rate of increase. . . . But contrasted with our belief in the fairly continuous march of economic progress, it raises a frequently overlooked question. Why is there an abatement in the growth of old industries? Why is not progress uniform in all branches of production, with the inventive and organizing capacity of the nation flowing in an even stream into the various channels of economic activity? What concentrates the forces of growth and development in one or two branches of production at a given time, and what shifts the concentration from one field to another as time passes?
>
> These questions can best be answered by an inspection of the historical records of industrial growth, focused upon the processes that underlie economic development.''

At this point Kuznets, having used a series of empirical observations to come to rest on the process of sectoral retardation, introduces some economic theory; but he slides it in with reference to ''factors discussed by economic historians'' and traces a path that permits him, like Schumpeter, to assert that changes in technique are the decisive factor in growth:[93]

> Of the numerous factors discussed by economic historians in connection with the history of an industry, three groups stand out as the dynamic, the pushing forces. They are: (1) growth of population; (2) changes in demand; (3) technical changes, including both mechanical or engineering progress, and improvement in business organization.
>
> These groups of factors are, of course, not independent of one another. The growth of population is conditioned to a large extent by the standard of living (demand) and the supply of means of subsistence, the latter in its turn depends upon the state of technical arts. Changes in demand usually follow changes in technique, while the volume of demand is in close and definite connection

with the size of the population. And technical progress comes to be realized in response to some felt needs, which may be brought about by the pressure of population or by changes in demand. . . .

While all three forces are interdependent, the changes in technique most clearly condition the movements in both population and demand, while the dependence of technical progress upon population and demand is less clear and immediate. In the chain interconnection of the three, this link seems to be most prominent.

Thus, a similar focus on innovation leads Kuznets to much the same hypothesis that had governed Schumpeter's *Economic Development* a generation earlier; but their conceptual framework differed rather sharply.

The second major difference between Schumpeter and the early Kuznets is much narrower. Schumpeter made the creative entrepreneur and the progressively lesser breeds that swarmed after him the center of the innovational process; for Kuznets, at the center were his logistic curves (or three constants Gompertz curves) capturing statistically the process of retardation that suffused the life of sectors in a dynamic economy. Retardation in a sequence of leading sectors was an observed statistical uniformity. He identified four reasons for retardation: the slowing down of technical progress; dependence of the innovational sectors on slower-growing sectors supplying raw material inputs; a relative decline in the funds available for expansion of the innovational sectors; and competition from the same industry in a younger country. Schumpeter's analysis of the waning contribution of an innovational sector to overall growth is not inconsistent with Kuznets's; but it is distinctively different in its emphasis on certain nonstatistical and sociological factors at work.[94]

A third difference between the two approaches to innovation and cycles concerns what might be called the technical or intermediate objective of their work. For Schumpeter, in *Business Cycles,* the major objective was to give substance to his innovational interpretation of the long, half-century (Kondratieff) cycle, suggesting also its linkage to sequences of strong and weak decennial (Juglar) cycles.

His selective evocation of history in *Business Cycles*—often impressionistic—was meant to provide evidence, statistical and otherwise, that amidst the clutter and noise of historical sequences, full of external intrusions, there was something to the three-cycle process by which he believed development went forward.

Kuznets was focused on a related but not identical set of problems: What were the secular and cyclical paths of output and prices in the major sectors? Kuznets was quite aware of the work of Kondratieff and others who interested themselves in economic movements that transcended conventional business cycles; but he was determined to proceed from a more solid statistical base than Kondratieff, even if that meant that all the phenomena Kondratieff identified could not be embraced in his conclusions. His method was to establish a long-run primary trend, by clearing his data of short-run cyclical and other movements; then to establish secondary movements in production and prices around the primary trend; and, finally, to examine the relation between the rate of growth of a sector and the amplitude of the cycles it experienced.

Kuznets found that primary trends in production and prices reflected systematically the life cycle of a given technical innovation (or opening up of a new territory or natural resource); that is, a phase of rapid, then decelerating, increase in output and of rapid, then decelerating, decrease in price.

The first thing Kuznets's analysis of primary trends demonstrated was that the cost-reducing effect of innovation was generally translated promptly into price reductions—a proposition Schumpeter failed to take into account. In fact, with the passage of time, price reductions were subject to retardation, just as were increases in output. In these paths of decelerating increases in output accompanied by diminishing rates of price decrease—and then price increase—Kuznets had the materials in hand to proceed to a more satisfactory explanation than Schumpeter was to provide for Kondratieff's long cycles in overall price indexes. But he did not take that route. He stayed with the sectors.

Kuznets exhibited a similar reserve with respect to overall production. He did not link his insights into sectoral retardation to statistical data on the course of national output during the time period with which he dealt. In dealing with secondary movements in production and prices, however, Kuznets came seriously to grips in aggregate terms with the relations among output, prices, labor productivity, and real wages. He first demonstrated that secondary expansions and contractions in production around the primary trends were systematically preceded by price increases and decreases, suggesting clearly the role of price movements as a mechanism for shifting the direction of investment. In a sustained theoretical passage of some fifty pages, Kuznets then poses the question of why a period of rising prices should be, at once, a period of rapidly expanding output and of constrained real wages. His answer is, essentially, that the downward relative shift in (urban) consumer income, due to rising prices, is compensated for by reduced savings and by enlarged opportunities for employment in the production of capital goods, whose financing is rendered easier by the shift in income distribution from wages to profits. Kuznets then explores why an expansion phase of this kind should come to an end. He adduces a decline in labor productivity, as the working force in the rapidly expanding sectors is increased, combined with monetary restraints, as rising prices reduce the incentive to mine gold under a gold standard regime. I would not wholly agree with this model, but it reflects a way of going about trend analysis highly germane to the phenomena confronted in the United States and in other advanced industrial economies in the period from the mid-1890s to 1914.

Kuznets then raised the question of whether these secondary movements in prices and production are to be regarded as cycles. He concluded that they are not: they are to be viewed as specific, historical occurences.

Finally, Kuznets explored how the rate of growth of a primary trend in production affected the amplitude of both secondary fluctuations and conventional cyclical movements. He found and sought to explain the expected positive correlation.

In general, Kuznets regarded his book as a preliminary reconnaissance of the issues that had to be faced if a general dynamic theory of production and prices was to be built. Nevertheless, in its analysis of primary trends in a succession of leading sectors and in the lagged linkage he established between secondary trend movements in prices and production, this germinal study had a grip on several of the key mechanisms basic to an understanding of secular trends.

The greatest difference between Schumpeter and the young Kuznets, however, concerns the ultimate problems to which their initial visions were addressed. From the final paragraphs of his youthful *Economic Development* to the final paragraphs of *Business Cycles* (and beyond to *Capitalism, Socialism, and Democracy*) Schumpeter's mind was focused on a very large problem indeed: would capitalism, as a social and political system, prove capable of maintaining a setting that would encourage and support the corps of innovating entrepreneurs on whom its growth and survival depended? Kuznets's ambition was a bit less grand but also ample: ". . . a complete and general theory of dynamic economics."[95] But, in both *Secular Movements* and his later work on economic growth (following, pp. 352–355) he cut his analysis down to what he could measure with more or less reputable data; and it turned out that all the empty boxes he perceived as essential for a general dynamic theory could not be filled.

For Schumpeter, innovation was the measure of a society's vitality; the innovating entrepreneur a kind of Hegelian hero. And he did not draw back from evoking the process in such human, societal terms, consciously breaching the conventional walls of his discipline as had the major classical economists, including Marx. But he was never able to link his evolutionary and essentially dynamic vision of whole societies to his commitment to conventional neo-Newtonian economic theory. Kuznets, in pursuing his goal of a firmly based dynamic economics did so within the framework of the old German dictum: "Mastery lies in limitation."[96] The limitations he accepted—long, reliable time series and modern statistical methods—proved insufficient for mastery. And, in effect, he abandoned his youthful vision. The central fact is, then, that neither Schumpeter nor Kuznets ever developed a full dynamic theory of growth although they made solid partial contributions to an understanding of growth.

Two Unorthodox Views:
Henry Adams and Thorstein Veblen

Schumpeter and Kuznets are, of course, not alone, but they are major figures between 1870 and 1939 in the relatively small band of economic professionals who explored the relation between major, discontinuous technological innovation, the economy, and, in Schumpeter's case, the fate of capitalist society. There were, of course, many others beyond the conventional boundaries of economics who reflected on the larger meaning of the sequence of technological revolutions that had been going on since the 1780s. One of the most memorable was Henry Adams, who captured his reflections on the Paris Exhibition of 1900 in an essay, "The Dynamo and the Virgin."[97] By 1900 the third great grouping of technologies was just emerging on the scene: the internal combustion engine, electricity, and a new array of chemicals, some linked to the motor vehicle (e.g., vulcanized rubber, refined gasoline). Adams—historian, professor, novelist, disenchanted commentator on post-1865 American society—was guided through the Exposition, embracing both art and technology, by a friend, the American scientist Samuel Langley. Here is the passage that builds up to his central analogy between the power of electricity and the power of Christian faith, crystallized in the cult of the Virgin.[98]

> . . . [T]o Adams the dynamo became a symbol of infinity. As he grew accustomed to the great gallery of machines, he began to feel the forty-foot dynamos as a moral force, much as the early Christians felt the Cross. . . . For Adams' objects its values lay chiefly in its occult mechanism. Between the dynamo in the gallery of machines and the engine-house outside, the break of continuity amounted to abysmal fracture for a historian's objects. No more relation could he discover between the steam and the electric current than between the Cross and the cathedral. . . . and thus it happened that, after ten years' pursuit, he found himself lying in the Gallery of Machines at the Great Exposition of 1900, his historical neck broken by the sudden irruption of forces totally new.

Since no one else showed much concern, an elderly person without other cares had no need to betray alarm. The year 1900 was not the first to upset schoolmasters. Copernicus and Galileo had broken many professorial necks about 1600; Columbus had stood the world on its head towards 1500; but the nearest approach to the revolution of 1900 was that of 310 when Constantine set up the Cross. The rays that Langley disowned, as well as those which he fathered, were occult, supersensual, irrational; they were a revelation of mysterious energy like that of the Cross; they were what, in terms of mediaeval science, were called immediate modes of the divine substance.

This insight leads to no prescriptions for policy but to a rather despairing passage—like much of his writing, more in sorrow than in anger—on the rich strands of Western culture somehow missing from American life:[99]

The force of the Virgin was still felt at Lourdes, and seemed to be as potent as X-rays; but in America neither Venus nor Virgin ever had value as force— at most as sentiment. No American had ever been truly afraid of either. . . . The Woman had once been supreme; in France she still seemed potent, not merely as a sentiment, but as a force. Why was she unknown in America?. . . .

The true American knew something of the facts, but nothing of the feelings; he read the letter, but he never felt the law. Before this historical chasm, a mind like that of Adams felt itself helpless; . . . On one side, at the Louvre and at Chartres, . . . was the highest energy ever known to man, the creator of four-fifths of his noblest art, exercising vastly more attraction over the human mind than all the steam-engines and dynamos ever dreamed of; and yet this energy was unknown to the American mind. An American Virgin would never dare command; an American Venus would never dare exist.

There is also an unlikely element of nostalgia in the reflections of Thorstein Veblen on the meaning of the new technology. He looked back not to the classics of the ancient world or to the creative force of mediaeval Christianity but to to what he called ''the instinct of workmanship.'' Veblen defines this concept as the characteristic of the human race over the ages that leads it to respond to challenges and problems with purposeful actions, guided by intelligence—actions that ''may be rated as purposeful by an observer, in the sense that they are seen to further the life of the individual agent or species, while there is no consciousness of purpose on the part of the agent under observation. . . .''[100] Thus, human societies gradually accumulate and pass along, from generation to generation, an expanding body of technology, induced by the requirements of society but, in turn, reshaping society.[101] Invention and innovation is an instinctive cultural reflex in Veblen, not a narrowly economic process.

Veblen was something of a philosopher, anthropologist, sociologist, psychologist, and historian who brought these multiple perspectives to bear on the American economy, its institutions, and their wider impact on the society. Adams's detachment was that of a member of a mainly superseded elite, a status he accepted with a sometimes gentle, often acid, philosophic pessimism. Veblen, with his Scandinavian heritage still strong, moved about the American academic establishment, a peripatetic outsider, acute critic of both mainstream economics of his day and of American society, propounding evolutionary rather than neo-Newtonian propositions about the workings of economies, past and contemporary.

Instinct of Workmanship is, essentially, a stylized history of technology from the life of primitive man forward. His climactic final chapter ("The Machine Industry") dramatizes the clash between the businessman and the engineer:[102] ". . .[U]nder the rule of the current technology and business principles, industry is managed by businessmen for business ends, not by technology experts or for the material advantage of the community." Veblen goes on to evoke the danger that the dynamics of business would lead to monopolies when "the material fortunes of the community would come to rest unreservedly and in all details in the hands of those larger businessmen who hold the final pecuniary discretion."[103]

It was directly from this line of thought that some of Veblen's disciples, viewing the Great Depression as the ultimate mismanagement of big business, advocated a planned economy operated by technocrats "for the material advantage of the community."

Evidently, Adams and Veblen contemplating the increasingly powerful technological potential of the society they were closely observing, had different posts of observation and drew different conclusions. But, in passing, it is worth noting that Veblen, in a quite different context, also evokes the mystical power of women—not unrelated to technology—in their role as divinities in primitive societies.[104]

> But if the magical-technological fitness and efficacy of women has led to the growth of institutions vesting the disposal of the produce in the women, in a more or less discretionary way, the like effect has been even more pronounced, comprehensive and lasting as regards the immaterial developments of the case. With great uniformity the evidence from the earlier peaceable agricultural civilisations runs to the effect that the primitive ritual of husbandry, chiefly of a magical character, is in the hands of the women and is made up of observances presumed to be particularly consonant with the phenomena of motherhood. . . . The deities, great and small, are prevailingly females; and the great ones among them seem invariably to have set out with being mothers.

Adams and Veblen shared another strand. They both accepted the new round of technology as an irreversible fact. They did not, in Veblen's phrases, "with a tincture of affectation and make-believe" seek "a remedy in a 'return to Nature,'" despite "a feeling of maladjustment and discomfort."[105] But they articulated in different ways an uneasiness about technology and society that has not abated as the twentieth century draws toward its close.

Formal Growth Models: Bickerdike (1876–1961) and Harrod (1900–1978).

In paying tribute to Marx's two-sector growth model (preceding, p. 138) Paul Samuelson observed that the distinguished horde of economists who tilled this field after the Second World War moved on not from Marx's work but "out of a marriage of the Clark–Bickerdike accelerator and the Keynes multiplier, and out of earlier works by Von Neumann and Frank Ramsey that show no Marxian influence." Without implying any derivation or dependence, those who preceded R. F. Harrod's 1939 formulation of a two-sector growth model were a bit more numerous than Samuelson suggests.[106] In his various papers relating to C. F. Bickerdike, Bruce Larson identifies, as predecessors, a considerable array of Marxists, plus Gustav Cassel, to say nothing of Quesnay; and Aftalion certainly belongs on the list of accelerator pioneers.[107]

I have decided to include in this section a brief sketch of Bickerdike's work on growth, as well as Harrod's, for four reasons: Sweezy has memorialized the Marxist growth theorists,[108] and their work had little impact beyond their own circle;[108] Bickerdike appears to be the first to formulate an algebraic as opposed to a simple arithmetic growth model and to incorporate the money supply (and the savings-investment balance) in his reckoning; he considered some disequilibrium aspects of the growth process not generally examined even by his successors; and, for reasons that will emerge, he deserves a bit more attention in the history of economic thought than he has been accorded thus far.[109]

Briefly, Bickerdike's rather frustrated but still fruitful professional career unfolded, from the little we know, as follows.[110]

Bickerdike went to Oxford (Merton) from Whitgift School in Croydon in 1895, studying mathematics and history, receiving his B.A. in 1899. In that year, he came under the influence of Francis Edgeworth, then Professor of Political Economy, a distinguished mathematical economist, and joint editor (with J. M. Keynes) of the *Economic Journal.* Bickerdike competed successfully for the 1902 Cobden Prize on land value taxation, a subject of particular interest to Edgeworth. Bickerdike moved on to London and sought a doctoral degree at the London School of Economics, his thesis being overseen by Professor Edwin Cannan, a nonmathematical economist of the older school. Bickerdike's thesis on *The Theory of Tariffs* yielded two articles, still remembered in the history of the field; but his thesis was turned down in 1906, presumably at Cannan's insistence, quite possibly reflecting his Thurberesque war against the kind of theory symbolized by Edgeworth. At that time Bickerdike was apparently supporting himself as a schoolmaster. In 1910, however, he was appointed a Lecturer at the University of Manchester; but he gave it up in 1912 to join the civil service in a unit within the Board of Trade that later became part of the Ministry of Labour. He received an O.B.E. in May 1937; and there is evidence of his employment as late as 1952, when he would have been 76 years old. He died 9 years later. Although he published nothing after 1929,[111] there is evidence suggesting that Bickerdike's writing in economic theory continued; but he shared his papers only with a small circle of friends. As nearly as we know, he died a bachelor. A collection of Bickerdike's papers is believed to exist (or to have existed); but they have not yet been run down.

Bickerdike's bibliography of published work includes fourteen articles, all but two of which appeared in *The Economic Journal;* and thirty-eight book reviews, virtually all done for the same publication.[112] They span the years 1902–1929. Bickerdike ranged over a wide spectrum of economic problems. He is best remembered for his writing on international trade, derived from his ill-fated doctoral thesis, and for his path-breaking 1914 article on the accelerator: "A Non-Monetary Cause of Fluctuations in Employment."[113]

Larson traces out a quite coherent three-stage progression in Bickerdike's work down to his 1924 and 1925 articles on growth.[114] It is, once again, a story of how an initial concern with welfare problems leads rather circuitously to insights into the growth process and, in this case, to its inherent instability.

Bickerdike's first phase, in the period between about 1907 and 1914, is one of intense concern with certain aspects of welfare economics under the influence of (but in occasional debate with) Pigou and Edgeworth. He focused, in particular, on positive and negative external effects ("co-operative" or "non-co-operative" conditions of production). These concepts covered cases where the pursuit of individual self-interest reduced costs or increased pleasure for other individuals—or the contrary. Work on specific micro-economic problems under this rubric involved systematically the distinction between individual and social points of view, emphasized notably by Pigou; and the distinction between the outcome in the long and short run, which Edgeworth elaborated out of Marshall.

Bickerdike shifted his focus from micro- to macrowelfare problems with the coming of war, retaining still his sensitivity to the distinction between individual and social perspectives and his interest in external effects. Along the way he became increasingly interested in the role of expectations. Although not set out in macro terms, Bickerdike's "A Non-Monetary Cause of Fluctuations in Employment" emerges as a kind of hinge on which he shifted from issues of micro- to macropolicy, as he perceived that the interplay of the accelerator and multiplier in a given sector might have a general impact on industrial fluctuations.

He begins with a bold reversal of the emerging awareness of the accelerator and suggests that what would later be called the multiplier effects of the large amplitude of fluctuations in durable goods production (including consumers durables) may be more important:[115]

> It has been observed for a long time that the trades connected with the construction of durable goods, such as buildings, ships, machinery, works of construction, &c., are liable to specially heavy fluctuations in employment. . . . [U]sually the argument has taken the line that if . . . there is a fluctuation in general trade . . . the producers of the instruments of production will be more particularly affected. . . . I would suggest . . . that perhaps we ought rather to put the argument the other way round, and find in the independently-caused fluctuations in the production of durable goods one at least of the principal factors in producing monetary disturbances and general fluctuations.

Focusing sharply on the degree of durability, with reference to Pigou and Robertson,[116] he then goes on to elaborate a cyclical sequence of interaction between accelerator and multiplier, with proposals for remedy:

- Because of their relative durability, changes in demand cause dramatically different changes in production as between consumers goods (e.g., woolen clothes) and capital goods (e.g., ships).
- On the other hand, the "exaggerated" variability of production of durable goods in response to small changes in demand is "one of the principal underlying causes of industrial fluctuations" to which the monetary system responds—as a result, not as a primary cause of fluctuations.
- The inputs to shipbuilding from engineering, iron and steel, and other sectors yield a "double exaggeration" and therefore "a considerable disturbance of purchasing power by the fluctuation in earnings of workmen and shareholders. . . ."[117]
- Thus, unemployment insurance is "a proper remedy to take and a way to check the extension of the disturbance."[118]
- Another damping device would be to permit a ship-owning trust, "which was governed by the interests of the public, and had to earn only a normal remuneration

of capital,'' to maintain an adequate reserve that ''would suffice to prevent the occurrence of any serious deficiency.''[119]

- The outcome for shipbuilding applies in lesser degree to other durable-goods sectors where ''there is a failure of competitive self-interest to tend towards maximum social interest.''[120]
- So far as period of gestation is concerned, self-interest would work toward ''checking that kind of irregularity'' that arose from incorrect forecasts of market conditions at the end of the period of production—taken in Bickerdike's example to be 5 years.[121] Efforts in this direction would not always succeed; but the magnitude of the problem would be much less than in the case of durable goods.

On these welfare economics foundations Bickerdike turned to problems of war finance and agricultural policy. One issue posed by war finance was the following:[122] Was it not possible (putting inequality of tax incidence aside) for individual savers to sustain their level of consumption during the war—that is, in the short run—by foregoing future interest and ceasing to save, so long as the war effort, on a macrolevel, was financed out of ''normal savings?''

In 1924 Bickerdike turned back to the social impact of the decisions of savers or nonsavers in his ''Individual and Social Interests in Relation to Saving.'' But this time the context was not the short-run framework of war but the long-run process of growth.

Here is how Bickerdike begins:[123]

A general survey of economic progress during the last two centuries certainly gives the impression that the capitalist system of private saving and investing has resulted in benefits not only to individuals who saved and invested (and their heirs) but also to the non-saving proletarians. These two centuries however, have been characterised in a marked degree by the discovery of new processes, and especially by cheapening of transport, and such discoveries are not necessarily an accompaniment of saving pure and simple [a distinction in the spirit of Colin Clark, preceding, pp. 213–214, and, Solow, following, p. 622]. The question whether and how saving as such benefits the non-savers cannot be settled merely by this kind of observation, therefore. It has to be examined analytically and is then seen to be not so very simple a matter when we take account of the fact that the saver gets interest and he or his heirs may ultimately spend both interest and capital.

So far as the incidence of saving is concerned, Bickerdike's conclusion is based on the effect of saving in the first instance—and the later disposal of interest and of capital—on the price level. His analysis is framed by assumptions that decree that savings yield lower prices by reducing the demand for consumers goods. Thus, so long as falling prices do not ''dislocate'' production, the nonsaver, with a constant money income, gains from saving via lower prices; and he continues to gain if interest and principal are plowed back in savings.

From the point of view of our concern with growth modeling, Bickerdike starts out essentially with Cassel's primary model (preceding, pp. 204–205), assuming for purposes of simplification a socialist state and banking system, a constant rate of growth, geared to a constant given rate of growth in population, with no technological change. Bickerdike then establishes that a constant price level can be maintained if ''the rate of money interest would be identical with the rate of growth of physical wealth and of money, and the aggregate amount of interest received by the State per unit of time would equal the total increase of money needed to finance increase as distinct from merely replacement production''—the latter a distinction Cassel firmly makes.

Bickerdike then proceeds to consider the equilibrium conditions required if one assumes a nonsocialist economy in which individual saving takes place. He concludes in a Harrodian vein:[124]

> In a *regime* of individualism it is mainly bank credit which takes the place of the State creation of money. . . .
>
> A smooth state of growth, with uniform price-level, is possible if the two conditions are fulfilled: (1) growth is uniform, (2) saving and the creation of bank credit always continually equal the amount required for financing growth as distinct from maintenance production. If these conditions are not fulfilled, there is almost inevitably involved not only disturbance of individual prices, but disturbance of the general level of prices and, under ordinary conditions of individualism, oscillation of trade activity. . . . [A] study of the conditions of uniform growth, even though that condition does not actually exist, is useful as a preliminary to the consideration of the effects of irregularity.

Bickerdike's 1925 article attempts to meet challenges posed by the analysis of ''irregularity'' by relaxing several assumptions governing the earlier essay and identifying various circumstances in which the growth rate would not be uniform; e.g., changes in the rate of population increase via increased immigration; acceleration in the rate of productivity increase; a rate of interest higher than the rate of growth in output due to discount of the future; a failure of private savings to match the investment required to sustain a constant growth rate; the consequences for prices and savings of an accelerated growth rate; the cyclical impact on prices and growth rates of investment in a major sector (e.g., housing) where the capital stock is highly durable and the period of production is long;[125] and the role of inflationary episodes—and forced savings—in providing the shift of income to profits and savings required for a high rate of growth. This is Bickerdike's large, final, almost Schumpeterian reflection:[126]

> What actually happens is that there are spurts of rapid growth, with extension of credit beyond the current rate of saving, and rising prices, which enable clever and fortunate men to make much more considerable gains than they would be able to do if prices were uniform, and they save a large part of such gains, and in that roundabout way the aggregate savings is made sufficiently great, taking the period of the boom and the depression together. It was not purely by normal savings that the rapid growth of wealth in England and America during the nineteenth century, in Germany from 1870 to 1914 was financed, but largely by extension of bank credit in excess, for the time being, of normal saving, resulting in periodical inflations. If the level of prices is to be kept much steadier, and if, in addition, there is to continue a high rate of super-tax and of death duties, there is real danger that the rate of growth of wealth might become very slow unless some other way of providing for it can be found.
>
> This is the most important practical consideration to which the discussion

leads. The "capitalist system" has imposed a fairly rapid rate of growth in developed communities, but through a high degree of inequality in the distribution of wealth, and by a financial system which tends to prevent the destruction of that inequality, by way of periodical inflationary periods. There is now a strong attack on the inequality of distribution through the system of taxation and much discussion, at least, of methods of checking the monetary fluctuations. The question how growth is to be maintained at a good rate requires also to be tackled, and, be it remembered, so far as this country is concerned, the growth of the outside territories, from which so large a part of our supplies is obtained, is included in the problem, because hitherto their growth has mainly been dependent on the supply of British capital. If the community determines not to allow the accustomed rate of growth to be forced upon it in the old way, or not to the extent which prevailed until recently, it has to be seriously considered whether there is any really practicable alternative other than a substantial slowing down of the rate of growth of wealth.

Except for some passages summarizing his own already published views in a critique of Foster and Catchings's *Profits,* Bickerdike never returned in print to the themes of his 1924–1925 articles.[127] In fact he only wrote five reviews after "Saving and the Monetary System." Between 1929 and his death in 1961 he published nothing although, as noted earlier, he set down and shared some of his thoughts with friends and regularly attended meetings of the Political Economy Club of London.[128]

Thus Bickerdike took over from Cassel a simple growth model that expanded in uniform proportions geared to the rate of growth of population; but Cassel did not explore the monetary implications of a constant growth rate. This is what Bickerdike did. He first established the conditions for the maintenance of a constant price level, assuming a monopolistic state bank under socialism, and he then examined an array of conditions in a regime of private saving and investment that would not only bring about alterations in the price level but also in growth rates and employment; i.e., differing periods of gestation and durability of capital instruments, the likelihood that the price-reducing effects of saving would lead to unemployment, and the unlikelihood that private savings would be exactly matched by private decisions to replace and expand the capital stock.

Each of the building blocks introduced by Bickerdike can be traced to or associated with one or another figure of his time; e.g., Marshall, Cassel, Pigou, Edgeworth, Robertson.[129] And the analysis of instability, unemployment, and slow growth was endemic in Britain of the mid-1920s. Moreover, in this pre-*General Theory* time, Bickerdike's analysis of saving and investment appears a bit antique and awkward. Nevertheless, in a quite original way, he wove together some important partial insights of his time; carried growth modeling forward far beyond J. B. Clark and Cassel; set out his exercises in algebraic form; and clearly anticipated the methods and "irregularity" concerns of Harrod–Domar and their neoclassical successors—adding a few with which they did not choose to grapple. In fact, his casual modesty about dynamic models in a steady equilibrium and acute consciousness that their proper use was merely as a prelude to the analysis of irregularity and disequilibrium might well have been emulated by some of his successors.

It should also be noted that Bickerdike was quite aware of the sectoral unevenness of productivity increases, which captured the imagination of both Schumpeter and the early Kuznets:[130]

> Growth of wealth has been regarded as due to corresponding growth of population. Suppose, now, it is due to the increasing productivity of labour, with, at first, a constant population. The increasing productivity may be the result of improving processes, or of economies of large-scale production, or of the conjunction of the two.
>
> Under actual conditions, increasing productivity does not affect all kinds of production alike, but we can consider the fundamental questions on the supposition that the improvement applies equally to all production, and continues at a uniform rate.

Thus, Bickerdike consciously set that problem aside to pursue, out of his early fixation on welfare economics, the implications for the common interest of the privately motivated and separate decisions to save and to invest, in a capitalist banking and monetary system.

Harrod makes no reference to Bickerdike, as one might expect from a regular reader (and later editor) of the *Economic Journal,* where Bickerdike mainly published. Perhaps, writing in the blinding light generated by Keynes's *General Theory,* other strands of thought and lesser figures from the past were temporarily lost from sight.

Nevertheless, despite its ample array of foreshadowing predecessors and progenitors, Harrod's ''An Essay in Dynamic Theory'' (1939) is likely to retain its present place as a landmark in economic analysis in general, growth analysis in particular.[131] Its status derives from the fact that it crystallized and rendered explicit a way of looking at growth and fluctuations toward which a number of economists were tending; and, despite its imperfections, it provided a base and point of reference for criticism and further refinements.

Proximately, Harrod's ''Dynamic Theory'' derives directly from his own *Trade Cycle* (1936).[132] That exercise, in turn, as Harrod points out, was built on the bringing together of three strands in economic thought.[133]

> . . . (i) There is a well-established relation,[134] vouched for by experience and the laws of arithmetic, between the demand for consumable goods and the demand for durable goods, the essence of which is that the absolute amount of the latter depends primarily on the rate of increase of the former. The implications of this for trade cycle theory are here explored. (ii) Mr. Keynes, in his recent volume, *The General Theory of Employment, Interest, and Money* has developed certain important ideas concerning the relations between the demand for capital goods, the propensity of the community to save, and its general level of activity and income. Full use is made of these. (iii) I have had occasion in the past to work upon the theory of imperfect competition; the object of this branch of economics has been to bring the general theory of value into closer relation with the facts. The doctrines so developed have proved of relevance to the trade cycle problem.

Harrod's 1936 conclusion was that the trade cycle ''results from the joint operation of the Relation [Accelerator] and the Multiplier.''[135] In a summary section, entitled ''The Inevitability of the Cycle,'' before he turns to possible remedies, Harrod anticipates his later approach to a growth model:[136] ''. . . [L]et us suppose a condition of a steady advance. Every batch of hostages to fortune (net investment) is precisely justified by the result, and on the basis of this experience the advance is maintained.'' He then goes on to examine the forces that might slow down the rate of increase in output during a trade expansion; concludes that outcome is, on balance, likely:[137] "And here is the crux of the matter. If there is any drop in the rate of advance, a recession must occur. At that point the Relation dominates the scene. A decline in the rate of advance involves a recession of investment. But then, in accordance with the Multiplier, consumption must recede.''

Clearly, then, Harrod's interest was not economic growth, but (like Bickerdike's "irregularities") cyclical fluctuations or high chronic unemployment—an understandable emphasis in Britain of the mid-1930s. He was led, nevertheless, by the nature of the question he posed—what prevents "steady advance"—to touch briefly on certain growth issues; e.g., the relation between cycles and the rhythm of technological innovation,[138] the capital or labor bias of the flow of innovations,[139] the prospects for the future increase in population and flow of innovations.[140] The latter passage introduces one of the key concepts in Harrod's 1939 growth model;[141] that is, the rate of advance "warranted by the normal increase in population and the normal increase in efficiency through inventions and improvements within the period.'' In fact Harrod introduces his 1939 excursion into a dynamic model of growth by linking it explicitly to the passages cited above from his 1936 *Trade Cycle* study.[142]

Putting aside refinements, Harrod's growth analysis proceeds in six stages.

1. *The Fundamental Equation.* In its simplest form, the warranted rate of growth (G_w) is determined by the following equation: $G_w = s/c$ where s is the proportion of income individuals and corporate bodies (private and public) choose to save; and C is the value of capital goods required for the production of a unit increment of output (the accelerator converted into the marginal capital-output ratio or capital coefficient). s and C are assumed to be independent of the value of output (G). In dynamic equilibrium the warranted rate of growth is "the one level of output at which producers will feel in the upshot that they have done the right thing, and which will induce them to continue in the same line of advance. Stock in hand and equipment available will be exactly at the level which they would wish to have them.''[143]

2. *Departures of Actual Growth Rate (G) from G_w.* If G exceeds G_w a capital shortage will assert itself; production for stocks and equipment will expand; G will depart further and further from G_w in a cumulative process of expansion, via the interaction of multiplier and accelerator. Similarly, if G falls below G_w, capital equipment and stocks are redundant, and a self-aggravating decline in output is set in motion. The inherent instability of the dynamic equilibrium path is fundamental for business cycle analysis.

3. *Endogenous Accelerator Investment versus Exogenous (or "Independent" or "Long-Range") Investment.* In fact, all investment is not determined by the rate of growth of output (the accelerator). Some components of investment may be determined by: (a) judgments about "prospective long-period increase of activity''; (b) new inventions calculated to revolutionize production costs or consumers' tastes; and (c) the *level* of income rather than the *rate of growth* of income (e.g., public works outlays by public authorities or even business firms sensitive to current profit levels). These refinements reduce the role of the accelerator principle in determining the dynamics of growth and fluctuations.

4. *The Role of the Foreign Balance.* G_w is raised by a rise in imports as a proportion of current income, lowered by a rise in exports or other foreign exchange earnings.

5. *The Natural Growth Rate.* Whereas G_w varies with phases of the business cycle and the level of activity, affecting s and C, the "natural rate of growth" is defined by Harrod

as "the maximum rate of growth allowed by the increase of population, accumulation of capital, technological improvement, and the work/leisure preference schedule, supposing that there is always full employment in some sense." Against this background a "proper" warranted rate is defined as the rate "which would obtain in conditions of full employment." If the latter is above the natural rate a chronic tendency to depression exists because, by definition, the natural rate sets a limit on the growth rate a given economy can, in fact, attain. If the proper warranted rate is below the natural rate, the system will experience a succession of booms marked by inflation and a shift of income to profits.

6. *Possible Implications for Policy.* If the proper warranted rate is substantially above the natural rate, a chronic rather than cyclical problem of underemployment is confronted and may require long-term anti-cycle measures. For example, a low interest rate encourages high values for investment independent of the accelerator and a high value for *C;* that is, capital-intensive investment. It may also reduce *s.* A virtually permanent public works supplement may also be required. On balance three factors suggested to Harrod that Great Britain as of the late-1930s was in such a state and required such remedies: (a) the decline in population growth; (b) the believed tendency of the more wealthy to save a larger fraction of their income; and (c) the possible tendency toward capital-saving innovations.

This kind of analysis, linking the multiplier and the accelerator, was, as Harrod noted (in a feeble but rare pun in the literature of economics) "rapidly accelerating" as the 1930s drew to a close.[144] Among the more famous such exercises, for example, was Paul Samuelson's multiplier–accelerator essay, virtually concurrent with Harrod's.[145] This form of economic analysis had many antecedents reaching back more than a century; and the pace of its development intensified with the contributions of a good many including the most nearly Harrodian, Bickerdike. Nevertheless, Harrod put it all into a neat bundle, focusing it with a touch of the Ricardian Vice on the problem of Britain in the 1930s as Keynesians saw it. Notably in the wake of the recession of 1937–1938, occurring long before the economy had attained anything approximating full employment—and like Hansen in the United States (following, pp. 321–323)—they took the British problem to be one of secular stagnation.

Looked at closely, virtually all elements in the classic growth equation were to be found somewhere in Harrod's equations except education and the quality of the working force. The rate of population increase was there, as were the investment rate and the productivity of investment. But neither Harrod (nor Samuelson) knew what to do with Schumpeter's insight that major innovations were endogenous and discontinuous, and that their ebb and flow were at the heart of cyclical fluctuations; nor did they know what to do with Kuznets's insight that the continuity of growth hinged on a sequence of leading sectors. Harrod (like Bickerdike) was aware that sectoral growth rates varied:[146] "Even in a condition of growth, which generally speaking was steady, it is not to be supposed that all the component individuals are expanding at the same rate." But the conveniences of highly aggregated growth and cyclical analysis were too great to forego; and without facing up to the inherently sectoral character of the innovation process, no satisfactory growth or cyclical analysis is possible.[147]

This, then, was the mainstream economist's vision of growth that emerged from the Keynesian Revolution on the eve of the Second World War and which was reaffirmed quite promptly in its wake once it was clear that reconstruction in Western Europe was likely to succeed and the United States not plunge again into deep depression. Evsey Domar's version of the growth equation was published in 1947–1948; Harrod's elaboration of his 1939 essay, *Towards a Dynamic Economics,* in 1948.[148] As a framework for viewing the macroperformance of advanced industrial economies this approach had the virtue of employing concepts capable of statistical measurement. The cumulative achievement of national income accounting provided usable approximations for G_w, s, and C. Moreover, it is possible to approximate Harrod's natural rate of growth; that is the approximate rate of advance that the increase in the working force and technological change will permit, at relatively full employment, given the full employment value of s. Some such path, when compared with the actual path of growth, measured the shortfall and proved useful for some public finance and other purposes. And, so long as the world economy—and especially its advanced industrial countries—moved forward with D. H. Robertson's "slooms and bumps" rather than pre-1914 decennial cycles or a repetition of the European interwar chronic unemployment levels, the refinement of such highly aggregated growth models did no great harm and afforded a substantial phalanx of talented mainstream economists a great deal of innocent pleasure in the 1950s and 1960s (see Chapter 15, to follow).

On the other hand, it is hard to conceive of a framework less likely to grip and generate understanding of the great boom of the 1950s and 1960s rooted as that boom was in four variables lost among the black boxes of Harrod–Domar and neoclassical growth models:

- The large backlog of technologies available to Western Europe and Japan already applied in the U.S. economy.
- A considerable pool of relatively new technologies available for rapid diffusion in all the more advanced industrial countries, e.g., television, synthetic fibers, plastics, a new batch of pharmaceuticals, atomic energy.
- An approximately 20% favorable shift for the advanced industrial countries in the terms of trade in the period 1951–1964.
- Despite a generally adverse shift in the terms of trade, an historically unexampled if somewhat erratic phase of growth in the developing regions.

Nor was it a framework that illuminated the growth problems of the 1970s and 1980s (following, pp. 350–351); and as Chapter 11 argues, it represented a setback rather than a stage of progress in the pre-1939 evolution of business-cycle analysis.

10

Business Cycles and Growth: From Juglar to Keynes

The period 1870–1939 was the heyday of business-cycle analysis in two respects: the problem attracted an extraordinary array of talent throughout the Atlantic world; and, from initial diversity and disarray, business-cycle analysis moved towards substantial consensus.[1] Combining the index of two major histories of economic theory, here is the list of names referenced under Business Cycles for this period: Fisher, Hawtrey, Hayek, Hobson, Juglar, Kitchin, Kondratieff, Kuznets, Mitchell (and the NBER), Mises, Moore, Panteleoni, Pigou, Robertson, Schumpeter, Spiethoff, Tinbergen, Wicksell. And the list is palpably incomplete; e.g., Burns, Haberler, Hansen, Harrod, Keynes, Myrdal, and Samuelson of the Multiplier–Accelerator (1939) failed to make it.

For reasons set out earlier I shall not attempt to identify the angle of approach of all these worthies, but will simply make two observations. First, it should be recalled that the business cycle was increasingly recognized as a recurrent phenomenon and a problem in the interval between Malthus–Ricardo (say, 1820) and Mill–Marx (say, 1870). The central theme of the period 1870–1939, as we have often noted, was welfare rather than growth; and periodic severe unemployment, its vicissitudes inadequately cushioned by private and public measures, emerged in democratic societies as a critically important welfare issue from the 1870s forward. Second, as the rhythm of the decennial cycle persisted between 1870 and 1914, in an environment where the volume of useful statistical data progressively improved, the opportunities for scientific study of the business cycle expanded and were increasingly seized upon by scholars on both sides of the Atlantic.

The number and quality of minds that turned to the study of business cycles thus resulted from a convergence of rising human and social concern and cumulatively expanding historical and currently collected evidence. From the special perspective of this book, however, the outcome of this rather grand international scientific effort proved anti-climactic. Just as the linkages between growth and cycles were emerging with increasing clarity—moving toward a convergence of Marshallian long- and short-period analysis—the depth and social pathology of the depression of the 1930s drove economists to put aside concern with the long period. The link with growth was attenuated or broken. Led by Keynes of the *General Theory* the operational focus for most economists became the expansion in short-period terms of output and employment. For these purposes highly aggregated analyses of the determinants of effective demand would do; and this tendency was heightened by the maturing of methods for the measurement of national income and its major components. Chapter 15 demonstrates that the character of the problems confronted (and not confronted) in the post-1945 world encouraged mainstream economists to persist along highly aggregated lines for almost 30 years: until the quadrupling of the oil price in 1973–1974.

I anticipate these judgments because they govern the organization of this chapter and the next whose sub-title might be: ''The Rise and Fall of Business-Cycle Analysis.'' I believe the application of the high-powered overaggregated theoretical tools and econometric exercises that dominated post-1945 macroeconomics have reduced rather than expanded our knowledge of the causes of fluctuations in real income in general, the cyclical process in particular. Some 40 years later I wholly agree with these gentle but acute observations of D. H. Robertson on business-cycle analysis as of 1948.[2] Referring to his youthful *Study of Industrial Fluctuations* (1915) he observed:

> Those long hours of wallowing in the Economist Annual Histories and similar material, however crude and amateurish their external fruits, had certain enduring internal consequences. To one so drenched with the vision of eternal ebb and flow, relapse and recovery, Keynes' final attempt in his *General Theory* to deal with the savings-investment complex in terms of a theory of static and stable equilibrium was bound to seem a step backwards, and his embrace, on the strength of one bad depression, of 100 percent stagnationism at least premature. As to stylised models of the cycle, of the kind now so fashionable, they doubtless have their uses, provided their limitations are clearly understood. We must wait with respectful patience while the econometricians decide whether their elaborate methods are really capable of covering such models with flesh and blood. But I confess that to me at least the forces at work seem so complex, the question whether even the few selected parameters can be relied on to stay put through the cycle or between cycles so doubtful, that I wonder whether more truth will not in the end be wrung from interpretative studies of the crude data of the general type contained in this volume, but more intensive, more scrupulously-worded and more expert.

Behind Robertson's conclusion is a more general judgment. Since the business cycle happens to be the form growth has assumed over the past two centuries at least, the separation of the two domains is inappropriate and has proved analytically costly; although it is theoretically quite possible if a sufficient number of unrealistic assumptions are made.

In any case, the reader should be aware of the narrow focus that governs the organization of this chapter. It examines a highly selected group of significant business-cycle analysts, focusing sharply on whether and, if so, how they linked cyclical analysis to the process of economic growth.

Juglar and Some Other Continentals

Schumpeter may have exaggerated somewhat in describing Clement Juglar (1819–1905) as ''among the greatest economists of all times''; but despite his predecessors, whom he consulted in a systematic and scholarly way, Juglar's *Des Crises Commerciales* remains a major benchmark in business-cycle analysis, and Schumpeter was just in using his name to designate the 9–10-year major cycle.[3]

Juglar, a medical doctor, began from an unusual angle: a study of population growth including fluctuations in marriages, births, and deaths.[4] After discounting for drought, wars, and epidemics he was led to reflect on the possibility that business fluctuations might have had an independent impact on these variables. A series of studies, starting out with Bank of France data from 1800, built up to the 1860 publication of *Des Crises Commerciales.* In subsequent editions, Juglar progressively extended the range of data he mobilized and came to embrace Britain and the United States. He dated accurately the cycles as well as times of crisis; surveyed various theories of causation, mainly focused on the expansion and contraction of bank credit; explored in detail the behavior of various value-denominated variables (e.g., prices, interest rates, exchange rates, components of central bank balance sheets); surveyed proposals for remedy (mainly financial and monetary); compared the same crises in the three countries, and analyzed comparatively the sequence of crises he identified (from 1696 to 1882 for Britain; 1800–1882, France; 1814–1882, U.S.A.); and, finally, he examined the impact of cyclical fluctuations on a wide array of economic (plus a few social) variables.

This orderly treatise, organized with impeccable French logic, closes in the spirit of a wise old doctor offering advice to an overvolatile—even manic—patient:[5]

> What we wished to demonstrate in this work and would be happy if we have succeeded in suggesting is: —to those who place excessive confidence in the future during a period of prosperity, *Prudence* in view of the inevitability of crisis and *the means for calculating the approach of crisis;*—[t]o those who permit themselves to become excessively depressed by the suffering imposed by the crisis, the hope of certain future *recovery;*—to those who employ or distribute that formidable but fragile power, credit, the *moderation* which would render it more stable and the *backbone* to maintain it;—to all those who are interested in human affairs a means to *explain* the facts of the past and, perhaps, the future in ways which would permit us if not to *eliminate* at least *soften* these terrible accidents we call *Commercial Crises.*

As Schumpeter points out, Juglar clearly anticipates those, like Wesley Mitchell—and, he might have added among others, Robertson, Pigou, and himself—who much later sought to combine systematically theory, history, and the orderly use of statistics to understand cyclical fluctuations.

But, Juglar, with all his pioneering virtue, is something of a washout so far as the relation between growth and fluctuations is concerned. He clearly perceived that crisis and depression were rooted in the excesses of prosperity; but, except for the need for moderation by all hands during the boom and for faith during depression, he had no clear definition of the variables that drove the economy forward along the path it would have followed, if perfect wisdom—or moderation—had prevailed. Like his contemporaries, J. S. Mill and Marx, he assumed economic progress was normal and, in a sense, automatic. Against that assumed background his view is well captured in the lines set out on the title page of *Des Crises Commerciales,* here translated: "The regular expansion of the wealth of nations does not take place without pain and resistance. In crises everything stops for a time, social life appears paralyzed; but it is only a passing stagnation (*torpeur*), prelude to happier times; in a word, it is a general liquidation."

But whatever the theoretical inadequacies of Juglar's insights, he asserted correctly and definitively that a more or less orderly cyclical process existed; and he demonstrated that it was subject to systematic exploration by the testing of theoretical hypotheses against statistical evidence.

One of the most obvious characteristics of cyclical behavior was the greater amplitude of fluctuations of statistical series linked to durable than nondurable goods; and the explicit linkage of cycles to economic growth takes its start—on the Continent as in Britain and the United States—with analyses that come to rest on the volatility of long-term investment. As Schumpeter put it bluntly:[6] "Most theories of cycles are nothing but different branches of that common trunk, 'plant and equipment.' "

At some risk of oversimplification, the Continental succession is from Tugan-Baranowsky to Spiethoff to Haberler's League of Nations synthesis (1937) and then Schumpeter's *Business Cycles* (1940).[7] Marx hovers explicitly or implicitly in the background throughout, not because he outlined a business-cycle theory others tested and refined but because he had insisted that the business cycle was an integral part of economic development under capitalism and that the cycle related somehow to the process of fixed capital formation.

Tugan-Baranowsky's study of British industrial crises was published in Russian in 1894, German in 1901, French in 1913.[8] Tugan-Baranowsky dramatizes his own cyclical theory in terms of the operation of a steam engine, an analogy Hansen summarizes as follows.[9]

> . . . It is the accumulation of loanable capital which plays the role of the steam in the cylinder; when the pressures of the steam against the piston attains a certain force, the piston is set in motion, and is pushed to the end of the cylinder; here the steam escapes and the piston returns to its former position. The accumulated loanable funds operate in the same manner in industry when they reach a certain volume. The funds are set in motion—i.e., expended on fixed capital goods. Once the loanable funds are exhausted, industry returns to its former position. In this manner crises recur periodically.

Loanable capital—the piston in this analogy—derives from idle balances built up during the depression; enlarged current savings generated during the boom, through the multiplier impact of increased investment on income; and the expansion of bank credit. The bottleneck is clearly on the supply side of the capital market: expansion proceeds until the sources of capital supply are exhausted.

But Tugan-Baranowsky goes a bit beyond. He devotes a considerable portion of his exposition to what might be called the real side of the cycle; that is, the demand for and production of capital goods, and the disproportions that can develop during the boom between requirements for consumers goods, working capital, fixed industrial capital, and infrastructure.[10] The linkage of these structural problems—evocative of Marx's analysis—to Tugan-Baranowsky's capital-supply piston is not lucidly and persuasively made; but it is clear that Tugan-Baranowsky took business-cycle analysis some distance beyond Juglar and Marx with the rudiments, at least, of a supply–demand analysis of capital formation.

Spiethoff moved forward on these foundations in two respects.[11] First, he linked cyclical expansion more explicitly to the growth process by underlining the importance of new inventions and the opening up of new territories; second, he attributed the cyclical crisis and depression primarily to "overproduction" although he did not exclude the operation of Tugan-Baranowsky's shortage of loanable capital as well.[12]

Spiethoff's concept of overproduction does, indeed, turn out to be quite complex, consisting of a long array of circumstances in which a "lack of balance between production and consumption" may exist.[13] The critical form of overproduction was, of course, what Spiethoff envisaged at the peak of the boom, i.e., the saturation of capital requirements brought about by the surge of investment in durable capital and consumers goods. For example:[14]

> The demand for productive equipment and durable consumers' goods is not continuous; and when an economy has been fully supplied with such goods, the plant and machines which produced them are thrown out of work. Once the iron industry of a country has produced the necessary railways, mere repair and upkeep are insufficient to keep the industry operating at capacity.

A less obvious aspect of Spiethoff's analysis is a question he poses from time to time but never clearly answers: what would the "ideal profitable balanced production" be like?[15] But he is content to specify the dynamic supply-and-demand forces in a modern capitalist economy that render imbalance the normal condition and to conclude almost wistfully:[16] ". . . balanced profitable production . . . as a contrast to overproduction is a phenomenon of short duration occurring only at the height of prosperity. Perhaps indeed it is only an ideal which is never actually realized."

It will be recalled that Schumpeter holds up the image of an economy in circular-flow equilibrium and describes it in professional detail, unlike Spiethoff's rather mystical "balanced profitable production." Like Spiethoff, he specifies the forces that render smooth dynamic equilibrium impossible under the broad rubric of "innovation" as he defines it. He then goes on (in *Business Cycles*) to argue that the inherently pioneering and, then, "swarming" character of the innovation process yields a three-cycle pattern of growth. His account of the Juglar cycle is distinguished from that of most of his contemporaries by his insistence (already articulated in *Theory of Development*) on the benign and constructive role of cyclical depression as the process of diffusing "the achievements of the boom over the whole economic system through the mechanism of the struggle for equilibrium."[17] But, like Spiethoff, Schumpeter never defined clearly the shape of the dynamic equilibrium from which capitalism deviated.

He did, however, provide us with a useful statement of the character of his agreement and disagreement with Spiethoff:[18]

> . . . I should only . . . add one thing, that capital investment is not distributed evenly in time but appears *en masse* at intervals. This is obviously a very fundamental fact. . . . The effect of the appearance of new enterprises *en masse* upon the old firms and upon the established economic situation, having regard to the fact . . . that as a rule the new does not grow out of the old but appears alongside of it and eliminates it competitively, is so to change all the conditions that a special process of adaptation becomes necessary.

Thus, Schumpeter placed himself firmly with the mainstream continental tradition but identified in one terse sentence the factor that most distinguishes his view from that of his predecessors and contemporaries; i.e., his recognition that innovations appear "*en masse* at intervals" and set in motion a painful as well as creative process of adaptation.

Gottfried Haberler's *Prosperity and Depression, A Theoretical Analysis of Cyclical*

Movements (1937) belongs, to a degree, with this brief survey of continental analyses of cycles and growth; but it is, in fact, a magisterial effort at analytic summation embracing cyclical theory throughout the advanced industrial world. It was a serious response to the challenge posed by its League of Nations sponsorship.[19] He summarizes the various existing business-cycle theories in reasonably clean-cut categories, with the continental overinvestment theorists given an ample but not overwhelming hearing, and he constructs a quite persuasive synthetic portrait of the cycle, as it moves through the four phases he defines. Prizes are awarded to all without the loss of analytic coherence.

But under the heavy weight of the depression of the 1930s and the governments' urgent search for short-run solutions, growth virtually disappears from Haberler's analysis. Reflecting the consensus that had emerged since 1870, investment takes over the center of the stage; but it is a rather abstract aggregate investment—essentially a component of effective demand rather than an engine of growth. Schumpeter's creative entrepreneurs make only a cameo appearance, and specific innovations are mentioned mainly as a force that raises the profit rate above the money rate of interest, thus inducing an increase in investment, effective demand, and employment.

Growth appears briefly disguised as "secular trend," a variable, like seasonal fluctuations, for which correction is required:[20] ". . . being primarily interested in cyclical movements of the order of magnitude of three to twelve years, we are concerned not so much with the 'Secular Trend' as with departures from it which our series exhibit." Focus on the depression and its remedy was so intense that the accumulating wisdom of the past several generations of business-cycle analysis was, for a time, lost from sight; i.e., the insight that the business cycle was simply the form growth assumed.

Three Cambridge Giants

A sequence somewhat similar to that we have traced on the continent was enacted in Cambridge over much the same period of time by three remarkable economists who came along in Marshall's wake: D. H. Robertson, A. C. Pigou, and J. M. Keynes, who is treated in Chapter 11.

D. H. Robertson

I begin the British story arbitrarily with the appearance of the 23-year-old Dennis Robertson at a session of the Royal Statistical Society on December 16, 1914, with Edgeworth in the chair.[21] The years preceding the First World War were particularly rich in major business-cycle studies. As Hutchison points out, Spiethoff's major work on business cycles was published in 1909; Pigou's *Wealth and Welfare* and Schumpeter's *Economic Development* in 1912, Irving Fisher's *Purchasing Power of Money* and Ludwig von Mises's *Theory of Money and Credit* were also published in 1912, with explicit application of their doctrines to business cycles; Wesley Mitchell and Albert Aftalion published massive works in 1913, and R. G. Hawtrey, his extreme articulation of a monetary theory of the cycle, *Good and Bad Trade*.[22] Cassel's Book IV on business cycles in his *Theory of Social Economy*, published accessibly in German in 1918, was, in fact, written in 1914. This was also the period when J. A. Hobson (*The Unemployed*, 1895), H. H. Davenport (1896), Thorstein Veblen (*Theory of Business Enterprise, 1904*), and Mentor Bouniatian (1908) were publishing their unorthodox, generally underconsumptionist cyclical doctrines. Writing of the period 1918–1929, Hutchison observes that:[23] "Most of the main contributions in these years took the form of revised and perfected versions of their theories by pre-war pioneers. . . ." He cites Spiethoff, Mitchell, Hawtrey, and Pigou, and he might well have included Schumpeter.

I introduce this lively and creative pre-1914 setting because young Robertson was clearly affected by it as well as part of it. There was evidently an intense, interactive international ferment underway, evocative of the 1930s on chronic unemployment and of the 1950s on economic development. Robertson by no means conformed to Myrdal's image of the parochial Anglo-Saxon economists engaged in "unnecessary originality": (p. 623, note 44). Robertson reflected a respectful knowledge of Spiethoff, Aftalion, and other continental figures, although his acknowledged weakness in German led to lags in his direct command of the literature.

At Robertson's presentation to the Royal Statistical Society in January 1914, his paper focused narrowly on the possible implications for cyclical fluctuations of the period of gestation of investment in a wide range of (mainly but not exclusively) British industries. Among others, he dealt with qualitative as well as statistical data relating to the British railway boom of the 1840s; a series of cycles in coal and pig iron; freight rates and shipbuilding; coffee, cotton spinning, and oil. With great—almost exuberant—energy, Robertson sought to evoke the institutional setting in which these sectoral investments took place; and, in accounting for year-to-year and cyclical movements in the time series he had collected, he sedulously consulted *The Economist Annual Reviews* and other contemporary sources. The whole was unified by incisive theoretical observations, some of which, as Robertson later noted, did not stand the test of time. But his central propositions were essentially correct: (a) the cycle was determined in part by investment decisions governed by current market indications of profit to which many responded without taking into account the consequences for supply and profitability of their collective decision, when the period of gestation had passed and new supplies came on the market, thus lowering radically the expected rate of return over cost in that sector; and (b) the cycle was also affected by the length of life of the capital good, notably ships, an element Bickerdike thought Robertson had inadequately stressed although it appears in his Royal Statistical Society paper.[24]

Robertson's 1914 paper is the basis for the first chapter in his *A Study of Industrial Fluctuations,* which, as Hutchison justly says, was "the first monograph devoted to the subject by an English academic economist combining historical, statistical, and theoretical analysis."[25]

So far as the linking of growth to cycles is concerned, I would rate Robertson's study among the few most original of the works published between 1870 and 1939.

After "wallowing" long hours in *Economist Annual Histories* and similar material, he emerged with an indelible sense of how and why one should begin the study of both growth and fluctuations in their full complexity, in the sectors, including all the major factors determining sectoral overinvestment and underinvestment. Part I of his study opens with three chapters on "Phenomena of Supply" followed by four on "Phenomena of Demand," including an exploration of the significance of crop fluctuations. After the experience of writing Part I, no one had to tell Robertson that Marshallian long-period forces were at work every day, shaping events over short periods of time, producing irreversible structural change.

Another distinguishing characteristic of Robertson's study is that he was forced by the logic of his initially sectoral approach to deal with the profound and inescapable interconnections within the international economy. This is a quite different matter than, say, studies, starting with Juglar's, that place national accounts of cyclical fluctuations side by side or, even, those that place emphasis on the macroeffects arising from the interconnection of money and long-term capital markets. Whether it was the impact on British shipbuilding in 1879 of the expected rise in British iron prices due to resumed U.S. railway building, or the recurrent impact of U.S. harvests and construction activity on the Yorkshire woolen trade, Robertson viewed the world economy as an intensely interconnected and interacting unit at the sectoral level.[26]

On the other hand, Robertson did not get lost among the trees. He quite explicitly linked sectoral and macroanalysis. For example, he notes in his 1948 Introduction:[27]

> . . . I should like to draw attention to the attempt (pp. 2–7), to define what the whole discussion is about. One feature of this attempt is the deliberate selection of *real national income* . . . rather than prices, profits or even employment, as the thing whose fluctuation is to be the primary object of study. . . .
>
> The next point for comment is the stress laid on the role of *invention* (including legal and geographical "invention") in moulding the course of investment and hence of general activity. . . . [T]here was nothing really new about this—though Schumpeter's work was not known to me till long after, and though I had to proceed in face of my master Pigou's then belief, afterwards handsomely reconsidered, that "specific inventions are like *enduring* booms in Nature's bounty, and are not, therefore, of first-rate importance for the study of *fluctuations*." I venture to hope that the passages in this book which attempt to trace the different consequences, for general activity, of the diverse natures and successive phases of the great innovations—railways, basic steel, electricity, oil—may still be worth searching for clues. Anyway, my explorations in this field, cursory as they were, have left me with an abiding sense of the difficulty of providing, in a world in which so many and such various changes may be wrought by the wand of Science, neat little models of the trade cycle and (*a fortiori*) neat little packets of therapeutic pills.

Although his analysis was tipped heavily to real factors, Robertson dealt with the monetary aspect of cycles as well in a chapter on "The Wage and Money Systems," that begins with this paragraph:[28] "The influence of a money, especially of a credit money, economy upon the course of trade is of such obvious importance that it has more or less completely hypnotised all but a very few of those who have contributed to the discussion of this problem."

He then proceeds to analyze how the banking system plays its part in each phase of the cycle. Along the way he rejects a strictly monetary argument for crisis and depression:[29] "Monetary influences, though they aggravate the severity of the crisis, are not its essential cause."

Robertson's conclusion is that the business cycle is the result of the peculiar way growth proceeds; that is, the way investment is conducted. In general, he is content to accept the limpid dictum of Marcel Labordère, a rich French eccentric whose pamphlet on the American crisis of 1907 made a deep impression on Robertson.[30] "La crise est venue . . . parce qu'on a voulu faire trop vite trop de choses à la fois."*

---

*"The crisis came . . . because people tried to do too quickly too many things at the same time."

In fact, Robertson argues that expansion can be halted by a reversal of any one of the forces that pulled the economy from "the nadir of depression in the first place."[31] The positive forces are defined as: (1) an increase in productivity due to more efficient methods adopted "under the stimulus of depression"; (2) good global harvests shifting the terms of trade favorably for industrial products and raising real incomes; (3) a rise in the expected productivity of capital goods due to the wearing out of "a large number of existing instruments," "the discovery of the industrial possibilities of a new country," or "some physical or legal invention"; and (4) an expansion of credit due to increased gold reserves or an increase in confidence otherwise caused. Robertson then specifies how the dynamics of the boom is capable of reversing each of these expansionary forces: the boom tends to induce increasing marginal costs and decelerated increases in productivity; bad harvests turn up after good; the expected rate of return on capital goods will decline as the period of gestation ends and new supplies come on the market; and rising prices and interest rates and a depletion of gold reserves may well erode confidence.

So far as growth and cycles are concerned it is clear that (3)—the rise and fall in the expected rate of return over cost (later Keynes's marginal efficiency of capital)—is what most matters in Robertson's analysis; and that factors (1) and (4) play their part via their impact on expectations and costs, as well.

From 1915 to the autumn of 1919 Robertson was in military service mainly in the Middle East. He resumed his Trinity fellowship and was assigned to write the book on money in the Cambridge Economic Handbook series, at a time, as Hicks notes, when money had become "important."[32] Chart 5.1 exhibiting the movement of British prices, unemployment, and real GNP for the period 1870—1939, suggests the basis for the pre-1914 sense of continuity among the major British (and other) economists, the interwar sense of discontinuity and vulnerability, and the underlying reason for a focusing of talent on problems of unemployment, sluggish growth, and (until the mid-1930s) price deflation.

Robertson, starting with his money textbook, emerged quickly as a major expert on monetary matters, his most substantial work being *Banking Policy and the Price Level* (1926), subtitled *An Essay in the Theory of the Trade Cycle*.[33] Although a good deal of Robertson's book is his contribution to an intense contrapuntal dialogue with Keynes on how to formulate the relation between savings and investment, both men (and others) having recognized that the two acts are often performed by different actors with differing motives. Out of this ferment Keynes, working with a circle that increasingly excluded Robertson,[34] was to emerge with the formulations in *The Treatise on Money* (1930) and *General Theory* (1936). Robertson's insistence on the continuity of his *Banking Policy* with his youthful *Study of Industrial Fluctuations,* with its strong emphasis on real as opposed to monetary factors, is of some interest. For example, the opening paragraph of the introduction to the first edition of *Banking Policy and the Price Level* includes this reaffirmation:[35] "I suspect that the minds of some modern writers are unduly influenced by certain exceptional features of the great post-war boom and slump: I hold that far more weight must be attached than it is now fashionable to attach to certain *real,* as opposed to monetary or psychological, causes of fluctuation. . . . "

And, looking back from 1949, Robertson makes even more explicit the link to his earlier work:[36]

> My object in writing the book was, first, to preserve and re-present some
> part of the analytical framework of my *Study of Industrial Fluctuation* (1915),

which had fallen out of print and which I could not bring myself to attempt to re-write; and secondly to interweave with the mainly "non-monetary" argument of that work a discussion of the relation between saving, credit-creation and capital-growth.

What, then, can we conclude about Robertson's view of growth and cycles? I would make four points.

First, Robertson's intellectual roots were, in the end, more in the continental than the British (i.e., Mill–Marshall) tradition of business-cycle analysis. In his introduction to *Banking Policy,* whom does this son of a schoolmaster and Anglican country parson, educated at Eton and as a classics scholar at Trinity, a bachelor whose only real home for all his life was his rooms at Trinity, reared on Marshall, taught by Pigou, influenced strongly and emotionally by Keynes—whom does this man cite in listing his obligations?[37] Aftalion (*Les Crises Périodiques de Surproduction*); Cassel (*Theory of Social Economy*); Labordère's pamphlet of 1907; and Spiethoff ("So far as I [D.H.R.] can judge without reading the original"). Pigou is often cited; and, in the 1926 introduction, the chapters on saving and investment (V and VI) are described as the product of "so many discussions with Mr. J. M. Keynes . . . that I think neither of us now knows how much of the ideas therein contained is his and how much is mine."[38] But it was an unflinching lifelong insistence on the role of real supply factors that most distinguishes Robertson and earns from Schumpeter considerable praise tempered by resentment at his imperfect grasp of the German language.[39]

Second, Robertson was clearly aware that each cycle had its own character, and its uniqueness had to be identified in part by the sectoral character of investment in the leading sectors of that cycle. There is, for example, an extended passage that begins: "The second aggravation arises from the fact that the invested resources are not as a rule equally distributed among all industries. . . ."[40] It is followed by references to booms in railroads, electric traction, rubber, oil, electric power, etc. Later, in *Banking Policy,* he has a blunt footnote which asserts simply: "The international boom of 1872 is in my view, to be particularly connected with railway building; that of 1882 with inventions in the steel trade; those of 1900 and 1907 with electricity; that of 1912 with oil-power."[41] This is as solid a linking of growth to cycles as one is likely to find. Moreover, Robertson, in returning to this theme in *Banking Policy,* comes closest of any economist of his time to the notion of sectoral optimum levels of output (and investment) with his concept of "Appropriate Fluctuations of Output" (Chapter II) and "Inappropriate Fluctuations of Output" (Chapter IV). Chapter II supplies criteria for defining dynamic sectoral equilibria but mainly in a cyclical context. Changes in output would be appropriate if they reflected accurately (1) changes in real operating costs that may reflect innovations in the sector of long-run significance or cyclical fluctuations in productivity; (2) changes in demand for both capital goods and durable consumers due to the operation of the accelerator or the period of gestation; and (3) intersectoral shifts in the terms of trade:[42] ". . . [T]hus [it] is that even in the simplified industrial world which we have constructed we should not expect the appropriate or optimum rate of industrial output to be constant, but to be subject to a succession of what may be called 'justifiable' increases and decreases, some at least of which are of a fairly rhythmical nature."

"Divergences between actual and appropriate output" (Chapter IV) derive from the following circumstances: (1) In many trades instruments of production are "very large, expensive, and durable" and, in addition, costly to adjust to decreased demand (e.g., the laying up of a ship, the damping down of a blast furnace, the closing of a coal pit); (2) the tendency for an excessive response to an increase in demand due to a convergence of response time lags and excessive estimates by each firm of its future share of the enlarged market; (3) the vulnerability to mutually reinforcing and excessive optimism (or pessimism) about the future in interconnected private markets; and (4) the money illusion—in which a seller is excited by the rise in his selling price but does not correctly estimate the likely rise in prices of the goods and services he purchases.

Robertson concludes:[43] "The aim of monetary policy should surely be not to prevent all fluctuations in the general price-level, but to permit those which are necessary to the establishment of appropriate alterations in output and to repress those which tend to carry the alterations in output beyond the appropriate point." Robertson does not pursue the full significance of his distinction between "appropriate" and "inappropriate" expansion of output for a simple reason we have encountered often in this parade of theorists: his interest is not the construction of a theory of growth but a theory of cycles or other lapses from full employment of the working force and of productive capacity. But of all the pre-1939 (and, I would add, post-1945) economists, he came closest to commanding the insights required to link a disaggregated sectoral-growth theory to the macroperformance of the economy.

Third, it was Robertson's view of the economic process—with its strands of dynamic real forces powerfully at work in the sectors and the increasingly strong but still limited powers of macropolicy instruments to moderate the impact of these real forces—that explains the difference between Robertson and Keynes, which came to a head with the publication of the *General Theory* and its aftermath. Here is Robertson's 1948 reflection on both Keynesian theory and policy:[44]

> . . . [T]o speak frankly, I think there is too great a disposition among the general public to believe that in the mid-'30s some revolutionary discovery was made about "effective demand" which has transformed the whole outlook. And the highly inflationary twist then given to that schematic statement of the whole problem which has won the widest measure of attention from the world seems to me to have had an unfortunate effect on policy, in England and the United States, since the end of the war.

Finally, one should note the manner in which Robertson wove together the short run and the long run in prescribing remedies for industrial fluctuations.[45]

> When fairly faced, the problem of the prevention of industrial fluctuation becomes nothing less formidable than the problem of maximising the community's aggregate of net satisfaction through time,—in other words of attaining the best distribution through time of its income of consumable goods which is practicable without undesirable restriction of the total of that income.
>
> In the light of this definition we may lay down the following propositions. The desired aim is likely to be furthered first . . . by anything which increases the tendency to inter-local and inter-temporal compensation in agriculture; secondly, by anything which, without sacrifice of efficiency, reduces the necessity for discontinuity in the process of investment; thirdly, by anything which diminishes the tendency of miscalculation either during the "boom" or the "depression"; and fourthly, by anything which mitigates those incidental

effects of over-investment during the boom which prevent it from being followed by a very large volume of consumption during the "depression."

He closes, after exploring remedies for "inappropriate fluctuations," in a mood of questioning evocative of J. S. Mill, but a good deal less confident of the right answer:[46]

> From some points of view the whole cycle of industrial change presents the appearance of a perpetual immolation of the present upon the altar of the future. During the boom sacrifices are made out of all proportion to the enjoyment over which they will ultimately give command: during the depression enjoyment is denied lest it should debar the possibility of making fresh sacrifices. Out of the welter of industrial dislocation the great permanent riches of the future are generated. How far are we bound to honour the undrawn bills of posterity, and to acquiesce in this never-closing hyperbola of intersecular exchange? Shall we sacrifice ourselves as willing victims to the
>
> > Urge and urge and urge
> > Always the procreant urge of the world?
>
> Or shall we listen to the words of one of the wisest of English philosophers, who counsels us to eat our grapes downwards, and who always washed up the knives first in case it should please God to take him before he got to the forks? The question is one of ethics, rather than of economics: but let us at least remember that we belong to an age which is apt to forget the ὅυ ἕνεκα among the ὧν ἄνευ οὔ, and immolate ourselves, if we must, with our eyes open and not as in a trance.*

A. C. Pigou (1877–1959)

Strictly speaking, Pigou should be accorded precedence in time over Robertson in a discussion of British analyses of the business cycle. He was 13 years older; became Marshall's successor as Professor of Political Economy in 1908; devoted a substantial section of his 1912 *Wealth and Welfare* to "the Variability of the National Dividend;" and supervised Robertson's *Study*.[47] On the other hand, Pigou came at the business cycle quite explicitly from the side of welfare. He conducted careful but also impassioned elaborations of Marshall. He demonstrated in a tradition reaching back to Hume that, if one granted the legitimacy of rough interpersonal comparison of utility, transfers of income and wealth from the rich to the poor could enlarge total satisfaction in a society. This possibility was at the center of his vision; and it found expression in his most famous and influential book, *The Economics of Welfare*.[48] The treatment of the business cycle in *Wealth and Welfare* is mainly focused on the burdens imposed on labor by fluctuations in income and employment, and on remedies, including "an efficient national labour exchange" and "regularized demand for labour." Analytically, Pigou concentrates on irregularities, in the "bounty of nature" and "the variability of error in business fore-

---

*In a world where the study of Greek is less common than in Robertson's youth, I should report that reliable authority informs me the two Greek phrases are reasonably translated, respectively, as "ultimate aims" and "inescapable necessities." In Richard Kahn's *The Making of Keynes' General Theory*, p. 20, the phrases are rendered: "Things which really matter among the things which we cannot do without."

casts'' as underlying causes of fluctuations. As noted earlier, Pigou then firmly held to a view later abandoned:[49] "Specific inventions are like enduring booms in Nature's bounty, and are not, therefore, of first-rate importance for the study of fluctuations.''

In the end, Pigou's view comes heavily to rest on the large amplitude of fluctuations in expectations. This turns out to be "a very great danger" because "[a] change in tune in one part of the business world diffuses itself, in a quite unreasoning manner, over other and wholly disconnected parts.''[50] Caught up in "sympathetic and epidemic panic, which so largely sways communities of men" [Kemmerer, *Money and Prices*] there comes into play a quasi-hypnotic system of mutual suggestion: "One with another, soul with soul they kindle fire from fire.'' Thus, ''. . . [t]hey rush in combined panic from side to side.'' As we have seen, successive errors of optimism and pessimism, with their impact on investment decisions, had long been recognized as part of the business-cycle process. But in his time Pigou dramatized that strand memorably.

The business cycle was dropped from the *Economics of Welfare* and pursued more systematically at book length in *Industrial Fluctuations,* a study which illustrates well Robert Skidelsky's *bon mot*[51]: ''. . . Pigou's way of learning a subject was to write a book on it. . . .'' And he wrote a book which, like Robertson's *Study,* seeks to combine theory, statistics, and frequent historical illustration. It is a bit like Haberler's League of Nations study in two respects: it embraces and seeks to integrate the major analytic hypotheses, including real, psychological, and monetary factors, with generous acknowledgments to the work of others; and it budgets about 150 pages for a critical examination of "remedies"—central bank and credit policy, wage policy, and a variety of devices to stimulate the demand for labor, including relief works, unemployment insurance, etc.

As for growth, Pigou, like most of his contemporaries, was quite well aware that cyclical fluctuations are a product of the process of growth; but his method is to isolate cycles from growth for purposes of both analysis and prescription. For example:

- In defining the problem of cyclical analysis, which he identifies in terms of fluctuations in employment, he focuses on "*deviations in the movement of the demand schedule away from its general line of trend*"; i.e., from the path of growth.[52]
- In introducing real causes of cycles, Pigou begins with a static norm or steady trend and then moves on:[53]

  In a non-stationary state . . . real causes *may* set going psychological causes: actual prosperity, for example, leading people to take an unduly optimistic view of the future. On the other hand, psychological causes *must* set going real causes, for an error of expectation made by one group of business men, leading to increased or diminished output on their part, alters the *facts* with which other groups are confronted. Nor is this all. The reactions set up may, when once started, be reciprocating and continuous . . .''

- In dealing with technological change, Pigou first introduces "minor inventions and improvements" that, "from the point of view of general industrial fluctuations [are] a minor factor that may safely be left out of account.''[54] He then goes on with this passage that draws a sharp Schumpeterian line between invention and innovation.[55]

  There are, however, from time to time large and dominating inventions, such as those associated with railway development, electrical development, and so on. . . . It is not the making of an invention or a discovery that sets up either the reactions of which we have just been speaking in the industry primarily concerned or the reactions in other industries: it is the *adoption and actual working* of the invention or discovery that does this.

- Some forty pages further on he evokes the pioneering entrepreneur:[56]

    In these circumstances [lower cyclical turning point] certain of the bolder spirits in industry begin to make preparations for an enlarged output, or to venture upon some hitherto untried type of enterprise, for which scientific advance has opened up the way. The pioneers, who thus undertake and expand enterprises, at once fill a social need and lay up treasure for themselves. Gradually, as no disaster happens to them, other less bold spirits follow their example; then others and yet others. . . .

    All these people are further encouraged by the fact . . . that, during the preceding period of depression, there has probably been an accumulation of technical improvements. . . . Advance thus takes place all along the line.

- These two passages—taken together—represent a considerable advance over Pigou's position in *Wealth and Welfare*. And, if read, as they can be, as simply emphasizing the distinction between the technological function of invention and the investment process of innovation, they stand as a legitimate part of the business cycle story.

I would thus conclude that Pigou carried forward in Britain in the 1920s with less originality but on a wider front the precocious prewar pioneering work of his student, Dennis Robertson. All the diverse essential elements were present in his work; but he did not begin with the process of economic growth and ask: What in that process made growth assume the form of cycles? He asked: How can I eliminate the trend (or growth) element from the data, so that I can isolate the purely cyclical elements in the process? The two questions are not quite identical; although it should also be noted that, in a footnote, Pigou quoted without criticism Schumpeter's central doctrine: "The recurring periods of prosperity of the cyclical movement are the form progress takes in a capitalistic society."[57] He did not, however, pursue the full implications of that proposition.

But in Britain as elsewhere, business-cycle analysis, as it had been evolving in the first third of the twentieth century towards an increasingly sophisticated linkage of cycles and growth, of the Marshallian short and long periods, was transformed and almost overwhelmed by the Keynesian Revolution.

11

Business Cycles and Growth: Keynes and After

J. M. Keynes (1883–1946)

So much has been written about Keynes and the Keynesian Revolution—the man was so multi-faceted, his impact on economics so ramified, his name associated with so many parallel or obliquely related developments—that it would be easy to be drawn at this point into one more spacious essay on his character as a personality and scientist, and on his times, ideas, and influence. What I have to say will be more useful if disciplined rather sharply to the narrow question that concerns us in this chapter; i.e., How if at all did Keynes's business-cycle analysis link to the analysis of growth? The answer, we shall find, is that there was a considerable retrogression between *A Treatise on Money* and *The General Theory*.

In both books his purpose was to use analysis of the trade cycle to exercise and illustrate his central themes. In *A Treatise,* he begins with an already familiar proposition; i.e., that saving and investment are functions performed by different persons or institutions for different purposes. The dynamics of *A Treatise* depends on definitions of income and saving that exclude windfall profits and losses of entrepreneurs.[1] Saving and investment are, therefore, unlikely to be equal. The difference between them drives the economic system into expansion (if investment exceeds saving) or contraction (vice versa); but each process is inherently limited.

Keynes begins his treatment of the trade cycle (which he calls the "credit cycle") by defining a dynamic equilibrium in which "the supply of money is being increased at the same steady rate as that of general output; e.g., (say) 3% per annum."[2] In this quantity-theory-of-money proposition, MV is increasing at the rate of $Q,$ and P is steady. Keynes then asks: "In what way can this state of equilibrium be upset?" Keynes responds by identifying potential sources of disequilibrium in monetary, investment, and industrial factors.

Against this background he traces out in generalized terms the "life-history" of a credit cycle, which takes its start as follows:[3]

> Let us suppose that circumstances have come about which lead en-
> trepreneurs to believe that certain new investments will be profitable; for
> example, a new technical discovery, such as steam or electricity or the inter-

nal-combustion engine, or a shortage of houses due to a growth of population, or more settled conditions in a country where previously the risks of normal development had been excessive, or a Capital Inflation due to psychological causes, or a reaction stimulated by cheap money from a previous period of underinvestment; i.e., a previous slump. If they are to put their projects into operation, they must either attract factors of production from other employments or employ factors previously unemployed.

Keynes then argues that this process (which can take various forms) is likely to set in motion a rise in both prices (Commodity Inflation) and costs of production (Income Inflation); but the former will exceed the latter, windfall profits will result, and, on his definitions, investment will exceed savings. All this implies compliance of the monetary authorities and an increase in interest rates not sufficiently great to destroy the mood of confidence that pervades what Keynes calls the Primary Phase of the credit cycle.

In the Secondary Phase, as expansion diffuses and full employment is approached, costs rise faster than prices of output (Income Inflation overtakes Commodity Inflation), and "sooner or later consumption goods will be coming on the market which can no longer be sold at the previously ruling price; so that the downward phase of the cycle now commences."[4] Other forces are likely to operate that also decree a falling expected profitability of investment, spreading loss of confidence, excessive interest rates, and credit contraction. All can be drawn together under the rubric of a shift to a period when entrepreneurial losses, by definition, yield an interval where saving exceeds investment.

Keynes concludes and draws one of the two major operational lessons of *A Treatise* as follows:[5]

> All this presumes of course that the Banking System has been behaving according to the principles which have in fact governed it hitherto, and that it lies either outside its purpose or outside its power so to fix and maintain the effective bank-rate as to keep Saving and Investment at an approximate equality throughout. For if it were to manage the Currency successfully according to the latter criterion, the Credit Cycle would not occur at all.

The second major lesson follows, namely, that a stable price level may not always be a correct overriding criterion for public policy because there may be circumstances where a protracted (as well as a temporary) Commodity (not Income) Inflation might prove salutary:[6]

> It should be noticed that the Commodity Inflation phase of a Credit Cycle cannot be of use for continuously raising the rate of wealth-accumulation. It is only useful for the purpose of producing a short, sudden spurt. . . .
>
> A prolonged Commodity Inflation due to progressive increases in the supply of money, as contrasted with a prolonged Commodity Deflation, is quite another thing . . . and may be a most potent instrument for the increase of accumulated wealth. . . .
>
> The advantages to economic progress and the accumulation of wealth will out-weigh the element of social injustice, especially if the latter can be taken into account, and partially remedied, by the general system of taxation;—and even without this remedy, if the community starts from a low level of wealth and is greatly in need of a rapid accumulation of capital.

Volume II of *A Treatise* extends his analysis of the volatility of investment and provides eight historical illustrations of his system and the policy doctrine he evolved from it.[7]

Once again, as we saw in Keynes's description of the possible initiating forces for the primary phase of the credit cycle, his analysis fully embraces the Marshallian long period and the factors making for growth. He focuses on the greater volatility and amplitude of movement of investment as the cause of disequilibrium between saving and investment, and he returns to the role of innovational investment with this reference to Schumpeter and the work of others who sought to link growth and cycles but weaving in an explicitly Robertsonian linkage of real and monetary factors.[8]

> In the case of Fixed Capital it is easy to understand why fluctuations should occur in the rate of investment. Entrepreneurs are induced to embark on the production of Fixed Capital or deterred from doing so by their expectations of the profit to be made. Apart from the many minor reasons why these should fluctuate in a changing world, Professor Schumpeter's explanation of the major movements may be unreservedly accepted. He points to "the innovations made from time to time by the relatively small number of exceptionally energetic business men . . . when a few highly-endowed individuals have achieved success, their example makes the way easier for a crowd of imitators. So, once started, a wave of innovation gains momentum."
>
> It is only necessary to add to this that the pace at which the innovating entrepreneurs will be able to carry their projects . . . will depend on the degree of complaisance of those responsible for the banking system. Thus whilst the stimulus to a Credit Inflation comes from outside the Banking System, it remains a monetary phenomenon in the sense that it only occurs if the monetary machine is allowed to respond to the stimulus. . . .
>
> Accordingly I find myself in strong sympathy with the school of writers— Tugan-Baranovski, Hull, Spiethoff and Schumpeter. . . . But none of these writers clearly apprehend the direct effect on prices of disequilibria between savings and investment and the part played by the Banking System. The pioneer work at this point is due to Mr. D. H. Robertson (*Banking Policy and the Price Level*). Moreover, lacking a version of the Quantity Theory of Money applicable to the problem of Credit Cycles, they have not got to the root of the matter or perceived that Cycles due to a growth of Working Capital are at least as "characteristic" as those primarily due to a growth of Fixed Capital.

And growth does not disappear from Keynes's eight historical illustrations which, at some risk of oversimplification, can be summarized tersely as follows:

- *Spanish Treasure*. The inflow of bullion to Europe starting early in the sixteenth century yields for Britain and France a greater rate of Commodity than Income Inflation and a salutary protracted increase in investment relative to saving. He concludes that even the working class, which experienced a fall in relative real income, was rewarded in the long run; but that the lesson for the present should not be hastily drawn.[9]
- *The Depression of the Eighteen Nineties*. Keynes takes this period to be a "perfect example of a prolonged Commodity Deflation" directly analogous to his view of Britain in the 1920s: prices fell more than costs, investment fell off radically;

savings and real wages for the employed were, respectively, well maintained and increased; interest rates were extraordinarily low. The Bank of England also wallowed in gold, a situation not typical of the 1920s. To deal with the case of relatively protracted and stubborn excess of saving over investment, Keynes counseled as follows:[10]

> . . . It may have been a case where nothing but strenuous measures on the part of the Government could have been successful. Borrowing by the Government and other public bodies to finance large programmes of work on Public Utilities and Government guarantees on the lines of the recent Trade Facilities and Export Credit Acts were probably the only ways of absorbing current savings and so averting the heavy unemployment of 1892–95. But any such policy was of course utterly incompatible with the ideas and orthodoxies of the period.

- *The War Boom, 1914–1918.* By trial and error, without an adequate theory of war economy or even war finance, Britain evolved a "virtuous" system:[11]

> . . . It is expedient to use entrepreneurs as collecting agents. But let them be agents and not principals. Having adopted for quite good reasons a policy which pours the booty into their laps, let us be sure that they hand it over in the form of taxes, and that they are not enabled to obtain a claim over the future income of the community by being allowed to "lend" to the State what has thus accrued to them. To let prices rise relatively to earnings and then tax entrepreneurs to the utmost is the right procedure for "virtuous" war finance. . . .
>
> Whilst I am not aware that the theory of the matter was ever expressed quite in this way, this is very nearly the system which the British Treasury had actually evolved by the method of trial-and-error towards the end of the war.

- *The Post-War Boom, 1919–1920.* Commodity Inflation (and investment in excess of saving) continued from the spring of 1919 to the middle of 1920; it then reversed with wages outrunning prices to the end of 1921. Keynes concludes:[12]

> Looking back, we see that the extreme prolongation of the slump was due to the Profit Deflation which occurred in the first half of 1921. This was doubtless inspired by the object of cancelling some part of the Income Inflation of the war and post-war periods—as was, indeed effected from the middle of 1921 to the end of 1922 and again subsequently to 1924. But from the standpoint of national prosperity it was a mistake. We might have avoided most of the troubles of the last ten years—and been, perhaps, just about as rich as the United States—if we had endeavoured to stabilise our monetary position on the basis of the degree of Income Inflation existing at the end of 1920, i.e., about 175 per cent up as compared with pre-war. Incidentally this would have left the real burden of the War Debt at less than two-thirds of its present figure. The policy actually adopted increased the severity of the Debt problem by 50 per cent, and gave us a decade of unemployment which may have diminished the production of wealth by more than £1,000,000,000.

- *Great Britain's Return to the Gold Standard [May 1925].* The Bank of England's return to the gold standard produced a fall in commodity prices and profits but not in costs (i.e., wages).[13]

The entrepreneur, faced with prices falling faster than costs, had three alternatives open to him—to put up with his losses as best he could; to withdraw from his less profitable activities, thus reducing output and employment; to embark on a struggle with his employees to reduce their money-earnings per unit of output—of which only the last was capable of restoring real equilibrium from the national point of view. . . .

The entrepreneur tried all three. . . .

. . . the loss of national wealth entailed by the attempt to bring about an Income Deflation by means of the weapons appropriate to a Profit Deflation was enormous. If we assume that only half the unemployment was abnormal, the loss of national output may be estimated at more than £100,000,000 per annum—a loss which persisted over several years.

- *British Home and Foreign Investment after the Return to Gold.* The post-May 1925 adjustment of the British economy was further complicated by a vicious circle. Profit deflation at home rendered capital exports more attractive at a time when Britain's overvalued exchange rate rendered it impossible to generate the surplus on trade account that should finance capital exports. The consequent pressure on the overall British balance of payments led to higher interest rates in London, prolonging the excess of domestic saving over investment, increasing further the attraction of foreign lending. Since the attainment of an adequate trade surplus appeared ruled out when Keynes wrote (1930) he advocated a series of familiar remedial measures of public policy plus the following:[14]

> It may be that the attainment of equilibrium in accordance with our traditional principles would be the best solution,—if we could get it. But if social and political forces stand in the way of our getting it, then it will be better to reach equilibrium by such a device as differential terms for home investment relatively to foreign investment, and even, perhaps, such a falling off from grace as differential terms for home-produced goods relatively to foreign-produced goods, than to suffer indefinitely the business losses and unemployment which disequilibrium means.

Thus, after about 175 years, the mainstream tradition of advocacy of free trade by British political economists came to an end.

- *The United States, 1925–1930.* The American boom and crash was a puzzle to Keynes and his *Treatise* system with which he felt impelled to grapple. He viewed the boom as marked by a rare maintenance of balance between saving and investment with commodity prices falling, down to its climactic phase (1928–1929). In part this equilibrium was due to a great expansion in corporate saving, about 60% of the U.S. total, despite the lack of Commodity Inflation and the windfall profits that thereby accrue to entrepreneurs. Keynes concluded that a Profit Inflation did occur in 1928–1929 in which, for corporations, high short-term money-market rates were outbalanced by high stock prices relative to dividend yields. Nevertheless, in the end, the protracted period of dear money preceding the stock market crash had its effect, reinforced by the depressing psychological effect of the crash itself on consumers' purchases of new motorcars and other "extravagances."

- *The "Gibson Paradox."* Why, systematically, did long- and intermediate-term trends in commodity prices move in the same direction as interest rates, all the way back to 1820? Keynes's central proposition was quite Wicksellian: the market rate of interest tended systematically to lag behind the natural rate; the lag induced a "prolonged tendency for investment to fall behind saving when this [natural] rate is falling . . . and to run ahead of saving when it is rising. . . . "[15] Thus he concludes again with a lesson for Britain in 1930:[16]

> In general, I am inclined to attribute the well-known correlation to . . . a failure of the market-rate of interest to fall as fast as the natural-rate. . . .
>
> . . . I repeat that the greatest evil of the moment and the greatest danger to economic progress in the near future are to be found in the unwillingness of the Central Banks of the world to allow the market-rate of interest to fall fast enough.

I have summarized these applications of the *Treatise* system for two reasons. First, I have long concluded that the simplest way to verify one's understanding of an economic theorist's concepts is to observe how he applies them to a familiar body of fact.[17] This is a particularly useful supplementary method in dealing with a rather complex treatise like Keynes's, full of special definitions, learned elaborations and detours, and the somewhat ponderous self-consciousness of a great book summarizing a quarter-century's study, experience, and reflection. I don't believe any one can read these eight illustrative homilies without understanding the essence of Keynes's *Treatise* system and its message.

A second reason is to suggest how closely geared Keynes's *Treatise* theory is to its message. Despite its scale, academic texture, references to the literature, and almost leisurely pace, the *Treatise* is quite as much a pamphlet for the times as the *General Theory*. It argued the sequence of consistent positions he had taken, starting in July 1923, opposing the return to the gold standard at prewar parity, proposing positively a mixture of monetary and fiscal policies, domestic and international, designed to free Britain from the tyranny of imposed deflation and chronic high unemployment that averaged 13% in 1921–1924 and 11% in 1925–1929.[18] The definitions of saving and investment, the distinction between Commodity and Income Inflation, and all the rest of the paraphernalia constitute, from the perspective of economic theory, one of a number of efforts in Keynes's generation to escape from the limitations of the quantity theory of money, with its obsessive focus on the price level rather than the rate of growth of output or level of unemployment. As one of Keynes's biographers has written:[19] "The history of the Keynesian revolution is largely a story of Keynes's escape from the quantity theory of money."

But more fundamentally, the theoretical structure Keynes devised between 1925 and 1930 was designed to provide a firm underpinning—and if possible, a professional consensus—for policy positions he felt were fundamental to the survival of a vital Britain.

This was, of course, also Keynes's purpose in *The General Theory*. What evoked a second heroic effort to remake the theoretical foundations of what we now call macroeconomic policy?

First, the *Treatise* failed to achieve Keynes's grand purpose. Along with testimony to the Macmillan Committee in 1930 and, indeed, all he had written and argued since 1923, Keynes contributed significantly to the consensus that shaped the radical revision of British domestic and foreign economic policy in 1931. But the *Treatise*, while widely respected, failed to rally the economics profession to the firm analytic consensus he judged necessary to force a radical change in public policy. Few of his fellow economists accepted even his critically important definition of saving and investment, although in imprecise, commonsensical form the notion of a gap achieved wide currency.

In a curious way Keynes's sense of frustration if not failure in the wake of the *Treatise* ranks in the history of economic doctrine with David Hume's reaction to what he judged to be the failure of his youthful *Treatise of Human Nature*. That reaction yielded Hume's brilliant and highly successful short policy essays in economics and politics. In Keynes's case it yielded a determination the next time round to capture the attention of his professional colleagues and the economically-literate public by hitting the sluggish mule of conventional wisdom with a 2×4. In the climax to one of the best passages in his biography of Keynes, covering the transition from *A Treatise* to the *General Theory*, Harrod states the point well:[20]

> It has been said, with some show of justice, that in this volume he went out of his way to stress differences from and find weaknesses in traditional economic theory. . . . To some he seemed to take a mischievous pleasure— perhaps he did—in criticising revered names. In fact this was done of set purpose. It was his deliberate reaction to the frustrations he had felt, and was still feeling, as the result of the persistent tendency to ignore what was novel in his contribution. He felt he would get nowhere if he did not raise the dust. He must ram in the point that what he was saying was inconsistent with certain lines of classical thought, and that those who continued to argue that he was merely embroidering old themes had not understood his meaning.

A second factor at work in the post-*Treatise* (post-1930) period was a worsening of the world (and British) economic situation. The average level of British unemployment in the 5 years 1930–1934 was over 19%, rising to a peak of 22% in 1932; but it was still 17% in 1934, at the end of which year *The General Theory* began to circulate for criticism. In the 1920s, whose problems generated *A Treatise,* the United States enjoyed great sustained prosperity, and France and Germany quite good times in the period 1925–1930 when *A Treatise* was written. It aimed primarily to stir Britain from what Keynes regarded as the costly perversity of Treasury and Bank of England policy. In the 1930s Keynes was concerned for the fate of the West and democratic civilization as a whole, palpably threatened from abroad by fascism and communism, and at home by the unwisdom of conventional political economy and the bedeviled politicians who had no other doctrines to turn to.

Third, in his escape from the Quantity Theory of Money to one that related money, prices, output, and employment in a better way, Keynes's *Treatise* proved to be a way station. He began immediately to move beyond, stimulated by the emergence as the 1930s began, of a lively circle of young economists. Their leader in relation to Keynes was Richard Kahn, who along with Dennis Robertson was cited by Keynes for important assistance in the final stages of *A Treatise.* Starting with his celebrated "Home Investment and Unemployment" (*Economic Journal,* June 1931), Kahn and his multiplier was a major actor in the process that yielded the *General Theory.* The multiplier related change in the level of investment directly to a change in the level of employment or income, the impact on the latter depending primarily on the proportion of income saved and spent. This eliminated the role of windfall profits and losses (and Commodity versus Income Inflations and Deflations) as the instruments driving the system to expand or contract. And, as every elementary student of economics now knows, Keynes argued that the level of investment (and thus employment and income) was determined by the intersection of a marginal efficiency of capital curve (essentially Fisher's expected rate of return over cost)

and the rate of interest; but interest was determined independently by the multiple demands for money (liquidity preference) and the supply of money provided by the banking
system. With the rate of interest thus determined by forces other than a simple equilibrium
clearing of demand and supply in the investment market, an explanation could be provided for chronically high levels of unemployment. Keynes's decade-old support for
active public policies to reduce interest rates and stimulate investment and consumption
had a new theoretical rationale.

In this formulation investment and saving were brought into equality by a dynamic
process in which, for example, intended saving in excess of investment so lowered
income as to yield, *ex post,* equality with investment.

Now, what about growth and cycles in the *General Theory?* It will be recalled that, in
the *Treatise* Keynes accepted, as descriptive background, the insights of his contemporaries who took into account changes in technology (preceding, p. 274). The investment
that exceeded or fell short of saving, as he then defined them, embraced quite explicitly
major discontinuous innovations. It is true that Keynes was much more at home in dealing
with the banking system, the capital markets, and international finance than with industrial investment and technology. Unlike Robertson, Keynes never slogged through the
Economist files or calculated periods of gestation for coal mines and ships, coffee and
railroads. Nevertheless, the Marshallian long-period real factors have a significant place
in the business-cycle analysis incorporated in *A Treatise on Money.*

Formally, at least, the *General Theory* is set up in strictly Marshallian short-period
terms:[21]

> We take as given the existing skill and quantity of available labour, the
> existing quality and quantity of available equipment, the existing technique,
> the degree of competition, the tastes and habits of the consumer, the disutility
> of different intensities of labour and of the activities of supervision and
> organisation, as well as the social structure including the forces, other than
> our variables set forth below, which determine the distribution of the national
> income. This does not mean that we assume these factors to be constant; but
> merely that, in this place and context, we are not considering or taking into
> account the effects and consequences of changes in them.

Robert Solow makes this point, although he is thinking of the long period in more
highly aggregated terms than I am:[22]

> Perhaps the largest theoretical gap in the model of the *General Theory* was its
> relative neglect of stock concepts, stock equilibrium, and stock-flow rela-
> tions. It may have been a necessary simplification for Keynes to slice time so
> thin that the stock of capital goods, for instance, can be treated as constant
> even while net investment is systematically positive or negative. But those
> slices soon add up to a slab, across which stock differences are perceptible.
> Besides, it is important to get the flow-relationships right; and since flow-
> behavior is often related to stocks, empirical models cannot be restricted to
> the shortest of short runs.

In dealing with the trade cycle, however, Keynes's narrow *General Theory* focus on the
short period did not prove wholly possible.

Like the analysis of the credit cycle in *A Treatise,* Keynes's "Notes on the Trade

Cycle'' in the *General Theory* is a self-conscious exercise in applying to complex reality his current theoretical system, which he summarized with admirable compression as follows:[23]

> Thus we can sometimes regard our ultimate independent variables as consisting of (1) the three fundamental psychological factors, namely, the psychological propensity to consume, the psychological attitude to liquidity and the psychological expectation of future yield from capital-assets, (2) the wage-unit as determined by the bargains reached between employers and employed, and (3) the quantity of money as determined by the action of the central bank; so that, if we take as given the factors specified above, these variables determine the national income (or dividend) and the quantity of employment.

He begins with the latter stages of the boom and onset of the ''crisis'' running briskly through the phases of the cycle with heavy emphasis on the ''three fundamental psychological factors.''[24] Keynes argues that the boom proceeds until overoptimistic expectations about the profitability of investment cease to offset the decline in the yield of capital goods due to their ''growing abundance [diminishing returns to the capital stock] and their rising costs of production [Cost Inflation in the language of *A Treatise*] and, probably, a rise in the rate of interest also.''[25] Thus, booms ''wear themselves out.''[26] The crisis and turn from prosperity to depression is not brought on primarily by a rise in the rate of interest—as prosperity increases two of the sources of liquidity preference (''for trade and speculative purposes'')—but by ''a sudden collapse in the marginal efficiency of capital'' [''the psychological expectation of future yield from capital assets'']. Keynes does not specify the triggering mechanism ''when disillusion falls upon an over-optimistic and over bought market''; but he notes that it precipitates ''a sharp rise in liquidity preference—and hence a rise in the rate of interest,'' which will aggravate a decline in investment primarily caused by a reversal of expectations about the expected rate of return over cost (i.e., the collapse of the marginal efficiency of capital). It is the convergence of the collapse of the marginal efficiency of capital and the rise in liquidity preference that ''renders the slump so intractable.'' But an end to the liquidity crisis and a fall in the rate of interest as depression takes hold (reducing the transactions demand for money) are insufficient foundations for the revival of the economy:[27]

> . . . [I]t is not so easy to revive the marginal efficiency of capital, determined, as it is, by the uncontrollable and disobedient psychology of the business world. It is the return of confidence, to speak in ordinary language, which is so insusceptible to control in an economy of individualistic capitalism. This is the aspect of the slump which bankers and business men have been right in emphasising, and which the economists who have put their faith in a ''purely monetary'' remedy have underestimated. . . .
>
> Unfortunately a serious fall in the marginal efficiency of capital also tends to affect adversely the propensity to consume. For it involves a severe decline in the market value of Stock Exchange equities. . . . With a ''stock-minded'' public, as in the United States to-day, a rising stock-market may be an almost essential condition of a satisfactory propensity to consume; and this circumstance, generally overlooked until lately, obviously serves to aggravate still further the depressing effect of a decline in the marginal efficiency of capital.
>
> . . . In conditions of *laissez-faire* the avoidance of wide fluctuations in

employment may, therefore, prove impossible without a far-reaching change in the psychology of investment markets such as there is no reason to expect. I conclude that the duty of ordering the current volume of investment cannot safely be left in private hands.

This argument evidently was designed to buttress Keynes's case for systematic state intervention both "to promote investment and, at the same time, to promote consumption, not merely to the level which with the existing propensity to consume would correspond to the increased investment, but to a higher level still."[28]

At several points in this systematic application of his system to trade-cycle analysis and remedy, Keynes breaks out of his formal structure with *ad hoc* observations of relevance to growth analysis.

He introduces repeatedly, for example, the notion that each boom is marked by certain sectors where overoptimism is particularly marked, the increase in investment particularly heavy, and the pattern of investment thus "misdirected."[29] It is in these sectors where overshooting is greatest that the dramatic collapse of the marginal efficiency of capital occurs, with its multiple spreading effects. This is a correct and powerful insight; but it cannot be realistically introduced into business-cycle analyses framed by Marshallian short-period assumptions. Moreover, Keynes does not define the sectoral levels of output and investment that would define a correct as opposed to a "misdirected" pattern of investment. He introduces the point merely to illustrate his basic conclusion that, at the peak of the boom, overinvestment exists in only a limited sense:[30]

> . . . [T]he term over-investment is ambiguous. It may refer to investments which are destined to disappoint the expectations which prompted them . . . or it may indicate a state of affairs where every kind of capital-goods is so abundant that there is no new investment which is expected, even in condi- tions of full employment, to earn in the course of its life more than its replacement cost. . . . [I]t is only in the former sense that the boom can be said to be characterised by over-investment. . . . It may, of course, be the case—indeed it is likely to be—that the illusions of the boom cause particular types of capital-assets to be produced in such excessive abundance that some part of the output is, on any criterion, a waste of resources. . . . It leads, that is to say, to *misdirected* investment.

In my view this is the critical insight; i.e., that "over-investment" in a boom is a sectoral and not an aggregate phenomenon. It was not pursued by Keynes or by his successors in business-cycle analysis. The link of growth to business cycles was thereby rendered much less realistic than if his insight into unbalanced sectoral distortion was sedulously pursued.

In expounding his view of the trade cycle Keynes was forced to slip out of the short period at several further points; for example, the declining yield from the capital stock as it expands during the boom is hard to fit into a short-period framework and, historically, the kind of sectoral surges yielding, for the time, gross investment distortion ("misdirec- tion") were associated with the introduction of major new technologies, the opening up of new territories, large waves of immigration, and other phenomena of the Marshallian long period. In addition, the *General Theory* moves explicitly into the long period as Keynes introduces his then rather depressing view of the long-term prospects for the marginal efficiency of capital under capitalism.[31]

During the nineteenth century, the growth of population and of invention, the opening-up of new lands, the state of confidence and the frequency of war over the average of (say) each decade seem to have been sufficient, taken in conjunction with the propensity to consume, to establish a schedule of the marginal efficiency of capital which allowed a reasonably satisfactory average level of employment to be compatible with a rate of interest high enough to be psychologically acceptable to wealth-owners. . . .

To-day and presumably for the future the schedule of the marginal efficiency of capital is, for a variety of reasons, much lower than it was in the nineteenth century. The acuteness and the peculiarity of our contemporary problem arises, therefore, out of the possibility that the average rate of interest which will allow a reasonable average level of employment is one so unacceptable to wealth-owners that it cannot be readily established merely by manipulating the quantity of money. . . .[,] time-honoured methods may prove unavailing.

The *General Theory* was not expounded in a lucid and felicitous way, despite Keynes's great stylistic gift; and, in addition, it met the kind of resistance any book is liable to meet that applies a new vocabulary to a familiar subject.[32] The relatively young were less affronted than their older colleagues; and a variety of efforts were made quite promptly to clarify, improve, or go beyond the *General Theory;* e.g., Harrod's *Trade Cycle* (1936) and Samuelson's bringing together of the multiplier and the accelerator. There were also elaborations, among others, by Michael Kalecki and Nicholas Kaldor.[33] What was lost in these elegant exercises in highly aggregated short-term income analysis was the growing pre-*General Theory* consensus—reflected within the book but not pursued—that perceived that cycles and growth were intimately interwoven; that the analysis of growth had to confront the process of innovation; that innovation had to be understood as initially a sectoral process; and, therefore, cyclical analysis had to be conducted in sectoral as well as macro terms. The setting aside of these insights in post-*General Theory* models drained both growth and cycles of their sectoral content and, thus, innovational substance.

W. C. Mitchell (1874–1948)

Wesley Mitchell's 1913 classic, *Business Cycles,* is one of a group of business-cycle studies that came to fruition at about the same time—on the Continent, in Britain, and in the United States. Despite important differences in method, style, and substance—and unquestioned "subjective" originality and independence—they constitute, in Schumpeter's phrases, work done "in a kindred spirit" bearing "a certain family likeness in their conceptions of the problem:"[34]

 . . .([A]s in the case of the discovery—or invention—of the calculus, and many similar ones) there is the fact that men's minds, at any given time, are apt to converge in similar views but in such manner as to make these men— and their pupils—see secondary differences between one another more clearly than the essential similarities. In the case before us, workers were under the impression that the number of different "explanations" [for the business cycle] was increasing, whereas the fact is that a certain family likeness in their conceptions of the problem—of cycles versus "crises"; their methods—involving increasing appeal to statistical material; and their results—such as emphasis upon a generalized form of what we call now the acceleration principle, became more strongly marked all the time. No one author led in this movement and none seems to have been greatly influenced by the others. But the date of Mitchell's volume assures to it an outstanding position in the history of the movement.

Like Keynes, Mitchell did not produce in his twenties a book that framed and fore-shadowed his life work. One can, it is true, find in Mitchell's doctoral thesis at Chicago, *A History of the Greenbacks* (1903)—published when the author was 29—an integrated analysis of monetary and real factors that constituted "a first step toward a general theory of the money economy of today, his real topic throughout his adult life."[35] Without question, his early studies of the greenback period did start him on the road of testing theoretical propositions against the facts—in the first instance, the quantity theory of money. But I would guess that it was Veblen's limited but powerful influence at Chicago that most strongly left its mark on Mitchell's business-cycle analysis, on which be began to focus in the period 1905–1908.

The Veblenian strand in Mitchell leads all the major commentators to spend some time sorting out his attitude toward and the relationship of his work to conventional economic theory.

On the one hand, unlike some institutionalists who proudly set aside mainstream economics of their day, Mitchell was a serious student of economic theory and lectured at Columbia University regularly on current types of economic theory. He had studied economics for a year in Germany and Austria; and he knew the literature written in German, although Hansen observes that "one carries away the strong feeling that the basic contributions of this group of thinkers [the Continentals] never fully registered on Mitchell's mind."[36] Nevertheless both his 1913 *Business Cycles* and 1927 *Business Cycles: The Problem and Its Setting* begin with a review of business cycle theories.

On the other hand, his commitment to institutionalism had a dual impact that separated his work from contemporaries of different methodological faith. First, he attributes the bulk of *Business Cycles*—an elegant book of over 600 quarto pages—to[37]

> . . . [m]y conviction that the quickest way to attain reliable results is to take great care in measuring the phenomena exhibited by business cycles. . . . Readers who look over the first chapter will find that many diverse theories about the causes of crises seem plausible when considered in the light of common knowledge. To determine which of these explanations are really valid, it is necessary to find out the regularity with which each alleged stress recurs, the scope which each attains. The elements which enter into each, and the consequences with which each is associated. To make progress toward the solution of these problems requires the collection and analysis of elaborate records of business experience in quantitative form.

This was the faith and method that controlled Mitchell's work and it was the rock on which the National Bureau of Economic Research was to be built.

But second, Mitchell accepted a quite explicit and powerful set of concepts from Veblen that provided his work with a central focus and institutional setting, but also tended to blind him to perspectives that might have led him to link growth and cycles more effectively than he did. His Veblenian strand derives explicitly from *Theory of Business Enterprise*.[38] Its flavor is captured in a passage like this:

> A business enterprise may participate directly or indirectly in the work of providing the nation with useful goods, or it may not. For there are divers ways of making money which contribute nothing toward the nation's welfare, and divers ways which are positively detrimental to future welfare. But, for the understanding of prosperity and depression, it is more important to observe that even the enterprises which are most indubitably making useful goods do so only so far as the operation is expected to serve the primary business end of making profits. Any other attitude, indeed, is impracticable under the system of money economy.

There is nothing intrinsically wrong or even remarkable about this statement. As Mitchell observes in a footnote: "Practically all the recent theories rest tacitly on this basis ['money-making' or profit-maximization]. Veblen is explicit on this point."[39] And the distinction he draws from Veblen between the criteria of "the well-being of the community," requiring "efficient industry and commerce," and the vastly less important criteria for "successful money-making" is, again, familiar, although not as fully developed as it was, for example, by Marshall and Pigou. What this Veblenian strand does supply is a large, never-fulfilled vision of capturing the dynamics of a "money economy" and a narrower, more conventional objective of tempering the amplitude of cyclical fluctuations.[40]

> . . . [T]he complicated machinery of the money economy has never been wholly under the control of its inventors. The workings of the system are not fully mastered even by the present generation of business men, and recurrently the financial machinery inflicts grave suffering upon us who use it. . . . [B]ecause our theoretical knowledge and our practical skill are deficient regarding these technical matters, we cannot maintain prosperity for more than a few years at a time.
>
> Nevertheless, within the past century, we have made incontestable progress toward mastery over the processes of the money economy . . . . By a combination of various agencies such as public regulation of the prospectuses of new companies, legislation supported by efficient administration against fraudulent promotion, more rigid requirements on the part of stock exchanges regarding the securities admitted to official lists, more efficient agencies for giving investors information, and more conservative policy on the part of the banks toward speculative booms, we have learned to avoid certain of the rashest errors committed by earlier generations. Again from hard experience, European banks at least have learned methods of controlling a crisis and preventing it from degenerating into a panic. The "integration of industry" has also done something, though less than is often claimed, toward steadying the course of business both by concentrating power in the hands of experienced officials, and by moderating the extreme fluctuations of prices.

Thus, Mitchell—like so many of his generation—approached cyclical analysis as a byproduct of a larger impulse to explore, in effect, welfare economics.

The technical organization of Mitchell's *Business Cycles* requires brief summary both because it cast a long shadow on subsequent U.S. business cycle research and because it is necessary to understand the unsatisfactory linkage of growth and cycles in Mitchell's work.

After establishing his theoretical perspective and his view of the institutional setting of the advanced industrial countries (the United States, England, and France) Mitchell's exposition proceeds in four parts:

- Some 45 pages of business annals covering the period 1873 to 1911 reflecting in more systematic form the lively sense of the unique character of each cycle to be found in Robertson's *Study*.
- Some 350 pages of well-organized statistical data, including analytic discussion of their movement, embracing commodity prices, money and real wages, interest rates, interest rate and stock prices, series reflecting variations in physical output and unemployment, data on the quantity of money and its velocity of circulation, and data bearing on saving, investment, profits, and bankruptcies.
- A stylized analytic description of the cyclical process (of about fifty pages) with great emphasis on "How Prosperity Breeds Crisis," embracing five major endogenous degenerative processes that operate during a boom ultimately to reverse the process.
- And, finally, reflections on the meaning of the cyclical process for human welfare with special emphasis, among proposed remedies, on the creation of better "business barometers," a function the NBER was, in time, to fulfill with distinction.

The fact that the analytic end product of Mitchell's effort was the stylized analytic description of the cycle (Part III) rather than a neat, highly aggregated theory, focused on a few key relationships, was the inevitable consequence of his immersion (like Dennis Robertson) in the business-cycle history of the period 1873–1912.[41] ". . . [I]n the real world of businessmen, affairs are always undergoing a cumulative change, always passing through some phase of a business cycle into some other phase. . . . In fact, if not in theory, a state of change in business conditions is the only 'normal' state."

Nonetheless, Milton Friedman's evaluation of the theoretical content of Part III is worth noting:[42]

> The business cycle theory . . . from Part III of Mitchell's 1913 volume contains practically every element that is significant in the business cycle theories that are currently prominent [1950]. Here are the multiplier process, the acceleration principle, the Pigovian cycles of optimism and pessimism, the Marshallian and Hawtreyan drain of cash from the banking system and the resultant tightening of the money market, a decline in the expected yield of new investment at the peak that is the counterpart of the Keynesian "collapse of the marginal efficiency of capital" except that it is a continuous decline rather than a discontinuous "collapse," the Keynesian changes in liquidity preference. Here, too, is an attempt at a reasoned explanation and integration of these phenomena.

Commenting on Friedman's evaluation, T. W. Hutchison observes:[43] "Whether or not this judgment inclines towards a generous hind-sighted interpretation, it certainly comes very much nearer the truth than does the view of Mitchell's work as a methodologically naive mass of statistical raw material."

I agree with Friedman and Hutchison on this point. Mitchell studied theory, understood it, used it, and taught it. There were nevertheless, two problems embedded in Mitchell's concept of the relationship between theory and facts. First, he did not recognize explicitly that the data he amassed in Part II—their grouping and analysis—already reflected a set of hypotheses about the nature of the business cycle that deserved more careful analysis than his one- and one-half-page note toward the close of the book citing the theoretical concepts he had accepted.[44] Veblen's "money economy" was not a sufficient framework for an empirical investigation of this kind. Second, the emphasis on quantitative evidence, in the form of reputable statistical series, tended to limit the range of hypotheses that might be explored. As we have already noted, both characteristics apply to Kuznets; and they were to remain typical—not universal—limitations in the work of the NBER.

The data as organized by Mitchell cry out for growth as well as cyclical analysis. The raw data are presented in tables; and the most important series are plotted in ample charts. Even over quite short periods, growth rather than fluctuations strike the eye (e.g., Figure 11.1). Moreover, Mitchell is quite conscious of the uniqueness of each cycle and the changing investment content of each period of expansion.[45] He is aware that "a decline of present or prospective profits [can occur] in a few leading branches of business . . . before that decline has become general."[46] He is also conscious that the flow of inventions is more continuous than the introduction of innovations whose introduction he believed was concentrated in the early stage of cyclical recovery.[47] But his mind was focused sharply on cycles and their mitigation. Growth he took for granted like almost all of his generation.

Mitchell's next major contribution to business-cycle analysis was published 14 years later, *Business Cycles: The Problem and Its Setting.* By 1927 NBER had settled down as a well-established institution. It had in hand a vastly increased number of statistical series; Willard Thorp had expanded the files of business annals from four to seventeen countries and published a much-used volume.[48] Above all, Mitchell's Preface could cite the staff support of able associates: Frederick C. Mills, Willford I. King, and Simon Kuznets, as well as Thorp, among others.

In structure, the new study was an update of the 1913 version:[49]

> I have not been able to devise a new way of conducting the inquiry which seemed better than the way followed in 1913. My earlier impressions that business cycles consist of exceedingly complex interactions among a considerable number of economic processes, that to gain insight into these interactions one must combine historical studies with quantitative and qualitative analysis, that the phenomena are peculiar to a certain form of economic organization, and that understanding of this scheme of institutions is prerequisite to an understanding of cyclical fluctuations—these impressions have been confirmed by my efforts to treat the subject in a simpler fashion. Hence the new version is not shorter or easier than its predecessor.

It summarized some new empirical data, discussed problems of statistical method, cited a wider array of business-cycle theorists than the 1913 volume, and held out the prospect of further study of "the Rhythm of Business Activity." But it was a disappointing interim book, with none of the sense of the creative vitality and unity of a youngish man's *tour de force* conveyed by the 1913 study. It left the impression that the study of business cycles was being pulled apart, specialized, and bureaucratized.

There was, nevertheless, a minor but interesting positive change. Listed in a rather elaborate classification of business-cycle theories, (among those "which trace business

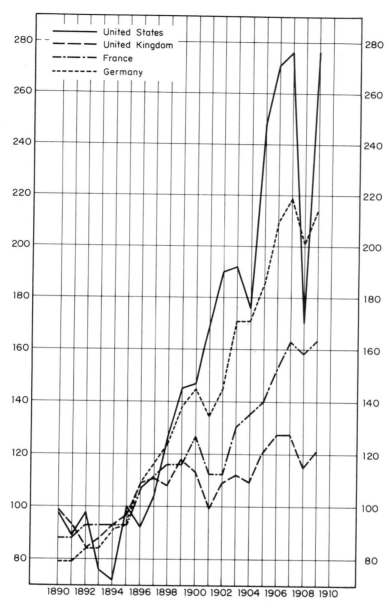

Figure 11.1. Relative Production of Pig Iron in the United States, United Kingdom, France, and Germany, 1890–1909. [Adapted from Wesley Clair Mitchell, *Business Cycles* (Berkeley: University of California Press, 1913), p. 234.]

cycles to institutional process") is: "Innovations come in waves, and initiate periods of activity followed by crises and depressions. Joseph Schumpeter, Minnie T. England"[50]; and Mitchell devotes several pages to paraphrasing theories rooted in "Innovations, Promotion, and Progress," including Schumpeter's.[51]

Much more serious, however, is an extended passage on secular trends, reflecting quite explicitly the work currently being conducted by Simon Kuznets.[52] Mitchell discusses the technical problems of measuring and interpreting secular trends; the logic of retardation; long-wave hypotheses (including Kondratieff's). His exposition leads him at last to pose sharply the problem of relating growth to cycles.[53]

> If we embark upon a search for causes of secular trends, we must expect to find not one cause peculiar to each series, but a peculiar combination of a multitude of interrelated causes. These causes may be classified as (1) causes related to changes in the number of population, (2) causes related to the economic efficiency of the population—its age, constitution, health, education, technical knowledge and equipment, methods of cooperation, methods of settling conflicts of interest, and many other matters; (3) causes related to the quantity and quality of the natural resources exploited by the population.

These are, evidently, causes related to basic growth variables. Mitchell then goes on:

> . . . One set of questions is particularly insistent. Is there a definite relation between secular trends and cyclical fluctuations? Are activities characterized by a rapidly rising trend subject to more frequent, or more violent, cycles than activities whose trend is nearer the horizontal? And more at large, can the trends of time series, after they have been measured, be discarded as of no further interest? Or must the trends themselves be brought into the explanations of cyclical fluctuations, as suggested by those theories which connect business cycles with ''progress''? Are the trends themselves generated by cyclical fluctuations. . . ? While these questions arise at this point, they cannot be answered by any process short of considering the pertinent evidence in detail. But the mere fact that such problems must be faced by the business-cycle theorist suffices to show that he cannot imitate the business-cycle statistician in merely eliminating secular trends.

There the matter ended so far as *The Problem and Its Setting* was concerned. The relation between cycles and growth does not appear in the final chapter devoted to NBER ''Results and Plans.''[54]

Some of Mitchell's Progeny

But, in fact, the NBER did conduct or inspire several studies relating growth and cycles. First, of course, was Kuznets's *Secular Movements* discussed at some length earlier (pp. 242–246). Four years later the NBER published Arthur F. Burns's *Production Trends in the United States since 1870.*

Burns's *Production Trends* is one of the major studies produced by the NBER since its founding in 1920. In part, it is a narrower and deeper study of one phenomenon probed in Kuznets's *Secular Movements in Production and Prices;* that is, it examines sectoral retardation in 104 physical-output series in the United States from the period 1870–1885 to 1920–1929.[55] But Burns departed from Kuznets's method of fitting curves to series over their whole length by measuring trend in terms of overlapping 11-year segments designed to eliminate conventional business cycle movements. The broad sweep of the segments, to which an exponential curve is fitted, constitute ''primary trends'' that are the basis for measuring the pace of retardation. Like Kuznets, Burns speculates on the multiple forces contributing to the virtually universal fact of sectoral retardation and concludes with a rough delineation of stages in this process and their relative duration.[56]

Table 11.1. Periods of Rapid and Slow Growth: United States, 1875–1929

General production shows exceptionally	
Rapid growth in	Slow growth in
1875–1885	1885–1895
1895–1905	1905–1915
1910–1920	1915–1925

SOURCE: A. F. Burns, *Production Trends in the United States since 1970,* (New York: National Bureau of Economic Research, 1934), p. xx.

More significant for the linkage of growth and cycles, Burns measured fluctuations in growth rates around the decelerating primary trend. He found a pervasive cyclical pattern in the overshoots and undershoots of his primary trends in both individual production series and in the production indexes he was prepared to examine with appropriate scepticism once he had, in Robertson's phrase, "wallowed" in the disaggregated series and their measurement. Here, in Table 11.1 and Figure 11.2, was the result:[57]

Now, what did Burns make of these laboriously achieved measurements? He arrived, essentially, at three significant conclusions and posed an important question. The conclusions, in his own words, were the following:

DISPERSION RATES AND GROWTH TRENDS

[Figure 11.3] presents, at each central decade year, measures of dispersion of the decade rates of two groups of production series. . . . It will be noticed that

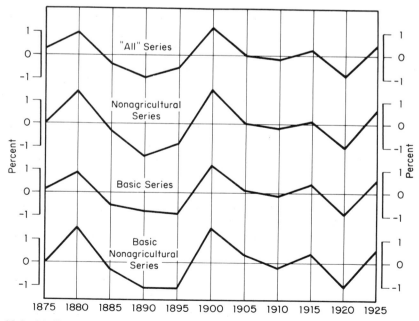

Figure 11.2. Medians of Trend-Cycles of Several Groups of Production Series. [Adapted from A. F. Burns, *Production Trends,* p. 181.]

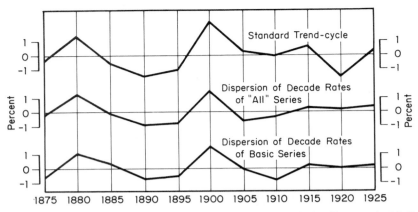

Figure 11.3. Cycles of Dispersion of Decade Rates of Production Series Compared with Standard Trend-Cycle. [Adapted from A. F. Burns, *Production Trends*, p. 243.]

the cyclical movements of the dispersion measures trace out patterns very similar to that of the standard trend-cycle. This correspondence means that when the trends of production have on the whole moved steeply upward, the degree of divergence of production trends has also been high; and that when the trends of production have on the whole moved only moderately upward, the degree of divergence of production trends has also been only moderate. In fine, the degree of divergence of production trends has varied with the degree of progressiveness of the economy.

DIVERGENCE AND ''NORMAL'' GROWTH.[59]

A certain degree of trend divergence is a necessary condition of smooth development in a progressive economy; for, in such an economy, the ratio of manufactured products to raw materials will tend to increase, as will the ratio of instrumental equipment to final consumers' goods, and of ''comforts'' and ''luxuries'' to ''necessaries.'' In actual experience, however, the degree of divergence of production trends will be generally either more or less than ''normal;'' . . . When during an upward trend-cycle movement the divergence exceeds what is ''normal'' for the time, a strain will develop in the economic system; this is likely to lead to a general crisis and to a curtailment in the rate of development of the system. The unique correspondence, then, between relatively sharp divergence of production trends and an upward trend-cycle movement in industry suggests that one of the factors serving to terminate an upward trend-cycle movement is a partial loss of industrial balance that develops during the upward movement.

. . . But when the divergence of production trends falls to a ''subnormal'' level during a downward trend-cycle movement, it is practically certain to be symptomatic of increasing readjustment; for the ''subnormal'' degree of divergence will then derive mainly from the sharp curtailment in the rates of development of those industries which had grown at a disproportionately rapid rate during the upward trend-cycle movement. . . . The unique correspondence, then, between relatively mild divergence of production trends and a downward trend-cycle movement suggests that a restoration of industrial balance develops during the downward movement, which creates conditions favorable to (or permissive of) the initiation of a new upward movement.

TREND-CYCLES AND BUSINESS CYCLES.[60]

. . . It is a matter of common knowledge that differences in rates of industrial growth were very considerable during the last decade. Some industries of large magnitude, such as automobiles, rayon, radios, and electrical household devices, grew at excitingly rapid rates; other industries, such as men's clothing, sole leather, boots and shoes, certain knit goods, and certain lumber manufactures, experienced little growth or actual decline; but none of these are included among the statistical records we have analyzed. It is highly probable, then, that the divergence of production trends during 1920–29 was much greater in fact than our long-term series suggest. This decade of rapid advance in production and curious contrasts in rates of expansion came to a close with what is . . . the severest depression in the history of the nation. . . . Apparently, our hypothesis is borne out also by the experience of the last decade. . . .

We may therefore conclude from our analysis of American experience since 1870: first, that periods of sharp advance in the trend of general production, which are characterized invariably by considerable divergence in production trends, have been followed invariably by severe business depressions; second, that most of the business depressions of marked severity have been preceded by a sharp advance in the trend of general production and considerable divergence in the trends of individual industries.

Clearly, in these propositions, Burns made a major contribution to the linking of growth and cyclical analysis. They strongly suggest that the dynamics of the economic system generates cycles by pulling certain sectors more or less strongly off optimum sectoral equilibrium growth paths, with powerful secondary consequences for other sectors and the aggregate performance of the economy; and the stronger the distortion during expansion the stronger the reaction is likely to be in the subsequent cyclical downswing.

There is an engaging passage in Schumpeter's essay on Wesley Mitchell:[61]

. . . I shall never forget his speechless surprise when I tried to show him that his great book of 1913, so far as the bare bones of its argument are concerned, was an exercise in the dynamic theory of equilibrium.

For what else are his "recurring readjustments of prices" to which he returned again and again but imperfect movements of the economic system in the direction of a state of equilibrium? If he failed to avail himself of the apparatus of equilibrium theory, so the (successors of the) builders of the equilibrium theory failed to avail themselves of his facts.

Unlike Mitchell, Burns did conduct—and, up to a point, quite consciously—"an exercise in the dynamic theory of equilibrium." He clearly posed but did not pursue the larger question raised by his study for growth analysis: How should one define a normal (or optimum, dynamic equilibrium) production trend for a sector? The reader will note that he provides a crisp definition in two clauses quoted above:[62] ". . .either more or less than is warranted by changes in the technical relations of commodities and in consumer's habits; more or less than is necessary for an uninterrupted rate of development, in the general economy." Thus, Burns's highly disciplined exercise in statistical analysis led him directly into—or at least to the edge of—the camp of those, of whom Malthus was an early pioneer, who sensed that a loss of "proportion" among dynamic sectors was the key to cyclical fluctuations.

In 1934 another quite different kind of study was published by the NBER which came sharply to rest on the question of dynamic balance and its relation to business cycles: John Maurice Clark's *Strategic Factors in Business Cycles*.[63] As Note 63 indicates, the tragic abnormality of the depression of the 1930s generated a study thus far untypical of the NBER. Clark's 234 pages do not contain a single statistical table or chart; although there is an Appendix focused on aggregate fluctuations of producers' goods, residential housing, and automobiles. The object of the study was explicitly operational rather than austerely "scientific"; that is, to find "factors about which something can be done, . . . [and] focus attention on them. . . . [64]

Clark proceeded by stating his theoretical presuppositions; summarizing from NBER data conclusions on the timing and amplitude of fluctuations in a wide range of variables; identifying the general and special features of cyclical movements in the period 1922–1929; and then a section that bears particularly on the central issue examined here: "Another Approach: The Meaning and Requirements of Balance."

Referring to the use of the concept of "balance" in a report of the Committee on Recent Economic Changes, Clark launches into a perceptive discussion of the possible meaning and implications of an economy moving forward in dynamic, sectorally disaggregated "balance"—a kind of rough "moving equilibrium," of the kind Allyn Young had earlier evoked and Burns had suggested:[65]

> . . . Can a condition be conceived and described which would deserve the name "balance," in which population is increasing, capital increasing more rapidly, product per capita increasing at still a different rate, perhaps in the long run intermediate between the other two, technical methods of production changing as they must to utilize the increasing supply of capital per worker, older methods being constantly rendered obsolete (though not constantly in every process at once), and new goods being developed as the consequence of increased spending power resulting from increased production? This is emphatically not a static condition, and it is one to which the conceptions of equilibrium and balance can be applied only in a special and limited sense.
>
> The term "balance" was used by the Committee on Recent Economic Changes only in the sense of a rough approximation, with the idea of a "zone of tolerance" beyond which disproportions become serious. The question remains, however, approximation to what? Tolerable degree of departure from what? . . .
>
> It is clear that business cycles in their very nature are departures from balance in the absolute sense.

Clark then proceeded to explore the following criteria for balance:

- Balance in the labor market yielding low average unemployment.[66]
- "A reasonably steady" rate of increase in production.[67]
- A balance between "savings and capital expenditures."[68]
- Keeping within reasonable bounds "the tendency of credit expansion to generate cumulative expansion."[69]
- Achieving an approximate balance between the role of high wages, as a means of

maintaining a high level of consumers expenditure and the danger of excessively high wages, as a cause of excessive unemployment—a dilemma best resolved by increases in labor income "in forms which do not constitute a wages-charge upon the employer's act of hiring [labor];" e.g., via profit-sharing arrangements;[70]

- With respect to the invention and marketing of new consumers goods, achieving "an amount and distribution of purchasing power as can make the demand effective and assimilate the new goods approximately as fast as we gain the power to produce them."[71]
- Finding the right, preferably flexible formula for hours of labor that would minimize total unemployment.[72]
- Solving, on an even wider basis, the problem of sectoral distortion Burns had identified in *Production Trends:*[73]

> One essential feature of balance is that no part of the economic system shall be working at a rate very much faster or slower than it can continue without outrunning or falling behind its proper proportion to the rest, as fixed by physical and economic forces. The rate of production of raw materials should equal the amount consumed in the production of finished goods (with allowance for slow growth of stocks as total volume of production grows). And the rate of production of equipment should be such as the volume of savings and the development of technical methods indicate can be maintained. . . . [T]here are very narrow limits on the rate at which existing capital can be increased without wasteful duplication and a defeating of the end in view. . . .
>
> The amount of consumers' goods the market can be geared to buy is elastic, and we have never reached its ultimate limits. But, like the amount of capital we can man, it can be increased only at a limited rate. The market will buy as much as it can produce if it produces just the commodities wanted by those among whom the income is divided, and if they spend for consumption all the funds not needed to finance a balanced supply of capital. But all this takes time to work out.

- Balance between prices and profits requires rough conformity to the following rules:[74]

> The ideal condition is one in which expanding industries receive just sufficient profits to stimulate the growth that will bring productive capacity into balance with demand; no more and no less. And contracting industries should suffer just sufficient losses to bring about a contraction in the productive capacity engaged in them adequate to restore the balance in the other direction by causing the least efficient producers to drop out, and others to defer expansion or to contract by failing to make full replacements.

On this basis, Clark proceeded to his identification of the operational strategic factors about which "something can be done," with considerable emphasis on the application of the accelerator, a concept he had helped pioneer, to automobiles, durable consumers' goods, and residential construction.[75]

The notion that the business cycle was the consequence of forces that systematically deranged balance and proportion in the economic system was, as we have seen, by no means new; but Clark's analysis of the array of balances that could go awry—and did go grotesquely awry in the 1920s and early 1930s—was more complete than that of any of his predecessors. Even more important, he tried to make explicit the criteria for dynamic, "tolerable" balance in an economy's sectors as it moved through time; and he built his recommendations for action around strategic factors that would hold the economy in such a rough dynamic equilibrium. In contrast to the oversimplified macroformulations of the business cycle that progressively gained vogue in the second half of the 1930s. Clark redoubtably insisted on introducing explicitly Marshallian long-period as well as short-period variables into his analyses and proposals for remedy.

Two further NBER studies should be briefly cited. First, there is Solomon Fabricant's book, *The Output of Manufacturing Industries, 1899–1937*.[76] Strictly speaking, as Fabricant made clear, this book does not belong in a chapter on business cycles.[77] It is more purely a study in the sectoral anatomy of growth than, say, Kuznets's *Secular Movements* or Burns's *Production Trends,* both of which focus substantially on links between sectoral growth patterns and cycles. In fact, Fabricant's study was part of a substantial series of books and occasional papers generated by the NBER in the area of Production, Employment, and Productivity—a series mainly published during and after the Second World War. The central result of Fabricant's effort is captured in Table 11.2. The extraordinary differences in sectoral growth rates presented in that table and the complex interconnections among them are analyzed with subtlety.

But cyclical analysis could not be wholly bypassed because more than 20% of the period covered consists of the cycle (peak-to-peak) 1929–1937. In fact, the first occasional paper published by the NBER was Fabricant's analysis of that cycle, in terms of sectoral (as well as aggregate) trends in manufacturing output.[78]

The major conclusions of that abnormal cycle—that still left 14.3% unemployed at its 1937 peak—were the following:

- There was a modest (about 3%) rise in total factory output.
- The pervasive operation of Marshallian long-period forces over a relatively short period of time is suggested by the following:[79]

> Even a cursory glance at the table reveals that many industries achieved important net gains in output during these troubled years. Of the 139 industries, 42 increased their output one-fifth or more. The output of another 15 industries rose between one-tenth and one-fifth, while 17 more made smaller gains, less than one-tenth. In other words, over half of the 139 industries increased their output by some amount, large or small; 2 had the same output in 1929 and 1937; that of the other 63 declined.

- In terms of growth rates:[80]

> New or revived industries head the list. The liquor industries shot up, of course, upon the repeal of prohibition. Also in the forefront are such obviously new industries as mechanical refrigerators, rayon, washing machines, and radios; and industries producing, in addition to well-established commodities, new products or products for which demand had recently been stimulated, including flavorings, glass (beverage and food containers), chemicals, compressed and liquefied gasses, and silk and rayon goods. . . . Older industries that cannot be said to have reached maturity also appear in the upper third of the list: tin cans, canned fruits, vegetables, and milk, cigarettes, carbon black, asbestos products, and petroleum refining. Among the declining industries at the lower end of the list are charcoal, locomotives, clay products (brick), pianos, carriages and wagons, lumber-mill products, ice, linen goods, and cigars.

Table 11.2. Individual Manufacturing Industries, Ranked According to Percentage Change in Physical Output, 1899–1937

Industry	Percentage change	Industry	Percentage change
Automobiles	+180,100	Cotton goods	+101
Cigarettes	+4,226	Cane-sugar refining	+101
Petroleum refining	+1,920	Fish, canned	+96
Milk, canned	+1,810	Hats, wool-felt	+90
Beet sugar	+1,688	Shoes, leather	+87
Hosiery, knit	+1,202	Salt	+82
Cement	+838	Cane sugar, not elsewhere made	+67
Fruits and vegetables, canned	+792	Meat packing	+66
Chemicals, not elsewhere classified	+741	Cottonseed products	+63
		Leather	+61
Ice	+668	Woolen and Worsted goods	+60
Silk and rayon goods	+512	Liquors, malt	+60
Pulp	+505	Underwear, knit	+52
Printing and publishing	+494	Carpet and rugs, wool	+52
Paper	+465	Lead	+51
Rice	+416	Cordage and twine	+38
Outerwear, knit	+393	Hats, fur-felt	+26
Paints and varnishes	+391	Gloves, leather	+16
Coke-oven products	+380	Cigars	0
Zinc	+318	Pianos	−5
Liquors, distilled	+315	Tobacco products, other	−6
Steel-mill products	+313	Flour	−8
Butter	+309	Clay products	−15
Tanning and dye materials	+292	Ships and boats	−17
Copper	+272	Cars, railroad, not elsewhere made	−22
Explosives	+267	Lumber-mill products, not elsewhere classified	−32
Wood-distillation products	+259		
Fertilizers	+248	Turpentine and rosin	−32
Blast-furnace products	+171	Linen goods	−44
Cheese	+158	Locomotives, not elsewhere made	−79
Jute goods	+134	Carriages, wagons, and sleighs	−95
Wool shoddy	+116		

SOURCE: Solomon Fabricant, *The Output of Manufacturing Industries, 1899–1937* (New York: NBER, 1940), p. 89.

• As one would expect, perishable goods did better than durable goods:[81]

> There are, of course, many exceptions, but in general output in the perishable goods industries increased. The semi-durable products industries are scattered through the ranks, but most are above the median point. The industry manufacturing silk and rayon goods is the highest representative of importance, followed by women's clothing, knit outerwear, hosiery, woollen and worsted goods, shoes and leather. Cotton goods and men's clothing declined fractionally. The tires and tubes industry was the only large one producing semi-durable goods whose output declined drastically. The most important durable goods industries—agricultural implements, steel-mill products, rail-road equipment, automobiles, nonferrous metals, ships and boats, lumber mill products, cement, planing mill products, and locomotives—all declined in output. Hardest hit were the industries manufacturing materials used in building.

Fabricant's observations on this and other cyclical passages,[82] make his study a useful addition to the literature relating growth and cycles.

A second study of this era—independent of but closely linked to the NBER—also deserves a word; A. D. Gayer *et al.*, *The Growth and Fluctuation of the British Economy, 1790–1850*.[83] Completed in February 1941, its two volumes were first published in 1953. Their subtitle suggests the large purposes of the enterprise: "An Historical, Statistical, and Theoretical Study of Britain's Economic Development."

I include reference to this study for several reasons. The concept was purely Arthur Gayer's, and his truly innovative enterprise deserves to be remembered. His Oxford doctoral thesis (1930), entitled "Industrial Fluctuations and Unemployment in England, 1815–1850," converged with later research at the NBER to suggest a rather romantic effort to fulfill Wesley Mitchell's grand dream of uniting sophisticated statistical analysis with historical, institutional, and theoretical perspectives, for a single national economy, over a substantial period of time. Full of youthful energy and methodological idealism, Gayer and his small team produced a fair working approximation of Mitchell's dream. It reflects accurately the hopes and aspirations of a good many American and British business-cycle analysts of the 1930s.

Growth and cycles were explicitly linked from the beginning of the study; but as Anna Jacobson Schwartz and I underlined in our 1952 joint prefatory addendum (written after Gayer's untimely death), the linkage was not, with hindsight, as effective as it might have been. In the cyclical history, the growth content of each boom is identified and, indeed, the strands of innovational change that persisted during slumps. In both historical and analytic portions of the study the business cycle emerges as the form in which growth unfolds, with the leading sectors of each cycle clearly identified. On the other hand, the theoretical portions of the text were focused rather more on trend-period (or long-cycle) analysis than on growth as it might have been dealt with in, say, the 1950s or 1960s—or 1980s. The compulsively detailed application of the NBER technique of cyclical and trend analysis did provide, however, measurements of growth for individual series that are discussed (along with cyclical patterns) in the portion of the study devoted to formal statistical analysis.

As noted in the 1975 Preface to the second edition:[84] "Since the 1930s, the historical study of business cycles has not flourished." For good or ill, the Gayer study is something of a period piece. But it remains one of a kind, the product in Gayer's words, of "a close harmonious co-operation" in pursuit of a large vision of how various methods of analysis can be made to converge in the analysis of growth and cycles.

Alvin Hansen (1887–1975) and the Young Paul Samuelson (1915–   )

But this chapter should not close with a nostalgic reference to a kind of analysis that did not flourish after 1945. More appropriate is an exercise already referred to several times: Paul A. Samuelson's "Interactions between Multiplier Analysis and the Principle of Acceleration," published in May 1939. Again for good or ill, it does indeed foreshadow a great deal of post-World War II macroeconomic analysis, including business-cycle analysis; and its elegant four pages are suffused with a talented young man's hope and excitement about the future prospects for mathematical economics and econometrics.

Samuelson underlines his debt to Alvin Hansen who "suggested" that it might be

Table 11.3. Hansen's Business Cycle Theory Categories: 1927

> *I. The Capitalistic Economy schools*
> A. The capitalistic system of distribution as cause of the business cycle
> B. The capitalistic process of production as cause of the business cycle
>   1. Inventions, discoveries, and innovations as impelling factors disturbing the economic equilibrium
>   2. Fluctuations in consumers' demand as impelling factor disturbing the economic equilibrium
> *II. The Exchange Economy school*
> *III. The Money Economy schools*
> A. The interrelations of the rate of interest, the prospective rate of profit, and the price level
> B. The interrelations of costs and prices, profit margins, and capitalization

SOURCE: Alvin H. Hansen, *Business Cycle Theory, Its Development and Present Status,* (Boston: Ginn, 1927) p. 10.

fruitful to formulate mathematically the relation between the multiplier and the accelerator, the linkage dramatized since Harrod's *The Trade Cycle* (1936). But, before returning to Samuelson's *tour de force,* Hansen deserves a prior word, for his contribution was more substantial than the spear-carrier role conventional texts sometimes assign him in the Keynesian Revolution.

Hansen began in 1921 with an analytic monograph on cyclical fluctuations in the United States, Great Britain, and Germany in the period 1902–1908;[85] and he went on to become, along with Wesley Mitchell, the leading business-cycle analyst in the United States, with a full command of the various types of business-cycle theory generated since, say, the days of Henry Thornton and David Ricardo. His classification of business-cycle theories in his second major study (1927) is indicated in Table 11.3.[86] After examining analytically this array of theories, Hansen sought to reconcile the major types of theory ("monetary, capital-production, consumer-demand") and to speculate temperately but skeptically on the likelihood that the business cycle would wither away in a dynamic capitalistic society.[87]

In the present context a general and a specific point should be noted. Hansen's 1927 study embraced the theories that looked on cycles as the form growth assumed in an economy subject to rapid and discontinuous technological change and capitalist investment methods. Moreover, Hansen's synthesis includes the mechanisms of what later came to be known as the multiplier and the accelerator; that is, the impact on income and employment of changes in investment, and the disproportionate impact on the demand for fixed and working capital of modest changes in consumer demand.[88] He cites, for example, how a 5% increase in consumer demand will give rise to a 50% increase in demand for fixed capital if the depreciation rate on fixed capital is taken to be 10%.[89] Hansen clearly had no difficulty in absorbing the refinements of Kahn, Keynes, and Harrod of the 1930s; and his encouragement of Samuelson to apply his mathematical virtuosity to the interactions of the multiplier and accelerator is easily understood. Hansen became in time a major Keynesian; but, like the post-Wicksell Stockholm school, he has a legitimate claim to have anticipated a good deal of the analysis and doctrine that evolved from and in the wake of *The General Theory.*

Specifically, Samuelson attributes to Hansen the breaking down of additions to national income to three components:[90] "(1) government deficit spending, (2) private consumption expenditure induced by previous public expenditure, and (3) induced private investment, assumed according to the familiar acceleration principle to be proportional to the time increase of consumption." Samuelson then proceeds to explore the implications for national income of different assumed values for the marginal propensity to consume (which determines the multiplier) and the proportionate relation between an increase in consumption and the induced increase in investment (which defines the accelerator). After first producing a model that exhibits cyclical behavior, he goes on to show more generally that, depending on the values chosen for the marginal propensity to consume and the relation between an increment in consumption and derived investment, only four types of solution are possible. For example, a single expenditure impulse will yield, after a surge, an asymptotic gradual approach to the original national income level; a constant continuing level of government expenditure will result in ever-increasing explosive oscillations; with high values chosen for the marginal propensity to consume and the relation, a constant level of government expenditure will cause a rise in national income that eventually approaches a compound interest growth rate. With a full employment ceiling on the economy assumed and a floor set by zero net investment, this kind of analysis evidently could be—and soon was—converted into a highly aggregated form of business-cycle analysis.[91]

Now, what happened to growth in this formulation? Two things. First, the full employment ceiling that reverses the direction in which the accelerator drives the economy was, dynamically conceived, a kind of full employment growth path of total output; but the implications of that fact were rarely taken into account, and business-cycle analysis was, in fact, treated in quasi–short-period terms, as in Keynes's *General Theory* (preceding, p. 279). Second, perceiving that the great Schumpeterian innovations were left out, the concept of exogenous (or autonomous) investment was added to investment induced by the accelerator when the latter was operating positively in a period of cyclical expansion. This procedure—denying the endogenous character of the great innovations, concealing their sectoral character, and separating growth from cyclical analysis—was a profoundly retrograde step. The painfully achieved and elaborated insights of several generations of economists—on the Continent, in Britain, and the United States—that the business cycle was the form that growth assumed and that expansion, crisis, contraction, and revival could only be fully understood in disaggregated terms, related to systematic sectoral distortions and their movement back toward dynamic sectoral equilibrium positions never in fact attained—all that knowledge and wisdom accumulated by wallowing in the statistical and qualitative evidence and reflecting upon its meaning was put aside.

But Samuelson was not primarily interested in the relation between growth and cycles. He drew more general conclusions highly appropriate to his age (24) and the vision of his "sacred decade"—a vision to which he subsequently remained loyal:[92] "Contrary to the impression commonly held, mathematical methods properly employed, far from making economic theory more abstract, actually serve as a powerful liberating device enabling the entertainment and analysis of ever more realistic and complicated hypotheses." To which he added in a footnote: "It may be mentioned in passing that the formal structure of our problem is identical with the model sequences of Lundberg, and the dynamic theories of Tinbergen. The present problem is so simple that it provides a useful introduction to the mathematical theory of the latter's work."

As Samuelson was later to write in honor of Joe S. Bain, who combined painstaking empirical research with theory:[93] "As a theorist, like Picasso, there is no afternoon when

I cannot contrive a new gemlet. But in the study of real world markets, one must collect and analyze data for years in order to make relevant contributions.'' The problem Samuelson does not confront is the pied piper effect of his virtuousity, which helped induce several generations of young economists, with less than Picassolike talents, to concentrate their efforts fruitlessly on the production of gemlets at the expense of ''the study of real world markets,'' past and present.

As far as business-cycle analysis was concerned, those drawn to multiplier–accelerator models did, indeed, produce theories of cycles. The problem was that they bore little relation to cycles as they occurred in the real world. They recalled the observation of the wife of an American academic on an aspect of life in Britain:[94] ''English women's shoes look as if they had been made by someone who had often heard shoes described, but had never seen any. . . . ''

The Emergence of Econometrics: Frisch and Tinbergen

But there were good reasons in the late 1930s for Samuelson's hopeful focus on the potential fruitfulness of mathematical economics and econometrics. The Econometric Society was set up in 1930, uniting an older generation of pioneers (e.g., Fisher, Schumpeter, Frisch) with a widening phalanx of younger enthusiasts, generating by January 1933 a house organ, *Econometrica*. Wassily Leontief came to America at about the same time (1931) and, after a short stint at the NBER, was hard at work expounding input–output analysis at Harvard. And, as noted earlier (pp. 209ff.) the emergence of national income accounting at about the same time as Keynesian income analysis encouraged a linking of statistics, economic theory, and mathematics that Frisch elegantly evoked as he defined the mission of econometrics:[95]

> Thus, econometrics is by no means the same as economic statistics. Nor is it identical with what we call general economic theory, although a considerable portion of this theory has a definitely quantitative character. Nor should econometrics be taken as synonymous with the application of mathematics to economics. Experience has shown that each of these three view-points, that of statistics, economic theory, and mathematics, is a necessary, but not by itself a sufficient, condition for a real understanding of the quantitative relations in modern economic life. It is the *unification* of all three that is powerful. And it is this unification that constitutes econometrics.

So far as this chapter is concerned, the major exercise in econometric analysis was Jan Tinbergen's two-volume League of Nations study, *Statistical Testing of Business Cycle Theories*.[96] The study is clearly a landmark in the evolution of econometric model-building—a major post-1945 sport—although it is at least equally remembered for Keynes's unbridled attack on the first volume in the *Economic Journal* for September 1939.[97] Keynes's response was not merely—or was hardly at all—as a business-cycle theorist but as a logician and expert on the theory of probability since his youth. His somewhat sadistic specification of the inherent ambiguities of multiple-correlation analysis (with which Tinbergen mainly agreed) retains its relevance.

In his first volume Tinbergen sought to identify by econometric methods the determinants of fluctuations in three variables: investment [iron and steel consumption], residential buildings, and net investment in rolling stock. Data are drawn from prewar France; pre- and postwar United Kingdom, Germany, Sweden, and the United States. The second volume aims to "explain" business cycles in the United States for the period 1919–1932.

Conscious of the partially methodological purpose of the exercise, Tinbergen took pains to explain the concepts and methods employed. In the first volume the treatment of each variable is broken down in three sections: the relation tested, the statistical material, and results. The results were not startling:[98] investment, on "fairly good evidence," was mainly "determined" by industrial profits earned in industry as a whole some months earlier; residential building was determined in the several countries by various combinations of rent, building costs, profits, and number of houses (in deviation from trend) lagged $3\frac{1}{2}$ years—the latter variable appearing particularly influential in the United States; rolling-stock investment also presented a somewhat confused picture with the privately owned U.S. railways apparently more responsive to profits, interest rates, and iron prices as compared to the greater role of the rate of increase of traffic [designated the "acceleration principle"] in the publicly owned European systems, notably that of Germany.

In his concluding chapter Tinbergen underlined that definitive "explanations" required that "a complete system be constructed in which the number of equations should be equal to the number of variates necessary to describe adequately the business cycle mechanism."[99] That was the objective of his second volume.

Although simple by later standards, Tinbergen's construct of the American economy is too detailed for description here. Briefly, he set up groups of demand, supply, and income-formation equations. Out of their interaction a set of "direct" and "indirect" relations are adduced, building up to Tinbergen's assessment of the categories of business-cycle theories set out in Haberler's twin League of Nations study.

Tinbergen's major conclusions were the following:[100]

- Short-term interest rates were found to have slight influence on investment, long-term rates a "moderate" influence; the monetary system was elastic and not a "chief factor" in fluctuations.
- Profits, with a lag, were the major determinant of investment; the acceleration principle was not confirmed.
- The period of production played a "rather important role" in rising costs during the boom, but as a cause of crisis was of "less importance." In this respect the behavior of prices in the boom peaking in 1929 was something of an exception.

Perhaps the most important substantive result of the study—still on Tinbergen's mind when he wrote the 1967 "Introduction" to its reprinting—is the apparently large role in the American business cycle of the 1920s played by stock-market speculation in 1928–1929—a question his method could pose but not answer.

Looking back on this and other pioneering econometric enterprises 30 years later Tinbergen said:[101]

> Some of the fits in our models never became very good, or, if finally they had been forced into a high correlation, broke down a few years later. I am afraid that the first subject I tackled in my work for the League of Nations, namely to explain the fluctuations in investment activity, never has become a great success. In the Netherlands Central Planning Bureau we found it safer, after some years, to ask industrialists for their investment programs rather than rely on an econometric explanation. Also government expenditures were

among the variables difficult to explain. In both cases we may account for the lack of success by the fact that a small number of decision makers determine the picture and that hence random deviations will be important.

The critical point to be noted, however, is that Tinbergen's model, like multiplier–accelerator analysis, required a clear break between growth and cyclical analysis. Trends are eliminated, major inventions as well as public policies are regarded as exogenous shocks to the system. Tinbergen reflected on the reasons for this procedure in his December 1969 Nobel lecture:[102]

> In a more general way many of us know that quite a few business cycle models were "forecasting" the turning points only *after* they had occurred. Ragnar Frisch was quite right when, at an early stage of model building, he introduced *random shocks* as an essential element of the business cycle, leaving the cumulative process between turning points rather than the latter themselves as a thing that really could be explained by the models.

From the perspective of this chapter the substitution of "random shocks" for the endogenous forces that decreed the cyclical path of growth is much more than a useful technical limitation in model building: it breaks the link between growth and cycles on which any valid theory of cycles must be constructed.

12

Relative Prices

Whereas an imposing array of distinguished economists wrestled with the analysis of business cycles in the period 1870–1939, only a small band examined the classic question: How did the prices of manufactures move relative to those for basic commodities, i.e., the net barter terms of trade for countries that were primarily exporters of manufactures and importers of basic commodities? The members of this select group mainly addressed three problems:

- The pre-1914 unfavorable movement of the British terms of trade that affected strongly Keynes's view of the Versailles Treaty in *The Economic Consequences of the Peace*.
- The sudden, subsequent excessively favorable movement of the British terms of trade and its role in the interwar debate on British economic policy.
- The problem of long cycles in the world economy: notably, Kondratieff's long-wave hypothesis; Colin Clark's hypothesis about successive "capital-hungry" and capital-sated" periods; and the analysis of foreign trade price and volume movements by Folke Hilgerdt in *Industrialization and Foreign Trade*. The latter two analyses were explicitly linked by their authors to relative price trends: Kondratieff's was not, although certain aspects of it—notably reference to bringing new agricultural areas into the world economy—lent itself to such a linkage.

Although there was a reasonable case for treating separately the transfer problem (Chapter 9) and the terms of trade, it is evident that a part of the argument there relates closely to the discussion here of relative prices.

British Anxiety about Unfavorable
Terms of Trade: 1903–1919

It will be recalled that Marshall was extremely sensitive to the impact on Britain—and, notably, on the real wages of British labor—of the relative price of British imports. On the basis of Arthur Bowley's data he noted the lift in British real wages in the last quarter of the nineteenth century, rooted essentially in cheap food from overseas; and, as early as 1903, he was aware that the trend had begun to reverse (preceding, pp. 182–184).

No doubt influenced by Marshall, Keynes and Robertson took seriously the post-1900 unfavorable shift in the terms of trade, echoing as it did pre-1813 classical economics, with its anxiety about diminishing returns to agriculture. Keynes published a note on the subject in the *Economic Journal* in 1912 noting that Britain was £37 million worse off than it would have been if import and export prices had moved equally between 1900 and 1911. It included the following passage:[1]

> The deterioration—from the point of view of this country—shown above is due, of course, to the operation of the law of diminishing returns for raw products which, after a temporary lull, has been setting in sharply in quite recent years. There is now again a steady tendency for a given unit of manufactured product to purchase year by year a diminishing quantity of raw product. The comparative advantage in trade is moving sharply against industrial countries.

In his *A Study of Industrial Fluctuations* Robertson explored for several pages various consequences of shifting relative prices for basic commodities, coming to rest on the same terms of trade data Keynes had used. He concluded forcefully as follows:[2]

> The general conclusion to which these figures, taken as a whole, lead is that the normal tendency for the ratio of exchange to alter against the manufacturing and in favour of the agricultural communities was in force in the seventies, was suspended in the eighties and nineties, and is now once more on the whole triumphing. This is perhaps the most significant economic fact in the world to-day. . . . But the fact is clearly of *secular* rather than cyclical importance.

This preoccupation was carried over directly by Keynes as a basis for Chapter II of the *Economic Consequences of the Peace,* where, thinking again of the prewar movement of the terms of trade, he wrote: ". . . taking the world as a whole, there was no deficiency of wheat, but in order to call forth an adequate supply it was necessary to offer a higher real price"; and, later, in summing up, he referred to "the increase in the real cost of food, and the diminishing response of Nature to any further increase in the population of the world" as one of two fundamental problems of post-1919 Europe.[3] It was in large part on these analytic foundations that Keynes contrasted the precariousness of western Europe's economic position in the world with the cavalier political surgery of the statesmen of 1919.

In their biographies of Keynes, neither Harrod nor Skidelsky focus explicitly on his pre-1914 conviction that, after being fended off by a century in which new lands were brought into cultivation, that old devil Diminishing Returns was at work and would remain at work corroding industrial Europe's terms of trade.[4] Thereby, they miss the drama with which Keynes was confronted in the immediate post-war years as the British terms of trade moved in a wholly unexpected favorable direction and oscillated in a high range down to 1938 when they were over 40% more favorable than in 1913 (Table 12.1).

There is something more to be said about the *Economic Consequences of the Peace* and Keynes's false assumption about the postwar prospects for the terms of trade. That essay remains a vivid self-portrait of Keynes, with virtually all his qualities of mind and character in play. There is, first of all, the convergence of a professional economist's analysis, focused sharply by a civil servant's sense of the operational issues, and a great stylist writing in white heat, at his best. Behind it all is a loyalty and commitment to the best values of pre-1914 Western civilization, clearly endangered by the short-sightedness of its leaders and the mixture of apathy and brutishness among its citizenry, but also hope

Table 12.1. Terms of Trade: United Kingdom, 1913–1938
(1938 = 100)

1913	70	1928	83
—	—	1929	83
1919	81	1930	90
1920	88	1931	100
1921	99	1932	100
1922	92	1933	103
1923	90	1934	100
1924	87	1935	99
1925	83	1936	97
1926	85	1937	92
1927	85	1938	100

NOTE: Export over import prices (average values).
SOURCE: *Board of Trade Journal*, August 4, 1951, reprinted in B. R. Mitchell and Phyllis Deane, *Abstract of British Historical Statistics*, (Cambridge: at the University Press, 1962), p. 332.

and a desire to recapture faith. In evoking Europe before the war (Chapter II) and Europe after the treaty (Chapter VI), Keynes moves effortlessly from economic to political to social and psychological arguments. He is addressing himself to the fate of an intimately interconnected group of national societies with an essentially common cultural base. And then there are his unforgettable portraits of the leaders—perceptive and, to a degree, bitchy—as he is driven on, in frustration and fury, by a sense of the gap between the statesmanship required and the pedestrian, parochial politics shaping the outcome.

Finally there is Keynes, the probability theorist, with an observation that bears directly on his terms of trade error and his brisk, unembarrassed adjustment to it:[5]

> We cannot expect to legislate for a generation or more. The secular changes in man's economic condition and the liability of human forecast to error are as likely to lead to mistake in one direction as in another. We cannot as reasonable men do better than base our policy on the evidence we have and adapt it to the five or ten years over which we may suppose ourselves to have some measure of prevision; and we are not at fault if we leave on one side the extreme chances of human existence and of revolutionary changes in the order of Nature or of man's relations to her.

Keynes and Robertson on the Interwar Terms of Trade: *Un Embarras de Richesse*

In 1919–1920 the high price of British coal exports cushioned the terms of trade against the high price of food and raw material imports; in the general price collapse of 1921 the fall in Britain's import prices substantially exceeded that of its export prices including coal, and the terms of trade stood 41% higher in that year than in 1913. In the period of relative world recovery down to 1929 the terms of trade fell somewhat; but, at their interwar trough, the terms of trade were still almost 20% more favorable than in 1913.

It was in the course of a protracted debate with William Beveridge (on the *Economic Consequences* thesis that the world faced Malthusian population pressure on the food supply), that Keynes confronted the fact that his projection into the postwar period of the 1900–1913 trend had been wrong. He, rather than Beveridge, noted that the volume of manufactured exports given for a uniform quantity of food imports had fallen from 97 in 1913 to 77 in 1922, reflecting a "vast improvement" in the terms of trade position, thus defined.[6] This change, however, was accompanied by a "disastrous falling off in the volume of British exports." In a typically swift adjustment to new circumstances Keynes then bridged the diverse movements of the terms of trade, prewar and postwar, with a concept that would define Britain's difficulties in both cases: "We are no longer able to sell a growing volume of manufactured goods (or a volume increasing in proportion to population) at a better real price in terms of food."[7]

With a general recognition of what had happened to the postwar terms of trade, interest among economists tended to concentrate on how the British economy should react to its sudden, and rather embarrassing, increase in real wealth. In his "Reply" to Beveridge Keynes discussed the probable elasticity of demand for British exports, concluding that an attempt to restore their volume, and thus to eliminate unemployment in the export industries, might involve a sufficiently serious deterioration in the terms of trade to cause a fall in real wages, a view symmetrical with his conclusions on the German reparations transfer problem.[8] Robertson continued this phase of the discussion by defining three alternative methods of adjustment: "a contrived fall in the ratio of interchange", as Keynes had proposed; a shifting of labor from export industries to production for the home market; or an increase in capital exports.[9] On the whole he leaned to stimulus to the home market.

In the course of his exposition Robertson underlined the critical role in the outcome of an economy's capacity to shift its resources rapidly from one sector and occupation to another:[10]

> The general conclusion is that if a country's resources in capital and labour were completely mobile between different occupations, an improvement in the ratio of interchange would be an unmixed blessing, even though it led to a reduction in the volume both of exports and imports. If we could costlessly erect a vast sausage-machine which would grind shipyards into cottages and cotton-spinners into plasterers, we should be wise to do so. I am not sure that even as it is we ought not, so far as labour is concerned, to take a leaf out of Germany's book, and make a far more decisive move in that direction than we have yet done.

The argument evokes something of Hume's commended response of an "industrious" nation to an up-and-coming challenger as well as the situation faced by Western Europe and the United States in the 1980s as they confronted a major technological revolution, progressively heightened competition with Japan, and an enlarging band of new industrial powers. And, indeed, Robertson, in his further probing reflections on an appropriate response to the embarrassment of excessively favorable terms of trade, concludes with a prescient passage on the possible narrowing of the gap between rich and aspiring countries:[11]

> If at some future time the terms of trade swing against us, it is likely to be as part of a more far-reaching change—namely, a partial closing of those gaps in the comparative capacities of different countries for following different pursuits on which the advantages of international trade depend. If that occurs, it will still be true that England will have to adapt her economy to a smaller

volume of export trade than she has been used to in the past—not, as at the present moment, because she is getting her imports so cheaply, but for the less agreeable reason that the circumstances in which it paid the world to let her be its workshop will have partially passed away.

The adjustment actually made in 1931 by the British government contained, in effect, elements of all three of Robertson's three alternatives; that is, Britain, in effect, devalued the pound, stimulated the domestic market (for example, by measures to encourage housing construction), and acted to encourage capital exports within the Empire. With respect to capital exports, it is of interest that Robertson regarded them as a rather special sort of short-run stimulant to the British export industries. He did not attempt to determine whether the causes for the favourable shift were likely to persist or whether capital exports, in their long-run effects, might be so directed as to cushion the British economy against a time of higher relative import prices. On the whole, contemporary economists tended to regard the terms of trade position during the interwar years as if that position were likely to persist. Policy discussion was addressed mainly to the most appropriate form and means of adjustment to it.

Pulling back from the role of terms of trade analyses in the effort of Britain to cope with the interwar pathology in the world economy, two aspects of this story are worth noting. First Keynes and Robertson were both conscious that they were evoking an old classical doctrine when they viewed with alarm the unfavorable pre-1914 movement in the terms of trade, but they did not review the historical oscillations of relative prices and the terms of trade over the previous century, nor explore the corrective mechanism that had operated in the past or ask whether that mechanism might again operate. When the pre-1914 trend was unfavorable, they assumed, implicitly at least, that trend would continue into the indefinite future. When the interwar trend was favorable they generally assumed that circumstance would persist over the time period relevant to current policy. They did not follow Marshall who, in giving written testimony on "Fiscal Policy of International Trade" (1908) devoted more than five pages to "wheat prices in England since 1820,"[12] and sought systematically to put his conclusions in such a long historical perspective.

Second, in a manner somewhat evocative of the international debt crisis of the 1980s, Britain learned something of a lesson about the intense interdependence of the world economy. The negative impact on Britain's overseas export markets of excessively favorable terms of trade was a puzzlement mainstream economists had not generally contemplated before; and they did not turn their minds to it again until the United States of the 1980s so behaved as to generate a dollar some 30% overvalued, which damped domestic inflation at home while contributing to a radical loss in U.S. export markets.

Three Longer Perspectives: Kondratieff, Colin Clark, and Hilgerdt

From a quite different perspective and an unexpected quarter—the Soviet Union—an historical analysis emerged during the interwar years reaching back from the 1920s to 1790: N. D. Kondratieff's definition and discussion of long waves. Although he acknowledged two Dutch predecessors, Kondratieff is properly regarded as the father of the notion that capitalist economies are subject to cycles some 50 years in length.[13] He established an empirical case by finding two and one-half cycles in a number of price, wage, interest-rate, and other value-affected series, with troughs around 1790, 1844–1851, and 1890–

1896, and peaks at 1810–1817, 1870–1875, and 1914–1920. Production data were both sparse and recalcitrant when set into this cyclical mold. Nevertheless, Kondratieff believed that long-run cycles in output accompanied his cycles in prices and other value data. His image was one of a dynamic world economy moving forward in long price and output oscillations around a more or less stable upward trend in production.

Kondratieff did not attempt directly to provide a theory of the long cycle, but he counterattacked critics who asserted that the phenomena he was examining reflected exogenous forces: changes in technology, wars and revolutions, the bringing of new countries into the world economy, and fluctuations in gold production. His counterattack asserted that none of these phenomena could be properly regarded as exogenous to the workings of a world capitalist system,[14] but he did not render them endogenous. He implied that a coherent explanation must exist; but, in his own phrase, he never developed "an appropriate theory of long waves." It is fair to say that his major net contribution was dual: to demonstrate long-period movements (or cycles) in prices, interest rates, and other value series, and to pose for others to contemplate his empirical assertions that the upswings of his cycles tended to contain more years of (conventional) cyclical prosperity than the downswings; that agricultural depressions accompanied the downswings; that large numbers of inventions and discoveries were made in the downswings to be applied fully in the upswings; that the beginnings of the upswings were accompanied by both expanded gold production and the effective absorption of new areas into the world economy; and that the latter phase of the upswings brought with them "the most disastrous and extensive wars and revolutions." Above all, what Kondratieff did was to dramatize, in the most vivid and persuasive of his charts, the two and a half cycles between 1789 and 1920 in commodity prices (Figure 12.1).

One of the most important consequences of Kondratieff's work was, of course, that it stimulated Schumpeter, in his *Business Cycles,* to try to link his earlier innovational

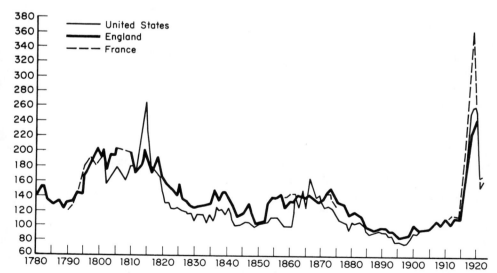

Figure 12.1. Index Numbers of Commodity Prices, 1780–1922: England, United States, and France (1901–1910 = 100). [Adapted from N. D. Kondratieff, "The Long Waves in Economic Life," *Review of Economic Statistics,* vol. 17, No. 6 (November 1935), p. 106.]

model to the pattern of price and interest-rate cycles Kondratieff isolated (preceding, p. 240).

As this summary indicates, Kondratieff addressed himself to overall price indexes, not relative price movements. Nevertheless two students of long cycles—W. Arthur Lewis and I—have concluded that the phenomena Kondratieff identified are to be explained in terms of periods of relative shortage and relative abundance of agricultural and other basic commodities, yielding movements in relative prices, the price level, interest rates, etc.[15] In fact I would argue that of the possible forces cited by Kondratieff, only relative price movements, thus conceived, fit the timing of Kondratieff's waves and cover the whole period from 1790 to, say, the late 1980s.

From the present perspective, however, Kondratieff's achievement was to assert firmly that long waves were to be regarded as one aspect of the process of capitalist development itself.

Colin Clark's observations on the terms of trade are also set in an historical context, in a rather remarkable chapter in his *National Income and Outlay*, "The Rate of Economic Progress."[16]

Clark's point of departure appears to have been his *ex post* measurement of the extent to which Britain, in the interwar period, had dissipated the potential advantages accruing from highly favorable terms of trade in a high average level of unemployment. After a somewhat schematic summary of partial historical evidence, he advances a Doctrine of Economic Indigestion:[17] "During the period when potentialities of real income production are rapidly increasing, either through a genuine increase in productivity, or through an improvement in the terms of trade, it seems inevitable that a large part of this improvement should be wasted in the form of unemployment." This notion appears later, with acknowledgments to D. H. Robertson's testimony before the Macmillan Committee, as an *ad hoc* historical hypothesis; namely, that modern economic history has been marked by successive capital-hungry and capital-sated periods.[18]

Specifically, Clark broke the post-1870 period into the following intervals: 1870–1876: low unemployment, rising retail prices, apparent prosperity, low rate of productivity increase;[19] 1877–1885: falling prices and interest rates, favorable terms of trade, but productivity gains canceled in part by higher unemployment; and 1900–1913: rising prices, stagnant real wages, stagnant productivity, but low unemployment. Evidently, Clark interpreted the interwar years as an extreme version of the obverse of 1900–1913; that is, a period in which a high rate of productivity increase and favorable terms of trade were dissipated in unemployment, notably in the export industries.

Clark's exposition was frankly exploratory; he pointed to certain anomalies in the story; and his historical data were incomplete and, in some cases, debatable. The major missing element in his pattern, however, is the role of capital exports. The periods of intense capital exports (e.g., 1871–1873, 1911–1913) were marked by inflationary pressures, retardation in productivity and real wage increases, and low unemployment. Thus the link Clark failed to make was between high and low relative prices for basic commodities and the usual (not universal) fluctuations in the flows of capital to basic commodity-producing regions.

Folke Hilgerdt added a useful dimension to the analysis of relative prices by calculating the connection between trends in relative price trends and trends in the relative volume of manufactured and primary goods in world trade (Figure 12.2). In a world in which manufactured exports were heavily concentrated in highly industrialized countries, primary exports in less developed countries, the elegant symmetry of Figure 12.2 down to

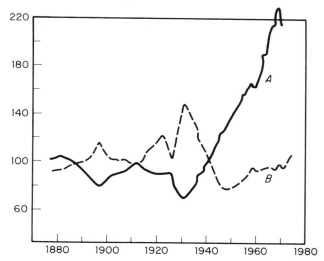

Figure 12.2. Relative Price Movements and World Trade, 1876–1880 to 1972. *A.* Quantum index of world trade in manufactured goods as percentage of that in primary goods. *B.* Price index of manufactured goods as percentage of that for primary goods. [Adapted from Folke Hilgerdt, *Industrialization and Foreign Trade,* p. 18, updated from *United Nations Statistical Yearbooks,* various years.]

1951 is almost tautological; that is, a shift in relative prices in favor of manufactures would, other things remaining equal, require a larger volume of primary products to be exchanged for a given volume of manufactured products. Table 12.2 exhibits the actual proportioning of trade between the "highly industrialized" and "other countries." Hilgerdt commented as follows, noting, in effect, that other things did not always remain equal:[21]

> It would be erroneous to assume that the failure of the quantum of trade in manufactured goods to keep pace with that in primary products has been due simply and directly to the fact that, as the terms of trade changed in favour of industrial countries, they could acquire a given quantity of primary products in exchange for the export of a declining quantity of manufactured goods. The relative decline in manufactured goods during the 1890's . . . was due in part to a reduction in the imports of these goods into certain relatively advanced industrial countries, such as the United States, France and Italy, that resulted from the increase in tariff protection about 1890. In the early 1930's the exchange of manufactured goods among industrial countries again declined as a result of import barriers, which this time took the form of quantitative controls rather than of tariffs. On both occasions barriers were raised after a fall in prices that had rendered barter terms more "favourable" to industrial countries, owing to the tendency of primary products to change more rapidly in price than manufactured goods.

I included the post-1950 movement of the two curves in Figure 12.2 to indicate that, for a sustained period, (say 1951–1971), once again other things did not remain equal.[22] That is, there was a large relative increase in trade in manufactured goods among advanced

Table 12.2. World Trade in 1935, in Old U.S. Gold Dollars (Billions)

	Imports			Exports		
	Primary products	Manufactured articles	Total	Primary products	Manufactured articles	Total
I. Highly industrialized countries						
Intra-trade	1.7	1.4	3.1	1.7	1.3	3.0
Trade with Group II	4.1	0.2	4.3	0.7	2.5	3.2
	5.8	1.6	7.4	2.4	3.8	6.2
II. Other countries:						
Intra-trade	1.2	0.4	1.6	0.9	0.4	1.3
Trade with Group I	0.8	2.6	3.4	3.6	0.2	3.8
	2.0	3.0	5.0	4.5	0.6	5.1
World	7.8	4.6	12.4	6.9	4.4	11.3

NOTE: The figures in this table have been adjusted so as to represent "frontier values" (imports c.i.f. and exports f.o.b.) in the case of all countries. This involved an addition to recorded world imports of 0.2 and to recorded world exports of 0.1.

The countries included in Group I are: Austria, Belgium, Czechoslovakia, France, Germany, Italy, Japan, Netherlands, Sweden, Switzerland, United Kingdom, United States.

SOURCE: *Industrialization and Foreign Trade*, p. 19.

industrial countries as well as a rise in the role of such countries as exporters of basic commodities.

In passing, it is worth noting that the issue of relative prices was a domestic as well as international issue during the interwar years, the foundation for which is suggested in Figure 12.3, which presents both the British terms of trade and the U.S. farm parity ratio. Their roughly inverse movement is apparent.

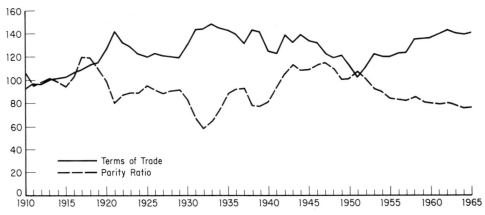

Figure 12.3. The Relationship between the British Terms of Trade and the U.S. Agricultural Parity Ratio. [Adapted from C. H. Feinstein, "Statistical Tables of National Income, and Output of the U.K., 1855–1965," 1972, p. T139. U.S. Department of Commerce, *Historical Statistics of the United States: Colonial Times to 1970,* Part 1, 1971, pp. 488–489.]

A Conclusion

Relative price movements in the period 1870–1939 clearly generated problems that captured the attention of several major economists of the period, just as large British pre-1914 exports of capital and the debate on the reparations-transfer problem generated studies bearing on the determinants of the terms of trade. Keynes and Robertson focused on the believed implications of both unfavorable and favorable terms of trade movements for the British economy and short-run British economic policy, as well as (in Keynes's case) for postwar policy toward Germany. Colin Clark looked a bit further back in history to illuminate three trend periods in the terms of trade (roughly 1873–1896; 1896–1920; and 1920–mid-1930s). He probed imaginatively but indecisively at possible links between terms of trade, productivity, unemployment, and capital-requirement trends. Folke Hilgerdt measured and analyzed relative price movements in relation to the relative volumes of manufactured and primary goods entering international trade. Kondratieff put effectively on the agenda the possible reasons for long waves in prices and other value-dominated series reaching back to 1790. He perceived these cycles ought to be treated as an aspect of the growth process; but never made a satisfactory linkage. The other analyses of cyclical movements in relative prices suffered the same basic weakness as most pre-1939 business-cycle analyses; that is, they did not begin with a sufficiently disaggregated, dynamic model of growth and then account for the systematic deviations of actual from dynamic equilibrium sectoral capacity. It was these deviations that yielded successive phases of distortion in relative prices and, thus, the terms of trade.[23]

13

Stages of
and Limits to Growth

The available analytic literature on the early stages of development is much thinner in the pre-1939 period than it should be. The import substitution takeoffs of Argentina and Brazil began in the 1930s, in constructive response to the devastation of their export earning capacity; and Mexico completed its preconditions for takeoff, after the end of its bloody civil war, in the period 1920–1940. There were significant parallel developments elsewhere in Latin America. The takeoff of Turkey also occurred in the 1930s after the rather tortured emergence of a nation state committed to modernization in the wake of the dismemberment of the Ottoman Empire. There were also important developments elsewhere short of takeoff, including India and China; although they were overshadowed by political and, in the latter case, military events.

Meanwhile, closer to the center of social science theorizing, Eastern Europe moved forward unevenly before 1914 and continued its modernization, despite the depressing impact of interwar circumstances in Western Europe and the world economy as a whole.

There was, nevertheless, somewhat more systematic reflection on the development process in the 1870–1939 period than most analyses suggest.[1] But, still, the literature conventionally available is meager as compared, for example, with that on the business cycle. This is the case for three reasons. First, the economists of the United States, Western and Central Europe who dominated the formal literature of economics were, with one notable exception (i.e., Marshall), a rather parochial crew obsessed with the problems of their own time and place.

Second, those actually engaged in the early stages of modernization in developing countries were too busy to reflect analytically on what they were doing and to set out their conclusions in a conventional way. For example, Raul Prebisch, one of the first economists from a developing region to find his voice, had this to say in retrospect:[2]

> When I started my life as a young economist and professor during the 1920s, I was a firm believer in neoclassical theories. However, the first great crisis of capitalism—the world Depression—prompted in me serious doubts regarding these beliefs. . . .
>
> During those hectic years of the Depression I had some influence on the economic policy of my country, Argentina, first as Under Secretary of Finance and later with the Central Bank. During the 1930s I recommended

orthodox anti-inflationary measures to eliminate the fiscal deficit and suppress inflationary tendencies, but at the same time I departed from orthodoxy when I had to face a serious balance of payments disequilibrium and advocated a resolute industrialization policy as well as other measures to this end.

My duties during this period did not permit me to devote time to theoretical activities. But after I left these responsibilities in the early 1940s, I spent some years trying to derive some theoretical views from my experience.

Third, there was an abiding problem that persisted into the post-1945 years when the analysis of economic development became fashionable. The serious study of development requires the systematic blending of economic and noneconomic analysis. In the period 1870–1939, when economics became a professional and specialized academic discipline, not many mainstream economists were willing and able to work on a multidimensional social science basis, in conformity with the older tradition of political economy.

Still, I would guess we could find a larger body of analytic reflection in and on the developing regions than we have yet mobilized if we were to dig deeper in government archives and local journals, as well as into the archives of the colonial powers. Unfortunately, that was a task I could not undertake as part of the present enterprise.

I shall, therefore, confine this chapter to five easily accessible approaches to the stages of and limits to growth as conceived in the period 1870–1939:

- Colin Clark's truly pioneering *Conditions of Economic Progress.*
- The country studies of Vera Anstey (India) and R. H. Tawney (China), along with Lillian Knowles's observations on developments in the British Empire.
- W. G. Hoffmann's highly original *Growth of Industrial Economies.*
- Folke Hilgerdt's rather striking generalizations on the development process in *Industrialization and Foreign Trade.*
- Reflections on the limits to growth stirred by the Great Depression of the 1930s: notably those of Hansen and Schumpeter.

The Conditions of Economic Progress

Although Colin Clark's title derives from Marshall,[3] it was rather remarkable that a study of the conditions of economic progress should have been written by an Englishman, caught up in the intractable problems of his country in the 1930s, focusing, apparently, on the laborious refinement of national income calculations and their analytic applications. In the course of planning this chapter I wrote and asked Clark how it happened. His beguiling reply (10 June, 1986):

> The first begetting of the idea of *Conditions of Economic Progress* came in 1935. I was engaged to be married, and my fiancée had just told me, in a good natured tone, that I was leading rather an idle life. On a bright sunny afternoon, unseasonable for the time of year (March), I canoed out on the River Cam, tied up under a tree, and sketched the whole outline of the book in less than an hour.

In *Pioneers in Development,* Clark explained some of the other strands that bore on his unorthodox interest.[4] Among them were two connections that drew him into the problems of India: The experiences there of Austin and Joan Robinson in 1926–1928, which they conveyed with enthusiasm to their Cambridge colleagues on their return;[5] and Clark's supervision of a brilliant Indian student (V.K.R.V. Rao) in writing his thesis *The National Income of British India, 1931–1932.* Clark's interest was broadened by a comparative study, begun in 1935, of agricultural output in developing countries.

The Conditions for Economic Progress was first published in 1940 and then, thoroughly rewritten, in 1951. It is the study that laid the foundations for the post-1945 studies of Kuznets, Hollis Chenery, and others who aimed to measure and compare the structural characteristics of economies at different levels of real income per capita either over long periods of time or, in cross-section, at a given time interval.

Although the 1940 edition contains somewhat less statistical data than its 1951 successor, it is totally a product of the period we are now examining rather than the post-1945 years dealt with in Part Three; and it contains certain features that one can regret were dropped from the second edition including, notably, a vivid and useful "Summary and Conclusions," a chapter on the terms of trade in relation to growth, and an effort to shift multiplier and accelerator analysis from a short- to a long-run basis.[6]

The heart of Clark's technical analysis in both editions consisted in these major features.

- Real income and its components are defined in terms of a standard "international unit" (I.U.) consisting of the amount of goods and services that could be purchased for $1 in the United States over the average of the decade 1925–1934. This permitted both systematic international comparison and, even, a bold effort to calculate global product and income distribution by countries at different average levels of real income.
- Clark's basic disaggregation was in terms of primary (agriculture, etc.), secondary (manufacturing), and tertiary (service) sectors. He examined relative productivity and manpower allocations among the three sectors at different levels of real income, and the changing proportions for particular countries with the passage of time, changing technology, and the rise in real income per capita. His analyses were the forerunners of both comparative cross-section and country studies of the post-1945 period.
- He grappled suggestively but indecisively with the problem of measuring and assessing the role of capital in economic progress; the distribution of incomes of individuals; changes in patterns of consumption at different income levels; and the rate of population increase in relation to national income growth rates.

As Clark's acknowledgments and references make clear, he had a good deal of data available for mobilization by the second half of the 1930s, but his assembly of the material and organization of it around a coherent and principled set of questions was an authentic path-breaking enterprise. Some of his conclusions have been altered as more data have become available; some of his analytic passages are debatable; and I, at least, would question the adequacy of real income per capita as a sufficient measure of degree of development and stage of growth. But *The Conditions of Economic Progress* is one of the few books that virtually created a new branch of economic analysis, despite Clark's self-denying assessment that some of his principal conclusions were foreshadowed by Sir William Petty,[7] to whose name he might have added those of Adam Smith and Alfred Marshall.

Anstey, Tawney, and Knowles

I had something to say about Vera Anstey's interwar study of India (first edition, 1929) and R. H. Tawney's of China (1932) in the course of the brief account of the evolution of demographic analysis in Chapter 7 (preceding, pp. 206–208). They are both distinguished studies of development problems and prospects set in a view of whole societies, worth reading more than a half century after they were written, although analyses of Indian and Chinese development have since become cottage industries.

At the time these analyses were conducted both India and China were in the complex transitional stage I call the preconditions for takeoff. They contained elements of a modern economy and relatively small groups of (mainly) men knowledgeable about Western methods of organization, and for one reason or another, motivated to expand the modern centers of activity. In Anstey's phrase, "[t]he educated English-speaking Indians . . . form a thin articulate layer covering the surface of the whole of Indian society."[8] A similar relatively small catalytic group existed in Chinese society. The two economies contained railway systems, cotton textile mills, iron and steel, engineering, and chemical plants, among others. But these enclaves were embedded in societies still essentially traditional with the round of life of most human beings untouched—or only marginally touched—by modern activities and attitudes. Anstey used explicitly the rough analogy of mediaeval Western Europe to illuminate the setting from which a modern India would have to evolve. She pointed to, among other features of Indian life, the pervasive influence of religion; the absence of the idea of progress; the nature of the sharp social divisions; the subordination of the individual to the group; the predominance of self-sufficient agriculture; the pervasive role of guilds. In both countries, the focusing of political life on the tasks of development was inhibited by the existence of problems of evident higher priority: in India's case, the achievement of independence; in China's case, a more equitable balance with intrusive external powers, the building of a vital central government, and the settlement of the civil war that existed from, at least, 1927.

The counterpoint between powerful old strands of religion, culture, social structure, and political behavior and the tasks of modernization is the central theme of both books, which end by arguing that economic development can only proceed successfully as these noneconomic obstacles are overcome, including those that decree excessive rates of population increase.

The bulk of Anstey's text is devoted to the modern economic enclaves within Indian society, to recent trends and policies, and prospects. It is a prototype of the kind of country study the World Bank was to conduct on a large scale, starting about a quarter-century later. But its linking of the technical economic analysis with the noneconomic forces at work is unforced, uninhibited, and more effective than in most highly professional economic development studies of a later time. When she comes, in the end, to identify the major "obstacles to a great forward movement" in the economy, she observes that none is to be sought "in the material, technical sphere, but in the sphere of social organization." She defines the "three fundamental obstacles" as "the tendency towards an excessive increase in population, the uneconomic outlook of the people, and the lack of co-operation between the government and the governed."[9]

Tawney's study of China (*Land and Labour in China*) is both narrower and broader than Anstey's. Less than two-fifths as long, it focuses, as its title suggests, primarily on the agricultural sector and rural life. It was originally written as a memorandum for a conference of the Institute of Pacific Relations held at Shanghai in November 1931, whose organizers had the wit to enlist one of the great analysts of Europe's transition from mediaeval to modern life. His discriminating analogies with strands of European experience and, even more, his underlining of what in China was unique, provide the framework for the book.

As for analogies, there are passages like this:[10]

> . . .[T]he disorders of Chinese agriculture . . . are acute in degree but [in part] not unique in kind. They are one species of a genus which has been widely diffused, and which is characteristic, not of this nation or that, but of a particular phase of economic civilisation. The persistence of an empirical technique based on venerable usage and impervious to science; the meagre output of foodstuffs which that technique produced; the waste of time and labour through the fragmentation of holdings; the profits wrung from the cultivator by middleman, usurer and landlord; the absence of means of communication and the intolerable condition of such as existed; the narrow margin separating the mass of the population from actual starvation and the periodical recurrence of local famines—such phenomena, if exception be made of a few favoured regions, were until recently the commonplaces of western economic life since men first reflected on it. . . .
>
> The forces which shifted the scene in the course of the last century need no lengthy explanation. The novelty of the age was the application of science to the productive arts.

The bulk of Tawney's text explores the possible relevance to China of remedies applied elsewhere: in communications; science and education; cooperative organizations; land tenure; drought and flood control; reduced birthrates and migration; and the development of modern industry, to which a chapter is devoted. Technically, Tawney concludes that the "fundamental economic needs of China . . . are, in order of their importance:[11]

> *(i)* an improvement in the means of communication, by the extension of roads, and, as circumstances allow, of railways; *(ii)* the improvement of agriculture, on the side, not only of productive methods, but of finance, marketing, and land tenure; *(iii)* the development, with adequate safeguards, of machine industry, and its extension beyond the small number of areas in which at present it is concentrated. Neither political stability nor economic progress, however, will be achieved automatically.

But he argues that politics has priority over economics:[12]

> They [the Chinese] must create a stable and unified political system, in the absence of which it is idle to talk either of national independence or of economic reconstruction. . . . He [a Western observer] hears much of China united under the Nationalist Government. Then he takes a map, goes through the provinces one by one, marks with a pencil those where the authority of Nanking is effective, those where it is nominal, those where it is openly defied. His perspective changes. The capital dwindles to a city effectively governing, perhaps, six or seven provinces out of thirty in a continent partly

friendly, partly indifferent, partly hostile. It is France in the twelfth century, on a scale immensely greater—Paris and the Ile de France, a little circle of light, in one corner, and, for the rest, a welter of liberties.

Like Anstey, Tawney turns for analogy to "mediaeval Christendom" to evoke the underlying structure of institutions and concepts that would have to change if a modern China were to emerge. But his operational focus remains on:[13] "[t]he first problem . . . ; To create an efficient system of government;" and he links that critical objective to development of a more modern and effective educational system.

His final chapter is addressed to "Education and Politics" as the critical determinants of the outcome; and to his final eloquent judgment that the Chinese themselves must reconcile the imperatives of modernization with the continuity of their culture—one of the wisest observations to be found in development literature.[14]

> Much talk of the Westernisation of China is remote from realities. . . . [T]he imitation of America or Europe, which has profoundly influenced Chinese education, offers no solution of the deeper problems of China. It was a necessary stage in her evolution; till she knew of the West, she could not fully know herself. . . . [T]hough a nation may borrow its tools from abroad, for the energy to handle them it must look within.

> Erquickung hast du nicht gewonnen,
> Wenn sie dir nicht aus eigner Seele quillt.*

> It is in herself alone, in her own historical culture, rediscovered and reinterpreted in the light of her modern requirements, that China will find the dynamic which she needs. The most fundamental achievements of her revolution are still to come. The problem is to translate political rejuvenation into the practical terms of social institutions, and to build with a modern technique, but on Chinese foundations. It is to her schools and universities that she must look for the builders.

Lillian Knowles's *Economic Development of the British Overseas Empire* is a quite different kind of book.[15] It is primarily a study of the tropical regions of the empire,[16] reflecting Knowles's pioneer teaching at the London School of Economics of a course on economic development of the British Empire required for the Bachelor of Commerce degree. As compared with the work of Anstey and Tawney, it is rather more a history of imperial policy than an analysis of development problems and prospects; although both strands are explored. Inevitably, it covers a wider range of circumstances in less detail. There is, also perhaps inevitably, an element of wonderment—even glorification—at "the underlying romance of the new British tropical empire. . . ," Britain's role as "the great civilizer, the bringer of law and order" and shock absorber between the "world-desire for produce and sale and the primitive races. . . ."[17]

It contains, however, important analytic insights; for example, the systematic impact on colonial policy of changing technology, including the capacity to suppress slavery. It deals in a forthright way with the "underlying commercialism of the British empire" but also the rise in priority of "the native interest" and a "sense of responsibility for the

---

*"One does not achieve rejuvenation unless it arises from one's own soul."

indigenous inhabitants. . . ."[18] And like her two contemporaries at LSE, she evokes Europe's transition from mediaeval times to illuminate the historical passage to be observed in the tropical empire and reflects:[19] "When one looks back in English history and sees how civilized persons [e.g., Roman occupiers] must have regarded us about 1,900 years ago one need not despair of the tropics."

It is also worth noting that there were British writers who peered beneath the surface of modernization under colonialism and captured with sensibility and compassion the ambivalence of both sides among those caught up in the process; e.g., E. M. Forster and Joyce Cary, the latter for some time a colonial civil servant in West Africa. *Passage To India* and *Mr. Johnson* belong with the literature of modernization along with more conventional texts.

Walther Hoffmann

Hoffmann's *The Growth of Industrial Economies* was published first in German in 1931 but did not become widely accessible in the West until published in translation in 1958.[20] Hoffmann does not explain fully how he came to write this highly original book but he suggests it arose from an effort to resolve the clash of two perspectives on the accelerated industrialization outside Europe during the First World War. One view was that the "war-babies" would be endangered by "the revival of European competition after 1918"; the other, that the spread of industry beyond Europe was similar to its earlier diffusion within Europe, that the latecomers had the "advantage of the prior experience of European countries," and their tendency toward industrial self-sufficiency would reduce exports "of some types of European manufactures."[21] To get at these matters Hoffmann proceeded in a straightforward, orderly manner. First he defines the determinants of the overall growth of the economy with his own version of a basic growth equation:[22]

> In each country, . . . there are considerable variations in the rates of growth of the three main sectors of the economy—the primary, the secondary, and the tertiary industries*—and of the rates of growth of particular industries *within* these three sectors. These differences have been due largely to the interplay of the following factors: (i) the relative amounts of the factors of production (natural resources, capital stock, labour force), (ii) the location of the productive resources in relation to home and foreign markets, (iii) the level of technological development, and (iv) factors of a non-economic character such as the skill of entrepreneurs, the tastes of consumers, and the political and social structure of the country concerned. These factors determine the growth of a national economy as a whole and of its various sectors. During the course of economic development these factors, however, are to a large extent the result of economic growth.

Hoffmann then narrows his focus to structural changes within the industrial sector that are "the result of different rates of growth of various branches of manufacture" and asserts that there are striking similarities in patterns of industrialization among countries in the process of growth.[23]

---

*This is Colin Clark's terminology.

Specifically he finds the following:[24]

> . . . [T]he structure of the manufacturing sector of the economy has always followed a uniform pattern. The food, textile, leather and furniture industries—which we define as "consumer-goods industries"—always develop first during the process of industrialization. But the metal-working, vehicle building, engineering and chemical industries—the "capital-goods industries"—soon develop faster than the first group. This can be seen throughout the process of industrialization. . . .

> For the purposes of our analysis we have divided this gradual process into the following four stages:

> - Stage I has a ratio of 5 (± 1) : 1
> - Stage II has a ratio of 2.5 (± 1) : 1
> - Stage III has a ratio of 1 (± 0.5) : 1
> - The fourth stage has a still lower ratio. . . .

> The main purpose of this book is to show that these stages of economic development can be identified for all free economies.

Hoffmann then tests his central hypothesis about industrial structure with respect to countries at similar stages of growth at different time periods. This leads him to identify the periods when modern industrialization began in various countries.[25] After a knowledgeable discussion, focused rather sharply on cotton textiles, he groups these beginnings in four periods: 1770–1820 (Britain, Switzerland, United States); 1821–1860 (Continental Western and Central Europe plus Russia); 1861–1890 (Italy, Netherlands, Denmark, Greece, Japan, Canada); post-1891 (Hungary, India, South Africa, Latin America, Australia, New Zealand, and China). These dates are generally earlier than my takeoff dates. Hoffmann is content with a modern textile industry. My criteria for takeoff are more complex and represent progress already achieved over a wider front. In only a few cases was the rise of a modern textile industry a sufficiently large and powerful phenomenon to fulfill my criteria for takeoff. But Hoffmann's dates are solidly based for his narrower purposes.

By seizing on and pursuing a measurable ratio—the proportion of value added in a selected group of consumers' goods industries relative to a similar group of capital goods industries—Hoffmann produced an original morphology of growth in four stages and, along the way, arrayed a wide spectrum of countries with respect to the timing of their entrance into industrialization. His work in this area—generally ignored in the literature on development—clearly belongs among the authentic pioneering efforts.

Hilgerdt

As a by-product of its main purpose (preceding, pp. 308–310), *Industrialization and Foreign Trade* generated two chapters that constitute not only a kind of brief manual on the tasks of industrialization in a developing country but also a sophisticated general essay on development and development policy.[26] Hilgerdt's analysis draws on a wide range of contemporary and historical experience of countries at different stages of modernization, but distinguishes his cases, in particular, with respect to population density; initial income per capita; size of country and its domestic market; climate and health of population; scale of installed infrastructure; availability of domestic and foreign capital; determinants of the dynamic relationship between rates of growth of population and industry; and the role of tariff policy.

The flavor of Hilgerdt's analysis is captured in these extracts from his "Summary of Findings:"[27]

14. . . . [D]istinction had to be made between nonindustrial countries in which the population is relatively sparse in relation to available natural resources, and those in which it is relatively dense.

15. In the sparsely populated countries the economy is frequently commercialized to a considerable extent even before industrialization, for exportable surpluses of primary products are likely to be relatively great and hence also the import of manufactured articles. The early growth of foreign trade in these countries [is] . . . likely to facilitate their industrialization.

16. The densely populated countries, which occupy about three-fourths of their population in agriculture, are usually handicapped by poverty, low productivity of labour and an old-fashioned and inert social organization. . . . Their industrialization would require, among other things, a radical change in social values and administration, reorganization and rationalization of agriculture.

17. Industrial development in countries with a relatively small population . . . presents a special difficulty on account of the fact that the domestic market in these countries is not large enough to absorb the production on an industrial scale of many manufactured articles.

18. Particularly during its early stages, industrial development in densely populated countries may be facilitated if the industry established is decentralized and the scale of production relatively small. . . .

19. In densely populated countries a successful programme of industrialization might have to be combined with measures intended to check excessive population growth.

20. In these countries, it is imperative that the existing natural resources should be exhausted as little as possible before progressive industrialization is undertaken. . . .

21. The influx of foreign capital is of great importance for the development of external trade and of public utilities which are prerequisites for industrialization. But experience shows that only limited amounts of such capital are likely to be available for building up a manufacturing industry. Hence, domestic savings must usually supply the bulk of the industrial capital. The possibility of raising such capital . . . is greater than it may appear at first sight.

22. Tariff protection cannot nowadays be relied upon as the only or chief means to bring about industrialization. A successful industrialization scheme must usually include a broad programme of social rejuvenation, of hygienic improvement, of general and technical education, of agricultural reform and of investment in transportation, power generation and other utilities.

Hilgerdt evidently anticipated a good deal in the postwar prescriptive literature on development.

Reflections on the Limits to Growth:
Hansen versus Schumpeter

There are, essentially, three kinds of perspectives on the limits to growth: one focused on diminishing returns and relatively rising prices for basic commodities; a second, on a possible failure of the economic system to generate sufficiently high levels of effective demand to avoid abnormally high and protracted unemployment; and a third, on the need to restrain growth in order to elevate the quality of life. To these we can add Schumpeter's vision of a clash between the dynamics of democracy and the imperatives of viable capitalism.

The first follows quite closely the rhythm of Kondratieff cycles when defined in phases of relative shortage and abundance of basic commodities.[28] The intervals of greatest anxiety about diminishing returns to production of basic commodities have been the pre-1813 concern of Malthus and Ricardo with the pressure of population increase on the food supply and its consequences for the prospects for growth and real income per capita; anxieties about food, cotton, and coal at various times in the period from the mid-1840s to 1873, including W. S. Jevons's reluctant conclusion that "our motion must be reduced to rest" because the $3\frac{1}{2}$%-per-annum rate of increase in British coal consumption could not be supported from thick, accessible, high-productivity seams;[29] and the reflections of Keynes and Robertson on the larger meaning of the pre-1914 European terms of trade. Parallel anxieties arose in 1945–1951 and 1965–1980—again, in response to relative price movements and, in the latter case, evidence of gathering pressure of population increase and accelerated industrialization on the physical environment.

Concern with high and apparently chronic unemployment and slow growth led some to propose radical changes in public policy. This was the context in which Malthus and Ricardo debated during the worst phases of structural adjustment after 1815; the acute depressions of the early and late 1840s stirred the Chartists (as well as monetary and other reformers) to intense activity in Britain, as well as the Socialists on the Continent; bimetallists emerged in the Britain of the mid-1880s and the United States of the mid-1890s; and advocates of strong Keynesian remedies asserted themselves in the 1930s. The outcome of the unease of the 1980s in the Atlantic world is still to define itself in political terms.

No such stately rhythm is to be discerned with respect to those who have advocated for positive reasons limits to growth, although from J. S. Mill to Dennis Meadows their views have been linked often to anxiety about resources and the environment in a regime of progressive industrial expansion.

Here the focus is a particular phase of the second type of anxiety—the heightened concern with "secular stagnation" that followed the sharp recession of 1937–1938 after a cyclical upswing that had failed to bring the economies of Western Europe (except Germany) and North America back to full employment. Alternative perspectives are provided by Alvin Hansen's Presidential Address at the fifty-first meeting of the American Economic Association, December 28, 1938, entitled "Economic Progress and Declining Population Growth,"[30] and Schumpeter's quite explicitly different view of the meaning of "the disappointing Juglar."[31]

Hansen perceived clearly that to grapple effectively with the problem of secular stagnation he had to bring together the tools of both growth analysis and Keynesian short-run income analysis, or, in Hansen's vocabulary, "structural change" and "fluctuations."[32]

Tersely summarized, Hansen's thesis was the following.

1. The 1930s represented a new era, not yet definable: "We are passing, so to speak, over a divide which separates the great era of growth and expansion of the nine-teenth century from an era which no man, unwilling to embark on pure conjecture, can yet characterize with clarity or precision."[33]

2. "Overwhelmingly significant" was the decline by one-half of the increase in U.S. population in the 1930s as opposed to the rate of increase in the 1920s and pre-1914 (preceding, p. 201).[34]

3. Taking a positive Smithian rather than negative Malthusian view of the role of population increase in economic growth, there are two additional "constituent elements of economic progress . . . (a) inventions, (b) the discovery and develop-ment of a new territory and new resources. . . . Each of these [including population increase] in turn, severally and in combination, has opened investment outlets and caused a rapid growth of capital formation."[35]

4. Since the late nineteenth century a group of economists have elaborated "the thesis that economic fluctuations are essentially a function of economic progress."[36] Wicksell, Spiethoff, Schumpeter, Cassel, and Robertson led the way.

5. In the nineteenth century "investment outlets were numerous and alluring." The business cycle was *par excellence* the problem of that century. Now we suffer from "secular stagnation—sick recoveries which die in their infancy and depressions which feed on themselves and leave a hard and seemingly immovable core of unemployment. . . [,] the main problem of our times. . . ."[37]

6. The fall in the rate of population increase has reduced the demand for investment and thus contributed to chronic unemployment by cutting requirements for housing, utilities, and manufactured consumer goods. Rough estimates suggest that in the last half of the nineteenth century the growth of population was responsible for about 40% of the total volume of capital formation in Western Europe, 60% in the United States.[38]

7. The proportion of new capital created in the nineteenth century as a direct conse-quence of the opening up of new territory cannot be even approximately estimated. But perhaps one-fourth of total British capital formation went abroad before 1914, one-seventh for France. The prospects in the twentieth century for such stimulus are narrow; and there is also not much stimulus to be expected from the likely indus-trialization of Russia, Eastern Europe, China, and the Orient.[39]

8. "Thus the outlets for new investment are rapidly narrowing down to those created by the progress of technology." We need an acceleration in the rate of progress of science and technology. We need the creation of large new industries; but that process is "discontinuous, lumpy, and jerky," as D. H. Robertson has said. "And when giant new industries have spent their force [e.g., railroads, motor cars] it *may* take a long time before something else of equal magnitude emerges. In fact nothing has emerged in the decade in which we are now living. This basic fact, together with the virtual cessation of public investment by state and local governmental bodies . . . explains in large measure the necessary rise in federal expenditures."[40]

9. Certain institutional and market rigidities reduce the potential contribution of new technology to enlarged investment and the reduction of unemployment.[41] But pro-gress in reducing these barriers cannot substitute for action on the central require-ment: large-scale governmental action to stimulate consumption and public invest-

ment on the scale necessary to avoid intolerable levels of unemployment and declines in real income.

Hansen estimated current full employment national income at $80 billion, suggested strong government action should it fall "materially below" $65 billion, and commended a "tapering off" of government stimulus at about $70 billion to avoid inflationary pressures.[42]

10. The pursuit of such a policy, Hansen recognized, posed major questions that economists as of 1939 could not answer.[43] He pointed, in particular, to the fact that government measures to stimulate consumption and public investment would confront not only political difficulties but also might diminish the incentives for private investment in various ways. He concluded: "The great transition, incident to a rapid decline in population growth and its impact upon capital formation and the workability of a system of free enterprise, calls for high scientific adventure along all the fronts represented by the social science disciplines."

Given the great global boom of the 1950s and 1960s, some of Hansen's analysis seems quaint and off the mark; and, evidently, he did not perceive the extraordinary interdependence that would evolve in the four post-1945 decades between the advanced industrial and developing regions. But his argument remains a rare bringing together of growth and short-run income analysis—multiplier, accelerator, and all. It also, of course, captures a perspective widely shared as the Second World War broke out.

But it was not shared by Joseph Schumpeter, who devoted the final chapter of *Business Cycles* to specifying the area and character of his disagreement, a view later elaborated in his *Capitalism, Socialism and Democracy.*[44]

Schumpeter's thesis was, in the end, simple enough:[45] ". . . The balloon shriveled, not from causes inherent to its structure [as Hansen argued] but because the air was being sucked out of it"—by the psychological impact on American capitalists, and their willingness to invest, of various New Deal policies and the hostile atmosphere they created. In short, Schumpeter was prepared to argue that Hansen's final question about the compatibility of a vigorous competitive capitalism and an active if selective interventionist government of the kind commended by Hansen had already been answered negatively.

Schumpeter's conclusion is less important than how he made his case; for he wove together not only growth and short-run analysis but also the sociology and psychology of capitalism.

1. Focusing like Hansen on invention and innovation, Schumpeter viewed the 1930s as a phase (like the 1880s) in which the economy is carried forward by the diffusion of the increasingly mature but still vigorously unfolding technologies of its long Kondratieff cycle: in this case, electricity, motor vehicles, and chemicals.[46] He concluded his interpretation of this Kondratieff downswing in terms quite different from Hansen's:[47]

> Having thus satisfied ourselves that the processes which in the past used to carry prosperities have not been absent in the present instance, we have established a right to speak of a Juglar prosperity and to infer from experience that it would have asserted itself without any external impulse being imparted to the system by government expenditure or any other factor. In particular, there is nothing to indicate that objective opportunities were smaller or capitalist motivation weaker than they had been, say, in 1925. The problem why that prosperity was so weak, and why it

should have been followed by so severe a slump now emerges in its proper setting.

2. After reviewing various monetary and fiscal developments he concludes that the government's role was ". . . singularly infelicitous—its high-water mark came exactly at the time when the economic process could most easily have done without it and its cessation exactly at the time when the economic process was in its most sensitive phase."[48] But he argues infelicity of fiscal and monetary policy does not account for the severity of the recession of 1937–1938.

3. After reviewing Hansen's thesis in typically judicious style, Schumpeter identifies two further areas of agreement with the secular stagnation doctrine: "[S]ometime in the future investment opportunities may vanish;" and they might vanish "through saturation."[49] This permits him to isolate lucidly his area of disagreement by questioning[50]

> . . . the relevance of those [long-run] considerations for the diagnosis of the situation of 1938. . . . We are less than ten years removed from as vigorous a prosperity as was ever witnessed and from a depression proba- bly due, in the main, to the pace of preceding "progress. . . ." [I]t did not differ in character from the comparable Juglar prosperities of the preceding Kondratieff downgrades, and therefore does not indicate any fundamental change in the working of the capitalist organism. . . .
>
> . . . [But] capitalism produces by its mere working a social atmo- sphere—a moral code, if the reader prefer—that is hostile to it, and this atmosphere, in turn, produces policies which do not allow it to func- tion. . . . This is what, to a certain extent and presumably not yet for good has happened in this country.

5. Schumpeter, now freed to expound his own thesis, argued that it was the sudden change in policy and attitude of the government toward American private capitalism that produced the radical inhibition of investment. Changes in tax, labor, utilities, and antimonopoly policy, which Schumpeter reviewed, explain part of the problem, because they "tended to reinforce each other."[51] Their combined effect was en- hanced by the suddenness of the change in 1933 and the manner of administration of the new measures.

6. Thus, Schumpeter concludes:[52] ". . . [T]here should not be left much doubt as to the adequacy of the factors external to our process to account both for the disap- pointing features in the current Juglar and for the weakness of the response of the system to government expenditure, in particular for the failure of the latter to affect investment and employment more than it did."

In a final footnote Schumpeter prepares the way for his next book (and foreshadows something of the rationale for the enormous deficits of the Reagan Administration):[53]

> . . . [T]he pattern resulting from the action of inhibiting factors would in all respects be similar to the pattern envisaged by the saving-investment theory; it would display the same lack of resilience and the same tendency towards sub- normal quasi-equilibria; in particular, it would always produce or reproduce extensive unemployment. Therefore, government spending would . . . al- ways suggest itself as a remedy for shortrun difficulties each application of which would impose, under penalty of breakdown, the application of the next

dose. Fear of such breakdowns may in the end become the dominant motive even among those who on principle are most strongly opposed to spending policies.

Two Perspectives on 1870–1939: A Coda for Part II

Pigou, quite as sensitive to the grave issues posed by the apparent secular stagnation of the 1930s as Hansen and Schumpeter, managed a somewhat longer and more philosophical perspective. In 1939 he delivered a presidential address of charm and nostalgia to the Royal Economic Association entitled "Looking Back from 1939."[54] He identified a considerable series of changes since he was a Cambridge undergraduate 40 years earlier; for example, the two-edged triumphs of the motorcar and airplane; the changed status of women and revolution in their mountain-climbing garments; an enormous expansion in the number of professionally trained economists, with a strong suggestion that diminishing returns had operated severely on their quality. He could name only eight "leading economists" of his undergraduate days, including Marshall and Edgeworth. He then asks:[55]

> What is the most important difference? There need be little doubt about the answer. Economists then had grown up in, and their whole experience was confined to, a world which, as regards politics and economics alike, was reasonably stable. . . . [T]he basic changes were gradual and slow-working. There were no catastrophes. How different is the experience of economists today! The 1914 War, with its aftermath of ruin; the period of unbalanced Budgets and astronomical inflations; the slow readjustment; the terrible relapse of the great depression and the political tensions that accompanied it! This fundamental difference of experience is, I think, largely accountable for the difference in the way in which the old generation of economists and the new approach their problems. Inevitably now the short run presents itself with far greater urgency relatively to the long run than it did then. The economists from, say, 1890 to 1910 did not, of course, ignore problems of transition or the great evils of fluctuating employment. But, relatively to the underlying forces by which production and distribution are governed, these things took second place. . . . In a period when our minds are attuned to sudden and violent changes, a different viewpoint is natural. In calm weather it is proper to reckon the course of a ship without much regard for the waves. But in a storm the waves may be everything. The problems of transition are the urgent problems. For, if they are not solved, what happens is not transition, but catastrophe; the long run never comes.

Pigou's evocation of the terrible urgency and uniqueness of the sequence of interwar problems helps explain the limited attention to economic growth in that period. In a sense Pigou was offering a rationale for Keynes's dictum that in the [Marshallian] long run we're all dead. As for 1870 to 1914, growth was pretty much taken for granted in the then advanced industrial regions of the world. Growth was part of the stable, slow-changing world in which Pigou matured; and, against that assumed background, he could devote his talents to essentially marginal improvements in welfare and the mitigation of the trade cycle.

Looking back from the 1980s, what is surprising is how many of the fundamental insights and methods on which post-1945 growth analysis of various kinds was based were generated in the two quite different settings on either side of the 1914 watershed: in demography; the analysis of investment and technology; the business cycle; relative price trends; and the stages of and limits to growth. Moreover, the quality of the major contributions to growth analysis—direct and oblique—was, like the giants of Pigou's youth, high: Marshall still and Robertson; Spiethoff and Schumpeter; Colin Clark and Kuznets; Arthur F. Burns and Fabricant; Anstey and Tawney; Bickerdike and Harrod; Hoffmann and Hilgerdt; and, in their way, Cassel, J. B. Clark, J. M. Clark, Fisher, Wicksell, and Allyn Young. And then Keynes and Hansen articulating the case for secular stagnation by linking rather classical growth analysis, dominated by diminishing returns, to the new income analysis, generating in response, out of Schumpeter's deeply rooted central European pessimism, an even gloomier Hegelian prospect.

Part Three demonstrates that growth analysis did not dominate mainstream economics in the four decades after 1945; but growth was directly addressed by large numbers of analysts in ways clearly foreshadowed in the 70 pre-1939 years, despite the interwar compulsion to focus on the short run.

III

GROWTH ANALYSIS POST-1945: A THREE-RING CIRCUS

14

Introduction

In turning now to the period 1945–1988 the challenges differ from those of Part II. Like all growth curves, the professional field of economics, after further expansion, decelerated in the Atlantic World; it generated all manner of specialized sports; its focus shifted in response to the unexpected, uniquely high, and relatively steady growth of the 1950s and 1960s, and shifted again, reluctantly and awkwardly, to try to deal with the inelegant turbulence induced by the two oil shocks between 1973 and 1981, and to the relatively slow average growth and high unemployment rates, deficits, and debts of 1982–1989.

This time growth analysis moved back on stage from the wings. But it did not return in the spacious classic mold of the 18th and 19th centuries. We are dealing here with three areas of growth analysis, all with roots in the inter-war period:

- formal growth models in the style crystallized by Harrod in 1939;
- statistical analyses of comparative growth patterns at different levels of real income per capita, of the kind pioneered by Colin Clark;
- development theory comprising a wide range of less methodologically rigid approaches to the analysis of growth in less developed countries, foreshadowed, among others, by Anstey, Tawney, and Hilgerdt.

There was some interaction among these three lines of endeavor, although their practitioners mainly pursued their insights and conducted their debates in separate terrains.

I should note parenthetically that one major study of growth in this period transcends these categories; that is, Ingvar Svennilson's *Growth and Stagnation in the European Economy,* published in Geneva in 1954 by the United Nations Economic Commission for Europe. It is quite free of any of the post-1945 theoretical or methodological fads. Its theoretical structure consciously unites macro- and sectoral analysis with full awareness of the achievements of and unresolved difficulties encountered by Marshall, Cassel, Schumpeter, Wicksell, Keynes, and Harrod. The author refuses to separate the long and short periods and weaves together cyclical and trend analysis. He devotes detailed attention to technological change in the key sectors and to the causes and impact of shifts in relative prices and the terms of trade. But his study was essentially unique. The focus, therefore, must be on those who dominated growth analysis in the first four decades after the Second World War.

Although growth analysis was distinctly more in vogue in post-1945 than pre-1939, only one type of growth analysis was part of mainstream economics as it defined itself in the wake of the Second World War; that is, the formal growth model. Its highly aggregated form, elaborated in mathematical terms, and its clear links to other branches of macroeconomic theory, made it natural for neo-Keynesians to enter growth analysis via the Harrod route. The other two types of growth analysis had little interest for mainstream economists of the immediate postwar generation.

With some exaggeration, it is fair to say that the tone of mainstream economics was set, the major problems defined, and the method laid down by Paul Samuelson's *Foundations of Economic Analysis* more than by any other single book.[1] Its first draft won the David A. Wells prize at Harvard in 1941; but most of the material dates back to 1937 when Samuelson was 22 years old. A part of the vision he defined for himself and his generation was explicitly directed against Alfred Marshall.[2]

> . . . I have come to feel that Marshall's dictum that "it seems doubtful whether anyone spends his time well in reading lengthy translations of economic doctrines into mathematics, that have not been made by himself" should be exactly reversed. The laborious literary working over of essentially simple mathematical concepts such as is characteristic of much of modern economic theory is not only unrewarding from the standpoint of advancing the science, but involves as well mental gymnastics of a peculiarly depraved type. . . .
>
> It is certainly true, notably in the writings of Marshall, that economists have made use of biological as well as of mechanical analogies, in which evolution and organic growth is used as the antithesis to statical equilibrium analysis. In general the results seem to have been disappointing; viz., the haziness involved in Marshall's treatment of decreasing cost.

Samuelson proceeded, on the basis of his vision, to publish in 1948 the first edition of his textbook, *Economics,* which, in effect, superseded J. S. Mill's and Marshall's *Principles* and, in its various editions (and, in time, imitators), constituted the fourth dominating economics textbook in the Anglo-Saxon world—and beyond—starting with *The Wealth of Nations.*

Samuelson was correct to choose Marshall as an antagonist; but he did not, at this early stage of his career at least, fully grasp Marshall's position. There was much more to Marshall's strictures on the adequacy of mathematics as a language for political economy than Samuelson's brief critique would suggest. Marshall was a trained mathematician who regarded the language of mathematics as a valuable but limited tool incapable of gripping either the full range of variables relevant to economic analysis or the great issues of political economy that always transcend economics in the narrow sense. Marshall did not harbor a "depraved" masochistic taste for translating easy, lucid mathematical formulations into English prose. He simply did not regard mathematics as an adequate language because he did not believe economics could be embraced in "simple mathematical concepts." He wrote prose in order to capture the full complexity of his insights. As for the case of decreasing cost, it is true Marshall never solved the problem neatly in mathematical terms; but, almost a century later, "modern economic theory" has still not found such a satisfactory solution. This is because a solution involves the Schumpeter Problem: the problem of large, discontinuous, but endogenous innovation from which contemporary mainstream economics has retreated by one abstract, evasive device or another.

But, to his credit, Samuelson was not primarily interested in launching a war about method. His object was to demonstrate the positive and exciting potentialities, as he saw them, of applying rigorous mathematical methods to the body of economic theory as his generation inherited it: the theory of consumers' behavior; of the firm; of welfare economics; of business cycles.

Thus, although Samuelson's substantive interests and technical contributions in economics were wide, the banner he raised, reflecting and greatly reinforcing the bias of two post-1945 generations, was not inscribed, like those of his great predecessors, with a large principle or objective of political economy, but with the single word: math. He defined himself unambiguously in the line running from Walras through Pareto to Frisch and others who accepted the discipline and reveled in the elegance of living by J. Willard Gibbs's dictum (on the title page of *Foundations*): "Mathematics is a language." Samuelson was quite aware that Marshall (and Hicks) belonged in this array of mathematical literates; but they made him a bit uneasy—almost traitors to their class—by "keeping formidable mathematical analysis below the surface of things and locked up in appendices. . . ."[3]

Two operational principles were laid down by Samuelson to guide mathematically articulated economic theory, given unity as "the study of maximizing behavior." First, in addition to definitions, all propositions must be articulated in terms of rules of behavior, parameters, and initial conditions that govern the variables that concern the practitioner. Second, having met these conditions, the objective of economic theory, whether in the form of comparative statics or dynamics, is to determine "how our variables change qualitatively or quantitatively with changes in explicit data. Thus, we introduce explicitly into our system certain data in the form of parameters, which in changing, cause shifts in our functional relations."[4] What Samuelson sought to expose and elaborate were the "striking formal similarities" underlying "seemingly diverse fields—production economics, consumers' behavior, international trade, public finance, business cycles, income analysis. . . ."[5] He did so by exploring various facets of the method of comparative statics, then moving over via the bridge of the correspondence principle to comparative dynamics.[6] The *Foundations* concludes with high hopes:[7] "The further development of analytical economics along the lines of comparative dynamics must rest with the future. It is to be hoped that it will aid in the attack upon diverse problems—from the trivial behavior of a single small commodity, to the fluctuations of important components of the business cycle, and even to the majestic problems of economic development."

One can not avoid sympathy with the young Samuelson's ambitious agenda for mathematics as a language; but the outcome also suggests regret that he and his followers did not take Francis Bacon more seriously: "It cannot be that axioms established by argumentation can suffice for the discovery of new works, for the subtlety of nature exceedeth many times over the subtlety of argument." But here the relevant question is narrower: How, in fact, did mainstream economists address themselves "to the majestic problems of economic development" over the past four decades?

In providing a response to that question and then examining the other two post-1945 schools of growth analysis defined here, my limited objectives will be these: First, to suggest in broad terms how each type of growth analysis evolved in the past two generations, including its links to events and circumstances in the world economy, but with special emphasis on how it dealt with—or failed to deal with—each of the dimensions of growth analysis identified throughout this book as critical; second, to assess the special strengths and deficiencies of each approach.

15

Formal Models of Economic Growth: Rise and Subsidence

A Half-Serious Statistical Note

There is a certain shapeliness to the story of formal growth modeling over the past half-century or so. It takes its start with Harrod's 1939 *Essay in Dynamic Theory,* gets a second-stage booster with Domar's articles of 1946–1947,[1] but generates no large-scale controversy or momentum until three papers are published in the mid-1950s by Tobin, Solow, and Swan. These challenge the knife's-edge instability of the initial formulations and launch the era of neoclassical as opposed to Harrod–Domar models.[2] Then the fun begins. Like business opportunists of lesser enterprise and imagination "swarming" into a new sector in the wake of three Schumpeterian innovative heroes who demonstrate profitability, the volume of talent allocated to formal growth modeling builds up to a peak in, say, 1965–1966; although as early as December 1964, Hahn and Matthews, in their majestic survey (see Note 4) announced ". . . the point of diminishing returns may have been reached." A subsidence follows into the 1970s. All passion is not quite spent; but it gradually became clear that about all the insight likely to be extracted from the exploration of and debate about neoclassical growth models had been accomplished. Figure 15.1, whose construction is explained in Note 3, captures the rise and subsidence of formal growth modeling over the period from the late 1930s to the early 1970s.[3] An interesting aspect of the Jones bibliography used to construct Figure 15.1 is that almost half the items for the period 1969–1973 are retrospective studies, textbooks, or collections of documents covering a field whose contours and limits appear to have been pretty well defined.[4] The interests of students who wish to learn about modern formal growth models have been well served. It is, therefore, unnecessary here to provide a full summary of how the growth-model literature evolved between 1939 and the early 1970s. Several of the works cited in Note 4 constitute or contain excellent summaries; e.g., Hahn and Matthews, Jones, Sen, Wan, and Solow's 1970 growth lectures.

The exposition proceeds, then, in four stages:

- An evocation of the setting in the world economy in which growth models were produced and the impact on them of the larger environment.
- A stylized account of the characteristics of the major types of growth models.

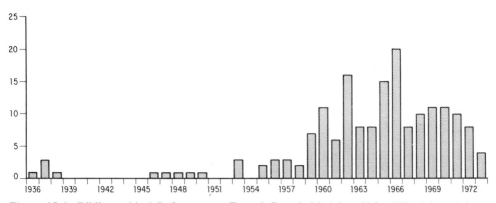

Figure 15.1. Bibliographical References to Formal Growth Models: 1936–1973. Adapted from Hywel Jones, *An Introduction to Modern Theories of Economic Growth*, (New York: McGraw-Hill, 1975), pp. 241–250.

- A brief survey of the extent to which the major models dealt with the key growth variables used throughout this study.
- An assessment of the achievements and deficiencies of the growth-model caper.

Growth Models in Three Phases of the World Economy

The state of the world economy helped shape the evolution of formal growth models in three fairly distinct periods. First, prewar and immediate postwar concern with the recurrence of deep depression strongly influenced both Harrod and Domar and, one can assume, rendered acceptable and *prima facie* realistic models with built-in possibilities for extreme instability. In his 1939 article, when Harrod drew policy conclusions, virtually all assumed the economic system was vulnerable either to lapsing into a slump before full employment is reached in the preceding boom (as in 1937–1938) or to chronic high unemployment due to a decline in the rate of growth of population or a rise in the savings rate or a tendency of technological change to be capital-saving.[5] In his 1948 *Towards a Dynamic Economics* Harrod discusses some positive postwar developments, but both his short-run and long-run prescriptions are still rooted in the interwar pessimism that shaped his system. Similarly, Domar's 1946 *Econometrica* article reflected the then-current consensus among most economists that the postwar world economy would soon lapse into depression unless rather heroic countermeasures were undertaken by the public authorities.[6] He is concerned explicitly with Hansen-type secular stagnation where "spontaneous" investment (induced by changes in technology, tastes, discoveries of new resources, etc.) is insufficient to maintain full employment via the multiplier; that is, the total employment generated by a given increase in investment. Domar proposes, therefore, that the growth of incomes be guaranteed by public authorities on a scale such that the volume of total investment required for full employment is generated via the accelerator; that is, the increase in investment generated by a given increase in income.

But, of course, the world economy did not lapse into a great postwar depression and, for a time, the growth-model business was a bit slow.

By the mid-1950s, the U.S. economy had emerged with vigor from the Korean war, post–Marshall-Plan Europe, with even greater vigor, into the age of private automobile and durable consumers goods on a mass basis, and the Japanese economy, from a surprising recovery to an astounding surge of sustained growth. In this setting it began to occur to a number of economists that the fragility of growth in the advanced industrial world may have been overdone; and several among them explored forces endogenous to the economy that might react to movements away from dynamic equilibrium in ways that more or less brought it back to a steady growth path. Thus the neoclassical growth models of which Tobin, Solow, and Swan are generally accounted the pioneers.

These self-correcting, dynamically fairly stable models were explored and debated for about a decade. The paradigm was pretty well exhausted by the time the world economy moved, in 1973–1974, into a protracted phase of the most acute instability since the 1930s. Moreover, the forces inducing this instability were of a kind that the Harrod–Domar models did not take into account and for which the neoclassical models provided no built-in correction. The palpable irrelevance of formal growth models to the central problems of the world economy from 1973 to 1989 account for the virtual disappearance of fresh work in this field much as the relatively steady course of the world economy from 1945 to 1972 greatly attenuated the allocation of analytic resources to the study of business cycles.

Growth Models: Variations on a Theme by Harrod–Domar

In seeking to move mainstream economics into a mold where growth was the central process and cycles and other irregularities were viewed as deviations from growth, analysts were severely constrained by the highly aggregated neo-Keynesian framework they took for granted and brought to bear. Here it is sufficient briefly to characterize the main strands in the formal growth model literature from Harrod's 1939 article down to the early 1970s; and to summarize the efforts of a handful of those who grappled more directly with the problem of relating growth and cycles.

1. *Harrod–Domar: On the Edge of the Abyss.* These models pose the questions: Is steady-state growth possible? If so, what are its characteristics? What conditions might yield instability? Harrod responded by defining warranted and natural growth rates, applying to growth the marriage of the multiplier and accelerator on which he had built his 1936 *Trade Cycle*. His system focused on the difficulty of keeping in harness the warranted (G_w) and natural (G_n) rates of growth. He thus builds up to this definition of the issues that concerned him:[7] "... [T]here are two distinct sets of problems both for analysis and policy, namely: (1) the divergence of G_w from G_n; and (2) the tendency of G to run away from G_w. The former is the problem of chronic unemployment, the latter the trade-cycle problem."

Domar worked out independently the problem of defining the inherent instability of a growing private enterprise economy in a somewhat different vocabulary but to the same effect. The equivalent of his warranted rate of growth is G; of the natural growth rate, s. His anxiety, in the end, is the unlikelihood that s will be high enough to match G, in which case, he concludes, heroic compensatory measures of public policy will be required to elevate s.

From the point of view of growth theory Domar stated with lucidity the formal gap in Keynesian analysis: because it was set up under Marshallian short-period assumptions, investment is treated as a determinant of the level of income via the multiplier, but not in its role in expanding productive capacity.

As with the theme of a symphony enunciated at the opening of the first movement with elegant simplicity, variations and even contrapuntal themes, not always harmonious, emerged in response to the Harrod–Domar analysis.

2. *Neoclassical Growth: Stability via Factor Substitution.* In 1956, with the publication of the Solow and Swan papers, the central theme of one branch of the growth modelers turned from an anxious minor to a major key. Solow enunciated the hopeful theme as follows:[8]

> The characteristic and powerful conclusion of the Harrod–Domar line of thought is that even for the long run the economic system is at best balanced on a knife-edge of equilibrium growth. Were the magnitudes of the key parameters—the savings ratio, the capital-output ratio, the rate of increase of the labor force—to slip ever so slightly from dead center, the consequence would be either growing unemployment or prolonged inflation. . . .
>
> But this fundamental opposition of warranted and natural rates turns out in the end to flow from the crucial assumption that production takes place under conditions of *fixed proportions.* There is no possibility of substituting labor for capital in production. If this assumption is abandoned, the knife-edge notion of unstable balance seems to go with it. Indeed it is hardly surprising that such a gross rigidity in one part of the system should entail lack of flexibility in another. . . .
>
> The bulk of this paper is devoted to a model of long-run growth which accepts all the Harrod–Domar assumptions except that of fixed proportions. Instead I suppose that the single composite commodity is produced by labor and capital under the standard neoclassical conditions.

Without entering into Solow's detailed exposition, his assumption of variable proportions between labor and capital combined with neoclassical assumptions about the behavior of competitive markets, permits him to conclude:[9]

> . . . [W]hen production takes place under the usual neoclassical conditions of variable proportions and constant returns to scale, no simple opposition between natural and warranted rates of growth is possible. There may not be—in fact in the case of the Cobb–Douglas function there never can be— any knife-edge. The system can adjust to any given rate of growth of the labor force, and eventually approach a state of steady proportional expansion.

3. *A Cambridge (England) Response to Neoclassical Growth Models: Stability via Changes in Income Distribution and the Saving–Consumption Ratio.* There is a considerable array of growth models in which an element of stability is provided by the difference in the marginal propensity to consume (and to save) as between those receiving wages and profits; the former including salaries, the latter including incomes of all forms of property owners, not merely entrepreneurs.[10] Shifts in the overall marginal propensity to consume are stabilizing if the proportion of income saved at the margin is higher for property owners than those receiving wages and salaries. As expounded by Kaldor (who evolved several versions of his central proposition) the system tended toward stability only if initial full employment was assumed.

The assumed mechanism of adjustment is simple enough: a tendency of the system to deviate toward a higher level of output (caused by, say, an increase in investment) yields a shift to an inflationary increase in prices and profits and therefore in savings, thus reducing effective demand and pushing the system back toward full employment equilibrium. A movement in the other direction is symmetrically self-correcting. This is how Kaldor, a central figure in this version of a neoclassical growth model, rooted in the Kahn–Keynes consumption function and multiplier, described how the central mechanism worked:[11]

> . . . [W]ith the assumption of "full employment" . . . a rise in investment, and thus in total demand, will raise prices and profit margins, and thus reduce real consumption, whilst a fall in investment, and thus in total demand, causes a fall in prices (relatively to the wage level) and thereby generates a compensating rise in real consumption. Assuming flexible prices (or rather flexible profit margins) the system is thus stable at full employment.

This approach to a stable growth model not only went through various modifications, but it was also the subject of lively controversy, well-documented like all other dimensions of the growth-modeling story.

Where, then, did the roles of invention, innovation, and technology fit in these enterprises?

4. *Invention, Innovation, and Technology in Growth Modeling.* What one might call the mainstream growth models used a variety of devices to cope with the role of invention, innovation, and technology. All were designed to evade Schumpeter's central insight; namely, his assertion that a significant number of innovations are large, endogenous, discontinuous, and have their initial impact on particular sectors; but, in their larger consequences, these grand innovations affect not only the structure of the economy as a whole but virtually all of its major variables; e.g., the rate of growth of output, the demand for credit, the price level, real wages, and the profit rate. The major growth modelers fastened their attention firmly on forces making for instability or stability in the overall growth path when the determinants of growth were defined in highly aggregated terms. The Schumpeter Problem was bypassed by the following major devices:

- Assume no technical progress and treat growth as a product of an expanding working force and capital stock.
- Assume technical progress is incremental, exogenous, and a function of the passage of time (disembodied).
- Assume technical progress is embodied in investment and a function of the rate of investment—a kind of return to Smithian incremental technological change in response to the expansion of the market.
- Assume all technical change is endogenous but incremental, induced by factor prices, cumulative experience in production, education and other improvement of human capital, and/or by R & D investment.

This world of incremental technological change, exogenous or endogenous, is rendered even more manageable by the generous use of the assumption of neutral technical progress, which is usually defined as an unchanged ratio of the marginal products of capital and labor so long as the overall capital–labor proportion is constant. But capital-saving and labor-saving forms of technical progress are, in some cases, introduced.

This terse evocation of the changes rung on formal growth models is incomplete. But I judge it unnecessary here to get into some of the other issues posed and debated; for example, the degree to which capital, once made and installed, is rigidly fixed or adjustable (putty–putty, putty–clay, clay–clay), and the consequent age (or vintage) composition of capital goods; the introduction, in a stylized way, of a monetary dimension to the growth process; two-sector (capital and consumers' goods) and maximum growth rate (Neumann) models. The heart of the mainstream growth-modeling exercise is best understood in the elegant formulation in Solow's 1970 lectures.[12] He focuses on three terms: the savings rate (s) 0; the capital–output ratio (v) 0; and the rate of growth of the labor force (n). The Harrod–Domar analysis asserts, essentially, that steady growth requires that $s = vn$ and, since each variable is independently determined, that stability condition is likely to occur only as "the merest fluke." The response of other economists was to generate models in which the determinants of v and s were defined in ways that tended to bring the economy back toward a steady growth path.[13]

> With this general kind of model [Harrod–Domar] there is only one way out of the box. At least one and perhaps more of the three numbers s, v, and n must be, not a given constant, but a variable capable of taking on a sufficiently wide range of values. That would be enough to establish the bare possibility of steady-state growth. Something more is needed, however, to account for the prevalence of steady or near-steady growth in actual economies. What is needed, ideally, is some plausible mechanism to drive the one or more variables among s, v, and n into a configuration in which the Harrod–Domar consistency condition is satisfied. One could settle for something less, a route by which the appropriate changes in s, v, and n could come about under favourable and not-too-implausible circumstances.
>
> Which among the three key parameters is the likeliest candidate for the role of the variable? It is interesting that the classical economists would presumably have agreed first on the one of the three that modern theorists tend to take as the only constant—the rate of population growth.

Thus, the exploration of the possible self-correcting characteristics of v, in particular, led to a sequence of complexities that were sedulously explored in the highly abstract world which, as a catalyst, the Harrod–Domar model brought into being; although one aspect of the exploration of v led back to income distribution and, by indirection, to s.

N. Kaldor

Not all growth analysts of this period were content with such elegant abstract manipulations of a few variables. One of the most unusual exercises by a model-builder of the 1950s, for example, was Kaldor's explicit effort to find a mode of reconciliation with Schumpeter's innovational theory of growth and cycles.[14]

Kaldor begins by giving Schumpeter a brisk brush-off:[15]

> The trouble with Schumpeter's theory is that it is descriptive rather than analytical. Although it is easy enough to see how one particular part of the story follows from the preceding part, it is not possible to make the story as a whole into a "model" . . . without incorporating into it elements which would suffice by themselves to explain the cycle—without recourse to Schumpeter's own stage army of initiators and imitators, or even the very

concept of technical progress. For the necessary "bunching" (in time) of innovating investment, which is essential to Schumpeter's theory, cannot be satisfactorily explained without bringing the Keynesian multiplier, and some variant of the output–investment relationship [accelerator] to one's aid.

Indeed, the development of trade-cycle theories that followed Keynes' *General Theory* has proved to be positively inimical to the idea that cycle and dynamic growth are inherently connected analytically—to the idea, that is, that the cycle is a mere by-product of, and could not occur in the absence of, "progress."

Kaldor then demonstrates that, with appropriate assumptions, a cyclical model with a static trend can be constructed. Recognizing the unrealism of the model he goes on to show that a trend can be incorporated in the model, thus belying Schumpeter's growth-cycle hypothesis:[16] "It is thus seen that all the 'dynamic' models that were recently presented to the world . . . are all variants of the same thing, and, essentially, all consist of the superimposition of a linear trend introduced from the outside on an otherwise trendless model without altering, in any way, its basic character."

Now Kaldor leaves the world of modeling and begins to get interesting:[17]

> . . . But is this situation, from an intellectual or analytical point of view, wholly satisfactory? The trend itself is not "explained"; it is introduced as a datum. There can be no pretence, therefore, of these theories providing the basis for a theory of economic growth. Yet the very fact that different human societies experience such very different rates of growth—in fact, differences in rates of growth in different ages or in different parts of the world in the same age are one of the most striking facts of history—in itself provides powerful support for the view that technical invention and population growth, the two factors underlying the trend, are not like the weather or the movement of the seasons, that go on quite independently of human action, but are very much the outcome of social processes.

On the basis of this central proposition, Kaldor argues that the rates of population growth, technical progress, and capital accumulation are the consequence of the relative strength of basic social forces rather than the initiating causes of growth; and[18]

> [t]he most plausible answer to the question why some human societies progress so much faster than others is to be sought . . . in human attitudes to risk-taking and money-making. . . .
>
> Here at last we find the inherent link between trend and cycle that we were searching for. For if the above analysis is correct, both the trade cycle and economic growth are the resultant of particular attitudes of entrepreneurs— more precisely, of the volatility of entrepreneurial expectations. . . . Schumpeter's hero, the "innovating entrepreneur," whom we dismissed so summarily and rather contemptuously at the beginning, is found, after all, to have an honourable place, or even a key role, in the drama—even though we prefer to endow him with a rather more variegated character. He is a promoter, a speculator, a gambler, the purveyor of economic expansion generally, and not just of the "new" techniques of production.

Although Kaldor's technical analysis of economic growth suffers, like those of the other model builders of his time, from excessive aggregation, and his evocation of noneconomic forces is evidently oversimple, the appearance of such considerations in the model-building desert is something of an oasis.

This interesting but somewhat untypical Kaldor paper raises two important points. First, I would underline a fairly narrow point of theory. Kaldor's earlier work on distribution and his case for the inherent stability of growth had depended on changes in the Keynesian marginal propensity to save (consume) as real income rises or falls. Here he introduces a somewhat different proposition:[19] "The re-investment of the profits of business enterprise always has been, and still is, the main source of industrial capital accumulation. . . ." This is an exceedingly important proposition because the rate of growth of particular sectors (and the profits earned)[20] is often a function of the rate at which new technologies are being absorbed. Kaldor did not pursue systematically this insight perhaps because the concept of technological change to which he was committed in most of his work was highly aggregated, incremental, embodied in the level of investment, and it did not allow for the notion of a technological backlog.[21]

Second, in the midst of his linkage of economic behavior to underlying social forces, Kaldor draws back and enunciates a self-denying ordinance:[22] "Economic speculation here trespasses on the fields of sociology and social history; and the most that an economist can say is that there is nothing in economic analysis as such which would dispute the important connection, emphasized by economic historians and sociologists, between the rise of Protestant ethic and the rise of Capitalism." This restricted view of the limits of economic analysis, quite conventional among mainstream economists of the twentieth century, does not conform to the scope of the field as envisaged in the line from David Hume to Alfred Marshall, or by the two authorities to whom Kaldor refers: Karl Marx and Joseph Schumpeter. More important, this perspective rules out any serious analysis of the economic development process or other analyses of why growth rates differ among national societies; for these questions, virtually without exception, involve noneconomic variables.

Joan Robinson

Joan Robinson was uneasy in a different way about the mainstream growth models. There is something at once chiding and intensely serious about her contribution to the growth literature of the 1950s and early 1960s. It was as if she concluded that the central figures in the exercise—especially the neoclassical growth modelers but to a degree also her friend and colleague Nicholas Kaldor—were dealing rather superficially with a serious subject. It was not enough to conclude from rather simple equations and assumptions that capitalism was either precariously unstable or held in relative full employment by factor substitution or, even, by the operation of the Keynesian consumption function in the face of changes in income distribution. It was as if she said: "Enough of this playfulness; let's get back to first principles."

And so she began by arraying the six fundamental variables judged relevant to the determination of the growth rate given the initial stock of capital goods and the state of expectations formed by past experience:[23] technical conditions (embracing the growth rate of the working force, the industrial arts, and natural resources); investment policy with an emphasis on "animal spirits" evocative of Hume, Marx, and Keynes; thriftiness conditions, including a Keynesian *ex post* savings equal to investment assumption; the degree of competition (with ambiguous observations on its relation to the growth rate); the wage bargain (money wages assumed constant except for cases of acute labor shortage and of unacceptable inflationary pressures on real wages); financial conditions (including the assumptions that all of capital replacement and much of net investment are financed from gross retained profits and that interest rates are given and partially determined by balance-of-payments and exchange-rate problems).

In a variation on Harrod's distinction between warranted and natural rates of growth—rooted, respectively, in the "animal spirits" of firms and the assumed "technical conditions"—Robinson proceeds to set out her eight well-known metallic cases, which she summarizes usefully as follows:[24]

> In golden ages the initial conditions are appropriate to steady growth. In true and limping golden ages the actual realized growth rate is limited only by the desired rate. (In a true golden age, the possible rate coincides with the desired rate and near full employment has already been reached.) In a restrained golden age, the realized growth rate is limited by the possible rate, and kept down to it. In a leaden age the possible rate is held down by the realized rate. In a bastard golden age the possible rate is limited in a different way—that is, by real wages being at the tolerable minimum. Both in a limping golden age and a bastard golden age the stock of capital in existence at any moment is less than sufficient to offer employment to all available labour. In the limping golden age the stock of equipment is not growing faster for lack of "animal spirits." In the bastard age it is not growing faster because it is blocked by the inflation barrier.
>
> In platinum ages the initial conditions do not permit steady growth and the rate of accumulation is accelerating or decelerating as the case may be.

She then proceeds to state tersely the general effect on the stability of growth models of variations in thriftiness and in the other determinants of growth arrayed earlier. She arrives finally at two conclusions:[25] First, all the growth models surveyed, including her own, are "too much simplified" and must be "judged on the *a priori* plausibility of their assumptions." Second, she reaffirms a Keynesian conclusion nearer Harrod–Domar than the neoclassicists: "There is an important difference in emphasis between them according as they exhibit some kind of inbuilt propensity to maintain full employment over the long run or as they follow Keynes in regarding it as dependent upon enterprise that cannot be relied upon, unassisted, either to achieve stability in the short run or to maintain an adequate rate of growth in the long run."

Robinson was, in my view, quite correct in her strictures on the highly aggregated, oversimple growth modeling of the period, and in her judgment that steady full employment growth was an unlikely outcome over long periods in a system of private investment. On the other hand, her analysis did not include the variables required to explain the extraordinary boom of the 1950s and 1960s; notably, relative price movements and the terms of trade, the backlog of technologies available to Western Europe and Japan, and the technologies that emerged from invention to innovation after 1945. One needs a highly disaggregated system to come to grips with these variables: "animal spirits" is not a macrophenomenon spread evenly across the sectors of the economy; and, as Salter and others have demonstrated (following, pp. 466–469), technological change and the plowback of retained earnings into plant and equipment tend to be heavily concentrated in relatively few technologically dynamic sectors at any given period.

In short, Robinson's critique of growth modeling is an important strand in the story of that period; but, as she was to a degree aware, her own overaggregated approach left her still some distance from "reality."

Solow Incorporates the Demographic Transition

Unlike most neoclassical growth modelers, Solow did render a more or less modern version of the demographic transition endogenous to his system. In his 1956 *Quarterly Journal of Economics* article the context is an examination of whether the interest rate and the related savings ratio might be so driven down by a sustained rise in the capital–labor ratio as to yield a classical stationary state. Solow points out that the continued rise in the population would bring down the capital–labor ratio if net investment stopped for a time. He then evokes the following possibility of a kind of Rosenstein–Rodan Big Push (following, p. 409) or Rostovian Takeoff:[26]

> Suppose, . . . that for very low levels of income per head the population tends to decrease; for higher levels of income it begins to increase; and that for still higher levels of income the rate of population growth levels off and starts to decline. The result may be something like [Figure 15.2]. The equilibrium capital–labor ratio r_1 is stable, but r_2 is unstable. The accompanying levels of *per capita* income can be read off from the shape of $F(r,1)$. If the initial capital–labor ratio is less than r_2, the system will of itself tend to return to r_1. If the initial ratio could somehow be boosted above the critical level r_2, a self-sustaining process of increasing *per capita* income would be set off (and population would still be growing). The interesting thing about this case is that it shows how, in the total absence of *indivisibilities* or of increasing

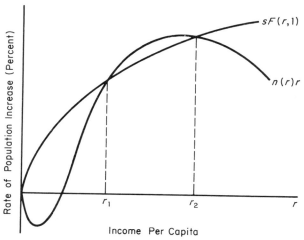

Figure 15.2. Income per Capita and the Rate of Population Increase. [Adapted from Robert M. Solow, "A Contribution to a Theory of Growth," in A. K. Sen (ed.), *Growth Economics* (Harmondsworth, Eng.: Penguin, 1970), p. 189.]

returns, a situation may still arise in which small-scale capital accumulation only leads back to stagnation but a major burst of investment can lift the system into a self-generating expansion of income and capital per head.

Thus, unlike those who built their case for a surge in public investment on the inescapably large scale of infrastructure outlays and the substantial indirect stimulus to private investment they provided, Solow argues that a jump in the investment rate might lift the aggregate capital-labor ratio, thereby slow the rate of population increase, and thus yield an accelerated, sustained increase in output *per capita*.

Investment and Technology: The Charles Kennedy–Paul Samuelson Debate and Some Uneasy Asides

The inherent limitations of the mainstream growth models with respect to investment and technology are illustrated by the well-known mutually reinforcing exchange between Charles Kennedy and Paul Samuelson on the relation of the character of inventions—their degree of capital or labor bias—to the alleged stability of shares of capital and labor in income distribution.[27]

The Kennedy–Samuelson exchange does, in a highly abstract way, relate a part of the process of innovation to the market process. But it suffers three weaknesses: First, innovation emerges, once again, as a diffuse incremental process, with no serious attention devoted to the relations among science, invention, and innovation, except for Samuelson's observation in "A Theory of Induced Innovation," that after some major breakthrough, creative scientists have an instinct as to where the next promising line of inventive activity lies.[28] Second, the character of invention and innovation is dealt with only as it relates to a capital- or labor-saving bias, leaving, as in other analyses of this type, a critical unexamined role for "exogenous technical changes." Third, the theoretical conditions for approximate long-run stability in distributive shares in a technically advancing economy with the supply of capital increasing faster than the supply of labor are explored with no empirical reference to the process by which that (very rough) stability has been achieved. In fact, the trend in distributive shares has varied significantly—for example, in Britain between, say, the periods 1873–1896 and 1896–1914, and the decisive force at work has been the trend in the urban cost of living in each period.

Nevertheless, it is the case that a good many economists engaged in growth modeling felt uneasy about leaving invention exogenous and a few, at least, sought to link the generation of innovations to the institutional structure of the economy.[30] As Karl Shell is reported to have said in opening the discussion of his paper referred to in Note 30: ". . . [I]n order to explain economic development satisfactorily, an endogenous theory of technical progress is required."[31] As suggested earlier, a number of devices were attempted, including the important efforts of Edwin Mansfield to measure the productivity of R & D as an investment subsector generating the flow of innovations in a modern economy.[32] Indeed, dissatisfaction with the handling of science, invention, and innovation yielded a special International Economic Association Conference in the early 1970s on "Science and Technology in Economic Growth."[33] The papers had (to this author) an appealing pragmatic quality, relating to both advanced and developing countries. On the other hand, links to model building were not effectively made; and E. A. G. Robinson's reported observation in the final session remains just:[34] "Professor Robinson asked whether there was something large in the explanation of economic growth which has defied economists. We can't have an amorphous residual factor for which there is no explanation, and yet this is the state in which I find myself at the end of the Conference." Chapter 20 returns to this problem.

Growth and Business Cycles:
Five Efforts to Go Beyond the Mainstream Consensus

In an engaging Foreword to a 1970 book on mathematical growth models by two of his former students, Robert Solow observes:[35] "It is a standard gambit—I have used it myself—to describe a topic as 'fit for text book treatment,' meaning it is played out, cut and dried." Whatever the state of growth models at that time, business-cycle analysis had long since become "fit for text book treatment" from the perspective of mainstream economics.

In the 1950s, however, there were at least four distinguished consolidating textbooks, each marked by strands of originality. The authors were J. R. Hicks (1950), Alvin Hansen (1951), James Duesenberry (1958), and R. C. O. Matthews (1959).[36] In addition, the last NBER effort at a grand business-cycle synthesis was published as early as 1947: Burns and Mitchell's *Measuring Business Cycles*.

It may be useful to summarize briefly what each of these five studies had to say about the relation between growth and cycles.

1. Hicks (1950). Hicks's *Trade Cycle* is an extraordinarily lucid and elegant elaboration of a multiplier–accelerator model with a painstaking elaboration of the upper ceiling and lower limits, as well as the asymmetry between expansion and contraction. Growth enters Hicks's story not only because, following Harrod, he places the cycle in a formal growth setting but also because he introduces autonomous investment in a quite particular way.

Hicks first sets out to define a condition of dynamic equilibrium (a "regularly progressive economy") in a model embracing both induced and autonomous investment. Autonomous investment is defined as:[37] "Public investment, investment which occurs in direct response to inventions, and much of the 'long-range' investment . . . which is only expected to pay for itself over a long period. . . ." Hicks is quite aware that such investments are unlikely to take place at a regular rate. He nevertheless sets out the stringent assumptions required for dynamic equilibrium, in a system including autonomous investment, in order to get at "the crucial question which a theory of the cycle has to ask . . . whether fluctuations are possible, and, if so, how are they possible, in the absence of exogenous disturbances."[38] Like Marx and Schumpeter he also sets out, as a preliminary benchmark, a stationary-state equilibrium model as "a standard of reference."[39]

Hicks then moves on, for purposes of formal exposition, to define one version of a progressive equilibrium in which the ratio of autonomous investment to output is constant. He then asks: In what sense is such investment autonomous? His answer is:[40]

> . . . [A]utonomous investment really is autonomous after all. The only condition which it must satisfy in order for the regularly progressive equilibrium to be possible, is that it must expand at a constant rate. Subject to that condition, its rate of growth and its "level" are both of them independent

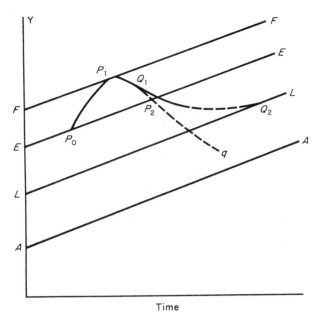

Figure 15.3. Abstract Cycle with Constant Rate of Growth of Autonomous Investment. CODE: *FF:* Full employment ceiling. *EE:* Equilibrium path of output. P_0: Initial equilibrium position from which output displaced upward by an external disturbance. *AA:* Path of autonomous investment at constant rate. *LL:* Lower equilibrium line during slump, taking account of multiplier effects of autonomous investment. [Adapted from J. R. Hicks, *A Contribution to the Theory of the Trade Cycle* (Oxford: at the Clarendon Press, 1950), p. 97.]

variables. It is the rate of growth of autonomous investment which determines the equilibrium rate of growth of the whole system; and it is its level which determines the equilibrium level of output.

With this formalized definition of a regularly progressive economy in hand Hicks builds up to his reasonably conventional version of a multiplier–accelerator model in which the continued upward slope of autonomous investment sets a limit to the slump and provides the basis for recovery (Figure 15.3).[41]

Against this background Hicks proceeds to relax the assumption of a constant rate of growth in autonomous investment and in the full employment ceiling. This yields the pattern in Figure 15.4 on which Hicks comments as follows:[42]

> . . . [T]he cycles of reality should be thought of as occurring against the background of an upward trend in output . . . ; and while that trend can fairly be regarded as being supported by an upward trend in autonomous investment, nevertheless, the actual course of autonomous investment cannot possibly be so very regular—it must experience autonomous fluctuations on its own account. These fluctuations, and their consequences, are superimposed upon the cycle which we have been studying. . . .

Fluctuations in autonomous investment will be reflected in corresponding fluctuations in the equilibrium lines—both in the upper equilibrium line *EE*

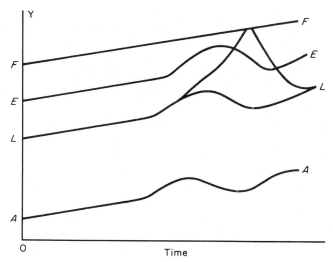

Figure 15.4. Abstract Cycle with Discontinuous Autonomous Investment. CODE: As in Figure 15.3. [Adapted from J. R. Hicks, *The Trade Cycle*, p. 121.]

and in the lower equilibrium line *LL*. With this amendment, the theory stands; it will still be true that the upper equilibrium is unstable, the lower stable. . . .

What can we make of this analysis in terms of the focus of this book? First, it represents a serious effort to relate growth and cyclical analysis and, especially, their interaction: the strength and course of cycles is dependent in good part on the underlying strength of autonomous investment; but a particularly sharp and steep cyclical decline can frustrate for a time the assertion of a strong underlying upward trend in autonomous investment.

Second, Hicks does, indeed, regard autonomous investment as autonomous and in no way induced by the market pressures or opportunities set up by the process of growth itself. Like most of the post-1945 model builders, Schumpeter's insights have no explicit place in his exposition. He does recognize the inherent discontinuity of autonomous investment, citing the railroad and automobile, but he does not recognize the endogenous forces that generate major inventions and innovations.

Third, the highly aggregated form of Hicks's model is not a satisfactory structure for linking realistically growth and cycles.[43] Specifically that model cannot grip three fundamental empirical phenomena:[44]

- The leading directions of new investment in each boom can in large part be related to disequilibria as between the optimum rates of growth in certain sectors and the levels of capacity existing just prior to the boom. . . .
- The persistent tendency for the expansion in capacity in the leading sectors to be carried too far, yielding, toward the end of the boom, a conscious prospect of a level of capacity higher than that which would be required in those particular sectors of the economy in terms of the optimum model.
- The role of the period of gestation of the leading forms of investment in determining the extent to which investment distortion proceeded in each boom.

Nevertheless, by taking autonomous investment seriously—as something more than a device for simplifying his model—Hicks captures more linkage of growth and cycles than most of his contemporaries.

2. *Alvin Hansen (1951)*. There is a great deal about both growth and cycles in Hansen's *Business Cycles and National Income* as well as discussion of various suggested linkages. There are sections placing U.S. post-1865 cycles in their historical context; on building cycles; on secular trends and business cycles; on investment in the business cycle. All contain passages linking growth and cycles. A lengthy review of business-cycle theories touches on the work of economists with important insights into the relation of the two processes. But at only two points do Hansen's own views on this matter break through the eclectic textbook character of his book.

First, in affirming the correctness of Schumpeter's basic insight:[45]

> It is possible to account for cycles in our system if we assume with Schumpeter that this innovational investment comes in swarms. The [investment] schedule is deformed to the right in a burst which begins slowly, then gathers speed, and finally ceases. Consequently, investment rises slowly and declines as all the possibilities are exhausted and the new products come on the market, forcing down prices and lowering the present values of the remaining possibilities. This process repeats itself with only a rough regularity and with a varying violence, depending on the historically given course of technological change. These facts must be incorporated in any cycle theory, and they are vital because in this way we may explain how, given a relatively unchanging economic structure and hence mechanism of response, each cycle is a historical individual, very unlike either its predecessors or its successors. It should be noted, however, that the essential explanation of the cycle, for this simple model, lies outside the model—in the Schumpeterian theory of the bunching of investment outlays—and that this theory is difficult to formulate in econometric terms.

And, again, in summation:[46]

> The modern analysis reveals that, so long as the economy remains dynamic, so long as the requirements of growth and progress call for large investment outlays, powerful forces will be at work to produce cyclical fluctuations. One cannot, therefore, regard the cycle as a pathological condition. It is inherent in the nature of the modern dynamic economy. "Built-in" institutional arrangements can indeed narrow the limits of oscillation. But only in a measure. A positive counter-cyclical program is necessary.

3. *James Duesenberry (1958)*. Duesenberry's textbook, *Business Cycles and Economic Growth,* was published only 7 years after Hansen's; but it reflects a gap of a full generation. The author is presenting his own version of a neoclassical growth model and explicitly regards himself in dialogue and, to a degree, in debate with Harrod, Hicks, Goodwin, Kaldor *et al.* Tougan–Baranowsky, Spiethoff, and Schumpeter; Cassel and Wicksell, Robertson and Pigou, Fisher and Mitchell, all are gone from the radar screen. Arthur Burns appears only as a critic of a point in Keynes's *General Theory*. This study is quite consciously part of the in-house mainstream growth-modeling debate of the 1950s.

Nevertheless, it deals with two aspects of the relation between growth and cycles worth noting.

First, Duesenberry designed a model based on a capital-adjustment process rather than a more volatile conventional accelerator. It links growth and cycles in ways that could yield both weak (Hansen) and strong (Hicks) expansion and contraction phases. Then, using Edwin Frickey's production index (1860–1914) and later data, he briskly surveyed American business cycles from the 1870s to the 1950s, in terms of that distinction.[47]

Second, Duesenberry set up initially a model dependent, like most such models of the period, on fixed initial conditions and parameters, designed to explore key interactions among the variables within that static framework. He then boldly confronted the complexities in generating a model that would "explain the actual movements of income:"[48]

> The occurrence of changes in the parameters will gradually change the characteristic behavior of the system. . . .
>
> A complete analysis of economic history would require an explanation of the parameter changes themselves. Such an explanation is at least as important as an elucidation of the consequences of the existence of a given set of behavior parameters, but it requires talents of a different type from those required to analyze models with given parameters.

Without pretending to create a model that would explain "actual movements of income" in their full complexity, Duesenberry makes a valiant effort to bring his theoretical framework closer to the history of American cyclical fluctuations in the post-Civil War period. It is sufficient to note here that this procedure forces him to confront the need for defining a multisector equilibrium;[49] and, as part of that exercise, to examine "Growing Industries and Autonomous Investment."[50] By this route Duesenberry is brought to deal directly with the relation between growth and cycles:[51]

> . . . To understand the real world we must take account of changes in production methods, the development of new products, growth of population, and the opening up of new areas of settlement. Those phenomena influence the economic system, but their occurrence is not primarily dependent on economic conditions. They are usually classified as exogenous events operating on the economic system.

After examining in broad, abstract terms the net effect on income of various types of autonomous investment—including the effects of anticipations, indivisibilities, and lags, he concludes:[52] "Sustained growth is certainly possible, but it is not likely to occur without the aid of outside driving forces, such as population growth and the relatively rapid growth of certain types of capital-intensive industries" [e.g., railroads, street railroads, telephones, and electric utilities].

In retrospect and in the sweep of this survey, Duesenberry's analysis is of considerable interest for a point of substance and a point of method. His determination to narrow the gap between his model and, in effect, economic history, forces him to disaggregate investment and the process of economic growth by key sectors. Second, Duesenberry's enterprise pushes him toward what might be called a Marshallian method. As he goes beyond a simple, conventional model—with given initial conditions, fixed parameters, and a single output—mathematics becomes decreasingly useful. In specifying the changed growth circumstances that may have determined the difference between pre-1914 and post-1918 cycles, he finds prose the required form of exposition.

4. R. C. O. Matthews (1959). Matthews's textbook in the Cambridge series, *The Trade Cycle,* is of special interest because he is also the author of a substantial historical study of a trade cycle.[53] Disaggregated by sectors in great detail, his analysis of the primarily Anglo-American cycle of the 1830s is, in addition, an account of growth in the two economies over a rather dramatic decade; cotton is still at the center of commercial, financial, and industrial affairs, but railroads are moving in from the wings on both sides of the Atlantic. And in his later text Matthews does, indeed, exhibit sensitivity to the problem of growth in relation to cycles.

Somewhat like Duesenberry, Matthews uses a stock-adjustment–multiplier version of a cyclical mechanism. But, as one would expect in a book written by an economist-historian, Schumpeter appears explicitly in an extended discussion of the role of innovation in both growth and cycles.[54]

He confronts the issue of growth as a whole in a penultimate chapter, "The Trend and the Cycle." It is an elegant essay whose main lines are worth summary. He states his central theme in a form that addresses directly the concern of this chapter:[55] "The difficulty of devising a theoretical apparatus capable of dealing with both trend and cycle arises largely because theories of the cycle have been mainly concerned with the causes of fluctuations in effective demand, whereas in discussions of growth the demand side has usually been less emphasised than the supply side."

Matthews then identifies the key analytic problem as requiring "an analysis of the demand side of the *growth* process that is consistent with the more familiar [short-period, Keynesian] type of *fluctuations* in demand."[56] He cites four possible hypotheses linking demand and supply, adopting the last:

- Say's law that supply creates its own demand.
- Multiplier–accelerator (or capital–stock adjustment) systems in which increases in income and investment stimulate each other *ad infinitum.*
- Expectations that lead entrepreneurs in a slump to believe that the current condition is transient and that the previous peak will be re-achieved or exceeded, because the capacity ceiling has been lifted beyond its previous level.
- The adaptation of Keynesian analysis to demonstrate how increases in population and technical progress communicate themselves somehow to aggregate demand:[57]

> What is required is to show that population growth and technical progress affect the consumption function and/or the inducement to invest in such a way as to give an upward trend to demand; fluctuations in income . . . can then take place around a rising trend. . . . Of these two effects that on investment may perhaps be considered the more fundamental. . . .
>
> . . . [A]lthough there is no guarantee of full employment, there is some guarantee against a cumulative increase in unemployment such as would result if the natural rate of growth persistently exceeded the actual rate of growth.

From here on Matthews is back in the world of highly aggregated growth models, examining different alleged adjustment mechanisms in a way that anticipates the later Hahn–Matthews survey. But he concludes with an evident sense of dissatisfaction and awareness that there was still much to be done in a quite different direction—the determinants of the rate of technical progress:[58]

> . . . [P]roblems of capital theory have been extensively studied by economists, but some doubts may be felt about their practical importance. The reverse is true of the influences affecting the natural rate of growth, especially

the influences affecting the rate of technical progress: these are of great practical importance for the understanding of growth, and possibly also for the understanding of fluctuations, but relatively little systematic work has been done on them.

The critical missing piece of the growth-cycle puzzle here is that, inherently, cyclical expansions violate sectoral optimum levels of capacity on a scale likely to lead to excess supply for a considerable period of time; that the downturn begins in and spreads from the leading sectors of the boom; but that the passage of time reveals potentially profitable avenues of investment in other directions that will be exploited when the trauma of financial crisis has passed and resources are disengaged from the leading sectors of the previous boom. Only rarely are the leading sectors of two successive booms the same. What Matthews's analysis does demonstrate—along with those of Hicks, Hansen, and Duesenberry—is the legitimacy of Mullineux's reflection on modern business-cycle modeling:[59] "It seems difficult to escape the conclusion that a full theory of dynamic economic development, capable of explaining both the cycle and growth and, perhaps, their inter-relationships, is required."

5. Burns and Mitchell (1947). Measuring Business Cycles is, of course, a quite different kind of book than the others cited here. As Mitchell's introduction makes clear, it is an interim summation in which Burns rather than the elderly Mitchell is the principal author. About 90% of the text is devoted to an authoritative description of the NBER method of cyclical and trend analysis and to reflections on certain technical problems in interpreting the results. Moreover, the work summarized was carried out mainly before or during the Second World War, well before post-1945 problems and perspectives were defined. The authors do, however, test against NBER data certain hypotheses linking conventional cycles to longer trends or aspects of growth. For example:

- They test a tentative 1926 hypothesis of Frederick C. Mills that the length of business cycles is relatively long in an early stage of growth, shortens with a phase of rapid growth, and lengthens again as the economy decelerates. On the basis of their improved reference cycle dates, they find the hypothesis gets "slight support" at best.
- Contrary to another hypothesis, they find no significant change in the timing or structure of cycles in the period 1914–1933 as compared to the pre-1914 decades.
- They reaffirm strongly the evidence suggesting a building cycle of 15–20 years; but find no systematic relation between the amplitude and duration of business cycles and periods of rising and falling building trend.
- They review the hypotheses of Kondratieff, Schumpeter, and Kitchin with respect to cyclical behavior in various time periods with indecisive results.

From the present perspective, the most important observation to be made on this volume is that it did not carry forward in the direction the NBER appeared to have been moving in the pre-1939 years; that is, no effort is made to link systematically growth and cyclical analysis along the suggestive paths earlier explored by Burns, J. M. Clark, Fabricant, and Kuznets.

This large gap is almost certainly the result of the interim and methodological character of this study, which includes a brief section on "plans for later work."[60] But it should be noted that the focus of the authors' thought at this time appears to have been conventional business cycles in relation to long cycles rather than to the process of growth itself.

A Conclusion

Growth modeling, in the 35 years or so surveyed here, attracted an extraordinary concentration of talent. It inevitably yielded some results of interest and value. Hahn–Matthews and Mirrlees have sought to specify those positive results. The former team, for example, identify as a "decisive contribution . . . the recognition that investing and technical progress may be Siamese twins" yielding Kaldor's technical-progress function and Kenneth Arrow's learning process;[61] although that recognition is, perhaps, less impressive to economic historians than to post-1945 mainstream theorists. Mirrlees, for example, generated a list of eight "uses to which growth models have been put:"[62] as a framework for conjecture about history; for reflection on the consequences of change in economic behavior or policy; for (sometimes conflicting) interpretations of economic relations with policy implications; to assert new propositions of theoretical significance; to pose inescapable philosophical or value problems; to illuminate the significance of institutional settings on optimum choices among policy alternatives; as a tool for estimating parameters as part of the process of policy formulation; and as a clarifying pedagogical device.

Despite this impressive array of believed contributions it is fair to say that, in retrospect, the results of this sustained virtuoso effort have been judged by friendly observers to be thin. At the close of their remarkable survey, for example, Hahn and Matthews are clearly dissatisfied:[63]

> . . . Nothing is easier than to ring the changes on more and more complicated models, without bringing in any really new ideas and without bringing the theory any nearer to casting light on the causes of the wealth of nations. The problems posed may well have intellectual fascination. But it is essentially a frivolous occupation to take a chain with links of very uneven strength and devote one's energies to strengthening and polishing the links that are already relatively strong.

Sen's conclusion is even more pungent:[64]

> . . . Interest in growth [after 1945] revived at first slowly and then by leaps and bounds. . . . Growth was everybody's concern and it is no wonder that in such a milieu growth theory was pampered by the attention of economists.
>
> With this immensely practical motivation it would have been natural for growth theory to take a fairly practice-oriented shape. This, however, has not happened and much of modern growth theory is concerned with rather esoteric issues. Its link with public policy is often very remote. It is as if a poor man collected money for his food and blew it all on alcohol.

There is in the reflective literature on growth modeling a pervasive sense of disproportion between the volume of scarce talent invested in the effort and its yield. What explains this retrospective malaise?

First, the anxieties about a recurrence of deep depression underlying the knife's-edge Harrod–Domar models were belied by the course of the world economy after 1945. The subsequent neoclassical phase of growth modeling was inspired by the relatively steady and unexpected growth of the advanced industrial countries after immediate postwar recovery; but none of the growth models, in fact, illuminated the causes of the great boom of the 1950s and 1960s. That boom was rooted in technological and terms-of-trade phenomena that literally have no place in the structure of the models elaborated by the various contenders.[65] As for entrepreneurship, they assumed all profitable inventions, whether exogenous or endogenous—embodied in gross investment or learnt by doing— were incorporated promptly into the capital stock.

Second, the application of simple profit maximization to innovation barred the modeling exercise from the essential notion of absorptive capacity. It is, of course, true that the study of absorptive capacity requires political, social, and cultural as well as economic analysis, as the great classic texts of political economy recognized. This deficiency denied the latter-day models relevance to the development problems of Latin America, Africa, the Middle East, and Asia. As Chapter 17 demonstrates, development economics evolved in a setting almost—not quite—independent of the concurrent growth-modeling effort that proceeded in an intense parochial world of its own, in another ring of the circus.

Third, when model builders sought to link their analyses to the longer sweep of history, they were forced to assert questionable propositions.[66] As Hahn and Matthews concluded:[67] "The historical patterns of economic growth . . . are too complex to be describable in terms of steady growth." Aside from the evidence of history, the convolutions of national economies and the world economy in the 1970s and 1980s violated most of the stylized facts that mainstream growth economists assumed, as well as the whole notion of a stable, self-correcting growth path—circumstances that delivered a kind of *coup de grace* to a field already exhibiting, by the early 1970s, distinct symptoms of diminishing returns.

All the participants in the growth-modeling effort did not accept as their mission the illumination of the large problems and prospects of national growth, past, present, or future. They entered the field to clarify certain more limited professional problems or, perhaps, for the simple fun of participating in the most popular game in town—a by-no-means unworthy motive in any science, rooted in the same human impulse that explains "clustering" and, therefore, sectoral overshooting in investment and inventions. And, besides, it is still too soon to pass final judgment on what the enterprise accomplished and failed to accomplish.

What can be said is that, whatever its attractions, formal growth modeling failed to dominate the field of growth analysis, or to illuminate significantly the political economy of growth in either the advanced industrial or developing countries. The post-1945 saga of growth theory turns, therefore, to two groups who approached the field with different sets of questions somewhat closer to "the infinitely more complex world of reality."[68]

16

Statistical Analyses
of the Structure of Growth:
from Morphology to Policy—Almost

The Great Enterprise of Simon Kuznets

The years 1955–1956 represent an important interval in the history of growth analysis. As noted earlier, it was then that Solow, Swan, and Tobin launched their neoclassical models, providing a third-stage booster to mathematical growth analysis. Reflecting a quite different approach, my takeoff article appeared in the March 1956 issue of *The Economic Journal*. For purposes of this chapter, however, the appropriate bench mark is the October 1956 issue of *Economic Development and Cultural Change*. It contained the first of ten lengthy monographs by Simon Kuznets under the rubric: *Quantitative Aspects of the Economic Growth of Nations*. The last monograph was published in October 1964.[1] Four major books that built on and extended these monographs followed.[2] In addition, the organization that supported Kuznets's remarkable effort from 1949 forward (The Committee on Economic Growth of the Social Science Research Council) helped finance major studies of national income and its determinants over time for eleven countries.

There is no authoritative account of how Kuznets came to conceive of and to mount this grand enterprise; but certain elements in the story can be discerned.[3] In terms of Kuznets's own evolution, his post-1945 work on growth can, to a degree, be seen in continuity with his earlier research, uniting as it did growth and national-income analysis. Growth was a central concern in his *Secular Movements* (1930) and, when drawn into national-income estimation, Kuznets did not remain a narrow statistician. His instinct and interest were to push his calculations back in time and to explain the movements of the time series that emerged. In that sense, Kuznets's international comparisons of the structure of growth follow naturally from his national-income work on the United States; notably, his *National Product Since 1869* and *National Income, A Summary of Findings* (both 1946).

Analytically, his later work is clearly distinguished from *Secular Movements* by his systematic exploitation of the rapid postwar extension of more or less reliable national-income data, both current and in the form of historical time series. The strengths and weaknesses of Kuznets's exercise in the comparative morphology of economic growth flow from his strategic research decision to build on national-income data and the highly aggregated elements into which such data were conventionally decomposed.

Although he envisioned it while still in Washington, Kuznets firmly crystallized his decision to concentrate on growth analysis when he returned to the NBER and joined in the intense immediate postwar discussion of the directions research in that institution should take. One of the priority areas considered was growth analysis, with Kuznets assuming leadership in its advocacy.

Aside from the inner logic of Kuznets's march from *Secular Movements* to the comparative analysis of the structure of growth, he (and some others at the NBER) may well have been affected by war and immediate postwar contact with parts of the world never before confronted; for example, in Kuznets's case, China; in Fabricant's, West Africa and Brazil. But Kuznets lost the battle to make the long-run contours of economic growth a major terrain of NBER effort, perhaps because of skepticism among some of his colleagues about the quality of the data likely to be available. Persisting, he found transitional support from Joseph Willetts at the Rockefeller Foundation and then an ample sustained base in the Committee on Economic Growth of the SSRC.[4] Seven years after the project was initiated in 1949 his results began to flow from the pipeline.

Kuznets's major conclusions may be summarized as follows:[5]

- Total product growth accelerated as nations entered "modern economic growth," starting with Great Britain in the late eighteenth century: the last one and one-half or two centuries represent a new economic epoch as compared to the longer past.
- With the important exception of Japan, currently, the developed countries are all in Europe or are European offshoots overseas.
- The currently less developed countries have failed to enter the developed group either because of the low initial levels of their per capita product (as they entered "modern economic growth") or because of low rates of growth in per capita product during the past century or so—or for both reasons. Their prospects should not be read off from pre-1914 European or Europe-derived experience. [The 1960s revealed more cases evoking the earlier Japanese experience than Kuznets's analysis would suggest; for example, India, China, South Korea, Taiwan; while some Latin American countries and Turkey had moved into "modern economic growth" (or takeoff) earlier.]
- Breaking out production and the working force under three gross headings (I, roughly, industry; A, roughly, agriculture; S, services), Kuznets emerges with findings most of which had been familiar since, at least, Colin Clark's pathfinding work in *The Conditions of Economic Progress* with foreshadowings by Marshall (preceding, p. 173). During modern growth the A sector declines in its relative contribution to product and its call on the working force; the I sector rises; and the S sector moves less consistently, showing a conspicuous rise in product share in certain of the richest countries. But the average lower productivity of the S than the I sector yields a marked increase in the proportion of the labor force in the S sector at high per capita product levels.
- The size of a country has a profound effect on the structure of its economy and particularly on the degree to which a country will be involved in foreign trade. Large countries in terms of population trade less than small countries.
- In the early stages of growth the rate of savings and capital formation as a percentage of national income and product rises, but after reaching a certain level those percentages no longer exhibit any clear trend that diverges significantly from the rise in GNP.
- There was a "U" shape to the way the size distribution of income changed as

average per capita income rose, that is, inequality tended to increase in the early stages of development and then decline slowly thereafter. The same phenomenon could be observed with regional differences in income.

- All nations undergoing modern economic growth go through what is now referred to as the "demographic transition"; that is, first the crude death rate falls sharply and is followed with a considerable lag by a fall in the birth rate. During this transition, therefore, the population growth rate accelerates markedly.
- There is some evidence of long swings in growth rates (over a span of some 20 years) in the few cases where continuous data exist for the period before 1914.
- Increases in productivity rather than in per capita man hours or material capital mainly account for the acceleration in product per capita during modern economic growth, stemming from the enlarging pool of science and technology.
- Conventionally calculated increases in product per capita overstate the growth rate for three reasons: some items listed as consumption should, in fact, be debited as costs of urban industrial life; other costs (for example, air pollution and noise) are not taken into account; education, to some extent hard to measure, is a capital cost as well as a form of consumption enriching the quality of life.
- Contemporary less developed countries show a less marked decline in the share of the working force in the *A* sector, with given increases in the *I* sector and per capita output, than historical data would suggest; whereas the post-1945 revolution in agricultural productivity in the developed countries yields more rapid decline than expected for the working force in agriculture. [Kuznets's data were from the 1950s. It is possible that the Green Revolution and subsequent improvements in agricultural productivity in important developing countries would somewhat alter these findings.]

In an accurate and candid statement, in the context of a paper relating historical Japanese data to the average performance of post-1945 developing countries, Chenery wrote:[6] "Our study does not get at the more basic determinants of growth: the level of savings, the adoption of new technology, the effects of specific resource endowments, or the importance of national policies. These factors only enter the analysis by inference." This observation has a major, quite direct bearing on Kuznets's work, of which he was quite aware. Kuznets did not confine himself to reporting the average behavior of growing economies at different levels of real income per capita. He analyzed the fundamental nature of accelerated modern growth itself. He concluded, like most analysts, that, at its core, it was caused by the application of modern scientific thought and technology to industry. Like Chenery, Kuznets also regarded the measurable statistical phenomena he cited as evidence of entrance into modern growth as a result of a deeper process. These secondary, measurable phenomena were, notably, an accelerated rate of urbanization (which he used to date entrance into modern growth); a sustained and rapid increase in real product per capita usually associated with high rates of population growth; a shift of the working force out of agriculture to industry and services; enlarged contacts with the outside world.

For the author of *Secular Movements*, some 30 years earlier, Kuznets's analytic emphasis on the application of modern scientific thought and technology to the economy is wholly comprehensible, focused as that book was on the sequence of leading sectors resulting from the diffusion of a succession of new technologies. But two aspects of Kuznets's massive exercise in statistical morphology denied him access to what he himself regarded as the central force at work in the story of modern economic growth; i.e., science and technology. First, his three basic categories (industry, agriculture, and services) were so broad that they could not be directly linked to the introduction and diffusion of major, particular technologies. Second, having made reasonably precise statistical measurability the overriding criterion for his work, Kuznets found it impossible to deal with technological change within the framework of his enterprise. In his 1971 *Economic Growth of Nations,* near the end of his most productive period, Kuznets, after some 300 pages of statistical and analytic summary of previous findings, suddenly expresses his frustration:[7]

> Since the high and accelerated rate of technological change is a major source of the high rates of growth per capita product and productivity in modern times and is also responsible for striking shifts in production structure, it is frustrating that the available sectoral classifications fail to separate new industries from old, and distinguish those affected by technological innovations. . . .

In the following twenty-eight pages, Kuznets illustrates the need for greater disaggregation, if growth is to be linked to the coming in of new technologies. He discusses leading sectors, old and new, and sets up a highly disaggregated table to capture their evolution in the United States over the period 1880–1948. Against that background he then outlines a model to illustrate the impact on aggregate growth rates of new rapid-growth sectors and new products. It is a joy to be back with the author of *Secular Movements* and to observe his sensitive appreciation of the innovational process hitherto masked by his overriding preoccupation with large national income aggregates and the three categories of production he derived from Colin Clark.

But, in fact, Kuznets was never able to resolve his fundamental dilemma: he defined modern growth in terms of the effective absorption of new technologies; but he measured it in terms of product per capita, a quite different, obliquely related variable. And his successors in comparative statistical growth analysis, productive in many ways, were also not able to break out of this prison of their own construction, although sectoral-development planners and growth accountants engineered a partial escape (following, pp. 359–362).

Chenery *et al.*

In his 1981 critical survey of international quantitative comparisons, Perkins characterizes the second post-Kuznets phase as "more data and disaggregation." Clearly, Hollis Chenery was its central figure.[8] I would distinguish his work from Kuznets's on somewhat different grounds. Kuznets was overwhelmingly concerned with the morphology of growth in Western Europe, North America, Russia, Japan, and Australasia, basing his analysis on the longest time series available, notably national income data. In my vocabulary he contrived a kind of highly aggregated statistical history of the countries that had graduated into takeoff before 1914. Chenery's primary (by no means exclusive) concern was contemporary developing countries and, ultimately, what statistical analysis could provide in the way of broad guidance for development policy.[9] As Perkins suggests, Chenery had more data available: the extraordinary gathering of post-1945 statistical series by the United Nations, the World Bank, and other specialized agencies. Of the nature of the case the time series available were usually short. Chenery's primary method in mobilizing and analyzing the data was, perforce, cross-sectional, usually drawing on the average behavior of countries at different levels of real income per capita during the 1950s and 1960s.

In his leading essay in the Chenery *festschrift*, Edward S. Mason states with his usual capacity for terse, definitive summary the three central issues in the analysis of development:[10]

> . . . [T]he extent to which uniformities among countries can be discerned. . . . Whether, if such uniformities are discovered, they conform to the patterns that characterized growth in the now-developed countries. . . . Whether, uniform or not, the development process in LDC's can be usefully attacked with the tools shaped in the analysis of growth in developed countries. Chenery has made large contributions to the discussions of all these questions. Perhaps his largest contribution has been in his examination of uniformities.

With respect to uniformities, his 1975 *Patterns of Development, 1950–1970,* written with Moises Syrquin, perhaps best captures his method and achievement. Chenery moved beyond in several major subsequent publications; and Table 16.1 (p. 360) is, in effect, a summary of his 1986 findings.

His cross-sectional method differs from Kuznets's comparison of long historical time series in several respects. Chenery and Syrquin use correlation analysis to establish their average patterns (or "stylized facts"); disaggregate systematically a bit beyond Kuznets's strictly economic categories; and helpfully include several social categories, notably education and the demographic transition.

Chenery went further in three major directions. First, in an article written with Lance Taylor, he disaggregated industries into "early, middle, and late."[11] These three roughly approximate the sequence of leading sectors that characterize my takeoff, drive to technological maturity, and high mass consumption, as well as Walther Hoffmann's industrial stages. Second, Chenery gave a great deal more attention to trade and capital flows (including foreign aid) than Kuznets and defined categories for developing countries according to the relative scale and composition of their foreign trade. Third, Chenery had the advantage of having worked intensively on the problems of particular countries, e.g., Italy, Japan, Pakistan, Israel. He was a substantial figure in policy-oriented development analysis from the late 1950s forward. He understood better than some the gap between average behavior (and average deviations) derived from correlation analysis and the kind of data unique to time and place required to render responsible policy recommendations. Analytically, he consciously sought to combine the virtues of historical and cross-sectional analysis with a sense of the particularity of each case. For example, his 1962 paper (written with Shuntaro Shishido and Tsunehiko Watanabe) is a systematic analysis of the structure of the Japanese economy in 1914, 1935, and 1954 set against "standard" behavior. The Japanese deviations are, for the most part, explained in a persuasive way.

As the 1980s wore on, those concerned with the statistical measurement of the structure and patterns of growth took stock. They were, in part, responding to criticisms from essentially friendly critics, in part reaching out for a new phase in their working agenda. The most authoritative statement of their past achievements and future hopes came appropriately from Hollis Chenery.[12] His assessment deserves summary.

Kuznets's contribution to structural analysis is defined as isolating "a consistent set of changes in the composition of demand, production, trade, and employment, each reflecting different aspects of the shifts in resource allocation that take place as income levels rise.''[13]

He identifies the major problems Kuznets left for his successors:

- the role of trade and capital flows in development;
- similarities and differences between cross-country and time series estimates of development patterns;
- the translation of ''speculations as to causal sequences into more formal models and testable hypotheses;'' and
- filling the gap left by ''the absence of policy analysis'' in Kuznets's work.

Chenery also notes the important contribution of Adelman and Morris in extending structural measurements to relations among economic, social, and political aspects of development.

He goes on to summarize the progress made, in good part under his leadership, in categorizing development patterns by form of market expansion (primary exports, manufactured consumers exports, exploitation of domestic markets); modeling typical relations among key development variables; refining the typologies within which developing countries are grouped; the use of modeling techniques to come to grips with policy problems where ''market forces may not lead to optimal results—as in population growth, urbanization, or income distribution.''[14]

As was inevitable and appropriate, these lines of approach, foreshadowed for some time but brought to a kind of climax in *Industrialization and Growth* (1986), have been subjected to what might be called respectful criticism. As early as 1976 Carlos Diaz-Alejandro argued that the ''. . . search for uniform patterns appears to hit sharply diminishing returns outside production and consumption structures, and related patterns in labour allocation and urbanization;'' and he found some important regression results ''disappointing.''[15]

Dwight Perkins's 1981 paper expressed uneasiness over a wider range:

- The relatively few new discoveries of statistical uniformities in the structure of growth beyond those established by Colin Clark and Kuznets.
- The limited guidance to planners provided by disaggregation into industrial groups.
- Uncertainty that input–output coefficients are stable over time and among countries at different stages of growth.
- The search for growth patterns that are stable over time and/or in cross-section conceals the extent to which such patterns were determined by the absorption of unique technological innovations, not dealt with.
- The quite appropriate search for cross-sectional uniformities in subgroups of countries has yielded unsatisfactory results.
- A critical question: Is it wise to throw India and China into measures of average behavior, containing as they do over half the population of the world's developing countries but rooted in quite different cultures?
- The national income and pricing data essential for Kuznets–Chenery structural analyses are seriously flawed, as demonstrated by Kravis's efforts at correction through relative purchasing-power analysis.

Perkins argued that refinements in structural analysis should enjoy lower priority than improvements in data; growth theory and data collection and analysis should be brought closer together; and that, somehow a whole range of critically important variables determining the growth performance of countries, now excluded for purposes of convenience, should be taken into account, notably, technological change and differences in technological absorptive capacity, the role of governments and public policy, the role of institutions, and the role of foreign and civil wars.

Perkins concludes as follows:[16]

> It is of no help to say that these issues belong properly within the scope of some other discipline such as political science or psychology because these disciplines aren't dealing with these issues as they relate to economic development either. International comparisons of economic growth have given us an important tool to work with, economic theory provides us with specific tools and a tradition of rigorous analysis, but we also need the more traditional skills and perspective of the broad-based historian.

One further commentary should be noted, that of Edward S. Mason in his essay in the *festschrift* in honor of Hollis Chenery.[17] After a lucid summary of Chenery's objectives and findings, he concludes:[18] "The studies pay little attention to the cultural, political, and administrative elements that also affect development. They are useful, indeed essential, in bringing economic policy alternatives to light, but they provide an incomplete picture of the sources of and limitations to growth." Mason then goes on to illustrate the centrality of these noneconomic variables by comparing the evolution of post-1945 Egypt and South Korea.

The most fundamental unsolved economic problem in the kind of analyses led by Chenery is the treatment of technological change. Here is Perkins's observation on the product of three decades of international quantitative comparisons.[19]

> There is general agreement that technological change, broadly defined, sometimes embodied in capital and sometimes not, is the main source of modern economic growth. Furthermore, the accumulated backlog of technology has much to do with why some of today's developing countries have managed to grow so much faster than their Western predecessors. And yet, economists know very little about either the nature of technological innovation as it relates to development or how and why innovations do or do not spread to other nations in the world.

It is, I believe, necessary to distinguish in this matter Kuznets's position from Chenery's. Kuznets accepted, out of his early work in *Secular Movements*, what might be called a Schumpeterian position; that is, modern economic growth was driven forward by the application of science to the economy, the result being, in part, a sequence of large, discontinuous leading sectors, each subject to retardation. He regarded his later work on the structural characteristics of growth based on long time series[20] as preliminary to a definitive explanation of growth; but he asserted often and without ambiguity that he already knew its root cause; that is, the systematic application of modern science to the production of goods and services. And he was quite capable of acknowledging his frustration that comparative statistical morphology did not come to grips with technological change and, therefore, his dream could not be fulfilled.

Chenery's work was primarily cross-sectional; and he had a strong professional interest in both the structure of developing countries and in development policy. His study of Japan had an historical dimension, but his work was overwhelmingly focused on the post-1945 world of developing countries. He also acknowledged the introduction of new technologies as fundamental to growth, but it was natural that he should approach the problem of technological change in a somewhat different way than Kuznets. He does so in his "prototype" model of industrialization by subsuming technological change in "growth of intermediate demand," one of the four factors identified as the source of increases in output.[21] The other three are: growth of domestic demand; growth of exports; and effects of import substitution. The "transformation" from lowest to highest level of development can then be presented, as in Table 16.1, as a highly simplified input–output table.

In a formal sense, technology is accounted for over the transformation, embodied as it is in the massive increase in intermediate manufactures. But this captures little of what is involved in measuring and reducing the technological backlog that virtually defines underdevelopment. It is one more of the considerable array of ingenious devices for evading the problem of accounting for the generation and diffusion of technology.

The Sectoral Planners

The ultimate purpose of Chenery's cross-sectional analyses, definition of types of developing countries and strategies, and prototype models of the transformation based on his stylized facts was operational. In effect, they were designed to help economic planners and other officials to define certain broad development policy options by identifying in which category their country belonged; isolating their deviations from average behavior; and deciding whether or not they wished to move toward the average, stay with their existing development pattern, or pursue some other course. This large purpose is most nearly fulfilled in his *Industrialization and Growth*. It is a major link between the structural analysis of average growth patterns and development policy. I shall discuss its conclusions, therefore, in dealing with the policy debate among development economists (following, pp. 422–423).

But in moving toward this practical objective, Chenery himself, and a good many others, ran into—and only partially escaped from—what I shall call the Gesell problem.[22]

Dr. Arnold Gesell was author or co-author of well over twenty books on the development of children from birth to 10 years. The heart of his work consists in a sequence of rather detailed portraits of average behavior as children move through their "transformation" with time rather than GNP per capita on the horizontal axis. Also, like Chenery, Gesell tried to find intermediate ground—between uniqueness and overgenerality—by defining three types of growth patterns.[23] Again, like Chenery, Gesell was, ultimately, interested in policy; that is, guidance in child-rearing for parents, teachers, etc. But like all serious analysts of growth (and every parent) Gesell understood that, ultimately, each child was unique and his or her individuality had to be respected in applying the lessons that appeared to flow from his portraits of average behavior and types of growth patterns. The conflict between the search for scientific averages and the uniqueness of the cases imparts a strand of uneasiness to his work.

Something like this sense of the limits of biological generalization has led to substantial literature of economic planning that applies sophisticated mathematical and econometric techniques to sectoral (and occasionally systemwide) planning in particular developing

Table 16.1. Structural Change during the Transformation, Income Level 5 Compared with Level 1 (Percentage of GDP)

Sector	Domestic demand (D)			Net trade (T)			Intermediate demand (W)			Gross output (X)[a]			Value added (V)		
	Initial	Final	Increment	Initial	Final	Increment	Initial	Final	Increment	Initial	Final	Increment	Initial	Final	Increment
Tradables															
Primary	18	4	−14	13	−2	−15	14	14	0	46	16	−30	38	9	−29
Manufacturing	28	34	+6	−14	0	+14	22	51	+29	36	85	+49	15	36	+21
Nontradables															
Social overhead	14	20	+6	−1	1	+1	5	7	+2	20	28	+8	11	16	+5
Services	42	42	0	−2	2	+1	9	10	+1	50	53	+4	36	39	+3
Total[b]	102	100	−2	−2	−1	+1	50	82	+32	151	182	+31	100	100	0

NOTE: Period 1 is defined by a GDP level of $140 per capita; period 5 is defined by a level of $2,100.

[a] $X = D + T + W$.

[b] Totals may not add because of rounding.

SOURCE: Hollis Chenery, Sherman Robinson, and Moshe Syrquin, *Industrialization and Growth: A Comparative Study* (New York: Oxford University Press, Published for the World Bank, 1986), p. 52.

countries with the purpose of generating specific policy recommendations.[24] The system-wide planning models are generally described as computable general equilibrium (CGE) models.

David Kendrick and Arthur MacEwan describe lucidly the purpose and structural character of planning as opposed to less policy-oriented growth models:[25]

> Planning models are designed to study the long-term consequences of policies affecting the allocation of resources, particularly the division of investment among sectors. They draw on the results of theoretical growth models but differ from them in that they (1) contain empirical estimates and are solved with numerical methods, (2) are usually disaggregated into many sectors, and (3) involve more complex specification of development processes and specific policy constraints. The net effect of these differences is to make theoretical models more useful for studying the general character of growth in an abstract setting and to make planning models more useful for studying more disaggregated and complex systems which include the instruments and constraints of government policy.

Planning studies of this type have been made for, among others, the following developing countries: Egypt, Chile, Greece, India, Israel, South Korea, Mexico, Pakistan, and Taiwan. In addition, Lief Johansen conducted a methodologically sophisticated analysis of Norway.[26] And these methods were applied less rigorously to characterize certain regional development problems; for example, in Latin America and Sub-Saharan Africa.

From the perspective of the present study, policy-oriented growth modeling has had several positive characteristics.[27] First, it has forced analysts ultimately concerned with optimum investment allocation to disaggregate down to the level at which new technologies are introduced into the economy. Analysis moves out of the frustrating world of "primary," "industry," and "service" sectors and into the arena where decisions have to be made about whether or when a steel mill or petrochemical plant is to be built and on what scale. And difficult as it is (it hasn't got easier since Marshall's time) analysts have to grapple with increasing returns and have found ways to do so.[28]

In general, then, the imperatives of investment planning in developing nations—combined with a sense that prototype modeling left one still too far from reality—have led to major advances in dynamic theory, which embrace some aspects of technological change, including significant aspects of the case of increasing returns and efforts to capture the dynamic impact of technological change on the input–output coefficients in the majestic tables pioneered by Wassily Leontief.

Important limitations, of course, remain. For example, the existing pool of technology is taken as given. These models do not deal with the dynamic interplay of science and technology. The quality of entrepreneurship is either not dealt with or embraced in interesting but rather abstract and overaggregated calculations of absorptive capacity. They do not analyze the forces that cause leading sectors suddenly to accelerate. They take into account backward and forward linkages but the lateral spreading effects that go with a fast-moving leading-sector complex are inadequately measured in present multisectoral models. But, in the long history of economic thought, the planning econometricians are beginning to make a serious dent on some problems long set aside or swept under the rug by empty devices of formal elegance.

As for their contribution to planning, it is too soon to make a dogmatic judgment, for the field is still evolving. David Kendrick, a major practitioner, casts up the interim account justly:[29]

> At least two views may be taken of the usefulness of the present models for economic planning. One view compares the present models to the more disaggregated and more generally specified models which may be built in the future and to the requirement of government planning offices for highly disaggregated results. This view finds the present models lacking and thinks of the present research effort as a long-run effort which will eventually produce tools which are useful for government policy analysis. A second view compares numerical models to other methods of analysis used in making economy-wide planning decisions and finds that the comprehensive nature of the models produces insights which cannot be obtained with less complex analytical means.
>
> The author's present opinion is closer to the first viewpoint than the second in the conviction that the models are still more useful in providing insight into how to build better models than they are in providing prescriptions for economic policies. However the models have the virtue of forcing the economic analyst into systematic thought about the problem under study and therein lies one of their most useful attributes.

A Conclusion

By way of conclusion it may be useful to suggest briefly what these studies of the morphology of growth have had to say about the key growth variables that have provided structure to this study.

Basic Growth Equation

As Chenery pointed out, the narrowly statistical analysis of structural changes that accompanied increases in real GNP per capita "does not get at the more basic determinants of growth . . . these factors only enter by inference." It is quite clear, however, that the "inferred factors" are those by now quite familiar: population and the working force; saving-investment; natural resource endowments. To these Chenery added "national policies." The character of the tripartite sectoral disaggregation initiated by Colin Clark made the impact of Engels's Law particularly important, decreeing as it did a relative shift of the working force from agriculture to industry and services with the increase in GNP per capita.

Rather more than their successors both Colin Clark and Kuznets were led to explore and to speculate about aspects of growth not actually measured in the data available to them. But it was inherent in their statistical approach to structural change that they would be dealing primarily with reflections of the growth process rather than "basic determinants."

Population and the Working Force

The statistical approach to growth analysis has brought into sharp focus historical and cross-sectional data on birth and death rates in relation to GNP per capita, permitting more soundly based analyses than in the past of the demographic transition. The deviations from average behavior, notably for birthrates, are, however, substantial (Figure 20.1). A considerable literature has evolved seeking to narrow the range of these deviations by correlating birthrates with additional variables; e.g., education, health, urbanization, mobility, income distribution.[30] Although these analyses of fertility have left a great many unanswered questions, they represent a rare and important example of the merging of economic and social analysis—an objective, in particular, of the work of Irma Adelman and Cynthia Taft Morris.

Investment and Technology

A great deal of additional evidence, both historical and cross-sectional, has been generated on the proportion of GNP invested associated with different levels of income per capita. It is now clear that, on average, the investment rate rises in what I would designate as the takeoff and drive to technological maturity and then levels off.[31]

On the role of investment in growth and the sources of investment perhaps the most interesting observations among the growth morphologists are Colin Clark's (preceding, pp. 213–214); i.e., that the rate of capital formation does not uniquely determine the rate of growth and that a high proportion of saving-investment in plant and equipment results from the plowback of profits rather than an overall Keynesian consumption–savings function conventionally conceived. It is in the latter terms, for example, that Chenery–Syrquin discuss the theoretical and empirical bases for their data on "accumulation processes."[32] On the other hand their mobilization of investment rates, systematic data on flows of capital imports, and allocations to investment in education are all extremely valuable.

With respect to technological change, Colin Clark and Kuznets underlined that the application of science to the economy was the foundation for modern growth; but as Kuznets finally underlined, their method proved an awkward instrument for grappling with this crucial linkage.[33]

Analyses of the Chenery type did not appear as concerned with the question of technology. The word *technology,* for example, appears only once in Chenery–Syrquin's conclusions along with two other exogenous variables.[34] But Chenery does introduce technology via a structural variable; i.e., the relative rise of "intermediate" industry, which he takes to be at the heart of the transformation.

In a study published a year earlier (1974), using much the same data sources as Chenery–Syrquin, Thorkil Kristensen arrived at similar conclusions on the pattern of growth rates through time (Tables 16.2 and 16.3); but his linkage to technology is more direct than Chenery's.[35]

Kristensen's fundamental propositions bearing on the rising and falling sequence of growth rates come to this: economic growth depends on the rate of absorption of the existing and unfolding stock of relevant knowledge; the rate of absorption depends on the availability of both trained men and capital; the reason for the accelerated growth among his middle-income countries is that they have built up the stock of trained manpower (including entrepreneurs) to a position where they can accelerate the rate of absorption of the existing stock of knowledge, so long as they generate at home or acquire from abroad the requisite capital to incorporate that knowledge; the reason for the subsequent slowdown in growth rates is that the high-income countries, having absorbed the backlog of existing knowledge, must rely for subsequent growth on the rate at which new knowledge

Table 16.2. Income Levels and Growth Rates, 1960–1970

	Population 1967 (millions)	GNP per capita 1967 U.S.\$	Average annual growth rate 1960–1970
United States	199	\$3,670	3.2%
Group 1 (\$1,750–\$3,670)	307	3,120	3.4
Group 2 (\$1,000–\$1,750)	238	1,490	3.5
Group 3 (\$700–\$1,000)	444	930	6.5
Group 4 (\$400–\$700)	161	550	4.4
Group 5 (\$200–\$400)	299	270	2.9
Group 6 (\$100–\$200)	376	130	2.6
Group 7 (\$50–\$100)	1,580	90	1.7
World	3,391	\$ 610	3.2%

SOURCE: Thorkil Kristensen, *Development in Rich and Poor Countries* (New York: Praeger, 1974), pp. 156–159.

is created. He concludes: "Thus, if there is something that can be called the typical growth curve for GNP per capita, it is not an exponential curve but rather an "S"-shaped curve that may or may not approach an upper limit."[36]

On the basis of this quantitative but not directly measurable hypothesis, Kristensen proceeds to indicate how his "S"-shaped path of technological absorption is reflected in a wide range of more or less measurable economic and social indicators that he associates with real income per capita—for example, the distribution of the working force, urbanization, income distribution, food and energy consumption, health services, demographic variables, education, foreign trade, and so forth.

The major analytic difference as between Kristensen's and Chenery's views of the process of growth centers on the role of technological progress: Kristensen regards the diffusion of old and new technological knowledge as fundamental to growth. Chenery regards the progressive absorption of new technologies, as one moves up the income per capita ladder, as a by-product of the expansion of manufactures of increasing sophistica-

Table 16.3. Annual Average Growth Rates per Capita GDP, 1960–1973

Stage	Per cent
A. Old developed	
1. United States	3.1
2. Other	3.7
Total	3.4
B. Newly developed	7.0
C. Transitional	3.9
D. Less developed	1.8
Total market economies	2.8
E. Centrally planned	3.6

SOURCE: Hollis Chenery, "Transitional Growth and World Industrialization," paper presented to the Nobel Symposium on the International Allocation of Economic Activity, Stockholm, June 8–11, 1976, Table 2b.

tion; and this perspective is understandable in cross-section analysis, with a given pool of working technologies assumed to exist accessibly in the old developed countries. From a historical perspective, Kristensen's emphasis on the critical role of the diffusion of technologies through time is more congenial to the analysis that underlies this book.

The econometric sectoral planners, of course, also approached technological change head on; but as they moved into the realm of dynamic, multisectoral equilibrium models they confronted problems that, up to the present, have required technological change to be introduced exogenously.

Business Cycles and Relative Prices

Inevitably, studies addressed primarily to long-term patterns of structural change systematically associated with substantial changes in levels of GNP per capita have had little to contribute to the analysis of business cycles or changes in relative prices.

The Stages of and Limits to Growth

Colin Clark and Kuznets were content to treat growth as a process that, once started, had a number of identifiable structural characteristics associated with different levels of real income per capita. It was natural that Chenery, building on foundations laid by Clark and Kuznets, dealing with structural change in a large number of countries in cross section, should evolve his own conception of the stages of growth defined in terms of those structural changes.

Here are the essentials of Chenery's view:[37]

1. Stages are defined in the broad literary terms indicated in Table 16.3, but they are rooted in the Chenery–Syrquin data on the average pattern of the transition set out in Table 16.1.

The transition can be usefully divided into an earlier and a later phase by measuring the halfway point in each development process. For example, on average, the share of industry (manufacturing plus construction) in GNP increases from an average of 12.5% for underdeveloped countries to 38% for developed ones. This process is half completed at an income level of about $450 [300 1967 U.S. $] which is close to the average for all processes. On the other hand, the rise in the share of manufactured exports in GDP [gross domestic product] (from 1.1% to 13%) takes place much later in the transition and is half completed only at an income level of $1000 [625 1967 U.S. $]. In the following discussion the countries that have completed more than half of the normal changes in the structure of production and trade will be classed as "transitional" and those that have not reached this point as "less developed."

By Chenery's reckoning the share of manufacturing in the "old developed" countries for 1973 is 30.7%; the "newly developed," 29.6%; the "transitional," 21.7%; the "less developed," 14.4%; the "centrally planned," 39.8%.

2. The transitional countries, in turn, are grouped in three categories: "large" coun-

tries, with populations of 15 million or more in 1960, substantial domestic markets for manufactures, and relatively low ratios of foreign trade to GNP; small countries relatively specialized in primary exports; small countries relatively specialized in the export of manufactured goods and services.

Chenery also embraces within the transitional category two further types of economies that exhibit higher growth rates than either the least-developed or old developed nations: "newly developed market economies" and "newly developed centrally planned economies." All had levels in 1973 of GNP per capita over $1000 (1967 U.S. $) and productive structures more or less typical of that real income level.

In thus defining the transition process, Chenery embraces nations in subcategories containing about 52% of the world's population as of 1973: newly developed market (7%), newly developed centrally planned (9%), transitional market economies (13%), transitional centrally planned (35%, including China, 23%). The old developed countries contained only 13% of the world population; the other developing countries, 35%.

3. In an article written with Lance Taylor, Chenery moved beyond the criterion of the aggregate share of GNP generated by industry to the association of GNP per capita with periods of acceleration and deceleration in certain "early," "middle," and "late" industry groups.[38]

This proposition is linked, in a general way, to Chenery's stages as follows: the "transitional" countries are in the process of absorbing the basic heavy industry sectors (steel, light engineering, chemicals); the "newly developed," the more sophisticated technologies associated with motor vehicles on a mass scale, durable consumer goods, heavy engineering, electronics, and so on.[39] Like virtually all post-1960 studies, Chenery's data and analysis confirm the reality of the once much-debated question of a substantial rise in the investment rate during take-off.[40]

There are however, several fairly important distinctions worth noting. First, Chenery regards the progressive absorption of new technologies, as one moves up the income per capita ladder, as a by-product of the expansion of manufactures of increasing sophistication. But from the historical perspective of a developing country struggling to move forward (or, even, the perspective of an advanced industrial country), the subtly interconnected world of science and technology must be regarded as an economic sector to which investment resources are allocated and that yields, like any other sector, a conceptually definable, if difficult to measure, rate of return over cost, with appropriate lags.

One reason for underlining the importance of technological generation and diffusion is that for two centuries it was essential in fending off diminishing returns in agriculture and raw material production, an aspect of the story of growth that falls out in a cross-sectional view of the complacent 1950s and 1960s, when the prices of basic commodities were relatively low. A cross-sectional analysis as of, say, the 1790s, the 1850s, 1900–1910, 1945–1951, or the mid–1970s could certainly not ignore the effects on income and growth rates of relative prices; and, indeed, the growth rates of the 1950s and 1960s in industrial countries and regions were abnormally high in part because of favorable terms of trade in the form of cheap energy, food, and raw materials.

Second, Chenery's method for capturing technological change within the manufacturing sector, even when disaggregated along Chenery–Taylor lines, misses the dynamics of a succession of leading sector complexes, with their backward, lateral, and forward linkages. The level of disaggregation in *Industrialization and Growth* is, at certain points, more detailed. But, in the end, the authors acknowledge their black box.[41]

Our empirical results on TFP [Total Factor Productivity] change thus should not be interpreted as measuring technical change only in the sense of a shift in the frontier of production possibilities because of the implementation of a new generation of technical knowledge. Instead, the measures must be interpreted quite broadly to include such factors as industrial and plant organization, engineering know-how or changes in response to disruptions in the production process that affect capacity utilization in the short run. The measures really treat production units as a black box. We measure the inputs and the outputs but make no real attempt to describe exactly what is going on inside the plant gate. Figuring out how the black box works is important, but it is beyond the scope of this book. We seek to delineate the stylized facts at a fairly aggregate level and will necessarily be modest in our attempts to generalize and to discern causal links.

Both of these points—the linkage of technological virtuosity to the scale of manufactures and the black-box approach to total factor productivity—relate to something lost in the statistical morphology of growth: the pain, complexity, and endless creativity inherent in the process of growth, including the strain, costs, and exhilaration of shifting from one set of leading sectors to another as (for the United States) in the 1840s (cotton textiles to railroads), 1900–1910 (steel to electricity, motor vehicles, chemicals), 1975–1985 (motor vehicles, etc., to microelectronics, etc.).

Growth analysis inherently consists of such successive phases of irreversible dynamic disequilibrium, each solving a problem but creating new problems to solve after, perhaps, a transient interval of relative stability. This approximates, I believe, what Albert Hirschman had in mind in his view of economic development (following, pp. 390–391); what Gesell perceived in his view of human development as the solving of an "endless succession of growth problems" via the pressures of disequilibrium;[42] and it is not far from the chaos theorist's view of the physical world as "a science of process rather than state, of becoming rather than being . . . [where] the disorderly behavior of simple systems acted as a creative process [that] generated . . . richly organized patterns, sometimes stable and sometime unstable. . . ."[43]

The practitioners of the craft of comparative structural analysis of economies fail to capture this process because the dynamic model implicit in their charting of transformation from poverty to affluence is one of general equilibrium.[44] Analyses flowing from Colin Clark's pioneering effort assert, in effect, that growing economies, viewed in cross-section, alter their structures and their allocations of resources in a roughly uniform way, once they begin to move forward in modern (or self-sustained) growth. The pattern that emerges reaches beyond conventional economic variables to birth rates and death rates, educational levels, social welfare allocations, and income distribution. The average cross-sectional pattern is, as one would expect, subject to considerable deviation; and, as Chenery's exploration of manufacture- and primary-oriented small countries indicates, some of those deviations are systematic. The range of variation within these categories is, however, wide. But what we have here is a rather grand assertion of the ultimate imperatives of balanced growth and dynamic equilibrium.

As Chenery and Syrquin correctly argue, such equilibrium models may well suggest "the interdependent changes in resource allocation which underlie the major development patterns."[45] But they do not explain the erratic course economic growth actually assumes;

and they can only reflect rather than capture the substantially noneconomic forces that initiate modern economic growth and drive it forward.

Noneconomic Factors

As noted earlier, a considerable and wide-ranging effort has been made to refine, through statistical analysis, knowledge of the determinants of birthrates beyond the broad familiar pattern that links them inversely to income per capita. Irma Adelman and Cynthia Taft Morris have pioneered and applied statistical methods for testing the association between economic growth and a wide range of social and political variables that do not lend themselves to straightforward time series.[46] They have exhibited imagination and ingenuity in finding statistical surrogates for (or methods for rough quantitative ranking of) the following thirteen sociocultural and seventeen political indicators for which conventional statistical data are only normally available for three (extent of urbanization, of literacy, and the crude birthrate):[47]

SOCIOCULTURAL INDICATORS

Size of the traditional agricultural sector
Extent of dualism
Extent of urbanization
Importance of the indigenous middle class
Extent of social mobility
Extent of literacy
Extent of mass communication
Degree of cultural and ethnic homogeneity
Degree of social tension
Crude fertility rate
Degree of modernization of outlook
Predominant type of religion
Level of socioeconomic development

POLITICAL INDICATORS

Degree of national integration and sense of national unity
Degree of centralization of political power
Extent of political participation
Degree of freedom of political opposition and the press
Degree of competitiveness of political parties
Predominant basis of the political party system
Strength of the labor movement
Political strength of the traditional elite
Political strength of the military
Political and social influence of religious organizations
Degree of administrative efficiency
Extent of leadership commitment to economic development
Extent of direct government economic activity
Length of colonial experience
Type of colonial experience
Recency of self-government
Extent of political stability

Such associational analysis of variables that evidently interact does not lend itself to clear-cut analytic or fine-grained policy conclusions. It did lead Adelman and Taft in their study of growth and social equity to a sense of shock at the failure of positive association between economic growth rates, more equal income distribution, and degree of political participation. They concluded that new economic and political development strategies were required to fulfill the objectives they judged desirable. But it did not require the elaborate quantitative exercise undertaken to come to that judgment.

Put another way, the uniformities in social and political life that accompany the development processes are, at their core, a sequence of problems solved by each society in its own way.[48] Averaging these solutions by some quantitative method may not be the optimum way either to identify the sequence of problems or to explain the deviations from average behavior.

But the most important weakness of this kind of analysis is the one it shares with the comparative statistical analysis of economic growth itself; i.e., the method inherently masks the dynamics of change—what Paul Rosenstein-Rodan called "the pursuit curve which shows the dynamic path toward equilibrium."[49] For example, none of these analyses captures the complex forces—of which fear of or reaction to external intrusion is the most powerful—which led quasi-traditional societies to accept the inherently painful and contentious changes required to enter takeoff or modern economic growth. None identifies the particular group or groups that emerge to lead the way. None specifies the prior historical experience with central government and administration that helps determine the ease or difficulty of the transition. And so also with the interplay of economic and noneconomic factors in all subsequent stages.

One should not, however, ask of a method more than it is capable of accomplishing. The comparative statistical analysis of growth and development has permitted the systematic organization of a vast amount of historical and cross-sectional data that all serious students of growth will continue to use even if they must look elsewhere for the dynamics of the "Transformation."

Growth Accounting: Edward F. Denison

Starting from a quite different approach to technical change and productivity than Chenery's "intermediate production," Edward F. Denison of the Brookings Institution has developed a method for analyzing changes in the determinants of growth on the basis of painstaking disaggregation. His method is incorporated in six books of his own (the first published in 1978) plus similar studies by others. Taken all together this literature embraces recent experience in the United States, Canada, Western Europe, Japan, India, and the Republic of Korea. Denison's most recent study (1985) is of the United States over the period 1929–1982.[50]

Table 16.4 indicates the extent of Denison's disaggregation as well as his estimate of the various sources of American growth over the 53 years for which he has developed comparable data. For present purposes, the key variable is quantitatively the most important: "advances in knowledge." It covers both technological change and improvements in "managerial and organizational knowledge."[51] Despite heroic efforts, including linkage to the estimates of the productivity of R & D by Edwin Mansfield and others, Denison has thus far been forced to settle for treating advances in knowledge as a residual.[52] Denison provides reasonably convincing reasons for believing his residual is a fair approximation

Table 16.4. United States: Contributions to 1929–1982 Growth Rates

	Potential national income				Actual national income			
	Total		Per person employed		Total		Per person employed	
	Whole economy (1)	Nonresidential business (2)	Whole economy (3)	Nonresidential business (4)	Whole economy (5)	Nonresidential business (6)	Whole economy (7)	Nonresidential business (8)
Growth rate	3.2	3.1	1.6	1.7	2.9	2.8	1.5	1.6
Percent of growth rate								
All sources	100	100	100	100	100	100	100	100
Labor input except education	34	25	-13	-23	32	20	-12	-25
Education per worker	13	16	26	30	14	19	27	34
Capital	17	12	15	10	19	14	20	13
Advances in knowledge	26	34	54	64	28	39	55	68
Improved resource allocation	8	11	16	19	8	11	16	18
Economies of scale	8	11	17	20	9	12	18	22
Changes in legal and human environment	-1	-2	-3	-4	-1	-2	-3	-4
Land	0	0	-3	-4	0	0	-3	-3
Irregular factors	0	0	0	0	-3	-5	-7	-8
Other determinants	-5	-7	-10	-13	-5	-8	-10	-13

SOURCE: Edward F. Denison, *Trends in American Economic Growth, 1929–1982*. (Washington, D.C.: The Brookings Institution, 1985), p. 30.

of improvements in knowledge for the period 1948–1973; but he finds the collapse in the rate of productivity increase after 1973 beyond the explanatory power of his analytic system.[53]

I find hopeful Denison's effort—and those of others similarly engaged—to break open the various black boxes in which modern theorists have blandly encased invention and innovation. I suspect, however, that a satisfactory explanation of the pre-1973 as well as the post-1973 period requires more disaggregation than Denison's method allows. For example, Denison explained the relatively higher productivity performance of Northwest Europe than the United States over the period 1950–1962 primarily in terms of the components of economies of scale. He associates this tendency with large increases in output of "income-elastic consumption components."[54] In all conscience this is a rather awkward and muscle-bound way of saying that Europe moved toward U.S. patterns of consumption; that is, toward the diffusion to a higher proportion of the population of the automobile, durable consumers' goods, etc. Via backward linkages this process made for the efficient larger scale absorption of familiar technologies earlier applied massively in the United States. The leading sector complexes, which expanded disproportionately, both drew capital on a large scale, including a high rate of plowback of profits, and used it with the greatest relative efficiency. The accelerator operated powerfully; that is, an expansion of consumption outlays led to rapid increases in investment in the sectors with high income elasticity of demand and in the subsectors to which they were linked. Put another way, Western Europe enjoyed and exploited in this period an asset usually associated with successful developing countries: a large backlog of hitherto unapplied technologies.

In the vocabulary of the stages of economic growth, Western Europe came—belatedly but fully—into the stage of high mass-consumption.[55]

An analysis of the marked post-1973 deceleration in American productivity is not offered here; but I am confident a persuasive treatment requires a great deal of disaggregation including the impact of the energy price increases of the 1970s on the leading sectors of the boom of the 1950s and 1960s via both income and price elasticities of demand, as well as the emergence from about the mid-1970s of the new round of technologies with quite uneven initial rates of diffusion in Japan, the United States, and Western Europe.

In short, growth accounting is a promising method for studying economic progress; but, like mainstream economic theory and the statistical morphology of growth of which it is a branch, it has not yet developed a grip on the process by which new technologies are generated and diffused.

A Final Reflection

My final reflection on this admirable, highly disciplined body of statistical and analytic literature is advanced tentatively because it so patently reflects my own biases and experience. As an economic historian I am, by profession, impressed with the uniqueness of each story of national growth, the large deviations from average behavior of the data that aim to define uniformities, and the critical character of the residual black boxes that statistical methods of the greatest sophistication give little promise of penetrating. As a development economist, asked to analyze and prescribe for nations in every developing region, over a period of more than 30 years, I know for certain how essential it is to examine the unique characteristics of each case rather than to read off prescriptions from statistical averages. And a critical part of uniqueness can only be established by a detailed knowledge of the developing nation's history—political, social, cultural, as well as economic.

What follows? In addition to educating our students in what the statisticians in the Colin Clark tradition can provide, economists should study and teach the histories of the major economies. Once that approach is taken, the kinds of questions that have troubled the friendly critics of Chenery's work become answerable: why Egypt's development performance differs from South Korea's; how Mason's "cultural, political, and administrative elements" enter into the development process; why technological absorptive capacity differs among societies at different periods of time; and what and why the sequence of absorption from the technological backlog was what it was.

Is this an impossible dream? I think not. In Part Five of *The World Economy* I tell tersely the story of twenty economies covering about two-thirds of the world's population as of the mid-1970s, perhaps 80% of gross global product. I have no doubt the job could be done differently and better. But I am sure it is not an exaggeration to assert that it is possible to get to know well some such group of countries and their development histories.

Indeed, it may well be that, with the passage of time, the analytic histories of national growth sponsored or inspired by Kuznets's SSRC project will be valued at least as highly as the assembly of statistics of average behavior. In any case, I believe it is only by getting to know these stories in their uniqueness and complexity, including the critical role of noneconomic variables, and the sequences of increasingly sophisticated leading sectors through which the major specific technologies were absorbed, and their changing relationship to the world economy, that we will be able to round out our knowledge of the growth process and its dynamics. Now, it is true, as thoughtful scholars and artists have long reminded us, that human beings, as well as countries, are unique; but there are many fewer countries than men, women, and children; and it is possible to get to know those countries containing the bulk of the world's population like old friends. Such knowledge will, I am confident, tell us vastly more than all the average statistical data, even data manipulated with sophistication, that we are likely to be able to mobilize.

17

Development Economics

To quote again Robert Solow's sardonic *bon mot* in another context, development economics in the first half of the 1980s—like growth modeling and the statistical morphology of growth—exhibited some of the signs of "being ripe for text book treatment." H. W. Arndt set the tone with his 1978 *The Rise and Fall of Economic Growth*.[1] Dudley Seers followed along with his "The Birth, Life, and Death of Development Economics" in 1979.[2] The first chapter in Albert O. Hirschman's *Essays in Trespassing* (1981) is "The Rise and Decline of Development Economics."[3] The Twentieth Century Fund commissioned I. M. D. Little to review the literature on economic development, yielding his 1982 *Economic Development: Theory, Policy, and International Relations*—a kind of critical memorial service—followed shortly by Deepak Lal's *The Poverty of Development Economics*.[4] In 1983 the World Bank, sensing that it stood at some kind of intellectual as well as policy crossroads, reached back to evoke from ten "pioneers in development" of the 1950s the story of how their views had emerged, their retrospective assessment of them, and how they viewed development problems and policy as of the early 1980s.[5] The resultant volume contains a historical survey of the emergence of development economics by Gerald Meier as well as an analytic postscript (if not post mortem) by Paul Streeten on "Development Dichotomies."[6] And, in the midst of this sense that momentum and direction had been lost, W. Arthur Lewis took note and took stock with his usual acute, temperate good cheer in a presidential address before the American Economic Association on December 29, 1983, entitled "The State of Development Theory." It set the stage as follows:[7]

> However defined, Development Economics is said to be now in the doldrums, after a couple of spirited decades. It seems to be true that the subject has been deserted by American Ph.D. students. Their antennae tell them where to find the best jobs. In this contest, Development Economics no longer competes. Foreign aid has been cut, the multilateral institutions cannot keep up with the inflation, and the Ford Foundation has changed its priorities.

Lewis went on gently to remind American economists that their rapid shifts in fashion and priority are not universally shared, and that development economics remain alive and well among third-world students.

The development economists who emerged in the post-1945 years came at the subject from many directions. What they shared was a concern for policy rooted, in turn, in a mixture of moral commitment and what might be called historical excitement at the drama of intensified efforts at modernization that began to unfold in Asia, the Middle East, Latin America, and Africa.

To a significant degree the policy-oriented aspects of the work of the statistical morphologists of growth and of the econometric planners converged with issues of development policy. And they were drawn to their work by much the same motives as the more conventional development economists. But there is a distinction to be drawn. The former group aimed to establish what particular methods might achieve in the analysis of and prescription for economic growth. The development economists were less inhibited. This does not mean they were free of methodological preconceptions or bias. No one is; and the contrary was the case for a quite specific reason. For almost all the major pioneering figures, development economics was a kind of second marriage or a liaison conducted in parallel with earlier and sometimes ongoing commitments in other directions. In a natural, even inevitable way, these earlier professional commitments and biases are reflected in their work on development. Nevertheless, their approaches to analysis and prescription were more direct and less rigidly constrained by loyalty to particular methods of analysis. And they were a variegated lot. They took hold of the elephant at many different points.

But there was also an important time sequence in the evolution of development economics; and, as one would expect in such an explicitly policy-oriented field, the cast of analysis was linked to events in the active world.

Six Phases in Development and Development Policy

At some risk of oversimplification, I would suggest that the story can be broken into six phases.

First, wartime planning for the postwar. In addition to Folke Hilgerdt's *Industrialization and Foreign Trade,* this phase yielded three other serious studies: Paul Rosenstein-Rodan's 1943 "Problems of Industrialization of Eastern and Southeastern Europe"[8] arising from his work at Chatham House; Eugene Staley's 1944 *World Economic Development: Effects on Advanced Industrial Countries,* commissioned by the International Labour Office;[9] and Kurt Mandelbaum's (later, Martin) 1945 *The Industrialisation of Backward Areas,* a product of a wider research project on problems of international reconstruction initiated in Oxford by a Joint Committee of Nuffield College and the Institute of Statistics.[10] Rodan's ten pages remain a justly famous pioneering contribution to the theory of development, to which we shall return (following, pp. 408–411). Staley's substantial monograph, rooted in a research program at the Fletcher School of Law and Diplomacy on "The Economics of Transition and Adaptation," remains a remarkably fresh and germane tract for the 1980s and beyond. He addressed an important part of his wide-ranging survey, without reference to Hume or Adam Smith, to the rich-country–poor-country problem. His objective was, in the end, to define policies that would yield the greatest mutual benefit to advanced industrial and developing countries. With the assistance of economists and statisticians in the U.S. Department of Commerce, Staley drove home with a barrage of historical data the first of the two basic truths Hume had recognized; i.e., growth in less advanced countries leads to an increased demand for imports from more advanced countries. He then analyzed the processes of industrial adaptation required in both groups of countries. His prescription for an "advanced industrial country,'' for example, might come from an enlightened Japanese, U.S., or Western European policy statement of 1989.[11]

The basic principles of a positive adaptation policy such as each advanced industrial country might apply to advantage within its own borders are:

1. To encourage expansion of the stronger and more promising industries and contraction of the weaker and less promising ones (unless the latter, by drastic enough changes in techniques, can so increase their efficiency and improve their prospects as to cease to be 'weaker' industries).
2. To assist the transfer of workers and capital from less promising to more promising lines. . . .
3. To protect persons and communities against serious loss of income and employment arising out of a reorientation of production which is in the social interest, but not to protect them against the necessity of making adjustments.

Mandelbaum's study, like Rodan's essay, takes the "backward areas" of Eastern and Southeastern Europe as its focus; i.e., Bulgaria, Greece, Hungary, Poland, Rumania, and Yugoslavia. But his objective—again like Rodan's—was wider: to use "this corner of Europe" to explore the pathology of "population pressure, poverty, and lack of industries" wherever they might be found.[12] Drawing on relationships roughly established by Colin Clark's *The Conditions of Economic Progress* and using a circular flow, Leontief input–output table, Mandelbaum provided a 5-year industrialization plan for the region. The plan includes capital requirements from domestic and foreign sources, that would absorb excess population as measured, notably, by concealed unemployment in the countryside. This *tour de force* was achieved by excluding the problem of carrying out the defined policy objective; by using Marshallian short-period assumptions (e.g., assuming fixed labor productivity and savings rate); and by neglecting changes in agriculture. Nevertheless, Mandelbaum's is an interesting pioneer exercise in development planning.[13]

On a larger stage, the pressure of a handful of developing countries represented at Bretton Woods succeeded in getting "Development" into the name and concept of the World Bank; the Food and Agriculture and International Trade Organizations came into being with an agenda of interest to developing countries; and, shortly after the war, the regional economic commissions for Asia and the Far East and Latin America were set up.[14]

Despite these institutional developments, the immediate focus of postwar attention among the advanced industrial countries of the Atlantic was Europe and, for economic policy and economists, the recovery of Europe. This preoccupation was resented in the developing continents; but large parts of the Middle East and Asia were caught up in civil war (e.g., China) and in various more or less violent forms of disengagement from colonialism. Meanwhile, Latin America was enjoying a phase of favorable terms of trade and was a good deal less vocal than it was to be after the post-1951 relative price shift.

The second phase in the evolution of thought and policy on economic development centers on the hinge period 1948–1949, when the setting for policy and thought swung away from European reconstruction toward the developing regions. A group of quite independent situations and events converged to heighten the priority accorded development policy in the United States and Western Europe and to enlarge the cast of characters engaged in development analysis:

- With the passage by the Congress of the Marshall Plan legislation in 1948 and the German currency reform, the recovery of Western Europe appeared assured. The Anglo-American airlift appeared a viable response to the Berlin blockade imposed by the Russians over the autumn and winter of 1948–1949.
- In Asia, however, Mao was clearly on his way to victory in China, and guerrilla warfare broke out in Malaya, Burma, the Philippines, and Indonesia, adding to the anxiety created by the war in Indochina that had begun in 1946.
- Meanwhile, India and Pakistan emerged as separate and independent states with development evidently high on their agendas.
- The sharp U.S. recession of 1948–1949, begun at the close of 1948, induced a relative decline in basic commodity prices, sending a tremor through Latin America and other basic commodity exporting areas.

All these strands, taken together, shifted, as it were, both the demand and supply curves for foreign aid. Just as the League of Nations and International Labor Office had led the way with wartime staff work, the United Nations General Assembly, with its global constituency, reflected the interests of the less developed countries at this critical juncture. The first response came at a wintry meeting in Paris, at the Palais de Chaillot late in 1948. While one group sought to keep the Soviet Union and the three Western powers in negotiation over the Berlin blockade, others, including ardent U.N. secretariat members, lobbied successfully for a small technical assistance program. On January 20, 1949, out of the same broad setting, came President Truman's Point Four, the first American initiative in support of development, also a technical assistance program. Its broad purposes as stated in the spacious language of an Inaugural Address, far outstripped the limited proposal itself and the still more limited action of the Congress. But it clearly constituted a turning point in Western policy and had a substantial resonance and influence. It was also in this turning-point phase that the World Bank made its first loans to developing countries: Chile (1948), Mexico and Brazil (1949). The Colombo Plan, an Australian concept embraced by London and the Commonwealth, was set in motion in 1950, providing modest but useful measures of technical assistance to a good many developing countries.

A protracted third phase began when momentum in policy was broken by the outbreak of the Korean War. That war not only yielded a large increase in military expenditures in the United States but also diverted foreign aid toward security as opposed to development purposes for the better part of a decade.[15] Paradoxically it was in this distorted setting that the most creative phase of thought about development and development policy began. It ran through the 1950s and can be viewed as comprising three elements: concepts and debates about foreign aid policy; development policy itself; and concepts and debates about development theory.

The accession to power in China of the Communists in October 1949 and Mao's lean-to-one-side policy of close association with the U.S.S.R. focused high-level thought on the economic as well as military and political aspects of containment, yielding thoughtful speeches by Secretary of State Dean Acheson on Asia in January and March 1950, before the outbreak of the Korean War. A committee headed by Gordon Gray, reporting in November 1950, examined sympathetically the case for development assistance outside the framework of military alliances. Nelson Rockefeller's March 1951 report "Partners in Progress" focused on Latin America in similar terms.[16]

At the United Nations, a succession of three expert international committees made the case for enlarged assistance to developing countries: *National and International Measure for Full Employment* (1949), in which development aid appeared in a secondary role; *Measures for Economic Development of Under-Developed Countries* (1951), providing a head-on case for greatly enlarged official lending to developing countries; and *Measures for International Economic Stability* (1951), focused on the poorer developing countries, including support for measures to reduce basic commodity price fluctuations as well as to enlarge capital flows from abroad.[17] Meanwhile, Raúl Prebisch, who set up shop for the Economic Commission for Latin America in Santiago, Chile, in 1950, had found his distinctive voice a year earlier in *The Economic Development of Latin America and Its Principal Problems.*[18]

Given its relative importance in international development policy in the 1950s—since greatly diminished—the United States was the scene of the crucial debate on assistance to the developing regions. Briefly, from the beginning to the end of the Eisenhower administration (1953–1961) a running bureaucratic and political battle over development policy occurred.[19] It engaged not only contesting personalities and agencies within the administration but also the Congress, the press, a wide array of voluntary associations, and, of course, a lively segment of the academic community. The debate was by no means confined to Americans. Barbara Ward and P. T. Bauer, for example, were distinguished participants at polar ends of the spectrum. Out of the protracted interaction of these groups came a good deal of what might be called analytic-policy literature of which the MIT Center for International Studies (CENIS) *A Proposal: Key to an Effective Foreign Policy* was one example and Bauer's polemic against development assistance to India another.[20]

In the latter years of the 1950s, under the impact of a complex set of circumstances, the policy of the Eisenhower administration, in the grip of Hamletian indecision since 1953, began to move toward support for enlarged development assistance. A shift of personalities within the administration, Sputnik, an initial romantic misinterpretation of Mao's Great Leap Forward, the cumulative corrosive effects on the developing regions of relatively falling basic commodity prices since 1951, the acute discomfiture of Vice President Nixon on a trip to Latin America, and, perhaps, at the margin, the long-winded doggedness of the development crusaders—all played a part. But the fact is that before the third phase ended, with the inauguration of John Kennedy, the U.S. Development Loan Fund existed, as well as the World Bank's soft-loan window, the International Development Association (IDA), the Inter-American Development Bank, and World Bank consortia in support of India and Pakistan. In addition, Eisenhower, as a departing act, perhaps influenced by the sight of and his reception in India, on his final trip abroad, sent a budget to the Congress with a 30% increase in development assistance—an act he had refused for 8 years—easing Kennedy's task.[21]

I would underline again that though the policy debate in the United States and its resolution, as the decade came to a close and Kennedy came to power, was crucial, neither the debate nor the policy outcome was purely American. In fact the trend of the 1950s was increasingly to engage Western Europe and then Japan in development aid. That was, for example, one explicit purpose of the Senate Resolutions of 1958–1959, sponsored by then Senator John Kennedy and his Republican colleague John Sherman Cooper in support of sustained development assistance to India and Pakistan. It was reflective of the trend and the future that the three wise men who were sent out to Asia in 1960 by the World Bank in the wake of the Kennedy–Cooper Resolution were a Briton (Oliver Franks), a German (Herman Abs), and an American (Alan Sproul); and, by common consent, Franks was the leader of the enterprise. A pioneering World Bank international consortium arrangement followed.

The period of intense policy conflict in Washington, yielding a modest positive result at its close, was also the period of greatest creativity in development theory. Hirschman notes the element of paradox; for development policy and growth rates accelerated in the fourth phase as the "liveliness" of development economics diminished:[22]

> The forties and especially the fifties saw a remarkable outpouring of funda-
> mental ideas and models which were to dominate the new field and to gener-
> ate controversies that contributed much to its liveliness. In that eminently
> "exciting" era, development economics did much better than the object of its
> study, the economic development of the poorer regions of the world, located
> primarily in Asia, Latin America, and Africa.

The fourth phase—the 1960s—was one of activism, progress, and to a degree, disap-pointment. With the extension of World Bank consortia arrangements along lines of the initial Indian model—the Alliance for Progress launched in March 1961 in support of Latin American development, the diffuse but not trivial initiatives of the United Nations Decade of Development, and, above all, President Kennedy's eloquent advocacy of support for development—there was a 27% rise in official development assistance by the OECD countries between 1960 and 1965, a 35% increase by the United States. In the second half of the decade the OECD total fell in part because of the impact on aid of the war between India and Pakistan, in part because the intensified war in Southeast Asia diverted American resources and attention from development, notably in the Congress. Nevertheless, the flow of U.S. aid to Latin America and growth rates there surged, led by Brazil's recovery from the morass into which it had fallen earlier in the decade. The second half of the decade also saw sharply enlarged relative contributions by Western Europe and Japan as well as an increased role for the World Bank and the regional development banks.

A quite substantial group of the intellectual pioneers of the 1950s were caught up in the exciting but sometimes chastening experience of applying their theories within national governments, international institutions, advisory missions, etc.

The fifth phase began with an intellectual revolt against what might be called the orthodox development position of the 1960s that became a political revolt from which the international community has still not recovered.

The intellectual revolt took the form of the "basic-human-needs" strategy. It arose, in turn, from two sources. First, and most important, because in a good many countries high, overall real growth rates were accompanied by considerable mass poverty, by unemploy-ment and partial unemployment, and by other social ills. Second, there was a strand within the "basic-needs" movement of limits to growth doctrine; that to preserve the human habitat, growth must stop, income be redistributed, and real income be stabilized at a level that would provide for basic human needs. There was also, sometimes, a touch of romanticism about Mao's China and Castro's Cuba in the exposition of this doctrine.

One of the best and most lucid articulations of the basic-needs doctrine came in response to the report of the Pearson Commission: *Partners in Development: Report of the Commission on International Development (1969).* That report, financed by the World Bank, was an effort to dramatize the need for continuing and even enlarged development assistance at a time when political support in the advanced industrial countries was weakening.

The Pearson Commission recommended that an average growth target for the developing countries of 6% be set for the 1970s; official development assistance be targeted at 0.7% of GNP for the advanced industrial countries with 20% allocated through multi-lateral agencies; and that the terms of ODA be limited to 2% interest (with a 25–40-year maturity). The quantitative target percentage of GNP was twice the current level. In that sense, the Pearson Commission report was quite ambitious.

The report was reviewed at an international conference organized by Columbia University and held at Williamsburg and New York, February 15–21, 1970. These gatherings yielded a document called the Columbia Declaration, which captures well the themes and mood of the basic-needs doctrine:[23]

> In incomes, living standards, economic and political power, one-third of the world has in recent decades been pulling steadily ahead, leaving the remainder of mankind in relative poverty, in many cases to live without clean water, education, basic medical facilities or adequate housing. Yet with modern technology and existing productive capacity, none of this need continue if mankind would develop the will and organization to use the resources at hand. . . . [n]ew objective criteria for effective development assistance are required. . . . Criteria are also needed which focus on the living standards of the bottom quarter of each country's population. We also suggest setting up of a special fund devoted specifically to the fulfillment of social objectives in the areas of education, health, family planning, rural and urban works housing and other related social programs. . . .
>
> Performance criteria should increasingly focus on income distribution, land and tax reform, ineffective trade and exchange rate policies, size of military expenditures, and the promotion of social justice. . . .
>
> International power must increasingly be shared democratically; and this objective can only be attained by strengthening the role of institutions in which the developing economies have a representative vote.

This doctrine was not ignored in the 1970s. The World Bank, for example, under Robert McNamara's direction, allocated increased resources for social purposes and conducted sophisticated analyses of the relationship of poverty and excessively skewed income distribution to aggregate and sectoral growth rates. A great deal of both poverty and abnormally skewed income distribution was, in fact, linked to excessive rates of population increase and inadequate attention of governments to agriculture and to the modernization of rural life. Inadequate tax collection and the diversion of governments' funds to a variety of dubious subsidies (thus constraining allocations for health, education, and other important social purposes) also played a role.

Where birthrates were rapidly declining and agricultural productivity and the modernization of rural life taken seriously, the lowest 20% of the population received proportions of total income comparable to distribution patterns in advanced industrial countries; e.g., South Korea and Taiwan.

Despite these deeper forces that largely determined the social outcome in developing nations, the rise of the basic-human-needs doctrine undoubtedly led to some reallocation of national and international development resources and, perhaps equally important, to intensified analyses of the anatomy of poverty in developing countries.

But the fact is that during the 1970s the governments of the advanced industrial countries rejected not only the high objectives and demands of the Columbia Declaration but also the targets of the Pearson Commission report. The proportion of collective OECD GNP allocated to ODA remained, essentially, static: it was .34% in both 1970 and 1979.

This outcome—part of the fifth phase—was the result of a sequence of traumatic events in the world economy and in North–South political relations:

- The breakdown of the Bretton Woods system followed by the explosion of grain and then oil prices in the period 1971–1974.
- The consequent phase of stagflation in the OECD world definitively ending the protracted boom of the 1950s and 1960s, diverting also the attention of economists of the North away from development to problems nearer home.
- A brief phase of euphoria among a good many economists and politicians of the South based on the hope that the transient success of OPEC in diverting enormous resources from the North via the rise in the oil price might be repeated in other sectors. This reached its peak in the April 1974 cacophonous special session of the United Nations General Assembly. The mood quickly gave way to sober second thoughts as it became apparent that the oil-importing countries of the South were the major victims of high oil prices as well as the sharp depression imposed by those prices on the North. But this interval left behind its legacy in the form of heightened emphasis on the New International Economic Order (NIEO), an enterprise which proved peculiarly sterile—even counterproductive—over the next generation of North–South diplomacy.
- Development in a good many countries of the South was nevertheless carried forward by their own resources, supported by continued purposeful efforts in a rather distracted international community by the World Bank and the Latin American and Asian development banks; but, even more, by radically expanded private lending by the banking system of the North based on the transfer of excess petrodollars that could not be productively invested in the rather sluggish OECD economies.

The sixth phase was launched with the second oil shock of 1979–1980 stemming from the Iranian revolution. The excessive rise in oil prices and subsequent radical decline dried up the flow of petrodollars as a basis of private lending to the South; and the sharp deceleration of the OECD economies and high U.S. interest rates further attenuated the capacity of some important economies of the South to maintain import levels consistent with high growth rates. In this setting of chronic crisis for some, slow growth or anxiety for all but a few others, the international development policy agenda was dominated by unsustainable debts, rising protectionism in the OECD countries, and other urgent specific problems.

As Hirschman and most others who have reflected on the evolution of development theory observed, the 1970s and 1980s did not generate much that was new and vital. But there were two quite distinct—even conflicting—elements in the literature: a heightened effort by dependency theorists, focused on the alleged dominance of the industrialized "core" over the less-developed "periphery," to drive home their quasi-Marxist propositions; and a progressive disabuse with central economic planning and a symmetrical heightening of respect for the virtues of allocation and pricing via competitive markets. The former strand was strengthened by frustrations of some developing countries with debt burdens, as well as slow growth and rising protectionism in the OECD world; the latter, by gathering lessons of painful experience in both socialist and nonsocialist societies, as well as the palpable increase in the difficulty of planning intelligently at the

Table 17.1. Average Performance of Industrial and Developing Countries, 1965–1985 (average annual percentage change)

Country group	1965–1973	1973–1980	1980–1985
Industrial Countries			
GDP	4.7	2.8	2.2
Inflation rate[a]	5.1	8.3	−0.3
Real interest rate[b,c]	2.5	0.7	6.7
Nominal lending rate[c]	5.8	8.4	12.0
Developing countries			
GDP growth	6.6	5.4	3.3
Low-income countries			
Africa	3.9	2.7	0.9
Asia	5.9	5.0	7.8
Middle-income oil exporters	7.1	5.8	1.4
Middle-income oil importers			
Major exporters of manufactures	7.6	5.9	2.1
Other oil-importing countries	5.4	4.5	1.7
Export growth	5.0	4.6	4.1
Manufactures	11.6	13.8	7.9
Primary goods	3.8	1.1	1.4
Import growth	5.8	5.9	0.9

NOTE: Projected growth rates are based on a sample of ninety developing countries.

[a]Industrial countries' weighted GDP deflator expressed in U.S. dollars. Inflation in the United States is 3.0% per year in the High case and 5.7% in the Low case. But for the industrial countries as a whole, it is higher in dollars because of an assumed depreciation of the dollar between 1985 and 1990.

[b]Average for 6-month U.S. dollar Eurocurrency rates deflated by the rate of change in the GDP deflator of the United States.
[c]Average annual rate.
SOURCE: World Bank, *World Development Report, 1986*, p. 43.

national level as many countries moved into the increasingly diversified and sophisticated sectors of the drive to technological maturity. Nevertheless, development itself did not stop.

I would note here three powerful trends: the high momentum of the 1970s as well as 1960s that took the more advanced developing countries beyond takeoff into the drive to technological maturity, (''middle income'' level in World Bank parlance, Tables 17.1 and 17.2); the dramatic expansion of technological absorptive capacity reflected in data on education (Table 17.3); and the evidently enlarged capacity of some developing countries to produce and export competitively increasingly diversified and sophisticated manufactures (Table 17.4). In addition, led by India and China, some developing countries came, at last, to understand the critical role of agriculture in modernization and radically altered farm policy with remarkably positive results. These tables suggest the division in the developing world between countries that have moved beyond takeoff into the drive to technological maturity and those that have not yet made it into takeoff.

Development Pioneers

The literature on economic development that burgeoned after 1945 is so extensive that, I will take as more or less representative nine of the ten ''pioneers in development'' chosen for the World Bank's first volume thus entitled.[24] The arbitrariness of the Bank's initial

Table 17.2. Growth of GDP per Capita, 1965–1985
(average annual percentage change)

Country group	1965–1973	1973–1980	1980–1985
Industrial countries	3.7	2.1	1.7
Developing countries	4.0	3.2	1.3
Low-income countries	3.0	2.7	5.2
Africa	1.2	−0.1	−2.0
Asia	3.2	3.0	5.9
Middle-income oil exporters	4.5	3.1	−1.1
Middle-income oil importers	4.5	3.2	−0.1
Major exporters of manufactures	5.2	3.7	0.2
Other oil-importing countries	2.8	2.1	−0.8

NOTE: Projected growth rates are based on a sample of ninety developing countries.
SOURCE: World Bank, *World Development Report, 1986*, p. 45.

selection is suggested by the fact that dissatisfaction with those left out of the first volume resulted in a second, featuring an additional five "pioneers."

This means that I will not deal at any length (or at all) with a good many economists who contributed important strands to the development literature.

There was, for example, Jacob Viner, who not only argued, as might be expected, the fundamental importance of agriculture and foreign trade in development but also brought to bear a less remembered strand in the classics: a passionate Marshallian revolt against poverty including the memorable statement: "The first requirements for high labour productivity under modern conditions are that the masses of the population shall be literate, healthy, and sufficiently well fed to be strong and energetic."[25] On trade there is also the work of Hla Myint arguing elegantly for the importance of exports on "vent for

Table 17.3. Secondary and Higher Education in Developing Nations:
1960 and 1982

	Number enrolled in secondary school as percentage of age group		Number enrolled in higher education as percentage of population aged 20–24	
	1960	1982	1960	1982
Low-Income Economies	15%	30%	3%	4%
India	20	30	5	9
China	—	35	—	1
Lower-Middle-Income Economies	10	35	4	10
Upper-Middle-Income Economies	20	51	5	14
Republic of Korea	27	89	6	24
Brazil	11	32	2	12
Mexico	11	54	4	15
Argentina	23	59	14	25
Hong Kong	20	67	5	11
Singapore	32	66	10	11
Industrial Market Economies	64%	85%	16%	37%

SOURCE: *World Bank Development Report, 1984*, pp. 266–267, and 1986, pp. 236–237.

Table 17.4. Change in Trade in Developing Countries, 1965–1985 (average annual percentage change)

Country group	Exports of goods			Exports of manufactures			Exports of primary goods			Imports of goods		
	1965–1973	1973–1980	1980–1985	1965–1973	1973–1980	1980–1985	1965–1973	1973–1980	1980–1985	1965–1973	1973–1980	1980–1985
Developing countries	5.0	4.6	4.1	11.6	13.8	7.9	3.8	1.1	1.4	5.8	5.9	0.9
Low-income countries	1.9	5.4	5.0	2.3	8.3	7.4	1.6	3.6	3.1	0.8	6.1	5.9
Africa	4.6	1.3	-1.5	5.4	2.0	-2.1	4.5	1.2	-1.5	3.4	2.1	-3.0
Asia	0.6	6.8	6.6	2.0	8.7	7.8	-0.6	5.2	5.4	-0.5	7.7	8.2
Middle-income oil exporters	4.3	0.0	1.2	10.7	8.0	15.4	4.2	-0.4	-0.1	3.7	9.1	-2.0
Middle-income oil importers	7.1	9.0	5.6	15.5	15.3	7.4	3.8	3.3	2.8	8.0	4.7	0.9
Major exporters of manufactures	9.2	10.6	5.9	15.6	15.9	7.0	5.5	3.8	3.6	9.6	4.8	1.1
Other oil-importing countries	2.4	3.5	4.3	14.8	9.1	13.0	1.2	2.4	1.4	3.6	4.3	0.0

NOTE: Historical growth rates of volume of international trade reflect revisions in the nominal trade figures, as well as revisions in the methodology of calculating trade deflators.
SOURCE: World Bank, *World Development Report, 1986*, pp. 48–49.

surplus'' rather than comparative-costs grounds.[26] Then there was Ragnar Nurkse's case for balanced growth rooted in J. S. Mill's interpretation of Say's Law.[27] J. R. Hicks's *A Theory of Economic History* in a different way also deals with how traditional societies become modern, using the primal case of Great Britain. In first approximation he makes the transition from handicraft to modern manufactures with a comfortable mainstream (but also Marxist) economist's distinction. He argues that it is the rise in the relative importance of fixed relative to working capital and the increased range of the former which defines ''the change we are considering.''[28] But he then brings himself up short:[29] ''Surely there is something more.'' It turns out to be science. The four best pages in the book (in my view) then follow as a first-rate mainstream theorist wrestles with the problem most of them ignore: the links between science, invention, and innovation. The result is indecisive and not wholly convincing. But it is a memorable moment.

There were, of course, a good many others with distinctive things to say. The objective point to be made here is that the author's—and no doubt the reader's—consciousness of what is left out of this portion of the book reflects a fact of some significance: the flowering of theories of development in the 1950s and 1960s yielded the richest body of growth literature since the eighteenth century.

Although the nine officially but arbitrarily chosen ''pioneers'' do not represent a full spectrum, they constitute a reasonable sample. Table 17.5, presented in the same only semi-serious mood as Table 1.1, suggests a few limited aspects of their professional lives.

Table 17.5. Nine "Pioneers of Development"

Name	Date of birth	Date of first publication on development	Pre-Development interests	Developing countries of influence
P. T. Bauer	1915	1946	Rubber industry in Southeast Asia and organization of trade in British West Africa.	Malaya and West Africa
Colin Clark	1905	1940[a]	National income estimates	India (1928)
Albert O. Hirschman	1915	1958[b]	Postwar reconstruction of Western Europe	Colombia (1952–1956)
W. Arthur Lewis	1915	1944	History of world economy since 1870[c]	Jamaica and Caribbean
Gunnar Myrdal	1898	1955	Welfare Economics	India
Rául Prebisch	1901	1951[d]	Neoclassical economics	Argentina and Latin America
Paul N. Rosenstein-Rodan	1902	1943	Conventional economic theory	Eastern and Southeastern Europe
Hans Singer	1910	1949	U.K. distressed areas, 1930s; welfare economics	Northeast Brazil
Jan Tinbergen	1903	1958	Econometrics; Economic planning in postwar Europe[e]	India (1951); Turkey, Egypt

[a]*Conditions of Economic Progress* written 1935–1939.

[b]Interest begins as result of 1951 conference.

[c]Concurrent with development interests.

[d]Advocated Argentine industrialization as Under Secretary of Finance, 1930–1932, otherwise "firm believer in neoclassical theories." Development views first published in 1950–1951 ECLA studies.

[e]Development interest foreshadowed by 1942 paper on trend movements.

Table 17.5 underlines a few characteristics, of uneven importance, perhaps worth noting:

- Colin Clark is the only economist born in Great Britain; although at least four others were strongly influenced by British economists and economics of the 1930s. There is no American among the nine.
- On the whole, development economics was not the central interest of the members of the group in Schumpeter's critical third, "sacred decade"; although Arthur Lewis, with his 1944 economic plan for Jamaica, is an exception and Peter Bauer comes close with his Colonial Office studies of the rubber industry in Malaya and trade in British West Africa begun in the 1940s.
- In virtually every case, one can trace a strand of continuity between each pioneer's later perspective on development and his prior professional interest, his initial experience in particular developing countries, or both.
- Without exception the problems directly observed in the developing countries of initial interest were those of preconditions for takeoff or of takeoff itself. This fact left definable marks on the pioneers' various development theories; but several of those who stayed with the field of development economics generated propositions relating to the post-takeoff stage—the drive to technological maturity.

Against this general background, notes follow on each of the pioneers in alphabetical order. Because his approach to development was more general, covers more variables, and is more explicitly grounded in classical growth theory and economic history, Arthur Lewis is treated at somewhat greater length than the others. But in all cases, the purpose is not to write a definitive scholarly essay. It is, first, to evoke something of each economist's unique approach to development, and to indicate briefly a view of his contribution from my own quite arbitrary perspective.

P. T. Bauer

The link between a formative experience in developing regions and subsequent development doctrine is nowhere more lucid than in the case of Peter Bauer. He observed closely and over substantial periods of time the positive effects on the real income of the inhabitants of rubber growing in Malaya and the raising of cocoa and other cash crops in West Africa. He observed also the flexibility and resilience of the trading networks that operated in those places. All this put him in head-on opposition to what he regarded as "the tenets of the development orthodoxy of the 1950s," which he defines as follows:[30]

> External trade is at best ineffective for the economic advance of less developed countries (LDCs), and more often it is damaging. Instead, the advance of LDCs depends on ample supplies of capital to provide for infrastructure, for the rapid growth of manufacturing industry, and for the modernization of their economies and societies. The capital required cannot be generated in the LDCs themselves because of the inflexible and inexorable constraint of low incomes (the vicious circle of poverty and stagnation), reinforced by the international demonstration effect, and by the lack of privately profitable investment opportunities in poor countries with their inherently limited local markets. General backwardness, economic unresponsiveness, and lack of enterprise are well-nigh universal within the less developed world. Therefore,

if significant economic advance is to be achieved, governments have an indispensable as well as a comprehensive role in carrying through the critical and large-scale changes necessary to break down the formidable obstacles to growth and to initiate and sustain the growth process.

By this route, going to war against his private definition of orthodoxy, Bauer became an ardent polemicist: first, in an assault on the marketing boards of the late British colonial era in West Africa taken over by the postcolonial governments. He regarded these boards as instruments of taxation to finance graft and low-productivity government expenditures. He then moved on to become the leading intellectual opponent of foreign aid and of virtually any public intervention in the market process, even with respect to limitation of family size.

In conducting his polemics, Bauer's method has been to isolate his targets by name, if possible, and to go after them hammer and tongs, using where available, selected quotations that incorporate the offending views in their most egregious and attackable form. He developed a gallery of favorite villains: Kwame Nkrumah (for his feckless and wastrel economic policies); Julius Nyerere (for his creation of a low-productivity collectivized agriculture); Professor P. C. Mahalanobis and the Indian Second Five-Year Plan (for its exaggerated emphasis on expansion of the capital goods industries); perhaps above all, the designers and supporters of the New International Economic Order, which incorporates just about all the major economic and political doctrines and attitudes that Bauer despises. I should note that among his villains are the "MIT development economists," of whom I was one in the 1950s; and he is quite correct in his judgment that although we also disagreed with most of his other villains, our image of the development process and an appropriate development policy differed substantially from his.

High-value plantation agriculture in Malaya and West Africa was not, of course, a sufficient base for generalizing a satisfactory theory of and program for development. But there are, evidently, serious and correct insights in the Bauer position; for example, the shrewd and quick responsiveness of farmers to incentives and disincentives, the superiority of competitive private over public trading systems. And, like a number of his contemporaries, he came increasingly to appreciate the tendency of politics and power in developing (as in developed) countries to enjoy higher priority than economic progress.

As a development theorist, Bauer exhibited an awareness of two kinds of complexity: the complexity of interactions within the economic system, and the complexity of interactions among the economic, social, and political sectors of society. And there are asides in his work that reflect an awareness of the power of tribe, race, caste, and culture in economic arrangements, notably in dealing with Africa and India. His knowledge of the other developing regions appears thin. But Bauer never organized his more subtle perceptions about societies as a whole and related them systematically to the economic process. There is a gap between the market economist and the wider but somewhat casual commentator on the human condition. In the end, Bauer seemed most comfortable as the neoclassical gadfly on the rump of what he regarded as the international liberal establishment.

As I wrote on another occasion:[31] "If Professor Bauer did not exist it would have been useful to invent him. . . . Surely, issues as inherently complex as growth theory and policy, as ramified in their linkage to politics, and as emotionally charged, needed a devil's advocate." On the other hand, he failed to take adequately into account the extremely large and inescapable role of the state in early phases of development in providing infrastructure investment and a rapidly expanding educational system; in encouraging enlarged agricultural output and foreign exchange; and in stimulating the emergence of a competent corps of private industrial entrepreneurs.

Colin Clark

I have already noted the oblique and somewhat casual way Colin Clark moved from his absorbing work on British national income statistics to pick up and carry forward Marshall's unfulfilled dream with his *Conditions of Economic Progress* (1940, 1951). His first pre-1939 vicarious acquaintance with the problems of a developing country was with India (via Austin and Joan Robinson and V. K. R. V. Rao); and his first direct, on-the-ground experience was also with India, as he responded in 1947 to an invitation of the Indian Planning Commission to report on that country's prospects for economic development. His subsequent direct knowledge was almost wholly derived from visits to India and other countries of the subcontinent.

As in his work on national income, Clark's controlling objective as a development economist was to enlarge and classify empirical knowledge.[32] In fact, he took the somewhat eccentric view that ''there is room for two or three economic theorists in each generation, not more.'' This inner commitment evidently did not prevent Clark from producing theoretical and speculative hypotheses about the determinants of the investment rate, the causes of business cycles, and trends in relative prices and the terms of trade. Similarly, despite the extraordinary energy and labor required to assemble, render roughly comparable, and analyze in formal statistical terms the data incorporated in the two editions of the *Conditions of Economic Progress,* Clark generated original, often controversial propositions about development. In his own way he was as much of a dissenter as, say, the self-proclaimed dissenter, Albert Hirschman.

Clark did not construct a general theory of economic growth and development. It was not his style. But it would not be difficult to link the following five substantive propositions into a reasonably coherent and unified theoretical framework.

1. *Increasing returns and the public-sector role in development.* Colin Clark was rooted in Pigou's welfare economics, based in turn on Marshallian analysis. Out of that tradition came, for example, G. T. Jones's excellent 1933 study, *Increasing Return,*[33] with which Clark had an important editorial connection. Thus, it was natural for Clark to argue a point that also figured significantly in the germinal propositions of Paul Rosenstein-Rodan; namely, that the existence of increasing returns may compromise the universal case for competitive private capitalism in both foreign and domestic economic policy.[34]

> What breaks down the *laissez-faire* argument is that economic fact which has also been one of the principal sources of the world's enrichment—namely the existence of Increasing Returns. . . .
>
> With Increasing Returns a valid case *may* arise for economic nationalism or protectionism. . . . [U]nder certain circumstances a country can enrich itself by interfering with the *laissez-faire* flow of international trade in order to build up increasing-returns industries. . . .
>
> There is no case for introducing public ownership or control into industries where competition is already functioning freely without causing the majority of businesses to operate below average cost unless we have good grounds for

believing that markedly increasing returns could be obtained by organising businesses on a scale so large as to be beyond the reach of any conceivable competitive enterprise.

2. *Agriculture and Industry in Economic Development*. Clark, more than most of the pioneers, had a lively sense of what agriculture was all about. His comparative study of agriculture in developing regions began as early as 1935 and continued over the next 20 years and beyond. In his *Pioneers* essay, for example, he quotes with evident relish the rather surprising views of Mahatma Gandhi:[35]

> Gandhi (nobody will believe this) proved to be a convinced free-market economist, strongly critical of the price controls, rationing, and compulsory purchase of farm crops which the Nehru government was then introducing. The right solution, he said, was to raise the price of food, then everyone would have to work harder. The source of India's troubles was that the people were thoroughly idle.

Clark also attacks the views of those who misread the operational meaning of the declining proportion of the working force in agriculture with a rise in per capita income to mean that the expansion of industrial employment (and neglect of agriculture) "would automatically enrich the country."[36] And in further thinly disguised attack on the Indian scientist-economic planner of the 1950s, P. C. Mahalanobis, he observed, when his opinion was sought, that the question of whether India should expand its steel capacity was "a problem in comparative religion."[37] Clark's positive view, which had evolved in quasi-mathematical form by the early 1960s, was that improvements in agricultural productivity were a necessary condition for industrial development.[38]

> Both international comparisons and time series indicated that a rising proportion of the labor force in nonfarm occupations was only possible if agricultural productivity not only rose, but rose at an increasing pace. . . . The only exceptions were when a developing country could produce what we labeled "food substitutes"—mineral or forest products, or occasionally manufactures, which could be exported to world markets—and would bring in food imports which could partially substitute for the productivity of the country's own agriculture. . . . You cannot employ an industrial population if you cannot feed them. In addition, economic development necessitates an increasing volume of imports (though many planners seem to have neglected this issue). These have to be paid for, and in most developing countries (apart from the exceptions mentioned above) the only possible exports are agricultural products.

3. *Idle Agricultural Labor*. One of Clark's most iconoclastic views was that in low-productivity agricultural countries there was, except seasonally, no surplus labor. With respect to China, for example, the data showed the normal situation was one of labor shortage except for the cold months of December and January:[39] "After all, to put it simply, if you are going to cultivate a country the size of China with hand hoes—very few draft animals and still fewer tractors were available—you are going to need the labor of something like 600 million people." He cites the cost to production and collection of the harvest by diversion of farm labor to industrial activity in the Great Leap Forward of 1958 as a dramatic demonstration of a widespread fallacy.

4. *The Maximum Rate of Increase in Nonfarm Employment.* One engaging characteristic of Colin Clark's professional performance is the ease with which he underlines prior error. He estimated in the early 1950s, for example, primarily on the basis of historical data on Japan, that the maximum sustainable rate of increase in nonfarm employment was 4% per annum. He later pointed out that the estimate proved ''much too cautious,'' citing a steady 8% rate in the Republic of Korea.[40]

5. *Population.* Perhaps the most controversial of Clark's positions is the view to which he came in the post-1945 years that a high rate of population growth could be advantageous to the rate of growth in the real income per capita in a developing country. In the 1940 edition of *The Conditions of Economic Progress* his view was that a high rate of population increase was ''disadvantageous'' in a poor agricultural country.[41] In the course of the 1950s he came to see some advantages in a high rate of population increase, no doubt enjoying yet another assault on the conventional wisdom:[42]

> Nearly everyone then, as indeed most people now, tended to regard population growth as an adverse factor. . . . A fundamental assault on this position was first made by Everett Hagen at the 1953 conference of the Association for Research on Income and Wealth. . . . International comparisons indicated that geographical density of population on the one hand, and its rate of growth on the other, both tended substantially to reduce per-head capital requirements. . . .
>
> Hagen made a further important point. Rapidly growing population has the effect, to use his curious phrase, of ''absolving'' the country from the consequences of errors in investment. . . . But with growing population a mistaken piece of physical investment is much more likely to find an alternative use than in a state of stationary population.

Colin Clark will be primarily remembered, as he would probably wish, for his extraordinarily bold, resourceful, and industrious pioneering in both national income and growth analysis, the bulk of which was ''left entirely to the unaided efforts of a single individual with a number of duties to perform, the only clerical assistance available being that which he cared to pay himself.''[43] A polar opposite to the postwar mainstream economists, he remained loyal to Francis Bacon's dictum on the title page of the first edition of *The Conditions of Economic Progress:* ''It cannot be that axioms established by argumentation can suffice for the discovery of new works, for the subtlety of nature exceedeth many times over the subtlety of argument.'' But his work was no body of shapeless empiricism. The questions he asked of the data arose directly from the line of Marshall and Pigou— and Keynes as well, who ''in reviving the Malthus–Ricardo controversy called in the nineteenth century to redress the balance of the twentieth.''[44] But his revolt extended to Adam Smith as well as Ricardo. In Clark's view, they had, between them, ''twisted out of shape'' the field of economics that ''was started on the right lines by Gregory King and Sir William Petty at the time of that astonishing flowering of the English scientific spirit in the later seventeenth century.''[45] It is certainly with the great political arithmeticians that Colin Clark belongs. And like them, his objective was large and practical:[46] ''To find the conditions under which we can hope for the greatest degree of economic progress in the future.'' But in pursuing this objective, he understood as a welfare economist in the Cambridge tradition not only the complexities of measurement that he confronted but also the inescapable hierarchy of values—philosophical and religious, ethical and political— that framed and properly controlled welfare considerations in all societies.[47]

Albert Hirschman

Hirschman, in the first World Bank *Pioneers* volume, proclaims himself a dissenter. His essay is entitled "A Dissenter's Confession: 'The Strategy of Economic Development' Revisited." His stance set me to reviewing the other nine essays in the volume. In one sense or another, all his co-authors of the major essays also regard themselves as dissenters. It is, therefore, important to define precisely against what Hirschman thought he was dissenting. His own description is the following:[48]

> I . . . saw myself as a rebel against authority, as a second-generation dissenter from the propositions that, while being themselves novel and heterodox, were rapidly shaping up in the 1950s as a new orthodoxy on the problems of development. . . . Viewed in perspective, my dissent, however strong, was in the nature of a demurrer *within* a general movement of ideas attempting to establish development economics as a new field of studies and knowledge. My propositions were at least as distant from the old orthodoxy (later called neoclassical economics) as from the new.

But what was the "new orthodoxy?" It turned out to be the guidance he received from World Bank headquarters when he first went to Colombia, where he was Financial Adviser to the Planning Board and then private consultant in 1952–1956:[49]

> . . . [W]ord soon came from World Bank headquarters that I was principally expected to take, as soon as possible, the initiative in formulating some ambitious economic development plan that would spell out investment, domestic savings, growth, and foreign aid targets for the Colombian economy over the next few years. All of this was alleged to be quite simple for experts mastering the new programming technique: apparently there now existed adequate knowledge, even without close study of local surroundings, of the likely ranges of savings and capital-output ratios, and those estimates, joined to the country's latest national income and balance of payments accounts, would yield all the key figures needed. I resisted being relegated to this sort of programming activity.

In one sense, then, Hirschman's dissent falls into the classic mold of a man in the field reacting against instructions from the ill-informed, insensitive center—one of the truly eternal aspects of bureaucratic history.[50]

The substance of Hirschman's dissenting doctrine is familiar and, in the end, quite simple—by no means a demerit. He perceived that what might be regarded as elements of irrationality or distortion (or lack of balance) in a developing economy might set up powerful incentives to solve problems, thus contributing elements of rationality to the growth process. In retrospect he cited these examples of the mechanism of his own version of the invisible hand.[51]

- Shortages and bottlenecks;
- Capital-intensive industrial processes in an apparently labor-surplus economy;
- pressures on decision makers induced by inflation and balance-of-payments deficits;

- pressures on those responsible for maintenance of a high-technology but potentially life-threatening form of transport (aircraft) versus, say, road transport.
- pressures set up by a commitment to produce a finished product to generate domestic inputs (backward linkages).

All this led to the definition of a Hirschman strategy, which he sets out as follows:[52]

> I now searched for a general economic principle that would tie them (and several related propositions) together. To this end, I suggested that underdeveloped countries need special "pressure mechanisms" or "pacing devices" to bring forth their potential. In my most general formulation I wrote: "development depends not so much on finding optimal combinations for given resources and factors of production as on calling forth and enlisting for development purposes resources and abilities that are hidden, scattered, or badly utilized" (*Strategy*, p. 5).

Hirschman exhibits an admirable sensitivity to the question inevitably posed by his elevation of the virtues and "hidden rationality" of imbalance and distortion:[53] "Would you actually advocate unbalanced growth, capital-intensive investment, inflation, and so on? The honest, if a bit unsatisfactory answer must be: yes, but of course within some fairly strict limits. There is no doubt that the unbalanced growth strategy can be overdone, with dire consequences. . . . But is it not unreasonable to ask the inventor of the internal combustion engine to come up immediately with a design for pollution control and airbags?"

Perhaps. But it is not unreasonable to ask an advocate of unbalanced growth to define his notion of the balance from which he counsels deviation. From Malthus to Arthur Burns and J. M. Clark, in the 1930s, thoughtful analysts have seen economies moving through time, in a quite erratic unbalanced way, marked by lack of balance among the sectors, these imbalances both driving the economy forward and, when excessive, setting in motion corrective responses. But Clark goes on to define 7 criteria for dynamic balance in the context of business-cycle analysis. Hirschman confines himself to implying that a dynamic pattern of sectoral balance exists that would assert itself, through both visible and invisible hands, in the face of imbalance:[54] "Because of the interdependence of the economy in the input–output sense, the expansion of one sector or subsector ahead of the other could be relied on to set forces in motion (relative price changes and public policies in response to complaints about shortages) that would tend to eliminate the initial imbalance."

The fact is that, in evoking his instructions from World Bank headquarters and the major battle he fought "against the then widely alleged need for a 'balanced' or 'big push' industrialization effort," Hirschman (like Bauer) is indulging in caricature. (It was quite possibly Paul Rosenstein-Rodan, then a substantial figure at the World Bank, who sent the offending headquarters cable to the understandably resentful adviser in Bogotá). I have never known a serious development planner who didn't understand that a 5-year plan had to be revised every year at least in the light of unexpected distortions and revealed possibilities and who did not live by the Chinese expression of the concept of crisis as embracing the characters for both danger and opportunity. Further, a good deal of Rosenstein-Rodan's doctrine was based on solid empirical evidence; i.e., that a high proportion of total investment in a developing country goes to infrastructure (say, 35%), much of which is in large discontinuous units (e.g., power plants, irrigation projects, ports) beyond the capacity of domestic private sectors to finance; and, as Adam Smith argued, these have important diffuse external-economy effects which make them profitable for "a great society" if not for the private investor.

There is an element of rediscovering the wheel in Hirschman's shock at finding that history does not move forward along smooth paths with all sectors in dynamic equilibrium. He exhibits little knowledge of the extensive literature on unbalanced growth reaching back to Malthus at least.

But never mind. Like Bauer—but in a quite different way—Hirschman's stance of dissent, evidently comfortable and stimulating for him, proved fruitful. Since the flowering of development economics was concurrent with the heyday of Harrod–Domar and neoclassical growth models, Hirschman's writings were an important reminder of the rather attractive inelegance of men and women performing as social animals. Indeed, as Hirschman reached for his own paradigm, he might well, with appropriate modification, have adopted Gesell's, who found in his insights into human disequilibrium also a bias for hope (preceding, p. 359).

W. Arthur Lewis

Arthur Lewis is unique among our nine pioneers in two major respects: economic development was his first love, the central interest of his sacred decade; and he consciously approached the problem of growth in the spirit of the classics from Adam Smith to J. S. Mill. As he makes quite clear, the two major concepts associated with his name are both rooted in the classics: the anatomy of growth with unlimited supplies of labor, and the fundamental role of increased agricultural productivity in the process of industrialization. The opening sentence of his "Economic Development with Unlimited Supplies of Labour" is worth recalling.[55] "This essay is written in the classical tradition, making the classical assumption, and asking the classical question."

Lewis became a development economist in his twenties. His first publication, at the age of 29, was "An Economic Plan for Jamaica."[56] Several other operational studies focused on the Caribbean followed, and then in 1951 his evidently substantial contribution to the collective United Nations document, *Measures for the Economic Development of Under-Developed Countries*.[57]

But Lewis's interests transcended development. Although he never lost his concern with development policy and, indeed, his loyalty to the Caribbean, he was a well-trained economist of wide interests and with more knowledge of the history of doctrine and of economic history than all but a few of his contemporaries. Three of his books are, in fact, concerned primarily with advanced industrial countries.[58] His approach to growth and development thus combined broadly based scholarship and the operational concern of one who wished to assist the aspiring nations of the postwar world. Lewis put it well in the Preface to his *Theory of Economic Growth*:[59] "It is partly irrepressible curiosity and partly the practical needs of contemporary policy-makers that have driven me to range over this enormous area. . . . Curiosity demands a philosophical enquiry into the processes of human history, while practical need demands a handbook of things to do."

It is wholly understandable that Lewis has written a chapter for a handbook on development economics summarizing how far forward, by standards of the 1980s, the field was taken from Adam Smith to J. S. Mill.[60]

Lewis is also unique among the development economists discussed in this chapter in another respect: his *Economic Growth* is the only study that touches on all the key growth variables. It may, therefore, be useful to indicate briefly how they are introduced.

A. *Population and the Working Force.* Chapter VI of *Economic Growth* is entitled "Population and Resources." It contains a sensitive analysis of the shape of the demographic transition in the post-1945 developing world, with comparative references reaching back to Malthus.[61] Virtually all the complex forces making for an inverse relation between income per capita and the birthrate are set out with considerable emphasis on a demographic variable judged critical since Adam Smith at least—the role of education. He then moves on to consider the balance between population and resources in the various regions of the world and the changing occupational structure of the working force. The latter passage closes on a theme, rooted in the physiocrats and the British classics, which runs, from beginning to end, through Lewis's work (as well as Colin Clark's); i.e., the centrality of a high rate of productivity increase in agriculture to a high overall rate of growth:[62] "The transfer from agriculture to other occupations which occurs with economic growth is the result and not the cause of growth. For it to take place without embarrassment there must be either increasing productivity in agriculture, or else increasing exports of non-agricultural commodities."

Forces determining the quality of the working force are dealt with elsewhere: the will and ability to work in Chapter II ("The Will to Economize"); the role of incentives and disincentives in Chapter III ("Economic Institutions"); the differing aptitudes for disciplined industrial work among societies and as between rural and urban folk in Chapter IV, ("Knowledge"). Education is dealt with, in one form or another, in virtually every chapter, reflecting Lewis's judgment on its critical function in the development process from primary schools to universities.[63]

B. *Capital and Technology.* The structure of *Economic Growth* is shaped by this proposition:[64] "The proximate causes of economic growth are the effort to economize, the accumulation of knowledge, and the accumulation of capital." Technology is treated in Chapter IV ("Knowledge"), capital in the following chapter of that title.

In dealing with knowledge Lewis sharply distinguishes pure science, technical research, development, and production. He also examines the forces making for the rapid or sluggish diffusion of new, commercially viable technologies, taking the story from ancient Greece and China, through the Renaissance, down to Britain of the early 1950s. Under each of his headings he examines major differences between the situation in advanced industrial and developing countries and the consequent differences in their appropriate priorities.

Lewis's section on knowledge closes with a passage in praise of competition as a goad to innovation evocative of J. S. Mill and Alfred Marshall:[65]

> Indeed commercial life itself will probably be more vigorous in countries where public administration is decentralized and democratic, where the people are used to managing their own affairs at every level, from the village upward, than in countries where political power is vested in an oligarchy. This is also one of the greatest arguments for competition, which similarly diffuses decision making and administrative experience in economic life.

Chapter V ("Capital") is the locus of one of Lewis's best known formulations foreshadowed earlier by Paul Rosenstein-Rodan (following, p. 409):[66] "All the countries which are now relatively developed have at some time in the past gone through a period of rapid acceleration, in the course of which their rate of annual net investment has moved from 5 percent or less to 12 percent or more. That is what we mean by an Industrial Revolution.''

Lewis arrived at this judgment by starting with measurements by Colin Clark and Kuznets of average and marginal capital–income ratios. After considering in some detail hypotheses about differences in those ratios by major sector, in advanced industrial and developing countries, he opted for an average marginal ratio between 3 and 4 to 1 for both. Taking India as an example, where the net investment rate in the early 1950s was perhaps 4% or 5% of national income and real income per capita virtually stagnant, he concluded that to achieve a 1½% to 2% increase in the standard of living a 12% net investment rate would be necessary—a figure achieved round about 1960.[67]

As a development planner as well as a macro-economist, Lewis then disaggregates the allocation of investment by roughly averaging the data from advanced industrial countries where gross investment was typically 20% of GNP.[68]

Housing	about	25 per cent
Public works and utilities	about	35 per cent
Manufacturing and agriculture	about	30 per cent
Other commerce	about	10 per cent
		100 per cent

After weighing each category (including stocks) in developing as opposed to advanced industrial countries, he concludes:[69]

> The great importance of construction is not generally realized; many people think of capital formation mainly in terms of installing machinery, while in truth it consists to a greater extent of building structures of one sort or another; civil engineering is the key industry in capital formation, with mechanical engineering following some distance behind. This has its corollaries. One is the point we have already made that, given finance, the real bottleneck which holds up a rapid acceleration of investment is the capacity of the building industry to extend itself. Another corollary is that in the earlier stages of economic development the greatest need for capital is for public works and public utilities, which in these days are not directly open to private foreign investors; so private foreign investment is of limited relevance to the capital needs of the less developed countries.

Against this background, Lewis then explores the sources of savings, concluding in classical style that profit is the most important:[70]

> This means that the fundamental explanation of any ''industrial revolution,'' that is to say, of any sudden acceleration of the rate of capital formation, is a sudden increase in the opportunities for making money; whether the new opportunities are new inventions, or institutional changes which make possible the exploitation of existing possibilities.
>
> If the process of converting an economy from a 5 to a 12 per cent saver is essentially dependent upon the rise of profits relatively to national income, it follows that the correct explanation of why poor countries save so little is not because they are poor, but because their capitalistic sectors are so small.

Thus, the rise in the investment rate in Lewis's Industrial Revolution, as in my takeoff, is a reflection of a deeper process, of which I would rate the rapid absorption of hitherto-unapplied technologies the most important. Lewis goes on to examine other sources of savings; notably, forced savings via inflation, public borrowing, taxation, and foreign borrowing.

C. *Business Cycles*. Lewis has written extensively about business cycles in other studies;[71] but *Economic Growth* contains a few pages that capture lucidly two of his basic hypotheses.

First, the role of the "irregularity of innovation" in determining the volatility of investment.[72] He views growth as rooted in a sequence of innovational leading sectors. The path of each follows, broadly, a logistic curve of acceleration and deceleration, but since investors cannot know that path *ex ante*, they systematically overshoot and under-shoot, imparting to the economic system as a whole powerful successive impulses toward expansion and contraction. Thus, having quite explicitly set aside the then-popular macro-growth models, Lewis brings growth and cycles together along lines of Schumpeter and the early work of Kuznets.

Second, investment in housing. Lewis systematically emphasizes the surprisingly large proportion of investment in all societies that goes to housing construction; and houses are long-lived. Despite fairly firm knowledge of the rate of family formation over, say, the next decade, investment in housing does not proceed smoothly. This volatility explains not merely the long (say, 20-years) housing cycle but also the tendency of strong and weak major cycles to follow one another in sequence:[73]

> A slump which occurs at a time when house-building or some major inno-
> vation is in full spate does not become serious, and does not last long.
> Whereas a slump which occurs during the off-period of the building cycle, or
> just after a major innovation has reached one of its peaks (e.g. motor cars in
> the U.S.A. in 1929) may be of serious magnitude and long duration. Since
> building averages 25 per cent of gross investment, and has a cycle of eighteen
> to twenty years, it is not surprising that decades of prosperity tend to alternate
> with decades of slower growth.

D. *Relative Prices*. Again like Colin Clark, Arthur Lewis has done some of his most original work on the course and impact of shifting trends in the terms of trade for both advanced industrial and developing countries.[74] In fact, his strong emphasis on the need to strive for "balanced development" comes mainly to rest on efforts to approximate optimum growth paths in agricultural and industrial sectors, thus damping, at least, terms of trade fluctuation that have subjected a good many developing countries to severe social and political as well as economic strains.[75] This relationship bears on Lewis's heavy emphasis on the need to raise agricultural productivity.[76]

Thus, as with business cycles, Lewis saw relative price trends as a product of growth itself under circumstances where uncertainty about the future yielded systematically irra-tional expectations and overshooting of optimum sectoral paths in agricultural as well as industrial production.[77]

E. *Stages of and Limits to Growth*. Like the eight other pioneers of the 1950s consid-ered here, Lewis's eyes were mainly fastened operationally on countries striving to enter or transit their industrial revolution; Kuznets would view as aiming to begin or carry forward in modern growth; and I would judge to be in the preconditions for takeoff or in takeoff.

Since Lewis's direct knowledge was primarily of the Caribbean, Africa, and India, his recommendations as of the early 1950s are addressed overwhelmingly to problems at the lower stages of growth. There are some but not many references to Latin America, where the takeoffs of Argentina and Brazil began in the mid-1930s, Mexico's round about 1940.

But, as an economist who took history seriously, and evokes it often in expounding his theory of growth, Lewis twice uses a concept of stages.

His first application is with respect to the growth of knowledge.[78]

> . . . [I]n considering the growth of knowledge one must distinguish three eras, the pre-literate, the era of writing without scientific method, and the era of scientific method. In the same way we must distinguish between societies according to whether they are illiterate, and according to whether their culture and philosophy are imbued with the scientific outlook.

Lewis divides the third stage into two parts: a long period, beginning in the Renaissance, when scientific knowledge is progressively enlarged but is not linked directly to invention:[79]

> The fact is that the great inventions of the eighteenth and the nineteenth centuries . . . were all invented by practical people who knew no science, or very little. It is only in the twentieth century that a scientific education has become essential for the would-be inventor, or that the discoveries of science have become the major source of further technological progress.

He then discusses at some length the organized close linkage of basic science and invention in the twentieth century.

Lewis's second evocation of stages is in a rarely examined subject, the relation between aggression and stage of growth. In the following passage he recognizes the dangerous "middle" years in the life of growing economies:[80]

> If there is any connection between dreams of glory and the stage of economic development, it is found in the 'middle' stages of economic growth. The richest countries tend to be peaceful, enjoying what they have, and envying none; and the poorest countries are too lethargic and disorganized for war. . . . The countries which are dangerous to world peace are more often those which think they have a great future ahead of them than those which are able to glorify their great past. And so the military leadership of the world tends to pass from one country to another in much the same way as leadership in international trade passes, and possibly for reasons of the same sort. . . .

As opposed to his rather thin treatment of stages, Lewis provides a quite complete discussion of the limits to growth in both its secular stagnation and resource-limitation versions.[81] In a philosophic mood evocative of David Hume, he also provides in the following passages a useful summary of what he has to say:[82]

> There are thus many pits into which a country may fall, as a result of prolonged growth: it may weary of material things, its entrepreneurs may behave less competitively, its public may create barriers to change, the distribution of income may alter unfavourably, it may exhaust its natural resources, it may lose its place in international trade, or it may run out of innovations. In addition, it may be a victim of natural disaster, or it may be

ruined by war, by civil strife or by misgovernment. None of these is inevitable. . . . But the expectation that a long period of growth is in due course succeeded by slower growth, by stagnation, or even by decline seems fairly well supported by the little we know of the economic history of the past four thousand years.

But he goes on to leave human beings and their societies a route of escape from this Toynbeeian prospect: "It is possible for a nation to take a new turn if it is fortunate enough to have the right leadership at the right time. In the last analysis history is only the record of how individuals respond to the challenge of their times. All nations have opportunities which they may grasp if only they can summon up the courage and the will."

F. *Noneconomic Factors.* One of the characteristics of the nine pioneers is that they all had some operational experience in formulating, administering, or advising on development policy. It will be recalled, for example, that Arthur Lewis's earliest work was on practical problems of development in Jamaica and Puerto Rico; and, from 1957 forward, he spent half his time in administration, including several United Nations posts; 4 years (1970–1974) as president of the Caribbean Development Bank.

In general, this kind of practical experience did not prevent the pioneers from developing strong, sometimes oversimplified analytic and/or policy propositions about development. They quite often appear to have lived by their own versions of Keynes's dictum:[83] "Words ought to be a little wild, for they are an assault of thought upon the unthinking. But when the seats of power and authority have been attained, there should be no more poetic licence. . . . When a doctrinaire proceeds to action, he must, so to speak, forget his doctrine. For those who in action remember the letter will probably lose what they are seeking."

In this respect, Arthur Lewis is, once again, something of an exception. In both his technical analyses as an economist and in his efforts to place development economics in its larger human and societal setting, he exhibits an ability to understand with sympathy and to take into account a wide spectrum of views without losing the capacity to emerge with a lucid, distinctive view of his own. In this respect, there is in Lewis something of J. S. Mill: a disciplined staff officer in the London headquarters of the East India Company; an economist dealing sympathetically with the work of his predecessors and contemporaries; but, in the end, capable of formulating distinctive and original economic propositions.

Behind Lewis's temperate approach to development economics and policy is a lively awareness of the complexity of human motivation and of the profound differences among societies and their cultures. More than almost all of his contemporaries, he was prepared not only to read beyond the conventional range of economics but also to reflect on and bring to bear insights from history, sociology, and anthropology.[84] Here, for example, is a statement of his approach to development economics capturing both the breadth of his view and his sense of the limits of the possible.[85]

> The most difficult problem . . . is to explain why people hold the beliefs they do. Economic growth depends on attitudes to work, to wealth, to thrift, to having children, to invention, to strangers, to adventure, and so on, and all these attitudes flow from deep springs in the human mind. There have been attempts to explain why these attitudes vary from one community to another. One can look to differences in religion, but this is merely to restate the

problem. . . . The experienced sociologist knows that these questions are unanswerable, certainly in our present state of knowledge, and probably for all time. . . .

It does not follow that we should cease to try to understand social change; man being a curious animal, it is beyond our nature to cease to try to understand. What follows is that we should be modest in our claims, and recognize how tentative is any hypothesis which we claim to base upon the study of history.

This was the spirit in which Lewis explored in the first 163 pages of his *Economic Growth* the noneconomic variables—"The Will to Economize" and "Economic Institutions"— that underlie the expansion (or failure to expand) of output per head of population.

Lewis's sense of the human condition also pervades his effort to answer a question usually taken for granted, "Is Economic Growth Desirable?" He begins, typically, with a proposition about the complexity of human beings:[86] "When growth begins, we are enthusiastic for it; but after a while it palls. We begin to long for stability; we reject materialism and return to spiritual preoccupations; and so on. Thus social attitudes alternate between favouring growth, and reacting against it, and social institutions alter in the same way." He then goes on to state the case for growth:[87]

> The case for economic growth is that it gives man greater control over his environment, and thereby increases his freedom.
>
> We can see this first in man's relations with nature. At primitive levels, man has to struggle for subsistence. . . . Economic growth enables him to escape from this servitude.
>
> Economic growth also gives us freedom to choose greater leisure. . . .
>
> Also, it is economic growth which permits us to have more services, as well as more goods or leisure. . . . The raising of living standards over the past century has widened the opportunity to appreciate and practise the arts, without necessarily affecting the quality of the best art one way or the other. . . . Relatively far more people hear the work of the best composers today than heard the work of Mozart or of Bach in their own times, or saw the work of Rembrandt or El Greco.
>
> Women benefit from these changes even more than men. . . . [F]or women to debate the desirability of economic growth is to debate whether women should have the chance to cease to be beasts of burden, and to join the human race.
>
> Economic growth also permits mankind to indulge in the luxury of greater humanitarianism. . . .
>
> Economic growth may be particularly important to societies where political aspirations are currently in excess of resources, since growth may forestall what might otherwise prove to be unbearable social tension.

Reviewing the various arguments against growth, he strikes a typically well-balanced view:[88]

> Three conclusions follow from this analysis. First, some of the alleged costs of economic growth are not necessary consequences of growth at all— the ugliness of towns or the impoverishment of the working classes, for instance. Secondly, some of the alleged evils are not in fact intrinsically

evil—the growth of individualism, or of reasoning, or of towns, for example. As in all human life, such things can be taken to excess, but they are not intrinsically any less desirable than their opposites. From this it follows, however, thirdly, that the rate of economic growth can be too high for the health of society.

As of 1984 Lewis's view of the balance sheet, quite unlike, say, Myrdal's or Prebisch's, remained temperately positive.[89]

> Taken as a group, governments of less developed countries (LDCs) have, in fact, passed reasonable tests. There are four times as many children in school as there were in 1950. The infant mortality rate has fallen by three-quarters. The multiplication of hospital beds, village water pipes, all-season village roads, and other mass services is faster than at any period in the history of the countries now developed. Much of the disillusionment with the results of the past three decades originates with people who do not understand the importance of the social wage, who have no idea what the conditions of the masses were like in 1950, or who have forgotten the extent to which LDC peoples live in semi-arid lands for which we have yet to make the technological breakthrough.

Gunnar Myrdal

Three strands distinguish Gunnar Myrdal's work on development. First, a matter of philosophy. His first postdoctoral book (1930) was *The Political Element in the Development of Economic Theory.*[90] In it he argued a basic theme that remained central to his work throughout his life; namely, that "the development of economic theory from earliest time . . . had been distorted by the biases of the time."[91] But he soon went beyond that proposition:[92]

> I found by further study . . . that value premises were needed already for establishing facts and not only for drawing policy conclusions. . . . The analysis of the doctrinal development of economic theory from earliest time, and the way it had been distorted by the biases of time, still stands. I had only to add my new insights that economic theory can never be neutral and, in the positivist sense, "objective."

This judgment had the salutary effect of making Myrdal sensitive to his own value premises and systematically explicit in sharing them with his readers.

Second, he came relatively late in life to development economics and carried over to that terrain values, technical judgments, and analytic methods he had evolved in dealing with Swedish (and, generally, Western European) problems of the 1930s and with the race problem in America.[93]

Third, Myrdal shared in heightened form a characteristic of virtually all the pioneers: the stance of a dissenter. Whether this is, in Myrdal's case, a matter of innate temperament, the imprint on his followers of that superdissenter Knut Wicksell, or a necessary concomitant of creativity, or all the above, is for others to assess. But, even in his most self-disciplined moments as a United Nations official of modest power dealing successfully on delicate, complex matters with foreign ministers of sovereign states, Myrdal never wholly lost the qualities of the brilliant *enfant terrible* who descended on Stockholm from Dalecarlia to *épater* the local bourgeoisie. *Against the Stream* is an apt title for a collection of his essays. For others, of course, Myrdal's advocacy of planning, Rosenstein-Rodan's "big push," and a large role for governments in the development process represented the orthodoxy or conventional wisdom from which they dissented.

Myrdal's positive development doctrine took its start from a proposition central to his rationale for the Swedish welfare state; namely, that movement toward equality of income within nations wholly converged with the requirements for a high rate of economic growth:[94]

> In the 1920s and 1930s, . . . I held the view that an equalization in favor of the lower-income strata was also a productive investment in the quality of people and their productivity. . . . It seemed clear that income equalization would have an even greater effect in this direction for underdeveloped countries, where the masses of people are suffering from very severe consumption deficiencies in regard to nutrition, housing, and everything else. . . .
>
> In underdeveloped countries such a redistribution of income cannot, however, be carried out by taxing the rich and transferring money to the poor via social security schemes and other such measures to raise their levels of living. The poor are so overwhelmingly many, and the wealthy so relatively few— and tax evasion among them so common. What is needed in order to raise the miserable living levels of the poor masses is instead radical institutional reforms. These would serve the double purpose of greater equality and economic growth. The two goals are inextricably joined.

This was the central theme of his three-volume *Asian Drama*.[95]

In method, as Myrdal notes, *Asian Drama* was a kind of "replica of an *American Dilemma*."[96] Like the latter study, *Asian Drama,* primarily an analysis of India, sees the tasks of development as one of supplanting a vicious with a benign, self-reinforcing process. The turnaround requires positive, simultaneous action in a number of sectors of the society, notably population policy, landownership and tenancy, public health, education, and politics; in all cases radical institutional change is necessary. The American Creed is the positive driving engine of "circular and cumulative causation" in the case of *An American Dilemma,* notably the ultimate commitment of American society to strive toward equality of opportunity. The emerging consensus in the developing regions on "the modernization ideals as epitomized in the desirability of development" drives *Asian Drama* with its assertion of the happy convergence of movement toward equality of income and high growth rates.[97]

Evidently the method of *Asian Drama* is also similar to Myrdal's still earlier approach to the prewar population problem in Sweden (preceding, pp. 199–200). In his 1938 Godkin Lectures he also took a subject normally treated by economists in primarily economic terms (i.e., the concept of an optimum population); shifted the argument to the social and institutional determinants of the size and quality of the population; and ended with a powerful reinforcing case for a welfare state including a radical shift in income distribution.

The continuity of income redistribution in Myrdal's work emerges once again in his (1970) *The Challenge of World Poverty*.[98] Arising from three lectures delivered at the Johns Hopkins School of Advanced International Studies (SAIS), *The Challenge*, in effect, summarizes *Asian Drama* and, in the words of its subtitle, presents "A World

Anti-Poverty Program in Outline.'' Its positive argument, extending the argument for the national welfare state to the international community, is that foreign aid should be expanded; and a series of measures should be taken that would strip both public and private lending to developing nations of what Myrdal regarded as their overbearing power content. He advocated, for example, increased use of multilateral aid, private management contracts with a terminal date, and U.S. governmental and World Bank collaboration in nationalizing U.S. private investments in Latin America. Aid should be granted at low concessionary interest rates to avoid the buildup of debt burdens. The political rationale in advanced industrial societies for enlarged aid should be moral rather than either long-run or short-run self-interest.[99] The enlarged Swedish aid program is presented as (almost) a prototype of this approach; the aid program and other U.S. relations with developing countries as a demonstration of all that required "purging."[100] ". . . In the future, we should try to move toward a common recognition of aid to underdeveloped countries as a collective responsibility for the developed countries, the burden of which should be shared in an agreed fair way, amounting to an *approach to a system of international taxation.*"

The SAIS lectures were delivered in 1969 in the disabused fifth stage of the global environment of development policy. It is in many ways a polemic against U.S. policy across a broad front, including its policy in Southeast Asia.

Myrdal then turned his attention to other problems. He was induced to write again about development policy in the early 1980s by the World Bank's request to write a chapter for the *Pioneers* volume. Its closing sections, while less enflamed, reflect an even wider disabuse than *The Challenge.* The immediate setting is the worldwide depression of 1979–1982, when progress ceased or reversed in a good many developing countries under the combined impact of reduced demand from the advanced industrial countries, the second oil price jump, increased debt burdens as global interest rates rose sharply, and a cutback in private lending. Myrdal responded by urging that aid be confined to basic needs (to increase food production, improve water supply, sanitation, schooling, and family limitation); and that aid be bilateral. Aid for large-scale industrial projects should be discontinued. And, in a remarkable reversal:[101] "The aid-giving governments should insist upon effectively controlling the use of aid in underdeveloped countries."

These recommendations were not merely a reaction to the human (or basic needs) crisis in the developing regions of that period but also a reflection of profound disappointment with the character of the governments that had emerged in many developing countries:[102]

> In the underdeveloped countries governments are everywhere in the hands of upper-class elites, even in countries that are not under military dictatorship. It is with the governments in power that all business deals have to be negotiated and concluded. And it is with them that even aid matters have to be settled. It has been pointed out that as a result poor people in developed countries are taxed to "aid" rich people in underdeveloped countries."

He comments without enthusiasm on the two Brandt Commission reports (of 1980 and 1983) and concludes with the following acerbic view of the New International Economic Order:[103]

> More recently the underdeveloped countries have raised their protest and demanded a 'new international economic order.' One world conference after another has been convened to consider that demand.
>
> Although the developed countries are not prepared to make any substantial

concessions in their economic relations with underdeveloped countries, they generally show their politeness by never asking whether the underdeveloped countries do not need a new order at home. . . .

[T]he underdeveloped countries have, I believe, turned demands for a new economic world order into a sort of alibi for not reforming the way in which they are governed. Any concessions they might win at these conferences are very small compared with what they should be able to win both economically and socially by the internal reforms I have emphasized in this paper."

I would guess that Myrdal's condemnation of the politics and politicians of the developing countries reflects not merely his own observations but also, in part, the frustrations experienced by the excellent band of Swedish aid administrators in carrying out the rather gallant unilateral enlargement of their country's contribution to official development assistance.[104] Like many others, they found themselves often, notably in the poorest developing countries, up against the following question: How in good conscience can we allocate Swedish resources to programs that are certain to fail, despite our aid, because of unwise local policies or corruption?

But there is a larger issue involved that we shall see again, in somewhat different form, in the five-stage pilgrimage of Raúl Prebisch. What can be realistically expected of the political process in developing countries? At one point in his *Pioneers* essay Myrdal evokes the hopes stirred by his visit to post-liberation India, led by Jawaharlal Nehru: a leader wishing to move "in the right direction of democracy and equalization"; a virtually uncorrupt civil service, at least at the higher levels, and good relations with Britain and the world community generally. Soon there was a Planning Commission and a First Five-Year Plan as well as projects for land and educational reform. For a good Northern European Social Democrat of the early postwar years, it was a heartwarming scene.

When Myrdal returned to India late in 1957 to begin work on *Asian Drama* he found a great deal to deplore: an ailing and discouraged leader; little if any progress toward equality of opportunity or more equal income distribution; political power in the hands of the rich; little progress toward land redistribution; a spread of corruption to higher levels of government; a general lack of social discipline. All this lay behind the large message of *Asian Drama* that the reform of India's "soft state" was the necessary condition for economic progress.

It will be recalled that, in the late 1950s, Mao's China, including the 1958 Great Leap Forward, captured the imagination of many Western intellectuals who had not carefully followed the evolution of affairs on the mainland since 1949. Myrdal was not exempt:[105]

Mao is, in the first place, the founder of a positive moral philosophy, embracing all social relations. Under the very singular circumstances that have existed in China for many decades . . . and working within equally singular national traditions in China since centuries, he has succeeded in molding his very large nation to become a "new people," diverging in their patterns of living and working from old China and, of course, from other nations.

. . . Also included [in Mao's moral doctrine] were certain general lines for economic development planning, which fitted conditions in China and—after many trials and errors—have had considerable success. They are without doubt intellectually superior to the planning directives of other very poor, underdeveloped countries.

I would guess that the contrast between what he perceived in India and this somewhat romantic view of Mao's harder state affected Myrdal's judgment on the former.

But the fundamental problem Myrdal confronted, common to all nine of the pioneers briefly examined here, is that there existed no accepted theory of political development to accompany, frame, suffuse, or dominate theories of economic development; and there is, in the end, no way to leave politics out of economic development.

There is inevitably, therefore, in Myrdal's disabuse something of a paraphrase of the famous question in *My Fair Lady:* "Why can't these people behave like Swedes?" Put more seriously, Myrdal's perception was correct that the Western ideology and value system of modernization have suffused much of the developing world, but it does not dominate in any simple overriding way. It interacts with strands of xenophobic nationalism, painful memories of relative inferiority, regional, tribal, and religious enmities, struggles for personal power, greed for money, and deeply ingrained social and political patterns that do not necessarily converge and often conflict with the imperatives of modernization.[106] It is the complexity of this heritage and, above all, the overriding power of nationalism that belied Myrdal's initial hypothesis that it was not only morally correct but realistic to carry over to the global community—to internationalize—the values and politics of domestic welfare states in advanced industrial societies. The story of the developing regions since the Second World War evokes much more of the tortured and violent story of early modern Europe from, say, the fifteenth to the eighteenth centuries, than the straightforward working out of the value system of modernization.

But when all this is taken into account Myrdal has the right proudly to affirm in the end, in a somewhat Marshallian mood, the positive operational role of philosophic idealism for which he stood for a stormy half-century.[107]

> The ideal is also a living force in our society and it is, therefore, part of the social reality we are studying. . . . The ideal works through people's valuations, their political attitudes. Whether we can hope for a gradual attainment of the ideal, and with what speed and to what degree, depends in great measure upon how strongly entrenched the ideal becomes in this sphere of human valuations. . . .
>
> People's striving are, indeed, among the most important social facts and they largely determine the course of history.

Myrdal's work can be—and has been—criticized on a number of grounds; for example, his unshakable pessimism in the face of a great deal of social and economic progress since 1950 in the developing regions; his overestimate of the potentialities of planning and underestimate of the positive social as well as economic uses of the competitive price system; and his failure to perceive the possibility of export-oriented development.

But Myrdal's contribution to development economics does not lie in how one strikes the balance in debate on these and similar issues. It lies in his insistence that the process of modernization be viewed as the performance of a whole society and whole people, not merely its economy and economic man.

Raúl Prebisch

Among the pioneers, Prebisch simplified the task of analysis for his readers by setting out his essay in precisely the way the editors requested; that is, the origins of his analytic and policy views of the 1950s and their subsequent evolution down to the 1980s. The title of his chapter: "Five Stages in My Thinking on Development."

Prebisch's five stages conform roughly to the six stages delineated at the beginning of this chapter. In effect he combines my last two stages (the 1970s and 1980s) in a somewhat cataclysmic critique of "peripheral capitalism."

Prebisch, by his own account, began as a neoclassical theorist drawn into politics when still under 30. As under secretary of Finance in the government of Argentina in 1930–1932 and later at the Central Bank, his orthodoxy was shaken by the radical decline in the volume and prices of Argentine exports. In a setting of acute shortage of foreign exchange, he came to advocate "a resolute industrialization policy" and was "converted to protectionism."[108] These pragmatic conclusions were, in Prebisch's view, essential background to his first stage (1943–1949), when, in relative tranquility, he developed a coherent rationale for his doctrine of industrialization via import substitution. But this familiar doctrine, with its asymmetrical assumptions about the relative elasticities of the demand for exports and imports of developing countries and its believed long-run degenerative relative price trend for basic commodities, was rooted in an effort to answer two deeper questions that he had generalized out of his experience with the intense crisis of Argentina in the 1930s:[109] "Why was it necessary for the state to play an active role in development? Why was it that policies formulated at the center could not be followed at the periphery?"

The second turning-point stage by my reckoning—1949–1950—turned out also to be Prebisch's. With his doctrine now coherently formulated, he assumed in 1949 responsibility as executive secretary for the United Nations Economic Commission for Latin America (ECLA), set up in Santiago, Chile. The first 2 years (1949–1951) were not propitious for Prebisch's doctrine. The Latin American terms of trade (1963 = 100) stood at 70 in 1938, 100 in 1948, and 124 in 1951, at the Korean War peak. (Excluding petroleum, the figures were, respectively, 67, 98, and 134.) Their subsequent subsidence to figures a bit above the 1948 level was, indeed, painful and evoked memories of the 1930s in Latin America and elsewhere among exporters of basic commodities. Prebisch summarized his initial view in these terms:[110]

> My diagnosis of the situation of the countries of Latin America was constructed on the basis of my criticism of the pattern of outward-oriented development, which I considered to be incapable of permitting the full development of those countries. My proposed development policy was oriented toward the establishment of a new pattern of development which would make it possible to overcome the limitations of the previous pattern. This new form of development would have industrializations as its main objective. In reality, my policy proposal sought to provide theoretical justification for the industrialization policy which was already being followed (especially by the large countries of Latin America), to encourage the others to follow it too, and to provide all of them with an orderly strategy for carrying this out.

But as the 1950s wore on, it became clear that the expansion of the initial group of import substitution sectors was decelerating quite rapidly.[111] The national markets were relatively small in a good many Latin American countries, and there were distortions of policy as well. Despite these and other problems of Latin American development in the 1950s, the technological absorptive capacity of the region was rising. The three major countries, especially, were beginning to move into a range of more diversified industries that marked the drive to technological maturity. Moreover, in its final few years, the Eisenhower Administration, against much initial inner resistance, shifted its stance toward development assistance as opposed to merely economic support of military allies; and before long the Kennedy administration was installed with a still more positive posture towards the developing regions.

Prebisch evokes the emerging mixture of problems and possibilities that shaped his third stage—the late 1950s and early 1960s:[112]

> . . . [T]he reconstruction of the world economy had been completed with the reorganization of the international system of trade and payments to improve its efficiency. New trade possibilities were visualized for the periphery, and I advocated a policy to stimulate exports of manufactures to the centers and to strengthen trade relations within the periphery. My reasoning was that industrialization had been asymmetrical, since it was based on import substitution through protection without corresponding promotion of exports of manufactures. Protection should be matched with selective export subsidies in order to face cost differentials with the centers. Furthermore, industrial policy had been improvised, principally to counteract the effects of a cyclical fall in exports. It was necessary to introduce rationality and correct exaggerations and abuses by reducing duties. Excessive duties not only distorted industrial production but also had adverse effects on exports of primary products.

Reflections of this kind—plus an increased sensitivity to skewed income distribution in developing regions—suffused Prebisch's work in the global arena provided by his role as secretary-general of the United Nations Conference on Trade and Development (UNCTAD). In this fourth stage (1964–1969), Prebisch sought to enlarge the flows of exports to the developed from the developing regions, and the flows of capital and technology in the other direction. Two major instruments he sought to have installed for this purpose were generalized trade preferences for developing countries and commodity price agreements that would reduce price fluctuations and, on average, improve the terms of trade for exporters. Prebisch looked back at this phase of his work with frustration and disappointment.[113] ". . . I did not succeed: clear proof that the North was not willing to act nor was the South inclined to engage in the very serious structural transformations needed to pave the way for development and social equity."

His final, fifth stage embraces the post-1973 decade with its two oil price jumps and the severe 1979–1982 depression. He regarded this period as the second great crisis of capitalism of the twentieth century. The politico-economic doctrine that emerged from his reflections is a weaving together of neo-Marxist, Leninist, and Schumpeterian strands. But, just as his import substitution industrialization model of the 1950s was a grand generalization of the pragmatic response of Argentina (Brazil and Mexico) to the foreign exchange catastrophe of the early 1930s, Prebisch's somber prognosis of the mid-1970s and early 1980s reflected the "frustrations of the last decade in Chile and Argentina. . . ."[114]

His argument begins by broadening his old basic concept of the center and the periphery in two respects: to embrace the failure of technology generated in the center to spread rapidly to the periphery because the latter's role was "mainly restricted to the supply of primary products";[115] and to characterize the élites of the periphery as imitators of the centers in "technologies and life styles"; "ideas and ideologies:"[116]

Against this background he shifts his argument to the disposition of "the economic surplus. . . ." He argues this surplus is not used as it should be to finance productive investment. It is dissipated in three directions:

- imitative high living of the social élite;
- increasing demands of the state due to its "spurious absorption" of unemployed manpower in activities of low or nil productivity; and
- pressure for redistribution of income from an increasingly skilled and assertive working force in the form of claims for both higher wages and increased social services.

The upshot is an inflationary crisis because the monetary authorities are faced with a choice of imposing depression or conniving at inflation. They generally choose the latter. This leads to the kind of political crises that Chile, Argentina, and other Latin American countries experienced in the last generation in which the "democratic process devours itself" and soldiers move eagerly or reluctantly, into the presidential palaces:[117]

> The other way to stop the spiral is to control wages and salaries by government intervention and let prices attain their "proper" level. In other terms, this involves restoring the surplus to the detriment of the labor force. . . .
>
> The state is then required to use force to overcome the political strength of the labor unions and the masses. Consider the paradox: the use of force by the state is justified by invoking the principle that the state should not intervene in the economy! Economic liberalism is strongly proclaimed at the tremendous social and political cost of destroying political liberalism, if we interpret these concepts in their original philosophic unity.

After arguing that the dominant groups are interested in only the maintenance of control over the surplus for their own excessive consumption Prebisch's remedy is:[118]

> The transformation of the system seems to me inevitable if we are to combine development with social equity and political advance. However, the most widely disseminated doctrinal options do not appear to be of much use for guiding this transformation. . . . I therefore believe that the time has come to search for a synthesis of both socialism and genuine economic liberalism, and thereby restore that essential philosophic unity of economic liberalism, with political liberalism. . . .
>
> Socialism is necessary to ensure the 'social use' of the surplus. . . . [E]conomic liberalism is necessary insofar as individual decisions to produce and consume should be left to the market.

Internationally, he argues, in particular, for reforms in the center that would enlarge export earnings by the periphery and, more generally, for policies which would exploit the potentialities that flow from long-run common interests:[119]

> We need a policy inspired with a long-term vision on both sides. But the long term starts now with regard to enlightened policy action involving a series of agreed convergent measures. The centers and the periphery are losing a great opportunity. Nothing important is being done to meet a tremendous historical responsibility with far-reaching economic, social, and political consequences for the whole world!

In casting up the accounts on Prebisch's contribution to development analysis and policy, it is not difficult to identify limitations, false leads, and even errors, as do the two distinguished commentators in the *Pioneers* volume (Albert Fishlow and Jagdish N. Bhagwati). For example, an import-substitution strategy was just about the only option open in the 1930s, but, as some of the countries of East Asia demonstrated, the potentialities for expanding exports other than basic commodities in the 1950s, 1960s, and even in the somewhat pathological 1970s and 1980s, proved much greater than Prebisch's analysis would suggest. For example, as acknowledged leader of UNCTAD he felt impelled to enunciate doctrines and policies, rooted in his perceptions of Latin American problems. He sought to apply these to the extraordinarily wide spectrum of what we call developing countries. The typical problems of Africa, the Middle East, and Asia differ from those of Latin America.[120] Even more important, the problems within these regions, including Latin America, differed greatly from country to country. In seeking common ground among his heterogeneous UNCTAD constituency, Prebisch was pressed by circumstances to move toward a stance of confrontation and a heightening of arguments that blamed the problems of developing regions on the policies of advanced industrial countries, past and present. The New International Economic Order (NIEO) strategy within the United Nations inherited and sharpened this rhetorically confrontational strategy. Its cost proved severe. The advanced industrial countries proved quite capable of fending off this kind of pressure. And, within developing countries, a gap opened up between those conducting rhetorical exercises and drafting empty resolutions in large international gatherings and those seriously at work on the domestic and international tasks of development. The coalitions supporting foreign aid in the parliaments of the advanced industrial countries—and the American Congress—were, in all conscience, rather fragile. They were not strengthened by the UNCTAD and NIEO strategy.

But there is a quite different way to regard Prebisch's contribution to development thought and policy. It is suggested by a comment, in passing, of Bhagwati:[121]

> . . . [F]or my generation of economists in the developing countries, preeminence of Raúl Prebisch in a field of obvious importance was a major source of inspiration. To see that one's own can be innovative, ingenious, and important is always, and was then especially, a matter of considerable psychological significance. For, among the colonial attitudes which afflicted our societies in those days was the belief that fundamental thinking required that one belong to the center, not the periphery, in Raúl Prebisch's splendid terminology. Prebisch and Lewis, among a few key figures, helped to shatter that myth decisively.

Prebisch was a sophisticated man. Those, like myself, who dealt with him professionally (as well as a friend and fellow crusader for development), knew that he understood fully that development was primarily a domestic task for each national society; that the major impediments lay in the history, culture, and institutions of the developing nations themselves; and that the so-called core countries could only help at the margin.[122] He also knew enough of history to understand that, in fact, "peripheral" countries were not doomed to perpetual second-class status. Such knowledge did not, however, ameliorate the pain of dependence in the short run. Thus, Prebisch's Hamiltonian stance gave effective psychological and political expression to the frustrations and resentments of latecomers confronting from day to day the often callous policies of the more advanced.

Paul N. Rosenstein-Rodan

No serious list of authentic development pioneers could be drawn up without including Paul Rodan. He was one of the remarkable band of young economists who made their way to Britain from central and Eastern Europe during the interwar years, greatly enriching university life, notably in London, but also in the world of political economy in general. Rodan taught at University College of the University of London from 1930 to 1947. Although a British citizen from the age of 28, he, like Schumpeter, never lost wholly—indeed, they cultivated—the style of their student years in Vienna.

Rodan's famous first article on Eastern Europe was published in 1943, when he was 41. But from that period until his death more than 40 years later, he focused his professional life with singular dedication on the theory and practice and teaching of development economics.

Looking back we tend to see the early work of economists—including our own work—with a hindsight shaped by later debates, events, and intellectual developments. It may, therefore, be useful to begin with a short summary of what Rodan's 1943 paper was in fact about. Foreshadowing much that was distinctive in his work of the 1960s at M.I.T., it is a quantitative outline of a 10-year postwar plan to lift the growth rate in Eastern and Southeastern Europe from virtual stagnation to over 4% by a combination of increased domestic savings, capital investment from abroad, German reparations in kind, and emigration, thus fully employing (40%–50%, in industry) a working force initially characterized by substantial unemployment and partial unemployment. Here are the essentials of Rodan's plan with its rather interesting arithmetic provided in our notes.[123]

> The aim of industrialization in international depressed areas is to produce a structural equilibrium in the world economy by creating productive employment for the agrarian excess population. It may be assumed that creditor countries will not be willing to enter into commitments for more than ten years. How much can be achieved in that period, and what is the rough order of magnitude of the capital required?
>
> . . . Even if we take account of the gradually rising national income, rates of savings beginning with 8 percent and leading at the end of a ten-year period to 15 percent would seem to represent the maximum one can plan for. Assuming a national income rising annually by 4 percent, and an average rate of investment of 12 per cent, the internal capital supply would only amount to 3,000 million. . . . At best 70–80 per cent of the unemployed workers could be employed. It follows that emigration will still have to supplement industrialization. Besides that, however, German reparations in the form of capital equipment might provide one part of the capital of the E.E.I.T. [East European Investment Trust]. . . . Germany can increase her consumption above the war-time standard, and transfer reparations *in natura* representing 25–50 per cent of what she used to spend on armaments.

The following points are worth noting about this precocious exercise:

- While building his calculations around a shift of labor from rural unemployment and partial employment to full employment (a kind of transfer of Keynesian concepts to development) Rodan also employs a Harrod capital-output ratio.[124]

- Rodan disaggregates capital requirements per employed worker by sector and, by implication, foreshadows his later concern with sectoral capital-output ratios.
- He applies to development economics the Keynesian notion of a marginal rate of saving rising with income per capita.
- He anticipates Arthur Lewis's rise in the investment rate during the transition with his estimate of the maximum possible rise in the domestic saving rate over 10 years from 8% to 15% (gross), with important additional resources required from abroad to round out his full employment target.

Behind this imaginative if primitive outline of a plan lay four conceptual "innovations," reflecting flaws in the working of private markets, which, in retrospect, Rodan defined as follows: a concern with disguised unemployment (or excess population) in the countryside; an elevation of Marshall's "pecuniary" external economies, yielding economies of scale; an emphasis on the indispensable role of large blocks of infrastructure investment as a necessary foundation for profitable industrialization; and a heightened emphasis on "technological external economies," notably public investment in education and training.

Taken all together, the reality of these forms of market failure constituted Rodan's case for planning the kind of "Big Push" he envisaged as necessary to lift a relatively stagnant underdeveloped country into sustained growth:[125]

> The market mechanism does not realize the "optimum" either in one nation or between nations because it relies on such unrealistic assumptions as linear homogeneous production functions, no increasing returns or economies of scale or of agglomeration, and no phenomenon of minimum quantum or threshold. This obscures the nature of the development process and the risks involved. Nothing in theology or technology ordains that God created the world convex downwards.

Rodan recognized the theoretical legitimacy of posing the question (as Kenneth Arrow did) whether perfect future markets for commodities and services might mitigate or eliminate these market failures.[126] His response:[127]

> In terms of contemporary theory, the essence of the 1943 article may seem to rest on the basic question whether perfect future markets can exist for all the commodities in the context of a future which is both open-ended and uncertain. Although I recognized that future markets and future prices could provide necessary additional signaling devices, I stated that "It is a moot point whether perfect future markets for all goods can exist. [My] suspicion (without proof) is that they cannot exist for the same reasons for which perfect foresight is impossible. In reality they certainly do not exist."

Rodan developed and refined these propositions in the course of his research and writing but, above all, as an adviser on development policy and plans. At the World Bank (1947–1953) he was assistant director of the Economics Department and head of the Economic Advisory Staff. His major enterprise was a stubborn crusade, ultimately quite successful, to shift World Bank lending from a project to a program basis. At M.I.T. (1953–1968) he carried forward work on Italy, India, and Chile. He was also a major figure in the crusade of the Center for International Studies, led by Max F. Millikan, to shift U.S. policy to large-scale sustained support for development.[128] He was among those who contributed substantially to the support of then Senator John F. Kennedy's effort (jointly with Senator John Sherman Cooper) to set in motion consortium arrangements in support of Indian and Pakistani development plans. He also played an important role in laying the foundations in the 1950s for what was to become the Alliance for Progress.

Aside from his analytic skills and cumulative experience, Rodan brought to these and other enterprises two distinctive qualities, one narrow, the other broad. First, skill in translating a policy proposal—and its analytic underpinnings—into rough but useful quantitative terms, much as he did in his 1943 article on Eastern Europe. He took the lead, for example, in designing the quantitative appendix for *A Proposal* (1957), with its rough calculations of necessary development aid levels; and he later refined these estimates for a major 1961 article in *The Review of Economic Statistics*.[129] Second, he contributed in a major way to the creation in the 1950s of a consensus among the development economists of the North and South on the analytic principles that should underlie a much enlarged international effort and on how such effort should be organized. Rodan's effectiveness derived from a special mixture of qualities and attributes: his evident total dedication to development; his stature as an acknowledged pioneer; his warm and lively personality; even his British citizenship at a time when the weight of American power was somewhat burdensome. Looking back, the existence of that consensus was a remarkable achievement of the period; and the lack of such a consensus on where to go from here, a major weakness in North–South relations of the 1980s.

Rodan returns in his *Pioneers* essay to the failure of one of his most cherished hopes. It was to leave in the hands of a kind of International Supreme Court of development economists the arbitration of differences among creditors and recipients concerning the appropriate volume and conditions for aid. The "Committee of Nine" in the Alliance for Progress was a first effort in this direction, destroyed by what Rodan regarded as a " 'trahison des clercs'—that is, the sabotage of the Alliance for Progress by both the U.S. and Latin American bureaucracies.''[130] Rodan's final observation on the concept is worth recording:[131]

> . . . [T]he very discussion by a credit-giving country of what the receiving country should do invariably raises objections that the latter's national sovereignty is being infringed upon. Under such circumstances, the discussion is either incomplete and not explicitly articulated or it is bound to give rise to mutual recrimination.
>
> The only way out of this vicious circle is to establish a committee, which is not appointed by and not responsible to either creditor or debtor governments, to make an independent evaluation of national development effort and a consequent recommendation of the amount of aid to be allocated. . . . It should evolve into a de facto "International Court of Economic Justice". . . .
>
> Today we have competence, finance, and no democracy in the international banks—and democracy and no finance in the United Nations*. . . . The Committee of IX of the Alliance for Progress was an attempt to apply such an international arbitration. It failed because of sabotage on both sides, but all

---

*As occasionally, Rodan's delight in a *bon mot* here strained reality. One country–one vote in the United Nations General Assembly can hardly be regarded as a "democratic" procedure.

great ideas first fail. All progress is first proclaimed to be impossible but is then realized.

Looking backward and forward, Rodan's final reflections, like those of a good many of his fellow pioneers, concern the larger than initially expected role of "non-economic" factors and objectives:[132]

> After some four decades of concerted attention to the challenge of development, we might ask how much economics can explain. Economic theory can determine the necessary, though not the sufficient, conditions of growth. The so-called noneconomic factors account for the gap between the necessary and the sufficient. . . .
>
> Data must . . . cover not only available material and human resources, technological possibilities, and psychological preferences but also attitudes of mind and the ability to change them. A good part of the last-named factors (social attitudes) are unknown rather than given quantities, so that the data are never available. And the objectives are largely subconscious—neither quite given nor quite unknown.

Like Myrdal and others, Rodan expressed his disappointments and regarded the early 1980s as a period when ". . . development is now passing through a low point."[133] But to the end (like Arthur Lewis) he refused to abandon his faith in the ultimate triumph of the sense of human community that suffused his commitment to development.[134]

> The original philosophy of aid is still correct, and present cynics are not justified. . . . The increase in life expectancy, the fall in infant mortality, the rates of growth, the achievements in any number of developing countries— nobody at the end of the Second World War would have expected so much. A billion people are still hungry, but it would now be 2 billion without the achievements that have been made.
>
> What got lost, however, in the 1970s was international solidarity. The objective of international full employment disappeared in cynicism after Vietnam. The transition from the national welfare state to the international level must still be made. . . . General cynicism is at least as unrealistic as naive idealism. We know what has to be done—we have to mobilize the will to do it.

Rodan's lucid, principled case for development planning, rooted in four specified failures of the competitive market process, moved to the center of the protracted debate on the appropriate role, if any, and appropriate limits of planning in the transition from relative stagnation to sustained growth. The debate did not always match the orderliness and precision of Rodan's argument or meet it head on; but, in building his case, on those requirements of "a great society" that "could never repay the expense to any individual or small number of individuals," Rodan linked his advocacy of planning and, indeed, his view of development economics in the early, critical stages of growth firmly to the classical tradition.

H. W. Singer

Like a number of his fellow pioneers, Hans Singer did his first professional work on acute problems of interwar Europe—in his case, on areas in Britain experiencing particularly high and protracted unemployment. And, again like a number of his fellows, he carried over into development policy not only the lessons he drew from an immersion in chronically depressed areas but also the ideology of the welfare state that the pathological interwar experience helped greatly to strengthen. In his essay for the *Pioneers* volume, Singer traces his intellectual roots to Keynes, Beveridge, and Schumpeter of what might be called the first modern generation (all born in the early 1880s) and to Colin Clark, Rosenstein-Rodan, Balogh, and Myrdal of the second (born about the turn of the century). Singer, born in 1910, rather belongs with Bauer, Hirschman, and Lewis (all 1915) who might be regarded as part of a third.

Singer's best-known contribution to development economics is, of course, his analysis of the terms of trade for developing countries incorporated in two papers published in the turning-point period (1949–1950).[135] Singer provides a detailed account of the influences that led him to focus on the long-run course of relative prices and the relative gains from trade of advanced industrial and developing countries.[136] But his underlying, larger interest was "distributive justice":[137]

> While mainstream economics concentrated on the problem of allocative efficiency (where comparative advantage ruled supreme), my interest was from the beginning more in the direction of distributive justice, or rather distributive efficiency as I saw it as a follower of Alfred Marshall, R. H. Tawney, and William Beveridge. This reflected a past concern with unemployment and the welfare state, and foreshadowed a future interest in basic needs and problems of children.

Thus, Singer, too, is a dissenter of one school just as, say, Bauer and Little are dissenters of a counter-school.

Looking back on his views of the 1950s, Singer conducts his defense on both technical and international welfare economic grounds. He depends heavily on an article (1980) by J. Spraos; his projections, on measurements that exclude oil prices and assume the decline in the relative prices of basic commodities of the mid-1980s will continue.[138]

In his commentary in *Pioneers,* Bela Balassa, in my view authoritatively refutes Singer's technical argument; and Lewis, in his essay, replies tersely to the Prebisch–Singer terms of trade perspective, along lines I find conclusive.[139] Moreover, in commending import-substitution industrialization, Singer failed to take into account the resultant egregious domestic terms of trade which resulted from excessively high prices of manufactures, exploitation of farmers on behalf of more politically volatile urban populations, and neglect of agricultural productivity—factors Prebisch came to appreciate only after a great deal of damage was done. The reversal of these distortions, requiring a shift of domestic terms of trade in favor of agriculture as well as encouragement for manufactured exports produced with greater efficiency, has proved a politically difficult—even explosive—process in a good many countries.[140] Singer also fails to consider my own and Lewis's arguments for the close interdependence of agricultural and industrial development.

Singer's second line of defense, put bluntly, is that, while noisy United Nations agitation for various devices to improve the terms of trade for developing countries did not yield significant results, they were a useful background to the effort to generate an institution that would enlarge the flow of soft loans to developing regions.

This argument is developed as followed: Singer first lists five lines of action that might mitigate or reverse worsening terms of trade:[141] "changing the underlying bargaining relations,'' for example, by ''pressure on multinationals and disseminating high productivity technologies;'' enlarging ''intra-LDC trade and intra-LDC investment''; autarchical import substitution delinking developing countries from trade with advanced industrial countries; expanding manufactured exports; increasing the volume of primary commodity exports and thus improving the income terms of trade (export revenue divided by import prices). He emerges with trade pessimism on all counts. This leaves him with the question: ''Aid not trade?''[142]

Singer then argues that the agitation of the ''wild men'' in the United Nations Secretariat for the Special United Nations Fund for Economic Development (SUNFED)—a proposed instrument for dispensing soft loans—played an important part in preparing the way for acceptance of the World Bank's International Development Association (IDA). There is an element of truth in this assertion, although the process that yielded IDA and other institutions and policies that enlarged development aid in the late 1950s was vastly more complex than Singer suggests.[143]

In a sense, all the pioneers, without exception, felt they were engaged in battle on behalf of the underdogs of this world,—i.e., the men, women, and children of countries that were latecomers—that did not get into takeoff until the 1930s or, indeed, were struggling to get into takeoff or in its early phases in the 1950s. They were sore beset with acute political and social as well as economic problems at a time when Western Europe and Japan, to the surprise of the bulk of the economics profession, with the help of a bit of American pump priming, had moved into the most rapid growth phase of their histories; and a United States, its economy rejuvenated by war, moved on to new levels of affluence in a world economy in which the dollar was the international currency and the American capital market was the uncontested center of global finance. The biases of Singer moving, as it were, from the distressed areas of Britain to the distressed areas of the world are not difficult to understand with sympathy. And the atmosphere of the United Nations, with its politics in nonsecurity matters run on the basis of one country–one vote, heightened those biases.

Against this background it was natural for Singer to think of his mission in terms of ''a global welfare state'':[144] ''As part of my concern with unemployment problems, I felt involved in the development of a social welfare state immediately after the war. . . . Obviously, a partisan of the social welfare state would be attracted by the thought and possibilities of a global welfare state represented by the United Nations in those hopeful first days of naive utopianism.'' To one degree or another, explicitly or implicitly, most— not all—the pioneers thought in some such terms. There was a strand of legitimacy in this perspective because the religions and cultures of Western societies were rooted in the ultimate brotherhood of man. Indeed, the language of the United Nations Charter reflected this strand in reality. It would be a naive cynicism wholly to deny the importance of this fact among the motives that moved the parliamentary bodies of advanced industrial countries, let alone the motives of men and women who committed a part of their lives and professional careers to the cause of development. And at least since David Hume there was also the proposition that an extra dollar of income for the poor added more than it took away from the rich.

But there were two important limitations that had to be respected if these elements in the equation were to be kept in proper proportion. First, for good or ill, the United Nations was an organization of sovereign nations, not a global government. Ultimate sovereignty was jealously guarded by all members, perhaps most jealously by the governments of developing countries, many freshly emerged from colonialism. This meant that only partnerships, as Paul Rodan pointed out, would work; and partnerships demand consensus.[145] Charters of rights and duties, in which all the rights are allocated to developing countries, duties to advanced industrial countries, proved in these circumstances unhelpful.

Second—and in my view more important—the welfare-state analogy was technically misleading. It encouraged the view that successful development hinged on an adequate flow of transfer payments from the rich to the poor. Thus, recommended targets were set in various international reports for foreign aid levels as a proportion of GNP in advanced industrial countries. But the proximate objective of international development policy is not income redistribution: it is to induce growth and development among the latecomers to modernization. Something approximating income redistribution occurs because the normal rate of growth in and beyond takeoff is higher for a developing country, with a large unexploited backlog of technology to absorb, than for an advanced industrial country. Foreign aid can certainly help if it is used well, but the correct criterion for aid (aside from humanitarian assistance at times of famine or other such transient crises) is an economy's capacity to absorb external resources in highly productive uses. This implies highly productive use of domestic resources, because foreign aid has always been a modest, marginal accretion of resources. Again to quote Rodan:[146] ". . . The basic purpose of aid is to catalyze additional national effort in developing countries. . . . Aid should continue to a point at which a satisfactory rate of growth can be achieved on a self-sustaining basis."

This perspective can be justified in terms of a partnership with common interests. The outcome would not be a fixed proportion of GNP in transfer payments to the poor from the rich but a declining flow as one country after another moved into self-sustaining growth and came to generate its capital requirements from its own resources plus conventional private borrowing from abroad.

Jan Tinbergen

In his comment on Tinbergen's essay in the *Pioneers* volume, Michael Bruno focuses sharply on the former's most distinctive contribution; that is, the conversion of the econometric planning techniques he pioneered in the postwar Dutch government to the planning of development—a conversion crystallized in his 1958 *The Design of Development.*[147] Although he had visited India in 1951, it was not until 1955, when Tinbergen was 52 years old, that he was freed of his governmental responsibilities and able to concentrate on problems of development. One senses in Tinbergen's *Pioneers* essay the moral as well as intellectual satisfaction he derived from this midlife commitment. He notes that he came to economics from physics in 1920 to struggle against the evil of poverty. He had seen on his 1951 trip to India poverty far worse and more widespread than any he had observed in Europe. One can understand the fulfillment he derived from his being able to turn wholeheartedly in the mid-1950s from an increasingly affluent Europe to the challenge of development and his joining the rapidly enlarging band of development economists, including those he generously describes as his teachers. They include, incidentally, three of his fellow pioneers: Raúl Prebisch, Paul Rosenstein-Rodan, and Hans Singer.

As noted earlier (pp. 300–301), Tinbergen himself, as well as Michael Bruno, underlines the frailty of formal econometric methods when applied to policy problems; and these lines from *The Design of Development* belong on every planner's wall:[148]

It must first be made clear that programming is not an alternative to common sense; it cannot replace common sense and it should not. It does supplement it, particularly with regard to the orders of magnitude of the phenomena involved. In the design of development all information and all methods available should be put to use. This seems the more desirable since information of the traditional type, the usual statistics, is often insufficient and inconsistent.

What distinguishes Tinbergen's reflections on his experience as a development economist is well captured in the title of his *Pioneers* essay, written when he was about 80: "Development Cooperation as a Learning Process." To capture the authentic and rare openness of mind his essay reflects, it is useful to go back to his first venture in growth analysis written in Holland during the German occupation and published in 1942.[149] It will be recalled that, in his pre-1939 work on business cycles, Tinbergen had sharply distinguished cycles from trends, regarding the latter essentially as exogenous phenomena. In his 1942 paper on trends, he virtually reverses the procedure, abstracting trends from cycles. He regards this procedure as legitimate so long as the "periodic [cyclical] components" of movement in the system are damped in such a way that the measured trend forms the "'center of gravity' of the short-term components" or "'general tendency' of the total movement" of the system.[150]

Against the background of this formal separation he states his purpose:[151]

The purpose of a theory of trend movements is to investigate economic movements extending over decades or even centuries. Such a theory must not overlook the development of population, capital etc., in fact it must make these the special subject of its analysis. Its central problem may be briefly expressed in the following question: how do production, employment, living standards and other factors change under the influence of population growth, technical development and capital formation?

After dismissing as an unsatisfactory basis for such an aggregated statement of the task the work of Kuznets (*Secular Movements*), Carl Snyder (on business cycles), Ernst Wagemann (on long waves), and Walther Hoffmann (on stages), he takes his start by combining Cassel's "uniformly progressing economy" with Paul Douglas's production function. He emerges with a quite straightforward version of the classic growth equation:

$$u = \epsilon^t \, a^\lambda \, K^{1-\lambda}$$

where u = total output of goods and services;

ϵ^t = a productivity factor increasing with time; i.e., "technical development"

a^λ = labor; $K^{1-\lambda}$ = capital; and $1-\lambda$ constant under the Douglas assumption of a linear homogeneous production function. He allows for the possibility of introducing land as a variable independent of capital. Douglas established that λ approximated $\frac{3}{4}$; but Tinbergen questioned Douglas's assumption that labor and capital were completely substitutable.

With this and some other modifications in his growth equation, Tinbergen proceeded to calculate over the period 1870–1914, for Germany, Great Britain, France, and the United States, comparative measures of wage flexibility; annual growth rates for total population, working population, real wages, production, and capital (including land); growth rates in labor productivity and overall "efficiency," and capital intensity. Perhaps the most interesting of these calculations is his effort to "explain" the increase in production in terms of the increase in inputs (capital and population) versus increases in efficiency.[152]

I evoke this bold, highly experimental exercise in comparative aggregate growth analysis not only because it was Tinbergen's point of departure from cycles to growth but also because it makes more vivid the reality of "the learning process" he evokes in the title to his *Pioneers* essay. He specifies, in particular, the following "shifts from less to more satisfactory approaches" to development:[153]

> . . . [F]rom the creation and transfer of physical capital to that of human capital; from foreign, capital-intensive technologies to appropriate, or adapted, less capital-intensive technologies, which in many cases implies a shift from large to smaller projects; and from employment creation in cities to its creation in villages or small towns. I also discussed a shift from external (intergovernmental) to internal policies and, somewhat related, from paternalism to self-reliance.

Although not formally listed by Tinbergen in his summation, I would add a further "shift" that he does, indeed, discuss; i.e., the need to link a broad general framework for planning to that "new industry: project appraisal."[154] Tinbergen describes in theory and, to a degree, in practice the conventional intellectual framework for project appraisal; i.e., the measurement of present value for all future yields. This demanded estimates of the project's construction cost and time, of annual yields and often (for markets in disequilibrium) estimates of shadow prices as well. He notes that the appropriate time discount—the value of present over future goods and services—is the most difficult variable of all to estimate, usually requiring, in the end, intuitive judgment or political compromises.

But something important is missing here: the criteria for sector rather than project appraisal. Theoretically establishing the highest present value for all future yields should settle the optimal sectoral as well as project allocation. The net marginal rate of return ought to be equal in all sectors. But, in fact, where private markets do not rule, the allocation process is and should be fought out in developing countries in terms of sectoral (or regional) rather than merely project terms; e.g., roads versus electric power versus agriculture versus education versus port development. Where these choices do not merely reflect the relative power of contending political interests, they imply an optimum sectoral pattern of development. Whether a sector is below or above its optimum dynamic path at a particular period of time (and, therefore, facing a current or foreseeable bottleneck or experiencing substantial excess capacity) profoundly affects the process of project appraisal.[155]

What marks Tinbergen's retrospective evaluation of his learning process is the ease with which he came to appreciate the rough-and-ready way development planning had to proceed in real life. There is no impulse to impose on a complex and opaque reality his virtuosity in econometric techniques:[156]

> Choosing concrete figures for each of the concepts implied a lot of arbitrariness, and striving for an "optimal" policy needed a number of heroic guesses. A logical start was, of course, to observe the recent past and then opt

for a somewhat higher figure. In practice, the narrowest of all the bottlenecks often determined its actual dimension. In many of the least developed countries this was the absorptive capacity (that is, the number of sufficiently concrete blueprints for projects); for many of the more developed countries the bottleneck was the donor's willingness to supply capital. But all sorts of other bottlenecks turn up during the execution of a given project: material supplies, certain types of skilled workers (from manual to managerial), and various bureaucratic shortcomings.

A similar pragmatic balance emerges in Tinbergen's discussion of the appropriate role of the public and private sectors in developing countries. In his 1958 *Design of Development,* for example, he argues that the line between private and public activity be drawn on the basis of the latter performing only where the former fails, after public encouragement, to fulfill an essential development function.[157] He identifies, within this rubric, the following essential tasks:[158]

(i) to create and maintain *healthy monetary conditions;*
(ii) to regulate the degrees of activity so as to *avoid mass unemployment;*
(iii) to *correct extreme inequalities* in income distribution; and
(iv) to *supplement private activity* in certain basic fields where for one reason or another that activity falls short of meeting legitimate requirements.

On top of these administrative, supervisory and supplementary tasks there is scope for some *direct participation* of the public sector in production. This is true of sectors so fundamental to the country's existence that direct control is needed, sectors safeguarding the country's security such as a system of flood control and military defense works.

Looking back in his *Pioneers* essay, he adds two further empirical observations: in the Netherlands, at least, the relative performance of public and private industries was primarily a function of the quality of management rather than the type of ownership; and that in Turkey public ownership came about in a good many industries because the private sector simply could not raise the requisite capital.[159]

Tinbergen's sturdy good sense and priority for relevance over elegance is well captured by Bent Hansen:[161]

For him the basic economic problems to be tackled have been so many and so large that frontal attacks on a broad scale by means of crude methods look much more rewarding than intensive studies of small isolated problems by means of highly refined methods. In the childhood of the automobile the French engineer Panhard once commented upon the newly invented manual (unsynchronized) gear box: "It is brutal, but it works." Although brutality is the last thing one would associate with Tinbergen, Panhard's comment certainly applies to Tinbergen's economic methods.

Behind Tinbergen's mixture of technological virtuosity and common sense, are qualities of humor, proportion, and awareness of the complexities of the human condition—all captured with rare candor and lack of pretension in his "My Life Philosophy."[161]

Two Conclusions about Development Policy: Time and Politics

As this review suggests, development economists after the Second World War, excepting Arthur Lewis, did not approach their field in the fundamental manner of the classical economists down to J. S. Mill and, I would argue, Alfred Marshall. Their focus was not the process of economic growth viewed as a terrain for systematic, general analysis. Nor did they accept the agenda of post-1870 mainstream economics overwhelmingly concerned with the workings of advanced industrial market economies that had successfully transited takeoff since the 1780s. The post-1945 development economists operated at the other end of the growth spectrum. They were concerned with an operational question: How could nations that had, for whatever reasons, been left behind in the previous two centuries catch up with the more advanced countries of North America, Europe, and Asia? More particularly, how could they move from slow, erratic, uneven progress to sustained growth accompanied by social progress and a place of dignity on the world scene? Many of the countries were newly independent; virtually all were stirred with fresh ambition as the course of the Second World War destroyed or fatally weakened the colonial framework and opened up options hitherto not judged to be realistic. The question was: What should these aspiring countries do? And, in the first instance, this meant: What should the governments of the aspiring latecomers do? And what should governments do that were interested and willing to help?

The orientation of development theory to clearly defined public policy issues was, of course, firmly in the tradition of classical economics. But its practitioners of the 1950s and 1960s were not seeking the natural laws for humanity to substitute for the arbitrary decisions of heavy-handed, power-seeking state bureaucracies. Shaped by previous experiences of interwar depression and war, when the role of the state was evidently critical, economists—with important exceptions—looked to public policies as fundamental instruments in the development process.

And, of course, they differed. Like virtually all its other branches since Hume and Adam Smith challenged mercantilist policy, modern development economics has been a quite contentious field. Of the various efforts to define the contending parties Paul Streeten's is certainly the most elaborate.[162] He begins with the following matrix:[163]

Table 17.6. Types of Development Theories

		Monoeconomics	
		Asserted	Rejected
Mutual benefit {	Asserted	Orthodox economics	Development economics
	Rejected	Marx?	Neo-Marxist theories

Source: Paul Streeten, see Note 163.

Evidently, he regards economists as split two ways: on whether or not they believe common interests exist between developed and developing countries; and on whether or not they judge a single corpus of economic analysis to be adequate for problems of developed and developing countries.

In elaborating the dual schism he argues that early development economists, who rejected the notion that neoclassical economics sufficed, identified specific structural problems in developing regions, some of which were later recognized as well in the advanced industrial world of the 1970s and 1980s. Thus, Streeten argues, development economics enriched mainstream economics and brought the two fields back towards unity ("Unity in Diversity").

He then canvasses in a somewhat cursory way the array of arguments asserting a convergence or conflict of interests between advanced industrial and developing countries and contrasts the insights of economists with those of "cranks, dissidents, 'poets,' journalists, and novelists" ("Formal Versus Informal Intellectual Sectors").[164]

Against this background, the battle on the central front, already introduced, is elaborated; that is, the battle of neoclassical economists versus the structuralists. Ian Little defined these categories as follows for Streeten:[165] ". . . [U]ntil fairly recently I see the story as one of a battle between structuralists who see the world as bounded and flat, and consisting of stick-in-the-muds, who have to be drilled—and neoclassicists who see it as round and full of enterprising people who will reorganize themselves in a fairly effective manner!"

Streeten then introduces two distinctions of his own: (1) between those who see a single obstacle to growth (e.g., lack of incentive to invest) or single objective (e.g., increase in GNP) versus those "pluralists" who see development as a product of multiple causation and an objective to be defined in terms of multiple values quite possibly differing among societies ("Hedgehogs versus Foxes"); and (2) "Linear versus Nonlinear Paradigms" which turns out to be his curious view that my concept of stages of economic growth asserts that Germany, Russia, Britain, and the contemporary developing countries followed identical ("Linear") development paths versus Streeten's version of the doctrine of *dependencia*.[166]

In a subsequent section ("Big versus Small") he sets P. C. Mahalanobis off against E. F. Schumacher. Polite to both, he sides nevertheless in the end with the former "with the major exception being his neglect of foreign trade opportunities."[167] Rather surprisingly he omits Mahalanobis's low priority for agriculture, a target for a good many of his other critics.

Streeten's final dichotomy consists of "Utopians versus Pedants." These are unnamed and unillustrated; but Streeten urges that their virtues be combined. In fact he struggles, rather gallantly in most cases, to identify the virtues of each approach and to suggest, sometimes incisively, sometimes vaguely, a benign synthesis.

Others undertaking Streeten's daunting task would emerge, no doubt, with different categories and biases. I would, in particular, commend the longer horizon and better balance of Gerald Meier's *Emerging from Poverty* (1988). But Streeten does suggest quite adequately the diversity of the perspectives brought to development economics. In concluding this survey of the field my purpose, therefore, will not be to redo his essay in my own fashion but to place the central issues in contention in two somewhat different perspectives than is conventional. The first concerns time; the second, politics.

I had the privilege of calling on two Thai economic planners at an interval of 22 years. The first visit in October 1961 was to Dr. Puey Ungphakorn, who was then not only chief economic planner in the government of Field Marshal Sarit Thanarat, but dean of the faculty of Thammasat University, Governor of the Central Bank, and, in the tradition of W. S. Gilbert's Pooh Bah, holder of several other high posts. Dr. Puey was one of the ablest development economists and public officials I ever met. We discussed a wide range of issues but came to rest on the problem posed for private entrepreneurship by the tradition that well-educated Thais enter the professions or public service rather than posts in commerce and industry. They thus left the field open to overseas Chinese, who, denied access to top political and social posts in Thai society, threw their extraordinary energies and talents into entrepreneurship in the manner observed by Sir William Petty some three centuries earlier as typical of the "heterodox party" (preceding, p. 211 and note 6). Dr. Puey noted that import-substitution industries were beginning to emerge initially to supply the Thai armed forces, then some of the local market. Entrepreneurship often took the form of somewhat awkward "marriages" between politically protective Thai military officers and Chinese businessmen.

Aided by policies that encouraged enlarged education, agriculture, and increased private capital imports, as well as by substantial official development aid, the Thai economy surged forward in the next quarter century in an extraordinary way. Real GNP more than quadrupled; strongly encouraged by a Promotion of Industrial Investment Act, value added in manufacturing rose from 14% in 1960 to well over 20% and greatly diversified; a new generation of well-educated Thais found their way into the economy. In the early 1980s Thailand was weathering the slowdown in the world economy better than virtually any other developing country and rapidly joining the Four Tigers of East Asia.

When I called on Dr. Snoh Unakul, president of the Economic Society of Thailand and secretary-general of the National Economic and Social Development Board in August 1983, he said that, at this stage of Thailand's history, the task of national planning consisted mainly of standing back and letting the private sector do the job.

The point is so important, in my view, that a second example is justified: the Republic of Korea, the first of the developing countries to emerge in the 1980s as well on its way to high-tech status across the board. Table 17.7 outlines the public-policy strategy that brought Korea to its present position.[168]

The policy objectives for the year 2000 are set out as follows by the vice-minister of Science and Technology:[169]

> The government of Korea has prepared a long-term technology development plan for the year 2000.
>
> The main goal of this long-term plan is to raise Korean technology to the level of the advanced countries by the target year. We identified five major technology fields to achieve this goal effectively.

The list includes microelectronics, genetic engineering, a range of industrial technologies, environmental protection, and health care. The report goes on:

> Key R & D projects will be carefully selected for development on the basis of their rate of return on investment, or feasibility based on Korean conditions. Our available resources will be invested intensively in these key projects.
>
> To support the development target, R & D investment will be increased sharply by the turn of the century. The master plan also aims at recruiting 150,000 R & D personnel by the target year, 10 percent of which will be of project manager caliber by international standard. . . .
>
> Consequently, the target setting will be transformed to concrete action programs of the Five-Year National Economic and Social Development Plans for actual implementation.

Table 17.7 and the extended quotation capture two essential points: the extraordinary transformation of the Korean economy in a quarter-century, including its switch from an

Table 17.7. Outline of Strategy: South Korea, 1960s–1980s

Period	Industrialization	Science and technology
1960s	1. Develop import-substitute industries 2. Expand export-oriented light industries 3. Support producer goods industries	1. Build S & T infrastructure 2. Develop skilled technical manpower 3. Promote adoption of transferred technology
1970s	1. Expand heavy and chemical industries 2. Shift emphasis from capital-import to technology-import 3. Strengthen export-oriented industry competitiveness	1. Strengthen S & T education at universities 2. Promote assimilation of imported technology in the private sector 3. Promote research applicable to industrial needs
1980s	1. Transform industrial structure to one of comparative advantage 2. Expand technology-intensive industry 3. Encourage manpower productivity of industries	1. Develop and acquire top-level scientists and engineers 2. Localize key strategic technology 3. Promote industry's technology development

SOURCE: *Korea Business World*, Vol. 3, No. 4, April 1987, p. 10.

import-substitution to an export-led growth pattern; and the extent to which that transformation was led and guided by an active government policy.

I cite these tales because much of the debate about development economics is peculiarly static, although the objects of the debate—the developing regions themselves—have been extraordinarily dynamic. Thailand, for example, entered takeoff (modern growth, its industrial revolution), in the 1960s; and was clearly in the drive to technological maturity (Lower-Middle-Income country) in the 1980s. More than a generation had passed with those coming to responsibility in the 1980s quite used to an environment of rapid growth and the voracious absorption of the large backlog of relevant technologies. In 1960 two percent of those between the ages of 20 and 24 were in institutions of higher education; in 1982, twenty-two percent—a truly revolutionary economic as well as social transformation.

The comparable statistics for the Republic of Korea over this span are even more remarkable. It was an even poorer country in 1961, at the time of the young officers' coup, but enjoyed a higher real income in the mid-1980s than Thailand (World Bank Upper-Middle-Income status). Its proportion of the relevant age group in higher education was 5% in 1960, 36% in 1985—a figure that compares with 22% in the United Kingdom. It is, evidently, well on its way to high mass consumption in my vocabulary, status as an "industrial market economy" in the vocabulary of the World Bank.

Although still societies living in continuity with their old cultures, Thailand and South Korea of the 1980s are different countries—economically, socially, and politically—from those of 1961. And the same can be said of virtually every other developing country although, of course the stories of Thailand, and Korea, like all others, have important unique features. Despite palpable negative and even pathological features, the per capita growth rates of developing countries in the 1950s and 1960s averaged over twice those of now-advanced industrial countries at equivalent stages.[170]

If one accepts, for a moment, Ian Little's definition of the dividing line among development economists as between structuralists and neoclassicists the distinction becomes highly sensitive to time and the historical stage of the economy or economies one has in mind. A country in what I call the preconditions for takeoff (say, Indonesia as of the 1960s) may not only lack, as did Thailand, an indigenous cadre of entrepreneurs, but also have a low level of literacy; a grossly inadequate secondary and higher educational system; a traditional agriculture essentially untouched by the productive methods available to modern labor-intensive farming; an infrastructure incapable of underpinning an efficient national market or a vital place in the international economy; a feeble if not obstructive and corrupt bureaucracy; and a flow of public revenues incapable of supporting the minimum irreducible functions of government, as defined, say, by Adam Smith.

The net investment rate may be 5% or less and concentrated in enclaves developed by foreign investors to expand raw material exports.

I cite this familiar array of the characteristics of underdevelopment to specify what I mean by "structural" problems, a term often used ambiguously.

A good many developing countries were, of course, further along in the 1960s than Indonesia. But the first and obvious point to be made—somehow lost in Little's structuralist-versus-neoclassical paradigm—is that a sensible policy prescription for a country will vary greatly with its stage of growth: where it stands in the preconditions for takeoff; in takeoff (which is always a phenomenon limited by sectors and, often, by regions); or how far beyond in the drive to technological maturity, also a dynamic process that takes time. The role of the state is bound to be greater relative to the private sector in the preconditions for takeoff than in, say, the drive to technological maturity. After all, the proportion of investment allocated to infrastructure (excluding housing) is normally above 30% in all societies. The development theorists of the 1950s and 1960s were visiting, staring at, prescribing for societies primarily at the lower end of the growth spectrum. Put another way, economies moving along well in the drive to technological maturity can, increasingly, be analyzed and prescribed for by the same techniques as those applied to more advanced industrial countries—although I would certainly not qualify neoclassical economics as adequate to either task.

The most rigorous formal effort to resolve the structuralist–neoclassical confrontation and the role of export-led versus import-substitution policies is to be found in Chenery's *Industrialization and Growth*.[171] Using an experimental computable general equilibrium model (CGE), Chenery and his colleagues compare export-oriented versus import-substitution strategies for stylized versions of Korean development on the one hand and Mexican and Turkish development on the other. An intermediate balanced strategy, more or less illustrated by Israel, is also explored.[172] One outcome is that while the export-promotion model performs best, the results are to a significant degree inconclusive because the model is, perforce, a highly simplified version of reality.[173]

> . . . We focus on market incentives and leave out exogenous factors whose links with policy are only imperfectly understood . . . [and] which could . . . only be explored by parametric variation. These elements are empirically very important. Endogenous effects working through incentives and market channels only explain a part of the differences in performance.
>
> Policies designed to "get the prices right" may be necessary to achieve rapid growth and structural change, but at this stage of our knowledge we cannot conclude that they suffice. . . .
>
> It may well be that all the associated elements follow naturally from a policy regime of sensible incentives in an environment of free markets. How-

ever, such a conclusion is certainly not obvious, and examination of the experiences of the countries which have successfully pursued export-led growth shows that their governments followed active interventionist policies, albeit with heavy reliance on market incentives. Our analysis has little to add to this debate directly, but it does suggest that a certain modesty in claims made for particular policy choices is called for.

In all conscience, one does not require—and may, indeed be confused by—a CGE model to explain why South Korea has done better than Mexico and Turkey since the early 1960s. Surely, differences in cultural attitudes toward education and family planning have been significant; the relative sense in which national security and independence are seen by the political leadership and the citizens to converge with the pace of development; the level of external assistance per capita; and other variables beyond the reach of the CGE model have been highly relevant to the outcome.

For present purposes, however, the following speculative dynamic conclusion is most relevant:[174]

> . . . [T]here may be a necessary sequence from growth dominated by import substitution to a shift to manufacturing exports as a major engine. It appears that an economy must develop a certain industrial base and set of technical skills before it can pursue manufactured exports. . . . There has been a sequencing at the sectoral level, with import substitution associated with low TFP [total factor productivity] growth rates followed in the same sectors with high export-led growth and high TFP growth. Whether these observed sequences are necessary or not cannot be determined by our data, but they are suggestive.

Without question, import substitution was overdone in a good many post-1945 developing countries. On the other hand, J. S. Mill's carefully delimited case for a transient tariff remains legitimate, with its lucid Humeian judgment: "The superiority of one country over another in a branch of production often arises only from having begun it sooner."

Now for the second observation: the critical role of politics in development. The fact is that from Djakarta through China and the Indian subcontinent to Rabat,[175] throughout Latin America, in Eastern Europe and the Soviet Union, and, indeed in Western Europe, a consensus has emerged that the weight of public intervention in the economy has become excessive and that greater reliance should be placed on private enterprise and the discipline of competitive markets. I believe it is the scope and consequences of public intervention in the economies of a good many developing countries that mainly account for the neoclassical attack on the structuralists. And, despite high aggregate growth rates, there is surely a great deal that justifies correction. Take for example, the following description of the situation in one developing country:[176]

> The Egyptian economy bears the legacy of economic policies dating from the 1950's which were motivated by concern for equity and assistance to the poor. These policies were characterized by price regulation, subsidization of consumer goods, a dominant public sector and state control. Subsequently the government has tried to insulate the average citizen from many of the shocks in the international economy and has not adjusted prices over the years. . . . [C]onsumers have not faced world prices for energy or many basic commodities. Both prices and wages of government workers in particular have

been held down significantly. As the gap between the market and the administered prices has grown, it has become more and more difficult and costly to maintain the current system.

This passage applies to a good many developing economies in Asia and Latin America as well as the Middle East. Other unresolved problems can be added with wide application in the developing regions; for example, agonizingly slow reductions in the birth rate, insufficient domestic competition behind excessive tariff barriers, and the emergence of "state bourgeoisies" often pursuing interests of their own that are rarely identical with those of the people as a whole.[177]

The bloated public sectors must be viewed as the outcome of an historic process. It resulted from the convergence of what might be called technical economic and political forces and certain strongly held attitudes in the developing countries of the 1950s.

On the economic side, there was the inability to earn or borrow, at tolerable rates, sufficient foreign exchange to avoid highly protectionist import substitution policies. These led directly to insufficient competition in domestic markets, damping the entrepreneurial quality of both the private and public sectors. Foreign exchange rationing was also a policy that required large powerful bureaucracies to decide what should be imported. In many countries that process was the heart of what passed for planning. On the political side there was the fear of explosions in the volatile cities and a decision, in effect, to exploit the farmer on behalf of the urban population. This had, of course, the effect of reducing incentives in the agricultural sector and slowing the rate of increase of agricultural production, forcing increased grain imports at the expense of capital goods for industry and transport.

With respect to attitudes, the 1950s were times when capitalism was an unpopular word and socialism a popular word in the developing regions. Capitalism was associated with colonial or quasi-colonial status, representing an intrusive external power, and it was systematically represented as such and denigrated by political leaders over a wide range. There was also considerable sentimental appeal in socialism during the 1950s: some of the European social democratic governments were doing quite well; Mao's Great Leap Forward and Chinese Communist policy in general generated a considerable appeal among those who did not investigate it too deeply; and even Khrushchev's boast that the U.S.S.R. would soon outstrip the U.S. in total output had a certain credibility in the late 1950s. To all this one can add that many of the emerging political leaders were often intellectuals or soldiers, both types inherently suspicious of the market process and inclined, for different reasons, to have excessive faith in the powers of government administration.

It is fair to ask to what extent, if any, structuralist development economists bear some responsibility for this outcome. Stripped of rhetoric the charges can be reduced to three:

- postwar "export pessimism" and excessive reliance on import substitution;
- inadequate incentives and support for agriculture combined with excessive subsidies to maintain low prices for "basic needs" in the cities; and
- excessive reliance on government ownership and control of industry and inadequate encouragement of domestic competition and foreign private investment.

With respect to the first charge, it should be recalled that import-substitution policies—if not traced back to Alexander Hamilton—were the product of a condition, not a theory; that is, the Great Depression of the 1930s. Prebisch, trained as a classical economist, supported such policies on pragmatic grounds in the face of the overwhelming balance-of-payments crisis that confronted Argentina and a great many other developing countries of the period. The later homilies of, say, Jacob Viner, Gottfried Haberler, or Peter Bauer would have sounded hollow, indeed, in Latin America of the 1930s. The ECLA doctrine, which in familiar pattern turned out to be fighting the last war, came later.

Export pessimism in the early postwar years was in part the result of a general expectation that global depression was likely to recur after a brief restocking boom. There was, moreover, a universal failure among economists to anticipate the pace of the global boom of the 1950s and 1960s: GDP per capita in the advanced industrial countries in the period 1950–1973 increased at an annual rate (3.8%) almost three times the highest previous sustained rate (1.4%, 1870–1913). Export pessimism suffused the view of prospects for certain advanced industrial countries (e.g., Italy, France, Japan) as well as the developing regions in the early postwar years. Other factors were, of course, also at work; for example, the judgment that the Soviet Union had managed to develop at a rapid rate on an autarchical basis and the shortage of foreign exchange.

In short, circumstances and the inaccurate expectations of economists combined to preserve or set in motion postwar import-substitution programs. Explicit positive professional doctrines of import substitution played a part; but, I would guess, an ancillary role. As Prebisch points out, his theories simply provided a rationale for policies the course of the world economy in the 1930s had forced Latin-American governments to adopt. As development economists observed the perverse influence of the vested interests that grew up around excessive tariff barriers, the rather narrow limits of import substitution as an impulse to industrialization, and the structural distortions that were generated (including perverse domestic terms of trade), they increasingly advocated remedy in the form of free trade areas, common markets, and efforts to expand manufactured exports.

As for the tilt of policy toward the cities at the expense of agriculture and rural life, development economists bear little or no blame. They did of course vary in the strength of their protests against these distortions, and Peter Bauer can argue legitimately that he should have been more strongly supported by his colleagues in protesting the damage to agriculture wrought by the African marketing boards. Moreover, most development economists did not appreciate fully the corrosive (as well as positive) consequences of U.S. agricultural products supplied by grant or subsidy under Pubic Law 480. But the relative neglect of agriculture and increasingly onerous subsidies to urban populations surely arose not from the propositions and prescriptions of development economists, but primarily from the political life of the developing regions and irrational reactions against real or believed distortions of the colonial (or quasi-colonial) past.

Similarly, the excessive reliance on government ownership and control of industry is primarily a product of political impulses and images combined with initially weak cadres of private entrepreneurs. Subsequently, the bureaucratic vested interests that grew up resisted the kind of shift to privatization the Japanese pioneered in the 1880s with such insight and skill.

I express these views not to defend the structuralists against the neoclassicists—whose relative virtues and demerits will gradually be sorted out with the passage of time—but for a larger reason. In my judgment the greatest weakness of development economics in the

1950s and 1960s in all its variants was its lack of a solid, analytic political base. Economic growth in the developing regions from Alexander Hamilton's 1791 *Essay on Manufactures* forward has been in good part—in some cases, wholly—a demand derived from a nationalist determination to achieve independence and dignity on the world scene in the face of remembered external intrusions of the past or of intrusions feared in the future.[178]

This strand was in many cases heightened by a judgment in the minds of responsible politicians that their most urgent task was to strengthen in one way or another the usually weak sense of nationhood. This often required a struggle to assert the power of the political center over the provinces or tribes; and it tempted a good many leaders to external adventure or xenophobic postures towards one or another major power.

The problem was brought home to President Kennedy in conversations with President Sukarno of Indonesia in April and September 1961.[179] In discussions on the former occasion Kennedy urged that development be given a high priority and offered to back such a commitment with U.S. support for a World Bank consortium of the kind that already existed for India and Pakistan. Sukarno's reply: "Development takes too long. Politics is everything. Mr. President, give me West Irian." For good or ill, Sukarno got West Irian; but, with Sukarno replaced by Suharto in 1965, an international consortium for Indonesia (The Hague Club) was organized later in the 1960s.

Kennedy saw Sukarno again in September 1961. This time he was accompanied by President Keita of Mali. The occasion was the visit of pairs of leaders from developing countries to the capitals of major advanced industrial countries to explain and defend the resolutions of the 1961 Belgrade conference of self-defined "neutrals," who gathered to assert their interests in the face of the U.S.–U.S.S.R. confrontation.

Keita, whose dignity and candor made a favorable impression on Kennedy, sought to explain a shadow from the past on U.S.–Mali relations. President Eisenhower had refused a Mali request for a few DC-3 transport planes and machine-gun armed jeeps. Keita subsequently acquired them from Czechoslovakia somewhat strengthening the hand of his left-wing advisers. He said: "I am responsible for a piece of real estate that calls itself a country. I needed some planes with our flag painted on them and some jeeps for our police to give a bit of substance to our nationhood."

And when some governments turned with highest priority and, even, with passion to development (e.g., South Korea, Taiwan), it was, as suggested earlier, for the Hamiltonian reason: the requirements for independence and security were perceived to converge with those for improved human and social welfare.

In short, politics was generally more important than economics in the developing world; and the critical political issues were substantially different from those of the advanced industrial countries. Here, I believe, is the reason for the inadequacy of, say, Bauer's plea that aid only be granted to those governments that relied on the market and thus moved toward democracy or, say, Myrdal's and Singer's easy transfer of the canons of the post-1945 social-democratic welfare state in Northwestern Europe to the developing world—a view that Myrdal finally recanted. It will be recalled that others among our pioneers ended up in puzzlement and disappointment at the extent to which politics frustrated the economic development outcomes they envisaged or hoped for. It is appropriate that Gerald Meier's final chapter in *Emerging from Poverty* ("The Under-development of Economics") is mainly about politics.

The politics of Latin America, whose countries acquired independence about a century and a quarter before 1945, was, of course, somewhat different from that of the other developing regions that contained many newly independent countries. But there, too, political leaders were in an endless struggle against fragmenting regional and class interests, including schisms derived from concepts rooted in the French Revolution. To establish somehow, in the face of limited resources, a majority national consensus and the requisite compromises to permit stable democratic rule was—and remains—extremely difficult.[180] Prebisch's ultimate disabuse with the Latin-American political process, does not, in my view, capture accurately the nature of the problem confronted in that region, nor does the prescription of his fifth stage suffice.

In any case, Part IV surveys the task ahead for political economy and public policy itself, and the primacy of noneconomic forces and policies will further emerge.[181]

18

Rostow's Theory
of Economic Growth

Presuppositions

The reader of this book is no doubt already reasonably clear about the biases I bring to the study of history and economics. But having felt free to pass judgment on the work of a good many predecessors and contemporaries, it may be useful to summarize explicitly, in a brief chapter, how I look at these matters.

This chapter is an exercise in summation, not intellectual autobiography. For these purposes all the reader needs to know is that I decided when I was 17 to combine history and economic theory in two senses: using economic theory both to illuminate economic history, then a rather descriptive, institutional field; and to explore the complex interactions of the economy with the noneconomic sectors of society. As an academic, this is what I have tried to do ever since.

I should, perhaps, add what is obvious. Trained from the beginning as a historian as well as an economist, my sympathy lies with Malthus in his assertion during the debate with Ricardo: "In political economy the desire to simplify has occasioned an unwillingness to acknowledge more causes than one in the production of particular effects. . . . The first business of philosophy is to account for things as they are. . . ." This was the aim in my early year-by-year, cycle-by-cycle studies of the British economy which covered every year from 1790 to 1914 except 1850–1868. Thus my evident sympathy for D. H. Robertson and others who disciplined themselves to establish how, with inelegant interactive complexity, and with long- and short-period factors simultaneously at work, economic life actually unfolded.

Because Chapter 20 and the joint mathematical Appendix, (with Michael Kennedy) will contain further technical and theoretical material reflecting my views, the summary here will focus on certain broad characteristics of my perspective.

People, Complexity, and Process

My unabashed delight with the thought, style, and values of David Hume is evident in Chapter 2. Quite particularly the following proposition is, in my view, the proper starting point for any historian, social scientist, novelist, or, indeed, anyone else dealing with human beings: "These principles of human nature, you'll say, are contradictory: But what is man but a heap of contradictions."

The inescapable complexity of people and, therefore, societies decrees that the assumption of maximizing behavior is often misleading.[1] Noneconomic forces can reinforce, dilute, or frustrate economic motives; for example, the fear of external intrusion (as with Alexander Hamilton and the Meiji reformers) can reinforce other impulses to modernize a society just as the wayward politics of many developing countries have frustrated the straightforward triumph of Myrdal's "modernization ideals." Take another example. The extraordinary and unpredicted revival of Western Europe after the Second World War cannot be fully understood without taking into account the linkage, as it were, of grandparents and grandchildren; that is, men who knew Europe before 1914 (e.g., Monnet, De Gasperi, Adenauer, Schuman) made common cause with the ardent young technocrats who emerged from the war. The interwar generation, burdened with a sense of failure, almost dropped from sight. Serious economic theory, history, and development doctrine must take this kind of complexity—including generational sequences—into account. In combination with the problem of increasing returns, the role of noneconomic factors demands, as Marshall perceived, that economics must ultimately be a biological rather than a neo-Newtonian subject. Thus, an understanding of the process of economic growth is a more appropriate objective than a theory of economic growth in the conventional sense. I was later to find in the images of a scientist, Ilya Prigogine, evoking his view of the physical world, phrases that capture quite precisely my view of how growth (and economic history) unfolds[2]: "instability, mutation, and diversification, where irreversible processes are constantly at work and nonequilibrium is itself a source of dynamic order."

These judgments in any case, explain *inter alia* the rather restrained enthusiasm of Chapter 15 for Harrod–Domar and neoclassical growth models as well as the title of my *Process of Economic Growth* (1952, 1960).

A Dynamic Disaggregated Theory of Production

The Process of Economic Growth is the basic statement of the theory I have subsequently elaborated and applied to a wide range of historical and policy problems. It was a kind of theoretical road map I felt impelled to lay out as I settled down to teach economic history at M.I.T. in 1950. I had concluded by that time that conventional economic theory suffered from four weaknesses that rendered it grossly inadequate as a framework for studying and teaching the history of the world economy as it had evolved since the mid-eighteenth century. First, conventional theory provided no mechanism for introducing noneconomic factors into the analysis of economic growth systematically when it was quite clear that economic growth—notably in its early phases but, in fact, throughout—could not be understood except in terms of the dynamics of whole societies. Second, it could not accommodate within its structure the process by which major new production functions were generated and diffused. It provided no linkage between science, invention, and the production process.

Third, mainstream theory provided no credible explanation for trend periods, longer than conventional business cycles, in the prices of basic commodities relative to manufactures. Fourth, it provided no credible linkage of conventional business cycles to the process of growth. For a historian it is palpable that cycles are simply the form growth historically assumed. The separation of cycle and trend—of the Marshallian short from the long period—is an act of intellectual violence that cuts the heart out of the problem of both cycles and growth. But it will be recalled that 1950 was a time when mainstream business-cycle theorists were ringing the changes on the interaction of the multiplier and the accelerator, thereby effectively separating growth from cycles, relegating innovation to exogenous investment.

The Process of Economic Growth responded to these four problems by an extended consideration of the interweaving of economic and noneconomic forces centered on propensities that summarize the effective response of a society to the economic challenges and possibilities it confronts (Chapters 2 and 3); by an analysis of the complex linkages among science, invention, and innovation that generate the flow of new production functions, including the sequence of majestic, innovational leading sectors that distinguish modern economic growth from all past human experience (Chapter 4); and by relating business cycles (Chapter 5) and secular trends (Chapter 6) to the process of growth thus conceived. I devoted a good deal of space, as in Chapters V and VI of my earlier *British Economy of the Nineteenth Century* (1948), to the forces that brought about change in the noneconomic framework of the economy (i.e., the propensities) including prior economic change. The balance of *The Process of Economic Growth,* in both its first and second editions, consisted of a set of illustrations and elaborations of this way of looking at the growth process.

At its core the process of economic growth as I conceived it implied that, within a given (or slowly changing) societal framework (the latter defined by the propensities), there existed a set of dynamic, optimum sectoral paths that, in a rough-and-ready way, an economy approximated with the passage of time. The deviations from the optimum paths were seen as setting up relative price and other incentives that, with varying lags, pulled the system back toward the sectoral optima. More than a quarter-century later, in writing *The World Economy: History and Prospect* (1978), that framework still seemed serviceable. This is how I defined *The World Economy's* underlying theoretical structure after noting its continuity with *The Process of Economic Growth:*[3]

> I believe it is possible to bring within the structure of a dynamic, disaggregated theory the forces making for population change, as well as the generation of scientific knowledge and invention, and the process of innovation. It is then possible to conceive of a dynamic equilibrium path for a peaceful, closed economy and all its sectors. Those overall and sectoral optimum paths imply that investment resources are allocated to the sectors without error or lag, taking into account changes in technology as well as demand. We can thus formulate abstractly a disaggregated, moving rather than static, equilibrium. In fact, of course, the economies we study were not closed; they were often at war or affected by war; and investment was subject to systematic errors and lags. Moreover, the coming of new technologies and the opening of new sources of food and raw-materials supply often took the form of large, discontinuous changes in the economy and its structure. And, even in the most capitalist of societies, the economic role of government was significant. What we observe, then, are dynamic, interacting national economies, trying rather clumsily to approximate optimum sectoral equilibrium paths, tending successively to undershoot and overshoot those paths.

If these various economies more or less regularly absorbed the technologies generated by the world's investment in science and invention, they grew; that is, with many irregularities and vicissitudes, their average income per capita tended to [follow] . . . an S-shaped path of acceleration and deceleration once take-off occurred. That process of growth, accompanied as it regularly was by increased urbanization, education, and other social changes, underlies the demographic transition. Where investment lags were particularly long, as they have historically tended to be in expanding output from new sources of food-stuffs and raw materials, the dynamics of growth yielded the trend periods . . . generally marked by rather massive undershooting and over-shooting of optimum sectoral paths. . . . [These oscillations reflect] my theo-ry of the cycles which Kondratieff identified but for which he offered no systematic explanation. When the lags were shorter, and investment errors more quickly corrected, [conventional business cycles] . . . emerged. When national growth is analyzed with particular attention to the effective absorp-tion of the lumpy sequence of major technologies, the stages of growth . . . move to the center of the stage.

Summarizing this perspective in *Pioneers in Development* I concluded:[4] "And so econo-mies made their way through history, overshooting and undershooting their optimum sectoral paths, like a drunk going home from the local pub on Saturday night."

My comments on the views of others at various points throughout this book suggest the importance I attach to the concept of a dynamic disaggregated optimum pattern of growth from which deviations can be assessed; for example, the respect expressed for J. M. Clark's extended analysis of the meaning of "balance" and Arthur Burns's measurement of cyclical distortion as well as my regret that Hirschman did not go beyond his praise of unbalanced growth to develop the notion of dynamic balanced growth that he acknowl-edged as an implicit norm in the course of his analysis.

The Emergence of the *Stages of Economic Growth*

As the preceding long quotation makes clear, the stages of economic growth, from my perspective, constitute merely one component of the general theoretical framework I have devised. The first virtually unnoticed appearance of the takeoff was in *The Process;* mainly in Chapter 4.[5] As in the present study, the stages of growth are dealt with there along with the limits to growth.

The takeoff arose as an inescapable discontinuity from my own research and the work of my seminar students at M.I.T. as together we turned around in our hands the stories not simply of Britain and the United States but also of Belgium, France, Germany, Japan, Sweden, Russia, Italy, Argentina, Brazil, Mexico, Turkey, Canada, Australia, and oth-ers. The discontinuity was inescapable because I began with the proposition that modern economic growth resulted from the generation and efficient absorption of increasingly sophisticated technologies. And if one studies the introduction into the economy of new technologies, one must disaggregate down to the level of the sectors, and sometimes even to particular factories (as with John Cockerill's seminal plant in Belgium), where the new technologies are introduced. The discontinuity induced in those sectors—and in related sectors—by the absorption of new technologies is then obvious; and it is quite possible to trace out, in rough approximation at least, the consequences for the aggregate performance of the economy induced by these multiple linkages.

By 1955 I was ready to write an article for the *Economic Journal* on "The Take-Off into Self-Sustained Growth."

Stages Beyond Takeoff

Up to this point I did not attempt to distinguish any stages beyond takeoff and the arrival of self-sustained growth. This, for example, is the formulation in my 1956 article:[6]

> . . . [T]he sequence of economic development is taken to consist of three periods: a long period (up to a century or, conceivably, more) when the preconditions for takeoff are established; the takeoff itself, defined within two or three decades; and a long period when growth becomes normal and relatively automatic. These three divisions would, of course, not exclude the possibility of growth giving way to secular stagnation or decline in the long term.

But two further definable stages emerged within the general rubric of self-sustained growth: the drive to technological maturity; and high mass computation.

The essentially noneconomic process permitting the drive to technological maturity to happen is, in antiseptic technical language, a progressive increase in technological absorptive capacity; that is, the buildup within the society of scientists and engineers, workers and entrepreneurs, and foremen and managers capable of absorbing—and motivated to absorb—the backlog of relevant, increasingly sophisticated, hitherto unapplied technologies. This implies not only an extension of education at every level and the emergence of a wide range of modernized institutions encouraging the process, but also a succession of generations each born into and taking for granted a technologically more complex and diversified world. The upshot is the progressive diffusion, beyond the relatively few leading sectors of takeoff (quite often confined to one or a few regions), of modern attitudes and motivations as well as modern technologies.

High mass consumption relates not to the buildup of a society's technological absorptive capacity but to its real income per capita and how men and women choose to spend it as they become more affluent. In economists' jargon it reflects a given phase in the income elasticity of demand; that is, the phase when people are rich enough to spend increases in income on a family automobile and the standard package of durable consumers' goods science and technology have provided for modern households in the twentieth century.

As I elaborated and refined the processes beyond takeoff, I directed a project and wrote *The United States in the World Arena* (1960), a rather long book focused on the interplay of American domestic life and foreign policy.[7] It included a substantial introductory historical section covering that interplay from the beginning of the American republic to 1940 and used the emerging, refined version of the stages of economic growth to help frame the analysis. (The other two concepts used for that purpose were the national style and the national interest.)

I delivered eight lectures to undergraduates at Cambridge University in the Michaelmas term of 1958 on "The Process of Industrialization," and I decided to pack what I had to say about the stages into those lectures.

The lectures were summarized by the London *Economist* in two issues in August 1959 and published in 1960 as *The Stages of Economic Growth*. With some eighteen reprintings in English and many translations, the book goes on having a lively career of its own, making new friends and stirring up controversy 30 years after the lectures were delivered.

Thus, I concluded that two centuries of growth had yielded five stages in the life of modern economies: the traditional society; the preconditions for takeoff; the takeoff itself; the drive to maturity; and the age of high mass consumption. Beyond we can detect elements of what I called, in *Politics and the Stages of Growth* (1971), the Search for Quality; but it remains to be seen if, in the wake of the turbulent 1970s and 1980s, it emerges as a definable stage.

The Stages of Economic Growth as Seen by the Author

It may be worth noting where *The Stages* fits in the elaboration of my own thinking about growth. Positively, it constituted a method for solving at least *ad interim,* two fundamental problems I identified, analyzed, and illustrated in *The Process*. First, how to relate economic and noneconomic factors as the process of growth unfolded. In large social science terms, this is the central question posed by Marxism and explains in large part why I accepted the suggestion of *Economist* editors and subtitled the book "A Non-Communist Manifesto." *The Stages* takes the view that the noneconomic sectors of society interact with the economy. They are not a superstructure determined simply by technology and property arrangements. The second problem I felt I had moved forward was how to use systematically in the analysis of economic growth the insights of economic historians—generalized notably by Schumpeter, the young Kuznets, and Hoffmann—about the succession of major innovational leading sectors that have given the period since the last quarter of the eighteenth century a unique place in human history.

With respect to economic and noneconomic factors, I found it fruitful to focus successively on that relationship in each stage (traditional society, preconditions, takeoff, drive to technological maturity, age of high mass consumption) rather than grapple with it in general. Every country is, of course, unique; and the relationship is one of interaction and is therefore immensely complex. But there were definable patterns and recurrent forces; e.g., the powerful role of xenophobic nationalism in the early stage of modernization stirred by intrusion or feared intrusion from abroad, and the assumption of leadership in modernization by an intermediate group denied access to the top of the traditional society but not denied education or money (e.g., the British nonconformists, the samurai, the parsees in India).

As for technology, the stages down to high mass consumption constituted a way of linking the degree of social modernization (in terms of education, enterprising entrepreneurs, nontraditional concepts of family, politics, etc.) to an important economic variable; i.e., technological absorptive capacity. Stages were thus defined not as is conventional in modern economics (e.g., the World Bank) in terms of real income per capita but in terms of the extent to which a society proved capable of absorbing efficiently (then) modern technology.

This technological approach, with its explicit linkage to large, powerful leading sectors, also cut across the conventional approach to saving-investment incorporated in Keynesian analysis. In *The Stages* the emphasis is on the importance to capital supply of entrepreneurs who plowed back profits in the rapidly growing, highly profitable leading sectors introducing a technology not hitherto efficiently incorporated in the economy. For example:[8]

> This view of the take-off is, then, a return to a rather old-fashioned way of looking at economic development. The take-off is defined as an industrial revolution, tied directly to radical changes in methods of production, having their decisive consequence over a relatively short period of time. . . .
>
> [T]his argument [asserts] that the rapid growth of one or more new manufacturing sectors is a powerful and essential engine of economic transformation. Its power derives from the multiplicity of its forms of impact, when a society is prepared to respond positively to this impact. Growth in such sectors, with new production functions of high productivity, in itself tends to raise output per head; it places incomes in the hands of men who will not merely save a high proportion of an expanding income but who will plough it into highly productive investment; it sets up a chain of effective demand for other manufactured products; it sets up a requirement for enlarged urban areas, whose capital costs may be high, but whose population and market organization help to make industrialization an on-going process; and, finally, it opens up a range of external economy effects which, in the end, help to produce new leading sectors when the initial impulse of the take-off's leading sectors begins to wane.

This was all very well, from my point of view; but the simple fact is that I failed almost totally to make my colleagues see the connection between *The Stages* and the wider framework of *The Process*. Summary Chapter 2 of *The Stages* contained four pages (entitled "A Dynamic Theory of Production") explicitly making the linkage that was so clear in my own mind.[9] My colleagues insisted on regarding the rise in the investment rate in the takeoff as a primal cause in the manner, say, of a Harrod–Domar growth model. As I have noted on other occasions, a part of the fault was certainly mine.[10] If I had it to do over again, I would state emphatically, right at the beginning, what I wrote in the "Introduction and Epilogue" summarizing the debate on takeoff organized at Konstanz in 1960 by the International Economic Association:[11] ". . . The emergence of a rate of net investment sufficient to outstrip the rate of increase of population and to yield a positive net rate of growth is at least as much the result of prior [sectoral] growth as a cause of growth." But, as I noted earlier, the takeoff appeared at just the time two alternative ways of looking at growth came on stage: the neoclassical growth model; and Kuznets's massive extension of Colin Clark's statistical approach to the morphology of growth. The takeoff was certainly not ignored; but its intellectual bone structure did not easily fit the other two approaches, although, as I noted at the time, it bore a family relation to Kuznets's earlier *Secular Trends*.

The Debate

For those who may be interested in the debate on The *Stages* and my response to it, Note 12 provides some references.[12] Here I would only make a few simple points:

- As already noted, in the course of the debate the concept of stages of growth was almost totally separated from the concept of a dynamic, disaggregated general theory of production from which it derived and of which it was, simply, one component.
- A great deal of the debate, with Simon Kuznets leading the attack, centered on whether the statistical evidence showed (or would show) a Rosenstein-Rodan–Lewis-Rostow rough doubling in the investment rate during takeoff. Data now available, some 30 years later, indicate that some such statistical discontinuity can be identified (following, p. 656 note 40); and Kuznets's dates for ''the beginning of modern economic growth,'' when he published them in 1971, closely approximated those given for takeoff in *The Stages*.[13]
- There was also debate at Konstanz—in general and with respect to particular historical cases—on a more profound issue; i.e., the degree of aggregation and disaggregation appropriate to the analysis of economic growth. Toward the end of his career, Kuznets, who vigorously made the case for aggregation at Konstanz, somewhat softened his view in the direction of the disaggregation of his youth (preceding, pp. 354–355, following, p. 669 note 12) and, François Crouzet's disaggregated annual production data have helped restore the 1840s as a key phase of the French takeoff, a view challenged at Konstanz.[14]

As Figure 18.1 suggests—comparing as it does the Smithian, neoclassical, and Rostovian growth models developed in the mathematical appendix—my approach to economic growth yields a quite distinctive formal result.

But, looking back over the 30 years since I defined the stages and their dynamics, I am

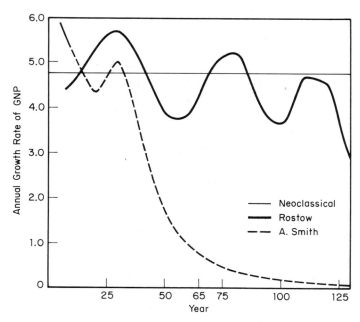

Figure 18.1. Annual GNP Growth Rates over Time in Three Systems (see Appendix, pp. 526 ff.).

inclined to conclude that the attention given to the concept stemmed primarily from its relevance for many readers to the problems of development policy and to the prospects for war and peace. Like a good many other theoretical works in economics it was a pamphlet for the times; perhaps because it was originally delivered as lectures to undergraduates, it communicated rather well, and it arrived at a moment when problems of development and the Cold War were high on the agenda of public concerns.

Applications in the 1950s: Development Policy

The reasonably orderly evolution of the concept of the stages from *The Process* to the Cambridge lectures was conducted in counterpoint to a protracted communal effort, starting in 1951, to generate a theory of development relevant to the problems of contemporary Latin America, Africa, the Middle East, and Asia, and, on that basis, to define and crusade for an appropriate policy of the advanced industrial countries towards the developing regions.[15] Although my research in the 1950s led to particular views about development policy, and I spoke and wrote a good deal on this matter as an individual, my most useful contribution to policy was, no doubt, as part of the collective effort mobilized in the 1950s at the Center for International Studies (CENIS) at M.I.T.

In 1952 CENIS's work on development began formally and included intensive studies of India, Indonesia, and Italy. Aside from Max Millikan and me, the members of the senior staff engaged on economic development problems were Everett Hagen, Benjamin Higgins, Wilfred Malenbaum, and P. N. Rosenstein-Rodan. Rodan had, of course, been at work on development problems longer than any of us. We were also closely in touch with our colleague Charles Kindleberger, whose wide portfolio of interests included the field of economic growth in both a historical and contemporary context. James E. Cross, Dan Lerner, Ithiel de Sola Pool, and Lucian Pye contributed insights from political science and sociology. Younger economists, including George Baldwin, Francis Bator, Richard Eckaus, and George Rosen, also got into the act, as did a then-junior political scientist, Donald Blackmer, and a remarkable former schoolmaster and novelist, Richard Hatch, who served as critic, editor, and conscience of CENIS.

The most complete synthesis of our collective argument was incorporated in a short book entitled *A Proposal: Key to an Effective Foreign Policy*, completed in August 1956.[16] With some oversimplification of a reasonably sophisticated exposition, the argument of *A Proposal* can be summarized as follows:

- The forces at work in the developing world inherently lent themselves to instability and violence: the tension between the modernizers and those still rooted in the values and institutions of the traditional society; struggles for power among the modernizers; various potentially disruptive forces unleashed by the intense often xenophobic nationalism that accompanied release from colonialism; frustration at the often slow pace of economic and social progress; and an urgent desire to assume a place of dignity and independence on a crowded and contentious world scene. The competition between communists and noncommunists merely added an extra dimension to and heightened these sources of instability.
- It was the interest of the United States that the developing societies evolve toward modernization rapidly but with minimum violence. A

concentration of limited talents and resources on the tasks of modernization rather than in external adventures or violent internal struggle appeared the most promising route to that objective.

- The United States could contribute to that objective most effectively by strengthening the hand of those who perceived that serious and sustained economic and social progress was the most effective path to the dignity and independence on the world scene almost universally sought; and this support could best be accomplished by assuring that the international community provided sufficient external capital to match the capacity of a developing society efficiently to absorb capital, while working via technical assistance and support for education to enlarge absorptive capacity.

Thus, our basic argument for development assistance was, in the widest sense, political. It was rooted in a judgment about the inevitably conflicting forces unleashed in a society at an early stage of modernization, and an assessment of what outsiders with only marginal influence might usefully do to tip the balance in what we judged to be a benign direction.

My colleagues accepted the legitimacy of the concept of stages of growth—an acceptance by no means automatic in that strong-minded lot, despite our friendship.

The introduction of the stages into the argument had two substantial political and psychological consequences. In the developing regions it provided an operational focus for efforts to accelerate economic growth that was manageable, as it were, within the lifetime of a human being. If one stared in the 1950s at the gap between income per capita in current prices of, say, $100 and $3000, one could conclude that the task of modernization was hopeless or, at least, irrelevant to one generation's efforts. If the task was defined as achieving takeoff and self-sustained growth, rather than the U.S. level of real income per capita, it was easier to roll up one's sleeves and go to work in reasonably good heart. Takeoff came to be accepted as a legitimate operational goal in a good many developing countries.

Within hard-pressed parliamentary bodies of the advanced industrial world, commitment to sustained development assistance was easier to achieve if it was believed such aid would level off and ultimately decline as takeoffs occurred in one country after another and the bulk of the developing world made its way to the stages beyond, relying increasingly on conventional sources of capital.

Against this background our proposal consisted of an international plan to generate sufficient resources to meet all requirements for external assistance that could be justified by absorptive capacity. The price tag was estimated at an additional $2.5 billion to $3.5 billion a year (about $10 billion to $14 billion in 1987 U.S. dollars), of which about two-thirds was judged to be then an equitable U.S. share.

Administratively it was proposed that the program be conducted mainly by existing institutions, but that the World Bank create a special instrument "to coordinate information, set the ground rules, and secure acceptance of the criteria for the investment program."

As for the linkage between economic development and the emergence of stable political democracies, we may, in retrospect, have been a bit too hopeful; although the assertion of the popular impulse toward democracy in many parts of the world as of 1989 might well have astonished as well as pleased the crusaders of the 1950s. And, on the whole, we were by no means naive. One CENIS publication of the 1950s posed and answered bluntly the question of linkage: "Is there any guarantee that the free Asian nations will emerge from rapid economic growth politically democratic? No such guarantee can be made. The relation between economic growth and political democracy is not simple and automatic."[17] We were, however, firmly convinced that a concentration of scarce resources, talents, and political energies on the task of development, undertaken with reasonable balance, was likely to maximize the chance that societies would move through the modernization process with minimum violence and human cost and yield governments whose policies increasingly approximated the will of the governed.

Early in this book I tried, in setting the stage for Hume and Smith, to evoke the large considerations that suffused their work: how a combination of "sympathy," as they defined it, and ruthless competition might heighten the good in human beings and discipline the evil; how the degradation of poverty might be mitigated; how enlarged affluence might be the friend of civil liberty and a civilizing agent over a wide front in the domestic life of societies; and how a wise economic policy might temper the barbarities of mercantilism abroad as well as at home.

However the concepts and policies generated by the development crusaders of the 1950s and 1960s may be judged in longer perspective, there was no time in the modern history of political economy when its practitioners had a better right to feel kinship with their classical progenitors.

Applications in the 1950s: War and Peace

I applied the concept of stages in two ways to issues of war and peace. Chapter 8 of *The Stages* ("The Relative Stages-of-Growth and Aggression") distinguished three kinds of wars related to the relative degree of technological virtuosity and economic power among societies. First, colonial wars embracing conflicts arising from the initial intrusion of a colonial power on a traditional society; from efforts of one colonial power to seize the colonial possession of another; or from the effort of colonial peoples to assert their independence of the metropolitan power. These were wars associated, on the colonial side, with societies in the preconditions for takeoff. Second, regional aggression, usually limited wars arising from the exuberance of newly formed national states as they looked backward to past humiliation and around them at opportunities to assert their nationalism. These were wars initiated by countries quite far along in the preconditions for takeoff (as in the case of the American effort to steal Canada in the War of 1812) or in takeoff (like Bismarck's Germany in 1864–1871). Third, struggles for the Eurasian power balance of which I cited the First and Second World Wars and the Cold War. Here the dangerous age came as nations completing the drive to technological maturity were tempted to seize and hold regional hegemonic power in Eurasia against others who had come to maturity earlier and appeared sluggish and ripe for the taking.

Against this background I asked what the prospects were for bringing the Cold War to a peaceful end in a chapter entitled "The Relative Stages-of-Growth and the Problem of Peace." The central concept I brought to bear was the diffusion of power away from both Moscow and Washington—a process I dated from 1948.

In the short run, the diffusion of power arose from the paradox that nuclear weapons were rationally unusable except to deter their use by others, and therefore, the proportionality between industrial power and usable military power had been violated.[18] ". . . [I]n different ways on different issues Nehru, Nasser, Ben-Gurion, Adenauer have found ways of exploiting this paradox within the non-Communist world; and Mao and Gomulka as well as Tito have done it within the Communist bloc.''

In the longer run, I argued, the diffusion of power would take on solidity.[19]

> Just as the forward march of the stages-of-growth in the latter half of the nineteenth century shaped the world arena of the first half of the twentieth— bringing Japan, Russia, Germany, France, and the United States into the arena as major powers—so sequences of change, long at work, and gathering momentum in the post-1945 years, are determining the somewhat different world arena now coming to life.
>
> For the central fact about the future of world power is the acceleration of the preconditions or the beginnings of take-off in the southern half of the world: South-East Asia, the Middle East, Africa, and Latin America. In addition, key areas in Eastern Europe (notably Yugoslavia and Poland), and, of course, China, are hardening up, as their take-offs occur. . . .
>
> And in Latin American the take-off has been completed in two major cases (Mexico and Argentina); and it is under way in others, for example, in Brazil and Venezuela.

Against this background I argued that the prospect for Russia was to see vast new nations come into the world arena that Russia could not control, and that its basic national interest, with respect to both the new weapons and the rise to maturity of new nations was a defensive interest essentially similar to that of the United States, Western Europe, and Japan. I concluded:[20]

> In the face of the diffusion of power being brought about by a new series of take-offs, the Russian national interest shifts closer to that of the United States and the West. . . . [I]t is not a realistic option to conceive of a continued bilateral or trilateral world of atomic powers blocking the others out, but continuing the competitive game of Cold War. . . .
>
> The diffusion of power can be rendered relatively safe or very dangerous; but it cannot be prevented. The process of growth and the stages at which various nations now stand rule out equally the notion of an American century, a German century, a Japanese century, or a Russian century.
>
> The rational policy for a nationalistic Russia would be, then, to exercise this moment of option to join the United States in imposing mutually on one another and on the world the one thing the world would accept from the two Great Powers; that is, an effective inter-national system of arms control.

I then turned to the difficulties Moscow confronted in accepting this vision and asked what we of the West could do to bring about what I called the Great Act of Persuasion:[21]

> Essentially we in the non-Communist world must demonstrate three things.
>
> We must demonstrate that we shall not permit them to get far enough ahead to make a temporary military resolution rational.
>
> We must demonstrate that the underdeveloped nations—now the main focus of Communist hopes—can move successfully through the preconditions into a well-established take-off within the orbit of the democratic world, resisting the blandishments and temptations of Communism. This is, I believe, the most important single item on the Western agenda.

And we must demonstrate to Russians that there is an interesting and lively alternative for Russia on the world scene to either an arms race or unconditional surrender.

But the great act of persuasion has an extra dimension: and that extra dimension is time. For this searching problem of transformation Russians must solve for themselves; and it will take time for them to do it.

Referring to Thomas Mann's novel of the generations, *Buddenbrooks,* I evoked in analogy the sequence that began with the old Bolsheviks, moved to the young engineer cadres who came to responsibility as Stalin purged his contemporaries, and hazarded the following about the future:[22]

> . . . [B]ut their children—taking a modern industrial system for granted— are reaching out for things that the mature society created by Stalin cannot supply. What is it we can detect moving in Soviet society? An increased assertion of the right of the individual to dignity and to privacy; an increased assertion of the dignity of Russia—as a nation and a national culture—on the world scene; an increased assertion of the will to enjoy higher levels of consumption, not some time in the future, but now; an increased appreciation of the way that modern science has altered the problem of power, including certain old and treasured military maxims, both Russian and Communist in their origins. . . . [T]here is no reason to believe that these underlying trends will automatically work themselves out smoothly and peacefully. On the other hand we should be aware that the dynamics of the generations within Soviet society—and notably the trends in the first post-maturity generation—combined with the diffusion of power on the world scene, could, in time, solve the problem of peace, if the West does its job.

Whatever Mikhail Gorbachev's fate may be in the time ahead, he will be remembered in part as the "first Soviet leader of the first post-maturity generation" (he was born in 1931). And his policies reflect a good many of the aspirations foreshadowed in the preceding quotation.

The application of the *Stages* to the theoretical and policy debate on development in the 1950s and 1960s is one strand in the public record of those lively times. The implications of the concept for U.S. policy toward the Soviet Union were transmitted as a consultant to the Eisenhower administration and a working member of the Kennedy and Johnson administrations.[23]

Five Applications for the 1980s and Beyond

The key questions addressed to each growth theorist, which provide bone structure and continuity to this study, derive directly from *The Process.* The continuity carries forward into Chapter 20 and the mathematical appendix. And it is also evident in Chapter 21, where I look ahead to the middle of the next century, that the stages of growth remains the matrix I use to identify the five critical future problems confronted by the human community. But in the time ahead it is the drive to technological maturity and its implications rather than the much-debated takeoff that comes to the center of the stage.

Put in the form of questions those problems can be stated quite simply:

- Will the diffusion of power in conjunction with the dynamics of Soviet society, both closely linked to the stages of economic growth, permit a peaceful resolution of the Cold War?
- Can the world community organize itself so as to absorb peacefully and equitably the countries of the Fourth Graduating Class (e.g., China, India, Brazil, Mexico) into takeoff as they come to technological maturity (see Figure 19.1)?
- Can the global community mount effective policies to sustain a livable physical environment as the enormous populations of the Fourth Graduating Class move to full industrialization; or will the strains already evident on the physical environment yield uncontrollable crises?
- Can the advanced industrial countries, having pretty well exploited and taken for granted the blandishments of high mass consumption, maintain, in Hume's phrase, "industrious and civilized" societies?—an issue posed in *The Stages*.[24]
- Can the global community, including the most advanced developing countries, mount patient, supportive policies to assist effectively the 20% or so of the human race that lives in countries that have not yet successfully completed the preconditions and moved into takeoff (e.g., Haiti, Africa south of the Sahara, Yemen, Afghanistan, Burma, and a good many of the Pacific islands)?

In the introduction to *The Stages* I underlined that it was a theory about economic growth and "a highly partial" theory about modern history as a whole.[25] I then quoted Benedetto Croce who wisely observed " . . . [W]hilst it is possible to reduce to general concepts the particular factors of reality which appear in history . . . it is not possible to work up into general concepts the single complex whole formed by these factors."[26] Returning to the initial theme of this chapter, I am quite aware of the limits and arbitrariness of any given set of concepts. That is one among several reasons that intellectual life, like other human pursuits, should be taken seriously but not too seriously. The concepts that emerged from my somewhat eccentric marriage of economics and history are valid only to the extent that they prove useful to others in perceiving and dealing with the elusive patterns of the past and in the life around them. But they have proved to have considerable predictive power.

IV

PROBLEMS AND PROSPECTS

19

Two Concluding Questions

Histories of economic thought and doctrine tend to come to an arbitrary, sometimes even an abrupt end. This is, in a way, inevitable. Such studies are, after all, analyzing the evolution of an ongoing field of considerable vitality and contention, whose continuous history reaches back to the seventeenth century at least, with mediaeval and classical antecedents as well. The story stops when the author decides to stop, with perhaps some final reflections on the sweep of the tale he has told, depending on his particular interests and biases.

The structure of this book suggests a way of closing out the story as of 1989, which is equally arbitrary but a bit unconventional. The method is to confront two questions: "What don't we know about economic growth?" (Chapter 20); and "Where are we? (An agenda in mid-passage.)" (Chapter 21).

The rationale for this method lies in this book's analytic structure. Parts I, II, and III are bound together not merely by the basic growth equation but also by a view of the key questions flowing from it with which, in my view, a growth theorist must deal. Specifically, I have tried to establish how a wide spectrum of theorists have viewed the determinants of: the size and quality of the working force; investment and the generation and absorption of technology; growth in relation to business cycles; growth in relation to relative price trends in manufactured goods and basic commodities; the stages of and limits to growth; and the role of noneconomic factors. These headings reflect, of course, a perspective elaborated in what I have published since 1938 on the subject of growth and fluctuations. And, although, I have tried in this book to capture with sympathy the perspectives of predecessors and contemporaries, my own point of view has not merely shown through but has also been occasionally stated quite explicitly, including Chapter 18 and the mathematical appendix. But I also decided it might be useful to define some of the unsolved problems still on the technical agenda of growth analysis, using once again the sequence of headings that has provided a bone structure for this book. That, in any case, is the objective of Chapter 20.

But the book has been bound together by another strand. It argues systematically that economists have been profoundly and sometimes permanently marked by the problems of their time and place—notably, but not exclusively, when they were young.

This linkage led me to pose the questions: What is our time and place in terms of the unfolding process of economic growth itself? Where does the human race stand in the story of growth as the 1980s—two centuries after the primal British takeoff—draws to a

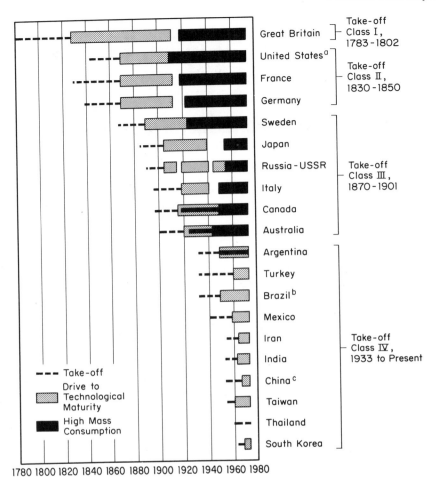

Figure 19.1. Four Graduating Classes into Takeoff: Stages of Economic Growth, Twenty Countries. [Adapted from W. W. Rostow, *The World Economy: History and Prospect* (Austin: University of Texas Press, 1978), p. 51 and Part Five.]

close? What broad implications flow from that assessment for the discipline of political economy and for public policy?

Once the British demonstrated that invention and innovation could become a flow rather than the sporadic contributions of Adam Smith's "philosophers," skill in the mechanic arts spread rapidly. A second graduating class into takeoff followed the unique British example (Figure 19.1); and a third followed the second. Each group moved forward more rapidly after takeoff than its predecessor because it had a larger backlog of technology to exploit. The latecomers closed on the earlier-comers, as those who debated the matter in the eighteenth century thought likely (Table 19.1). A Fourth Graduating Class has now emerged whose absorption into the world economy and polity is taken to be the central feature of the coming several generations.

For the century 1815–1914, balance of power diplomacy permitted the diffusion and redistribution of industrial power and military potential without major war, excepting the

Table 19.1 Per Capita Growth Rates, Takeoff to 1967: Fourteen Countries (1967 U.S.$)

Takeoff date	Takeoff date	Approximate GNP per capita: beginning of takeoff	GNP per capita 1965–1969	Number of years	Annual average growth rate
Great Britain	1783	$183	$2,018	184	1.31%
United States*	1843	451	3,995	124	1.77
France	1830	173	2,343	137	1.92
Germany	1850	249 (1851)	2,148	116	1.87
Sweden	1868	239	3,244	99	2.67
Japan	1885	158 (1886)	1,207	81	2.54
Russia–USSR	1890	246	1,594	77	2.46
Italy	1895	300	1,333	72	2.09
Canada	1896	796	2,962	71	1.87
Australia	1901	923	2,106	66	1.26
Argentina	1933	418	741	34	1.70
Brazil*	1933	144	323	34	2.40
Mexico	1940	224	545	27	3.35
Turkey	1934	171	331	33	2.02%

*Regional takeoffs are judged to have occurred beginning in the 1820s in New England, and in the São Paulo region from 1900 to 1920.

SOURCE: W. W. Rostow, *Why the Poor Get Richer and the Rich Slow Down*, (Austin: University of Texas Press, 1980), p. 261 and Appendix I.

American Civil War and the even bloodier civil war in China (the Taiping Rebellion), each related, in different ways, to the diffusing process of technological modernization. Part of the price for this century of transient relative peace was a phase of colonial rule that generated a considerable explosive potential released by the Second World War. But the story since 1914 has been, at its core, a demonstration of what a dangerous age completion of the drive to technological maturity can be. Look back for a moment to 1870 when Bismarck rounded out the German Empire with his three small wars. Britain accounted for 32% of the world's industrial production; Germany, 13%; France, 10%; Russia, 4%; and across the Atlantic, the United States, 23%. The Japanese, only 2 years beyond the Meiji Restoration, when the modernizers definitively seized power, were not in this company.

The German takeoff began in the 1840s; the Japanese in the 1880s; the Russian, in the 1890s. By 1914 Germany had acquired all the then-existing major technologies, as had Japan and the Soviet Union by 1941. These three challengers had come, in my vocabulary, to technological maturity, which, in that era, required some 60 years beyond the takeoff. By 1936–1938 the shares of world industrial production reflected the relative decline of Britain and France, the rise of Russia, and the appearance of Japan in the arena of power: Britain had 9%; Germany, 11%; France, 5%; Russia, 19%; the United States, 32%; Japan, 4%. World War II canceled out for a time Germany and Japan, gravely weakened Britain and France, and left a proud, ambitious but war-torn Soviet Union and an undamaged United States economically rehabilitated from the Great Depression.

There is a great deal more to the coming of the First and Second World Wars and the Cold War; but this relative growth sequence is certainly a fundamental part of the terrible saga.

In the midst of the turmoil of the interwar years and the Cold War, the Fourth Graduating Class came on stage, embracing countries with the bulk of the population of Latin America, Asia, and, potentially, the tortured Middle East. They are, in my view, mainly beyond takeoff, in the drive to technological maturity.

Growth in these regions is damped by all manner of problems, external or self-inflicted; but the old rule still appears to hold, that those who graduate into takeoff late move ahead faster than their predecessors; and in Chapter 20 some quite specific reasons will be adduced that suggest why this is likely to be the case in the several generations ahead.

The central question on the global agenda is, therefore, can we complete in peace the continued transformation from poverty to affluence that has been going on since the eighteenth century? In an age where the capacity to make nuclear weapons is diffused far beyond the present ample number of nuclear weapons powers, a Third World War must be regarded as a potential definitive disaster for all humanity.

There are many further questions, no doubt, beyond our capacity now to define, that lie further down the road, and I am quite conscious of the strand of legitimacy in Keynes's dictum, writing as a probability theorist rather than an economist:[1] "The inevitable never happens. It is the unexpected always." But the critical and central character of the adjustment to the rise of the Fourth Graduating Class has emerged with increasing clarity and insistence in recent years. The first approximation of an analysis of the adjustment proved to have a good many dimensions embracing not merely the peaceful defusing of the Cold War between the Soviet Union and the West, but also, among others, the reorganization of the terms of domestic politics in the Atlantic world and Japan; the finding of regional methods for regular cooperation among the nations of Asia and the Pacific, the Western Hemisphere, and other regions with countries at different stages of growth; the definition of new rules of the game for trade and finance under circumstances: (1) where no single country has the power to lead; but (2) all have vital stakes in the viability of the system; and (3) all must, therefore, assume, depending on their stage of growth and other relevant circumstances, duties as well as rights with respect to the international system. I have explored these matters elsewhere[2] and I shall not repeat in Chapter 21 the detailed arguments found there. But I shall try roughly to measure where we are in the great transformation that was modestly gathering momentum in the days when David Hume and Adam Smith were young. Assuming that, in the end, nations containing the bulk of the human race will, in their own ways, try to apply the fruits of modern science and technology to their societies, how far along in the process are we? What problems are clearly on the agenda? What kind of wisdom and luck will be required to get us through to a time of relatively universal affluence without global frustration or catastrophe of one kind or another? These are the issues probed in Chapter 21. They exhibit striking similarity to, as well as stark differences from, those that concerned the founding fathers of modern political economy in the eighteenth century.

An appendix follows that is the result of a second collaboration between Dr. Michael Kennedy of the Rand Corporation and myself. The first presented various views of the Kondratieff cycle in mathematical terms, and analyzed their differences and their relation to the flow of history.[3] The success of that venture led directly to this appendix, which is an attempt to see how much of the bone structure of the underlying argument of this book could be captured in formal mathematical terms.

Part II of the mathematical appendix consists of a systematic comparison from a common analytic matrix of three growth theories: a Smithian preindustrial revolution model; a neoclassical model; and a somewhat simplified version of the growth theory that underlies this book and includes as endogenous three essential features of the growth process: the demographic transition; the bunching of major innovations at intervals of, say, 55 years; and Kondratieff cycles in the generation of supplies of basic commodities (and in relative prices) of, say, 40 years. (The full array of distinctive assumptions entering into this model are set out on p. 543, following). Rather striking differences emerge in the aggregate growth paths that result from differences in the assumptions that underlie these three models.

20

What Don't We Know about Economic Growth?

Population and the Working Force

With hardly a respectful bow to Adam Smith, Colin Clark proudly traces his intellectual ancestry to "Political Arithmetick": to John Gaunt, Gregory King, William Petty, and others who began to measure the size of populations and the wealth of nations in the heated mercantilist setting of the late seventeenth century, thus launching the field of demography. But despite a history reaching back three centuries, despite the vital and various interests of governments in population data, the analysis of population changes remains somewhat elusive, notably, the determinants of fertility. In dealing with the demographic transition, for example, Chenery and Syrquin observed:[1]

> Given the crucial impact of population growth on the level of per capita income, it is important to show the extent to which the two are related and to indicate the linkages between them. Although these relations are the subject of active research by demographers and economists, there are wide areas of disagreement as to the nature and relative importance of the various factors involved. . . .
> While the causes of the world-wide fall in death rates are well understood, the interrelations among the socioeconomic processes related to fertility— education, health, urbanization, mobility, etc.—are still subjects of active debate.

In analyzing the cross-sectional data available, they fell back primarily on standard regression analysis. Figure 20.1 captures the result, with the scatter provided for birth rates.

The SEE (standard error) measurements indicate greater deviation among birth than death rates, and an enormous initial spread among birth rates narrowing as per capita income rises. Among richer countries of the world, birth and death rates appear to be relatively insensitive, after a certain point, to levels of GNP per capita.[2]

A great deal of analysis has been conducted to establish the relative weight of the factors determining the dispersion of birth rates at different levels of income,[3] but statistical analyses have not yet yielded firm or agreed results, and they have been systematically awkward in dealing with cultural and religious forces that have clearly helped shape the outcome in a good many cases. What has emerged is a policy rather than an analytic consensus: that the most effective programs to reduce birth rates in developing regions have combined determined public education in contraception with development programs that yielded not only rapid growth but also enlarged educational and health facilities and improved income distribution. All hands would agree that while the existence of this consensus is useful, it leaves a great deal to be learned about fertility and fertility policy, as the vicissitudes with family planning of the Indian and Chinese governments, among others, suggest.

It is worth noting, as a matter of substance as well as paradox, that the current conventional wisdom about the determinants of lower birth rates in developing countries closely relates to the Myrdal doctrine of the 1930s for elevating the birth rate; namely, that only wide-ranging programs of economic and social welfare would create a setting in which Swedish families were likely to have more children. The reason for recalling that proposition is that the trend in the net reproduction rate had fallen by the 1970s below 1.0 in seventeen advanced industrial countries; by 1986, of the nineteen industrial market economies listed by the World Bank, all but one (Ireland) had total fertility rates under 2.0.[4] A figure of 2.1 is roughly required for long run population stability. From such data the World Bank has provided, under stylized arbitrary assumptions, the hypothetical size of a stationary population for each country and the assumed date at which it will be reached. Such estimates are further examined in Chapter 20. But the fact is that the 1980s has seen the emergence of the strongest surge of anxiety and analysis of the implications of population decline since the 1930s;[5] and the beginning of pronatalist public policies in some advanced industrial countries.

For the moment it is sufficient to note that the world community is likely to confront simultaneously in the several generations ahead anxieties centered, in different parts of the world, on excessive increase and excessive decrease in population; that the richness of contemporary statistical data is not yet matched by firm knowledge of the determinants of fertility; and it is likely—perhaps certain—that the old unresolved issue of how to define an optimum population level will arise again, if it is not already upon us.[6]

Technology and Investment

I begin with a quotation that captures a major theme of this book:[7]

> While neoclassical economic theory has many important applications, it is poorly related to what really happens in the long run. It suffers from this deficiency mainly because it makes no provision for changes in technological knowledge. . . . [T]echnological change has to be introduced into the analysis from the outside. It is assumed, not explained. Thus what is certainly one of the most important determinants of price and output in the long run is entirely outside the range of the theory.

One of the major areas where knowledge of growth is imperfect centers on technology: its generation, including the oblique as well as direct links of science to invention; its diffusion and the role in that process of the quality of entrepreneurship; its links to the investment process as a whole and, therefore, to the macro performance of economies; and the determinants of the pace at which countries which have fallen behind absorb efficiently the backlog of relevant technologies. As the references suggest in the discus-

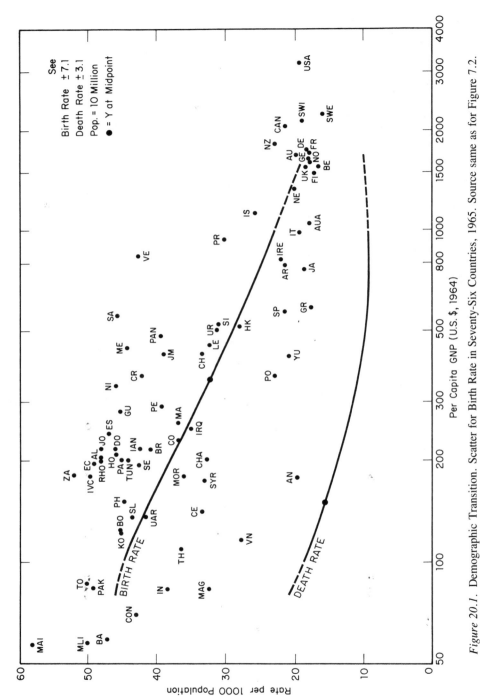

Figure 20.1. Demographic Transition. Scatter for Birth Rate in Seventy-Six Countries, 1965. Source same as for Figure 7.2.

Key to Country Codes

Country	Code	Country	Code	Country	Code
1. Afghanistan	AF	35. Haiti	HA	69. Papua	PNG
2. Algeria	AL	36. Honduras	HO	70. Paraguay	PA
3. Angola	AN	37. Hong Kong	HK	71. Peru	PE
4. Argentina	AR	38. India	IN	72. Philippines	PH
5. Australia	AU	39. Indonesia	IND	73. Portugal	PO
6. Austria	AUA	40. Iran	IRN	74. Puerto Rico	PR
7. Belgium	BE	41. Iraq	IRQ	75. Rhodesia	RHO
8. Bolivia	BO	42. Ireland	IRE	76. Saudi Arabia	SAU
9. Brazil	BR	43. Israel	IS	77. Senegal	SE
10. Burma	BA	44. Italy	IT	78. Sierra Leone	SL
11. Cambodia (Khmer)	CB	45. Ivory Coast	IVC	79. Singapore	SI
12. Cameroon	CM	46. Jamaica	JM	80. Somalia	SO
13. Canada	CAN	47. Japan	JA	81. South Africa	SA
14. Central African Republic	CA	48. Jordan	JO	82. Spain	SP
15. Ceylon (Sri Lanka)	CE	49. Kenya	KE	83. Sudan	SU
16. Chad	CD	50. Korea (South)	KO	84. Sweden	SWE
17. Chile	CH	51. Lebanon	LE	85. Switzerland	SWI
18. China (Taiwan)	CHA	52. Liberia	LBR	86. Syria	SYR
19. Colombia	CO	53. Libya	LBY	87. Tanzania	TA
20. Congo (Zaire)	CON	54. Malagasy	MAG	88. Thailand	TH
21. Costa Rica	CR	55. Malawi	MAI	89. Togo	TO
22. Dahomey	DA	56. Malaysia	MA	90. Tunisia	TUN
23. Denmark	DE	57. Mali	MLI	91. Turkey	TU
24. Dominican Republic	DO	58. Mexico	ME	92. Uganda	UG
25. Ecuador	EC	59. Morocco	MOR	93. U.A.R. (Egypt)	UAR
26. El Salvador	ES	60. Mozambique	MOZ	94. United Kingdom	UK
27. Ethiopia	ET	61. Netherlands	NE	95. U.S.A.	USA
28. Finland	FI	62. New Zealand	NZ	96. Upper Volta	UV
29. France	FR	63. Nicaragua	NI	97. Uruguay	UR
30. Germany (West)	GE	64. Niger	NIR	98. Venezuela	VE
31. Ghana	GH	65. Nigeria	NGA	99. Vietnam (South)	VN
32. Greece	GR	66. Norway	NO	100. Yugoslavia	YU
33. Guatemala	GU	67. Pakistan	PAK	101. Zambia	ZA
34. Guinea	GUI	68. Panama	PAN		

sion that follows, a good deal of work is going forward on these problems heightened over the past decade by an awareness that the early stage of one of the great technology revolutions of modern history is now underway.[8] But all hands concerned with these issues would, I suspect, agree that much current research and analysis is exploratory, fragmented, and not yet adequately woven into the principal conventional areas of economic analysis. The unfulfilled task in this terrain is, therefore, both the integration of technological analysis itself and its linkage with mainstream economics.

One of the ironies of the story told in this book is that the formulation of marginal analysis round about 1870, generally regarded as a decisive, creative breakthrough in the life of the profession, broke the rather easy, unembarrassed linkage of technological and economic analysis that had existed for a century.[9] Hume and Adam Smith, Malthus and Ricardo, J. S. Mill and Marx (educated by Charles Babbage)—all had a good deal to say about problems posed by technology in their time. So did Marshall, D. H. Robertson, and Allyn Young; but they could not find a way to reconcile their insights with post-1870 formal theory. Marshall, above all, saw with striking clarity the incompatibility of conventional equilibrium analysis and the rigorous treatment of the case of increasing returns, a conflict bound to arise in any serious formal analysis of the diffusion of new technologies.

I recall these efforts to confront an exceedingly intractable problem at this late stage of the argument for three reasons. First, the subsequent history of mainstream economics is, essentially, a story of successive evasions designed to protect a method by avoiding the problem: to render innovation exogenous or embody it in gross investment; to treat it as an incremental consequence of widening the market or learning by doing; to bury it in the "residual," or the marginal capital-output ratio, or "intermediate production." Except for the handful of exceptions noted along the way, the mainstream literature is set out as if Joseph Schumpeter and the young Simon Kuznets of *Secular Movements* had never written.[10]

Second, Michael Kennedy and I decided that if we were to construct for our Appendix an Adam Smithian preindustrial revolution growth model to contrast with models of a modern economy, a central problem to be solved was to capture the shift of inventions occasionally generated by Smith's "philosophers" and creative machine makers into a flow; for that is what modern economic growth is all about.

Third, in Chapter 21, the phenomenon defined as The Fourth Industrial Revolution will be seen to suffuse virtually all the major problems the global community will confront in, say, the next half-century. And its four major dimensions—microelectronics, genetic engineering, new industrial materials, and lasers—are all subject to discontinuous new developments as well as sustained incremental progress.

The balance of this section aims, therefore, to identify the problems that must be solved and the broad characteristics of an approach to technology and investment that might contribute to bringing back together again the two roads that went their separate ways after 1870. The argument takes the form of eight related propositions.

1. *Research and Development is a complex interacting spectrum yielding as an end product profitable inventions and innovations.* The creation and profitable introduction of a new technology into the economy is the result of a complex spectrum of activities ranging from basic science, through invention, to the pioneering complex business operations we call innovation that, in turn, is likely to involve high-risk finance, labor training or retraining, and imaginative marketing. Occasionally—for example, Edwin Land and the Polaroid camera—all three activities have been conducted by a single person. But

even with respect to the primal inventions of the First Industrial Revolution, each of the three phases was, in itself, not an event but a complex, frustrating process.[11]

As for basic science, as it evolved from Copernicus to Newton and beyond, its fields have had a life of their own, sometimes closely and directly linked to the process of invention, sometimes distant and oblique.[12] In different ways neither Schumpeter nor the early Kuznets were particularly helpful in making clear the complexities that lay behind one of the former's heroic innovations or the creation of one of the latter's leading sectors. Schumpeter's references to the origins of inventions were candidly derivative. It is the innovator and the economic consequences of large discontinuous innovations that mainly concerned him.[13] Kuznets's work, of course, contains many references to the fundamental role of modern science in economic growth; but he also did not explore in a serious way the varying character of the linkage of science to invention at different times and with respect to different specific inventions.

For present limited purposes it is sufficient to note that three conceptually distinguishable but interacting creative activities are involved in the R & D spectrum; that there is still much to be learned of how they relate to each other; and that the linkages and interactions have never been as close as they are in the Fourth Industrial Revolution now underway.

2. *It is useful if oversimple to regard inventions and innovations as made up of two broad types: incremental and discontinuous.* Adam Smith made this distinction, as did Schumpeter. The latter sharply distinguished technological change so small that managers could do the job, from great structural breakthroughs requiring entrepreneurial heroes. In fact he rather overdid this point. His own analysis suggests that one is, in fact, dealing at a moment of time, with a spectrum of degrees of creative entrepreneurship among sectors and firms (preceding, pp. 238–239). Rosenberg takes this point head-on.[14]

> Schumpeter accustomed economists to thinking of technical change as involving major breaks, giant discontinuities or disruptions with the past. . . . But technological change is also (and perhaps even more importantly) a continuous stream of innumerable minor adjustments, modifications, and adaptations by skilled personnel, and the technical vitality of an economy employing a machine technology is critically affected by its capacity to make these adaptations.

Carried along by the logic of his argument, Rosenberg, discussing the important pre-Watt role of Newcomen's engine, draws back from a *reductio ad absurdum* and finds a fair balance:[15]

> . . . One might almost be tempted to say of James Watt that he was "just an improver," although such a statement would be comparable to saying of Napoleon that he was just a soldier or of Bach that he was just a court musician. That is to say, Watt's improvements on the steam engine transformed it from an instrument of limited applicability at locations peculiarly favored by access to cheap fuel, to a generalized power source of much wider significance.

There are, in fact, two types of incremental invention and innovation. First, even with respect to the greatest and most powerful innovations, an incremental process, involving many hands and minds, is almost certain to have preceded the critical breakthrough and continued to operate to refine the new instrument or method as it moved along its inevitably decelerating Kuznetsian path as a leading sector. But, second, incremental invention and innovation go forward every day—probably with less élan—in less rapidly expanding, stagnant, or even declining sectors of a modern economy.

In short, while agreeing substantially with the emphasis—from Adam Smith to Nathan Rosenberg—on the importance of incremental technological change, I would also re-affirm the legitimacy of Schumpeter's dramatization of the three great industrial revolutions on which he focused in *Business Cycles:* that of the 1780s, with its convergence of the new textile machinery, Watt's steam engine, and Cort's method of fabricating good iron with coke; the railroad revolution, starting modestly in the 1830s but helping induce before long the steel revolution to overcome the high obsolescence rate of iron rails; and the breakthroughs in electricity, chemicals, and the internal combustion engine round about the turn of the century. The fourth, asserting itself from, say, the mid-1970s, after long incubation, embraces four large fields: microelectronics; genetic engineering; the development of new industrial materials (e.g., ceramics, optical fibers, a new round of plastics); and the laser. The process of incremental refinement goes forward more or less regularly in these highly diversified areas, punctuated as one would expect in a still-early stage of a technological revolution by sporadic major breakthroughs, e.g., recent progress toward superconductivity at higher temperatures.

3. *Both types of R & D—incremental and discontinuous—are forms of investment; that is, they represent the current allocation of human talent and other resources to achieve an expected future rate of return over cost that, taking risk and appropriability into account, at least matches allocations in other directions.* As wise economists from Hume to Keynes have observed, investment constitutes a creative adventure to which people are drawn by motives that transcend the conventional profit motive; and this is, perhaps, even more true of R & D than more conventional forms of investment. Nevertheless, the social value of invention was reflected even before the First Industrial Revolution by, say, the British patent system and various forms of subsidy and reward for invention offered by the French government in the eighteenth century.[16] But it has been only recently that serious professional efforts have been made to measure the profitability of investment in R & D as a subsector of the investment process in a modern economy. Three major pioneering figures associated with this effort are Jacob Schmookler, Edwin Mansfield, and Zvi Griliches. The deceleration of the American rate of productivity increase since, say, the mid-1960s—and its possible connection with a deceleration in civilian R & D expenditures—has enlarged and heightened work along lines initiated by the three pioneers.[17]

As Schumpeter perceived, the extent and manner in which the R & D process relates to familiar economic incentives is complex. At the scientific or research end of the spectrum there has, in fact, been some debate, with Marxists straining to embrace even Newton's *Principia* as a response to the felt needs of the bourgeoisie.[18]

The view here is somewhat more complex. In tracing the evolution of growth theories, two contrapuntal strands became apparent: an impulse to try to solve the problems of the active world; and a continuity of concept, debate, and elaboration in what might be called the inner life of the discipline. This is evidently also true of the evolution of the natural sciences. Moreover, both the social and natural sciences have been shaped, in part, by the capacity to measure and to calculate, as, for example, Keynesian income analysis was greatly strengthened by the emergence of national income and product calculations in categories that linked concept and numbers.[19] What needs to be emphasized here (and in Chapter 21) is that, with the passage of time and the four successive concentrations of innovations over the past two centuries, the linkage of basic science to invention and innovation has become progressively more direct. The Fourth Industrial Revolution is intimately linked to areas of basic science that themselves are experiencing revolutionary change. The inventor, innovating entrepreneur, and the working force have, for two centuries, always been a team—harmonious, despite frictions, if innovation was to succeed. Now the scientist must be increasingly a working member of that team; and to be successful the entrepreneur must understand something of what he is about. There are unlikely to be any great breakthroughs in the times immediately ahead based (like Henry Ford's moving assembly line) on a slaughterhouse.

But the oldest distinction between basic and applied science still remains. While immensely fruitful, in varying different ways, the social profits generated by basic science are hard to predict or to entrap for the creator. Therefore, as British scientists argued with Charles II in 1661 and Colbert with Louis XIV on behalf of French scientists, including Pascal and Huygens, a few years later, the state must subsidize basic science in its own interests on what Adam Smith was later to define as "great society" grounds. The rationale for the British Royal Society and the French Academy, reinforced in the nineteenth century by Babbage and J. S. Mill among others, thus set the pattern for public subsidy to basic research that continues down to the present.

Putting military technology aside and certain important civil enterprises too uncertain or expensive for the private sector to undertake (e.g., fusion power), a more easily recognizable market process has generated the great as well as small inventions of the past several centuries. In a good phrase related to Hirschman's "inducement mechanisms," Rosenberg cites three types of "compulsive sequences" which, by posing sharply defined problems, attracted creative talent to their solution:[20] technical imbalances brought about by disproportionate progress in one phase of an interconnected economic process; labor strikes or other threats to the continuity of production; and wartime shortages brought about by interruption or sharply increased costs of supply. All three of these forcing mechanisms operated, of course, on profits or expected profits; but Rosenberg is asserting more than this obvious linkage. He is arguing that the channels in which inventive talent are, in fact, concentrated, can be powerfully influenced by disequilibrium situations endogenous to the unfolding of technology itself, or exogenous to the economic system.

These are valuable insights; but it is evident that there is still much to sort out as we come increasingly to treat the whole R & D process as an endogenous part of the working of modern economies.

4. *Scientific and inventive as well as entrepreneurial talent tends to cluster; but why?* As demand-oriented macrotheories—Keynesian, monetarist, or both—demonstrated their inadequacy for analytic or prescriptive purposes in the 1970s and 1980s, there was something of a revival of interest in theories of long cycles, including especially, Schumpeter's innovational version of the Kondratieff cycle. This has led inevitably to a reexamination of Schumpeter's assertion that major innovations have historically tended to distribute themselves irregularly through time in bunches, swarms, or clusters.

The central figures in the revived debate on this issue have been Gerhard Mensch, an academic figure in both Germany and the United States; Christopher Freeman, who has led a distinguished team of analysts at the University of Sussex; and a Dutch economist, Alfred Kleinknecht.[21]

It should be said right off that the discussion has been complicated because three reasonably distinct definitions of (as well as hypotheses about) clustering are involved. First, Schumpeter appeared to have in mind in his *Theory of Development* a pioneering innovational breakthrough in a single major sector, followed by a strong bandwagon effect bringing into that sector a large number of new firms, with entrepreneurs of lesser breed, to exploit the demonstrated profitability of the innovation. Second, Mensch, relying heavily on the dating of invention and innovation in Jewkes's *The Sources of Invention* (1958) argues:[22] (1) that groups (or clusters) of major innovations in different sectors have tended to be set in motion during cyclical depressions, when the lag is shortened between invention and innovation, and their diffusion accounts for subsequent powerful booms; and (2) that a phase of "technological stalemate" follows the exploitation of these innovational clusters until depression generates and unleashes a new batch of inventions and innovations.

After a careful and temperate analysis of Mensch's data and findings, Freeman concludes as follows—a view I would generally support:[23]

> (*i*) Basic *inventions* do show a tendency to cluster at certain periods, including a big cluster in the early 1930s, but these clusters are apparently not systematically related to depressions.
>
> (*ii*) Neither does the available evidence consistently support the Mensch–Kleinknecht theory of heavy clustering of basic *innovations* in periods of deep depression, although there is some evidence of a cluster in the late 1930s.
>
> (*iii*) Nor does it support the acceleration hypothesis of reduced lead-times for innovations launched in deep depressions.
>
> (*iv*) There is however evidence of a falling off in basic innovations at the tail-end of long booms.
>
> (*v*) Firms tend to reduce both their R and D activities and their patenting during the more severe depressions.

Freeman's own hypothesis—the third—links science, invention, and innovation—as well as large discontinuous and small incremental innovations—in a somewhat different way:[24]

> We are interested in "constellations" of innovations which have a relationship to each other and not just in the more or less accidental statistical grouping of the innovations of a particular year or decade. The important phenomenon to elucidate if we are to make progress in understanding the linkages between innovations and long waves is the birth, growth, maturity and decline of *industries and technologies*. The introduction of a major new technology into the economic system can take a matter of decades and affect many industries but the process has cyclical aspects which can give rise to long wave phenomena.

Freeman then adds a conclusion, bringing him back to Schumpeterian orthodoxy at least as of the latter's *Business Cycles:*[25]

> . . . If the S-curves were randomly distributed for a fairly large number of discrete basic innovations, and if, too, the shape of the curves varied quite a lot, then there might be a series of ripple effects in the larger economy but there would not have to be big waves.
>
> Big wave effects could arise either if some of these innovations were very large and with a long time span in their own right (e.g., railways) and/or if some of them were interdependent and interconnected for technological and social reasons or if general economic conditions favoured their simultaneous

growth. Thus we are interested in what we shall call "new technology systems" rather than haphazard bunches of discrete "basic innovations." From this standpoint, which we believe was essentially that of Schumpeter, the "clusters" of innovations are associated with a technological web, with the growth of new industries and services involving distinct new groupings of firms and with their own "subculture" and distinct technology, and with new patterns of consumer behaviour. Schumpeter spoke of the first Kondratiev as based on a cluster of textile innovations and the widespread applications of steam power in manufacturing, the second as the railway and steel Kondratiev, and the third as based on electricity, the internal combustion engine and the chemical industry.

Freeman proceeds then to examine in some detail two technological systems that became of great importance in the world economy after the Second World War: synthetic materials and electronics.

Out of these and other analyses that are part of the economic historian's lore, three clues emerge, suggesting, perhaps, the shape of an answer to the question:[26] Why should there have been in the past two centuries four clusters of major technological systems?

The first clue is that the working out and refinement of a given innovational breakthrough is clearly a long-term process. In Part Five of my *World Economy: History and Prospect* I sought to dramatize the role of leading-sector complexes with a simple device. I charted the rate of growth of each leading sector, in a 5-year moving average, against the rate of growth of an overall industrial production index. Initially, of course, the growth-rate curve of the leading sector greatly exceeded that of the industrial index. After a time the rate of growth of the leading sector settled down to (or fell below) the rate of growth of the overall index. For Great Britain this is roughly how long it took:[27]

Table 20.1. Approximate Timing of Leading Sectors: Great Britain, 1783–1972

Sector	Maximum rate of expansion (1)	Estimated time sector became leading sector (2)	Estimated time sector ceased to lead (3)	(3) − (2) (in years, approximate)
Cotton textiles	1780s	1780s	1840s	60
Pig iron	1790s	1780s	1860s	80
Railroads	1830s[a]	1830s	1870s	40
Steel	1870s[b]	1870s	1920s	50
Electricity	1900–1910	1900–1910	—	—
Motor vehicles	1900–1910	1920–1929	1960s	40

[a]Figures for mileage added in each decade are as follows: 1825–1830, 71; 1830–1840, 1,400; 1840–1850, 4,586; 1850–1860, 4,493; 1870–1880, 2,001; 1880–1890, 1,718.

[b]Estimate begins in 1871 with 329,000 tons. Maximum growth rate may have come earlier, at very low levels of production.
SOURCE: W. W. Rostow, *The World Economy* (Austin: University of Texas Press, 1978), p. 379.

Freeman charts the life history of the U.S. plastics industry suggesting, once again, the stately decelerating rhythm of the life cycle of a technological system as captured earlier in Kuznets's *Secular Movements* (Figure 20.3 and 20.4). Conventional business cycles are the form this long-term process assumed, not the matrix which triggered this process into existence.

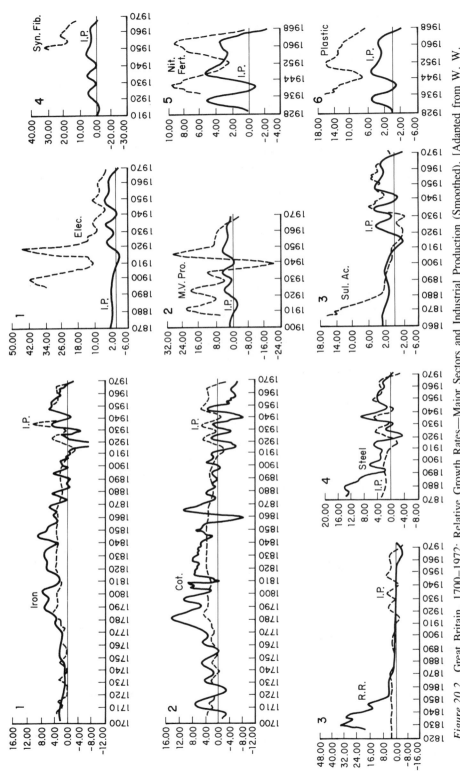

Figure 20.2. Great Britain, 1700–1972: Relative Growth Rates—Major Sectors and Industrial Production (Smoothed). [Adapted from W. W. Rostow, *World Economy: History and Prospect* (Austin: University of Texas Press, 1978), pp. 376–377.]

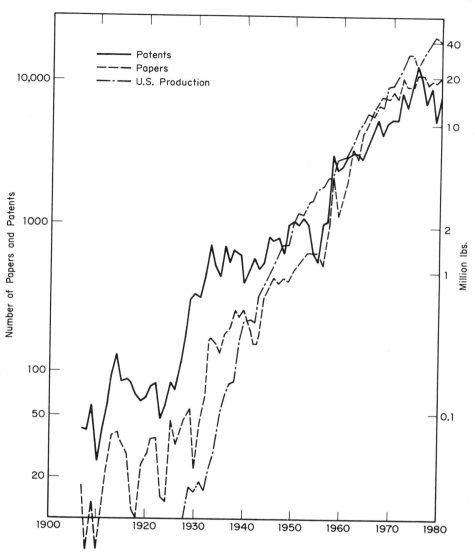

Figure 20.3. Plastics Patents, Papers, and U.S. Production (1907–1980). Adapted from V. Walsh *et al.,* "Trends in Invention and Innovation in the Chemical Industry," Report to Social Science Research Council (mimeo), Science Policy Research Unit, in C. Freeman, John Clark, and Luc Soete, *Unemployment and Technical Innovation* (Westport, Conn.: Greenwood Press, 1982), p. 86.

A second clue is that, as a system approaches its peak, its creative corps bails out first. This is apparent in Figure 20.3 where papers and patents peak out before production and, even more vividly, in Figure 20.4 covering the Japanese polymer chemistry industry: research funds turn down first, then, in order, research papers, patents, production, and researchers. The polymer chemistry departments of universities march implacably on for a time. The life cycle of a given technological system (or leading-sector complex) is likely

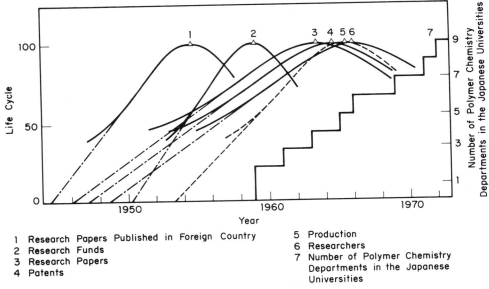

Figure 20.4. Life Cycle of Polymer Chemistry and the Number of Polymer Chemistry Departments in Japanese Universities. [Adapted from K. Yamada, "A Study on Time Lag between Life Cycle of a Discipline and Resource Allocation," *Research Policy* (1982) in Freeman, *Unemployment and Technical Innovation,* p. 92.]

to contain more than one major innovational breakthrough; but each is likely to be governed by diminishing returns. Creative men and women move to where they perceive the action is. Thus, for example, as the cotton textile industry settled down in the United States of the late 1830s, the machine makers who supplied that industry shifted over to building locomotives. To take a more recent case, in writing *Getting from Here to There* in the 1970s I tried to answer the question then widely posed: Is human creativity on the wane?[28] Private and public R & D expenditures were being cut, the rate of productivity increase was rapidly decelerating, and serious analysts were, after 40 years, raising again the specter of secular stagnation. I finally concluded that we were in transition from one set of leading sectors and technological systems to another and that J. M. Clark's dictum still held:[29] "Knowledge is the only instrument of production not subject to diminishing returns."

This kind of switch in the direction of creative effort in the science–invention–innovation spectrum can also, of course, be influenced from the supply side by a new scientific breakthrough (e.g., DNA, the laser, the microcomputer) as well as from the demand side, by the slowing down of technological momentum and interest in an old leading sector.

A third clue is that these clusters of apparently independent technological systems may not be quite as independent as they look. For example, Watt's steam engine proved essential to the success of Cort's iron fabrication process as well as to the ability to move cotton factories away from waterfalls. For example, the railroad not only set up a Rosenbergian "compulsive sequence" yielding cheap steel and all that followed from it but also greatly stimulated the machinery and other metalworking industries. For example, the internal combustion engine represented a bringing together of the chemical and electricity, steel, and machinery industries. And when we gain better perspective on the current,

Fourth Technological Revolution, we may find that at the root of apparently quite separate technological systems is the impact on basic science, in all its forms, of the still rapidly evolving computer.[30]

There is still much to learn as research breaks open that black box "technological change," but it is already clear that, while the scale of invention and innovation in a modern society is a function of noneconomic as well as economic variables, the composition of the stream of invention and innovation is substantially determined by profit incentives. Further, if one assumes that the yield on refinements to individual inventive breakthroughs is subject to diminishing returns, the profitability of concentrating R & D talent in a given direction will gradually diminish. This means the incentive will increase with the passage of time for R & D talent to be drawn in new directions of more profitable creativity. Some such process may explain why, with appropriate time lags, new profitable inventions and innovations emerge as old leading sectors decelerate. Such engagement and reengagement in new directions is, of course, similar to that of the pattern of investment in general, and it is one reason for treating basic research, invention, development, and innovation as part of the investment process.

5. *Technology generated by requirements in one sector often found application in others.* The notion that manufactures would better lend themselves to technical progress than would the production of basic commodities is one of the oldest in economics. It appears, even in David Hume's *History of England* (preceding, pp. 25–26); and it persists through Marshall to recur in virtually every period of substantial protracted relative rise in the prices of basic commodities.

The two points to be made tersely here are: (a) so far as modern history is concerned nature has proved a good deal less niggardly than many political economists thought it would;[31] and (b) innovations in manufactures have not only had powerful positive effects on basic commodity production but innovations in the latter have also played an important part in industrial development. Thus, the evolution of technology in the two sectors was intimately connected. The net result of this interaction has been that, by and large, diminishing returns has been held at bay; the globe's population has increased (since 1750) by almost 6 times, industrial production, by, perhaps, 430 times, real GNP per capita, as a global average, by something like 10 times. Clearly, in an era when the rate of population increase is only slowly decelerating from unprecedented levels, and the peoples and governments of virtually all of the nations of Latin America, Africa, the Middle East, and Asia are determined to move forward in industrial growth, the creative interaction of food and raw material supply on the one hand and technology on the other, will have to continue into the future if large scale Malthusian and/or Ricardian crises are to be avoided.

A few illustrations underline the reality of this useful dynamic interaction between the two sectors.

a. *Mining and Watt's steam engine.* Newcomen's steam engine had existed since the beginning of the eighteenth century, a response to the need in Britain to pump water out of mines. Watt's more efficient engine, once created, found many more uses than initially envisaged (including important manufacturing uses); and its efficiency was incrementally but rapidly improved.

b. *The timber price and iron from coke.* Between 1750 and 1790 the proportion of pig iron made from coke rose in Britain from 5% to 86% of the total because of the rise in price of timber and charcoal relative to coal. The process of transformation from charcoal to coke was completed with Henry Cort's method for using coke to puddle and roll iron, permitting the concentration of the fabrication stage of the industry. The use of the steam engine proved essential to Cort's major innovation.

c. *Cotton machinery, the cotton price, the cotton south—and guns with interchangeable parts.* The new cotton textile machinery diffused rapidly after 1785, yielding a sixfold increase in raw cotton imports by the end of the century. The financial incentive to solve the problem of removing the seeds from U.S. long-staple cotton by machine sharply increased. Responding to this incentive Eli Whitney created the cotton gin in 1793. Its use spread rapidly (without the benefit of patent royalties to Whitney), yielding a surge in production in the American South and, tragically, an increased demand for slaves. But Whitney's failed effort to mass produce and market a piece of agricultural machinery contributed to his subsequent successful effort to mass produce guns with interchangeable parts.

d. *The railroads, agriculture, and raw materials.* The first railroads were induced by the profitability of moving bulky raw materials cheaply to factories from ports: Manchester and Boston in the first instance. As the use of the railway spread, however, it became, on a worldwide basis, a principal instrument for expanding the supplies of agricultural products and raw materials from farms, mines, and forests.

e. *Railroads, steel ships, and freight rates.* The rapid diffusion of railroads, notably in the 1840s and 1850s, dramatized the high rate of obsolescence of iron rails. The incentive rose to find a way to produce cheap, high-quality steel. The inventors broke through in the 1860s and the steel industry emerged rapidly in the 1870s with the railroads their major customer. By the 1880s, as railway building decelerated, new uses for steel were soon found in machinery, bridges, urban construction, and shipbuilding. Freight rates in the mid-1890s were about half the level of the early 1870s, thus cheapening for Europe the prices of imported agricultural products and raw materials.

The array of complex interactions between industrial innovation and the supply of basic commodities could be indefinitely extended; electricity, modern dairy farming, and the refrigerator ship; chemistry, chemical fertilizers and pesticides; the internal combustion engine and the tractor; space flight and photovoltaic cells; and so on.

What one observes, then, over the past two centuries are inventions and innovations that responded initially to an agricultural or raw material requirement (often in a phase of rising or high relative prices for basic commodities), then finding other highly productive industrial or transport uses; but one also observes inventions and innovations that responded initially to a profit possibility in industry or transport, then finding other highly productive uses in expanding the supply of basic commodities.

This reassuring lesson from the past is a useful antidote to the simpler forms of limits to growth arguments, but it by no means guarantees the completion of the transformation of the world economy to full modernization without further strain on natural resources and the environment.

6. *It is essential to find a way to deal systematically with the phenomenon of a technological backlog: its size and the circumstances that determine whether and at what pace that backlog can be efficiently absorbed.* In the early post-1948 days of international concern in the advanced industrial North for economic growth in the South one spoke without embarrassment about "underdeveloped" countries. That phrase implied correctly that a pool of technologies existed that could be—but had not yet been—productively and

profitably applied in the South; and the task of development in such countries was not only to make relevant technologies available but to help build up their absorptive capacity.

The notion that a technological backlog might exist capable under proper circumstances of fairly rapid absorption by latecomers goes back at least to the eighteenth century debate on the rich-country–poor-country problem. In the nineteenth century the rise of Germany and the United States *vis à vis* Britain stirred considerable discussion of the costs of pioneering and the benefits of latecoming; and, of course, the twentieth century relative rise of Russia and Japan, let alone the new giants now stirring in the wings, have driven the point home quite convincingly.

Technological backlogs and their absorption are an awkward subject for mainstream economics for three reasons.

First, the degree of development is conventionally measured in terms of GNP per capita (or some such income measure) rather than in terms of the more correct but difficult index: the degree of efficient absorption of the relevant pool of existing technologies. And it doesn't help much to apply the Chenery measure: the relative scale of intermediate industrial production. A low figure for that index simply reflects a society's weak capacity to absorb the technological backlog.

Second, if one leans to the Ian Little view that conventional mainstream economics is a sufficient intellectual framework for analyzing the development process, the problem disappears: his ''enterprising people'' will promptly absorb all the relevant technologies from the existing pool. But, in fact, it's not quite that easy. The build-up of technological absorptive capacity is a process requiring the allocation of resources (for example, to education) just as the generation of inventions is an investment subsector.

Third, if one breaks open yet another black box and asks what, in fact, does the technology absorption (or transfer) process look like, one is immediately in a world of enterprising buccaneers, intelligence agents, itinerant foremen, peripetetic workers, educational institutions, transnational companies, etc.[32] Since, say, an uneasy French government, sensed that a new and dangerous challenge was stirring in Britain in the third quarter of the eighteenth century, set in motion an enlarged system of technological espionage, and, a bit later, Francis Cabot Lowell stole from the British not only the design of big textile machines but also Mr. Moody, a skilled and proven foreman, technology transfer has been a highly human, institutional enterprise not easily embraced by either the differential calculus or United Nations' resolutions.

One of the difficulties with Schumpeter's formulation of the innovation process is that he did not capture sensitively the degree of creativity involved in successfully transferring to another society even a technology well-proven in a different setting. Much United Nations' rhetoric on technology transfer also misses this point. The challenge may be less than that confronted by the primal innovator, but it is not a simple task of replication capable of being carried out by the faceless managers of Schumpeter's initial Walrasian circular-flow system. From, say, the setting up of the first big imitative American cotton textile mill in Lowell, Massachusetts, to, say, the successful transfer of wheat strains from Chapingo, Mexico, to the Punjab, a great deal of creative adaptation has been required.

Nevertheless, the pace of the transfer can be very brisk indeed, as, for example, Taiwan and South Korea have demonstrated. What are required, above all, are large numbers of literate, well-trained men and women, a competent corps of entrepreneurs, government policies designed to encourage the transfer of technologies from abroad, and sufficient infrastructure investment (in transport, power, etc.) to render the economy a reasonably efficient, interconnected market. What is always involved in a successful transfer is not merely the installation of a given technology but also the creation of surrounding institutions and services (including labor-force training) required for the technology system (or leading-sector complex) to take hold. In some cases (e.g., Belgium, France, Germany) the transfer of the railroad yielded a wide-based, diversified surge of industrialization in the second and third quarters of the nineteenth century. In India and China, where the supporting infrastructure did not exist or was not promptly created, the spreading effects from railways were much more limited.

I have emphasized at a number of points in this book that technological backlogs can build up for advanced industrial as well as developing countries. A notable example was the backlog of technologies associated with the mass production and diffusion of the automobile and durable consumers' goods that built up for Western Europe and Japan during the interwar years, when the United States moved (until 1929) much more strongly ahead in these directions. After phases of postwar recovery, both Western Europe and Japan were able voraciously to absorb (and in some cases, refine and further develop) these technologies because the supporting infrastructure and incentives existed or were quickly created.

The Soviet Union now represents the most dramatic case of an advanced industrial society confronted with an immense backlog of unapplied, relevant technologies; and, in terms of trained human beings alone, it commands an objective capacity to absorb the backlog and surge ahead as, say, Western Europe and Japan did in the post-1945 quarter-century. Whether or when this happens depends on political, institutional, and psychological changes within Soviet society that would release its evidently ample human, scientific, and technological potential. This is the issue Gorbachev has posed to his peoples and the world. Whether his view of the required changes is sufficient; whether, if it is, his policies will prove acceptable to the present elite; whether the elite, if persuaded, can carry the people forward effectively—all this is still to be decided.

But what needs underlining here are the kinds of deep societal and institutional issues ultimately at play in the process of technology absorption and transfer. Of all such issues in the contemporary world, the most important, perhaps, is the extent of secondary and higher education. As the frustrated story of Argentine development and the present *cul de sac* of the U.S.S.R. indicate, a strong educational base may be a necessary but is not a sufficient condition for rapid absorption of the technological backlog. Nevertheless, Table 17.3, the prelude to the further consideration of this matter in Chapter 21, suggests that the potential technological absorptive capacity of the developing regions may have been radically increased by the little-noticed educational revolution of the past quarter-century.

7. *Clarification is required on the extent to which the pace of technological absorption determines, directly and indirectly, the investment rate.* One of the unresolved challenges still before economists in the analysis of investment is to reconcile conventional neo-Keynesian, highly aggregated treatment of the operation of the consumption function (and the *ex post* equality of saving and investment) with two solid pieces of empirical knowledge: (a) in advanced industrial societies up to 70% of industrial investment is financed from internal sources:[33] and (b) the rate of growth, profits, and plant and equipment investment tend to be disproportionately high in sectors rapidly diffusing a new technology or rapidly absorbing a hitherto unapplied backlog of relevant technology.[34]

When surveying twentieth-century data on U.S. manufacturing and mining, Sergei Dobrovolsky found that retained profit plus depreciation in fact approximated total gross plant and equipment expenditure; but he noted immediately that some companies generated internal funds in excess of requirements which, in one way or another, helped finance dynamic firms which required external financing.[35]

One can go further. The rate of growth of the economy as a whole is extremely sensitive to the momentum of sectors absorbing new technologies; and, therefore, at one remove, infrastructure investment (usually responsive to the increase or decrease in public revenues) and residential housing investment (usually responsive to business cycles), may also be substantially determined by the pace of technological absorption.

Both these ways of looking at the consumption–saving–investment problem go far back in political economy; but they have not yet been brought satisfactorily together. For example, without understanding the accelerated increase in the ability of developing countries to absorb efficiently the backlog of relevant technologies, one cannot explain the peaking of both investment and growth rates in the drive to technological maturity (upper-middle-income countries).[36]

Take a narrower and more familiar case: the distribution of investment in relation to technology in the great postwar Western European boom of the 1950s and 1960s. M. M. Postan addressed the linkage most directly.[37]

> In almost every European country the industries . . . with the largest infusion of capital, were the "modern" or the modernized industries. The chemical and petro-chemicals, plastics, and man-made fibres, developed a voracious appetite for new capital as they grew and renewed their equipment. Equally voracious for capital were the engineering and metal-working industries, especially their newer branches, such as electro-mechanical, electronic, and motorcar.

Postan then points out that investment was low relative to output in an array of large but old and sluggish industries.

The general point from which the importance of the innovation–plowback link derives is the critical role of the pace of innovation in determining the overall rate of growth, employment, and price trends in an economy. Here W. E. G. Salter's analysis of the dynamic impact of innovation on the structure and performance of the British economy is most helpful.[38] He demonstrates (Table 20.2) that five technologically dynamic industries in a sample of twenty-eight industries account for 79% of the increase in output for the

Table 20.2. Changes in Total Output, Employment, Output per Head, and Prices, in Twenty-Eight Industries, United Kingdom, 1924–1950
1924 = 100 (weight base = 1935)

	Output	Employment	Output per head	Net prices
1. All industries in sample	185	94	196	158
2. Excluding the five industries with the largest increases in output	118	82	145	209
3. Excluding the ten industries with the largest increases in output	103	77	134	236

NOTE: These figures should not be taken as representative of all industry.
SOURCE: W. E. G. Salter, *Productivity and Technical Change* (Cambridge: at the University Press, 1969), p. 149.

Table 20.3. Changes in Shares of Branches of Manufacturing in Output and Capital of Total Manufacturing Grouped by Rapidity of Growth in Initial Period, United States, 1880–1948

I. Shares in value of output in 1929 prices (%)			
	1880	1914	(1948)
	(1)	(2)	(3)

Group A. Share in 1880 of 0.6% or less; growth factor, 1880 to 1914, of 6 or more

	1880 (1)	1914 (2)	(1948) (3)
Total, group A	3.2	13.0	35.6
(a) Automobile subgroup	0.5	3.2	19.4
(b) Other	2.7	9.8	16.2

Group B. Share in 1880 of more than 0.6%; growth factor, 1880 to 1914, of 6 or more

Total, group B	15.3	30.8	26.3

Group C. Growth factor, 1880 to 1914, of less than 6 but more than 3

Total, group C	24.8	25.9	22.9

Group D. Lagging industries (all other); growth factor, 1880 to 1914, of less than 3

Total, group D	56.7	30.3	15.2

Growth factors	*1880 to 1914*	*1914 to 1948*	*1880 to 1948*
Total output	4.33	3.51	15.17
Group A	17.59	9.61	168.77
(a) Automobile subgroup	27.71	21.28	588.60
(b) Other	15.72	5.80	91.02
Group B	8.72	3.00	26.08
Group C	4.52	3.10	14.01
Group D	2.29	1.76	4.07

II. Shares in total capital in 1929 prices (%)			
	1880	1914	1948
	(1)	(2)	(3)
Group A	6.0	16.2	39.2
(a) Automobile subgroup	1.0	4.2	22.6
(b) Other	5.0	12.0	16.6
Group B	21.3	33.0	26.5
Group C	29.8	27.7	23.2
Group D	42.9	23.1	11.1

Growth factors	*1880 to 1914*	*1914 to 1948*	*1880 to 1948*
Total capital stock	8.18	2.16	17.68
Group A	22.09	5.23	115.50
(a) Automobile subgroup	34.36	11.62	399.57
(b) Other	19.63	2.99	58.70
Group B	12.67	1.73	21.99
Group C	7.60	1.81	13.76
Group D	4.40	1.04	4.57

NOTE: The underlying data are from Daniel Creamer, Sergei P. Dobrovolsky, and Israel Borenstein, *Capital in Manufacturing and Mining: Its Formation and Financing* (Princeton: Princeton University Press for the National Bureau of Economic Research, 1960), table A-10, pp. 252–258, for value of output; table A-8, pp. 241–247 for total capital (both in 1929 prices).

period 1924–1950, and for 53% of the productivity increase. Prices would have been 32% higher without the five industries.

Salter's is one of the few serious efforts to link sectoral change brought about by invention and innovation to aggregate growth and structure. Another, based on an NBER study, is contained in Simon Kuznets's late return to technology on a disaggregated basis in his 1971 *Economic Growth of Nations* (Table 20.3). As in Salter's analysis of the British data, the engine of growth in Kuznets's analysis[39] is clearly in sectors

> . . . of quite recent or impending technological changes. This is certainly true of rubber products (increasingly dominated by automobile tires), petroleum (increasingly dominated by the demand for automobile fuel), and motor vehicles—which have been combined into an automobile subgroup. But it is also true of most of the other branches in A: canned foods, silk and rayon (because of recent emergence of rayon), chemical fertilizers, chemicals proper, metal building materials, electrical machinery, metal office equipment, and locomotives. On the other hand, the large but lagging Group D includes the older food products, textiles, and wood industries, in which any technological innovations made had too limited an effect to induce average growth. The second aspect is that in 1948 well over a third of the value of product of total manufacturing was in branches that did not exist in 1880, or were so small that they accounted in all for about 3 percent of manufacturing output.

In short, a modern economy is not driven forward by some sort of productivity factor operating incrementally and evenly across the board. It is driven forward by the complex direct and indirect structural impact of a limited number of rapidly expanding leading sectors within which new technologies are being efficiently absorbed and diffused. And it is this process of technological absorption that substantially generates, directly and indirectly, the economy's flow of investment via the plowback of profits for plant and equipment, enlarged public revenues for infrastructure, and enlarged private incomes for residential housing. Clearly, macroeconomics as conventionally expounded requires revision to take these realities into account.

8. *We have not yet solved the problem of how to measure employment generated by a specific technology: The International Standard Industrial Classification versus leading-sector complexes.*

Economists have been arguing about the net effect on employment of the introduction of new technology since Malthus and Ricardo debated the matter in the post-1815 adjustment process in Great Britain, and, in the next generation, Marx seized on part of Ricardo's argument to create his "reserve army of the unemployed." The coming of what I (not Freeman) regard as the Fourth Industrial Revolution since, roughly, the mid-1970s, has brought this old debate alive again in a heightened form. Many economists have argued that the high concentration of sophisticated skills required in the production and use of computers, the products of genetic engineering, etc., combined with the fact that they do not appear to require massive infrastructure investment, like the railroad and the internal combustion engine, would limit the scale of employment created by these technologies; and that the problem of employment would be heightened by the diffusion of robots, assumed by most commentators to be, on balance, destructive of jobs.

The simple point to be made in this catalog of ignorance is that statistical data are now organized in forms that make it virtually impossible to deal systematically with issues of this kind. A great deal of further analysis and data collection are required to measure the size and rate of growth of a whole leading-sector complex. We need not merely output, employment, and productivity data for final output of the kind provided by the International Standard Industrial Classifications but also data on the whole array of inputs required to create that output and employ it productively in the economy. We need, in effect, a highly disaggregated annual input–output matrix.

Data are collected to answer specific questions; and neither governments nor mainstream economists have been concerned at high priority with the macro effects of sectoral complexes incorporating new rising or old fading technologies. Thus, conventional instruments and methods for measuring economic activity fail to provide satisfactory estimates of the rise and fall of technologies on the overall course of the economy and, thereby, fail to make the sectoral bridge between conventional micro- and macroanalysis.

In the end the challenge is to give substance to one of the several major still undeveloped insights in Allyn Young's presidential address:[40]

> . . . The mechanism of increasing returns is not to be discerned adequately by observing the effects of variations in the size of an individual firm or of a particular industry, for the progressive division and specialization of industries is an essential part of the process by which increasing returns are realized. What is required is that industrial operations be seen as an interrelated whole.

But to solve the problem one must add to Young's final sentence, which is much in the spirit of Leontief, another of Young's insights; namely, that what is required is a "moving equilibrium," which input–output analysis has never been quite able to supply.

Relative Prices:
Have Kondratieff Cycles Passed into History?

This section returns to one of the oldest questions in political economy: prospects for the prices of basic commodities relative to manufactures. Earlier observations bore on the manner in which the impulses for invention and innovation in the two sectors interacted in such a way as to hold off for two centuries a sustained trend toward a relative increase in basic commodity prices. The only substantial exception is the trend in the relative price of timber, which rose quite steadily, inducing an ample supply of substitutes as well as other methods of timber economy.[41]

On the other hand, some historians interpret the rough long cycles in the price level, money wages, and interest rates dramatized by N. D. Kondratieff as having as their root cause periods of relative scarcity and therefore relative high prices for basic commodities.[42] These relatively high prices rendered profitable increased investment in the supply of basic commodities, usually involving in the pre-1914 world the opening up of new territories. The multiple lags embedded in this process, often requiring large infrastructure investment and flows of international capital and migrants, were longer than for conventional industrial investment.[43] Therefore, investment and basic commodity production capacity tended substantially to overshoot their optimum dynamic equilibrium norms, yielding, in the wake of the basic commodity booms, protracted periods of falling or low prices.[44]

Behind the question of capital movements and price fluctuations in foodstuffs and raw materials lay deeper questions: What were the equilibrium levels of world output for foodstuffs and the various raw materials; what determined these levels; and what determined departures from them? International capital movements did not generally launch periods of expansion in foodstuff- and raw-material–producing areas. They moved in to exploit and support waves of prosperity already under way, triggered by the increased profitability of expanding output of particular foodstuffs and raw materials. But they were palpably part of the process of balancing population expansion, urbanization, and the pace of industrialization with requisite increases in inputs. Changing relative prices were thus critical to the whole clumsy effort to maintain dynamic sectoral equilibrium in the face of substantial lags.

Writing about this sequence in *The Process of Economic Growth* (completed in October 1951) I raised the question of whether such cycles would persist in the future.[45] After noting the marked rise in the relative prices of basic commodities as between 1938 and 1948, I observed that in the second half of the twentieth century the response "would consist less in the opening up of new territories than in the improvement of productivity in existing territories, with less likelihood of substantial overshooting." I also noted that political forces, conscious of the extraordinarily low prices of the great depression years, were seeking to damp the supply response to relatively high postwar prices and thus avoid overshooting.

But I was, at most, only half right. There was, indeed, no opening up of major new agricultural regions in response to relatively high postwar basic commodity prices; but there was a powerful surge in agricultural productivity in North America, Australia, and rapidly reviving Western Europe. There was also the rapid development of the oil reserves of the Middle East.

As Table 20.4 shows, the surge in agricultural output and exports in North America and Australia was sufficient for some time to cover the rising deficits in all the other regions of the world. Meanwhile, as the mass automobile age seized Western Europe and Japan, and consolidated its dominance over the round of life in North America, the international trade in oil rose in importance; but, for a time, the control over oil output and prices of the international oil companies, against the background of enormous Middle East reserves, kept the oil price relatively low.

The upshot was the classic Fourth Kondratieff downswing of 1951–1972 followed by the classic explosive entrance into the Fifth Kondratieff upswing of 1972–1974. Table 20.5 demonstrates that such disproportionately large price increases marked the beginning of three other Kondratieff upswings.[46] For present purposes, the relevant questions to be

Table 20.4 The Changing Pattern of World Grain Trade

Region	1934–1938	1948–1952	1960	1966	1973 (Prel.)
	(Million Metric Tons)				(Fiscal Year)
North America	+5	+23	+39	+59	+88
Latin America	+9	+1	0	+5	−4
Western Europe	−24	−22	−25	−27	−21
Eastern Europe and USSR	+5	—	0	−4	−27
Africa	+1	0	−2	−7	−4
Asia	+2	−6	−17	−34	−39
Australia	+3	+3	+6	+8	+7

SOURCE: Lester R. Brown, *In the Human Interest* (New York: W. W. Norton, 1974), p. 81. Based on U.S. Department of Agriculture Data.

NOTE: Plus = net exports; minus = net imports.

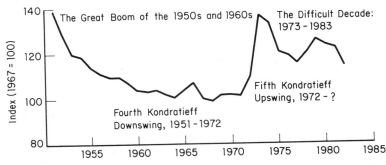

Figure 20.5. Relative Prices, 1951–1982. (Period characterizations are the author's.) [Adapted from *Economic Report of the President to the Congress, February 1983,* pp. 227–228.]

answered as background to Chapter 21 are these: will the relative rise in basic commodity prices resume in, say, the early 1990s, after a period of remission in the 1980s, yielding a Kondratieff upswing of normal length (say 1972–1997)? Will the recent downward trend in the relative prices of basic commodities continue yielding, for whatever reasons, an abnormally short fifth Kondratieff upswing (say, 1973–1981)? Put another way, are we already in the fifth Kondratieff downswing? Or, have the forces making for more or less systematic long cycles in relative prices disappeared—as I suggested was possible in 1951—and the Kondratieff cycle passed into history after a run of about two centuries?

No one can provide simple, confident responses to these questions; but it is possible to suggest some of the key variables that will, in fact, determine the outcome for relative prices.

The case for a resumed relative rise in basic commodity prices round about 1990 hinges in good part on the future course of the international oil price and its implications for energy prices in general. Although the fifth Kondratieff upswing was launched in December 1972 with an explosion in grain prices—and the subsequent course of agricultural prices has continued to influence significantly the course of overall and relative price indexes—oil prices have played since 1973 a role more like grain prices in the pre-1914 world. Moreover, the continued high energy use in agriculture has linked to some extent the trends in the two types of basic commodity prices.

But the case for a resumed rise in the real price of oil depends not on conventional supply–demand analysis but on an assessment of OPEC's capacity to maintain production

Table 20.5. Short Intervals of Disproportionate Price Increase: Great Britain, 1793–1913

Trend period	Price increase	Interval	Price increase	Percentage short interval increase to trend period increase
1793–1815*	75%	1798–1801	44%	59%
1850–1873	44	1852–1854	31	71
1897–1913	37%	1898–1900	21%	57%

*1813, rather than 1815, is peak year. Range to peak year rather than 1815 is measured.
SOURCE: B. R. Mitchell with collaboration of Phyllis Deane, *Abstract of British Historical Statistics* (Cambridge: at the University Press, 1971), pp. 470 (Gayer Domestic and Imported Commodities index) and 472–473 (Rousseaux overall index).

discipline within the cartel (and to coordinate policy with non-OPEC oil producers) under circumstances where about 56% of the world's known oil reserves are in the Middle East, of which almost half are in Saudi Arabia, which must produce far under capacity in order to avoid a deep further decline in oil prices. Evidently, as all hands recognize, the degree of political and military stability in the region is relevant, too.

There are also unknowns on the demand side. For example, will the increase in miles per gallon in automobiles continue or simply level off at a higher level when the automobile pool of the early 1970s is completely turned over? Will a high rate of growth be resumed in Latin America and other relatively stagnant developing regions which—given their energy-intensive leading sectors and pace of urbanization—have much higher marginal energy–GNP ratios than the advanced industrial societies?[47]

Whereas the conventional wisdom is that we shall see some rise in the relative price of energy in the years ahead, prediction runs in the opposite direction for raw materials. As this passage is drafted I have before me the *IMF Survey* for July 13, 1987, with the feature headline: "Sustained Price Weakness Forecast for Non-Fuel Primary Commodities." Aside from the protracted demand sluggishness of the world economy, there is a solid supply-side reason: technological innovations in new materials such as optical fibers, ceramics, and light, strong plastics. If one stares only at conventional industrial raw materials one could well conclude we are in a period of long-term decline in relative prices. On the other hand, the depreciation of the dollar has had an inflationary effect in the short run that helped lead *The Economist* to ring an inflationary alarm bell 2 weeks after the IMF evaluation. And before indulging in excessive generalization the doubling in the price of aluminum and surge of copper prices in 1987 should be noted, behind which lies a protracted period of subnormal investment in production capacity.

So far as agriculture is concerned one can observe in Table 20.6 a decline during the 1960s in grain stocks, idle U.S. cropland, and proportion of reserves as a share of annual production. This erosion of excess reserves—a typical late Kondratieff downswing process—was the prelude to the grain-price explosion of 1972–1973 as the Russian and other harvests failed (Fig. 20.6). The resultant surge of production reflected a new seriousness about agricultural production and productivity in India, China, and some other developing countries involving improved incentives, increased fertilizer application, and the diffusion of new seeds. Against this background the continued productivity rise of heavily subsidized agricultural output in Western Europe and North America yielded unmanageable surpluses, but in Africa notably, and also in some countries in other developing regions as well, per capita grain production declined (Fig. 20.7).

Thus, as with human fertility, agricultural problems and policies are likely to diverge in various parts of the world community in the time ahead; biotechnology is likely to yield important new means for raising agricultural productivity; and agricultural acreage is likely to decline.[48] And, so vigorous was the response to the global food crisis of the early 1970s that one might well conclude that the system overshot, and, for a while, at least, a period of relatively low agricultural prices would persist.

As with industrial raw materials, however, the signals are mixed; for in Indonesia and elsewhere in developing Asia there are signs that the diffusion of the new rice and wheat strains may, after a time, yield a plateau in production rather than a progressive expansion—a tendency compounded in China by the higher profitability of market gardening for urban centers and rapidly expanding industrial employment in rural industry. Further, the widespread drought of 1988 brought prospective grain stocks in storage for 1989 down to less than 60 days' supply, the lowest level since the grain crisis of 1973.

Table 20.6. Index of World Food Security, 1960–1986

Year	World carryover stocks	Grain equivalent of idled U.S. cropland (million metric tons)	Total	Share of annual world consumption (days)
1960	199	36	235	103
1965	142	70	212	81
1970	165	71	236	75
1971	183	46	229	71
1972	143	78	221	67
1973	148	25	173	49
1974	140	4	144	43
1975	148	3	151	44
1976	201	3	204	57
1977	201	1	202	55
1978	231	22	253	64
1979	207	16	223	56
1980	191	0	191	56
1981	227	0	227	57
1982	262	14	276	67
1983	191	97	288	67
1984	240	33	273	62
1985	316	38	354	82
1986	339	51	390	87

SOURCES: Carryover stocks and world consumption derived from U.S. Department of Agriculture (USDA), *Foreign Agriculture Circular,* FG-5-86, May 1986; idled cropland estimates from Orville Overboe, USDA Agricultural Stabilization and Conversation Service, private communication, June 2, 1986; grain equivalents derived from idled cropland data by assuming a yield of 3.1 metric tons per hectare. From Lester R. Brown *et al., State of the World, 1987* (New York: W. W. Norton for the World Watch Institute), p. 134.

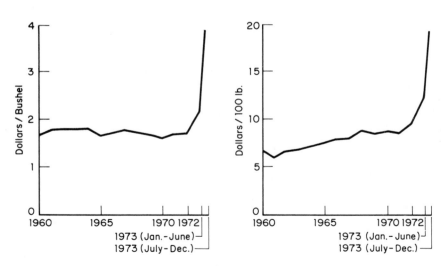

Figure 20.6. World Wheat and Rice Prices, 1960–1973. *Upper left:* World Wheat Price, 1960–1973 (Unit Value of U.S. Exports). *Upper right:* World Rice Price, 1960–1973 (Unit Value of U.S. Exports). [Adapted from Lester Brown, *In the Human Interest, 1974,* pp. 55, 57, and 58. Based on U.S. Department of Agriculture data.]

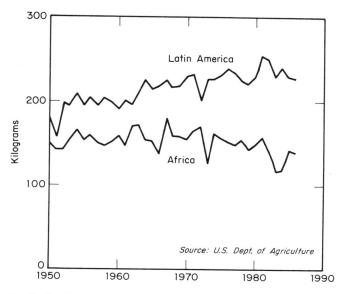

Figure 20.7. Per Capita Grain Production in Africa and Latin America, 1950–86. [Adapted from Lester Brown *et al.*, *State of the World, 1987* (New York: W. W. Norton for the World Watch Institute), p. 135.]

The midterm prognosis for the environment and requirements for investment in the control of environmental degradation appear less ambiguously pessimistic. The four major dangers appear to be: an attenuation of the ozone layer; an elevation of temperatures brought about by excessive emissions of carbon dioxide (the greenhouse effect), with possibly important net negative consequences for the food supply; the progressive destruction of the forests; and the consequences for human beings of increasing concentrations of harmful chemicals in the environment, including acid rain. In no case has scientific knowledge permitted firm predictions of the pace of deterioration or the timing of acute regional or even global crises. Nevertheless, even temperate analyses suggest that net deterioration in the environment continues in all four dimensions.[49]

To return to the questions posed earlier, there appear to be elements of validity in all the hypotheses defined. A resumed substantial rise in the real price of oil could produce an overall rise in relative prices and accelerated overall inflation. But, until Middle East oil reserves are much further drawn down, this outcome is likely to be the result of a disciplined cartel action or Middle East crisis rather than the abnormally lagged expansion of capacity that marked the Kondratieff expansions of the past. The second hypothesis—of a foreshortened upswing—has a good deal to commend it. The quadrupling of the oil price in 1973–1974 and the doubling again in 1979–1980 clearly set in motion extraordinarily powerful efforts at oil conservation and an intensified search for oil and other energy sources. Combined with the slowdown of the world economy these two shocks helped to produce, energy prices broke, yielding for most of the 1980s a phase of relatively cheap oil.

Something of the same is true of the supply response to the grain price, although it remains to be seen if the American drought of 1988 was a random event or part of an emerging environmental trend.

But, even more than weather prospects, it is the deep involvement of governments in policy that distinguishes contemporary world agricultural markets from those of the pre-1914 world. Against the background of widespread anxiety over the Indian food crisis of 1965–1967 and other warning events of the 1960s, agricultural output surged as India and China proceeded to render themselves, for the time being, independent of net agricultural imports by at last according agriculture the priority it deserved. Politics and politicians are equally responsible for the curious agricultural policies pursued in North America, Western Europe, and Japan, on the one hand, and the perverse policies pursued in much of Africa and the Soviet Union, on the other.

One other exogenous factor should be noted. Since 1985 the devaluation of the dollar has raised the relative prices of basic commodities denominated internationally in dollars. The sharp decline in relative prices from 1981 to 1986 began to reverse in 1987.

The argument for a requiem for Kondratieff cycles rooted in relative price terms is heightened if one moves to what might be called the environmental markets. There the policies of governments—including allocations of public resources to research and pollution control—are, once again, likely to prove decisive. At the moment the affluent nations on both sides of the Atlantic appear to be as profligate in living off their capital in the form of forests and waterways as the United States has been in the 1980s in sustaining its level of consumption by borrowing abroad at the cost of its accumulated capital stock.

I would guess that one will be able to trace in the future, as in the past, the impact of long investment lags on prices and output of basic commodity prices. After all, it required a decade to open up oil production in the North Sea and the north slope of Alaska. But the role of governments, whether exercised via international cartels or nationally, combined with the probably substantial impact of the new technologies, has probably altered once and for all the stately rhythm of Kondratieff cycles that, interwoven with other rhythms and stochastic events, can be traced quite persuasively from, say, 1790 to the grain and oil price explosions of 1972–1975. I would emphasize, however, that I merely suspect this outcome, as I did in 1951; but I am by no means sure and am quite prepared in this matter to accept Keynes's dictum on the inevitability of the unexpected.

By standing back from this analysis and viewing it in the long perspective of history, a few observations are possible. All basic commodity prices have, of course, not moved together.[50] Nevertheless, it is roughly true that from the late eighteenth century to 1914, the prices of basic commodities relative to manufactures were strongly affected by and at times dominated by fluctuations in wheat and other agricultural prices that carried a heavy weight in price indexes and exhibited high volatility. The pathological interwar years were marked, of course, by abnormally low basic commodity prices over a wide front, which concealed a progressive rise in the relative importance of energy prices as the electricity revolution matured and the automobile revolution gathered momentum and diffused. From 1950 to 1972 global energy consumption increased at an average annual rate of 5.3%; 3.4% per capita. This compares with a 3.1% annual rate of increase in grain production.[51] In both the period of relatively declining or low basic commodity prices (1951–1972) and of rising or high prices (1972–1981), fluctuations in energy prices evidently played an extremely large and, at times, a dominating role.

As one looks ahead, it may be that, in succession to grain and energy, outlays to maintain a viable environment—the cost of clean air, clean water, sustainable forests and arable land, the control of dangerous forms of pollution, and the avoidance of undesirable changes in climate or levels of radiation—may become, in effect, the dominating dimension of the relative price problem.

Growth and Business Cycles

One of the judgments that has palpably shaped the analysis of growth theories in this book is that the business cycle is the form growth has assumed once takeoff has begun. Certainly the initiation of the modern business cycle—with its long-term investment rhythm of about 9 years—cannot be dated later than the great British boom that peaked in 1792. There were fluctuations earlier in the eighteenth century in which war and the harvest played a large role; and there was also a strand of inventory fluctuations in foreign trade. From 1792 to 1914, however, one can quite easily identify the leading growth sectors in national economies and the world economy that gave a distinctive character to each boom as the major cycles succeeded each other in orderly procession in a world economy that widened out, over this century and a quarter, to embrace all the continents and that saw Britain joined by the United States and Canada, Western Europe, Russia, parts of Eastern Europe, Japan, and Australia in modern economic growth.

Since the end of the First World War the world economy experienced a series of phases, each quite different from the others, but none constituted a full return to the remarkably consistent pre-1914 pattern.

- The 1920s, with inflationless prosperity in the United States but high chronic unemployment in much of Western Europe.
- The 1930s, when the trade and financial structure of the world economy fell apart, leading to unemployment on an unexampled scale, followed by the recovery that peaked in 1937 long before conventional full employment was reached in most countries of the Atlantic community.
- The unique and unanticipated postwar quarter-century, when growth rates per capita in the advanced industrial countries rose at almost three times the maximum rate previously achieved:[52] 3.8% for 1950–1973 as compared to 1.4% for 1870–1913, 1.6% for the whole span, 1820–1979. These were the times when some economists asked whether the business cycle was a relic of the past; cycles in growth rates rather than employment could be found in most advanced industrial countries; and self-correcting full employment equilibrium growth models were in vogue.
- The two oil-shock cycles of 1973–1982, with growth rates in the developing regions quite well maintained by the recycling of petrodollars in the form of loans from private banks in the advanced industrial countries.
- The curious and complex period 1983–1988 marked by three quite diverse forces: the unintended conversion of the American economy to a massive net debtor position via the impact of the 1981–1982 tax cuts in raising the federal deficit, the relative U.S. growth rate, relative real interest rates, and the value of the dollar; the emergence on stage in full force of the Fourth Industrial Revolution, with differential rates of diffusion among countries and by sectors; the persistence of abnormally high rates of unemployment in Western Europe and, to a somewhat lesser degree, in the United States; virtual stagnation in some developing countries and regions, but the maintenance of relatively high growth rates in the Pacific Basin taken as a whole.

Against this background two observations are worth making before I comment tentatively on the uncertainties of the future.

The first concerns discontinuity. Why did the cyclical regularities of the pre-1914 era give way to these five curiously dissimilar phases? The direct and indirect impact of two world wars was, of course, partly responsible. But technically what happened is that, except for two intervals, the linkage mechanisms that had kept the pre-1914 economy in harness were broken or weakened. There were, essentially, three linkages:

- Massive international trade conducted in relative freedom, despite varying tariff barriers, including, especially, trade in certain basic commodities of heavy weight in virtually all domestic price indexes (e.g., cotton, wool, and wheat).
- The existence of a network of large capital markets, among which short-term funds shifted sensitively in response to interest-rate differentials or other factors determining expectations of profit.
- The commitment of the major banking systems to buy and sell gold at fixed prices and to maintain a gold reserve that varied (relative to liabilities) as among the major countries, varied over time within countries, but nevertheless constituted a variable whose change affected domestic interest rates, the supply of credit, and the rate of expansion or contraction of the economy.

In addition, of course, there was considerable freedom to migrate.

These are the characteristics that, in a rough-and-ready way, kept the national economies in step with respect to the business cycle. But there was also a political assumption underlying this system; namely, that the citizens of each country would accept cyclical depressions as a fact of life beyond the capacity of their governments to correct.

The two successful post-1914 intervals illustrate these technical and political propositions: 1925–1929; and the years of the Bretton Woods regime, 1945–1971. The first was an interval of relative global prosperity, with the gold standard restored, the volume of world trade surging ahead at almost 7% per annum, underpinned by U.S. capital exports to Germany that permitted reparations and war-debt payments to be made. The Great Depression destroyed not only the mechanisms of international order in the world economy but also the will of national polities to accept cyclical depressions passively.

The second exception—the Bretton Woods system—built on the overwhelming immediate postwar relative strength of the American economy and the dollar, gradually eroded between the late 1950s and 1971. It did not erode because of severe depression; for this was an era of apparently effortless, chronic, relatively full employment. Nor did it erode because of a rise of protectionism or a breakdown in the mechanisms of finance. The system did call for the fixing of exchange rates in terms of the dollar, but formal changes were permitted in the face of balance of payments crises. The external discipline was not onerous.

The system broke down because a weakening in the U.S. balance of payments, as Europe and Japan recovered and improved their competitive positions, rendered the dollar significantly overvalued at its Bretton Woods linkage to gold; and the major nations of the world, encouraged by simplistic propositions drawn from macroeconomic theory, preferred the somewhat illusory freedom of floating exchange rates to a formal modification of the Bretton Woods system in which responsibility would be more evenly shared.

My second comment concerns a strand of continuity. Although the pre-1914 business cycle has given way to a series of disparate phases, the fundamental characteristic of the investment process that underlay the business cycle is still operative; that is, expectations are systematically irrational, yielding distortions in the inherently lagged process of investment away from its optimum sectoral paths. Thus, phases in which capacity exceeds current requirements or falls short of them follow each other. It is these lags and distortions that continue to impart instability to growth patterns and also, in time, set in motion corrective forces.

As for the old-fashioned business cycle, it appears to have become so entangled with the policies of governments that, like the old-fashioned Kondratieff cycle, we may never again see it in its classic form. Put another way, the Keynesian Revolution, in its widest sense, may constitute a permanent loss of innocence in the sense that governments know a great deal about how to manipulate effective demand; and they are held accountable by their electorates. But it does not follow that all is well. The profound watershed represented by the Keynesian Revolution has broken the links and disciplines within the world economy that acceptance of the old-fashioned business cycle once supplied. The grotesque trade surpluses and deficits, the unsustainable debt burdens that characterize the world economy as of 1988 are the product of that de-linkage and undiscipline. There is, of course, no going back to a time of innocence. It will, therefore, require increasingly close international cooperation and the explicit acceptance of new international rules of the game to avoid breakdowns in the world economy reminiscent of cyclical depressions at their worst.

The Stages of Economic Growth

Countries other than pioneering eighteenth- and early-nineteenth-century Great Britain all faced in their pretakeoff phase the existence of an unapplied backlog of relevant technologies. The story of their stages of economic growth is the saga of why and how they transformed their institutions and educational systems to build up their technological absorptive capacity and to bring efficiently into their economies, in a sequence of progressively greater sophistication, the relevant technologies available in the global pool. The existence of that pool explains why growth rates accelerated for latecomers, as their technological absorptive capacity increased, exceeding those of the early-comers.[53] In time, if the process proceeded far enough, the latecomers exhausted what awaited them in the global backlog and became dependent on the current flow of new technologies from the global R & D process, to which a good many societies came to contribute. Their growth rates subsided as they completed the process of catching up.

Looked at in this way, the preconditions for takeoff constitute the period of most profound transformation for an initially traditional society.[54] Its political institutions and social structure, as well as educational system, require transformation before the technological backlog can be absorbed efficiently and regularly. That process has proved almost universally painful. Depending on a good many circumstances, including the character of the traditional society's culture, the period of preconditions for takeoff could be long or short. The precocious Japanese, with many advantages embedded in their traditional society, moved from the shock of Commodore Perry's intrusion at the point of cannon on his seven black ships to takeoff in about 30 years (say, 1854–1885). For Mexico the period from independence to takeoff was about 120 years (say, 1820–1940); for China, from the Opium Wars, about 110 years (say, 1842–1952). Once takeoff begins—the beginnings of Kuznet's modern growth, Chenery's transformation[55]—the absorption of technologies does not proceed painlessly or, necessarily, swiftly. The takeoff is usually a process confined to a relatively few sectors and regions. Moreover, as the leading sectors decelerate, the absorption of the next round of more sophisticated technologies may involve not only widened creative effort but further political and social conflict and institutional change. At the end of the process—the drive to technological maturity—a national society will have absorbed all the major technologies from the global backlog. For the countries whose takeoffs occurred before 1914, it required something like 40 years from the end of takeoff to the end of the drive to technological maturity. A few of the most precocious performers for the fourth graduating class into takeoff—notably, Taiwan and South Korea—have moved more briskly.

In the sweep of this book and the view it suggests of future prospects, the largest problem arising from stages of growth is the adjustment of the early-comers to takeoff to the rise of the latest batch of latecomers—notably those in Latin America and Asia. I shall consider the broad policy implications of this process in Chapter 21. But, having together isolated this as a central issue, little examined in recent times, Michael Kennedy and I decided that a model dramatizing its bone structure might be useful. Kennedy's exercise—consistent with the reflections on this issue of Hume, Hilgerdt, and Staley—appears on pp. 564–569, following.

The question of the limits of growth, which this book traces for more than two centuries, is also broadly discussed in Chapter 21 as an issue of policy. Here it is merely necessary to recall the rather wide variety of forces envisaged by various economists that might bring about a stationary state or secular stagnation:

- Diminishing returns to land and natural resources.
- A neo-Malthusian population policy yielding as a matter of positive objective high real wages with an unspoiled physical environment.
- A decline in birth rates leading to a stagnant or declining population yielding a lowered Keynesian marginal efficiency of capital and thereby a succession of progressively weaker business expansions and deeper and more protracted contractions.
- A decline in the productivity of science and invention yielding an attenuation of profitable outlets for investment and a deceleration of productivity increase.
- The Schumpeterian prediction that the rise of a powerful government role in the economy would sap the zeal and energy of entrepreneurs, reduce the absorption of potentially profitable innovations, decelerate the rate of growth, and ultimately, destroy capitalism.

Noneconomic Factors

The greatest of the unsolved problems in the analysis of economic growth is how to bring to bear in a systematic way the inescapable noneconomic dimensions of the problem. In the subsections addressed to noneconomic factors in the first three parts of the book, I made no effort to impose a uniform pattern on those subsections because noneconomic factors enter into the analysis of economic growth in quite different ways; and there is no agreed convention for dealing with the various linkages between the economy and the sectors of society related to it. I simply focused on the linkages that engaged the interest of the economists examined.

Here, as the focus shifts to major unsolved problems, I attempt to provide a higher degree of order, by distinguishing four reasonably distinct dimensions of this large terrain:

- The impact on economic behavior of noneconomic human motives and objectives.
- The impact of economic change on the noneconomic dimensions of society.
- The appropriate role of public policy in economic matters.
- The economy as it relates to the ideal concept of the individual in relation to society.

Noneconomic Motives and Objectives

Hume and Smith exhibited a lively sense that the economic behavior of individuals was often governed by noneconomic human motives and objectives; and they also understood that the weaving of such elements into economic analysis had to be quite precise if it were to be useful. Hume, for example, rooted the impulse to invest in the creative impulse within human beings rather than merely the profit motive. Smith took the view that the backward sloping supply curve for portions of the working force was caused by a failure to perceive the full range of options open to those with higher incomes—a failure that might be corrected by expanded popular education. The work of both economists is shot through with this kind of lucid and relevant linkage from the motives for having children to the deficiencies of country gentlemen as entrepreneurs.

Malthus's observations on such linkages are mainly confined to his work on population; and there is still less in this vein to be found in Ricardo. Both, however, saw the education and encouragement of the working force to aspire to higher levels of real income as fundamental to the limitation of family size and, in effect, as an elevation of the subsistence wage required to induce the working force to perpetuate itself.

The linkages of the economy to society are less *ad hominem*, more generalized in Mill and Marx; although the latter's image of the capitalist possessed by the compulsion to accumulate until he destroys the system he made goes beyond the profit motive and cash nexus.

In Marshall, the old classical tradition revives from his evocation of the strength of family affections among the motives for saving to his hopes for the civilizing possibilities of Economic Chivalry among business leaders. And Schumpeter, too, did not hesitate to build his case for the decline and fall of capitalism on the noneconomic compulsions of democratic societies. But that broad strand fades in mainstream economics to Kaldor's self-denying ordinance: "Economic speculation here trespasses on the fields of sociology and social history. . . ."

Perhaps most impressive was the extent to which the nine pioneers of development in Chapter 17 ended with frustrated reflections—bitter or philosophical, wrong-headed or wise—on the primacy of often disruptive noneconomic motives and aspirations in developing countries, notably those that shaped politics.

The great unsolved problem here is that posed by Auguste Comte: because economic behavior is embedded in the larger setting and more complex motivations of human beings in society, we require a general social science before adequate economic analysis can be conducted. Marshall responded: "It is vain to speak of the higher authority of a unified social science. No doubt if that existed Economics would gladly find shelter under its wing. But it does not exist; it shows no signs of coming into existence. There is no use waiting idly for it; we must do what we can with our present resources."

A century beyond Marshall we are, in all conscience, no nearer Comte's vision of a general social science. The disciplines, self-conscious and increasingly specialized, may, indeed, be further from one another now than then. What, then, can one do "with our present resources?'' I conclude that one should take the problem in all its complexity as the discipline and bring to bear around it relevant insights from whatever branch of knowledge that appears to have something to offer. There is little to be said for those who—as analysts or teachers—cut the problem down to the size of the method or discipline to which they are committed. Positively, Myrdal's *An American Dilemma* represents as good an example as I know of the acceptance of the problem as the discipline.

The subject clearly belongs in a chapter entitled "What Don't We Know about Economic Growth?" The interweaving of economic and noneconomic factors in the analysis of a given problem is a difficult art, still to be mastered. On the other hand, it was the art that David Hume and Adam Smith sought to practice; Malthus and, in the totality of his performance, also Ricardo; and, in quite different ways, J. S. Mill and Marx, Marshall and Schumpeter. Evidently, Arthur Lewis worked in this tradition as well as Myrdal. It is important to recall each of them; for none fully solved the major problems he addressed. But their insights—with respect to economic growth as it relates to noneconomic forces at work in human beings and society—are a rich and permanent part of the common social science heritage; and it is within that broad tradition that further striving is likely to yield most fruitful results. But, as I argued in *The Process of Economic Growth,* one must accept, in consequence, a biological theory of irreversible process rather than a neo-Newtonian theory of equilibrium.[56]

Economic Change and the Noneconomic Dimensions of Society

Hume and Smith viewed economic change in the directions they commended as an essential instrument for creating the kind of peaceful, civilized domestic and international society they hoped would come about. This was not merely a matter, in Smith's phrase, of defining one part of "the system of natural liberty." They saw and articulated clearly a set of connections between an increase in the wealth of nations, the expansion of a middle class, the strengthening of civil and political freedom, and the elevation of the quality as well as material level of life for the workers. Unlike Marx, but like the later Engels, they viewed society not simply as a superstructure reflecting the property relations and institutions flowing from changing methods of production but also as caught up in a dynamic interacting process in which social and political change, while affected by the contours of the economy, also played back on the economy.

Rather more than Hume, Smith perceived that some of the social changes brought about by an increase in the wealth of nations were not necessarily benign. He evoked, for example, the human costs as well as benefits from specialization of function as markets expanded.

Malthus and Ricardo focused before 1812 on a narrower, urgent problem; the disheartening pressure of expanding population on a national agricultural system subject to diminishing returns. They perceived a hopeful outcome in the possiblity of a self-reinforcing dynamic process in which a rise in wages plus popular education would lead workers and their wives to decide to have fewer children, and by respecting themselves "obliging the higher classes to respect them" (Malthus); or, in Ricardo's phrases "all legal means" should be used by "the friends of humanity" to stimulate the workers' taste for "comforts and luxuries." With brightening prospects for the food supply, their attention shifted in the period of postwar adjustment to a different urgent problem and its remedy, i.e., industrial unemployment.

In Mill and Marx the costs, as well as benefits, of industrialization are at the center of the stage in broader terms, especially the extent to which progress was shared by the urban workers. The capitalist system itself became the subject of debate and of net assessment. The debate continued in the democracies of the advanced industrial countries for a century; but with the victory of the democratic welfare state—as cumulatively envisaged by Mill, Marshall and Pigou, with the full employment addendum of Keynes—what might be called the mainstream political process settled at the margin the pace at which increasing resources would be allocated to render industrial societies more humane, offering along the way a better approximation to equality of opportunity and a more equitable distribution of income. Indeed, it was the latter issue that initially stimulated professional work on national income measurement and analysis in the first quarter of the twentieth century.

Meanwhile, the debate about systems was taken up in the third quarter of the twentieth century in and with respect to the developing regions: democracy versus communism; capitalism versus socialism. Much of that dialectic came ultimately to rest on another noneconomic dimension of the growth process discussed below; i.e., the appropriate role of public policy in the economic process. But Mill's "question of labour" had its counterpart in the "basic needs" debate in development policy of the 1970s, which arose from a sense that the palpable overall progress in the developing regions of the previous generation had not been equitably shared.

This quick evocation of some major human and social issues posed over two centuries of growth analysis leads on naturally to the great unanswered questions, half philosophical, half pragmatic: Is further economic growth a good thing? If so, can it go on without endangering the human habitat? If so, for how long and under what conditions? The philosophic dimension of the question—again posed by Mill—will evidently yield different net assessments in different societies at different stages of growth. The pragmatic questions are upon us and are likely to assert themselves increasingly in the time ahead (following, pp. 499–500).

The Appropriate Role of Public Policy

For more than two centuries the most continuous subject of debate in the literature of growth analysis is the appropriate role of government in the economic process. Understandably, the terms of the debate tend to follow the perceived impact of growth on the wider life of the society.

Thus we begin with Hume's and Smith's resistance to the apparatus of mercantilist objectives, policies, and controls, but also Smith's definition of three substantial legitimate areas for government action. Within that accepted framework, Malthus and Ricardo, in the second generation, focus on the Poor Laws, the Corn Laws, and, to a degree, on monetary and fiscal policy. With Mill and Marx we find advocates of alternative routes of transition to socialist societies—but socialist societies of quite different character.

In the advanced industrial democracies, the century of expansion of the welfare state—say, 1870s to the 1970s—yielded an extraordinary widening of Smith's "great society" proviso, a widening resisted by some at every step along the way. But the straitened times of the 1970s and 1980s rather than a shift in the relative persuasiveness of the debaters set limits on and in some cases forced a degree of retraction in welfare allocations.

In development economics and policy a somewhat parallel debate proceeded from the 1950s forward: to what extent and for what purposes should public authorities intervene in the economy at early stages of the development process? Having canvassed this matter at some length toward the close of Chapter 17 I shall simply note here three conclusions. First, the outcome in most developing countries was initially shaped rather more by political attitudes and policies than development theories. Second, the outcome proved sensitive to the setting provided by the state of the world economy and by each country's stage of growth. Third, the rising prestige of the competitive market in developing countries in the 1980's is, essentially, a pragmatic response to relative success stories and failures to be observed in the world economy plus the movement of a good many developing countries beyond takeoff into the more diversified and technologically sophisticated stage, the drive to technological maturity. In that stage the requirements for rapid adjustment to the market and rapid technological obsolescence have made government ownership and operation of means of production peculiarly inefficient.

The appropriate path ahead is reasonably clear for the more advanced developing countries if their debt problems can be sharply reduced; but what pattern of public policy is appropriate for the older industrialized countries as they confront a sustained period of revolutionary technological change and intensified competition from the emerging industrial powers? No clear challenging doctrine, let alone political consensus, has yet emerged in the OECD world. Chapter 21 considers a possible response.

The Individual and Society

It is on the question of the individual in relation to society that Marx is to be most fundamentally distinguished from others in the classical tradition. By and large, that tradition was committed to a society that provides "men the opportunity to take into account the inevitable alternatives posed by the diversity and paradox in their own natures" suffused by an "intense concern for the relationship of a man to himself and the next man to him. . . ."[57] Operationally, this vision of human beings permitted to be as autonomous as they could be led to a profound concern for means rather than ends—notably, means that could constrain the powers of the state; e.g., *habeas corpus,* electoral reform, competitive markets, free trade. In this perspective the abiding and acknowledged moral problems posed by the existence of the poor would be solved primarily by increasing the wealth of nations and providing an approximation of equality of opportunity rather than by the use of the state's power to level incomes.

For Marx, this vision of the appropriate relation of the individual to society was itself to be regarded as the outgrowth of "bourgeois production and bourgeois property": the individual could only be correctly defined in his relation to the course of history as driven forward by dialectical materialism.

Fundamental differences on this matter run through the protracted but sometimes desultory debate since the 1840s on capitalism versus socialism. It reemerges with considerable vitality in the development literature with a pragmatic rather than moral or philosophical cast around the question of which system is likely to do the best job of modernizing a society at an early stage of growth. But that pragmatic debate was, in its essence, foreshadowed and linked to the larger moral issue by J. S. Mill's definition of the decisive consideration: ". . . which of the two systems is consistent with the greatest amount of liberty and spontaneity."

On this matter history has not rendered a final judgment, but believers in democracy and competitive capitalism have no grounds for despair as of 1989.

21

Where Are We?
An Agenda in Midpassage

The First Takeoff:
The Entrance into Modern Economic Growth

In Adam Smith's model, a widening of the market leads, after a transient surge in productivity and affluence, to a surge in population and, finally, to a rather miserable stationary state with a minimum subsistence wage. In Smith's analysis, major technological change is possible but takes the form of an occasional breakthrough; in the end, however, that old devil Diminishing Returns prevails over incremental productivity improvement.

Michael Kennedy and I were pleased with the simplicity of our perception of what was required to convert an Adam Smithian into a modern dynamic growth model, with an unlimited horizon of per capita affluence.[1] One need change only three assumptions (following, pp. 563–564). First, one has to assume that the number of Smith's philosophers and creative toolmakers—and pioneering entrepreneurs, as well—grows within the society to a critical mass that yields a flow of major innovations sufficiently productive— if not necessarily smooth—to overcome various forms of diminishing returns in manufactures including limitations on the expansion of the market. Second, one has to assume that investment (including R & D) relevant to basic commodity sectors will fend off diminishing returns in that sector; or, more formally, that "land" will grow indefinitely. Third, one has to assume that, after a point, a rise in real income per capita yields via one economic-social-psychological route or another, a decline in birthrates sufficient to reduce the rate of increase in population permanently below the rate of increase in output; that is, an increase in output per capita becomes a permanent feature of the system. And, indeed it is historically as well as analytically the case that the removal of these three Smithian barriers in progressively wider regions of the world economy did clear the way for sustained, if erratic, growth since the 1780s.

As with most mathematical formulations in the social sciences, this one may usefully fasten attention on certain key variables and relationships, but its simplicity is purchased at a high price. The dynamic historical process, stretching over three centuries, that prepared the way for and then yielded this result was exceedingly complex. It embraced the interaction of the Commercial Revolution, the Renaissance, the protracted mercantilist struggles of the emerging nation states, and, above all, the Scientific Revolution. Taken together, they set in motion throughout Western Europe (and, to a degree, in the American colonies) a fermentation that changed irreversibly the way we view ourselves in relation to the physical world and to society. The process also set in motion policies, public and private, that, in effect, created the preconditions for takeoff; that is, improvements in transport and in agricultural supply to the cities, accelerated commercial expansion and urbanization, the refinement of banking and other economic institutions, the evolution of increasingly strong and competent central governments, and, then, from mid–eighteenth-century Britain, a quite sudden surge in the inventions that were to emerge as major innovations in the 1780s.

In particular, it was the oblique consequences of the Scientific Revolution that impart to this period its special character and explain why, in a good many earlier times and places, phases of commercial and urban expansion as well as the bloody competition of sovereign states for power and profit failed to generate an industrial revolution.[2] An equivalent of the Scientific Revolution was the missing ingredient. Thus, without exaggeration, Whitehead could observe of the sequence from Copernicus to Newton:[3] "Since a babe was born in a manger, it may be doubted whether so great a thing has happened with so little stir."

The Fourth Graduating Class:
The Central Phenomenon in the Time Ahead

The reasons for Britain's pioneering role in converting the widespread European and North American ferment of the seventeenth and eighteenth centuries into an industrial revolution are still debated; although they need not concern us here.[4] But clearly those initially beaten out of the starting gate by Britain did not have to wait long after the coming of peace in 1815 to emulate the British takeoff in their own ways, for the preconditions for takeoff were far advanced in the countries included in the Second Graduating Class of Figure 19.1 to which Belgium should certainly be added and, perhaps, Switzerland as well.

The central phenomenon of the period down to say, 2050 will be the coming to technological maturity—to a command over all the then-existing major technologies—of the Fourth Graduating Class incompletely represented in Figure 19.1.[5] This group includes China and India; Mexico, Brazil, Argentina and perhaps other countries of Latin America; a considerable group of countries in the Pacific Basin; Turkey; and, potentially, some countries of the Middle East now caught up in the tragic pathology of the region.

Here is how I defined the drive to technological maturity in *The Stages of Economic Growth*.[6]

> After take-off there follows a long interval of sustained if fluctuating progress, as the now regularly growing economy drives to extend modern technology over the whole front of its economic activity. Some 10–20% of the national income is steadily invested, permitting output regularly to outstrip the increase in population. The make-up of the economy changes unceasingly as technique improves, new industries accelerate, older industries level off. The economy finds its place in the international economy: goods formerly imported are produced at home; new import requirements develop, and new export commodities to match them. The society makes such terms as it will with the requirements of modern efficient production, balancing off the new

Table 21.1. Proportions of GDP in Industry and Manufacturing,
by Stages: World Bank Categories, 1985

	Industry	Manufacturing
Low Income (excluding India and China)	19%	12%
Lower-Middle Income	32	17
Upper-Middle Income	35	n.a.*
Industrial Market Economies	36	23

*Data not systematically available. Some significant individual 1985 percentages: Domini-
can Republic, 19%; Thailand, 20%; Peru, 20%; Turkey, 25%; Brazil, 26% (1965); Hong
Kong, 24%; Republic of Korea, 25%.
SOURCE: World Bank, *World Development Report, 1987*, pp. 206–207.

against the older values and institutions, or revising the latter in such ways as
to support rather than to retard the growth process.

Some sixty years after take-off begins (say, forty years after the end of
take-off) what may be called maturity is generally attained. The economy,
focused during the take-off around a relatively narrow complex of industry
and technology, has extended its range into more refined and technologically
often more complex processes; for example, there may be a shift in focus
from the coal, iron, and heavy engineering industries of the railway phase to
machine-tools, chemicals, and electrical equipment. This, for example, was
the transition through which Germany, Britain, France, and the United States
had passed by the end of the nineteenth century or shortly thereafter. But there
are other sectoral patterns which have been followed in the sequence from
take-off to maturity. . . .

A close examination of the structure of the economies of the Fourth Graduating Class
indicates that its members have moved beyond the usually light industries of the takeoff to
diversified metalworking, increasingly sophisticated chemicals, and, at least, the simpler
stages of electronics. China and India have developed nuclear weapons capabilities.
Others in the group evidently command that potential. In terms of structure they tend to
generate over 30% of GDP in industry, 20% or more in manufacturing.[7] Table 21.1
exhibits the World Bank averages for its stage categories suggesting the rough equiv-
alence of its middle income countries and my concept of the drive to technological
maturity.

Between 1965 and 1980 the middle-income countries, taken as a whole, sustained an
astonishing almost 15% per annum increase in the export of manufactures.[8]

Looking to the future, I am inclined to place even more weight on the summary data in
Table 21.2 reflecting the revolution in secondary and higher education referred to in
Chapter 20 (p. 466). To put these figures in perspective, it is useful to recall that the 1960
higher education proportion for Japan was 10%, for Britain, 9%.

These figures suggest a remarkable surge in technological absorptive capacity. There is
little doubt, for example, that South Korea's extraordinary drive to high-tech status is
rooted in the fact that its 1984 proportion in secondary schools was 91%, in higher
education, 26%. This compares with 66% and 20%, respectively, for the United
Kingdom.

There has been, moreover, a shift toward science and engineering in the more advanced

Table 21.2. Number Enrolled in School as Percentage of Age Group, by Stages: World Bank Categories, 1965 and 1984

	Secondary education		Higher education	
	1965	1984	1965	1984
Low Income (excluding India and China)	9	23	1	3
Lower-Middle Income	16	40	5	12
Upper-Middle Income	29	56	7	15
Industrial Market Economies	63	90	21	38

Source: World Bank, *World Development Report 1987*, pp. 262–263.

developing countries. In Mexico, for example, the annual average increase in Mexican graduates in Natural Science was about 3%, in Engineering, 5%, in the period 1957–1973. From 1973 to 1981 the comparable figures were 14% to 24%, respectively— an extraordinary almost fivefold acceleration.

I place special emphasis on technological absorptive capacity in looking ahead because the next several generations are likely to be substantially shaped by the unfolding of the potentialities of the Fourth Industrial Revolution that moved into an innovational stage in, roughly, the mid-1970s. The pace at which societies in the drive to technological maturity pick up and apply efficiently the relevant dimensions of this revolution depends heavily on their technological absorptive capacity, including in that concept not only the scale and quality of their pool of relevant personnel but also their ability to organize and motivate the men and women in that pool.

But what about India and China? The uniqueness in scale of the transition ahead envisaged here surely stems from the fact that the Fourth Graduating Class includes the two largest populations on earth. Evidently, they remain among the poorest countries in GNP per capita: $270 (1985) for India, $310 for China by World Bank calculations.[9] These figures, weighed down by vast low-productivity rural regions, do not correctly reflect the absolute scale and degree of sophistication of their rather diversified industrial establishments. Even then, the proportions of GDP generated in industry and manufacturing in India approximate the figures for lower-middle-income rather than low-income countries: 27% and 17%, respectively. For the period 1984–1987 the annual rate of increase of industrial production average 7%. The proportions of the relevant age groups in secondary and higher education are also disproportionately high for India's average income per capita: 34% and 9%. The most striking index of its potential technological absorptive capacity, however, is the increase in its pool of scientists and engineers from 190,000 in 1960 to 2.4 million in 1984—a critical mass exceeded only in the Soviet Union and the United States.

World Bank estimates for Chinese GDP generated in industry and manufacturing in 1985 are much higher than in India, although quite possibly distorted by the still-unreformed Chinese industrial price system: 46% for China, 29%, for India. The percentage of the relevant age group in secondary school is similar to India's (34%); but the percentage for higher education, set back severely during the Cultural Revolution, is much lower (1%). The Chinese authorities are, of course, extremely conscious of this setback and seeking to make up for it, although the tragic confrontation between the citizenry and the government in June 1989 may, once again, postpone the development of an intellectual and technical base adequate for China's full modernization.

Even discounting for problems of educational quality, the potential absorptive capacity for the new technologies in the more advanced developing countries is high. Their central problem—like that of most advanced industrial countries—is how to make effective the increasingly abundant scientific and engineering skills they already command. This requires, in turn, an ability to generate and maintain effective, flexible, interactive partnerships among scientists, engineers, entrepreneurs, and the working force.

I conclude, then, that despite current severe vicissitudes, the developing countries of the Pacific Basin (including China), India, and those containing most of the population of Latin America, will absorb the new technologies and, on balance, move rapidly forward over the next several generations. Much the same would happen, I believe, if the Middle East could find its way from its chronic, tragic bloodletting to a twentieth-century version of the Treaty of Westphalia.

As the latecomers continue to gain ground, the world economy and polity face an adjustment familiar in character but unprecedented in scale. The advanced industrial countries (including the U.S.S.R. and Eastern Europe) now constitute about 1.1 billion people, or, say, 24% of the world's population. At least 2.6 billion people, or about 55%, live in countries that are likely to acquire technological virtuosity within the next half-century. Moreover, population, in the decades ahead, will increase more rapidly in the latter than the former group. We are talking, then, about a great historical transformation.

How Far through the Transformation Are We?

It is by no means certain that the world economy will continue the generation and diffusion of technological virtuousity on an approximation of the pattern of the past two centuries. But it is useful to begin by assuming that this process will proceed at a pace and productivity that continues to overcome diminishing returns for the global economy as a whole. Cross-sectional data on expenditures in advanced industrial countries do not suggest that the human race faces formidable difficulties spending its income as its affluence increases. The time is not yet in sight when diminishing relative marginal utility for real income itself decrees that all (or a substantial majority) will be satisfied with their level of affluence; and some version of J. S. Mill's quasi-stationary state universally prevails by common consent. In fact, a few countries—or at least their governments— may turn their backs on high-technology modern life, as, to a degree, Burma and Western Samoa have done over the past several generations. Others may lack the physical or other capacity to achieve takeoff and self-sustained growth. In addition, growth could be aborted or grossly distorted by the real-enough dangers of nuclear war; a mercantilist fragmentation of the world economy generating nonnuclear conflicts as well as suboptimal use of resources; a frustration of growth by diminishing returns to resources or acute problems in the physical environment; and AIDS has reminded humanity that it is still potentially vulnerable to epidemic. But, on the assumption of a more benign future, it is worth asking how far forward the world economy is in movement toward virtually universal affluence arbitrarily defined.

First, population. Assuming that the demographic transition maintains the form it has assumed in recent decades, how close has the human race come to a more or less stationary global population?

Tables 21.3 and 21.4 dramatize a point made in Chapter 20: the extraordinary diver-

Table 21.3. Estimate of Population and Percentage Distribution by Region and Income Group, 1980–2100

Region	Population (millions)							Percentage of world population					
	1980	1984	1990	2000	2025	2050	2100	1980	1984	2000	2025	2050	2100
World total	4,435	4,750	5,253	6,145	8,297	9,778	10,869	100.0	100.0	100.0	100.0	100.0	100.0
Less developed	3,297	3,584	4,048	4,882	6,939	8,398	9,462	74.3	75.5	79.5	83.6	85.9	87.1
More developed[1]	1,138	1,166	1,205	1,263	1,358	1,380	1,407	25.7	24.5	20.5	16.4	14.1	12.9
Africa total	478	540	652	898	1,631	2,276	2,821	10.8	11.4	14.6	19.7	23.3	26.0
East, West, South	369	419	510	714	1,339	1,898	2,381	8.3	8.8	11.6	16.1	19.4	21.9
North Africa	109	121	142	184	292	378	440	2.5	2.6	3.0	3.5	3.9	4.1
America total	610	653	720	827	1,054	1,179	1,244	13.7	13.8	13.5	12.7	12.1	11.5
Latin America	356	390	444	535	731	854	919	8.0	8.2	8.7	8.8	8.7	8.5
North America	254	263	276	292	323	324	325	5.7	5.6	4.8	3.9	3.4	3.0
Asia total	2,575	2,768	3,068	3,570	4,698	5,383	5,835	58.1	58.2	58.0	56.6	55.0	53.6
East, Southeast Asia	1,533	1,622	1,754	1,968	2,415	2,600	2,696	34.6	34.1	32.0	29.1	26.5	24.7
East, Southeast (excluding China and Japan)	436	475	538	644	874	1,021	1,107	9.8	10.0	10.5	10.5	10.4	10.2
South Asia	943	1,035	1,183	1,434	2,023	2,453	2,760	21.3	21.8	23.3	24.4	25.1	25.4
South Asia (excluding India)	256	286	339	439	715	942	1,128	5.8	6.0	7.1	8.6	9.6	10.4
Southwest Asia	99	111	131	168	260	330	379	2.2	2.3	2.7	3.1	3.4	3.5
Europe total	749	765	787	821	879	901	928	16.9	16.1	13.4	10.6	9.2	8.5
Europe (excluding U.S.S.R.)	484	490	499	515	540	543	552	10.9	10.3	8.4	6.5	5.6	5.1
Oceania total	23	24	26	29	35	39	41	0.5	0.5	0.5	0.4	0.4	0.4
Oceania (excluding Australia and New Zealand)	5	5	6	8	11	14	15	0.1	0.1	0.1	0.1	0.1	0.1
By income group[2]													
Low	2,189	2,362	2,632	3,110	4,293	5,101	5,712	49.3	49.7	50.6	51.7	52.2	52.6
Low (excluding China)	1,209	1,332	1,537	1,913	2,883	3,652	4,250	27.3	28.0	31.1	34.8	37.4	39.1
Lower-middle	642	708	820	1,034	1,587	2,018	2,339	14.5	14.9	16.8	19.1	20.6	21.5
Upper-middle	492	539	617	752	1,052	1,253	1,372	11.1	11.4	12.2	12.7	12.8	12.6
High (oil exporters)	16	19	24	34	59	79	95	0.4	0.4	0.6	0.7	0.8	0.9
Industrial market	718	732	753	785	831	827	829	16.2	15.4	12.8	10.0	8.5	7.6
East European nonmarket	378	390	407	430	475	500	522	8.5	8.2	7.0	5.7	5.1	4.8

[1] More developed regions include Europe, U.S.S.R., North America (U.S.A. and Canada), Australia, New Zealand, and Japan. Less developed regions include all the rest of the world.
[2] Income groups criteria as of 1982 as indicated in World Bank, World Development Report 1984 (New York: Oxford University Press, 1984).
SOURCE: My T. Vu, World Population Projections 1984 (Washington, D.C.: The World Bank, 1984), p. xviii.

Table 21.4. Estimate of Annual Population Increase and Growth Rates by Region and Income Group, 1980–2100

Region	Annual population increase (millions)						Annual growth rates (percent)					
	1980	1984	2000	2025	2050	2100	1980	1984	2000	2025	2050	2100
World total	77.4	81.9	93.5	77.6	44.1	8.7	1.73	1.71	1.51	0.93	0.45	0.08
Less developed	70.3	75.0	89.2	75.5	43.8	8.5	2.13	2.07	1.81	1.08	0.52	0.09
More developed[1]	7.1	6.9	4.3	2.1	0.3	0.2	0.64	0.59	0.41	0.17	0.04	0.01
Africa total	14.4	17.0	27.5	29.4	22.7	3.0	2.98	3.08	3.03	1.79	0.99	0.11
East, West, South	11.5	13.7	23.0	25.4	19.9	2.5	3.07	3.20	3.17	1.88	1.04	0.11
North Africa	2.9	3.3	4.5	4.0	2.8	0.5	2.61	2.64	2.47	1.38	0.73	0.11
America total	10.6	11.1	10.2	7.3	3.2	0.7	1.74	1.68	1.24	0.70	0.27	0.06
Latin America	8.3	8.8	8.9	6.8	3.2	0.7	2.31	2.23	1.65	0.94	0.37	0.08
North America	2.3	2.3	1.3	0.5	0	0	0.92	0.84	0.50	0.18	0	0
Asia total	48.1	49.6	52.7	39.1	17.4	5.0	1.87	1.77	1.47	0.83	0.32	0.09
East, Southeast Asia	23.1	22.6	23.5	13.7	2.4	1.4	1.51	1.38	1.19	0.57	0.09	0.05
East, Southeast (excluding China and Japan)	9.6	10.2	10.4	8.2	3.9	0.9	2.18	2.13	1.60	0.93	0.38	0.08
South Asia	22.3	23.9	25.4	22.0	12.8	3.2	2.36	2.28	1.76	1.08	0.52	0.12
South Asia (excluding India)	7.0	8.1	10.9	10.7	7.9	1.2	2.70	2.78	2.45	1.49	0.83	0.11
Southwest Asia	2.7	3.1	3.8	3.4	2.2	0.4	2.81	2.78	2.31	1.31	0.66	0.10
Europe total	4.0	3.9	2.8	1.7	0.7	0	0.54	0.51	0.37	0.20	0.08	0.01
Europe (excluding U.S.S.R.)	1.6	1.6	1.3	0.7	0	0	0.34	0.33	0.28	0.12	0	0
Oceania total	0.3	0.3	0.3	0.1	0.1	0	1.32	1.30	1.01	0.57	0.23	0.03
Oceania (excluding Australia and New Zealand)	0.1	0.1	0.2	0.1	0.1	0	2.10	2.13	1.99	1.16	0.57	0.08
By income group[2]												
Low	42.7	44.4	51.6	43.1	23.4	5.5	1.94	1.86	1.65	1.00	0.46	0.10
Low (excluding China)	30.1	32.6	39.4	37.4	24.6	5.1	2.46	2.42	2.04	1.29	0.67	0.12
Lower-middle	15.8	17.6	22.5	21.1	13.7	2.2	2.45	2.44	2.16	1.33	0.68	0.10
Upper-middle	11.4	12.4	13.5	10.5	5.7	0.9	2.32	2.28	1.79	1.00	0.46	0.08
High (oil exporters)	0.7	0.8	1.1	0.8	0.6	0.1	4.60	4.17	3.12	1.53	0.88	0.11
Industrial market	3.7	3.7	2.7	0.7	0	0	0.54	0.50	0.36	0.09	0	0
East European nonmarket	3.1	3.0	2.1	1.4	0.7	0	0.85	0.77	0.49	0.31	0.16	0.02

[1]Same as Table 21.3, p. 491.
[2]Same as Table 21.3, p. 491.
SOURCE: Same as Table 21.3, p. 491.

gence in population prospects between presently less developed and more developed nations.[10]

The approximate and hypothetical character of these estimates should, of course, be underlined. They are rooted in arbitrary assumptions; for example, that populations will, in time, settle at a stationary level, not progressively decline. They do not attempt to take into account war, famine, and plague. They exploit patterns and relationships that have some empirical basis in past performance; but demography, like all the other social sciences, has had its surprises despite the comforting abundance of numbers available for manipulation.

By these calculations the hypothetical stationary population of the world is 11.2 billion. Population in the more developed nations approximates constancy from 2025; for the presently less developed nations constancy is achieved round about the year 2100. The proportion of the total population in presently more developed countries declines by half between 1980 and 2100: from 26% to 13%. This is a revolutionary shift. Since 1650 that proportion is estimated to have moved in the range 34%–26%.[11] The greatest percentage increase among the presently developing regions is calculated for East, West, and South Africa; from 8% to 22%, with Nigeria exceeding 500 million when stability is reached. The peculiarly powerful impact of AIDS on parts of Africa is not taken into account.

The years when the net reproduction rate (NRR) equals 1 come, of course, much earlier [2000–2045] with the interval between that date and a stationary population determined by prior population growth rates and the consequent age structure of the population— formally, by the total fertility rate (TFR) at the time the NRR = 1.

What of the prospects for GNP per capita? A good deal evidently depends on the annual average rates of growth assumed for each stage of growth or level of GNP per capita.

Table 21.5 provides estimates of the length of time required to achieve U.S. GNP per capita (1985) for four groups of countries, under two patterns of growth rates: the average for 1960–1980; the lower averages for 1965–1985. The upper-middle-income countries achieve current U.S. levels of affluence round about 2050 depending on the pattern of growth rates assumed; the lower-middle-income countries, in the fourth quarter of the next century. India and China take longer, starting as they do from low income levels; but, if they find it politically possible to release the potentialities of their private sectors, and use their pools of scientific and engineering manpower efficiently, they may achieve higher growth rates than in the past, as India appears to be doing; and, in any case, they are likely by, say, the middle of the next century to have achieved command over all the then-current technologies.

All of the present middle-income countries will have achieved or gone beyond the maximum proportion of manufacturing in GNP, say, 25% (Table 21.1).

Only the broadest conclusions can be drawn from these precarious exercises in projective arithmetic, but they are not trivial.

- Barring major catastrophes, the global population is likely to more than double by 2050, with marked deceleration down to the end of the twenty-first century.
- If present growth patterns persist, the more advanced developing regions will achieve or surpass present U.S. levels of GNP per capita by the mid–twenty-first century, the lower-middle-income countries somewhat later in the century, with proportions of GNP derived from industry and manufacturing at or beyond the present conventional maxima, giving way to the relative rise in services that appears to characterize affluence.

Table 21.5. Real per Capita Income Projected: Rich, Middling, and Poor Countries

Type of Economy	Population mid-1985 (millions)	GNP per capita (1985 US $)	Percentage of U.S.	Average annual per capita growth rate (1960–1980)	Average annual per capita growth rate (1965–1985)	Number of years to attain the U.S. 1985 per capita using 1960–1980 rates	Number of years to attain the U.S. 1985 per capita using 1965–1985 rates
Low-income ($110–$390)	2,439.4	270	.016	1.2	2.9	347	146
China	1,040.3	310	.019	NA	4.8	NA	87
India	765.1	270	.016	1.4	3.1*	298	137
Low-middle-income ($420–$1570)	1,242.1	820	.049	3.8	2.6	82	103
Upper-middle-income ($1640–$7420)	567.4	1,850	.111	3.8	3.3	60	69
Industrial market ($4290–$16,690)	737.3	11,810	.708	3.6	2.4	11	16
United States	239.3	16,690	1.000	2.3	1.7	—	—

*As reported by the Indian Embassy (US) 10 August, 1987.
SOURCE: Calculated from data in World Bank, *World Development Report* (New York: Oxford University Press), 1982, pp. 110–111, and 1987, pp. 202–203.

- The period from the present to the mid–twenty-first century is likely to be the time of the maximum strain on resources and the environment and the interval of maximum readjustment in the locus of population, economic potential, and political stature in the whole sweep of the period since the mid-eighteenth century.

Five Great Issues of Policy

If this broad portrait of where the world economy stands in terms of its evolution is more or less correct, and if we take as the common objective the successful transit through the stages of growth (or Chenery's Transformation), five massive challenges to policy—to the collective good sense of the human race—can be discerned.

First, a peaceful soft landing from the cold war.[12] Such an outcome is conceivable because the progressive diffusion of economic, political, and usable military power away from the Soviet Union (as well as from the United States) makes the dream of hegemony in Eurasia, which briefly appeared conceivable to Moscow after 1945, increasingly unrealistic. The revival of Western Europe and Japan, backed by a United States shaken out of its immediate postwar sleepwalking by the shocks of 1947–1950, the Sino-Soviet schism, and then the movement toward technological maturity of the Fourth Graduating Class all contributed to this outcome, as did the demonstration, in Eastern Europe and elsewhere, that culture, religion, and nationalism have great staying power even in the face of obsessive totalitarian rule. These events and processes have been heightened by progressive evidence that two of J. S. Mill's judgments were essentially correct. The public ownership and operation of economic units proved to be "hobbling, careless, and ineffective"; and, with the passage of time, the decision between socialism and capitalism appeared to be tipping toward the latter on the basis of "one consideration, *viz.* which of the two systems is consistent with the greatest amount of human liberty and spontaneity." These are societal qualities of peculiar importance in economies of increasing diversification, driven forward at high rates of technological obsolescence by rapidly evolving and linked revolutions in science and technology. Competence in mass production of standardized and relatively stable forms of capital goods (e.g., steel, cement, electricity) does not suffice. The explicit or implicit assumption that suffused much of Western intellectual life after the First World War—that socialism in one form or another was the wave of the future—appears to be dissipating in the century's fourth quarter as one after another of the more dynamic societies revolts against the inefficiencies and inequities of a self-interested "state bourgeoisie."

These powerful forces were masked in the 1970s as the Soviet Union enjoyed significant tactical gains during a period of acute American confusion in foreign policy. But in the 1980s Soviet authorities, without an ideological message of resonance, confronted an increasingly resistant external environment, dominated by still-gathering forces of nationalism. Simultaneously, they confronted gathering long-term domestic pressures radically to alter their dispositions and to move the society they led toward what the West would reckon as more liberal norms.

But it is one thing to perceive—as many Soviet analysts do—that Eurasian or global hegemony is an impossible dream. It is quite another matter to bring the Cold War to a peaceful resolution. A working agenda for ending the Cold War must embrace three critical areas.

The first—but not necessarily the most important—is, of course, the nuclear arms race.

Here three conditions would have to be satisfied: a thoroughly inspected U.S.–U.S.S.R. nuclear balance sufficient to guarantee, at lower overall force levels, secure second-strike capabilities but no capacity for nuclear blackmail; agreements on nuclear force ceilings with other nuclear weapons powers; and against this background, a drive to implement more firmly the Nonproliferation Treaty. The path of wisdom may alter as R & D unfolds; but I would be skeptical of solutions that eliminated nuclear weapons, which wholly relied on the Strategic Defense Initiative or totally eliminated elements of SDI as part of stable deterrent systems. Evidently, problems of immense complexity are embedded in these conditions, even under circumstances of maximum goodwill among the parties.

The second area would be reorganization of NATO and the Warsaw Pact in ways that allowed an increased scope for national political freedom in Eastern Europe and guaranteed agreed force levels, securely inspected, for residual NATO and Warsaw Pact forces. The most complex issue certain to arise is the degree and character of German unity. But the objective can be simply stated: the Soviet Union would have to decide to accept a balance of power rather than a hegemonic solution to its legitimate security interest in Eastern Europe; that is, a solution guaranteeing that no other major power dominates Eastern Europe, rather than Soviet domination of the region. On this proposition basic U.S. and Soviet interests firmly overlap.

Finally, the third condition: the settlement of regional conflicts with a cold-war dimension and the development of new longer-run rules of the game. In the short run, intimate Soviet ties to Hanoi, Havana, Managua, Kabul, and other regions in contention might provide the basis for settlements in which the existing government would remain but would be effectively confined within its own border without the presence of external military forces. But, clearly, no guarantees can be given to Moscow or Washington regarding the long-term political orientation of the countries concerned. This kind of solution would work only if the United States and the Soviet Union agreed that henceforth they would live with outcomes determined by strictly local historical forces—an evidently difficult condition to accept given habits built up over the past 40 years. The Middle East would, of course, be extremely difficult to sort out in these terms, given the limited powers of the United States and the Soviet Union in the region. But, as elsewhere, those powers would be formidable if rooted in a joint conviction that the Cold War was no longer a sensible framework for the conduct of U.S.–U.S.S.R. relations or the super-powers' respective relations with others.

In all cases, the U.S.–U.S.S.R. understandings would be basic to a successful outcome, but the interests of many other states would be involved. Negotiations would therefore be complex. Moreover, the outcome would be stable only if new common rules were established and validated by the successful experience. But once the expectation was established that all were engaged in transforming the Cold War into something more desirable, the process might move forward quite briskly.

Second, a challenge of equal magnitude will be to absorb the new industrial powers of the Fourth Graduating Class into the world system without major war. As noted earlier, the achievement of technological maturity by latecomers has proved to be a dangerous age.[13] A sense of glories denied by their late arrival at technological virtuousity has tended to unite with real or believed openings for expansion granted by the apparent slackness and complacency of the early-comers. The outcome has been a great deal of trouble and tragedy.

If the human race is extremely lucky, nuclear weapons may continue to play the stabilizing role they have played since 1945; that is, they have so raised the potential costs of all-out war as to permit an unexpected passage of more than four decades without military conflict among the nuclear weapons powers. Ironically, the existence of nuclear weapons has given lesser powers a leverage quite disproportionate to their military potential, conventionally measured. In an Inaugural Lecture at Oxford in November 1946 I remarked:[14] "In a happier day students of history may be entertained by the irony of America's final acts in a victorious war, which compromised perhaps fatally the two great props of military security—distance and a preponderance of economic resources." From Korea to the Persian Gulf to the Caribbean this proposition has been validated since 1950 in circumstances that were by no means entertaining; that is, lesser powers have found ways of pursuing their interests against major nuclear powers by techniques difficult or costly to contain. In the long pull, however, as new industrial powers emerge the nuclear constraint may operate to the advantage of the older industrial states.

Clearly, the two greatest potential industrial powers are India and China. Looking ahead, the stability and peace of Asia and the world will depend heavily on whether these two great nations decide to forego a phase of contentious rivalry, like the protracted historical rivalry between France and Germany, and conclude on the basis of history and weaponry and an increasingly crowded arena of technologically competent powers, that there are more realistic and rewarding goals to pursue than regional hegemony.[15] The prospects are now uncertain. Under circumstances where both countries would benefit greatly from cooperation, they have found it impossible to settle a border dispute of essentially symbolic significance and otherwise act to pacify rather than enflame the region. On the other hand, they have been blessed with a more forbidding frontier than France and Germany; and their underlying strategic interests *vis-à-vis* the Soviet Union overlap a good deal more than the rhetoric from New Delhi and Beijing would suggest.

But the decisive determinant of the outcome may well prove to be the kind of world the older industrial powers create or fail to create in the decades ahead, while important powers of decision still lie in their hands.

The third challenge, therefore, is whether, in David Hume's evocative phrase, the nations of the Atlantic and Japan, not inconceivably joined at some stage by the Soviet Union, remain "industrious and civilized." This book virtually begins and ends (following, p. 569) with Hume's treatment of the rich-country–poor-country problem. His prescription of 1758 remains the most relevant guidance for the passage of the world system down to the middle of the next century.[16]

> Nor need any state entertain apprehensions, that their neighbours will improve to such a degree in every art and manufacture, as to have no demand from them. Nature, by giving a diversity of geniuses, climates, and soils to different nations, has secured their mutual intercourse and commerce, as long as they all remain industrious and civilized. Nay, the more the arts increase in any state, the more will be its demands from its industrious neighbours.

This third task has several dimensions. The first is to mount and sustain policies that bring the countries of the Fourth Graduating Class into the world economy in a civilized way. As Hume suggests, there are positive advantages for the older industrial states to be derived from the rise of the latecomers. Given the latter's potential for rapid growth, exports to the more advanced developing countries should be a leading sector in the several generations ahead—a consideration that bears on an appropriate resolution of debt and trade imbalance problems that now bedevil the world economy.

To manage this dynamic process of mutual support and adjustment in a civilized way to the common advantage, global rules of the game in trade and finance will, in my view, require a sturdy underpinning of regional organization.[17] That should be the central mission for an intergovernmental Pacific Basin organization, the subject of endless symposia but virtually total governmental inaction. This is also the next task for the Organization of American States and the Inter-American Development Bank—not to try out of nostalgia to recreate the old Alliance for Progress but to assure that Latin and North America move forward with steady mutual support as the former makes the transition to full technological maturity, coming to grips along the way with debt and other acute, urgent problems.

Now what about remaining industrious? The first condition is that the United States, Western Europe, and Japan explore the possibilities opened up by the new technologies and apply them across the board to basic industries, agriculture, and the services including the containment of environmental degradation. Only by so doing will they be able to maintain economies of sufficient productivity and flexibility to support and enlarge their affluence in the face of the sustained competitive test ahead. I believe this requires a historic shift in the pattern of domestic politics in the Western World. The shift is away from a more or less decorous struggle over how real national income, assumed to be automatically expanding, should be distributed. It can be argued that this has been the dominant pattern of politics since Bismarck initiated his welfare legislation in the 1870s. The required shift is toward a cooperative effort that embraces business, labor, and government, as well as the scientific, engineering, and entrepreneurial sectors to ensure that real national income in the advanced industrial countries continues to expand in an arena increasingly crowded with technologically competent powers.

For historical reasons, Japanese politics appears, for the moment, well oriented for the task ahead. Since Commodore Perry turned up in Tokyo Bay some 130 years ago with his squadron of black ships, the interaction of the external world with Japanese pride and ambition has yielded a succession of crises that have strengthened the nation's sense of unity and common purpose; and since the mid-1950s Japan's economic position in the world has been the focus of that sentiment. Japan's challenge will be to maintain a sense of clear, common purpose when it shifts, as it inevitably must, from an obsessive focus on maximizing its export surplus to a wider spectrum of domestic and external objectives. The two Maekawa Reports of 1986–1987 outline this process extraordinarily well.

But it is one thing for a group of wise men to define persuasively new directions for Japanese society, a different and vastly more difficult matter to bring about the necessary changes, in the face of deeply rooted habits and vested interests, before Japan and the rest of the world community are engulfed in a major corrosive crisis. Such a crisis is wholly possible if the pace of adjustment on trade and Third World debts is not greatly accelerated.

If a mercantilist fragmentation—likely to intensify rather than end the Cold War and set the newer against the older industrial states—is to be avoided, something new and difficult, but not impossible, will be required. Western Europe, Japan, and the United States will have to generate collectively the leadership none can now provide alone. This means designing and abiding by new rules of the game for trade, capital movements, and domestic policy in the extraordinarily internationalized economy that has emerged. On the basis of such rules, they will have to work with each other and with the developing regions to exploit the new possibilities and make the peaceful adjustments cooperation could render realistic and mutually profitable. And, I would add, as the latecomers move forward, they must gradually assume an increasing degree of responsibility for the viability of the international system as a whole. The United States grossly failed this test between the two world wars—with tragic results. Japan now confronts this test, and before long so will South Korea, Taiwan, Brazil, and the other aspiring, fast-moving latecomers, especially India and China. In fact, Taiwan, with its fantastic reserves and modest external indebtedness, already confronts the rite of passage to responsibility.

A final aspect of the task relates to diplomacy and military policy rather than economics, although success in its pursuit depends on the effectiveness of the presently advanced nations in dealing with their complex economic agenda. While offering to the newer industrial states civilized economic relations and roles of increasing responsibility and authority in collective enterprises, the older industrial nations will have to maintain military strength, maximum unity, and common purpose if the chances of a peaceful transformation are to be maximized. The Second World War came about when the Atlantic world lost both a grasp on its economic and social problems and its unity on the raw issues of military security. Churchill was quite correct in calling the conflagration "the unnecessary war." In seeking to avoid such wars in the future I would merely suggest the possibility—not argue the case—that, contrary to much current conventional wisdom, closer ties as among the United Sates, Western Europe, and Japan will be required in the future than in the past or at present. The Cold War helped create the existing networks across the Atlantic and Pacific. An ending of the Cold War by no means guarantees peace. It could easily yield chaos if Trans-Atlantic and Trans-Pacific ties are weakened or broken. The movement from Cold War to a reasonably solid institutionalized peace will require great sustained common effort.

The fourth challenge is how to meet the strains on resources and the environment that may be posed by the effort to complete the transformation—or to move virtually all the globe's societies into their own versions of high mass consumption. As Chapter 20 suggests, no one can now estimate with confidence the degree or generality of the strains this effort is likely to entail. Certainly, the dogmatism of the standard computer run in *Limits to Growth*—with its injunction promptly to cease the further diffusion of industrial growth or face cataclysm early in the twenty-first century—was not well founded in either theory or the data.[18]

But effective criticism of the *Limits to Growth* doctrine did not constitute proof that sustainable growth, on present patterns, with existing technology, can go forward without regional or, possibly, general resource or environmental crises. Indeed, Sub-Saharan Africa is already experiencing limits-to-growth crises, and they have been none the less real because brought on substantially by unwise governmental policies.

When I surveyed the prospects for continued growth a decade ago while completing *The World Economy,* I isolated certain then-unanswerable technical questions that might well affect the outcome; for example, the likelihood of producing in, say, the first half of the twenty-first century an essentially infinite, nonpolluting source of relatively cheap energy or the possibility of drastic changes in the climate via the greenhouse effect. These and other large questions (e.g., the significance of the attenuation of the ozone layer) remain unanswered. But I concluded then—and would conclude again—that the critical issues are likely to be decided by national and international policies rather than inexorable laws of nature. That conclusion—if correct—offers only limited comfort, given the long record of human fallibility and the tendency of governments to await acute crisis before acting. But it offers some comfort by setting challenges in technology and policy that do not appear beyond the reach of human performance at its best. Put another way, with a bit of luck, there is no reason to judge it beyond the capacity of the human race to struggle through to a time when population growth in the developing continents has been sharply reduced and adequate food, shelter, and clothing, education, and the considerable amenities a mature industrial civilization can provide are available for the overwhelming majority of the world's men, women, and children.

There are, evidently, values to be cherished beyond material progress: the joys of family, the arts, religion, and the full expression of unique personalities. And these deserve cultivation, in the South as well as the North, as governments and their citizens struggle through the challenging agenda of the next several generations. But only those who do not know what the round of life is like in an impoverished village or an over-crowded urban slum, whether in eighteenth-century Europe or contemporary developing regions, will fail to appreciate how material progress has improved the quality of life and can continue to do so.

Surely there will be surprises along the way. In the first instance, responses must come from national societies; but whether the issue is a cure for AIDS, or the achievement of commercially viable fusion power, or preservation of lakes and forests by the reduc-tion of acid rain, or controlling pollution in the Mediterranean—the international dimen-sion of the task of preserving the human race and its habitat will remain critical, in-creasingly expensive, and demanding intensified international cooperation.

The fifth challenge centers on policy toward the approximately 20% of the human race that lives in poor countries that have not entered modern or self-sustained growth.[19] This group includes, *inter alia,* most of Sub-Saharan Africa, Bangladesh, Burma, Haiti, Yemen, Afghanistan, Vietnam, and some of the Pacific islands. This illustrative list suggests the variety of circumstances that may have forestalled entrance into takeoff: historical and cultural heritage; partial or total rejection of modernity as an objective; resource limitations; war; endemic political instability; perverse public policies; or vary-ing combinations of these circumstances.

The first and most important thing to be said about international development policy in relation to this array of countries flows from the conclusion drawn at the close of Chapter 16; namely, that, in the end, the analysis of growth must come to rest on each society, with all its unique features. No one can state with confidence how many will enter the Fifth Graduating Class in takeoff. Some may turn a corner fairly soon and move ahead rapidly, as South Korea did in the 1960s. Others may be frustrated for decades by problems of resource constraints and/or aspects of their political, social, or cultural heritage, and/or bad policy.

Evidently, the development problems of Sub-Saharan Africa are currently the most challenging, both because of their scale and because the popular desire for development, as nearly as one can judge, appears authentic. The plight of these aspiring but frustrated countries was made vivid by a question put to me by an African agricultural technician attending an international center in India where I spoke in 1983. He said, in effect: "Many African countries became independent 20 years ago but have not entered takeoff. What's wrong with your theory?" When laughter had subsided I discussed the wide range of mainly noneconomic forces that have historically determined the length of the precon-ditions for takeoff; short for Japan (32 years from Commodore Perry's arrival, only 17 from the Meiji Restoration); long for China (110 years from the Opium Wars), even longer for Mexico (120 years from Independence). Evidently no uniform time period could be defined for developing the preconditions for takeoff. I concluded that, basically, the people of each country, suffused with their respective cultural, social, and political heritages, would determine if, when, and how their entrance into sustained growth would begin; each case would be different; but the advanced countries—especially their development economists—owed the lagging aspirants more thought and attention than they had been thus far given plus a good deal of patience. The African heritage—including strong tribal attachment and arbitrary boundaries derived from colonial history that violated tribal locations—was likely to make the interval between independence and takeoff rather long but, I would guess, shorter than for China or Mexico.

A part of the challenge posed by these hard cases is that we economists cannot usefully come to grips with them unless we are willing to make cultural, social, and political factors—as well as history—a living part of our analyses. We paid a price in our studies of and prescriptions for more advanced developing countries when we set these factors aside, as we have often done. But still we could find areas of usefulness. This is much less likely to be the case in analyses of and prescriptions for the preconditions for takeoff.

But so far as development-aid policy is concerned, the major conclusion is that, while each country, like each student or doctor's patient, is unique, we need, broadly, two types of policy: one addressed to pre-takeoff countries, the other to countries in the drive to technological maturity.

The latter group of developing countries has, in my view, an important role to play in helping patiently to nurse along those laggard countries that desire to move forward. They are closer to the early phases of development and should be able to provide effective technical assistance as, indeed, Taiwan has done to a number of African countries. The assumption of that responsibility would be easier and more natural if the regional structures of the world economy were to be strengthened, each embracing nations at different stages of growth. As indicated earlier, the Pacific Basin appears ripe for such an effort, and the Western Hemisphere ripe for a renewed and heightened collective effort. As for Africa, a parallel regional effort appears appropriate, with Western Europe taking the lead among the advanced industrial countries, the United States and Japan as junior partners, the World Bank working in collaboration with the African Development Bank. Some such purposeful, collective effort may have to await the subsidence of certain political and diplomatic problems, but in terms of the fate of the men, women, and children of Africa, the effort is long overdue.

The Short Run and the Long Run

This terse definition of a five-point global agenda underlines one of the recurrent themes of this book, namely, that it is unwise to separate the analysis of the long run and the short run. Growth, cycle, and trend are inextricably interconnected. To take a self-evident case, the trend relative decline of basic commodity prices from 1920 to the mid-1930s helped cause—and was, in turn, exacerbated by—the damped cyclical expansion to 1929 and the subsequent extreme depression. As we peer ahead to 2050 and try to define the long-range agenda from the perspective of 1989, it is clear that the present interwoven crises of U.S. deficits, trade imbalances, burdensome debts, and relative stagnation in much of the developing world could, if poorly handled, make constructive action on that long-run agenda virtually impossible. Such a failure could, by fragmenting the alliances across the Atlantic and Pacific, frustrate whatever favorable prospects there may be for a withering away of the Cold War; render unlikely a peaceful and collaborative adjustment to the strains of the arrival at technological maturity of the Fourth Graduating Class; and attenu-

Table 21.6. Real GNP Growth in Developing Countries
[average annual percent change]

Region	1970 to 1980	1980 to 1986[1]
Western Hemisphere	5.8	1.0
Africa	3.7	1.0
Middle East	6.4	−.4
Asia	5.2	4.7

[1]Preliminary estimates.
SOURCE: International Monetary Fund, reproduced in *Economic Report of the President* (Washington, D.C.: United States Government Printing Office, 1987), p. 105.

ate cooperative efforts both to cope with strains on resources and the environment and to nurture those thus far left behind in the process of growth.[20]

I evoke these immediate problems not only because of their influence on the long-run prospect but also because the choice of guiding principles before the major nation states in the short run depends on the answer to the central question also confronted with respect to the long-run agenda outlined here. The question is: Shall the political process—domestic and international—recognize and act systematically on the interdependencies that have grown up in a global community within which power has now so diffused that domination by a single nation or coalition is impossible? The choice is to build increasingly on these interdependencies or to permit raw national impulses, in the form of intensified protectionism, to render the world arena a neomercantilist bear pit. It is quite possible to write the scenario for the next several generations either way.

It would be inappropriate to elaborate here a detailed description of a short-term policy to avoid the latter outcome. But its headings and principles can be suggested.

1. Concerted measures by the major economic powers and international organizations to ease substantially the debt burden of the developing regions. Table 21.6 reflects not merely the economic, social and political strain experienced in the 1980s by the developing regions, other than most of Asia, but also one major source of the U.S. trade deficit and the sluggishness of the European economies.
2. Concerted measures by the major economic powers and economic organizations to cushion the international banking system from the adjustments required to ease those debt burdens.
3. Measures to increase the rate of growth in chronically surplus countries, notably Japan and the Federal Republic of Germany, accompanied by strong import liberalization measures. Japan has been moving in these directions to a degree in partial response to the recommendations of the Maekawa Reports, but the FRG has thus far pursued an exceedingly parochial policy, inappropriate to its economic stature and chronic foreign exchange surplus.
4. Enlarged official and private lending to developing regions, the former by concerted action to enlarge resources available to the World Bank and the regional development banks. Capital exports to the United States should be diverted to the developing regions as the U.S. trade deficit and real interest rates are brought down. In the short run, the present surplus countries bear a special responsibility for such lending, notably Japan, which country, for historical reasons, is not making a proportionate contribution to its own defense.

5. In this environment, including accelerated growth in Western Europe, Japan, and the developing regions, the United States ought to be able to recapture its capacity to match its imports with exports if the following policies are followed: a balanced federal budget, permitting an easing in monetary policy and interest rates; accelerated application of the new technologies; and a rigorous incomes policy to contain the inflationary effects of post-1985 devaluation of the dollar.
6. Prompt movement toward the definition of new international rules of the game to supplant the Bretton Woods system that would once again link a nation's domestic economic policy to its international accounts.

International concert is essential for two reasons: because no single power commands the stature and resources to lead the international community as the United States briefly did after the Second World War; and because such concert is necessary for each national leader to cope with the domestic vested interests likely to oppose the courses of action necessary to transit the immediate crisis.

In a study that embraces a good deal of modern economic history as well as theory it is perhaps worth noting a fairly close analogy out of the common past to the present distorted state of affairs: the transfer problems confronted in 1928–1930 by Germany (with respect to reparations), and Britain and France (with respect to war debts), when the flow of U.S. capital was diverted from Germany to the New York stock market starting in the second half of 1928. The outcome was a cumulative breakdown in the international trade and financial system that drove the depression to unexampled depths and helped bring on the Second World War.

With hindsight we can say with reasonable confidence that this outcome could have been avoided if in, say, early 1930, a series of actions were taken quite analogous to those now required:

• If reparations and war debts [like Third World debts] had been cut down, stretched out, or canceled by international agreement;
• If concerted international action had been taken to cushion short-run strains in the banking system;
• If the United States, Britain, France, and Germany had agreed to conduct simultaneously strong expansionary fiscal and monetary policies;
• If the United States [like contemporary Japan and the FRG], with an exceedingly strong gold and foreign exchange position, had moved toward radically liberalized trade and the provision of enlarged capital exports.

The heart of a solution lay in intensified international cooperation, and that, of course, didn't happen.

Returning to the great unresolved transfer problem of the 1980s, it is evident that the world economy is confronted by the need for large adjustments. It would be unwise to underestimate the scale of the national and international effort required. But it is also easy to overestimate the magnitude of the challenge the current crisis represents. It is the lesson of the past half-century that modern economies are extraordinarily resilient if the political leadership and the citizenry are determined to act; for example, the wartime adjustments of the British and American economies; the postwar recovery of Western Europe and Japan including their shift from dollar-shortage to dollar-surplus status; and the adjustment of the highly vulnerable Japanese economy to the two oil shocks of the 1970s. In the end the adjustments required in the world economy are primarily a matter of politics and will, rather than economics, in the narrow sense. This, by itself, does not make these adjustments easier. But it would be a good deal less difficult for Japanese politicians to move more rapidly in the direction of the Maekawa Reports, for American politicians to face up to balancing the federal budget and other measures required to bring its international accounts into balance, and for German politicians to launch a more expansionist policy at home if these and the other courses of action required were part of the reestablishment of an orderly, disciplined international system than the outcome of sporadic bilateral negotiations in which merely raw domestic special interests and conventional nationalisms were in play.

The whole process could be eased if the almost accidental windfall brought about by measures taken in 1983 to assure the viability of the American Social Security system down to the middle of the twenty-first century were used, not only as at present, as a means to accelerate the balancing of the federal budget but increasingly to expand investment in research, education, infrastructure, and control of environmental degradation.[21]

A Conclusion: "All on a Razor's Edge It Stands, either Woeful Ruin or Life"*

It is peculiarly appropriate that this book come to a close on the choice between nationalist fragmentation and human solidarity; for in their time David Hume and Adam Smith saw the choice in quite similar terms. Recall Hume's argument for "enlarged and benevolent sentiments" as the guide for relations among nation states:

> I shall therefore venture to acknowledge, that, not only as a man but as a British subject, I pray for the flourishing commerce of Germany, Spain, Italy and even France itself. I am at least certain, that Great Britain and all those nations, would flourish more, did their sovereigns and ministers adopt such enlarged and benevolent sentiments towards each other.

Behind this proposition lay Hume's more general perception that closely knit societies depend ultimately for their stability on "sympathy"—a vivid perception of the emotions, interests, and views of the world held by others.

Adam Smith, perhaps a shade more disabused about the human condition and more inclined to rely on "self-love" than "humanity," nevertheless also evoked sympathy as a civilizing force and railed "very violently" against mercantilism, including colonialism: "Commerce," he wrote, "which ought naturally to be among nations, as among individuals, a bond of union and friendship, has become the most fertile source of discord and animosity." And, more generally, the remarkable first sentence of his *Theory of Moral Sentiments:* "How selfish so ever man may be supposed, there are evidently some principles in his nature which interest him in the fortune of others, and render their happiness necessary to him. . . ." On such principles the nations will have to build to come through successfully.

Hume, Smith, and others in the same tradition did not succeed in their own time. The endemic Anglo–French struggle of the eighteenth century continued, climaxed by the great war of 1793–1815. The American colonies achieved their independence not because the British government accepted the new maxims of political economy but only after 8

*Homer, *Iliad,* Book X, line 173.

frustrated years of bloody conflict and with essential assistance to the United States from monarchical, mercantilist France.

Nevertheless, Hume and Smith left a tradition for political economy that has never been more relevant as the twentieth century moves to a close, and "a step away" a new century beckons.[22] Looking back and at where we are, that tradition has had its victories, if not a definitive triumph. There is in the restless, often combative, global community more recognition that interdependent societies demand mutual "sympathy" than we often credit: The World Bank and IMF; the regional development banks; some $30 billion annually in official development assistance; spontaneous outpourings of assistance throughout the global community in the face of famine and natural disasters, dramatized in December 1988 by the global response to the Armenian earthquake.

In a quite different dimension, there was "sympathy" too as Nikita Khruschev drew back from the hard-knotted crisis he created by putting missiles and nuclear warheads in Cuba; and John Kennedy tried to make that drawing back as easy as possible. And there were other occasions when the nuclear Sword of Damocles—the most compelling form of interdependence—helped hold off major war.

These real-enough reflections of a sense of common humanity are now joined with a resurgent recognition of another dimension of the classical tradition in political economy: the virtues of individual initiative and competition. If it were merely a question of long-run trend, optimism would be justified.

But in a nuclear age the global community must do better than rely on a benign long-run trend. The men, women, and children of our community cannot afford an equivalent of the French Revolutionary and Napoleonic Wars or the kind of breakdown of affairs that occurred between the two world wars of this century.

If we economists are to make a maximum contribution to humanity's coming down on the right side of the razor's edge, I believe we would do well—without giving up the technical virtuousities we have generated—to build on the spacious principled tradition of the classical economists with which many of the young have lost touch. In phrases from Adam Smith's early *Theory of Moral Sentiments,* we too must try—in a post-Cold War world—to help rethink "the general principles which ought to run through and be the foundation of the laws of all nations." As Keynes once reminded us, we are not the trustees of civilization but of the possibility of civilization. In a sense we are jugglers; but like the medieval *Jongleur de Notre Dame,** we must make sure we juggle for large purposes.

*Since readings in elementary French may have changed since my days in New Haven High School, the legend of *Le Jongleur de Notre Dame* is the following: A juggler goes to a chapel to express his religious devotion in the only way he knows. Alone, before a statue of the Virgin Mary, he juggles until he falls exhausted. The statue comes to life, steps down from its pedestal, and mops his brow.

Appendix:
Models of Economic Growth

MICHAEL KENNEDY AND W.W. ROSTOW

Prefatory Note (WWR)

This Appendix is the result of a collaboration between Michael Kennedy and myself. Dr. Kennedy, now at the RAND Corporation, is a quantitative economist who is comfortable in mathematics. I am merely a reader of mathematical economics with some capacity to pose issues and roughly outline formal models in terms capable of translation into mathematical terms. I had envisaged from the beginning of this enterprise an effort to drive home in mathematical terms certain key propositions in my view of economic growth. I respected from the beginning of my training as an economist the power of mathematics as a device to dramatize with clarity certain key assumptions or relationships, at the cost of two kinds of simplification: the elimination or freezing of significant relevant variables, and the treatment of dynamic, nonreversible processes, in constant disequilibrium, as if they yielded equilibrium. I believe economic growth—like other forms of growth—is a biological process. Scientifically, it yields patterns, like chaos theory, rather than logical equilibrium sequences, like Newtonian physics. But I am quite prepared to exploit the virtues of mathematical formulations so long as the drastic simplification of reality they entail is clearly understood and so long as critically important variables are not eliminated or fixed for reasons of convenience. My collaboration with Kennedy was ultimately made possible because his views on these fundamental matters and mine are quite similar. Although we collaborated closely in the evolution and drafting of this Appendix, the mathematical exposition is, of course, Michael Kennedy's.

Introduction

We proceed by presenting a series of formal models that identify those key assumptions that produce significant, qualitative differences in portrayals of the growth process that are associated with different authors or schools analyzed in the text.

We begin with a single-sector model of growth that attempts to capture in analytical terms the primary determinants of the growth process as described in Adam Smith's *Wealth of Nations*. This is followed by a comparative exercise in which we develop successively formal models that represent three views of the growth process: the neoclassical model; the model associated with Rostow's work; and the Adam Smith model, this time appearing in multisectoral form. These three models are embedded in a common multisectoral framework so that the assumptions that lead to their distinctly different results can be clearly identified. Finally, we present some results of modeling the rich-country–poor-country relationship; that is, the dynamics of growth and interaction in an international system in which different countries are at different levels of development. This is the problem first explored by David Hume, by Folke Hilgerdt and Eugene Staley about two centuries later, and that lies at the heart of Chapter 21.

Appendix Part I:
A One-Sector Adam Smith Model of Growth

A Verbal Account

We begin with a verbal account of the Smithian growth process, and then proceed with a formal presentation of a one-sector model. The simplicity of the one-sector approach enables us to identify clearly the key assumptions that drive the model, although Smith's exposition was, in fact, quite disaggregated, as the text of Chapter 2 makes clear.

The level of output in the Smith model depends, as it does in contemporary growth analysis, on inputs of three factors of production—labor, capital, and land; and on the level of technology. Smith also took account of certain noneconomic factors; for example, the degree of political stability, the security of private property, and the role of laws, institutions, and customs in determining attitudes toward commerce and the social status of merchants. These can be introduced into formal models exogenously as factors that frustrate, damp, or heighten the working of strictly economic variables.

At its core, a model of growth representing a Smithian system must, therefore, account for changes in supplies of the factor inputs; and it must account as well for the evolution of technology. In the model presented here, supplies of the factors of production are assumed to evolve over time in the following ways:

- Change in the labor force is determined by the level of the real wage relative to a subsistence wage. If the real wage is above the subsistence wage, labor supply is assumed to grow; if it is below, labor supply is assumed to fall. This subsistence wage may be thought of as either a true physiological subsistence wage, or as some psychological minimum below which workers choose not to expand their numbers and above which they do. For simplicity, we do not introduce the lags that would, in fact, enter this linkage.
- The capital stock grows as a result of net investment. In this system, only owners of capital are assumed to invest, and thus to be a source of gross additions to the capital stock. Both landlords and workers are assumed to consume all of their income. Thus, investment is determined by the level of profits, which is the income of the owners of capital.
- In our model the supply of land is assumed to be fixed. Smith's full exposition is not that simple. He devotes considerable space to specifying which basic commodities (''rude materials'') are fixed in supply and suggesting the degree of elasticity of supply for others where increases in output are judged possible (preceding, p. 40). But there is no doubt that, on balance, Smith believed diminishing returns applied to basic commodities; and that diminishing returns is built into his definition of a country's growth ceiling: the ''full complement of riches which the nature

of its soil and climate, and its situation with respect to other countries, allowed it to acquire. . . .'' There is an implication here of a geographical limit to the profitable expansion of the market as well as diminishing returns to the production of ''rude produce;'' in a single-sector model the assumption of fixed land is the best analogue to this set of assumptions.[1] Without violating Smith's analysis this assumption gives a somewhat pre-1813 Malthusian and Ricardian cast to our one-sector exposition.

In short, growth of the two nonfixed factors depends on the level of their associated factor reward. Growth of the labor force depends explicitly on the real wage; growth of the capital stock depends on the level of profits, and thus on the rate of return to capital.

Three kinds of technological progress can be identified in Smith's work.

First, there is Smith's most famous proposition stated, like the theme of a symphony, in the opening sentences of the first and second chapters of *The Wealth of Nations:* (1) the greatest force making for the increase of labor productivity is the division of labor that, in turn, (2) arises from a propensity in human nature to truck, barter, and exchange one thing for another. Essentially, Smith asserts that what is now called increasing returns to scale arises from the expansion of the market; that is, an improvement of output per unit input occurs as the economy grows because there are increased opportunities for division of labor, and thus specialization, in a larger economy. This incremental improvement in productivity accompanying specialization is attributed to three forces: the worker's increase in dexterity; reduced waste of the worker's time; and the encouragement of invention of machines to take advantage of specialization possibilities, including the products of creative machine-builders ''combining the powers of the most distant and dissimilar objects'' (preceding, p. 41 and following p. 580 n. 98).

The second is less well known, less discussed, and rather Schumpeterian; that is, an occasional dramatic increase in the state of knowledge, associated with a ''philosopher's'' [scientist's] discovery of a new product or method of production. There is, thus, in the Smithian model an overlay of irregular, large spurts in knowledge, derived from the inventions of philosophers, atop the regular, small-scale accretion of productivity derived from the specialization of function induced by the expansion of the market and associated improvement in the workers' tools.

One can even deduce a third form of technological change. There are passages in *The Wealth of Nations* that seem to imply that there are incremental improvements in technology associated with a system of specialized function but not directly linked to increased specialization associated with current expansion of the market. Put another way, one gets the impression that Smith had in mind that specialization of function yielded the regular allocation of talent to the improvement of technology as a habit.

Using these assumptions about the development of factor inputs and technology, we can construct the following verbal portrait of the growth process as represented by Smith. The economy begins in an ''original rude state,'' which in today's terms is a stationary equilibrium. In this state the real wage is at the subsistence level; i.e., that level at which the labor force does not change. The rate of profit is at such a level that gross investment is just equal to replacement investment, or depreciation, so that the capital stock does not change. In addition, the economy is assumed to be below the minimum size at which economies of scale can be exploited. In the absence of any autonomous technical change or expansion of the market (internal or external) the economy would stay at this level.[2] In fact, Smith had the force of expansion in foreign trade primarily in mind as an instrument for moving the economy away from its original rude state. Historically, the commercial revolution of the previous two and one-half centuries was a powerful living reality to Smith's generation; but no technological change wrought by philosophers had yet been powerful enough to set in motion a sustained movement from the low-level equilibrium trap.

Theoretically, however, if either some incremental technical progress or a philosopher's invention or opening up of a new market by, say, discovery were to occur, causing an upward shift in the level of technology, some economic growth would begin. Output would be immediately higher, of course, due to the higher level of technology acting on the original level of factor inputs. Factor rewards would be higher as well, for the same reason. The labor force would grow due to the higher real wage, and the capital stock would grow due to the higher level of profits, yielding, in turn, increased investment. With the level of land fixed, however, this growth of labor and capital supplies would begin pushing the real wage and the rate of profit back down again, and these factor rewards would continue to fall until they reached their original levels. At the original levels of factor reward labor and capital supplies would remain constant at their new higher levels. There are more workers and more capital, but each worker and unit of capital receives the same reward as before the change in technology. The return to land, in contrast, has grown for two reasons: the original increase in technology, and the increase in the level of the other two factors. Landlords are the only ultimate beneficiaries of the increase in knowledge. The assumption that labor and capital grow when their rewards are above the original level inexorably drives their rewards back to those levels. Growth serves only further to enrich the landowning classes.

The end result of this growth process is thus a new steady state. Labor and capital supplies are higher, but their reward is at the original level. Land supply, at the original level by assumption, gains a higher reward.

This first growth case is the adjustment of the system to a single positive shock, causing a movement from one static equilibrium position to another. But Smith's analysis assumes that at some point, as the economy grows, it reaches the size at which a phase of increasing returns sets in. Let us imagine an economy that has just reached that size; i.e., at a point at which the level of output per unit input would begin to increase, solely due to specialization, or the division of labor, at any larger size. The economy still needs some initial exogenous shock to begin its growth, such as the opening up of trade with the Western Hemisphere or the East Indies. The growth process of this economy will differ from the one described above because of the specialization (and thus technical improvement) that is induced at larger sizes of the economy. Labor and capital still grow when their factor rewards are above the original level, and this tends to push those rewards back down. But counteracting this effect is the increase in productivity—output per unit input—that results from the larger size of the economy and thus the multiple effects of specialization of function. This tends to push factor rewards back up. Which force prevails? It is evident from Smith's comments on the Dutch, British, and French economies, as well as the North American colonies, that he envisaged that increasing returns might prevail for some time. But following his concept of a "full complement of riches," we assume that there is in his system an upper limit to possibilities for expansion of the market and specialization of function, and that at some size of the economy the phenomenon of increasing returns gives way to diminishing returns. As a result, wages and profits are still driven back to their original levels, and landlords become the sole beneficiaries of the prior phase of increasing returns as well as of the technological progress that initiated the expansion.

We now turn to the formal development of the model. Our strategy is to build up to the full-blown model through a series of simpler models, so that the important features of the model are added one by one, and their role in shaping the ultimate results becomes clear.

Formal Exposition

We began with a model with only two sectors, capital and labor, and with no technical progress. We initially focus on the implications of the Smithian assumption that the growth of factor supplies depends on the levels of factor rewards.

Our initial point of departure is then the familiar two-factor production function.

$$Y_t = F(K_t, L_t) \tag{AI.1}$$

where Y_t is output, K_t is capital input and L_t is labor input. t refers to the time period, which we take to be a year. F is assumed to exhibit constant returns to scale. Factor rewards are assumed to be related to factor inputs through the marginal productivity relations

$$w_t = F_L(K_t, L_t) \tag{AI.2}$$

$$r_t = F_K(K_t, L_t) \tag{AI.3}$$

where w_t is the wage rate, r_t is the gross rate of return to capital, and F_K and F_L represent partial derivatives.

Our assumption concerning capital accumulation is that only owners of capital save. In particular, the capital accumulation relations are

$$K_{t+1} = (1 - \delta) K_t + I_t \tag{AI.4}$$

$$I_t = s F_K (K_t, L_t) K_t = s r_t K_t \tag{AI.5}$$

Here I_t is the level of gross investment, and s is the saving rate of capitalists. Equation (AI.4), in which δ is the depreciation rate, represents a one-year gestation lag of new investment. Equation (AI.5) simply says that capitalists invest a fraction s of their income, their income being equal to the marginal product of capital times the level of capital. Combining equations (AI.3) to (AI.5) leads to the relation

$$\frac{K_{t+1} - K_t}{K_t} = (s r_t - \delta) \tag{AI.6}$$

which says that the growth of the capital stock depends on the saving rate of capitalists, the rate of return to capital, and the depreciation rate. In particular, given the saving rate of capitalists and the depreciation rate, the rate of capital accumulation depends on the rate of return to capital. The capital stock will increase, stay constant, or decrease as

$$r_t \gtreqless \delta/s \tag{AI.7}$$

If the rate of return to capital just equals the depreciation rate divided by the saving rate, the level of the capital stock will remain constant.

Since r_t depends on K_t and L_t, the familiar capital–labor diagram can be used to illustrate the capital-accumulation situation. Figure AI.1 shows the capital–labor space. This space is ordinarily used with production isoquants and equal budget lines to illustrate cost-minimizing choice of inputs. But since the rate of return to capital (r_t) depends on the level of capital and labor in the economy [equation (AI.3)] each point in this capital–labor

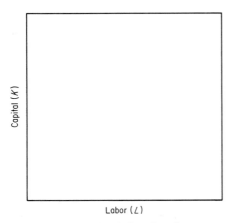

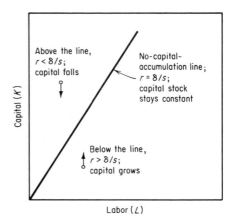

Figure AI.1. Capital–Labor Space.

Figure AI.2. No-Capital-Accumulation Line.

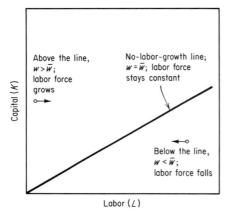

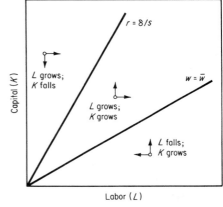

Figure AI.3. No-Labor-Growth Line.

Figure AI.4. Steadily Expanding Economy. NOTE: "$r = \delta/s$" is the no-capital-accumulation line. "$w = \bar{w}$" is the no-labor-growth line.

space will be associated with a given r_t. Just as one can define production isoquants, that is, loci of points at which output is equal to some constant level, one can also define rate of return isoquants, that is, loci of points at which the rate of return is equal to some constant level. In particular, we can find that locus of points at which $r_t = \delta/s$, or at which the level of capital stock stays constant. This locus is illustrated in Figure AI.2. (Since the production function is assumed to exhibit constant returns to scale, the level of factor rewards depends only on the ratio of capital to labor, so the locus of points at which $r_t = \delta/s$ is a ray through the origin.) At any point above this "no-capital-accumulation" line, the rate of return is below that needed to maintain the capital stock, so the capital stock falls. At any point below the line, capital stock rises. Thus the dynamics of capital accumulation moves the economy toward the "no-capital-accumulation" line in a direction parallel to the capital axis.

The reader can verify that an increase in the savings propensity of capitalists shifts the no-capital-accumulation line counterclockwise (up), as does a Hicks-neutral increase in total factor productivity [i.e., an upward multiplicative shift in equation (AI.1)].

We next assume that changes in the labor force are determined by the wage rate. In particular, we assume that there is a "subsistence" wage, $\bar{w}$, at which the labor force stays constant over time, and that the labor force grows when the wage is above $\bar{w}$, and falls when the wage is below $\bar{w}$. We represent labor force growth as

$$\frac{L_{t+1} - L_t}{L_t} = g(w_t/\bar{w}) \tag{AI.8}$$

$$g(1) = 0$$

$$g' > 0$$

The functional form can remain arbitrary at this point. Formulation (AI.8) was chosen to be parallel to equation (AI.6).

Labor force growth can be represented in the capital–labor graph in a way precisely analogous to the representation of capital stock growth. The locus of points of capital–labor pairs at which $w_t = F_L(K_t, L_t) = \bar{w}$ is that locus at which labor force growth is zero. Such a "no-labor-growth" line is illustrated in Figure AI.3. (This locus is a ray through the origin for the same reason that the no-capital-accumulation line was.) At points above this no-labor-growth line the market wage rate is above the subsistence wage, and thus the labor force grows. At points below the line, the labor force shrinks. Thus, the economy moves toward the no-labor-growth line in a direction parallel to the labor axis. The reader can verify that a decrease in the subsistence wage shifts the no-labor-growth line clockwise (down), as does a Hicks-neutral increase in total factor productivity.

How does the economy described so far evolve over time? Do capital and labor approach steady-state long-run equilibrium values? The answer is, in general, no. In general, the economy will be steadily growing or steadily shrinking, depending on the relative position of the no-capital-accumulation and no-labor-growth lines. The steady growth situation is shown in Figure AI.4. Here, the no-capital-accumulation line lies above the no-labor-growth line. The factor growth relations propel the economy toward the northeast, and it grows without bound. If the relative position of the lines is reversed, however, as in Figure AI.5, the situation is the opposite. Here the economy shrinks without bound toward the origin. The economy is not sufficiently productive to allow factor supplies to grow.

Only in the razor's-edge case of the two lines being coincident is it possible to attain nonzero finite steady-state equilibrium levels of capital and labor.

We now introduce the third factor of production, land, into the model. As described above, we assume that land is fixed in supply. The economy is assumed to exhibit constant returns to scale in the three factors capital, labor, and land combined. The production function is

$$Y_t = F(K_t, L_t, N_t) \tag{AI.9}$$

where N_t denotes land. (Given that land is fixed, the economy exhibits diminishing returns in capital and labor combined. Thus this addition to the model might also be interpreted as a generalization of the first model in which the original assumption of constant returns is replaced by one of diminishing returns. In order to distinguish this model from the first model, we will refer to it as a "decreasing returns" model, and the first as a "constant returns" model.)

We again assume marginal product pricing of factors of production so that

$$w_t = F_L(K_t, L_t, N_t) \tag{AI.10}$$

$$r_t = F_K(K_t, L_t, N_t) \tag{AI.11}$$

$$n_t = F_N(K_t, L_t, N_t) \tag{AI.12}$$

where n_t is the rent on land.

Our assumptions concerning accumulation of labor and capital are the same as in the first model: *viz.*

$$\frac{K_{t+1} - K_t}{K_t} = (s\, r_t - \delta) \tag{AI.6}$$

$$\frac{L_{t+1} - L_t}{L_t} = g(w_t/\bar{w}) \tag{AI.8}$$

Land is assumed to be fixed in supply, so N_t is an exogenous variable in the system, and its growth is zero.

Given N_t fixed, equations (AI.10) and (AI.11) define w_t and r_t as functions of K_t and L_t, exactly as they did in the constant returns model. Thus, we can define loci of constant wage rates and constant rates of return to capital in the capital labor diagram, just as we did above. Figure AI.6 illustrates a constant rate of return locus, which is a no-capital-accumulation line if the rate of return is chosen equal to δ/s. This no-capital-accumulation line is concave rather than linear. An illustration of the concavity of the line is given in Figure AI.7. Take a point A on the no-capital-accumulation line, and construct a ray from the origin through point A. Now consider a point B on the ray, chosen northeast of point A. Point B represents a constant percentage increase in capital and labor from point A. In a constant returns world, such a constant percentage increase would leave the rate of return unchanged. In the situation we are considering, however, such a change is the equivalent (for r_t) of a decrease in the amount of land available. We assume that a decrease in land available will decrease the marginal return to capital. An increase in labor will be necessary to raise the marginal product of capital back to the level that prevailed at point A. (The increase in labor needed is illustrated at point C in Figure AI.7.) Thus the no-capital-accumulation line, or the locus of points at which the marginal return to capital is constant at δ/s, is a concave curve as illustrated in Figure AI.6.

By a similar course of logic the no-labor-growth line, or the locus of points at which the wage rate is constant at $\bar{w}$, can be illustrated with a convex line as shown in Figure AI.8.

The steady-state equilibrium can then be illustrated by combining the no-capital-accumulation and no-labor-growth lines, as shown in Figure AI.9. The arrows show how the factor levels in the economy will evolve in each region of the graph. For example, in region A (above both the no-capital-accumulation and no-labor-growth lines), capital will fall and labor will grow. As the diagram shows, the economy moves toward the point of intersection of the two lines, which represents the steady-state equilibrium of the economy. This equilibrium is denoted by factor levels L° and K°. To repeat, at this point capital and labor supply are such that $r = \delta/s$ and $w = \bar{w}$.

We pause here to show some numerical results of changes in exogenous parameters of

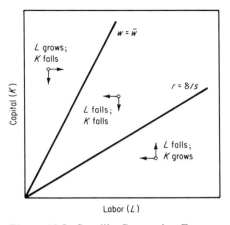

Figure AI.5. Steadily Contracting Economy.

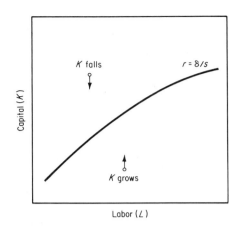

Figure AI.6. No-Capital-Accumulation Line. (Fixed land supply.)

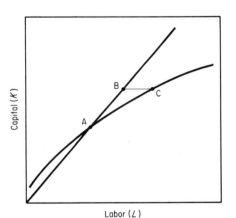

Figure AI.7. Derivation of No-Capital-Accumulation Line with Land Fixed.

NOTE: A movement from A to B increases labor and capital proportionately. With fixed land, this lowers the marginal product of capital. An increase in labor, represented by a movement to point C, is needed to restore the original rate of return to capital.

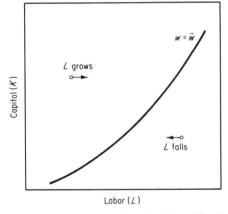

Figure AI.8. No-Labor-Growth Line. (Fixed land supply.)

this growth model. We now illustrate the effect of two kinds of change: an increase in technical efficiency, and an increase in land supplies.

As described earlier, the Smithian system admits two kinds of autonomous change in technical efficiency: incremental progress and the "philosopher's" leaps in knowledge. The two are analytically identical, and the effects of either are illustrated in the following exercises.

The effect of an increase in technical efficiency is illustrated in Figure AI.10. [An increase in technical efficiency is represented by a multiplicative upward shift in the production function (AI.9).] The initial steady-state equilibrium is represented by the no-labor-growth line w_o, and the no-capital-accumulation line r_o. These lead to equilibrium levels of capital and labor K^o and L^o. An increase in technical efficiency shifts the no-capital-accumulation line upward (to r', for example), and the no-labor-growth line outward (to w', for example). We illustrate the logic of these shifts for the no-capital-accumulation line. By definition, it is the set of points for which $r = \delta/s$, and before the change in technology the point K^o, L^o lay on it. An upward technical shift (Hicks neutral) will increase the rate of return to capital at factor levels K^o, L^o. An increase in capital would be necessary to return capital's reward to the equilibrium level, δ/s. Thus the no-capital-capital-accumulation line shifts upward. Similar logic applies to the no-labor-growth line. The new steady-state equilibrium of capital and labor (i.e., the levels at which factor rewards again equal $\bar{w}$ and δ/s so that no further change occurs) will be at K', L', the intersection of the new no-factor-change curves.

We now show some numerical results of changes in technical efficiency, based on some reasonable values for parameters that govern the economy. The numerical assumptions that are held constant across the results we show include

$$K^o = 300$$

$$\delta = 0.05$$

$$s = 0.50$$

$$L^o = 100$$

$$\bar{w} = 0.50$$

Here K^o and L^o are the levels of capital and labor that exist in the initial (pre–technical-change) situation, as shown in Figure AI.10. The equilibrium (no-factor-accumulation) levels of the wage rate and gross return on capital are 0.5 and 0.1, respectively.

We show results for six different forms of the production function, equation (AI.9). This production function is assumed to be of the constant elasticity of substitution form, that is, to have the functional form

$$Y_t = \gamma(aL_t^{-\rho} + bK_t^{-\rho} + cN_t^{-\rho})^{-(1/\rho)} \tag{AI.13}$$

We show results for three levels of the elasticity of substitution; namely, 0.5, 1.0, and 1.5; and for two levels of land's share of output in the initial equilibrium situation; namely, 0.2 and 0.4.

Results are given in Table AI.1. Before discussing the results, we briefly describe the dynamics of the process by which an increase in the level of technology affects this economy. (The discussion refers to a 10% increase in the level of technology for concreteness. This translates into an increase of γ in equation (AI.13) by a factor of 1.1.) In the initial equilibrium, the wage rate is $\bar{w}$ and the rate of return is δ/s. After technology increases 10%, both factor rewards are immediately increased 10%. This causes both factors to grow, to new levels where factor rewards are depressed to the original levels. Land enjoys a double increase in its rent level: first the 10% increase due to technology, then additional increases due to increases in factor supplies of capital and labor. Output will grow both as a result of the increase in technology and the growth in factors. Table AI.1 shows, for each of the six cases, the increases in factor supplies needed to return the factor rewards to the initial equilibrium levels, and the associated increases in output and

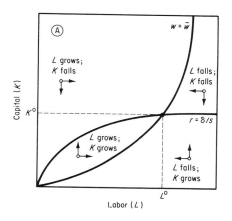

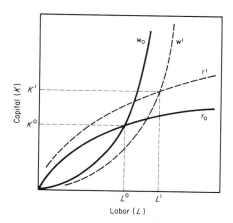

Figure AI.9. Steady-State Equilibrium in Fixed Land Supply Case.
NOTE: L^o, K^o are equilibrium factor levels. The economy tends to move toward equilibrium values from all four regions of diagram.

Figure AI.10. Effect of an Increase in Technical Efficiency on Equilibrium Factor Levels.
NOTE: K^o, L^o are initial equilibrium factor levels; w_o and r_o are initial no-factor-change lines. w' and r' are new no-factor-change lines after increase in technical efficiency; K' and L' are new equilibrium factor levels.

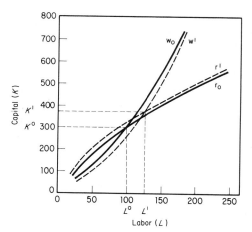

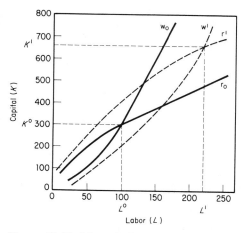

Figure AI.11. Numerical Example of Effect of Technical Change on Equilibrium Factor Levels.
NOTE: $\sigma = 0.5$, $s_N = 0.2$.

Figure AI.12. Numerical Example of Effect of Technical Change on Equilibrium Factor Levels.
NOTE: $\sigma = 1.5$, $s_N = 0.2$.

Table AI.1. Results of Numerical Simulations
10% Hicks-Neutral Increase in Technology

Case		Percent increase in			
		Y	K	L	n
$\sigma = 0.5$	$s_N = 0.2$	31	24	24	55
$\sigma = 0.5$	$s_N = 0.4$	18	12	12	26
$\sigma = 1.0$	$s_N = 0.2$	61	61	61	61
$\sigma = 1.0$	$s_N = 0.4$	27	27	27	27
$\sigma = 1.5$	$s_N = 0.2$	111	121	121	70
$\sigma = 1.5$	$s_N = 0.4$	38	45	45	28

land rent. (In the Case column, σ refers to elasticity of substitution and s_N refers to the initial share of land in output.)

Table AI.1 shows that the new equilibrium levels of factor supplies, output, and return to land will be higher, the higher is the elasticity of substitution. This situation is illustrated in Figures AI.11 and AI.12, which show the before and after steady-state situations for elasticities of substitution 0.5 and 1.5, respectively. (Land's initial share is 0.2 in these cases.) A comparison of Figures AI.11 and AI.12 illustrates clearly that factor supplies must grow more in the high-elasticity case to restore initial factor-reward levels than they must in the low-elasticity case. The reason is straightforward: When the elasticity of substitution is relatively low, relatively modest increases in factor supplies lead to relatively large decreases in factor rewards. At a low elasticity of substitution, not much increase in K and L is needed to push factor rewards down 10%, and thus back to their initial equilibrium levels. These numerical simulations also produce the result that landlords benefit most from technical progress when land as a factor is relatively easy to substitute for.

Figures AI.13 and AI.14 illustrate the cases of land's initial share, s_N, equal to 0.2 and 0.4, holding elasticity of substitution constant at 1.0 (the Cobb–Douglas case). Figure AI.13 is simply intermediate between Figures AI.11 and AI.12. Figure AI.14 illustrates that, for a given technical change, less increase is needed in a factor to reduce its reward to the original level if the factor's original share in output is lower. This simply says that the lower a factor's share in total output, the less elastic is demand for that factor, and thus the less of an increase is needed to reduce the factor's reward to a given level. These results recall Marshall's observation that low price elasticity of demand will result from either low substitution possibilities or low budget share. These exercises in technical progress form a useful background when we extend the model to the increasing returns world.

Another useful conceptual exercise to undertake with this decreasing returns model is to increase the supply of land. What occurs in this case? Marginal returns to labor and capital are increased at first, causing supplies of these factors to grow. Given that factor returns are a function of the labor–land and capital–land ratios only, however (a consequence of the linear homogeneity of function (AI.9) in all three of its arguments), the new steady-state equilibrium will be where labor–land and capital–land ratios have returned to their initial values. Thus, capital and labor will grow just as much as land did, and all factor rewards will be at the initial values, including rent. A consideration of the dynamics of the process is illuminating. An increase in land increases the return to capital and labor initially, causing them to grow. The return to these factors will be above the equilibrium return (and thus the factors will continue to grow) as long as the factors are applied less intensively to land than they were in the initial equilibrium situation. The new equilibrium can only be where the factors capital and labor are applied exactly as intensively to all land as they were in the initial equilibrium, which is the equivalent of a situation where capital and labor have grown precisely as much as land has. The new equilibrium is simply a proportionate expansion of the old equilibrium, with all factor rewards the same as in the initial situation.

We now introduce the third kind of technical progress, namely increasing returns, to the model. (This model is called an "increasing returns" model to distinguish it from the first two models.) Our basic notion of increasing returns is that total factor productivity is a function of the overall size of the economy, due primarily to the specialization of labor. An increase in total factor productivity is defined as an upward multiplicative shift in the general production function (AI.9), which would be translated into an increase in γ in the specific functional form of equation (AI.13). Thus, we can rewrite the general production function (AI.9) as

$$Y_t = p(\text{size}) \, F(K_t, L_t, N_t) \tag{AI.14}$$

where p represents total factor productivity. The precise definition of the size of the economy will be left unspecified for the moment.

The relationship between total factor productivity and the size of the economy is postulated to take the form shown in Figure AI.15. Total factor productivity is constant (at, say, unity) below some minimum critical size of the economy, shown as s_0 in Figure AI.15. Below this size, no opportunities for specialization of labor exist. As the economy moves beyond this size, however, expansion of the market presents opportunities for increased division of labor, so that total factor productivity increases. At some larger size of the economy, say, s_1, opportunities for further division of labor are exhausted, and the economy's total factor productivity remains constant at the higher plateau. This level is indicated by the symbol p^m in Figure AI.15 (m for maximum). If the economy grows beyond this point, the additional resources (capital, labor, and land) will simply duplicate what the existing resources had been doing, leading to higher output but no productivity change. This contrasts with growth of the economy between sizes s_0 and s_1, where the expansion of the market allowed by the additional resources leads to increased opportunities for division of labor, and thus to a physical change in the way resources are used.

We must now define the metric by which to measure the "size" of the economy. We choose the size of the capital stock as this metric, based on the notion that new capital will embody the division of labor opportunities. Other metrics (such as labor or the production function $F(\ )$ itself) are also reasonable, however, and we see no compelling argument for choosing one over the other in an aggregate model such as this. We write the basic production function as

$$Y_t = p(K_t) \, F(L_t, K_t, N_t) \tag{AI.15}$$

$$p(K_t) = 1 \text{ if } K_t \le K^0$$

$$p(K_t) = p^m \text{ if } K_t \ge K^1$$

K^0 and K^1 are constants here that define the range of increasing returns.

There is a well-known difficulty in factor pricing in this sort of model: if factors are rewarded with their marginal products total factor payments will exceed total output. We assume here that land and labor are paid their marginal products, and that capital is paid its

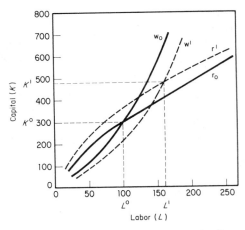

Figure AI.13. Numerical Example of Effect of Technical Change on Equilibrium Factor Levels.
NOTE: $\sigma = 1.0$, $s_N = 0.2$.

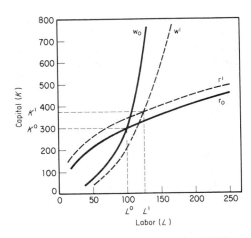

Figure AI.14. Numerical Example of Effect of Technical Change on Equilibrium Factor Levels.
NOTE: $\sigma = 1.0$, $s_N = 0.4$.

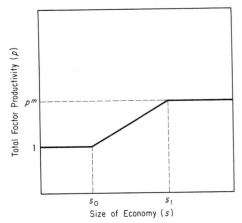

Figure AI.15. Relation Between Size of Economy and Total Factor Productivity.

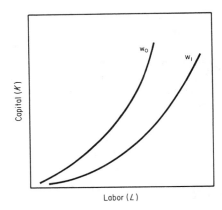

Figure AI.16. No-Labor-Growth Lines for Two Diminishing Returns Economies.
NOTE: w_0 is the no-labor-growth line for an economy in which total factor productivity equals 1. w_1 is no-labor-growth line for an economy in which total factor productivity equals p^m.

"marginal product" ignoring the effect of capital on total factor productivity. Thus the factor reward relations are

$$w_t = p(K_t) \, F_L \, (L_t, \, K_t, \, N_t) \qquad (AI.16)$$

$$r_t = p(K_t) \, F_K \, (L_t, \, K_t, \, N_t) \qquad (AI.17)$$

$$n_t = p(K_t) \, F_N \, (L_t, \, K_t, \, N_t) \qquad (AI.18)$$

There are two reasonable justifications for the assumption on capital factor pricing. The first is that the effect of additional capital on expanding the size of the market is an economywide effect, and that at the level of the individual enterprise this effect is negligible. That is, any increment an individual enterprise makes to its own capital stock has such a small effect on the overall size of the economy that entrepreneurs simply ignore it. A second justification is that owners of capital are assumed to hire labor and rent land. Competition among owners of capital will assure that land and labor are paid their marginal products, and owners of capital will receive the residual output. This residual will indeed be represented by equation (AI.17) due to Euler's Law.[3]

The capital accumulation and labor growth relations are the same in this model as previously, and land is again assumed to be fixed. How does such an economy behave? Let us first consider the no-labor-growth line. We begin by considering two different economies: one in which p is fixed (independent of K) at unity, and one in which it is fixed (independent of K) at p^m. These are simply two cases of our diminishing-returns economies at different levels of technical efficiency, whose characteristics were discussed above. Figure AI.16 shows the no-labor-growth lines associated with each of these two economies, marked w_0 and w_1. At levels of K below K^0, w_0 will also be the no-labor-growth line in our increasing-returns economy because at levels of K below K^0 our increasing returns economy is formally identical to the diminishing-returns economy with total factor productivity fixed at unity. Similarly, at levels of K above K^1, w_1 will be the no-labor-growth line. At levels of K between K^0 and K^1, the no-labor-growth line will fall between w_0 and w_1. This is demonstrated in Figure AI.17. Choose a level of capital between K^0 and K^1, say, K^*. At labor level L^0, and capital level K^*, the wage rate equals $\bar{w}$ if $p = 1$, because this point lies on the line w_0. But in the increasing returns economy, $p > 1$ (since $K^* > K^0$), so the marginal product of labor must be above $\bar{w}$, and thus labor must be growing. Thus, the no-labor-growth line for the increasing returns economy must lie to the right of w_0 at capital levels between K^0 and K^1. A similar argument at the point (K^*, L^1) will show that the no-labor-growth line must lie to the left of w_1 at capital levels between K^0 and K^1. Thus, we can derive the no-labor-growth line for the increasing returns economy as shown in Figure AI.18. Figure AI.19 shows the no-capital-accumulation line for the increasing returns economy. It is derived in precisely the same way as the no-labor-growth line. Our assumption that total factor productivity depends on the level of capital only affects the derivation of the no-factor-change curves in that the capital axis is used to determine the segments of the lines; the symmetric nature of factor pricing assumptions [equations (AI.16) and (AI.17)] means that symmetric techniques to derive the two lines can be employed.

This completes the essence of the increasing-returns economy. Such an economy has a no-capital-accumulation and no-labor-growth curve just as the diminishing-returns economy has, and where they cross will be steady-state equilibrium levels of capital stock and the labor force. Figure AI.20 shows the intersection of the no-factor-change curves derived in Figures AI.18 and AI.19, and thus their determination of equilibrium capital and labor levels. Diminishing returns (represented by the fixed stock of land) is assumed to prevail over increasing returns (due to the specialization of labor) at high levels of capital because the scope for increasing productivity due to increasing the specialization of labor is assumed to be finite.

An interesting possibility of multiple equilibria arises in this model. Consider the no-labor-growth curve derived in Figure AI.21 and the no-capital-accumulation curve derived in Figure AI.22. When the two no-factor-change curves are joined in Figure AI.23,

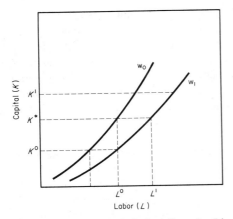

Figure AI.17. The No-Labor-Growth Line for the Increasing Returns Economy Must Lie between w_0 and w_1 if Capital Stock is between K^0 and K^1.

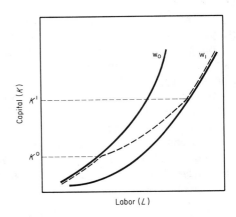

Figure AI.18. Derivation of No-Labor-Growth Line for Increasing Returns Economy.

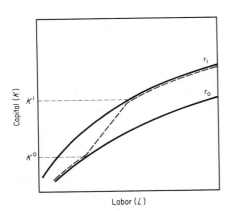

Figure AI.19. Derivation of No-Capital-Ac-cumulation Line for Increasing Returns Economy.

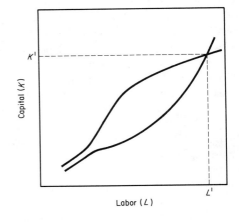

Figure AI.20. Steady-State Equilibrium in In-creasing Returns Case. K' and L' Are Steady-State Levels of Capital and Labor.

they show an economy with three equilibria. Equilibria A and C are stable, while B is unstable. A represents a low-level equilibrium trap of the type often discussed in develop-ment economics. If the economy is nudged upward slightly away from equilibrium A, it will fall back to point A. This is because the economy is not yet large enough to allow economies of scale to increase factor rewards so that factors will continue growing. However, if the economy can be increased to the region northeast of point B, the in-creased productivity, and thus increased factor rewards, will induce further capital and labor growth to point C. (Depending on the precise form of the function $p(K_t)$, economies with more than three equilibria can be constructed.)

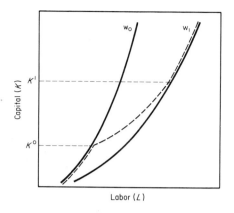

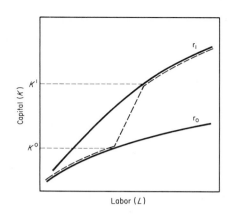

Figure AI.21. Derivation of Another No-Labor-Growth Line for an Increasing Returns Economy.

Figure AI.22. Derivation of Another No-Capital-Growth Line for an Increasing Returns Economy.

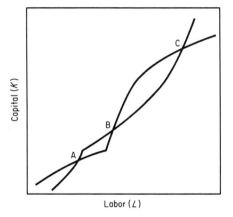

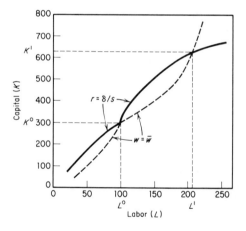

Figure AI.23. Multiple Equilibria Resulting from the Combination of No-Factor-Change Lines from Figures AI.21 and AI.22.

Figure AI.24. Transition from One Steady-State Equilibrium to Another.
NOTE: $\sigma = 0.5$, $s_N = 0.2$, $K^0 = 300$.

This completes all the parts of our one-sector Adam Smith model. We have illustrated the implications of the assumption that factor supplies depend on factor rewards, and shown how the introduction of the three kinds of technical progress affects the results. We now illustrate a Smithian growth sequence, in which an economy moves from a low-level steady-state equilibrium (an "initial rude state"), through a region of increasing returns, to a new steady-state equilibrium where increasing returns have been exhausted (the point of the "full complement of riches").

This growth sequence is illustrated in Figure AI.24. In this economy, capital and labor levels K^0 and L^0 represent a steady-state equilibrium, and K^0 is assumed to be the point at which increasing returns begin to affect the economy. (Letting N^0 represent the constant level of land, we assume the following relations

$$p(K^0) = 1 \tag{AI.19}$$

$$p(K) - p(K^0) > 0 \text{ if } K > K^0 \tag{AI.20}$$

$$F_L(K^0, L^0, N^0) = \bar{w} \tag{AI.21}$$

$$F_K(K^0, L^0, N^0) = \delta/s \tag{AI.22}$$

This is an economy that is sitting in stationary-state equilibrium, but has just come to the verge of being large enough to begin to exploit the potential division of labor and thus economies of scale. (We begin the growth story here for convenience. Before an economy reaches the verge of the increasing-returns region, that is, when it has total capital supply less than K^0, it can enjoy capital and labor growth only if some form of autonomous technical progress occurs, as illustrated in Figure AI.10. We can conceive of such an economy gradually growing as these episodes of technical change occur. We begin our analysis at the point where these episodes have just moved the economy to a capital stock level of K^0.) Figure AI.24 illustrates a case where, if nudged upward away from the initial equilibrium K^0, L^0, the economy will grow through the increasing-returns phase to a new plateau at K^1, L^1.

We illustrate one such numerical growth process, using the parameters to characterize the economy that were used in the decreasing-returns case. We choose the case $\sigma = 0.5$; $s_N = 0.2$. (This is in fact the case illustrated in Figure AI.24.) We pick a linear form for $p(K)$

$$p(K) = 1 \qquad\qquad K < 300 \tag{AI.23}$$

$$p(K) = 1 + 0.6 \frac{(K - 300)}{300} \qquad 300 \leq K \leq 550$$

$$p(K) = 1.5 \qquad\qquad K > 550$$

In words, increasing returns are presumed to occur through a region of almost a doubling of the capital stock from the initial level, and total factor productivity is assumed to reach 50% more than its initial level as a result of the capital stock doubling.

We must also choose a functional form for the relation of labor force growth to the wage rate for this exercise; we choose

$$L_{t+1} = (w_t/\bar{w}) L_t \tag{AI.24}$$

which says that labor force growth is proportional to the ratio between the real wage and the subsistence wage. (The subsistence wage is assumed to be 0.5, as given above.)

Table AI.2 shows the path of the economy from the initial equilibrium to the new equilibrium, assuming a 10% increase in capital and labor to get things started. As shown there and in Figure AI.24, the higher steady-state equilibrium is

$$Y = 260$$
$$L = 212$$
$$K = 637$$
$$n = 90$$
$$w = 0.5$$
$$r = 0.1$$

Table AI.2. Transition from One Steady State to Another

Year	Y	K	L	Rent
0	100	300	100	20
10	119	336	114	26
20	124	345	118	28
30	130	356	122	30
40	137	369	128	33
50	147	387	135	37
60	159	408	143	41
70	175	435	154	48
80	196	469	168	57
90	222	511	184	69
100	246	560	200	81
110	252	594	206	85
120	256	613	209	87
130	258	624	210	89
∞	260	637	212	90

Capital and labor are both approximately twice their initial levels, while output is about 2.5 times its initial level. Rent of land has increased by almost fivefold! (Return to capital and wages are at the no-factor-change levels, of course.) The economy reaches its new equilibrium in about the year 100. Between years 1 and 100, capital and labor have grown about 1% per year, and total factor productivity has grown about 0.5% per year. During the transition to equilibrium, wages and the return to capital are driven back to their original levels, and the rent of land grows dramatically, just as in the technological increase case in the diminishing-returns world.

In the spirit of Adam Smith, we interpret the new equilibrium (K^1, L^1) as the point of "full complement of riches" of the economy.

Figure AI.25 shows the time path of output in this case.

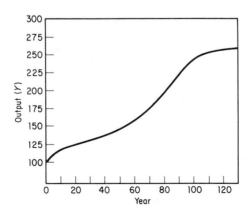

Figure AI.25. Time Path of Output (*Y*) during Transition from One Steady State to Another.

Appendix Part II:
Three Models of Economic Growth Compared

Introduction

In this part of the Appendix we present three formal models of economic growth, in order: a neoclassical model; a model representing the work of Rostow; and a model in the Adam Smith tradition. All three models are embedded in a common economic framework as much as possible, so that the key assumptions that lead to their different results can be clearly differentiated.

The first model is our version of the neoclassical models that emerged in the 1950s as an alternative to the pioneering Harrod–Domar model. As Chapter 15 makes clear, the neoclassical model was explored in many variations down to the early 1970s.

Like the predecessor Harrod–Domar model, the neoclassical growth models had a completely different purpose than Rostow's, which we shortly examine. The Harrod-Domar model aimed to explore the inherent stability or instability (or degree of instability) of growth in advanced industrial societies. The question addressed was whether the mechanisms and institutions of such societies would or would not generate a volume of expenditures (consumption, investment, and government expenditure) sufficient to approximate relatively steady noninflationary full employment of the working force; that is, without generating either chronic unemployment or price increases. The argument, therefore, came to rest on the existence and/or sufficiency of real or believed macroeconomic equilibrating mechanisms; notably, capital–labor ratios or changing proportions of income spent or saved.

For those purposes—in the midst of the most powerful sustained period of expansion in the whole sweep of modern economic history—there was no particular reason in advanced industrial countries to explore the shape of the demographic transition. The population anxieties of the 1930s were forgotten in the midst of the post-1945 baby boom. A wide range of new inventions were coming forward ripe for innovation, while Western Europe and Japan had, in addition, quite large technological backlogs to absorb. The terms of trade shifted in a radically favorable direction for the advanced industrial world after 1951. Some economists worried about the impact of this trend on the developing regions. But it is wholly understandable that the mainstream economists of the advanced industrial world, released from fears of a return to the deep depression of the 1930s, should have constructed highly aggregated models in which population and the flow of technology were treated as exogenous variables and that permitted them to apply their now highly polished neo-Keynesian tools of income analysis to explaining the unexpected stability of a remarkable boom.

The second model reflects Rostow's view of the minimum variables and relationships required to capture the story of economic growth as well as the processes going forward in the contemporary world in societies at different stages of their evolution. His view underlies the structure and judgments that suffuse this book; and its character is made explicit in Chapter Eighteen. Specifically, it has these characteristics:

- The demographic transition is treated as an endogenous aspect of the growth process—a relationship recognized by a good many analysts but difficult to specify especially because the determinants of fertility rates are not well established.

- The whole R & D process is treated as endogenous and, essentially, as a complex investment subsector or group of subsectors.
- As in Adam Smith and Schumpeter the distinction is recognized between incremental innovations and large-scale, discontinuous innovations with significant structural and macroeconomic consequences for the economy. Therefore, a considerable degree of sectoral disaggregation is required to capture the role of innovation because, in the first instance, innovation is inherently a sectoral process.
- The tendency for major innovations to cluster in time is recognized as a characteristic of the history of the past two centuries. Some insights can be formulated into why this tendency has existed (preceding, pp. 457–463); but we have evidently more to learn.
- The capacity of a society's entrepreneurs to absorb efficiently potentially profitable inventions is judged not only a function of prior investment in education and training but also of a society's institutions and the incentives (or deterrents) to innovation the society provides. In short, so far as innovation is concerned, an exogenous flow of technical change that is uniformly absorbed does not suffice as an assumption in the analysis of economic growth. Instead, a society's capacity for technological absorption must be specified.
- Linked to the concept of absorptive capacity and its complex determinants is the need to take into account the existence, for some advanced as well as most developing societies, of backlogs of potentially profitable technologies those societies have not yet put themselves into a position to absorb.
- The disproportionate role of rapidly expanding leading sectors in the growth process is taken into account, including the direct role of the plowback of profits in such sectors in determining the scale of plant and equipment expenditures and its indirect role in determining the overall rate of growth and thus infrastructure and residential housing investment.
- One must introduce the historical role of short- and medium-run relative price trends as between basic commodities and manufactures in inducing corrective changes in the direction of investment yielding, on one definition, and with appropriate lags, the phenomenon of Kondratieff cycles with their consequences for the price level, interest rates, income distribution, and overall as well as sectoral growth rates.
- The wide-ranging consequences of major innovations in one sector for productivity in others, plus the availability or generation of substitutes, has thus far prevented the classical prospect of long-term relative terms of trade deterioration against manufacturing products (relative to basic commodities) from asserting itself as a secular phenomenon. Put another way, there is no historical basis for assuming Adam Smith's land (an input into the production of "rude produce") any more fixed than the inputs into manufactures; although Chapter Twenty-one argues that excessive population and industrial growth and improvident policies could alter this benign outcome in the future (preceding, pp. 499–500).
- The view is accepted that business cycles have been the historic form that economic growth assumed from the late eighteenth century to, say, 1938; and that it is counterproductive to separate growth and fluctuations in modern economies whether the latter are regularly cyclical or not.

As argued in Chapter Eighteen this set of propositions and relationships can be woven into a dynamic disaggregated growth model, from which flows, *inter alia,* the concept of stages of economic growth defined primarily in terms of the degree to which a society has or has not absorbed the available pool of then-existing relevant technologies rather than in terms of real income per capita.

The second model in this section of the Appendix captures in sequence most of these characteristics. Where a proposition listed above is not pursued, that fact is noted and the reason for the omission explained. For example, for purposes of simplicity and to drama-tize less familiar features of the model we decided not to introduce conventional business cycles or inventory cycles.

The largest omission, however, is the complex interacting set of relationships between the economic and noneconomic dimensions of society. Our professions have not yet met Comte's challenge of a fully integrated social science within which economics could be one component. We must, therefore, try to deal with those crucially important rela-tionships via the study of problems specific to time and place where the pattern of interactions can be at least partially perceived. Or we can simply introduce noneconomic factors exogenously as Adam Smith did when he asserted that China's "full complement of riches" was lower than it would have been if it did not neglect and despise foreign commerce.

Despite their many differences, the Rostovian and neoclassical models share two char-acteristics that distinguish them from a Smithian world: they both produce rising real wages as a matter of trend; and they provide roughly constant long-run returns to land and other natural resources. We characterize a model with such properties as a model of "modern" economic growth, in contrast to a Smithian model of a "primitive" world, to which we now turn.

The Smithian, or premodern, world is characterized in the long run by constant real wages and growing land and other natural resource rents, whereas modern economic growth is characterized by steadily growing real wages and a roughly constant return to land and other natural resources. There are three key differences between the kinds of assumptions made in a modern growth model and those made in a Smithian growth model. They concern the availability of land (or natural resources in general); the reg-ularity of technical progress; and the relation of growth of the labor force to the level of real wages.

Since we have built both a modern model and a Smithian model in the same economic framework, we can produce a model representing either world by simply choosing the appropriate set of assumptions. We can also look at hybrid worlds, which contain some assumptions appropriate to each approach. The concluding exercise of this part of the Appendix starts with a Smithian model. We then change the key assumptions to their modern counterparts one at a time. This exercise shows how important each assumption is in determining whether the growth process that results is like modern sustained growth, or like the Smithian world of eventual decreasing returns and the stationary state.

We begin, now, by describing the economic framework in which all of the models will be embedded. We then present the neoclassical model first, since its properties should be familiar to most readers. Our account of the Rostow and Smith models follows.

Economic Framework of the Models

The economy represented by the models is assumed to consist of three production sectors:

- Primary

- Industry
- Services

This is a common disaggregation of economic activity in growth analysis. The economy is assumed to be closed, that is, there are no exports or imports. (Some issues of international relations in economic growth will be explored in the third part of the Appendix.)

We begin by defining the following variables. In each definition, the index i (and j, where it appears) is understood to run from 1 to 3.

$X(i)$ Gross output of the ith sector
$Y(i)$ Net output of the ith sector
$X(i,j)$ Output of the ith sector used as intermediate input to production in the jth sector.
$a(i,j)$ $X(i,j)/X(j)$; that is, amount of sector i's product used as input to sector j, per unit output of sector j.
$L(i)$ Labor employed in the ith sector.
$K(i)$ Capital employed in the ith sector.
$N(i)$ Land employed in the ith sector.
$A(i)$ An index of the state of technology in the ith sector.

Production relations in the model are represented by the following equations. The input–output coefficients $a(i,j)$ are taken as fixed parameters in any given time period, so the relation between gross and intermediate output can be written as

$$X(i,j) = a(i,j)X(j) \qquad\qquad i = 1,3 \qquad\qquad (\text{AII.1})$$

Net output in each sector is simply equal to gross output of that sector less use of that sector's output as intermediate input.

$$Y(i) = X(i) - \sum_{j=1}^{3} X(i,j) \qquad\qquad i = 1,3 \qquad\qquad (\text{AII.2})$$

The level of gross output is determined by the input of factors of production. This is represented as

$$X(i) = f_i[A(i), L(i), K(i), N(i)] \qquad\qquad i = 1,3 \qquad\qquad (\text{AII.3})$$

where f_i is the production function relating inputs of factors of production and the level of technology to output in the ith sector. Together, relations (AII.1) to (AII.3) imply that levels of net output are determined by levels of factor input and technology. (A non-negativity constraint must also be put on the $Y(i)$ to ensure economically meaningful results.)

Net output can be used for either consumption or for capital formation (investment). $C(i)$ is defined as consumption of net output of sector i. We assume that only the output of sector 2 (industry) can be used for capital formation, or investment, so the level of gross investment can be written simply as I, without a sector of origin designation. The sector of destination of investment, that is, the sector whose capital stock is being built up, is of interest because sector-specific capital stocks are arguments in equation (AII.3). The following variables are therefore defined.

$C(i)$ Consumption of net output of sector i, $i = 1,3$.
I Investment in capital stock, composed of output of sector 2.

$I(j)$ Investment in capital stock used in production of sector j's output, $j = 1,3$.

They are related to each other and to other variables in the model through the following equations:

$$C(1) = Y(1) \tag{AII.4}$$

$$C(2) + I = Y(2) \tag{AII.5}$$

$$C(3) = Y(3) \tag{AII.6}$$

$$I = \sum_{j=1}^{3} I(j) \tag{AII.7}$$

The representation of accumulation of factors of production over time and the course of technical progress are generally specific to the individual models. All of the models share a basic representation of capital formation, however. For this dynamic relationship a subscript on variables to represent time is introduced. The basic capital accumulation relation is

$$K_t(i) = (1 - \delta)K_{t-1}(i) + I_{t-1}(i) \qquad i = 1,3 \tag{AII.8}$$

This says that capital stock available for production of good i in year t equals the depreciated value of the capital stock in place in the previous year, plus gross additions to that stock in the previous year. The parameter δ represents the depreciation rate of capital. Equation (AII.8) implies a one-year gestation period for capital.

There are resource constraints for labor and land as well, of course. Overall availability of these resources is defined by the following variables.

L labor force
N available land

The expressions that relate labor use and land use to factor availability are simply

$$\sum_{i=1}^{3} L(i) = L \qquad\qquad i = 1,3 \tag{AII.9}$$

$$\sum_{i=1}^{3} N(i) = N \qquad\qquad i = 1,3 \tag{AII.10}$$

(The equalities in relations (AII.9) and (AII.10) could of course be replaced by in-equalities in underemployment analyses.)

The relation of prices and factor rewards in the model is now discussed. We define the following variables.

$p(i)$ Price of output of the ith sector
$q(i)$ Unit value added of the ith sector
w Wage paid to labor
n Rent of land
r Rental of capital

By omitting the i subscript from the factor returns, we are implicitly assuming that returns to factors equilibrate across production sectors. In long-run analyses of the sort we are doing, this is reasonable.

A simple accounting relation among the variables of the model is

$$p(i)X(i) = q(i)X(i) + \sum_{j=1}^{3} p(j)X(j,i) \qquad i = 1,3 \qquad \text{(AII.11)}$$

This equation can be simply interpreted as the definition of unit value added. Value added, in turn, can be broken down into factor-related components.

$$q(i)X(i) = wL(i) + nN(i) + rK(i) \qquad i = 1, 3 \qquad \text{(AII.12)}$$

This equation can be simply interpreted as the definition of the gross return to capital. A relation that holds true when equation (AII.3), the production function, exhibits constant returns to scale in $L(i)$, $K(i)$, and $N(i)$ is

$$q(i) = g_i(A(i), w, r, n) \qquad i = 1,3 \qquad \text{(AII.13)}$$

This relation is called the unit cost function, and it gives the lowest unit value added that can be attained given the factor prices w, r, and n. It is commonly referred to as the "dual" function to the production function (AII.3). We assume constant returns to scale in all three factors in the models developed in this Appendix.[4]

The following macroeconomic accounting identities relate all of the above variables. In these identities, the variable GNP represents the value of gross national product.

$$\text{GNP} = \sum_{i=1}^{3} p(i)Y(i)$$

$$= \sum_{i=1}^{3} (wL(i) + rK(i) + nN(i)) \qquad \text{(AII.14)}$$

If we now define the variable K (total capital stock) as

$$K = \sum_{i=1}^{3} K(i), \qquad i = 1,3 \qquad \text{(AII.15)}$$

equation (AII.14) can be rewritten more simply as

$$\text{GNP} = \sum_{i=1}^{3} p(i)Y(i)$$

$$= wL + rK + nN \qquad \text{(AII.16)}$$

This is the familiar relation that the value of net output, or GNP, equals the value of factor inputs.

Each of the three models we now present is set into this overall economic framework. The general way that the models are implemented, and their solution framework, is first discussed now. In any short-run period, which we take to be a year, the total supply of factors of production and the level of technology is fixed. Relations (AII.1) to (AII.3), (AII.9), (AII.10), and (AII.15) define a production possibility frontier over net outputs. A set of final demand relations must be added to complete the model. The specific forms of the final demand relations are different among the models, but they are all special cases of the following general equation:

$$F(i) = F_i(p, w, r, n, K, L, N, \Theta) \qquad\qquad i = 1,3 \qquad (AII.17)$$

Here $F(i)$ is final demand for output of the ith sector, p is the vector containing the three $p(i)$, and Θ is some vector of parameters. $F_i(. . .)$ is assumed to be homogeneous of degree zero in its arguments p, w, r, and n; that is, it is assumed not to display "money illusion." This final demand relation is really quite general. Through equation (AII.16), for example, it includes functions in which demand depends on GNP. Final demand relations in which saving, and thus investment, depend on GNP, its functional distribution, and the return to capital, and in which the remainder of income is used to purchase consumption goods, are also subsets of the general relation (AII.17). In each of the three models presented below we explicitly set out the final demand relations assumed for the model.

Equations (AII.1) to (AII.3), (AII.9) to (AII.15) and (AII.17), together with the "supply-equals-demand" relation

$$Y(i) = F(i) \qquad\qquad i = 1,3 \qquad (AII.18)$$

determine the values of all quantities and prices in any given year. (Prices are only determined up to a constant of proportionality.) This general equilibrium system is sufficiently regular that no existence or multiple equilibrium difficulties have been encountered.

So far we have discussed how the levels of output in the models are determined in any given year, when factor supplies and the level of technology are fixed. We must next consider how factor supplies and the level of technology evolve over time. These relations are quite different among the three models, so we proceed now to our discussion of each model.

A. The Neoclassical Model

Assumptions. The first model we consider is the neoclassical model of economic growth. This is the most common framework in which growth analysis is done by contemporary mainstream economists. Indeed, there are so many exercises done in this tradition that one can hardly write of *the* neoclassical model. We therefore incorporate a specific set of assumptions into the framework developed in the preceding subsection to produce a growth model in the neoclassical tradition. We then perform some numerical parametric simulations of the model to illustrate its basic properties. As just discussed, there are two major areas where further assumptions must be added to the basic economic framework developed above in order to produce a specific model. These are the final demand relations and the evolution of factor supplies and technology.

In our neoclassical model, the nominal value of saving is assumed to be a constant proportion of nominal GNP, and the difference between nominal GNP and nominal saving is assumed to be spent for consumption goods. Consumption purchases are assumed to maximize some underlying utility function, subject to prices and total expenditure. Letting σ be the saving rate, and V the value of consumption expenditures, the final demand relations are

$$p(2)I = \sigma GNP \tag{AII.19}$$

$$V = (1 - \sigma)GNP \tag{AII.20}$$

Consumption demand is then determined through solving the problem

$$\max U[C(1), C(2), C(3)] \tag{AII.21}$$

$$\text{subject to } \sum_{i=1}^{3} p(i)C(i) = V$$

where U is some utility function. This demand scheme is consistent with equations (AII.17). Two different examples of utility functions, and thus demand patterns, will be given later in this subsection.

There are three basic assumptions concerning factor growth and technology development that we add to the basic economic framework to produce a neoclassical model.

- The total labor force, L, grows at a constant percentage rate every year.
- The level of technology in each sector, $A(i)$, grows at a constant percentage rate every year.
- Land growth occurs at a rate that leaves the real level of rents unchanged.

Exposition. We now perform some numerical exercises with this neoclassical model. In order to do this, we must construct a hypothetical economy, whose course over time we can track as we apply our growth assumptions to it. We have constructed such an economy, and Table AII.1 shows its structure in the first time period under consideration. The growth of the economy from this point forward will be the subject of our analysis.[5]

Table AII.1 is cast in the familiar input–output tableau format. The first three rows show the total uses of output of each of the three production sectors. The first three columns show intermediate uses of output, that is, uses of output for input into other production sectors. (In the notation used above, the (i,j)th element of the tableau is $X(i,j)$.) The next two columns show uses of the output for consumption and investment, respectively. The sixth column shows total final demand, and is the sum of columns 4 and 5. Finally, the seventh column shows total use of output of a sector, and corresponds, in the ith row, to the variable $X(i)$ defined above.

Table AII.1. Structure of Economy in Period One

From sector	Deliveries to Sector						
	1	2	3	C	I	Y	Total
1	0.0	20.0	0.0	30.0	0.0	30.0	50.0
2	15.0	0.0	12.1	10.0	20.0	30.0	57.1
3	0.0	8.6	0.0	40.0	0.0	40.0	48.6
L	12.7	14.8	22.5				50.0
K	19.6	114.5	115.9				250.0
N	20.0	0.0	0.0				20.0
X	50.0	57.1	48.6				

The columns of Table AII.1 show the inputs that go into production of the output of each of the sectors. Each of the first three columns shows the input of intermediate goods, and then of factors of production. The last row shows the total value of output of each of the sectors, which is by definition equal to the corresponding entry in the last column of Table AII.1.

The prices of output of all sectors, and the wage of labor and the rent of land, are defined to be equal to 1 in the first period. The rental price of capital is defined to be equal to 0.12. Total GNP is thus 100.0. The share of labor is 0.5; of capital, 0.3; and of land, 0.2.

The first scenario examined using the neoclassical version of the model is a balanced-growth expansion of the economy. A balanced-growth path is defined as one in which all gross and net levels of output, and all intermediate uses of output, grow at a constant rate (say, g). It follows from this that GNP grows at rate g. The level of the capital stock and of land use also grow at rate g. All prices of output, and the return to capital and the rent of land, stay constant. Labor input grows at some lower rate, say ℓ. The difference between g and ℓ, say τ, equal to the growth of GNP per worker, is also equal to the growth of the wage rate. Since the growth of the capital stock and the growth of GNP are the same, the capital–output ratio, say k, must be a constant. As stated previously, in the neoclassical model considered here the ratio of saving to GNP, σ, is constant. A final relation implied by balanced growth is

$$g = \sigma/k - \delta \qquad\qquad (AII.22)$$

The following numerical assumptions have been introduced into the model to generate a balanced-growth path.

- The saving rate (σ) is 0.20.
- The annual depreciation rate (δ) is 0.03 (i.e., 3% per year).
- The annual growth of the labor force (ℓ) is 0.02 and of land is 0.05.
- The annual rate of growth of technology in each sector is 0.03. This is the parameter τ, and is defined in the model as the annual percentage change in $A(i)$, equal for all sectors i.
- Technical progress is Harrod neutral; i.e., the production function (AII.3) can be written as

$$X(i) = f_i[A(i)L(i), K(i), N(i)] \qquad\qquad i = 1,3 \quad (AII.23)$$

We choose Cobb–Douglas productions in this model, with coefficients given by the factor shares of Table AII.1.
- Input–output coefficients [i.e., the $a(i,j)$] stay constant at the levels implied in Table AII.1.
- The proportions of each of the three sectors of output in consumption stay constant at the levels implied in Table AII.1 at all levels of income. (These implied consumption proportions are 0.375, 0.125, and 0.50 respectively.) This is equivalent to choosing any utility function (AII.21) which is homothetic (i.e., implies unitary income elasticities) since relative prices do not change.

These assumptions imply that all quantities in the economy (in particular, GNP) will grow at a rate of 5% per year, except labor, which by assumption is growing at 2%. All prices stay constant, except the wage rate, which grows at 3% per year.

This balanced-growth path is illustrated in Figure AII.1. Figure AII.1 is the basic format with which the results of this Appendix will be illustrated. The top portion of the figure shows the growth path of three key quantities of the economy: GNP, labor force, and capital stock. The bottom portion shows the path of three key prices in the economy: the real wage, the return to capital, and the rent of land. The figure covers 100 years of growth, the basic time period over which results will be presented.

The results of a balanced-growth path are strikingly dissimilar to historical experience with economic development in that in balanced growth the composition of net output by sector of the economy remains constant. This result violates the well-established law of Engel that the proportion of foodstuffs in final consumption falls as GNP rises. A modification will therefore be made to the balanced-growth neoclassical model so that the relative proportions of the three sectors in net output will reflect the actual historical experience of development. This modification is a new utility function (AII.21) over consumption of output of the three sectors. In the balanced-growth case the utility function was such that the proportions of the sectors in consumption were constant at any level of total consumption. In the modified version of the neoclassical model, these proportions are assumed to vary with total consumption as shown in Figure AII.2. In order to generate this result, we choose the utility function

$$U = \min \left[\left(\frac{C(1)}{c + dC(3)} \right) C(3), \left(\frac{C(2)}{a + bC(3)} \right) C(3), \quad C(3) \right] \quad \text{(AII.24)}$$

$$C(3) \le \bar{C}(3)$$

$$= \min \left[\left(\frac{C(2)}{eC(3)} \right) C(3), \quad C(3) \right]$$

$$C(3) \ge \bar{C}(3)$$

This is a "moving fixed proportions" utility function in which consumption ratios vary with the level of real income but not, real income held constant, with relative prices.[6] Thus, there are nonunity income elasticities, but no compensated price effects.

If only this change is made to the model, the overall macroeconomic results are not too different from the balanced-growth case; real GNP in year 100 is about 95% of balanced growth GNP. This amounts to a change in the average growth rate of about one-half of one-tenth of a percent. However, the distribution of this GNP among factors of production is dramatically different: the rent of land falls sharply, to about 25% of the balanced growth level. (This level is reached in about year 50, and then levels off.) This implies that the 5% growth rate of land is too high for a constant level of rent on land to result. The reason for this is illustrated in the structure of the economy hypothesized in Table AII.1. Land is only directly used in the production of the output of sector 1, and the Engel curves of Figure AII.2 show that the proportion of sector 1 in the economy falls with economic growth. (Since there is intermediate input in the structure of the economy under consideration, this does not prove that demand for land will grow less quickly than GNP as a whole. In the input–output structure of the economy hypothesized in Table AII.1, however, this is the case.)

The economy just described violates our neoclassical premise that the rent of land remains constant as development occurs, and therefore a slightly different economy was constructed. In it, the only change made from the economy just described was that the supply of land was adjusted until the equilibrium rent turned out to be unity. (This is, of

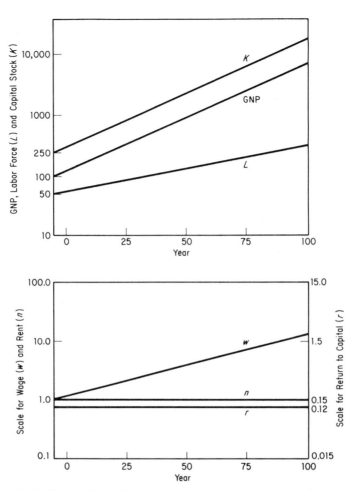

Figure AII.1. Growth Path of the Economy. Balanced growth neoclassical model.

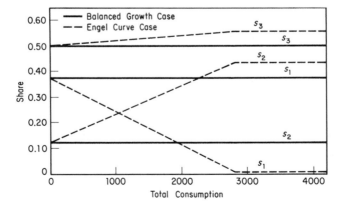

Figure AII.2. Shares of the Three Sectors in Consumption.
NOTE: s_i = share of ith sector in consumption.

Table AII.2. Structure of Economy in Period 100

From sector	Deliveries to Sector						Total
	1	2	3	C	I	Y	
1	0.0	1,944.4	0.0	0.0	0.0	0.0	1,944.4
2	583.3	0.0	1,013.0	2,529.0	1,430.1	3,959.2	5,555.5
3	0.0	833.3	0.0	3,218.8	0.0	3,218.8	4,052.1
L	42.0	130.1	164.3				336.4
K	609.5	9,445.0	7,950.9				18,008.8
N	751.7	0.0	0.0				751.7
X	1,944.4	5,555.5	4,052.1				

course, equivalent to making the supply of land infinitely elastic at a real rent level of unity.) The macroeconomic results of this economy are shown in Figure AII.3. (The results of this model are overlaid on the balanced growth results of Figure AII.1.) They do not differ greatly from those of the economy of Figure AII.1 in their macroeconomic characteristics.

How much of a change in land supply was needed to stabilize the rent of land? Land use in the balanced growth case grows at 5% per year, of course. Land use in the Figure AII.3 case grows more slowly, at a 4% average annual rate. It also grows at a nonconstant rate, averaging 3.6% in the first 50 years, (as sector 1 output is diminishing in importance in the economy), and 4.7% in the second 50 (as sector proportions stabilize).

An interesting (and well-known) point about the feasibility of balanced growth is illustrated in these results. It is not in general possible to have all three of: Engel curves with nonunitary income elasticities, constant rewards to factors of production, and constant growth rates of factors of production.

Table AII.2 shows the structure of the neoclassical economy of Figure AII.3 in the year 100. It should be contrasted with Table AII.1, which shows the structure of the economy in the first year. In the 100-year history of this economy (illustrated in Figure AII.3), GNP and the capital stock grow at a 4.8% average annual rate, and the real wage grows at a 2.6% average annual rate. The return to capital enjoys a slight increase, from 12% to 14%. This is because the sectors that grow relatively rapidly are somewhat more capital intensive than sector 1.[7]

The economy of Figure AII.3 is the baseline for excursions using the neoclassical model. For convenience, it is called the "base neoclassical case." These results are the background against which the results of simulations using different parameter assumptions are contrasted. These simulations are designed to illustrate important properties of the neoclassical model.[8] These properties are well known; the results are presented here to set the stage for results of alternate modeling approaches which are given later.

The first set of simulations that is presented illustrates the effect of a change in labor supply. In the base neoclassical case, the labor force grows at a 2% average annual rate. Figure AII.4 shows the results of a 1% growth rate. (The results from this case are overlaid on the base neoclassical case results from Figure AII.3.) This change leads to a decrease in the GNP growth rate from 4.8% to 3.9%, and a decrease in the capital growth rate from 4.8% to 4.1%. An increase in the capital–output ratio in year 100 from 2.5 to 3.0 results from this. The return on land falls steadily to about a quarter of its base-case value; the return to capital by year 100 falls from 0.14 to 0.13. The wage rate grows at 2.9% per year in this case compared to 2.6% in the base case.

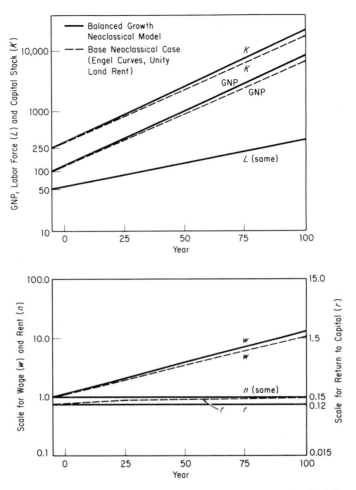

Figure AII.3. Growth Path of the Economy. Base Neoclassical Case.

The only surprising result here is the relatively sharp impact on the return to land relative to the impact on wages and capital returns. Since the specific functional form of the production functions (AII.3) used in this analysis is Cobb–Douglas, one might expect land's share in national output to remain the same. Since land growth is unchanged, and GNP in year 100 is about half in this case what it was in the base case (a simple result of compounding 3.9% instead of 4.8% over 100 years), this would account for a fall of about one-half in land's return. Instead, the share of land in GNP falls from about 10% to about 5%, consistent with the fall of land's return by three-quarters. This occurs because land is only used in production of output of sector 1, and the relative price of that sector falls by about one-half between the base simulation and this simulation. The other factors of production (capital and labor) are used in all sectors, so changes in sectoral terms of trade tend not to have so great an impact on their return. Land is in essence doubly inelastic in supply: it is literally fixed in total supply, and it cannot switch into production of other sectors when its reward falls in sector 1. Since there is no price effect in the utility function (AII.24) that we have chosen, when the relative price of sector 1's output falls, there is no offsetting increase in consumption. A utility function with more substitutability would of course have moderated the fall in land rent.

We also carried out a case in which the growth rate of the labor force is assumed to increase to 3% per year. The results, as one would expect, are roughly symmetric with the previous case, although somewhat less in magnitude. Table AII.3 summarizes the results of the two cases.

The next exercise done with the neoclassical model was a variation in the assumed saving rate. Figure AII.5 shows the results of an assumed decrease in the saving rate from 20% of GNP to 10%. As one would expect, the rate of growth of the capital stock falls dramatically in the early years, averaging less than 2% per year in the first 30 years. By the second half of the century, however, the capital stock is again growing at nearly 5% per year. This is a well-known result of neoclassical growth theory: in the long run, growth rates are independent of saving rates. In the hypothetical economy considered here, the "long run" for a change in saving rates of this magnitude is on the order of half a century. GNP growth follows a similar pattern; growth is below 4% for the first 25

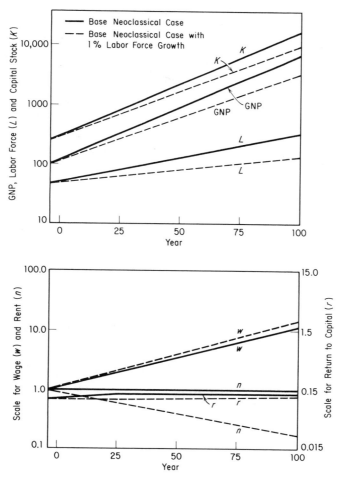

Figure AII.4. Growth Path of the Economy. One Percent Labor Force Growth.

Table AII.3. Results of Labor Force Cases

Growth of labor force	Growth* of				Level of K/GNP
	GNP	K	w	n	
1.0	3.9	4.1	2.9	−1.4	3.0
2.0 (base case)	4.8	4.8	2.6	0.0	2.5
3.0	5.5	5.3	2.2	1.2	2.1

*All growth figures in percent.

years, but recovers to a near 5% level by the end of the period. The return to capital rises dramatically, to 0.30, in the first 50 years, and stays at that level throughout the period. The real return to land is depressed to about a quarter of its base-case level, for the same reasons that depressed it in the lower labor-growth case.

What does it pay this hypothetical economy to lower its saving rate? We can compare

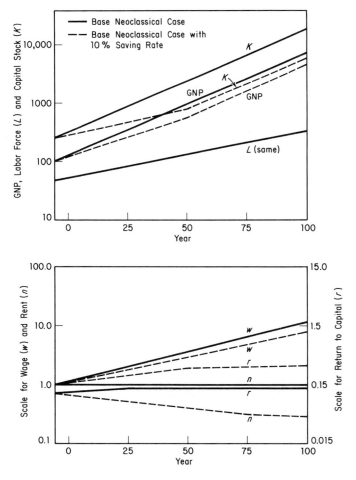

Figure AII.5. Growth Path of the Economy. Ten Percent Saving Rate.

the path of consumption in the base case and in the 10% saving case. Consumption is (naturally) initially higher in the lower saving case, but quickly falls (by year 15) to a lower level than in the base case. Between years 50 and 100 consumption is between 75% and 80% of its base-case levels in the lower saving case, whereas in year 1 it is (by definition) 12.5% higher. These results are of interest when we compare them to another investment option, the R & D option, in the Rostow model.

We also considered the results of an increase in the saving rate, to 30%. Once again, the results are symmetric with the preceding case, although not so large in magnitude. Table AII.4 summarizes the results of the two saving cases.

The final neoclassical case examined is a "Ricardian" case of no growth in the supply of land. Figure AII.6 shows the results. The initial impacts on GNP and capital stock are relatively modest, knocking about half a point off of growth rates in the first 25 years. By the end of the period, the impacts are considerably more severe; GNP and capital growth rates are reduced to about 2.5% per year. Thus the GNP and K lines of Figure AII.6 show the characteristic concave form of decreasing growth rates. Wage rate growth is reduced to less than 1% over the entire period, and the return to capital is lowered to 0.05. Rents of course grow dramatically, and the share of land in GNP in year 100, which is 10% in the base case, grows to 45%. Once again, this occurs despite the Cobb–Douglas structure assumed throughout the economy, and is a result of the fact that land is used in production of the output of only one sector, and that demand for that sector's output is assumed insensitive to relative price changes. Indeed, the relative price of this sector, sector 1, increases by a factor of about 3 over the base case. Results of this Ricardian case are summarized in Table AII.5.

B. The Rostow Model

Special Characteristics. This subsection presents a model incorporating major aspects of Rostow's view of the process of modern economic growth. As already noted, it shares with the neoclassical model certain broad assumptions about the availability of natural resources, the flow of technology, and the behavior of population growth when real wages change; but the process of growth envisaged is quite different. Continuing with our plan described earlier, we embody the Rostow model in the same economic framework as the neoclassical model so that comparisons among the approaches are facilitated. We introduce the differences between the Rostow approach and the neoclassical approach one at a time as we proceed through this subsection, and discuss the implications of each for the interpretation of modern economic growth.

Table AII.4. Results of Saving Rate Cases

Level of saving rate	Growth* of				Level of K/GNP
	GNP	K	w	n	
0.10	4.3	3.5	2.2	−1.2	1.3
0.20 (base case)	4.8	4.8	2.6	0.0	2.5
0.30	5.0	5.5	2.8	0.6	3.6

*All growth figures in percent.

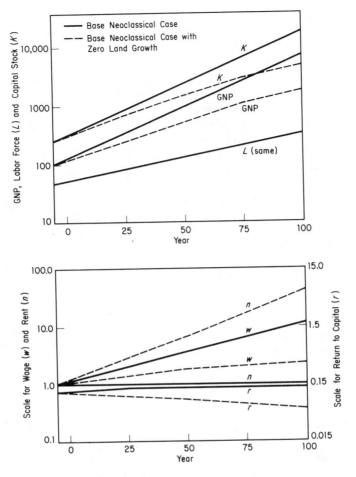

Figure AII.6. Growth Path of the Economy. Zero Land Growth.

The primary elements that characterize the Rostow model are the following:

- Investment spending, or capital formation, depends on the level and rate of change of profits rather than on the level of GNP. This is due to the phenomenon of reinvestment of profits. (This relation will be seen to have important interactions with the leading sector structure of the economy whose description follows.)

Table AII.5. Results of No-Land-Growth Case

Growth of land	Growth* of				Level of K/GNP
	GNP	K	w	n	
4.0 (base case)	4.8	4.8	2.6	0.0	2.5
0.0	3.1	3.3	0.8	4.1	2.7

*All growth figures in percent.

- The generation of technical progress is essentially an economic activity that uses resources rather than an autonomous process acting exogenously on the economy. Devotion of resources to the production of technical advance can be done only at the expense of an opportunity loss of other kinds of output, and is thus an activity analogous to investment. The productivity of resources devoted to technical advance depends upon many factors, including the backlog of available technology in the world that can be adopted, and the capacity of the economy to absorb new technology. This absorptive capacity is in turn a function of several factors, including previous investments in education, general attitudes in the managerial class toward innovation and risk, and the degree to which public policy and institutions encourage innovation and risk.
- The overall industrial sector can be usefully disaggregated into several components. The specific sectors associated with each of the great industrial (or technological) revolutions are included in a separate component. These sectors include the traditional leading sectors of the several industrial revolutions of the past two centuries, as well as the associated supporting sectors, including forward, backward, and lateral linkages. These components are characterized by rates of development that vary greatly over time, and it is the sum of their individual expansion histories that makes up much of the history of the advance of the economy.
- Technological change takes place in both small, incremental steps in virtually all sectors, but also in large, discontinuous steps, with major structural consequences. Our representation of these major technological jumps is associated with the industrial disaggregation described in the preceding point.
- The growth of the labor force depends on the stage of the economy. Beginning at low levels of per capita income, the rate of growth of the labor force decreases as the real wage increases. At some higher level of the real wage the rate of growth of labor stabilizes. This phenomenon is often referred to as the "demographic transition."
- New land (again interpreted here to represent all natural resources) is provided neither autonomously nor smoothly to the economy. Resources must be devoted to the development of new land supplies, and new land is often introduced into the world economy in irregular surges; i.e., in large units rendered profitable by investment with longer periods of gestation than investment yielding incremental changes in the capital stock.

Before turning to the discussion of each of these aspects of the model, we provide an overview of the structure of the Rostow model in the context of the common economic framework that has been developed. The assumptions that must be added to that framework to produce a specific model concern final demand patterns and factor and technology accumulation. We briefly review those assumptions made for the Rostow model and contrast them with the corresponding assumptions made for the neoclassical model. In the Rostow model, we assume that saving and investment are a function of the level and growth rate of profits, rather than GNP as in the neoclassical model. Consumption patterns are assumed to be the same as in the base neoclassical model, incorporating the Engel curves shown in Figure AII.2. Increases in technology and in land supplies are assumed to depend on resources devoted to their growth, as well as on exogenous factors, whereas in our neoclassical framework such increase is totally exogenous. Labor-force growth is constant in our neoclassical framework, whereas its pace varies with the level of

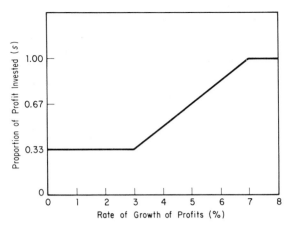

Figure AII.7. Proportion of Profit Invested as a Function of Rate of Growth of Profits.

economic development in the Rostow framework, first (i.e., at low levels of per capita income) falling with income, and then stabilizing. We now turn to a discussion of the individual features of the Rostow model.

Investment as a Function of Profit. Investment, or capital formation, is assumed to be a function of the level and rate of change of profits in the Rostow model rather than a function of the level of overall GNP. The rationale for this is that the plowback of profits by business firms into plant and equipment is the major source of investment funds. The amount of investment is assumed to depend positively on the rate of growth of profits as well as on their level. There are two rationales for this assumption. First, a high rate of growth of profits will be a signal to business of increasing future profit opportunities, and thus an inducement to invest more. In addition, if businesses are accustomed to distributing a relatively fixed level of profits, in periods of high growth higher proportions of profits can be retained. We represent these considerations by making investment proportional to the level of profits, where the proportion depends on the rate of growth of profits. The formal representation of this assumption is a new saving function, replacing relations (AII.19) and (AII.20). The new relations are

$$p(2)I = srK \qquad (AII.25)$$

$$V = GNP - p(2)I \qquad (AII.26)$$

The proportion of profit invested, s, is assumed to be a function of the rate of growth of profits as shown in Figure AII.7. At a rate of growth of 5%, the average rate of profit growth in the economy we have constructed, investment is 67% of profits. Given that profit is 30% of income in this economy, this corresponds to 20% of GNP invested, and is thus analogous to our base-case neoclassical assumption.

Making investment a function of the rate of profit growth as well as of the level of profits has an important implication for the analysis of growth; namely, a boost to the economy, say, through a major technological breakthrough, will in itself raise the rate of saving and investment for some period of time.

The result of the simple substitution of the assumption "saving depends on profits" as shown in Figure AII.7 for the assumption "saving is 20% of GNP" is shown in Figure AII.8. (The state of the economy is assumed to be the same in the first year as in the neoclassical case, and is, therefore, represented again in Table AII.1.) The base neoclassical case is shown in solid lines, and the new (*I* depends on profit) case shown in dashed lines. The primary difference between the cases is the stabilization of the profit rate at the 0.12 level (the year 1 level) in this case, compared to the increase of the profit rate to the 0.14 range in the neoclassical case. The explanation of this difference is straightforward. When investment is a function of profits, an increase in the profit rate will tend to extinguish itself. If the profit rate rises, profits rise; and as profits rise, investment (and investment as a share of GNP) rises. Thus, an increase in the profit rate will lead to an acceleration of the rate of growth of the capital stock, and this pushes the profit rate back down.

Associated with this increase in the capital stock is a modestly higher rate of GNP growth, and as a result a somewhat higher level of rent on land compared with the neoclassical model. These effects are also illustrated in Figure AII.8.

In general, changes in exogenous variables show a similar impact on growth trends in this case as they do in the neoclassical model. Table AII.6 shows the effects of changes in exogenous variables on the growth rates of key variables in both the case where saving is a

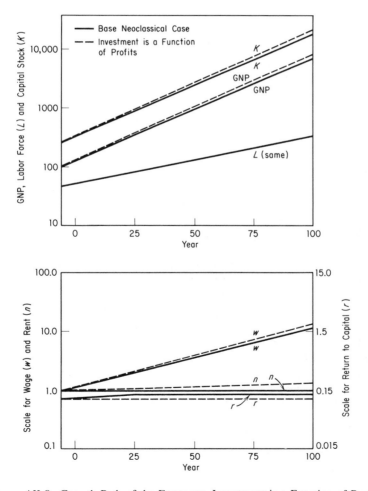

Figure AII.8. Growth Path of the Economy. Investment is a Function of Profits.

Table AII.6. Results of Changes in Exogenous Conditions on Growth

Case	Investment a function of	
	GNP	Profits
Labor grows 1%:		
Change in growth of		
GNP	−0.9	−1.0
K	−0.7	−0.8
w	+0.3	+0.2
n	−1.4	−1.5
Labor grows 3%:		
Change in growth of		
GNP	+0.7	+0.7
K	+0.5	+0.6
w	−0.4	−0.5
n	+1.2	+1.2
Saving falls 50%:		
Change in growth of		
GNP	−0.5	−0.3
K	−1.3	−1.0
w	−0.4	−0.4
n	−1.2	−1.0
Saving increases 50%:		
Change in growth of		
GNP	+0.2	+0.1
K	+0.7	+0.6
w	+0.2	+0.1
n	+0.6	+0.5

function of GNP and where it is a function of profits. (When saving is a function of profit, "saving falls 50%" means the graph in Figure AII.7 shifts downward by 0.33; "saving increases 50%" means the graph shifts upward by 0.33.) There is in fact a modest but discernible pattern to the relation of the changes across the two models. In the saving cases, the profit-related-saving model shows somewhat less change in the variables because (say) a decrease in the saving rate causes an increase in the rate of profit which, by somewhat increasing the ratio of investment to GNP, partially offsets the saving rate fall. In the labor-force growth cases, on the other hand, the profit-related-saving model shows somewhat more change. This is because (say, in the labor growth increase case) the increased GNP growth leads to higher profit growth rates, thus causing a higher proportion of profits to be saved, thus reinforcing the impact on growth.

Resource Cost of Technical Advance. A second new assumption in the Rostow model is that technical advance is not autonomous (exogenous), but is the result of economic activity devoted to its production. In this model, it is assumed that a certain portion of society's resources must be devoted to the production of technical advance if any is to occur. The activities that produce technical progress will be loosely referred to as the "R & D" sector, but they are meant to include the whole spectrum of activities that are necessary both (1) for new technology to be developed, and (2) for it to be efficiently incorporated into the general production processes of the economy. Thus, we distinguish two particular types of activities: first, the production of inventions themselves; and second, the buildup of absorptive capacity and other factors necessary for the incorporation of inventions into the economy as efficient innovations. The second type in reality makes the bulk of its contribution with a time lag, but for simplicity all inputs to the R & D sector in this analysis are assumed to have an instantaneous effect on technical progress. An obvious example of use of inputs to improve absorptive capacity with a lag would be education expenditures.

Another factor is assumed to affect the rate of technical progress in this model. This is the size of the backlog of existing, but not currently utilized, technologies that exist in the world. In any sector, the country that is currently the most advanced in the world will have no backlog to draw on; whereas a relatively backward country will have a relatively large backlog to draw on. [The size of the backlog for any given country, for any given sector *i*, might be defined as the difference between the *A(i)* that exists in the world's most advanced country, and the *A(i)* that exists in the country in question. This formulation makes clear that no one country is necessarily the world leader in all sectors.]

Since resources must be devoted to the production and absorption of new technology, a fourth sector must be added now to the Rostow model, namely, the R & D sector. It is assumed that the annual percentage change in the technological level of the country [i.e., in the *A(i)*] is related to the percentage of the total of the factors of production labor and capital that are employed in the R & D sector. In particular, for the base case, it is assumed that if 5% of the country's labor and capital are employed in the R & D sector, a technical progress rate of 3.0% per year occurs.[9] (This is the exogenous rate of technical progress in the base neoclassical case.) That is, the Rostow model allows the same rate of technical progress as the neoclassical model, but at a price that 5% of *K* and *L* must be employed in producing that progress.

The question now arises as to how the level of technical progress would change if the level of resources devoted to it changed. It is assumed here that the output of technical change [defined as the annual growth of the *A(i)*] is related to the inputs of resources for its production through a constant elasticity equation. This assumption is primarily made for convenience, since elasticities have clear intuitive interpretations. Figure AII.9 shows such a function for elasticities of 0.1 and 0.2. Larger elasticities seem to make technical progress too cheap.

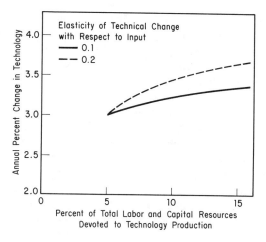

Figure AII.9. Relation of Technical Change to Resource Inputs.

Any technical progress production function of the sort shown in Figure AII.9 depends also on the available backlog of technologies. This backlog is held constant (and thus the function in Figure AII.9 is assumed stable) in the one country analysis to be carried out in this section. In the third part of this Appendix that deals with relations among nations, the backlog issue is considered further.

One can identify other factors that might shift the technology production function, which represents the efficiency with which resources devoted to technology production are utilized. In particular, one aspect of the "absorptive capacity" of a nation might be its ability to translate capital and labor devoted to technical advance into actual effective technical improvements. By "effective technical improvements" we mean literally changes in the $A(i)$, the technical progress variables in the economy's production functions. Factors influencing this ability might include the effectiveness of mechanisms that communicate new scientific knowledge to economic managers, and the factors that affect the willingness of economic managers to adopt new techniques. Anecdotal evidence about the Soviet Union, for example, indicates that incentives for adoption of new techniques are low in that centrally controlled economy, and we might interpret this as a relatively low technology production function of the type shown in Figure AII.9. That is, for any given level of resources used in the R & D sector, a relatively low level of technical improvement in the economy will result due to the poor absorptive capacity. (This is of course a different sense of the term "absorptive capacity" than was used when considering resource inputs into activities such as education that lead to more technical progress in later years.)

An interesting issue of GNP accounting arises when the R & D sector is included in a formal model. Is the production of technical progress considered a final or an intermediate production activity? That is, if resources are transferred out of sectors 1 through 3, and redirected to the R & D sector, does GNP go down? It is assumed here that R & D is a final good, and, thus, that the answer to the immediately preceding question is no. This decision is based on the similarity of using resources in the R & D sector to produce technology to using resources in sector 2 to produce capital stock. Both might be considered investment activities; they use resources that could be producing consumption goods to produce something that will increase productive capacity in the future. (In current U.S. GNP accounting, privately financed R & D is not considered a final good.)

Given this accounting assumption, a hypothetical economy, with a given level of resources in any given year, will have the same GNP in that year regardless of how much of its resources are devoted to R & D. (Just as an economy's GNP in any given year does not change as it transfers resources from consumption to investment.) The implications for future years' GNP are substantial, of course.

These points are illustrated with a new hypothetical economy. It is based on the economy just discussed (Figure AII.8), but an R & D sector is added. It is first assumed that this economy devotes 5% of its capital and labor to the R & D sector every year. Given the technical progress production function of Figure AII.9, the economy will grow just as did the economy of Figure AII.8.[10] That is, given that 5% of capital and labor are devoted to R & D, and given the technical progress production function of Figure AII.9, technology will advance 3.0% per year. The growth of technology and of GNP will be the same as in the preceding case of autonomous technical progress. The composition of GNP will be somewhat different, of course. Between 4% and 5% will be output of the R & D sector, and the remainder will be consumption and investment.

What is the effect of changing the amount of resources devoted to R & D? Figure

AII.10 illustrates the effect on non-R & D GNP of increasing the proportion of resources devoted to R & D to 10% and 15%, given that the elasticity of the technical progress production function is assumed to be 0.2. The visual impact is not large, but the numbers are not negligible. The level of non-R & D GNP is 25% higher in year 100 in the 10% case, and 43% higher in the 15% case. These increments come at a cost of about 4% and 8% in year 1; the non-R & D GNP lines cross around year 25. The decision as to which of these lines society should choose is an intertemporal valuation problem exactly equivalent to the decision of how much society should save.

The analysis just described was repeated assuming an elasticity of 0.1. The impact of increasing production of R & D is of course less; non-R & D GNP is 10% higher in year 100 in the 10% case, and 15% higher in the 15% case. The crossover year is around 40.

The Role of Industrial (or Technological) Revolutions. One striking aspect of the neoclassical model is its generally steady and regular growth patterns. There is none of the historically observed rise of whole new industries, whose internal growth leads and dominates the rest of the economy, in the course of what has come to be called "industrial revolutions." An integral part of Rostow's approach to analyzing economic growth is the prominent role of the periodic birth, rapid expansion, and gradual deceleration of new industrial complexes in shaping and accounting for observed patterns of aggregate economic growth.[11]

We briefly recount here the "stylized facts" of the historical episodes whose basic pattern we will attempt to capture in the Rostow model. [The story as a whole is set out in W. W. Rostow, *The World Economy, History and Prospect* (University of Texas Press, 1978).] We delineate four historical periods, beginning in the late eighteenth century, each with a similar overall economic growth pattern. Each of these periods lasts about two-thirds of a century. The periods begin with the generation from the R & D sector (one might loosely say "discovery") of a new set of products, which we call the "leading sector" complexes of the period. These sectors are characterized in the early years of the period by very rapid growth in output, and as they grow they come to make up a substantial part of the economy. Toward the end of the period, these sectors slow down in growth, and the pace of the economy as a whole slows as well. It is not until the advent of a new leading sector, or one might say until the dawn of a new industrial revolution, that growth picks up again and the economic growth pattern roughly repeats itself. The historical dating of these periods for Great Britain, and their associated leading sectors, are:

Time span[12]	Leading sectors
I. 1780s–1830s	Cotton textiles, Watt's steam engine, iron from coke
II. 1840s–1900s	Railroads,[13] steel
III. 1900s–1960s	Automobile, electricity, chemicals
IV. 1970s–	Microelectronics, biotechnology, new industrial materials, lasers

The last of the revolutions is of course still underway.[14]

The question then arises: how should we model such recurring patterns? One could simply vary the rates of technological progress through each period to mimic the observed swells and ebbs of growth rates, but this seems a bit contrived. Disaggregation is an attractive route, with the products associated with each industrial revolution combined into one sector. One could then distinguish five industrial sectors: a "primitive" sector, including the products generally existing before the first industrial revolution, and four additional sectors, each containing the products associated with one of the four periods in the preceding list. We could then represent each industrial revolution as a period of rapid growth in the technology level of the appropriate sector.

The representation of demand patterns then becomes an issue. What was the demand for computers in 1783? A simple solution would be to impose Engel curves with the property that the output of each new sector was demanded when it became available, but this is artificial. There presumably was a demand for computational power in 1783, since there was employment of clerks, but the price of computers was simply too high. (One might say infinite, but this leads to some arcane issues of just what an infinite price means. It suffices to stipulate that the price of the computational power associated with a modern computer was more than anyone could pay.) Our approach is to impose a stable demand function over time, and to represent the introduction of new sectors into the economy as occurring due to a falling supply price associated with improving levels of technological knowledge.

Each industrial revolution is then represented as a period in which, due to technical progress in the associated sector, the price of its output fell to the point where it was purchased along with the outputs of the other (previous) sectors. The exogenous changes that led to observed cycles of economic growth are changes in technology levels that enter the sectoral production functions, while the parameters of the demand functions are stable over history. Prices are not at all stable, of course, and it is their fall, driven by sector-specific technical progress, that causes the demand levels for the products of the individual sectors to rise through the historical periods. Industrial revolutions are interpreted as supply driven, and changing the timing of the improvement in technology levels would simply change the timing of the advent of the period associated with a new leading sector.

We represent the demand pattern for the output of the five industrial sectors in the following way: Let the variables $Z(k)$ be the output of each of the sectors, and let the unindexed variable Z be a measure of "effective output" of the industrial sector as a whole.[15]

$$Z = \left[\sum_{k=1}^{5} Z(k)^{-\phi} \right]^{-1/\phi} \tag{AII.27}$$

We thus define the measure of "effective output" to be a constant elasticity of substitution aggregation of the outputs of all five sectors. Given any set of prices for the outputs of the individual sectors, say $\pi(k)$, a cost-minimizing purchaser of a bundle of outputs will purchase them in the proportions

$$\frac{Z(k)}{Z(\ell)} = \left[\frac{\pi(k)}{\pi(\ell)} \right]^{-1/(1+\phi)} \tag{AII.28}$$

More generally, given a budget B to be spent on the output of these sectors, the amounts of each that will be purchased will be

$$Z(k) = B \left(\sum_{\ell=1}^{5} [\pi(\ell)]^{\phi/(1+\phi)} \right)^{-1} [\pi(k)]^{-1/(1+\phi)} \tag{AII.29}$$

Our general approach to this problem is then to disaggregate the industrial sector into five subsectors, and to represent effective output of the industrial sector as the C.E.S. aggregation (AII.27). This means literally that we replace the expressions $X(2)$, $Y(2)$, $X(2,j)$, $C(2)$, and I with their C.E.S. aggregations over the five subsectors. The levels of technology of five subsectors can then vary independently.

Before showing some empirical implications of this disaggregation, we discuss the choice of the value of the elasticity of substitution. (The elasticity of substitution, defined to be positive, is related to the parameter ϕ through the relation

$$e = 1/(1 + \phi) \tag{AII.30}$$

where e is the elasticity of substitution.) Clearly a choice of e below unity would be inappropriate, because it implies that the budget share of each subsector would increase as its price increased. But the whole point of this exercise is to represent not yet invented goods as having effectively very high prices, and effectively zero expenditure. Experimenting with various values of e shows that values of 2 or above lead to results that accord well with the verbal depiction of the introduction of new sectors given above.

The specific assumptions that we make about the rates of technical advance of the various sectors over the long run are shown in Figure AII.11. This figure shows the levels of the $\alpha(k)$, or the levels of the states of technology, for each of the industrial subsectors. [We use $\alpha(k)$ to represent the levels of technology of the five industrial subsectors; it is to be distinguished from $A(i)$, the technical levels of the three major economic sectors.] The 130-year time span represented in Figure AII.11 is divided into two 65-year periods, each representing the lifetime of one of the great industrial revolutions. (We limit the diagram to two periods for simplicity.) The primitive sector, called sector 1, shows steady technical advance at a rate somewhat below the rate of advance of the economy as a whole for the entire time period. The other sectors show very low levels of technology until the advent of their period of advance, and then they grow rapidly to catch up with the rest of the economy. The timing of Figure AII.11 shows that the period of rapid advance of each new technology ends 55 years after its introduction, after which that sector grows at the same pace as the other sectors.

Figure AII.12 shows the implications of these assumptions for the growth of the industrial sector as a whole over two industrial revolution periods. It shows that output of the industrial sector grows fastest at the time of introduction of each new technology, and then tapers off as the new technology grows to maturity. The first implication of this approach is that the overall growth of the industrial sector is dependent on the recurring appearances of new industries that grow rapidly as they are diffused throughout the economy, and thus bring up the level of growth of the sector as a whole. If such new industries were to stop recurring (as appears to happen for the last 10 years of each period, the lowest growth years) then industrial and overall economic growth would settle into a lower secular rate. To illustrate this point, Figure AII.12 also shows the path of growth that would occur if the second industrial revolution were not to occur; that is, if the $\alpha(3)$ technology level, associated with the second set of new industries, were to not grow from its initial low level starting in year 65.

The assumption of the Rostow model that saving is a function of profits has an interesting interaction with the industrial disaggregation. The rapidly growing industries generate more profits during the early years of each period than they generate investment needs, and so serve as a source of capital formation for the economy as a whole. Figure AII.13 shows, for one industrial revolution period, the time path of profits and gross investment demand in the leading sector. It illustrates that the leading sector generates profits in excess of its investment needs, and thus provides investment resources to other

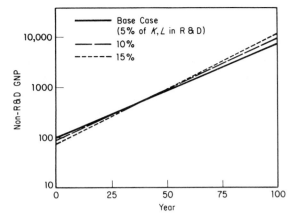

Figure AII.10. Path of Non-R & D GNP.
NOTE: Elasticity of technical change with respect to resource input assumed to be 0.2.

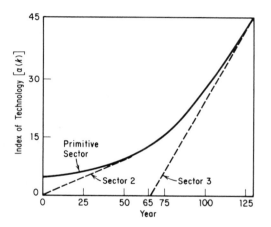

Figure AII.11. Technology Levels over Two "Industrial Revolution" Periods.

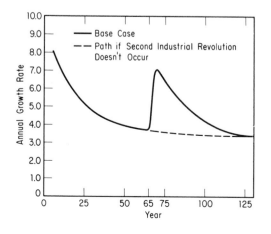

Figure AII.12. Rate of Growth of Industrial Sector over Two "Industrial Revolution" Periods.

sectors of the economy. There is thus a second role of leading sectors in the process of growth beyond being a source of new technology; they are also a source of saving.

The Demographic Transition. As described in the text, there is substantial historical evidence that growth of the labor force is not independent of wage rates, but that it tends to be negatively related to wages at low wage levels, and to become relatively constant at higher levels. One can introduce a modified labor-growth equation into the model, representing the kind of empirical relation shown in Figure 20.1 in the main text. It would say that the growth of the labor force in any period is a function of the real wage prevailing in that period. Figure AII.14 shows such a relation that we incorporate into the model.[16]

The Rostow Model Integrated. We now begin to put together the pieces of the Rostow model thus far independently presented. We construct a scenario in which the saving function of Figure AII.7 is used, in which technical progress occurs in the various industrial sectors as in Figure AII.11, and in which labor force growth behaves as in Figure AII.14. The results, over 130 years (two industrial revolution periods) are shown in Figure AII.15. Results are shown in growth rates of GNP and GNP per capita. Growth rates of GNP show a downward very long run trend, due to the falling growth rate of the labor force as real wages rise. Figure AII.15 also shows a growth-rate cycle due to the bunching of innovations in the early years of each industrial revolution. The magnitude of these changes is less than in Figure AII.12 because we assume that the cycles in technical

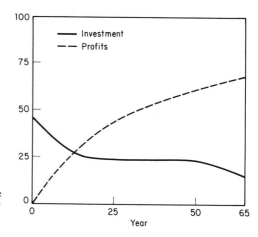

Figure AII.13. Profits and Investment in the Leading Sector over an "Industrial Revolution" Period. (Index Numbers)

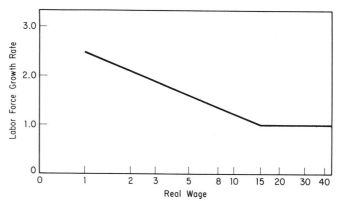

Figure AII.14. Relation of Labor Force Growth to Real Wage.

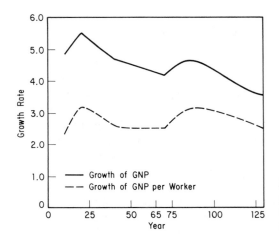

Figure AII.15. Growth of GNP and GNP per Worker through Two Industrial Revolutions. Demographic Transition from Figure AII.14 Included.

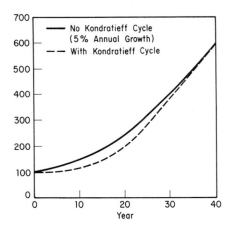

Figure AII.16. Availability of Land over the Kondratieff Cycle. (Index Numbers)

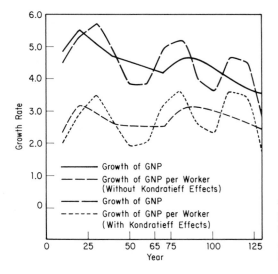

Figure AII.17. Growth of GNP and GNP per Worker through Two Industrial Revolutions. Demographic Transition from Figure AII.14 Included. Kondratieff Cycle from Figure AII.16 Included.

progress occur only in the industrial sector; in the primary and services sectors steady technical progress over time is assumed to occur. GNP per capita shows the technical cycle effects without the trend in labor force growth.

The interaction of the saving function with technical progress occurs in this simulation. The ratio of net investment to GNP rises by 50% in the first 20 years of each industrial revolution, from 12% to 18%, due to the dependence of saving on profit growth rates.

The Kondratieff Cycle Added. Rostow's work has emphasized the lumpiness of the accretions of land (or, more generally, natural resources) to the economy, and the role of capital investment in making them productive. We have already formulated a model of this phenomenon.[17]

We introduce this phenomenon into the model here in a way analogous to our earlier work. We introduce the factor of production land into the economy in an irregular way, as opposed to the smooth introduction in the neoclassical model that stabilizes the rent of land. Figure AII.16 shows the time path of land supply in both the smooth case (shown here as 5% steady growth), and in the irregular case, in which land supply grows more slowly at the beginning of each cycle period, and more rapidly afterwards. The phenomenon we are trying to capture is one of exhaustion of readily accessible natural resources early in the period, leading to increases in land rents (natural resource prices in general), leading to investments in new sources of natural resource supply, leading eventually to rapid increases in supply. The cycle is assumed to repeat every 40 years, as in our earlier work.

Figure AII.17 shows the result of adding this land supply assumption to the results of Figure AII.15. A 40-year growth cycle corresponding to natural resource scarcity is superimposed on the secular labor force growth decline and the technical innovation swings associated with the industrial revolutions.

C. The Adam Smith Model Revisited

The Multisector Framework. In this subsection the basic economic framework described in the beginning of this section is adapted to represent the Adam Smith model. A one-sector version of the Smith model was presented in the first section of this Appendix. The version discussed here follows the general multisector framework used for the neoclassical and Rostow models. The primary purpose of this discussion is to contrast the Smith model and the modern models, in particular, to identify precisely which changes in assumptions lead to the striking changes in results between the two kinds of models.

Both the neoclassical and the Rostow models describe a world whose stylized facts are those of modern economic growth; namely, limited growth of the labor force, more or less regular technical progress, and growing supplies of natural resources, all of which lead to rising real wages. Hence, these models will be referred to as the ''modern'' models. The Smith model, on the other hand, leads to substantially different long-run behavior than the modern models, and it is this difference that we analyze in this subsection.

Method. The method for the subsection will be as follows. The specific assumptions that, when incorporated into the general economic framework given previously, lead to a Smithian world are presented. The general character of the results of the model using these assumptions is described. Then the specific assumptions of the Smith model are changed, one by one, to the assumptions of the modern model, in order to illustrate the importance of each of the assumptions in determining whether the outcome of an economic growth process resembles a modern or a Smithian world.

As we have discussed before, specific assumptions concerning final-demand patterns, factor accumulation, and technical progress must be added to our general economic framework to produce a specific model. The final-demand relations of the Smith model are: saving is assumed to be a function of (specifically, proportional to) the level of profits. This is represented by relations (AII.25) and (AII.26), where the parameter s is taken to be constant. (This is a direct analogue of the assumption made about saving in the one-sector Smith model of the first section.) Consumption follows the Engel curves of Figure AII.2, which are algebraically represented by equation (AII.24). This is the same consumption-pattern assumption that was made in both the previous models. The assumptions concerning factor accumulation and technical progress are described next. These are directly analogous to the assumptions made in the one-sector model of the first section, so their treatment here is brief. A summary comparison of the assumptions in the Rostow and neoclassical models is also given.

Labor. Growth of the labor force in the Smith model is assumed to be determined by the relation of the real wage to some reference level of the real wage. Specifically, when the real wage is above this reference level, the labor force is assumed to grow, and when the real wage is below the reference level, the labor force falls. (Incidentally, Smith hoped that the reference wage would rise with increased education of the labor force [preceding, p. 47].) In the Rostow model, in contrast, the rate of growth of the labor force is assumed to depend on the real wage, but in a different fashion. At low levels of the real wage, the rate of growth of the labor force depends negatively on the real wage, while at some higher level the growth rate becomes constant. In the neoclassical model the rate of growth of the labor force is assumed to be constant, and independent of other economic variables.

The specific functional form we give to the labor force growth relation in the Smith model for numerical simulations is

$$L_{t+1}/L_t = w_t/\bar{w} \qquad\qquad\qquad \text{(AII.31)}$$

where $\bar{w}$ is the reference real wage.

Capital Stock. The physical accumulation rule for the capital stock, given as equation (AII.8), is common to all models. It is

$$K_t(i) = (1 - \delta)K_{t-1}(i) + I_{t-1}(i) \qquad\qquad i = 1,3 \qquad \text{(AII.8)}$$

The issue between models is, then, how is I, or the level of investment, determined? As just discussed, in the Smith model I is assumed to be related to the level of profits in the economy. Specifically, it is assumed that I is proportional to profits. In the neoclassical model, I is assumed to be proportional to GNP. In the Rostow model, I is assumed to be determined by both the level and the rate of growth of profits.

Land. Land is assumed to be fixed in the Smith model. Land is assumed to grow at a rate approximating the growth rate of GNP in the neoclassical model. The growth of land in the Rostow model is more irregular, giving rise to long swings in relative land prices. (The reader should recall here once again that "land" is a general term for natural resources, and so can represent agricultural land, or mineral- or energy-bearing properties, as well as critically important components of the physical environment.)

Technological Progress. There are three forms of technical progress included in the Smith model. [The reader will recall that technical progress is represented as increases in the $A(i)$ variables of the model.] The first is increasing returns to scale. Due to the advantages of specialization, output per unit of input will be higher if the overall size of the market is larger. The second is discrete, irregularly timed, large increases in technical knowledge that represent breakthroughs in technology. These have been characterized in the text as the contributions of "philosophers." Finally, there is "incremental" technical progress, a slow, regular accretion of knowledge that occurs independently of other economic conditions. In the particular model developed in this subsection, the following specific assumptions are made about technical progress:

- Incremental technical progress is ignored. The general sense of its character is that it is small, and including it would add little to the overall exposition. (There is a case later in this subsection in which regular technical progress is added to the Smith model; this result indicates the general impact of incremental progress.)
- One large technical breakthrough, which increases all technology levels [the $A(i)$] by 33%, occurs in the model. How the economy plays itself out after such a change is one subject of the growth analysis.
- The level of returns to scale is related to the size of the total capital stock, which is the index of the size of the market chosen for this exercise. Figure AII.18 shows the assumed relation of capital stock to technology levels $A(i)$. In this formulation there is a maximum level of returns to scale; this represents an assumed exhaustion of the possibilities for increasing specialization.

An important summary observation about the Smith system is that there is no continuing engine of regular progress. Returns from specialization are finite, and the intervention of philosophers is not allowed to recur regularly. Therefore, diminishing returns in one form or another triumphs in the end.

In the neoclassical system, by contrast, technical progress is assumed to be very regular. It is assumed to occur as a constant percentage increase in the $A(i)$ each year, and to occur autonomously regardless of the state of other economic variables. It is the same in nature as the "incremental" technical progress of Smith, but its sense is that it is relatively large, accounting for in fact all the technical progress of the economy.[18] In the modern world, this implies annual increases of the $A(i)$ of between one and about three to four percent. These autonomous increases in the state of technology in neoclassical theory

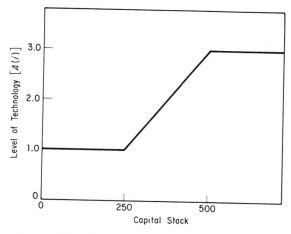

Figure AII.18. Returns to Scale in the Smith Model.

can be identified with the "residual" factor in empirical growth accounting. This residual factor has been discussed in the work of Denison and his associates.

It is important to note that a series of "philosophical" (i.e., scientific) breakthroughs in a Smithian model could lead to precisely the same long-run effects on technology as a neoclassical pattern of steady progress. The neoclassical and Smithian "philosophical" increases in technology share the characteristic that they are completely exogenous to their models, and their average impact on the level of technology is only a function of their size and frequency. A Smithian technical breakthrough of 33% every 15 years would have exactly the same long-run effect on technology as a neoclassical annual technical progress rate of 2%. The pattern of the former would of course be steplike rather than smooth, but in 100 years the difference in technology between these two worlds would be small. Thus, it is the characterization of the breakthroughs of the philosophers of Smith as nonrecurring that differentiates them from the neoclassical representation of technical progress, not their size.

In the Rostow system the level of technical progress depends on two factors, one autonomous to the economic system and one endogenous to it. The autonomous factor is the backlog of the technological advances available to a given economy.[19] This backlog would be literally zero for the most technically advanced country in the world, and relatively high for relatively backward countries. (The existence of multiple sectors implies that no one country might be unambiguously the "most advanced.") The endogenous factor is the level of resources devoted to advancing technology, which we loosely call resources employed in the R & D sector. Both these factors have a positive effect on technical progress. For any given backlog (including zero), the higher the level of resources devoted to R & D, the higher the level of technical advance. By the same token, for any given level of resources devoted to R & D, the higher the available backlog, the faster the rate of technical advance.

Manipulation of the Model. In summary, the assumptions that characterize the Adam Smith model are these:

- Changes in the labor force depend on the real wage. If it is above the reference level, the labor force grows; and if it is below the reference level, the labor force declines.
- Saving is proportional to the level of profits.
- Land is fixed.
- Returns to scale increase with the size of the market, as indexed by the level of the capital stock, up to a maximum level. Discrete technical jumps of the "philosopher" kind are allowed.

Specific numerical values to characterize the Smithian economy must be chosen. To facilitate comparisons, the condition of the economy in year 1 is chosen to replicate the year 1 condition of the earlier models, as shown in Table AII.1. Table AII.7 shows some summary characteristics of the economy in year 1.

For the Smith calculations, the reference real wage is chosen to be 1.00; i.e., if the real wage does not increase from its year 1 level, the labor force will not grow. The fixed level of land is chosen to be 20.0, the year 1 level. As shown in Figure AII.18, increasing returns to scale are assumed to begin at a capital stock level of 250, the year 1 level. Thus, we assume that in year 1 the economy is just large enough to begin to take advantage of the increased specialization that larger size will allow.

We first ask whether a steady state can obtain in this economy. If the model excludes

Table AII.7. Summary Characteristics of the Economy in Year 1

	GNP = 100.0		
Factor	Factor supply	Factor price	Share in GNP
Labor	50.0	1.00	0.50
Capital	250.0	0.12	0.30
Land	20.0	1.00	0.20

both discrete "philosophical" jump shifts in the level of technology and the phenomenon of increasing returns to scale (i.e., if it literally assumes no technical progress), then a steady state will exist if saving is just enough to replace depreciating capital. If the proportion of profits used for capital formation is 0.25, saving will be equal to the depreciation of capital, and a steady state will occur.[20] (Since gross profits are 30, saving will be 7.5. Since the capital stock is 250, and the depreciation rate is 0.03, the demand for replacement capital is also 7.5. Thus, a steady state obtains.) Such a steady state is illustrated in Figure AII.19. It is not very interesting.

Before going on to the full-blown Smithian model, we examine an instructive excursion from the steady-state case. The assumption of absolute technical stagnation is maintained, and the only change from the steady-state case is that the proportion of profits saved is increased to 0.67.[21] The results are shown in Figure AII.20, overlaid on the steady-state results.

The economy begins growing at $1\frac{1}{2}$%–2% rate for the first third of the century. This is due to two factors. The capital stock is growing because of the increase in investment. As the capital stock grows, the wage of labor is driven above the reference level, and the labor force also grows. Growth of the labor force increases the profitability of the capital stock, and this further fuels investment and capital formation. The expansion cannot be continually sustained, however, because the growth of the labor force drives the wage back to unity, and this puts a brake on further labor force growth. The last half of the century approaches the steady state once again, but at higher levels of capital, labor, and GNP. For the century as a whole, GNP grows at an average annual rate of 0.9%, as does labor. Capital grows at 1.7%, which leads to a capital–output ratio in the last year of 4.9, almost double the year 1 value.

The history of factor rewards over the century parallels the growth story told above. The real wage increases slightly, then is pushed back toward unity. The rent on land grows at 1.2% a year, since land supplies are fixed while capital and labor are growing. The return to capital falls from 0.12 to 0.05 due to the increase in capital intensity.

What is the overall message of this scenario? An increase in saving, or reinvestment, in the economy does not lead to sustained growth. Technology and land are fixed by assumption, and growth in labor extinguishes itself by driving the wage rate back to the subsistence level. Owners of land are the only beneficiaries of this activity. This is a theme that is repeated in the Adam Smith model.

The Adam Smith base case is presented now. Two kinds of technical change are included in it; namely, increasing returns to scale and an exogenous, quantum jump in technology that occurs just after the first period. [This jump is assumed to increase all the $A(i)$ parameters by 33%.] The proportion of profit saved is assumed to be 0.25 in the Adam Smith base case. Thus, in the absence of the "philosopher's" contribution in the beginning of the history described here, this Smithian economy would be mired in

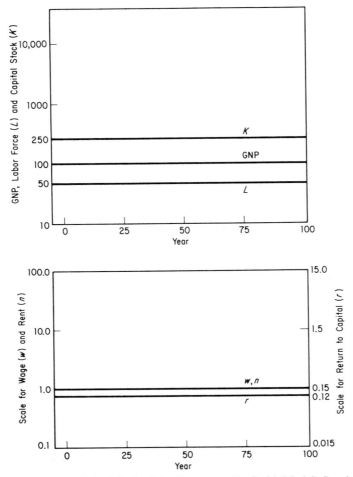

Figure AII.19. Growth Path of the Economy. (A. Smith Model) Steady State.

the steady state. The Smith base case shows, then, how the economy responds to the upward jump in technical proficiency bestowed upon it by the philosopher. Its response reflects the interplay of the key factors in the Smithian world; namely, fixed land; labor that grows when the wage grows beyond the subsistence level; increasing returns for a finite range of the size of the economy; and reinvestment of a fixed portion of profits.

Figure AII.21 shows the results of this base case. (They are superimposed on the results of the steady modern growth case from Figure AII.8; comparisons between the cases will be noted below.) GNP grows sharply in the first 40 years or so, at an average rate of over 6%. This is due to four causes:

1. The jump in technology that occurs just after the first year, an exogenous increase due to the invention of some "philosopher."
2. The increase in capital stock that occurs when profits rise, (and thus investment rises), due to the increase in the level of technology.
3. The increase in the productivity of inputs that occurs when the capital stock increases, which represents a widening of the market that allows increased specialization.

4. The growth in the labor force that occurs when the wage rate rises above the subsistence level, which is also caused by the increase in technology.

The economy slows toward the middle of the period, and approximates a steady state again in the last quarter century. Growth comes to a halt because the philosopher does not regularly repeat his inventive contribution to knowledge; because specialization and thus increasing returns are played out; because labor force growth has driven the real wage back to the subsistence level, so labor grows no more; and because capital has grown to the point at which 25% of profits approximates replacement investment, so capital grows no more.

The time path of factor rewards in Figure AII.21 is informative. The real wage initially blips up, but the induced labor force growth forces it back down. The profit rate rises to about 0.30 as a result of the improved technology and the increase in the labor force, but with investment a function of profits, this drives up the capital stock, which eventually pushes the profit rate back down. Only the rent of land steadily rises, because land is fixed

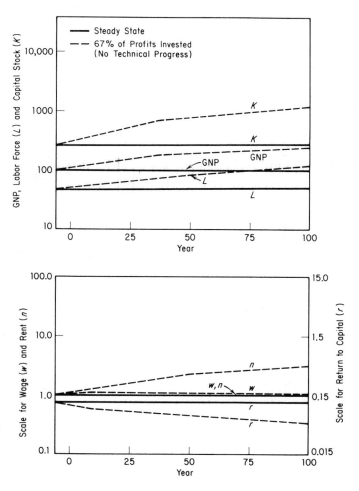

Figure AII.20. Growth Path of the Economy. (A. Smith Model) 67% of Profit Invested.

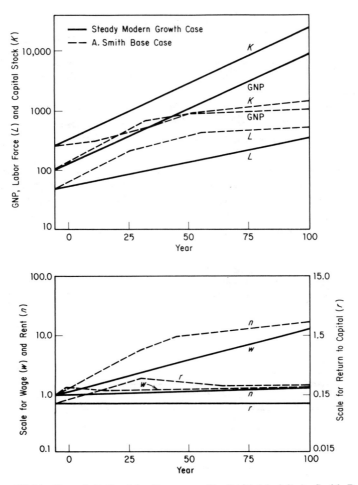

Figure AII.21. Growth Path of the Economy. (A. Smith Model) A. Smith Base Case.

and all other factors are growing. The comparison of the steady-growth case in Figure AII.21 with the Adam Smith case is informative in this regard. Rents in the Adam Smith case approximate wages in the modern growth case, and wages in the Adam Smith case approximate rents in the modern growth case.

Thus the full-blown Adam Smith case, with its philosopher's intervention and its increasing returns, is not especially different in kind from the case of Figure AII.20, which merely had an increase in saving. The wage of the workers never permanently rises above the subsistence level, and the landlords reap the benefit of any increase in either the size or the productivity of the economy.

Since these results are so strikingly different from those of the modern model, the question arises as to exactly which assumptions of the Smith model lead to the stagnation of the income of the workers, and the steady increase in wealth of the landlords, and which changes in them will lead to the reversed results of the modern model. We carry out a series of exercises in which the assumptions of the Smith model are transformed into the assumptions of the modern model, so that the importance of the various assumptions can be identified.

Three differences in assumptions will be explored. They are:

Smith model	*Modern model*
Labor force grows when wage is above unity.	Labor force grows at 2% regardless of wage.
Land is fixed.	Land grows at 4%.
Technical progress is the "philosopher's" contribution, and (finite) increasing returns.	Technology grows regularly (at 3.0% in this case).

Conclusion: Three Necessary Conditions for Sustained Growth

Table AII.8 shows some summary results of differences in assumptions. It indicates that no one change in a single assumption can produce a result in which real wages grow significantly over the century. If the technology or land assumptions are relaxed (that is, replaced with the modern counterpart assumptions), the assumption that the labor force grows whenever the wage is above the subsistence level inexorably drives the wage back down. When a 2% average labor force growth rate is imposed, the wage does rise in the middle part of the century, peaking at a level of 1.75 in the fortieth year. However, at this point technology has hit its maximum, and GNP growth starts falling markedly, to just over the 1% range. In fact, (as Table AII.8 indicates) overall GNP growth over the entire century is only 2.3%, and with 2% labor force growth, this leaves little room for increases in the real wage. Given that land is not growing at all, rents absorb a large part of the increase in GNP, and the real wage falls to near its original level by the end of the period. (A simulation was done in which the labor force was kept constant in a Smith model. In

Table AII.8. Alternate Growth Cases in the A. Smith Framework

Case	100-Year Wage	(Growth)	100-Year Rent	(Growth)	100-Year Profit	GNP Growth
A. Smith base case	1.01	0.0	17.0	3.1	0.17	2.5
2% labor growth	1.17	0.1	12.3	2.8	0.19	2.3
4% land growth	1.25	0.2	5.2	1.8	0.37	6.2
Regular technical progress	1.12	0.1	52.9	4.5	0.27	3.6
4% land growth, regular technical progress	1.41	0.3	26.7	3.7	0.54	7.6
2% labor growth, regular technical progress	2.02	0.7	26.8	3.7	0.25	2.9
2% labor growth, 4% land growth	3.50	1.3	0.1	−2.7	0.21	3.3
All three above measures	7.84	2.1	0.3	−1.2	0.31	4.3
All three above, plus 67% saving of profits (the modern steady growth case)	12.10	2.7	1.3	0.3	0.12	4.9

NOTE: "100-year wage" is wage rate in year 100. (Wage rate in year 1 is 1.00.) "Growth" is average annual growth rate. Rent figures are analogous. (Rent in year 1 is 1.00). Profit rate in year 1 is 0.12.

this case, the real wage grew 1% per year on average over the entire period. The rent of land grew about the same rate, so the two absolutely limited factors in this case equally divided the increase in GNP, which was also about 1%.)

Thus, changing only one assumption in the Smith model cannot get labor an increase in its reward. Next a set of simulations were done in which two assumptions at a time were changed. These are also summarized in Table AII.8. As might be guessed from the results of changing just technology and just land, changing these two together does little for labor. This is again because labor's assumed behavior of increasing itself any time its reward increases ultimately drives its reward back to the no-growth level. The two cases in which labor's growth is limited to 2% and another assumption is relaxed begin to produce some meaningful growth in the real wage. Regular technical progress along with 2% labor growth lets the real wage rise 0.7%, although landlords get the bulk of the GNP increase in this case. Adding 4% land growth to 2% labor growth permits the wage to grow 1.3% per year on average over the century. The great bulk of this wage growth occurs in the early part of the period, however. (Average wage growth is 2.4% for the first 40 years, 0.6% thereafter.) This is of course because technology is increasing during this early part of the century, and has become stagnant after that. There will be only very minor real wage gains after the end of the century in this case.

Thus the conclusion is reached that *any one* of the Smithian assumptions is sufficient drastically to reduce the real wage prospects for labor. Table AII.8 shows that when all three assumptions are relaxed, a familiar modern growth path is established. Indeed, if all three assumptions are changed to their modern counterparts, and the proportion of profits assumed to be saved is increased from 25% to 67%, exactly the modern steady growth picture of Figure AII.8 results. Thus, the Smith model has been transformed into the modern model with these four changes in the structure of assumptions.

If a model is to avoid the gloomy prospect of relatively stagnant real wages, it must incorporate three crucial features of the modern economy: restraint on labor force growth, regular increase in technology, and regular increase in land supplies.[22] A violation of any one of these assumptions leads us to a world more like the stagnating long-run wage picture of the primitive world than the regularly progressing wage result of the modern model.

Appendix Part III:
A Rich-Country–Poor-Country Model
The Framework

This final part of the Appendix presents a model of two countries growing, but at different stages of growth, defined in terms of technological sophistication, capital per worker, and real income per worker. It aims to show how their trade and technology transfer relations affect their absolute and relative rates of economic growth. The two countries included in the model represent a rich and a poor country in the sense of Hume (preceding, pp. 26–31). The model is meant to illustrate his points about how "civilized" relations between the two could make each better off, if they both remain "industrious." It also captures the problem examined during the Second World War by Hilgerdt and Staley (preceding, pp. 374–375).

Much of this discussion is simply an example of the well-known model of trade and comparative advantage. The examples will illustrate some properties of that model that relate to the relative "richness" and "poorness" of the two countries. The technology-transfer aspects of the model embody some of the determinants of technical progress discussed previously in the second subsection of Part II; namely, resources inputs into technology production and absorptive capacity, and the size of the technological backlog for the less technically advanced country.

Our discussion of the model begins with the static relations; that is, with the relations that determine the equilibrium values of the variables of the model in any single year. We choose the familiar two-country, two-good, two-factor framework in which to work. This framework was chosen rather than a more complex one, such as the one in the second subsection, because all the essential results can be shown in it. We first define the variables of interest. The index c will run over the two countries ($c = 1,2$) and the index j will run over the two goods ($j = 1,2$). The time index is suppressed for the moment. The variables are:

$P(j,c)$ Price of good j in country c.
$Q(j,c)$ Production of good j in country c.
$C(j,c)$ Consumption of good j in country c.
$I(j,c)$ Investment of good j in country c. (It is assumed that only good 2 is invested, so $I(1,c) = 0$.
$L(j,c)$ Labor used in production of good j in country c.
$LS(c)$ Total labor supply available in country c.
$K(j,c)$ Capital used in production of good j in country c.
$KS(c)$ Total capital supply available in country c.
$Y(c)$ The nominal value of GNP in country c.

Production relations are the following. We assume Cobb–Douglas production functions, and write them as

$$Q(j,c) = \gamma(j,c)L(j,c)^{\alpha(j,c)}K(j,c)^{[1-\alpha(j,c)]} \quad j = 1,2; c = 1,2 \quad \text{(AIII.1)}$$

where the α's are the factor shares, and the γ's are the levels of technology. We will later characterize the relative poorness of a poor country both in terms of its capital stock per worker and in terms of its γ's. Production in each country c is assumed to be at the point where the value of GNP is maximized; i.e., at the point that solves the problem

$$\max Y(c) = P(1,c)Q(1,c) + P(2,c)Q(2,c) \quad \text{(AIII.2)}$$

$$\text{subject to production functions} \quad \text{(AIII.1)}$$

$$KS(c) = K(1,c) + K(2,c) \quad \text{(AIII.3)}$$

$$LS(c) = L(1,c) + L(2,c) \quad \text{(AIII.4)}$$

This maximization problem represents the result of profit maximization and competitive markets in each country, and parametrically varying (say) $P(1,c)$ while holding $P(2,c)$ constant traces out the production possibility frontier of the country.

Demand relations are the following for each country c, where $V(c)$ is the value of consumption.

$$I(2,c) = \sigma(c)Y(c)/P(2,c) \quad \text{(AIII.5)}$$

$$V(c) = [1 - \sigma(c)]Y(c) \quad \text{(AIII.6)}$$

$$C(1,c) = \beta(c)V(c)/P(1,c) \tag{AIII.7}$$

$$C(2,c) = (1 - \beta(c))V(c)/P(2,c) \tag{AIII.8}$$

This says that investment is a constant proportion of GNP, and that the rest of GNP is consumed so as to maximize a Cobb–Douglas utility function with share parameter $\beta(c)$.

A Static Solution

The solution of the model is then to find prices $P(j,c)$ for which demand equals supply. One can derive both an autarkic and a trade solution to the model. The autarkic solution is really two problems, because it requires that we find the equilibrium set of prices in each country. In each country, the equilibrium prices are simply those for which, given relations (AIII.1) through (AIII.8)

$$Q(1,c) = C(1,c) \tag{AIII.9}$$

$$Q(2,c) = C(2,c) + I(2,c) \tag{AIII.10}$$

(I.e., supply equals demand.) These prices in general are different between the two countries. The trade solution is the set of prices (common between the two countries) for which

$$Q(1,1) + Q(1,2) = C(1,1) + C(1,2) \tag{AIII.11}$$

$$Q(2,1) + Q(2,2) = C(2,1) + C(2,2) + I(2,1) + I(2,2) \tag{AIII.12}$$

These relations, to repeat, are all familiar from the well-known model of comparative advantage in international trade theory. All the usual caveats (no transportation costs, shiftable capital, etc.) are appropriate. We now show some quantitative results of choosing specific numerical values for the parameters that are meant to illustrate a rich-country–poor-country situation.

We assume that the α's, β, and σ are the same in the two countries, and that the ratio $\gamma(1,c)/\gamma(2,c)$ is also the same.[23] Thus the only differences between the countries are in the levels of factor availability and in the overall level of technical progress, represented by the ratio of γ in the rich country to γ in the poor country, where this ratio is the same in both sectors by assumption.

Table AIII.1 shows the specific values assumed for the parameters of the model.

Table AIII.1. Numerical Parameter Values

Parameter	Assumed value
$\alpha(1,c)$*	0.65
$\alpha(2,c)$	0.35
$\gamma(1,1)$	1.10
$\gamma(2,1)$	0.67
$LS(1)$	50
$KS(1)$	250
$LS(2)$	50
$KS(2)$	100
$\sigma(c)$	0.15
$\beta(c)$	0.60

*When 'c' appears as a country indicator, the values are the same for both countries.

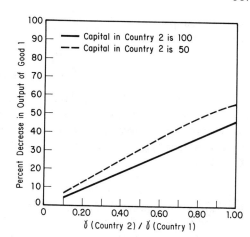

Figure AIII.1. Adjustment Needed by Large Country When Trade Is Opened. (Percentage Decrease in Output of Good 1)

(Country 1 is the rich country.) Given these values, the relative price of good 1 is 1.00 in the rich country and 0.75 in the poor country in the autarky case. (Good 2's price is taken as the numeraire in the model.) We now open the model to trade, and show the results as a function of the size of the poor country, as represented by the ratio of its γ's to the rich country's γ's. (Even if the ratio of the γ's is unity, the poor country is still poorer due to its lower capital stock.)

Figure AIII.1 illustrates the decrease that Country 1 (the rich country) must make in its production of good 1 when trade is opened up. (Since the autarkic price of good 1 is higher in Country 1 than in Country 2, as a result of trade Country 1 will import good 1 and export good 2. Good 2 is interpreted here as the industrial good, both since it is the investment good, and since it has a higher capital share.) Country 1's decrease in production of good 1 is a function of the "poorness" of Country 2, represented by the ratio of its γ's to Country 1's. As can be seen, the less poor (i.e., the larger) Country 2, the larger the adjustment that Country 1 must make. (By the same token, the larger Country 2, the larger Country 1's gains from trade, although they are never more than 5% in real income.)

Figure AIII.1 also shows, however, that if Country 2 is poorer in a different sense, that of having less capital, Country 1's adjustment will be larger rather than smaller. This is because when Country 2 has less capital, its autarkic price for good 1 is lower, and there is more opportunity for trade. (An equal multiplicative change in both γ's, on the other hand, does not change autarkic prices at all.) At any rate, Figure AIII.1 illustrates in this

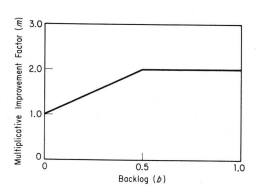

Figure AIII.2. Relation of Multiplicative Technology Generation Improvement Factor to Backlog.

simple example the need for "civilized behavior" on the part of Country 1 in making its adjustments to trade.

Three Dynamic Solutions

We now turn to the dynamic behavior of the model. In order to make the static model discussed so far dynamic, we must specify how factor supplies (labor and capital) and technology grow. Labor and capital growth are straightforward. Labor is simply assumed to grow 1% per year in each country. Capital stock is augmented in each country through the relation

$$KS(c)_{t+1} = (1 - d)KS(c)_t + I(2,c)_t \qquad (AIII.13)$$

where d is the depreciation rate, and time subscripts are added. (The depreciation rate is assumed to be 3% in both countries.) This accumulation relation is similar to those used above. We assume that Country 2's γ's are one half those of Country 1's in these growth simulations.

Our specification of technical progress is in the same framework discussed in the Rostow model. Figure AII.9 there shows the assumed relation between resource inputs to the generation of technical progress (including absorptive capacity), and actual technical progress. We adopt the same kind of relation for Country 1 in this subsection. The assumed numerical parameters of the relation are different for this example; we assume in particular that if 5% of Country 1's capital and labor resources is devoted to the generation of technology, then technical progress (Harrod neutral) of 1% per year will result. We assume an elasticity of 0.4 of output of technology with respect to inputs of resources. So in equation form, if Country 1 devotes a percentage $a(1)$ of its capital and labor resources to the generation of technical progress, it will enjoy (Harrod neutral) technical progress of

$$h(1) = 0.01[a(1)/0.05]^{0.4} \qquad (AIII.14)$$

where $h(1)$ is the rate of Harrod-neutral technical progress in Country 1. Given that technical progress is Harrod neutral (labor augmenting), the γ's will grow according to the relation

$$\gamma(j,c)_{t+1} = [1 + h(c)]^{\alpha(j,c)}\gamma(j,c)_t \qquad (AIII.15)$$

Country 2 is assumed to have somewhat different potential for generating technical progress. It depends on the backlog of technology available for it to absorb from Country 1 as well as on the resources it devotes to the process. We define the backlog available to Country 2 as

$$b = [\gamma(j,1) - \gamma(j,2)]/\gamma(j,1) \qquad (AIII.16)$$

where b is the backlog. It is simply defined as the percentage by which Country 1's technology levels exceed Country 2's. (By the assumptions made above, equation (AIII.16) will give the same result for j of 1 or 2.) Our modeling assumption is that the higher b, the more effective are resources devoted to technology generation in Country 2, due to the larger backlog of existing technology that it has to draw on. In particular, we modify equation (AIII.14) for Country 2 by introducing a multiplicative factor m; *viz.:*

$$h(2) = m0.01[a(2)/0.05]^{0.4} \qquad (AIII.17)$$

where m is defined as a function of b in Figure AIII.2.

Table AIII.2. Three Economic Growth Simulations

Case	Growth rate of	
	Country 1	Country 2
No backlog phenomenon $a(1) = a(2) = 0.05$	2.0	2.0
With backlog $a(1) = a(2) = 0.05$	2.0	2.5
With backlog $a(1) = 0.10; a(2) = 0.05$	2.3	2.65

Let us now consider growth patterns in this model; Table AIII.2 shows the results of three growth simulations. Case 1 is one in which the backlog phenomenon is assumed not to occur, so that each country has a technology-production function as shown in equation (AIII.14). Each country is assumed to devote 5% of its overall resources to technology production. As Table AIII.2 shows, this leads to growth of 2% in both countries, and no closing of the gap between the two. (The simulations shown in Table AIII.2 were done over 100 years.) Case 2 is also one in which each country devotes 5% of its resources to knowledge production, and in which the backlog phenomenon is assumed to occur as in equations (AIII.16), (AIII.17), and Figure AIII.2. Country 1 still grows at 2%, while Country 2's growth has increased to 2.5%. This 0.5% increase will allow it to catch up to Country 1 in 140 years. Case 3 is a case in which the backlog is still operative, and in which Country 1 increases its proportion of resources devoted to technology production to 10%. This leads to an increase of 0.3% in Country 1's growth rate, and 0.15% in Country 2's. The backlog phenomenon has transferred benefits from Country 1's production of knowledge to Country 2.

However, in Case 3 the increased attention in generating and absorbing technology in Country 1 not only increases its rate of growth but also narrows the rate of closure of Country 2 on Country 1's GNP per capita while, nevertheless, raising Country 2's growth rate as well as Country 1's. This provides concrete meaning to Hume's injunction to remain "industrious" as well as "civilized" in the face of the rich-country–poor-country problem; that is, the best a front-runner can do is to assure that it maximizes its technological absorptive capacity (education, quality of innovational entrepreneurship, incentives, etc.) and brings promptly and efficiently into its economy all the relevant output generated by its own R & D sector and the R & D sectors of others.

Thus endeth the lesson for the United States (and other advanced industrial countries) for the 1990s and beyond.

Notes

Chapter 1

1. W. W. Rostow, *The Process of Economic Growth* (New York: W. W. Norton, 1952; Oxford: at the Clarendon Press, 1953, 1961), pp. 10–11.

2. Irma Adelman, *Theories of Economic Growth and Development* (Stanford: Stanford University Press, 1961), especially pp. 8–24.

3. Warren Weaver, "Science and Complexity," *American Scientist*, Vol. 36, 1948.

4. J. K. Whitaker (ed.), *The Early Economic Writings of Alfred Marshall, 1867–1890*, Vol. 1 (London: Macmillan, 1975), p. 98.

5. Norman St. John Stevas (ed.), *The Collected Works of Walter Bagehot*, Vol. II (London: *The Economist*), p. 339; and John Maynard Keynes, *The General Theory of Employment, Interest and Money* (London: Macmillan, 1936), pp. 383–384. I owe the Bagehot reference to C. P. Kindleberger. Informed of my interest in this human phenomenon, Zhang Ruizhuang, with the aid of his wife Shen Xiaoli in Shanghai, was good enough to run down and make the following fresh translation of a passage from Confucius:

> The Master said, "I'd got the aspiration for learning when I was fifteen. At the age of thirty I was established,* then at forty no longer bewildered, knowing Providence at fifty, being discreet and judicious on whatever I heard at sixty, never behaving improperly even following every inclination of my own at seventy."

(Translation from Chapter IV, Part II, *The Practice of Government, An Interpretation and Notes on Lungyu* by Yang Bejun [The Chinese Book Company First Press, 1956, Beijing]). *Comment by Zhang Ruizhuang: "To my understanding, the assertion implies an establishment of both the way of thinking and also one's career." Joseph Schumpeter refers casually to Wilhelm Ostwald as the author of the "theory that thinkers conceive their truly original ideas before they are 30" (*History of Economic Analysis,* [New York: Oxford University Press, 1954], p. 388n). A considerable effort failed to run down Ostwald's original reference, which Schumpeter did not provide. My learned colleague Professor Eisig Silberschlag adds as a kind of inverse example of maturity defined at the age of 30: "St. Jerome mentions a Jewish tradition that forbids the study of 'the beginning and the end of the Book of Ezekiel' before the thirtieth year." These are the "mystical" passages in the Old Testament.

6. The evidence is to be found in Piero Sraffa and M. H. Dobb (eds.), *The Works and Correspondence of David Ricardo,* Vol. X, *Biographical Miscellany* (Cambridge: at the University Press, 1955), pp. 6–7, 34–37.

7. William Robert Scott, *Adam Smith as Student and Professor* (Glasgow: Jackson, Son and Company, 1937), pp. 55–59, 111–114. See, also, John Rae, *Life of Adam Smith* (London: Macmillan, 1895), p. 36, who identifies 1749 as the year when Smith drafted a course of lectures in economics advocating the "doctrine of commercial liberty."

8. Sir Peter Medawar, *Pluto's Republic* (Oxford: Oxford University Press, 1982), p. 263. This passage was also quoted in *The New York Times Book Review,* Sunday, June 22, 1986. Schumpeter's characterization of Quesnay is to be found in *History of Economic Analysis,* p. 224.

Chapter 2

1. The image is from Carl L. Becker, *The Heavenly City of the Eighteenth-Century Philosophers* (New Haven: Yale University Press, 1932), p. 49.

2. *Ibid.,* pp. 6–7.

3. Although written without apology from a strongly held, explicit point of view, Peter Gay's *The Enlightenment: An Interpretation. The Rise of Modern Paganism* (New York: Knopf, 1967) contains a well-balanced bibliographical essay, pp. 423–555.

4. *Ibid.,* p. 3.

5. *Ibid.,* pp. 401–403.

6. Louis E. Loeb, *From Descartes to Hume: Continental Metaphysics and the Development of Modern Philosophy* (Ithaca: Cornell University Press, 1981). See, for example, the discussion of Hume on "substance," pp. 86–109.

7. J. G. A. Pocock, *The Machiavellian Moment* (Princeton: Princeton University Press, 1975). See also his "Cambridge Paradigms and Scotch Philosophers: A Study of the Relations Between the Civic Humanist and the Civil Jurisprudential Interpretation of Eighteenth-Century Social Thought," Chapter 9 in Istvan Hont and Michael Ignatieff (eds.), *Wealth and Virtue: The Shaping of Political Economy in the Scottish Enlightenment* (Cambridge: at the University Press, 1983). This volume resulted from a conference inspired substantially by Pocock's central theme.

8. J. G. A. Pocock, *Machiavellian Moment,* p. 493. The tension between this concept of civic virtue and Christian morality is set out as follows in Pocock's "Cambridge Paradigms and Scotch Philosophers," p. 236:

> . . . it is worthwhile to note the important tensions between civic and Christian morality. The citizen (or 'patriot') did not forgive or love his city's enemies, and Machiavelli had carried this distinction so far that even the public character of virtue began to appear morally ambivalent. In a universe where everything was civic, the practice of religion would be a function of citizenship and there would be no room for an autonomous clergy; the possibility fascinated post-Puritan Erastians and deists, but such worship might be directed towards the gods of a classical city rather than the creator of the *civitas Dei.* . . . The anti-Christian possibilities latent in the civic ideal help account for its role in the Enlightenment, but only begin to account for the profound ambivalences of the Enlightenment's vision of the self.

9. "Cambridge Paradigms and Scotch Philosophers," p. 240.

10. *Ibid.,* p. 251.

11. *Ibid.,* p. 246. Istvan Hont makes an interesting link between Samuel Pufendorf's reconstruction of Grotius's jurisprudence and Adam Smith's theory of commercial society in "The Language of Sociability and Commerce: Samuel Pufendorf and the Theoretical Foundations of the Four Stages Theory," in Anthony Pagden (ed.), *Languages of Political Theory in Early Modern Europe* (Cambridge: at the University Press, 1986).

12. "Cambridge Paradigms and Scotch Philosophers," p. 251.

13. *Heavenly City,* pp. 30–31.

14. At least half of Gay's study is concerned with the complex relationship, as he sees it, between Christianity and the Enlightenment; notably, Chapters 4 to 7, pp. 207–419.

15. *Ibid.,* pp. 322–323.

16. *Ibid.,* pp. 418–419. Gay's Preface notes that he "discovered" Hume as an undergraduate in 1944 at the University of Denver and that his work on the Enlightenment dates from that occasion.

17. "Needs and Justice in the *Wealth of Nations:* An Introductory Essay," Chapter 1 in *Wealth and Virtue,* p. 7. Although he does not deal with Hume, Barry Schwartz captures well the complexity of Adam Smith's view of human beings and the critical tempering role of "love, gratitude, friendship, and esteem" in his *The Battle for Human Nature: Science, Morality, and Modern Life* (New York: W. W. Norton, 1986) especially, pp. 57–66. Schwartz's is a thoroughgoing study of the gross inadequacy of the psychological assumptions underpinning neoclassical economic theory.

18. Albert O. Hirschman has traced out an elaborate generalized version of this proposition from St. Augustine to Adam Smith in *The Passions and the Interests: Political Arguments for Capitalism Before Its Triumph* (Princeton: Princeton University Press, 1977). His basic argument is straightforward enough; namely, that an important strand of thought emerged from medieval origins asserting that men's wicked or disruptive passions could be tamed by their pursuit of rational self-interest. His thesis is summed up by Montesquieu: "And it is fortunate for men to be in a situation which, though their passions may prompt them to be wicked (méchant), they have, nevertheless, an interest in not being so." The portrait drawn by Hirschman of post-Platonic thought is of a bipolar clash in man between passion and reason (p. 43). Reason being judged an inadequate counterweight to passion (pp. 46 and 73n), interest is wedged in, notably rational economic interest, to achieve balance. Thus, capitalism acquires a high-level rationale. What is missing in this interesting exercise is the third strand in, say, Plato, Hume, and Freud: the tempering instinct in man to protect the continuity of the community via reason (in the full Platonic sense), "sympathy" as in Hume and Adam Smith, and Freud's super-ego.

19. David Hume, *Philosophical Works*, T. H. Green and T. H. Grose, eds. (London: Longmans Green, 1912 ed.), Vol. III, p. 238.

20. *David Hume, Writings on Economics*, edited and introduction by Eugene Rotwein (Madison: University of Wisconsin Press, 1955), pp. 52 and xxii–liii, where Rotwein reviews from all sources Hume's economic psychology.

21. *Ibid.*, especially pp. 21–22. Hume's view of the complexity of the human motives entering into economic decisions is echoed by Keynes's dictum: "If human nature felt no temptation to take a chance, no satisfaction (profit apart) in constructing a factory, a railway, a mine or a farm, there might not be much investment merely as a result of cold calculation" (*General Theory*, p. 150). As noted in the text, Karl Marx also regarded the process of investment "accumulation" under capitalism as the result of motives and compulsions transcending the search for profit. Among more modern economists, Joan Robinson is virtually alone in her effort to introduce "animal spirits" into the determination of investment, quoting Keynes's use of the phrase in a context much like that quoted above (*General Theory*, pp. 161–162). References are to be found in Joan Robinson, *Essays in the Theory of Economic Growth* (London: Macmillan, 1962), pp. 36–38 and 87.

22. E. Rotwein (ed.), *David Hume*, pp. 15 and 21–22. For a detailed application of the concept of diminishing relative marginal utility to politics, see W. W. Rostow, *Politics and the Stages of Growth* (Cambridge: at the University Press, 1971), especially pp. 7–25. For the spacious foundations of classical political economy, see, especially, Lionel Robbins, *The Theory of Economic Policy in English Classical Political Economy* (London: Macmillan, 1952), especially Lecture I, "The System of Economic Freedom."

23. I have arbitrarily defined this period of crystallization from Hume's brief autobiographical sketch included in William Bell Robertson's edition of *Hume's Political Discourses* (London and Felling-on-Tyne: Walter Scott Publishing Co., 1906), pp. xiv–xxii. The years indicated begin with Hume's abandonment at the age of 23 of the quiet study of the classics in Edinburgh for a brief interlude in Bristol and then a longer period in France. It closes with the publication of his *Essays Moral and Political* when he was 31. The interval could, of course, be extended a decade to the publication of his *Political Discourses*, which includes the bulk of his economic writing.

24. See, for example, T. S. Ashton, *Economic Fluctuations in England, 1700–1800* (Oxford: at the Clarendon Press, 1959), p. 187. Ashton provides a useful table exhibiting annually the number of men in the armed forces. The peak figure for the War of Spanish Succession (1711) was 186,000; for the War of Austrian Succession (1746), 136,000; the Seven Years' War (1762), 205,000; the American War of Independence (1782), 237,000. The peak level during the French Revolutionary and Napoleonic Wars was approximately 500,000. In the relatively peaceful interval 1713–1738 the British armed forces rarely exceeded 50,000. See Figure 2.1, this volume.

25. Phyllis Deane, *The First Industrial Revolution* (Cambridge: at the University Press, 1967), p. 7. The British agricultural surplus down to the mid-eighteenth century—in fact, to the late 1760s and 1770s—may explain, in part, the limited impact of physiocratic doctrines on Hume and Adam

Smith. Hume did not think well of the physiocrats, but Smith respected the French theorists and their emphasis on the importance of agriculture; but neither Hume nor Smith shared the French view that public policy was distorted at the expense of agriculture. On physiocratic (and earlier) theories of economic growth see, for example, Joseph Spengler "Mercantilist and Physiocratic Growth Theory," Chapter I in Bert Hoselitz (ed.), *Theories of Economic Growth* (Glencoe, Ill: The Free Press, 1960).

26. E. Rotwein (ed.), *David Hume*, p. 112.

27. Phyllis Deane, *First Industrial Revolution*, pp. 11 and 21–22. The rise in grain prices from about mid-century and the shift of Britain toward a net grain import position are well established by reasonably firm statistics. But the path of agricultural output in the course of the eighteenth century, of real wages, and the role of agriculture in the protracted dynamic process yielding the takeoff after 1783 are still the subject of lively debate. That debate is reviewed and some new propositions asserted in R. V. Jackson, "Growth and Deceleration in English Agriculture, 1660–1790," *Economic History Review*, Vol. XXXVII, No. 3, August 1985. Briefly, Jackson argues that the increase in agricultural output down to the 1740s was greater than Deane and Cole allowed, [Phyllis Deane and W. A. Cole, *British Economic Growth, 1688–1959* (2d ed.) (Cambridge: at the University Press, 1967)] and the subsequent expansion slower. He argues that the abundance in the first half of the century yielded the population surge in the second half at just the time agricultural output decelerated. His conclusion, which is quite consistent with grain price and foreign trade data, is clearly relevant to the shift from complacency about the food-population balance in Hume and Smith to the acute but transient anxiety of pre-1813 Malthus and Ricardo (p. 351):

> Finally, the major swings in agricultural output and the population during 1660–1790 are a fitting backdrop to the gloomy scenarios devised by Malthus and the classical economists. Here is a sequence in which rising living standards are followed by accelerated population growth and, in the long run, by a lack of supply response in agriculture. The classical doctrines of long-run subsistence wages and of diminishing returns in agriculture imposed by a fixity of resources may have turned out to be a poor guide to the future, but they are not out of place when seen in the context of the secular deceleration in English agricultural output growth, and of the half of a century of slowly falling levels of per capita output and consumption of agricultural products identified in this paper.

28. Measured from the beginning of the century to the average for 1748–1752, industrial production rose at an annual rate of .8%; the volume of exports at 1.3%; re-exports, .9%; imports, .6%. See W. W. Rostow, *How It All Began* (New York: McGraw-Hill, 1975), p. 43.

29. Deane and Cole, *op. cit.*, p. 80. See also N. F. R. Crafts, "English Economic Growth in the Eighteenth Century: A Reexamination of Deane and Cole's Estimates," *The Economic History Review*, Vol. XXIX, No. 2, (May 1976), pp. 226–235. Crafts' calculations would question the acceleration of growth after 1740 exhibited in the Deane and Cole figures. While sharing Crafts' scepticism of any eighteenth century GNP or GNP per capita calculations, I am inclined to believe an acceleration of sorts occurred on the basis of quite firm disaggregated foreign trade and industrial production series.

30. T. S. Ashton, *The Industrial Revolution, 1760–1830* (London: Oxford University Press, 1948), p. 57.

31. *Ibid.*, p. 58. See also W. W. Rostow, *How It All Began*, pp. 157–160. The number of English patents granted in the 1750s was 92, not much above the figure for the 1720s (89). The figure jumped to 205 in the 1760s and was 647 for the 1790s.

32. E. Rotwein (ed.), *David Hume*, p. 77.

33. *Ibid.*, pp. 10–11.

34. *Ibid.*, pp. 11–13, In this passage Hume goes on to argue that dynamic manufacturing and agricultural sectors generate a surplus that can be diverted by taxation to support military operations "without depriving anyone of the necessaries of life. The more labour, therefore, is employed beyond mere necessaries, the more powerful is any state. . . ." (p. 11).

35. *Ibid.*, p. 13.

36. See W. W. Rostow, *How It All Began,* p. 181.

37. E. Rotwein (ed.), *David Hume,* pp. 52–53.

38. *Ibid.,* pp. 49 and 53.

39. Piero Sraffa and M. H. Dobb capture vividly what Hume had in mind in the following passage contrasting David Ricardo's and Nathan Rothschild's views of money making and the joys of business (*Works and Correspondence of David Ricardo,* Vol. X, *Biographical Miscellany,* [Cambridge: at the University Press, 1955], p. 90):

> There could hardly have been two more contrasting types. It was in the *making* of money that Rothschild found the main enjoyment of life: not so much prizing the money for what it could buy, as "finding intense delight in the scrambling and fighting, the plotting and tricking, by means of which it was acquired." A story is told that, when someone said to him: "I hope that your children are not too fond of money and business, to the exclusion of more important things. I am sure you would not wish that," Rothschild replied: "I am sure I should wish that. I wish them to give mind, and soul, and heart, and body, and everything to business; that is the way to be happy." Ricardo, however, brought up his sons to be country gentlemen, and as for himself had no craving for the bustle of the City and viewed financial success as a means of retirement into the country, to the quiet pursuit of his "favourite science." When he first went to Gatcomb he wrote Malthus: "I believe that in this sweet place I shall not sigh after the Stock Exchange and its enjoyments."

40. E. Rotwein (ed.), *David Hume,* p. 48.

41. *Ibid.,* p. 17.

42. *Ibid.,* p. 146.

43. *Ibid.,* pp. 128–129. In commenting on this reference A. W. Coats notes correctly that "it made little or no impact."

44. *Ibid.,* p. 28.

45. *Ibid.*

46. *Ibid.,* p. 24.

47. Deane and Cole, *British Economic Growth,* p. 263.

48. E. Rotwein (ed.), *David Hume,* pp. 17–18. The context of this dictum is typical of both Hume and eighteenth-century Europe. It occurs in a passage commenting on the failure of societies in the tropics, unchallenged by the necessity to struggle for food, shelter, and clothing, to generate the sophisticated advances of societies set in more temperate climates.

49. David Hume, *The History of England* (London: Strahan [printer], 1802). References to prices are to be found in Vol. II, pp. 36–37, 224–225, 501; Vol. III, pp. 402–403; Vol. IV, pp. 326–329, 446–449; Vol. VI, pp. 23–25, 46–51, 180–183; Vol. VII, pp. 328–331.

50. *Ibid.,* Vol. III, pp. 402–403 (1508); Vol. IV., p. 327 (1549).

51. E. Rotwein (ed.), *David Hume,* pp. 5–6.

52. For an account of the application of this phrase to Hume's analysis of economic development and the subsequent controversy, see Istvan Hont, "The 'rich country–poor country' debate in Scottish classical political economy," in Hont and Ignatieff (eds.), *Wealth and Virtue,* p. 274, n7. Hont's essay is clearly the most sophisticated and illuminating analysis of the debate now available. In the vocabulary of my stages of economic growth Hume was dealing here with economies at early and later stages of the preconditions for takeoff. The fullest discussion of that distinction is my *Politics and the Stages of Growth,* Chapter 3, especially pp. 54–63. There can be—indeed must be—considerable economic progress in the preconditions stage. Such progress is distinguished from the surge in takeoff by the absorption of major new technologies in one or more sectors generating not only high momentum in that sector but strong spreading effects in sectors linked to the leading sector (or sectors), including accelerated urbanization, the criterion Kuznets used to date the onset of modern economic growth. For the economic dynamics of the preconditions see also *The Stages of Economic Growth,* Chapter 3.

53. This summary owes a good deal to Istvan Hont's account, Hont and Ignatieff, *Wealth and Virtue,* pp. 271–294.

54. Smout's essay is Chapter 2 in Hont and Ignatieff (eds.), *Wealth and Virtue*, pp. 45–72. A valuable bibliography on Scottish economic history is provided on p. 45n. and in other footnotes.

55. *Ibid.*, pp. 71–72.

56. Hont traces this strand in Western thought back to Aristotle and Machiavelli (*ibid.*, p. 272).

57. E. Rotwein (ed.), *David Hume*, pp. 80–82.

58. *Ibid.*, pp. 34–35.

59. *Ibid.*, pp. 190–205, for textual reflections of the debate, including letters to Lord Kames, the recipient of communications from both Hume and Tucker. Also, Istvan Hont, Hont and Ignatieff, *Wealth and Virtue*, pp. 275–276.

60. E. Rotwein (ed.), *David Hume*, p. 200.

61. *Ibid.*, pp. 14–15. See also p. 80 and Rotwein's discussion, p. cviii n.

62. *Ibid.*, p. 38. See also his formulation of the same point in a letter to Oswald, pp. 197–198.

63. *Ibid.*, p. 198.

64. *Ibid.*, pp. 108–109.

65. For a discussion of the tripartite view of man on which Plato built his *Politics* and Freud his *Civilization and Its Discontents*, see W. W. Rostow, *Politics and the Stages of Growth*, pp. 7–12 and related notes on pp. 361–364.

66. *David Hume*, pp. c and cii.

67. *Ibid.*, p. lii.

68. The following passage extracted from *ibid.*, pp. 22–29, captures Hume's view of the larger human and social benefits of a prosperous mercantile and manufacturing economic system.

> Another advantage of industry and of refinements in the mechanical arts, is, that they commonly produce some refinements in the liberal arts; nor can one be carried to perfection, without being accompanied, in some degree, with the other.
>
> The more these refined arts advance, the more sociable men become: nor is it possible, that, when enriched with science, and possessed of a fund of conversation, they should be contented to remain in solitude, or live with their fellow-citizens in that distant manner, which is peculiar to ignorant and barbarous nations. They flock into cities; love to receive and communicate knowledge; to show their wit or their breeding; their taste in conversation or living, in clothes or furniture. Curiosity allures the wise; vanity the foolish; and pleasure both. Particular clubs and societies are everywhere formed: Both sexes meet in an easy sociable manner: and the tempers of men, as well as their behaviour, refined apace. So that, beside the improvements which they receive from knowledge and the liberal arts, it is impossible but they must feel an encrease of humanity, from the very habit of conversing together, and contribute to each other's pleasure and entertainment. Thus *industry, knowledge,* and *humanity,* are linked together by an indissoluble chain, and are found, from experience as well as reason, to be peculiar to the more polished, and, what are commonly denominated, the more luxurious ages. . . .
>
> But industry, knowledge, and humanity are not advantageous in private life alone: They diffuse their beneficial influence on the *public,* and render the government as great and flourishing as they make individuals happy and prosperous. The encrease and consumption of all the commodities, which serve to the ornament and pleasure of life, are advantageous to society; because, at the same time that they multiply those innocent gratifications to individuals, they are a kind of *storehouse* of labour, which, in the exigencies of state, may be turned to public service. In a nation, where there is no demand for such superfluities, men sink into indolence, lose all enjoyment of life, and are useless to the public, which cannot maintain or support its fleets and armies, from the industry of such slothful members. . . .
>
> Laws, order, police, discipline; these can never be carried to any degree of perfection, before human reason has refined itself by exercise, and by an application to the more vulgar arts, at least, of commerce and manufacture. . . .
>
> Knowledge in the arts of government naturally begets mildness and moderation, by instructing men in the advantages of humane maxims above rigour and severity, which drive subjects into rebellion, and make the return to submission impracticable, by cutting off all hopes of pardon. When the tempers of men are softened as well as their knowledge improved, this humanity appears still more conspicuous, and is the chief characteristic which distinguishes a civilized age

from times of barbarity and ignorance. Factions are then less inveterate, revolutions less tragical, authority less severe, and seditions less frequent. Even foreign wars abate of their cruelty; and after the field of battle, where honour and interest steel men against compassion as well as fear, the combatants divest themselves of the brute, and resume the man. . . .

The liberties of England, so far from decaying since the improvements in the arts, have never flourished so much as during that period. And though corruption may seem to encrease of late years; this is chiefly to be ascribed to our established liberty, when our princes have found the impossibility of governing without parliaments, or of terrifying parliaments by the phantom of prerogative. Not to mention, that this corruption or venality prevails much more among the electors than the elected; and therefore cannot justly be ascribed to any refinements in luxury.

If we consider the matter in a proper light, we shall find, that a progress in the arts is rather favourable to liberty, and has a natural tendency to preserve, if not produce a free government.

The lower house is the support of our popular government; and all the world acknowledges, that it owed its chief influence and consideration to the encrease of commerce, which threw such a balance of property into the hands of the commons.

69. Adam Smith's account is included in William Bell Robertson's introduction to Hume's *Political Discourses,* pp. xxii–xxvii; Hume's "My Own Life," pp. xiv–xxii. Following is a memorable anecdote, as reported by Smith, that captures a good deal of Hume's character and style:

He said . . . when he was reading a few days before, Lucian's *Dialogues of the Dead,* among all the excuses which are alleged to Charon for not entering readily into his boat, he could not find one that fitted him: he had no house to finish, he had no daughter to provide for, he had no enemies upon whom he wished to revenge himself. "I could not well imagine," said he, "what excuse I could make to Charon in order to obtain a little delay. I have done everything of consequence which I ever meant to do; and I could at no time expect to leave my relations and friends in a better situation than that in which I am now like to leave them; I therefore have all reason to die contented." He then diverted himself with inventing several jocular excuses, which he supposed he might make to Charon, and with imagining the very surly answers which it might suit the character of Charon to return to them. "Upon further consideration," said he, "I thought I might say to him, good Charon, I have been correcting my works for a new edition; allow me a little time that I may see how the public receives the alterations." But Charon would answer, "When you have seen the effect of these, you will be for making other alterations. There will be no end of such excuses; so, honest friend, please step into the boat." But I might still urge, "Have a little patience, good Charon; I have been endeavouring to open the eyes of the public. If I live a few years longer, I may have the satisfaction of seeing the downfall of some of the prevailing systems of superstition." But Charon would then lose all temper and decency, "You loitering rogue; that will not happen these many hundred years. Do you fancy I will grant you a lease for so long a term? Get into the boat this instant, you lazy, loitering rogue."

70. For a successful effort to evoke Hume as a human being, see Ernest Campbell Mossner, *The Forgotten Hume, le bon David* (New York: Columbia University Press, 1943).

71. The quoted phrases are, respectively, from J. Hill Burton, a biographer of Hume (1846), and R. B. Haldane, a biographer of Adam Smith (1887), both quoted in W. B. Robertson (ed.) "Introduction," *Political Discourses,* pp. viii and xi. The ironic streak in Hume and his systematic use of irony as a literary and expositional device is fully developed in John Vladimir Price, *The Ironic Hume* (Austin: University of Texas Press, 1965). Price's study transcends the narrow central theme and yields a persuasive general portrait of Hume as a personality.

72. *The Works and Life of Walter Bagehot,* edited by Mrs. Russell Barrington (London: Longmans Green, 1915), Vol. VII, p. 8. T. W. Hutchison, *On Revolutions and Progress in Economic Knowledge* (Cambridge: at the University Press, 1978), p. 5, makes the same point:

Smith remained a philosopher from the beginning to the end of his life. He would never have regarded his work as a whole, as primarily economic or political economics, he thought of economics as only one chapter, and not the most important chapter, in a broad study of society and human progress which involved psychology and ethics (in social and individual terms), law, politics and the development of the arts and sciences.

73. Adam Smith, *Essays* (London: Alex Murray, 1869), pp. 48–49.

74. *Ibid.*, p. 161.

75. *Ibid.*, p. 163. Samuel Hollander's reference and discussion in his *The Economics of Adam Smith* (Toronto: University of Toronto Press, 1973), pp. 248–249. See, also, Jacob Viner, "The Invisible Hand and Economic Man," Chapter III in *The Role of Providence in the Social Order* (Philadelphia: American Philosophical Society, 1972), especially pp. 81–84. A further reference is in *The Essential Adam Smith* (edited and with introductory readings by Robert L. Heilbroner with the assistance of Laurence J. Malone; New York: W. W. Norton, 1986), pp. 60–61. Albert O. Hirschman in his *The Passion and Interests* also considers a number of examples of the workings of the "invisible hand," a doctrine that evidently relates to his own theory of unbalanced growth. William Baumol correctly pointed out to me that Smith's use of the "invisible hand" in *The Theory of Moral Sentiments* is generally broader than in *The Wealth of Nations;* but it should be noted that the latter also contains a phrase suggesting the "invisible hand" is more widely at work (p. 423): ". . . he is in this, as in many other cases, led by an invisible hand to promote an end which was no part of his intention." Like many writers of his time Adam Smith tended to avoid direct reference to the Deity with phrases such as "the Author of nature," "the great Director of nature," etc. (*The Theory of Moral Sentiments*, Dugald Steward, ed. [London: G. Bell, 1911]), pp. 109–110. Following is the context of Smith's use of the "invisible hand" in *Theory of Moral Sentiments* (pp. 264–265).

> The rich only select from the heap what is most precious and agreeable. They consume little more than the poor; and in spite of their natural selfishness and rapacity, though they mean only their own conviency, though the sole end which they propose from the labours of all the thousands whom they employ be the gratification of their own vain and insatiable desires, they divide with the poor the produce of all their improvements. They are led by an invisible hand to make nearly the same distribution of the necessaries of life which would have been made had the earth been divided into equal portions among all its inhabitants; and thus, without intending it, without knowing it, advance the interest of the society, and afford means to the multiplication of the species. When providence divided the earth among a few lordly masters, it neither forgot nor abandoned those who seemed to have been left out in the partition. These last, too, enjoy their share of all that it produces. In what constitutes the real happiness of human life, they are in no respect inferior to those who would seem so much above them. In ease of body and peace of mind, all the different ranks of life are nearly upon a level, and the beggar, who suns himself by the side of the highway, possesses that security which kings are fighting for.

76. The *bon mot* is often attributed to Walter Bagehot; but he quotes it from an unnamed source in his essay "Adam Smith and Our Modern Economy," in Norman Stevas (ed.), *Walter Bagehot*, Vol. II, p. 177.

77. See, for example, Irma Adelman, *Theories of Economic Growth and Development*, Chapter 3, "Adam Smith," pp. 25–42; John R. Hicks, *Capital and Growth* (Oxford: at the Clarendon Press, 1965), pp. 36–42; D. P. O'Brien, *The Classical Economists* (Oxford: at the Clarendon Press, 1975), pp. 206–214; W. A. Eltis, "Adam Smith's Theory of Economic Growth," in Andrew S. Skinner and Thomas Wilson (eds.), *Essays on Adam Smith* (Oxford: at the Clarendon Press, 1975), pp. 426–454; Paul A. Samuelson, "A Modern Theorist's Vindication of Adam Smith," *American Economic Review*, Vol. 67, No. 1 (February 1977). A more generalized model embracing the whole line from Smith to Marx is Samuelson's "The Canonical Classical Model of Political Economy," *The Journal of Economic Literature*, Vol. XVI, No. 4 (December 1978), in which once more he observes: "So to speak, within every classical economist there is to be discerned a modern economist trying to be born." Samuel Hollander has written a long commentary on "Professor Samuelson's Canonical Political Economics," mainly confirmatory in *Journal of Economic Literature*, Vol. XVIII (June 1980), pp. 559–574. While emphasizing quite correctly the difficulty of representing accurately Smith's theory of growth in symbolic terms, due to ambiguities in his definition of key terms, Joseph Spengler also tries his hand in "Adam Smith's Theory of Economic Growth" Parts I and II, *The Southern Economic Journal*, Vol. XXV, No. 1, and Vol. XXVI, No. 2 (April

and July 1959). Bringing to bear then contemporary development theory as his matrix, Spengler's analysis of Smith's growth theory is more elaborate than those that simply apply the terms of Harrod-Domar or neo-classical growth models. To the best of my knowledge, the first effort to render Adam Smith's theory of economic growth into mathematical terms was an elegant three-page paper of Alain Enthoven's, "A Brief Summary of *The Wealth of Nations*," written for my graduate seminar in economic history at M.I.T. in the autumn of 1954.

78. Smith's failure to reflect the arrival of the industrial revolution is the subject of some analysis and speculation. See, for example, R. Koebner, "Adam Smith and the Industrial Revolution" *Economic History Review*, Vol. XI, No. 3 (April 1959), pp. 381–391; Charles P. Kindleberger, "The Historical Background: Adam Smith and the Industrial Revolution," Chapter 1 in A. S. Skinner and Thomas Wilson (eds.), *The Market and the State* (Oxford: at the Clarendon Press, 1976), pp. 1–41, including comments by Asa Briggs and R. M. Hartwell; and Hiram Caton, "The Pre-Industrial Economics of Adam Smith," *Journal of Economic History*, Vol. 45, No. 4 (December 1985), pp. 833–853. For a somewhat more positive view of Adam Smith's awareness of the process of technological change, see Hollander, *Economics of Adam Smith*, pp. 208–217. Hollander makes clear, however, the distinction between the kind of incremental technological change that Smith mainly had in mind as a result of the widening of the market and the "radical changes in process" associated with Schumpeterian innovation (p. 212). He associates Smith's failure to capture fully the emerging innovational drama to his apparent lack of knowledge of what was going on in the cotton industry.

79. Adam Smith, *The Wealth of Nations*, edited by Edwin Cannan, with an introduction by Max Lerner (New York: Random House, 1937), p. 7. Smith's full exposition of his central proposition about the division of labor is presented, like the theme of a symphony, in a sustained opening passage: pp. 3–10.

80. Smith (*ibid.*, p. 76) asserts that the price of grain was "dearer in the last century" than at "present," and he adduces a table (pp. 256–258) concerning the wheat price in the Windsor Market for the period 1595–1764, drawn from Charles Smith, *Tracts on Corn Trade, 1766*, pp. 97–102. Like other such data, it exhibits a trough in the 1740s. It is a bit surprising that Smith did not update the table beyond 1764 and thereby missed the rising price trend after mid-century. See, for example, T. S. Ashton, *Economic Fluctuations*, p. 181.

81. *Wealth of Nations*, Chapter VIII ("Of the Wages of Labour"), pp. 64–68, contains most of Smith's discussion of the determinants of the size of population.

82. *Ibid.*, pp. 69 and 81.

83. Edwin Cannan (ed.), *Lectures by Adam Smith* (Oxford: at the Clarendon Press, 1896), pp. 255–258.

84. *Wealth of Nations*, pp. 81–82.

85. *Ibid.*, p. 737. For Smith's full exposition of his views on education, see "Of the Expence of the Institutions for the Education of Youth," *ibid.*, pp. 716–740. For an analytic dissection of Smith's views on education see Margaret G. O'Donnell, *The Educational Thought of the Classical Political Economists* (Lanham, Maryland: University Press of America, 1985).

86. *Wealth of Nations*, pp. 734–735.

> In the progress of the division of labour, the employment of the far greater part of those who live by labour, that is, of the great body of the people, comes to be confined to a few very simple operations, frequently to one or two. But the understandings of the greater part of men are necessarily formed by their ordinary employments. The man whose whole life is spent in performing a few simple operations, of which the effects too are, perhaps, always the same, or very nearly the same, has no occasion to exert his understanding, or to exercise his invention in finding out expedients for removing difficulties which never occur. He naturally loses, therefore, the habit of such exertion, and generally becomes as stupid and ignorant as it is possible for a human creature to become. The torpor of his mind renders him, not only incapable of relishing or bearing a part in any rational conversation, but of conceiving any generous, noble, or tender sentiment, and consequently of forming any just judgment concerning many even of the ordinary duties of

private life. Of the great and extensive interests of his country he is altogether incapable of judging; and unless very particular pains have been taken to render him otherwise, he is equally incapable of defending his country in war. The uniformity of his stationary life naturally corrupts the courage of his mind, and makes him regard with abhorrence the irregular, uncertain, and adventurous life of a soldier. It corrupts even the activity of his body, and renders him incapable of exerting his strength with vigour and perseverance, in any other employment than that to which he has been bred. His dexterity at his own particular trade seems, in this manner, to be acquired at the expence of his intellectual, social, and martial virtues. But in every improved and civilized society this is the state into which the labouring poor, that is, the great body of the people, must necessarily fall, unless government takes some pains to prevent it.

87. *Ibid.*, pp. 314–315. For a lucid analysis of the complexities of Smith's distinction of productive from unproductive labor, see, especially, W. A. Eltis, *Adam Smith's Theory*, pp. 433–435. One of the best contemporary expositions of the distinction between productive and non-productive labor is in Turgot's *Reflections on the Formation and the Distribution of Riches* (New York: Augustus Kelley, Reprints of Economic Classics, 1963), pp. 1–17. Turgot distinguished his views from physiocratic dogma, but was, essentially, of that school.

88. *Wealth of Nations*, p. 315.

89. *Ibid.*, For an elaboration of one interpretation of this aspect of Smith's theory of growth, see J. R. Hicks, *Capital and Growth*, pp. 36–42. Smith, however, clearly included manufactures as well as agriculture in his plowback model, which Hicks does not recognize (*Wealth of Nations*, pp. 316–319). For Ricardo and the corn growth model, see Chapter 2, notes 117, 118.

90. *Wealth of Nations*, p. 326.

91. The characterization is from Alexander Gray, *The Development of Economic Doctrine: An Introductory Survey* (London: Longmans Green, 1931), p. 123.

92. *Wealth of Nations*, p. 242.

93. *Ibid.*, pp. 321–323.

94. *Ibid.*, pp. 330–332.

95. *Ibid.*, p. 326.

96. *Ibid.*, p. 341.

97. *Ibid.*, pp. 245–246.

98. *Lectures*, pp. 167–168; *The Wealth of Nations*, pp. 9–10. The meaning of "philosophers" in Smith's usage, "whose trade it is not to do anything, but to observe every thing," is suggested by his listing of their several areas of specialization (*Lectures*, p. 168); "mechanical, moral, political, chemical." In *The Wealth of Nations* Smith also allows for creative inventions by specialized "makers of machines" (p. 10). In this passage Smith's terse evocation of the creative process is just and memorable: "combining together the powers of the most distant and dissimilar objects."

99. The evidence on this period is presented and discussed in W. W. Rostow, *The World Economy: History and Prospect* (Austin: University of Texas Press, 1978), pp. 311–313. See, also, Julian Hoppit, "Financial Crises in Eighteenth Century England," *Economic History Review*, Vol. XXXIX, No. 1, (February 1986), pp. 39–58. Hoppit argues persuasively that "loss of confidence arising from the onset or progress of war" was the primary cause of eighteenth-century financial crises even after 1770 when the private credit structure had attained reasonably mature status (pp. 56–57).

100. *Ibid.*, p. 769, note 10.

101. *Wealth of Nations*, p. 406. There is another passage (*ibid.*, p. 291) in which Smith exhibits sensitivity to the importance of time lags in the credit process. He warns that bankers should lend only for moderate periods of time and, especially, eschew the financing of fixed capital:

> Still less could a bank afford to advance him any considerable part of his fixed capital; of the capital which the undertaker of an iron forge, for example, employs in erecting his forge and smelting-house, his work-houses and warehouses, the dwelling-houses of his workmen, &c.; of the capital which the undertaker of a mine employs in sinking his shafts, in erecting engines for

drawing out the water, in making roads and waggon-ways, &c.; of the capital which the person who undertakes to improve land employs in clearing, draining, enclosing, manuring and plough-ing waste and uncultivated fields, in building farm-houses, with all their necessary appendages of stables, granaries, &c. The returns of the fixed capital are in almost all cases much slower than those of the circulating capital; and such expences, even when laid out with the greatest prudence and judgment, very seldom return to the undertaker till after a period of many years, a period by far too distant to suit the conveniency of a bank.

Time lags in the expansion of fixed capital are, of course, central to any useful explanation of the intermediate, 9-year business cycle.

102. *Ibid.,* pp. 242–243.

103. *Ibid.,* p. 217. Smith actually begins his analysis of basic commodities on pp. 174–175; but he then breaks off for over forty pages in his famous digression on the value of silver over the previous 4 centuries.

104. *Ibid.,* p. 356.

105. *Ibid.,* pp. 357–360.

106. *Ibid.,* p. 358.

107. *Ibid.,* p. 359.

108. D. P. O'Brien comments on Smith's dual view of the historical sequence, attributing to Hume's influence an awareness that the requirements of kings had generated urban concentrations prematurely, in terms of Smith's natural sequence (*The Classical Economists,* p. 210). For an interesting model of physiocratic doctrine and its implications, see, especially, G. Vaggi, "A Physiocratic Model of Relative Prices and Income Distribution," *Economic Journal,* Vol. 95, No. 380, (December 1985), pp. 928–947.

109. *Wealth of Nations,* p. lix.

110. Hont's discussion of Smith's views in the debate is to be found in Hont and Ignatieff (eds.) *Wealth and Virtue,* pp. 298–306.

111. *Wealth of Nations,* p. 91. In his discussion of levels of real income per capita in relation to rates of growth, Smith observes: "France, though no doubt a richer country than Scotland, seems not to be going forward so fast. It is a common and even popular opinion in the country, that it is going backwards; an opinion which, I apprehend, is ill-founded even with regard to France, but which nobody can possibly entertain with regard to Scotland, who sees the country now, and who saw it twenty or thirty years ago." Smith judged that Scotland was advancing slower than England (*ibid.,* pp. 90 and 189); although the precise periods for which he was making the comparisons of Scotland with France and England are not specified.

112. The quotations are to be found, respectively, in Istvan Hont, Hont and Ignatieff (eds.), *Wealth and Virtue,* p. 300 (where original sources are provided), and *The Wealth of Nations,* p. 462. It might be noted in passing that, in the discussions within the United States government on post-1945 economic policy, one strand was articulated (notably by Will Clayton) in terms almost identical with the second quotation. Clayton argued that the United States could not live in either prosperity or safety as the rich man on the hill surrounded by impoverished peoples. He deployed this argument against those who asserted, in a mercantilist spirit, that United States assistance to Europe would only foster dangerously strong trading rivals.

113. *Ibid.,* pp. 94–95.

114. *Ibid.,* p. 96. Holland was experiencing the expected decline in interest rates that, in Smith's view, had the wholesome effect of driving rentiers into commerce or manufactures where profits were higher than the safe rate of interest. But Holland was not yet experiencing a decline in wages.

115. Hont and Ignatieff (eds.), *Wealth and Virtue,* p. 300.

116. *Wealth of Nations,* pp. 14–15.

117. *Ibid.,* pp. 736–738.

118. *Ibid.,* pp. 384–385.

119. *Wealth of Nations,* pp. 249–250.

120. *Ibid.,* p. 651. In *Politics and the Stages of Growth* (pp. 11–16 and 361–365, notes 1, 4, 5,

11, 14, 16–19) I link this tripartite approach to government to: (1) the Plato–Freud tripartite conception of man and Plato's "state within us"; (2) other, similar tripartite formulations of the tasks of government; and (3) the tradition in public finance, flowing directly from Smith's tripartite formulation, which divides expenditures under the headings of defense; law, order, and administration; and economic and social services. See, for example, Richard A. Musgrave, *Fiscal Systems* (New Haven: Yale University Press, 1969), Table 4-1, pp. 94–95.

121. D. P. O'Brien, *The Classical Economists*, pp. 206–207 and 275, usefully summarizes Smith's views on the legitimate positive functions of public policy in relation to the economy under his tripartite breakdown. See also S. Hollander, *Economics of Adam Smith*, pp. 262–267.

122. Milton Friedman, *Adam Smith's Relevance for 1976* (Los Angeles: International Institute for Economic Research, original paper 5, December 1976), pp. 11–15.

123. *Wealth of Nations*, p. 423.

124. Vol. II, p. 304. See also the reference to this passage in Lionel Robbins, *The Theory of Economic Policy*, pp. 112–114.

125. *Wealth of Nations*, p. 308. Lionel Robbins comments on this passage in *The Theory of Economic Policy*, pp. 30–31.

Chapter 3

1. Hume's letter is to be found in John Rae, *Life of Adam Smith* (London: Macmillan, 1895), pp. 286–287.

2. Piero Sraffa and M. H. Dobb, *Works and Correspondence of David Ricardo, Vol. VI, Letters 1810–1815,* (Cambridge: at the University Press, 1952), p. xiv.

3. *Ibid.* Vol. II, *Notes on Malthus's Principles of Political Economy.*

4. *Ibid.,* Vol. I, pp. 5–7.

5. T. R. Malthus, *Principles of Political Economy,* 2d ed. (New York: Augustus Kelley, 1951), pp. 310–311.

6. Piero Sraffa and M. H. Dobb, *Works and Correspondence: Ricardo,* Vol. II, *Notes on Malthus's Principles,* p. vii.

7. Keynes's tribute is worth quoting. (*Essays in Biography,* London: Macmillan, 1933, pp. 133–135):

> The most important influence of his [Malthus's] later years was his intimacy with Ricardo, of whom he said:
>
> > I never loved anybody out of my own family so much. Our interchange of opinion was so unreserved, and the object after which we were both enquiring was so entirely the truth, and nothing else, that I cannot but think we sooner or later must have agreed.
>
> As Maria Edgeworth, who knew both well, wrote of them:
>
> > They hunted together in search of Truth, and huzzaed when they found her, without caring who found her first; and indeed I have seen them both put their able hands to the windlass to drag her up from the bottom of that well in which she so strangely loves to dwell.
>
> The friendship between Malthus and David Ricardo began in June 1811, when Malthus "took the liberty of introducing himself" in the hope "that as we are *mainly* on the same side of the question, we might supersede the necessity of a long controversy in print respecting the points in which we differ, by an amicable discussion in private." It led to a long intimacy which was never broken. Ricardo paid repeated week-end visits to Haileybury; Malthus seldom came to London without staying, or at least breakfasting, with Ricardo, and in later years was accustomed to stay with his family at Gatcomb Park. It is evident that they had the deepest affection and respect for one another. The contrasts between the intellectual gifts of the two were obvious and delightful. In economic discussions Ricardo was the abstract and *a priori* theorist, Malthus the inductive and

intuitive investigator who hated to stray too far from what he could test by reference to the facts and his own intuitions.

8. J. A. Schumpeter, *History of Economic Analysis* (New York: Oxford University Press, 1954), pp. 472–473. Ricardo evidently stirred strong, ambivalent feelings in Schumpeter. He states (*ibid.*, p. 471) that Ricardo "had no philosophy at all. . . . Similarly, he had not an inadequate sociology, but none at all." He asserts that Ricardo, like American university students, lacked "the historical *sense* that no amount of factual study can give. That is why it is so much easier to make theorists of them than economists" (*ibid.*, p. 472, n. 2). In short, Schumpeter regarded Ricardo as the polar opposite of the kind of economist he himself aimed to be. On the other hand, Schumpeter praises Ricardo as a leader, a system builder, a man of integrity and generosity (*ibid.*, pp. 473–475). A footnote to this passage in Schumpeter makes clear that he regarded Keynes also as seized of "the Ricardian Vice."

9. T. R. Malthus, *Principles of Political Economy*, pp. 4–12. It should be recalled, however, that it was Malthus, trained in mathematics, who foreshadowed quite explicitly the possible relevance of the calculus to the formulation of economic theory (J. A. Schumpeter, *History of Economic Analysis,* p. 481).

10. The estimate is from G. Talbot Griffith, *Population Problems in the Age of Malthus* (Cambridge: at the University Press, 1926), p. 18. Griffith's figures for the eighteenth century are given along with six other estimates in B. R. Mitchell, with the collaboration of Phyllis Deane, *Abstract of British Historical Statistics* (Cambridge: at the University Press, 1971), p. 5. This array includes Malthus's estimates for 5-year intervals between 1780 and 1800 from the fifth edition (1817) of his *Essay on Population.* All estimates exhibit the post-1780 acceleration but differ with respect to population growth rates over the 5-year intervals. The first official British census was taken in 1801.

11. Phyllis Deane and W. A. Cole, *British Economic Growth, 1688–1959,* 2d ed. (Cambridge: at the University Press, 1969), p. 91.

12. These movements can be traced in A. D. Gayer *et al., The Growth and Fluctuations of the British Economy* (Oxford: at the Clarendon Press, 1953): Vol. I, pp. 27–29, 37–38, 50, 54–57, for detailed movements, 1794–1801; Vol. II, Chapters IV and V for trend movements, 1790–1850.

13. See, for example, *ibid.,* Vol. I, pp. 25–27.

14. *Ibid.,* Vol. II, Chapters I, II, and III present systematically the evidence on cyclical fluctuations in Britain from 1790 to 1850 and provide a theoretical explanation of them.

15. See, for example, D. P. O'Brien, *The Classical Economists* (Oxford: at The Clarendon Press, 1975), pp. 229–232; also, the useful review in Henry William Spiegel, *The Growth of Economic Thought* (Englewood Cliffs, N.J.: Prentice-Hall, 1971), pp. 292–306, on "The Concern with Demand."

16. See, for example, Charles P. Kindleberger, in *Economics In the Long View* (eds. C. P. Kindleberger and Guido di Tella), Vol. 3, (London: Macmillan, 1982), pp. 105–120. Also Michael D. Bordo and Anna J. Schwartz, "Money and Prices in the Nineteenth Century: An Old Debate Rejoined," *Journal of Economic History,* Vol. XL, No. 1 (March 1980), pp. 61–72; and "Money and Prices in the 19th Century: Was Thomas Tooke Right?" *Explorations in Economic History,* Vol. 18, No. 2 (April 1981), pp. 97–127. For the amiable disagreement that developed after our initial concord on this matter as collaborators on the Gayer study of 1790–1850 see A. D. Gayer *et al., Growth and Fluctuation,* "New Preface (1975)," 2d ed. (Hassocks nr. Brighton: Harvester Press, 1975), pp. v–xiv.

17. *Essay on Population,* pp. 309–437.

18. *Ibid.,* p. 310.

19. *Ibid.,* p. 360. For the most recent effort to capture the distinctive characteristics of Malthus's growth theory in a formal model, see Lilia Costabile and R. E. Rowthorn, "Malthus's Theory of Wages and Growth," *Economic Journal,* Vol. 95, No. 378 (June 1985), pp. 418–435. A useful listing of relevant references is to be found on pp. 436–437.

20. *Ibid.,* pp. 313–314.

21. *Ibid.*, pp. 226–227.

22. *Ibid.*, pp. 224–225. For discussions of a similar lagged interplay between economic and noneconomic forces, see Chapter VI in the author's *British Economy of the Nineteenth Century* (Oxford: at the Clarendon Press, 1948, reprinted 1981 by Greenwood Press, Westport); also Chapter 2 in *The Process of Economic Growth* (Oxford: at the Clarendon Press, 1953, 1960). See also, Alfred Marshall's doctrine of the interplay of environment and social behavior, preceding, pp. 169–170.

23. *Principle of Population*, 6th ed., Vol. II (London: John Murray, 1826), pp. 355–359. Margaret G. O'Donnell comments on Malthus's views on education, *The Educational Thought of the Classical Political Economists*, pp. 37–38, 41, 74, 95, 107, 119–120, 145.

24. *Principles of Political Economy*, p. 314.

25. The literature on Malthus's theory of underconsumption (or overproduction) is voluminous and, in my view, often inappropriately condescending. For example, Harry G. Johnson, Introduction to "Malthus on the High Price of Provisions," reprinted in *The Canadian Journal of Economics and Political Science*, Vol. 15, No. 2 (May, 1949), pp. 190–192; George J. Stigler, "Sraffa's Ricardo," *American Economic Review*, Vol. 43 (September–December 1953), pp. 591–599. Although less condescending than Johnson and Stigler, I would also put Lord Robbins's brisk characterization of Malthus's view in this category (*The Theory of Economic Development in the History of Economic Thought* [London: Macmillan, 1968], pp. 57–60).

26. Sraffa and Dobb, *Works and Correspondence: Ricardo*, Vol. IX, Malthus to Ricardo, p. 20, Ricardo's reply, p. 25. The letters are dated, respectively, July 16 and July 21, 1821.

27. *Political Economy*, pp. 355 and 423–424. The quotation is from the latter pages.

28. See Gayer *et al.*, *Growth and Fluctuation*, Vol. I, especially Chapter III (1812–1821), pp. 110–170.

29. *Ibid.*, pp. 136–137 and 169–170.

30. Sraffa and Dobb, *Works and Correspondence: Ricardo*, Vol. II, p. 449. Ricardo's notes on the whole of this section of Malthus's *Principles* extend from p. 421 to p. 452.

31. Malthus, *Principles*, pp. 422–423 and 416, respectively.

32. For data on agricultural rents see pp. 53–54 and note 12.

33. *Principles*, p. 418.

34. *Ibid.*, pp. 431–432. See Thomas Tooke, *History of Prices*, (London: Longman, 1838) Vol. 1, pp. 1–6, for a lucid statement of his general perspective; Vol. 2, pp. 346–349, for a quite detailed summary of his conclusions on the causes of the period of rising or high prices (1793–1814) and the subsequent protracted phase of falling or low prices. For Phillip Cagan's view that short-run movements in the monetary variables responded to business conditions, *Determinants and Effects of Changes in the Stock of Money, 1875–1960* (New York: Columbia University Press, 1965), notably p. 272.

35. *Ibid.*, p. 432.

36. *Ibid.*, p. 425.

37. *Ibid.*

38. *Ibid.*, pp. 429–430. For Richard Kahn's comments on the Malthus–Ricardo debate on this issue see *The Making of Keynes's General Theory* (Cambridge: at the University Press, 1984) pp. 4–7. Kahn modulates Malthus's stature as a pre-Keynesian heretic by noting that he begins by assuming that all savings are invested before allowing for the possibility of idle capacity due to a disproportion between saving and consumption. He also finds Malthus's attachment to *laissez-faire* excessive.

39. See, for example, Gayer *et al.*, *Growth and Fluctuation*, Vol. I, pp. 146–210.

40. *Ibid.*, Vol. II, pp. 623–627. See also, Deane and Cole, *British Economic Growth*, pp. 80, 170, and 172, for rough calculations of pre- and postwar calculations of real product and real product per capita.

41. See, for example, discussion, *ibid.*, Vol. II, pp. 532–534.

42. Malthus's most extensive and detailed discussion of machinery is in *Principles*, pp. 351–361.

For the emergence and unfolding of "the machinery question" in the wake of the Napoleonic wars, see especially Maxine Berg, *The Machinery Question and the Making of Political Economy, 1815–1848* (Cambridge: Cambridge University Press, 1980).

43. *Principles*, p. 351.

44. *Ibid.*, p. 352.

45. *Ibid.*, p. 354.

46. *Ibid.*, pp. 356–357 and 360.

47. Gayer *et al.*, *Growth and Fluctuation*, Vol. II, pp. 534–540.

48. Sraffa and Dobb, *Works and Correspondence: Ricardo*, Vol. VII, p. 120 (January 24, 1817). Malthus's reply (26 January) is on pp. 121–124.

49. *Principles*, p. 437.

50. See preceding note 26 that includes reference to Ricardo's reply rejecting Malthus's argument and asserting that reduced demand for labor "must mean a diminished reward for the labourer, and not a diminished employment of him."

51. Stigler's comment on hoarding is in "Sraffa's Ricardo," p. 596. In support of his contention, Stigler quotes Malthus (*Principles*, p. 38) as stating that: "No political economist of the present day can by saving mean mere hoarding. . . ." That assertion does not rule out hoarding as a process that sterilizes income, as in Malthus's quotation given in the text (pp. 137–138). Stigler is correct, however, in asserting that Malthus's theory of effective demand and of the inadequacy of Say's Law did not depend on hoarding.

52. Thomas Robert Malthus, *First Essay on Population 1798*, with notes by James Bonar, reprinted for the Royal Economic Society (London: Macmillan, 1926), p. 284. Malthus is here contrasting the "frugal man" of Adam Smith whose saving "is always added to stock" with "the avaricious man of Mr. Godwin" who hoards. For further discussion of Malthus's views on the possibility of saving that does not yield investment, see H. W. Spiegel, *Growth of Economic Thought*, pp. 296–297. See also L. Costabile and R. E. Rowthorn, *Malthus's Theory*, p. 423, n. 5, who review the debate on whether Malthus did or did not recognize the possibility of an *ex ante* inequality between saving and investment and side with the former view.

53. Sraffa and Dobb, *Works and Correspondence: Ricardo*, Vol. VIII, p. 260. See also George Stigler, "Sraffa's Ricardo," p. 598. The extent to which Malthus accepted Say's Law as opposed to a Keynesian view of *ex ante* saving and investment is the central concern of two articles: B. A. Corry, "Malthus and Keynes—A Reconsideration," *Economic Journal*, Vol. LXIX, No. 276, (December 1959), pp. 717–724; and S. Hollander "Malthus and Keynes: A Note," *ibid.*, Vol. 72, No. 286, (June 1962), pp. 355–359.

54. *Principles*, p. 420.

55. H. W. Spiegel, *Growth of Economic Thought*, p. 296. The quotation from Malthus is from *Principles*, pp. 6–7. Lange's "optimum propensity to consume" is set out in his "The Rate of Interest and the Optimum Propensity to Consume," *Economica*, Vol. V (New Ser.), No. 17, (February 1938), pp. 12–32, accessibly reprinted in *Readings in Business Cycle Theory*, Gottfried Haberler (ed.), (Philadelphia: Blakiston, 1944), Chapter 8. L. Costabile and R. E. Rowthorn, *Malthus's Theory*, pp. 434–435, present an equation for an optimum savings rate that is designed to define Malthus's "intermediate point."

56. *Classical Economists*, pp. 230–232.

57. For a brief evaluation of the relation between Malthus's concepts and business cycle theory, see J. A. Schumpeter, *History of Economic Analysis*, pp. 738–740.

58. "Sraffa's Ricardo," p. 599.

59. My view of trend periods (or Kondratieff cycles) can be traced through my books: *The British Economy of the Nineteenth Century*, especially Chapter 1; A. D. Gayer *et al.*, especially Vol. II, Chapters IV and V; *The Process of Economic Growth*, especially Part III and Chapters 6, 8, and 9; *The World Economy: History and Prospect*, especially Part III; *Why the Poor Get Richer and the Rich Slow Down* (Austin: University of Texas Press, 1980), especially Chapters 1 and 2; *The Barbaric Counter Revolution: Cause and Cure* (Austin: University of Texas Press), especially pp.

8–11 and 62–69, and 102–115, which deals with recent phases of Kondratieff cycles and their policy implications. W. Arthur Lewis's view is most explicitly stated in his *Growth and Fluctuations, 1870–1913* (London: Allen and Unwin, 1978), especially Chapter 3.

60. The indexes were calculated by Glen Hueckel, "War and the British Economy, 1793–1815: A General Analysis," *Explorations in Economic History*, Vol. 10, No. 4 (Summer 1973), p. 388. For discussion, see my *World Economy: History and Prospect*, pp. 111–115.

61. *Principles*, p. 188. In the first edition of his *Essay on Population*, Malthus (pp. 90–91) draws a related but not identical distinction between food and "wrought commodities."

> A demand for these last [manufactures] will not fail to create them in as great a quantity as they are wanted. The demand for food has by no means the same creative power. In a country where all the fertile spots have been seized, high offers are necessary to encourage the farmer to lay his dressing on land, from which he cannot expect a profitable return for some years. And before the prospect of advantage is sufficiently great to encourage this sort of agricultural enterprize, and while the new produce is rising, great distresses may be suffered from the want of it. The demand for an increased quantity of subsistence is, with few exceptions, constant everywhere, yet we see how slowly it is answered in all those countries that have been long occupied.

62. *Principles*, p. 288.

63. *Ibid.*, p. 289.

64. *Ibid.*

65. *Ibid.*, pp. 289, 297, and 413–437.

66. *Ibid.*, p. 286.

67. *Ibid.*, p. 288.

68. *Ibid.*, p. 280.

69. *Why the Poor Get Richer*, Chapter 2.

70. Colin Clark's views can be traced through his *National Income and Outlay* (London: Macmillan, 1937), *The Conditions of Economic Progress* (London: Macmillan, 1940), and *The Economics of 1960* (London: Macmillan 1942).

71. *Principles*, pp. 288–289.

72. Sraffa and Dobb, *Works and Correspondence: Ricardo*, Vol. II, p. 284.

73. *Principles*, pp. 281–282.

74. On Malthus's travels (1802), see, notably, Patricia James (ed.), *The Travel Diaries of Thomas Robert Malthus* (Cambridge: at the University Press for the Royal Economic Society, 1966). For the wider background of the first and second editions of the *Essay on Population*, see Patricia James, *Population Malthus, His Life and Times* (London: Routledge and Kegan Paul, 1979), especially pp. 55–115.

75. *Essay on Population*, 2d ed. (London: J. M. Dent, 1914, 1952), Vol. I, pp. 154–163.

76. *Essay on Population*, 1st ed., pp. 231–239.

77. *Ibid.*, Vol. II, pp. 79–96.

78. *Population*, 2d ed., Vol. II, p. 79.

79. *Ibid.*

80. *Ibid.*, pp. 95–96.

81. See, notably, Frederic R. Kolb, "The Stationary State of Ricardo and Malthus: Neither Pessimistic nor Prophetic," *Intermountain Economic Review*, Vol. 3, (1972), pp. 17–30; the reinforcing comment of M. A. Akhtar, "The Stationary State of Ricardo and Malthus: Comment," *ibid.*, Vol. 4 (1973), pp. 77–79; and Kolb's "Reply," *ibid.*, p. 80.

82. *Ibid.*, especially Kolb's "Reply." Even so sedulous a scholar as Schumpeter fails to capture the post-1812 transition of Malthus and Ricardo to, at least, quasi-optimisim (*History of Economic Analysis*, pp. 270–271).

83. A. D. Gayer *et al.*, *Growth and Fluctuation*, Vol. I, p. 61.

84. Frederic Kolb, in his initial exposition, persuasively offsets relatively optimistic quotations from Ricardo and Malthus against pessimistic characterizations to be found in various histories of

economic thought, but all of Kolb's quoted optimistic references are drawn from writings in the period 1815–1822 ("Stationary State," pp. 20–25.)

85. *First Essay on Population 1798,* p. 4.

86. *Ibid.,* p. 11.

87. *Ibid.,* pp. 63–69.

88. *Essay on Population,* 2d ed., Vol. I, p. 315.

89. Patricia James, *Population Malthus,* notes (p. 55):

> Before considering the first *Essay on Population,* modern readers must face three difficulties. The first is the air of unreality that for us, pervades all early British works on the subject, since the writers argue as if there were no such thing as contraception. For all practical purposes this was truly the case: it simply would not, *could not,* have occurred to more than a handful of men that contraceptives might ever be in general use as a means of controlling the size of families.

The other two difficulties noted by James are that Malthus was born before the age of specialization and must not be thought of as a professional economist or demographer; and a general lack of reliable statistics and "an attitude of mind that set a low value on ascertained facts."

90. *Essay on Population,* pp. 226–227.

91. Dugald Stewart, "Biographical and Critical Memoirs of Adam Smith," Introduction to *The Theory of Moral Sentiments* (London: G. Bell, 1911), pp. lx and lxiv.

92. There is something deeply understood, and perhaps autobiographical, in this passage from the *First Essay on Population* (pp. 64–65):

> A man of liberal education, but with an income only just sufficient to enable him to associate in the rank of gentlemen, must feel absolutely certain, that if he marries and has a family, he shall be obliged, if he mixes at all in society, to rank himself with moderate farmers, and the lower class of tradesmen. The woman that a man of education would naturally make the object of his choice, would be one brought up in the same tastes and sentiments with himself, and used to the familiar intercourse of a society totally different from that to which she must be reduced by marriage. Can a man consent to place the object of his affection in a situation so discordant, probably, to her tastes and inclinations?

93. Patricia James, *Population Malthus,* p. 443. The characterization is from a letter of William Whewell to his sister shortly after Malthus's death.

94. James explores admirably the various facets of the controversy, *ibid.,* p. 116–159. William Petersen's study, *Malthus* (Cambridge, Mass.: Harvard University Press, 1979), deals systematically with contemporary and subsequent controversies centered on Malthus's views (or believed views) on population.

95. Sraffa and Dobb, *Works and Correspondence,* Vol. X, pp. 1–5. The account is part of the brief memoir of David Ricardo's brother Moses.

96. *Ibid.,* pp. 4–5.

97. *Ibid.*

98. *Ibid.*

99. *Ibid.,* pp. 36–43.

100. *Ibid.,* p. 280, including footnote.

101. *Ibid.,* pp. 168–169.

102. *Ibid.,* p. 171.

103. *Ibid.,* pp. 67–68 and 104–106.

104. *Ibid.,* p. 90; full text of letter, Vol. VI, p. 115.

105. For example, *ibid.,* Vol. X, pp. 113–115 (J. H. Wilkinson) and 129–132 (Jacob Ricardo).

106. *Ibid.,* pp. 133–135.

107. *Ibid.,* p. 113.

108. *Ibid.,* pp. 119–123.

109. *Ibid.,* p. 157.

110. *Ibid.*, pp. 277–280. Mary Ann Carlile and her husband Richard also impinge on the life of the young John Stuart Mill at this time in his brief phase of open advocacy of birth control. See, for example, Michael St. John Packe, *The Life of John Stuart Mill* (New York: Macmillan, 1954), pp. 53–55 and 58.

111. See, for example, Sraffa and Dobb (eds.), *Works and Correspondence: Ricardo*, Vol. V, pp. 112–113, Ricardo's statement in support of a reform bill defeated on April 18, 1823.

112. *Ibid.*, pp. 495–503 (Parliamentary reform) and 504–512 (voting by ballot).

113. For example, *ibid.*, Vol. VII, pp. 219–221 (10 December, 1815).

114. *Ibid.*, Vol. VI, pp. 343–344 (25 December, 1815). Ricardo then adds, as theorists are wont to do: "But granting all this does not affect the theory of the bullionists."

115. *Ibid.*, Vol. I, p. 5.

116. For Ricardian growth models, see, especially, Irma Adelman, *Theories*, pp. 43–59; J. R. Hicks, *Capital and Growth*, pp. 42–48; and D. P. O'Brien, *op. cit.*, pp. 37–45.

117. I shall not attempt to trace out here in detail the course of the debate on Ricardo's corn model. It starts with Piero Sraffa's effort to construct from circumstantial evidence (primarily in Ricardo's *Essay on Profits*) the existence of a pure Ricardian corn model in which corn is both capital (in the form of food supplied to labor) and output, the profit rate being a fraction of the net difference between the two, divided by output. The fraction is independent of price or wage rates since the numerator and denominator are both reckoned in corn. (Sraffa and Dobb (eds.), *Works and Correspondence: Ricardo*, Vol. I, pp. xxx–xxxiii). Samuel Hollander challenged Sraffa's reconstruction in "Ricardo's Analysis of the Profit Rates, 1813–15," *Economica*, Vol. 40, (1973), pp. 260–282; John Eatwell commented on Hollander's paper in "The Interpretation of Ricardo's *Essay on Profits*," *Economica*, Vol. 42, (1975), pp. 182–187 and Hollander replied to Eatwell, "Ricardo and the Corn Profit Model: Reply to Eatwell," *ibid.*, pp. 188–202. Finally, Terry Peach provides strong independent support for the view that the corn model was "a figment of Sraffa's imagination" in "David Ricardo's Early Treatment of Profitability: A New Interpretation," *Economic Journal*, Vol. 94, No. 376 (December 1984), pp. 733–751. Of the formal models cited in n. 20, Adelman builds her model on Ricardo's *Principles* rather than the *Essay on Profits*. Hicks, writing initially before Hollander's challenge to Sraffa's interpretation, produces an elegant diagrammatic version of the corn model (*Capital and Growth*, pp. 44–46). D. P. O'Brien provides a similar but not identical diagrammatic model (*Classical Economists*, pp. 38–41), ignoring Hollander's 1973 paper. For Hollander's later (1977) confrontation with Hicks and the latter's second thoughts, see John Hicks, *Classics and Moderns, Collected Essays on Economic Theory*, Vol. III, (Cambridge, Mass.: Harvard University Press, 1962), Chapter 4, pp. 34–59.

118. Sraffa and Dobb, *Works and Correspondence: Ricardo*, Vol. I, p. xxxii.

119. References will be to the reproduction in *ibid.*, Vol. IV, pp. 3–41, including the editor's note (pp. 3–8).

120. See A. D. Gayer *et al.*, *Growth and Fluctuation*, pp. 113–115.

121. Sraffa and Dobb, *Works and Correspondence: Ricardo*, Vol. IV, p. 41.

122. *Ibid.*, pp. 9–10. In his *Principles* (*ibid.*, Vol. 1, pp. 5–6), first published in 1817, Ricardo acknowledges Malthus as the author of the theory of rent he brings to bear in making his case; although he differs with Malthus on agricultural protection. Ricardo acknowledges Edward West of Oxford as well as Malthus as virtually simultaneous and independent authors of the correct doctrine of rent.

123. *Ibid.*, p. 12.

124. *Ibid.*, pp. 22–23.

125. *Ibid.*

126. *Ibid.*, pp. 23–26.

127. *Ibid.*, p. 9.

128. *Ibid.*, Vol. 1, pp. xiii–lx, provides a detailed account of the evolution of the *Principles* including variations as it moved from its first (1817) to its second (1819) to its third (1821) edition.

129. *Ibid.*, Vol. IV, p. 23. D. P. O'Brien, *Classical Economists*, p. 40, provides a diagram

resulting from capital and population "alternately taking the lead" as profits respond to periods when market wages rise above and fall back to the subsistence level. The diagram is a variant of W. J. Baumol in *Economic Dynamics,* 2d ed. (New York: Macmillan, 1959), p. 19.

130. *Ibid.,* Vol. I, pp. 96–97. The editors note a similarity of this passage to one in Robert Torrens's *Essay on the External Corn Trade,* p. 68.

131. Sraffa and Dobb, *ibid.,* Vol. I, pp. 30–33.

132. *Ibid.,* pp. 131 and 166.

133. See preceding (*ibid.,* Vol. V, p. 122), Ricardo's famous dictum: ". . . no one accumulates but with a view to make his accumulation productive. . . ."

134. *Ibid.,* pp. 125–126.

135. *Ibid.,* p. 126.

136. *Ibid.,* p. 120. See also pp. 94 and 132, where "the extension of foreign trade and the exploitation of natural advantage" joins the list of factors helping to sustain the profit-saving process and thus the momentum of the economy.

137. *Ibid.,* Chapter XXXI, "On Machinery," pp. 386–397. For a somewhat disabused discussion of Ricardo's position, see Joseph H. Schumpeter, *History of Economic Analysis,* pp. 680–687. John Hicks provided a kind of vindication of Ricardo's position in his *A Theory of Economic History* (Oxford: at the University Press, 1969), pp. 151–154 and 168–171. For a meticulous account of the evolution of Ricardo's view, see Samuel Hollander, "The Development of Ricardo's Position on Machinery," *History of Political Economy,* Vol. 3, No. 1 (Spring 1971), pp. 105–135. E. F. Beach challenges Hicks's position on Ricardo as theoretically interesting but historically irrelevant, and Hicks replies in *The Economic Journal,* Vol. 81, No. 324 (December 1971), pp. 916–925 ("Hicks on Ricardo on Machinery" and "Reply to Professor Beach). D. P. O'Brien, *Classical Economists,* pp. 224–228, summarizes the classical literature on the machinery question, providing a useful bibliography, pp. 238–239. Shlomo Martal and Patricia Haskell, "Why Did Ricardo (Not) Change His Mind? On Money and Machinery," *Economica,* Vol. 44, (1977), pp. 359–368, speculate somewhat playfully on why Ricardo recanted on machinery but not on his equally flawed monetary doctrine. A 1981 article resurrects Ricardo on machinery in an interesting context (L. Jonung, "Ricardo on Machinery and the Present Unemployment: An Unpublished Manuscript by Knut Wicksell" [*Economic Journal,* Vol. 91, No. 361 (March 1981)], pp. 195–205). Wicksell, troubled by the extraordinarily high levels of unemployment after the First World War in Sweden and elsewhere in Europe, canvassed various remedies in several articles written in 1922–1923. They mainly advocated migration to America and a reduced birthrate. In the course of his work on this problem he also wrote a short piece criticizing Ricardo's logic. The essence of Wicksell's argument was that Ricardo did not take into account the effects of the wage reduction that would follow the introduction of machinery. Over time, the wage reduction would lead to the employment of labor in other functions and, in a dynamic sequence, it would make it possible for output and profits to increase and wage rates to be restored. He suggested this sequence might provide a way of reducing current unemployment, adding, however, that, if wage cuts yielded workers' income below the subsistence level, government might subsidize workers' income until the dynamics of the process yielded its benign results.

Wicksell submitted the article early in 1924 to the editor of the *Economic Journal* (J. M. Keynes) who turned it down—an act that may well have increased Wicksell's chronic irritation with English economists. The *amende honorable* awaited the passage of 57 years.

138. *Ibid.,* pp. 389–392.

139. *Ibid.,* pp. 390–395.

140. T. R. Malthus, *Principles,* pp. 351–354.

141. This passage paraphrases D. P. O'Brien's useful summary, *Classical Economists,* pp. 226–227.

142. Sraffa and Dobb, *Works and Correspondence: Ricardo,* Vol. 1, pp. lvii–lx, deal with the transition of Ricardo to the "revolutionary change" on machinery and unemployment in the third edition. Sraffa and Dobb find evidence of the beginnings of a shift in two of Ricardo's notes on

Malthus's *Principles* (Vol. II, pp. 234–236 and 237–239). (I would add note 151, pp. 237–239, to Sraffa and Dobb's notes 149 and 153 as evidence of the transition.)

143. T. R. Malthus, *Principles,* pp. 217–261, especially pp. 236–240.

144. *Ibid.,* p. 237.

145. Sraffa and Dobb, *Works and Correspondence: Ricardo,* Vol. II, p. 239.

146. J. R. Hicks, *A Theory of Economic History,* pp. 150–154 and 164–171.

147. A. D. Gayer *et al., Growth and Fluctuation,* Vol. I, pp. 169–170 (1819–1820), pp. 208–210 (1822–1826).

148. *Ibid.,* p. 210.

149. See, for example, W. W. Rostow, "Trade Cycles, Harvests, and Politics: 1790–1850," Chapter V in *British Economy of the Nineteenth Century.* An annual social-tension index is presented on pp. 123–125, combining trade fluctuations with fluctuations in the British wheat price.

150. Sraffa and Dobb, *Works and Correspondence: Ricardo,* Vol. I, pp. 265–267.

151. Without pretending to compulsive and complete scholarship on the history of economic thought, and putting aside Malthus's fragmentary insights, I am inclined to date serious cyclical analysis from the publication in 1823 of Thomas Tooke's *Thoughts and Details on the High and Low Prices of the Last Thirty Years.* Thomas Atwood, even earlier (1817–1819), had couched some of his argument for a postwar reflationary policy in terms that suggested consciousness of a cyclical process, as did Thomas Joplin, whose first work in economics (as opposed to banking) was published in 1823. (See, for example, Joseph A. Schumpeter, *History of Economic Analysis,* pp. 708–715, and Robert G. Link, *English Theories of Economic Fluctuations, 1815–1848* (New York: Columbia University Press, 1959), pp. 6–33 (Attwood), pp. 73–102 (Thomas Joplin), and pp. 127–147 (Thomas Tooke).

152. A. D. Gayer *et al., Growth and Fluctuation,* Vol. I, pp. 44–54.

153. The controversy, in fact, continues into the present. See, preceding, Malthus note 16.

154. Sraffa and Dobb, *Works and Correspondence: Ricardo,* Vol. 1, pp. 93–94.

155. *Ibid.,* pp. 80–83 and 120.

156. *Ibid.,* pp. 80–82.

157. *Ibid.,* Vol. II, p. 332.

158. *Ibid.,* p. 337.

159. *Ibid.,* p. 347.

160. *Ibid.,* Vol. VI, p. 147. I owe reference to this point to Irma Adelman, *Theories of Economic Growth,* p. 54 and note 39, p. 151.

161. Sraffa and Dobb, *Works and Correspondence: Ricardo,* Vol. I, p. 395.

162. Krishna Chandra Roychowdhury, "Ricardo and Development Planning," *The Indian Economic Journal,* Vol. 25, No. 1 (1977), pp. 257–264. This conclusion derives from the view that, so long as the stock of new machines is being built up, employment will expand in the machine-building industry. This will require additional allocations from consumption goods to support the expanded work force in machine building. But production has not yet been augmented in the consumption-goods sector by the expanding increment of capital goods. Thus, an inflationary impulse is imparted to the economy. Additional domestic or foreign savings are required, therefore, to preserve the real wage during the period until the increment of new machines comes into production yielding an increase in productivity and production of consumers goods.

163. Sraffa and Dobb, *Works and Correspondence: Ricardo,* Vol. I, pp. 98–100.

164. *Ibid.,* Vol. VI, pp. 315–316.

165. *Ibid.,* Vol. IV, p. 179. For quotations—some from distinguished economists—asserting that Ricardo was pessimistic about the economic prospect, see Frederic R. Kolb, "Stationary State," pp. 17–20.

166. Sraffa and Dobb, *Works and Correspondence: Ricardo,* Vol. VII, pp. 16–17.

167. *Ibid.,* Vol. IV, p. 179, from Ricardo's article on the funding system for the *Encyclopedia Britannica.*

Chapter 4

1. One cannot be sure that Mill never read any of Marx's works, for he notes in his autobiography that, in the wake of the publication of the first edition of his *Principles*, in 1848, and of the French Revolution of that year, he devoted much time "to the study of the best Socialistic writers on the continent. . . ." (J. S. Mill, *Autobiography*, with a preface by John Jacob Coss [New York: Columbia University Press, 1924, 1944], p. 164). But, we have no evidence that the *Communist Manifesto* came to Mill's attention. Professor John M. Robson supplies further elucidation in a letter to the author:

> . . . It might be worth mentioning that the question of Mill's command over German is moot, and almost nothing of Marx's appeared in English during Mills' lifetime. Though he says in the *Autobiography* (normally very reliable as to fact) that he learned it by the Hamiltonian method (and under Sarah Austin's tutelage he would not be slack), and in his library there are several German volumes (most notably a full set of Goethe in quite unreadable type), I have found very little evidence of his using German texts. The most promising evidence, in the *Principles*, is tarnished by the discovery that several of the quoted passages are marked in George Grote's copies of the sources; the marks may of course be Mill's (they are no more than marks), but they more probably are Grote's made for Mill's guidance.

2. Karl Marx, *Capital* (Moscow: Foreign Languages Publishing House, 1954), Vol. I, pp. 610–611, n. 2 ("herd of vulgar apologists"), and 518. This is the 1887 edition incorporating, however, some changes made by Engels in the 1890 German edition.

3. For Gladstone's characterization of Mill, see Michael St. John Packe, *The Life of John Stuart Mill* (New York: Macmillan, 1954), p. 455.

4. I should note immediately that others have been intrigued by the linkages and differences between Mill and Marx. See, notably, Bela A. Belassa "Karl Marx and John Stuart Mill," *Weltwirtschaftliches Archiv*, Vol. 83, No. 2 (1959), pp. 147–167, and Graeme Duncan, *Marx and Mill* (Cambridge: at the University Press, 1973). Belassa argues persuasively that Marx on several important points was influenced by Mill and "it is not inappropriate to speak about Mill's influence on the formation of the Marxian Theory." See, also, Joseph A. Schumpeter, *History of Economic Analysis*, (New York: Oxford University Press, 1954), p. 574 on similarities between Mill's Stationary State and Marx's Communism.

5. M. St. J. Packe, pp. 55–58, describes the incident well and its subsequent echoes during Mill's life and even beyond. See, also, Norman E. Himes, "John Stuart Mill's Attitude Towards Neo-Malthusianism," *Economic History*, No. 4 (Supplement to *The Economic Journal* [January 1929]), on which much of Packe's account is based. See also Francis E. Mineka, "John Stuart Mill and Neo-Malthusianism, 1873," *The Mill News Letter*, Vol. VIII, No. 2, pp. 3–10. Mineka's article is mainly focused on the controversy following Mill's death; but n. 1 (p. 8) goes beyond Hime's article, citing three Mill letters on the need to control population published in *The Black Dwarf* in 1823–1824. Samuel Hollander includes a brief but useful appendix on Mill's "Attitudes Towards Birth Control" in *The Economics of John Stuart Mill*, (Toronto: University of Toronto Press, 1955), Vol. II, pp. 968–970.

6. Charles Babbage, *On the Economy of Machinery and Manufactures* (London: Charles Knight, 1841), fourth edition enlarged, p. vi (Preface to second edition, dated November 22, 1832).

7. *History of Economic Analysis*, p. 531.

8. *Autobiography*, p. 162. Mill here describes his "third period" view linked to his close association with Mrs. Harriet Taylor. The two earlier "periods" were his phase of more or less pure Benthamism and a phase that included a reaction against it.

9. J. S. Mill, "The Claims of Labor," in *Dissertations and Discussions*, Vol. II (New York: Henry Holt, 1882), p. 261.

10. A good deal of Mill's year in France was spent in continued intense study broadly under the wing of Jeremy Bentham's brother Sir Samuel: naval architect, mineralogist, explorer, inventor, ex-Brigadier General in the army of Catherine the Great, ex-Inspector General of His Majesty's Naval Work. Operationally, Lady Bentham directed Mill's studies with Sir Samuel's son, George Bentham, aged 20, keeping a still closer eye on his routine, his French, etc. Despite Mill's continued precocious labors, there were lessons in fencing, riding, and dancing, considerable travel, 6 months in Montpelier that Mill remembered as the happiest time of his youth, friendships made on his own. See, notably, Anna Jean Mill (ed.), *John Mill's Boyhood Visit to France, Being a Journal and Notebook Written by John Stuart Mill in France, 1820–21* (Toronto: University of Toronto Press, 1960). Aside from acquiring a good working knowledge of the French language, this year left a permanent residue of connection with France and French ideas, adding an important dimension to Mill's life.

11. *Autobiography*, pp. 19–21.

12. *Ibid.*, p. 47. Samuel Hollander has traced out in great detail Mill's complex and changing views of the utilitarian propositions in Chapter 8 of *The Economics of John Stuart Mill* ("On Utility and Liberty," Vol. II, pp. 602–676).

13. *Ibid.*, p. 61. Mill writes of Ricardo as follows (p. 38): "My being an habitual inmate of my father's study made me acquainted with the dearest of his friends, David Ricardo, who by his benevolent countenance, and kindliness of manner, was very attractive to young persons, and who after I became a student of political economy, invited me to his house and to walk with him in order to converse on the subject." Samuel Hollander (*Economics of John Stuart Mill*, Vol. I, pp. 26 and 347n.) notes that Ricardo did not regard Mill's initial public appearance as an economist as impressive.

14. *Ibid.*, p. 93.

15. *Ibid.*, p. 94. The most complete and persuasive account of Mill's famous crisis is John M. Robson's "Mental Crisis and Resolution", Chapter 2 in his *The Improvement of Mankind* (Toronto: University of Toronto Press, [London: Routledge and Kegan Paul], 1968), pp. 21–49. For another sensitive well-balanced effort to reconstruct Mill's crisis and its possible causes see M. St. J. Packe, *Life of John Stuart Mill*, pp. 74–80.

16. *Ibid.*, p. 96.

17. *Ibid.*, p. 99.

18. *Ibid.*, p. 113. M. St. J. Packe goes, I believe, a bit too far when he concludes (p. 81): "He remained as he had been before, a reformer of the world: but he now went after emotion like an addict after drugs."

19. *Ibid.*, p. 177. In this passage Mill credits Harriet Taylor with keeping this eclectic tendency from going too far.

20. *History of Economic Analysis*, p. 528.

21. For an account of Mill's activities while writing *The Principles*, see the textual introduction by J. M. Robson in V. W. Bladen and J. M. Robson (eds.), *Principles of Political Economy* by John Stuart Mill (Toronto: University of Toronto Press [London: Routledge and Kegan Paul], 1965), pp. lxv and lxvi. Subsequently referred to as *The Principles*. Also M. St. J. Packe, *Life of John Stuart Mill*, pp. 295–296.

22. *The Principles*, p. 97. See also, A. D. Gayer *et al.*, *Growth and Fluctuation of the British Economy, 1790–1850,* (Oxford: at the Clarendon Press, 1953), pp. 315–318 and 331–333. For a thorough account of Mill's "Transition to the *Principles*" see Chapter Three in Samuel Hollander, *The Economics of John Stuart Mill*, Vol. I.

23. A. D. Gayer *et al.*, *Growth and Fluctuation*, p. 307.

24. Bladen and Robson (eds.), *The Principles*, p. xcii.

25. Typical of the longevity of Mill's *Principles* is the 1898 American (Appleton) edition "abridged, with critical, bibliographical and explanatory notes, and a sketch of the history of political economy" by J. Laurence Laughlin, Professor of Political Economy at the University of Chicago. Laughlin not only pruned out a good deal of "Sociology and Social Philosophy" but

inserted contemporary U.S. illustrations of Mill's propositions, charts, maps, etc. He also occasion-ally interpolates views that differ from Mill's. This book happens to be in the family library because it was used early in this century as a textbook at the University of Chicago by my wife's father, Milton J. Davies.

26. Quoted M. St. J. Packe, *Life of John Stuart Mill*, p. 81.

27. *History of Economic Analysis*, pp. 531–532. See also John Hicks's appreciation of Mill "From Classical to Post-Classical: The Work of J. S. Mill," *Classics and Moderns: Collected Essays on Economic Theory*, Vol. III (Cambridge, Mass.: Harvard University Press, 1983), pp. 60–70.

28. I owe this image to W. H. Auden, who once described T. S. Eliot not as a man but as a household: a high church archdeacon, a wise and passionate old peasant grandmother, and a young boy given to slightly malicious practical jokes, all living somehow together (*New Yorker*, April 23, 1949).

29. It should be underlined, of course, that this statement of the bureaucrat's creed was counter-balanced for Mill by his remarkable freedom to engage in propaganda and controversy, as well as exalted intellectual exercise of various kinds (*Autobiography*, pp. 59–60). Mill's reflections on the disciplines of bureaucracy recall J. M. Keynes's observation:

> Words ought to be a little wild, for they are an assault of thought upon the unthinking. But when the seats of power and authority have been attained, there should be no more poetic licence. . . . When a doctrinaire proceeds to action, he must, so to speak, forget his doctrine. For those who in action remember the letter will probably lose what they are seeking. ("National Self-Sufficiency," *Yale Review*, xxii (1933), p. 755).

30. *Principles*, p. 154.

31. *Ibid.*, p. 173.

32. *Ibid.*, p. 174.

33. *Ibid.*, p. 177.

34. *Ibid.*, p. 182.

35. *Ibid.*, p. 183.

36. *Ibid.*, p. 184.

37. *Ibid.*, pp. 186–187.

38. *Ibid.*, p. 337.

39. *Ibid.*, p. 415.

40. *Ibid.*, p. 199.

41. See, for example, Alexander Gray, *The Development of Economic Doctrine*, (London: Longmans Green, 1931), pp. 280–281. But even as thoughtful and temperate an analyst as Eric Roll writes (*A History of Economic Thought*, 3d Ed. [Englewood Cliffs, N.J.: 1956], p. 363): "The central propositions of Mill's theory—those relating to value and to production—show his endeav-or . . . to cast them in such terms that they have no connection with the laws of distribution." But in a vein similar to mine, see, also, Samuel Hollander, *The Economics of John Stuart Mill*, Vol. I, pp. 216–223 and 246–247.

42. *Ibid.*, p. 159.

43. *Ibid.*, p. 378.

44. *Ibid.*

45. Quoted, Alexander Gray, *Development of Economic Doctrine*, p. 279. Samuel Hollander has called my attention to the views on population of Thomas Chalmers as supportive of Malthus, anticipatory of J. S. Mill. He summarizes Chalmers in his *Economics of John Stuart Mill*, Vol. I, pp. 58–60.

46. *Ibid.*, Book One, Chapter X, especially pp. 154–159.

47. *Ibid.*, Book Two, Chapters XI, XII, and XIII, especially pp. 343–360, 343–360, and 367–379.

48. *Ibid.*, Book Four, Chapter VI, especially pp. 752–757.

49. *Ibid.*, Book Four, Chapter VII, especially pp. 758–769.

50. *Ibid.*, Chapter VI, pp. 756–757.

51. J. M. Keynes, *Essays in Persuasion* (London: Macmillan, 1933), pp. 358–373.

52. *Principles*, pp. 351–352.

53. Norman E. Himes, "Attitude Toward Neo-Malthusianism," p. 484. Speculating on the reasons for Mill's failure to be more outspoken on birth control, Himes evokes the following (pp. 481–483):

> (1) He was intensely preoccupied with other matters. He may well have felt that if he ever publicly took up such a position it would have needed much explanation in his day, when the discussion of sex matters was studiously avoided. (2) As matters stood, his relations with Mrs. Taylor were the subject of gossip, and were very much misunderstood even by members of his family and by rather intimate friends. Had he been a public advocate of birth-control, what extraordinary credence would have been lent to the accusations already afloat! (3) A public advocacy of Neo-Malthusianism would have impeded the realisation of many of the other objectives and reforms for which Mill cared intensely in later life, e.g., woman suffrage and the emancipation of women. (4) Mill had a keen sense of the delicate; he did not like to offend even when he thought he was right. . . . (5) I think Mill was definitely in favour of the artificial check, but I do not think that he held the opinion strongly. He was the reverse of the dogmatist and tended toward the eclectic. He was probably aware of certain limitations in the doctrine. . . . (6) Moreover, Mill may have thought that the time had not yet arrived when he could usefully take up a firm stand publicly. I think he realised that after all public opinion had not advanced much since 1823. . . . And would it not have rendered nugatory his promotion of other equally useful ends? Who can say that such reflections did not influence Mill?

54. *Ibid.*, p. 477.

55. *Ibid.*, pp. 480–481.

56. William Petersen, *Malthus*, p. 194 and subsequent discussion.

57. Norman E. Himes, "Attitude Toward Neo-Malthusianism," p. 462.

58. *Principles*, pp. 102–106.

59. *Ibid.*, pp. 107–111.

60. *Ibid.*, pp. 112–115.

61. *Ibid.*, pp. 116–130.

62. *Ibid.*, pp. 765–766.

63. *Ibid.*, pp. 769–775.

64. *Ibid.*, pp. 775–794.

65. For full reference to Babbage on machinery and manufactures, see note 6, this chapter. John Rae, *Statement of Some New Principles on the Subject of Political Economy*, Vol. II of R. Warren James, *John Rae, Political Economist* (Toronto: University of Toronto Press, 1965). For a positive evaluation of Rae's work and J. S. Mill's role in acknowledging its quality, see J. A. Schumpeter, *History of Economic Analysis*, pp. 468–469.

66. *Principles*, p. 162.

67. *Ibid.*, pp. 170–172.

68. *Statement on Some New Principles*, pp. 208–264.

69. *Principles*, pp. 918–919.

70. *On the Economy of Machinery*, p. iii.

71. Babbage, aside from filling the Lucasian Professorship of Mathematics at Cambridge (1828–1839) played an important part in founding the Astronomical (1820) and Statistical (1834) societies. He published papers on mathematics, statistics, physics, machine design, and geology.

72. Edward Baines, *History of Cotton Manufacture* (London: Fisher and Jackson, 1835); Andrew Ure, *The Philosophy of Manufactures*, (London: H. G. Bohn, 1835). Ure's 1835 volume was confined to the cotton industry. It was the product of a quarter-century's teaching in "a public seminary . . . to practical men, as well as to youth, the application of mechanical and chemical science to the arts. . . ." It is analytically less sophisticated than Baines's, let alone Babbage's

study, but full of accurate information on the cotton industry. In 1861 P. L. Simmonds published an edition that extended Ure's analysis of cotton to 1860 and embraced the flax, silk, and wool industries as well (*The Philosophy of Manufactures* [London: H. G. Bohn, 1861], 3d Ed.).

73. A. D. Gayer *et al.*, *Growth and Fluctuation*, Vol. I, pp. 221–222.

74. This idea is developed in Rae's *New Principles* Book II, Chapter V, pp. 109–117.

75. *Ibid.*, Chapter X, "Of the Causes of the Progress of Invention, and the Effects Arising from It," pp. 109–118; Babbage, *On the Economy of Machinery*, Chapters XXVII and XXXV pp. 260–267 and 334–341. It should be recalled that Adam Smith gave some thought to the process of invention (preceding, p. 41).

76. *Principles*, p. 969.

77. *Ibid.*, p. 107.

78. See, for example, A. D. Gayer *et al.*, *Growth and Fluctuation*, Vol. I, pp. 295–296. Also R. C. O. Matthews, *A Study in Trade Cycle History, Economic Fluctuations in Great Britain 1833–1842*. (Cambridge: at the University Press, 1954), p. 32.

79. *Principles*, p. 413.

80. *Ibid.*, pp. 750–751.

81. J. A. Schumpeter, *History of Economic Analysis*, pp. 571–572. Samuel Hollander has called to my attention passages in both Ricardo and J. S. Mill that, if not exactly Schumpeterian, make clear an awareness that profitability and investment can be enlarged by technological "improvements." See Hollander's *Economics of John Stuart Mill*, Vol. I, pp. 26 and 428.

82. See, for example, Mill's reference to Tooke in his "Paper Currency and Commercial Distress," originally published in *Parliamentary Review, Session of 1826* (London: Longman, Rees, Orme, Brown, and Green, 1826), pp. 630–632, reprinted in *Collected Works of John Stuart Mill* (J. M. Robson, ed.), Vol. IV, *Essays on Economics and Society* (Toronto: University of Toronto Press, Routledge and Kegan Paul, 1967), p. 74. Also many references to Tooke in *Principles* are listed, pp. 1150–1152. Aside from Tooke, Babbage had the clearest grasp on the cyclical process (see, especially, *On the Economy of Machinery*, Chapter XXIV, "On Overmanufacturing," pp. 231–241). Babbage's view is unique for its time because his perspective is rooted in the industrial sector rather than commodity markets or the monetary system.

83. *Essays on Some Unsettled Questions*, pp. 47–74. These essays were written in 1829–1830.

84. "Paper Currency and Commercial Distress," p. 77. See also J. R. Hicks, *Classics and Moderns*, pp. 63–65. Hicks respectfully summarizes Mill's view of commercial crises and the possibilities of general overproduction as elaborated in *Essays on Some Unsettled Questions*. He does not refer to Mill's 1826 essay.

85. "Paper Currency and Commercial Distress," pp. 74–76.

86. *Ibid.*, pp. 75–76.

87. A. D. Gayer *et al.*, Vol. I, pp. 215–216.

88. Mill, *Essays*, p. 48. For Hicks's analysis of Mill on "gluts," *Classics and Moderns*, pp. 62–64.

89. Mill, *Essays*, p. 56.

90. *Ibid.*, pp. 69–74.

91. After the major cycle peak in 1836 there was a year of acute depression followed by a minor cycle recovery (1836–1838). For the subsequent period of chronic idle capacity, unemployment, and social difficulty, see A. D. Gayer *et al.*, pp. 276–303. John Hicks states (*Classics and Moderns*, p. 64) that "the internationalizing of fluctuations, spreading from one industrialized country to another, did not occur before the end of the nineteenth century." The crisis of 1836 was clearly an international affair engaging Britain and the United States, and the severe crisis of 1847–1848 engaged not only Britain and the United States but also Belgium, France, and Germany where railroadization had begun.

92. *Principles*, pp. 542–544.

93. *Ibid.*, p. 574.

94. *Ibid.*, p. 576.

95. *Ibid.*, pp. 650–651.

96. *Ibid.*, pp. 741–742. See also p. 750, where quite specifically Mill cites "the railway gambling of 1844 and 1845" as having "saved the country from a depression of profits and interest."

97. *Ibid.*, p. 174.

98. *Ibid.*, pp. 176–177.

99. *Ibid.*, pp. 178–180.

100. *Ibid.*, pp. 711, 713–714.

101. *Ibid.*, p. 185.

102. *Ibid.*, p. 713.

103. *Ibid.*, pp. 10–21.

104. *Ibid.*, pp. 18–21.

105. *Ibid.*, p. 968. Also, see preceding, p. 106.

106. *Ibid.*, p. 21.

107. *Ibid.*, p. 189.

108. *Ibid.*, p. 705. John M. Robson, in *The Improvement of Mankind,* notes that Book IV bears, to some controversial extent, the mark of Harriet Taylor Mill (pp. 58–61), and that Auguste Comte influenced Mill, *inter alia,* with his distinction between Statics and Dynamics, although Mill's interpretation differed from Comte's (pp. 87–100).

109. Mill, *Principles*, pp. 706.

110. *Ibid.*, p. 729.

111. *Ibid.*, pp. 706–707.

112. *Ibid.*, pp. 719–732.

113. *Ibid.*, p. 722.

114. *Ibid.*, p. 731.

115. *Ibid.*, pp. 731–732.

116. *Ibid.*, p. 754.

117. *Ibid.*, p. 754 n.a–a 48.

118. J. R. Hicks, *Classics and Moderns*, p. 68.

119. *Principles*, p. 755.

120. See, for example, J. A. Schumpeter, *History of Economic Analysis,* pp. 571–572. Samuel Hollander justly points out that Mill did not wholly rule out diminishing returns to "wholly or partially exhaustible" natural resources such as coal and most metals (*Economics of John Stuart Mill*, Vol. I, p. 450); and he was much impressed by W. S. Jevons, *The Coal Question,* 2nd edition (London: Macmillan, 1966). For a critical passage relevant to Mills' stationary state see pp. 370–376. Hollander concludes, therefore, that (*ibid.*) "[t]he full-fledged stationary state—constant technology, population, and capital with unchanged wages and profit rates—was thus an approximation."

121. See especially, Hont and Ignatieff, *Wealth and Virtue,* pp. 1–4, and *Wealth of Nations,* p. lviii. The key passage in Smith is the following:

> Among the savage nations of hunters and fishers, every individual who is able to work, is more or less employed in useful labour, and endeavours to provide, as well as he can, the necessaries and conveniencies of life, for himself, or such of his family or tribe as are either too old, or too young, or too infirm to go a hunting and fishing. Such nations, however, are so miserably poor, that from mere want, they are frequently reduced, or, at least, think themselves reduced, to the necessity sometimes of directly destroying, and sometimes of abandoning their infants, their old people, and those afflicted with lingering diseases, to perish with hunger, or to be devoured by wild beasts. Among civilized and thriving nations, on the contrary, though a great number of people do not labour at all, many of whom consume the produce of ten times, frequently of a hundred times more labour than the greater part of those who work; yet the produce of the whole labour of the society is so great, that all are often abundantly supplied, and a workman, even of the lowest and poorest order, if he is frugal and industrious, may enjoy a greater share of the necessaries and conveniencies of life than it is possible for any savage to acquire.

122. In *American State Papers, Encyclopaedia Britannica* (Chicago: University of Chicago Press, 1952), p. 271.

123. *Principles,* pp. 913–971.

124. *Ibid.,* p. 963.

125. *Ibid.,* p. 199. The bulk of Mill's discussion of socialism is to be found on pp. 199–234. But an important additional comment on socialism and competition is on pp. 794–795.

126. *Ibid.,* p. 202.

127. *Ibid.,* pp. 204–205.

128. *Ibid.,* p. 207.

129. *Ibid.,* pp. 207–208.

130. *Ibid.,* pp. 208–209.

131. *Ibid.,* pp. 794–795.

132. Joan Robinson, *An Essay on Marxian Economics* (London: Macmillan, 1942), p. 6.

133. Robert C. Tucker (ed.), *The Marx–Engels Reader,* 2d ed. (New York: W. W. Norton, 1978), p. 220. The passage is from a letter written on March 5, 1852, by Marx to his friend Joseph Weydemeyer, who had emigrated from Germany to the United States.

134. Robert C. Tucker (ed.), *ibid.,* pp. 4–5. The passage is from the preface to Marx's *A Contribution to the Critique of Political Economy.* For an evocation of Marx's transition from radical Hegelianism to political economy, and Engels's important role, see, for example, Peter F. Bell and Harry Cleaver, "Marx's Crisis Theory as a Theory of Class Struggle," *Research in Political Economy,* Vol. 5, (1982), especially pp. 195–208.

135. Marx, in a speech at Amsterdam on September 8, 1872, reaffirmed that for most countries on the Continent "the lever of our revolution must be force," but a peaceful transition to socialism might take place in Britain, the United States, and, perhaps, Holland. Tucker, *ibid.,* p. 523.

136. The first quotation is from *The Manifesto of the Communist Party* (1848) (*ibid.,* p. 491); the second, from *Critique of the Gotha Program* (1875) (*ibid.,* p. 531).

137. The adjectives are from this passage in Isaiah Berlin, *Karl Marx: His Life and Environment* (London: Oxford University Press, 1939), p. 137: "For Marx, no less than for earlier rationalists, man is potentially wise, creative, and free."

138. *Ibid.,* pp. 262–263. See, also, J. A. Schumpeter, *History of Economic Analysis,* p. 387: ". . . with every fact, with every argument that impinged upon him *in his reading,* he wrestled with such passionate zest as to be incessantly diverted from his main line of advance."

139. C. J. S. Sprigge, *Karl Marx* (London: Duckworth, 1938), p. 27.

140. I. Berlin, *Marx: Life,* p. 33. Berlin speculates tentatively on the link between Marx's "smouldering sense of resentment" and his family's ambiguous position as half-accepted converted Jews (pp. 25–28). Berlin describes the increased freedom for Jews initially granted by Napoleon; the subsequent retraction; the choice faced by Jews of either returning to the ghetto or converting to Christianity; the decision of Marx's father, Heinrich, to enter the Lutheran church in 1817, a year before the birth of his son Karl. The elder Marx found this framework for his life congenial; but in 1834 he confronted a crisis of conscience (p. 28):

> After his baptism he adopted the Christian name of Heinrich, and educated his family as liberal protestants, faithful to the existing order and to the reigning King of Prussia. Anxious as he was to identify that ruler with the ideal prince depicted by his favourite philosophers, the repulsive figure of Frederick William III defeated even his loyal imagination. Indeed, the only occasion on which this tremulous and retiring man is known to have behaved with courage, was a public dinner at which he made a speech on the desirability of moderate social and political reforms worthy of a wise and benevolent ruler. This swiftly drew upon him the attention of the Prussian Police. Heinrich Marx at once retracted everything, and convinced everyone of his complete harmlessness. It is not improbable that this slight but humiliating *contretemps,* and in particular his father's craven and submissive attitude, made a definite impression on Karl, then sixteen years old, and left behind it a smouldering sense of resentment which later events fanned into a flame.

141. I owe this reference to Ronald Hayman. It is also quoted in Jerrold Seigel, *Marx's Fate* (Princeton: Princeton University Press, 1978), pp. 367 and 386.

142. Alvin Johnson's autobiography (*Pioneer's Progress* [New York: Viking Press, 1952]; passages here taken from pp. 282–283) contains several further anecdotes on Veblen's affectation.

143. For Schumpeter's somewhat similar evaluation, see *Ten Great Economists: From Marx to Keynes* (London: Allen and Unwin, 1952), pp. 53–55.

144. *Capital*, Vol. I, p. 171.

145. For example, see Bell and Cleaver, *Marx's Crisis Theory*, pp. 254–255.

146. For a presentation and explanation of Marx's view of the determination of wages, see William J. Baumol, "Classical Economics: The Subsistence Wage and Demand–Supply Analysis: Marx and the Iron Law of Wages," *AEA Papers and Proceedings* (May 1983), pp. 303–308.

147. In the simple algebraic terms Marx used, the fall of the rate of profits is a matter of definition, as follows: Let V = variable capital (wage payments); C = constant capital (plant, machinery, raw material); S = surplus value (interest, profits, and rent). S/V is the rate of exploitation. C/V is the organic composition of capital. $S/(C + V)$ is the rate of profit. If the rate of exploitation is constant as Marx asserted, and the organic composition of capital is rising (that is, fixed capital per worker is increasing) the rate of profit must fall. As indicated elsewhere (pp. 128–129), this proposition got Marx into a dilemma he was never able to resolve. The profit rate could fall only with the increase in the organic composition of capital if real wages rose; and his system forbade him (or made it exceedingly difficult for him) to admit a rise in real wages.

148. For a terse but precise comparison of Marx (as opposed to Ricardo) on diminishing returns—and other departures of Marx from the classics—see Nicholas Kaldor, "Alternative Theories of Distribution," *The Review of Economic Studies*, Vol. XXIII (2), No. 61 (1955–1956), pp. 87–88.

149. Perhaps more significant of Marx's basic character as a "city boy" with virtually no knowledge of how food is produced is his praise of the bourgeoisie for having "rescued [via urbanization] a considerable part of the population from the idiocy of rural life" (Robert C. Tucker (ed.), *Marx–Engels Reader*, p. 477). For my views on some of the consequences of Marx's myopia about agriculture, see "Marx Was a City Boy or Why Communism May Fail," *Harpers Magazine* (February 1955), reprinted as Chapter 3 in my *Essays on a Half-Century* (Boulder: Westview Press, 1988).

150. See notably, Engels's letters to Joseph Bloch, Franz Mehring, and H. Starkenburg in Robert C. Tucker (ed.), *Marx–Engels Reader*, pp. 760–768.

151. From the *Communist Manifesto*, Robert C. Tucker (ed.), *Marx–Engels Reader*, p. 475.

152. *Capital*, Vol. I, p. 632.

153. The comments of Marx and Engels on Malthus are collected in Ronald L. Meek (ed.), *Marx and Engels on Malthus* (New York: International Publishers, 1954). The description of Malthus as a baboon is from *The Grundrisse*, in Robert C. Tucker (ed.), *Marx–Engels Reader*, p. 276. Samuel Hollander has written an effective critique of Marx's treatment of real wages in relation to population: "Marx and Malthusianism: Marx's Secular Path of Wages," *American Economic Review*, Vol. 74, No. 1 (March 1984), pp. 139–151.

154. From Engels's *Outline of a Critique of Political Economy*, in Ronald L. Meek (ed.), *Marx and Engels on Malthus*, p. 62.

155. From Engels's letter to Lange, in *ibid.*, p. 82.

156. The most extensive—but not the only—debate centering on this issue concerns the so-called transformation problem. It takes its start from the publication in 1894 of the first German edition of the third volume of *Capital*, put together by Engels from Marx's notes. The book opens with four chapters on the relation between surplus value and profit. Volume I of *Capital* opened with an exposition of value defined in terms of labor directly or indirectly embodied in commodities with surplus value expressed in terms of labor units and sometimes, even, hours of work. In effect, Marx undertook to transform his argument, initially presented in terms of use-value calculated in terms of

standard labor units, into conventional market values. The meaning (and technical correctness) of this transformation has been discussed in a literature well reviewed (down to 1971) by Paul A. Samuelson in "Understanding the Marxian Notion of Exploitation: A Summary of the So-Called Transformation Problem Between Marxian Values and Competitive Prices," *The Journal of Economic Literature,* Vol. IX (June 1971), pp. 339–431. One result of the explorations and debates on this issue is agreement that Marx's initial Volume I formulation would be valid only if capital–labor proportions (the organic composition of capital) were uniform throughout the economy—a most unlikely circumstance. For a contrary view, elaborated with erudition and subtlety, but which I find unpersuasive, see William J. Baumol, "The Transformation of Values: What Marx 'Really' Meant: An Interpretation," *Journal of Economic Literature,* Vol. XII (March 1974), pp. 51–62.

157. William Fellner, "Marxian Hypotheses and Observable Trends Under Capitalism: A 'Modernized' Interpretation," *Economic Journal,* Vol. LXVII, No. 265 (March, 1957), p. 22.

158. Joan Robinson, *Essay on Marxian Economics,* pp. 24–25.

159. Paul M. Sweezy, *The Theory of Capitalist Development* (New York: Oxford University Press, 1942) pp. 128–129.

160. Paul A. Samuelson, "Wages and Interest: A Modern Dissection of Marxian Economic Models," *American Economic Review,* Vol. XLVII (December 1957), p. 892. It should be noted, however, that in this and other writings on Marx, Samuelson scrupulously seeks to isolate what he regards as legitimate insights in Marx's formulations.

161. Robert C. Tucker (ed.), *Marx–Engels Reader,* pp. 479 and 483.

162. For example, *Capital,* Vol. I, p. 645:

> . . . within the capitalist system all methods for raising the social productiveness of labour are brought about at the cost of the individual labourer; all means for the development of production transform themselves into means of domination over, and exploitation of, the producers; they mutilate the labourer into a fragment of a man, degrade him to the level of an appendage of a machine, destroy every remnant of charm in his work and turn it into a hated toil; they estrange from him the intellectual potentialities of the labour-process in the same proportion as science is incorporated in it as an independent power; they distort the conditions under which he works, subject him during the labour-process to a despotism the more hateful for its meanness; they transform his lifetime into working-time, and drag his wife and child beneath the wheels of the Juggernaut of capital. But all methods for the production of surplus-value are at the same time methods of accumulation; and every extension of accumulation becomes again a means for the development of those methods.

> It follows therefore that in proportion as capital accumulates, the lot of the labourer, be his payment high or low, must grow worse. The law, finally, that always equilibrates the relative surplus-population, or industrial reserve army, to the extent and energy of accumulation, this law rivets the labourer to capital more firmly than the wedges of Vulcan did Prometheus to the rock. It establishes an accumulation of misery, corresponding with accumulation of capital. Accumulation of wealth at one pole is, therefore, at the same time accumulation of misery, agony of toil, slavery, ignorance, brutality, mental degradation, at the opposite pole, i.e., on the side of the class that produces its own product in the form of capital.

163. *Ibid.,* p. 619.

164. *Ibid.,* p. 639.

165. A useful bibliography on the standard-of-living question is to be found in Phyllis Deane, *The First Industrial Revolution* (Cambridge: at the University Press, 1967), pp. 285–286. Some further contributions to the debate are:

J. E. Williams, "The British Standard of Living, 1750–1850," *Economic History Review,* Vol. XIX, No. 3 (1966), pp. 581–589.

G. N. Von Tunzelman, "Trends in Real Wages, 1750–1850, Revisted," *Economic History Review,* 2d series, Vol. XXXII, No. 1 (February 1979), pp. 41–45.

Peter H. Lindert and Jeffrey G. Williamson, "English Workers' Living Standards During the

Industrial Revolution: A New Look,'' *Economic History Review,* Vol. XXXVI, No. 1 (February 1983), pp. 1–25.

M. W. Flinn, ''A Comment'' [on Lindert and Williamson, and their reply], *Economic History Review,* Vol. XXXVII, No. 1 (February, 1984), pp. 88–94.

L. D. Schwarz, ''The Standard of Living in the Long Run: London (1700–1860),'' *Economic History Review,* Vol. XXXVIII, No. 1 (February 1985), pp. 24–41.

166. Quoted in *Capital,* Vol. I, p. 371, from Mill's *Principles,* p. 756.

167. See especially, A. D. Gayer *et al., Growth and Fluctuation,* Vol. II, pp. 939–940 and discussion pp. 949–970. By National Bureau of Economic Research methods the average amplitude of money wage movement in specific cycles was 16.0 for textile wages, 14.7 for agricultural wages, and 3.6 for London artisans. The figure was 33.2 for cost of living.

168. The liveliest and most sophisticated exploration of the Marxian dilemma is Paul A. Samuelson's *Wages and Interest.* His footnotes embrace the considerable modern literature on this problem. For a later Marxian model of economic growth, see David Laibman, ''Toward a Marxian Model of Economic Growth,'' *Radical Economics* in *American Economic Review* (February 1977), pp. 387–392.

169. *Ibid.,* p. 895.

170. *Capital,* Vol. I, extracted, in order, from pp. 631–633, 624–628, 638–640.

171. Franz M. Oppenheimer called to my attention the following affirmation that Marx once visited a German factory but never set foot in a British factory. Ricard Friedenthal, *Karl Marx, Sein Leben und Seine Zeit,* (Munich: Deutscher Taschen Verlag, 1983), p. 417: ''Marx hat, was oft berkmerkt worden ist, nie eine englische Fabrik aufgesucht und nur einmal, auf der Badereise nach Karlsbad, in eine deutsche Fabrik flüchtig hineingeblickt.'' (''As has been often noted, Marx never visited an English factory and only once made a casual visit to a German factory in Badereise near Karlsbad'').

172. K. Marx, *Grundrisse: Foundations of the Critique of Political Economy* (in a rough draft), translated with a foreword by Martin Nicolaus (London: Allen Lane, 1973), p. 704. For a somewhat revisionist view, see Donald Mac Kenzie, ''Marx and the Machine,'' *Technology and Culture,* Vol. 25, No. 3 (July 1984), pp. 473–502. Mac Kenzie argues that Marx's simpler formulations of the role of machinery in shaping society are inadequate and that a complex interaction occurred. Typically, he is able to cite passages from Marx of both types.

173. *Capital,* Vol. I, pp. 506–507.

174. See, especially, ''Genesis of the Industrial Capitalist,'' Chapter XXXI of *Capital,* Vol. I, pp. 750–760.

175. For precise references and discussion, see W. W. Rostow, *How It All Began* (New York: McGraw-Hill, 1975), pp. 148–151 and 251. These passages and references include G. N. Clark's reply to Hessen's interpretation of Newton. This gap in Marxism was not filled until B. Hessen, a Soviet historian of science, delivered a paper in London in 1931. Hessen argued that Newton ''was the typical representative of the rising bourgeoisie,'' and that ''the scheme of physics was mainly determined by the economic and technical tasks which the rising bourgeoisie raised to the forefront.''

176. It should be noted that Marx's fascination with machinery led to considerable discussion of the inner logic and dynamics of what he called ''a machinery system''; that is, by a group of machines systematically related to each other. See, especially, *Capital,* Vol. I, pp. 378–386.

177. For an analysis of this characteristic of conventional economic theory, see W. W. Rostow, ''Technology and the Price System,'' Chapter 4 in *Why the Poor Get Richer and the Rich Slow Down* (Austin: University of Texas Press, 1980).

178. Paul A. Samuelson, ''Marxian Economics as Economics,'' *American Economic Review,* Vol. 57, No. 2 (May 1967), reprinted in *The Collected Scientific Papers of Paul A. Samuelson,* edited by Robert C. Merton (Cambridge: M.I.T. Press, 1973), Vol. 3, pp. 268–275. Wassily Leontief's depression-conditioned evaluation of 1937 should also be noted (''The Significance of

Marxian Economics for Present-Day Economic Theory,'' *American Economic Review* (March 1938 supplement), pp. 5 and 8–9):

> However important these technical contributions to the progress of economic theory, in the present-day appraisal of Marxian achievements they are overshadowed by his brilliant analysis of the long-run tendencies of the capitalistic system. The record is indeed impressive: increasing concentration of wealth, rapid elimination of small and medium-sized enterprise, progressive limitation of competition, incessant technological progress accompanied by the ever-growing importance of fixed capital, and, last but not least, the undiminishing amplitude of recurrent business cycles—an unsurpassed series of prognostications of fulfilled, against which modern economic theory with all its refinements has little to show indeed. . . .
> Marx had also his rational theories, but these theories in general do not hold water. Their inherent weakness shows up as soon as other economists not endowed with the exceptionally realistic sense of the master try to proceed on the basis of his blueprints.

179. See, for example, Ernest Mandel, *Late Capitalism,* translated by Joris De Pres (London: [Verso Ed.]. 1978). I reviewed this study in *The Journal of Economic History,* Vol. XXXIX, No. 3 (September 1979), pp. 849–850.

180. Walter Ellis, *The Classical Theory of Economic Growth* (New York: St. Martin's Press, 1984), p. 306.

181. See, especially, *Capital,* Vol. II, Chapters XX and XXI, the latter unfinished.

182. *Ibid.* Quesnay is one of the exceedingly few economists for whom Marx expressed virtually unreserved praise and respect. On the linkage between Quesnay and Marx's reproduction model, see, P. Sweezy, *Capitalist Development,* p. 75; all of the Chapters V and X; and Appendix A (by Shigeto Tsuru), pp. 365–374, ''On Reproduction Schemes, Relating Quesnay, Marx and Keynes.'' For further observations on Marx and Quesnay, see J. A. Schumpeter, *History of Economic Analysis,* pp. 238–243, 391, and 566, n. 25. See, also, *Quesnay's Tableau Économique,* edited, with new material, translations, and notes, by Marguerite Kuczynski and Ronald L. Meek (London: Macmillan, 1972).

183. See, for example, Paul M. Sweezy's discussion of Michael Tugan-Baranowsky, Rosa Luxemburg, Bulgakov, Lenin, and Otto Bauer, *Capitalist Development,* pp. 162–189; also Joan Robinson, *Essay on Marxian Economics,* pp. 57–60, who supplies her own version of the theory Marx ''intended to work out'' from his extended reproduction system.

184. Paul A. Samuelson, (''Marxian Economics as Economics''), p. 269.

185. ''Marx's Crisis Theory,'' pp. 191–192.

186. Isaiah Berlin, *Marx: Life* p. 215. Berlin goes on to observe that the crisis of 1857 had a severe negative consequence for Marx: it reduced Engels's income (and thus Marx's) ''at a moment when he could least afford it.''

187. P. F. Bell and H. Cleaver (''Marx's Crisis Theory,'' pp. 209–210) note that the first volume of *Capital* was completed before the crisis of 1866. They note also, however, that Marx delivered two lectures in June 1865 that bear on the cyclical process (published as *Wages, Price and Profit*). Marx argued strongly that labor should struggle for higher wages, at a time of prosperity and strong labor market leverage, as in 1865, even if success should help bring on crisis, depression, and unemployment.

188. W. W. Rostow, *World Economy: History and Prospect,* (Austin: University of Texas Press, 1978), pp. 315 and 324–325.

189. *Capital,* Vol. I, p. 20. The reference is to the afterword to the second German edition, dated January 24, 1873. The monthly cyclical peak for Britain came as early as September 1872. The text of Marx's observation follows:

> The contradictions inherent in the movement of capitalist society impress themselves upon the practical bourgeois most strikingly in the changes of the periodic cycle, through which modern industry runs, and whose crowning point is the universal crisis. That crisis is once again approaching, although as yet but in its preliminary stage; and by the universality of its theatre and

the intensity of its action it will drum dialectics even into the heads of the mushroom-upstarts of the new, holy Prusso-German empire.

190. Isaiah Berlin, *Marx: Life*, p. 234.

191. Joan Robinson, *Essays on Marxian Economics*, p. 59. On precisely this point see also Henry Smith, "Marx and the Trade Cycle," *The Review of Economic Studies*, Vol. IV, No. 3 (June, 1937), pp. 192–204.

192. *Capital*, Vol. III, pp. 244–245 and 484. For Joan Robinson's discussion of these passages, *Essays on Marxian Economics*, pp. 56–60. Also P. Sweezy, *Capitalist Development*, pp. 156–189, and Maurice Dobb, *On Economic Theory and Socialism* (London: Routledge and Kegan Paul, 1955), pp. 197–198.

193. *Capital*, Vol. II, p. 410.

194. *Capital*, Vol. I, pp. 453–454.

195. See also Marx's chronology for the cotton industry, 1845–1865, *Capital*, Vol. III, pp. 124–137.

196. Gerhard Mensch, *Stalemate in Technology: Innovations Overcome Depression* (Cambridge, Mass.: Ballinger, 1979, first published in German in 1975).

197. *Capital*, Vol. II, p. 186.

198. Thomas Kuczynski, "Marx and Engels on 'Long Waves,' " Institute of Economic History of the Academy of Sciences of the GDR, Berlin. (Unpublished paper delivered at the International Meeting on Long-Term Fluctuations in Economic Growth: Their Causes and Consequences, Weimar, GDR, June 10–14, 1985, sponsored by International Institute of Applied Systems Analysis, Laxenberg, Austria.)

199. For a typically aggressive and abusive footnote of Marx's on diminishing returns, focused mainly but not exclusively on J. S. Mill, see *Capital*, Vol. I, p. 506.

200. *Grundrisse*, p. 107. For further argument along these lines, see pp. 252–253 and 275–278.

201. For references and discussion of this point, see P. Sweezy, *Capitalist Development*, p. 67; J. A. Schumpeter, *Economic Analysis*, pp. 569 and 647–654.

202. *Capital*, Vol. I, pp. 504–507.

203. *Capital*, Vol. III, pp. 614–813. These passages deal with rent derived from mines, favorably located building sites, etc., as well as rent for agricultural land.

204. *Ibid.*, p. 781.

205. *Ibid.*, p. 643.

206. *Ibid.*

207. *Ibid.*, pp. 105–141.

208. *Manifesto of the Communist Party* in Robert C. Tucker, (ed.), *Marx–Engels Reader*, p. 475.

209. *Ibid.*, p. 481.

210. Paul Sweezy, *Capitalist Development*, p. 192. For a lucid study of Marx's thin portrait of the breakdown of capitalism and subsequent efforts to fill the gap, see F. R. Hansen, *The Breakdown of Capitalism, A History of the Idea in Western Marxism, 1883–1983* (London: Routledge and Kegan Paul, 1985), especially (on Marx) pp. 1–31.

211. F. Engels, "Socialism: Utopian and Scientific," a pamphlet derived from his *Herr Eugen Dühring's Revolution in Science* (or *Anti-Dühring*), accessibly reprinted in Robert C. Tucker (ed.), *Marx–Engels Reader*, p. 713.

212. *Ibid.*, p. 715.

213. Marx's notes are to be found in Karl Marx and Friedrich Engels, *Werke*, Vol. 18 (Berlin: Dietz Verlag, 1962), pp. 599–642. Robert C. Tucker (ed.), *Marx–Engels Reader*, includes brief passages in English, pp. 542–548.

214. Robert C. Tucker (ed.), *ibid.*, p. 545.

215. J. A. Schumpeter, *Economic Analysis*, p. 392.

216. Marx wrote two articles on India, the first, from which the present quotation comes, being

published on June 25, 1853 in the *New York Tribune,* reprinted in Robert C. Tucker (ed.), *Marx–Engels Reader,* p. 653.

217. I. Berlin, *Marx: Life,* pp. 257–258.

218. Herbert Dingle, "Copernicus and the Planets," in *The History of Science, a Symposium* (Glencoe, Ill.: Free Press, 1951), p. 37.

219. George Santayana, *Character and Opinion in the United States* (London: Constable, 1920), pp. 167–168. The context of the quoted phrases is the following:

> . . . human discourse is intrinsically addressed not to natural existing things but to ideal essences, poetic or logical terms which thought may defined and play with. When fortune or necessity diverts our attention from this congenial ideal sport to crude facts and pressing issues, we turn our frail poetic ideas into symbols for those terrible irruptive things. In that paper money of our own stamping, the legal tender of the mind, we are obliged to reckon all the movements and values of the world.

220. Robert C. Tucker (ed.), *Marx–Engels Reader,* p. 489.

221. *The Stages of Economic Growth* (Cambridge: at the University Press, 1960, 1971), pp. 149–150. Marx understood well the critical analytic importance of the question of the individual and society. The *Grundrisse* begins, in fact, with this issue (pp. 83–85). Marx argues that in the long sweep of history man was always a dependent social animal, rather than an individual—dependent on family, clan, and larger units. He views the eighteenth century as an exceptional period when "various forms of social connectedness confront the individual as a mere means towards his private purposes, as an external necessity." He regards this perspective as inappropriate in the inherently intensively socialized setting of a modern industrial society, where man is "an animal which can individuate itself only in the midst of society." What Marx misses here is the insistence of human beings on asserting in significant ways their uniqueness, despite acceptance—within families and larger collective units—of the inescapable disciplines of life as a social animal, even the disciplines of an industrial society.

222. Quoted, Jerrold Seigel, *Marx's Fate,* p. 387.

223. *Ibid.,* pp. 387–389. In a considerable *tour de force,* Seigel traces the continuity in the pattern of Marx's life from his relations with his parents, his doctoral dissertation on Democritus, his recurrent self-induced illnesses ["aggression against his own body"], his incapacity to complete *Capital* as "reality failed to fulfill [his] expectations."

Chapter 5

1. H. W. Arndt:

> The classical economists from Adam Smith to Ricardo had been intensely interested in economic growth because they thought it desirable and because they advocated government policies which they believed would promote it, chiefly policies of *laissez-faire,* of less government interference. By the mid-nineteenth century, these policies had been substantially adopted, with spectacular success. It did not need economists to advocate material progress which was conspicuously under way. Instead, economists, apart from pursuing the scientific task of improving and perfecting the analytical work of the classics on the working of a market economy, felt it increasingly necessary to direct their attention to the evils, or at least the blemishes, of the existing system—inequality in the distribution of income and wealth, the growth of monopolies and combines, the trade cycle and unemployment.

(H. W. Arndt, *The Rise and Fall of Economic Growth* [Melbourne: Longman Cheshire, 1978], p. 14.)

Mark Blaug:

> Whether we look at Smith, Ricardo or John Stuart Mill, the economic problem is seen in essence as a contrast between nonaugmentable land and augmentable labor, with capital subsumed under

the latter as stored-up wealth. The function of economic analysis is to reveal the effects of changes in the quantity and quality of the labor force upon the rate of growth of aggregate output. . . .

After 1870, however, economists typically posited some given supply of productive factors, determined independently by elements outside the purview of analysis. The essence of the economic problem was to search for the conditions under which given productive services were allocated with optimal results among competing uses, optimal in the sense of maximizing consumers' satisfactions. . . . For the first time, economics truly became the science that studies the relationship between *given* ends and *given* scarce means that have alternative uses. The classical theory of economic development was replaced by the concept of general equilibrium within an essentially static framework.

(Mark Blaug, *Economic Theory in Retrospect* [Homewood, Illinois: Richard D. Irwin, 1968], pp. 299–300.)

Phyllis Deane:

> . . . [T]he work of Jevons, Walras and Menger marked the beginnings of a major change in economists' views on the scope and methodology of their discipline. . . .
>
> The marginal revolution had significant implications for both the scope and methodology of orthodox economic theory. For in providing the theorist with a convenient set of analytical tools that were easily and effectively applied over a wide range of uses it changed the problem orientation of economic orthodoxy and (in the process though not necessarily by design) associated with that orthodoxy significant philosophical and ideological tendencies. . . . Within the conventional assumptions of the marginal analysis it can be logically shown that perfect competition leads to equimarginal allocation of expenditures and resources.

(Phyllis Deane, *The Evolution of Economic Ideas* [Cambridge: at the University Press, 1978], pp. 97–98.)

Robert Heilbroner:

> . . . [T]he great intellectual bombshell that Marx had prepared went off in almost total silence; instead of a storm of abuse, Marx met the far more crushing ignominy of indifference.
>
> For economics had ceased to be the proliferation of world views which now in the hands of a philosopher, now a stockbroker, now a revolutionary seemed to illuminate the whole avenue down which society was marching. It became instead the special province of professors whose probings were more in the nature of pinpoint beams than the wide searching beacons the earlier economists had thrown out over the misty seas ahead.
>
> "". . . [T]he Victorian boom gave rise to a roster of elucidators, men who would examine the workings of the system in greatest detail, but who would no longer ask penetrating questions as to its basic merits or cast troublesome doubts over its eventual fate. In the new professordom, men like Alfred Marshall, Stanley Jevons, John Bates Clark, Leon Walras, Taussig, Menger—a whole faculty of economists—took over the main line of economic thought. Their contributions were often important, yet they were not vital.

(Robert Heilbroner, *The Worldly Philosophers: The Lives, Times, and Ideas of the Great Economic Thinkers* [New York: Simon and Schuster, 1961], p. 145.)

John Hicks:

> The sixty years from 1870 to 1930 were in Britain the time of the rise of the Labour Movement; thus it is not surprising that the British post-classics (Marshall, Edgeworth and Pigou in particular) should have had labour problems very much on their minds. It seemed to them that their marginal utility analysis was well fitted to deal with such problems; nowadays this may seem more doubtful.

(John Hicks, *Classics and Moderns*, Vol. III [Cambridge: Harvard University Press, 1983], p. 71.)

Karl Pribram:

> Until the fourth decade of the present [twentieth] century, problems of economic growth were ignored by almost all post-Ricardian economists. Their theories had been built around the prob-

lems of pricing and allocating scarce resources in an optimal way, and they remained true to the essentially static Ricardian approach to economic analysis. . . .

The indifference to the problems of economic growth shown by the post-Ricardian and marginalist economists provides a good example for the overwhelming influence of methodological considerations on the choice of scientific problems. No tools appeared to be available to analyze long-range developments. The economic movements which were taken into consideration were almost exclusively of the short-range type. . . .

(Karl Pribram, *A History of Economic Reasoning* [Baltimore: John Hopkins University Press, 1983], p. 550.)

Eric Roll:

It has been customary to regard the changes made in the apparatus of economic analysis in the 'seventies as marking a complete revolution in economics. . .

One interpretation of the marginal school has proclaimed it as the economics of the rentier class. It links the development of a subjective and "unhistorical" method in economics (which takes consumption as its starting point) with the rise of a class of people who live by "clipping coupons." This leisure class, it is said, is no longer a part of the process of production and is interested exclusively in the disposal of the income from its investments. It is Veblen's class of absentee owners, and it is natural that it should consider economic activity solely from the point of view of consumption.

(Eric Roll, *A History of Economic Thought*, 3d ed. [Englewood Cliffs, New Jersey: Prentice-Hall, 1956, 1957], pp. 368–369.)

Joseph Schumpeter:

. . . [I]t was around 1870 that a new interest in social reform, a new spirit of "historicism," and a new activity in the field of economic "theory" began to assert themselves. . . . [T]here occurred breaks with tradition as distinct as we can ever expect to observe in what must always be fundamentally a continuous process. . . .

But all the qualifications that are necessary in order to prevent periodization from becoming misleading—or downright nonsense—should not blind us to the fact that the period we are about to discuss [1870–1914] actually forms a real unit, which would have to be recognized quite irrespective of the claims of expository convenience. The breaks with tradition around 1870 were meant to be breaks by the men whose names are associated with them: they may have looked to those men more abrupt and more important than they do to the historian, but this does not mean that they were wholly imaginary.

(Joseph A. Schumpeter, *History of Economic Analysis* [New York: Oxford University Press, 1954], p. 753.)

Henry Spiegel:

Conventional economics as exemplified by John Stuart Mill's writings, against which Marx and his followers launched their attack, did not stand still but underwent during the closing decades of the nineteenth century a profound transformation often designated as the "marginal revolution." When this revolution had run its course at the turn of the century, both the structure of economics and its method differed sharply from the political economy of the classics. The labor theory of value was shed, and with the help of a new unifying principle there was accomplished the integration of the theories of the consumer and of the firm, as well as the integration of the theories of value and distribution, which had been only loosely connected in classical thought. . . . There was less emphasis on economic growth, with which Adam Smith had been so greatly concerned. Instead, the attempt to locate equilibrium positions was made within a framework in which the total quantity of resources was given. Economics became the science treating of the allocation of a given quantum of total resources, which meant that little attention continued to be devoted to the question of how this quantum was determined and how it could be increased. . . .

The economic discussion thus shifted its attention from total quantities to small changes in these totals. One of its central concepts became the equilibrium which equated certain variables and maximized others. Since the equilibrium was primarily employed in microeconomics and centered around the consumer and the firm, such matters as the macroeconomics of national income determination and the economics of growth and development were not among the themes that ranked prominently in this discussion. They had to wait until attention was eventually accorded to them as the twentieth century progressed.

(Henry William Spiegel, *The Growth of Economic Thought* [Englewood Cliffs, N.J.: Prentice-Hall, 1971], pp. 505–506.)

Although it does not lend itself to summary quotation, perhaps the best evocation of the turning point of the 1870s is the first chapter in T. W. Hutchison, *A Review of Economic Doctrines, 1870–1929* (Oxford: at the Clarendon Press, 1953): "Political Economy in England after 1870," pp. 1–31. See also Hutchison's *On Revolutions and Progress in Economic Knowledge,* especially Chapter 3, "The Decline and Fall of English Classical Political Economy and the Jevonian Revolution," pp. 58–93. Hutchison argues (pp. 92–93) that by overthrowing Ricardian distribution theory the Jevonian analysis "opened up the whole question of poverty and social reform," while the principle of diminishing utility was to be evoked in support of progressive taxation.

2. John Williams, "The Theory of International Trade Reconsidered," *Economic Journal,* Vol. XXXIX, No. 154, (June 1929), pp. 195–209.

3. The adjectives set off by quotation marks are from John F. Kennedy's often repeated definition of the group that had to be won over by a victorious candidate in an American presidential election. For context, see my *Diffusion of Power* (New York: Macmillan, 1972), p. 129.

4. See "Explanations of the Great Depression," Chapter VII in my *Essays on the British Economy of the Nineteenth Century* (Oxford: at the Clarendon Press, 1948), pp. 145–160. Schumpeter also dealt with the falling price trend in the context of his analysis of Kondratieff cycles (discussed, *ibid.,* pp. 28–30). See also pp. 176–178 and 181–182, above.

5. J. M. Keynes, *Essays in Biography,* p. 201.

6. For further discussion in a wider context, see W. W. Rostow, *The World Economy: History and Prospect* (Austin: Texas University Press, 1978), pp. 58–61 and 729–731 (notes 9–12).

7. For elaboration, see *ibid.,* Chapter 14, especially pp. 163–178.

8. See, for example, A. W. Coats, "The Origins and Early Development of the Royal Economic Society," *Economic Journal,* Vol. LXXVIII, No. 310 (June 1968), pp. 349–371; and A. W. Coats and S. E. Coats, "The Changing Social Composition of the Royal Economic Society, 1890–1960 and the Professionalization of Economics," *British Journal of Sociology,* Vol. 24 (1974), pp. 165–187. For the more complex story of the creation of the American Economic Association and the conflicts of ideology and method that marked its early days, see A. W. Coats, "The First Two Decades of the American Economic Association," *American Economic Review,* Vol. L, No. 4 (September 1960), pp. 555–574.

Chapter 6

1. Gerald M. Meier and Dudley Seers (eds.), *Pioneers in Development* (New York: Oxford University Press, 1984), pp. 229–261.

2. Alfred Marshall, *Principles of Economics,* 8th ed. (London: Macmillan, 1930), p. 461.

3. *Ibid.,* pp. 805–812. See also Marshall's treatment of the case of Exceptional Supply, paras. 8–10, Appendix J, *Money Credit and Commerce* (London: Macmillan, 1903), pp. 351–356.

4. J. K. Whitaker (ed.), *The Early Economic Writings of Alfred Marshall, 1867–1890* Vol. I, (London: Macmillan, 1975), pp. 97–98.

5. Quoted *ibid.,* p. 84. The context is a letter to L. C. Colson, written in 1908 or 1909.

6. *Principles,* pp. xv and xvii.

7. *Early Writings: Marshall,* Vol. I, pp. 4–5.

8. *Principles,* pp. x–xi. One of the best statements of Marshall's view of mathematics and (unlike Jevons) his determination to combine formal theory with empirical data and a historical perspective

is that of G. F. Shove, "The Place of Marshall's *Principles* in the Development of Economic Theory," *Economic Journal*, Vol. LII, No. 208 (December 1942), especially pp. 307–309.

9. J. K. Whitaker, *Early Writings: Marshall*, pp. 106–107.

10. See, notably, J. M. Keynes, "Alfred Marshall, 1842–1924," in A. C. Pigou (ed.), *Memorials of Alfred Marshall* (London: Macmillan, 1925), pp. 9–11. It is perhaps appropriate to note that, while the seriousness of Marshall's moral commitments was unquestionable, he lacked a sense of humor in matters of morality and could be sententious. See, especially, his nephew's testimony, Claude W. Guillebaud, "Some Personal Reminiscenses of Alfred Marshall," *History of Political Economy*, Vol. 3, No. 1 (Spring 1971), especially pp. 2–4.

11. Clark Kerr, *Marshall, Marx, and Modern Times* (Cambridge: at the University Press, 1969), p. 7.

12. Quoted, J. M. Keynes, "Marshall," p. 9.

13. Quoted, *ibid.*, p. 10.

14. Quoted, *ibid.*

15. J. K. Whitaker, *Early Writings: Marshall*, Vol. I, p. 8. The phrase is used in a letter to James Ward, the Cambridge psychologist.

16. Quoted in Roy Harrod, *The Life of John Maynard Keynes* (New York: Harcourt Brace, 1951), pp. 193–194.

17. *Principles*, pp. ix, xiii, and xiv. Modern science is less confident that nature never makes a jump. See, for example, James Gleick, *Chaos: Making a Science* (New York: Viking, 1987), pp. 160–174, on "phase transitions" and other discontinuities.

18. *Early Writings: Marshall*, Vol. 2, p. 352.

19. Lionel Robbins, *The Theory of Economic Development in the History of Economic Thought* (London: Macmillan, 1968), p. 17.

20. J. M. Keynes, "Marshall," pp. 18–21.

21. *Early Writings: Marshall*, p. 306.

22. Whitaker's summary is at *ibid.*, pp. 305–309; Marshall's text pp. 309–316. Whitaker elaborated his analysis of Marshall's thought at this early, formative period (probably 1881–1882) in "Alfred Marshall: the Years 1877 to 1885," *History of Political Economy*, Vol. 4 (Spring 1972), and "The Marshallian System in 1881: Distribution and Growth," *Economic Journal*, Vol. 84, No. 333 (March 1974). For a rare reference to Marshall's early version of a neoclassical growth model, see Sukahamoy Chakravarty, *Alternative Approaches to a Theory of Economic Growth: Marx, Marshall and Schumpeter* (Calcutta: Longman, 1980), pp. 8–11. The following equations are from Marshall's text in Whitaker, *ibid.*, pp. 309–316.

> If g be the gross real income of the country, n the number and e the average efficiency of the workers in it, w the amount of wealth in it, F the fertility of its natural resources above and below the surface of the ground (this fertility being regarded as itself a product of the extent, the average richness and the convenience of situation of these resources), A the state of the arts of production, and S the state of public security, then we have:

$$g = f_1(n,e,w,F,A,S) \qquad (1)$$

> If s be the net incomes available for saving, $f_2(e)$ the average necessaries of a population whose average efficiency is e, [and] T the taxes that have to be paid for the maintenance of public security, [we have]:

$$s = g - T - nf_2(e) \qquad (2)$$

> Since w is the wealth of the country therefore dw/dt is the rate of saving. [If] D is the rate of discount at which people on the average discount future enjoyments, A' the strength of the family affections, and i is the rate of interest, then:

$$\frac{dw}{dt} = f_3(s,D,A',i) \qquad (3)$$

If E be the evenness of distribution of incomes, [then]:

$$\frac{dn}{dt} = f_4(n,e,g,E,A',D) \qquad\qquad (4)$$

$$\frac{de}{dt} = f_5(n,e,g,E,A',D)$$

E may perhaps be regarded provisionally as measured by the ratio which the aggregate of the incomes bears to the sum of the differences between each individual income and the mean income: it depends so largely on causes which are not properly economic that in this stage at all events it must be accepted by the economist as an ultimate fact from the statistician or the historian.

23. *Ibid.*, pp. 309–312.
24. *Ibid.*, p. 309.
25. *Principles*, p. 203.
26. *Ibid.*, p. 322.
27. *Ibid.*, p. 223.
28. *Ibid.*, pp. 136–137.
29. *Ibid.*, p. 321n.
30. Marshall consistently draws a distinction between material progress (or rate of real earnings) and standard of life, which implies ''an increase of intelligence and energy and self-respect'' (for example, *ibid.*, p. 688). He argues that an increase in the latter will yield a rise in ''the national dividend'' as well as a rise in real wages.
31. *Ibid.*, pp. 714–715.
32. *Ibid.*, p. 722.
33. *Ibid.*, p. xxxii.
34. *Ibid.*, pp. 173–219. To a degree, these passages are foreshadowed in Alfred Marshall and Mary Paley Marshall, *The Economics of Industry* (London: Macmillan, 1879), pp. 8–12 and 27–35. The treatment in the *Principles* is more elaborate, introduces a much wider range of empirical material, and is less didactic.
35. *Principles*, p. 173.
36. *Ibid.*, p. 192.
37. *Ibid.*, p. 197.
38. *Ibid.*, p. 201.
39. On this theme Marshall ends up (*ibid.*, p. 205, n. 2) with a passage that anticipates, to a degree, both J. M. Keynes's peroration to the *General Theory* and Schumpeter on early and late stages of innovations.

> In this connection it is worth while to notice that the full importance of an epoch-making idea is often not perceived in the generation in which it is made: it starts the thoughts of the world on a new track, but the change of direction is not obvious until the turning-point has been left some way behind. In the same way the mechanical inventions of every age are apt to be underrated relatively to those of earlier times. For a new discovery is seldom fully effective for practical purposes till many minor improvements and subsidiary discoveries have gathered themselves around it: an invention that makes an epoch is very often a generation older than the epoch which it makes. Thus it is that each generation seems to be chiefly occupied in working out the thoughts of the preceding one; while the full importance of its own thoughts is as yet not clearly seen.

40. *Ibid.*, p. 212.
41. *Ibid.*, pp. 217–218.
42. *Ibid.*, p. 180n.
43. *Ibid.*, pp. 314 and 317.
44. *Ibid.*, p. 151, n. 2, Marshall notes that ''most of the migrations of which history tells'' were caused by diminishing returns, beginning with Abraham's departure described thus in Gen. 13:6:

"The land was not able to bear them, that they might dwell together; for their substance was great, so that they could not dwell together."

45. *Ibid.*, p. 153.

46. *Ibid.*, pp. 229–230.

47. *Ibid.*, pp. 232–233.

48. *Ibid.*, p. 236.

49. *Ibid.*, pp. 298–300. *Buddenbrooks*, published in 1901, is of about the same vintage as Marshall's *Principles*, although there is no suggestion of any influence running from one book to the other. Modern industry was, however, an old-enough phenomenon in Germany as well as Britain for a generational cycle to be noted.

50. *Ibid.*, p. 304.

51. *Ibid.*, p. 277 n. 1.

52. *Ibid.*, pp. 274–277.

53. *Ibid.*, pp. 315–316.

54. *Ibid.*, p. xiii.

55. In *Principles* Marshall refers back and quotes from the business cycle passage in *The Economics of Industry* on pp. 711–712, including the note that begins on the former page; in his submission to the Royal Commission on The Depression of Trade and Industry, he again quotes the critical passage (*Official Papers by Alfred Marshall*, J. M. Keynes [ed.], [London: Macmillan, 1926], pp. 7–9; and in *Money, Credit, and Commerce*, pp. 247–251). The passage does not appear in *Industry and Trade* (London: Macmillan, 1919; reprinted New York: Augustus M. Kelley, 1970, Reprints of Economic Classics).

56. For comments on Mill in relation to Marshall's view of the business cycle, see J. A. Schumpeter, *History of Economic Analysis*, p. 747. For a detailed account and analysis of the major cycle 1868–1879, see W. W. Rostow, *British Trade Fluctuations, 1868–1896* (New York: Arno Press, 1981) (1940 doctoral thesis), pp. 15–176.

57. *Economics of Industry*, pp. 152–155.

58. *Ibid.*, pp. 155–167.

59. *Ibid.*, pp. 156–157.

60. See W. W. Rostow, *British Trade Fluctuations, 1868–1896*, pp. 165–180 and 542–566 for relevant data and analysis.

61. *Economics of Industry*, pp. 162–163.

62. *Ibid.*, pp. 165–167.

63. *Ibid.*, p. 155n.

64. J. M. Keynes (ed.), *Official Papers*, especially pp. 90–101.

65. *Ibid.*, pp. 98–101.

66. *Principles*, pp. 711–712.

67. *Money, Credit, and Commerce*, pp. 238–253.

68. A. C. Pigou (ed.), *Memorials of Alfred Marshall*, pp. 60–65.

69. *History of Economic Analysis*, p. 747. But see also Schumpeter's more substantive observation in his *Ten Great Economists* that is similar to my conclusion that Marshall failed to translate the insights of his aggregate growth model and those of Book IV into a growth concept capable of linkage to his concept of the business cycle. Schumpeter points to Book VI rather than Book IV (p. 106):

> Well, I suppose we have got to recognize a third type of theory [in addition to partial and general static equilibrium analysis]—in my own workshop it is called "aggregative." Of course, he did not link up his treatment of such aggregative quantities with money. His failure to do so, in spite of his many and important discoveries in monetary theory . . . is perhaps the only fundamental criticism that I should level against him. But really, if one starts from partial analysis and then wishes to say something about the economic process as a whole, is it not natural that, despairing of the possibilities of the unwieldy idea of general equilibrium, one should turn to aggregative

theory? And would not then the theory of money automatically come in, to use Mrs. Robinson's phrase, as the theory of total output and employment?

70. *Principles,* pp. 317 and 342–343. See also references on pp. 342–350, 377, and 459–460.

71. Marshall had, in fact, formulated the concept of Normal Value as determined by Normal Expenses of production in the late 1870s. His passage on the business cycle in *The Economics of Industry* concludes as follows (pp. 166–167):

> When the wages of any class of labourers have been raised by a rise in the price of the commodity produced by them, the rapidity with which an additional supply of labour comes into the trade depends on the relation in which these wages stand to those of other trades. If the wages in this trade are abnormally high relatively to others, the rise is likely to attract so much additional labour, as to prevent the upward movement of wages from going very far, and to make them fall fast and far when the time of depression comes. On the other hand, if, before the rise came, the wages were below their Normal level relatively to other trades, the rise may go on for a long time without bringing in much additional labour, and whatever rise is gained will probably be maintained.
>
> Thus we see how the Law that Normal value is determined by Normal Expenses of production is consistent with the fact that market fluctuations of value are the cause and not the consequence of market fluctuations of Expenses of production. If Ricardo and Mill had taken more pains to make clear the distinctions between the theory of Normal value and that of Market value, there could not have been as much controversy as there has been on the question whether value is governed by Expenses of production, or Expenses of production by value.

72. *General Theory,* p. 292. For discussion in the context of the post-1873 price decline, see W. W. Rostow, *British Economy of the Nineteenth Century* (Oxford: at the Clarendon Press, 1948), pp. 61–63.

73. *Ibid.,* pp. 295–296. Keynes then modifies the underlying assumptions, concluding less sharply (*ibid.,* p. 296):

> Thus we must first consider the effect of changes in the quantity of money on the quantity of effective demand; and the increase in effective demand will, generally speaking, spend itself partly in increasing the quantity of employment and partly in raising the level of prices. Thus instead of constant prices in conditions of unemployment, and of prices rising in proportion to the quantity of money in conditions of full employment, we have in fact a condition of prices rising gradually as employment increases.

Here, in fact, is how production, prices, and unemployment moved in the upswing 1868–1873, conforming rather well to Keynes's stylized case of rising output-falling unemployment–static prices followed by almost pure price inflation.

N.1 Movement of Major Variables, U.K., 1868–1873

	Capital goods production	Consumers goods production	Unemployment percentage	General prices
1868	43.4	60.7	6.75%	132
1869	47.9	58.1	5.95	131
1870	49.8	63.5	3.75	128
1871	51.2	69.2	1.65	133
1872	55.3	68.8	.95	145
1873	55.3	68.8	1.15	148

NOTE: 1900=100 except where otherwise indicated.

SOURCE: W. W. Rostow, *British Trade Fluctuations, 1868–1896,* p. 70; sources specified, pp. 7–13.

74. *Ten Great Economists*, p. 104.

75. These points are elaborated in W. W. Rostow, *British Trade Fluctuations, 1868–1896*, pp. 422–430, and also in *British Economy of the Nineteenth Century*, pp. 151–154.

76. *Official Papers*, p. 5.

77. *Ibid.*, pp. 5–6.

78. *Ibid.*, p. 126.

79. These four points are elaborated *ibid.*, pp. 127–131. Marshall's view on the long-term rate of interest was that a decline had been caused by "a thinning out of the field for the investment of capital relatively to the supply of capital." (*Ibid.*, p. 130).

80. *Ibid.*, p. 128.

81. The annual average percentage rate of growth of Gross Domestic Product per man-year in the U.K. was 1.2% for the period 1873–1899 (R. C. O. Matthews, C. H. Feinstein, and J. C. Odling-Smee, *British Economic Growth, 1856–1873* [Stanford: Stanford University Press, 1982], p. 31). The rate of growth of real wages as calculated in Bowley's table quoted by Marshall (p. 411) is 2.4% for the period 1864–1873 to 1884–1893.

82. *Official Papers*, p. 287.

83. B. R. Mitchell with the collaboration of Phyllis Deane, *Abstract of British Historical Statistics* (Cambridge: at the University Press, 1971), p. 489.

84. *Historical Statistics of the United States: Colonial Times to 1970*, Vol. I, (Washington, D.C.: U.S. Department of Commerce, 1975), pp. 200–201.

85. C. H. Feinstein, *Statistical Tables of National Income, Expenditure, and Output of the U.K., 1855–1965* (Cambridge: at the University Press, 1976), Table 65, p. T140.

86. *Principles*, pp. 672–673.

87. *Official Papers*, pp. 366–420. The paper includes (pp. 394–395) a terse and precise summary of the six major arguments for British protectionism that Marshall systematically but temperately refutes.

88. *Ibid.*, pp. 383–384. See also Marshall's understanding in this period (1907) of the decelerating effect on British real wages of capital exports designed to expand food and raw materials production (*Memorials*, p. 324):

> Wages in Britain are now but very little affected by the rate of growth of population and the pressure on the means of subsistence. The restraining forces which prevents their rise from being even faster than it is, is the fact that countries whose large expanse offers very high returns on investments in railways, in building, in developing mines and new agricultural land can outbid British enterprise in the demand for Capital.

89. *Ibid.*, p. 402.

90. *Industry and Trade*, p. 7.

91. *Economics of Industry*, pp. 43–48.

92. *Ibid.*, p. 47.

93. *Principles*, p. 738.

94. *Ibid.*, pp. 743–744.

95. *Ibid.*, p. 747n.

96. *Ibid.*, p. 775.

97. *Industry and Trade*, pp. 681–699.

98. *Economics of Industry*, pp. 27–31.

99. *Ibid.*, pp. 60–61.

100. *Ibid.*, pp. 187–190.

101. For example, *Principles*, pp. 173–180 (population and population doctrine); pp. 220–226 (the growth of wealth in the course of the stages of growth); pp. 267–277 (the evolution of industrial organization); pp. 582–587 (attitudes toward and doctrines concerning interest); and pp. 637–645 (land tenure).

102. *Industry and Trade*, Chapters III–V, pp. 32–106.

103. *Ibid.*, p. 104.

104. *Ibid.*, pp. 95–98.

105. *Ibid.*, p. 98.

106. *Ibid.*, pp. 99–102.

107. *Ibid.*, pp. 102–103.

108. *Ibid.*, pp. 104–105 and 157–159.

109. *Ibid.*, pp. 161–162.

110. *Memorials*, pp. 11–12.

111. *Ibid.*, p. 12.

112. *Ibid.*, pp. 41–46.

113. *Ibid.*, p. 43.

114. *Ibid.*, pp. 45–46.

115. "The Present Position of Economics" (1885), Marshall's inaugural lecture as professor at Cambridge, *Memorials*, pp. 163–164.

116. *Ibid.*, p. 155.

117. Marshall attributed a good deal of this parochialism among early nineteenth-century economists to Ricardo (*ibid.*, pp. 153–156). So far as Ricardo was concerned the charge is somewhat misdirected. Ricardo's parochialism consisted not in extending his propositions unthoughtfully to other times and societies but in focusing narrowly on certain specific problems confronted by Britain in his time (preceding, p. 88). But it must be allowed that his technique of argument and exposition, via simple, abstract, strong constructs, lent itself to misinterpretation. It should also be noted that Schumpeter accused Marshall of applying to the world the parochial values of a Cambridge professor (*History of Economic Analysis*, p. 129n). Like all sets of moral values, Marshall's were, indeed, arbitrary; but they derive, I believe, from a wider and longer tradition than Schumpeter's observation would suggest.

118. *History of Economic Analysis*, p. 888.

119. For example, see Schumpeter's comments on John A. Hobson and Beatrice and Sidney Webb, *ibid.*, pp. 823–824 and 833.

120. *Memorials*, p. 11. See also pp. 69–72 and 82–83.

121. *Ibid.*, p. 162.

122. For example, *ibid.*, pp. 16, 20, 34, and 156.

123. *Ibid.*, p. 20.

124. *Ibid.*, p. 166.

125. *Ibid.*

126. *Principles*, p. 587. Marshall goes on to argue his denial of the labor theory of value as follows (*ibid.*):

> It is not true that the spinning of yarn in a factory, after allowance has been made for the wear-and-tear of the machinery, is the product of the labour of the operatives. It is the product of their labour, together with that of the employer and subordinate managers, and of the capital employed; and that capital itself is the product of labour and waiting: and therefore the spinning is the product of labour of many kinds, and of waiting. If we admit that it is the product of labour alone, and not of labour and waiting, we can no doubt be compelled by inexorable logic to admit that there is no justification for Interest, the reward of waiting; for the conclusion is implied in the premiss. Rodbertus and Marx do indeed boldly claim the authority of Ricardo for their premiss; but it is really as opposed to his explicit statement and the general tenor of his theory of value, as it is to common sense.

127. *Memorials*, pp. 323–346.

128. *Ibid.*, p. 173.

129. *Principles*, p. 722.

Chapter 7

1. For an invaluable survey of the history and current state of population studies as of the late 1950s, see Philip M. Hauser and Otis Dudley Duncan, *The Study of Population: An Inventory and Appraisal* (Chicago: University of Chicago Press, 1959). References to John Gaunt, his achievement and influence, are at pp. 124–130 and 190. The Hauser and Duncan volume contains for each chapter a valuable bibliography.

2. *Ibid.,* and Charles Henry Hull (ed.), *The Economic Writings of Sir William Petty,* together with the *Observations upon the Bills of Mortality More Probably by Captain John Gaunt* (Cambridge: at the University Press, 1899), pp. lxxvii–lxxix.

3. For a full account of Süssmilch, see Frederick S. Crum, "The Statistical Work of Süssmilch," Publications of the American Statistical Association, Vol. VII, New Series, No. 55 (September 1901), pp. 335–380. This article is based on Crum's Cornell doctoral thesis. See also the vivid evocation of Süssmilch and his pro-natalist doctrines in Theodore M. Porter, *The Rise of Statistical Thinking, 1820–1900* (Princeton: Princeton University Press, 1986), pp. 21–23.

4. P. M. Hauser and O. D. Duncan (eds.), *Study of Population,* in Chapter 6 (Frank Lorimer, "The Development of Demography"), pp. 127–128.

5. *Ibid.,* pp. 141–142.

6. *Ibid.,* p. 181 (Chapter 7, Alfred Sauvy, "Development and Perspectives of Demographic Research in France"). See also *ibid.,* p. 137 (Frank Lorimer).

7. *Ibid.,* F. Lorimer, "The Development of Demography," p. 137–138.

8. *Ibid.,* A. Sauvy, "Demographic Research in France," p. 180.

9. E. Castelot, "Stationary Population in France," *Economic Journal,* Vol. XIV, No. 54 (June 1904), pp. 249–253. Castelot discusses briefly pro- and anti-natalist views and policies in various countries.

10. *Ibid.,* p. 250. For a more recent, detailed review of German strategic hopes and French and British anxieties in this period see Michael S. Teitelbaum and Jay M. Winter, *The Fear of Population Decline* (New York: Academic Press, 1985), Chapter 2, "Demography and International Politics," pp. 13–44.

11. E. Castelot, "Stationary Population," pp. 252–253.

12. For a brief discussion and references, see W. W. Rostow, *The World Economy: History and Prospect,* pp. 18–20 and 720. For the international multiplier effects of this controversy on population research, see Hauser and Duncan, *Study of Population,* pp. 145–146 (Frank Lorimer).

13. Imre Ferenzi (ed.), *International Migrations* (New York: National Bureau of Economic Research, 1929).

14. A. M. Carr-Saunders, *World Population: Past Growth and Present Trends* (London: Oxford University Press, 1936).

15. F. Lorimer, in Hansen and Duncan, *Study of Population,* p. 153.

16. Hauser and Duncan (eds.), *ibid.,* in Chapter 14 (Rupert B. Vance, "The Development and Status of American Demography"), p. 297.

17. *Ibid.,* p. 291. Vance's more detailed comment on American demography is worth quotation, suggesting both the heightened urgency of social analysis in the Depression and the coming to fruition of efforts with a longer period of gestation (*ibid.,* p. 293):

> Strangely enough, the impetus demography needed to attain maturity in the United States came from the impact of the depression. Population as human resources took its place at the forefront of analysis, and policy-making gave impetus to the work of scholars, government agencies, and foundation programs. Demography in this period reached a new level of creative scholarship, and the pattern which emerged made distinctive contributions to analysis and theory.

18. In Chapter 32 (Joseph Spengler, "Economics and Demography"), in Hauser and Duncan, *Study of Population,* p. 796.

19. Note Schumpeter's comment on this period, *History of Economic Analysis*, pp. 890–891.

20. John Maynard Keynes, *The General Theory of Employment, Interest, and Money* (London: Macmillan, 1936), p. 318. M. S. Teitelbaum and Jay M. Winter, *Fear of Population Decline*, survey other strands in the population debate in Chapter 3 ("Demography and Internal Politics, 1870–1945"), notably concerns with eugenics and the "quality" of populations.

21. J. M. Keynes, "Some Economic Consequences of a Declining Population," *The Eugenics Review*, Vol. XXIX, No. 1 (April 1937), pp. 13–17.

22. W. B. Reddaway, *The Economics of a Declining Population* (London: Allen and Unwin, 1946 [2d impr.]).

23. *Ibid.*, p. 152.

24. *Ibid.*

25. See Johannes Overbeek, "Wicksell on Population," *Economic Development and Cultural Change*, Vol. 21, No. 2 (January 1973), pp. 205–207. Three pages contain a useful account of the origin of Wicksell's views on population as an introduction to a translation of a 1910 speech he gave in The Hague to a neo-Malthusian gathering on "The Optimum Population." Overbeek's translation is helpful because Wicksell dropped from the English edition of his *Lectures* the chapter on population that appeared in the first two Swedish editions. This is the only English text of Wicksell's views. For brief observations on Wicksell in the course of expounding his own rather grim view of population prospects, see R. M. Goodwin, *Essays in Dynamic Economics* (London: Macmillan, 1982), Chapter 14 ["Wicksell and the Malthusian Catastrophe," pp. 173–182], originally published in *The Scandinavian Journal of Economics*, 1978). See also K. Wicksell, "The Theory of Population, Its Composition and Changes," in Goran Ohlin, *Some Unpublished Works* (Lund: 1977). For an authoritative essay on Wicksell, including reference to his views on population, see Erik Lindahl (ed.), Knut Wicksell, *Selected Papers on Economic Theory*, Reprints of Classics (New York: Augustus M. Kelley, 1969), pp. 9–48. (Lindahl's Introduction).

26. Introduction to Knut Wicksell, *Lectures on Political Economy*, Vol I, translated by E. Classen (New York: Macmillan, 1934), pp. xl–xii.

27. *Ibid.*, p. 211.

28. Gunnar Myrdal, *Population, A Problem for Democracy*, The Godkin Lectures, 1938 (Cambridge: Harvard University Press, 1940). Alva Myrdal, *Nation and Family* (New York: Harper, 1941).

29. G. Myrdal, *Population, A Problem for Democracy*, pp. 26–27. Myrdal asserts that the theory of optimum population "stands mainly as an excuse for, and also as an actual inhibition of, the proper posing of the problem of the economic effects of population changes."

30. *Ibid.*, p. 203.

31. Alvin H. Hansen cites these figures in *Business Cycles and National Income* (New York: W. W. Norton, 1951), p. 76, n.23.

32. *Ibid.*, pp. 74–76. In Hansen's view the Second Industrial Revolution centered on the railroads; the Third, on the automobile (and related sectors), electricity, the street railroad, and telephone.

33. A chapter in T. W. Schultz (ed.), *Food for the World* (Chicago: University of Chicago Press, 1976), pp. 36–57.

34. A. M. Carr-Saunders, *World Population* (Oxford: at the Clarendon Press, 1936), pp. 59–128.

35. J. K. Whitaker (ed.), *The Early Economic Writings of Alfred Marshall, 1862–1890*, Vol. II (London: Macmillan, 1975) p. 311.

36. *Ibid.*, p. 315.

37. J. B. Clark, *Essentials of Economic Theory* (New York: Augustus M. Kelley, 1968; Reprints of Economic Classics), p. 557.

38. *Ibid.*, especially pp. 321–335.

39. *Ibid.*, pp. 335–336 (as follows):

> *The Working of Malthusianism in Short Periods as Contrasted with an Opposite Tendency in Long Ones.* There is little doubt that by a long course of technical improvement, increasing capital, and rising wages, the laboring class of the more prosperous countries have become accustomed to a standard of living that is generally well sustained and in most of these countries tends to rise. There is also little uncertainty that a retarded growth of population has contributed somewhat to this result. One of the facts which Malthus observed is consistent with this general tendency. Even though the trend of the line which represents the standard of living be steadily upward, the rise of actual wages may proceed unevenly, by quick forward movements and pauses or halts, as the general state of business is flourishing or depressed. In "booming" times wages rise and in hard times they fall, though the upward movements are greater than the downward ones and the total result is a gain.
>
> Now, such a quick rise in wages is followed by an increase in the number of marriages and a quick fall is followed by a reduction of the number. The birth rate is somewhat higher in the good times than it is in the bad times. Young men who have a standard income which they need to attain before taking on themselves the care of a wife and children find themselves suddenly in the receipt of such an income and marry accordingly. There is not time for the standard itself materially to change before this quick increase of marriages takes place. . . .

40. *Ibid.*, pp. 338 and 317–318.

41. Gustav Cassel, *The Theory of Social Economy* (New York: Harcourt Brace, revised from the fifth German edition, translated by S. L. Barrow, 1932), pp. 27–41 and 148–152.

42. *Ibid.*, pp. 39–40.

43. Cassel's further references to population are to be found in *Theory* pp. 241–249. This aspect of Wicksell's sustained polemic begins (p. 241): "This book contains no chapter on the theory of population—only a couple of pages in the chapter on wages are devoted to it out of sheer necessity—and the author's own views on the subject seem to be hopelessly vague."

44. The classic studies of business cycles in relation to marriage, birth, and death rates are: Dorothy Swaine Thomas, "An Index to British Business Cycles," *Journal of American Statistical Association*, Vol. XXI, No. 153 (1926); and (with V. L. Galbraith) "Birth Rates and Inter-war Business Cycles," *ibid.*, Vol. XXXVI (1941). On migration, also by Thomas, *Social and Economic Aspects of Swedish Population Movements* (New York: Macmillan, 1941). Walter W. Willcox (ed.), *International Migrations, Vol. II, Interpretations* (New York: National Bureau of Economic Research, 1931), is shot through with references to the sensitivity of migration flows to economic push and pull, including the role of business cycles. The chapters, written by scholars from different countries, analyze twenty cases of significant migration flows.

45. C. Chandrasekaran, "Survey of the Status of Demography in India," Chapter 12 in Hansen and Duncan, *Study of Population*, p. 249. Censuses in different parts of India were taken between 1865 and 1872. Efforts have been made to correct the results in ways that render them consistent with the regular decennial censuses beginning in 1881.

46. *Ibid.*, p. 250.

47. *Ibid.*, p. 251.

48. Vera Anstey, *The Economic Development of India* (London: Longmans, Green, 3d ed. , 1936).

49. See, especially, *ibid.*, pp. 38–58 and 474–475.

50. *Ibid.*, pp. 39–41.

51. *Ibid.*, p. 59.

52. *Ibid.*, p. 474.

53. See, for example, *ibid.*, p. 2.

54. R. H. Tawney, *Land and Labour in China* (New York: Harcourt Brace, 1932).

55. *Ibid.*, pp. 103–104.

56. L. C. A. Knowles, *The Economic Development of the British Overseas Empire*, (London: George Routledge, 1924).

Chapter 8

1. Sir Josiah Stamp, *The Statistical Verification of Social and Economic Theory* (London: Oxford University Press, 1927), Sidney Ball Lectures November 5, 1926; Barnett House Papers No. 10, p. 1.

2. Theodore M. Porter, *The Rise of Statistical Thinking, 1820–1900*, especially pp. 23–36. (Princeton: Princeton University Press, 1986)

3. *Ibid.*, p. 31.

4. For the best reconstruction in modern form of Gregory King's social accounts of England and Wales in 1688, see Phyllis Deane and W. A. Cole, *British Economic Growth, 1688–1959*, second edition (Cambridge: at the Cambridge University Press, 1969) p. 2 and discussion, pp. 1–4. On Petty, see Charles Henry Hull (ed.) *The Economic Writings of William Petty* (Cambridge: at the University Press, 1899). The most complete—almost compulsively detailed—history of national income estimates is that of Paul Studenski, *The Income of Nations*, Part One: History (Washington Square, N.Y.: New York University Press, 1961). Studenski notes (p. 13) that Boisguillebert and Vauban in France were quick on the heels of Petty and his popularizer, Charles Davenant.

5. C. H. Hull, *William Petty*, p. lxi.

6. *Ibid.*, p. 264. Petty's observation on the "heterodox" in various societies follows: (*ibid.*, pp. 263–264)

> . . . [I]t is to be observed that Trade doth not (as some think) best flourish under Popular Governments, but rather that Trade is most vigorously carried on, in every State and Government, by the Heterodox part of the same, and such as profess Opinions different from what are publickly established: (that is to say) in *India* where the *Mahometan* Religion is Authorized, there the *Banians* are the most considerable Merchants. In the *Turkish* Empire the *Jews*, and Christians. At *Venice, Naples, Legorn, Genoua*, and *Lisbone, Jews*, and Non-Papist Merchant-Strangers: but to be short, in that part of *Europe*, where the *Roman* Catholick Religion now hath, or lately hath had Establishment; there three quarters of the whole Trade, is in the hands of such as have separated from the Church (that is to say) the Inhabitants of *England, Scotland*, and *Ireland*, as also those of the *United Provinces*, with *Denmark, Sueden*, and *Norway*, together with the Subjects of the *German* Protestant Princes, and the *Hans* Towns, do at this day possess three quarters of the trade of the World; and even in *France* it self, the *Hugonots* are proportionably far the greatest Traders; Nor is it to be denied but that in *Ireland*, where the said *Roman* Religion is not Authorized, there the Professors thereof have a great part of the Trade. From whence it follows that Trade is not fixt to any Species of Religion as such; but rather as before hath been said to the Heterodox part of the whole, the truth wereof appears also in all the particular towns of greatest Trade in *England*. . .

7. See Deane and Cole, *British Economic Growth*, p. 82. For greater detail, see P. Deane, "The Implications of Early National Income Estimates for the Measurement of Long-Term Economic Growth in the United Kingdom," *Economic Development and Cultural Change*, (November 1955).

8. These estimates, along with parallel estimates for British national wealth, are reviewed in the supplementary microfilmed material (Part IV. British Basic Statistical Data) to A. D. Gayer *et al.*, *The Growth and Fluctuation of the British Economy, 1790–1850*, (Oxford: at the Clarendon Press, 1953) pp. 705–725. The microfilmed material is to be found at University Microfilms International, 300 N. Zeeb Road, Ann Arbor, Michigan 48106.

9. Reprinted in Robert Giffen, *Economic Inquiries and Studies*, Vol. I (London: George Bell, 1904), pp. 382–422.

10. For example, *ibid.*, pp. 419–420.

11. Michael G. Mulhall, *The Dictionary of Statistics* (London: George Routledge, 1892), pp. 320–323. Mulhall also supplies wealth figures for nineteen European and five extra-European countries (pp. 589–595). Here is Mulhall's brisk account of his unorthodox but not wholly irrational method of calculating national earnings (*ibid.*, p. 320):

> It is compiled thus: 90 per cent. of agricultural values, 90 per cent. of mining, 60 per cent. of manufactures. Transport is computed at 10 per cent. on the gross value of agriculture, mining, and manufactures; house-rent, according to the assessed valuation or the nearest estimate; commerce, 10 per cent. on imports and exports; shipping, 30s. per ton yearly of carrying power; banking, 5 per cent. on banking power; and furthermore an allowance of 10 per cent. on the total of the preceding eight items, to cover the earnings of domestic servants, learned professions, army, police, civil service, &c. This is, of course, a conventional method for estimating the earnings of nations, but will answer fairly well for the sake of comparison.

Later, more professional national income statisticians, including Simon Kuznets, have generally come to respect Mulhall's rough-and-ready method and feel for numbers. See, for example, the reference in Paul Studenski, *op. cit.*, pp. 140–141. But Mulhall was also capable of serious error. (See, for example, my *World Economy: History and Prospect*, [Austin: University of Texas Press, 1978], p. 664.) Mulhall did not systematically cite sources for each statistic used; but he supplied an impressive general list of references at the end of his *Dictionary* (pp. 618–620). Mulhall was a member of the Royal Statistical Society; and in my view, a statistician, unorthodox in many respects, but farsighted as well as compulsively industrious. Except for Studenski's reference, he appears in none of the histories of economic thought or doctrine known to me; but he is memorialized at the University of Texas at Austin in Project Mulhall, a computerized economic history data base.

12. *Ibid.*, p. 464. See also Mulhall's detailed analysis of the use of steam power in various forms from 1840 to 1888 for fifteen countries, *ibid.*, pp. 554–549.

13. *Ibid.*, p. 589.

14. Among the conventional historians of economic thought, Eric Roll is virtually unique in treating the emergence of national income accounting *A History of Economic Thought* (Englewood Cliffs, N.J.: Prentice-Hall, 1956), pp. 509–518).

15. A. L. Bowley, *Wages and Income in the United Kingdom since 1860* (Cambridge: at the University Press, 1937). J. C. Stamp's major independent study was *British Incomes and Property: The Application of Official Statistics to Economic Problems* (London: P. S. King, 1916).

16. Colin Clark, "Development Economics: The Early Years," in Gerald M. Meier and Dudley Seers (eds.), *Pioneers in Development* (New York: Oxford University Press for the World Bank, 1984), p. 59.

17. A. C. Pigou, *The Economics of Welfare* (London: Macmillan, first published in 1920). References are to the 4th (1932) ed.; reprinted in 1978 (New York: AMS Press).

18. *Ibid.*, See, especially, Chapter IX, which begins as follows:

> In general industrialists are interested, not in the social, but only in the private, net product of their operations. . . . [S]elf-interest will tend to bring about equality in the values of the marginal private net products of resources invested in different ways. But it will not tend to bring about equality in the values of the marginal social net products except when marginal private net product and marginal social net products are identical. When there is a divergence between these two sorts of marginal net products, self-interest will not, therefore, tend to make the national dividend a maximum; and, consequently, certain specific acts of interference with normal economic processes may be expected, not to diminish, but to increase the dividend. It thus becomes important to inquire in what conditions the values of the social net product and the private net product of any given (r^{th}) increment of investment in an industry are liable to diverge from one another in either direction. There are certain general sorts of divergence that are found even under

conditions of simple competition, certain additional sorts that may be introduced under conditions of monopolistic competition, and yet others that may be introduced under conditions of bilateral monopoly.''

19. See, especially, *ibid.*, Chapters III–VIII, pp. 31–97.

20. Colin Clark, *National Income and Outlay* (London: Macmillan, 1937).

21. Colin Clark, ''Development Economics: The Early Years,'' p. 60.

22. *The National Income, 1924–1931* (London: Macmillan, 1932).

23. All four of these strands of analysis are reflected in *National Income and Outlay,* although Clark's full analysis of economic growth awaited the publication of *The Conditions of Economic Progress* (London: Macmillan, 1940, 1970).

24. Colin Clark, *National Income and Outlay,* p. 273.

25. Colin Clark, ''Development Economics: The Early Years,'' p. 59.

26. *National Income and Outlay,* p. 272.

27. *Ibid.,* Chapter XII, pp. 248–261.

28. R. F. Kahn, ''The Relation of Home Investment to Unemployment,'' *Economic Journal,* Vol. 41, No. 162, (June 1931).

29. *National Income and Outlay,* pp. 250, 253–255.

30. *General Theory,* see especially, pp. 52–65 and 74–85.

31. See, for example, R. F. Harrod, *The Life of John Maynard Keynes* (New York: Harcourt, Brace, 1951), pp. 484–503, which covers the period down through the April 1941 White Paper on National Income (*Analysis of the Sources of War Finance and Estimate of the National Income and Expenditure in 1938 and 1948*). Keynes's *How to Pay for the War* (New York: Harcourt Brace, 1940) argued that half the required national reduction in consumption should be brought about by increased taxes, half by deferred pay; the increase in national debt would be liquidated after the war by a capital levy; exemption for those with minimum incomes and family allowances; further changes in money wages, pensions, etc., to be linked to changes in cost of a limited group of essentials, which would be rationed and subsidized if necessary. Ludo Cuyvers has noted the important role of Erwin Rothbarth in developing the national income calculations at the base of Keynes's argument (''Keynes's Collaboration with Erwin Rothbarth,'' *Economic Journal,* Vol. 93, No. 371 [September 1983], pp. 629–636. Cuyvers argues persuasively that the Keynes–Rothbarth calculations are ''a true 'missing link' '' between the work of Colin Clark and the 1941 contributions of Meade and Stone in the Treasury.

32. For a contemporary evaluation see Nicholas Kaldor, ''The White Paper on National Income and Expenditure,'' *Economic Journal,* Vol. LI, Nos. 202–203, (June–September 1941), pp. 181–191. The analysis of national income and expenditure was done primarily by Richard Stone and James Meade, in frequent consultation with Keynes. The latter's detailed interest in the fine points of national income definition and estimation at this time is reflected in two notes in the *Economic Journal:* ''The Concept of National Income'' (March 1940) and ''The Measurement of Real Income'' (March and June–September 1940)—the latter involving triangular debate with A. L. Bowley and Colin Clark.

33. C. K. Hobson, *The Export of Capital* (London: Constable, 1914). Douglas's paper was published in the *Journal of Business History,* Vol. II (August 1930), pp. 659–684.

34. *Export of Capital,* especially pp. 234–236.

35. *Growth of Capital,* p. 684 n. 7.

36. *Ibid.,* pp. 682 and 684.

37. *Dictionary of Statistics,* p. 322. Carol S. Carson (''The History of the United States National Income and Product Accounts: The Development of an Analytic Tool,'' *The Review of Income and Wealth,* Series 21, No. 2 [June 1975, p. 153] cites estimates of national income by George Tucker published in 1855 as well as 1843. For a summary of Tucker's method and finding, see Paul Studenski, *op. cit.,* pp. 129–132.

38. *Ibid.,* pp. 593–594. Mulhall's presentation of the census data includes the following imaginative calculations for the period 1850–1880

N.2 The Accumulations per U.S. Inhabitant in 30 Years' Average £205 Sterling, or Nearly £7 per Annum, *viz.*:

States	Increase, million £	Annual average, £	Mean population	Annual accumulation per head		
				(£)	(s.)	(c.)
New England	842	28,070,000	3,400,000	8	4	0
Middle	2,749	91,630,000	9,500,000	9	13	0
South	713	23,800,000	11,700,000	2	1	0
West	3,287	109,600,000	12,200,000	9	0	0
Union	7,591	253,100,000	36,800,000	6	17	0

This is a prodigious growth of wealth in thirty years, and without parallel in the history of the human race. Nevertheless the accumulation per head is less than in Australia.

39. Willford I. King, *The National Income and Its Purchasing Power* (New York: NBER, 1930), p. 9. See also citations of Carol S. Carson, *National Income and Product*, p. 153.

40. Carol S. Carson, "National Income and Product," p. 156.

41. Solomon Fabricant, *Toward a Firmer Basis of Economic Policy: The Founding of the National Bureau of Economic Research* (Cambridge, Mass.: NBER, 1983), p. 5. The story of the invention and innovation of the NBER, as told by Fabricant, is worth quoting at length (pp. 3–5):

> The crucial question was how to attain objective knowledge and—also essential—how to assure that the public would accept it as objective. Suppose, the founders reasoned, they were to form an organization for this purpose—one devoted to the scientific investigation of controverted social facts and to the dissemination of the findings in a scrupulous manner. Could such a union be established under a constitution and with the procedures and goodwill that would hold it together when inevitable difficulties arose? No less vital: Could financial support for its work be obtained and retained, although the aim was to serve only the general welfare, not to provide a specific *quid pro quo* in the way of business service or support for particular views? If these difficulties could be overcome, the enterprise would constitute a significant contribution "to the working methods of intelligent democracy."
>
> What was required? The question was raised when the idea was first discussed in 1916 by two men deeply concerned with economic policy, even though their views on what it should be were wide apart. One was Malcolm C. Rorty; the other, Nahum I. Stone. Rorty was an engineer turned statistician (later, chief statistician) in the American Telephone and Telegraph Company and author of a pioneer contribution on "The Application of the Theory of Probability to Traffic Problems." Among other things, he was writing a monthly letter on business conditions for his company and was taking an active interest in social and economic problems generally. Stone was an economist who had taken the trouble, when he was young, to translate Karl Marx's *Critique of Political Economy,* which he felt made a contribution, still "timely and useful," to thinking on the free-silver issue that had been disturbing the country for many years. In 1904 he had become a tariff expert for what was then the U.S. Department of Commerce and Labor and later, chief statistician of the U.S. Tariff Commission. In 1916 he was earning his living as an arbitrator of wage disputes and a consultant to governmental committees.
>
> Rorty and Stone had met the year before, in 1915, at a hearing of the New York State Factory Investigating Committee. Stone told the story at the 25th anniversary of the National Bureau:
>
>> Having made a study and prepared a report for the Committee on Minimum Wage Legislation, I was testifying before the committee in favor of the adoption of such legislation by the State of New York. Rorty was strongly opposed.
>> Our next contact (or conflict) took place across the table of the Mayor's Unemployment Committee in New York City. . . . In advocating the expediting of as many public works projects as the city could undertake as an alternative or supplement to public soup kitchens, I again clashed with Rorty. He formed a definite impression of me as a dangerous radical.
>
> In 1916 Scott Nearing published his pioneer study on the distribution of national income. He divided all income into service and property income and after an elaborate analysis of

statistical data, in which he displayed considerable originality and ingenuity, came to the conclusion that national income was divided roughly 50–50 between the two types. Harry Laidler, at that time editor of the *Intercollegiate Socialist,* a socialistic monthly intended chiefly for circulation among college students, asked me to review Nearing's book. My review grew into an article in which I took Nearing to task for his pseudo-scientific approach to the subject, and pointed out several large items of service income that Nearing ignored in his estimate. I arrived at the conclusion that the division between service and property income was approximately in the ratio of two to one (as the first publication of the National Bureau of Economic Research subsequently confirmed).

My article in the *Intercollegiate Socialist* caught the eye of Malcolm Rorty who made it his business to follow current labor and socialist publications. In line with his impression and the character of the magazine, he expected to find a "red hot" diatribe on the unjust distribution of income under capitalism. Instead, my article gave him a new slant on the "dangerous radical" and he invited me to lunch to talk things over. This was followed by several conferences which culminated in a warm friendship, although we continued to differ strongly on many public questions.

At our second meeting, Rorty said: "Here we are considering a most important question which deeply affects the lives of every man, woman, and child in this country, and despite a large fund of statistical data, there is no agreement on the purely arithmetical question of what part of the national income goes to each element of society. Would it not be a great step forward if we had an organization that devoted itself to fact finding on controversial economic subjects of great public interest?" I agreed that it would, provided the organization could command public confidence so its findings were accepted as conclusive by all parties to the controversy.

He assented to my proviso and asked for suggestions. I said the organization should be started by a group of well-known economists representing every school of economic thought from extreme conservative to extreme radical who should associate with them representatives of all the important organized interests in the country: financial, industrial, agricultural, labor, etc.

Rorty thought that some such plan would have to be adopted and believed he could raise the funds. . . . Rorty lost no time in pushing toward the realization of the project, which filled his thoughts to the exclusion of everything except his official duties.

The economists Rorty first approached were Edwin F. Gay, Wesley C. Mitchell, and John R. Commons.

42. *Ibid.*

43. *Income in the United States, Its Amount and Distribution, 1909–1919,* by Willford I. King, Oswald Knauth, and Frederick R. Macaulay (assisted by the Staff of NBER), edited by Wesley C. Mitchell. Volume I: *Summary* (New York: Harcourt, Brace, 1921); Volume II, *Detailed Report* (New York: NBER, 1922).

44. *National Income and Outlay,* p. VII.

45. *Toward a Firmer Basis,* p. 14.

46. Kuznets's study was published not by the NBER, where he then worked, but by Houghton Mifflin in Boston. The Hart, Schaffner, and Marx Committee consisted of Lawrence Laughlin of the University of Chicago, John B. Clark and Wesley C. Mitchell of Columbia, Edwin F. Gay of Harvard, and Theodore E. Barton of Washington, D.C.

47. *Ibid.,* p. 5.

48. For discussions of Kuznets's dilemma and his acknowledgement of it, see, for example, my review of his *Economic Growth of Nations. Total Output and Production Structure* (Cambridge, Mass.: The Belknap Press of Harvard University Press, 1971), in *Political Science Quarterly,* Vol. LXXXVI, No. 4 (December 1971), pp. 654–657. Kuznets's discussion of the problem is on pp. 314–343 of his *Economic Growth of Nations..*

49. *Congressional Record,* 72d Cong., 1st Session, Vol. LXXV, p. 12285. Passage of the Resolution is recorded on June 13, 1932, p. 12749.

50. S. Fabricant, *Toward a Firmer Basis,* p. 14.

51. Carol S. Carson, "National Income and Product," p. 156.

52. *National Income, 1929–1932* was filed with the Senate on January 3, 1934, by John Dickson, Acting Secretary of Commerce (Washington, D.C.: GPO, 1934, 73d Cong., Document 124). For acknowledgement of the role of Kuznets and the NBER, see p. xi.

53. The story is well told by Robert R. Nathan in his "Remarks Intended for Simon Kuznets' 80th Birthday, April 25, 1981," which Nathan made available to me. See, also in more detail, Carol Carson, "National Income and Product" pp. 156–159.

54. Carol S. Carson, "National Income and Product," p. 163.

55. The most complete account of "The Feasibility Dispute" is John Brigande, *The Feasibility Dispute: Determination of War Production Objectives for 1942 and 1943,* Committee on Public Administration Cases, Washington, D.C., 1950. Also Carol S. Carson "National Income and Product," pp. 174–175. Robert R. Nathan, a major belligerent, summarizes his view of the matter in his "Remarks" for Kuznet's eightieth birthday and, more formally, in his testimony and statement prepared on "World War II and the Problems of the 1980s," Hearing before the Committee on Banking, Finance and Urban Affairs, House of Representatives, Ninety-Sixth Congress, Second Session, September 23, 1980, Serial No. 96-66, (Washington, D.C.: G. P. O., 1980), especially pp. 5–7 (testimony); pp. 17–19 (prepared statement). Nathan's prepared statement was submitted on behalf of David Ginzburg and J. Kenneth Galbraith as well as himself. All three of these battle-scarred veterans of the war economy struggles in Washington sought lessons from their experiences that might be applied to the energy problem as it appeared in 1980.

56. Edwin R. A. Seligman (editor-in-chief), Alvin Johnson (associate editor); (New York: Macmillan, 1933), pp. 205–224.

57. *Ibid.,* pp. 206 and 224.

Chapter 9

1. Eugen V. Böhm-Bawerk, *Capital and Interest: A Critical History of Economical Theory* (William Smart, ed.), (London: Macmillan, 1890). The German edition of *Kapital und Kapitalizmus* was first published in 1884.

2. For an outline and terse summary of Böhm-Bawerk's interest theory, see *ibid.,* pp. 257–259 and 421–428. *The Positive Theory of Capital* was published in German in 1889 and in William Smart's English translation in 1891 (New York: G. E. Streehert).

3. Joseph A. Schumpeter, *Ten Great Economists,* (London: Allen and Unwin, 1952) p. 176.

4. *Ibid.,* p. 177.

5. The debate over Bohm-Bawerk's concept of roundaboutness and the period of production and its evolution is well summarized in Mark Blaug, *Economic Theory in Retrospect* (Homewood, Illinois: Richard D. Irwin, 1981) pp. 501–543.

6. For an elegant summation, see Irving Fisher, *The Theory of Interest* (New York: Macmillan, 1930) [accessibly available in Reprints of Economic Classics (New York: August M. Kelley, 1961)], p. 451.

7. W. W. Rostow, *British Economy of the Nineteenth Century,* (Oxford: at the Clarendon Press, 1948) p. 145.

8. For my comments on Keynes's interpretation of the 1873–1896 price decline in *The Treatise, ibid.,* pp. 155–157.

9. *The Theory of Interest,* Reprints of Economic Classics (New York: August M. Kelley, 1961: original publisher New York: Macmillan, 1930), p. 451.

10. Irving Fisher, *The Purchasing Power of Money* (New York: Macmillan, 1926), pp. 242 and 246–247. I should, perhaps, report an exceedingly minor moment in the history of economic theory. When I was a graduate student at Yale in 1938–1939, Professor Fisher, then retired, invited me to lunch at his home. Afterwards he showed me the annex in which was housed his voluminous historical and contemporary files, mainly of price and monetary data, as well as his famous hydraulic model of the economy, then down for repairs. He finally came to the point: if I would commit my professional research to "tracing the gilden strand" through history (that is, the relation

of gold to prices) he would bequeath me his files. I greatly respected Professor Fisher as a theorist then, as I do now, and I sensed a certain sadness that he had not generated at Yale a disciple to carry forward his vision of long-term price analysis. But I had already concluded that the supply of bullion was not a decisive determinant of price trends in history and that the quantity theory of money was a grossly inadequate instrument for price analysis. I refused his offer as gently as I could.

11. *Purchasing Power*, pp. 242–245.

12. *Ibid.*, p. 247. For Friedman's view and my comment on it see my *Why the Poor Get Richer and the Rich Slow Down*, (Austin: University of Texas Press, 1980), pp. 220–232.

13. *Theory of Interest*, Chapter XVI, pp. 341–355.

14. *Ibid.*, p. 503.

15. Knut Wicksell, *Interest and Prices*, translated from the German by R. F. Kahn, with an introduction by Bertil Ohlin, (London: Macmillan, 1936), pp. 1–7. The preface of the first edition of *Interest and Prices* is dated 1893. Myrdal's lucid definition of Wicksell's "normal or equilibrium rate of interest" is the following (*Monetary Equilibrium* [London: William Hodge, 1938], pp. 37–38).

> Wicksell, as is well known, defined the equilibrium position by specifying the level of the "money rate of interest" which brings about monetary equilibrium. This equilibrium interest rate Wicksell calls the "normal rate of interest" and determines it with reference to quantities in three different spheres of price formation:
>
> (1) Productivity of the roundabout process of production;
> (2) Conditions in the capital market;
> (3) Conditions in the commodity market.
>
> The "normal rate of interest" must now, according to Wicksell, (1) equal the marginal technical productivity of real capital (i.e., the "real" or "natural" rate of interest); (2) equate the supply of and the demand for savings; and, finally (3) guarantee a stable price level, primarily of consumption goods.

Myrdal then adds:

> Wicksell assumes that these three criteria for the normal rate of interest are equivalent—i.e., never mutually inconsistent; but he cannot prove it. His formulations are, indeed, too loose and contradictory for this purpose. In the following I will prove that they cannot be identical: Only the first and the second of the equilibrium conditions are even consistent; they are interrelated in such a way that the first is conditioned by the second and otherwise not determined. They both correspond to the main argument which is implicit in the whole theory. But this is so only after they have been corrected in essential points and more precisely formulated. With respect to the commodity market however, the fulfillment of these two monetary equilibrium relations means something quite different from an unchanged price level.

16. *Ibid.*, Chapter 11, pp. 165–177. For a reconsideration of Wicksell's historical chapter, see J. R. T. Hughes, "Wicksell on the Facts: Prices and Interest Rates, 1844 to 1914," in J. N. Wolfe (ed.), *Value, Capital and Growth, Papers in Honour of Sir John Hicks,* (Chicago: Aldine Publishing Company and Edinburgh University Press, 1968), pp. 215–255.

17. *Ibid.*, pp. 174–175.

18. *Ibid.*, pp. xxiii–xxv, where Wicksell, in his 1898 Preface, lucidly states his purpose.

19. *Ibid.*, especially Chapter 12, pp. 178–196.

20. G. Myrdal, *Monetary Equilibrium*, pp. 178–180.

21. G. Myrdal, *An American Dilemma* (New York: Harper and Brothers, 1944), especially pp. 75–78 and Appendix 3, "A Methodological Note on the Principle of Cumulation," pp. 1065–1070, where Myrdal refers explicitly to his own *Monetary Equilibrium* and other dynamic economic analyses.

22. This passage is from a letter Keynes wrote me on February 2, 1940, at the time he accepted for publication in *Economic History*, an article on theories of the Great Depression.

23. J. M. Keynes, *The Economic Consequences of the Peace* (New York: Harcourt, Brace, and Howe, 1920), especially pp. 22–26 and 229–30.

24. John H. Williams, "The Theory of International Trade Reconsidered," *Economic Journal*, Vol. XXXIX, No. 154 (June 1929), pp. 195–197.

25. The historical studies of the transfer process, include: John H. Williams, *Argentine International Trade under Inconvertible Paper Money* (Cambridge: Harvard University Press, 1920); Frank D. Graham, "International Trade under Depreciated Paper. The United States, 1862–79," *Quarterly Journal of Economics* (1922); Jacob Viner, *Canada's Balance of International Indebtedness, 1900–1913,* (Cambridge, Mass.: Harvard University Press, 1924); Gordon Wood, *Borrowing and Business in Australia* (Oxford: at the Clarendon Press, 1930); Roland Wilson, *Capital Imports and the Terms of Trade* (Melbourne: Melbourne University Press in association with Macmillan, 1931); Harry D. White, *The French International Accounts, 1880–1913* (Cambridge, Mass.: Harvard University Press, 1933); C. Bresciani-Turroni, *Inductive Verification of the Theory of International Payments* (Egyptian University Publications of the Faculty of Law, No. 1, Cairo, n. d.—about 1933). The work of A. G. Silverman, as reflected in two articles in the *Review of Economic Statistics* ("Monthly Index Numbers of British Export and Import Prices, 1880–1913" [1930] pp. 139–148; and "Some International Trade Factors for Great Britain, 1880–1913" [1931] pp. 114–124), is to be distinguished by the eclectic character of his approach to the terms of trade. Silverman is less concerned with the verification of classical hypotheses than with a direct accounting for changes in the terms of trade. Taussig's own conclusions are incorporated in his *International Trade* (New York: Macmillan, 1927.)

26. John A. Williams, *Argentine International Trade*, p. 4.

27. *Ibid.*, p. 27.

28. *Ibid.*, p. 239. n. 1. In his conclusions Williams notes that the association in conventional theory of a depreciated paper exchange with a "dislocated" exchange does not hold for Argentina, since a gold exchange rate existed virtually throughout the period examined. He also notes the emphasis on the matter is misguided given its "incidental importance" (*ibid.*, p. 258).

29. *Ibid.*, pp. 256–257.

30. See Note 19, preceding.

31. A. K. Cairncross, *Home and Foreign Investment, 1870–1913* (Cambridge: at the University Press, 1953), p. xiii. Sir Alexander was good enough to provide me with an explanation for his interest in the transfer problem in a letter of 7 April, 1986:

> I wish I could rise to your suggestion and produce some esoteric explanation of my interest in the transfer problem in 1930. But the fact is that it had nothing to do with long-run growth initially. My undergraduate thesis is chiefly concerned to turn Taussig's explanations round the other way and show, case by case, that investment responded to the terms of trade rather than pushed them this way and that. When I got to Cambridge I applied this idea to British experience over a long stretch of time. I don't think that the word "growth" occurs anywhere in my dissertation although "development" certainly does.
>
> I moved from the transfer problem to the theory of investment as expounded by Keynes, trying to work out the relationship between home and foreign investment but without making much impression on anybody by my theoretical chapters. When I began to dig in to the statistics I found Colin Clark very helpful and he seemed to move along much the same intellectual path as I did, trying to understand investment in quantitative and historical terms instead of sinking into a conceptual bog.
>
> If you look at Chapter[s] 2–4 of my *Home and Foreign Investment* you will see that the interest lies in fluctuations rather than growth, in the impact of domestic investment on the balance of payments, and in the interconnection between capital movements and labour movements. Chapter 2 was written in 1934 at Cambridge and Chapters 3 and 4 in 1937/8 at Glasgow. They don't really show much concern with growth (especially as I was always inclined to play down the role of capital accumulation in growth). My explicit interest in growth really developed in the war when I became alive to the full significance of technical change.

Like Colin Clark, Cairncross also became skeptical that the tight linkage between investment rates and growth was justified. The closing paragraph of his postwar paper on "The Place of Capital in Economic Progress" captures well the emphasis he came to place on technology as opposed to capital inputs, (*Economic Progress,* Leon Dupriez (ed.) [International Economic Association Louvain, Institut de Recherches Economiques et Sociales, 1955], pp. 235–248):

> On the whole, there is a greater danger that the importance of capital in relation to economic progress will be exaggerated than that it will be underrated. How many successful firms, looking back over their history, would single out difficulty of access to new capital as the major obstacle, not to their growth, but to the adoption of the most up-to-date technique? How many countries in the van of technical progress have found themselves obliged to borrow abroad? It is where there has been a lag, where technical progress has been too slow, that capital is called upon to put matters right. No doubt where capital is plentiful, more risks can be taken and development is speeded-up, so that rapid development and rapid accumulation go together. But the most powerful influence governing development, even now, is not the rate of interest or the abundance of capital; and the most powerful influence governing capital accumulation, even now, is not technical progress.

Cairncross's 1955 paper can lay legitimate claim to status among the better known pioneering analyses of the role of technological change (as opposed to capital investment) in economic growth; i.e., Fabricant (1954), Abramovitz (1956), and Solow (1957). See note 50, Chapter 16, below.

32. See, for example, *Home and Foreign Investment, 1870–1913,* pp. 189–194.

33. *Ibid.,* pp. 65–83 and 209–221.

34. *Ibid.,* pp. 84–102.

35. *Ibid.,* pp. 103–186.

36. *Ibid.,* pp. 187–208.

37. *Ibid.,* pp. 189–197.

38. *Ibid.,* pp. 37–49.

39. *Ibid.,* pp. 37–64.

40. *Ibid.,* pp. 222–235.

41. Loring Allen, *Opening Doors: The Life and Work of Schumpeter* (unpublished). Professor Allen was kind enough to make available a semi-final draft of his book from which I have greatly profited.

42. Joseph A. Schumpeter, *The Theory of Economic Development,* translated from the German by Redvers Opie (Cambridge: Harvard University Press, 1955), p. ix, in the Preface to the English edition.

43. The phrase "sacred decade" appears in 1914 and 1921 in obituary essays for Böhm-Bawerk and Menger written by Schumpeter in *Zeitschrift für Volkswirtschaft, Sozialpolitik und Verwaltung,* cited by Loring Allen, *Opening Doors,* mss. Chapter III, p. 7.

44. *Theory of Economic Development,* Chapter I, pp. 3–56 and 158–159. One hesitates to impute motives in such circumstances, but one feels that Schumpeter was paying respects to his teachers, as he did explicitly in the essays incorporated in *Ten Great Economists;* whereas Myrdal, at the cost of partially concealing his originality, was underlining the importance of the Swedish school and thereby strengthening his tart criticism of the British economic tradition:

> The English school of theorists has only slowly arrived at Wicksell's statement of the problem. Not only Marshall, but also Pigou and Hawtrey do not seem to be really familiar with Wicksell's work. D. H. Robertson's significant little book, *Banking Policy and the Price Level,* contains many of the new ideas, but he, too, obviously lacks a thorough knowledge of the content of the monetary studies of Wicksell and his pupils, and he has therefore been forced unnecessarily to think for himself. J. M. Keynes's new, brilliant, though not always clear, work, *A Treatise on Money,* is completely permeated by Wicksell's influence. Nevertheless Keynes's work too, suffers somewhat from the attractive Anglo-Saxon kind of unnecessary originality, which has its roots in certain systematic gaps in the knowledge of the German language on the part of the majority of English economists.

45. On the whole, Schumpeter leaned to the proposition that in one way or another the perceived possibility of profit (if not quite raw necessity) was the mother of invention. This has been the predominant view among historians of technology; although all agree that the assertion of any single overriding rule poses complexities and suggests exceptions. Schumpeter (*Business Cycles,* [New York: McGraw-Hill, 1939] Vol. 1, p. 85, note) allows for the existence of inventions and innovations induced by necessity; but also for inventions not related to any particular requirement or not related to the requirement met by the particular innovation that incorporates them. Schumpeter states:

> It might be thought that innovation can never be anything else but an effort to cope with a given situation. In a sense this is true. For a given innovation to become possible, there must always be some "objective needs" to be satisfied and some "objective conditions"; but they rarely, if ever, uniquely determine what kind of innovation will satisfy them, and as a rule they can be satisfied in many different ways. Most important of all, they may remain unsatisfied for an indefinite time, which shows that they are not themselves sufficient to produce an innovation.

While admitting, of course, the possibility that nature may not always be fruitful and that the form of the innovational response to a necessity is not determinable *ex ante,* I would continue to attach a considerable formal importance to the link between necessity, invention, and innovation, as I did in *The Process of Economic Growth.* The link is judged essential to a formal explanation of the changing character of investment in the course of growth and from cycle to cycle. While admitting the possibility of highly productive sports and total failure in meeting necessities, this argument would regard the character of the effort expended in applying science to the economy and the character of the potentialities accepted into the economy as reflecting the response of the society to challenges and opportunities created by the process of growth pressing against existing resources and techniques, revealing themselves in profit opportunities. The processes of scientific endeavour and of efforts to seek applications for the economy are thus viewed as a part of the normal investment process in the economy. It is the lack of such an analytic link that gives to Schumpeter's major innovations an exogenous element.

46. Loring Allen points out that there are foreshadowings of *The Theory of Economic Development* in Schumpeter's first book *Das Wesen und der Hauptinhalt Der Theoretischen Nationaloekonomie* (Munchen and Leipzig: Duncker and Humbolt, 1908). In his most vivid comment (pp. 182–183), Schumpeter argues that statics and dynamics are completely different fields, with different problems, methods, and subject matter. He notes that his current work is within the terrain of statics; but he concludes: "Dynamics still in its infancy [Anfangen], is a 'Land of the Future.'"

47. For Loring Allen's judicious evaluation of Marx's influence on Schumpeter, mss. Chapter V, *Opening Doors,* pp. 18–19. See also Nathan Rosenberg's excellent "Schumpeter and Marx: How Common a Vision?" in *Technology and the Human Prospect, Essays in Honour of Christopher Freeman,* Roy M. MacLeod (ed.), (London and Wolfeboro, N.H.: Francis Pinter, 1986), pp. 197–213. Sukhamoy Chakravarty also discusses the Marx–Schumpeter connection in *Alternative Approaches to A Theory of Economic Growth: Marx, Marshall, and Schumpter,* pp. 23–28 (Calcutta: Orient Longman, 1980).

48. *Economic Development,* p. 5.

49. *Ibid.,* p. 62.

50. *Ibid.,* pp. 61 and 64 n. 1.

51. *Ibid.,* pp. 63–64 and 66. For further discussion of the five types of innovation see pp. 132ff.

52. *Ibid.,* p. 63 n.1. The reference to Marshall is in the later English edition. It is unclear whether Marshall's bold confrontation of the problem of increasing returns—and failure fully to solve it— influenced Schumpeter's thought when initially formulating *The Theory of Economic Development.*

53. *Ibid.,* pp. 84–94. The quotation in the text is from p. 85.

54. *Ibid.,* pp. 128–130.

55. Ibid., pp. 131ff. and 197–198 ("clustering"); for example, pp. 156 and 252–253 ("creative destruction").

56. For example, *ibid.,* p. 154.

57. *Ibid.,* p. 157.

58. *Ibid.*

59. *Ibid.,* p. 158.

60. *Ibid.,* pp. 183ff.

61. See, especially, p. 191.

62. *Ibid.,* p. 215.

63. *Ibid.,* In his *Theory of Economic Development* Schumpeter accepts from Spiethoff that the first modern British business cycle occurred in the 1820s (*ibid.,* p. 215). By the time he wrote *Business Cycles* he had concluded correctly that the first major cycle (Juglar) in Britain peaked in 1792–1793 (*Business Cycles* [New York: McGraw-Hill, 1939], Vol. I, pp. 296–297.)

64. *Ibid.,* p. 230.

65. *Ibid.,* p. 232

66. *Ibid.,* pp. 232–233. Schumpeter notes that the length of the boom is determined by "the average time which must elapse before the new products appear"; an interval jointly determined by the period of gestation and "the tempo in which the multitude follow the leaders" in the innovative sectors.

67. *Ibid.,* p. 233.

68. *Ibid.,* p. 236. Schumpeter uses the term "normal" here in a special sense: to abstract from the "abnormal" intrusion of crisis with its "panic, breakdown of the credit system, epidemics of bankruptcies," and severe unemployment (*ibid.,* pp. 236 and 249–250).

69. *Ibid.,* pp. 243–245.

70. *Ibid.,* pp. 249–250.

71. *Ibid.,* p. 255. I assume this passage and his critical remarks about the countercyclical ameliorative proposals "associated with the names of Keynes, Fisher, and Hawtrey and the policies of the Federal Reserve Board" (p. 252) were inserted in the second German edition of 1926 from which the English translation of *The Theory of Economic Development* was made (p. ix). The third edition was merely a reprint of the second.

72. See, for example, Schumpeter's somewhat irritated reply to critics that he neglected all historical factors of change except "the individuality of entrepreneurs" (*ibid.,* p. 61 n. 1). I would guess this line of criticism helped push Schumpeter from the rather stylized but powerful theory of *The Theory of Economic Development* into *Business Cycles,* with its extensive historical sections.

73. Quoted, Alexander B. Trowbridge, *Private Leadership and Public Service* (Washington, D.C.: National Academy of Public Administration, 1985), pp. 14–15.

74. *Business Cycles,* Vol. I, p. v.

75. *Ibid.*

76. *Ibid.* Two examples come to mind: Adam Smith's *Lectures* (delivered 1748–1751) in relation to *The Wealth of Nations* (1776); and Karl Marx's *Communist Manifesto* (1848) in relation to the first volume of *Capital* (1867).

77. *Ibid.,* pp. 212–219 with charts on pp. 213–214.

78. See, for example, *Essays in the British Economy of the Nineteenth Century* (Oxford: at the Clarendon Press, 1948), pp. 28–30; A. D. Gayer *et al., Growth and Fluctuation of the British Economy, 1790–1850* (Oxford: at the Clarendon Press, 1953), Vol. II, pp. 632–638; my *Why the Poor Get Richer,* pp. 5–8 and 76–78. Perhaps the best review of Schumpeter's *Business Cycles* is Simon Kuznets's in *American Economic Review,* Vol. 30, No. 2 (June 1940), pp. 257–271. Its substance and flavor are captured in Kuznets's own summary (pp. 270–271):

> The critical evaluation . . . of what appear to be important elements in Professor Schumpeter's conclusions, viewed as a systematic and tested exposition of business cycles, yields disturbingly destructive results. The association between the distribution of entrepreneurial ability and the cyclical character of economic activity needs further proof. The theoretical model of the four-phase cycle about the equilibrium level does not yield a serviceable statistical approach. The three-cycle schema and the rather rigid relationship claimed to have been established is without a

serviceable statistical procedure. The core of the difficulty seems to lie in the failure to forge the necessary links between the primary factors and concepts (entrepreneur, innovation, equilibrium line) and the observable cyclical fluctuations in economic activity.

And yet this evaluation does injustice to the treatise, for it stresses the weaknesses of the discussion and overlooks almost completely its strength. Granted that the book does not present a fully articulated and tested business-cycle theory; that it does not actually demonstrate the intimate connection between economic evolution and business cycles; that no proper link is established between the theoretical model and statistical procedure; that historical evidence is not used in a fashion that limits the area of personal judgment; or that the validity of three types of cycles is not established. Yet it is a cardinal merit of the treatise that it raises all these questions; that it emphasizes the importance of relating the study of business cycles to a study of the underlying long-term movements; that it calls for emphasis on the factors that determine the rate and tempo of entrepreneurial activity; that it demands a statistical procedure based upon a clearly formulated concept of the business cycle; and that it valiantly attempts to use historical evidence. In all these respects the volumes offer favorable contrast with many a book published in recent years on business cycles, whether of the type in which abstract reasoning is unsullied by contact with observable reality or of the opposite category in which mechanical dissection of statistical series is the sum total of the author's achievement.

Furthermore, both the summary and the critical discussion above necessarily fail to show the achievements of the treatise in providing illuminating interpretations of historical developments; incisive comments on the analysis of cyclical fluctuations in various aspects of economic activity; revealing references to an extraordinarily wide variety of publications in directly and indirectly related fields; thought-provoking judgments concerning the general course of capitalist evolution.

79. *Business Cycles,* p. 164.

80. *Ibid.,* p. 164.

81. For an effort to demonstrate and then correct for this kind of bias see my *British Economy of the Nineteenth Century,* pp. 43–50.

82. *Business Cycles,* pp. 166–167.

83. *Ibid.,* pp. 213–214 and 1051, where the mathematics of the combined curve is specified with the Juglar taken as 9 1/2 years, the Kitchin at 3 1/6 years.

84. *Ibid.,* p. v. In 1940 I was recruited by Professors James Angell and Arthur D. Gayer, of Columbia and Barnard, to reply formally to Schumpeter's exposition of *Business Cycles* to the New York Political Economy Club. They knew of my reservations concerning Schumpeter's historical analysis based on a year-by-year, cycle-by-cycle study of the period 1788–1914 I had conducted over the previous 5 years. I was urged to respond with vigor. With the enthusiasm of a 23-year-old I did. Schumpeter replied that his schema was meant only as a rough way of looking at history. I ended the evening regretting the exuberance of my charge, as I do 48 years later; for, on balance, I regard Schumpeter as one of the most creative economists of the twentieth century and still underrated by mainstream economists.

85. *Ibid.,* pp. 319–325.

86. The final section of *Business Cycles* bears this title, pp. 1011–1050.

87. *Ibid.,* p. 1037.

88. *Ibid.,* p. 1050.

89. Kuznets, born in 1901, was 29 when *Secular Movements* was published. Prefatory notes indicate that it was submitted for the Hart, Schaffner, and Marx prize 2 years earlier and that he had been at work in the study over the 3 previous years; that is, since 1925.

90. Kuznets (*ibid.*), pp. 299–300, includes a brief paraphrase of Schumpeter's development theory in a section entitled "Innovations, Progress, and the Cyclical Fluctuations." He notes that it is among the theories he is using "as a point of departure for our reasoning" (*ibid.,* p. 300 n. 1). Schumpeter has numerous references to Kuznets in *Business Cycles,* mainly, however, with respect to his national income estimates.

91. *Theory of Economic Development,* p. 10.

92. *Ibid.,* pp. 1–5.

93. *Ibid.*, pp. 5, 6, and 9.

94. Schumpeter, *Business Cycles*, pp. 497–500. There is a certain grudging character to Schumpeter's references to Kuznets on retardation. He refers to it as an "old idea" (*ibid.*, p. 497, n.2;) and characterizes Kuznets's analysis as a "partial success."

95. *Ibid.*, p. 329. The context of Kuznets's statement of his grand objective deserves quotation:

> One visualizes the dynamic theory of economics arising from the long vision of a statistician and the penetration of a theoretical analyst, framing a complete account of economic reality as it presents itself to our eye. It will give us a complete account of why and how economic phenomena are as they are, and what brought them to the form in which we conceive them. We shall know not only the current state of economic reality, but the more or less stable sequences and interrelations which underlie its changes. The stability of these interrelations will be only relative. The process of long-time movement would seem a condition of stability of those factors which come prominently into play in the cyclical fluctuations. But the interesting part in the study of these conditions would be not to show them in their stability, where their composition becomes a matter of conjecture, but in their movement and flux where the hypotheses concerning their mechanism and forces can be tested. If we have a theory of economic changes in their different, discernible types we shall have a complete and general theory of dynamic economics.

96. *Ibid.*, p. 3.

97. *The Education of Henry Adams*, with an introduction by D. W. Brogan (Boston: Houghton Mifflin, Sentry Ed., 1916), Chapter XXV, pp. 379–390.

98. *Ibid.*, pp. 379–383.

99. *Ibid.*, pp. 383–385.

100. Thorstein Veblen, *The Instinct of Workmanship and the State of the Industrial Arts*, 1st ed. 1914 (New York: The Viking Press, 1943), p. 5.

101. This theme was to be systematically elaborated in great detail by C. E. Ayres. For my discussion of this perspective and its limitations see "Technology and the Price System," in William Breit and William Patton Culbertson, Jr. (eds.), *Science and Ceremony, The Institutional Economics of C. E. Ayres* (Austin: University of Texas Press, 1976), pp. 75–113.

102. *Instinct of Workmanship*, p. 351.

103. *Ibid.*, p. 354.

104. *Ibid.*, pp. 96–97.

105. *Ibid.*, p. 319.

106. R. F. Harrod "An Essay in Dynamic Theory," *Economic Journal*, Vol. XLIX, No. 193 (March 1939), pp. 14–33. As Harrod notes, this essay moves on from his 1936 *Essay on the Trade Cycle*, notably the bringing together of the multiplier and the accelerator. I considered seriously also dealing in this section with Allyn A. Young's famous Presidential Address to Section F of the British Association for the Advancement of Science (Glasgow: September 10, 1928) published as "Increasing Returns and Economic Progress" (*Economic Journal*, Vol. XXXVIII, No. 152, [December 1928], pp. 527–542). It does, indeed, deal with technology and economic growth; and at one point (p. 535) he notes that economic progress could come via the endogenous working of the economic system and "that the appropriate conception is that of a moving equilibrium. . . ." On the other hand Young confines himself to an emendation of Adam Smith's assertion that the division of labor depends on the extent of the market to include the possibility that the extent of the market depends on the division of labor and to certain observations on the inadequacy of Marshall's handling of increasing returns. Young does not grapple with Schumpeter's endogenous, discontinuous major innovations, nor does he try to deal with the stability of a consumption-savings model. For further discussion see my *Why the Poor Get Rich*, pp. 162–163.

I also considered F. P. Ramsey's equally famous "A Mathematical Theory of Saving" which was published in the same issue of *The Economic Journal* as Young's address (Vol. XXXVIII, No. 152, [December 1928], pp. 543–559). Ramsey carried forward Marshall's speculations of the early 1880's "On Utilitarianism: A Summum Bonum" reflecting issues posed still earlier by Sidgwick and Edgeworth. [For Marshall's hitherto unpublished note and its setting, see, especially, J. K.

Whitaker (ed.), *The Early Economic Writings of Alfred Marshall, 1867–1890* (London: Macmillan for the Royal Economic Society, 1975), Vol. II, pp. 316–325.] Ramsey's elegant paper poses important issues in welfare economics, intergenerational equity, and political morality which have been subsequently elaborated and indecisively debated. Ramsey's analysis does, indeed, relate the saving rate to the rate of growth and the pace at which Bliss is approached. But his interests led him explicitly to fix by assumption the variables most relevant to economic growth and its stability. His model may well have influenced later growth model builders; but, for purposes of this book, I concluded Bickerdike was a more relevant predecessor of Harrod-Domar and their successors.

107. Bruce Dean Larson, *The Analysis of Interests in the Economics of Charles Frederick Bickerdike* (doctoral thesis, Chapel Hill: University of North Carolina, 1983). See also Larson's "Bickerdike's Life and Work," *History of Political Economy* Vol. 19, No. 2 (Summer 1987). I am greatly in Professor Larson's debt for making available before publication his thesis, his article on Bickerdike, and an unpublished note, as well as for criticizing portions of the manuscript of this book. The major Marxists cited by Larson are Michael Tugan-Baranovsky, Rosa Luxemburg, and Otto Bauer; but he notes that Karl Kautsky, L. B. Boudin, and Ant. Bannekock also contributed to the development and elaboration of Marx's model. In his authoritative array of pre-1939 expositors of the accelerator, Gottfried Haberler adds to the list—aside from Aftalion, J. M. Clark, and Bickerdike—Bouniatian, Carver, Marco Fanno, Kuznets, Mitchell, Pigou, and Robertson (*Prosperity and Depression* [Geneva: League of Nations, 1937], p. 82).

108. Paul Sweezy, *Capitalist Development*, especially pp. 190–213. B. D. Larson, *Analysis of Interests*, p. 164 and unpublished "Notes on Early Mathematical Models of Economic Growth" (1982).

109. There are no index references to Bickerdike in the well-known histories of economic theory of Blaug, Roll, or Schumpeter; the briefest possible references to his analysis of the accelerator are in Hutchison and Pribram, and a similarly terse reference to a refinement of Mill on tariffs and the terms of trade are in Spiegel. Hansen's early study of the business cycle (*Business-Cycle Theory, Its Development and Present Status* [Boston: Ginn, 1927]), written closer to the time when Bickerdike was publishing regularly in *The Economic Journal,* contains eleven index references and three footnote citations.

110. Aside from my own reading of Bickerdike's articles and reviews, this brief account of Bickerdike is based mainly on Larson's work; but see also Harold Pilvin, "C. F. Bickerdike on Economic Growth," *The Canadian Journal of Economics and Political Science,* Vol. 20, No. 2 (May 1954), pp. 238–242; and Vincent Tarascio, "Bickerdike's Monetary Growth Theory," *History of Political Economy,* Vol. 12, No. 2 (Summer 1980), pp. 161–173. Here is Larson's more complete evaluation of Bickerdike's contribution to economic thought, fully annotated in the original ("Bickerdike's Life and Work," *History of Political Economy,* Vol. 19, No. 1 [Summer 1987], pp. 1–21. The following quotation is from pp. 1–2.):

> Today he is best known for his contributions to international trade, in which he was the first to employ comparative static analysis to consider the welfare implications of a tariff, and to derive the optimal tariff formula, and growth theory, in which he was the first to formulate an algebraic growth model and consider it in relation to the money supply.
>
> Bickerdike's place in the history of economic thought would be secure if he had only accomplished the above, but he accomplished more. His work has drawn notice for its early use of the acceleration principle and the multiplier, and some of his papers have been reprinted in recognition of their importance for public finance. Beyond these contributions are Bickerdike's generalized concept of external effects and the theory of local expenditures which he built upon it, and the attention that he gave to the role of expectations in economic affairs. His work also sheds light on the theory of monopolistic competition.

111. As pure conjecture, one can surmise that Edgeworth's death in 1926, ending his joint editorship of the *Economic Journal,* may have reduced Bickerdike's interest in publication.

112. B. D. Larson, *"Life and Work,"*, p. 1.

113. C. F. Bickerdike, "A Non-Monetary Cause of Fluctuations in Employment" *Economic Journal,* Volume XXIV, No. 95 (September 1914), pp. 357–370.

114. B. D. Larson, *"Life and Work"* pp. 5–16. Bickerdike's two key growth articles are "Individual and Social Interests in Relation to Saving," *Economic Journal,* Volume XXXIV, No. 135 (September 1924), pp. 408–422, and "Saving and the Monetary System," *ibid.,* Volume XXXV, No. 139 (September 1925), pp. 366–378.

115. "A Non-Monetary Cause. . . ," p. 357.

116. *Ibid.*

117. *Ibid.,* p. 361.

118. *Ibid.*

119. *Ibid.,* p. 363.

120. *Ibid.,* p. 367. In at least one case a longer view of the shipbuilding market led to a rather remarkable convergence of self-interest and social interest; that is, the countercyclical method of Sir William Burrell (1861–1958), a Glasgow shipowner that ultimately yielded for his native city a splendid museum and art collection (Richard Marks, "Sir William Burrell" in Richard Marks *et al., The Burrell Collection* [London and Glasgow: Collins, 1983]), p. 10:

> The Burrell brothers undoubtedly had the Midas touch. George kept abreast of developments in marine engineering while William specialized in the commercial side. Their fortunes were based on a steady nerve, foresight and breathtaking boldness. The formula was quite simple. In times of depression they would order a large number of ships at rock-bottom prices, calculating that the vessels would be coming off the stocks when the slump was reaching an end. Burrell and Son was then in a position to attract cargoes because it had ships available and could undercut its rivals. Then, after several years of highly profitable trading, the brothers would sell the fleet in a boom period and lie low until the next slump occurred, at which point the cycle would begin again. It sounds easy, and Burrell himself described it as making money like slatestones, but none of the firm's competitors was bold enough to take such risks.
>
> The operation was repeated twice on a large scale. In 1893/4 twelve new ships were built for the fleet of Burrell and Son at a time when the industry was in a very depressed state. A few years later, advantage was taken of the current high prices obtainable for shipping and every vessel flying the Burrell house flag was sold. After going into semiretirement for several years, in 1905 William and George rocked the shipping world by ordering no fewer than twenty steamers; a further eight were delivered in 1909/10. After a few years of prosperous trading the brothers once again decided to capitalize on the rise in the market values of ships, a rise which became dramatic after the outbreak of the First World War. Between 1913 and 1916 almost the entire fleet was sold, including vessels which were still on the stocks. With his share of the proceeds shrewdly invested, William Burrell devoted the remainder of his long life to what became an all-consuming passion, the amassing of a vast art collection.

121. "A Non-monetary cause . . . ", pp. 369–370.

122. See B. D. Larson, *Analysis of Interests,* mss. pp. 104–105 and 115–121. Also, "Life and Work" pp. 15–16.

123. "Individual and Social Interest in Relation to Saving," p. 408.

124. *Ibid.,* pp. 421–422.

125. Bickerdike's brief summary of this case approximates my view of the Kondratieff cycle, implying the existence of a dynamic optimum sectoral stock level ("Saving and the Monetary System"), pp. 372–380. See my *Why the Poor Get Rich,* Chapters 1 and 2.

126. "Saving and the Monetary System," pp. 377–378.

127. Essay by C. F. Bickerdike in *Pollak Prize Essays, Criticisms of Profits,* a book by William Trufant Foster and Waddill Catchings (Newton, Mass.: Pollack Foundation, 1927), pp. 72–78, 83–84, 87–88.

128. Both John Hicks and Nicholas Kaldor recalled Bickerdike's regular attendance at meetings of the Political Economy Club in London; but neither remembered any specific interventions.

129. See, for example, B. D. Larson, "Life and Work," pp. 18–19.

130. "Saving and the Monetary System," pp. 366–367.

131. *Economic Journal,* Volume XLIX, No. 193 (March 1939), pp. 14–33. H. Phelps Brown, in a supplementary note to his memorial essay on Harrod (*Economic Journal,* Vol. 91, No. 361, [March 1981], p. 231) observes that Erik Lundberg as well as Gustav Cassel may be regarded as having anticipated, to a degree, Harrod's growth equation.

132. R. F. Harrod, *The Trade Cycle, An Essay* (Oxford: at the Clarendon Press, 1936). As Harrod underlines, his *Trade Cycle* is a post-*General Theory* study. In his biography of Keynes, Harrod makes clear that he knew the *General Theory* intimately before its publication: *John Maynard Keynes* (New York: Harcourt Brace, 1951), pp. 452–453 and 456.

133. *Trade Cycle,* p. vii.

134. Harrod initially called this link the Relation, but abandoned it reluctantly in his "Dynamic Theory" in favor of the inaccurate but more popular Accelerator (p. 14n).

135. *Ibid.,* p. 102.

136. *Ibid.*

137. *Ibid.,* p. 104.

138. *Ibid.,* pp. 60–61, where references are made to the views of Kuznets and Schumpeter.

139. *Ibid.,* pp. 102–103.

140. *Ibid.,* p. 105.

141. *Ibid.*

142. "Dynamic Theory," p. 14.

143. *Ibid.,* p. 22.

144. *Ibid.,* p. 14n.

145. P. A. Samuelson, "Interaction between the Multiplier Analysis and the Principle of Acceleration," *Review of Economic Statistics,* Vol. XXXI,(May 1939), pp. 75–78.

146. *Ibid.,* p. 16.

147. This is not the place in our story to elaborate and defend this *obiter dicta.* But see preceeding, p. 231. For an earlier critique of Harrod's and similar models, see my *Process of Economic Growth,* Chapters IV and V.

148. E. D. Domar, "Expansion and Employment," *American Economic Review,* Vol. 37, No. 1 (March 1947); also "The Problems of Capital Accumulation," *ibid.,* Vol. 38, No. 4 (December 1948), R. F. Harrod, *Towards a Dynamic Economics* (London: Macmillan, 1948).

Chapter 10

1. The most complete business-cycle bibliography covering the period 1870–1939, of which I am aware, is to be found in Gottfried Haberler (ed.), *Readings in Business Cycle Theory* (Philadelphia: Blakiston, 1944), pp. 443–487. The opening sentences of D. H. Robertson's *A Study of Industrial Fluctuations* evokes both the scale and diversity of pre-1914 analyses of the business cycle (London: P. S. King, 1915, reprinted by the London School of Economics and Political Science, Reprints of Scarce Works on Political Economy, No. 8, 1948), pp. 1–2:

> The causes of crises and depressions alleged before the various committees of Congress in the eighties amounted to some 180 in number, and included the issue of free railway passes and the withholding of the franchise from women. This list remained undefeated until M. Bergmann in 1895 was able to publish an exhaustive discussion in the German tongue of 230 separate opinions, arranged in eight categories. Indeed, the problem of industrial fluctuation has exercised the minds of business men, economic writers and practical reformers of all schools throughout the past century: and within the last five years alone six weighty works, varying in length from 280 to 742 pages, have been published upon it in England, America and France. In these circumstances it might seem a presumptuous and superfluous undertaking to add to an already voluminous literature: nevertheless I conceive that no apology is needed.
>
> For on the one hand, in spite of the obvious futility of many of the minor explanations that have been given, this does appear to be a case in which, in the deathless words of the Dodo, everybody has won and must have prizes. . . .

2. *Ibid.*, pp. xvi and xvii.

3. For Schumpeter on Juglar, see *History of Economic Analysis*, (New York: Oxford University Press, 1954), especially pp. 1123–1124. The full title of Juglar's major study is *Des Crises Commerciales et Leur Retour Periodique en France, en Angleterre, et aux États-Unis* (Paris: Librarie Guillaumin, 1860, 1889 2d ed.). Page references here will be to the second edition.

4. *Des Crises Commerciales*, pp. v–vi. Juglar's demographic studies were published in 1851–1852.

5. *Ibid.*, p. 558. Translation is mine.

6. *History of Economic Analysis*, p. 1128.

7. Schumpeter's business-cycle analysis in his *Theory of Economic Development* (Cambridge: Harvard University Press, 1955), Chapter VI contains a number of supportive references to Spiethoff's views, but he draws (pp. 215–216) a lucid line of distinction between his formulation and Spiethoff's. Alvin Hansen argues persuasively that Gustav Cassel's business-cycle theory, to be found in Book IV of his *Theory of Social Economy*, derives substantially from Tugan-Baranowsky and Spiethoff; and, indeed, that Spiethoff owes a good deal to Tugan-Baranowsky (A. Hansen, *Business Cycles and National Income*, [New York: W. W. Norton, 1953]), pp. 292 and 310. The following quotation is from the latter page:

> That Cassel was profoundly influenced by the writings of Tugan-Baranowsky and Spiethoff appears plainly evident, though he fails to mention either one in his book. We are reminded of Tugan-Baranowsky when we read that "the movements of the trade cycle are merely expressions of the fluctuations in the production of fixed capital." Both Tugan-Baranowsky and Spiethoff come to mind when we learn that the "production of iron represents the entire production of fixed capital." Cassel defines periods of boom and depression precisely as follows: "A period of boom is one of special increase in the production of fixed capital; a period of decline or a depression is one in which this production falls below the point it had previously reached." He marks off these periods from a chart of world pig-iron production, which reflects, he believes, the world production of fixed capital. The alternation between periods of advance and periods of decline is fundamentally a variation in the production of fixed capital. But the production of consumption goods varies relatively little in relation to the movements of business cycles.

Hansen goes on to specify some original features of Cassel's cyclical analysis.

8. The references here are to the French edition, *Les Crises Industrielles en Angleterre* (Paris: Giard and Briére, 1913).

9. *Business Cycles and National Income*, pp. 289–290. The heart of Tugan-Baranowsky's exposition of his own theory is to be found in *Les Crises Industrielles*, Part II, Chapter III, "Le Cycle Industriel et L'Explication de la Périodicité des Crises," pp. 247–279. The steam-engine image is on p. 273.

10. *Les Crises Industrielles*, especially pp. 271–277.

11. Although it does not bear on the main theme of our analysis here, Spiethoff's background may be worth noting briefly. Born in 1873, he was led to study business cycles by a traumatic event in his boyhood: his father's firm in Westphalia went bankrupt in the depression of the 1870s. (Arthur Schweitzer, "Spiethoff's Theory of the Business Cycle," [Laramie: University of Wyoming Publications, Vol VIII, No. 1, April 1, 1941], p. 1.) He studied under Gustav Schmoller, a leader of the German Historical School, and Adolph Wagner, the statistician who analyzed the tendency for the proportion of national income expended by governments to increase with the rise in income. Leaning to Wagner's (and Juglar's) more disciplined empiricism, he set about trying to identify and describe in detail a "typical cycle" (*Musterkreislauf*). In 1902, at the end of his "sacred decade," he enunciated the doctrine of overproduction for which he is best known in "Vorbemerkungenzueiner Theorie der Ueberproduktion," *Schmollers Jahrbuecher*, Vol. XXVI, No. 2 (1902), pp. 271–305, where it is noted that the essay was delivered as a lecture on December 17, 1901, before the Political Science Association in Berlin. In addition to Juglar and Tugan-Baranowsky, he is said to have been influenced by Eugen Von Bergmann (A. Schweitzer, "Spiethoff's Theory," p. 2):

What is Spiethoff's position in economics and his attitude in business cycles theory? We can answer this by reference to the writings of three men: Juglar, Bergmann and Tugan-Baranowsky, and consider Spiethoff's reactions to them. A close study of Juglar's books revealed to Spiethoff that there are not just irregular crises but cycles; every upswing will lead to a downswing. This important observation led Spiethoff to the formulation of his "typical cyclical pattern." Bergmann, in his history of the theories of crises, tried to prove that the Classical theory could only explain the partial crises, but that general crises are necessarily in contradiction to the so-called "Law of the Markets." Spiethoff accepted Bergmann's explanation, rejected Say's law of the markets and concluded that it was impossible to explain the business cycles in terms of an equilibrium theory. Tugan-Baranowsky, on the other hand, convinced Spiethoff that a correlated factual and theoretical study of the business cycle is feasible and will lead to a satisfactory result. Thus we see that Spiethoff comes from the Historical School and does not favor the Classical and Neo-classical theory, yet in his own investigation he goes far beyond the boundary of Schmoller in attempting to give a theory in which the facts are the foundation for the explanation of the cycles.

Schweitzer's evaluation is based on his *Speithoffs Konjunkturlehre* (Basel: Helbing and Lichtenhahn, 1939). For references to Bergmann's work, notably his survey of business-cycle theories, see J. A. Schumpeter, *History of Economic Analysis,* notes on pp. 739, 740, 745, 1123, and 1134. T. W. Hutchison, (*A Review of Economic Doctrines, 1870–1929* [Oxford: at the Clarendon Press, 1953], p. 381), usefully oversimplifies the major distinction between Tugan-Baranowsky's emphasis and Spiethoff's: "Spiethoff's description of the cycle is in terms rather of a cycle of investment outlets as contrasted with Tugan-Baranowsky's description in terms of a cycle of gradual accumulation and sudden exhaustion and shortage of savings."

12. The most mature statement of Spiethoff's overproduction doctrine is in *Encyclopedia of the Social Sciences,* Vol. XI (New York: Macmillan, 1933), pp. 513–517. The article is reproduced in Alvin H. Hansen and Richard V. Clemence, *Readings in Business Cycles and National Income,* Chapter 9, pp. 108–115.

13. *Ibid.,* p. 109. The following passage suggests how Spiethoff defines his central concept (pp. 109–110):

> Lack of balance between production and consumption may be caused by forces operating on either side or on both and resulting in an increase in production or a decrease in consumption. On the production side there are three chief sets of causes for overproduction: first, natural occurrences such as particularly good crops, either of raw materials or of foodstuffs, which greatly augment production without any widening of the area under cultivation; second, technical inventions which make possible increasing productivity; and third, actual increase of the means of production—cultivation of additional land, more intensive exploitation of natural resources, the construction of new or the enlargement of capacity of old manufacturing plants—with the resultant disproportional increase of output.
>
> On the consumption side the causes of overproduction are even more numerous. Changing fashion . . ., the effect of technical changes . . . as central heating, for instance, displaced tiled stoves. Again, changes of locality may affect consumption. . . . Emigration of consumers . . . the transfer of workmen, officials or troops. . . . In the same way the transfer of an industry to a new location can cause a shutdown of the local industries dependent upon it. Furthermore consumption may fall off as a result of the saturation of demand.

14. *Ibid.,* pp. 110 and 114.

15. *Ibid.,* p. 114.

16. *Ibid.,* p. 113.

17. J. A. Schumpeter, *Theory of Economic Development,* p. 251.

18. *Ibid.,* pp. 214–216. See also Hansen's statement of the characteristics of Schumpeter's cyclical analysis that distinguishes him from Spiethoff (*Business Cycles and National Income,* pp. 301–308). Another effort of this period to link growth and cycles should be noted: Johan Äkerman, *Economic Progress and Economic Crisis* (trans. Elizabeth Sprigge and Claude Napier), (London: Macmillan, 1932), [Swedish edition, 1931]. Äkerman's analysis is governed by the judgment that

economics, if it was to be useful, had to break out of the static mold of Ricardo, Walras, and Jevons and "combine the study of conditions of equilibrium with that of the changes wrought by time" (pp. 16–17).

19. As A. Loveday's Preface reports, Haberler's study arose from a 1930 resolution adopted by the Assembly of the League of Nations launching an effort "to co-ordinate the analytical work then being done on the problem of the recurrence of periods of economic depression" (p. iii). The first stage, represented by Haberler's study, was meant to identify areas of consensus and differences of opinion about the cause of business cycles.

The next stage was planned as a confrontation of the various theories with historical facts. This task was undertaken by Jan Tinbergen, *Statistical Testing of Business-Cycle Theories*, Volume I, *A Method and Its Application to Investment Activity*, and Volume II, *Business Cycles in the United States of America, 1919–1932* (Geneva: League of Nations, 1939). These studies are briefly considered preceding, pp. 299–301.

20. *Prosperity and Depression*, p. 174.

21. "Some Material for a Study of Trade Fluctuations", *Journal of the Royal Statistical Society*, No. 77, New Series, (January 1914), pp. 159–178. Robertson's paper was drawn from work on his *A Study of Industrial Fluctuations* (1915) which, in an earlier draft, won the Cobden Club Prize at Cambridge in 1913. The *Journal* article is a condensed version of his paper and of the subsequent discussion.

22. T. W. Hutchison, *Economic Doctrines, 1870–1919*, pp. 379–404.

23. *Ibid.*, p. 404. Schumpeter's more direct dictum is (*History of Economic Analysis*, pp. 1134–1135): ". . . The essential of both the methods and the explanatory principles that serve in today's business-cycle analysis, barring refinements of technique, date from before 1914. . . ."

24. "Some Material for a Study of Trade Fluctuations," pp. 167–168.

The discussion of Robertson's paper, as summarized, was generally supportive but restrained. D. A. Thomas politely called the paper "exceedingly interesting and suggestive," but responded head-on to Robertson's suggestion that his (Thomas's) 1903 paper on investment in coal pits may have been in error. He also suggested that annual data were inadequate to test Robertson's linking of periods of gestation to cyclical fluctuations. R. G. Hawtrey's intervention eschewed monetary matters, but covered the monetarists' flanks implicitly by expressing doubt on several grounds that "the harmonics" of investment, as shaped by periods of gestation, could play the large role in overall cyclical fluctuations Robertson attributed to that process. (It is doubtful that Hawtrey was aware of the rather rude observations in the full text of Robertson's *Study* on extreme monetarists in general, on Hawtrey in particular.) Flux, a distinguished statistician, underlined inadequacies in Robertson's annual data, which he had already acknowledged. Edgeworth concluded that Robertson's ideas were more important than his data (which Flux had suggested) and characterized the paper as an exercise in "[t]hat fundamental distinction between long periods and short periods which Dr. Marshall had first of all pointed out clearly."

25. *Ibid.*, p. 402. Since the text will deal with Robertson's monograph mainly in terms of its relation to growth rather than business-cycle analysis, in the narrower sense, Hutchison's excellent summary of its contents is worth including here (pp. 402–403):

> Methodologically it provides a synthesis of theoretical analysis with historical and statistical material, . . . Over-investment and capital shortage, deficiency of consumption demand, inventions, errors in investment, and crop fluctuations, are all given a place, either as working together or as alternative possibilities in the various phases of different cycles.
>
> Robertson's over-investment analysis was similar to that of Spiethoff, but is combined with elements emphasized by Aftalion. The virtual impossibility of stable and correct forecasts by entrepreneurs of the marginal utility of capital goods, as contrasted with consumption goods, is emphasized, and it is the variations in these forecasts "which furnish the key to the most important aspects of modern industrial fluctuations." (p. 157) Special stress is laid on the rise in costs as a factor tending to bring the boom to an end. An actual "real" shortage of consumable goods as described by Spiethoff . . . is recognized as a possible ground for the breakdown of an investment boom, but is not held to be the only possible ground:

> The relapse in constructional industry is seen to be due to the existence or imminence of an over-production of instrumental as compared with consumable goods. Whether or not this over-production is indicated by an actual shortage of consumable goods which renders it impossible to maintain investment on the scale which has prevailed during the preceding years or months, or whether it is due to miscalculation or to the inevitable characteristics of modern large-scale production, its essential nature is the same, a failure to secure the best conceivable distribution through time of a community's consumption of consumable goods. (p. 187.)

Particularly detailed attention is given to the role of fluctuations in crop values in the trade cycle, a subject which had been much studied, but with highly ambiguous and diametrically conflicting conclusions as to the processes involved. (Part I, Chapter 5–7.)

> The remedies discussed include "a more centralized investment policy" and Fisher's plan for stabilizing the general price-level, which is approved with reservations, . . . Wage reductions in the slump are considered to be of very doubtful aid:
> > It must be remembered first that if the men are employed in constructional industry, the demand for their labour at such a time is likely to be inelastic, and the aggregate income of members therefore lessened, even though unemployment be avoided, by the acceptance of lower wages. . . . On the whole I cannot help feeling, that, in spite no doubt of errors of judgment, the trade unions have known their own business in this matter better than is always admitted. (p. 249)
> "Cordial support" is given to the public-works proposal of the Minority report of the Poor Law Commission, and "Mr. Hawtrey's attack upon the proposal scarcely deserves formal refutation." (p. 253.) The final emphasis of the book is somewhat similar to Schumpeter's , being on the clash of progress and security in the existing economic order: "What is meant" it is asked "by the most desirable distribution of the community's income through time?" Under the existing order "out of the welter of industrial dislocation the great permanent riches of the future are generated." (p. 254.)

Richard Kahn notes, in my view correctly, that immediately before and, indeed, immediately after the First World War the "thinking of Dennis Robertson was in advance of that of Keynes . . . . [He] had developed his economic thinking well ahead of Keynes" (*The Making of the General Theory*, p. 15, see also pp. 49 and 185). The two men collaborated closely down through the publication of *The Treatise on Money* (1930) when leadership shifted, by most evaluations, to Keynes; although I would judge Robertson's command over the real factors operating in the economy remained superior. Keynes evidently emerged as a far more effective expositer and negotiator of new policies at home and abroad.

26. *Study*, pp. 61 and 104–105.

27. *Ibid.*, pp. ix–x.

28. *Study*, pp. 211–212.

29. *Ibid.*, p. 218. Robertson's section on "Gold—Medicine, Poison, and Intoxicant" (pp. 228–235) remains a useful antidote against simplistic interpretations of the workings of the monetary system.

30. Labordère's essay first appeared in *La Revue de Paris,* February 1, 1908, and was published separately under the title *Crise Americaine de 1907 ou Capitaux -réels et Capitaux-apparents*. It is reprinted as an appendix in the reprint of Robertson's *Study*. The quoted sentence in the text is to be found on p. 14 of Labordère's essay which, along with other arguments for overinvestment as the cause of crises, made a sufficient impression on Keynes for him to present a paper to the London Political Economy Club (December 3, 1912) entitled "How Far Are Bankers Responsible for the Alternations of Boom and Depression?"

31. *Study*, pp. 239–241.

32. J. R. Hicks, "A Memoir: Dennis Holme Robertson, 1890–1963," in Dennis Robertson, *Essays in Money and Interest* (London: Collins, The Fontana Library, 1966), pp. 12–13.

33. *Banking Policy and the Price Level,* initially published by Staples Press, London, appeared in

a second edition in 1932 later issued in 1949 as No. 8 in the London School of Economics series of reprints of "scarce works" (New York: Augustus M. Kelley).

34. For a reflection of Robertson's discomfiture—evidently more deeply felt than formally expressed—with Keynes's drift from what the former regarded as their basically harmonious intellectual partnership of the 1920s, see the 1949 Preface to *Banking Policy*, p. xiii. For example:

> For these and other reasons, including the treatment by Pigou in his *Industrial Fluctuations* (1927) of the monetary causes of changes in output, it is bound to remain to me a source of some bewilderment that at some time in the period following 1930 the idea that monetary analysis . . . is concerned with the behaviour of output as well as of prices should apparently have struck Keynes, or at any rate the able little group who were then advising him, with the force of a new discovery.

On the other hand see Richard Kahn's well-documented account of the limited character of the Keynes–Robertson estrangement during Keynes's work on *The General Theory* and their cheerful, effective, occasionally playful collaboration during the Second World War and at Bretton Woods (*The Making of Keynes' General Theory*, pp. 185–188).

35. *Ibid.*, p. 1.
36. *Ibid.*, pp. vii–viii.
37. *Ibid.*, p. 5.
38. *Ibid.*
39. *History of Economic Analysis*, pp. 1127–1128.
40. *Study*, pp. 175–187.
41. *Banking Policy*, p. 11 n. 1.
42. *Ibid.*, p. 18.
43. *Ibid.*, p. 39.
44. *Study*, pp. xvi–xvii. Robertson (like Davidson in Sweden in response to Wicksell) was conscious that, in a time of rapid cost-reducing innovation, the optimum objective of macropolicy might be a falling rather than constant price level. In discussing wage policy in the *General Theory*, Keynes also explored the case of constant money wages with prices falling with the progress of technique and equipment (p. 271).
45. *Study*, pp. 241–242.
46. *Ibid.*, p. 254.
47. A. C. Pigou, *Wealth and Welfare* (London: Macmillan, 1912), Part IV, pp. 401–486. John R. Presley, *Robertsonian Economics* (London: Macmillan, 1978), provides the following account of Pigou's influence on Robertson's *Study* (pp. 9–10):

> His [Robertson's] first approach to the study of industrial fluctuation had in fact been to summarise a number of theories and to test these against empirical evidence. He was diverted from this course by A. C. Pigou, who wrote: "You have collected an astonishing amount of material and have made comment on it in such a way that I feel sure you will eventually make something very good indeed. But, of course, at present, the thing is mainly a great mass of raw material. Marshall used to instruct one that the *bones* of a piece of work, which was really one's own production, grew gradually and then the whole thing came together round them. You haven't yet got the bones; you haven't thought through the material. The next stage is to set and stew on all these facts and partial explanations until some coherent unity grows up and the separate facts fall into their proper place." Whether or not this advice did provide the direction for his future work is difficult to determine in retrospect; there may have been other, unknown influences; but the approach adopted by Robertson does bear a striking resemblance to this counsel. Robertson was recommended to take a *positive* rather than a critical line in his study. In particular, and this is very significant, Pigou instructed, though with some reservation: "You ought more consistently and thoroughly to dig down behind money appearances to real facts" . . . and to "distinguish more between causes of a *general* kind affecting industry as a whole and special causes affecting particular industries."

48. A. C. Pigou, *The Economics of Welfare* (Macmillan: London, 1920), (1st ed.).

49. *Wealth and Welfare*, p. 447, n. 1. See also Robertson's comment, *Study*, p. ix.
50. *Wealth and Welfare*, p. 460, from which following two sentences in the text are also drawn.
51. Robert Skidelsky, *John Maynard Keynes*, Vol. I, *Hopes Betrayed, 1883–1920* (London: Macmillan, 1983), p. 211.
52. *Industrial Fluctuations*, p. 22.
53. *Ibid.*, pp. 35–36.
54. *Ibid.*, p. 49.
55. *Ibid.*, pp. 49–50.
56. *Ibid.*, pp. 92–93.
57. *Ibid.*, p. 93 n. 2 carried over from p. 92.

Chapter 11

1. For a convenient summary statement see *A Treatise on Money* (London: Macmillan, 1930), Vol. I, pp. 171–184. R. F. Harrod (*Life of John Maynard Keynes*, [New York: Harcourt Brace, 1951, pp. 407–408]), provides a lucid rational for Keynes's rather curious definitions in *A Treatise:*

> He excluded from saving what may be called excess profit and did not deduct from it business losses. Excess profit is defined as such profit as causes the producer to increase output, and loss is defined as the difference between what he actually gets and what he would have to get in order to make him willing not to decrease output; if loss in this sense occurs, he decreases his operations in the next round. Thus if we add excess profit to saving, we get the book-keeping identity that investment is equal to saving, and if we deduct realised loss from saving the remainder is equal to investment. Keynes' reason for segregating this particular item of income (or loss) is that it is the dynamic element which causes the economy to move towards expansion and inflation on the one hand or depression and deflation on the other. It seems quite reasonable to distinguish between savings which arise in the ordinary prudent conduct of business life by an individual or a company and those savings which are windfall, unexpected, and the result of a disequilibrium in the economy.

2. *A Treatise*, Vol. I, p. 258.
3. *Ibid.*, pp. 282–283.
4. *Ibid.*, p. 289.
5. *Ibid.*, p. 291.
6. *Ibid.*, pp. 294, 297–298.
7. *Ibid.*, Vol. II, Book VI, "The Rate of Investment and Its Fluctuations," pp. 195–210.
8. *Ibid.*, pp. 95–96, 100–101. While Schumpeter no doubt appreciated Keynes's reference to his work he must have been infuriated by the fact that Keynes quotes "the convenient summary" from Wesley Mitchell's *Business Cycles*, p. 96, n. 1, rather than the original in German.
9. *Ibid.*, pp. 162–163.
10. *Ibid.*, p. 170.
11. *Ibid.*, p. 174.
12. *Ibid.*, pp. 180–181.
13. *Ibid.*, pp. 182–184.
14. *Ibid.*, p. 189.
15. *Ibid.*, p. 204.
16. *Ibid.*, pp. 206–207.
17. For my first exercise in this method see "Explanations of the Great Depression," Chapter VII in *British Economy of the Nineteenth Century*, (Oxford: at the Clarendon Press, 1948). Harrod (*Life of Keynes*, pp. 338–345) evokes persuasively the winter of 1922–1923 as the critical turning point in Keynes's evolution as he moved from a concern with reparations to domestic financial problems. He dramatizes the passage with a note by Keynes in the *Nation*, July 14, 1923, protesting a rise of the bank rate on July 7, at a time of falling prices and rising unemployment. It was,

presumably, a conscious deflationary step on the road to the return of sterling to the gold standard at prewar parity. Keynes's "Note on Finance and Investment," followed in November 1923 by his *A Tract on Monetary Reform,* set him on the path that led directly to *A Treatise, The General Theory,* and, indeed—the Bretton Woods institutions and the British loan of 1946.

19. R. Skidelsky, *John Maynard Keynes,* (Macmillan: London, 1930) Vol. I, p. 214.

20. R. Harrod, *Keynes,* p. 451. See also A. C. Pigou, "John Maynard Keynes, Economist" in memorial statements from Proceedings of the British Academy,1946, *John Maynard Keynes, Baron Keynes of Tilton, 1883–1946,* (London: Geoffrey Cumberledge), p. 19:

> After Marshall's main work was finished economic thought on fundamental issues moved little, at all events in this country. We were pedestrian, perhaps a little complacent. Keynes's *Treatise on Money* and, later, his *General Theory* broke resoundingly that dogmatic slumber. Whether in agreement or in disagreement with him, discussion and controversy sprang up and spread over the whole world. Economics and economists came alive. The period of tranquillity was ended. A period of active and, so far as might be, creative thought was born. For this the credit is almost wholly due to Keynes. Even should all his own ideas presently be rejected—which, of course, will not happen—for this inbreathing of the spirit he would still rank among the foremost architects of our subject.
>
> He had, of course, as all have, the defects of his qualities. By defining common words in uncommon senses, as with "savings" and "income," in his earlier book, and "full" employment—which was compatible with a large volume of unemployment!—in his later one, he caused much confusion among persons less agile-minded than himself. Maybe too, had he been less ready to hoist the flag of intellectual revolution, stressing agreement more and disagreement less, he would have obviated some misunderstanding and some unfruitful debate, thus freeing himself to produce even more constructive work than he actually did. But there are two sides to this. Had he acted so, in a more Marshallian manner, not only must he have proved a less effective catalyst, but also—and this to him would have meant much—his influence upon immediate public policy in these times of urgency must inevitably have been far smaller than it was.

21. *General Theory,* p. 245.

22. David Worswick and James Trevithick (eds.), *Keynes and the Modern World, Proceedings of the Keynes Centenary Conference, King's College, Cambridge* (Cambridge: Cambridge University Press, 1983), p. 164. This point is made also in A. C. Pigou, *Keynes' General Theory: A Retrospective View* (London: Macmillan, 1950), p. 4: "These restricting assumptions exclude from consideration the consequences of gradual increase in the stock of capital equipment consequent on successive investments made over a series of years."

23. *General Theory,* pp. 246–247. This is the passage Pigou isolated as containing "Keynes's main and very important contribution to economic analysis." *Retrospective View,* p. 20.

24. *General Theory,* p. 315.

25. *Ibid.*

26. *Ibid.,* p. 250.

27. *Ibid.,* pp. 317 and 319–320.

28. *Ibid.,* p. 325.

29. See, for example, *ibid.,* pp. 316, 322–323.

30. *Ibid.,* pp. 320–321.

31. *Ibid.,* pp. 306–309. For Richard Kahn's comments on the emergence of the Marshallian long period for certain limited purposes in a book overwhelmingly geared to the short period see *The Making of the General Theory,* pp. 122–123.

32. W. W. Rostow (ed.), *The Economics of Take-off into Sustained Growth,* proceedings of a conference held by the International Economics Association (New York: St. Martin's Press, 1963), pp. xiii–xiv. I made this observation with respect to the concept of take-off in the course of the Konstanz debate: ". . . the introduction of a new concept—especially a new term—is an act of aggression against respected colleagues and friends."

33. Michael Kalecki, "A Theory of the Business Cycle," *Review of Economic Studies,* Vol. IV,

No. 2 (February 1937); Nicholas Kaldor, "A Model of the Trade Cycle," *Economic Journal, Vol. L, No. 197* (March 1940), accessibly reprinted in Alvin H. Hansen and Richard V. Clemence, *Readings in Business Cycles and National Income* (New York: W. W. Norton, 1953, Chapter 23. Kaldor explicitly relates his cyclical theory to Keynes's *General Theory,* but J. R. Hicks argued that it was more Robertsonian than Keynesian ["The Monetary Theory of D. H. Robertson," *Economica,* Vol. IX, No. 33 (February 1942), p. 55]. Hicks linked Kaldor's essay explicitly to Robertson's "Industrial Fluctuations and the Natural Rate of Interest," Chapter V in D. H. Robertson, *Essays in Monetary Theory* (London and New York: Staples Press, 1940).

34. J. A. Schumpeter, *Ten Great Economists,* p. 251 and n. 1.

35. *Ibid.,* p. 249.

36. Alvin H. Hansen, *Business Cycles and National Income,* p. 406.

37. Wesley Clair Mitchell, *Business Cycles* (Berkeley: University of California Press, 1913), p. vii.

38. See, for example, *ibid.,* pp. 22–26.

39. *Ibid.,* p. 26.

40. *Ibid.,* pp. 585–586.

41. *Ibid.,* p. 398.

42. Milton Friedman, "Wesley Mitchell as a Theorist," *Journal of Political Economy* (December 1950), p. 487.

43. T. W. Hutchison, *A Review of Economic Doctrines, 1870–1929* (Oxford: at the Clarendon Press, 1953), p. 401.

44. *Business Cycles,* pp. 578–581.

45. For example, *ibid.,* pp. 387–421 and 581–583.

46. *Ibid.,* p. 503.

47. *Ibid.,* pp. 567 and 598.

48. Willard L. Thorp, *Business Annals* (New York: NBER, 1926). Other pre-1927 monographs published by the NBER bearing on cyclical fluctuations were: *Business Cycles and Unemployment* (1923), the NBER staff and collaborators; Willford I. King, *Employment, Hours, and Earnings in Prosperity and Depression, United States, 1920–22* (1923); and Harry Jerome, *Migration and Business Cycles* (1926).

49. *The Problem and Its Setting,* p. x.

50. *Ibid.,* p. 50. Minnie T. England's work focused on waves of "promotion"; the degenerative forces that develop during a boom undermining the expected profit in the sectors under promotion; and the mechanism of crisis. See, for example, her "Economic Crises," *Journal of Political Economy,* (April 1913), pp. 345–354; and "An Analysis of the Crisis Cycle," *ibid.,* (October 1913), pp. 712–734.

51. *The Problem and Its Setting,* pp. 20–23.

52. *Ibid.,* pp. 213–233. Mitchell states (p. 213 n. 1): "So far as I know, the only one working upon secular trends as a problem in its own right is Dr. Simon S. Kuznets. . . ."

53. *Ibid.,* pp. 230–233. The substance and style of this passage suggests that it may have been, in fact, drafted by Kuznets.

54. This chapter does foreshadow the NBER technique for clearing statistical series of trend and isolating cyclical patterns unique to each series (specific cycles) and patterns in relation to general cyclical movements (reference cycles) (*ibid.,* pp. 472–474). This is accomplished by recalculating each statistic relative to the trend average for the cycle. This form of clearance yields, via the sequence of average standings, a trend measurement. Mitchell does not deal with the potentialities for trend (i.e., growth) measurement implicit in this method except for the following vague reference (p. 474): "The analysis of what happens in [cycles] must be supplemented by discussions in which certain hypotheses are tested with respect to long periods of time . . . in which statistical series are taken as wholes instead of segments."

55. Arthur F. Burns was good enough to explain the interesting origins of this study in a long telephone conversation with the author on April 23, 1986. He began in the late 1920s by studying

the relationship between cyclical movements in production and prices in the course of U.S. business cycles. After analyzing a new index of business activity, Burns's preliminary conclusions ''collapsed.'' He then paused to reflect on the problems implicit in any effort to measure the physical volume of production over substantial periods of time, including multiple facets of the index-number problem. The result was a classic article ''The Measurement of the Physical Volume of Production,'' *Quarterly Journal of Economics,* Vol. XLIV, (February, 1930), pp. 242–262. *Production Trends* reflects his subsequent acute sensitivity to possible distortions resulting from the use of indexes over long periods of time. The book is shot through with implicit or explicit references to the *QJE* article, notably Chapters I, II, and VI. For example, he observes (p. 256): ''. . . any so-called index series of the physical volume of production in a changing economic system is inherently ambiguous. . . ; and that ambiguity is apt to increase with the length of the period covered by the index.'' He then notes the proposition is given fuller discussion in the 1930 article.

56. *Production Trends,* pp. 172–173. Burns's analysis of sectoral retardation, which he takes to be generally related to an economy's dynamism, is elaborated in Chapter IV, pp. 96–173.

57. *Ibid.,* pp. xx, 180–181.

58. *Ibid.,* pp. 242–243.

59. *Ibid.,* pp. 244–245.

60. *Ibid.,* pp. 248–251. Burns includes in his exposition the following historical passage:

> . . . [T]he decade rates furnish an instructive tentative approach to the problem.
>
> The first peak in the standard trend-cycle and in the cycle of divergence in production trends comes in the decade 1875–85. In April 1882, a severe business depression set in, which lasted through May 1885. . . . The statistical record in the present case is therefore roughly consistent with the hypothesis that the severity of business depressions is connected with the magnitude of the preceding secular advance in general production and the divergence in the rates of secular advance of individual industries.
>
> The second peak in the standard trend-cycle of production and in the cycle of divergence in production trends comes in the decade 1895–1905. This decade experienced extraordinarily rapid and almost uninterrupted growth. . . . The setbacks in 1900 and 1903–04 are almost imperceptible in annual production data, and are of a quite different order of magnitude from the decline during the depression of 1907–08. Though this depression was of rather brief duration, running over some thirteen months from June 1907 through June 1908, it was of very considerable depth. Again, the statistical record confirms the hypothesis that a severe depression tends to follow a period during which the secular trends of production move sharply upward while the divergence in the rates of expansion is exceptionally large. . . .
>
> The next peak in the standard trend-cycle comes in the decade 1910–20. The peak for this period is not quite so significant as for other periods, since a considerable number of individual industries, especially those connected with construction, registered troughs. A more important characteristic of this period is the considerable diversity in the rates of industrial expansion—a natural consequence of the shifts in the economy from a peace to a war basis. . . . For the present purpose it suffices to state that the statistical evidence again satisfies our hypothesis; for this decade terminated with a crisis of extraordinary severity, the downturn lasting from February 1920 to September 1921.
>
> The following and final peak in the standard trend-cycle and in the cycle of the dispersion in the rates of secular expansion comes in 1920–29. . . . Though we cannot be certain that a peak actually occurs in 1920–29, the statistics of production since 1925 suggest strongly that the level of the standard trend-cycle for the central decade year 1930 will compare unfavorably with that for the central decade year 1925. . . .

61. *Ten Great Economists,* p. 248 and n. 9.

62. *Production Trends,* p. 244.

63. J. M. Clark's study was, in fact published by the NBER in cooperation with the Committee on Recent Economic Changes. It includes an Introduction by the Committee describing its origins in the midst of the initial post-World War I depression of 1921; its subsequent evolution including systematic collaboration on ''a comprehensive fact-and-figure picture of the results of the working

of economic forces during a major business cycle. . . .''; its concentration after 1929 on intense analyses of the pathology of the great depression and, to a degree, a search for remedies. Clark, who participated in the sessions of the Committee and the presentation of the data by experts, was asked to view "the whole picture objectively . . . make an appraisal and draw certain conclusions."

64. J. M. Clark, *Strategic Factors*, pp. 5–7. Clark's effort to balance theory and induction yields a nice definition of the middle ground Malthus and Ricardo sought vainly to establish in their exchanges on method (p. 6):

> Theoretical studies give us causes that are too few and too simple, such as over-production, under-consumption, over-saving, or failure to distribute to laborers their whole product or enough of the whole product of industry to enable them to buy the things they have produced. Inductive studies, on the other hand, reveal so many factors at work, so completely interrelated, that we are likely to come to the conclusion that everything is both cause and effect, and everything is the result of nearly everything else, or that all features of modern industrialism are jointly responsible for the business cycle. The attempt in the present study is to steer a course between these two extremes, including anything which a well-rounded survey of the facts can suggest, but selecting those factors which seem to have the greatest strategic importance, if any can be picked out. A factor may be said to have strategic importance if it has real power to control other factors, and to determine the general character of the result; and it has a peculiar strategic importance if, in addition, we have power to control it; if it is not, like the weather, beyond the reach of anything we can now do.

65. *Ibid.*, extracted from pp. 127–131. The phrase "moving equilibrium" is from Allyn A. Young's "Increasing Returns and Economic Progress," *Economic Journal,* Vol. XXXVIII, No. 152 (December 1928), p. 535.

66. *Strategic Factors*, pp. 131–134.

67. *Ibid.*, pp. 134–136.

68. *Ibid.*, pp. 136–137.

69. *Ibid.*, pp. 138–139.

70. *Ibid.*, pp. 139–142.

71. *Ibid.*, pp. 143–144.

72. *Ibid.*, pp. 144–147

73. *Ibid.*, pp. 151–154. Clark does not make explicit reference to Burns's roughly concurrent study.

74. *Ibid.*, p. 155. In a final, catchall section (pp. 155–158), Clark cites other potential sources of imbalance; e.g., sluggish adaptation of manpower in agriculture to productivity increases, and tariff and other distortions of foreign trade and payments.

75. Clark's initial exposition of the accelerator is to be found in his "Business Acceleration and the Law of Demand," *Journal of Political Economy,* Vol. XXV, (March 1917), pp. 217–235.

76. Solomon Fabricant, *The Output of Manufacturing Industries, 1899–1937* (New York: NBER, 1940).

77. *Ibid.*, p. 3.

78. Solomon Fabricant, *Manufacturing Output, 1929–1937,* (New York: NBER, Occasional Paper No. 1: December 1940).

79. *Ibid.*, p. 6.

80. *Ibid.*, pp. 9–10.

81. *Ibid.*, p. 12.

82. See, for example, *Manufacturing Output, 1899–1937*, pp. 43–46.

83. Oxford: The Clarendon Press, 1953. A second edition was published by the Harvester Press (Hassocks *nr.* Brighton, Sussex) in 1975. In addition to Gayer, authors were W. W. Rostow and Anna Jacobson Schwartz, with the assistance of Isaiah Frank. The study was financed by the Columbia University Council for Research in Social Sciences but conducted with the cooperation of Wesley C. Mitchell, Arthur F. Burns, and the NBER staff.

84. *Ibid.*, 2d ed., p. v.

85. Alvin H. Hansen, *Cycles of Prosperity and Depression in the United States, Great Britain and Germany. A Study of Monthly Data, 1902–1908* (Madison: University of Wisconsin Press, 1921). In his later *Business-Cycle Theory*, (Note 86, following) Hansen observes that his earlier study was more "dogmatic" than he had become by 1927. His early work was unabashedly monetarist: ". . . The cycle of prosperity is at bottom a question of money, credit, and prices. . .," p. 110.

86. Alvin H. Hansen, *Business-Cycle Theory, Its Development and Present Status,* (Boston: Ginn, 1927) p. 10.

87. *Ibid.,* pp. 187–206.

88. *Ibid.,* see especially pp. 191–196.

89. *Ibid.,* p. 193.

90. P. A. Samuelson, "Interactions between the Multiplier Analysis and the Principle of Acceleration", *Review of Economic Statistics* (May 1939), p. 75.

91. For a useful terse exposition of Samuelson's and subsequent multiplier–accelerator models see, A. W. Mullineux, *The Business Cycle after Keynes;* (Totowa, New Jersey: Barnes and Noble, 1984).

92. *Ibid.,* p. 78, including Note 1.

93. P. A. Samuelson, "Foreword," in Robert T. Masson and P. David Quall (eds.), *Essays on Industrial Organization in Honor of Joe S. Bain* (Cambridge, Mass.: Ballinger, 1976), p. xviii.

94. Margaret Halsey, *With Malice Toward Some,* (New York: Simon and Schuster, 1938), pp. 99–100.

95. This definition appears in the first issue of *Econometrica,* Vol. I (January 1933), p. 2. The large hopes and enthusiasm that went with the emergence of econometrics as an explicitly defined field (and international fellowship) is suggested by the names of some of those who contributed papers to the first issue of *Econometrica:* Johan Åkerman, A. L. Bowley, Alfred Cowles, III, Mordecai Ezekiel, Irving Fisher, Ragnar Frisch (in addition to his opening "Editorial"), Alvin Hansen, Harold Hotelling, Joseph Schumpeter, Jan Tinbergen. In addition, a note of Alfred Marshall's was published: "The Mathematician, as Seen by Himself."

96. Geneva: League of Nations, 1939. Vol. I, *A Method and Its Application to Investment Activity;* Vol. II, *Business Cycles in the United States, 1919–1932.* Both works are reproduced in a single volume (New York: Agathon, 1968), with a special introduction by Tinbergen.

97. This review, Tinbergen's reply, and Keynes's comment are accessibly reprinted in A. H. Hansen and R. V. Clemence, *Readings,* pp. 330–356.

98. The chief results are summarized in *Statistical Testing,* Vol. I, pp. 49, 98, 130.

99. *Ibid.,* pp. 131–132. The notably rigorous and self-disciplined Tinbergen could not resist, however, drawing conclusions about the British economy in, for example, 1883 and 1887 on the basis of exceedingly frail correlations, errors he could have avoided by "wallowing" a bit, like D. H. Robertson in, for example, *The Economist Annual Reviews* for the relevant years.

100. *Ibid.,* pp. 184–193.

101. Jan Tinbergen, "The Use of Models: Experiences and Prospects," *American Economic Review* (Special Ed., December 1981), p. 17 (Nobel Lecture, December 1969). Paul Samuelson's reflections on the yield from econometrics is more bluntly disappointed ("My Life Philosophy," *The American Economist,* Vol. XXVI, No. 2 [Fall 1983], p. 9.):

> Let me make a confession. Back when I was 20 I could perceive the great progress that was being made in econometric *methods.* Even without foreseeing the onset of the computer age, with its cheapening of calculations. I expected that the new econometrics would enable us to narrow down the uncertainties of our economic theories. We would be able to test and reject false theories. We would be able to infer new good theories.
>
> My confession is that this expectation has not worked out. From several thousands of monthly and quarterly time series, which cover the last few decades or even centuries, it has turned out not to be possible to arrive at a close approximation to indisputable truth. I never ignore econometric studies, but I have learned from sad experience to take them with large grains of salt. It takes one

econometric study to calibrate another: a priori thought can't do the job. But it seems objectively to be the case that there does not accumulate a convergent body of econometric findings, convergent on a testable truth.

For a more favorable assessment of the fruits of econometric and other forms of quantitative analysis see Richard Stone, "Political Economy, Economics, and Beyond," *Economic Journal*, Vol. 90, No. 360 (December 1980), pp. 719–736.

102. *Ibid.*, The point is driven home in Jan Tinbergen and J. J. Polak, *The Dynamics of Business Cycles* (Chicago: University of Chicago Press, 1950), based on Tinbergen's *Economische Bewegingsleer* (Amsterdam: North Holland Press, 1942). Here Tinbergen includes a chapter of fifteen pages on "Long-Run Developments" another on "Interruptions and Sudden Changes in Structure," a third on "The Process of Long-Run Development." But he regards cycles as "superimposed on the general long-run tendencies in the economy" (p. 60); and, in the heart of his analysis, he separates cycles from trend (p. 159). Tinbergen reflects at various points an uneasiness at this procedure; and in a "Theoretical Postscript" acknowledges that endogenous factors may yield an upturn from depression as well as growth factors (e.g., "a new invention or the opening up of new markets," p. 257); but the latter he regards as exogenous. The separation of growth and cyclical analysis remains analytically complete despite the various references to growth in the book.

Chapter 12

1. "Official Papers, 'Return of Estimated Value of Foreign Trade of United Kingdom at Prices of 1900,' " *The Economic Journal*, Vol. XXII, No. 88 (Dec. 1912), pp. 628–632.

2. D. H. Robertson, *A Study of Industrial Fluctuations* (London: P. S. King 1915 reprinted by the London School of Economics, Reprints of Scarce Works on Political Economy, No. 8, 1948) p. 169 n. 1.

3. J. M. Keynes, *The Economic Consequences of the Peace* (New York: Harcourt Brace, 1920), pp. 9–26 and 254–255. The following passage (pp. 9–10), not only captures the link between Keynes's 1912 and 1919 positions on the terms of trade but also the vivid rhetoric of his evocation of economic history:

> After 1870 there was developed on a large scale an unprecedented situation, and the economic condition of Europe became during the next fifty years unstable and peculiar. The pressure of population on food, which had already been balanced by the accessibility of supplies from America, became for the first time in recorded history definitely reversed. As number increased, food was actually easier to secure. Larger proportional returns from an increasing scale of production became true of agriculture as well as industry. With the growth of the European population there were more emigrants on the one hand to till the soil of the new countries, and, on the other, more workmen were available in Europe to prepare the industrial products and capital goods which were to maintain the emigrant populations in their new homes, and to build the railways and ships which were to make accessible to Europe food and raw products from distant sources. Up to about 1900 a unit of labor applied to industry yielded year by year a purchasing power over an increasing quantity of food. It is possible that about the year 1900 this process began to be reversed, and a diminishing yield of Nature to man's effort was beginning to reassert itself. But the tendency of cereals to rise in real cost was balanced by other improvements; and— one of many novelties—the resources of tropical Africa then for the first time came into large employ, and a great traffic in oil-seeds began to bring to the table of Europe in a new and cheaper form one of the essential foodstuffs of mankind. In this economic Eldorado, in this economic Utopia, as the earlier economists would have deemed it, most of us were brought up.
>
> That happy age lost sight of a view of the world which filled with deep-seated melancholy the founders of our Political Economy. Before the eighteenth century mankind entertained no false hopes. To lay the illusions which grew popular at that age's latter end, Malthus disclosed a Devil. For half a century all serious economical writings held that Devil in clear prospect. For the next half century he was chained up and out of sight. Now perhaps we have loosed him again.

4. The relevant passages are: R. F. Harrod, *John Maynard Keynes* (New York: Harcourt Brace, 1951) pp. 280–281; Robert Skidelsky, *John Maynard Keynes* (London: Macmillan, 1983) Vol. I, pp. 384–388.

5. *Economic Consequences* p. 204. I would note here that Keynes's view of the theory of probability would cause him to accept an error of the kind he made without excessive brooding. Skidelsky (*John Maynard Keynes* pp. 390–391) comments in this vein on Keynes's response in the *Economic Consequences of the Peace* to French critics of his estimates of the German capacity to pay reparations:

> The fact that all things are *possible* is no excuse for talking foolishly. . . . The fact that we have no adequate knowledge of Germany's capacity to pay over a long period of years is no justification . . . for the statement that she can pay ten thousand million pounds.

For an effort to evoke the complex and rather unusual strands that came together to form Keynes's character in his third decade, see David Felix, "The Early Keynes: Logician and Applied Economist," *Challenge* (September–October, 1986), pp. 51–54. Felix perceives three strands in Keynes: "The Perverse, The Practical, The Transcendent" (*ibid.,* p. 54). Felix arrives at this summation by identifying the following specific influences: G. E. Moore's neoplatonist philosophy leading Keynes to revolt against his father's commitment to "objective" logic and to build his *Treatise on Probability* on Moore's view of the primacy of intuition and subjectivity; the discipline of his experience in the India Office, and the writing of *Indian Currency and Finance;* and a willingness to propose at certain critical moments visionary solutions transcending the disciplined civil servant he also could be. Felix's triad evokes something of Auden's young boy, peasant grandmother, and high church official, in describing T. S. Eliot and my tripartite characterization of J. S. Mill (preceding p. 97 and p. 591, note 28).

6. For a summary of the Keynes–Beveridge debate see my *Process of Economic Growth* (Oxford, at the Clarendon Press, 1953), pp. 186–188.

7. "A Reply to Sir William Beveridge," *Economic Journal,* Vol. XXXIII, No. 132 (December 1923), pp. 476–477.

8. *Ibid.,* p. 482.

9. D. H. Robertson, "Note on the Real Ratio of International Interchange," *Economic Journal,* Vol. XXXIV, No. 134 (June 1924), pp. 286–291, reprinted in A. C. Pigou and Dennis H. Robertson, *Economic Essays and Addresses* (London: P. S. King, 1931). It is in this piece that Robertson teased Keynes for his swift adjustment to the favorable shift in the terms of trade with the phrase: "a raven not thus easily to be balked of his croak." (Pigou and Robertson, p. 163).

10. Pigou and Robertson, *Economic Essays,* pp. 168–169.

11. *Ibid.,* p. 136.

12. *Official Papers,* pp. 380–385.

13. N. D. Kondratieff, "The Long Waves in Economic Life," *Review of Economic Statistics,* 17, No. 6 (November 1935), pp. 105–114. See also George Garvy, "Kondratieff's Theory of Long Cycles," *Review of Economic Statistics,* 25, No. 4 (November 1943), pp. 203–220; and the discussion of Kondratieff's views in Simon Kuznets, *Secular Movements in Production and Prices* (Boston: Houghton Mifflin, 1930), pp. 263–265. Kondratieff published his views in three versions between 1922 and 1928. His concept of capitalist economies oscillating around a long-run dynamic-equilibrium position came to be regarded, in Stalin's time, as anti-Marxist heresy. In 1930 he was sent to a Siberian prison camp where, according to Solzhenitsyn's *Gulag Archipelago,* he died. Kondratieff is reported to be rehabilitated in the Soviet Union in 1987 (*Science* [9 October, 1987], p. 149).

14. Kondratieff, "The Long Waves in Economic Life," pp. 112–115.

15. Lewis's views are set out fully in his *Growth and Fluctuations, 1870–1913* (London: George Allen and Unwin, 1978). Lewis's current views are foreshadowed in his *Economic Survey 1919–1939,* (London: Allen and Unwin, 1949). For a recent evocation of relative price cycles, see John Levi, "Omens from the Terms of Trade—Expectations about the Next Few Years," In *Inter-*

Economics, No. 3 (May–June 1983), pp. 120–124. My views are to be found in *Essays on the British Economy of the Nineteenth Century* (Oxford: at the Clarendon Press, 1949), especially Chapters 1 and II where the analyses of both Kondratieff and Schumpeter are discussed. My subsequent work on long cycles can be found in A. D. Gayer, W. W. Rostow, and Anna Jacobson Schwartz, *Growth and Fluctuations of the British Economy, 1790–1850* (Oxford: at the Clarendon Press, 1953), especially Vol. II, Chapters IV and V; *British Trade Fluctuations, 1868–1896* (New York: Arno Press, 1981 [actually written in 1939–1940]); *The Process of Economic Growth* (Oxford: at the Clarendon Press, 1951 and 1960), especially Part Three and Chapters 6, 8, and 9; *The World Economy: History and Prospect* (Austin: University of Texas Press, 1978), especially Part Three; and *Why the Poor Get Richer and the Rich Slow Down* (Austin: University of Texas Press, 1980), especially Chapters 1 and 2. Chapter 1 discusses views of the Kondratieff cycle other than my own. It should be noted that the opening up of new areas with railroads could take place in a period of falling prices for mixed political-economic reasons; e.g., the Argentine Pampas and Western Canada. This point is discussed and illustrated in "The Terms of Trade and Development," my contribution to *Perspectives on Economic Development,* essays in the honour of W. Arthur Lewis, edited by T. E. Barker, A. S. Downes, and J. A. Sackey (Washington, D.C.: University Press of America, 1982), pp. 256–258.

16. Colin Clark, *National Income and Outlay* (London: Macmillan, 1937) Chapter XIII, pp. 262–273. The foundation for Chapter XII is Chapter X (pp. 210–235), which is a pioneering reconstruction of British national income statistics from Gregory King to the 1930s.

17. *Ibid.,* pp. 270–271.

18. D. H. Robertson's testimony (April, 1930) before the Macmillan Committee on Finance and Industry (reported June 1931) is to be found in Pigou and Robertson, *Economic Essays,* pp. 116–138. The Macmillan Committee Report has been reprinted in *British Parliamentary Reports on International Finance,* (New York: Arno Press, 1978). Clark almost certainly found Robertson's testimony suggestive by combining two passages. First, the initial section entitled "The Gluttability of Wants," then the section on the appropriate response to a radically favorable shift in the terms of trade.

The first passage argues that it was of the nature of a depression that production had exceeded requirements for both consumers and capital ("instrumental") goods, at a particular period of time and, therefore, the view that the banking system could be content with supplying the legitimate "needs of trade" was inadequate. In an economy with an underlying high growth rate, the demands for capital and consumers' goods would revive the economy fairly soon. But he added (*ibid.,* p. 124): "At the present time the need for such a policy seems to me more urgent than in the typical slump of pre-war days, . . . with a retarded rate of growth of population and of world-trade, instrument-gluts are liable to last longer than of old: the tail of one depression, so to speak, does not so easily get bitten off by the head of the next boom." Later in his testimony Robertson evoked the swings in the terms of trade with their powerful effects on British export markets.

19. In fact, the years on either side of the international crisis year, 1873, must be dealt with in different terms. After 1873 prices fell, real wages rose, but unemployment remained low due to a postcrisis building boom down to 1876, responding to lowered interest rates as the demand for capital exports fell away in the city of London after the cyclical peak.

20. Folke Hilgerdt, *Industrialization and Foreign Trade,* (New York: League of Nations, distributed by Columbia University Press, 1945), pp. 14–20.

21. *Ibid.,* pp. 16 and 18.

22. For explanation see, W. W. Rostow, *World Economy,* pp. 98–99.

> A number of factors account for the significant structural change after 1951: the diminishing role of the less-developed nations in the grain trade, which came to be dominated by the United States, Canada, and Australia; the extraordinary rise of trade in manufactures among the industrialized nations centered on automobiles, television sets, and other paraphernalia of high mass-consumption; economies in the use of raw materials in manufacturing plus a shift to industrial

sectors using a lower proportion of raw materials; the increasing role of petroleum in world trade, responding to demand and supply conditions somewhat different from the classic circumstances governing trade in primary products between industrialized and nonindustrial countries. Between 1938 and 1971 trade in fuel rose in volume from 7.2 percent of total world trade to 10.3 percent (from 8.1 percent to 9.7 percent in value). In the same period, trade in food and raw materials declined from 49.1 percent to 23.4 percent in volume (from 46.4 percent to 22.9 percent in value).

Between 1972 and, say, 1980, the pattern of both relative prices and world trade altered dramatically. The terms of trade shifted sharply in favor of oil exporters and against importers of both oil and (for a time) food. The trade among industrialized countries, whose expansion dominated the post-1945 world, was constricted by two recessions which also affected the volume and prices of trade in industrial raw materials. The proportion of world trade conducted by the oil exporters rose to an extraordinary degree. The course of events in 1972–1980, while in many ways unique, bears a family relation to four previous periods over the past two centuries when major changes in relative prices occurred. In all these cases, including the most recent experience, these shifts in relative prices flowed from gross distortions in the balance between demands of industry and consumers and the supply of raw materials and food necessary to match them.

23. See, especially, my *Why the Poor Get Richer,* Chapter 2.

Chapter 13

1. See for example, Gerald M. Meier and Dudley Seers (eds.), *Pioneers in Development,* (New York: Oxford University Press for the World Bank, 1984), pp. 3–6, (Gerald M. Meier, "Introduction").

2. *Ibid.,* p. 175. In fact, import substitution development doctrines can be traced back to the mid-nineteenth century at least in Latin America. See, for example, Francisco Calderon, "El Pensamiento Economico de Lucas Aleman," *Revista Historia Mexicana,* Colegio de Mexico, Vol. XXXIV (July 1984), pp. 435–459. Lucas Aleman wrote hopefully about the first industrial fruits of protectionism in Mexico in 1845. His views sank from view in the subsequent wave of economic liberalism to be revived in the depression of the 1930s and post–World War II development policy. For a survey of Mexican development thought, see Jesus Silva Herzog, *El Pensamiento Economico, Social y Politico de Mexico, 1810–1964* (Mexico: Fondo de Cultura Economica, 1974).

3. J. M. Keynes reports as follows in the concluding section of his essay on Marshall (*Memorial of Alfred Marshall*), p. 65:

> "Although old age presses on me," he [Marshall] wrote in the Preface to *Money, Credit and Commerce,* "I am not without hopes that some of the notions which I have formed as to the possibilities of social advance may yet be published." Up to his last illness, in spite of loss of memory and great feebleness of body, he struggled to piece together one more volume. It was to have been called "Progress: Its Economic Conditions." But the task was too great.

4. *Pioneers in Development,* pp. 62–65.

5. The Robinsons went to India on their honeymoon in 1926 where Austin was tutor to the Crown Prince of Gwalior. I can attest that they jointly recalled that interval with unabated enthusiasm as late as 1949.

6. C. Clark, *The Conditions for Economic Progress* (London: Macmillan, 1940), pp. 1–16 ("Summary and Conclusions"); pp. 448–469, Chapter XIV, "The Terms of Exchange"), and pp. 470–484 (Chapter XV, "The Relation Between Investment and Income").

7. *Pioneers in Development,* p. 70.

8. Vera Anstey, *The Economic Development of India* (3d ed., 1936), p. 3.

9. *Ibid.,* pp. 470 and 473–478.

10. R. H. Tawney, *Land and Labour in China* (New York: Harcourt Brace, 1932), p. 79.

11. *Ibid.,* p. 182.

12. *Ibid.*, pp. 162–163 and 167.

13. *Ibid.*, p. 169.

14. *Ibid.*, pp. 193–195.

15. L. C. A. Knowles, *The Economic Development of the British Overseas Empire* (London: George Routledge, 1924).

16. *Ibid.*, p. viii.

17. *Ibid.*, pp. 510–511.

18. *Ibid.*

19. *Ibid.*, p. 509.

20. The 1931 edition, entitled *Stadien und Typen der Industrialisierung,* was published in Kiel by the Institut für Weltwirtschaft of the University of Kiel. The 1958 edition, *The Growth of Industrial Societies,* translated from the German by W. O. Henderson and W. H. Chaloner, was published in Manchester by the Manchester University Press.

21. *The Growth of Industrial Economies,* pp. xi–xii. There is evidently a family relation between Hoffmann's initial focus and Folke Hilgerdt's in *Industrialization and Foreign Trade.*

22. *Ibid.*, pp. 1–2.

23. *Ibid.*, p. 2.

24. *Ibid.*, pp. 2–3 and Chapter II ("The Process of Industrialization"), pp. 24–41.

25. *Ibid.*, see especially p. 3 and Chapter III ("The Historical Phases of Industrialization"), pp. 42–66.

26. *Industrialization and Foreign Trade,* Chapters III and IV, pp. 30–75. See also Chapter VII ("Summary of Findings), pp. 116–121.

27. *Ibid.*, pp. 120–121.

28. For discussion of this linkage, see, for example, W. W. Rostow, *Getting from Here to There* (New York: McGraw Hill, 1978), pp. 13–16.

29. William Stanley Jevons, *The Coal Question,* 2d ed. (London: Macmillan, 1866), p. vii.

30. Hansen's paper was published in *The American Economic Review,* Vol. 29, (March 1939), No. 1, Part I, pp. 1–15. In 1938 Hansen also published a more spacious version of his thesis in *Full Recovery or Stagnation.*

31. *Business Cycles,* Vol. II, pp. 1011–1050.

32. Hansen, *"Economic Progress",* p. 1.

33. *Ibid.*

34. *Ibid.*, p. 2.

35. *Ibid.*, p. 3.

36. *Ibid.*

37. *Ibid.*, p. 4.

38. *Ibid.*, pp. 8–9.

39. *Ibid.*

40. *Ibid.*, pp. 9–11.

41. *Ibid.*, pp. 11–12.

42. *Ibid.*, pp. 13–14.

43. *Ibid.*, pp. 12 and 15.

44. *Capitalism, Socialism and Democracy,* (New York: Harper and Row, 1942).

45. *Business Cycles,* Vol. II, p. 1050.

46. *Ibid.*, pp. 1020–1026.

47. *Ibid.*, p. 1026.

48. *Ibid.*, p. 1032.

49. *Ibid.*, pp. 1034–1035.

50. *Ibid.*, pp. 1036–1038.

51. *Ibid.*, p. 1045.

52. *Ibid.*, p. 1050.

53. *Ibid.*, p. 1050, n. 1.

54. Chapter 1 in A. C. Pigou, *Essays in Economics* (London: Macmillan, 1952), pp. 1–9. (Reprinted from *Economic Journal,* Vol. XLIX, No. 194 [June 1939]).

55. *Ibid.,* pp. 3 and 4.

Chapter 14

1. P. A. Samuelson, *Foundations of Economic Analysis* (Cambridge: Harvard University Press, 1947).

2. *Ibid.,* pp. 6 and 311–312.

3. *Ibid.,* p. 141. Samuelson's *Principles* is, in effect, an exercise in precisely the method he attributes to Marshall and Hicks. For a later, somewhat more nuanced exposition of the role of mathematics in the social sciences, see Samuelson's "Economic Theory and Mathematics—An Appraisal", *American Economic Review,* Vol. 62, No. 2, [May 1952 (*Papers and Proceedings*)], pp. 56–73.

4. *Foundations,* p. 7.

5. *Ibid.,* p. 3.

6. Samuelson defines the correspondence principle as demonstration that the comparative statical behavior of a system is seen to be closely related to its dynamical stability properties (pp. 351–352):

> The central notion of *comparative dynamics* is simple enough. We change something (just what need not concern us at the moment), and we investigate the effect of this change on the whole motion or behavior over time of the economic system under investigation. It will be seen that comparative statics involves the special case where a "permanent" change is made, and only the effects upon final levels of stationary equilibrium are in question.

Evidently this approach approximates Ricardo's position in his debate with Malthus.

7. *Ibid.,* p. 355.

Chapter 15

1. E. D. Domar, "Capital Expansion, Rate of Growth, and Employment," *Econometrica,* Vol. 14 (1946), pp. 137–147; and "Expansion and Employment," *American Economic Review,* Vol. 37, No. 1 (March 1947), pp. 34–55.

2. James Tobin, "A Dynamic Aggregative Model," *Journal of Political Economy,* Vol. LXIII (April 1955), pp. 103–115; R. M. Solow, "A Contribution to the Theory of Economic Growth," *Quarterly Journal of Economics,* Vol. 70 (February 1956), pp. 65–94; and T. W. Swan, "Economic Growth and Capital Accumulation," *Economic Record,* Vol. 32 (November 1956), pp. 334–361. A critique of the Harrod model is included in my *Process of Economic Growth* (Oxford: at the Clarendon Press, 1953), pp. 86–96. See also R. Sato, "The Harrod–Domar Model vs. the Neo-Classical Model," *Economic Journal,* Vol. LXXIV, No. 294 (June 1964), pp. 380–387. Sato argues that the adjustment process assumed in the neoclassical model may be, in fact, so slow as to produce Harrod–Domar-style instability.

3. Figure 15.1 was constructed from the 278-item reference bibliography in Hywel G. Jones, *An Introduction to Modern Theories of Economic Growth* (New York: McGraw-Hill, 1975), pp. 238–247. I arbitrarily eliminated references not directly related to the modeling work of recent decades; e.g., studies by J. B. and J. M. Clark, Milton Friedman, J. M. Keynes, P. H. Wicksteed, etc. I then arrayed the remaining 182 items by year of publication.

4. The first of such surveys comes in the midst of the most intense and exciting stage of the growth-modeling effort and is something of a classic: F. H. Hahn and R. C. O. Matthews, "The Theory of Economic Growth: A Survey," *Economic Journal,* Vol. LXXIV, No. 296 (December 1964), pp. 779–902. Among the later surveys, syntheses, or compendia are E. Burmeister and A.

R. Dobell, *Mathematical Theories of Economic Growth* (New York: Collier-Macmillan, 1970); F. H. Hahn, *Readings in the Theory of Economic Growth* (London: Macmillan, 1971); A. K. Sen (ed.), *Growth Economics* (Harmondsworth, Eng.: Penguin, 1970); K. Shell (ed.), *Essays on the Theory of Optimal Economic Growth* (Cambridge: M.I.T. Press, 1967); R. M. Solow, *Growth Theory: An Exposition* (Oxford: Oxford University Press, 1970, 1988 enlarged); J. E. Stiglitz and H. Uzawa (eds.), *Readings in the Modern Theory of Economic Growth* (Cambridge: M.I.T. Press, 1969); and H. Y. Wan, Jr., *Economic Growth* (New York: Harcourt Brace and Jovanovich, 1971). H. G. Jones, *Introduction to Modern Theories,* also belongs, of course, on this list.

5. R. F. Harrod, *Towards a Dynamic Economics* (London: Macmillan, 1948) p. 33.

6. Domar's 1946 essay is accessibly reprinted in Amartya Sen's *Growth Economics,* pp. 65–77. Domar's discussion of "Guaranteed Growth of Income" is on pp. 74–77.

7. R. F. Harrod, *Towards a Dynamic Economics,* pp. 81–82.

8. R. M. Solow, "A Model of Growth." This piece, originally published in the *Quarterly Journal of Economics* (1956), is accessibly available in A. Sen, *Growth Economics,* pp. 161–162.

9. *Ibid.,* p. 169.

10. For an exposition of various versions of this type of growth model see, for example, F. H. Hahn and R. C. O. Matthews, "Theory of Economic Growth," pp. 793–801; A. Sen, *Growth Economics,* pp. 16–18 and 79–157; H. Y. Wan, Jr., *Economic Growth,* pp. 63–93; and H. Jones, *Introduction to Modern Theories,* pp. 143–152.

11. This passage is from N. Kaldor's "Alternative Theories of Distribution," *Review of Economic Studies,* Vol. 23 (1955–1956), pp. 94–100, accessibly reprinted in A. Sen, *Growth Economics.* The quotation is on p. 84 (Sen). The roots of the Cambridge (England) point of view can be discerned in Joan Robinson's critique, "Mr. Harrod's Dynamics," *Economic Journal,* Vol. LIX, No. 233 (March 1949), pp. 68–85.

12. *Growth Theory,* pp. 8–12. For Solow's later reflections on his 1956 model and his Radcliffe Lectures, see his 1987 Nobel lecture reprinted in the 1988 edition of *Growth Theory: An Exposition.*

13. *Ibid.,* p. 12.

14. Nicholas Kaldor, "The Relation of Economic Growth and Cyclical Fluctuations," *Economic Journal,* Vol. LXIV, No. 253 (March 1954), pp. 53–71, originally delivered as a lecture to the Institut de Science Economique Appliquée in Paris on May 23, 1953.

15. *Ibid.,* pp. 53–54.

16. *Ibid.,* pp. 61–63.

17. *Ibid.,* p. 65.

18. *Ibid.,* pp. 67, 68–71.

19. *Ibid.,* p. 66.

20. See, for example, Leif Johansen, "A Method for Separating the Effects of Capital Accumulation and Shifts in Production Functions upon Growth in Labour Productivity," *Economic Journal,* Vol. XXXI, No. 284 (December 1961), pp. 775–782. Johansen's analysis employs data from W. E. G. Salter's *Productivity and Technical Change* (Cambridge: at the University Press, 1960).

21. See, for example, my discussion (and references) in "Technology and the Price System" in *Why the Poor Get Richer and the Rich Slow Down,* (Austin: University of Texas Press, 1980), pp. 166–168.

22. "Economic Growth and Cyclical Fluctuations," p. 67.

23. Joan Robinson, *Essays in the Theory of Growth* (London: Macmillan, 1962), p. 34–50. In the most elaborate examination of Robinson's growth system I have come across (*Economic Growth,* pp. 63–82), Henry Y. Wan Jr., points out that this fundamental, complex, open-ended approach reflects virtually all the dimensions of "the panoramic vista of the Robinsonian World":

> One can understand Mrs. Robinson's view better by considering the sources of her theory. From Marx she obtained the schema of "expanded reproduction" which may be traced all the way to Quesnay. Marx has a two-sector (two department) model complete with the resource flows

in the economy. Following Marx, Mrs. Robinson's theory also takes account of the incentive to invest. Marx regards the impulse to accumulate as inherent in the capitalist system. From Keynes, Mrs. Robinson inherited the "income theory" approach, including concepts such as "effective demand," "inflationary gap," "hoarding," etc.; the "animal spirit" explanation of investment which regards the readiness for risk-taking as more important than profit calculations in investment decisions; and what later became known as the Kalecki saving function: capitalists save all and workers spend all. To Keynes, this latter feature justified capitalism as a means of speedy accumulation. From Harrod she received the concepts of balanced growth and Harrod-neutral technical progress. Besides these, the long-run/short-run dichotomy of Marshall, the capital theory of Wicksell, and the heterogenous capital goods model of Sraffa all contribute to the panoramic vista of the Robinsonian world.

24. Joan Robinson, *Theory of Economic Growth*, p. 59.

25. *Ibid.*, p. 98.

26. R. M. Solow, "A Contribution to a Theory of Growth," in A. Sen, *Growth Economics*, pp. 188–189. For a more complex argument, with a family relation to Solow's, see Harvey Leibenstein, "Population Growth and the Take-off Hypothesis" and "Technical Progress, the Production Function, and Development," in W. W. Rostow (ed.), *The Economics of Take-off into Sustained Growth* (London: Macmillan, 1963), pp. 170–200. For discussion of such models, see, notably, F. H. Hahn and R. C. O. Matthews, "Theory of Economic Growth," pp. 835–836.

27. Charles Kennedy, "Induced Bias in Innovation and the Theory of Distribution," *Economic Journal*, Vol. 74 (September 1964), pp. 541–547; Paul A. Samuelson, "A Theory of Induced Innovation along Kennedy–Weisacker Lines," *Review of Economics and Statistics*, Vol. 47 (November 1965), pp. 343–356; Charles Kennedy, "Samuelson on Induced Innovation," and Paul A. Samuelson's "Rejoinder," Review of *Economics and Statistics*, Vol. 48 (November 1966), pp. 442–448.

28. P. A. Samuelson, "A Theory of Induced Innovation," pp. 353–355.

29. See W. W. Rostow, *British Economy of the Nineteenth Century* (Oxford: Clarendon Press, 1948), Chapter 4, "Investment and Real Wages, 1973–86," and the Appendix, "Mr. Kalecki on the Distribution of Income, 1880–1913."

30. See, for example, Karl Shell, "Inventive Activity, Industrial Organization, and Economic Growth," Chapter 4 in James A. Mirrlees and N. H. Stern (eds.), *Models of Economic Growth*, Proceedings of a conference of the International Economic Association (New York: John Wiley, 1973), pp. 77–96. For a later Solow reevaluation see his "Second Thoughts on Growth Theory," Chapter 1 in Alfred Steinherr and Daniel Weiserbs (eds.) *Employment and Growth: Issues for the 1980s* (Dordrecht: Kluwer Academic Publishers, 1987), pp. 13–45.

31. *Ibid.*, p. 97.

32. See, for example, E. Mansfield, "Rates of Return from Industrial Research and Development," *American Economic Review*, Vol. 55, No. 2 (May 1965), pp. 310–322.

33. B. R. Williams (ed.), *Science and Technology in Economic Growth* (London: Macmillan, 1973). This volume is a report of a conference held by the International Economic Association.

34. *Ibid.*, p. xi.

35. Edwin Burmeister and A. Rodney Dobell, *Mathematical Theories*, p. vii. Solow goes on to deny that formal growth models had run their course and were pretty well "played out." I would judge, with hindsight, that, as of 1970, when Burmeister and Dobell's book was published, the field was closer to that stage than Solow then thought.

36. J. R. Hicks, *A Contribution to the Theory of the Trade Cycle* (Oxford: at the Clarendon Press, 1950); Alvin Hansen, *Business Cycles and National Income* (New York: W. W. Norton, 1951); James B. Duesenberry, *Business Cycles and Economic Growth* (New York: McGraw-Hill, 1958); R. C. O. Matthews, *The Trade Cycle* (Cambridge: at the University Press, 1959). Significantly, all but Hicks's study are explicitly textbooks. Hicks presents his contribution as a synthesis built on three "progenitors": Keynes, J. M. Clark, and Harrod. But, it also bears a family relation to Marx's and Schumpeter's dynamic growth formulations, although Hicks might be surprised at the

suggestion. I would underline that these studies were by no means the only efforts of the period to grapple with the problem of trends (or growth) and cycles, to cite only three: R. M. Goodwin, "The Problem of Trend and Cycles," *Yorkshire Bulletin of Economic and Social Research,* Vol. 5 (August 1953), pp. 89–97: William Fellner, *Trends and Cycles in Economic Activity* (New York: Henry Holt, 1956); Arthur Smithies, "Economic Fluctuations and Growth," *Econometrica,* Vol. 25, No. 1 (January 1957), pp. 1–52.

37. J. R. Hicks, *The Trade Cycle,* p. 59.

38. *Ibid.,* p. 63.

39. *Ibid.,* pp. 56–57.

40. *Ibid.,* pp. 60–61.

41. *Ibid.,* p. 97.

42. Hicks's figure is at *ibid.,* p. 121; his comment and elaboration are on pp. 120–123.

43. These points are elaborated in W. W. Rostow, "Some Notes on Mr. Hicks and History," *American Economic Review,* Vol. XLI, No. 3 (June 1951), pp. 316–324.

44. *Ibid.,* pp. 319–321.

45. A. Hansen, *Business Cycles and National Income,* p. 446.

46. *Ibid.,* p. 497.

47. J. S. Duesenberry, *Business Cycles,* pp. 281–294.

48. *Ibid.,* pp. 199–201.

49. *Ibid.,* p. 222.

50. *Ibid.,* pp. 225–239.

51. *Ibid.,* p. 225.

52. *Ibid.,* p. 239.

53. R. C. O. Matthews, *A Study in Trade-Cycle History, Economic Fluctuations in Great Britain 1833–1842* (Cambridge: at the University Press, 1954).

54. *The Trade Cycle,* pp. 68–84. Matthews's review article indicates the substantial area of agreement (as well as some disagreement) with Duesenberry ("Duesenberry on Growth and Fluctuations," *Economic Journal,* Vol. LXIX, No. 276 [December 1959], pp. 749–765).

55. *Ibid.,* pp. 227–228.

56. *Ibid.,* p. 228.

57. *Ibid.,* pp. 233–235.

58. *Ibid.,* pp. 253–254.

59. A. W. Mullineux, *The Business Cycle after Keynes: A Contemporary Analysis* (Totowa, New Jersey: Barnes and Noble, 1984), p. 89.

60. Burns and Mitchell, *Measuring Business Cycles,* pp. 464–465.

61. Hahn and Matthews, *Economic Growth: A Survey,* pp. 888–889.

62. Introduction to Mirrlees and Stern (eds.), *Models of Economic Growth,* pp. xii–xvi.

63. Hahn and Matthews, *Economic Growth: A Survey,* p. 890.

64. Sen, (ed.) *Growth Economics,* p. 9. The quotations cited here reflect a general unease among the model builders themselves. See, for example, "The Summary of the Final Discussion" in Mirrlees and Stern (eds.), pp. 361–367. D. H. Robertson's typically lighthearted but sharp-edged comment in the 1960 Marshall Lecture is worth noting (*Growth, Wages and Money,* Cambridge: at the University Press, 1961, p. 4.):

> . . . [I]n this matter of growth theory I have fallen too far behind. And anyway you need no help from me. Rumour has it that there is not one of you who could not, in his or her first or at latest second year, tackle undaunted such a question as this: "Compare and contrast the growth models of Harrod, Domar, J. Robinson, Kaldor Mark I, Kaldor Mark II, Kaldor Mark III, Hahn, Matthews, Goodwin, Champernowne, Hicks, Little, Duesenberry, Tobin, Fellner, Solow and Swan. Which seems to you the biggest nonsense, and why?"

65. I elaborate this theme in "The World Economy Since 1945: A Stylized Historical Analysis," *Economic History Review,* Vol. XXXVIII, No. 2 (May 1985), pp. 252–275.

66. N. Kaldor, "Capital Accumulation and Economic Growth," in F. A. Lutz and D. C. Hague

(eds.), *The Theory of Capital* (London: Macmillan, 1965), pp. 178–179. For example, in a heroic effort to render his model relevant to the modern history of advanced industrial countries, Kaldor adduced six "stylized facts":

(1) The continued growth in the aggregate volume of production and in the productivity of labour at a steady trend rate; no recorded tendency for a *falling* rate of growth of productivity.

(2) A continued increase in the amount of capital per worker, whatever statistical measure of "capital" is chosen in this connection.

(3) A steady rate of profit on capital, at least in the "developed" capitalist societies; this rate of profit being substantially higher than the "pure" long-term rate of interest as shown by the yield of giltedged bonds. . . .

(4) Steady capital–output ratios over long periods; at least there are no clear long-term trends, either rising or falling. . . .

(5) A high correlation between the share of profits in income and the share of investment in output; a steady share of profits (and of wages) in societies and/or in periods in which the investment coefficient (the share of investment in output) is constant. . . .

(6) Finally, there are appreciable differences in the rate of growth of labour productivity and of total output in different societies. . . .

Of these propositions (6) is unambiguously true for advanced industrial societies once takeoff has begun, but as Kaldor was explicitly aware, his model (and others) did little or nothing to explain growth differentials in different societies; (1) and (2) are true, although the rates of growth and increase are not steady; (3) and (4) are not true; (5) implies a questionable analytic linkage.

67. Hahn and Matthews, "Economic Growth: A Survey", p. 890.

68. *Ibid.*, p. 889.

Chapter 16

1. The titles of Kuznets's monographs follow: *Quantitative Aspects of the Economic Growth of Nations:*

    I. Levels and Variability of Rates of Growth
    II. Industrial Distribution of National Product and Labor Force
    III. Industrial Distribution of Income and Labor Force by States, United States, 1919–1921 to 1955
    IV. Distribution of National Income by Factor Shares
    V. Capital Formation Proportions: International Comparisons for Recent Years
    VI. Long-Term Trends in Capital Formation Proportions
    VII. The Share and Structure of Consumption
    VIII. Distribution of Income by Size
    IX. Level and Structure of Foreign Trade: Comparisons for Recent Years
    X. Level and Structure of Foreign Trade: Long-Term Trends

These studies were published successively in the following issues of *Economic Development and Cultural Change,* Vol. 5 (October 1956); Vol. 5 (July 1957 Suppl.); Vol. 7 (April 1959, Part II); Vol. 8 (July 1960, Part II); Vol. 9 (July 1961, Part II); Vol. 10 (January 1962, Part II); Vol. 11 (January 1963, Part II); Vol. 15 (October 1967, Part IV).

2. Simon Kuznets, *Economic Growth and Structure* (New York: W. W. Norton, 1965); *Modern Economic Growth: Rate Structure and Spread* (New Haven: Yale University Press, 1966); *Economic Growth of Nations: Total Output and Production Structure* (Cambridge: The Belknap Press of Harvard University Press, 1971); and *Population, Capital, and Growth* (New York: W. W. Norton, 1973).

3. In constructing this account I was greatly assisted by conversations with two of Kuznets's friends and colleagues: Moses Abramovitz and Solomon Fabricant. They bear, of course, no responsibility for the conclusions I have drawn.

4. On Kuznets's death in July 1983 the SSRC published a note summarizing his long and fruitful connection with that foundation, which is worth quoting at length given the strategic importance of Kuznets's role as chairman of the SSRC Committee on Economic Growth. (*Items,* Social Science Research Council, Vol. 39, No. 3 [September 1985], pp. 49–50.)

> Mr. Kuznets became an active participant in Council activities soon after it was founded in 1923 and immediately after he received a Ph.D. in economics from Columbia University in 1926. He was a research fellow of the Council in 1925–26, the first year of the Council's fellowship program, devoting himself to research on secular movements in production and prices. For six years, 1938–43, he was a member of the Council's board of directors, designated by the American Economic Association, and he continued to participate in various Council activities. His major contribution to the Council's program was as chairman of the Committee on Economic Growth throughout its 20 years of existence, 1949–1968.
>
> . . . A substantial portion of his research was developed in collaboration with and with the support of the Committee on Economic Growth, which had its origins in a memorandum that he submitted to the Council in 1948. In it, Mr. Kuznets proposed:
>
>> . . . a committee for the purpose of exploring possible directions of study of economic growth, the latter defined as long-term increase (or decline) in magnitude and changes in structure of larger social units (nation-state primarily). The aim of such exploration is to establish how fruitful empirical study of economic growth can best be planned; and, in areas in which the groundwork is not ready for empirical studies, to stimulate thinking and discussion leading toward formulation of the necessary intellectual framework.*
>
> Mr. Kuznets urged that the committee concern itself not only with economic studies but also with factors affecting economic growth such as science and technology, natural resources, the efficiency of the state, and other social mechanisms, cultures, and social structures. He noted that the committee should include members from a variety of disciplines other than economics.
>
> In the two decades that followed appointment of the committee, major studies of long-term economic growth were initiated in Australia, Canada, Denmark, France, Germany, Italy, Japan, the Netherlands, Norway, Sweden, and the United Kingdom. Mr. Kuznets and other scholars in the field used these studies in comparative analyses of economic growth and in strengthening the empirical foundation for theoretical and policy analysis.
>
> Mr. Kuznets guided and inspired a great deal of the committee's work. He visited economists abroad and at home to recruit their interest in the committee's plans, advised the often nascent attempts at empirical study, and maintained an overarching strategy of research planning and of communication among scholars. Few committees in the Council's history have had a chairman who worked with such dedication and such skill in joining the efforts of many, often quite disparate, scholars. Members of the Committee on Economic Growth have testified that their greatest rewards came from their association with the committee's chairman.
>
> In addition to his central role in the work of the Committee on Economic Growth, Mr. Kuznets helped to organize the work of the Council's Committee on the Economy of China, which constituted in many senses a special case in the analysis of problems of economic growth. He was chairman of this committee throughout its existence, 1961 to 1970.

5. Kuznets himself provides several summaries of his major findings at different levels of generality; for example, in his *Economic Growth of Nations,* in considerable detail (pp. 303–314), and in *Population, Capital, and Growth,* pp. 165–184 (Kuznets's 1971 Nobel Lecture), at a higher level of abstraction. See also Dwight Perkins, "Three Decades of International Quantitative Comparison," paper prepared for the eightieth birthday of Simon Kuznets, 1982 (unpublished), pp. 4–7, who defines eight "important discoveries that have stood up well over time." Perkins's "discoveries" include a few by Kuznets's disciples using his methods. I have here combined in the text items from my own selective list in the review of Kuznets's *Economic Growth of Nations* (*Political Science Quarterly* [December 1971], pp. 654–657) with Perkins's.

---

*Social Science Research Council, Committee on Problems and Policy, Minutes of the meeting of January 8, 1949, Appendix 1, "Memorandum on Setting up of a Social Science Research Council Committee on a Study of Economic Growth," prepared by Simon Kuznets, December 8, 1948.

6. Hollis B. Chenery, Shuntaro Shishido, and Tsunehiko Watanabe, "The Pattern of Japanese Growth, 1914–1954," *Econometrica,* Vol. 30, No. 1 (January 1962), pp. 98–139.

7. *Economic Growth of Nations,* p. 315. One of Kuznets's final scientific papers is focused substantially on the same theme; i.e., the centrality of technological innovation and its structural sequences: "Driving Forces of Economic Growth: What Can We Learn from History?" in Herbert Giersch (ed.), *Towards an Explanation of Economic Growth* (Tubingen: J. C. B. Mohr, 1981), pp. 37–58. This paper was presented at a 1980 symposium at the Institut für Weltwirtschaft, Kiel.

8. Chenery's principal publications are the following:

With Tsunehiko Watanabe, "International Comparisons of the Structure of Production," *Econometrica,* Vol. 26 (October 1958), pp. 487–521.

With Paul G. Clark, *Interindustry Economics* (New York: John Wiley and Sons, 1959).

"Patterns of Industrial Growth," *American Economic Review,* Vol. 50, No. 4 (September 1960), pp. 624–654.

With Lance J. Taylor, "Development Patterns Among Countries and over Time," *Review of Economics and Statistics,* Vol. 50 (November 1968), pp. 391–416.

With M. S. Ahluwalia, C. L. G. Bell, J. H. Duloy, and R. Jolly, *Redistribution with Growth* (London: Oxford University Press, 1974).

With Moshe Syrquin, *Patterns of Development, 1950–1970* (London: Oxford University Press, 1975).

With Sherman Robinson and Moshe Syrquin (with contributions by Gershon Feder, Yuji Kubo, Jeffrey Lewis, Jaime de Melo, and Mieko Nishimizu) *Industrialization and Growth* (New York: Oxford University Press for the World Bank, 1986).

9. A complete bibliography of Chenery's publications (1949–1981) is to be found in the volume organized in his honor: Moshe Syrquin, Lance Taylor, Larry E. Westphal (eds.), *Economic Structure and Performance* (New York: Academic Press, 1984), pp. xxi–xxvi. Perkins's paper contains a selected list of Chenery's major publications bearing most directly on the quantitative comparative analysis of structural change in the course of modern economic growth. See also, the excellent general economic growth bibliography in *Industrialization and Growth,* including Chenery items, pp. 361–377.

10. Syrquin, Taylor, and Westphal (eds.), *Economic Structure,* p. 3.

11. "Development Patterns: Among Countries and Over Time." Chenery's "Patterns of Industrial Growth" foreshadowed to a degree the conclusions of the later (1968) article (1971 ed.), pp. 230–234.

12. "Structural Transformation: A Program of Research," Development Discussion Paper No. 323 (Cambridge: Harvard Institute for International Development, June 1986).

13. *Ibid.,* p. 5.

14. *Ibid.,* p. 22.

15. *Economic Journal,* Vol. 86, No. 342 (June 1976), pp. 401–403, in a review of Chenery and Syrquin, *Patterns of Development, 1950–1970.*

16. Perkins, "Three Decades", p. 36.

17. "The Chenery Analysis and Some Other Considerations," in Syrquin, Taylor, and Westphal (eds.), *Economic Structure,* pp. 3–21. I should perhaps note that I, like Chenery, had the great privilege of both working closely with Mason and being also the target of quite sharp criticism in a *festschrift.*

18. *Ibid.,* p. 7.

19. Perkins "Three Decades", p. 35.

20. Kuznets on one occasion did present a cross-sectional analysis as of 1958, embracing countries from under $100 U.S. (1958) per capita to over $1000 (*Modern Economic Growth Rate, Structure, and Spread*), pp. 402–408.

21. Chenery usefully summarizes his method in "Structural Transformation," pp. 13–18. For

greater detail see *Structural Change and Development Policy,* Chapter 3 and *Industrialization and Growth,* especially Chapters 2 and 3.

22. The study, which I shall use to illustrate the Gesell problem, is Arnold Gesell and Francis L. Ilg, in collaboration with Janet Learned and Louis B. Ames, *Infant and Child in the Culture of Today, The Guidance of Development in Home and Nursery School* (New York: Harper, 1943).

23. *Ibid.,* especially ''The Individuality of Growth Patterns,'' pp. 43–46.

24. David Kendrick assembled 117 references in his (unpublished) handbook, *Mathematical Methods in Economic Planning.* Among them the following are representative.

Adelman, I. (ed.). *Practical Approaches to Development Planning: Korea's Second Five-Year Plan* (Baltimore: John Hopkins University Press, 1969).

Adelman, Irma, and Erik Thorbecke (eds.). *The Theory and Design of Economic Development* (Baltimore: John Hopkins University Press, 1966).

Bowles, Samuel, and David Kendrick, in collaboration with Lance Taylor and Marc Roberts. *Notes and Problems in Microeconomic Theory* (Chicago: Markham Publishing Co., 1970).

Brown, M. *On the Theory and Measurement of Technological Change* (London: Cambridge at the University Press, 1966).

Chakravarty, S. *Capital and Development Planning* (Cambridge: M.I.T. Press, 1969).

Chenery, Hollis B. (ed.). *Studies in Development Planning* (Cambridge: Harvard University Press, 1970).

Johansen, Lief. *A Multisectoral Study of Economic Growth* (Amsterdam: North Holland Publishing Co., 1964).

Kendrick, David A., *Programming Investment in the Process Industries* (Cambridge: M.I.T. Press, 1967).

Malinvaud, E., and M. O. L. Bachrach. *Activity Analysis in the Theory of Growth and Planning* (London: Macmillan; and New York: St. Martin's Press, 1967)

Sen, Amartya Kumar. *Choice of Techniques* (Oxford: Basil Blackwell, 1960).

Sengupta, Jati K., and Karl A. Fox. *Optimizing Techniques in Quantitative Economic Models* (Amsterdam: North Holland Press, 1969).

Shell, Karl (ed.), *Essays on the Theory of Optimal Economic Growth,* (Cambridge: M.I.T. Press, 1967).

Westphal, Larry E., ''A Dynamic Multi-Sectoral Programming Model Featuring Economies of Scale: Planning Investment in Petrochemical and Steel in Korea,'' unpublished Ph.D. thesis, Department of Economics, Harvard University, Cambridge, Mass. (June 1968).

25. Introduction to H. B. Chenery (ed.), *Studies in Development Planning,* p. 7.

26. Lief Johansen, *A Multisectoral Study.*

27. For an earlier analysis and assessment of this branch of modeling, see my *Why The Poor Get Richer and the Rich Slow Down* (Austin: University of Texas Press, 1980) pp. 183–185.

28. See, for example, H. M. Markowitz and A. S. Manne, ''On the Solution of Discrete Programming Problems,'' *Econometrica,* Vol. 25, No. 1 (January 1957), pp. 19ff., and application of this method to the steel industry in David Kendrick, *Programming Investment in the Process Industries.*

29. *Mathematical Methods in Economic Planning,* pp. 11–12.

30. For discussion and bibliography, see H. Chenery and M. Syrquin, *Patterns of Development, 1950–1970,* pp. 56–63; see also my *World Economy: History and Prospect,* (Austin: University of Texas Press, 1978) pp. 39–42 and 726–727.

31. For a mobilization of the existing historical and cross-sectional data on this point and an analysis of reasons for this pattern, see my *Why the Poor Get Richer,* Chapter 6, especially pp. 267–281.

32. *Patterns of Development, 1950–1970,* pp. 23–25.

33. S. Kuznets, *Economic Growth of Nations,* pp. 314–384.

34. *Patterns of Development*, 1950–1970, pp. 135–136.

35. Thorkil Kristensen, *Development in Rich and Poor Countries* (New York: Praeger, 1974), pp. 156–159.

36. *Ibid.*, p. 29.

37. H. B. Chenery, "Transitional Growth and World Industrialization," pp. 5–6.

38. H. B. Chenery and L. Taylor, "Development Patterns: Among Countries over Time," *Review of Economic Statistics*, Vol. 50. No. 4 (November 1968) pp. 391–416.

39. Chenery explicitly links his "early industries" to my leading sectors in takeoff in his "Patterns of Industrial Growth," p. 651. In the conclusion to *Patterns of Development, 1950–1970* he notes (p. 136n): "Although this formulation has some elements in common with Rostow's (1956) 'Take-off' we have shown that the periods of more rapid change occur at different levels of income for different processes and vary with the strategy being followed." There is nothing in the *Stages of Economic Growth* that would deny the possibility of surges in growth rates in post-takeoff stages or the possible influence of growth strategies on growth rates. On the contrary.

40. For summary of post-1960 evidence, see *Stages of Economic Growth*, 2d ed. (1971), Appendix B, pp. 233–235. It might also be noted that, after a fashion, Kuznets quietly capitulated on this point in his 1971 *Economic Growth of Nations* (pp. 61–65). He observed that historical evidence suggested a premodern growth net investment rate of 5% or 6%; a characteristic terminal figure of 15%. Although Kuznets was inclined to suggest a long, gradual rise in the investment rate, detailed historical and cross-sectional data suggests a sharp initial rise (covering, in my view, the drive to technological maturity as well as takeoff) followed by a marked deceleration. In the Chenery–Syrquin analysis, the deceleration comes after $300 (1964) per capita. (*Patterns of Development, 1950–1970*, p. 20.) For Chenery's latest investment-rate data associated with initial, intermediate, and final positions in the "Transformation" see *Industrialization and Growth*, pp. 49–52.

41. *Industrialization and Growth*, p. 288.

42. See, especially, *Infant and Child in the Culture of Today*, pp. 45, 293, 354.

43. James Gleich, *Chaos: Making a New Science* (New York: Viking, 1987), pp. 5 and 43. In a quite limited analogy—the rise of foreigners in British economic, intellectual, and political life— Sir James Goldsmith, the Anglo-French financier, observes: "Dynamism is usually the result of disequilibrium." (*The Economist* [24 Dec., 1988–6 January, 1989], "New Blood," p. 73.)

44. H. B. Chenery and M. Syrquin, *Patterns of Development*, p. 10: "Since we are concerned with interrelated changes in the structure of the whole economy, the model implicit in our analysis is one of general equilibrium."

45. *Ibid.*

46. See, especially, I. Adelman and C. T. Morris, *Society, Politics, and Economic Development*, rev. ed. (Baltimore: John Hopkins Press, 1971); and *Economic Growth and Social Equity in Developing Countries* (Stanford: Stanford University Press, 1973).

47. *Economic Growth and Social Equity*, pp. 15–16.

48. My *Politics and the Stages of Growth* (Cambridge: at the University Press, 1971) is an exercise in this approach to relating economic and political development.

49. P. Rosenstein-Rodan, "Natura Facit Saltum," in Gerald M. Meier and Dudley Seers (eds.), *Pioneers in Development*, (New York: Oxford University Press for the World Bank, 1984), p. 208. In a note Rodan explains the concept of "the pursuit curve" and its origin as follows:

> A dog pursues a hare, without anticipation, along the shortest distance at which he sees him (a straight line). Meanwhile the hare runs from point 1 to point 2. When the dog sees him again in this new position he again runs along the shortest distance (a straight line) in which he sees him. Meanwhile the hare runs to point 3, and so on. The line along which the dog runs is what we want to explain. It is determined by a straight-line distance wherever the dog sees the hare. The overwhelming majority of the points of the pursuit curve are disequilibrium points. It may be called "state of equilibrium" if the dog ultimately catches the hare.
>
> (Pareto had mentioned it but never worked it out.)

50. Edward F. Denison, *Trends in American Economic Growth, 1929–1982* (Washington D.C.: The Brookings Institution, 1985). The work of Denison, John Kendrick, and others in growth accounting has a considerable intellectual background including the following: J. Schmookler, "The Changing Efficiency of the American Economy, 1869 to 1938," *Review of Economics and Statistics* (August 1952), pp. 214–213; S. Fabricant, "Economic Progress and Economic Change" in *36th Annual Report,* (New York: NBER, 1954); A. Cairncross, "The Place of Capital in Economic Progress," in *Economic Progress,* Léon H. Dupriez, ed. (Louvain: Institut de Recherches Economiques et Sociales, 1955) pp. 235–248, (1955); M. Abramovitz, "Resources and Output in the United States since 1870," *American Economic Review, Proceedings,* Vol. 46 (May 1956); and R. M. Solow, "Technical Change and the Aggregate Production Function," *Review of Economics and Statistics,* Vol. 39 (August 1957). See also, a critical response to emphasis on technology rather than total physical inputs as the source of productivity increase, D. W. Jorgenson and Z. Griliches, "The Explanation of Productivity Change," *Review of Economic Studies,* Vol. 34 (July 1967).

51. *Ibid.,* p. 28.

52. See, especially, *ibid.,* pp. 27–32, including notes on Edwin Mansfield and others.

53. *Ibid.,* pp. 29–30.

54. Edward F. Denison, *Why Growth Rates Differ* (Washington, D.C.: The Brookings Institution, 1967), pp. 301–302.

55. For a more complete analysis of comparative U.S.–Western European–Japanese growth rates in this period, see my *World Economy: History and Prospect,* Chapter 17. On Europe, see notably M. M. Postan's admirably disaggregated treatment of new consumption patterns, technology, and investment: *An Economic History of Western Europe, 1945–1964* (London: Methuen, 1967), especially Chapters 5, 6, 8, and 11.

Chapter 17

1. The full reference to Arndt's volume is *The Rise and Fall of Economic Growth, A Study in Contemporary Thought* (Sydney: Longman Cheshire, 1978). This study is mainly addressed to disabuse with growth in advanced industrial countries; but its argument is evidently relevant to development economics as well.

2. In *Development and Change,* Vol. 10, No. 3 (July 1979), pp. 707–718.

3. The full title of Hirschman's book is *Essays in Trespassing: Economics to Politics and Beyond* (Cambridge: at the University Press, 1981). His first chapter was originally delivered at a symposium on Latin America in 1980.

4. Little's study was published by Basic Books, New York, 1982. Lal's *The Poverty of "Development Economics"* was initially published by the Institute of Economic Affairs, London, in August 1983 and republished in Cambridge: Harvard University Press, 1985.

5. Gerald M. Meier and Dudley Seers (eds.) *Pioneers in Development* (New York: Oxford University Press for the World Bank, 1984).

6. Meier's historical introduction, "The Formative Period," is at *ibid.,* pp. 3–22; Streeten's postscript, pp. 337–361. The essays by each of the "pioneers" are followed by critical commentaries by one or two younger commentators. Meier has subsequently written a more spacious analytic account of the evolution of development theory including his own policy recommendations, *Emerging from Poverty: The Economics That Really Matters* (New York and Oxford: Oxford University Press, 1984).

7. *American Economic Review,* Vol. 74, No. 1 (March 1984), p. 1. For another measured but by no means complacent assessment see A. K. Sen, "Development: Which Way Now?" *Economic Journal,* Vol. 93, No. 372 (December 1983), pp. 745–762. Professor Claudia Goldin tells me, however, that as of the autumn of 1987 she detects a revival of interest in development economics, and my view is out of date.

8. *Economic Journal*, Vol. 111, Nos. 210–211 (June–September 1943), pp. 202–211.

9. Montreal: International Labour Office, 1944.

10. Oxford: Basil Blackwell (Institute of Statistics Monograph No. 2) 1945.

11. *World Economic Development*, pp. 185–186.

12. *Industrialisation of Backward Areas*, p. iii.

13. Mandelbaum (*ibid.*, p. 5, n. 6) notes and draws data from Sir P. Thakurdas and others, *A Plan of Economic Development of India* (London: Penguin, 1944). He also notes among early planning studies A. Bonne, *The Economic Development of the Middle East: An Outline of Planned Reconstruction* (London: Kegan Paul, 1945).

14. Gerald M. Meier and Dudley Seers (eds.), *Pioneers in Development*, pp. 8–10. See also, my *United States in the World Arena* (New York: Harper, 1960), pp. 133–139; and *Eisenhower, Kennedy, and Foreign Aid* (Austin: University of Texas Press, 1985), pp. 70–80. On the origins of the United Nations regional economic commissions, see my *The Division of Europe after World War II: 1946* (Austin: University of Texas Press, 1981), pp. 70–75.

15. For data and discussion, see my *Eisenhower, Kennedy, and Foreign Aid*, pp. 80–83.

16. The title of the report of the Gordon Gray Commission is *Report to the President on Foreign Economic Policies* (Washington, D.C.: G.P.O., 1950); of the Rockefeller Report, U.S. International Development Advisory Board, *Partners in Progress: A Report to President Truman* (New York: Simon and Schuster, 1951). Acheson's speeches dealing with foreign aid in Asia are summarized accessibly in McGeorge Bundy (ed.), *The Pattern of Responsibility* (Boston: Houghton Mifflin, 1952), pp. 171–200.

17. For a more complete summary of these reports and authors, see Gerald M. Meier and Dudley Seers (eds.) *Pioneers in Development*, pp. 11–13.

18. New York: United Nations, 1950.

19. *Eisenhower, Kennedy, and Foreign Aid* is, essentially, a book about the multidimensional debate on development policy of the 1950s.

20. *A Proposal* (New York: Harper, 1957) was written by Max F. Millikan and me, in collaboration with Paul Rosenstein-Rodan and eleven other members of the CENIS staff. Bauer's study was *United States Aid and Indian Development* (Washington, D.C.: American Enterprise Institute, November 1959).

21. See, for example, *Eisenhower, Kennedy, and Foreign Aid*, Chapters 9 and 10.

22. *Essays in Trespassing*, p. 1.

23. Barbara Ward, J. D. Runnalls, and Lenore d'Anjou (eds.), *The Widening Gap: Development in the 1970's* (New York: Columbia University Press, 1971), pp. 11–13. For a more professional pro–basic-human-needs study about a decade later, see Paul Streeten *et al.*, *First Things First* (New York: Oxford University Press for the World Bank, 1981).

24. Although honored to have been included among the ten, I shall deal with my own views in Chapters 18–21 and the joint Appendix with Michael Kennedy.

25. Jacob Viner, *International Trade and Economic Development* (Oxford: at the Clarendon Press, 1953) p. 100. This passage is included in the chapter from Viner's volume reprinted in A. N. Agarwala and S. P. Singh (eds.), *The Economics of Underdevelopment* (New York: Oxford University Press, 1963), p. 17.

26. "The 'Classic' Theory of International Trade and the Underdeveloped Countries," *Economic Journal*, Vol. 68, No. 270 (June 1958), pp. 317–337.

27. See, Nurkse's "Some International Aspects of the Problem of Economic Development" *American Economic Review*, Vol. 42, No. 2 (May 1952, *Papers and Proceedings*), pp. 571–583; also, more generally, *Equilibrium Growth in the World Economy*, (Cambridge: Harvard University Press, 1961).

28. J. R. Hicks, *A Theory of Economic History* (Oxford: Oxford University Press, 1969) pp. 142–143.

29. *Ibid.*, p. 145.

30. *Pioneers*, pp. 27–28.

31. From my review of Bauer's *Equality, The Third World and Economic Delusion* (Cambridge: Harvard University Press, 1981), published in *Transaction/Society*, Vol. 20, No. 1 (November/December 1982), pp. 88–89. This review contains a specification of my areas of agreement and disagreement with Bauer, which does not belong in this chapter.

32. *Pioneers*, p. 60. See also Clark's attack on English economists as excessively speculative and theoretical in the Preface to the 1940 edition of *The Conditions of Economic Progress* (p. vii).

33. G. T. Jones, *Increasing Return*, (Cambridge: at the University Press 1933). Colin Clark edited Jones's book for publication after the latter's premature death. See, *The Conditions of Economic Progress* (1940), pp. 291ff and 340–341.

34. *Conditions of Economic Progress* (1951), pp. viii–xiii.

35. *Pioneers*, p. 63.

36. *Ibid.*, p. 64.

37. *Ibid.*

38. *Ibid.*, pp. 76–77.

39. *Ibid.*, p. 65.

40. *Ibid.*, p. 73.

41. *Conditions of Economic Progress*, p. 6.

42. *Pioneers*, pp. 75–76.

43. *Conditions of Economic Progress* (1940), p. ix.

44. *Ibid.*, p. ix.

45. *Ibid.*

46. *Ibid.*, p. vii.

47. See, especially *Conditions of Economic Progress* (1951), pp. 1–5.

48. *Pioneers*, p. 87.

49. *Ibid.*, p. 90.

50. For a more subtle interpretation of Hirschman's dissent as a protracted fight against "vulgar recipes imposed on the weak or the vanquished" see Carlos Diaz Alejandro, *ibid.*, pp. 112–113.

51. *Ibid.*, pp. 91–110. Although a study that stands on its own feet, Hirschman's *The Passions and the Interests* is clearly related to his theory of unbalanced growth with its "remarkable unintended effects." See, notably, in *The Passions and the Interests*, pp. 130–131, for echoes of his development theory earlier formulated.

52. *Pioneers*, p. 94.

53. *Ibid.*, pp. 92 and 96.

54. *Ibid.*, p. 105.

55. *Manchester School* (May 1954), accessibly reprinted in A. N. Agarwala and S. P. Singh, *The Economics of Underdevelopment*, p. 400.

56. *Agenda*, Vol. 3, No. 4 (November 1944).

57. On the Caribbean, Lewis published "Industrialization of Puerto Rico," *Caribbean Economic Review* (December 1949), and the more general *Industrial Development in the Caribbean* (Port-au-Spain, Trinidad: Caribbean Commission, 1949). Lewis's colleagues in writing the 1951 United Nations report on development were: Alberto Baltia Cortez (Chile), D. R. Gadgil (India), George Hakim (Lebanon), and T. W. Schultz (United States).

58. The books referred to are *Economic Survey, 1919–1939* (London: Allen and Unwin, 1949) which includes some materials on developing countries, notably the impact on them of interwar terms of trade movements; *The Principles of Economic Planning* (London: Allen and Unwin, 1949) concerned primarily with planning in advanced industrial countries, although it includes an appendix "On Planning in Backward Countries"; and *Overhead Costs* (London: Allen and Unwin, 1949), a collection of essays mainly addressed to problems of monopolistic competition in advanced industrial countries.

59. It should be noted that Lewis was not alone in London academic life in his concern with economic development. Among others, Paul Rosenstein-Rodan was there, as well as Kurt Martin, R. H. Tawney, Vera Anstey, Eileen Power, and Michael Postan.

60. "The Roots of Development Theory," Chapter 2 in H. B. Chenery and T. N. Srinivasan (eds.), *Handbook of Development Economics*, Vol. I. (Amsterdam: North Holland Press, 1968).

61. *Economic Growth*, pp. 304–319.

62. *Ibid.*, p. 340.

63. *Ibid.*, p. 183.

64. *Ibid.*, p. 164.

65. *Ibid.*, p. 200.

66. *Ibid.*, p. 208. I later used a similar formulation in my takeoff article and have often referred to such an increase in investment as "pure Arthur Lewis behavior." I confess that it was only in writing this book and re-reading afresh Paul Rodan's pioneering article on Southeastern Europe that I discovered he originated the concept. I suspect I picked it up as part of the M.I.T. development economists' conventional wisdom in the early 1950s. For my expression of some regret at the preeminence accorded this feature of takeoff, see *Pioneers*, pp. 234–236 and pp. 433–434, preceding.

67. *World Development Report, 1983*, p. 156.

68. *Economic Growth*, p. 210. The most detailed estimates of the distribution of investment and of sectoral, marginal capital-output ratios that I'm aware of are those of Paul Rodan. They were reproduced on a faded old-fashioned mimeographed sheet and are unpublished so far as I know. I include also the estimates in Chenery, *Industrialization and Growth*, p. 49. (See Tables N.3, N.4, N.5.)

69. *Ibid.*, p. 213.

70. *Ibid.*, pp. 233–235.

71. Lewis deals with interwar cycles in *Economic Survey* and, more systematically, in *Growth and Fluctuations* (London: Allen and Unwin, 1978).

72. *Economic Growth*, pp. 284–286. Lewis cites three other factors that help determine the unsteadiness of investment: the flexibility of bank credit, the unstable relation between investment and the growth of income, and changes in the distribution of income.

73. *Ibid.*, p. 286.

74. See, notably, *Economic Survey*.

75. See, for example, *Economic Growth*, pp. 289–292.

76. *Ibid.*, p. 279.

77. Lewis and I are the major proponents of the notion that the price, money-wage, and interest-rate phenomena identified by Kondratieff as subject to long cycles are to be explained by successive trend periods in the intersectoral terms of trade between basic commodities and manufactures. See, for example, Lewis's *Growth and Fluctuations*, pp. 69–93.

78. *Economic Growth*, p. 165.

79. *Ibid.*, p. 169. For emphasis on the important oblique rather than direct linkage of science and invention in the eighteenth and nineteenth centuries, see my *How It All Began* (New York: McGraw Hill, 1975), especially Chapters 1 and 4.

80. *Ibid.*, p. 371. For a somewhat different but not inconsistent discussion of this subject, see Chapter 8, "Relative Stages of Growth and Aggression," in my *Stages of Economic Growth*.

81. On both types of secular stagnation, see Lewis's *Economic Growth*, pp. 292–302 and 408–415, the latter a catalog of nine ways in which the policies of governments may retard economic growth. There is some discussion of the possibilities of secular stagnation in a section entitled "Institutional Change," pp. 145–162.

82. *Ibid.*, pp. 302, 415, 418.

83. J. M. Keynes, "National Self-Sufficiency," *Yale Review*, Vol. XXII (1933), p. 755.

84. See, for example, the bibliography at the close of the Introduction to *Economic Growth*, pp. 21–22. This and Lewis's other bibliographical notes at the end of chapters are a vivid reminder of how limited—but still rich—the literature on development was in the early 1950s.

85. *Ibid.*, pp. 14–16.

86. *Ibid.*, p. 159. For a more general application to politics of this doctrine—rooted in Plato's

Table N.3. Distribution of Investment in Underdeveloped (A) and Developed (B) Countries

Sector	(A) Percent of total investment	(A) Sectoral capital output ratio	(A) Contribution to output	(B) Percent of total investment	(B) Sectoral capital output ratio	(B) Contribution to output
I. 1. Social overhead capital	34.0%	8 : 1	4.25	32.0%	7 : 1	4.6
2. Education	1.0	10 : 1	0.1	1.5	8 : 1	0.2
3. Housing	24.0	10 : 1	2.4	24.0	10 : 1	2.4
II. Agriculture						
1. "Old"	7.5	1.33 : 1	5.6	4.5	1.7 : 1	2.6
2. "New"	3.0	6 : 1	0.5	2.0	5 : 1	0.4
3. X			1.5			
III. Industry						
1. Heavy	7.5	4.5 : 1	1.7	8.5	4.25 : 1	2.0
2. Light	8.5	2.5 : 1	3.4	9.5	2.25 : 1	4.2
3. Handicrafts	1.5	1.2 : 1	1.25	1.0	1.5 : 1	0.7
4. Construction residual			1.5			1.8
5. X						2.5
IV. Services	13.0%	1.1 : 1	11.8	17.0%	1.5 : 1	11.4
			34.00			32.8
Aggregate marginal capital-output ratio	100 : 34.0 = 2.9			100 : 32.8 = 3.0		

Source: Paul Rosenstein-Rodan (no other source).

Table N.4. Standard Solution to the Cross-Country Model, Income Level 5 ($2100/1970/per capita), (dollars per capita)

Sector	Consumption	Investment	Percentage of total investment	Government	Total demand	Percentage of total demand
Domestic final demand						
Primary						
1. Agriculture	64	0		4	68	3%
2. Mining	19	0		4	23	1
Subtotal[a]	83	0		8	91	4
Manufacturing						
3. Food	186	0		19	205	10
4. Consumer goods	202	0		15	217	10
5. Producer goods	104	0		6	110	5
6. Machinery	15	172		4	191	9
Subtotal[a]	507	172	36%	44	723	34
Nontradables						
7. Social overhead	115	283	59	26	424	20
8. Services	549	25	5	300	874	42
Total[a]	1,254	480	100%	378	2,112	100%
Percentage of total final demand	59	23		18	100	

NOTE: [a]Totals may not add because of rounding.

SOURCE: Hollis Chenery et al., Industrialization and Growth (New York: Oxford University Press for the World Bank, 1986), p. 51 (World Bank Data).

Table N.5. Standard Solution to the Cross-Country Model, Income level 1 ($140/1970/per capita) (dollars per capita)

Sector	Domestic final demand					
	Consumption	Investment	Percentage of total investment	Government	Total demand	Percentage of total demand
Primary						
1. Agriculture	25.5	0		0.5	26	18%
2. Mining	0	0		0.5	1	0
Subtotal[a]	26.0	0		1.0	270	18
Manufacturing						
3. Food	15	0		1	16	11
4. Consumer goods	11	0		0	11	8
5. Producer goods	3	0		0	3	2
6. Machinery	0	7	33%	1	8	6
Subtotal[a]	29	7		2	38	27
Nontradables						
7. Social overhead	7	12	57	1	20	14
8. Services	41	1	5	16	58	40
Total[a]	102	21	95%	20	143	100%
Percentage of total final demand	71	15		14	100	

NOTE: [a]Totals may not add because of rounding.
SOURCE: Hollis Chenery et al., *Industrialization and Growth* (World Bank Data), p. 49.

Republic—see my *Politics and the Stages of Growth* (Cambridge: at the University Press, 1971), pp. 8–16 and 248–250.

87. *Economic Growth*, pp. 421–423.

88. *Ibid.*, pp. 429–430.

89. *Pioneers*, p. 132.

90. This study was first published in Sweden in 1930, in English in 1958 (London: Routledge and Kegan Paul).

91. Gunnar Myrdal, *Against the Stream: Critical Essays on Economics* (New York: Pantheon Books, 1972), p. vi. Myrdal begins by paraphrasing his earlier study.

92. *Ibid.*

93. Myrdal notes that his direct introduction to development problems arose from his work (1947–1957) as executive secretary of the United Nations Economic Commission for Europe (ECE). U.N. regional economic commissions for the Far East (ECAFE) and Latin America (ECLA) were promptly created in its wake. Myrdal established fraternal relations with those institutions and traveled extensively in Asia and the Middle East. His first reflections on development were published in 1956 when Myrdal was 58: *An International Economy: Problems and Prospects*, stemming from a lecture at Columbia University in May 1954 on the occasion of the University's bicentennial; and *Economic Theory and Underdeveloped Regions*, derived from lectures at the Central Bank of Egypt in 1956, and published separately the next year. The former views the world economy as a whole from the perspective of "integration"; but roughly two-thirds of the text is devoted to development problems. The latter is wholly addressed to development.

94. *Pioneers*, p. 154.

95. *Asian Drama: An Inquiry into the Poverty of Nations* (New York: Pantheon, 1968).

96. *Pioneers*, p. 153.

97. *Asian Drama*, p. 1536 (Vol. 3).

98. *The Challenge of World Poverty, A World Anti-Poverty Program in Outline* (New York: Pantheon Books, 1970).

99. *The Challenge*, p. 365.

100. *Ibid.*

101. *Pioneers*, p. 162.

102. *Ibid.*

103. *Ibid.*, pp. 164–165.

104. From a figure of .19% of GNP Sweden raised its level of official development assistance to a peak of 1.02% in 1982. The figure for 1985, .85%, was exceeded only by the Netherlands. *World Development Report, 1986* (New York: Oxford University Press for the World Bank, 1986), Table 20, p. 218.

105. *Against the Stream*, p. 312.

106. For further discussion of the complex politics of modernization, see preceding, pp. 418–427.

107. *International Economy*, p. ix.

108. *Pioneers*, pp. 175 and 178.

109. *Ibid.*, p. 176. Prebisch's summary of his doctrine is lucid as well as authoritative (*ibid.*, pp. 176–180).

110. *Ibid.*, p. 177.

111. See, for example, my *World Economy*, pp. 381–283, for a consideration of reasons for this phenomenon.

112. *Pioneers*, p. 181.

113. *Ibid.*, p. 183.

114. The reference here is from Albert Fishlow's commentary on Prebisch's essay, *ibid.*, p. 196. Prebisch was provided a base for his analyses in this final phase of his life by his editorship of the *CEPAL Review*. His major publications of this period are listed, *ibid.*, p. 183 n. 6.

115. *Ibid.*, p. 184.

116. *Ibid.*
117. *Ibid.*, pp. 188–189.
118. *Ibid.*, p. 191.
119. *Ibid.*
120. For an acute critique of Prebisch on this and other points see, for example, M. J. Flanders, "Prebisch on Protectionism: An Evaluation," *Economic Journal,* Vol. LXXIV, No. 294 (June 1964), pp. 305–326.
121. *Pioneers,* p. 197.
122. My closest professional dealings with Prebisch took place when he was Director-General of UNCTAD and I chairman of the Policy Planning Council at the State Department. In a private conversation I recall questioning whether generalized preferences would constitute a powerful enough force to overcome the bad habits built up in the phase of excessively protected import-substitution industrialization in Latin America. He agreed that significant domestic changes of attitude and policy would be required to generate greatly enlarged exports of competitive, diversified manufactures and doubted that generalized preferences would be accepted by the OECD countries; but he thought the pressure exerted on them via UNCTAD would lead to enlarged foreign aid. I said I thought his strategy, in the old British phrase, was "too clever by half," but wished him well.
123. "Problems of Industrialization" as reprinted in A. N. Agarwala and S. P. Singh (eds.), *The Economics of Underdevelopment* pp. 254–255. The exposition of the EEIT (East European Investment Trust) is a rough approximation of the kind of enterprise into which the World Bank was to evolve (*ibid.,* p. 254):

> The Institutional implementation of this programme must be left over to another occasion. Its main outlines are: At least 50 percent of the capital required must be supplied internally. "Creditor" and "debtor" countries acquire each 50 percent shares of a trust formed of all the industries to be created in the region. They will plan and proceed as business partners with Government representatives on the board. The creditors acquire shares in the trust which are redeemable after twenty years at 10 percent above parity if an average dividend service of $4\frac{1}{2}$ percent at least has been maintained in the past. An *average* dividend service of 3 per cent is guaranteed by Governments on the shares subscribed in their countries. Private investments in Eastern and South-Eastern Europe requiring foreign credits are licensed. Shares may be acquired by contributions *in natura:* for instance, the establishment of branch factories. Guarantees of nondiscrimination in the internal taxation policy will be obtained from Eastern European authorities."
>
> Industrial employment has to be found for (a) 20 million of the agrarian excess population + (b) 7–8 million = 40–50 per cent of the increase in population during the next decade (assuming that 50–60 per cent will be absorbed by agriculture) = 28 million people = 9 million active men and 3 million active women = 12 million workers. Up to 2 million workers can be employed in idle capacity. Capital has to be found for 10 million workers. Since the available capital is scarce, labour-intensive—i.e., light industries—will prevail. According to such statistics as are available, the following classification of industries is proposed: (1) light industries—capital equipment per head £100–£400; (2) medium industries—capital equipment per head £400–£800; (3) heavy industries—capital equipment per head £800–£1,500. Since some heavy industries cannot be avoided, let us assume that £300–£350 per head will be required, including housing, communications and public utilities. That amounts to £3,000 million, to which has to be added £1,800 million on maintenance of old and new capital for ten years, giving a total of £4,800 million. Eastern Europe would have to supply at least 50 percent—i.e., £2,400 million. Another £1,200 million of capital will be necessary for the improvement of agriculture, of which we assume that the bulk would have to be provided internally,[1] so that Eastern and Southeastern Europe would have to supply £3,600 million capital internally between, say, 1945 and 1956.[2] Since its total income is £2,000 million per annum, that would represent a rate of investment of 18 per cent (equal to that of Russia).

[1] A small part of it may be borrowed from abroad, but in this case in the form of bond credit.
[2] The immediate transition period of the first two years after the war is not included in these calculations, so that *de facto* it is a twelve years plan, not a ten-years plan.

124. In a footnote to his article in *Pioneers* (p. 207), Rodan cites as "important predecessors of the theory of development Harrod–Domar, Joan Robinson, Keynes, and Colin Clark."

125. *Pioneers*, p. 209.

126. See Kenneth J. Arrow, "Limited Knowledge and Economic Analysis," *American Economic Review,* Vol. 64, No. 1 (March 1974), pp. 1–10. Arrow concluded that the imperfection of investment markets was, essentially, irremediable. For discussion in the context of T. N. Srinivasan's reply to Peter Bauer, see *Pioneers,* pp. 54–55. Also, Sikhamoy Chakravarty, "Paul Rosenstein-Rodan: an Appreciation," *World Development,* Vol. 11, No. 1 (January 1983).

127. *Pioneers,* p. 210. Rodan quotes here from a paper of the M.I.T. Center for International Studies, prepared for the Special Committee to Study the Foreign Aid Program, *The Objectives of U.S. Economic Assistance Programs* (Washington, D.C.: Government Printing Office, 1957), p. 70.

128. See, for example, my references in *Pioneers,* pp. 240–245 and in *Eisenhower, Kennedy, and Foreign Aid,* pp. 41–50.

129. Max F. Millikan and W. W. Rostow with the collaboration of P. N. Rosenstein-Rodan and others, *A Proposal: Key to an Effective Foreign Policy* (New York: Harper, 1957), "Appendix: The Estimation of Capital Requirements for Development," pp. 153–170. Rodan's article was "International Aid for Underdeveloped Countries," *The Review of Economics and Statistics,* Vol. XLIII, No. 2 (May 1961), pp. 107–138.

130. *Pioneers,* p. 212. Having observed with sympathy and closely the experiment with the Committee of Nine, I feel impelled to report that its failure, in my view, was for somewhat more complex reasons than the instinctive antagonism of entrenched Latin American and U.S. bureaucrats. The Nine proved to be a rather contentious egocentric group. They might have been knit together under Rodan's leadership if other legitimate claims upon his time and presence in Washington were not so pressing. The Nine overlapped with and were finally superseded by CIAP (Inter-American Committee on the Alliance for Progress) a group of seven Latin-American members (also government officials), plus a Latin-American Chairman (Carlos Sanz de Santamaria) plus one member (*not* representative) from the United States. For a time, before its dissolution, the Nine advised CIAP. The American Congress stipulated that Alliance for Progress loans had to be made on the basis of CIAP recommendations. Unfortunately, in my view, the CIAP machinery progressively weakened in the latter years of the 1960s.

131. *Ibid.,* pp. 218–219.

132. *Ibid.,* pp. 219–220.

133. *Ibid.,* p. 220.

134. *Ibid.,* pp. 220–221.

135. Singer's two basic papers were: "Relative Prices of Exports and Imports of Underdeveloped Countries" (New York: United Nations, Department of Economic Affairs, No. 1949, II, B.3); and "Distribution of the Gains Between Investing and Borrowing Countries," *American Economic Review, Papers and Proceedings* (May 1950).

136. *Pioneers,* pp. 279–280. Singer cites, from different perspectives, the work of Keynes, Meade, Hilgerdt, Carl Major Wright, and Gunnar Myrdal. He later (p. 285) notes that he carried over into international economic relations Schumpeter's notion that the innovation of new technologies carried with it quasi-monopolistic profits.

137. *Ibid.,* p. 280, text and Note 13.

138. *Pioneers,* especially pp. 282–283 and 288–293. Spraos's article is "The Statistical Debate on the Net Barter Terms of Trade between Primary Commodities and Manufactures," *Economic Journal,* Vol. 90 (March 1980).

139. *Ibid.,* pp. 123–124 (Lewis) and pp. 304–311 (Balassa).

140. I should note that Singer (*ibid.,* p. 288) does acknowledge that: "With the benefit of hindsight . . . I would agree that the limits of the ISI [Import Substitution Industrialization] were not fully realized."

141. *Ibid.*, pp. 293–295.

142. *Ibid.*, pp. 296ff.

143. See, for example, my *Eisenhower, Kennedy, and Foreign Aid,* especially Chapters 8–10.

144. *Pioneers,* p. 276.

145. *Pioneers,* pp. 220–221.

146. *Ibid.*, pp. 218, 217.

147. Jan Tinbergen, *The Design of Development* (Baltimore: Johns Hopkins University Press, for the International Development Institute of the World Bank, 1958). For a more general evaluation of Tinbergen's career, see, notably, Bert Hansen, "Jan Tinbergen. An Appraisal of his Contributions to Economics," *Swedish Journal of Economics* (1969), pp. 325–336.

148. *Design of Development,* pp. 9–10. Bruno's commentary on Tinbergen as a development economist is in *Pioneers,* pp. 332–334.

149. First published as "Zur Theorie der Langfrisrigen Wirtschaftentwicklung," *Weltwirtschaftliches Archiv,* Vol. 55 (1942), pp. 511–549. Translated and reprinted as "On the Theory of Trend Movements," in L. H. Klassen, L. M. Koyck, and H. J. Wittereen (eds.), *Jan Tinbergen: Selected Papers* (Amsterdam: North Holland Press, 1959), pp. 182–221.

150. L. H. Klassen *et al.* (eds.), p. 189.

151. *Ibid.*, p. 183.

152. Here is Tinbergen's later account of his assumptions in this exercise (*Pioneers,* p. 316):

> Production, and hence real income, was assumed to depend on the supply of labor and of capital. The relationship determining production was assumed to be a Cobb–Douglas function with disembodied exponential technological development; the exponents of labor and capital were three-fourths and one-fourth respectively. The supply elasticity of capital with regard to its price (interest) was assumed to be zero; labor supply was given values ranging from -1 to infinity. The supply of labor was also assumed to depend proportionally on population, itself growing exponentially. Capital formation was taken to be a fixed proportion of real income. Other assumptions with regard to the supply elasticity of capital and the development of population over time were considered. For the central case described in the preceding sentences two main results were offered: (1) the time shape of production and (2) the growth rates, for the middle of the period considered, of capital, labor, and product for four different values of labor supply elasticity.
>
> The whole exercise was meant as a supplement to business cycle theory and was typically inspired by the situation in developed countries and by the absence of massive unemployment in the phase of prosperity.

153. *Ibid.*, p. 330.

154. *Ibid.*, p. 320.

155. There is discussion of the sectoral structure of planning that borders on this point in *The Design of Development,* pp. 47–49 and 81–84; but I, at least, do not regard it as adequate.

156. *Pioneers,* p. 320.

157. *The Design of Development,* pp. 63–67.

158. *Ibid.*, p. 65. Tinbergen notes (*Pioneers,* p. 325, n. 19) that his citing of Dutch government financing of the steel industry sufficiently disturbed the president of the World Bank (Eugene Black) to postpone publication of his monograph for several years.

159. *Pioneers,* pp. 325–326. Tinbergen fails to note that as the private sector generated an enlarged corps of vigorous entrepreneurs in Turkey some initially government owned plants were sold off, a procedure also followed in Japan, beginning in the 1880s.

160. "Jan Tinbergen: An Appraisal," p. 331.

161. Jan Tinbergen, "My Life Philosophy," *The American Economist,* Vol. XXVIII, No. 2 (1934), pp. 5–8.

162. Paul Streeten, "Postscript: Development Dichotomies," *Pioneers,* pp. 337–361.

163. *Ibid.*, p. 338.

164. *Ibid.*, p. 342.

165. *Ibid.*, p. 345. The distinction has been elaborated in I. M. D. Little, *Economic Development*.

166. The editor of *Pioneers*, G. M. Meier, asked me to reply to Streeten's *dependencia* doctrine, which I did, *ibid.*, pp. 250–253. A reading of *The Stages of Growth*, detailing the multiple routes to, through, and beyond takeoff, and Part V of *The World Economy*, should dispel the (to me) incomprehensible notion that nations have passed through identical development experiences. But, as noted above, development economists, peculiarly drawn to postures of "dissent," tend to conduct their controversies against caricature straw men.

167. *Ibid.*, p. 257.

168. Kwon Won-Ki, Vice Minister of Science and Technology, "Science and Technology Vital to Nation's Modernization," *Korea Business World*, Vol. 3, No. 4 (April 1987), p. 10. On the essential catalytic role of the South Korean bureacracy in that country's remarkable post-war economic development see the short but authoritative essay by Lee Hahn-Been, "Korean Development: Lessons, Problems, and Prospects," Chapter 8 in his *The Age of the Common Man in Korea*, (Seoul: Bak Young Sa, 1987), pp. 258–267.

169. *Ibid.*, p. 11.

170. See my *Why the Poor Get Richer*, especially pp. 268–271, Tables 6-7 and 6-8.

171. Hollis Chenery, Sherman Robinson, and Moshe Syrquin, *Industrialization and Growth* (New York: Oxford University Press, 1986). See especially Chapter 11 ("Alternative Routes to Development") and 12 ("Growth and Structure: A Synthesis"). For important underlying data and analysis see also Chapter 6 ("Trade Strategies and Growth Episodes") and Chapter 7 ("Interdependence and Industrial Structure").

172. The computable general equilibrium (CGE) models, pioneered by Johansen, are described by Chenery (*ibid.*, p. 314) as follows:

> In the development literature, CGE models trace their lineage back to the multisector input–output models widely applied to problems of planning in developing countries in the 1960s. While firmly based on the foundation of Walrasian general equilibrium theory, CGE models can also be seen as a logical culmination of a trend in the literature on planning models to add more and more substitutability and nonlinearity to the basic input–output model. The models tend to be highly nonlinear—to have neoclassical production and expenditure functions—and to incorporate a variety of substitution possibilities in production, demand, and trade.
>
> CGE models applied to developed countries have generally stayed relatively close to the Walrasian paradigm. In applications to developing countries, however, most researchers have introduced certain structuralist features into CGE models to capture the stylized facts characterizing these countries.

173. *Ibid.*, pp. 339–340 and 358–359.

174. *Ibid.*, p. 358. For a similar conclusion see Martin Fransman, *Technology and Economic Development* (Brighton: Wheatsheaf Books, 1986), especially Chapter 8, "Infants, Exports and Technical Progress," pp. 75–93.

175. I cite Djakarta to Rabat because, during a year off from July 1983 to July 1984, my wife and I spent the first $4\frac{1}{2}$ months traveling through the Pacific to Asia and the Middle East. In virtually every one of the dozen developing countries we visited (including both China and India), high officials were attempting to focus their citizens on the need to reduce the role of government and expand the scope of private enterprise in the economy. The first such country was Indonesia; the last, Morocco.

176. This passage comes from an unclassified U.S. government document written by an anonymous U.S. public servant. I quoted it in a lecture at the National Bank of Egypt in November 1983 (*Prospects for the World Economy*).

177. The phrase is quoted in William P. Glade, "Economic Policy-making and the Structures of

Corporation in Latin America," (Offprint Series No. 208, Institute of Latin American Studies, The University of Texas at Austin, 1981).

178. See, especially, my *Stages of Economic Growth,* especially pp. 26–30; *Politics and the Stages of Growth,* especially, Chapters 3 and 4, also *Pioneers,* pp. 232–233.

179. For a more complete account see my *Diffusion of Power* (New York: Macmillan, 1972), pp. 192–196.

180. For an elaboration of this argument see my *Politics and the Stages of Growth,* pp. 289–295.

181. As this book was being put to bed, the Winter 1989 edition of *Daedalus* arrived, "A World to Make: Development in Perspective" (Vol. 118, No. 1). It is a wide-ranging review and critique of post-1945 development theory and practice in which some 38 scholars participated. A good many drew policy conclusions in their papers or discussion. For our present purposes, it is relevant to note that, from beginning to end, the volume is shot through with reflections—in many moods—on the inescapable, often overriding, often distorting, occasionally reinforcing, role of politics in the development process of the past four decades.

Chapter 18

1. See, in particular, *Politics and the Stages of Growth,* (Cambridge: at the University Press, 1971), pp. 7–16. for an elaboration of some implications of the tripartite view of human beings including the relevance to individual and collective behavior of the economist's principle of diminishing relative marginal utility.

2. The phrases are from Professor Prigogine's "Order out of Chaos," an unpublished public lecture delivered at the University of Texas at Austin, November 18, 1977, on the occasion of the announcement of his Nobel Prize Award.

3. *The World Economy: History and Prospect* (Austin: University of Texas Press, 1978), pp. xi–xli.

4. *Pioneers in Development,* Gerald M. Meier and Dudley Seers (eds.) (New York: Oxford University Press for the World Bank, 1984), p. 238.

5. *The Process of Economic Growth,* (Oxford: at the Clarendon Press, 1953, 1960), pp. 17, 71, 103–108.

6. *Economic Journal,* Vol. LXVI, No. 26 (March 1956), pp. 25–48.

7. *The United States in the World Arena* (New York: Harper and Row, 1960).

8. *The Stages of Economic Growth,* (Cambridge: at the University Press, 1960, 1971) pp. 57–58.

9. *Ibid.,* pp. 12–16.

10. *Pioneers,* pp. 234–237.

11. W. W. Rostow (ed.), *The Economics of Take-off into Sustained Growth* (New York: St. Martin's Press, 1963), p. 16.

12. See, especially, *ibid.,* pp. xiii–xxvi and Chapter 1, pp. 1–21; *The Stages of Economic Growth,* 2d ed., 1971, Appendix B, pp. 172–241; *The World Economy,* pp. 778–779; *Pioneers,* pp. 234–238 and 250–253.

13. *The World Economy,* pp. 778–779, where the two sets of dates are given and minor differences discussed, including the case of Japan, where we were both a bit early.

14. For the relevance of Crouzet's work to this issue see *Stages,* 2d ed., p. 214. I should add that David H. Pinkney's *Decisive Years in France, 1840–1847* (Princeton: Princeton University Press, 1986) makes the case, mainly in prose, for the critical importance of the 1840s in French modernization more effectively than either Crouzet's or my statistics.

15. This collective adventure is described at some length in my *Eisenhower, Kennedy, and Foreign Aid* (Austin: University of Texas Press, 1985), Chapters 3 and 4; and in my essay "Development: The Political Economy of the Marshallian Long Period," in Gerald M. Meier and Dudley Seers (eds.), *Pioneers,* especially pp. 240–247.

16. New York: Harper, 1957.

17. *An American Policy in Asia,* (Technology Press of M.I.T. and John Wiley, 1955), p. 50. The palpable lack of automatic short-run linkage between real income per capita and the capacity to sustain democracy was one factor that led me to write *Politics and the Stages of Growth* (Cambridge: at the University Press, 1971).

18. *Stages,* p. 125.

19. *Ibid.,* pp. 126–127.

20. *Ibid.,* p. 130.

21. *Ibid.,* pp. 133–134.

22. *Ibid.,* p. 135.

23. There were some reflections of these lines of thought in, for example, President Eisenhower's peroration of his talk before the United Nations General Assembly on August 13, 1958, and President Johnson's talk with Prime Minister Kosygin in Glassboro on June 23, 1967 (see my *Diffusion of Power,* [New York: Macmillan, 1972], p. 390). I also had an occasion to assert my view of the relation of the diffusion of power to peace in Moscow, at a Pugwash conference in November–December 1960. For the setting and relevant text see my *Essays on a Half-Century* (Westview: Boulder: Colo., 1988) pp. 58–59 and 158–159.

24. See, especially, *The Stages,* pp. 90–92 and pp. 165–167.

25. *Ibid.,* p. 1.

26. *Ibid.;* The quotation is from Croce's *Historical Materialism and the Economics of Karl Marx,* tr. C. M. Meredith (London: Allen and Unwin, 1922), pp. 3–4.

Chapter 19

1. Milo Keynes, *Essays on John Maynard Keynes* (Cambridge: at the University Press, 1975), p. 3. The quotation is from a letter of August 26, 1938, to Kingsley Martin, editor of *The New Statesman and Nation.* The text is to be found in Donald Moggeridge (ed.), *The Collected Writings of John Maynard Keynes,* Vol. XXVIII., *Social, Political, and Literary Writings* (London and Basingstoke: Macmillan and Cambridge University Press, for the Royal Economic Society, 1982).

2. *Rich Countries and Poor Countries: Reflections from the Past, Lessons for the Future* (Boulder, Colo.: Westview, 1987).

3. See, *Why the Poor Get Richer and the Rich Slow Down* (Austin: University of Texas Press, 1980), Chapter 1.

Chapter 20

1. Hollis Chenery and Moshe Syrquin, *Patterns of Development, 1950–1970,* (New York: Oxford University Press for the World Bank, 1975), p. 56.

2. *The World Economy: History and Prospect* (Austin: University of Texas Press, 1978), p. 17

3. For discussion and bibliographical references, *ibid.,* pp. 38–44 and related notes on pp. 726–727. Also see the demographic references in Chenery and Syrquin's excellent bibliography, *Patterns of Development,* pp. 215–222.

4. *World Development Report 1988* (New York: Oxford University Press for the World Bank, 1988) Table 28, p. 277. Both the net reproduction rate and the total fertility rate are designed to foreshadow future population trends and levels. They are defined as follows by the World Bank (*ibid.,* p. 301);

> The *net reproduction rate* (NRR) indicates the number of daughters a newborn girl will bear during her lifetime, assuming fixed age-specific fertility and mortality rates. The NRR thus

measures the extent to which a cohort of newborn girls will reproduce themselves under given schedules of fertility and mortality. An NRR of 1 indicates that fertility is at replacement level: at this rate child-bearing women, on average, bear only enough daughters to replace themselves in the population.

The *total fertility rate* represents the number of children that would be born per woman, if she were to live to the end of her child-bearing years and bear children at each age in accordance with prevailing age-specific fertility rates.

5. See, for example, John C. Caldwell, *The Theory of Fertility Decline* (New York: Academic Press, 1982); Michael S. Teitelbaum and Jay M. Winter, *Fear of Population Decline* (Orlando: Academic Press, 1985); and Ben J. Wattenberg, *The Birth Dearth* (New York: Pharos, 1987). Also, Sidney L. Jones, "Demographic Trends in America: Squaring the Population Pyramid," *Forum Report* (Washington, D.C.: The Washington Forum, September 30, 1987). Jones analyzes in some detail the implications for the economy, social security, etc., of apparent trends in the size and structure of the American population down to 2050.

6. See, for example, Julian L. Simon, *Theory of Population and Economic Growth* (Oxford: Basil Blackwell, 1986), Chapter 7, "The Optimum Rate of Population Growth," Gunter Steinmann and Julian L. Simon, pp. 15–139. This book is distinguished by its sophisticated linkage of population growth to technological change.

7. Jacob Schmookler, *Patents, Invention, and Economic Change* edited by Zvi Griliches and Leonid Hurwicz, (Cambridge: Harvard University Press, 1972), p. 70.

8. The bibliographical references at the close of each chapter of Paul Stoneman's *The Economic Analysis of Technological Change* (Oxford: Oxford University Press, 1983), provide a useful sense of the scale and directions of recent analytic work on the economics of technological change. Stoneman's book is a valuable stocktaking as of the early 1980s. To Stoneman's bibliography should be added Burton H. Klein, who has done interesting work on the economic determinants of technological change; e.g., *Prices, Wages, and Business Cycles: A Dynamic Theory* (Elmsford, N.Y.: Pergamon Press, 1984). Klein evokes the "hidden foot" (i.e., the intensity of competition in a given sector) as a supplement to the profit blandishments of the hidden hand as a determinant of pace of technological diffusion. An earlier serious effort to reconcile the processes of invention and innovation with neoclassical mainstream economics is William D. Nordhaus, *Invention, Growth, and Welfare, A Theoretical Treatment of Technological Change* (Cambridge: The M.I.T. Press, 1969). A full bibliography as of the late 1960s is on pp. 155–164. On pp. 55–59, Nordhaus underlines the three critical unrealistic assumptions required to conduct his enterprise: certainty, nonincreasing returns to scale, and perfect competition. Of equal unreality is the assumption that the product of R & D (productivity improving technical knowledge) is incremental.

Technology has been a area of analysis where economic historians and economists focusing on technological change have not managed very well to communicate in mutually reinforcing ways. For a lucid statement of the inevitable clash between technological analysis and neoclassical economics—and the inescapable need to evoke history—see Paul A. David, *Technical Choice Innovation and Economic Growth* (Cambridge: Cambridge University Press, 1975), "Introduction: Technology, History and Growth," pp. 1–16. For an effort to bridge the gap between mainstream economics and economic history, including considerable discussion of problems posed by technology, see William N. Parker (ed.) *Economic History and the Modern Economist* (Oxford: Blackwell, 1986).

9. This is the central theme of my "Technology and the Economic Theorist," an unpublished paper presented to a conference in honor of David Landes's sixty-fifth birthday, held August 30–September 4, 1987, at the Villa Serbelloni, Bellagio, Lake Como.

10. For a critique of mainstream economics in much the same spirit as that which suffuses this book, see R. R. Nelson and S. G. Winter, "Neoclassical v. Evolutionary Theories of Economic Growth: Critique and Prospectus," *Economic Journal*, Vol. 84, No. 336 (December 1974), pp.

886–905. For the full array of restricting assumptions required to deal with invention using neo-classical tools, see William D. Nordhaus, *Invention, Growth, and Welfare*, p. 27. After devoting a chapter to efforts to relax these assumption, Nordhaus concludes (p. 59): "The problems we have raised in this section are clearly important and cannot be assumed away if it is to be hoped that the results can be applied to real markets. However, a complete discussion and resolution of the problems is not within the scope of this study."

11. For an exploration of these complexities, see Chapter 4 ("Science, Invention, and Innovation") in my *How It All Began,* (New York: McGraw-Hill, 1975).

12. For discussion of the links of science to invention, see, notably, Jacob Schmookler, *Invention and Economic Growth* (Cambridge: Harvard University Press, 1966), and Nathan Rosenberg's comments, in *Perspectives on Technology* (Cambridge: at the University Press, 1976), Chapter 7 ("Karl Marx on the Economic Role of Science"); and Chapter 15 ("Science, Invention and Economic Growth"). The latter is, in part, a critique of Schmookler's study. My own views are incorporated in the references previously given to *The Process of Economic Growth* (Oxford: at the Clarendon Press, 1953) and *How It All Began* as well as in Chapter 4 of *Why the Poor* ("Technology and the Price System").

13. For an important critique of Schumpeter and his influence in these terms, see Nathan Rosenberg, *Perspectives on Technology,* pp. 66–68.

14. *Ibid.,* p. 166.

15. *Ibid.,* p. 192.

16. The British and French methods for encouraging inventions are discussed and compared in my *How It All Began,* pp. 173–189.

17. See, for example, Edward Denison, *Trends in American Economic Growth 1929–1982* (Washington, D.C.: The Brookings Institution, 1985), pp. 40–44, including footnote references. In addition to his *Invention and Economic Growth,* cited in note 12, see also Jacob Schmookler, *Patents, Invention, and Economic Change,* especially "Technological Change and the Law of Industrial Growth," pp. 70–84.

18. For discussion of the debate on this matter, see *How It All Began,* pp. 148–150. In his rather sympathetic essay on Marx's view of science, Rosenberg sums up usefully:

> There are several possible meanings which can be attached to the statement that "the origin and development of the sciences has been determined by production."
>
> 1. Science depends upon industry for financial support.
> 2. The expectation of high financial returns is what motivates individuals (and society) to pursue a particular scientific problem.
> 3. The needs of industry serve as a powerful agent in calling attention to certain problems (Pasteur's studies of fermentation and silkworm epidemics).
> 4. The normal pursuit of productive activities throws up physical evidence of great importance to certain disciplines (metallurgy and chemistry, canal building and geology). As a result, industrial activities have, as a byproduct of their operation, provided the flow of raw observations upon which sciences have built and generalized.
> 5. The history of individual sciences, including an account of their varying rates of progress at different periods in history, can be adequately provided by an understanding of the changing economic needs of society.

> I believe that Marx and Engels subscribed to propositions 1–4 without qualification. I believe they often sounded as if they subscribed to the fifth proposition. However, I think . . . they subscribed to the fifth proposition only subject to certain qualifications—qualifications which strike me as being, collectively, more interesting than the original proposition.

The qualifications to which Rosenberg refers relate to the emergence of complex, highly differentiated machinery and the application to its design and manufacture of scientific principles.

19. For discussions of the role of the capacity to measure in the early days of the modern physical sciences and more currently, see my *How It All Began*, p. 154, and *Getting from Here to There* (New York: McGraw-Hill, 1978), pp. 160–162.

20. *Perspectives on Technology*, Chapter 6 ("The Direction of Technological Change: Inducement Mechanisms and Focusing Devices").

21. Mensch's hypothesis is incorporated in his *Stalemate in Technology: Innovations Overcome the Depression* (New York: Ballinger, 1979), English translation of the 1975 German edition. Freeman's views are fully elaborated in C. Freeman, John Clark, and Luc Soete, *Unemployment and Technical Innovation* (Westport, Conn.: Greenwood Press, 1982). The references in the latter (pp. 203–210) list the principal recent work on long cycles as well as the older literature, although work on long cycles has continued to swarm in the 1980s. My evaluation of the Mensch–Freeman debate is in my review of the latter's study in *The Journal of Economic Literature*, Vol. XX (March 1983), pp. 129–131. See also Alfred Kleinknecht, foreword by Jan Tinbergen, *Innovation Patterns in Crisis and Prosperity; Schumpeter's Long Cycle Reconsidered* (New York: St. Martin's, 1987), and my review in *The Journal of Economic Literature*, Vol. XXVI (March 1988), pp. 111–113.

22. J. Jewkes *et al.*, *The Sources of Invention* (London: Macmillan, 1958, 1969).

23. C. Freeman *et al.*, *Unemployment and Technical Innovation*, p. 63.

24. *Ibid.*, pp. 64–65.

25. *Ibid.*, pp. 67–68.

26. One intellectual issue exists between Freeman's analysis and mine: Where does the world economy stand in terms of the rhythm of innovation—if, indeed, there is a rhythm? Accepting Schumpeter's three pre-1914 technological revolutions, Christopher Freeman and his colleagues identify a post-1945 "Fourth Long Wave" (Chapters 6–8). It peaks out in the mid-1960s and is linked to plastics, synthetic fibers, and premicrochip electronics, including television—sectors analyzed by Freeman in an original and fruitful way. He is quite aware of the extremely important role of motor vehicles and durable consumers goods in the great postwar boom; and these sectors were (excepting television) evidently far beyond an innovational stage, clearly belonging with the Third Industrial Revolution. But Freeman chooses to dramatize the rise and deceleration of a batch of technologies, long germinating, that clearly did emerge into large-scale production after 1945.

I am inclined to regard the leading sectors of the postwar boom (including plastics, synthetic fibers, and television) as the rounding out of the Third Industrial Revolution, placing more emphasis than Freeman on the diffusion in the 1950s and 1960s of the automobile and durable consumers' goods revolution to Western Europe and Japan, sectors that, incidentally, absorbed significant proportions of the output of synthetic materials and light electronics. I would identify microelectronics, genetic engineering, new synthetic materials, and the laser as the Fourth Wave, dated from the mid-1970s.

The point I would make here is not that my view is correct and Freeman's incorrect: it is that, while the phenomenon of bunching is a real feature of modern economic history, our groupings and dating are inherently arbitrary. They should be taken seriously but not too seriously, as we recall that many important innovations occurred outside the intervals of cluster and that the clusters can be grouped in different ways.

A quite different approach to innovational bunching is taken by Wilhelm Krelle ("Long-Term Fluctuation of Technical Progress and Growth," *Journal of Institutional and Theoretical Economics*, Vol. 143, No. 3 [September 1987], pp. 379–401.) He adduces a cycle in "entrepreneurship," defined as a "latent variable—that measures the degree of economic activity in the population," to explain the waning of innovation in the United States, the Federal Republic of Germany, and Japan in, roughly, the decade 1965–1975 and the subsequent revival. While I would take a less generalized approach to the phenomenon, Krelle is one of the few who has recognized the deceleration of innovation in that decade and subsequent revival.

27. *World Economy*, p. 379.

28. *Getting from Here to There,* Chapters 8 and 9.

29. J. M. Clark, *Economics of Overhead Costs* (Chicago: University of Chicago Press, 1923), p. 120. This splendid affirmation is affixed to the wall of the Old Regents Room at the University of Texas at Austin. My colleague, Michael Kennedy, points out, however, that Clark's use of diminishing returns in this context is a bit colloquial or, even, suspect. He argues that it is unlikely that a doubling of outlays on R & D would double the annual increment to the stock of usable knowledge, somehow measured.

For a thoughtful examination of the Kuznets–Burns–Salter hypothesis (diminishing returns to invention and innovation in a given sector) versus the Schmookler hypothesis (enlarged demand and production increase the volume of inventions and innovations in a given sector), see Michael Gert and Richard A. Wall, "The Evolution of Technologies and Investment in Innovation," *Economic Journal,* Vol. 96, No. 383 (September 1986), pp. 741–747. The authors conclude indecisively that both forces are at work and the outcome cannot be predicted a priori.

30. This point, made in *Getting from Here to There,* pp. 161–162, is elaborated by W. O. Baker in "Computers as Information-Processing Machines in Modern Science," in *The Making of Modern Science: Biographical Studies,* (Fall, 1970), Vol. 99, No. 4, *Daedalus,* pp. 1088–1120.

31. For general reflections on this subject see Nathan Rosenberg, *Perspectives on Technology,* Chapter 13 ("Technological Innovation and Natural Resources: The Niggardliness of Nature Reconsidered"). See also, for historical and policy review, my *World Economy,* Part Six (especially Chapters 49–53) and *Getting from Here to There,* Chapters 4–7.

As of the 1980s the IC^2 Institute at The University of Texas at Austin has evolved as a major center for the exploration of technological innovation and diffusion. A few of its many monographs in this terrain are:

Abetti, Pier A., Christopher W. LeMaistre, Raymond W. Smilor, and William A. Wallace (eds.), *Technological Innovation and Economic Growth* (Austin: IC^2 Institute, The University of Texas at Austin, 1987).

Abetti, Pier A., Christopher W. LeMaistre, and Raymond W. Smilor (eds.), *Industrial Innovation, Productivity, and Employment* (Austin: IC^2 Institute, The University of Texas at Austin, 1987).

Konecci, Eugene B., George Kozmetsky, Raymond W. Smilor, and Michael D. Gill, Jr. (eds.), *Commercializing Technology Resources for Competitive Advantages* (Austin: IC^2 Institute, The University of Texas at Austin, 1986).

Konecci, Eugene B., George Kozmetsky, Raymond W. Smilor, and Michael D. Gill, Jr. (eds.), *Technology Venturing: Making and Securing the Future* (Austin: IC^2 Institute, The University of Texas at Austin, 1985).

Konecci, Eugene B., and Lawrence Kuhn (eds.), *Technology Venturing: American Innovation and Risk-Taking* (New York: Praeger Publishers, 1985).

Kozmetsky, George, *Transformational Management* (Cambridge, Mass.: Ballinger Publishing Company, 1985).

Mahajan, Vijay, and Yoram Wind (eds.), *Innovation Diffusion Models of New Product Acceptance* (Cambridge, Mass.: Ballinger Publishing Company, 1986).

32. In a bold but thoughtful essay Aaron Segal has not only set out criteria for the institutionalization of a capacity to absorb modern technologies in a developing country but also arrayed thirty-two countries in the following table ("From Technology Transfer to Science and Technology Institutionalization," Chapter 6 in John R. McIntyre and Daniel S. Papp [eds.], *The Political Economy of International Technology Transfer* [Westport, Conn.: Greenwood, Press, 1986], pp. 95–115).

Segal's essay concludes with a useful set of references to technology-transfer problems and initiatives in various parts of the developing world (pp. 114–115).

N.6 Developing Country Science and Technology Capabilities, 1984

I. Fully institutionalized
India

II. Semi-institutionalized

Brazil	Singapore
China	South Korea
Hong Kong	Taiwan

III. Partly institutionalized

Argentina	Pakistan
Malaysia	South Africa
Mexico	

IV. Partly institutionalized petroleum dependent

Algeria	Saudi Arabia
Iran	Trinidad and Tobago
Iraq	Venezuela
Kuwait	

V. Longshots

Barbados	Sri Lanka
Colombia	Thailand
Costa Rica	Turkey
Jamaica	

VI. Apparent failures

Chile	Nigeria
Cuba	Philippines
Egypt	Vietnam
Indonesia	

VII. Others

SOURCE: Aaron Segal, "From Technology Transfer to Science and Technology Institutionalization," Chapter 6 in John R. McIntyre and Daniel S. Papp (eds.), *The Political Economy of International Technology Transfer* (Westport, Conn.: Greenwood Press), pp. 95–115.

33. See, for example, Sergei P. Dobrovolsky, *The Economics of Corporate Finance* (New York: McGraw Hill, 1971), pp. 329–333. See also his earlier *Corporate Income Retention, 1915–1943* (New York: National Bureau of Economic Research, 1951), which found (p. 97): "The relative importance of retained income and external financing absorbed by manufacturing corporations during the years of 1915–1943 varied with the rate of their asset growth."

34. See, for example, W. E. G. Salter, *Productivity and Technical Change* (2d ed. with an addendum by W. B. Reddaway [Cambridge: at the University press, 1966], especially Chapter XI ["Productivity and Technical Change"], pp. 147–155). On the pattern of capital in U.S. manufacturing industries, 1880–1948, see notably Daniel Creamer, Sergei P. Dobrovolsky, and Israel Berenstein, *Capital in Manufacturing and Mining: Its Formation and Financing* (Princeton: Princeton University Press, 1960). For a summary of recent U.S. data confirming Salter's and Dobrovolsky's earlier findings, see Donald L. Losman and Shu-Jan Liang, *The Industrial Sector* (Washington, D.C.: National Defense University, 1987), especially pp. 43–54.

35. *Economics of Corporate Finance*, pp. 331–332. Direct quotation may be helpful on this important point:

> It is also possible to compare [for manufacturing and mining] gross internal financing (retained profit plus depreciation allowances) with gross plant and equipment expenditures. The ratio of the former to the latter is found to be as follows:

N.7. Retained profit plus depreciation as percentage of gross plant and equipment expenditure

1900–1914	87.1%
1919–1929	107.8
1936–1940	92.2
1946–1958	109.9

One is tempted to conclude from the above that plant and equipment expenditures were essentially financed with internal funds and that external funds were required only to finance relatively small investments in other assets: inventories, receivables, and marketable securities. On the basis of aggregate data, however, one cannot justifiably match individual sources with individual uses of funds. Some corporations that were engaged in substantial plant modernization or expansion programs doubtless required large amounts of external funds in addition to the funds generated internally. At the same time, other companies generated internal funds well in excess of their own expenditures on plant and equipment. Nevertheless, it is interesting to observe that, for the industry as a whole, the amount obtained from the internal sources was approximately equal to the amount required to finance the most important type of expenditures.

36. See, for example, my "World Economy Since 1945: A Stylized Historical Analysis," *Economic History Review,* Vol. XXXVIII, No. 2 (May 1985), especially pp. 256–257. Also *World Economy,* especially pp. 561–563.

37. *An Economic History of Western Europe, 1945–1964* (London: Metheun, 1967), p. 128. The argument, which is close to the central thesis of Postan's study, is extended on pp. 129–132, 163–166, and p. 364 (Note 7).

38. The references in the text are drawn from W. E. G. Salter, *Productivity and Technical Change,* pp. 147–151. For an extended group of references on this point, see *The World Economy,* pp. 762–763, note 198. On Japan, for the period 1960–1971, see Miyohei Shinohara, *Industrial Growth, Trade, and Dynamic Patterns in the Japanese Economy* (Tokyo: University of Tokyo Press, 1982), "Technical Progress and Production Function by Industry," pp. 203–237. This supplementary chapter relates, for twenty-one Japanese industries, the rate of growth of output, capital, the labor force, and productivity over the period 1960–1971. The annual average growth rates table indicates the extraordinary range of increases in output, capital, labor, and, by implication, productivity as between, say, automobiles and cotton spinning (see p. 677).

39. Simon Kuznets, *Economic Growth of Nations* (Cambridge: The Belknap Press of the Harvard University Press, 1971), p. 319. Kuznets's full discussion is on pp. 314–343. Kuznets uses for this exercise data from Daniel Creamer, Sergei P. Dobrovolsky, and Israel Borenstein, *Capital in Manufacturing and Mining.*

40. Allyn Young, "Economic Returns and Economic Progress" *Economic Journal,* Vol. XXXVIII, No. 152 (December 1928), p. 539. For background to Young's address, see Charles P. Blitch, "Allyn A. Young: A Curious Case of Professional Neglect," *History of Political Economy,* Vol. 15, No. 1 (Spring 1983). Blitch's essay provides a useful biographical sketch of Young's life and work.

41. See, for example, *The World Economy,* pp. 611–612.

42. Arthur Lewis and I are the major advocates of this interpretation of the Kondratieff cycle. Lewis's view is most fully developed in his *Growth and Fluctuations, 1870–1913;* mine in *The World Economy* and the first two chapters of *Why the Poor Get Richer.*

43. One aspect of Kuznets's *Secular Movements* was the measurement of the lags between changes in basic commodity prices and output by calculating and smoothing deviations from trend lines. For discussion and specific references see my *Why the Poor Get Richer,* pp. 21–25.

44. Mathematical models of this process are presented and related to the course of history in Chapter 2 of *Why the Poor Get Richer.* The mathematical portions of that chapter are the work of Michael Kennedy. We jointly designed the chapter as a whole.

45. *Process of Economic Growth,* pp. 134–136.

46. I call these movements classic because Kondratieff cycles did not unfold in history in the smooth, stylized sine curves evoked by Schumpeter (*Business Cycles,* Vol. 1, p. 213). There were three typical irregularities: first, on the downswing, basic commodities initially fell rapidly relative to prices of manufactures, then decelerated or, as in the late 1960s, leveled off; second, as Table 20.b indicates, a high proportion of the total—and relative—price increase tended to be concentrated in the early stage of the upswing; and third, the second Juglar (to use Schumpeter's designation) often exhibited countertrend movements of the kind to be observed in the mid-1980s.

N.8. Annual Average Growth Rates of Output, Capital and Labor:
Japan, 1960–1971

	Output (Y)	Capital (K)	Labor (L)
Flour milling	11.3	12.0	1.4
Edible oil	9.1	12.7	2.2
Cotton spinning	7.6	7.6	−1.0
Synthetic textiles	15.2	12.6	0.0
Paper and pulp	9.0	9.4	−0.9
Chemicals	14.2	14.5	−1.3
Drugs and medicines	17.9	15.8	5.5
Glass	14.9	13.2	3.0
Cement	8.8	10.7	−0.9
Petroleum refining	9.5	14.0	1.1
Blast furnace	12.7	15.2	2.0
Open and electric furnaces	10.6	17.0	2.6
Special steel	10.8	12.9	1.0
Non-ferrous metals	7.6	11.9	−5.6
Electric wire and cable	11.0	14.3	1.5
Machine tools	9.2	12.3	1.8
Bearings	14.8	15.4	0.7
Automobiles	22.8	24.3	10.0
Heavy electric equipment	15.3	11.8	4.5
Light electrical appliances	22.0	17.2	5.0
Optical instruments	23.3	21.1	7.1
Total	14.1	14.2	2.2

NOTES: K and L are adjusted by the utilization rate of equipment and manhours, respectively.

Annual average growth rates are computed from mere comparison of 1960 and 1971 by compound interest calculation. "Blast furnance" and "open and electric furnaces" designate types in the iron and steel industry.

SOURCE: Miyohei Shinohara, *Industrial Growth, Trade, and Dynamic Patterns in the Japanese Economy* (Tokyo: University of Tokyo Press, 1982), p. 206.

47. See, for example, *BP Statistical Review of World Energy* (London: British Petroleum Company, June 1984), pp. 28–30.

48. See the excellent discussion by Edward C. Wolf, "Raising Agricultural Productivity," Chapter 8 in Lester R. Brown *et al., State of the World, 1987* (New York: W. W. Norton for the World Watch Institute), pp. 139–156.

49. See, for example, Sandra Postel, "Stabilizing Chemical Cycles," Chapter 9 in Lester R. Brown *et al., State of the World, 1987.*

50. See, for example, *Process of Economic Growth,* pp. 197–201 and 358–359.

51. For data and discussion see *World Economy: History and Prospect,* pp. 586–588 (grain), pp. 594–598 (energy).

52. Angus Maddison, *Phases of Capitalist Development* (Oxford: Oxford University Press, 1982), p. 44.

53. See *Why the Poor*, pp. 259–288 ("Growth Rates at Different Levels of Income and Stage of Growth). See also Moses Abramovitz, "Rapid Growth Potential and Its Realization: The Experience of Capitalist Economies in the Post-War World" in Edmond Malinvaud (ed.), *Economic Growth and Resources, Volume One: The Major Issues* (London: Macmillan, 1979), pp. 1–51, also available as Reprint No. 221, Center for Research in Economic Growth, Department of Economics, Stanford University. Abramovitz extends his analysis in "Catching Up, Forging Ahead, and Falling Behind," *Journal of Economic History*, Vol. XLVI, No. 2 (June 1986), pp. 1–22. In a similar vein, see William J. Baumol, "Productivity Growth, Convergence, and Welfare: What the Long-Run Data Show," Research Report #85-27 (August 1985), C. V. Starr Center for Applied Economics, New York University.

54. Readers of *The Stages of Economic Growth* may recall that, in this context, I distinguished traditional societies from those "born free," that is, offshoots of a Great Britain already well along in the modernization process. Intermediate cases (e.g., Latin America, Quebec) are also identified (pp. 17–18).

55. Kuznets used an acceleration in urbanization to date the beginnings of modern growth; Chenery begins his transformation with countries at the lowest levels of per capita real GNP in a 1960s' cross-section. One would expect a tendency for Kuznets's dates to be somewhat earlier than mine, since an acceleration of urbanization normally begins in the preconditions for takeoff. And when his dates and mine are compared for the eight cases where comparison is possible, his initial date is slightly earlier in five cases (see *World Economy*, pp. 778–779). Chenery's cross-sectional analysis does not permit the dating of stages. But there were no national societies in the 1960s that could properly be called traditional in that decade, even if, for some, modernization was limited, proceeding slowly, and take-off a distant prospect at best.

56. Pp. vii–viii. Chapter 14 in the second edition of *The Process of Economic Growth* is a reasonably full exposition of this perspective.

On the general inadequacy and misleading consequences of the assumption of profit maximization see Barry Schwartz, *The Battle for Human Nature, Science, Morality, and Modern Life*, (New York: W. W. Norton, 1986). For a narrower examination of the impenetrable complexity of the motives of entrepreneurs and a positive proposal for bypassing that complexity operationally, see William J. Baumol, "Entrepreneurship and Economic Theory," *American Economic Review*, Vol. 58, No. 2 (May 1968).

The distinction between neo-Newtonian and biological approaches to economic analysis can be traced back, at least, to the protracted effort of Malthus and Ricardo to identify the source and character of their fundamental disagreement. It is paralleled at the present time by the two fundamental approaches to artificial intelligence and the dialogue between their practicioners (plus comments from friendly observers of their dilemma). See, for example, the Winter 1988 issue of *Daedalus*, devoted wholly to *Artificial Intelligence* (Vol. 117, No. 1, Proceedings of the American Academy of Arts and Sciences, Cambridge, Mass.) The nineteen authors characterize the approaches in different but roughly harmonious ways. For example, logic versus biology; information processing versus connectionism; reliance on algorithms versus network modeling; rationalist reductionism versus holistic neuroscience; solving puzzles versus classifying patterns; symbol manipulation versus modeling of the brain. Also like economics, artificial intelligence runs into two fundamental and inescapable problems. First, human intelligence cannot be usefully separated from the background cultural world within which individual human beings have evolved. Intelligent human calculation is intimately linked to the evolution of the social, political, and economic concepts and institutions that surround them, suffuse their thought, and through which they must act. Thus, like Plato's "state within us," one of the major figures in artificial intelligence (Marvin Minsky) evokes the concept of the society of mind and uses it as the title of a book (New York: Simon and Schuster, 1986). In less elevated language, this dimension of reality leaves the artificial intelligence expert with the problem of modeling "common sense"—a fact often acknowledged and a challenge yet unmet. Second, like a serious economist who does not blindly accept profit or utility maximization as adequate assumptions, the expert on artificial intelligence confronts a closely related but distinguishable puzzlement: the human being is a mightily complex unit who acts in terms of desires and goals—and internalized constraints as well—that transcend rational thought and behavior as conventionally defined. Put another way, human intelligence is much more than an abstract information-processing system.

An awareness of these problems has led some experts to despair of achieving their goal of fully replicating human intelligence by either approach or by some synthesis of approaches.

The ultimate question they confront is that which Auguste Comte posed and which Alfred Marshall addressed bluntly (preceding, p. 190). The question is: Since the behavior of an economy reflects forces derived from a whole society, should we not concentrate on developing a general theory of society before refining economics on an evidently flawed, excessively narrow basis? Marshall replied: "It is vain to speak of the higher authority of a unified social science. No doubt if that existed Economics would gladly find shelter under its wing. But it does not exist; it shows no sign of coming into existence. There is no use waiting idly for it; we must do what we can with our present resources." And a great deal of practical and theoretical work in artificial intelligence goes forward in a Marshallian spirit. But the mythic adventure of understanding and reproducing the whole process of human intelligence still beckons to a good many.

57. *Stages of Economic Growth*, p. 165.

Chapter 21

1. For a more formal model of this case see Appendix, pp. 561–562.

2. This is the central theme of *How It All Began* (New York: McGraw-Hill, 1975). See, especially, Chapters 1 and 4.

3. A. N. Whitehead, *Science and the Modern World* (New York: Macmillan, 1925), p. 3.

4. For continued debate on this matter, see, for example, N. F. R. Crafts, "Industrial Revolution in England and France: Some Thoughts on the Question 'Why Was England First?' " *Economic History Review*, Vol. XXX (1977), pp. 429–441, and W. W. Rostow "No Random Walk: A Comment on 'Why Was England First?' " *ibid.*, Vol. XXXI (1978), pp. 610–612.

5. For an extended analysis of this stage, going beyond earlier expositions, see my "Reflections on the Drive to Technological Maturity," *Banca Nazionale del Lavoro Quarterly Review*, No. 161 (June 1987), pp. 115–146.

6. *The Stages of Economic Growth*, (Cambridge: at the University Press, 1960, 1971), p. 9.

7. See for example Table 3 (pp. 206–207) in *World Development Report 1987* (New York: Oxford University Press for the World Bank, 1987).

8. *Ibid.*, p. 175.

9. *Ibid.*, p. 202.

10. My T. Vu, *World Population Projections 1984* (Washington, D.C.: The World Bank, 1984), Tables 2 and 3, pp. xviii and xix. The methods used by Vu to generate these projections are set out on pp. ix–xvii. A good deal of the basic data is drawn from United Nations sources. See, for example, *World Population Prospects* (as assessed in 1984), (New York: United Nations, 1986).

11. Donald J. Bogue, *Principles of Demography* (New York: Wiley, 1969), p. 49.

12. The argument summarized in the paragraphs that follow is elaborated in "On Ending the Cold War," *Foreign Affairs* (Spring 1987), pp. 831–851.

13. The relation between war and stages of growth is explored at some length in Chapters 8 and 9 of my *Stages of Economic Growth*.

14. *The American Diplomatic Revolution*, An Inaugural Lecture delivered before the University at Oxford, 12 November 1946 (Oxford: at the Clarendon Press, 1946), p. 8.

15. *The United States and the Regional Organization of Asia and the Pacific, 1965–1985,* (Austin: University of Texas Press, 1986), pp. 158–161.

16. David Hume, in Eugene Rotwein (ed.), *Writings on Economics* (Madison: University of Wisconsin Press, 1955), p. 80. For a post-1945 discussion of the rich-country–poor-country problem see Albert O. Hirschman, "Effects of Industrialization on the Markets of Industrial Countries," in B. F. Hoselitz (ed.), *The Progress of Underdeveloped Areas* (Chicago: University of Chicago Press, 1952), pp. 270–283. Writing in the wake of the success of the Marshall plan, Hirschman is full of praise for the "carefree attitude" of U.S. policy in reviving potential competitors and extending the process via the Point Four program. He contrasts this policy with pre-1914 and interwar German policy. Although his argument as of the late 1980s would probably not be quite so optimistic, he enunciates what I would regard as the correct principle (p. 283): ". . . [T]he only way in which any nation can hope to maintain industrial leadership is through a continuous process of economic growth and technological improvement."

17. The case for regional organizations as a supplement to inevitably cumbersome global institutions is argued in my *The United States and the Regional Organization of Asia and the Pacific: 1965–1985* especially Chapters 3 and 7 and Appendices D and E.

18. For a critique of the original *Limits to Growth* analysis, see my *The World Economy: History and Prospect,* (Austin: University of Texas Press, 1978), pp. 571–578.

19. This estimate is, distinctly, not one for the number of poor people in the world. It excludes, for example, China and India, but includes quite arbitrarily other lower- and middle-income countries up to $790 GNP per capita, 1985. For an imaginative effort to estimate the proportion of the world's population living in poverty in 1975, see Hollis Chenery, with Montek S. Ahlowalia and Nicholas G. Carter, "Growth and Poverty in Developing Countries," Chapter 11 in Hollis Chenery, *Structural Change in Development Policy,* pp. 456–495. The authors found that, depending on method of calculation, 35%–38% of the population lived in poverty in a sample of thirty-six developing countries at different income levels.

20. Here is a typical statement of the issue at stake:

> The economic legacy of the first half of the 1980s threatens to create enormous disruption in the short run and will produce a fundamentally different global structure for the 1990s. These developments may have significant effects on international political and security arrangements, and could erode today's alliance systems much as they are eroding the trade regime and international finance.

The quotation is from C. Fred Bergsten, "Economic Imbalances and World Politics," in *Foreign Affairs* (Spring 1987), p. 793.

21. For a useful analysis of the major options see the testimony of Barry Bosworth before the Budget Committee of the United States Senate, March 24, 1988, and Henry J. Aaron, Barry P. Bosworth, and Gary Burtless, *Can America Afford to Grow Old?* (Washington, D.C.: The Brookings Institution, 1989).

22. The phrase is from the welcoming address on July 20, 1987, of the Prime Minister of Western Samoa, Va'ai Kolone, at the Global Community Forum 1987, Apia, Western Samoa.

Appendix

1. As becomes clear in the following formal exposition of the model, our assumption of fixed land supply leads to diminishing returns in the application of the factors labor and capital, and this leads ultimately to a steady state, given our factor growth assumptions. In the multisectoral version of the Smith model presented later, the relations among land, other factors, and basic and other commodities are made more precise.

2. The Smithian model developed in this subsection is of a closed economy. The expansion of the market in *The Wealth of Nations* evidently embraces both domestic and foreign trade. The third part

of this Appendix, focused on the rich-country–poor-country problem, permits analysis of an open economy.

3. Euler's Law implies that any function that is homogeneous of degree one (i.e., which exhibits constant returns to scale) can be written as the summation of its arguments times its partial derivatives with respect to those arguments. In particular, if $F(L,K,N)$ exhibits constant returns to scale, Euler's Law implies

$$F(L,K,N) = F_L L + F_K K + F_N N.$$

4. The reader will note that in the industrial sector of the Smithian model there is a region of increasing returns. As discussed in Part I of this Appendix, we assume that producers ignore this economywide effect in their production decisions, so the unit cost function (AII.13) still exists. The increasing-returns factor, called $p(...)$ in Part I, is incorporated into the $A(i)$ term in the cost function.

5. Some major aspects of this economy were based on the "Income Level I" economy presented in Table 3–4 of Hollis Chenery, Sherman Robinson, and Moshe Syrquin, *Industrialization and Growth, A Comparative Study* (Oxford University Press, 1986), p. 49. Several modifications were made to that economy to derive the economy of Table AII.1 (such as introducing land as an explicit factor), so we are not attempting to replicate it. We do acknowledge it as our original data source.

6. The particular values of the parameters of equation (AII.24) that lead to the Engel curves of Figure AII.2 are

$$a = -22.1, \quad b = 0.802, \quad c = 30.9, \quad d = -0.0221,$$
$$e = 0.786, \quad \bar{C}(3) = 1568.$$

7. The time path of the return to capital could have been stabilized in the model by modifying saving rates in an analagous manner to the way land supply was modified to stabilize the time path of rent. It was decided that a constant saving rate was more in the neoclassical spirit than a constant return to capital. Given changing proportions of the individual sectors in total output, and different capital shares in these sectors, one cannot construct a model that displays both a constant saving rate and a constant return to capital.

8. The reader should recall that in all simulations using this model, the time path of the supply of land will be held constant at levels that lead to unity land rent in the base neoclassical model.

9. Conventionally measured, R & D is much less than 5% of GNP in advanced industrial countries. We have chosen a higher figure to take roughly into account two components of R & D, as we have defined it, for which we currently have no measure: (1) labor and capital devoted to incremental technological change outside the formal R & D sector, and (2) that element in the education process that more or less directly contributes to enlarging or maintaining technological absorptive capacity.

10. Since the production of technical progress is assumed to use only labor and capital, and the proportions of labor, capital, and land change during the growth process, there will be minor adjustments in the relative sectoral prices in the model that includes the R & D sector. These differences make negligible changes in the aggregate growth picture.

11. This phenomenon has been described by economic historians and analyzed by Schumpeter, the young Kuznets, Fabricant, Salter, Freeman, and others.

12. These intervals measure roughly the period between the time a sector became a leading sector and the time it ceased to lead; that is, the time when its growth rate approximated or fell below the average industrial growth rate of the economy as a whole.

13. Railroads ceased to be a leading sector in Britain by the 1860s, but steel in all its multiple uses, notably shipbuilding, carried forward with high momentum. The peaking out of the railroad boom comes later in some other advanced industrial countries; e.g., the 1870s for Germany, the 1880s for the United States, and the 1890s for Russia.

14. Straightforward evidence for this dating of the cycles can be seen in the marked deceleration in economic growth in Britain in the late 1830s and early 1840s; in the decade before the First World

War; and in the decade 1965–1975. (See *World Economy,* pp. 375–377). Of course, many other forces affect aggregate growth rates.

15. For the moment we ignore the issue of whether Z represents gross, net, or intermediate output. The aggregation procedure described here applies to all measures of output.

16. This relation is based on Figure 20.1 in Chapter 20. The wage rate of unity in Figure AII.14 corresponds to $100 of real GNP per capita (1964 prices) in Figure 20.1. This corresponds to $360 in 1987 prices. 1987 U.S. GNP per capita was $18,000, equivalent to a real wage of 50 in Figure AII.14.

17. See reference in Chapter 19, note 2.

18. The sense of incremental change in the Smithian system, by contrast, is that it is relatively small, accounting for little of the total improvement in the overall state of technology.

19. This backlog, as discussed above, might be defined as the difference (for each sector i) between the $A(i)$ of the most technically advanced country in the world and the $A(i)$ of the country in question.

20. Of course, if saving is only 25% of profits, the initial state of the system is not quite as shown in Table AII.1. Given the saving pattern of 25% of profits, final demand for the output of sector 2 is lower than in Table AII.1 (19.1 vs. 30). This is because investment is a lower proportion of GNP in the steady state than in the 5% growth base neoclassical case. Thus, the relative price of sector 2 is somewhat lower in this case, and the steady state actually comes to rest at a GNP of about 106. For the purpose of the argument here, this is negligible.

21. This then leads us to precisely the first-year situation shown in Table AII.1.

22. The reader should recall once again that ''land'' in this analysis means all natural resources; so fixity of supply means literally a finite amount with no substitutes available.

23. The reader will note that the consumption equations (AIII.7) and (AIII.8) (preceding), derived from a Cobb-Douglas utility function, assume unitary income elasticities and thus cannot represent Engel curve phenomena. This decision was made for simplicity, and all the points we wish to make are not affected by it.

Subject Index